Law

for Business *and* Personal Use

18e

JOHN E. ADAMSON

SOUTH-WESTERN
CENGAGE Learning

Australia • Brazil • Japan • Korea • Mexico • Singapore • Spain • United Kingdom • United States

SOUTH-WESTERN
CENGAGE Learning™

Law for Business and Personal Use, 18th Edition

John E. Adamson

Vice President of Editorial, Business: Jack W. Calhoun

Vice President/Editor-in-Chief: Karen Schmohe

Executive Editor: Eve Lewis

Senior Developmental Editor: Enid Nagel

Marketing Manager: Valerie Lauer

Marketing Coordinator: Kelley Gilreath

Content Project Manager: Jennifer A. Ziegler

Production Manager: Patricia Matthews Boies

Senior Technology Project Editor: Sally Nieman

Website Project Manager: Edward Stubenrauch

Manufacturing Coordinator: Kevin Kluck

Editorial Assistant: Virginia Wilson

Production Service: ICC Macmillan Inc.

Senior Art Director: Tippy McIntosh

Internal Designer: Trish Knapke, Ke Design

Cover Designer: Trish Knapke, Ke Design

Cover Image: Kelly Redinger/Design Pics/Corbis

For product information and technology assistance, contact us at
Cengage Learning Academic Resource Center, 1-800-423-0563

For permission to use material from this text or product,
submit all requests online at www.cengage.com/permissions
Further permissions questions can be emailed to
permissionrequest@cengage.com

ExamView® and **Exam**View Pro® are registered trademarks of FSCreations, Inc. Windows is a registered trademark of the Microsoft Corporation used herein under license. Macintosh and Power Macintosh are registered trademarks of Apple Computer, Inc. used herein under license.

The Career Clusters icons are being used with permission of the:

States' Career Clusters Initiative, 2007, www.careerclusters.org

ISBN-13: 978-0-538-44588-7
ISBN-10: 0-538-44588-2

South-Western Cengage Learning
5191 Natorp Boulevard
Mason, OH 45040
USA

Cengage Learning products are represented in Canada by Nelson Education, Ltd.

For your course and learning solutions, visit **school.cengage.com**

Printed in the United States of America
2 3 4 5 6 7 11 10 09

Reviewers

Brenda Albright-Barnhart
Digital Academy
Career Tech Department
Bolton High School
Alexandria, Louisiana

Judith Kay Binns
Teacher, Business Department
Bryant High School
Bryant, Arkansas

Dawna Carter
Business Education Teacher
Puxico R-8 School
Puxico, Missouri

Leo Dunn
Instructor, Business and Technology
Greater Lowell Technical High
    School
Tyngsboro, Massachusetts

Nancy Everson
Chair, Business Education
Sun Prairie High School
Sun Prairie, Wisconsin

Christine Ferreira
Business Teacher
Algonquin Regional High School
Northboro, Massachusetts

Richard T. Gordon
Lead Teacher, Business & Applied
    Tech Department
Bloomington High School
Bloomington, Illinois

Linda Hughes
Business Educator
Rapides High School
Lecompte, Louisiana

Kristine Labbus
Business Education Instructor
Neenah High School
Neenah, Wisconsin

Jallane Link
Business Office Technology
    Instructor
Canadian Valley Technology Center
Chickasha, Oklahoma

Catherine McDonald
Senior Teacher, Business
Ridgefield High School
Ridgefield, Connecticut

Vicki Noss
Business Teacher
Beloit Memorial High School
Beloit, Wisconsin

Jeanne Robinson
Teacher, Business Department
South Technical High School
Sunset Hills, Maryland

Thomasine Montoya
Teacher/Coordinator
Cibola High School
Albuquerque, New Mexico

Tammy Savage
Business Department Chair
Spain Park High School
Hoover, Alabama

Janice B. Shelton
Business Teacher
Mills E. Godwin High School
Richmond, Virginia

Lynn M. Taillon
Business Educator
Cheshire High School
Cheshire, Connecticut

Caroline Janovec Tassone
Business Teacher
Waynesboro Area High School
Waynesboro, Pennsylvania

Tamara M. Tucker
Teacher, Business Department
Columbia High School
Columbia, South Carolina

Grant Pierce Williams
Business Instructor/FBLA Adviser
Harrison High School
Harrison, Arkansas

Kevin W. Willson
Business Education Chair
York Suburban Senior High School
York, Pennsylvania

About the Author

John E. Adamson is Emeritus Professor of Business and Law in the Department of Finance and General Business at Southwest Missouri State University. Adamson received a B.S. from the U.S. Military Academy at West Point, New York; an M.A. from Georgetown University; and an M.B.A. and J.D. from the University of Virginia at Charlottesville. A decorated, disabled veteran and past mayor and school board member of Miller, Missouri, Adamson is author of numerous business law publications.

Mock Trial Consultant

Melissa A. Marcin
Attorney at Law
Milford, Ohio

Contents

Unit 1 Law, Justice, and You 2

Planning a Career in Law: Trial Lawyer   3
Entrepreneurs and the Law: Law, Justice, and You   102
Community Action: Get Out the Vote   103

Winning Edge: FBLA Emerging Business Issues 103
Mock Trial Prep: Concepts of Advocacy   104

Features in Unit 1

A Question of Ethics   17, 29, 57, 65, 87
Cyberlaw   8, 86
Economic Impact   66
Global Issues   6, 32, 71
Hot Debate   4, 24, 48, 64, 80
In This Case   11, 16, 42, 54, 70, 73, 83, 85, 93

Law Brief   9, 29, 58, 74, 94
Legal Research   10, 38, 50, 69, 91
Net Bookmark   19, 32, 53, 72, 95
Online Research   97
What's Your Verdict?   5, 6, 10, 12, 13, 16, 25, 28, 31, 33, 36, 39, 49, 52, 55, 57, 65, 67, 68, 71, 72, 74, 81, 82, 83, 85, 89, 91, 93, 94, 96

Chapter 1 Laws and Their Ethical Foundation   4

1-1   Laws and Legal Systems   5
1-2   Types of Laws   10
1-3   Ethical Bases for Laws   16
       Chapter 1 Assessment   20
       Sports & Entertainment Law   23

Chapter 2 Constitutional Rights   24

2-1   Foundations of the U.S. Constitution   25
2-2   Division and Balance of Governmental Powers   31
2-3   The Internet and Constitutional Rights   36
       Chapter 2 Assessment   44
       Sports & Entertainment Law   47

Chapter 3   Court Systems   48

3-1   Forms of Dispute Resolution   49
3-2   The Federal Court System   52
3-3   State Court Systems   55
       Chapter 3 Assessment   60
       Case For Legal Thinking   63

Chapter 4 Criminal Law and Procedure   64

4-1   Criminal Law   65
4-2   Criminal Procedure   71
       Chapter 4 Assessment   76
       Sports & Entertainment Law   79

Chapter 5 Civil Law and Procedure   80

5-1   Private Injuries vs. Public Offenses   81
5-2   Intentional Torts, Negligence, and Strict Liability   85
5-3   Civil Procedure   93
       Chapter 5 Assessment   98
       Sports & Entertainment Law   101

Unit 2 Contract Law 106

Planning a Career in Law: Franchisee 107
Entrepreneurs and the Law: Contract Law 222
Community Action: Positive Peer Pressure 223

Winning Edge: FBLA Multimedia
  Presentation 223
Mock Trial Prep: Case Scenario 224

Features in Unit 2

A Question of Ethics 112, 133, 148, 159, 183, 193, 216
Cyberlaw 134, 161
Economic Impact 115, 171
Global Issues 116, 132, 143, 157, 180, 207
Hot Debate 108, 126, 140, 156, 170, 190, 206
In This Case 109, 115, 119, 127, 130, 142, 147, 159, 163, 173, 177, 181, 182, 193, 199, 208

Law Brief 120, 132, 150, 158, 173, 193, 215
Legal Research 110, 134, 150, 164, 178, 200, 210
Net Bookmark 111, 133, 145, 158, 175, 198, 209
Online Research 217
What's Your Verdict? 109, 110, 114, 116, 118, 127, 128, 130, 131, 133, 141, 145, 147, 149, 157, 160, 162, 163, 164, 171, 174, 177, 179, 181, 191, 192, 197, 199, 207, 208, 210, 213, 214

Chapter 6 Offer and Acceptance 108

6-1	Creation of Offers	109
6-2	Termination of Offers	114
6-3	Acceptances	118
	Chapter 6 Assessment	122
	Sports & Entertainment Law	125

Chapter 7 Genuineness of Assent 126

7-1	Duress and Undue Influence	127
7-2	Mistake, Misrepresentation, and Fraud	130
	Chapter 7 Assessment	136
	Case For Legal Thinking	139

Chapter 8 Consideration 140

8-1	Types of Consideration	141
8-2	Questionable Consideration	145
8-3	When Consideration Is Not Required	149
	Chapter 8 Assessment	152
	Sports & Entertainment Law	155

Chapter 9 Legal Capacity to Contract 156

9-1	Contractual Capacity of Individuals and Organizations	157
9-2	Limits on the Rights of Those Without Capacity	162
	Chapter 9 Assessment	166
	Sports & Entertainment Law	169

Chapter 10 Legal Purpose and Proper Form 170

10-1	Illegal Agreements	171
10-2	The Statute of Frauds	177
	Chapter 10 Assessment	186
	Sports & Entertainment Law	189

Chapter 11 Contractual Obligations and their Enforcement 190

11-1	Transfer and Discharge of Obligations	191
11-2	Remedies for Breach of Contract	197
	Chapter 11 Assessment	202
	Sports & Entertainment Law	205

Chapter 12 Contractual Aspects of Marriage and Divorce 206

12-1	Marriage and the Law of Contracts	207
12-2	Divorce and the Law of Contracts	213
	Chapter 12 Assessment	218
	Case For Legal Thinking	221

Unit 3 The Law of Sales 226

Planning a Career in Law: Border Patrol
  Agent   227
Entrepreneurs and the Law: The Law of
  Sales   278

Community Action: Become a Consumer
  Activist   279
Winning Edge: FBLA Public Speaking I   279
Mock Trial Prep: Case Law: Search and
  Seizure   280

Features in Unit 3

A Question of Ethics   230, 250, 270
Cyberlaw   251, 264, 271
Economic Impact   252, 268
Global Issues   231, 244
Hot Debate   228, 242, 258
In This Case   232, 236, 244, 248, 270

Law Brief   232, 249, 261
Legal Research   230, 251, 260
Net Bookmark   233, 251, 261
Online Research   273
What's Your Verdict?   229, 232, 234, 235, 243,
  245, 247, 249, 259, 260, 263, 266, 268

Chapter 13 Sales Contracts   228

13-1 Sales	229
13-2 Special Rules for Sales Contracts	234
Chapter 13 Assessment	238
Case For Legal Thinking	241

Chapter 14 Ownership and Risk of Loss in Sales   242

14-1 Transfer of Ownership	243
14-2 Risk of Loss and Insurable Interest in Sales	247
Chapter 14 Assessment	254
Case For Legal Thinking	257

Chapter 15 Consumer Protection   258

15-1 Protection through Governmental Action	259
15-2 Protection through Action by the Consumer	266
Chapter 15 Assessment	274
Case For Legal Thinking	277

Unit 4 Property Law 282

Planning a Career in Law: Title Examiner   283
Entrepreneurs and the Law: Property Law   372
Community Action: Protect Your
  Environment   373

Winning Edge: BPA Presentation
  Management   373
Mock Trial Prep: Opening Statements   374

Features in Unit 4

A Question of Ethics   291, 307, 326, 349, 365
Cyberlaw   286, 320, 349
Economic Impact   346
Global Issues   290, 306, 325
Hot Debate   284, 300, 314, 334, 356
In This Case   286, 290, 301, 307, 319, 324, 338,
  344, 348, 359, 365

Law Brief   287, 306, 318, 345, 361
Legal Research   293, 305, 317, 348, 366
Net Bookmark   290, 303, 321, 343, 364
Online Research   367
What's Your Verdict?   285, 289, 292, 301,
  302, 305, 307, 315, 319, 323, 325, 335,
  336, 338, 340, 343, 347, 348, 357, 360,
  364, 366

Chapter 16 Property and Its Acquisition 284

16-1 Types of Property 285
16-2 How Property Is Acquired and Held 289
    Chapter 16 Assessment 296
    Case For Legal Thinking 299

Chapter 17 Bailments 300

17-1 Bailments 301
17-2 Bailor and Bailee Duties 305
    Chapter 17 Assessment 310
    Case For Legal Thinking 313

Chapter 18 Ownership and Leasing of Real Property 314

18-1 Ownership and Transfer of Real Property 315
18-2 Leasing Real Property 323
    Chapter 18 Assessment 330
    Case For Legal Thinking 333

Chapter 19 Insurance Law 334

19-1 Insurance Fundamentals 335
19-2 Property and Casualty Insurance 340
19-3 Life and Social Insurance 347
    Chapter 19 Assessment 352
    Case For Legal Thinking 355

Chapter 20 Wills, Trusts, and Estates 356

20-1 Property Distribution Upon Death 357
20-2 Trusts 364
    Chapter 20 Assessment 368
    Case For Legal Thinking 371

Unit 5 Agency and Employment Law 376

Planning a Career in Law: Pension Investigator 377
Entrepreneurs and the Law: Agency and Employment Law 458
Community Action: Homeland Security at School 459

Winning Edge: BPA Human Resources Management 459
Mock Trial Prep: Direct and Cross Examination 460

Features in Unit 5

A Question of Ethics 385, 404, 414, 436, 450
Cyberlaw 429, 446
Economic Impact 436
Global Issues 388, 402, 420
Hot Debate 378, 394, 410, 426, 442
In This Case 381, 387, 398, 404, 414, 417, 428, 433, 444, 449

Law Brief 384, 403, 412, 428, 452
Legal Research 380, 402, 416, 430, 447
Net Bookmark 381, 396, 411, 434, 451
Online Research 437
What's Your Verdict? 379, 380, 384, 386, 387, 395, 396, 401, 404, 411, 413, 416, 417, 427, 429, 432, 434, 435, 443, 447, 449

Chapter 21 Agency Law 378

21-1 Creation and Operation of Agencies 379
21-2 Agency Duties 384
    Chapter 21 Assessment 390
    Case For Legal Thinking 393

Chapter 22 Employment Law 394

22-1 Making and Terminating Employment Contracts 395
22-2 Duties of Employers and Employees 401
    Chapter 22 Assessment 406
    Sports & Entertainment Law 409

Chapter 23 Unions and the Employment Relationship 410

23-1   Establishment of Unions   411
23-2   Employment Relations in a Unionized
       Workplace   416
       Chapter 23 Assessment   422
       Sports & Entertainment Law   425

Chapter 24 Discrimination in Employment 426

24-1   Legal versus Illegal Discrimination   427
24-2   Proving Illegal Discrimination   432
       Chapter 24 Assessment   438
       Sports & Entertainment Law   441

Chapter 25 Employment-Related Injuries 442

25-1   Safety on the Job   443
25-2   Employer's Liability for Work-Related
       Injuries   447
       Chapter 25 Assessment   454
       Sports & Entertainment Law   457

Unit 6 Legal Forms of Business Organization 462

Planning a Career in Law: Corporate
   Attorney 463
Entrepreneurs and the Law: Legal Forms of
   Business Organization 524

Community Action: Ethical Business
   Conduct 525
Winning Edge: FBLA Business Plan 525
Mock Trial Prep: Evidentiary Questions:
   Objections 526

Features in Unit 6

A Question of Ethics 467, 498, 512
Cyberlaw 494, 516
Economic Impact 488, 514
Global Issues 473, 490
Hot Debate 464, 486, 508
In This Case 467, 472, 477, 487, 495, 502,
   509, 516

Law Brief 480, 498, 518
Legal Research 471, 501, 518
Net Bookmark 466, 494, 517
Online Research 503
What's Your Verdict? 465, 469, 473, 476, 479,
   487, 490, 493, 496, 500, 501, 509, 511, 514, 517

Chapter 26 Forms of Business Organization 464

26-1   Main Forms of Business Organization 465
26-2   Creating and Terminating Partnerships 469
26-3   Operating Partnerships   476
       Chapter 26 Assessment   482
       Case For Legal Thinking   485

Chapter 27 The Law of Corporations 486

27-1   Founding a Corporation   487
27-2   Shareholders, Directors, and Officers 493
27-3   Corporate Powers and Termination   500
       Chapter 27 Assessment   504
       Sports & Entertainment Law   507

Chapter 28 Organizational Forms for Small Business 508

28-1   Traditional Small Business Forms   509
28-2   New and Evolving Small Business
       Forms   514
       Chapter 28 Assessment   520
       Sports & Entertainment Law   523

Unit 7 Borrowing Money and Paying Bills 528

Planning a Career in Law: Forensic
   Accountant   529
Entrepreneurs and the Law: Borrowing Money
   and Paying Bills   614
Community Action: Protect Against Identity
   Theft   615

Winning Edge: BPA Extemporaneous
   Speaking   615
Mock Trial Prep: Closing Arguments   616

Features in Unit 7

A Question of Ethics   534, 554, 563, 578, 602
Cyberlaw 539, 570
Economic Impact   581, 604
Global Issues   538, 548
Hot Debate   530, 544, 560, 576, 592
In This Case   533, 546, 553, 561, 569, 578, 584,
   594, 601

Law Brief   531, 547, 568, 577, 605
Legal Research   538, 551, 570, 584, 606
Net Bookmark   534, 548, 564, 582, 599
Online Research   609
What's Your Verdict?   531, 532, 537, 545, 546,
   551, 552, 561, 562, 564, 568, 577, 578, 581,
   586, 593, 597, 601, 604, 606

Chapter 29 Commercial Paper   530

29-1   Basic Types of Commercial Paper   531
29-2   Specialized Types of Commercial
       Paper   537
       Chapter 29 Assessment   540
       Case For Legal Thinking   543

Chapter 30 Negotiability and Negotiation of Commercial Paper   544

30-1   Requirements of Negotiability   545
30-2   Proper Indorsement and Negotiation   551
       Chapter 30 Assessment   556
       Case For Legal Thinking   559

Chapter 31 Discharge of Commercial Paper and Electronic Fund Transfers   560

31-1   Discharge of Commercial Paper   561
31-2   The Law of Electronic Fund Transfers   568
       Chapter 31 Assessment   572
       Case For Legal Thinking   575

Chapter 32 Secured and Unsecured Credit Transactions   576

32-1   What Is a Secured Credit Transaction?   577
32-2   How Are Security Interests Perfected
       and Terminated?   581
       Chapter 32 Assessment   588
       Case For Legal Thinking   591

Chapter 33 Creditors, Debtors, and Bankruptcy   592

33-1   Legal Protection of Creditors   593
33-2   Legal Protection of Debtors and
       Credit Card Users   597
33-3   Bankruptcy   604
       Chapter 33 Assessment   610
       Case For Legal Thinking   613

Appendix A Constitution of the United States   618

Appendix B The Declaration of Independence   630

Glossary of Legal Terms   633

Case Index   649

Index   652

To the Student

You will soon find business law is one of your most valuable subjects. You will study true situations that show how business and personal law impacts not only business, but the lives of young people and adults as well. The learning package will help you achieve an understanding of legal principles you will use throughout your life. Use the following plan to help you effectively study *Law for Business and Personal Use*.

How to Study the Textbook

- Each chapter opens with a *Hot Debate*. Read the *Hot Debate* scenario and then discuss with your class the questions that go along with it.

- Each chapter is divided into two or three lessons. Each lesson has a list of *Goals* at the beginning. Read the *Goals* and then scan the lesson to see where each goal is addressed.

- Read each lesson slowly and carefully. Make notes of important points. In the *Student Activities and Study Guide,* there is an outline of every lesson to help you take notes.

- Each main topic heading is followed by a *What's Your Verdict?* scenario. Try to answer the question. Then read the following paragraphs to learn the law that applies to *What's Your Verdict?* before you go on to the next topic.

- As you read, apply what you learn to your own experiences or those of your family and friends. Think about situations within your own experience to which the law applies.

- At the end of each main topic section, ask yourself the *Checkpoint* question to review the material.

- After you have carefully studied the lesson, complete the exercises in *Think About Legal Concepts* and *Think Critically About Evidence*.

- After you complete all the lessons in a chapter, read the *Concepts in Brief* to refresh your memory. Then complete *Your Legal Vocabulary, Review Legal Concepts, Write About Legal Concepts, Make Academic Connections,* and *Analyze Real Cases*.

- The exercises in *Think Critically About Evidence* help you apply what you learned in the chapter. *Analyze Real Cases* allows you to work with the facts from real lawsuits related to the topics in each chapter.

Special Features

- **A Question of Ethics** presents ethical issues that arise within the legal framework.

- **Cyberlaw** discusses emerging legal aspects of the Internet and e-commerce.

- **Economic Impact** discusses a situation in which the law is affected by a certain economic circumstance.

- **Global Issues** illustrates legal procedures and issues in other nations.

- **Hot Debate** promotes thoughtful discussion of important legal issues.

- **In This Case** demonstrates legal principles and concepts through hypothetical situations.

- **Law Brief** provides unusual or interesting facts or ideas related to the law.

- **Legal Research** helps you investigate issues relating to federal, state, and local laws using Internet and library resources.

- **Net Bookmark** encourages you to use the Internet for research. Find the URLs you need to complete the research on the Xtra! web site at school.cengage.com/blaw/lawxtra.

- **Planning a Career in Law** introduces you to seven law-related careers within various career clusters.

- **Online Research** gives you a scenario and then instructs you to use the Findlaw web site to answer questions about it.

- **What's Your Verdict?** motivates you to learn new legal concepts.

Mock Trial Competitions

- **Mock Trial Prep** features in each unit cover court and trial procedures to prepare you for participation in mock trial competition.

Real-World Cases

- **Case for Legal Thinking** presents important real-world cases for analysis and discussion.
- **Sports & Entertainment Law** presents cases involving sports and entertainment figures.

Projects

- **Entrepreneurs and the Law** allows you to apply the law to a start-up business situation.
- **Community Action** provides ideas for getting involved and making a difference in your local, national, and global communities.
- **Winning Edge** helps you prepare for business law-related FBLA and BPA competitive events.

How to Analyze Legal Situations

Following each lesson and each chapter you will find a number of legal situations in *Think Critically About Evidence*. You also will find actual cases that have been decided by courts in *Analyze Real Cases, Case for Legal Thinking,* and *Sports & Entertainment Law.* You may use the same method to analyze all of these exercises. To answer the question raised, first read it carefully. Be sure you understand the question and the facts involved. Then determine the rule of law involved and reach a decision. You will find it helpful to answer these questions.

- What are the facts?
- What is the disputed point?
- What rule of law is involved?
- How does this rule apply to the facts?
- What is the answer or decision?

How to Analyze Ethical Situations

An ethical dilemma is posed in A Question of Ethics. You can use the ethical frameworks described in Lesson 1-3 to analyze these dilemmas.

To analyze the dilemmas using ethical reasoning based on consequences,

- Describe alternative actions that would improve the situation.
- Forecast consequences that would flow from each alternative described.
- Evaluate the consequences for each alternative by selecting a standard for judging right or wrong consequences.

To analyze the dilemmas using fundamental ethical rules,

- "Universalize" the action in question.
- Determine whether the action is irrational, illogical, or self-defeating.

How to Read Case Citations

Law cases are referenced in a way that makes them easy to find. There are three parts to a citation. For example, 28 A2d 309 identifies (1) a series of law books, (2) one volume in that series, and (3) the page where the case begins. In the example, A2d identifies the series of books that report the decisions of certain courts. The A stands for Atlantic Reporter, a series that reports the cases of appellate courts in the North Atlantic Region. The 2d indicates that the case appears in the second series of the Atlantic Reporter. The 28 in this example citation refers to Volume 28 in the series. The case begins on page 309.

Legal Advice

Consult a lawyer if you have any doubts about your rights or duties when your property, life, or liberty is endangered or if significant changes occur in your circumstances.

- Familiarize yourself with local, state, and federal laws to help avoid violations. Ignorance of the law normally is no excuse.
- Remember that as a minor you generally are liable for crimes and torts and bound by contracts.
- If you are involved in a legal dispute, try to learn the other person's version and honestly seek a friendly solution out of court. In every court action at least one person loses and often both find the costs burdensome.
- If someone injures you or your property, do not rush to sign a statement releasing the person from liability in exchange for some payment of money. The damages may be greater than they appear at first. Consult your attorney immediately.
- Although oral agreements can be legally binding, you should write out all contracts that involve significant time, money, or detail and have both parties sign and receive copies.

Unit 1
Law, Justice, and You

Chapters

1 Laws and Their Ethical Foundation

2 Constitutional Rights

3 The Court System

4 Criminal Law and Procedure

5 Civil Law and Procedure

Planning a Career in Law

Trial Lawyer

Are you good at arguing and debate? Do you like to defend others? Are you passionate about justice being served for the good of society? If so, you might consider a career as a trial lawyer.

Trial lawyers are needed in both criminal and civil law courts. Trial lawyers must be able to think quickly and speak with ease and authority. Knowledge of courtroom rules and strategy is particularly important in trial work. Trial lawyers spend most of their time outside the courtroom, conducting research, interviewing clients and witnesses, and handling other details in preparation for a trial. Criminal trial attorneys work as defense attorneys or for the local, state, or federal government as a prosecutor.

EMPLOYMENT OUTLOOK

- Employment opportunities for trial lawyers are expected to grow steadily through 2014, primarily as a result of growth in the population and in the general level of business activities.

- Competition for job openings should continue to be keen because of the large number of students graduating from law school each year. Graduates with superior academic records from highly regarded law schools will have the best job opportunities.

- The willingness to relocate may be an advantage in getting a job, but to be licensed in another state, a lawyer may have to take an additional state bar examination.

NEEDED SKILLS AND EDUCATION

- Prospective lawyers should develop proficiency in writing and speaking, reading, researching, analyzing, and thinking logically. A multidisciplinary background is recommended.

- Students interested in a particular aspect of law may find related courses helpful.

- Courses in English, foreign languages, public speaking, government, philosophy, history, economics, mathematics, and computer science, among others, are useful.

- The required college and law school education usually takes seven years of full-time study after high school—four years of undergraduate study, followed by three years of law school. Law school applicants must have a bachelor's degree to qualify for admission.

How you'll spend your day

As a new trial lawyer you'll put in long hours assisting senior lawyers. The work involves fact gathering and legal research. The amount of information you'll need to organize and sort before trial can be daunting, but the work is excellent training. After awhile you'll sit in on trials, participate in conferences with judges, and prepare arguments.

Eventually you will represent your own clients in court. In a criminal case you may represent the prosecution or the accused. In a civil case you'll take the side of your client in a private dispute. Your job will be to persuade a jury of the facts in the case. You'll present the facts in a way that best supports your client's position, using evidence to prove your case.

When not in court you'll review files, contact witnesses, take depositions, and talk to your client. Preparing for a trial can take weeks or months. Many cases settle before they ever reach trial. In these instances you'll work for the best settlement for your client. On court days you'll meet with judges, select jurors, and argue your case.

What about you?

Does the job of trial attorney interest you? Why or why not? Which aspects of the job would you most enjoy? Which aspects would you least enjoy?

Chapter 1
Laws and Their Ethical Foundation

1-1 Laws and Legal Systems

1-2 Types of Laws

1-3 Ethical Bases for Laws

HOT DEBATE

With her stereo system blasting, Clarisse began her drive home from school in her small pickup. She was soon pulled over by a police officer. The officer cited her for violation of the city's noise ordinance. As he did so, his voice was partially drowned out by the sound of jack hammers from a nearby construction site. Clarisse asked the officer why he had not cited the construction company as well. He replied that, even though the company was in violation, the noise ordinance had been put on the books to stop people from playing loud music in public, not to stop honest work.

WHERE DO YOU STAND?

1. Is the ordinance fair?
2. Has the ordinance been fairly applied?
3. Can you suggest some changes in the ordinance that might make it a better law?

© GETTY IMAGES/PHOTODISC

1-1 Laws and Legal Systems

What Is Law?

WHAT'S YOUR VERDICT? Two archeologists, Professor DiPalermo and Professor Shuster, were deciphering some stone law tablets from the Middle East dating back before 2000 B.C.E. Looking up from his work, Professor DiPalermo commented that, while the amount of knowledge held by humanity had increased dramatically, its basic nature had not changed. Professor Shuster agreed, saying, "Just compare the laws they had way back then with the ones we have now. We're still making the same mistakes and still need the same protections from the conduct of others."

Do you think their observations are correct?

The **laws**, or enforceable rules of conduct in a society, reflect the culture and circumstances that create them. Laws may be grouped into an organized form referred to as a **code**. When you compare one civilization's code with the codes of other civilizations, you see many similarities. For example, the law code set down about four thousand years ago by Hammurabi, King of Babylon, had sections on criminal law, property law, business law, family law, personal injury law, labor law, and others. Such coverage is similar to that found in the U.S. law codes today.

The professors in *What's Your Verdict?* were correct. The need for law has not changed much over recorded history. People still make the same mistakes and still need the same protections from the conduct of others.

Stages In the Growth of Law

Most societies go through four distinct stages in forming their legal systems:

1. Individuals are free to take revenge for wrongs done to them
2. A leader acquires enough power to be able to force revenge-minded individuals to accept an award of goods or money instead
3. The leader gives this power to a system of courts
4. The leader or central authority acts to prevent and punish wrongs that provoke individuals to seek revenge

© NORTH WIND PICTURE ARCHIVES

The law code set down by King Hammurabi of Babylon contained sections or categories similar to those found in modern U.S. law codes. How do you think the *specific content* of Hammurabi's codes compares to that of U.S. law codes today?

In the first stage, injuries inflicted on one human being by another are matters for personal revenge. Those who are wronged feel that justice can be done only through personally punishing the wrongdoers. Gang wars in the inner cities often result from this type of attitude. Whether they occur in a big city or in a developing society, such events usually disrupt the normal productive routine of the people and result in harm to innocent bystanders.

The situation often leads to one individual taking power and exerting control to bring peace to the society. To achieve this peace, the powerful leader or authority, often called the *sovereign,* hears and resolves disputes between the people. The sovereign then forces the injured parties to accept awards of money or goods as a substitute for their taking revenge. This is the second stage in the growth of law.

In many civilizations, the sovereign ultimately becomes faced with more cases than one person can handle. As a consequence, the sovereign sets up a system of courts and gives them powers to decide certain types of disputes. Elders or priests generally preside over these courts. However, the sovereign still presides over the most important matters.

In the fourth and final stage, the sovereign takes a step beyond being merely a passive authority working only to resolve disputes after they occur. Instead the sovereign tries to prevent breaches of the peace before they can occur. The sovereign does this through enforcing a set of laws and matching punishments.

Common Law versus Positive Law

Laws reflect the wisdom—or lack thereof—of their creators. In any society laws should be both predictable and flexible. A system of laws that is not predictable will not produce a stable society. Chaos, unrest, and the replacement of the system by one that can exercise control and restore peace will follow.

A legal system that is too controlling and too rigid to change with the wants and needs of the people also will be overthrown. The best system of laws always evolves slowly towards a form that is most appropriate to the current standards of the people.

Law based on the current standards or customs of the people is called **common law**. Common law usually is formed from the rules used by judges to settle people's disputes. However, as noted earlier, some laws are set down by a sovereign or other central authority to prevent disputes and wrongs from occurring in the first place. Law dictated from above in this fashion is called **positive law**.

CHECKPOINT How does common law differ from positive law?

What Is the Origin of the U.S. Legal System?

WHAT'S YOUR VERDICT? LaBonne, from Louisiana, was visiting his cousin in St. Louis, Missouri. While they were talking about the differences in traffic laws in the two states, LaBonne told his cousin that Louisiana's legal system was different from that used in Missouri and all the other states.

Is LaBonne correct?

The world's two great systems of law are the English common law and the Roman civil law. Countries with systems patterned after the Roman civil law have adopted written, well organized, comprehensive sets of statutes in code form. The laws in these codes are typically only changed by the central government, not by the

GLOBAL ISSUES

Napoleonic Code

The territory that is now Louisiana was claimed for France by the explorer Lasalle in 1682. French settlers brought many French influences to the state of Louisiana—customs, food, language, and law. Louisiana's legal system was developed using the French Code Napoléon (or Napoleonic Code) as a foundation. However, regardless of the legal system it uses, over the years Louisiana has modified its laws to correspond with those of the other 49 states. The Napoleonic Code was derived from Germanic customs and Roman law. The Napoleonic Code also was the model for the civil law codes of Italy, the Netherlands, Spain, and the Canadian Province of Quebec.

judges who administer them. Only one state in the United States—Louisiana—has a civil law system. The legal system used in the other 49 states is based on the English common law. Therefore, in *What's Your Verdict?*, LaBonne was correct.

Colonists from England brought the common law system to this continent. To understand how this system works, you must look back to England to see how it was developed.

English Common Law

Before the English common law system developed, feudal barons acted as judges within their territories. Disputes were settled on the basis of local customs and enforced by the barons' power. Because of this, the laws of England differed from region to region. Such differences were difficult for people to follow. They also made it hard for a central government to maintain control.

KING'S BENCH Around 1150 King Henry II decided to improve the situation. He appointed a number of judges from a group of trusted nobles. King Henry gave these judges the power to order that wrongdoers pay with money or goods the parties they injured.

In good-weather months the judges would "ride circuit" into the countryside, holding court in the villages. During bad-weather months, the judges stayed in London and sat together as a court to hear cases on appeal that might have been decided unwisely on circuit. This court so formed by the circuit-riding judges came to be called King's Bench—or Queen's Bench if the regent was female.

The baron's courts, which heard local cases before the King's courts were created, kept the power to decide some of the minor cases. However, the King's courts always had **jurisdiction**—the power to decide a case—over the most important cases.

JURY King Henry recognized that it was important to decide the court cases in harmony with the customs of the people. To do otherwise would cause unrest, if not revolution. The judges were instructed to choose citizens from each region to help interpret that region's customs for the court. This panel of citizens evolved into what we know today as the *jury.* The jury is an institution unique to the English common law system.

AN EXAMPLE The early system of English common law worked something like this. Imagine that a farmer named William is on his way to

Because he could not resolve all the disputes in the nation by himself, King Henry appointed a group of judges to decide them for him. What personal qualities do you think he looked for in these judges?

market one morning in his ox cart. He is traveling through an unfamiliar region. As he approaches an intersection, he sees another person in a similar ox cart coming into the intersection from his right.

In William's home region the right of way at an intersection goes to the person on the left. So he continues on, expecting the other person to rein in. The other party, a local resident named Gwen, does not yield and a collision results. Both William and Gwen are injured. Their oxen are gored. Their carts and other property are destroyed. As a consequence, the next time the circuit-riding judge comes into Gwen's region, both people appear in court and request damages (a monetary award) for their losses.

The judge needs to know who is at fault in the case in order to decide who must pay. To find out, the judge chooses a jury of 12 residents. These people must decide which person, according to their customs, acted improperly. The jury determines that, because the right of way customarily goes to the person on the right in their region, William is at fault and must pay Gwen damages. The judge accepts the decision and orders William to pay.

The decision, however, upsets William. He knows that throughout most of his travels the right of way is given to the person on the left. Therefore, he decides to take his case to the higher, or appellate, court—King's Bench in London—on appeal. That court will not be in session for several months yet, so William uses the time to collect information on the law used in other courts in England that have ruled on the issue of right of way. Finally, the time comes to appear before King's Bench. The judges listen to William's appeal and Gwen's defense of the lower court's decision.

The appellate court judges review the information presented to them by both parties, including the laws used by other courts to settle like issues. They decide that it would be wisest to reverse the holding in the lower court (that the right of way should go to the person on the right). Instead, says King's Bench, the right of way will be given to the person on the left. They send the case back down to the lower court with instructions to enter a judgment for damages in William's favor.

From that point on, anyone in the kingdom will need to give the right of way to the person on the left. If any lower court, including the one in Gwen's region, decides a case using a different rule, the result can be appealed to King's Bench, where it will be reversed.

ADVANTAGES OF ENGLISH COMMON LAW The judicial process described in the example was repeated over and over in England throughout the centuries. As a result, a uniform web of custom-based common law developed across the whole of England. The process used to achieve this end is called the English common law system. The English common law system achieves uniformity while maintaining an ability to adapt to changes in society. It has been a model for legal systems worldwide, including that in the United States.

Equity: An Alternative to Common Law

The common law courts carefully follow *precedent*. This means the courts use prior cases as a guide for deciding similar new cases as would be done with the decision in *William v. Gwen* above. Following precedent helps to provide stability in the law. However, if overdone it can have the disadvantage, as came to be the situation in old England, of requiring a rigid adherence to proper form. For example, a misplaced period or misspelled word could nullify, or void, the effect of a document.

Another disadvantage of the early common law system was that its courts could only grant the remedy of damages. This meant that common law courts had to wait until the harm actually occurred before they could take action.

For example, if a farmer decided to dam up the stream that watered the neighbor's crops and animals, the courts of law had to wait until the harm had occurred and then award the neighbor damages for what the farmer did. The courts of law could not order the farmer to stop building the dam. This inability to stop a wrong before it inflicted actual harm often resulted in a waste of resources from the perspective of the country as a whole.

However, if the neighbor were a noble, he might be able to get around the courts and directly petition the king for help. The king would refer the matter to his chancellor, who was usually a high clergyman respected for his **equity**, or fairness.

CyberLAW

Ah, the joys of e-mail—instant communication of thoughts. You feel it. You say it. You send it. But, if your message is perceived as a threat, you could be prosecuted and convicted for it. In the first conviction of an online hate crime, a 21-year-old Los Angeles man was found guilty in federal court. He sent death threats by e-mail to more than 50 Asian students. The case set a precedent, as it put Internet communications on equal legal ground with telephone calls and postal mail. It also addressed civil rights violations committed online—hate crimes in this case. The defense team argued this was a "stupid prank" and that so-called flames or abusive messages are commonplace with Internet culture and discussion groups. The jury thought otherwise and took the threats seriously. At first the Net was considered to be a fantasy land where users could be anonymous. This case shows that the legal system will not treat the Net differently from other forms of communication.

THINK ABOUT IT

Do you think people should be held accountable for threats they make online? Why or why not?

The chancellor would conduct a hearing under rules different from those of a common law court. There would be no jury, for example, and the remedies the chancellor could impose in the king's name were different from those available to the law courts.

The chancellor might issue an order to compel that something be done. Or, he might issue an *injunction,* which stops something from being done. For example, the chancellor could issue an injunction to stop the dam from being built. However, if the neighbor were not a noble, he would not have been able to petition the king. The harm would be allowed to occur.

Eventually the king sensed a need for access to equitable remedies for all citizens. He created a system of equity courts and placed them under the chancellor's control. These courts were given the power to issue injunctions or to compel

LAW BRIEF

Three states in the United States administer law and equity separately. In Delaware and Mississippi equity is administered in chancery courts. In Tennessee equity is administered in law-equity courts.

specific actions. In the United States today, law courts and equity courts generally are merged. Consequently, most American courts can award damages or issue orders or both.

CHECKPOINT On which early legal system is the U.S. legal system based?

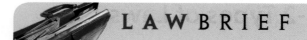

1-1 Assessment

school.cengage.com/blaw/lawxtra

THINK ABOUT LEGAL CONCEPTS

1. Substitution of damages for revenge is the first stage in the evolution of law. **True or False?**

2. The two systems of law in use today are the English common law and the (a) American Constitution (b) French legal code (c) Roman common law (d) none of the above.

3. A remedy of the English Courts of Equity was the (a) injunction (b) court order (c) disputation (d) none of the above.

4. Louisiana is the only one of the 50 states whose legal system was not originally based on the English common law system. **True or False?**

5. Most American law courts can use either damages or an injunction or both as remedies in civil cases. **True or False?**

THINK CRITICALLY ABOUT EVIDENCE

Study the situation, answer the questions, and then prepare arguments to support your answers.

6. You are on your daily jog when a car negligently pulls out in front of you. Unable to stop, you run into it and injure yourself. Should you be able to recover damages for the harm done to you?

7. The driver of the car in exercise 6 becomes abusive towards you after your recovery. The driver follows you on your jogs and yells threats at you. He has recently taken to driving very close to you as you jog. What can you do legally to make him stay away from you?

8. Cracked Mirror, a local rock group, contracts to play for your high school prom. A week before

the dance, the group cancels its appearance. A teacher finds out that the band booked a concert that will pay them $800 more. The class president's mother is an attorney and offers her services to the school. If you sue the band for damages, what would be an appropriate amount and why?

9. For the situation in exercise 8, fashion an equitable remedy that might encourage Cracked Mirror to decide to keep its commitment to play at your prom.

1-2 Types of Laws

GOALS

■ Identify the four sources of law
■ Discuss how conflicts between laws are resolved
■ Compare and contrast criminal and civil law, and substantive and procedural law

KEY TERMS

constitution	administrative agencies
statutes	civil law
ordinances	criminal law
case law	procedural law
stare decisis	substantive law

What Are the Sources of Law?

WHAT'S YOUR VERDICT? The federal Constitution guarantees the citizens of the United States many rights. These include freedom of speech, of press, of assembly, to petition, to bear arms, against unreasonable searches and seizures, and more.

What part of the U.S. Constitution contains most of these guarantees?

Laws in this country are created at all three levels of government—federal, state, and local. The forms that these laws can take include constitutions, statutes, case law, and administrative law.

Constitutions

A **constitution** is a document that sets forth the framework of a government and its relationship to the people it governs. When constitutions are adopted or amended, or when courts interpret constitutions, *constitutional law* is made. You are governed by both the Constitution of the United States and the constitution of your state. The Supreme Court of the United States is the final interpreter of the federal Constitution.

Constitutions are the highest sources of law, and the federal Constitution is "the supreme law of the land" (U.S. Constitution, Article VI). This means that any federal, state, or local law is not valid if it conflicts with the federal Constitution. Similarly, within each state the state constitution is supreme over all other state laws.

Federal and state constitutions are concerned primarily with defining and allocating certain powers in our society. Constitutions allocate powers (1) between the people and their governments, (2) between state governments and the federal government, and (3) among the branches of the government.

ALLOCATION OF POWER BETWEEN PEOPLE AND THEIR GOVERNMENTS The federal Constitution is the main instrument for allocating powers between people and their governments. It does this primarily with its first ten amendments, called the *Bill of Rights*. The Bill of Rights protects people from actions of their governments. This is the section of the federal Constitution referred to in *What's Your Verdict?* The Bill of Rights will be discussed in detail in Chapter 2.

LEGAL *Research*

The Fraudulent Online Identity Sanctions Act (H.R.3754) was signed into law in December 2004. It increased prison sentences by up to seven years for someone who provided "material and misleading false contact information to a domain name registrar, domain name registry, or other domain name registration authority." It was intended to prevent online scams and also make it much easier for the recording studios and movie producers to track down copyright violators and obtain the $150,000 per violation damages. However, opponents of the law saw it as a danger to the exercise of several Constitutional rights. They also claimed it would be ineffective in achieving its intended results. Research and assess the accuracy of these criticisms. Does the Act achieve its intended goals?

Railroads often are used to transport goods over long distances. What type of commerce, interstate or intrastate, does this represent, and which level of government most likely regulates it?

ALLOCATION OF POWER BETWEEN FEDERAL AND STATE GOVERNMENTS The federal Constitution also allocates powers between the federal and state governments. For example, many governmental powers over business are divided between state governments and the federal government on the basis of commerce. In general, the Constitution gives the federal government the power to regulate both foreign and interstate commerce. *Interstate* commerce occurs between two or more states. The power to regulate *intrastate* commerce, which occurs within one state, is left with that state.

ALLOCATION OF POWER AMONG THE BRANCHES OF GOVERNMENT State and federal constitutions also allocate governmental powers among the three branches of government: executive, legislative, and judicial. Traditionally these powers are distributed so as to create a system of checks and balances between the branches of each government. This ensures that no branch of government becomes too powerful. For example, the U.S. Constitution gives the federal courts the authority to determine which laws passed by Congress are constitutional. However, in turn it gives Congress the power to ordain and establish the courts in the first place.

Statutes

The federal Constitution created the Congress of the United States. State constitutions created the state legislatures. These state and federal legislatures are composed of elected representatives of the people. Acting for their citizens, these legislatures enact laws called **statutes**.

In addition, all states delegate some legislative authority to local governments. Thus, towns, cities, and counties can legislate on matters over which the state has given them authority. These pieces of legislation created by a town or city council or by a county board or commission are typically referred to as **ordinances**. They are only effective within the boundary of the local governments that enacted them.

Case Law

The judicial branch of governments creates **case law**. Case law usually is made after a trial has ended and one of the parties has appealed the result to a higher court. This appeal will be based on legal issues arising from rulings made by the lower court in deciding the case.

When the appellate court publishes its opinion on a case, that opinion may state new or more appropriate rules to be used in deciding the case and others like it. These rules are referred to as case law at either the federal or state level.

The effectiveness of case law arises out of the doctrine of **stare decisis**. This is Latin for "let the decision stand." This doctrine requires that lower courts must follow established case law in deciding similar cases. Generally, case law doctrines are carefully established and seldom revoked. However, the doctrine of *stare decisis* generally does not bind supreme courts.

IN THIS CASE Carol borrowed her stepfather's car without his express permission. The police stopped her and discovered the car was not registered in her name. They then phoned her stepfather. When he said he did not know where his car was, Carol was arrested. At her trial, Carol and her stepfather testified that she had his permission to use the car without asking each time. The trial judge nevertheless found Carol guilty of auto theft, which, the judge stated, occurs when one person takes the car of another without expressly asking permission. Carol appealed to the state supreme court. That appellate court issued an opinion stating implied permission is enough, and, therefore, Carol was innocent. This rule then became state case law to be applied in similar cases.

Administrative Law

Federal, state, and local legislatures all create administrative agencies. **Administrative agencies** are governmental bodies formed to carry out particular laws. The federal Social Security Administration, your state's division of motor vehicles, and your county's zoning commission are examples of administrative agencies.

Although created by legislatures, administrative agencies usually are controlled by the executive branch of government. Thus, the president, governor, or mayor will supervise the agency's activities. Legislatures sometimes give administrative agencies legislative powers and limited judicial powers. Legislative power means the agency is authorized to create administrative laws, also called *rules* and *regulations.* For example, the federal Social Security Administration might establish rules for determining when a student is depending on support from a widow or widower and thereby qualified to receive Social Security payments.

If an agency has judicial power, it can hold hearings, make determinations of fact, and apply the law to particular cases. In the above example, the Social Security Administration might hold a hearing to judge whether a *particular* student is in fact a dependent. Once this determination is made, the Social Security Administration would use its executive powers to carry out the rules on payments to dependents of widows or widowers.

CHECKPOINT What are the four sources of law?

What Happens When Laws Conflict?

WHAT'S YOUR VERDICT? When adopted, the U.S. Constitution provided that there could be no income tax. So when Congress levied a 2 percent income tax in 1894, the U.S. Supreme Court declared it unconstitutional. Many people wanted the federal government to raise money by taxing incomes because the burden imposed would be based on one's current ability to pay.

What did the people do to override the Supreme Court decision?

Sometimes laws created by different levels of government conflict. For example, a city ordinance setting a speed limit of 35 mph on a state highway near an elementary school may conflict with a state statute setting 45 as a minimum speed limit on state roads. Different types of laws created by the same level of government also may conflict. A federal administrative regulation requiring the phase-out of coal-fired electric-generating plants may conflict with a federal court decision holding that such regulations are unconstitutional.

In these situations, legal rules are used that determine which statement of the law is superior to the other and should therefore be enforced. Generally, these *supremacy* rules hold that federal law prevails over state law and state law prevails over local (city and county) law. Within the state and federal systems, constitutional law prevails over statutory law and statutory law over administrative law. Finally, within the state and federal court systems, a higher court's decision prevails over a lower court's.

CONSTITUTIONS AND VALIDITY Constitutions are the highest sources of law, and the federal Constitution is "the supreme law of the land" (U.S. Constitution, Article VI). This means that any federal, state, or local statute, case law or administrative decision is not valid if it conflicts with the federal Constitution. Within each state's legal jurisdiction, the state constitution is supreme to all other state laws.

When any type of law is declared invalid by a state or federal court because it conflicts with a constitution, it is said to be *unconstitutional.* Such a determination may be appealed to the highest court within the state and federal systems. Within the federal system, the U.S. Supreme Court has the final say. The highest state court wins out on state issues. Of course, even when interpreting constitutions, courts are not the ultimate authority. The people have the power to amend constitutions if they disagree with the courts' interpretations.

In answer to *What's Your Verdict?* the people's response to the Supreme Court decision was the Sixteenth Amendment to the U.S. Constitution. Adopted in 1913, it gave Congress the power to lay and collect an income tax. This in effect nullified the U.S. Supreme Court decision.

STATUTES AND VALIDITY As discussed, statutes or ordinances must be constitutional to be valid. In addition, when needed in a particular case, courts also examine the statutes and ordinances involved to see whether or not the law's enactment exceeded the scope of the powers of the body that authored it.

ADMINISTRATIVE REGULATIONS AND VALIDITY Administrative regulations also can be reviewed by courts to determine whether they are constitutional. The courts also may invalidate a rule or regulation if it is outside the scope of powers delegated to the agency by the legislature that created it.

CASE LAW AND VALIDITY A case law decision by a court holding a statute invalid is not always the end of the issue. A legislative body has the power to nullify a court's interpretation of a statute or ordinance by rewriting the statute. Administrative agencies also can revise their regulations when challenged.

CHECKPOINT Which source of law in the United States is the highest authority?

What Are the Main Types of Laws?

WHAT'S YOUR VERDICT? Bolyston was steering her 18 wheeler down a steep hill in the outside lane of westbound I–44. Gradually her speed built up to over 85 mph. On the right-angled curve at the bottom of the hill, the truck's speed carried it into the inside lane where it side-swiped JJ's car and forced it into a guard rail. JJ lost control and his car veered across both eastbound lanes and into a concrete barrier. Thanks to a seat belt, an air bag, and quick avoidance by other traffic, JJ's injuries were minor, but his car was demolished.

Did Bolyston violate civil law or criminal law or both?

Laws may be classified in various ways. Common classifications include civil law, criminal law, procedural law, substantive law, and business law.

Civil and Criminal Laws

When the private legal rights of an individual are violated, the matter is governed by civil law. The use of the term **civil law** within the common law system refers to the group of laws that allows individuals to seek legal remedies for wrongs done to them. (Civil law in this sense does not refer to the comprehensive system of law mentioned in Lesson 1-1.)

For example when a tenant fails to pay the rent as promised, the landlord has the right to sue the tenant. (The police do not take action in civil matters.) If a defendant loses a civil case, that defendant is liable. This means that she or he must pay compensation to the plaintiff for his or her loss. This is typically done by the payment of money in civil matters. In addition to enforcing legal promises, civil law also applies whenever one person is injured by another. Such private wrongs (civil offenses) against people or organizations are referred to as *torts.*

A *crime* is an offense against society rather than individuals. It disrupts the stable environment that we all depend upon to make civilization work. So, when the citizens' right to live in peace is violated by such activity, the offense is governed by **criminal law.** Acting in the name of all the people, the government investigates an alleged wrongdoing. If a crime has been committed and the person responsible can be found, the government will prosecute. Conviction of a crime can result in a fine, imprisonment, and in some states, execution.

Usually when a crime occurs, private injuries may be inflicted as well. A result may be both a crime and a civil offense. Thus, the civil law may also apply, and the victim of the crime may sue the wrongdoer.

In *What's Your Verdict?* Bolyston committed both a crime and a civil offense. Exceeding the

© GETTY IMAGES/PHOTODISC

Is shoplifting a crime or a tort? Explain your answer.

speed limit was a crime for which Bolyston could be arrested, convicted in a criminal trial, and fined. In addition, Bolyston committed a civil offense when she carelessly allowed her truck to smash into the side of JJ's car. JJ could probably win a civil lawsuit against Bolyston for compensation for his injuries and the value of his car.

Procedural and Substantive Laws

Procedural law sets forth how rights and responsibilities can be legally exercised and enforced through the legal system. Procedural laws, for example, determine what remedies are available in a lawsuit and how those remedies are to be secured. They determine whether equitable remedies, such as an injunction, are available. The doctrine of *stare decisis* is a procedural law. Rules for determining the supremacy of conflicting laws are procedural laws.

In contrast, **substantive law** defines rights and duties. It is concerned with all rules of conduct except those involved in enforcement. Substantive laws define offenses, such as murder, theft, breach of contract, and negligence.

There are two types of procedural law: civil procedure and criminal procedure. *Criminal procedure* defines the process for enforcing the law when someone is charged with a crime. *Civil procedure* is used when a civil law has been violated. Civil law is concerned only with private offenses. When a civil law is violated the injured party is entitled to protect his or her rights. Police and public prosecutors generally do not involve themselves in the dispute.

Business Law

Business law covers rules that apply to business situations and transactions. This book's table of contents shows that the scope of business law is broad. Business law is important for all students—not just those planning careers in business or law. Most business transactions involve a merchant and a consumer. As you study business law, you will gain legal knowledge that will make you a better consumer.

Business law mainly is concerned with civil law, especially contracts. The area of the law pertaining to commercial torts is another category of business law. Such torts are distinct from breaches of contracts. For example, torts may occur when manufacturers make defective products that injure users. Business activities are at times also governed

© GETTY IMAGES/PHOTODISC

Assume that the woman in this photo is a public prosecutor giving her closing argument in a case to a jury. Is this most likely a civil trial or a criminal trial? Justify your answer.

by criminal law. For example, criminal law would punish a firm that conspires with competitors to fix prices or an employee who steals company tools.

UNIFORM BUSINESS LAWS Laws of our various states do not have to be alike as long as they are constitutionally valid. However, with the growth of interstate commerce and large business firms, more uniformity among state laws governing business and commercial transactions is important.

Committees of legal experts have written model laws covering such areas as sales, certain credit transactions, and business forms. Sets of these model laws were then offered to the states for adoption in place of their current statutes covering the areas. The result has been more uniformity in state commercial laws. The *Uniform Commercial Code (UCC)* is a widely adopted uniform business law. It governs such areas as sales of goods, certain aspects of banking, and leases of goods. You will learn more about the UCC throughout this book.

CHECKPOINT Compare and contrast criminal and civil law and substantive and procedural law.

TYPES OF LAW	
Constitutional law	Based on constitutions
Statutory law	Enacted by legislative bodies
Administrative law	Rule-making by administrative agencies
Civil law	Addresses wrongs done to individuals
Criminal law	Addresses wrongs done to society
Procedural law	Deals with methods of enforcing legal rights and duties
Substantive law	Defines legal rights and duties
Business law	Rules that apply to business transactions

1-2 Assessment

Xtra!
Study Tools
school.cengage.com/blaw/lawxtra

THINK ABOUT LEGAL CONCEPTS

1. The first ten amendments to the U.S. Constitution are known as the _ ?_.

2. Which of the following would not be considered civil law? (a) contract law (b) tort law (c) felonies (d) All of the above would be considered civil law.

3. Legislative enactments by a city government are called _ ?_.

4. *Stare decisis* is the doctrine that requires lower courts to adhere to existing case law in their decisions. **True or False?**

5. Torts are private wrongs committed against individuals or organizations. **True or False?**

6. Business activities are at times governed by criminal law. **True or False?**

7. Businesses cannot commit torts. **True or False?**

8. The statutory definition of murder is a (a) substantive law (b) procedural law (c) prohibitive law (d) none of the above

THINK CRITICALLY ABOUT EVIDENCE

Study the situation, answer the questions, and then prepare arguments to support your answers.

9. Suppose the principal of your public school required all students to recite a prayer at the start of each school day. What level of government (federal, state, or local) would most likely determine whether or not the principal's action was constitutional?

10. In exercise 9, what governmental body would make the determination?

11. Sonoma County passed a law making it legal to drive 65 mph on freeways inside the county. A state law limited all vehicles anywhere in the state to 55 mph. What is the valid speed limit on freeways inside this county?

12. In 1896, the U.S. Supreme Court held in *Plessy v. Ferguson,* 163 U.S. 537, that equal treatment of different races is provided when public and semipublic facilities, even though separate,

are substantially equal in quality. For years, railroad cars, buses, schools, and other facilities had separate and supposedly equal facilities for blacks. In 1954 black plaintiffs in Delaware, Kansas, South Carolina, and Virginia sought admission for their children to public schools on an integrated basis. Does the doctrine of *stare decisis* bar the U.S. Supreme Court from changing the law declared in *Plessy v. Ferguson?* (*Brown v. Board of Education,* 347 U.S. 483)

13. On a two-week vacation in a neighboring state, you buy several large firecrackers and take them home. A police officer notices them in your car on a routine traffic stop. She cites you for possession of an illegal explosive device, which is a felony in your state. Possession of fireworks in the neighboring state is not a crime. Can this be a defense for you?

1-3 Ethical Bases for Laws

GOALS

- Define ethics
- Compare and contrast consequences-based ethics with rule-based ethics
- Discuss ways in which ethics are reflected in laws

KEY TERMS

ethics

civil disobedience

Ethics and the Law

WHAT'S YOUR VERDICT? In the early 1960s, Dr. Martin Luther King, Jr., wanted to lead a march into Birmingham, Alabama, to protest racial segregation in that city. When he applied for a parade permit, his request was denied. Dr. King, knowing that his conduct was illegal, led the nonviolent march anyway. He was at the front of the line and allowed himself to be arrested, although he could have escaped easily. He went to jail. Community leaders were highly critical of Dr. King because he had violated the law.

Was there sufficient ethical justification for Dr. King's violation of the law?

Ethics is a practice of deciding what is right or wrong in a reasoned, impartial manner. To involve ethics, a decision must affect you or others in a significant way. An ethical decision is one that is reasoned out typically by referring to an established authority that provides consistency. The law is such an authority. So are religious texts such as the Torah, the Bible, and the Koran. For example, a person might reason, "I believe that God is the source of the Bible, and the Bible tells me not to lie. Therefore, it would be wrong, or unethical, for me to lie." To make ethical decisions, we usually must base our decisions on reason, not on emotion.

In addition to being reasonable, ethical decisions should be impartial. *Impartiality* is the idea that the same ethical standards are applied to everyone. The reason you are learning about ethics in general is to prepare you to apply ethical concepts to business decision making. *Business ethics* are the ethical principles used in making business decisions.

All too often, however, ethics are not considered when business decisions are made. The reason can be summarized in two words: profit maximization. The idea of profit maximization is supported by those who need a justification for actions that would hurt the general welfare. These actions might include moving factories offshore, having skilled jobs done overseas instead of by American workers, and buying solid, conservatively run companies only to close them down and sell the company's assets piecemeal. To move toward a more ethically motivated economy, the profit maximization justification for such actions will need to be replaced by more humane ethical standards.

Basic Forms of Ethical Reasoning

Ethical reasoning about right and wrong takes two basic forms. One form is based on consequences. In this style of ethical reasoning, rightness or wrongness is based only on the results of the action. Particular acts have no ethical, or moral, character.

IN THIS CASE As Gabriella was pulling out of her parking spot at the mall, her tires slipped on the coating of ice and snow left by a recent winter storm. Her car slid sideways, causing her bumper to crunch into the back fender of the car parked next to her. Gabriella's car was undamaged by the impact, but the bumper left a large dent and deep scratches on the other car. Gabriella realized she could just drive off without anyone knowing. Then she considered that the damage would probably cost more than a thousand dollars to repair. Consequently, she flagged down a mall security car and had the other owner paged so as to take appropriate responsibility.

An act that produces good consequences is good. An act that produces bad consequences is bad.

The other form of moral reasoning is based on ethical rules. In this style of reasoning, acts are either right or wrong. For example, telling the truth is always right, and lying is always wrong. In rule-based ethics, good consequences do not justify wrong or bad acts. For example, in rule-based ethics, you cannot justify lying by showing that it produces good consequences.

For almost all ethical decisions, these two forms of reasoning reach the same conclusion. In the decision of whether to lie or to tell the truth, for example, both forms usually conclude that one should not lie.

CONSEQUENCES-BASED ETHICAL REASONING

Consequences-based reasoning first looks for alternative ways to alter the current situation. Then it attempts to forecast the consequences that will arise from each alternative. Finally, it evaluates those possible consequences to select the alternative that will generate the greatest good. This last criterion often is very subjective as to how one defines the good—financial reward, pleasure, love, justice. Who will be receiving "the good" often is a major consideration in this reasoning process.

RULE-BASED ETHICAL REASONING
With fundamental ethical rules, the acts themselves are judged as right or wrong. The standard for judging usually comes from one of two sources—a recognized authority or human reasoning.

The authority, frequently a religious source, often clearly prescribes what is correct by time-tested rules such as those found in the Ten Commandments. Human reasoning also can

show what is basically wrong or right. A test, called *universalizing,* has been developed to help in this effort. In universalizing, you picture everyone doing the action and then ask yourself, "Would the result be irrational, illogical, or demeaning?" If so, the action is considered ethically wrong.

Ethics Reflected in Laws

Under the U.S. system of democracy, representatives must vote for laws that are acceptable to the

Universalize cheating on tests. Is it unethical? Why or why not?

© PHOTODISC/GETTY IMAGES

majority of people if the representatives expect to be reelected. Because this system is grounded on majority rule, it uses many of the features of consequences-based ethics. In this system, laws are judged to be right or good when they affect the majority of the people positively. Laws are judged to be wrong when they affect the majority negatively. Thus the government, empowered by the U.S. Constitution, seeks to ensure that the federal lawmaking system provides the greatest good for the greatest number.

On the other hand, the Constitution also seeks to protect the well-being of minorities that might be taken advantage of by the wrong actions of the majority. This is done primarily through the rights preserved in the first ten amendments to the Constitution. Such protection of basic human dignity afforded by the Bill of Rights and other civil rights laws reflect ethics based on rules.

Both ethics based on consequences and ethics based on rules conclude that we are obligated to obey the law. According to consequences-based reasoning, when the law is violated, many more people are injured than are benefited. With rule-based reasoning, if we say that we have agreed to obey the law but violate it, we are breaking our promise. If we universalize promise breaking by imagining that everyone always breaks promises, there would be no point to promising. In this universalized state, promise breaking is illogical or pointless and thus wrong.

Even if unethical, the ease with which laws can be broken, especially by those with superior abilities or knowledge, such as a computer programmer, makes such behavior tempting. Aware of this, employers often purchase fidelity bonds for persons who handle large sums of money, such as cashiers, managers of movie theaters, or supervisors of restaurants. A *fidelity bond* is an insurance policy that pays the employer money in the case of theft by employees.

Unethical, lawbreaking behavior does not always occur on a large scale, however. Often, individuals do not obey even minor laws. These individuals are termed *scofflaws*. These are persons who do not respect the law at all. They simply assess the risk of being caught and punished against the benefits they obtain by breaking the law. They lack personal *integrity*, or the capacity to do what is right in the face of temptation or pressure to do otherwise. They think they are smart because they frequently violate valid laws without being caught. A scofflaw is never ethically justified in violating the law.

In contrast to the self-serving behavior of scofflaws, some people care passionately about ethical behavior, human rights, and justice. Their concern for justice sometimes compels them to violate what they consider to be an unjust law—a law they believe to be in conflict with ethical reasoning. They violate the law by engaging in acts of civil disobedience.

Civil disobedience is an open, peaceful, violation of a law to protest its alleged, or supposed, injustice. The goal of those who engage in civil disobedience is not to advance their self-interest but rather to make the legal system more just. The participants may be willing, or even eager, to be arrested in order to test the validity of the law in court.

In *What's Your Verdict?* Dr. Martin Luther King, Jr., engaged in civil disobedience. Dr. King believed that civil disobedience is justified only in very limited circumstances. He and others conclude that civil disobedience is ethical when

■ a written law is in conflict with ethical reasoning

■ no effective political methods are available to change the law

- the civil disobedience is nonviolent
- the civil disobedience does not advance a person's immediate self-interest
- the civil disobedience is public and one willingly accepts the punishment for violating the law

As a result of Dr. King's efforts, many human rights were extended for the first time to several minority groups in this country.

CHECKPOINT In the U.S. system of democracy, how are ethics reflected in laws?

Access school.cengage.com/blaw/lawxtra and click on the link for Chapter 1. Read the excerpt from Dr. Martin Luther King's autobiography. How did Henry David Thoreau's essay on "Civil Disobedience" influence Dr. King's development as a civil rights activist?

school.cengage.com/blaw/lawxtra

1-3 Assessment

school.cengage.com/blaw/lawxtra

THINK ABOUT LEGAL CONCEPTS

1. Ethics is a practice of deciding what is right or wrong in a reasoned, _?_ manner.
2. The two forms of ethical reasoning almost never reach the same conclusions. **True or False?**
3. Which of the following best describes the elements involved in civil disobedience? (a) violating the law (b) violating the law openly (c) violating the law openly and peacefully (d) violating the law openly, peacefully, and accepting punishment for the violation
4. Majority rule usually involves which of the following types of ethical reasoning? (a) reasoning based on consequences (b) rule-based reasoning

THINK CRITICALLY ABOUT EVIDENCE

Study the situation, answer the questions, and then prepare arguments to support your answers.

5. Conner walked past the candy section in the grocery store and quickly stuffed a handful of candy bars into her purse. A store security guard saw her do it, and she was arrested. Her parents came to the police station after her arrest to take her home. Did Conner's shoplifting significantly affect anyone? If so, who? Was Conner basing her conduct on emotion or reason? Was she treating herself and the other customers and stockholders of the store equally?

6. Sharon knows about tax laws and how the Internal Revenue Service (IRS) audits tax returns. She knows a way to cheat on her tax return that would save her almost $2,000. She thinks her chance of being caught is about one in 100. Can this cheating be justified by reasoning based on ethical rules? Can it be justified by ethics based on consequences?

7. An ordinance of Walker County provided that all automobiles must pass a smog emissions test once a year. Ross was ticketed because his car had not been inspected and approved at a testing center. Ross claimed to be a skilled mechanic who kept his car well tuned and cleaner than the law required. According to Ross, the law violated his natural rights. Explain why you agree or disagree with Ross.

8. If a legislature enacted a law that made it illegal to shout "fire" in a movie theater, would the dominant ethical character of the law reflect consequences-based or rule-based reasoning?

9. Assume a state legislature enacted legislation which budgeted more money to educating rich children than to educating poor children. Also assume that the majority of children are poor. Would complying with the law reflect more of a rule-based or a consequences-based ethic?

Chapter 1 Assessment

CONCEPTS IN BRIEF

1-1 Laws and Legal Systems

1. Laws are the enforceable rules of conduct in a society.

2. The two great systems of law in the world are the English common law and the Roman civil law. The legal systems of all the states except Louisiana are based on the English common law.

3. Sources of law include constitutions, statutes, cases decided by appellate courts, and regulations and rulings of administrative agencies.

1-2 Types of Laws

4. Civil law is concerned with the private legal rights of individuals and governs relations between individuals. Criminal law deals with crimes (offenses against society) and governs the behavior of individuals in relation to the laws of a society.

5. Procedural law deals with methods of enforcing legal rights and duties. Substantive law defines those rights and duties.

1-3 Ethical Bases for Laws

6. Business law is concerned with the rules that apply to business situations and transactions.

7. Ethical reasoning should be applied to reach reasonable and impartial decisions that affect people.

8. Ethics are either based on consequences or on fundamental rules.

9. Civil disobedience is the open, peaceful violation of a law to protest its alleged injustice or unfairness. It is only justified in rare and extraordinary circumstances.

YOUR LEGAL VOCABULARY

Match each statement with the term that it best defines. Some terms may not be used.

1. Doctrine requiring lower courts to adhere to existing case law in making decisions
2. Group of laws that set forth how rights and responsibilities can be legally exercised and enforced through the legal system
3. Enforceable rules of conduct in a society
4. Law based on the customs of a group of people
5. Legislative enactment by a city
6. Group of laws defining and setting punishments for offenses against society
7. An open, peaceful, violation of a law to protest its alleged injustice
8. Power of a court to decide a case
9. Law enacted by state legislatures or federal legislatures
10. Law made when an appellate court endorses a rule to be used in deciding court cases
11. The practice of deciding what is right or wrong in a reasoned, impartial manner
12. Document that sets forth the framework of a government and its relationship to the people it governs
13. Group of laws that allows individuals to seek legal remedies for wrongs done to them
14. Laws grouped into an organized form
15. Fairness
16. Law dictated from above

a. administrative agency
b. case law
c. civil disobedience
d. civil law
e. code
f. common law
g. constitution
h. criminal law
i. equity
j. ethics
k. jurisdiction
l. laws
m. ordinance
n. positive law
o. procedural law
p. *stare decisis*
q. statute
r. substantive law

REVIEW LEGAL CONCEPTS

17. Louisiana is the only one of our 50 states whose law was not originally based on the English common law system. What system was its law based on? How did this system come to be used?

18. Why should a constitution be considered the highest law of a nation or a state?

19. What does the phrase "interstate commerce" mean to you? Would you consider growing vegetables in your garden for your own consumption interstate commerce? Why or why not?

20. Why does the doctrine of *stare decisis* not bind supreme courts?

21. Why are most fines the courts assess for criminal behavior paid to the government and not to the victim of the crime?

22. Explain how both rule-based ethical reasoning and consequences-based ethical reasoning conclude that people are obligated to obey the law.

23. Identify a situation in your life where someone used rule-based ethical reasoning.

24. Describe the three steps involved in making a decision using consequences-based ethics.

WRITE ABOUT LEGAL CONCEPTS

25. Would you rather be under the control of a system of common law or positive law? Write a paragraph to explain your answer.

26. Why is it important to have uniform state laws governing business? Write a paragraph to list and discuss at least four reasons.

27. Use one to three words to identify a current event that others will quickly recognize. Next, write a paragraph evaluating someone's conduct in the current event using the ethics of reasoning based on consequences.

28. Use one to three words to identify a current event that others will quickly recognize. Next, write a paragraph evaluating someone's

conduct in the current event using the ethics of rule-based reasoning.

29. Create and write a scenario which raises an ethical issue. Try to create a scenario where something is wrong in rule-based reasoning but right in reasoning based on consequences.

30. **HOT DEBATE** Clarisse is convicted of a violation of the noise ordinance. Her appeal is dismissed. As a consequence, she organizes a group of friends with cars to drive through the neighborhoods of the city with their stereos going at full volume as an act of civil disobedience. Is she ethically justified in so doing? Why or why not?

THINK CRITICALLY ABOUT EVIDENCE

Study the situation, answer the questions, and then prepare arguments to support your answers.

31. You are in France and are accused of a crime. You ask for a trial by jury. Why is one not available?

32. Your friend Bill has shared with you his dream of getting rid of the income tax. He says that if the people wanted to, they could pass a constitutional amendment that would eliminate the tax. Is he correct?

33. Juana was trying to decide whom to vote for in an upcoming election. After reviewing the candidates, she said, "I've decided to vote for Gary because I just feel better about him." Is Juana's decision based on ethics? If not, why?

34. Staub, Conly, and Winfield were employees of the Prime Time Restaurant. They were aware that the owner never checked the totals on the sales checks against the cash in the register. Therefore, it would be very easy to steal from the cash register. However, they did not steal. When asked why, they gave the following reasons. Staub said he did not take the money because he was afraid of being caught. Conly said she did not take the money because she felt obligated to obey the law. Winfield said he did not take the money because of his religious beliefs. To which person do you best relate? Why?

MAKE ACADEMIC CONNECTIONS

35. **MEDICINE** As medical science moves forward, major ethical issues are developing that are likely to be encountered in the courts and legislative bodies. Identify such issues in medical fields such as cloning, cryogenic preservation, organ marketing and farms, etc. Choose one of these issues, and apply both consequences-based and rule-based ethical reasoning to determine whether it is ethical or not. Write a paragraph summarizing your findings.

ANALYZE REAL CASES

36. Alaska enacted a statute known as "Alaska Hire." It required employers in the state to hire qualified Alaskan residents in preference to nonresidents. Hicklin, a nonresident, sued Orbeck, the state official charged with enforcing the statute. After the Supreme Court of Alaska found the statute constitutional, Hicklin appealed to the U.S. Supreme Court, which found the statute to be in conflict with the U.S. Constitution. Which supreme court is the final authority in this case? (*Hicklin v. Orbeck,* 437 U.S. 518)

37. The city of Chicago sued to stop the operation of the Commonwealth Edison Company's coal-burning, electricity-generating plant in nearby Hammond, Indiana. Chicago claimed that the plant emitted too much smoke, sulfur dioxide, and other harmful substances. The city also claimed that the plant was a common-law public nuisance because it caused "an unreasonable interference with a right common to the general public" to clean air. Edison argued that it had spent much money to reduce harmful emissions and that the emissions were now well below the levels prescribed by federal clean air regulations and by the city of Hammond. Edison also pointed out that "unpleasant odors, smoke, and film" already characterized the area in which the plant was located. The trial court refused to issue an injunction. Therefore, the city of Chicago appealed to a higher court, which affirmed (upheld) the trial court. How can this legal action be ethically justified? (*City of Chicago v. Commonwealth Edison Company,* 321 N.E.2d 412, Ill.)

38. On March 30, 1981, as then President Ronald Reagan left the Washington Hilton Hotel after giving a speech, he was wounded by one of a series of bullets allegedly fired by John Hinckley. Three other men also were wounded, including James Brady, the President's press secretary, who received a severe wound to the head. President Reagan underwent surgery shortly thereafter at the hospital. Hinckley was arrested at the scene literally with the smoking gun. Soon after the criminal process was begun against him, he underwent two psychiatric examinations by order of the magistrate and then the chief judge involved in the case. Both examinations found him to be competent. On August 28, after being indicted by a federal grand jury, Hinckley pled not guilty to a battery of charges, including the attempted assassination of the President of the United States. Hinckley's lawyers then began their work. In two very important rulings they were able to suppress the use of evidence that would have been very damning to the defendant. They first had thrown out all answers he had given to questions prior to having his attorney present. This was done even though he had been read his Miranda rights three times before agreeing to answer those questions. Then Hinckley's attorneys were able to suppress allegedly incriminating material in the form of a diary gathered by the jailers when they checked Hinckley's cell for contraband and instruments useful in a potential suicide attempt. These rulings by the court were based on the constitutional rights to counsel and to protection against improper searches and seizures. Do you consider their use in this case a proper application of such rights? Is the exclusion of the evidence the only possible remedy, or could you come up with another one? If so, what is it, and why would it be an improvement over the current policy? (*United States v. John W. Hinckley, Jr.,* 525 F. Supp. 1342)

Sports & Entertainment Law

2 Live Crew Raps Roy Orbison's "Oh, Pretty Woman"

ACUFF-ROSE MUSIC INC. V. CAMPBELL
972 F. 2D 1429

BACKGROUND The hit song for singer Roy Orbison in 1964, "Oh, Pretty Woman" also was the theme song for "Pretty Woman," a hit movie three decades later. Orbison became famous for his rendition of the song. After eight more top-ten hits, he was inducted into the Rock and Roll Hall of Fame in 1987. Orbison died a short time later at age 52.

FACTS When "Pretty Woman" was recorded in parody form by 2 Live Crew in the early 1990s, the holder of the copyright, Acuff-Rose Music Inc., brought suit for infringement. 2 Live Crew had faced similar conflicts before. Manager-performer Luke, through his company Luke Records, previously had paid George Lucas $300,000 for using the name of Lucas' *Star Wars* character Luke Skywalker. The U.S. Supreme Court, which already had overturned a Florida court's declaration of another 2 Live Crew recording as obscene, was called upon to rule in the "Oh, Pretty Woman" case. Here are some comparative first-stanza lyrics:

Roy Orbison's version
Pretty Woman, walking down the street
Pretty woman, the kind I like to meet
Pretty woman

I don't believe you, you're not the truth
No one could look as good as you

2 Live Crew's version (Luke rapping, entire group's words in parentheses)
(Pretty woman)
Ha haaa, walkin' down the street
(Pretty woman)
Gir, girl, you look so sweet
(Pretty woman)
You, you bring me to the knees
(Pretty Woman)
You make me wanna beg please
(O-o-o-o-oh, pretty woman)

THE LAW Section 107 of the Copyright Act allows the "fair use" without permission of copyrighted material for criticism, comment, news reporting, teaching (including classroom use in the form of multiple copies), scholarship, and research without being considered infringement.

THE ISSUE Does the publication of a parody for commercial gain fall within the protection afforded by Section 107?

HOLDING The Court held that 2 Live Crew's version of the song was a ridiculing commentary on Orbison's work and deserving of protection against the infringement charges. As long as the work was intended as a parody and not for advertising for the group or its products, the fact that it was a commercial success for 2 Live Crew does not bar the Crew from using the Section 107 defense.

PRACTICE JUDGING

1. Assess the Court's holding from a consequences-based ethical standpoint.

2. Assess the Court's holding from a rule-based ethical standpoint.

© RUNN WOLFSON/TIME LIFE PICTURES/GETTY.IMAGES

Chapter 2
Constitutional Rights

2-1 Foundations of the U.S. Constitution

2-2 Division and Balance of Governmental Powers

2-3 The Internet and Constitutional Rights

HOT DEBATE

The original draft of the Declaration of Independence condemned the slave trade and criticized the English people. Both passages were edited out by the delegates of the Continental Congress before the Declaration was approved.

WHERE DO YOU STAND?

1. Why do you think the passages were omitted?
2. Was omitting them a good or bad idea? Why?

© GETTY IMAGES/PHOTODISC

2-1 Foundations of the U.S. Constitution

GOALS

- Identify the documents written in the course of the nation's founding
- Explain how the U.S. Constitution addresses and protects citizens' civil rights

KEY TERMS

Declaration of Independence

Articles of Confederation

U.S. Constitution

Bill of Rights

civil rights

due process of law

The Documents That Formed a Nation

WHAT'S YOUR VERDICT? When the Constitutional Convention sent the proposed Constitution to the states for ratification, it met with strong opposition. Patrick Henry, James Monroe, and John Hancock, for example, all opposed it. When the Constitution was put into effect in 1789, two colonies had yet to ratify it. The ratification did not become unanimous until 1790.

What caused the opposition to the Constitution? What action resolved the dispute?

Declaration of Independence

On July 4, 1776, delegates from the 13 original American colonies to the second Continental Congress, meeting in Philadelphia, formally adopted the **Declaration of Independence**. Thomas Jefferson of Virginia drafted the Declaration in less than a month. The document asserted the rights the colonists desired. It charged King George III of England with "a history of repeated injuries and usurpation" for the purpose of establishing an "absolute tyranny. . . ." It declared that "all men are created equal, that they are endowed by their Creator with certain unalienable rights, that among these are life, liberty, and the pursuit of happiness." (See the full text of the Declaration of Independence in Appendix B on page 630.)

© NORTH WIND/NORTH WIND PICTURE ARCHIVES

This image is a reproduction of a famous painting by John Trumbull entitled "Declaration of Independence." The painting has been criticized for showing a scene that never took place. That is, according to historians, all 48 men shown in this picture were never gathered in the same place at the same time. Despite this criticism, do you think the picture is historically valuable? Why or why not?

The authors of the Declaration of Independence believed that to secure these rights, they would need to have their own government. This new government would draw its power from the people.

At the time the Declaration was adopted, fighting between British troops and colonists had already begun. The American War of Independence that followed lasted more than eight years, with the colonies claiming ultimate victory.

Articles of Confederation

The 13 former colonies, each with its own independent form of government, united in 1781 under a charter called the **Articles of Confederation**. The Articles of Confederation contained the following provisions:

- the government was to be conducted by a one-house legislature (the "United States in Congress") with two to seven representatives from each state; each state, however, had only one vote on issues before the Congress

- strict term limits (no person could serve more than three years in a 6-year period) placed on members of Congress, who were subject to recall by their states

- the legislature had only the power to declare war, make peace, enter into treaties and alliances, manage relations with Indian nations, coin money, settle differences between states, establish a postal system, and appoint a Commander in Chief; all other powers were reserved to the states

- paying for the common defense or general welfare came from a common treasury funded by the states in proportion to the value of all land within each state

- paupers, vagabonds, fugitives from justice, and slaves were not entitled to the privileges and immunities of free citizens of the states

- major legislation, including bills relating to finance, would require a two-thirds vote for passage

- amendments to the Articles would require a unanimous vote of the states

Many people felt a need for a stronger central government than the one the Articles provided. Disagreement among the states regarding the Articles ultimately led to the calling of a special convention of delegates from the original 13 states.

ORDER OF RATIFICATION OF THE U.S. CONSTITUTION	
1. Delaware	December 7, 1787
2. Pennsylvania	December 12, 1787
3. New Jersey	December 18, 1787
4. Georgia	January 2, 1788
5. Connecticut	January 9, 1788
6. Massachusetts	February 6, 1788
7. Maryland	April 28, 1788
8. South Carolina	May 23, 1788
9. New Hampshire	June 21, 1788
10. Virginia	June 26, 1788
11. New York	July 26, 1788
12. North Carolina	November 21, 1789
13. Rhode Island	May 29, 1790

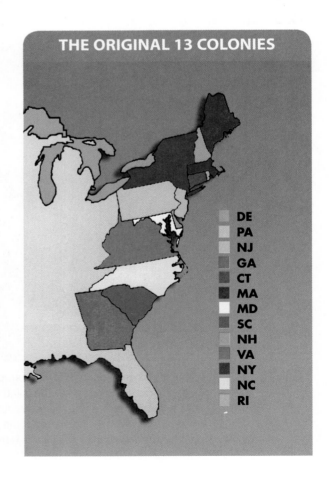

THE ORIGINAL 13 COLONIES

DE
PA
NJ
GA
CT
MA
MD
SC
NH
VA
NY
NC
RI

U.S. Constitution

The special convention, held in Philadelphia in the summer of 1787, drafted the initial **U.S. Constitution**. The seven articles of the U.S. Constitution provided a workable framework for a federal government. By June 21, 1788, the Constitution had been ratified by delegates to special conventions held in nine of the original 13 colonies. (See the full text of the U.S. Constitution in Appendix A on page 618.)

As specified in Article VII of the Constitution, ratification by at least nine prospective states was enough to put the Constitution in force. Consequently, March 4, 1789, was selected as the date the government of the United States of America was to begin operation under the new Constitution. Ratification took so long to be approved in all the states because critics felt the wording of the Constitution failed to provide adequate protection of the human rights proclaimed in the Declaration of Independence. In *What's Your Verdict?* North Carolina and Rhode Island took longer to ratify because they felt this fundamental problem with the Constitution—the failure to protect human rights—had to be corrected. The situation was resolved by the adoption of the Bill of Rights.

The Bill of Rights

The first ten amendments to the Constitution, known as the **Bill of Rights**, were adopted to ensure that U.S. citizens would enjoy the human rights proclaimed in the Declaration of Independence. Three documents that helped secure the rights of individuals in England contributed greatly to our own Bill of Rights. These were: The Magna Carta, the Petition of Right of 1628, and the Bill of Rights.

The amendments in the U.S Bill of Rights shown below are in the words of the founding fathers.

AMENDMENT I Congress shall make no law respecting an establishment of religion, or prohibiting the free exercise thereof; or abridging the freedom of speech, or of the press, or the right of the people peaceably to assemble, and to petition the Government for a redress of grievances.

AMENDMENT II A well regulated Militia, being necessary to the security of a free State, the right of the people to keep and bear Arms, shall not be infringed.

AMENDMENT III No Soldier shall, in time of peace be quartered in any house, without the consent of the Owner, nor in time of war, but in a manner to be prescribed by law.

AMENDMENT IV The right of the people to be secure in their persons, houses, papers, and effects, against unreasonable searches and seizures, shall not be violated, and no warrants shall issue, but upon probable cause, supported by oath or affirmation, and particularly describing the place to be searched, and the persons or things to be seized.

AMENDMENT V No person shall be held to answer for a capital, or otherwise infamous crime, unless on a presentment or indictment of a Grand Jury, except in cases arising in the land or naval forces, or in the Militia, when in actual service in time of War or public danger; nor shall any person be subject for the same offense to be twice put in jeopardy of life or limb, nor shall be compelled in any criminal case to be a witness against himself, nor be deprived of life, liberty, or property, without due process of law; nor shall private property be taken for public use without just compensation.

AMENDMENT VI In all criminal prosecutions, the accused shall enjoy the right to a speedy and public trial, by an impartial jury of the State and district wherein the crime shall have been committed, which district shall have been previously ascertained by law, and to be informed of the nature and cause of the accusation; to be confronted with the witnesses against him; to have compulsory process for obtaining witnesses in his favor, and to have the assistance of counsel for his defense.

AMENDMENT VII In Suits at common law, where the value in controversy shall exceed twenty dollars, the right of trial by jury shall be preserved, and no fact tried by a jury shall be otherwise re-examined in any Court of the United States, than according to the rules of the common law.

AMENDMENT VIII Excessive bail shall not be required, nor excessive fines imposed, nor cruel and unusual punishments inflicted.

AMENDMENT IX The enumeration in the Constitution of certain rights shall not be construed to deny or disparage others retained by the people.

AMENDMENT X The powers not delegated to the United States by the Constitution, nor prohibited by it to the States, are reserved to the States respectively, or to the people.

Civil Rights

★ **WHAT'S YOUR VERDICT?** One afternoon, during a class break, Bill and Santos were talking. Bill complained that his parents had been monitoring the web sites he had visited on his computer. "I can't believe they can do that. What about my civil right of privacy?" Santos replied, "I went through the same thing with my parents. When I complained about it, my dad said there was no mention of a right of privacy in the Constitution."

Was Santos' father correct?

The First Amendment protects your right to practice the religion of your choice. If the founding fathers believed that freedom of religion was important, why do you think they opted for separation between church and state?

Through the Bill of Rights and other amendments that were to follow, the Constitution became a shield for the personal, natural rights of the individual. These rights are referred to as **civil rights**. The most vital of these rights are those protected by the First Amendment: freedom of speech, freedom of the press, and freedom to assemble.

The First Amendment also protects the people's rights to practice the religion of their choice. Religion has inspired men, women, and children to noble and caring conduct. However, misguided religious zeal also has caused great violence and destruction. The founders of the republic recognized this deep-seated religious impulse but wisely imposed a role of neutrality for the government. They created a wall of separation between church and state. The government tolerates all religions but supports none in any strictly religious efforts.

Due Process of Law

Another significant amendment in the Bill of Rights is the Fifth Amendment. It states, "No person shall be . . . deprived of life, liberty, or property, without due process of law . . ." Unlike the Declaration of Independence, the Constitution does not mention "the pursuit of happiness." However, respect by others for one's life, liberty, and property surely helps one to be secure and content, if not consciously happy.

The Constitution does not spell out what is meant by due process. The term has, however, come to be defined through various U.S. Supreme Court decisions. At the present time **due process of law** is taken to mean that, at a minimum, a defendant over whom jurisdiction has been established must be provided adequate notice and a proper hearing. Due process of law requires fundamental fairness in compliance with reasonable and just laws. If convicted, the criminal may be deprived of property by fine, of liberty by imprisonment, and even of life by lawful execution.

Due process of law is a concept embodied throughout the Constitution. It is assured by guaranteeing

■ the right to be secure against unreasonable searches and seizures (Fourth Amendment)

■ the right not to be a witness against yourself in any criminal case (Fifth Amendment)

■ in criminal prosecutions, the right for the accused to a speedy and public trial by an impartial jury of the state and district where the crime was committed, and to be informed of the nature and cause of the accusation;

© GETTY IMAGES/PHOTODISC

the right to be confronted with the witnesses against him; to have a set process for obtaining witnesses in his favor, and to have the benefit of a defense counsel (Sixth Amendment)

■ trial by jury in civil suits where the value in controversy exceeds $20 (Seventh Amendment)

■ that excessive bail will not be required nor excessive fines imposed, nor cruel and unusual punishment inflicted (Eighth Amendment)

The Abolition of Slavery

Originally the practice of slavery was enabled under the Constitution. In particular, the Constitution provided that Congress could not prohibit, prior to 1808, the "migration or importation of such persons. . . ." Slaves were further dehumanized by a provision in Article I that counted them as only three-fifths of a person for the purpose of apportioning representatives to Congress. Under Article IV, a slave who escaped to another state had to be returned to "the party to whom such service or labor may be due."

Finally, as a consequence of the Civil War, these provisions were negated by the Thirteenth Amendment, which states in part, "Neither slavery nor involuntary servitude, except as a punishment for a crime whereof the party shall have been duly convicted, shall exist within the United States, or any place subject to their jurisdiction."

The Right to Vote

The Fifteenth Amendment provided the newly freed slaves the legal right to vote. It decreed, "The right of citizens of the United States to vote shall not be denied or abridged by the United States or by any State on account of race, color or previous condition of servitude." Although the Thirteenth Amendment abolished slavery, and the Fifteenth guaranteed the former slaves the right to vote, racial discrimination continued in both the North and the South. Some southern states enacted a *poll tax.* This was a fixed payment per person required before the person could vote. Many former slaves could not afford to pay a tax in order to vote.

In 1964, more than 100 years after the Civil War began, the Twenty-Fourth Amendment guaranteed that the right to vote in federal elections "shall not be denied or abridged . . . by reason of failure to pay any poll tax or other tax." The Supreme Court subsequently applied the same rule to all state elections, declaring such

taxes unconstitutional under the Fourteenth Amendment.

DENIAL BY GENDER The exclusion of "gender" in the Fifteenth Amendment was a deliberate denial of voting rights to women of all races. This injustice was removed in 1920 with the passage of the Nineteenth Amendment. It provided "The right of citizens of the United States to vote shall not be denied or abridged by the United States or by any State on account of sex."

DENIAL BY AGE Students protested during the Vietnam War, in part, because they objected to being eligible to fight in a war at the age of 18— but not vote until age 21. One result of these student protests was the hasty enactment of an amendment that gave all citizens age 18 or older the right to vote. The Twenty-Sixth Amendment was approved overwhelmingly by the Senate and House in March 1971. It was ratified by 38 states within three months.

A Question of ETHICS

The Emancipation Proclamation by President Abraham Lincoln is looked upon as a landmark in the struggle against slavery. Many historians, however, see it purely as a political ploy. They point out that it actually freed only a handful of individuals, if any at all. By its wording it did not apply in the border states where slaves were held but who were fighting on the union side. Nor did it apply in the areas of the Confederacy held by union forces. Of course, the Confederate states did not act in compliance with it. Do you think that Lincoln acted ethically by limiting his proclamation to a strictly political position? Why or why not?

Peripheral Rights

Some rights are not explicitly mentioned in the U.S. Constitution or Bill of Rights, but courts have recognized them as necessary to protecting the rights that are mentioned. The *right of privacy* is such a peripheral right—it is not specifically mentioned in the Constitution or Bill of Rights. In the 1960s the U.S. Supreme Court acknowledged the right of privacy as a separate right. The right of privacy has since been reinforced by several federal acts.

In *What's Your Verdict?* even though Santos' father was technically correct, the civil right of privacy does exist. However, concurrent with that right is the right of parents to control the health and welfare of their children. Therefore, such monitoring of web-site visits of underage children is legally permissible.

CHECKPOINT How does the Constitution address and protect citizens' civil rights?

2-1 Assessment

school.cengage.com/blaw/lawxtra

THINK ABOUT LEGAL CONCEPTS

1. The Declaration of Independence was adopted on (a) July 4, 1776 (b) July 4, 1789 (c) July 4, 1861

2. The "inalienable rights" mentioned in the Declaration of Independence are "life, liberty, and the pursuit of _ ?_."

3. The American War of Independence lasted about (a) two years (b) four years (c) eight years (d) ten years

4. The 13 colonies originally created a common government under the "Articles of Incorporation." **True or False?**

5. Opponents of the ratification of the original Constitution claimed the wording failed to protect human _?_.

6. _ ?_ was the thirteenth state to ratify the U.S. Constitution.

7. Which of the first 10 amendments guarantees freedom of the press? (a) First (b) Second (c) Third (d) freedom of the press is not guaranteed in the Bill of Rights

8. The original Bill of Rights contains the right of peaceful assembly. **True or False?**

9. Paupers, vagabonds, fugitives from justice, and slaves were not entitled to the privileges and immunities of free citizens under the Articles of Confederation. **True or False?**

10. The right of privacy was not acknowledged as a separate right until the 1960s. **True or False?**

THINK CRITICALLY ABOUT EVIDENCE

Study the situation, answer the questions, and then prepare arguments to support your answers.

11. It is 1793 and you are a citizen and editor of a newspaper in one of the original states. Your newspaper regularly carries stories about corruption in state government. Finally, the state prosecuting attorney brings charges against you for criticism of government officials, a violation of state law, and closes your newspaper. You maintain that your freedom of the press under the U.S. Constitution has been violated. The prosecutor replies that the Bill of Rights does not protect you from state actions. Is the prosecutor correct?

12. You are a citizen of one of the 13 colonies. The time is mid-July 1776. You have just heard of the issuance of the Declaration of Independence. What reasons might cause you to withhold your support of the Declaration?

13. As a protest against overseas military action by the government, about 600 sign-carrying students from a local school gathered peacefully at a major road intersection. As curious drivers slowed to observe, traffic came to a standstill. Within minutes, the police moved in and forced the crowd to break up. Several individuals who dropped their signs and "went limp" on the pavement were arrested. Did the police action violate the protesters' First Amendment constitutional right "peaceably to assemble"?

2-2 Division and Balance of Governmental Powers

GOALS

- Describe the system of checks and balances in the U.S. government
- Explain how the power to govern is divided between the federal and state governments

KEY TERMS

system of checks and balances

impeachment cases

political party

amendment

democracy

republic

sovereignty

interstate commerce

intrastate commerce

A System of Checks and Balances

WHAT'S YOUR VERDICT? Thomas was critical of the U.S. Constitution because he said it had not been ratified by a democratic vote of the people. Shakira said in response that of course it had been.

Who is correct?

Warren E. Burger, former Chief Justice of the U.S. Supreme Court, has pointed out that at the time the Constitution was drafted and adopted, "There was not a country in the world that governed with separated and divided powers providing checks and balances on the exercise of authority by those who governed." The 55 delegates who drafted the U.S. Constitution displayed great foresight in devising a unique **system of checks and balances**. This system is based upon the creation of a balance of power between governmental branches by having the powers given one branch check the powers given another.

Branches of Government

The three branches of the U.S. government are the legislative, the executive, and the judicial.

LEGISLATIVE BRANCH The legislative branch makes the laws. At the federal level, the heart of the legislative branch is the Congress. When the Constitution was drafted, the convention delegates were concerned with equal representation in Congress. States with small populations worried they might lose some of the independence they enjoyed under the Articles of Confederation. States with large populations feared they would be dominated by the less populous states (of which there were many more), if each state had an equal number of votes.

The solution? The national legislature would consist of two bodies:

1. a Senate, with two members from every state—regardless of population, and
2. a House of Representatives, with seats allocated to the states in proportion to their population.

The existence of two bodies allows for various checks and balances. For instance, all bills for taxing or appropriating funds must originate in the House. However, a majority vote of both bodies is required for passage of any bill, including tax and appropriations bills.

Even the checks the legislative branch can exercise on the abuse of power by the executive or judicial branches are divided between the two houses of Congress. For example, the House has the power to impeach or accuse any civil officer of the United States—including the President and Vice President—of treason, bribery, or other high crimes and misdemeanors. However, the Senate has the sole power to try all impeachment cases. **Impeachment cases** are criminal proceedings against a government official for misconduct in office. Conviction in such cases requires a two-thirds vote of the Senate members present.

Finally, the people may vote for their representatives in elections to the House (for a two-year term), the Senate (for a six-year term), and the executive office (for a four-year term).

EXECUTIVE BRANCH The executive branch is headed by the President and the Vice President. These officers are elected by a vote of the people.

In the electoral process, citizens vote for the electors who are pledged to support candidates selected by political parties. Because the President and the Vice President are not elected directly by the people, the candidate who receives the greatest popular vote for president may not always win the office. This has occurred four times, in 1824, 1876, 1888, and 2000.

A **political party** is a private organization of citizens who select and promote candidates for election to public office. Party members agree with these candidates on important governmental policies and legislation. Political parties are not mentioned in the Constitution.

JUDICIAL BRANCH The third branch of government is the judiciary. It is headed by the Supreme Court of the United States. Ultimately, the Supreme Court decides on the constitutionality of a statute passed by the legislative branch and signed by the President as head of the executive branch. The Supreme Court also may decide if a particular action or decision exceeds the powers granted to the executive branch or legislative branch under the Constitution. If so, the action or decision is void.

Changing the Constitution

A major check is provided by the power of constitutional **amendment** meaning to change or alter. The Constitution may be amended in two ways. The first way has been used for all amendments adopted to date. The amendment is proposed by a two-thirds majority vote in both the Senate and the House. The second way requires the legislatures of two-thirds of all the states to call a convention of all the states. The convention may propose one or more amendments. Under either method of proposal, the amendment becomes a valid part of the U.S. Constitution only if it is ratified by the legislatures of three-fourths of the states, or if it is ratified by conventions in three-fourths of the states.

The U.S. Form of Government

In a pure **democracy**, every adult citizen may vote on all issues. This is almost impossible to make happen in a nation of more than 300 million-people. Instead, the United States is a **republic** or a representative democracy. Voters select their representatives to the legislative, executive, and judicial branches of government.

Although representatives make the day-to-day decisions, the sovereign power ultimately resides in the people. This means that the highest final authority to decide what the law shall be rests with the citizens who exercise their right and duty to vote. In many elections only a minority of the total number of voters who are eligible actually exercise this right.

NETBookmark

Access school.cengage.com/blaw/lawxtra and click on the link for Chapter 2. Check out the "failed amendments"—amendments that never received the level of support needed to ratify them—or amendments recently proposed by Congress. Choose one of the failed or proposed amendments. Write a paragraph describing the amendment, and then explain whether you agree or disagree with it.

school.cengage.com/blaw/lawxtra

GLOBAL ISSUES

Democratic Representation in Hungary

The history of democratic representation in Hungary is long and complicated. For nearly a thousand years, the only form of representation was an assembly of nobles called the Diet which met infrequently at different places around the country. Finally, due to the reforms introduced in the nineteenth century, a parliament was formed. Unfortunately, the parliament was relatively weak, and Hungary was dominated by outside powers. In 1867, the parliament gained considerable powers when the Austrian emperor Franz Joseph agreed that Hungary should be administered as a separate nation within the empire.

The parliament continued into the twentieth century as a semi-representative body. After the collapse of Communism in 1989, Hungary gained its first parliament that truly represented all Hungarians.

In *What's Your Verdict?* Thomas is correct. The Constitution was proposed, ratified, and has since been amended only by representatives of the people in Congress, in conventions, and in the state legislatures. There has never been a purely democratic vote on the Constitution.

CHECKPOINT How did the Constitution create a system of checks and balances?

The Power to Govern

WHAT'S YOUR VERDICT? Several thousand people had assembled in the park for the annual Fourth of July celebration. The state's senior U.S. senator opened the ceremonies. He said, "I am proud and pleased to be a citizen of the United States of America and of this great state. But, before I am a citizen of either state or country, I, like all of you, am a human being. Our humanity precedes our citizenship. Government exists only by the will and consent of the people. The people control the government. Any control by the government of the people occurs because the people have granted permission for that control."

Does the senator's analysis conform to the governmental structure created by the framers of the Constitution?

The Constitution and the Bill of Rights were written by representatives of the people elected by voters in the 13 original states. These documents place a priority on the basic rights of human beings. This priority exists whether people act as individuals or together. The Ninth Amendment recognizes this priority by stating, "The enumeration in the Constitution of certain rights, shall not be construed to deny or disparage others retained by the people."

Sovereignty of the States

The Tenth Amendment acknowledges the continued sovereignty of all of the states to govern their own citizens within their own borders. **Sovereignty** in this sense means supreme political authority free from external control. The Tenth Amendment declares, "The powers not delegated to the United States by the Constitution, nor prohibited by it to the States, are reserved to the States respectively, or to the people." Here it is evident that the Constitution is a shield against the consolidation of unlimited power by the federal government.

Article VI recognizes the Constitution to be "the supreme law of the land." It prevails over any possible contrary state constitution or law. At the same time, every state's constitution and statutes are supreme on matters over which the federal government has not been given authority. Powers kept by the states include control over most business law and contract law, most criminal and tort law, real property and probate law, and domestic relations law.

Limiting States' Powers

The Fourteenth Amendment opens with these sweeping provisions: "All persons born or naturalized in the United States and subject to the jurisdiction thereof, are citizens of the United States and of the state wherein they reside. No state shall make or enforce any law which shall abridge the privileges or immunities of citizens of the United States; nor shall any State deprive any person of life, liberty, or property, without due process of law; nor deny to any person within its jurisdiction the equal protection of the laws."

Recall that the Fifth Amendment had previously applied such limitations only to the powers of the federal government. The Fourteenth Amendment subjects the states to the same restraint. Due process, as outlined in the Fifth Amendment, is not the only constitutional protection that state governments are required to respect.

Other relevant amendments in the Bill of Rights also have been applied to the states. As a result, today the shield of the Constitution is effective against abuse of power by both the federal and state governments. At both levels, statutes have been enacted to provide comparable protection against abuse of power by private individuals and corporations.

Powers of the Federal Government

The federal government has the duty to protect every state against invasion. It may raise and support armies, a navy, and an air force for national defense. The federal government alone may establish post offices, coin money, and tax imports and exports. Both federal and state legislatures may impose other taxes—on sales and

SELECTED FEDERAL REGULATORY AGENCIES AND THEIR POWERS

Federal Reserve System's Board of Governors Determines economic policies involving the money supply, credit availability, and interest rates.

Federal Trade Commission (FTC) Assists the antitrust division of the Justice Department. Enforces laws against anti-competitive business activities. It also is involved in protecting consumer rights, preventing monopolistic behavior, and eliminating unfair and deceptive trade practices.

Securities and Exchange Commission (SEC) Enforces laws regulating the disclosure of information related to the buying and selling of stocks and bonds. It also regulates the stock exchanges themselves.

National Labor Relations Board (NLRB) Charged with preserving employees' rights to join labor unions and to participate in collective bargaining. It also is charged with eliminating employer, employee, and union unfair labor practices.

Federal Communications Commission (FCC) Controls all interstate channels of communication and channels of communication between the United States and foreign nations. This includes satellite, telegraph, telephone, radio, and television forms of communication.

Equal Employment Opportunity Commission (EEOC) Charged with the elimination of workplace discrimination based on race, religion, sex, color, national origin, age, or disability.

Occupational Safety and Health Administration (OSHA) Governs health and safety in the workplace.

Consumer Product Safety Commission (CPSC) Researches the safety of various consumer products, including toys. It also collects data on mishaps with products and has banned various products including toys, baby cribs, and fireworks.

Food and Drug Administration (FDA) Enforces a number of pure food and drug acts. Tests and reviews any new drug before it can be marketed to the American public. The FDA also conducts food product inspections and regulates the availability and use of medical devices such as prosthetics and pacemakers.

Environmental Protection Agency (EPA) Enforces antipollution acts (the Clean Air and Clean Water Acts, for example) and regulates the creation, marketing, and use of various hazardous chemicals. Also handles cleanups of toxic dumpsites around the country.

Nuclear Regulatory Commission (NRC) Charged with insuring the safety of nuclear power plants in the United States.

Department of Homeland Security (DHS) Controls an agency formed by the merger of 22 separate agencies into one with the mission of protecting the American homeland from terrorist attack.

on incomes. The federal government has exclusive power to regulate **interstate commerce,** or commerce that affects trade between states, and foreign commerce. Each state retains authority to regulate **intrastate commerce,** or trade within its own borders.

As a result of the nationwide, or interstate, impact of the Great Depression in the 1930s, the federal government assumed more and more power in the regulation of business. Today this power is exercised through its many agencies. The figure above lists and describes some of the major federal agencies. When a federal agency properly makes regulations to control its

commercial area of responsibility, those regulations have the force of federal law. The states often have similar agencies with jurisdiction only within their boundaries.

Congress has the power to make detailed laws it considers appropriate for executing the powers given to it in the Constitution. The people, through their votes, ultimately control the entire governmental structure. Each adult retains power over choice of a place to live and to work, a career, friends, travel, holiday activities, and many other personal lifestyle factors.

In *What's Your Verdict?* the senator's comments do accurately reflect the reality of the relationship between citizens and the government today. However, even after the Bill of Rights was added to the Constitution, certain deficiencies existed in the Constitution and in the resulting life of the nation. Additional amendments have been ratified through the years to correct these problems.

CHECKPOINT How is the power to govern divided between the federal and state governments?

2-2 Assessment

THINK ABOUT LEGAL CONCEPTS

1. Under the U.S. Constitution, all spending bills must originate in the _ ?_.

2. Which of the following powers was not retained by the states? (a) power to define and apply tort (personal injury) law (b) power to define and apply criminal laws (c) power to define and apply probate laws (d) the states retained all of the above powers

3. Individual states in the United States can coin money. **True or False?**

4. According to the Constitution, the legislative powers of the federal government are vested in the __?__ of the United States.

5. The U.S. Senate is made up of _ ?_ members from every state.

6. The U.S. House of Representatives is made up of the same number of members from each state. **True or False?**

7. The U.S. Senate has the power to initiate impeachment proceedings against a U.S. President. **True or False?**

8. The _ ?_ branch of government is headed by the President.

THINK CRITICALLY ABOUT EVIDENCE

Study the situation, answer the questions, and then prepare arguments to support your answers.

9. You are a member of the legislature of a large Midwestern state. Your state is running short of money to carry out some much needed programs. As a possible solution you suggest that the state government issue its own currency to people who work for it. The currency can be exchanged for dollar bills at a rate that is to be fixed by the state the first of every month. Is your idea constitutional?

10. Later in the legislative session mentioned in exercise 9, you become disenchanted with your fellow citizens when you learn that only 28 percent of those eligible to vote actually did so in the last election. Consequently, you pass a law requiring that everyone vote in every election.

What arguments can you make in support of such a measure? Against?

11. The Equal Rights Amendment (ERA) was formally proposed in 1972. It provided: "Equality of rights under the law shall not be denied or abridged by the United States or by any state on account of sex." For more than ten years, supporters and opponents conducted campaigns in all states. When the time limit for approval elapsed in 1982, only 35 of the required state legislatures had voted in favor. Women in a sorority at a nearby college now wonder if another campaign should be launched to pass the ERA. How would you advise them?

2-3 The Internet and Constitutional Rights

GOALS

- Understand the issues of jurisdiction that arise with Internet usage
- Identify the various constitutional issues involved in the use of electronic communication

KEY TERMS

cyberlaw

browser

Who Controls the Internet?

WHAT'S YOUR VERDICT?
Sharksinthepool.biz Inc. is a Nevada manufacturing company that sells an elbow-stiffening device for pool players. The device holds the elbow in the proper position for a smooth and accurate follow through while cueing a ball. The device has been very popular for several years and has only been sold on the Internet to customers throughout the United States as well as in Japan, Canada, Mexico, Europe, and South America. Recent research into the use of this device has found that even moderate use may cause a pinched-nerve syndrome somewhat like carpel tunnel but in the user's elbow. You are the founder and president of the company. You are extremely concerned about the lawsuits that may be filed against your company.

Where may these suits be filed? What jurisdiction's law will be used to decide these cases once filed?

Foundations of Cyberlaw

Literally right in front of your noses an entire new area of law is being formed. **Cyberlaw**—law that is intended to govern the use of computers in e-commerce and, more generally, the Internet—is developing at a previously unheard of pace. Legal issues born in this advancing wave of technology are testing the courts and established law to the maximum. The cases in which these issues are developed involve the computer and subject areas such as jurisdiction, trademarks, copyrights, contracts, privacy, obscenity, defamation, security of data, and crime.

Often the opinions in these cases do not fully decide the issues, but clarify them. The judges in the cases leave it to Congress, the state legislatures, and federal and state administrative agencies to actually create the lasting cyberlaw.

An example can be found in the complex area of jurisdiction, where states have competing laws to determine where a case is to be tried. The courts often are faced with the choice of either duplicating the work of other courts in other jurisdictions or accepting the result determined in the other courts without adequate review.

The Birth of the Internet

The U.S. Department of Defense laid the groundwork for the Internet in the late 1960s during the so-called Cold War. It did so by having its

One of the most difficult issues in cyberlaw is determining jurisdiction, or where a case will be tried. Based on what you know about the Internet, why do you think this is so difficult?

© GETTY IMAGES/PHOTODISC

Advanced Research Projects Agency (ARPA) tie together computers on various academic campuses and research centers around the country in a network called ARPANET. The idea was to increase the pace of development of defense projects by empowering the sharing of defense-related information between researchers through the use of electronic mail, file transfers, and online chats. The success of the idea was immediate and, as a result, this defense network was expanded and even connected to overseas networks.

Soon academics outside of the defense establishment began to take notice of the usefulness of the medium. As a consequence, in the late 1980s the National Science Foundation (NSF) built its own network. This more advanced NSF network—or Internet—took over the functions of the defense network and continued to grow and gain in popularity among the academics and students who had the expertise to use it.

Eventually, commercial interests began to inquire about the Internet. Their requests to use it for business purposes, however, were turned down. This was primarily because the NSF Internet, like the defense network before it, was never intended to serve a commercial purpose. In fact, until 1991, all the users of the NSF network had to agree to a contract that explicitly disallowed the use of the Internet for business purposes.

The World Wide Web

In 1990, after 20 years of scientific and academic use, the Internet was opened up to new users through the creation of hypertext. *Hypertext* is a nonlinear format for the publishing of information used to send e-mails, transfer mountains of data, and converse in chat rooms. These new users were seeking specialized information in subject areas in which they did not have a great deal of background.

The access these new users desired was developed chiefly through the work of one person, Tim Berners-Lee. Working at the European Laboratory for Particle Physics, Berners-Lee developed the World Wide Web (WWW) Program mainly in his spare time. This program's effect was to simplify the Internet to allow almost universal access to anyone with the use of a computer. Berners-Lee, who has not earned a profit from his development, is currently director of the World Wide Web Consortium, the coordinating body for Web development. His vision is that of open access to as wide a body of information as possible for every user. This access is accom-

plished through the use of a scanning program called a **browser**. A browser utilizes the attributes of hypertext to allow immediate access to any and all subjects and the background information necessary to comprehend them.

To quote Berners-Lee, "there is power in arranging information in an unconstrained, web-like way." To that end, he created hypertext markup language (HTML) and hypertext transfer protocol (HTTP). HTML dictates the format of standard Web documents, while HTTP provides the standard for exchanging files in the HTML format. Note that in this web-like arrangement of information, there are a multitude of connecting points and, therefore, a multitude of paths and storehouses for information. Shut down one path or storehouse and many more spring up in its place. The very decentralization of the Internet makes it nearly impossible to exercise legal control over it and what goes on within it.

Evolving Legal Issues in Cyberspace

Cyberlaw is developing in many separate areas at once. Contracts, privacy, obscenity, defamation, security of data, trademarks, copyrights, and crime all have been the focus of many decisions intended

Information on the Internet is arranged in a web-like fashion. How does this affect government's ability to exercise legal control over it?

to resolve the legal issues raised by computer usage and the Internet. These issues will be explored in the remainder of this lesson and in the Cyberlaw features in the chapters that follow.

THE ONGOING ISSUE OF JURISDICTION Final answers to the legal questions in all of the areas mentioned above can only be arrived at after the court responsible for giving them is determined. Traditionally, the state courts have been given jurisdiction over cases between their citizens. Cases with relatively large amounts of money at stake and between citizens of different states, along with cases that involve questions of federal law, have been left to the federal courts to decide. (See Lessons 3-2 and 3-3 in the text for more information on this topic.)

Regardless of whether or not a case is filed in state or federal court, however, the vital issue soon becomes whether or not the case is to be decided within the state where it was filed or in the state where the e-business is physically located. For example, would a corporation physically located in New Jersey and incorporated there have to fund a defense against a case filed against it in California?

The answer to this question of jurisdiction is based on two vital legal considerations. First of all, the laws of the state in which the case is filed must allow suits against non-resident defendants. Most states do have statutes—referred to as "long-arm statutes" for the long arm of the law—that, for the good of their citizens, permit such cases to be heard. However, the standards the state's long-arm statute sets for the involvement of the non-resident defendant in the state must be met or the suit will be dismissed for lack of jurisdiction. These standards vary from state to state.

Some standards require a concrete presence in the state in the form of an office, a traveling salesperson, a mailing address, etc. Others simply require a reasonable presumption that the defendant is doing business in the state by its level of involvement there.

The second legal consideration relating to jurisdiction is whether or not allowing the state or federal court (the latter using the state rules) to decide the case would be a violation of the due process requirements of the U.S. Constitution. As discussed earlier in this chapter, these requirements are embedded in the Fifth and Fourteenth Amendments to the Constitution. The Fifth Amendment, originally meant to apply to the actions of the federal government, prohibits the taking of life, liberty, or property without the

due process of law. The Fourteenth Amendment extends this same prohibition to the states.

According to the latest decisions regarding cyberlaw issues, the establishment of jurisdiction by a state over a nonresident defendant is only proper if the defendant has either a "substantial, continuous, and systemic presence" in the state or has "minimum contacts" with the state. Most e-businesses lack the former and, therefore, are judged by the minimum contacts rule.

Soliciting business from a web site available in the state generally has been held to be a minimum contact. Accordingly, it is reasonable to presume that a lawsuit (over contracts, product liability, warranty, etc.) might be generated as a result of such activity. Simply providing an informative web site has been held not to be a minimum contact, however. In other words a car company merely providing pictures and characteristics of its cars on its web site but not providing a means by which one can be purchased through the web site itself would be free of the threat of suit based strictly on it as a "minimum contact." There must be something more to indicate that the defendant intended to serve the market in the state.

In *What's Your Verdict?* Sharksinthepool.biz Inc. most likely would have to defend against the product liability suits wherever they were filed in the United States. Should they not defend and suffer a default judgment or defend and lose, the judgment may be entered and enforced against them in a Nevada court without substantial review by the Nevada court.

INTERNATIONAL JURISDICTION International cases are governed by international law, which is currently under serious revision due primarily to e-commerce. An established, pre-e-commerce principle is that a country may exercise jurisdiction

LEGAL *Research*

Imagine that you are a member of the governing body of the Internet. Help to set up a system of rules and a procedure for enforcement to prevent the appearance of web sites that you consider unethical. These may include sites that contain instructions on how to make bombs or how to assist or commit crimes. Research and appraise the rules that are currently in place for this purpose.

Internet-Related Constitutional Issues

What action can an e-business take to remove the uncertainty involved in both international and domestic jurisdiction issues?

WHAT'S YOUR VERDICT? A respected Internet news service carried on its web site a picture of the U.S. Secretary of State provided by the Secretary's publicity staff. The picture depicted the Secretary of State shaking hands in front of a foreign embassy next to a statue of a nude woman. The web site does not have the controls required to ensure that minors do not have access to it. In fact, it promotes itself as a source of information for school-age children.

Would the news service be in violation of federal statutes against online pornography accessible by minors? Would the Secretary of State or the Secretary's office be in violation of the statute?

only over activities with a substantial effect on or in that country. However, new standards under consideration would impose a country-of-origination selection principle on business-to-business transactions and a country-of-residence-of-the-consumer principle on consumer transactions. The reviewability of decisions made overseas and then entered in the domestic courts of the United States for enforcement currently is covered mainly by treaties between individual countries.

Most of the uncertainty involved in the jurisdiction issue can be removed if the e-business puts a notice on its web site and clarifying section in its contracts. This notice or clause should state, in effect, that all legal issues shall be resolved in a particular jurisdiction (hopefully its home state) with favorable laws. If the laws of a particular jurisdiction do not allow such limits on suits, then the e-business should not do business in that jurisdiction.

CHECKPOINT What characteristic of the Internet makes exercising legal control over it nearly impossible?

Freedom of Speech

The legal cornerstone of any defense against governmental action that would place limitations on freedom of speech are the rights protected by the First Amendment to the U.S. Constitution. This protection against federal governmental action is extended by the Fourteenth Amendment against similar state actions.

Note that these basic means of expression—speech, press, religion, assembly, and petition—are jealously protected not only in their fundamental forms but also in the extension of those forms. Such extensions may include flag burnings, anti-government publications, or what the vast majority would label obscene. The theme of this extended protection is that censoring these questionable forms of expression would ultimately have a chilling effect on more generally acceptable forms.

However, even these fundamental rights are not absolute. Certainly the freedom of speech does not condone your shouting "fire" in a crowded theater or a newspaper maliciously publishing lies about a celebrity. In the case of obscenity, for example, the basic law was formulated by the U.S. Supreme Court in the mid-1950s.

Freedom of speech is an important right protected by the First Amendment. Besides communicating orally, what other means of expression are protected under the umbrella of freedom of speech?

ROTH V. UNITED STATES In Roth the Court determined that obscenity did not have the protection of the First Amendment. To reach this conclusion the court noted that the protections given speech and the press were to ensure the open exchange of ideas that would allow necessary political and social change. Therefore, to quote the Court in *Roth v. United States,*

> All ideas having even the slightest redeeming social importance—unorthodox ideas, controversial ideas, even ideas hateful to the prevailing climate of opinion—have the full protection of the guaranties, unless excludable because they encroach upon [interfere with] the limited area of more important interests. But implicit in the history of the First Amendment is the rejection of obscenity as utterly without redeeming social importance.

Obviously, it is vital to be able to determine what is or is not obscene in order to apply the court's decision. The standards used to determine

that issue have varied through the years. The Roth decision, quoted above, indicated that the key question was whether or not the questionable material had any redeeming social importance. If it did not, then it could be regulated or banned totally by the federal or state government.

MILLER V. CALIFORNIA In the 1960s the standard became whether or not the questionable material was "utterly without redeeming social value." This standard was much more difficult to prove and resulted in much greater latitude for those publishing material arguably obscene. Finally, in a 1973 case, *Miller v. California,* the Supreme Court toughened the standards by deciding that the questionable materials were to be judged by the standards of the community affected.

Unfortunately, the Miller standards proved inadequate when applied to the Internet environment. Slowly, however, case law has begun to fill in the necessary gaps. For example, the issue of "community standards" raises the question, "Which community?" The answer to the question often determines whether or not someone will spend years in jail. Currently, the case law holds the sender to the standards of the recipient's community. This tends to put the responsibility on the party profiting from such an exchange to know those standards and refuse to send the material to areas in which the community standards would make such an act illegal.

Local community standards also are applicable in determining whether or not the material has any literary, artistic, political, or socially redeeming value when taken as a whole. Certainly, what is of such value will vary greatly from an urban to a suburban setting. Because of the unpredictability of the interpretation of the laws it has been suggested that the "community" be considered to be the Internet community rather than any particular geographical region. Thus far, the courts have declined to adopt this perspective.

Supreme Court decisions of the last 50 years have held that once material is determined to be obscene, it can be regulated by the local, state, and federal governments. The types of regulation and their extent, however, have been open to challenge. See "Landmark Decisions in Cyberlaw," on the next page.

COMMUNICATIONS DECENCY ACT In 1996, Congress passed the Communications Decency Act (CDA). One purpose of CDA is to control the knowing transmittal of obscene material through the Internet. The statute provides heavy fines and imprisonment for up to five years for first-time violators with even stronger penalties for subsequent offenses. Upon passage, the CDA came under immediate legal attack from the American Civil Liberties Union and others. The result, due mainly to the legally ambiguous term "indecent" used in the statute, was the declaration that the statute was overbroad and chilling of protected speech. Consequently, the statutory portions relying on that term were declared unconstitutional.

Currently, another section of the Act aimed at protecting Internet sites from lawsuits for carrying content created by others is under attack. A lawsuit filed in Illinois in late 2006 targeted a housing ad site that allegedly carried racially discriminatory content created by the parties advertising properties for sale. The section of the CDA under attack has in the past even protected employers whose employees have used computer systems at work to violate the CDA's own provisions in threatening and harassing others. However, the carrying of discriminatory housing ads violates another federal statute, the Fair Housing Act, which prohibits such third-person-created ads in print media. Internet companies such as Google, Yahoo, AOL, eBay, and Amazon have filed briefs in the case in support of the immunity provided by CDA.

CHILD ONLINE PROTECTION ACT The Child Online Protection Act (COPA) of 1998 required commercial sites to use up-to-date methodology to restrict access to their sites containing material harmful to children. This Act was amended due to the alleged inability of site operators to afford

the necessary equipment and the overbroad definition of "harmful material" so that it would have arguably included legitimate art works and scientific information about sex. As access-control technology continues to become more accurate and cheaper, the Act's potential for enforcement by the federal government has increased. If convicted of violating the Act, commercial web sites face fines of up to $50,000 per incident and web-site operators face jail terms of up to six months. See the figure on page 43 for a summary of the statutes relating to free speech issues and citations to these statutes.

In *What's Your Verdict?* the Child Online Protection Act of 1998 might have made criminal both the actions of the news site in posting it and the actions of the Secretary of State's staff in circulating the picture.

The Right of Privacy

The right of privacy was legitimized as a right by the U.S. Supreme Court in the late 1960s. Ever since then, it has been based on a person's reasonable expectations as to whether his or her actions, communications, beliefs, and other personal attributes deserve protection from those who would improperly use them. For example, a recent case involved an employee's privacy regarding personal e-mail sent at work. The court held that the employee had no true expectation of privacy on a company's e-mail system. Therefore, the employee's personal e-mails were not protected by the right of privacy.

Other issues of privacy remain unresolved. For example, *spamming*—the practice of sending unrequested bulk e-mailings to hundreds of thousands of potential customers via the Internet—is supported by the ability to generate address lists. This generation typically is performed by popular web sites compiling the "cookies" that are left behind every time such a site is visited by a web user. A cookie is a packet of information containing the Internet address and other personal information about a web site visitor, such as buying patterns. This information is then sold without the user's knowledge or permission.

Existing federal law rightfully protects against such information being gathered on the videos and cable programs you rent or purchase. But, no such law exists in the United States that covers gathering information about users while they are online. The European Union (EU) has passed a directive that requires its member nations to pass legislation protecting consumers—not companies—against such practices.

The European Union Directive forbids member nations from permitting the transfer of personal data to companies and other entities in a nation, like the United States, that does not provide an adequate level of personal privacy protection. Should U.S. firms doing business in the European Union, especially in the areas of credit and insurance, transfer data back to the United States they could be in violation of the directive and subject to penalties and civil suits. To address this problem, the Department of Commerce negotiated with the European Union to produce a list of precautions that a U.S. firm should take in order to comply with the EU directive.

IN THIS CASE BigBro Inc. assured its employees that any e-mails they sent over the company's computer system would be confidential and that no action, such as reprimand or termination, would ever be taken based on such communications. However, Gulli Bell, an employee, sent several e-mails to a fellow employee complaining about management decisions and stating that the company president was "twice as smart as an ox." She was dismissed soon thereafter, and the e-mails were cited as the primary reason. The state where BigBro was located was an employment-at-will state, meaning that Bell could legally be fired without statement of cause. Bell brought suit against BigBro for breach of her right of privacy but lost.

CHECKPOINT What are the constitutional issues related to use of the Internet?

Whenever you visit a web site, personal information about you may be collected and then sold by the web site operator. What is your opinion of this practice? Do you think it should be outlawed? Why or why not?

STATUTES OF IMPORTANCE TO CYBERLAW

Lanham Act of 1976 (Title 15 U.S.C. Section 1051 et. seq.) Provides for the registration and protection of trademarks and copyrights.

Trademark Dilution Act of 1996 (Title 15 U.S.C. Section 1125) Attempts to protect the holders of famous trademarks from the effects of domain-page registrations that tend to confuse and dilute the trademark's goodwill.

Computer Fraud and Abuse Act (Title 18 U.S.C. Section 1030) An often-amended act that pioneered the treatment of computer-related crimes as unique offenses in the United States Code.

Telecommunications Act of 1996, also known as **The Communications Decency Act of 1996 (CDA)** (Title 47 U.S.C. Section 223, Title V) Makes it criminal to knowingly transport obscene material through interactive computers or interstate or foreign commerce for sale or distribution. In addition Section 230 of the CDA gives protection from defamation suits to Internet service providers.

Child Online Protection Act of 1998 (Title 47 U.S.C. Section 231) Makes it a crime for site operators to fail to use proper technology and methodology to prevent minors from accessing "harmful" material.

Fraudulent Online Identity Sanctions Act of 2004 Increased potential prison sentences by up to seven years for someone who provided "material and misleading false contact information to a domain name registrar, domain name registry, or other domain name registration authority."

2-3 Assessment

Xtra!
Study Tools
school.cengage.com/blaw/lawxtra

THINK ABOUT LEGAL CONCEPTS

1. Typically, when citizens of the same state sue one another, their case will be handled by (a) the state courts (b) the federal courts

2. What is obscene is now determined by one uniform national standard. **True or False?**

3. An employee's personal e-mail, composed and sent at work, is protected by the right of privacy. **True or False?**

4. The Act that would offer protection to an employer whose employee used the computer system at work to harass his ex-girlfriend is the (a) CDA (b) COPA (c) FTCA (d) none of the above

5. Statutes that allow a citizen of one state to file suit against a non-resident of the state are called (a) Jurisdictional Reach Acts (b) long-arm statutes (c) Interstate Commerce Acts

THINK CRITICALLY ABOUT EVIDENCE

Study the situation, answer the questions, and then prepare arguments to support your answers.

6. Sy Bore has been receiving spam mail advertisements from adult-oriented web sites that contain pictures. Some of the pictures are very similar to ones that have been termed obscene in his state, and the senders were punished at criminal law there. However, the senders of the pictures he is receiving in the spam mail are located in states other than Bore's. Bore persuades the local prosecutor to bring charges against the senders based on the obscene nature of the pictures. At trial, the senders defend themselves by showing the material is not obscene in their home states. Can they still be convicted?

7. Consider the effects of making the European Union's privacy standards federal law here in the United States. What groups would support a movement to do so? What groups would oppose the move? What would be the effects on business?

Chapter 2 Assessment

CONCEPTS IN BRIEF

2-1 Foundations of the U.S. Constitution

1. The documents that helped form the U.S. government include the Declaration of Independence, the Articles of Confederation, and the U.S. Constitution, including the Bill of Rights.

2. The First Amendment protects free speech, free press, free exercise of any private religion, freedom to assemble peaceably, and the right to petition the government for redress if one is wronged.

3. Civil rights are personal, natural rights of individuals guaranteed by the Constitution.

4. Although the Constitution does not spell out what is meant by "due process," U.S. Supreme Court decisions have come to define it as a defendant being provided, at a minimum, adequate notice and a proper hearing. Due process of law is assured by the First, Fourth, Fifth, Sixth, Seventh, and Eighth Amendments.

5. Voting rights were extended to freed slaves by the Fifteenth Amendment and to women through the Nineteenth Amendment. The voting age for all citizens was lowered to eighteen by the Twenty-Sixth Amendment.

2-2 Division and Balance of Governmental Powers

6. A vigorous and useful balance of power exists among the three basic branches of government: legislative, executive, and judicial.

7. The Tenth Amendment allows states the freedom to govern their citizens. However, the Constitution limits states' powers through the Fourteenth Amendment.

2-3 The Internet and Constitutional Rights

8. Cyberlaw is developing at a rapid pace as the underlying technology advances.

9. Freedom of speech and the right of privacy are the two main constitutional issues related to Internet use.

YOUR LEGAL VOCABULARY

Match each statement with the term that it best defines. Some terms may not be used.

1. Personal, natural rights guaranteed by the Constitution

2. Internet scanning program

3. Governmental system wherein each citizen may vote directly to decide issues

4. Division and allocation of the powers of government between its various branches

5. Governmental systems wherein citizens elect representatives to decide issues

6. Supreme political authority free from external control

7. Charter for common government for the 13 colonies prior to the adoption of the Constitution

8. Document that provides a framework for the federal government, consisting of 7 articles and 27 amendments

9. Concept of fundamental fairness in compliance with reasonable and just laws

10. The first ten amendments to the U.S. Constitution

11. Law that is intended to govern the use of computers in e-commerce

12. Change or alteration

a. amendment
b. Articles of Confederation
c. Bill of Rights
d. browser
e. civil rights
f. cyberlaw
g. Declaration of Independence
h. democracy
i. due process of law
j. impeachment cases
k. interstate commerce
l. intrastate commerce
m. political party
n. republic
o. sovereignty
p. system of checks and balances
q. U.S. Constitution

REVIEW LEGAL CONCEPTS

13. The Constitutional Convention of 1787 was meant to make changes in the Articles of Confederation instead of create a new document. Why do you think the Articles were discarded?

14. Can you foresee a time when the U.S. might become a true democracy? If so, how could this occur?

15. While the system of checks and balances works to prevent the accumulation of too much power by any one branch of the government, it also causes problems in the functioning of government. What do you think some of these problems might be?

16. Could you get your friends and neighbors to sign the Declaration of Independence today?

During the Vietnam era, young people around the country tried to do just that. Most citizens who read the document but were not told that it was the Declaration, refused to sign and, in some cases, reacted violently to its content. Why is that?

17. Susan, a manager in a local company, became romantically involved with one of her subordinates at work. They sent love messages back and forth by using the company's Internet connection. The company regularly monitored its employee's on-the-job e-mails and had a policy against such personal involvements. As a consequence, Susan was fired. She brought suit for invasion of privacy. Will she win?

WRITE ABOUT LEGAL CONCEPTS

18. Write an essay on how the framers of the Constitution and the Bill of Rights could justify the maintenance of slavery and the denial of voting rights to women.

19. Write a paragraph stating your opinion about which is the most important right preserved by the Bill of Rights.

20. The Bill of Rights is presented in this book in the language the founding fathers used. Rewrite the Bill of Rights in your own words.

21. **HOT DEBATE** While the passages denouncing the people of England and the slave trade were cut from Jefferson's draft of the Declaration, numerous direct accusations against the King of England were left in the document. Why was the King singled out for criticism and not the people? Was this a wise move on the part of the Continental Congress?

MAKE ACADEMIC CONNECTIONS

22. **HISTORY** Rhode Island was the last of the 13 colonies to ratify the Constitution. Using the Internet and the library, determine what caused them to pause for so long. Write a one-page paper summarizing your findings.

23. **SOCIAL SURVEY** Apply the standards of the Child Online Protection Act to works of art, advertisements, and other such displays easily visible to the young in your community. What conclusions can you draw about the Act and its enforcement as a consequence?

THINK CRITICALLY ABOUT EVIDENCE

Study the situation, answer the questions, and then prepare arguments to support your answers.

24. Jennifer let her cousin use her computer during a recent visit. Without Jennifer's permission the cousin visited several web sites that sold pornography. Now Jennifer is receiving spam from similar sites all around the world. No matter how often she reports the objectionable nature of the material, it keeps appearing. Evidently, the site her cousin visited sold her web address to others in the same line of business. It makes

her very upset, but she cannot change her web address for some time. What practical and legal means can Jennifer use to solve this problem?

25. In 1919 the Eighteenth Amendment outlawed "the manufacture, sale, or transportation of intoxicating liquors...." This law led to widespread illegal traffic in liquor by criminals. The controversial law also led to unspoken approval of the illegal trade by many citizens

who continued to buy and consume liquor. The Eighteenth Amendment was repealed by the Twenty-First Amendment, but individual states were permitted to continue to enforce Prohibition within their borders. By 1966, all individual states had abandoned Prohibition. According to experts, abuse of alcoholic beverages is the most serious drug problem in overall harmful effect on society. Should Prohibition be reinstated? If not, what, if anything, should be done?

ANALYZE REAL CASES

26. A Champaign County, Illinois, board of education granted permission to religious teachers to give religious instruction in public school buildings in grades four to nine. Subject to approval of and supervision by the superintendent of schools, the teachers were employed by a private religious group and included representatives of the Catholic, Jewish, and Protestant faiths. Only pupils whose parents requested religious instruction were required to attend the religious classes. McCollum, a resident with a pupil who was enrolled in one of the public schools, sued for a writ, or court order, to end the religious instruction as a violation of the First Amendment to the Constitution. The writ was denied, and the Illinois Supreme Court upheld the denial. The parent appealed to the U.S. Supreme Court. Should the writ have been granted to end the practice as a violation of the First Amendment? Why or why not? (*McCollum v. Board of Education,* 333 U.S. 203)

27. In 1964, a motel owner in Atlanta restricted its clientele to white persons, three-fourths of whom were interstate travelers. U.S. government attorneys charged that this policy violated the Civil Rights Act of 1964, which forbids such discrimination against blacks. The trial court ordered the motel to stop refusing blacks as guests. The motel owner appealed to the U.S. Supreme Court, claiming the Civil Rights Act was unconstitutional. Was it? Why or why not? Does the federal government have the power to regulate matters that might in any way affect interstate commerce? (*Heart of Atlanta Motel, Inc. v. United States,* 379 U.S. 241)

28. Cleveland police had received information that a person wanted for questioning about a recent bombing was hiding in a particular two-family dwelling. There was said to be a large quantity of illegal lottery materials hidden in the home. Upon arrival, three officers knocked on the door and demanded entrance. Mapp, who lived on the top floor with her daughter, telephoned her attorney and then refused to admit the officers without a search warrant. Three hours later, reinforced by additional officers, the police returned. When Mapp did not answer immediately, they tried to kick in the door, then broke its glass pane, reached in, unlocked it, and entered. Meanwhile Mapp's attorney had arrived, but the officers would not let him see his client or enter the house. Mapp demanded to see a search warrant. When an officer held up a paper claiming it to be a warrant, Mapp grabbed the paper and placed it in her bosom. A struggle ensued during which the officer recovered the paper. Mapp was handcuffed for resisting the officer. The entire house was searched, but all that was found were certain allegedly "lewd and lascivious books and pictures." Mapp was convicted of knowingly having them in her possession. At the trial, no search warrant was produced nor was the failure to produce one explained. Mapp appealed to the U.S. Supreme Court for a reversal of her conviction because it was based on a search that was illegal under the U.S. Constitution. Was the evidence for conviction obtained in violation of the U.S. Constitution? If so, was it admissible in the trial against the defendant Mapp? (*Mapp v. Ohio,* 367 U.S. 643)

29. Weber was injured while staying in a hotel in Italy. When he returned to the United States, he filed suit against the hotel in a New Jersey court. Weber based his claim that the New Jersey court had jurisdiction on the fact that the hotel's web site advertising for rooms for rent was available in that state. Was Weber correct in maintaining that the New Jersey court had jurisdiction? (*Weber v. Jolly,* 977 F. Supp. 327)

30. When a company began sending literally millions of unsolicited e-mails per day to its subscribers, America Online (AOL) blocked the transmissions. The sender then sued claiming an abridgement of its First Amendment rights by the action and requested an injunction preventing AOL's actions against its spamming. How should the court decide? (*Cyber Promotions, Inc., v. America Online, Inc.,* 948 F. Supp. 436)

Sports & Entertainment Law

Seinfeld's "George" a Plagiarization?

COSTANZA V. SEINFELD 693 N.Y.S.2D 897

BACKGROUND Remember George Costanza, the character in *Seinfeld* portrayed for laughs as an inept, petty failure in business, romance, and other ventures? The plaintiff in this lawsuit, Michael Costanza, was not amused.

FACTS Michael Costanza sued comedian Jerry Seinfeld, NBC, and others for invasion of privacy and defamation. The cause of action was based upon the use of the character over the successful TV show's long run. George Costanza had Michael Costanza's character and last name. Michael alleged that George, bald and obese, even looked like him. Michael also noted that, like himself, the show's character was portrayed as knowing Seinfeld from college and being from Queens, New York. Michael alleged that the character's personality, including the traits of being self-centered, unreliable, and generally incompetent, have been imputed to him by the similarities and have humiliated him. He also noted that the co-creator of *Seinfeld* called him a "flagrant opportunist" for publishing a book alleging his connections with and handling by the defendants during the highly publicized timeframe of the show's last episode. He sought damages in the amount of $100 million because he believed the interplay with George Costanza was one of the main reasons for the show's successful and very lucrative run. Jerry Seinfeld, NBC, and other defendants offered as defenses that Michael Costanza waived any right to sue by accepting a minor role on a Seinfeld episode aired in

the middle-1990s, that he made the similarities public in a book on the subject, and that the label "flagrant opportunist" was a statement of opinion and was, therefore, not actionable as being defamatory.

THE LAW Defamation requires a false written or oral statement to a third party or parties that brings the victim into disrepute, contempt, or ridicule by others.

THE ISSUES (1) Was Michael Costanza defamed by the portrayal of George Costanza on Seinfeld? (2) Was he defamed by being called a flagrant opportunist for his lawsuit and publication?

HOLDING Because Michael Costanza's actual image was not associated with the character portrayed on television, the Court held that defamation was not a viable cause of action. In addition, giving the timing of the book and lawsuit, the label "flagrant opportunist" was considered a statement of opinion, not fact. Consequently it could not base a lawsuit for defamation.

PRACTICE JUDGING

1. Do you consider Michael Costanza a public figure? Why or why not? What would be the consequences for the lawsuit if he were considered a public figure?

2. Ethically, do you feel that Michael Costanza was defamed? Why or why not?

Chapter 3
Court Systems

3-1 Forms of Dispute Resolution

3-2 The Federal Court System

3-3 State Court Systems

HOT DEBATE

Anthony Destin works as a junior designer at a large fashion house called Berentinos. After two years on the job, Anthony learns that his co-worker Sarah Blake earns 35 percent more than he does. Anthony and Sarah were hired at the same time and have exactly the same job. Anthony has five more years experience in the field than Sarah does. Anthony discussed his concern with Tom Sortee, one of his colleagues. Tom commented that such discrimination against males has long been the rule at Berentinos. Anthony loves his work but can't help feeling he is being treated unfairly.

WHERE DO YOU STAND?

1. What alternative courses of action, other than filing suit in court, might Anthony utilize to bring about a resolution of the issue?
2. Does Anthony have a duty to anyone, legally or morally, to bring a lawsuit instead of using alternative forms of dispute resolution?

© GETTY IMAGES/PHOTODISC

3-1 Forms of Dispute Resolution

GOALS

- Explain how disputes can be settled without going to court
- Name the different levels of courts and describe their jurisdictions and powers

KEY TERMS

litigate

mediator

arbitrator

court

trial court

verdict

original jurisdiction

appellate court

transcript

appellate briefs

Dispute Resolution

WHAT'S YOUR VERDICT?

Odeen and Dva Click ran the Clickety-Clack Garage in a suburb of Boston, Massachusetts. Part of their standard repair contract reads that any and all disputes arising out of their repair work were to be settled by arbitration rather than by a court of law.

Is this clause enforceable?

How Can Disputes Be Resolved Without Going to Court?

Many people decide too quickly to **litigate**—or to allow a court to resolve their disputes. When one person injures another or fails to keep a binding agreement, often the best solution is for the parties to negotiate a settlement themselves. Together, they often can reach a mutually acceptable solution.

As an alternative to face-to-face negotiations, the parties may invite an independent third party to act as a mediator. The **mediator** tries to develop a solution acceptable to both sides of the dispute. The actions of a mediator are advisory (not legally binding on the parties). In other cases, the parties may retain an arbitrator. An **arbitrator** usually holds an informal hearing to determine what happened. The arbitrator's decision, unlike that of a mediator, is binding on both parties. The decision can be enforced by court order if necessary. Sometimes a provision for arbitration is included in the original agreement between the parties. In *What's Your Verdict?*,

the clause is enforceable. If both parties agree to the contract then either party can require a dispute over the repairs to be resolved by arbitration.

How Do Courts Settle Disputes?

A **court** can be defined as a governmental forum that administers justice under the law. Courts decide disputes between private individuals and try criminal cases. A court may award damages or order other appropriate relief in resolving private disputes and impose punishment (fine and/or imprisonment) in the criminal cases.

Courts follow impartial and thorough procedures to make decisions. Witnesses are in some cases compelled to give testimony. The accused party is allowed equal opportunity to argue her or his side of the case. Typically, two levels of courts are involved in deciding a dispute. These two levels are trial courts and appellate courts.

© GETTY IMAGES/PHOTODISC

Disputing parties may retain a mediator or an arbitrator to develop a solution. What is the difference between a solution offered by a mediator and a solution offered by an arbitrator?

TRIAL COURTS The court in which a dispute is first heard is called a **trial court**. The trial court hears the witnesses testify and reviews the other pertinent evidence firsthand so as to determine the facts of a case. The trial court will then apply what it selects as the appropriate law to the facts to reach a **verdict**, or decision, in the case. Because it has the power to make these initial decisions of fact and law, a trial court is said to have **original jurisdiction** over the case.

A trial court consists not only of a judge but also of lawyers, who are officers of the court. Other court personnel necessary for its operation include clerks, sheriffs or marshals, bailiffs, and jury members.

Clerks enter cases on the court calendar, keep records of proceedings, and often compute court costs. Sheriffs or their deputies serve as bailiffs. Bailiffs summon witnesses, keep order in court, and take steps to carry out judgments in the state court systems. Marshals have these duties in the federal court system. Juries are citizens sworn by a court to decide issues of fact in court cases.

APPELLATE COURTS An **appellate court** reviews decisions of lower courts when a party claims an error of law was made during the lower court's proceeding. Because appellate court judges were not present to evaluate firsthand the truthfulness of the witnesses, their testimony, and other evidence, they do not make determinations of

LEGAL *Research*

Contact the clerks of your local courts—city, county, and state—to find out the types of cases over which each court has jurisdiction.

fact. Instead appellate jurisdiction is concerned solely with errors of law.

Appellate courts examine the **transcript**, which is a verbatim record of what went on at trial. They also read **appellate briefs**, or written arguments on the issues of law, submitted by the opposing attorneys. Appellate courts also often listen to attorneys' oral arguments in support of these briefs. During such oral argument the appellate judges question attorneys about the case. Finally, appellate courts decide whether the decision of the lower court should be affirmed (upheld), reversed (overturned), amended (changed), remanded (sent back to the trial court for corrective action or possibly a new trial), or a combination of these.

CHECKPOINT What are the two levels of courts, and what is the function of each?

Which type of court, trial or appellate, is pictured here? Justify your answer.

THINK ABOUT LEGAL CONCEPTS

1. Which of the following means of dispute resolution may be enforced by a court order? (a) The parties invite a mediator to develop a solution. (b) The parties retain an arbitrator to prescribe a solution. (c) The parties call the police in to resolve the dispute.

2. There is no difference between mediation and arbitration. **True or False?**

3. A trial court has _?_ jurisdiction over a case.

4. Courts (a) award damages in criminal cases (b) hear witnesses at the appellate level (c) decide questions of fact at the trial level (d) enforce mediators' decisions (e) all of the above

5. Appellate courts review decisions of lower courts when one or more of the parties appeal, claiming an error of law was made during the lower court's proceeding. **True or False?**

6. Appellate court review of trial court decisions is normally confined to errors of _?_.

7. Which of the following are involved in appellate court proceedings? (a) bailiffs (b) juries (c) judges (d) witnesses

8. To _?_ means to allow a court to resolve a dispute.

9. When an appellate court sends a case back down to a trial court for a new trial, it is said to have _?_ the case. (a) affirmed (b) reversed (c) remanded (d) none of the above

10. A decision of the lower court that has been overturned by an appellate court is said to have been (a) affirmed (b) reversed (c) amended (d) remanded

11. A decision of the lower court that has been upheld by an appellate court is said to have been affirmed. **True or False?**

12. A decision of the lower court that has been changed by an appellate court is said to be (a) affirmed (b) reversed (c) amended (d) remanded

THINK CRITICALLY ABOUT EVIDENCE

Study the situation, answer the questions, and then prepare arguments to support your answers.

13. Your boss at Swift Electronics is getting ready to enter into a series of contracts with a new group of suppliers. She is concerned with avoiding the delays and high costs of any litigation that might result from the new agreements. She asks you for your recommendations. You suggest putting a binding arbitration clause in the contracts. Why?

14. Your boss at Swift Electronics decides against the recommendations you made (see exercise 13). Six months later, a supplier sends the wrong projection device in response to your order. The supplier then refuses to correct the mistake. Your boss hires an attorney at $250 per hour and takes you to lunch to admit she made a mistake in not following your ideas. Ultimately, the case is set for trial. What type of jurisdiction will this court have? What will be done during the trial?

15. In exercise 14, who may be present during the trial? If there is an appeal, which of these parties will not have to appear again?

16. Don Long is convicted of second-degree murder for killing a woman he had been seeing over the last few months. The court sentenced him to 30 years in jail. One year after his trial, Don admits that he withheld evidence that would have cleared him. He states he did so to protect his twin brother, who actually committed the crime, but who was dying of cancer at the time. He further states that he did not want his brother to spend the last years of his life behind bars. His brother has since died. The evidence is conclusive as to Don's innocence. Should the court set aside his conviction due to the new evidence? What policies would support the court in not doing so?

3-2 The Federal Court System

GOALS

- Identify the source of power of the federal courts
- Name the major federal courts and describe their jurisdictions and powers

KEY TERMS

general jurisdiction

specialized jurisdiction

writ of certiorari

Origin of the Federal Court System

WHAT'S YOUR VERDICT? Tom and Martina were discussing how the various federal courts were empowered to decide cases. Tom said that federal courts received their power from the U.S. Constitution. Martina maintained that Congress had created and empowered them.

Who is correct?

Through Article III of the Constitution, the people conferred the power to judge certain criminal and civil matters on a system of federal courts:

> Section 1. The judicial Power of the United States shall be vested in one Supreme Court, and in such inferior Courts as the Congress may from time to time ordain and establish.

The Articles of Confederation did not allow for a Supreme Court, and some citizens did not think a Supreme Court would be needed under the Constitution. As a result, after George Washington's inauguration as the nation's first president, it took nearly six months for Congress to utilize the power it was granted under Article III and pass the Federal Judiciary Act. This act "ordained and established" the U.S. Supreme Court (USSC) and thirteen district courts. In 1891, approximately a century after passing the initial Federal Judiciary Act, Congress passed a Judiciary Act that established the federal Courts of Appeal. Certain specialized courts, such as those concerned primarily with tax or bankruptcy matters, also were created as the need for them arose.

In *What's Your Verdict?* both Tom and Martina are correct. Ultimately, the federal courts receive their power to adjudicate cases from the Constitution.

However, the Constitution left to Congress the power to ordain and establish these courts if and when it deemed them necessary.

CHECKPOINT What is the source of power of the federal courts?

Jurisdiction of the Federal Courts

WHAT'S YOUR VERDICT? Susan Bean, a citizen of Illinois, sued Wallis Turk, a citizen of the state of Colorado, for the breach of a construction contract on Bean's new Chicago residence. More than $600,000 was at stake. Bean filed the suit in Illinois state court. Turk filed a motion to remove the case to the federal courts.

Will the case be heard in federal or state court?

Currently there are three levels of federal courts with general jurisdiction. These are federal district courts, federal courts of appeals, and the U.S. Supreme Court. A court with **general jurisdiction** can hear almost any kind of case. A court with **specialized jurisdiction** hears only one specific type of case. The chart on page 53 illustrates the three levels of the federal court system.

Federal District Courts

The federal (or U.S.) district court is the lowest level of federal court with general jurisdiction. This is the trial court (the first court to hear the dispute) of the federal system. It has the power to determine the facts and to make initial determinations of the law to use in deciding the case.

In general, district courts have original jurisdiction over (a) federal questions, or cases that arise under the Constitution, U.S. law, and U.S. treaties; and (b) lawsuits between citizens of different states, between a U.S. citizen and a foreign nation, or between a U.S. citizen and a citizen of a foreign nation. These parties are said to have *diversity of citizenship.* More than $75,000 must be in dispute for a federal court to hear a diversity of citizenship lawsuit. Otherwise a state court will decide the case.

Bean v. Turk in *What's Your Verdict?* will be tried in the federal courts. As the case has more than $75,000 in question and is between citizens of different states, it falls within the jurisdictional limits of the federal courts. These courts, when at least one of the parties requests their exercising it, have priority jurisdiction over state courts in such diversity cases.

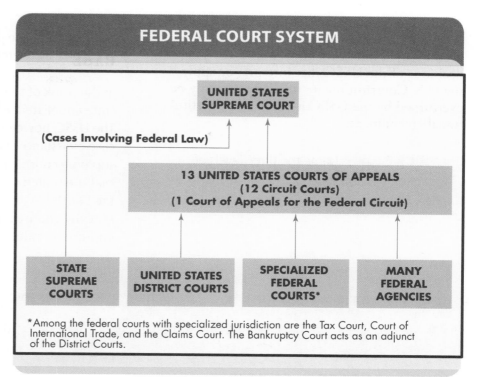

FEDERAL COURT SYSTEM

UNITED STATES SUPREME COURT

(Cases Involving Federal Law)

13 UNITED STATES COURTS OF APPEALS
(12 Circuit Courts)
(1 Court of Appeals for the Federal Circuit)

STATE SUPREME COURTS **UNITED STATES DISTRICT COURTS** **SPECIALIZED FEDERAL COURTS*** **MANY FEDERAL AGENCIES**

*Among the federal courts with specialized jurisdiction are the Tax Court, Court of International Trade, and the Claims Court. The Bankruptcy Court acts as an adjunct of the District Courts.

Federal Courts of Appeals

The federal courts of appeals have appellate jurisdiction over the district courts, certain specialized federal courts, and many federal administrative agencies. Such power is exercised when the result of a case in a lower court is appealed by one or more of the parties to the case.

Appellate courts do not accept any new evidence or call witnesses. Instead, they review the trial transcripts, appellate briefs, and oral arguments of the attorneys to reach a decision. No appellate court, not even the USSC, can change the factual determinations of a jury.

There are 13 federal courts of appeal. Twelve of these are circuit courts, each of which is responsible for an assigned geographic area. The thirteenth is dedicated to the "federal circuit." As such, it handles patent cases appealed out of the district courts and appeals from federal courts with specialized jurisdictions.

United States Supreme Court

The U.S. Supreme Court (USSC) has both original and appellate jurisdiction. Its original jurisdiction, according to the Constitution, is over "cases affecting ambassadors, other public ministers and consuls and those in which a state shall be party." The most important function of the USSC, however, is the exercise of its appellate jurisdiction. This jurisdiction is exercised over cases on appeal from the U.S. Courts of Appeals or from the highest courts of the various states. If the Supreme Court believes that a case contains a constitutional issue sufficiently important to be decided by it, the Supreme Court will issue a **writ of certiorari** to the last court that heard the case. This "writ" or order compels the lower court to turn over the record of the case to the Supreme Court for review.

Access school.cengage.com/blaw/lawxtra and click on the link for Chapter 3. Click on one of the topics on the home page of the official web site of the U.S. Supreme Court. Write a one-paragraph summary of your findings.

school.cengage.com/blaw/lawxtra

Jurisdiction over state supreme court cases is limited to those in which a federal question has been brought out at the trial court level. The decisions of the USSC that interpret or apply the U.S. Constitution are final and can only be overturned by the USSC itself or by a constitutional amendment.

CHECKPOINT Name the three levels of federal courts and describe the jurisdiction of each.

IN THIS CASE The jury in Martin's case convicted him of grand larceny partially based on evidence found in the trunk of the car he was driving. The state appellate courts upheld his conviction. The USSC, however, took jurisdiction over the case by issuing a writ of certiorari to the state supreme court. The USSC on appeal then held that the search of his trunk that discovered the items was improper. The USSC overturned his conviction, as the jury could have been improperly influenced by such evidence.

3-2 Assessment

Xtra! Study Tools
school.cengage.com/blaw/lawxtra

THINK ABOUT LEGAL CONCEPTS

1. A Supreme Court did not exist under the Articles of Confederation. **True or False?**

2. There are _ ?_ levels of courts with general jurisdiction in the federal system.

3. The federal trial courts are known as (a) district courts (b) federal county courts (c) common law courts (d) all of the above

4. Cases involving citizens of different states in which less than $75,000 is at stake must be tried in the state courts. **True or False?**

5. An appeal to the federal court system of a ruling of a federal agency initially would be taken to (a) a federal district court (b) a federal court of appeals (c) the USSC

THINK CRITICALLY ABOUT EVIDENCE

Study the situation, answer the questions, and then prepare arguments to support your answers.

6. Ms. Tant of New York City recently sued Mr. Bloom, also of New York City. She claimed that he had run into and injured her while he was jogging. She asked for $50,000 in damages. When she filed her suit in federal district court, Mr. Bloom's attorney immediately moved for the case to be dismissed from the federal court for two reasons. What were they?

7. Ms. Tant's case (see exercise 6) was thrown out of federal court. She later filed it in the New York state court solely as a case involving Mr. Bloom's negligent jogging. When she lost, she appealed all the way to the highest New York state court but still lost. She then sought to appeal to the U.S. Supreme Court. Will the U.S. Supreme Court hear her case? Why or why not?

8. Paul Stone sued his employer for assault and battery due to the actions of several of his female co-workers. While gathered around the coffee machine each morning, they would whistle at him, make lewd comments, and touch and pinch him. When the case was dismissed from the state circuit court, Stone appealed. The intermediate court of appeals sustained the result in the lower court, and Stone appealed to the state supreme court. When the state supreme court also sustained, Stone sought to appeal to the U.S. Supreme Court. Are there any federal issues in this case that would allow the U.S. Supreme Court to take jurisdiction? What might prevent the nation's highest court from so doing?

3-3 State Court Systems

GOALS

- Compare the structure of a typical state court system with the structure of the federal courts
- Explain the jurisdictions of the specialized courts in a typical state system

KEY TERMS

court of record

associate circuit courts

county courts

municipal courts

small claims courts

juvenile courts

probate courts

A Typical State Court System

WHAT'S YOUR VERDICT? Sheila had a beautiful apartment with a view of the harbor. After she had lived there several years, her landlord gave her and the other tenants of the apartment building 30 days notice to vacate. Sheila sued to prevent the mass evictions. After losing in the state trial court, she vowed to appeal the issue directly to the U.S. Supreme Court.

Can she do so?

The typical state legal system resembles the federal system. The state legislature makes the laws. The state executive branch enforces those laws in the courts of the state judicial branch.

The courts of a typical state's judicial branch are organized into three tiers. In the bottom tier is a geographically based set of trial courts with either general or specialized jurisdictions. An appellate tier of courts is next. This appellate tier is then capped by a state supreme court as the ultimate level of appeal. Both the trial and appellate courts are controlled and supervised by this supreme court. In *What's Your Verdict?* Sheila could not take her appeal directly to the U.S. Supreme Court. Generally, there is no guaranteed right to be heard on appeal by even the state supreme court, with the exception of capital murder convictions.

State Trial Courts

In most states trial courts—those courts with general original jurisdiction over both criminal and civil matters—are known as circuit courts.

Other states refer to them as superior courts, district courts, or courts of common pleas. Regardless of their name, these trial courts are the courts of record in the state system.

A **court of record** keeps an exact account of what goes on at trial. The accuracy of this "record" is vital, as any appeal filed depends on it. The record may include a transcript of what was said, the evidence that was submitted, statements, the determinations of the court officials, and the judgment of the court.

State trial courts also review the decisions of courts of more specialized jurisdiction, such as the small claims courts, which are not courts of record. Where necessary, state trial courts retry such cases to make a proper record for the purpose of potential appeals.

Because a state trial court has original jurisdiction over cases before it, it makes determinations

If the parties to a case do not request a jury, a judge will preside over the case. Do you think it is always in the best interest of the parties to request a jury? Why or why not?

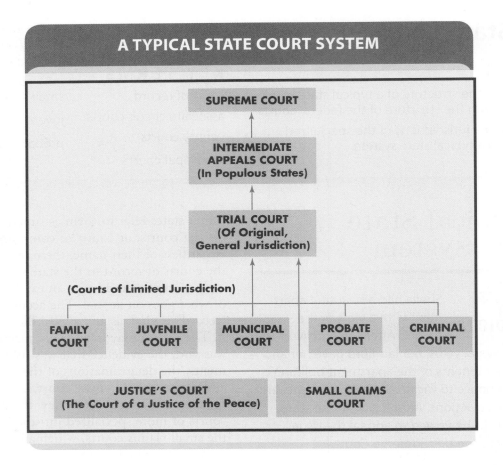

A TYPICAL STATE COURT SYSTEM

SUPREME COURT

INTERMEDIATE APPEALS COURT (In Populous States)

TRIAL COURT (Of Original, General Jurisdiction)

(Courts of Limited Jurisdiction)

FAMILY COURT | JUVENILE COURT | MUNICIPAL COURT | PROBATE COURT | CRIMINAL COURT

JUSTICE'S COURT (The Court of a Justice of the Peace) | SMALL CLAIMS COURT

of the facts in the case often by using a jury. If a jury is not requested by the parties in the case, the judge will determine the facts. Once the facts have been determined, the judge will select and apply the law to the facts to reach a verdict.

State Courts of Appeals

An appeal from a court of record is typically reviewed by a panel of judges in a state court of appeals. The panel of judges from the state court of appeals usually consists of no more than three judges. The state court appellate procedure is very similar to that of the federal courts of appeals. In particular, the state appellate panel evaluates the record of the case and the appellate briefs submitted by the attorneys for the parties. It also may hear oral arguments by those attorneys in the case. No new evidence can be introduced at this level. The judges at the appellate level check to be sure that the lower court used the correct law to conduct and resolve the case. If the correct law was used, the result in the case will be upheld.

If court of appeals judges conclude that the trial court used the incorrect law, they may apply the correct law themselves to reach a new result. If, however, they conclude that the use of the incorrect law interfered with the proper determination of the facts of the case, they may send the case back down for a new trial.

State Supreme Courts

Generally, in whatever legal issue you confront, you are entitled to a trial and to one appeal, if filed in a timely manner and in the proper form. In states with the intermediate level of courts of appeals, only cases that involve the most vital and complex legal issues are taken to the justices of the state supreme court. (*Justice* is the title given to judges who sit on state supreme courts and the federal Supreme Court.) Typically, at the state supreme court level, a panel of three or more justices reviews the cases on appeal in the same manner as the lower appellate courts.

State supreme courts issue the final decision on matters of law appealed to them. If a U.S. Constitutional or other federal question of law is involved, however, a further appeal can go to the U.S. Supreme Court. In several states, in addition to its appellate jurisdiction, the state supreme court has original jurisdiction over most state impeachment cases.

CHECKPOINT What does a typical state court system have in common with the federal court system?

State Courts with Specialized Jurisdictions

WHAT'S YOUR VERDICT? Chase, age 15, violated his state's anti-hacking law. He was caught and referred to a juvenile court.

Will he be treated differently under the juvenile court's jurisdiction than under a regular trial court's jurisdiction?

Below the main circuit court level in most states are courts with specialized jurisdictions. These courts include the associate circuit, municipal, small claims, juvenile, and probate courts.

Associate Circuit Courts

Many states have a layer of courts below their main courts of general original jurisdiction. These lower courts are referred to as **associate circuit courts** or **county courts**. Such courts hear minor criminal cases, state traffic offenses, and lawsuits in which relatively small amounts are involved (usually no more than $25,000). Generally, these courts are not courts of record. However, they take a significant burden off the higher courts, even though appeals from their decisions can be taken to a state trial court for a trial on the record.

City or Municipal Courts

Cities typically have courts that administer their ordinances. These **municipal courts** are usually divided into traffic and criminal divisions. As city ordinances often overlap with or duplicate state laws, less serious violations occurring within city limits are brought before such municipal courts for their first trial. The result can then be appealed to the state trial court level if necessary.

Although the penalties for violating ordinances can be as severe, ordinances are not considered criminal laws. Only state and federal governments can make an act criminal.

Small Claims Courts

Minor individual suits would not often be heard if not for the **small claims courts**. These courts handle disputes in which small amounts, generally $2,500 or less, are involved. Attorneys generally are not required in small claims courts. The judge hears the case without a jury or formal rules of evidence. Decisions of small claims courts also can be appealed to a state trial court.

Juvenile Courts

Younger members of society—those over 13 and under 18 years of age in most states—are referred to as juveniles. The map on page 58 shows the minimum age at which each state tries an individual as an adult. Society typically believes that juveniles should not be held as responsible as adults for their criminal acts. To carry out this policy, special **juvenile courts** have been set up. In these courts the juvenile is entitled to his or her full constitutional rights, including the right

A Question of ETHICS

At age 17, Horace Samuels was brought before the juvenile court charged with child molestation. He was convicted and, as a juvenile, was sentenced to probation in a foster home. While in the home, he was again caught and tried for the same offense. Again, he was tried as a juvenile. Now he is 18 and about to live on his own in an area in which many children of the same age that he has been charged with molesting also live. Horace's probation officer realizes that Horace has not been rehabilitated and is a potential danger to the neighborhood's young. The law requires that the juvenile's record remain closed so that the individual may begin a new life free and clear of past mistakes. What should the probation officer do?

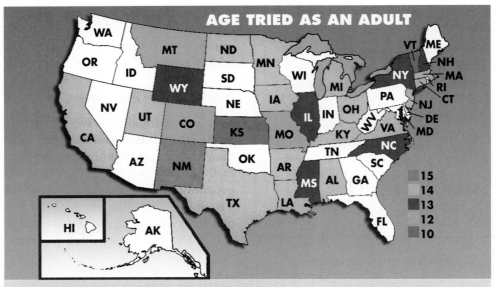

AGE TRIED AS AN ADULT

15
14
13
12
10

Washington, D.C., and 22 states do not have a set minimum age for a child to be tried as an adult. Twenty-eight of the states do have a set minimum age—the range is 10 to 15 years of age.

to be represented by an attorney. If the juvenile is found guilty of the charges brought, the court has wide powers in determining what should be done.

However, the emphasis for juveniles generally is on rehabilitation, not punishment. Possibilities open to the court include release into the supervision of parents, guardians, or governmental officials; placement in foster homes; and detention in correctional facilities. These courts ensure that most of the criminal cases involving juveniles do not become public knowledge. The courtroom is closed while an

informal hearing into the charges is conducted. Any records made on juvenile cases are not open to the public.

If rehabilitation fails or is shown to be impossible, the young offender can be tried and punished as an adult. This occurs only in cases involving a very serious offense. For example, murder and certain other crimes may bring about trial and punishment through the criminal law system. Appeals from actions of the juvenile courts are directed to the circuit courts.

In *What's Your Verdict?* Chase would be treated far differently under the juvenile court's jurisdiction. He would be entitled to a juvenile court hearing where his age, level of maturity, and potential would be considered in determining how he is to be treated.

Probate Courts

When individuals die, their property and other interests must be divided according to their wishes and the appropriate laws. The courts that administer wills and estates to accomplish this task are called **probate courts**.

LAW BRIEF

A juvenile offender's rehabilitation is a priority with society to prevent the loss of the productive resources that youth could someday provide. Juveniles are capitalized by society through education and supported by various health systems and programs. Instead of sending them off to jail and pushing them into the cycle of crime and punishment, society seeks to protect its investment by assisting them to get back on a productive path.

CHECKPOINT Name the typical state courts that have specialized jurisdiction.

THINK ABOUT LEGAL CONCEPTS

1. Which of the following is generally not included in the "record" of a case? (a) verbatim transcript (b) physical and documentary evidence (c) media coverage (d) all of the above are generally included

2. Attorneys generally are not required in a small claims court. **True or False?**

3. A state trial court has the power to hear some appeals. **True or False?**

4. A dispute between neighbors involving property damage of $750 would probably be heard in (a) federal district court (b) probate court (c) small claims court (d) associate circuit court

5. A state supreme court can make its own determinations of the facts in a particular case. **True or False?**

THINK CRITICALLY ABOUT EVIDENCE

Study the situations, answer the questions, and then prepare arguments to support your answers.

6. Gwendolyn Hunt was driving while intoxicated when she hit and killed Felicia Meyers, a seven-year-old, in a school crosswalk. Gwendolyn was 16 years old at the time. However, she was on probation from a reduced sentence for driving 62 in a 35 mph residential speed zone. Should Gwendolyn be tried as an adult for vehicular manslaughter?

7. You are driving along a residential city street when you are stopped by a city police officer for speeding. You are given a citation and a summons to appear before a particular court. What court would that most likely be and why?

8. You are driving along the interstate highway headed for a ballgame in a nearby city. A state highway patrol car suddenly appears in your rearview mirror, lights flashing. You pull over and are cited for doing 80 in a 65 mph zone. Your receive a summons to a particular court. What court would that most likely be and why?

9. After a long illness, your uncle dies. He leaves a sizeable estate but no will is found for several weeks. Finally, one of his ex-wives appears with a document she claims to be a valid will. It shows her and her children by him receiving most of his property. Your parents and the deceased's other children contest the will. Should the federal or state courts handle this case? Why? Which court in which system is most likely to hear it?

10. Jean Marie of Bangor, Maine, ordered a new laptop computer from a company in California. The computer was advertised as having cutting-edge technology and the fastest computing speed in its class. When Jean received the laptop, he found it ran much slower than expected. Upon further examination, he discovered that the computer chips utilized were out of date and their speed less than 25 percent of the current ones. The laptop cost $499 plus shipping. The company refused to refund Jean's money. Should he sue? What court would be available to him? Will he receive justice in the matter?

Chapter 3 Assessment

CONCEPTS IN BRIEF

3-1   Forms of Dispute Resolution

1. Mediation and arbitration offer dispute resolution alternatives to litigation. Using these alternative methods of dispute resolution helps to avoid the costs, delays, and difficulties of a court trial.

2. The levels of courts are trial courts, which have original jurisdiction, and appellate courts, which review decisions of lower courts.

3-2   The Federal Court System

3. The federal courts receive their power from Article III, Section 1, of the U.S. Constitution.

4. Federal courts can have either general or specialized jurisdiction. Courts with general jurisdiction include federal district courts, federal courts of appeals, and the U.S. Supreme Court. Courts with specialized jurisdiction hear only one specific type of case.

3-3   State Court Systems

5. The typical state court system is similar to the federal court system. Both the federal and most state court systems have trial courts, appellate courts, and a supreme court.

6. Associate circuit courts, or county courts, hear minor criminal cases, state traffic offenses, and lawsuits involving small amounts of money.

7. Municipal or city courts usually feature two divisions, one to handle traffic and another to handle violations of all other ordinances. Penalties for ordinance violations (which are not considered crimes) are less severe than federal and state criminal law penalties.

8. Small claims courts feature relaxed rules of evidence and do not require representation by an attorney. The dollar amount that can be adjudicated usually is limited to around $2,500.

9. In every state, there are juvenile courts with specialized jurisdiction over persons under a certain age. These courts emphasize rehabilitation over punishment. In certain instances, juveniles can be bound over for trial as adults.

10. Probate courts settle the estates of decedents who die with or without a will.

YOUR LEGAL VOCABULARY

Match each statement with the term that it best defines. Some terms will not be used.

1. Verbatim record of what went on at trial

2. Court that reviews trial court decisions to determine if a significant error of law was made during trial

3. Court in which an accurate, detailed report of what went on at trial is made

4. Independent third party who develops a binding, court-enforceable dispute resolution

5. Order to a lower court to produce the record of a case for the Supreme Court to review

6. Power to hear a case in full for the first time

7. Court that hears cases involving individuals generally between the ages of 13 and 18

8. To place a dispute before a court of law for resolution

9. Court that hears cases involving violations of ordinances

10. Power to hear only cases of a specific type

a. appellate brief
b. appellate court
c. arbitrator
d. associate circuit court (or county court)
e. court
f. court of record
g. general jurisdiction
h. juvenile court
i. litigate
j. mediator
k. municipal court
l. original jurisdiction
m. probate court
n. small claims court
o. specialized jurisdiction
p. transcript
q. trial court
r. verdict
s. writ of certiorari

REVIEW LEGAL CONCEPTS

11. What is the fundamental difference between arbitration and mediation?

12. Why are appeals heard by higher courts?

13. Why should the federal courts handle cases involving private matters between citizens of different states (for example, cases involving diversity of citizenship with more than $75,000 at stake)?

14. Why shouldn't the USSC be able to substitute its own factual determinations for those of a jury in a lower court?

WRITE ABOUT LEGAL CONCEPTS

15. Wherever you go you are charged with knowing all the laws, ordinances, rules, and regulations that apply to you. "Ignorance of the law is no excuse." Because of the confusion this causes, there has been a movement in the last 50 years to make state laws more uniform. From sales law to various parts of the criminal code, the effect has been positive. Should state court systems be made more uniform? What are the advantages and disadvantages of such an idea?

16. Judges cost an extraordinary amount of money. To attract competent personnel to the judiciary, salaries must be comparable to what an exceptional lawyer would earn in private practice. A way to provide the necessary salary levels is to save money elsewhere in the system. To that end, many states use extensively trained non-lawyers to preside over municipal courts and hold other minor judiciary positions. Do you think this is a good idea? Why or why not?

17. **HOT DEBATE** Write a paragraph discussing the following question: If Anthony decides to file suit in state court against his employer, what federal court might ultimately claim jurisdiction? Under what circumstances?

MAKE ACADEMIC CONNECTIONS

18. **BIOLOGY** The jurisdictional shield of the juvenile courts ends at age 18. Research the maturation process of homo sapiens and determine whether or not, according to the scientific evidence, 18 is a good cutoff age. What implications does the result of your research have for driving age, voting age, age to enter the military, and age to drink in your state.

THINK CRITICALLY ABOUT EVIDENCE

Study the situation, answer the questions, and then prepare arguments to support your answers.

19. Gomez wanted to sue Shapiro for failure to complete work under their contract but could not afford the expenses and time delays associated with litigation. What alternatives are available to resolve this matter?

20. If you were called to testify as a witness in a friend's criminal trial, would you have the moral strength to tell the complete truth even if your friend might be convicted as a result?

21. June lost her case in trial court. She thought that the plaintiff, Sid, had lied during the trial. On appeal, she requested that she be allowed to appear and explain why she thought Sid had lied. Will her request be granted?

22. Suppose someone has injured you. Do you have a duty to sue them for the injury even when the costs of bringing suit may be more than you can recover?

23. On May 7, Bart Masters turned 18. The evening of that day, he was caught stealing a woman's purse. "Don't worry," he told his friend Julia, "I just turned 18 today, they won't try me as an adult. I'm too close to being a juvenile." Is he correct?

24. Priscilla is being sued in small claims court by her landlord for past due rent. "Just wait," she exclaims. "Once I get in front of that jury, they won't award him the money. After all, he shut off the water several times and didn't even have heat in the building for over a month last winter." What is wrong with Priscilla's estimate of the situation?

ANALYZE REAL CASES

25. In April of 2004, the U.S. Supreme Court refused to hear the appeal of a case involving Virginia Military Institute (VMI). The case centered on the issue of whether or not, at a public supported college such as VMI, a prayer traditionally offered before the evening meal should be prohibited as a violation of the constitutional mandate requiring the separation of church and state. In an unusual step, two of the Justices of the Court criticized the other Justices for avoiding the responsibility of rendering a clear decision with attendant guidelines on the matter. Failing to take the case left in place a lower court's decision against having the prayer. The two Justices pointed out that, although there were previous decisions against such prayer in the public schools where attendance was enforced, colleges were voluntary institutions. Should the court have taken the case? How do you feel the court should rule on the mandatory recital of the pledge of allegiance, with the phrase "Under God" therein, in public schools or colleges? (*Bunting v. Mellen*, USSC 03-863, 181 F. Supp. 2d 619)

26. Taylor and Fitz Coal Company had a dispute over the amount of money due under a mineral lease. They submitted the dispute to arbitration according to the provisions of the lease. The arbitrators awarded the lessor, Taylor, $37,214.67. Taylor did not like the amount awarded and filed suit in court. Will the court conduct a trial to determine whether the amount is fair? (*Taylor v. Fitz Coal Company*, 618 S.W.2d 432, Ky.)

27. A 17-year-old boy first appeared in juvenile court to answer charges of vehicular homicide. The incident had occurred when he was 16. By the time the case actually went to trial the boy was 18. Should he be tried as an adult? Why or why not? (*Commission v. A Juvenile*, 545 N.E.2d 1164)

28. When a tip was received that marijuana was being grown in his greenhouse, Michael Riley's property was observed from a helicopter by an investigating officer. The helicopter flyover was deemed necessary because the items within the greenhouse could not be observed from a nearby road. Riley was subsequently arrested and tried for offenses stemming from his cultivation efforts. The defense challenged the use of the information acquired by the helicopter flyover saying that it was an illegal search under the Fourth Amendment to the U.S. Constitution. The Florida Supreme Court agreed with the defense. Could the State of Florida appeal the decision to the U.S. Supreme Court? Why or why not? (*Florida v. Riley*, 102 L.Ed. 2d 835)

29. Colleen Donnelly filed charges with the Equal Employment Opportunity Commission (EEOC) against her employer, Yellow Freight, for sex discrimination. After she filed the charges, Colleen received notice from the EEOC that she had 90 days to bring suit. This 90-day period was a procedure for claims under the federal Civil Rights Act of 1964. Within that period Donnelly did indeed file suit but in an Illinois state court under an Illinois statute that also prohibits such discrimination. After the 90-day period had expired, however, she tried to transfer the suit to a federal court. Yellow Freight defended claiming that she could not make such a transfer as the 90-day period had expired for federal actions. Should she be allowed to go forward with her suit? Why or why not? (*Donnelly v. Yellow Freight System, Inc.*, 874 F.2d 402)

30. A government-owned P-51 fighter plane landed at a Los Angeles airport and waited on a runway for a tow truck, on instructions from the tower. Shortly thereafter, a plane owned by Douglas Aircraft Company began approaching the airfield to land. The Douglas aircraft struck the P-51, which was parked on the runway. The United States brought suit against Douglas, claiming that the Douglas pilot was negligent. During the trial, evidence was introduced indicating that the Douglas pilot was careless in not seeing the parked P-51, but that the airport was covered with a haze and the P-51 was painted in camouflage colors. Also, the Douglas pilot had "zigzagged" his plane while taxiing in order to improve his forward vision. The trial was conducted before a jury. The government claimed that the issue of whether the Douglas pilot was negligent was an issue of law for the judge to decide. Douglas claimed that it was an issue of fact for the jury to decide. Which one is correct? (*United States v. Douglas Aircraft Company*, 169 F.2d 755, 9th Cir.)

Case For Legal Thinking

TEXAS V. JOHNSON
USSC, 109 SUPREME COURT REPORTER 2533

BACKGROUND In 1984, during the Republican National Convention in Dallas, Texas, a political demonstration was held. The point of the demonstration was to protest the policies of the President of the United States, Ronald Reagan. Mr. Reagan was to be re-nominated by the convention for a second term. The demonstration also targeted several Dallas-based corporations for their government-related activities.

FACTS As the demonstration was being conducted, a protestor took an American flag from a pole outside one of the buildings. The protestor passed the flag to another protestor, Johnson, who subsequently doused it with kerosene and set it afire. As the flag of the United States of America burned, the protestors chanted, "America, the red, white, and blue, we spit on you." The protestor who set the flag afire was ultimately charged with a crime and tried in a Texas trial court.

LOWER COURT The trial court found Johnson guilty of violating a state statute which prohibited the desecration of state or national flags. The statute defined desecration as the physical mistreatment of such objects so as to seriously offend individuals likely to observe or discover the act.

APPEAL Johnson appealed his conviction on the basis of the First Amendment's guarantee of freedom of speech. A Texas Court of Appeals affirmed the conviction even after noting that such a statute, which might have a potentially chilling effect on speech, deserved close scrutiny in its application. However, said the court, the conviction could be upheld in this instance as being necessary to guarantee the peaceful nature of the assembly due to the highly inflammatory nature of a flag burning. The case was then appealed to the Texas Court of Criminal Appeals. The Court of Criminal Appeals reversed the decisions of the inferior courts and sent the case back to the trial court with instructions to dismiss the charges. The Court, in so doing, indicated that the statute was too broad in its reference to protecting against a breach of the peace. The U.S. Supreme Court then took jurisdiction by a writ of certiorari.

ISSUE Was the conviction of Johnson justifiable by the state of Texas as an attempt to protect against breaches of the peace, or did the flag burning have overriding elements of communication that the state statute failed to protect?

DECISION The United States Supreme Court, in an opinion written by Justice Brennan, held that the First Amendment freedom of speech had indeed been violated by the application of the statute.

PRACTICE JUDGING

1. Should the court affirm or reverse as a consequence?

2. The record did not contain any evidence indicating that a breach of the peace had indeed occurred. How do you think this affected the decision?

3. There is an exception for "fighting words" provided for governments who want to enforce statutes that might chill public speech. Could this exception have been applied to this situation in order to uphold the conviction?

Chapter 4
Criminal Law and Procedure

4-1 Criminal Law
4-2 Criminal Procedure

HOT DEBATE

While sitting in his pickup waiting to cross South Street in Springfield, Missouri, Thomas, an infantryman on leave from the war in Iraq, was hit and killed by Hercule, a 45-year-old intoxicated driver. At the time, Hercule was driving at high speed trying to evade pursuing police cars. Hercule was arrested at the scene. At trial, his attorneys were able to have the blood-test evidence that showed a 0.20 level of intoxication (double the legal limit) thrown out. Hercule was convicted only of second-degree manslaughter, served a week of "shock" jail time, and was set free on two years probation. Outraged at what he termed the failure of the legal system, Mark, Thomas's younger brother, took his parent's car and ran Hercule over in the street as he left the jail. Hercule, a married father of four, was crippled for life as a result.

WHERE DO YOU STAND?

1. Was Mark morally justified in his actions?
2. What action should the law take against Mark?

4-1 Criminal Law

GOALS

- Understand the three elements that make up a criminal act
- Classify crimes according to the severity of their potential sentences
- Identify the types of crimes that affect business

KEY TERMS

crime

vicarious criminal liability

felony

misdemeanor

white-collar crimes

Crimes and Criminal Behavior

WHAT'S YOUR VERDICT? O'Brien, a vice president at the Del Norte Credit Union, cleverly juggled the company books over a period of years. During that time, he took at least $135,000 belonging to the credit union. When the theft was discovered by outside auditors, O'Brien repaid the money with interest.

Has he committed a crime despite the repayment?

The most fundamental characteristic of a **crime** is that it is a punishable offense against society. When a crime occurs, society—acting through police and prosecutors—attempts to identify, arrest, prosecute, and punish the criminal. These efforts are designed to protect society, not the victim of the crime. As a consequence, it is up to society's chosen representatives to determine what action to take against the person who committed the crime. The victim can sue identified criminals for civil damages. However, victims seldom do so because few criminals have the ability to pay judgments.

A Question of ETHICS

Not more than two centuries ago society routinely imposed a single punishment for a felony. That punishment was death. What do you think was happening at that time in history that required such a level of punishment?

Crimes should be carefully defined by statutes, or laws enacted by state or federal legislatures. A well-worded criminal statute clearly and specifically defines the behavior it prohibits. It does not interfere with protected individual rights in so doing.

Elements of Criminal Acts

Before you can be convicted of a crime, the prosecution must prove three elements regarding your behavior at the trial. These elements are

1. whether you had a duty to do or not to do a certain thing
2. whether you performed an act or omission in violation of that duty
3. whether or not you had criminal intent

DUTY Generally, under our system everyone has a legally enforceable *duty* to conform his or her conduct to the law's requirements. To establish a specific legal duty in a trial, the prosecutor cites to the judge a statute that prescribes the duty owed in the case at hand.

VIOLATION OF THE DUTY The *breach of duty*—the specific conduct of the defendant that violates the statute—is the *criminal act.* For example, all states have statutes that make battery a crime. These statutes often define criminal battery as "the intentional causing of bodily harm to another person." A breach of this duty could be proved in a trial by the testimony of a witness who saw the defendant punch the victim.

CRIMINAL INTENT The third element, criminal intent, also must be proven in most cases. Criminal intent generally means that the defendant intended to commit the specific act or omission defined as criminal in the controlling statute.

Note that intent and motive are separate in the eyes of the law. Intent refers strictly to the state of mind that must be present concurrently with the alleged criminal act or failure to act. Motive refers to what specifically drives a person to act or refrain from doing so.

In *What's Your Verdict?* O'Brien owed a duty, defined by state statute, to not take the credit union's money. Violation of this duty, the criminal conduct of taking another's property or money by a person to whom it has been entrusted, is *embezzlement*. This act could be proved with the testimony of the auditors. O'Brien's criminal intent, to wrongfully deprive others of the money, can be inferred from his conduct. So O'Brien did commit a crime. His return of the money does not alter this fact.

Criminal intent creates two issues related to corporations. First, can a corporation, which is an organization, form criminal intent the way humans can? The answer is yes. If the corporation's employees have criminal intent, their employer may be judged to have criminal intent. If the employees were doing their assigned duties and the criminal act benefits the organization, most courts will hold that the organization had criminal intent.

The second issue relates to corporate presidents, treasurers, and other officers. When a corporate employee commits a crime, can officers be held criminally responsible? Again, the answer often is yes. In some situations, the officer will be held criminally liable under the doctrine of **vicarious criminal liability**. Vicarious means substituted. The criminal

intent of the employee is used as a substitute for the requirement of criminal intent for an officer.

Criminal intent also is related to age. Under early common law, children under age 7 were considered incapable of forming the criminal intent necessary for crimes. Those over age 14 were presumed capable of recognizing the difference between right and wrong and so were as accountable as adults for their acts. For children ages 7 through 14, such ability had to be proved.

Today, statutes in most states fix the age of criminal liability at 18, but the figure ranges from 16 to 19. State statutes provide that minors as young as 7 may be tried and punished as adults if they are accused of serious crimes such as murder. Generally, however, what is a crime for an adult is *juvenile delinquency* for a minor.

The lack of the mental capacity to know the difference between right and wrong can be a defense to being held responsible for the commission of criminal acts. Accordingly, insane persons are not held responsible for their criminal acts. However, people who voluntarily become intoxicated or drugged are held responsible.

Some minor crimes do not require the element of criminal intent. Traffic offenses are an example. A driver may be exceeding the speed limit without noticing, yet still be in violation of the law. In addition, in certain circumstances extreme carelessness may be considered the same as criminal intent. Suppose you drive 80 miles per hour through a residential neighborhood while drunk and kill a

Economic Impact

ADA ACCESSIBILITY GUIDELINES

The Americans with Disabilities Act (ADA) is a comprehensive federal civil rights statute that outlaws discrimination on the basis of disability. On July 23, 2004, after years of planning and evaluation, the Architectural and Transportation Barriers Compliance Board (Access Board) issued several amendments to the Americans with Disabilities Act Accessibility Guidelines (ADAAG) to cover newly constructed and altered recreation facilities. These rules were intended to provide access for the disabled to facilities such as amusement park

rides, marinas, golf courses, physical fitness facilities, recreational camps, etc.

THINK CRITICALLY

Evaluate these new rules based on their stated cost to the owners of such facilities. (Access lawxtra.swlearning.com for a link to a detailed listing of estimated costs per type of facility.) If you were the president of a company in the recreational field, what impact might these rules have on your decision to update or build new facilities?

Imagine that the person in this photo killed a pedestrian while driving under the influence of alcohol. Do you think the law should treat the intent of this person as criminal? Why or why not?

Crimes can be classified in many different ways. One method of classification is to identify against whom or what they are committed. The table below lists and gives examples of this classification method. Crimes also can be classified as either felonies or misdemeanors according to the severity of their potential sentences.

Felony

A **felony** is a crime punishable by confinement for more than a year in a state prison or by a fine of more than $1,000, or both—or even death.

Murder, kidnapping, arson, rape, robbery, burglary, embezzlement, forgery, theft of large

pedestrian. You may not have intended to strike the pedestrian with your car. However, your conduct was so careless that in many jurisdictions courts will treat it the same as criminal intent. You could be convicted of the crime of vehicular homicide.

CHECKPOINT What three elements must be proven at trial before someone can be convicted of a crime?

Classifications of Crimes

WHAT'S YOUR VERDICT? Murdock was a witness at a civil trial for damages. Before testifying, he took an oath "to tell the truth, the whole truth, and nothing but the truth." Nevertheless, while being questioned by one of the attorneys, Murdock deliberately lied, hoping to help the defendant.

What crime has Murdock committed?

Classification of Crimes by Party, Interest, or Property Injured	
Crimes against . . .	**Type of Crime**
a person	assault and battery kidnapping rape murder
property	theft robbery embezzlement
government and administration of justice	treason tax evasion perjury
public peace and order	rioting disorderly conduct illegal speeding
realty	burglary arson criminal trespass
consumers	fraudulent sale of securities violation of pure food and drug laws
decency	bigamy obscenity prostitution

sums, and perjury are examples of felonies. People who lie under oath (as Murdock did in *What's Your Verdict?*) commit the felony of *perjury*.

Misdemeanor

A **misdemeanor** is a less serious crime. It usually is punishable by confinement in a county or city jail for one year or less, by a fine of $1,000 or less, or both. Crimes such as disorderly conduct and speeding usually are misdemeanors.

Some states classify lesser misdemeanors as *infractions*. Persons convicted of infractions can only be fined. Because there is no risk of being jailed, the defendant charged with an infraction is not entitled to a jury trial. Parking violations and littering are examples of infractions.

CHECKPOINT Name the two categories of crimes classified by the severity of their potential sentences.

Littering in this beach town carries a fine of $1,000. Research to find out the fine for littering in your area.

© GETTY IMAGES/PHOTODISC

Business-Related Crimes

WHAT'S YOUR VERDICT? Officers of the major competing DRAM memory chip manufacturers met at a trade convention. All of the officers agreed to use the same wholesale prices in bids to supply computer retailers with the chips. They also agreed to follow the lead of the biggest company in making future price changes. Each officer agreed to promote sales by concentrating only within an assigned geographical region.

Have the officers and their companies committed any crime?

Like people, businesses are subject to general criminal law. Offenses committed in the business world typically are referred to as **white-collar crimes**. These crimes do not involve force or violence and do not cause physical injury to people or physical damage to property.

Common examples of white-collar crimes are not paying income taxes, stock fraud, using false weighing machines, conspiring to fix prices, making false fire insurance and auto insurance claims, engaging in false advertising, committing bribery, engaging in political corruption, and embezzling. Because physical violence is not involved, courts tend to be more lenient with white-collar criminals. Punishments usually include fines or short prison sentences.

In *What's Your Verdict?* the corporate officers and their corporations were guilty of violating criminal portions of the antitrust laws. *Antitrust laws* state that competing companies may not cooperate in fixing prices or in dividing sales regions. Antitrust laws require that business firms compete with one another. Some of the more common business-related crimes follow.

LARCENY *Larceny*, commonly known as *theft*, is the wrongful taking of money or personal property belonging to someone else, with intent to deprive the owner of it. *Robbery* is a variation of larceny. It is the taking of property from another's person or immediate presence, against the victim's will, by force or by causing fear. *Burglary* is another variation of larceny. It is entering a building without permission when intending to commit a crime. Other types of larceny include shoplifting, pick pocketing, and purse snatching.

Larceny may be either a felony or a misdemeanor. The classification is determined by the value of the property stolen and other circumstances. Robbery and burglary are always felonies. A thief who sells the stolen goods is guilty of the separate crime of *selling stolen property*.

RECEIVING STOLEN PROPERTY Knowingly receiving stolen property consists of either receiving or buying property known to be stolen, with intent to deprive the rightful owner of the property. One who receives stolen property is known as a *fence*.

FALSE PRETENSES One who obtains money or other property by lying about a past or existing fact is guilty of *false pretenses*. This crime differs from larceny because the victim parts with the property voluntarily. False pretenses is a type of fraud.

FORGERY *Forgery* is falsely making or materially altering a writing to defraud another. The most common forgeries are found on checks when one signs another's name without permission to do so. Forgery also includes altering a check, such as changing "$7" to "$70" and "Seven" to "Seventy." Forgery usually is a felony. Of course, if others authorize you to sign their names, there is no forgery.

BRIBERY *Bribery* is unlawfully offering or giving anything of value to influence performance of an official in the carrying out of his or her public or legal duties. Soliciting or accepting the bribe is also criminal. In many states, bribing nongovernmental parties is also a form of bribery called commercial bribery. Thus, paying a private company's purchasing agent to obtain a sale may be bribery. It is usually bribery when a professional gambler pays an athlete to lose a game intentionally. The federal Foreign Corrupt Practices Act of 1977 prohibits most instances of bribery in foreign countries by U.S. companies. Unlike the United States, many other nations do not make criminal or prosecute such actions by their companies.

© GETTY IMAGES/PHOTODISC

What is the evidence that this man is committing a burglary? Is there any evidence that a robbery is in process? If so, what is it?

COMPUTER CRIME The computer revolution has created a range of problems for criminal law. For example, larceny is "the wrongful taking of the personal property of others." This traditional definition of the crime made it difficult to prosecute those who steal computer data. Many courts concluded that there was not a "taking" if an intruder merely copied the information in the computer. Even if an intruder copied and erased computer information, some courts concluded that there was no taking of "personal property"

LEGAL *Research*

Search the Internet for state and federal laws that prohibit computer-related crimes. An example would be to research electronic identity theft in all its forms from credit card fraud to invasion of accounts.

but only the loss of electrical impulses, which no one really owns. In response, the federal and state governments have created new criminal laws, such as the federal Computer Fraud and Abuse Act (Title 18 U.S.C. Section 1030) specifically targeting computer-related crimes.

EXTORTION *Extortion* (commonly known as *blackmail*) is obtaining money or other property from a person by wrongful use of force, fear, or

---

IN THIS CASE

Intercomp is a U.S. company that routinely buys surplus computers in this country and markets them overseas. Intercomp agreed to reimburse its agent for gifts given to a foreign government official. The official decided which companies were to be placed on a list of those authorized to do business in the country. Intercomp's non-U.S. competitors all gave similar gifts to the official. However, for doing so, Intercomp was prosecuted in the United States under its Foreign Corrupt Practices Act, convicted, and fined $500,000.

---

the power of office. For example, the extortionist (blackmailer) may threaten to inflict bodily injury. At other times, the threat may be to expose a secret crime or embarrassing fact if payment is not made.

CONSPIRACY An agreement between two or more persons to commit a crime is called *conspiracy*. Usually the agreement is secret. The conspiracy is a crime separate from the crime the parties planned to commit. Depending on the circumstances, conspiracy may be either a felony or a misdemeanor. Business executives of competing corporations sometimes conspire to fix prices or to divide markets.

ARSON *Arson* is the willful and illegal burning or exploding of a building. Arson occurs when someone intentionally starts a fire or causes an explosion that damages or destroys a building or other property without the owner's consent. In some states, arson also occurs if you burn your own building to defraud an insurer.

CHECKPOINT Name the types of business-related crimes.

4-1 Assessment

Xtra!
Study Tools
school.cengage.com/blaw/lawxtra

THINK ABOUT LEGAL CONCEPTS

1. Legally, a crime is considered an offense against (a) the victim (b) society (c) the court (d) none of the above

2. Ben is convicted and sentenced to two to five years in jail. The crime he has committed is a (a) misdemeanor (b) felony

3. In some situations, an officer of a corporation will be held criminally liable for the acts of an employee under the doctrine of _?_.

4. Falsely making or materially altering a writing to defraud another is known as the crime of false pretenses. **True or False?**

THINK CRITICALLY ABOUT EVIDENCE

Study the situation, answer the questions, and then prepare arguments to support your answers.

5. Phillips developed a scheme to generate funds by sending bogus bills for small amounts for District Sanitation Services to residents of affluent areas. Enough people paid these bills to make the practice quite profitable. What crime has Phillips committed?

6. A corporation was cited and charged with illegal pollution for dumping chemical wastes

into a river. The dumping happened when an employee mistakenly opened the wrong valve. The company pleaded not guilty because the dumping was not intentional. Neither the company nor the employee knew of the ban on dumping this particular chemical. Is either argument a good defense? Why or why not?

4-2 Criminal Procedure

GOALS

- Know the rights people have when arrested and their potential criminal liability for the actions of others
- Name and describe the two types of defenses to criminal charges
- Understand appropriate punishments for crimes

KEY TERMS

probable cause

defense

procedural defense

substantive defense

self-defense

immunity

contempt of court

punishment

plea bargaining

Rights and Responsibilities

WHAT'S YOUR VERDICT? During a routine traffic stop of a small truck for speeding, an officer became suspicious of the cargo the truck contained due to a smell coming from inside. When his request to search the truck was refused, the officer radioed for the assistance of a drug dog. Unfortunately, the dog was unavailable. Finally, he ordered the driver to open the cargo area. When the driver did so, the officer found more than a ton of marijuana. At trial, the defense attorney maintained that it was an illegal search and seizure and that the marijuana should not be allowed to be used as evidence.

Do you agree? Why or why not?

One of the major objectives of the framers of the Constitution of the United States was to protect individuals from the powers of the federal government. The constitutional limitations created as a consequence have been extended over the years so as to also apply to the state and local governments. The authors of the Constitution believed it was better for society to give individuals too much liberty than to allow the government too much power. Thus, in this country, people suspected or accused of criminal conduct have rights that are not available in many other countries. For an example of this, see the Global Issues feature on this page.

Rights of the Accused

The constitutional right to due process requires fundamental fairness in governmental actions. It requires fair procedures during an investigation and in court. As discussed in Chapter 2, criminal defendants may not be compelled to testify against themselves. Evidence presented against them cannot be developed by unreasonable searches and seizures by the authorities. For example, in *What's Your Verdict?* the police officer's sense of smell was not as keen as the police dog's. Therefore, the search was deemed unreasonable as it lacked **probable cause** (a reasonable ground for belief) and the marijuana could not be used as evidence.

Perhaps the most important right is the right of the accused criminal to be represented by a lawyer. The state will provide a lawyer for a person who cannot afford to hire one.

GLOBAL ISSUES

Criminal Procedure in France

Criminal procedure in France—and most other European countries—is significantly different from criminal procedure in the United States and Great Britain. A few examples from the French system are

- persons accused of crimes are not presumed innocent until proven guilty
- victims and their families can become parties to investigations
- judges take an active role in trials, including examining and cross-examining witnesses
- persons accused of crimes have no protection from self-incrimination and can be compelled to testify
- testimony based on hearsay and opinion is allowed.

To convict a person of a crime, the evidence must establish guilt with proof "beyond a reasonable doubt." This means that there must be no sufficient basis placed in evidence at the trial that would logically indicate that the defendant did not commit the crime. Defendants have a constitutional right to a trial by jury. There will be a jury if either the state prosecutor or the defendant requests one. In criminal jury trials, the defendant usually is found guilty only if all the jurors vote to convict.

Responsibility for the Criminal Conduct of Others

A person who knowingly aids another in the commission of a crime also is guilty of criminal wrongdoing. For example, one who acts as a lookout to warn a burglar of the approach of the police is an accomplice in the burglary. Similarly, one who plans the crime, or otherwise intentionally helps, is guilty of the same crime. In most jurisdictions, if someone is killed during the commission of a felony, all the people who participated are guilty of the crime of felony murder.

As discussed previously in this chapter, corporations can be held vicariously liable for the conduct of their employees. Also, officers of corporations may be criminally liable for their actions as managers.

CHECKPOINT What constitutional rights would you have if you were accused of a crime?

Defenses to Criminal Charges

WHAT'S YOUR VERDICT? Will and Zack were arrested for stealing a car. Both signed confessions at the police station. At their trial, they claimed that their right to due process had been violated. They said they had not been advised of their right to remain silent and to have a lawyer present when questioned.

If true, are those good defenses?

To insure the fair application of laws, a criminal defendant may often be able to avoid conviction in court by the use of one or more defenses. In criminal law, a **defense** is a legal position taken by an accused to defeat the charges against him or her. In court the state must prove that the defendant is guilty beyond a reasonable doubt. Even when the prosecution has conclusive evidence to

Why would it be important to be represented by an attorney if you were accused of a crime?

show such guilt, all too often that evidence cannot be introduced due to procedural defenses. In addition, even if there is sufficient admissible evidence to show guilt, defendants also may use substantive defenses to excuse their conduct.

Procedural Defenses

Procedural defenses are based on problems with the way evidence is obtained or the way an accused person is arrested, questioned, tried, or punished. For example, a defendant who had confessed to a crime might say that she signed the confession only because she was threatened by the police. This would be a procedural defense.

Ignorance of the law is not a defense. The legal system assumes everyone knows the law. Thus, if you park in a no-parking area because you did not see the sign, you have no defense. In *What's Your Verdict?* if Will and Zack could prove they were not so advised, such a violation of their procedural rights under the Constitution would be a valid defense to any attempt by the prosecution to use their confessions as evidence against them. Because of the likelihood of such claims by defendants, however, most police departments videotape the rendering of the Miranda warning. They also obtain signed acknowledgements from suspects that the warning has been given.

Why must police officers be very careful in the way that they arrest and question accused individuals?

Substantive Defenses

Substantive defenses disprove, justify, or excuse the alleged crime. Most substantive defenses discredit the facts that the state sought to establish. In other words they discredit the very substance of the prosecution's case against the defendant. For example, an eyewitness may have placed the defendant at the scene of the crime. The defendant may establish a substantive defense by showing that he was in the hospital at the time of the alleged crime. Self-defense, criminal insanity, and immunity are other examples of substantive defenses.

Self-defense is the use of the force that appears to be reasonably necessary to the victim to prevent death, serious bodily harm, rape, or kidnapping. This defense also extends to members of one's family and household and to others whom one has a legal duty to protect. You may not use deadly force if non-deadly force appears reasonably sufficient. Only non-deadly force may be used to protect or recover property. You may not set deadly traps to protect unoccupied buildings. In addition, a civilian may not shoot a thief who is escaping with stolen property.

Criminal insanity generally exists when, because of a verifiable mental disease or defect, the accused does not know the difference between right and wrong. If the accused is criminally insane, there is no criminal intent and therefore no crime. At a trial, the defendant must prove the criminal insanity.

Immunity is freedom from prosecution even when one has committed the crime charged. Sometimes one criminal may be granted immunity

IN THIS CASE A state law makes "hit-and-run" driving a crime. The law requires drivers of motor vehicles involved in an accident to stay at the scene, give their names and addresses, and show their driver's licenses. Barlow, who was arrested for violating this law, claimed that the law was unconstitutional. He said that the law violated his Fifth Amendment right against self-incrimination. In concluding the law was constitutional, the court said that the right against self-incrimination applies only to statements that would implicate a person in a crime. Merely identifying oneself as a party to an accident does not indicate guilt.

A law passed in Oklahoma in the late 1980s, known as the "Make My Day" gun law, is credited with cutting burglaries in that state in half since its passage. The law was enacted after 66-year-old Dr. Frank Sommer was charged with a criminal act for shooting a burglar in his own home. The state senator who sponsored the law said that its purpose is to protect the victim of crime who defends his home and his family against unlawful intrusion from any criminal prosecution or civil action.

in exchange for an agreement to testify about the criminal conduct of several other criminals. In other instances, there is no agreement. Instead, the government grants immunity to a reluctant witness to remove the privilege against self-incrimination. A witness who refuses to testify after the grant of immunity is in contempt of court. **Contempt of court** is action that hinders the administration of justice. It is a crime punishable by imprisonment.

CHECKPOINT Name the two defense categories and give an example of each.

© GETTY IMAGES/PHOTODISC

Why do you think society regards contempt of court a crime punishable by imprisonment?

Punishments for Crimes

WHAT'S YOUR VERDICT? To conserve water, a city ordinance prohibited the watering of gardens, flower beds, and yards after the declaration of a drought emergency. Gill was on vacation when the declaration was issued. As soon as she returned from the trip, she began to water her lawn. Gill was caught and cited for violating the ordinance.

What is an appropriate penalty for this type of offense?

"Let the punishment fit the crime" is more easily said than done. Any penalty provided by law and imposed by a court is called a **punishment**. The purpose is not to remedy the wrong but rather to discipline the wrongdoer. If reasonably swift and certain, punishment should also deter others from similar behavior. Punishment also may remove criminals from society and, in some cases, criminals may be rehabilitated during their sentences. Punishments for crimes range from fines to imprisonment, and in some cases, death.

In *What's Your Verdict?* Gill was guilty of an infraction, which did not require criminal intent. Nevertheless, her conduct was illegal so she would probably be fined. Criminal statutes ordinarily set maximum limits for punishment, but allow a judge discretion within those limits.

An accused person may agree to plead guilty to a less serious crime in exchange for having a more serious charge dropped. This is called **plea bargaining**. The accused voluntarily gives up the right to a public trial to avoid the risk of a greater penalty if convicted. Plea bargains must be approved by the judge of the court with the criminal jurisdiction over the case.

CHECKPOINT What is the purpose of punishment for a crime?

4-2 Assessment

THINK ABOUT LEGAL CONCEPTS

1. The authors of the Constitution believed it was better for society to give individuals too much liberty than to allow the government too much power. **True or False?**

2. An individual who helped in a car jacking in which someone was killed by another car jacker can be charged with felony murder. **True or False?**

3. Which of the following is not a substantive defense? (a) self-defense (b) immunity (c) criminal insanity (d) All of the above are substantive defenses.

4. Ignorance of the law is a procedural defense. **True or False?**

5. Immunity is never granted to someone who has committed the crime. **True or False?**

6. A deal in which the prosecutor offers an accused an opportunity to plead guilty to a lesser charge in return for the accused testifying against other involved parties is called a _?_.

THINK CRITICALLY ABOUT EVIDENCE

Study the situation, answer the questions, and then prepare arguments to support your answers.

7. Sharon spent the weekend with her friend Amelia. Amelia proposed a plan for shoplifting CDs from a local music store. Sharon was to go to the store clerk, say she felt ill, and then pretend to faint. This distraction would allow Amelia, at the other end of the store, to place CDs in her shopping bag without risk of being seen. At first Sharon said she could not do something like that because it is against the law. Amelia argued that Sharon would not be breaking the law, only Amelia would. Is Amelia right? If a person can think of a way to profit by violating the law without risk, what reasons are there for not breaking the law?

8. Art is charged with kidnapping. After listening to all the evidence, 11 of the 12 jurors found him guilty. The twelfth juror voted he was not guilty. Has Art been convicted of the crime?

9. Rosa shot a burglar in her home when he was about to enter her bedroom with a knife in his hand. What would be a good defense for her?

10. John left his home state of Missouri early one afternoon to drive to New Mexico. Eventually the sun set, but John continued on. Hours later, while driving 70 mph on an interstate highway east of Amarillo, he was pulled over by the Texas highway patrol. The last speed limit sign John had seen had been in Oklahoma and had read 70 mph. As she issued the ticket, the officer noted that the speed limit in Texas on interstates is 70 during the day but drops to 65 at night. John protested he was unaware of the change. Was he still guilty of speeding?

CONCEPTS IN BRIEF

4-1 Criminal Law

1. A crime is a punishable offense against society. In order to convict, the prosecution must establish a duty, an act or omission in violation of the duty, and, in most cases, criminal intent.

2. Crimes are generally categorized as felonies or misdemeanors. Some states classify minor misdemeanors as infractions.

3. Some crimes in which a business may be the victim are robbery, burglary, shoplifting, employee theft, passing bad checks, vandalism, receiving stolen property, and embezzlement.

4. Some crimes in which a business person or firm may be the perpetrator are income tax evasion, price fixing, false advertising, and bribery.

5. Generally, any adult capable of knowing the difference between right and wrong is considered sane under the law.

4-2 Criminal Procedure

6. Anyone accused of committing a crime has certain due process rights. These rights include freedom from arrest without probable cause; the right to be represented by a lawyer; the right to cross-examine witnesses; the right to not testify against oneself; and the right to a speedy, public, fair trial.

7. Procedural defenses relate to the way evidence is obtained or the way the accused person is arrested, questioned, tried, or punished. Substantive defenses disprove, justify, or excuse the alleged crime. Common substantive defenses are self-defense, criminal insanity, and immunity.

8. Crimes are punishable by fine, imprisonment, or both. Some states execute certain criminals.

YOUR LEGAL VOCABULARY

Match each statement with the term that it best defines. Some terms may not be used.

1. Legal position that disproves, justifies, or otherwise excuses an alleged criminal act

2. Accused person admitting guilt to a less serious crime in exchange for having a more serious charge dropped

3. The use of the force that appears to be reasonably necessary to the victim to prevent death, serious bodily harm, rape, or kidnapping

4. Punishable offense against society

5. Action that hinders the administration of justice

6. Crime punishable by either a fine of more than $1,000 or by confinement for more than one year in a state prison or both or by death

7. Substituted criminal liability

8. Freedom from prosecution even when one has committed the crime charged

9. Any penalty provided by law and imposed by a court

10. Crime punishable by confinement in a county or city jail for one year or less, by fine of $1,000 or less, or both

11. A criminal defense based on how the evidence was obtained or how the accused was arrested, questioned, or tried

a. **contempt of court**
b. **crime**
c. **defense**
d. **felony**
e. **immunity**
f. **misdemeanor**
g. **plea bargaining**
h. **probable cause**
i. **procedural defense**
j. **punishment**
k. **self-defense**
l. **substantive defense**
m. **vicarious criminal liability**
n. **white-collar crime**

REVIEW LEGAL CONCEPTS

12. Why must criminal statutes carefully and clearly define the prohibited behavior?

13. Why are certain acts crimes in one state but not in another? Why are there varying levels of punishment for the same crime in different states?

14. Explain the significance of the main steps in a criminal prosecution. Is the cause of justice served when a defense attorney gets his client off because of a "loophole" in the law? Consider both the short-term and the long-term consequences.

WRITE ABOUT LEGAL CONCEPTS

15. An old adage of the law states, "As society becomes less secure, criminal punishments become more severe." Write a paragraph relating this to the United States' experience with the death penalty and other punishments in the last few decades.

16. **HOT DEBATE** Write a paragraph debating whether or not the protections afforded those accused of criminal activity by the Constitution are mainly used by individuals who are truly guilty to avoid their deserved punishment.

MAKE ACADEMIC CONNECTIONS

17. **SOCIAL STUDIES** As a result of a U.S. Supreme Court decision in the early 1960s, improperly or illegally obtained evidence cannot be used to convict an accused in the court system. This is referred to as the "exclusionary rule," as the evidence is excluded from consideration by the court. The rule was put into place to stop police from using the wrong tactics to obtain incriminating evidence. Other developed countries handle such actions by their police force in a different manner. Research how England and two other European countries discipline improper or illegal attempts to gather evidence by their police and whether or not the evidence developed thereby can be used against the accused at trial.

THINK CRITICALLY ABOUT EVIDENCE

Study the situation, answer the questions, and then prepare arguments to support your answers.

18. Elton had three children. As they grew up and became eligible to drive, Elton bought each a car. To avoid paying high premiums for their car insurance, Elton titled each car in his name. He then stated to his insurance company that he and his wife were the primary drivers on the vehicles. When the youngest child totalled "his" car by hitting a large deer, the insurance company paid to replace the car. What could Elton be charged with should his deception be uncovered?

19. Bif was in Gail's office waiting to go to lunch with her. Gail owned a business in competition with Bif's business. When Gail excused herself to go to the restroom, Bif looked at her computer screen and saw part of a customer list. Bif had a blank diskette which he inserted into the computer. He quickly copied the file onto his diskette. Then he put his diskette in his pocket. The entire action took only 20 seconds. Bif finished long before Gail returned. Has Bif committed a crime? If so, what crime?

20. Paula's boyfriend moved to her home town, Oklahoma City, from Houston, Texas. Two weeks after he arrived, he asked her to phone his bank in Houston and inquire about his balance. She did so as a favor to him and found out the balance was more than $40,000. As soon as she told him, he left and drove to Houston to remove it from his account. In Houston, he was arrested by the FBI for fraud and several related crimes. Paula was then charged with the federal crime of making a phone call across state lines for the furtherance of a fraudulent scheme. Her boyfriend only knew the scheme had been successful by Paula's report of the large balance in his old account. What would be a possible defense for Paula?

ANALYZE REAL CASES

21. The Royal Scotsman Inn built a motel that did not comply with the building code. Therefore, Scotsman was refused an occupancy permit. The chair of the county council approached a representative of the motel and offered to have "everything taken care of" in exchange for the payment of $12,000. Scotsman was faced with the possibility of a large loss of revenue. Therefore, Scotsman agreed to pay the money. The Federal Bureau of Investigation arrested the council chairperson after tape recording the discussion and seeing the exchange of the money. What crime did the council chairperson commit? (*United States v. Price,* 507 F.2d 1349)

22. Basic Construction Company was engaged in the road-paving business. Two of its lower-level managers rigged bids by giving competitors the prices that Basic would bid for work. That is a criminal violation of the Sherman Antitrust Act. Will Basic be criminally liable for the conduct of its manager? (*United States v. Basic Construction Company,* 711 F.2d 570)

23. Citrin was an employee of International Airport Centers (IAC). As such he was responsible for identifying properties that IAC might want to buy. To help in his work, IAC loaned Citrin a laptop computer on which to store the data he collected. Citrin eventually decided that he would branch off on his own and start a competing firm. Before quitting IAC and turning in his laptop, Citrin downloaded a computer program that wiped out the hard drive which contained the data IAC had paid him to collect as well as evidence of his misconduct. What statute was Citrin convicted of violating? (*Int'l Airport Ctrs. L.L.C. v. Citrin,* No. 05-1522, 7th Cir., 2006)

24. Pack was the president of Acme Markets, Inc., a large national retail food chain. Both Pack and Acme were charged with violating criminal provisions of the federal Food, Drug, and Cosmetics Act. They were charged with allowing interstate shipments of food contaminated by rodents in an Acme warehouse. Pack defended himself by stating that although he was aware of the problem, he had delegated responsibility for the sanitary conditions of food storage to responsible subordinates. Can Pack be criminally liable in these circumstances? (*United States v. Pack,* 95 S. Ct. 1903)

25. Feinberg owned a cigar store in a poor neighborhood of Philadelphia. He sold cans of Sterno, which contains about 4 percent alcohol, to people in the neighborhood who mixed it with water and drank it to become intoxicated. After conducting this business for some time, Feinberg purchased a quantity of Institutional Sterno. It contained 54 percent alcohol. The cans were marked "Danger—Poison," and had a picture of a skull and crossbones; Feinberg did not warn customers of the difference. As a result, 33 people died from alcohol poisoning. Did Feinberg commit a crime? (*Commonwealth v. Feinberg,* 234 A.2d 913, Pa.)

26. To help attract convention business to the city, a group of hotels, restaurants, and various other businesses in Portland, Oregon, formed an association. The association was funded by contributions. To provide incentives for contributions to the association, its members agreed to stop doing or curtail doing business with those who did not contribute. As a part of this effort, the Portland Hilton Hotel's purchasing agent threatened a Hilton supplier with the loss of the hotel's business unless such a contribution was forthcoming. Such activities and the agreement behind them are criminal violations of the federal antitrust laws. As a result, the federal government charged Hilton accordingly and a guilty verdict was returned at the trial. Hilton appealed, as it had been shown in court that the manager and assistant manager of the hotel had, on at least two occasions, told the purchasing agent not to participate in the boycott. He was instead to follow corporate policy and purchase supplies only on the basis of price, quality, and service. Should the decision be reversed on appeal given the employee's actions were clearly against corporate policy and directions by corporate executives? (*United States v. Hilton Hotels Corporation,* 467 F.2d 1000)

Sports & Entertainment Law

Criminal Intrusion or Protected Freedom

GALELLA V. ONASSIS 353 F. SUPP. 196, 487 F.2D 986

BACKGROUND The involvement of the paparazzi in the death of Princess Diana of England brought cries that they were guilty of criminal manslaughter. The incident brought to mind the actions of the man who is said to have given the paparazzi their original bad reputation, Ronald E. Galella. Paparazzi (Italian for "buzzing insects") became known for their intrusive behavior as a result of documentation in the court records of the many incidents related to the case of *Galella v. Onassis*.

FACTS Jacqueline Onassis was the remarried widow of President John F. Kennedy and mother of the two Kennedy children, John and Caroline. Photos of Mrs. Onassis and the children, especially those exposing emotions or questionable behavior, were drawing a premium from publishers in the early 1970s. As a consequence, Galella began a campaign of intrusive behavior likely to provoke marketable snapshots. In her deposition, a ten-year-old Caroline Kennedy said, "Unlike the many other photographers, Mr. Galella often rushes at me, snaps flash bulbs in my face, trails me closely and uses other

© BILL RAY/TIME LIFE PICTURES/GETTY IMAGES

techniques that I find dangerous and threatening…. I fear I will be hurt." On September 24, 1969, Galella allegedly jumped out of some bushes in Central Park in front of John's oncoming bicycle. The nine-year-old boy swerved to miss the photographer and crashed his bike, injuring himself and causing the Secret Service Agent accompanying the Onassis party to say, "Look what you almost did, you almost killed John." Ultimately, because of his alleged criminal and tortious behavior, an injunction was issued by a federal district court preventing Galella from coming within 50 yards of Mrs. Onassis. In this action, Mr. Galella wants the injunction to be dismissed.

THE LAW The First Amendment through its interpretation by the U.S. Supreme Court sanctifies and renders almost inviolate the right of the press to report on the actions of public figures.

THE ISSUE Does this right provide immunity from all criminal and civil actions levied against the press for their actions in pursuing a story?

HOLDING No, it does not. Said the court, "… the First Amendment does not immunize all conduct designed to gather information about or photographs of a public figure. There is no general constitutional right to assault, harass, or unceasingly shadow or distress public figures." The injunction was upheld that the "plaintiff, his agents, servants, employees and all persons in active concert and participation with him from, *inter alia,* approaching within 100 yards of the home of defendant and her children, 100 yards of the schools attended by the children; at all other places and times 75 yards from the children and 50 yards from defendant; from performing surveillance of defendant or her children; from commercially appropriating defendant's photograph for advertising or trade purposes without defendant's consent; from communicating or attempting to communicate with defendant or her children."

PRACTICE JUDGING

1. Do you think the court could have achieved its objective by simply enjoining Galella from selling any photos he took of the subjects? Why or why not?

2. Do you think the injunction as issued above was effective? Why or why not?

Chapter 5
Civil Law and Procedure

5-1 Private Injuries vs. Public Offenses

5-2 Intentional Torts, Negligence, and Strict Liability

5-3 Civil Procedure

HOT DEBATE

Every time Chanelle's science teacher asked her a question during class, the teacher walked over to her desk, squatted down, and placed a hand on Chanelle's thigh. Chanelle found this behavior extremely offensive. Finally, in private, she politely asked the teacher to stop. Although the teacher seemingly agreed, the next time Chanelle raised her hand the teacher behaved the same way. However, this time when the teacher extended her hand to place it on Chanelle's leg, Chanelle twisted violently away and slammed her knee into the other side of her desk.

WHERE DO YOU STAND?

1. What corrective action could Chanelle take within the school structure?
2. Regardless of whether or not she tries to resolve the problem within the school's structure, has Chanelle received a personal injury for which she could bring suit in court?

5-1 Private Injuries vs. Public Offenses

GOALS

■ Distinguish a crime from a tort

■ Identify the elements of torts

■ Explain why one person may be responsible for another's tort

KEY TERMS

tort

damages

negligence

How Do Crimes and Torts Differ?

WHAT'S YOUR VERDICT? When he applied for his license as a ferry pilot for the city, Jerone failed to tell the Coast Guard about his high blood pressure and prescription drug use. Some three years later, while operating the ferry, Jerone passed out at the controls. As a consequence, the ferry crashed into the dock killing 18 commuters and injuring dozens more. At the time Jerone was also taking two medications for back pain. Both the pain medications list drowsiness as a possible side effect.

Does Jerone's conduct represent a criminal or civil wrong or both?

One act can be both a tort and a crime. In *What's Your Verdict?* Jerone committed two crimes—the crime of manslaughter (18 counts) and the crime of failing to disclose his drug use and blood pressure status in applying for the position.

Jerone also committed a tort by his negligent conduct in piloting the ferry. Manslaughter is punishable in most states by up to 10 years in prison for each count. Damages for negligence will be awarded appropriate to the claims of the injured and the families and estates of the deceased passengers.

CHECKPOINT What is the difference between a crime and a tort?

A crime is an offense against society. It is a public wrong. A **tort**, in contrast, is a private or civil wrong. It is an offense against an individual. If someone commits a tort, the person injured as a result can sue and obtain a judgment for **damages**. This is a monetary award intended to compensate the injured party for the harm done to her or him. From society's standpoint, the money is meant to restrain the injured individual's desire to exact revenge by taking the law into her or his own hands. Doing so would cause chaos.

What is the purpose of an injured party's receiving money damages for a tort committed against him or her?

Elements of a Tort

Like criminal law, tort law is a broad legal category. Just as there are many specific crimes, there also are many specific torts. Certain elements are common to most torts. In a trial, these elements must be proved to establish liability (legal responsibility).

The elements of most torts include

1. duty (a legal obligation to do or not to do something)
2. breach (a violation of the duty)
3. injury (a harm that is recognized by the law)
4. causation (proof that the breach caused the injury)

DUTY By law, you have certain rights. You also have certain duties related to respecting the rights of others. The following are the duties created by tort law:

1. the duty not to injure another (including bodily injury, injury to someone's reputation, or invasion of someone's privacy)
2. the duty not to interfere with the property rights of others, for example, by trespassing on their land
3. the duty not to interfere with the economic rights of others, such as the right to contract

Whether or not a duty exists in a certain situation is a question of law for the judge to decide. A judge will make this decision by consulting state case and statutory law and, on occasion, federal law.

VIOLATION OF THE DUTY A violation (or breach) of the duty must be proved before the injured party can collect damages. Whether a breach of a tort duty has occurred is almost always a question of fact for a jury or a judge, if no jury is requested, to decide.

Many torts acknowledge a breach only when the defendant actually intended to inflict harm by her or his action. These are classified as *intentional torts*. In other torts, the intent to inflict harm is not required. It is enough that the harm occurred as a result of the neglect or carelessness of the defendant. Such a tort is generally termed **negligence**.

In still other torts, even carelessness is not required. Liability is imposed simply because a person acted in a certain way, and this caused injury. The last classification, where neither intent nor carelessness is required, is classified as strict liability.

INJURY Generally, injury resulting from the breach of duty must be proved. Thus, if you act recklessly, but no one is injured, there usually is no tort.

© GETTY IMAGES/PHOTODISC

Apply the elements of a tort to determine whether Mason in *What's Your Verdict?* committed a tort in allowing the fire to occur. Check your answer against the explanation on the next page.

CAUSATION Causation means that breach of the duty caused the injury. There are degrees of causation. For example, one could argue that the first people on earth are the ultimate cause of every injury that occurs in the world today. However, when the amount of causation is great enough for it to be recognized by the law, it is called *proximate cause.* Generally, proximate cause exists when it is reasonably foreseeable that a breach of duty will result in an injury.

Applying these elements to *What's Your Verdict?* Mason committed a tort because (1) he owed a duty to the neighbors not to injure their property; (2) he breached the duty when he left the fire unattended so it spread to the neighbor's property; (3) the injury occurred when the neighbor's house was burned; and (4) leaving the fire unattended was a proximate cause of the loss of the fence, the tool shed, and the house. Therefore, the neighbor can obtain a judgment against Mason for the value of the loss.

CHECKPOINT Name the four elements of a tort.

Responsibility for Another's Torts

WHAT'S YOUR VERDICT? Hunt was taking riding lessons from Saddleback Stables. Patterson, the Saddleback instructor, was a skilled rider although only 15 years old. Nevertheless, during a lesson while leading the horse Hunt was riding, Patterson negligently dropped the bridle. As a result, the horse bolted and Hunt was thrown to the ground and injured.

Who was liable for Hunt's injuries?

With few exceptions, all persons, including minors, are personally responsible for their conduct and are therefore liable for their torts. Even children or insane persons may be held liable for injuring others. Certainly, in *What's Your Verdict?*

Patterson's negligence would result in his being liable to Hunt for Hunt's injuries. In addition, Saddleback Stables can be held liable for the negligence of its employee Patterson. In such cases, the injured party may sue both employer and employee.

When one person is liable for the torts of another, the liability is called *vicarious liability.* For example, parents may be liable if they give their children "dangerous instrumentalities," such as guns, without proper instruction. Similarly, parents may be liable for their children's continuing dangerous habits. For example, if a child continues to throw rocks at trains and vehicles, the parents may be liable if they fail to stop the child's behavior.

In some states parents are liable, by statute, up to a specified amount of money for property damage by their minor children. This is usually designed to cover vandalism and malicious destruction of school property. Most states also provide that parents are liable, up to the limits of financial responsibility laws, for damages negligently caused by their children while operating motor vehicles.

CHECKPOINT What parties might be held responsible for another person's tort?

IN THIS CASE Bottomless Barges, Inc. (BBI), contracted with a coastal city to barge the city's untreated sewerage some 300 miles into the ocean and dump it. This activity was permitted by the federal government due to the city's lack of funds needed to build an adequate treatment facility. Ollee Facktory, an employee of BBI, dumped an afternoon run only 35 miles offshore in order to get back to land in time for a date. Various diseases, including minor cases of cholera, broke out in several coastal towns. As a result, BBI was sued by individual plaintiffs and the government and recovered against due to its vicarious liability for Facktory's actions.

THINK ABOUT LEGAL CONCEPTS

1. A single act can be both a tort and a crime. **True or False?**

2. The degree of causation of a tort great enough to be recognized by law is called (a) proximate cause (b) intimate cause (c) incidental cause (d) none of the above

3. A tort is considered to be an offense against society. **True or False?**

4. In order to establish liability for a tort, all of the following must be proved except (a) duty (b) breach of duty (c) harm recognized by law (d) vicarious liability

5. An insane person cannot be held liable for a tort. **True or False?**

6. When one party is held responsible for the tort of another, the liability is called _ ?_ liability.

7. The three classifications of torts are intentional torts, negligence, and _ ?_ . (a) manslaughter (b) strict liability (c) vicarious liability (d) none of the above

THINK CRITICALLY ABOUT EVIDENCE

Study the situation, answer the questions, and then prepare arguments to support your answers.

8. Philip drove a tractor-trailer rig onto a ferry boat. He left the rig in gear because of a problem with its brakes. Posted regulations prohibited the starting of engines before docking, but when the ferry was about 50 feet from the dock, Philip started his engine. That caused the tractor-trailer to jump forward and strike Herrick's car, which in turn hit Patton's car. Patton's car, at the head of the line, crashed through the ferry's barricades and plunged into the water. The car could not be recovered. What was the tort duty in this case? Where was the breach of the duty? What were the injuries? What was the proximate cause of the injury to Patton's car?

9. Felicia carelessly left a campfire before it was completely extinguished. The fire spread through the woods and caused the destruction of a nearby lodge. Is Felicia liable to the owners of the lodge for the building? Is she liable to the lodge owners for the loss of income until the lodge can be restored? Is she liable to the persons who had reservations for the lodge but whose trips are now ruined?

10. The driver of a rental car lost control while passing another vehicle. The car crossed the median of the four-lane highway and slammed head-on into Todd's truck. The truck then flipped over and caught fire. Todd suffered extensive burns and his son, who had been riding with him, suffered traumatic brain injuries. The dollar value set on their injuries was more than $4 million. Against whom can they recover?

11. As a police officer, Maureen was authorized to carry her handgun with her. While darting into a store to pick up her dry cleaning, she left the gun in her car hidden under the seat. Her 9-year-old son found the pistol and accidently shot his friend in the leg. Is Maureen liable for the injury?

12. Patrick borrowed his friend John's car to impress a young lady he was dating. It was a new luxury car that John had saved four years to purchase. The paint on the car turned colors under various climatic and light conditions. While on the date, Patrick drove the car down a public road that had just been repaved with hot oil and gravel. The result was streaks of hot oil glued to the sides of the car and several nicks in the paint from flying rocks. Patrick then parked in front of his favorite restaurant, a sports pub on the far side of town. While in the restaurant, Patrick heard a special weather report that a thunderstorm with large hail was sweeping across the area and would arrive over the restaurant in ten minutes. Unfortunately for John's car, the date was going too well to break off and move the car under cover. Consequently, the hail left a multitude of pock marks on the top of the car. Is Patrick legally responsible for the damage done by the gravel, oil, and hail? Why or why not?

5-2 Intentional Torts, Negligence, and Strict Liability

GOALS

■ Identify common intentional torts

■ Recognize the elements of negligence

■ Explain the basis for strict liability

KEY TERMS

intentional torts

assault

battery

false imprisonment

defamation

invasion of privacy

trespass to land

conversion

fraud

strict liability

What Are the Most Common Intentional Torts?

WHAT'S YOUR VERDICT? During deer-hunting season, Hart drove miles into the country in search of game. He parked his pickup truck along a dirt road, climbed a fence, and hiked into the woods. Hart thought the land was part of a national forest. However, it actually belonged to Quincy, who had posted "No Trespassing" signs. Confronted by Quincy, Hart apologized for his mistake and left.

Had Hart committed an intentional tort?

Intentional torts are torts in which the defendant possessed the intent or purpose to inflict the resultant injury. These torts contrast with negligence and strict liability, where intent to produce the injury is not required. There are numerous intentional torts. The most common of these include assault, battery, false imprisonment, defamation, invasion of privacy, trespass to land, conversion, and fraud.

Assault

The tort of **assault** occurs when one person intentionally puts another in reasonable fear of an offensive or harmful bodily contact. An assault can be based on words or gestures. However conveyed, the threat must include a display of force indicating a present ability to carry it out. In addition, to be considered

IN THIS CASE Spencer, elderly and totally blind, thought Wills had swindled him. Spencer told Wills that he was going to "beat your face to a pulp." Because it was obvious that Spencer could not carry out his threat, there was no assault.

"reasonable" from the viewpoint of the potential victim, the threat must be believable. The threatened injury can be physical: a person may raise a fist threatening to punch you. Or the threatened injury can be offensive: a person might threaten unwanted sexual touching by attempting to kiss you.

Battery

A person has a duty to refrain from harmful or offensive touching of another. An intentional breach of the duty is a **battery**. Shooting, pushing in anger, spitting on, or throwing a pie in another's face are all batteries. An assault frequently precedes a battery.

Angrily raising a clenched fist and then striking someone in the face involves first an assault (the raised fist) and then a battery (the blow to the face). When the victim is hit without warning from behind, there is a battery without an assault.

Even though there is harmful or offensive touching, there may be no battery if the contact is not intentional. This could occur, for example, when someone sneezes and their spittle inadvertently strikes another. Also, the contact may be justified. For example, when you act in self-defense, you have not committed a battery. Further, there may be consent to the contact. Thus, in a boxing match, there is no battery because the boxers consent to the harmful touching.

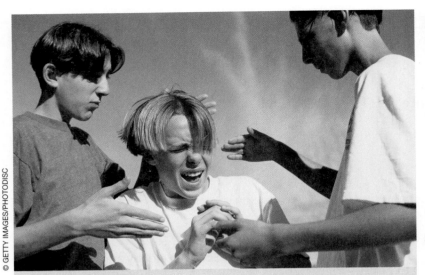

Is the action in this photo an example of assault or battery? Justify your answer.

When the police have probable cause to arrest people, they are privileged to imprison them. Privilege justifies the imprisonment. But if the police mistake the identity of one person for another, they may commit false imprisonment in the course of the arrest. Merchants in many states have a privilege to detain a person if they have a reasonable basis for believing the person was shoplifting. If they detain persons against their will without a reasonable basis, they falsely imprison them.

False Imprisonment

False imprisonment is the intentional confinement of a person against the person's will and without lawful privilege. People may be deprived of freedom of movement in many ways. For example, they may be handcuffed; locked in a room, car, or jail; told in a threatening way to stay in one place; or otherwise denied their liberty. Consent occurs when they agree to being confined. For example, when a burglary suspect sits voluntarily in a police car to describe his actions over the last hour, the suspect consents to being detained.

Defamation

Statements about people can injure them. If a false statement injures a person's reputation or good name, it may constitute the tort of **defamation**. If the defamation is spoken, it is *slander*. If the defamation is written or printed, it is *libel*. To be legally defamatory, the statement must

1. be false (truth is a complete defense)
2. be communicated to a third person (your reputation is not harmed if no other person hears or reads the lie)
3. bring the victim into disrepute, contempt, or ridicule by others

In slander suits, you must show that you have suffered an actual physical loss, or damages, as a

CyberLAW

Defamatory statements published on Internet bulletin boards, e-mails, and the like, are considered libel due to the somewhat permanent nature of the medium. This often is vital to a successful suit for defamation as damages are presumed to exist in the case of libel and do not have to be proven to the court. The remaining question becomes who should be sued. This is the hard part. Sections of the Communications Decency Act of 1996 and several court decisions provide protections to Internet service providers and bulletin board operators. Such parties

generally are considered to be immune from suits brought to make up for the harm done by such statements. However, they may be held liable if it can be shown that they exercised editorial or full control of the material posted or transmitted or, at least, had knowledge of the specific defamatory contents. Such a showing has proven very difficult to accomplish.

THINK ABOUT IT

Why do you think it has been so difficult for people to win libel suits against Internet bulletin board operators or Internet service providers?

result of the slanderous remark. Exceptions to this occur in cases where the oral statements are to the effect that the plaintiff committed a serious crime, has a loathsome disease, or injures someone in his or her profession or business. In libel cases, you are presumed to have suffered a loss, and so these damages do not have to be shown to the court.

Exceptions are made to the law of defamation in order to encourage open discussion of issues of public concern. For example, legislators' statements, even those made with malice, are immune from liability if made during legislative meetings. Judges, lawyers, jurors, witnesses, and other parties in judicial proceedings are also immune from

liability for statements made during the actual trial or hearing. Similarly, liability for defamatory statements about public officials or prominent personalities does not exist unless the statements were made with malice. That means the statement when issued was known to be false or was made with a reckless disregard for its probable falsehood.

Invasion of Privacy

People are entitled to keep personal matters private. This is the right to privacy. Congress has stated that "the right of privacy is a personal and fundamental right protected by the Constitution of the United States." **Invasion of privacy** is a tort defined as the uninvited intrusion into an individual's personal relationships and activities in a way likely to cause shame or mental suffering in an ordinary person.

An invasion of privacy also can result from unnecessary publicity regarding personal matters. So, unlike the law regarding the tort of defamation, publication of even a true statement about someone may be an invasion of privacy. This is because, as the U.S. Supreme Court put it, you should be protected when you have a reasonable "expectation of privacy." Thus, two-way mirrors

© BLEND IMAGES

What are some situations related to the right to privacy that affect your life?

in the women's restroom of a gas station would constitute an invasion of privacy.

The right to privacy also includes freedom from commercial exploitation of one's name, picture, or endorsement without permission. The right to privacy bans illegal eavesdropping by any listening device, interference with telephone calls, and unauthorized opening of letters and telegrams. However, the right of privacy is not unlimited. For example, the police are permitted to tap telephone lines secretly if they have a warrant to do so. Also, public figures, such as politicians, actors, and people in the news, give up much of their right to privacy when they step into the public domain.

In order for the tort of trespass to occur, what would have to be proven about the person who enters this property without the owner's permission?

Trespass to Land

The tort of **trespass to land** is entry onto the property of another without the owner's consent. However, trespass may consist of other forms of interference with the possession of property. Dumping rubbish on the land of another or breaking the windows of a neighbor's house also are trespasses. Intent is required to commit the tort of trespass. However, the only requirement is that the intruder intended to be on the particular property. If a person were thrown onto another's land, there would be no intent and no trespass. If a person thought she was walking on her own property, but was mistaken, there would be a trespass because she intended to be there. Thus, in *What's Your Verdict?* Hart was guilty of trespass, even though he thought he was in a national forest.

Conversion

People who own personal property, such as diamond rings, have the right to control their possession and their use. This right is violated if the property is stolen, destroyed, or used in a manner inconsistent with the owner's rights. If that happens, a **conversion** occurs. A thief is always a converter.

Conversion occurs even when the converter does not know that there is a conversion. So, the innocent buyer of stolen goods is a converter. The party injured by the conversion can receive damages. Or the converter can, in effect, be compelled to purchase the converted goods from their owner.

Interference with Contractual Relations

Generally parties who breach a contract to which they are a party must pay damages under contract law for the injury suffered by the other party. However if a third party encourages the breaching party in any way, that third party may be liable in tort to the non-breaching party. This is called the tort of *interference with contractual relations*.

Fraud

Fraud occurs when there is an intentional or recklessly made misrepresentation of an existing important fact. The misrepresentation must be made with the intent of inducing someone to enter into a contract. Finally, the other party, relying on the misrepresentation, must actually enter into the contract.

To be able to recover damages in court for fraud, the person alleging it must not have been able to check on the truth of the statement by exercising due diligence. In addition, ordinarily a statement of opinion is not considered fraudulent. This is because the hearer should recognize that the statement is the speaker's personal view.

CHECKPOINT Name at least six of the most common intentional torts.

What Constitutes Negligence?

WHAT'S YOUR VERDICT? Britt was driving home late one rainy night after drinking alcohol all evening. With only one working headlight, she raced down residential streets at speeds up to 60 miles per hour. Meanwhile, Yee was slowly backing her station wagon out of her driveway, but she failed to look both ways when she should have. Britt rammed into the right rear end of Yee's car. Both Yee and Britt were injured in the collision and their vehicles severely damaged.

Who will have to pay damages for the injuries and property damage sustained in the accident?

Negligence is the most common tort. Intent to injure is not required for this tort. Only careless behavior is required for negligence. Negligence is proven in court by the showing of a duty of due care owed by the defendant to the plaintiff, a breach of that duty, causation, and injury.

Duty Imposed by Negligence

The general duty imposed by negligence law is defined by the reasonable-person standard. This standard requires that you act with the care, prudence, and good judgment of a reasonable person so as not to cause injury to others. In court, the trier of fact (typically a jury) is asked how the reasonable person would have behaved under the circumstances. The answer to this question sets the standard of due care against which the defendant's actions will be compared.

For certain individuals, a different degree of care is applied. For example, children under age seven are held to be incapable of negligent conduct. Children seven through fourteen are only required to act with the care that a reasonable child of like age, intelligence, and experience would act. If, however, a child undertakes an adult activity, such as driving a boat or a car, the child is held to the adult standard.

Professionals and skilled tradespersons are held to a higher degree of care in their work. These persons are required to work with the degree

If the driver of this aquacycle is ten years old, would she be negligent if she ran into a swimmer? Why or why not?

© GETTY IMAGES/PHOTODISC

of care and skill that is normally possessed by members of the profession or trade. Thus, an attorney must act with the care and skill normally possessed by other attorneys in his or her community. Similarly, a plumber must perform work with the care and skill normally exercised by other plumbers in the community.

Breach of Duty

The "reasonable-person" standard defines the duty of due care in any specific case. A defendant's actual conduct, such as Britt's in *What's Your Verdict?* is then compared with this specific duty to determine whether a violation of it has occurred. You could conclude that a reasonable person would drive a car only at a safe speed, only when sober, and at night only when the car's lights work. Because Britt engaged in speeding, driving while intoxicated, and driving at night without proper lights, she clearly breached the duty of due care set by the reasonable-person standard.

Causation and Injury

As with other torts, the violation of the duty must be the proximate cause of the injury. In *What's Your Verdict?* Britt's speeding in an unsafe

vehicle while impaired was a breach of the duty, and it is reasonably foreseeable that speeding will cause injury. In fact, speeding was a partial cause of the property damage to the station wagon and the personal injury to Yee.

Defenses to Negligence

In several states a plaintiff cannot recover for loss caused by another's negligence if the plaintiff also was negligent. This is the old common law defense of *contributory negligence*. For example, in *What's Your Verdict?* Yee was also negligent because she backed into the street without looking left or right. That and Britt's speeding were causes of the accident. So Yee was contributorily negligent. If she lived in a state that allows contributory negligence as a defense, she could not recover anything from Britt. Under this legal rule, it does not matter that one party, like Britt, was very negligent and primarily responsible for causing the collision while the other, like Yee, was only slightly negligent.

Most states have substituted comparative negligence for contributory negligence. *Comparative negligence* applies when a plaintiff in a negligence action is partially at fault. In such a case the plaintiff and defendant are awarded damages in proportion to their percentage of

Bart broke his leg while playing tennis at night on a dark city tennis court. Do you think he would win a judgment against the city for his injury? Why or why not?

responsibility for the accident. The percentages of responsibility are assigned by the trier of fact in the case. Some states do not allow a plaintiff whose negligence was greater than the defendant's to recover.

Assumption of the risk is another defense to negligence. If plaintiffs are aware of a danger, but decide to subject themselves to the risk, that is a defense. Suppose you take a shortcut across a suburban lot where a three-story house is being constructed. The perimeter of the lot is clearly marked with signs stating "Danger. No Trespassing. Construction Area." A sudden gust of wind blows a section of plywood off the top floor and into your back. You are seriously injured. The defense of assumption of risk could be raised against you in any later lawsuit that you might bring against the construction company and the property owner to recover for your injuries.

CHECKPOINT Name the four elements of the tort of negligence.

Why Is Strict Liability Necessary?

WHAT'S YOUR VERDICT? While grocery shopping, Mrs. Lamm placed a large glass container of a new drain cleaner in her shopping cart. Later, when she set the container on the check-out counter, it exploded. The flying glass cut her in several places.

Can she collect in tort from the grocery store or the bottler?

Sometimes the law holds a party liable in tort on the basis of absolute or **strict liability**. Under the doctrine of strict liability a defendant can be held liable if he or she merely engaged in a particular activity that resulted in injury, regardless of whether or not he or she was negligent. In strict liability, proof of both the activity and the injury substitutes for proof of a violation of a duty.

Strict liability is only applied when someone has engaged in abnormally dangerous activities, such as target practice, blasting, crop dusting with

Imagine you are the owner of this dog, and the dog just bit your young neighbor. Could you be held liable on the basis of strict liability? Why or why not?

© GETTY IMAGES/PHOTODISC

dangerous chemicals, or storing flammable liquids in large quantities. If you engage in activities of this type and someone is injured as a result, you will be liable regardless of the precautions you take.

Ownership of dangerous animals also subjects you to strict liability. Domesticated animals (dogs, cats, cows, and horses) are not considered dangerous unless the owner knows that the particular animal has behaved in such a way. Bears, tigers, snakes, elephants, and monkeys are examples of wild or dangerous animals. If the dangerous animal causes injury, the owner is strictly liable.

A third strict liability activity is the sale of goods that are unreasonably dangerous. If the goods are defective, the defect makes them dangerous. If the defect causes an injury, any merchant who sells those goods is strictly liable, as is the manufacturer. Under strict liability, the manufacturer and any sellers in the chain of distribution are liable to any buyer of the defective product who is injured by it.

Without strict liability, the victim might not receive any compensation because negligence may be difficult to prove. In *What's Your Verdict?* Mrs. Lamm could collect from either the store, the bottler, or both under strict liability. The bottle was defective, and this defect made the product unreasonably dangerous.

CHECKPOINT What is strict liability and why is it necessary?

5-2 Assessment

school.cengage.com/blaw/lawxtra

THINK ABOUT LEGAL CONCEPTS

1. An actual harmful or offensive touching must be shown to prove the tort of assault. **True or False?**

2. A person who has consented to be detained by another cannot recover for the tort of false imprisonment. **True or False?**

3. Spoken defamation is (a) libel (b) label (c) slander (d) none of the above

4. An uninvited intrusion into a person's personal relationships or activities in a way likely to cause shame or mental suffering in an ordinary person is the basis of the tort of _?_.

5. An innocent buyer of stolen goods cannot be liable for conversion because the buyer had no intent to keep the goods from their rightful owner. **True or False?**

6. Which of the following is not a defense to negligence? (a) contributory negligence (b) comparative negligence (c) violation of reasonable person standard (d) assumption of risk

7. Strict liability may exist even when a defendant is not negligent. **True or False?**

THINK CRITICALLY ABOUT EVIDENCE

Study the situation, answer the questions, and then prepare arguments to support your answers.

8. Betty was at a baseball game seated one row behind a famous movie star. When Betty stood up to cheer, she was bumped by the person beside her. She lost her balance and fell into the lap of the movie star. He sued her for the tort of assault. Who prevails?

9. Every morning on the way to work, Sharon rides an elevator up 14 floors. Sometimes, when it is crowded, the elevator operator intentionally bumps into her in an offensive way. What can Sharon do legally? What would be a likely defense for the operator?

10. Ham asked to borrow Lane's car to go to a movie with his girlfriend. Lane gave him permission. After the movie, Ham decided to drive to a city some 50 miles away to see a friend. Has he committed the tort of conversion?

11. Ashleigh has a pet boa constrictor named Pauline. She keeps it in the most expensive, escape-proof cage she can find. Regardless, the boa escapes and kills the neighbor's famed show cat which was valued at more than $5,000. Will Ashleigh be liable?

5-3 Civil Procedure

GOALS

- State the legal remedies that are available to a tort victim
- Describe the procedure used to try a civil case

KEY TERMS

injunction

evidence

testimony

witness

subpoena

verdict

judgment

Remedies Available in a Civil Suit

WHAT'S YOUR VERDICT? Horsley, the owner of a dry cleaning store, lived next door to Eardly, who ran a competing dry cleaning store in the same town. The two quarreled frequently and became enemies. One summer night Eardly composed, printed, and secretly posted around town a flyer accusing Horsley of dealing drugs out of Horsley's store. The accusation was untrue and defamatory. Several witnesses saw Eardly posting the flyers.

What kind of damages could Horsley collect from Eardly in a lawsuit?

Two types of remedies are generally available in a civil lawsuit for a tort, breach of contract, or other private injury. These two types are injunctions and damages. An **injunction** is a court order for a person to do or not do a particular act. An injunction may be issued to prevent a private injury, to stop it from continuing, or to undo it.

As discussed earlier, damages are a monetary award by the court to a person who has suffered loss or injury because of the act or omission of another. Generally damages fall into two categories, compensatory (also known as actual damages) and punitive (also known as exemplary damages). *Compensatory damages* are meant to place the injured party in the position he or she was in prior to the injury or loss. Under tort law these damages are the sum of the injured party's lost wages, doctor's fees, and a monetary amount to compensate for the injured party's pain and suffering. Damage amounts are usually determined by the trier of fact in each case.

Punitive damages are a type of damages generally only awarded in intentional tort cases. They are meant to punish the person who inflicted the injury. As a consequence, they are set by the trier of fact at an amount that would accomplish this objective. So, if a person is willfully injured by a large corporation, the punitive damage award can run into the millions of dollars.

Lawyers at times handle a civil lawsuit for a percentage of the recovery. This is referred to as taking the case on a *contingency fee* basis. Common percentages are 25 percent if the case is settled before a trial, 33 percent if the case is won at trial, and 40 percent or more if the case is won on appeal.

In *What's Your Verdict?* Horsley could recover both compensatory damages (for any provable loss of business) and punitive damages (to punish Eardly for his conduct).

IN THIS CASE Grimshaw sued the manufacturer of his auto after being burned severely in a collision. He was able to show that the manufacturer willfully kept a defective gas tank in Grimshaw's model of car even after it knew of the problem. The jury awarded him nearly $7 million in actual damages and another $100 million in punitive damages. The punitive damage award was set so high because a smaller amount would not be enough to punish an auto maker making billions each year.

CHECKPOINT Name the two remedies available in a civil suit.

What Procedure Is Used to Try a Civil Case?

WHAT'S YOUR VERDICT?

When their cars collided at an intersection, Claxson and DaLucia sued each other. Claxson claimed that DaLucia caused the accident by failing to stop for his stop sign. DaLucia claimed he had stopped and then moved through the intersection. He said he had not yet reached five miles per hour when Claxson ran his stop sign and slammed into him. Two witnesses saw the accident and could testify, but they have conflicting stories.

How can the court determine what really happened?

The procedure used to try a civil court case follows a set sequence.

Judge or Jury

First of all, if a jury is to be used, it is selected. Remember that judges and juries play different roles in trials. Judges always decide any issues of law. The issues of fact are left to the jury to decide, if a jury is sitting. By its Seventh Amendment, the U.S. Constitution provides for the right to a jury trial in civil cases involving more than $20. However, the states generally do not have such a guarantee in their constitutions. Even when there is a right to a civil trial by jury, both the *plaintiff* (the party that initiates the lawsuit by filing a complaint) and the *defendant* (the party complained against in a criminal or civil proceeding) may decide to forgo this right. When there is no jury, the judge decides the issues of both law and fact. In *What's Your Verdict?* the trier of fact, be it judge or jury, would listen to the testimonies of Claxson, DaLucia, and any other witnesses, and evaluate them for truth and accuracy. The trier of fact also would weigh any other evidence such as sobriety tests, skid marks, and location of debris to determine what happened.

Civil juries are made up of 6 to 12 citizens who listen to witnesses, review physical evidence, and reach their decisions. In most states, jury decisions in civil trials do not have to be unanimous.

Opening Statements and Testimony

After the jury for a specific case has been selected, the attorneys make opening statements. These statements briefly outline what the plaintiff and the defendant will try to prove. The evidence is then presented to the jury, first by the plaintiff and then by the defendant. **Evidence** includes anything that the judge allows to be presented to the jury that helps to prove or disprove the alleged facts. Evidence may consist of testimony, written documents, records, charts, sobriety test results, photographs of skid marks and debris location, and other relevant material.

Testimony is the most common form of evidence. **Testimony** consists of statements made by witnesses under oath. A **witness** is someone who has personal knowledge of the facts. Sometimes an *expert witness* will give an opinion. An expert witness possesses superior knowledge about important facts. For example, an engineer may be utilized as an expert witness to testify that skid marks indicate a car was going 70 miles per hour before a collision.

Witnesses often are summoned into court by subpoena. A **subpoena** is a written order by the judge commanding a person to appear, give testimony, and perhaps present other evidence.

LAW BRIEF

Expert witnesses generally are hired first as "consultants." Only after the lawyer feels comfortable with the potential of their testimony is the "consultant" designated to the court and the opposition in a case as an expert witness. All information and material provided to a potential expert witness while merely a consultant is confidential. However, after he or she is designated an expert witness, the other side in the case can find out everything the expert witness knows including everything disclosed to him or her while a consultant.

Willful, unexpected failure to appear after receipt of such an order is contempt of court. The judge can punish persons guilty of contempt of court by fine or jailing them without a trial.

Closing Arguments and Instructions to the Jury

Following the presentation of the evidence, the attorney for each side gives a closing argument. During closing arguments, each attorney summarizes the case, trying to persuade the judge (and the jury if there is one) to favor his or her side. After consultation with the attorneys, the judge then gives instructions to the jury. These instructions tell the jury what rules of law apply to the case. They also tell the jury what issues of fact they must decide.

Jury Deliberation and the Verdict

For example, in a civil case involving an auto accident, the judge might instruct the jury that exceeding the speed limit in bad weather is negligence (a rule of law). The judge also may tell the jury to decide if the weather was bad at the time of the accident (a question of fact) and whether the defendant was exceeding the speed limit at the time of the accident or driving faster than a reasonable speed given the weather (questions of fact). The jury then retires to the jury room for deliberation in secret to decide the case. In deciding, each juror must determine whether a preponderance (superior weight) of the evidence supports the plaintiff's case. In a civil action, a unanimous vote of the jurors is not required. Usually, 10 out of 12 or, in a few states having smaller jury panels, 5 out of 6 voting for the plaintiff will be enough to find for the plaintiff. The jury's decision is called the **verdict**.

After the verdict has been returned, the judge renders a judgment. The **judgment** is the final result of the trial. It will normally be for a sum of money if the plaintiff wins. If the defendant wins, the judgment will merely be "judgment for the defendant." If either party believes the judge made a mistake of law in any part of the trial, an appeal may be made to a higher court.

Examples of judicial error include incorrect instructions to the jury, admission of evidence that should have been rejected, or exclusion of evidence that should have been admitted. When there has been an error, the appellate court may modify or reverse the judgment of the lower court. Or it may order a new trial. If there is no error in the record, the reviewing court will affirm the judgment of the lower court.

CHECKPOINT List the steps in the procedure used to try a civil case.

© GETTY IMAGES/PHOTODISC

What is this defense attorney trying to do with his closing argument to the jury?

How are Civil Damages Collected?

Ordinarily, when a civil judgment for the plaintiff becomes final, the defendant will pay the judgment. If the defendant does not pay, the plaintiff may obtain a *writ of execution.* Execution here means the process by which a judgment for money is enforced. The court directs that the defendant's property (for example, a savings account or car) be seized or sold. The proceeds, after deducting the costs of seizure and sale, are used to pay the judgment.

CHECKPOINT How does a plaintiff collect damages if the defendant refuses to pay?

© GETTY IMAGES/PHOTODISC

Would the possibility of losing a prize possession influence you to pay a judgment against you in a civil suit?

5-3 Assessment

Xtra!
Study Tools
school.cengage.com/blaw/lawxtra

THINK ABOUT LEGAL CONCEPTS

1. Damages meant to punish the person who has committed a tort are called compensatory damages. **True or False?**

2. Compensatory damages are also referred to as __?__ damages.

3. A jury never determines a matter of law. **True or False?**

4. In deciding the amount of compensatory or actual damages to pay a plaintiff, the jury decides on a figure that would equal lost wages and medical bills plus a more arbitrary amount for the plaintiff's __?__.

5. A witness who was at the scene of the crime and who is very sure about what happened is referred to as an expert witness. **True or False?**

6. An order that a judge issues commanding a witness to appear and give testimony is called a(n) __?__.

7. In a civil case, the judge renders a judgment after hearing the jury's (a) determination (b) resolution (c) verdict (d) none of the above

8. If a defendant refuses to pay a damage award, the court may issue a writ of __?__ ordering the defendant's property be seized and/or sold to pay the amount due.

THINK CRITICALLY ABOUT EVIDENCE

Study the situation, answer the questions, and then prepare arguments to support your answers.

9. Stone had secretly criticized the large chemical company she worked for over a span of several years. Her inside information had led to many accurate stories in the local papers about toxic releases into the environment. Finally, the company discovered what she was doing and hired two thugs to rough her up. They did a very thorough job, and she had to be hospitalized for several weeks. Because she immediately reported her beating to the police, the thugs were captured. In a plea bargain with the prosecutor, they confessed who had hired them. Stone brought suit against the chemical company. For what types of damages could she sue? Why?

10. Stone lost $14,000 in salary and owed $30,000 in medical bills as a result of the beating in exercise 9. She had sustained a concussion and had a broken leg with numerous lacerations and abrasions. Thereafter, she consistently walked with a limp. The chemical company averaged $72 million in annual profits over the last five years. What damage award for each type of damages you selected in exercise 9 would be appropriate? Why?

11. Presume that the damage awards that you deemed appropriate in exercise 10 were awarded by the jury. If the company refused to pay, even after the appeals went against them, how could Stone go about collecting?

12. In preparing for the suit, Stone's attorney subpoenaed several witnesses. After they were served with the subpoenas, the company immediately assigned them to distant locations in the country. If they willfully fail to appear at the trial, what sanctions can the court utilize to punish them?

13. Presume that, because the evidence against it was overwhelming, the chemical company decided to settle the case out of court for $16 million. Typically, what would be an attorney's contingency fee percentage share of this amount? If the case had to be won at trial and $20 million was awarded by the jury, how much would Stone's attorneys receive under a typical fee arrangement? If the chemical company appealed but lost, what would be Stone's attorney's typical share of the $20 million?

 Online Research> **Becky's Battle**

It is early December and Becky is an 18-year-old high school senior trying to sign up for her final semester's courses. She comes from a poor family that did not own a car until a month ago, when Becky bought one with her savings from work. Because she did not have access to a car until a few weeks ago, Becky had not even considered taking the driver's education course offered by her school. Her auto insurance agent told her that her rates would be significantly reduced if she took such a course, so she is trying to enroll in it.

Unfortunately, her application has been rejected. Because of limited funding for the program and a large number of applicants, the school has a rule that it only allows 16 and 17 year olds to take the course. Becky claims this is a form of age discrimination prohibited by law.

THINK CRITICALLY

Does Becky's claim have merit? Does the school's position have legal support? Explain your answers to both questions. Is Becky likely to win if she sues to gain admission to the program?

GO TO FINDLAW.COM TO FIND THE ANSWERS

To find the material in FindLaw on this issue, go to Findlaw.com and click on the following sequence of hyperlinks: Civil Rights, Civil Rights: More Topics, Age Discrimination, Age Discrimination in Education. Read the material including the questions and answers.

Chapter 5 Assessment

Xtra! Quiz Prep
school.cengage.com/blaw/lawxtra

CONCEPTS IN BRIEF

5-1   Private Injuries vs. Public Offenses

1. A tort is an act that causes private injury to the person or property of another.

2. Torts may be broadly classified as intentional torts, negligence, or strict liability. The most common tort is negligence.

3. Generally every individual is personally responsible for damage resulting from any torts committed by him or her.

4. Employers are liable for the torts of their employees if the torts are committed within the scope of the employees' employment.

5-2   Intentional Torts, Negligence, and Strict Liability

5. With intentional torts, the defendant possesses the intent or purpose to inflict the resultant injury.

6. In some states, if the injured person was also negligent and the negligence contributed to the injury, the injured person may be barred from recovering damages. In many states today,

however, some recovery may even then be obtained by the plaintiff under the doctrine of comparative negligence.

5-3   Civil Procedure

7. A person injured by a tort is entitled to damages—monetary compensation for the loss or injury suffered. The amount of damages is typically determined by the trier of the fact in the case.

8. If a jury is present, it will determine the issues of fact in a civil trial. The issues of law will be determined by the judge.

9. For a civil case, lawyers can either be hired on an hourly basis or, if the case promises an adequate award to the client on a contingency fee basis, for a percentage of the prospective award. However, if the client's case is lost, the attorney working on a contingency fee basis receives nothing.

YOUR LEGAL VOCABULARY

Match each statement with the term that it best defines. Some terms may not be used.

1. Person who has personal knowledge of the facts in a case

2. Deprivation of freedom of movement without consent or privilege

3. Final result of a trial

4. Using property in a manner that is inconsistent with its owner's rights

5. Tort based on carelessness

6. False statement that injures a person's reputation

7. Intentionally made threat to physically or offensively injure another

8. Harmful or offensive touching

9. Written court order compelling a person to appear in court and to testify

10. Materials or statements presented in a trial to prove or disprove alleged facts

11. A monetary award by the court to a person who has suffered loss or injury because of the act or omission of another

a. assault
b. battery
c. conversion
d. damages
e. defamation
f. evidence
g. false imprisonment
h. fraud
i. intentional tort
j. invasion of privacy
k. judgment
l. negligence
m. strict liability
n. subpoena
o. testimony
p. tort
q. trespass to land
r. verdict
s. witness

REVIEW LEGAL CONCEPTS

12. If certain acts are both crimes and torts, why couldn't you let the prosecutor both bring criminal charges against the defendant and bring suit for damages for the victim at the same time?

13. In most cases, in order to recover damages for emotional harm, a person also must show physical harm. Why would society want to establish an additional barrier to someone who has been harmed by the commission of a tort?

14. The Japanese have a popular belief that any defendant who risks his fate on the opinions of untrained laymen in a jury is almost certainly guilty. Do you agree with this contention? Why or why not?

15. Under the doctrine of strict liability, the manufacturer and any sellers in the chain of distribution are held liable for the injuries of a buyer of a defective product. Given the complexity of many modern products, is it fair to hold the sellers liable especially when the manufacturers have gone out of business and cannot pay?

WRITE ABOUT LEGAL CONCEPTS

16. Make an outline of what takes place in each of the main steps of a civil lawsuit from the filing of the complaint to the execution of the judgment. Is justice done when the process is halted by a settlement between the parties?

17. **HOT DEBATE** What parties would Chanelle likely sue over the assault? What type of relief would she likely seek?

MAKE ACADEMIC CONNECTIONS

18. **PSYCHOLOGY** The selection of favorable jury members by the parties to a lawsuit was once conducted according to near legendary rules. For example, clergy, school teachers, lawyers (and their spouses) were considered bad risks in the jury box because they were opinionated and could not be swayed by the lawyer's arguments. Good jury selections included retired businesspeople and reasonably well-educated laborers. Today, however, jury selection in important cases is done on a scientific basis utilizing psychological insights. Research and comment on the new methods and criteria for picking jurors.

THINK CRITICALLY ABOUT EVIDENCE

Study the situation, answer the questions, and then prepare arguments to support your answers.

19. Martin asked Gabrielle on a date. They went to a movie and then drove around for a while. As he drove, Martin grabbed Gabrielle, pulled her to him, and tried to kiss her. After a moment she was able to break his grip and demanded he let her out of the car. Instead, Martin sped up and kept driving at a high rate of speed, saying he would only let her out if she would kiss him. What torts has Martin committed?

20. McDonald and Beck were sitting in a bar watching a professional football game. When she discovered McDonald was not rooting for her team, Beck hit McDonald in the face, breaking McDonald's glasses and nose. McDonald called the police, who arrested Beck. What legal causes of action does McDonald have against Beck? What type of damages can he recover?

21. Jackson was a lawyer, respected by his peers. He successfully represented several persons who were charged with income tax evasion. All three defendants were reputed to be leaders of an organized crime syndicate. The local newspaper then printed an editorial calling for the tightening of tax laws "to protect society against mobsters and shyster lawyers like Jackson who would sell their souls to the devil for 30 pieces of silver." Was this statement a tort?

22. Yardly and Whiple, ages 12 and 13, intentionally threw stones which smashed 57 windows in an old warehouse. The warehouse had been

standing vacant for nine months. Yardly and Whiple were caught and disciplined by the juvenile court. Then the owner of the warehouse sued them and their parents for damages. The girls said they were "just having fun and not hurting anyone because the place was empty." Who, if anyone, is liable and why?

ANALYZE REAL CASES

23. Town Finance Corporation (TFC) foreclosed on a mortgage following a dispute with Hughes as to whether a loan had been repaid. TFC had a locksmith remove the locks of Hughes' dwelling. When no one was home, TFC personnel then entered the house, seized household goods, and left the inside of the house in disarray. Hughes filed suit over the debt. The court held that the finance company had been paid and thus had no further right of action against Hughes. Hughes thereupon filed this action, which claimed malicious and willful trespass and asked both actual (compensatory) and punitive damages. Was Hughes entitled to judgment? (*Town Finance Corporation v. Hughes*, 214 S.E.2d 387)

24. Lewis, an undercover police officer carrying a concealed pistol, went shopping in a Dayton Hudson department store. There, a security officer became suspicious that he was a shoplifter. Lewis took some clothing into a fitting room, where there were signs stating, "This area is under surveillance by Hudson's personnel." In fact, the security guard observed Lewis from a grille in the ceiling. After he saw Lewis place the gun on a chair, he called the police. Eventually, Lewis was identified as an undercover officer. But he sued Dayton Hudson claiming that the spying in the fitting room was an invasion of his privacy. Will he recover? (*Lewis v. Dayton Hudson Corporation*, 128 Mich. App. 165)

25. A train stopped at the defendant's railroad platform. As it started up again, a man carrying a small package jumped aboard. He appeared unsteady and about to fall. Therefore a guard on the train, holding the door open, reached out to help him. Another guard, standing on the platform, pushed the man from behind. The man made it onto the train, but he dropped the package, which was about fifteen inches long. The package was wrapped in newspaper and contained fireworks that exploded when the package hit the rails. The shock of the explosion caused several scales at the other end of the platform, many feet away, to fall down. As they fell, they struck the plaintiff, injuring her. She sued the railroad, claiming the guards were negligent. Is the railroad liable? (*Palsgraf v. Long Island Railroad Company*, 162 N.E. 99, N.Y.)

26. David Allen, age two, was attacked and severely bitten in the face and ear by a dog owned by Whitehead. Whitehead admitted that the dog barked a lot, was large, looked mean, and chased cars. On the other hand, no one had ever complained about the dog, it had never bitten anyone before, and it frequently played with other children. Is Whitehead liable for the injuries to David? (*Allen v. Whitehead*, 423 So. 2d 835, Ala.)

27. When a statement appeared on its financial bulletin board claiming that individuals from a securities investment firm committed criminal and fraudulent acts during an initial public offering of a stock, Prodigy and the anonymous poster of the statement were sued for defamation. Prodigy had previously maintained that the content of its bulletin board was monitored and edited by Prodigy. Can Prodigy be held liable for the comments of the anonymous poster on its bulletin board? (*Stratton Oakmont, Inc. v. Prodigy Services Co.*, 5 Alb L J Sci & Tech 229, 237 [1996])

Sports & Entertainment Law

As The Wheel of Fortune Turns

WHITE V. SAMSUNG ELECTRONICS AM., INC.
971 F.2D 1395 (9TH CIR.)

BACKGROUND One category of invasion of privacy involves the misappropriation of a person's name, likeness, or other identifying features. These are looked upon by the law as having commercial value and labeled the "right to publicity." This right can be transferred only by proper licensing or other formal or informal assignment.

FACTS A landmark case defining the scope of this right occurred when the hostess of the very popular game show *Wheel of Fortune* sued Samsung Corporation for infringement because they had used her likeness in an advertisement without permission. The scene depicted in the ad was easily recognizable as a futuristic version of the *Wheel of Fortune* set. Vanna White's image was conveyed by a robot costumed in a wig, dress, and jewelry to resemble her and staged in White's characteristic stance. The caption for the ad read, "Longest-running game show, 2012 A.D." and conveyed the message that the Samsung products being promoted would still be in use at that time. The federal district court dismissed the case without trying it, and White appealed to the 9th circuit federal court of appeals.

THE LAW Prior to this case, the law had focused mainly on the appropriation of a plaintiff's name and likeness as grounds for a suit for a violation of the so-called "right of publicity." Samsung in its defense cited previous restrictive rulings in cases involving Bette Midler, Clint Eastwood, and Johnny Carson.

THE ISSUE Should the "right to publicity" be expanded to protect more than just the name and likeness of a plaintiff?

HOLDING The court pointed out that the right of publicity was identified and developed to protect the commercial value of a celebrity's identity. Therefore, it was not important how the defendant has appropriated the identity of the plaintiff but whether the defendant had done so. Only by an analysis of the latter question can the right of publicity be utilized in the proper manner to defend the legitimate interests of plaintiffs in their very identity. Using this expanded logic, the court reversed the district court's holding and sent the case back down to the lower court to be tried.

PRACTICE JUDGING

1. What are the essential elements of a person's recognizable identity? Pick a celebrity and identify, if possible, what would convey his or her identity without using a name or likeness.

2. In what situations would being able to convey such a person's identity be of value?

Entrepreneurs
AND THE LAW

Project 1   Law, Justice and You

THE IDEA   Stacy Jean Meyer had worked for her state's Department of Transportation for more than two years when the accident occurred. In midsummer, her DOT section had been doing an asphalt surfacing job on a state road. The temperature had peaked at 95 degrees. That meant the temperature on the paving machine Stacy operated was above 120 degrees for most of the day. Finally, her shift ended. Air conditioner roaring, she drove her car onto the parkway and headed home. A few miles from her turnoff, it happened. A tire on a flatbed truck ahead of her started to come apart. Huge parts of the tire's outer bands, with metal reinforcing webbing exposed, were thrown backwards at Stacy's car. One end of the largest piece caught under her car's bumper. The other end slammed down onto the hood. Barely able to steer, Stacy hit the brakes and finally eased onto the shoulder of the road. With the help of another motorist, Stacy removed the fragment of the tire. As she did so, Stacy noted that the tire had been a recap—a tire created by gluing a new outer portion of tread onto the worn inner core of old tires. "Ironic," she said to the other driver. "My father is co-owner of a retread manufacturer. A lot of trucks use recaps because they're half as expensive as new tires."

Before she left the scene, Stacy called her insurance company and the highway patrol to report the accident. She guessed that damage to her car would cost more than $2,000 in body work of which she'd have to pay a $500 deductible. While taking the report, the insurance company representative noted that accidents caused by blown recaps added a great deal to the cost of auto insurance.

Later that evening, Stacy started researching. She discovered that recaps are 50 to 70 percent less expensive than new tires. Also, the tire cores can be recapped three times for high-speed usage and up to ten times for low-speed (city) usage. Problems arose when the temperatures caused by the friction and conduction of heat from the road contact exceeded the glue's tolerance. Stacy thought about that, and it occurred to her that there was a similar problem at her work. It involved asphalt adhering to the underlying road surfaces to which it was applied. If the surface and the asphalt did not bind securely, the asphalt would be quickly moved by the constant pressure of the vehicle tires until it formed ridges in the road's surface. To prevent this, the underlying road surfaces often were deeply grooved by machine before the asphalt was applied. Then the idea hit her: If you could groove the cap on its underside before gluing, it might be possible to prevent the tire separation and extend the life of the recap. She reached for the phone to call her dad.

THE PROTOTYPE   Her dad listened carefully and then suggested that she come by the shop that weekend. Bright and early Saturday, Stacy met her father with a big hug and a set of drawings of possible patterns for the grooves. She also had done extensive research to try and find a machine that could do the grooving without damaging the caps but was unsuccessful. Over the next several months, Stacy and her dad, Joe, worked together on the idea. Eventually, by repeatedly grooving the caps by hand, gluing them, and then testing them for longevity, they evolved an angular cross-hatch design that increased the life and resiliency of the recap by more than 60 percent. Tracy designed a machine to do the grooving that would function like the one used to assist in the changing of big truck tires. It would flatten 10 percent of the cap at once, groove it to pattern, and then rotate the cap until the groove pattern was applied to the entire item. Joe took her design to a mechanical engineer to draft plans. He then sent the plans to a nearby metalworking shop to fabricate the prototype and fronted the $30,000 cost of manufacturing.

ACTIVITIES

Divide into teams and perform one or more of the following activities, as directed by your teacher.

Analyze

Assess the safety and environmental consequences of Stacy's activities. What are the problems and potential of the process and device? What hurdles must be overcome before Stacy and her dad's work can be a success?

Role-Play

Divide the class into two groups. Have one group represent Stacy's interests and the other represent Joe's. Have each group define those interests and announce them to the class. Anticipate potential conflicts and propose solutions.

GET OUT THE VOTE Did you know that in a recent presidential election only 51 percent of potential voters under age 30 actually cast their ballots? Overall the voter turnout in the United States mocks the description of participatory democracy often applied to this country. In that election, only about 60 percent of the eligible voters exercised their right to determine who makes the decisions in this land. Shocking? Actually, that was up more than 8 percent from the previous presidential election. You can help change that with a campaign to get out the vote.

DO YOUR PART

1. Research the appropriate laws on registration and alternative means of voting. Contact your courthouse or city hall for information.

2. Devise a plan to inform potential voters how to exercise their right to vote. Often people want to vote but do not know the basics. Language barriers, employment hours, and handicaps all can be overcome with proper planning. You can provide information to assist potential voters in overcoming barriers.

3. Determine resources for assistance for those with problems getting to the polls, locations of the appropriate polling station, and so on.

4. Develop a plan to make personal contact with potential voters. It is far and away the most effective means of getting out the vote. Experience shows that it also is beneficial to recontact the potential voters before the election.

5. Create a handout, in appropriate languages, with a map of polling stations, answers to frequently asked questions, and resources.

Emerging Business Issues

This event for two- or three-member teams challenges FBLA members to develop and demonstrate research and presentation skills for an emerging business issue. Your research should find both affirmative and negative arguments for each topic.

- Setting Award Limits for Malpractice Lawsuits
- The Death Penalty
- Lemon Laws for Automobile Purchases
- Making Home Builders Accountable for Their Work

Performance Indicators Evaluated

- Understand the given emerging business issue.
- Present a relevant affirmative or negative argument for the topic.
- Conduct research to support your argument.
- Demonstrate persuasive speaking and oral presentation skills.
- Involve all team members in the research and presentation. Fifteen minutes before your presentation time, you will draw to determine whether you will present an affirmative or negative argument for your emerging business issue. Each presentation may last no more than five minutes. Following each oral presentation, the judges have five minutes to ask questions.

For more detailed information about performance indicators, go to the FBLA web site.

THINK CRITICALLY

1. Why must consumers conduct major research before receiving medical treatment or making major purchases?

2. List two strategies during the presentation that will hold the attention of the judges.

3. Does *caveat emptor* mean that the consumer is accountable for purchases even when defective?

4. List a pro and con for setting award limits on malpractice lawsuits.

www.fbla-pbl.org

Mock Trial Prep

CONCEPTS OF ADVOCACY

WHAT IS MOCK TRIAL?

Mock trial is a trial based on a hypothetical case where students play the roles of attorneys, witnesses, and other courtroom participants. Mock trial competitions take place at the junior high and high school levels, as well as at the collegiate and law school levels. The purpose of mock trial is to help students gain a working knowledge of the judicial system, develop analytical skills, and explore various aspects of roles of legal professionals.

What is the National High School Mock Trial Competition?

Each year, teams from states and territories of the United States gather together to compete in the National High School Mock Trial Competition. The competition is held in a different state each year. For more information, please see their web site at www.nationalmocktrial.org.

What Happens in a Mock Trial?

A mock trial begins with the opening of the court by a student bailiff. The bailiff will stand and say,

> All rise. Hear ye. Hear ye. The Court of
> _____ (city or county) is now in session.
> Honorable Judge _____ presiding.

There are two opposing sides in a mock trial, the prosecution in a criminal case, or plaintiff in a civil case, and the defendant. Generally, there are two attorneys for each side. One attorney for each side will present an opening statement explaining what the case is about, what evidence will be presented, and what the evidence will prove.

Each side will then present its case-in-chief, which is the stage of the trial where the parties present their evidence to support their case. Evidence is presented through the testimony of each party's witnesses. Testimony is the evidence given by a witness under oath or affirmation. Witnesses are called to testify during the case-in-chief and may be either lay witnesses or expert witnesses.

Before each witness takes the stand, the student bailiff will swear in the witness. The bailiff will approach the witness and ask the witness to stand and raise his or her right hand. The bailiff will ask the witness,

Do you promise that the testimony you are about to give will faithfully and truthfully conform to the facts and rules of the mock trial competition?

Each witness called is asked a series of questions by the attorney who called that witness to the stand. This is called direct examination. After the direct examination, the witness is then cross-examined by the opposing attorney. Cross examination generally is limited to the scope of the direct examination. In other words, the questioning on cross examination is limited to matters addressed in the direct examination.

After a party has completed its case-in-chief, that party rests its case.

The mock trial concludes with the closing arguments. One attorney for each side reviews the evidence presented and asks the judge or jury for a ruling in his/her client's favor. If there is a jury in the mock trial, then the judge will read jury instructions to the jury. Jury instructions are statements made by the judge to the jury concerning the applicable law. The final steps in a mock trial include the deliberation and the decision.

How to Prepare for Mock Trial

The first step in preparing for a mock trial is to read the case scenario and the case law sections which follow. In a mock trial competition, the case materials often are quite lengthy. The case summary, witness statements, case law, exhibits, motions, rules of evidence, and rules of the mock trial competition are included in the case materials.

Assign the roles of attorneys and witnesses. In a mock trial competition, the roles of jury members (optional) and the bailiff also need to be filled. Months of preparation and practice, assisted by teachers and legal advisors, are expected in a mock trial competition.

Attorneys should begin drafting direct-examination and cross-examination questions for each witness. The witnesses should assist the attorneys in drafting questions. This will help the witnesses to memorize their witness statements and delve into the character they are playing. Further, it will help ensure that the witnesses know their testimony thoroughly so that their testimony will not be inconsistent with their statements. When the witness's

testimony in court is inconsistent with the witness statement, the questioning attorney may impeach the witness. Impeachment occurs when an attorney calls into question the veracity, or truthfulness, of a witness by suggesting that the witness is contradicting a prior statement, is biased, is changing his testimony, or is not credible. A witness may be rehabilitated after impeachment with evidence supporting his credibility. It is best to avoid any chance of impeachment by the opposing side by mastering the facts in the witness statements.

Direct examinations should be rehearsed by the attorney and the witness being examined. However, the attorney and the witness need to take care to avoid presenting an examination that seems too rehearsed. The witness should listen to the question asked, pause before answering, and then deliver an answer that is responsive to the question and sounds unrehearsed. Memorized responses to questions are obvious. Mock trial competitions are as much about acting realistic as they are about knowing the materials.

Cross-examination questions should be drafted and rehearsed. One strategy is to end your cross examination with your strongest argument or point.

The closing argument is challenging to prepare because it must be a flexible presentation. The attorney responsible for the closing argument must review not only the evidence presented for his or her own side but also the weaknesses and inconsistencies of the other side's case which came during the trial proceedings.

Prepare a Trial Notebook

A three-ring binder containing the case materials, case law, copies of the exhibits, opening statement, direct-examination and cross-examination questions for each witness, and closing statements should be assembled. Organizing your trial materials for easy access and reference is essential for a successful trial.

General Mock Trial Rules

Generally, the following rules apply.

1. Teams may refer only to materials included in the case materials supplied.

2. No photographs, charts, graphs, or other visual aids of any kind may be used, unless provided in the case

packet. The only exhibits permitted are included in the case packet. No enlargements or alterations of the case materials will be permitted.

3. Absolutely no props or costumes are permitted unless specifically authorized in the case materials. Costuming is defined as hairstyles, clothing, accessories, and makeup which are case-specific.

4. Teams may not communicate with their teachers or legal advisers during the competition.

5. Witnesses may not use their witness statements or any notes while testifying.

6. Time limits generally are imposed on each portion of the trial. For example, the opening and closing statements may be limited to five minutes per side.

7. No motions may be made to the judge during the trial.

8. No objections may be made during opening or closing statements.

TEAMWORK

Trials should reflect a process that indicates a fair treatment by the law in determining the guilt or innocence of the accused. Work together in teams to arrange the following steps of a trial in the proper order.

Arraignment

Arrest

Charge to the jury by the judge

Closing statement by the prosecution

Closing statement of the Defense

Cross examination of defense witnesses

Cross examination of prosecution witnesses

Direct examination of defense witnesses

Direct examination of prosecution witnesses

Jury deliberation

Jury selection

Opening statement by the defense

Opening statement by the prosecution

Pre-trial hearings

Verdict/Sentencing

Unit 2
Contract Law

Chapters

6 **Offer and Acceptance**

7 **Genuineness of Assent**

8 **Consideration**

9 **Legal Capacity to Contract**

10 **Legal Purpose and Proper Form**

11 **Contractual Obligations and Their Enforcement**

12 **Contractual Aspects of Marriage and Divorce**

Franchisee

Marketing, Sales & Service

Are you interested in owning a business that has proven to be successful in other areas of the country or the world? Would you be willing to own the business even if you didn't have complete decision-making control? If so, you may be interested in purchasing a franchise.

H&R Block, MerryMaids, Ace Hardware, and Arby's are all examples of franchised businesses. For the right amount of money, typically varying from thousands to millions depending on the type and scale of operation one wishes to own, a franchise businesses can be yours. The purchaser, called the franchisee, must follow strict guidelines set down by the franchisor which may include how the business can be decorated, what prices can be charged, or how to advertise the business.

EMPLOYMENT OUTLOOK

Although the employment outlook with a franchised operation is directly dependent on the success of the business, some general guidelines should be noted. Employment of business executives—including chief executives and general and operations managers—is expected to grow about as fast as average for all occupations through 2014. Some industries are projected to grow faster than others. For example, employment growth is expected to be much faster than average in professional areas such as law. Other areas with growing employment opportunities include scientific, and technical services and in administrative and support services. However, employment is projected to decline in some manufacturing industries.

NEEDED SKILLS AND EDUCATION

- A bachelor's degree in business is helpful to any business owner, but it is generally not a requirement for becoming a franchisee.

- Many franchise owners are active in managing day-to-day operations. These franchisees must have the skills needed to hire, train, supervise, and discharge workers. They also purchase supplies, deal with vendors, keep records, and help whenever an extra hand is needed. Other franchisees hire managers to run the day-to-day operations. These franchisees oversee the operation and are only involved in specific tasks, like record keeping.

- Successful franchisees must have the willingness to: conform to standards set by others; make unpopular decisions at times; ask for help; work long hours.

How you'll spend your day

Although the typical franchise business is a restaurant, for those with the proper legal training owning a franchise that provides basic legal services like a simple will, name change, or uncontested divorce is also a possibility.

As the owner of a franchised law firm, you'll hire lawyers and administrative staff to run your business. Your day will begin by checking e-mails and handling phone calls from your franchise headquarters. You'll talk about your business's progress and how to improve it. Are you following the agreed-upon rules established by the franchisor?

You'll also resolve any problems with your clients or employees. In order to build your business, you'll arrange for advertising as outlined in your franchise agreement. You'll meet with prospective clients to discuss how your law firm can address their needs. On some days you'll complete the payroll and perform other administrative work.

You and your staff will meet daily with clients who have sought your help in a variety of legal matters. Your work probably will be limited to cases that can be resolved efficiently. The franchise headquarters will advise you on which cases are best to accept, and how to go about completing each case. If you own more than one franchise location, you'll frequently travel to check on progress. When necessary, you'll step in to do the work yourself.

What about you?

Does the job of franchisee interest you? Why or why not? Which aspects of the job would you most enjoy? Which aspects would you least enjoy?

Chapter 6
Offer and Acceptance

6-1 Creation of Offers

6-2 Termination of Offers

6-3 Acceptances

HOT DEBATE

© GETTY IMAGES/PHOTODISC

Trenton and Elisa were college students taking a class on movie production. Knowing that the final movie in the *Alien Cheerleader* trilogy was about to come out, Trenton camped out overnight at the theater. He bought two tickets, and then asked Elisa to go with him. Elisa agreed. To be able to go, however, she had to call in sick to her evening job as a waitress. Not working that evening would cost her more than $100 in wages and tips. Nonetheless, she made the call. When Trenton did not show up to get her, she confronted him. He admitted he had sold the tickets to someone else for $50 each.

WHERE DO YOU STAND?

1. Should Elisa be allowed to sue Trenton for not taking her to the movie?
2. Would your answer change depending upon whether or not Trenton knew Elisa would lose income by going?

6-1 Creation of Offers

GOALS

■ List the elements required to form a contract

■ Describe the requirements of an offer

KEY TERMS

contracts

offeror

offeree

offer

What Must Be in a Contract?

WHAT'S YOUR VERDICT? Juan and Susan were talking one day after school. Juan would turn 16 on the upcoming July 13 and wanted to buy Susan's car. Susan, 17, had been working and saving her money to buy a new car. Selling her old car for $2,800 would give her enough to do so. She offered it to Juan for that amount, and he accepted.

Did the two friends create a legally enforceable contract?

Because of its limited resources, the court system is very selective in what it will enforce. Criminal laws and laws allowing recovery for certain private injuries (torts) are highest on the list for enforcement as they are necessary for keeping peace in society. However, when it comes to **contracts**, generally defined as agreements between two or more parties that create obligations, the courts are far more selective.

In particular, there are six major requirements that must be satisfied before courts will treat a transaction as a legally enforceable contract. These are offer and acceptance, genuine assent, legality, consideration, capacity, and writing.

1. **OFFER AND ACCEPTANCE** There must be an agreement composed of an offer and an acceptance upon which to base the contract. The person who makes the offer is termed the **offeror**. The person to whom it is made is the **offeree**. The terms of the offer must be definite and accepted without change by the party to whom it was intended to be offered.

2. **GENUINE ASSENT** The agreement must not be based on one party's deceiving another, on an important mistake, or on the use of unfair pressure exerted to obtain the offer or acceptance.

3. **LEGALITY** What the parties agree to must be legal. An agreement to commit a crime or tort cannot be a legally enforceable contract.

4. **CONSIDERATION** The agreement must involve both sides receiving what the law considers value in some form as a result of the transaction.

5. **CAPACITY** To have a completely enforceable agreement, the parties must have the legal ability to contract for themselves. For example, in *What's Your Verdict?* if the minimum age to form a legally enforceable contract is 18 as it is in almost every state, the courts would not enforce Juan and Susan's contract against either of them.

6. **WRITING** Some agreements must be placed in writing to be fully enforceable in court.

CHECKPOINT What elements are required to form a legally enforceable contract?

IN THIS CASE When you told Sheila how nice the paint job was on her car, she responded that she painted cars in her garage for a second income. She took a close look at your vehicle. Then she said that, if you agreed, she would do a similar job on it with the color of your choice in the next week for $1,800. In this situation, Sheila is the offeror and you are the offeree.

Requirements of an Offer

An **offer** is a proposal by an offeror to do something, provided the offeree does or refrains from doing something in return. The offer is the basis of the bargain. If it is not valid, there can be no contract for the courts to enforce. As a consequence, the law examines would-be offers carefully. There are three tests that an offer must pass to be legally enforceable:

1. Contractual intent must be present in the offer.
2. The offer must be communicated to the offeree.
3. The essential terms of the offer must be complete and definite.

Contractual Intent Must Be Present

Often, although the words themselves may indicate an offer, a reasonable person would disregard them because of the facts and circumstances under which they were spoken. When a teacher says to a business law class, "I will sell you my new car for $3,000," this probably isn't an offer but an example. Words that take the form of offers but which are spoken in jest (as a joke), in extreme terror or anger, or as a preliminary negotiation or social agreement would not be enforced.

JESTS The law is not concerned with what is actually in the mind of a person making what might be considered an offer. Rather, it is concerned with the appearance of this action. If you think you are joking, but a reasonable person would interpret your conduct as indicating that you intend to contract, you have made an offer. On the other hand if you are serious, but a reasonable person would interpret your conduct as a joke, then no legally enforceable offer is made.

STATEMENTS MADE IN ANGER OR TERROR Yelling after someone who has just stolen your watch, "Stop thief—I'll pay anyone who stops her $100," is not looked upon as being a valid offer by the law. It does not have the reasoned basis necessary for enforceable offers. So if someone ran after the person, captured her, and returned your watch, you would not, in a legal sense at least, owe the $100.

© GETTY IMAGES/PHOTODISC

Imagine that this man just told his two friends that he would gladly sell his motorcycle to the first one of them who could scrape together $100 in cash to pay for it. Judging from the expression on his face, has he made a legally enforceable offer? Why or why not?

PRELIMINARY NEGOTIATIONS Information often is communicated merely to induce someone to initiate bargaining. Such statements are not seen by the law as indicating an intent to contract. You might casually say, "Would you pay $800 for my laptop computer?" without intending to be bound if he says yes. (This contrasts with a valid offer which might take the form, "Look Jeff, I'll sell you my laptop computer today for $800.") Statements of this nature, including putting signs on merchandise with a certain price or ads in newspapers to the same effect, are *invitations to negotiate.* They are not offers. The offer in such circumstances would typically come from the party responding to the ad.

In *What's Your Verdict?* Anchors Aweigh advertised boats. When would-be buyers tendered (presented for acceptance) the purchase price of the cabin cruiser, the would-be buyers were the ones making an offer. Thus, Anchors Aweigh was not bound by contract to the seven would-be buyers who came to purchase the boats after they were out of stock. To promote good customer relations, businesses try to deliver advertised merchandise to all who want to buy. Statutes prohibit false or misleading advertising. However, prosecuting an advertiser—who might be fined or imprisoned as a consequence under such a statute—does not get someone the bargain in the ad.

Advertisements may occasionally be offers. This can occur in one of two ways. First, the ad must be clearly worded in ways that address the problem of numerous people receiving the ad for a limited amount of product. Someone selling a car could create an offer by writing a complete and clear ad, and in addition, writing that the car will be sold only to the first person to accept the terms contained in the offer. Or an ad may state "subject to stock on hand."

Second, an ad may become an offer if it asks the offeree to perform an act as a way of accepting. An ad which states that a clearly described new power lawnmower will be sold for $20 "to the first person to appear at the main door of a shopping mall on Saturday morning after 6:00 A.M." will be a valid offer.

SOCIAL AGREEMENTS If two friends agree to go to the movies, no contract is intended. The friends don't think of this agreement as creating legal obligations. If either breaks the

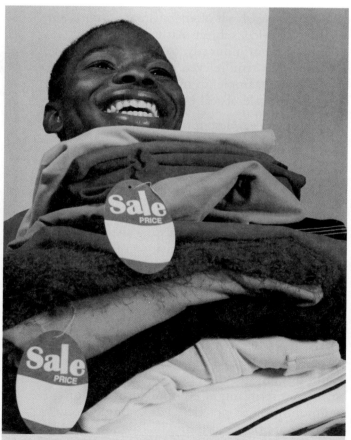

The salesperson in this photo is about to mark the sale prices on these tags. Are these invitations to negotiate or offers?

date, the other may be offended but cannot file suit for breach of contract. Social arrangements do not create legal obligations.

Offer Must Be Communicated to the Offeree

A person who is not the intended offeree cannot accept the offer. Nor can a person accept an offer without knowing it has been made. That is because any action taken would not have been a response to the offer. Thus, an offer of a reward that is made to certain persons or even to the general public cannot be accepted by someone acting as required by the reward offer but who has never seen or heard of it.

Essential Terms Must Be Complete and Definite

The terms of an offer must be sufficiently complete and definite to allow a court to determine what the parties intended and to identify the parties' legal rights and duties.

COMPLETE Nearly all offers must, at a minimum, identify the price, subject matter, and quantity, either directly or indirectly, to be legally effective.

Some offers require even more information to be valid. For example, in most states the essential terms for the sale of real estate would include

1. a proper legal description of the real estate
2. price
3. full terms for payment
4. date for delivery of possession
5. date for delivery of the deed

If one of those terms were missing there would not be a valid offer. In contrast, an offer for the sale of a candy bar by a friend who identifies price, subject matter, and quantity (as many as are on the shelf) is a valid offer.

DEFINITE Each essential term must be identified clearly. If a seller owned several cars but only stated that she would sell "my car," the courts would not enforce the offer. In some contracts, however, a term might be implied by law or common business practice. For example, some contracts are between individuals who regularly deal in the goods, such as televisions and cars, being bought or sold. In these contracts, when

the price is not specified, current market price is used as the basis for the contract.

CHECKPOINT What are the requirements of an offer?

What do you think would be the essential terms in a contract for a used car?

© GETTY IMAGES/PHOTODISC

THINK ABOUT LEGAL CONCEPTS

1. If the offer that was accepted to form a contract is invalid, the courts will not enforce the contract. **True or False?**

2. Which of the following is not an essential element of a contract? (a) offer and acceptance (b) genuine dissent (c) legality (d) all of the above are essential elements.

3. In some cases a person may be held to an offer that she only intended as a joke. **True or False?**

4. All agreements must be in writing to be enforceable in court. **True or False?**

5. A newspaper ad that specified "first come, first served out of our limited stock" would be treated as an invitation to negotiate. **True or False?**

THINK CRITICALLY ABOUT EVIDENCE

Study the situation, answer the questions, and then prepare arguments to support your answers.

6. The owner of a small color television set offers to sell it to a neighbor for $75. As the neighbor stands there thinking about the offer, a bystander says, "That's a bargain. I'll take it!" Is there a contract between the bystander and the owner?

7. Bill spent most of his month's allowance for expensive tickets to a rock concert after Lorene said she would go with him. On the morning of the event, Lorene phoned and said she was terribly sorry, but Tony, the high school's star fullback, had also asked her to go and she "just couldn't say no." Did she breach a contract? Could Tony be held legally liable if he knew Lorene had already promised to go with Bill? Was Lorene's conduct ethical? If Tony knew Lorene had already promised Bill she'd go with him, was Tony's conduct ethical?

8. After reviewing her application, the Nationwide Credit Union notified Heidi that she was qualified to borrow up to $10,000. Nothing was specified as to the length of the agreement, the rate of interest the credit union would charge, or the terms of repaying any loan. The credit union did not make a loan of $8,000 to Heidi when she requested it four months later. Is the credit union liable for breach of contract?

9. G. Whiz Sports Shop published this advertisement in the local newspaper: "Congratulations to the winners of the Tour de France! Now YOU TOO can be a champ! Get an 18-speed Blue Lightning bicycle for only $2,295—marked down from $2,795, the manufacturer's suggested retail price. What a bargain! Come and get it!" Baxter visited the discount store the following day and said, "I'll take one of the Blue Lightning bikes." The clerk replied, "Sorry, we had only ten bikes in stock and they've all been sold." Was the advertisement an offer?

6-2 Termination of Offers

GOALS

■ Describe the various ways to end offers
■ Explain how an offeree can ensure an offer will remain open

KEY TERMS

revocation   option
counteroffer   firm offer

How Can Offers Be Ended?

WHAT'S YOUR VERDICT?

On May 15th, Melissa offered to sell her collection of baseball cards for $3,000 at anytime before the first of the next month to her friend and fellow collector, Raoul. While Raoul was trying to raise the money, Melissa had second thoughts. So she called Raoul and said, "I've changed my mind, I'm not interested in selling the cards." Raoul responded, "It's too late, you said the offer would be open for this whole month. This is just the 20th, and I've got the money so I accept."

Was Melissa's offer terminated before Raoul's attempted acceptance?

Once made, an offer does not last forever. It may be terminated in a variety of ways.

Revocation by the Offeror

After an offer has been made, the offeror can generally revoke it anytime before it is accepted by the offeree. This is true even if the offeror promised that the offer would remain open for a particular period. In *What's Your Verdict?* because Melissa revoked first, there was no offer for Raoul to accept. The fact that she had promised to keep it open until the end of the month was not legally binding on her. Therefore there was no contract. The right to withdraw an offer before it is accepted is known as the right of **revocation**. A revocation is not effective until communicated to the offeree.

Time Stated in the Offer

In making an offer, the offeror may state how and when the offer must be accepted. For example,

on October 10, the Mercantile Bank sent a letter to Boggs, who had applied for a loan. In the letter, Mercantile offered to lend $50,000 on specified terms and stated that the acceptance had to be in writing and received no later than October 18. Boggs mailed an acceptance on October 17, but the letter did not arrive until October 20. As Mercantile did not receive Boggs's reply by the time specified, the offer expired. There was no contract.

Reasonable Length of Time

When nothing is said in the offer about how long it will remain open, it will end after a reasonable length of time. What is a reasonable length of time depends on all the surrounding circumstances. For example, a produce broker in New Jersey telephones a customer in Florida offering to sell a truckload of tomatoes. If the offer to sell the tomatoes is not accepted within an hour, it probably will terminate automatically. That is because tomatoes are perishable produce which rot and therefore must be marketed and shipped quickly. The seller

Why does the length of time an offer will remain open vary with the type of goods to be sold?

Economic Impact

may be in touch with many prospective buyers, and they understand they must accept quickly.

In contrast, an offer to sell expensive durable equipment, such as a bulldozer, would not terminate until a longer time had elapsed. At least several days would be reasonable. If the parties had bargained about the sale over a period of months, a week or longer might be appropriate. To avoid misunderstandings, the time available for acceptance should be specified at the outset.

Rejection by the Offeree

When an offeree clearly rejects the offer, the offer is terminated. Unless renewed by the original offeror, the offeree can no longer accept the original offer. For example, in *What's Your Verdict?*, if Raoul had immediately declined the offer after Melissa made it, he could not have shown up with the $3,000 later in May and accepted it, because the offer no longer existed. His rejection ended the offer immediately. His subsequently producing the previously mentioned sales price of $3,000 would be treated as an offer that Melissa could accept or reject. An offer is terminated by an offeree's rejection even if a time limit set by the offeror has not expired.

Counteroffer

Generally an offeree accepting an offer must accept it exactly as made. If the offeree changes the offeror's terms in important ways and sends it back to the offeror, a **counteroffer** results. In making a counteroffer, the offeree says in legal effect, "I refuse your offer; here is my proposal." The counteroffer terminates the original offer. The counteroffer then becomes a new offer.

Death or Insanity of Either the Offeror or Offeree

Contracts are agreements voluntarily entered into by the parties and subject to their control. Death or insanity eliminates such control. Therefore the law acts for these parties when they can no longer act and terminates their offers.

Destruction of the Specific Subject Matter

If the offer refers to unique subject matter, such as Melissa's card collection, and it is subsequently

---

IN THIS CASE

If, in *What's Your Verdict?* Raoul had said, "I will pay you $2,000 for them and not a penny more," his counteroffer would have terminated Melissa's original offer at that moment, even though she had promised to keep it open for the month. If, seeing that Melissa was not going to take the $2,000, Raoul immediately said he'd pay the $3,000, he would be making another offer, not accepting Melissa's original.

destroyed, for example in a fire, the offer is automatically terminated.

CHECKPOINT Explain two ways in which offers can be terminated.

How Can an Offer Be Kept Open?

WHAT'S YOUR VERDICT? Adamssen, a well-known non-fiction author, sent a fiction book manuscript entitled The Endtimes Project to Hardcover, Inc., a publisher in New York City. Adamssen offered to let Hardcover publish it if he received an advance of $50,000 and 15 percent of gross sales. Sorrento, an editor at Hardcover, thought the manuscript would be a sure best seller, but the subject matter was out of the area of the material in which Hardcover specialized. Wanting approval from the editorial board at Hardcover before accepting Adamssen's offer, Sorrento offered Adamssen $1,000 to keep his offer open solely to Hardcover for 30 days. Adamssen agreed.

Is Adamssen now legally bound to keep his offer to Hardcover open for the 30 days?

As mentioned, an offeror is not legally obligated to keep an offer open for a specified time even if the offeror has promised to do so. This may cause the offeree not to pursue the offer or to act without proper consideration to close the deal. Such uncertainty may be eliminated in the following ways.

Options

If the offeree gives the offeror something of value in return for a promise to keep the offer open, this agreement is itself a binding contract. It is called an **option**. The offer may not be withdrawn during the period of the option. In *What's Your Verdict?* with the $1,000 Sorrento bought an option to acquire Adamssen's manuscript for publishing. Thus, Adamssen could not legally withdraw the offer or sell to another publisher during the 30 days.

Firm Offers

A special rule that works the same result as an option applies to merchants (individuals who regularly deal in the goods being bought or sold) who make offers in writing. If such a written offer contains a term stating how long it is to stay open, it is called a **firm offer**. The Uniform Commercial Code (UCC) makes firm offers binding for the time stated, but not more than three months. This is true even when nothing is paid by the offeree.

CHECKPOINT How could an offeree insure that an offer will stay open for a set period of time?

Do you think China's foreign trade has increased since the passage of the two law codes mentioned in the Global Issues feature? Why or why not?

THINK ABOUT LEGAL CONCEPTS

1. If a time for the offer to expire is not stated, it will expire in a reasonable time under the circumstances. **True or False?**

2. If an offeree clearly rejects the offer, the offer is termed (a) suspended (b) revoked (c) expired (d) terminated

3. When an offeree changes the offeror's terms in important ways, the offeree makes a(n) _ ?_.

4. Which of the following does not describe an event that will terminate an offer? (a) revocation by the offeror (b) purchase of an option by the offeree (c) counteroffer (d) death of the offeree

5. An offeree who rejects an offer can later accept it if the acceptance occurs within a reasonable time after the original offer. **True or False?**

6. If an offeree gives the offeror something of value to keep an offer open, the contract thereby created is called a(n) _?_.

7. If either the offeror or offeree is deemed insane, the law will (a) uphold any offers made (b) terminate any offers made

8. If a hardware store salesclerk said, "This price on the lawnmowers is good for 30 days," would this be a firm offer? **Yes or No?**

9. A written offer between merchants that contains a term stating how long it is to stay open is called a _?_ offer.

10. If a beauty salon hair designer said to a customer, "This price on the cut and dry is good for 30 days," and then wrote it down on a piece of paper and signed it, would this be a firm offer? **Yes or No?**

THINK CRITICALLY ABOUT EVIDENCE

Study the situation, answer the questions, and then prepare arguments to support your answers.

11. While her car was in Prescott's garage for repairs, Wood noticed a large, seemingly unused, metal tool chest in the corner, complete with about 400 standard and metric tools. Wood offered to buy it for $3,000 and said, "You can take a week to think about it before you decide whether to accept." Four days later, before Prescott had responded, Wood told Prescott that she was withdrawing her offer as she had found a better set for less money. Can Prescott still accept Wood's original offer? If Wood had put the offer in writing, could she have withdrawn it before the week was over?

12. Frank saw a wheelchair advertised in the paper for sale for $900. When he called Tom, the offeror, who had bought it to use while he was recovering from a skiing accident, Tom said it had not yet been sold. Frank drove out to see it but found it needed work. So Frank offered $700. Tom seemed insulted, and said he wasn't interested at that price. Frank left. About an hour later, he went back and found the wheelchair had not been sold. He then offered the $900 specified in the ad. However, Tom refused to sell it to him. Frank became upset and sued to

get the court to force Tom to sell it to him for $900. Will Tom have to do so? Why or why not?

13. Gus walked into his local hardware store to buy exterior paint for his house. It was on sale for $35 a gallon. Gus wanted to check around but didn't want to lose the chance to buy at the sale price. In response to Gus's request, the manager of the paint department wrote Gus a note stating, "Gus Almondson may buy up to 15 gallons of Old Dutch Exterior Grade paint for $35 per gallon anytime within the next two weeks." The manager signed and dated the note. Is this offer binding?

14. Phil was talking with Sharon about Opie, his Springer Spaniel dog. Phil explained that Opie has a strong personality, loves to snuggle up to people, likes to eat "people food," and is a good watchdog. Sharon liked Opie a lot and needed a dog. As she knew Phil needed money at the moment, she offered him $1,000 for Opie. Phil said, "It's a deal but I have to have him back during hunting season." Is there a contract between Phil and Sharon for the sale of Opie?

6-3 Acceptances

GOALS

- Discuss the requirements of an effective acceptance
- Determine at what point in time an acceptance is effective

KEY TERMS

acceptance

mirror image rule

bilateral contracts

unilateral contracts

What Is Required of an Acceptance?

WHAT'S YOUR VERDICT?

Jan, an entertainer, borrowed a computerized keyboard from his friend, Arturo. Jan needed the instrument to use in an upcoming jazz concert tour. When the tour was cancelled half-way through, Jan sent Arturo the following message in a letter: "Am stuck in San Jose. Need to sell the keyboard to pay for the trip home. If I don't hear from you by the 13th of the month, will do so and treat the proceeds of the sale as a loan at 10 percent from you to be repaid within a year." Arturo did not respond by the 13th.

Did Arturo's silence indicate he had legally agreed to Jan's contractual proposal?

Acceptance occurs when a party to whom an offer has been made agrees to the proposal. To create an enforceable contract, the acceptance must

1. come from the person or persons to whom the offer was made
2. match the terms in the offer
3. be communicated to the offeror

Only Offerees May Accept

An offer made to one person cannot be accepted by another. Sometimes, however, an offer is made to a particular group or to the public and not to an individual. For example, a reward offer may be made to the general public. Any member of the general public who knows of the offer may accept it.

The Acceptance Must Match the Offer

The **mirror image rule** requires that the acceptance must exactly match the terms contained in the offer. This is true even as to when and how the acceptance must be made and even if the change is advantageous to the original offeror. If the attempted acceptance is not identical to the offer, it is a counteroffer.

Currently, courts in most states apply the mirror image rule only when the term altered in the attempted acceptance is material (important) and related to the providing of services or the sale of real property. Even in these states, however, if the offeror requires that acceptance must exactly match the terms contained in the offer, then any variation is legally a counteroffer.

© GETTY IMAGES/PHOTODISC

What three characteristics of acceptances must be present in order for the contract these men are concluding to be enforceable?

Under the UCC, absent such a requirement for identity in the offer, an attempted acceptance of an offer for a contract for a sale of goods can be valid even if it does include new or conflicting terms. In these cases, there is a contract on the terms where the offer and acceptance agree. Then the new or modified terms are treated as follows:

1. If a party is a consumer, not a merchant, then the new or changed terms are mere proposals and not a part of the contract unless agreed to by the original offeror.

2. If both parties are merchants, the new or changed terms are not a part of the contract if the original offeror objects, or in the absence of an objection, if the terms are material.

3. If the parties are merchants, the new or changed terms are part of the contract if the original offeror is silent and the terms are minor (not material).

Acceptance Must Be Communicated to the Offeror

An acceptance must be more than a mental decision. It must be communicated to the offeror.

SILENCE AS ACCEPTANCE One is not obligated to reply to offers made by others. An offeror's attempt to word the offer so that silence would appear to be an acceptance will not work. In *What's Your Verdict?* no contract would result from Arturo's silence.

BILATERAL ACCEPTANCE Most offers are bilateral. This means the offer implies that it can be accepted by giving a promise instead of performing the contracted-for act. For example, a seller promises to deliver a load of topsoil in exchange for a homeowner's promise to pay $65. Offers for **bilateral contracts** require that the offeree accept by communicating the requested promise to the offeror. Until this is done, there is no contract. The promise can be implied from the offeree's conduct as well as from words.

UNILATERAL ACCEPTANCE In some offers, the offeror requires that the offeree indicate acceptance by performing his or her obligations under the contract. Contracts offered under these conditions are **unilateral contracts**. The offeror in a unilateral contract promises something in return for the offeree's performance and indicates that this performance

is the way acceptance is to be made. For example, the offeror may publicly promise to pay a $100 reward to anyone who returns a lost camera. Many people learn of the offer. All may join the search. A promise to look for the camera does not create a contract. Only by the finding and returning of the camera, the specific performance required in the offer, can the reward be earned.

Note that if the person performing the act does not know of the reward, that person is not legally entitled to it. Also, if the words used are not clear as to whether an offer is unilateral or bilateral, courts will presume that the offer is for a bilateral contract.

IN THIS CASE Stirrup found Buster, Fenton's lost dog and returned the animal to Fenton. After doing so, Stirrup noticed several reward posters by which Fenton offered $500 for the return of the dog. As he did not know of the reward prior to returning Buster, Stirrup was not entitled to it.

MODES OF CONTRACTUAL COMMUNICATION
Contractual communications such as offers, acceptances, rejections, revocations, and counteroffers may generally be communicated in person

Imagine that you tell your brother that you will pay him $100 if and when he paints your fence. If he agrees, have you formed a bilateral contract or a unilateral contract with him? Explain your answer.

or by other effective means. These means include by telephone, text messaging, mail, delivery service, e-mail, facsimile (fax) machine, or other methods.

The UCC provides that an acceptance of an offer to buy or sell goods may be made "in any manner and by any medium reasonable in the circumstances" unless otherwise clearly "indicated by the language or circumstances."

How are these stock exchange floor traders communicating offers and acceptances? Do you think this is an efficient communication method in this market? Why or why not?

WHEN ACCEPTANCES ARE EFFECTIVE When the communication takes time, for example when sent through the surface mail, the question of when the communication is effective can become very important. All forms of contractual communications but one take effect only when received. The exception to this is the acceptance, which often is effective when sent.

The offeror may require the offeree to use a certain communication method to accept. If a different method is used, then it is treated as a modification of the offer. Business custom often implies a method to be used in an acceptance. On some stock and commodity exchanges, hand signals are used to communicate offers and acceptances. In many industries, next-day delivery service is the custom. When the required or the customary method is used, the acceptance is effective when sent unless the offeror specified the acceptance would be effective when received.

Often there is no specified or customary method for communicating acceptances. Most courts then say the acceptance is effective when sent by the same means used for the offer, or by faster means.

Under the UCC, if the acceptance of an offer for the sale or purchase of goods is by a reasonable means, it is effective when sent. A "reasonable"

method incorporates all of the above rules but opens the door for a slower means to be reasonable in some situations.

It often becomes important to determine even more precisely when acceptance is effective. Oral acceptances are effective at the moment the words are spoken directly to the offeror. Acceptances sent by mail generally take effect when properly posted. That is, they are placed, with correct address and sufficient postage, under the control of the U.S. Postal Service. A telegram takes effect as an acceptance when it is handed to the clerk at the telegraph office or telephoned to the telegraph office. A fax transmission is instantaneous when the transmission lines are open and both sending and receiving

LAW BRIEF

To facilitate proof of your acceptance of a contract by mail, use certified mail with return receipt requested. Also, keep a copy of your acceptance letter and other documents, including the offer. These items will be useful as evidence in court to establish a particular contractual communication.

equipment work properly. Therefore the effect is similar to instantaneous oral communication, but in a more durable form that is easier to prove in court.

The offeror may specify that an acceptance will not be binding until it is actually received. This avoids the confusion that arises when an acceptance is mailed yet never reaches the offeror because it is lost in the mail. It also avoids the requirement for using the rules above.

CHECKPOINT What are the requirements of an effective acceptance?

6-3 Assessment

Xtra!
Study Tools

school.cengage.com/blaw/lawxtra

THINK ABOUT LEGAL CONCEPTS

1. A(n) _ ? _ is an offeree's agreement to an offeror's proposal.

2. If an offeror specifies in the offer that the acceptance must be made by fax, an e-mailed acceptance will not be effective. **True or False?**

3. All forms of contractual communication take effect only when received. **True or False?**

4. If the parties to a contract have mutual obligations to perform it, the contract is termed (a) unilateral (b) bilateral (c) biliteral (d) none of the above

5. When there is no specified or customary means for communicating acceptances, a faster means than that employed by the offeror to make the offer would be considered effective by the courts. **True or False?**

THINK CRITICALLY ABOUT EVIDENCE

Study the situation, answer the questions, and then prepare arguments to support your answers.

6. To help pay for housing renovations, Jeanne placed an ad on the bulletin board at the public golf course showing a picture of her prized set of golf clubs, her phone number, and the figure $2,000. Eve, after seeing the ad, called Jeanne and then drove to her house with $2,000 in hand. When she presented the $2,000 to Jeanne, the latter refused it, stating that she had received several calls wanting the clubs for that price, so she was raising it to $2,500. Can Eve sue and force Jeanne to accept her $2,000 for the clubs. Why or why not?

7. Jonas wrote to Smith offering to sell 42 acres of farmland at $5,000 per acre with the purchase price to be paid at the closing. Smith replied, "I accept for the 42 acres, for the $5,000 per acre, but will pay the purchase price two days after closing." Is this an acceptance?

8. Office Suppliers, Inc., ordered 2,000 reams of 20-lb. paper from Dimension Paper for $1.75 per ream to be delivered at the Office Suppliers warehouse on or about April 24. Dimension responded that 2,000 reams would be delivered on April 25 at the price of $1.75 per ream. Office Suppliers made no further response. Has a valid contract been formed? If so, what are the terms? If not, why not?

Chapter 6 Assessment

CONCEPTS IN BRIEF

6-1   Creation of Offers

1. Contracts are agreements between two or more parties that create obligations.

2. To be legally enforceable contracts require a valid offer and acceptance, genuine assent, legality, consideration, and capacity. In addition, some contracts must be placed in writing to be enforceable.

3. The party making the offer is the offeror. The party to whom the offer is made is the offeree.

4. An offer must (a) be made with the offeror's apparent intention to be bound by it, (b) be complete and definite, and (c) be communicated to the offeree.

6-2   Termination of Offers

5. If not accepted, an offer is ended (a) by revocation of the offeror, (b) at the time stated in the offer, (c) at the end of a reasonable time if no time is stated, (d) by rejection of the offeree, (e) by counteroffer, (f) by death or insanity of either of the parties, or (g) by destruction of the specific subject matter.

6. In general, an offeror is not obliged to keep an offer open for a specified time even if the offeror has promised to do so.

7. The offeree may give the offeror something of value in return for a promise to keep the offer open. The contract so formed is called an option.

8. A firm offer, made between two merchants, is an offer that contains a term stating how long the offer is to stay open. The Uniform Commercial Code (UCC) makes firm offers binding for the time stated, but not for more than three months.

6-3   Acceptances

9. In contracts for the sale of services or realty, the offeree must accept the offer unconditionally and in the exact form and manner indicated by the offeror. In contracts for the sale of goods, acceptances can vary the terms of the offer.

10. Contractual communications are carried out by a constantly increasing variety of means including phone, text messaging, fax, e-mail, face-to-face negotiations, ground mail, and hand signals.

11. Although most contractual communications are effective when received, acceptances are generally effective when sent.

YOUR LEGAL VOCABULARY

Match each statement with the term that it best defines.

1. Binding agreement created by an offer that is accepted by a promise of performance

2. Offeror's withdrawal of an offer before it is accepted

3. Party to whom an offer is made

4. A contractual proposal in writing, signed by a merchant, and stating how long it is to stay open

5. Response by offeree, with new terms, which ends the original offer

6. Requirement that the terms in an acceptance exactly match the terms in the offer

7. Affirmative response necessary to transform an offer into a contract

8. Contract to leave an offer open for a period of time in exchange for other consideration

9. A unilateral or bilateral agreement that is legally effective and enforceable in court

10. The person who makes the offer

a. acceptance
b. bilateral contract
c. contract
d. counteroffer
e. firm offer
f. mirror image rule
g. offer
h. offeree
i. offeror
j. option
k. revocation
l. unilateral contract

REVIEW LEGAL CONCEPTS

11. It is vital for a businessperson to be able to review a contract quickly to see if it is likely to be legally enforceable. This means being certain that the six essential elements of a valid contract are present. Without consulting the material in the book, list these elements, and give a short description of each.

12. Imagine you have made an offer to buy your friend's mountain bike. Make a list of the different ways your offer could be terminated.

WRITE ABOUT LEGAL CONCEPTS

13. Imagine that you are a portrait painter. Create an ad for your services to be placed in a local paper.

14. Write a reward offer for the return of your missing pet skunk. It has not been deodorized.

15. **HOT DEBATE** Assume that Elisa were allowed to bring a lawsuit against Trenton and was successful. Write a paragraph examining possible remedies that might be appropriate, such as damages or court orders.

MAKE ACADEMIC CONNECTIONS

16. **HISTORY** The feudal period in Europe did not have the level of trade and commerce that is such a part of our lives. Read about the quality of life during this period. Make a list of businesses and transactions that were not allowed or severely limited during that time.

17. **ENVIRONMENTAL SCIENCE** Could you pass a law requiring that every contract have a term in it requiring all parties to it to not hurt the environment in any way? What would be the economic consequences of such a requirement? Write a paragraph explaining your answer.

THINK CRITICALLY ABOUT EVIDENCE

Study the situation, answer the questions, and then prepare arguments to support your answers.

18. Caryn offered to tutor Dottie in business law for six hours on the day before the final exam in return for $100. Dottie responded, "Let me think about it for a day, okay?" Two hours later Jim offered Caryn $150 to tutor him on the day before the final and she accepted. Dottie called Caryn an hour later and said, "I accept." Caryn said, "I'm sorry but I've already agreed to tutor Jim that day so I can't tutor you." Was there a contract between Caryn and Dottie?

19. Sam advertised his ski boat for sale, priced at $4,500, complete with outboard engine and trailer. Barbara paid Sam $100 for a ten-day option, the money to be applied to the purchase price if she exercised her right to buy. Two days later, Sam was killed. Is Barbara's option still valid?

20. On Monday, Abner offers to sell his trained golden retriever, Track, to Bob for $300 cash. "My offer is open until we go hunting next Saturday." On Tuesday, Carl offers Abner $400 for Track, in eight equal monthly payments of $50. Abner says "Sorry, my price is $300 cash." On Wednesday, Dan learns that Abner has offered to sell Track. Dan tells Abner, "I'll pay $300 cash when you deliver the dog at the end of this year's duck hunting season. But you can keep Track until then." Abner says, "Sounds like a good deal. Okay, you now own Track." He phones Bob and tells him of the sale. On Thursday, Carl phones Abner and says, "I accept your offer. I'll pay $300 cash. When can I pick up Track?" Abner replies, "Sorry, but Track's been sold." Has Abner breached a contract with Bob or Carl? Has he been ethical in his conduct?

21. For several months Lambi repeatedly made offers to Atkins to buy his Santa Fe Apartments. Finally Atkins wrote Lambi a letter containing the following statement: "Here is my suggestion. Clearly $4.2 million isn't nearly enough. Between your sales fee and my closing cost, I'd be out of pocket $200,000 which would mean I'd only net $100,000. After taxes I'd have been better off saving my time and waxing my car. $4.4 million is better, but again with the owner financing you've suggested, it would take me years to recoup my out-of-pocket expense, let alone realize some cash profit. With that in mind, here is my suggestion: Price: $4.6 million." Ultimately, Lambi attempted to conclude an agreement with Atkins at $4.6 million. However, Atkins refused to sell at that price. Lambi then brought suit to enforce the transaction. Was there a binding contract? (*Lambi v. Atkins,* 130 S.W.3d 607)

22. Scheck wanted to sell a parcel of his real property. He made an offer to pay a commission to Marchiondo, a real estate broker, if Marchiondo caused the sale of the property to a particular buyer within six days. However, Scheck revoked his offer to Marchiondo on the morning of the sixth day. Later that day, Marchiondo obtained the prospect's acceptance of Scheck's offer, but Scheck refused to pay the commission. Marchionado sued, claiming the offer could not be revoked because he had begun performance. The trial court dismissed the complaint, stating that Scheck could revoke his offer at any time before completion of the requested act. Marchiondo appealed. Who should win the case? (*Marchiondo v. Scheck,* 78 N.M. 440, 432 P.2d 405)

23. On December 23, the First National Bank had its sales agent, Wyman, mail a written offer to Zeller to sell a parcel of real property for $240,000. On January 10, Zeller had his purchasing agent mail a written offer to buy the property for $230,000. The same counteroffer was made in a telephone conversation on that day to Wyman, but Wyman told Zeller's agent that the offer to sell the land was no longer in effect. When Zeller's agent reported this news to Zeller, he promptly told his agent to wire an acceptance of the original offer at $240,000.

Zeller's agent did as ordered and the telegram of acceptance arrived before the letter containing Zeller's counteroffer. The bank refused to sell, reminding Zeller that the offer to sell had been revoked and that its agent Wyman had so informed Zeller's agent in the telephone conversation on January 10. Nevertheless, Zeller sued the bank for specific performance and for damages. Who should win? (*Zeller v. First National Bank,* 79 Ill. App. 3d 170, 398 N.E.2d 148)

24. Epton orally bargained for an option to buy a 54 percent share of the ownership of the Chicago White Sox baseball club for $4.8 million from the defendant, CBC Corporation. The option, which was to have been reduced to writing, was to last one week in exchange for the payment of $1,000 by Epton. To exercise the option within the week, Epton was supposed to give CBC a certified or cashier's check for $99,000 as a down payment. Epton was also to notify the corporation in writing that he was exercising his option. Twice during the week, Epton orally assured CBC of his intent to exercise the option and he also offered to pay the $99,000 as soon as the option was signed by CBC. After the week had passed, CBC refused to sell, and Epton sued. He claimed that his oral notice of intent to exercise the option was sufficient. He said that failure of CBC to sign a written option agreement excused both the requirement of a written exercise of the option by him and the necessity of the $99,000 deposit. Who should win? (*Epton v. CBC Corporation,* 48 Ill. App. 2d 274, 197 N.E.2d 727)

25. A brokerage sued its customers to recover for the purchase price of certain uranium stock. The brokerage contends it was directed to buy the stock "as close to two cents as possible," while the customers contend the price was to be two cents per share. Pursuant to the order, the brokerage purchased the stock and several days thereafter sent a confirmation listing purchase of the stock at two and one-eighth cents per share. The trial court found the order to buy was given at two cents per share which plaintiff executed by purchasing the stock at two and one-eighth cents per share. Is there an enforceable contract? (*Baldwin v. Peters, Writer & Christensen,* 41 Colo. 529)

Sports & Entertainment Law

Put Me In Coach

FORTAY V. UNIVERSITY OF MIAMI
UNITED STATES DISTRICT COURT FOR THE
DISTRICT OF NEW JERSEY, CIVIL ACTION NO. 93-3443

BACKGROUND Bryan Fortay was a consensus high school All-American quarterback at East Brunswick High School in New Jersey. He was recruited by most of the major college football programs starting in his junior year.

FACTS Fortay received personal letters from University of Miami (Miami) personnel touting its football program's ability to develop NFL quarterbacks. He also was visited at home by Jimmy Johnson, then head football coach at Miami, and other coaches in the program. During his meeting with Coach Johnson, Fortay and other members of his family allege Johnson promised that the school would cease recruitment efforts of other quarterbacks in his class upon Fortay making a commitment to play for the school. Subsequently, Fortay and his father met with the Miami quarterback coach and signed a letter of intent to play at Miami. Fortay did so with the belief that he would be the starting quarterback at the university and that the team would be built around him. Regrettably for Fortay, shortly after his signing the Letter of Intent, Coach Johnson left Miami to coach the Dallas Cowboys of the NFL. Fortay then sought release from his letter, but the new university of Miami coach allegedly assured Fortay and his father that he would be a starter for at least two years. Rather than transfer and lose two years of eligibility, Fortay honored his commitment to the University. During two disappointing years

at Miami in which he only played in two games, Fortay became involved in a fraudulent scheme by a University advisor to procure Pell Grants for the University's athletes and other students. Ultimately, after Fortay's transfer to Rutgers University, he avoided prosecution by entering a pre-trial probation program which required him to make restitution for the monies illicitly received. Fortay then filed a 25-count complaint against the University of Miami. The complaint sought actual, compensatory, and punitive damages for the breach of promises made by the University representatives and for the humiliation resulting from involving him in the Pell Grant scandal.

THE LAW Although not adopted by the NCAA, the Letter of Intent is used by the Collegiate Commissioners Association of college programs to lessen the competition for recruits among its members. When signed by a prospective player, all other schools in the organization must cease their recruitment efforts of that athlete. The Letter is binding on the player as long as it contains a promise of financial aid from the institution. The Letter limits the player's athletic eligibility unless she or he transfers to another school after being released from his Letter by the original university.

THE ISSUE Could the promises of stardom at the University and in the NFL made to Fortay, if provable as alleged, be considered a part of an enforceable contract?

HOLDING The federal district court for the Southern District of Florida dismissed the entire case but allowed Fortay the right to refile the portion relating to negligence of the University as to involving him in the Pell Grant scandal. Subsequently, the University and Fortay arrived at a settlement in the latter matter which was undisclosed.

PRACTICE JUDGING

Presume that Fortay could prove that the promises of the starting quarterback position and future NFL stardom were made. Should Fortay be able to sue for their breach? Why or why not?

© GETTY IMAGES/PHOTODISC

Chapter 7
Genuineness of Assent

7-1 Duress and Undue Influence

7-2 Mistake, Misrepresentation, and Fraud

© GETTY IMAGES/PHOTODISC

HOT DEBATE

Yelling, "I've got to get the first one," your friend Jack jumped off the couch in response to a TV ad during a championship football game. The ad touted a cell phone that also incorporated a PDA, a foldout keyboard, word processing program, Internet access, and a 4 megapixel camera for "only" $600. Jack phoned immediately and bought the cell phone with its dedicated portable printer and attachable full-sized "natural" keyboard. As she took Jack's credit card information, the salesperson did not mention that the keyboard and printer are optional and not a part of the $600 package. However, that information was displayed clearly in large print in the ad. Jack receives the phone the next day via "overnight" shipping, rips it out of the package, slips his Sim card in, and begins using it. However, when his credit-card statement arrives at the end of the month listing the total purchase price of $998, he objects.

WHERE DO YOU STAND?

1. State two reasons why it would be fair to allow Jack to withdraw from the contract.
2. State two reasons why it would be fair for Jack to be bound to the contract.
3. Which reasons are more persuasive?

7-1 Duress and Undue Influence

GOALS

- Recognize when genuine assent is not present
- Identify the two key elements in undue influence

KEY TERMS

genuine assent   ratification

voidable   duress

rescission   undue influence

Genuine Assent and Duress

WHAT'S YOUR VERDICT? Cameron owned a promising racehorse that Link had offered to buy for undisclosed parties. When Cameron refused to sell, Link lowered his voice and slowly said, "Listen, the people I represent don't take 'no' for an answer. If you don't sell, they'll hurt you. They'll hurt your family. Like a good friend, I'm telling you to sell. You're getting a fair price, just sign the contract." Cameron, who had secretly recorded the conversation, sold. Then he called the police.

Can he now rescind and get his horse back?

IN THIS CASE Steven inspected a 5-year-old car with the intention of buying it. He asked the owner, Allan, how many miles were on the engine. Allan said, "As you can see from the odometer, it only has 30,000 miles on it, and I'm the only one who has ever owned it." A written contract was executed and Steven took the car to the local automobile dealer to be inspected. The dealer informed Steven that the car had often been serviced there, and that the odometer had been replaced at about 100,000 miles. This was a fraudulent misrepresentation on Allan's part, making the contract voidable by Steven. However, if Steven continued to make his monthly payments to Allan after discovering the truth, this would ratify the contract and Steven would lose his ability to rescind.

Whether oral or written, an agreement will be treated as valid (legally binding and enforceable) as long as it meets all the proper legal requirements. One of the most important of these requirements is genuineness of assent. **Genuine assent** (true and complete agreement) is at times shown to be lacking in court. This is due to a variety of causes such as duress, undue influence, mistake, misrepresentation, and fraud. Without genuine assent a contract typically is **voidable**. This means that, if the injured party desires, that party can cancel the contractual obligation. The party then has the legal right to get back what has already been put into the contract. This latter action is referred to as a **rescission**.

To be effective, an avoidance must be prompt. It must occur shortly after you discover that there is no genuine agreement. In addition, it must occur before you ratify the contract. **Ratification** is conduct that confirms you intend to be bound by the contract.

Duress

Certainly, most parties are subject to duress in the form of apprehension and pressure when negotiating a contract. However, the law only allows a contract to be undone because of it in a few instances. Actionable or legal **duress** only occurs when one party uses an improper threat or act to obtain an expression of agreement. The resulting contract is voidable. Much of the law of duress focuses on the nature of the threat.

THREATS OF ILLEGAL OR TORTIOUS CONDUCT
The threat to engage in illegal or tortious conduct, such as a crime or tort, to win agreement is always duress. Committing an act of violence (for example, stabbing), threatening a crime (threatening to stab), committing a tort (for example, unlawful detention), or threatening a tort to obtain a signature on a written contract is duress. The actual crime or tort, or the threat,

may be to the physical life, liberty, or property of the victim, the victim's immediate family, or the victim's near relatives. In *What's Your Verdict?* Cameron acted under duress in making the contract and therefore could rescind it.

THREATS TO REPORT CRIMES If you observe a crime, you have a duty to report it to the proper authorities. If you use a threat of reporting to force the criminal to contract with you, this is duress. It may also be the crime of extortion.

THREATS TO SUE The law encourages parties to settle conflicts without a suit. An important part of this process involves communicating a threat that you will sue if the other side doesn't settle. This happens frequently. When the threat to sue is made for a purpose unrelated to the suit, this may be duress.

For example, during divorce negotiations, a husband threatens to sue for custody of the children if the wife doesn't sign over valuable shares of stock. Because he doesn't really want custody of the children, this threat to sue makes the contract for the stock voidable. If the threatened suit is completely groundless, a resulting contract may be voidable for duress.

ECONOMIC THREATS Often when parties are bound by a valid contract, they will seek to modify it. Parties then are tempted to use the economic power they have over one another to negotiate a favorable modification or settlement. If a manufacturer has a contract to pay a supplier $15 for a special computer part needed to maintain production, the supplier might threaten to withhold the parts unless the manufacturer agrees to a price of $20 each. If a disruption in the flow of parts would cause substantial injury to the manufacturer, then the courts would find the agreement on the new price an economic threat voidable for duress.

In economic duress cases, the courts look at both the threat and the alternatives available to the threatened party. If the threatened party had no choice but to enter into or modify a contract, then duress exists.

CHECKPOINT List the various forms of legal duress.

Undue Influence and Assent

Explain under what circumstances a court might find a price increase in factory parts voidable due to duress.

WHAT'S YOUR VERDICT? Albert had cancer and was being treated by Dr. Bennington. He had carefully followed the doctor's advice, and the treatment had been successful. One day, during a periodic checkup, Dr. Bennington said to Albert, "To prevent the cancer from recurring, you need to reduce the stress in your life. Long drives in the country are great for that. Come to think of it, I'm selling my convertible right now. You should buy it." Without investigating, Albert followed the doctor's directions and contracted to buy the car. Later he found the price he'd agreed to pay was nearly double the market value.

Could Albert avoid the contract due to undue influence?

Undue influence occurs when one party to the contract is in a position of trust and wrongfully dominates the other party. The dominated person then does not exercise free will in accepting the contractual terms. The two key elements in undue influence are the relationship and the wrongful or unfair persuasion. When a contract arises because of undue influence, the contract is voidable by the victim.

The Relationship

A relationship of trust, confidence, or authority must exist between the parties to the contract. This relationship is presumed to exist between an attorney and client, wife and husband, parent and child early in the child's life and child and parent late in the parent's life, guardian and ward, physician and patient, or minister and congregation member. In *What's Your Verdict?* the contract would be voidable by Albert. Although more difficult to prove when it is not present, a formal relationship is not necessary. The type of relationship that fosters the exercise of undue influence could arise between a housekeeper and her elderly employer. It also could arise between a disabled person and his neighbor.

Unfair Persuasion

Often the best evidence of unfair persuasion is found in the terms of the contract. For example, an elderly person, who is dependent on one child for daily care, may sell her home to that child for half its value. This is strong evidence of lack of free will.

To prevent a claim of undue influence, the stronger party should act with total honesty, fully disclose all important facts, and insist that the weaker party obtain independent counsel before contracting. Persuasion or nagging do not necessarily substantiate undue influence. Whether action rises to the level of undue influence is a difficult question of fact for a jury.

CHECKPOINT What are the key elements in undue influence?

7-1 Assessment

THINK ABOUT LEGAL CONCEPTS

1. Avoidance of contracts affected by legal duress must be timely and occur before ratification. **True or False?**

2. Contracts created or modified by duress are rescindable. **True or False?**

3. Which of the following is a threat that can create duress? (a) threat to shoot the contracting party if she doesn't sign the contract (b) threat to sue (without grounds) the contracting party if she doesn't modify the contract (c) threat to report the contracting party to the IRS for tax evasion if she doesn't sign an agreement (d) all of the above

4. In economic duress cases the courts look at the _?_ and the victim's alternatives.

5. A formal relationship between parties to the contract must always be shown to prove undue influence. **True or False?**

6. Which of the following need not be done by the dominating party to prevent a claim of undue influence? (a) act with total honesty (b) fully disclose all important facts (c) insist the weaker party seek independent legal advice before contracting (d) submit the contract to a judge for review

7. Claims of duress, undue influence, mistake, fraud, misrepresentation, and others place the genuineness of _?_ to a contract's provisions in doubt.

THINK CRITICALLY ABOUT EVIDENCE

Study the situation, answer the questions, and then prepare arguments to support your answers.

8. Manuela rented an apartment and later discovered that the roof leaked. She asked the landlord to make repairs, but he refused. Manuela said that she would move out unless the landlord either made the repairs or lowered the rent. The landlord lowered the rent. Does Manuela's conduct make the modification to the contract voidable due to duress?

9. Evelyn was 86 years old and of sound mind. However, she relied upon her nephew Jamal, an accountant, to advise her in business matters.

During one of Jamal's visits, he persuaded her to sell him a valuable painting for about 80 percent of its true value. Evelyn agreed and signed a contract. Then she had the painting appraised and learned its true value. She continued with the transaction by accepting payment for the painting. About a year later she died. Her estate sued for rescission of the contract. Jamal defended by claiming that Evelyn had ratified by accepting payment after learning of the value of the painting. Who prevails, Evelyn's estate or Jamal?

7-2 Mistake, Misrepresentation, and Fraud

GOALS

■ Recognize the types of mistakes that can make a contract voidable or void

■ List the criteria for a statement to be treated as a misrepresentation

■ Define fraud and describe the remedies for it

KEY TERMS

unilateral mistake

mutual mistake

material facts

void

innocent misrepresentation

fraudulent misrepresentation

fraud

What Are the Types of Contractual Mistakes?

WHAT'S YOUR VERDICT? Bugliosi saved more than $25,000 to buy the new car of his dreams. At the dealership, the sales staff convinced him to purchase option after option until his $25,000 was totally exhausted. When he went to register the vehicle, he found that the state expected him to pay an 8% sales tax on the purchase price. Bugliosi thought the $2,000 in sales tax had been included in the $25,000 paid at the dealership, just as it is with purchases at other retail stores.

Is the contract voidable by Bugliosi because of his mistake?

Generally, mistakes are categorized as either unilateral or mutual. A **unilateral mistake** occurs when only one party holds an incorrect belief about the facts or law related to a contract. Generally, this does not affect the validity of the contract. In *What's Your Verdict?* Bugliosi made a unilateral mistake of law, so the contract is valid.

A mistake from failure to read a contract before signing is the most prevalent example of a unilateral mistake of fact. Such a mistake still leaves the contract valid and enforceable. The same is true of a misunderstanding from a hurried or careless reading. Similarly, signing a contract written in language you don't understand will bind you even if you are mistaken about some of the contract's content.

When there is a **mutual mistake** (also called a *bilateral mistake*) both parties have an incorrect belief about an important fact or the applicable law. Important facts that influence the parties'

decisions about a contract are called **material facts**. If a mutual mistake of fact occurs, the contract is **void** (without legal effect). For example, suppose both a buyer and seller think that a property is 41 acres in size and they contract for the sale based on this belief. Later they learn that it is only 28 acres. This is a mutual mistake of fact. Their agreement is not binding.

When the mutual mistake is about the applicable law, the contract is still valid. For example, if both parties to a sale of raw land mistakenly believe that local zoning laws permit construction of duplexes on the lot, the contract would be valid though there was a mutual mistake and the duplexes could not be constructed. This is because all persons are presumed to know the law. Similarly, unilateral mistakes of law (such as Bugliosi's in *What's Your Verdict?*) generally have no effect upon the validity of the contract for the same reason.

IN THIS CASE Falkhausen, owned two Spitzmobile classic luxury cars. Both cars were the famous Nordic Blue color, but one was the rare 1927 model and the other, the far more common 1928 model. Firenzi had seen Falkhausen driving the 1927 and fell in love with it. A week later, thinking Falkhausen only owned one such car, she made him a low offer for his "Nordic Blue Spitzmobile." Falkhausen, judging from the size of the offer, thought Firenzi was wanting to buy the far less expensive 1928 model and accepted the offer. Because of the mutual mistake of fact as to the subject matter, there was no contract.

CHECKPOINT Name the types of mistakes that can make a contract voidable or void.

What Is Misrepresentation?

WHAT'S YOUR VERDICT?

Nutri-Life offered a dietary supplement for sale. The package contained a statement that clinical studies at a nationally known university had shown the drug reduced the risk of cancer by more than 30 percent if taken regularly. In actuality, the expert who had conducted the tests had been bribed to make the claim on the package even though the clinical studies were inconclusive.

Can customers get their money back if they learn of the deception?

In many contract negotiations, the parties make statements that turn out to be untrue. For example, in the sale of a car, a seller, unaware that a previous owner replaced the odometer, might say that it has 70,000 miles on it when in fact it has 150,000 miles on it. This is an **innocent misrepresentation**. If the seller had known the statement was untrue, the seller would have engaged in **fraudulent misrepresentation**. In both of these situations the contract that results is voidable by the party to whom the misrepresentation is made. Statements are treated as misrepresentations by the law only if

1. the untrue statement is one of fact or there is active concealment
2. the statement is material to the transaction or is fraudulent
3. the victim reasonably relied on the statement

Untrue Statement of Fact

In misrepresentation, the statement must be one of fact rather than opinion. Therefore the statement must be about a past or existing fact. If someone says, "This car will suit your needs well for at least the next year," this is a statement about the future and therefore must be an opinion. It cannot be the basis for misrepresentation. A seller's statement that, "I'm sure land values will increase at least 15 percent a year for the next three years," is a statement of opinion.

Opinions also can be distinguished from facts based on how concrete they are. Saying, "it really runs well," is a statement of opinion about the condition of the car. Statements like "This is the best tasting cola on the market" are mere sales talk. In contrast, if the seller said, "the engine was rebuilt 7,000 miles ago," this is the expression of a concrete fact. If untrue, it would be considered a misrepresentation.

Note, however, that when an expert expresses an opinion, the law will treat the statement as a statement of fact which can be the basis for misrepresentation. If an expert auto mechanic says, "The engine is in A-1 shape," and this is not true, it is a misrepresentation and the buyer could avoid the contract. The packaging of the Nutri-Life dietary supplement in *What's Your Verdict?* involved an expert's opinion that, therefore, constituted misrepresentation.

ACTIVE CONCEALMENT Active concealment is a substitute for a false statement of fact. If the seller of a house paints the ceiling to cover stains which indicate the roof leaks, this is active concealment. Similarly, if a seller places the price sticker on the TV screen to cover a wide scratch, this is active concealment.

SILENCE While in many situations the seller may remain silent about defects, there are three important situations where disclosure is required. The first is where a statement about a material

With what you just read about active concealment, what would you do if you were interested in buying the vehicle in this picture?

fact omits important information. If a seller says, "I only drove this car once a week," then the seller also must disclose that this occurred while racing the car at the local drag strip. Half-truths cannot be used to conceal or mislead.

The second duty to break silence arises when a true statement is made false by subsequent events. A seller says, "No, the roof of the house doesn't leak." Later that night, it begins leaking and the seller ends up sleeping under an umbrella. This seller must break silence and disclose the defect to correct the buyer's misimpression.

The third situation arises when one party knows the other party has made a basic mistaken assumption. For example a buyer may assume that a foundation is solid, but the seller knows of a defect allowing water to flood the basement each spring. The seller knows repairs will cost 25 percent of the sale price. This mistaken assumption must be corrected.

Materiality

There are three ways an untrue statement can be determined to be material. First, a statement is material if the statement would cause a reasonable person to contract. Statements about total miles on a car and the number of miles since an engine was rebuilt probably would cause a reasonable person to enter the contract. A statement that a star's signature on a baseball card is his authentic autograph, is a statement that would be material to a reasonable person who collects such memorabilia.

Second, a statement can be material if the defendant knew this plaintiff would rely on the statement. Suppose a seller says the oil in the car was changed every 3,000 miles when it was only changed every 4,000 miles. This slight discrepancy would probably not be material to a reasonable person. If, however, a buyer says that the frequency of oil changes is very important to her, then statements about the frequency of oil changes would be material.

Third, if the defendant knew the statement was false, this makes the statement material. Therefore, if a seller lies about an otherwise non-material fact, this is material. If a seller says, "I always had the car serviced at the local Chevrolet dealership," when in fact he had it serviced at the local gas station, this statement would be material.

Reasonable Reliance

Even though the statement is material, there is no misrepresentation unless the victim reasonably relied on it. A buyer may be told by an art gallery owner that an oil painting was created by "one of the great masters of the Renaissance era." She then learns from an art appraiser that it is a mere imitation. If the buyer still completes the sale, the buyer isn't relying upon the statement. If a car dealer says the tires are new, but the buyer responds, "Two are as bald as you," there is no reliance.

LAW BRIEF

American contract law is built on the principle that individuals can take care of themselves when contracting. This attitude is inherent in the traditional advice "caveat emptor" or "let the buyer beware." The American approach generally allows silence as to material facts the seller knows that might adversely affect his or her bargaining position. It is up to the buyer to ask the seller about specific product attributes. Then, if the seller's answer is factually inaccurate, the basis for active concealment, fraud, and the potential avoidance of the contract is laid.

GLOBAL ISSUES

In contrast to the principle on which American contract law is built, as explained in the Law Brief on this page, European law imposes a duty to inform. Revealing problem areas in adherence to this requirement helps ensure an informed genuine assent to contracts. Failure to inform of defects in a timely manner allows the contract to be avoided when the problems present themselves.

CHECKPOINT What are the three criteria for a statement to be treated as a misrepresentation?

You are told by a jewelry store salesperson that the diamond you are looking at is a perfect stone. After you purchase the diamond, you learn from an appraiser that it is not perfect after all. Would you have relied on the salesperson's statement in making your purchase decision? Did a misrepresentation occur as a consequence?

Fraud and Remedies for Fraud

WHAT'S YOUR VERDICT? Graffter sold a used car to Camacho for $16,000. Graffter told her that the car had been driven only 50,000 miles, had never been in an accident, and had the original paint. In fact, Graffter had stolen the car, set back the odometer from 90,000 miles, and repainted the exterior in the original color. Graffter stood between Camacho and the right rear end of the car to prevent her from seeing a crudely repaired fender that had been damaged in the accident. Later Camacho learned the truth.

What remedies are available to Camacho?

Fraud is based on misrepresentation. All the elements of misrepresentation must be proven to show fraud plus two additional elements: intent and injury. If a victim can show fraud, courts will grant the victim assistance beyond the rescission available for misrepresentation.

NETBookmark

Some businesspeople are tempted to commit acts of fraud with regard to paying taxes. Access school.cengage.com/blaw/lawxtra and click on the link for Chapter 7. Read the examples of tax fraud cases on the Internal Revenue Service web page. Choose one of the cases and write a summary of the facts involved.

school.cengage.com/blaw/lawxtra

The Misrepresentation Must Be Intentional or Reckless

Fraud clearly exists when a person deliberately lies or conceals a material fact. Fraud also exists if a person recklessly makes a false statement of fact, without knowing whether it is true or false. To constitute fraud, in addition to intending to deceive, the misrepresentation also must be intended to induce the victim to contract.

The Misrepresentation or Concealment Must Injure

To establish fraud, there must be proof of injury. If there is an intentional misrepresentation, but no injury, there is no liability for fraud. Suppose you are looking at an antique motorcycle.

A Question of ETHICS

Paul, a tax protestor, refused to pay income taxes. Although he only had a daughter, he listed so many children as dependents that his employer did not withhold any federal taxes from Paul's paycheck. Each April 15, Paul would appear on local TV holding up a blank 1040 Internal Revenue Service form and state his belief that the income tax was only intended for corporate income. He would then cite Congressional debate at the time of the passage of the Constitutional amendment allowing the income tax in support of his position. Is Paul's behavior illegal, unethical or both?

The seller says, "It is a 1938 Indian." The seller knows it is a 1937 Indian but intentionally lies, thinking the newer bike is more valuable. If you buy it for $9,000 and it turns out to be worth $14,000, you haven't suffered an injury. While you could rescind based on misrepresentation, you could not establish fraud.

Remedies for Fraud

If a seller innocently misrepresents a material fact, the buyer may avoid the contract. This remedy also is available for fraud. If a victim can establish fraud, courts also will allow recovery of actual damages and punitive damages.

In *What's Your Verdict?* Graffter was a criminal who intentionally lied about the car and actively concealed the damaged rear fender. The deception injured Camacho because the car was not worth $16,000. Accordingly, as Camacho could establish fraud, she could have her contract rescinded and be awarded compensatory and punitive damages.

RESCISSION As mentioned, contracts entered into as a result of misrepresentation or fraud are voidable by the injured party and can be rescinded. Normally when you rescind, anything you received must be returned. A deceived party who has performed part of the contract may recover what has been paid or given. A deceived party who has done nothing may cancel the contract with no further obligation. If sued on the contract, the deceived party can plead fraud or misrepresentation as a defense.

DAMAGES Damages are available if fraud is proven. Should a defrauded party nonetheless choose to ratify the contract, the defrauded party may seek damages for loss created by the fraud. In *What's Your Verdict?* if Camacho decided to keep the car and ratified the contract, she could recover the difference in value for a car with 50,000 miles on it (the fraudulent misrepresentation) and one with 90,000 miles on it (the truth). Note that, under the UCC, damages are available when there is only an innocent misrepresentation in a sale of goods (tangible personal property).

LEGAL Research

Elect a class representative to contact your local police department and inquire as to whether any fraudulent schemes have occurred in your area. Possibilities include "con games" such as the pigeon-drop scenario as well as the techniques of short-change artists, pickpockets, and others. Discuss the findings in class.

CyberLAW

Fraud is one of the fastest-growing threats facing consumers today. Because many consumer transactions now take place over the Internet, consumers also face the prospect of online fraud. In 1996, the National Consumers League started the Internet Fraud Watch project and the National Fraud Information Center web site. Consumers can access the web site to get tips on how to avoid scams and fraud 7 days a week, 24 hours a day. Many of the scams involve travel fraud. Travel fraud is growing quickly and involves bargain vacation packages, travel vouchers, and prize trips "for a small fee." In Operation Trip-Up, the Federal Trade Commission and 12 other law enforcement agencies brought 36 separate actions against travel-related scams. Attorneys general in many states have established special task forces to handle Internet fraud. To curb Internet fraud, education is the key to protection. Before you purchase, check it out!

THINK ABOUT IT

Type "National Fraud Information Center" into an Internet search engine to check out this web site. Click on "Internet Fraud" and then "Internet Fraud Tips." Choose one tip that you think is especially helpful to share with your class.

PUNITIVE DAMAGES If fraud is proven, then punitive damages also become available. Punitive damages are a form of punishment. For instance, a judge might award a victim $5,000 in addition to actual damages as a way to punish the party who committed fraud.

CHECKPOINT What are the remedies available for fraud?

7-2 Assessment

school.cengage.com/blaw/lawxtra

THINK ABOUT LEGAL CONCEPTS

1. Which type of mistake may give both parties the right to rescind? (a) unilateral mistake of law (b) bilateral mistake of law (c) mutual mistake of fact (d) mutual mistake of law.

2. Unilateral mistakes of law generally have no effect on the rights of the parties under the resultant contract. **True or False?**

3. A statement of opinion by an expert _?_ be treated as fact. (a) will (b) will not

4. Misrepresentation is an element in both innocent misrepresentation and fraud. **True or False?**

5. For misrepresentation, which of the following elements need not be proven? (a) a false statement of fact (b) the fact must be material (c) the statement must be relied upon (d) all of the above must be shown

6. Punitive damages may be awarded if _?_ can be proven. (a) misrepresentation (b) mistake (c) fraud (d) all of the above

THINK CRITICALLY ABOUT EVIDENCE

Study the situation, answer the questions, and then prepare arguments to support your answers.

7. Anne was shopping for a used washing machine. She found one she thought was in good condition. She asked the seller what shape it was in and the seller replied, "It is in great shape." In fact it needed major repairs. Is the seller's statement a misrepresentation?

8. Chip was shopping for a used computer. He found one and asked the seller if the processor's speed was greater than 3 megahertz. The seller said, "Yes, it runs at 3.4 megahertz." In fact it was a much slower chip. Is the seller's statement a misrepresentation?

9. Glenna found a cell phone she wanted, but she wanted to be sure it had a camera with at least 3 megapixel resolution. When asked the seller said, "Certainly it does. In fact it's rated at 5 megapixels." In fact, the seller wasn't even

sure the cell phone had a camera. Glenna later found that it merely had a one megapixel camera. Has this seller committed misrepresentation? Has this seller committed fraud?

10. For years, Salazar, the lead mechanic at the Pull On In gas station, saved his money and eventually bought the business. Two weeks after the purchase, he found out that, a month previous, the Environmental Protection Agency had passed a regulation that would make the dispensing of petroleum-based fuels within a mile of a drinking water reservoir illegal. The station was only a few blocks from such a reservoir. Salazar also discovered that the previous owners knew of the regulation when they sold but did not inform him. Can he get the transaction rescinded?

Chapter 7 Assessment

CONCEPTS IN BRIEF

7-1 Duress and Undue Influence

1. One of the most important legal requirements for a valid contract is genuineness of assent.

2. Genuine assent is at times shown to be lacking due to a variety of causes such as duress, undue influence, mistake, misrepresentation, and fraud.

3. Duress consists of either an improper act or threat that induces the victim to make an unwanted contract. Such contracts are voidable by the victim.

4. Undue influence exists when one person, with the trust of, confidence of, or authority over the victim, uses that position to cause the victim to enter into a contract heavily favorable to the dominating party. The contract is voidable by the victim who acted without free will.

7-2 Mistake, Misrepresentation and Fraud

5. Generally a unilateral mistake of fact does not affect the validity of a contract.

6. Generally a mutual or bilateral mistake of material fact makes the agreement void.

7. Generally a unilateral or mutual mistake concerning applicable law leaves the contract valid.

8. Misrepresentation occurs if a victim reasonably relied on a material or fraudulent misstatement of fact or a material fact was actively concealed. Misrepresentation leaves the contract voidable by the victim.

9. Fraud exists when there is a deliberate false representation or a deliberate concealment of a material fact which influences the decision of the other party, causing injury. Contracts induced by fraud are voidable by the victim.

10. If a contract is voidable, the injured party must avoid shortly after the discovery that there is no genuine agreement. The injured party also must not engage in any activity that might ratify the contract.

YOUR LEGAL VOCABULARY

Match each statement with the term that it best defines. Some terms may not be used.

1. Of no legal effect

2. Consent not clouded by fraud, duress, undue influence, or mistake

3. Contract in which the injured party can withdraw from the transaction

4. One party holds an incorrect belief about the facts related to a contract

5. Deliberate false representation or concealment of a material fact, which is meant to and which does induce another to make an unfavorable contract

6. Approval of a voidable contract

7. Overpowering of another's free will by taking unfair advantage to induce the person to make an unfavorable contract

8. Use of an improper act or threat to obtain an expression of agreement

9. The process of restoring to the parties what they have put into the contract

a. duress
b. fraud
c. fraudulent misrepresentation
d. genuine assent
e. innocent misrepresentation
f. material fact
g. mutual mistake
h. ratification
i. rescission
j. undue influence
k. unilateral mistake
l. void
m. voidable

REVIEW LEGAL CONCEPTS

10. Describe the concept of mutual mistake of fact.

11. Distinguish the effect of the passage of time on the potential for avoiding the contract versus the effect of time on the potential for the contract's ratification.

12. What does reliance mean?

13. Explain all the elements that must be proven to establish fraud.

14. How is innocent misrepresentation different from fraud?

WRITE ABOUT LEGAL CONCEPTS

15. Write a short paragraph explaining why undue influence would be presumed in certain cases, such as the attorney and client relationship, but not in others.

16. Describe in writing a scenario where a mutual mistake of a material fact might cause a contract to be void.

17. Write a paragraph describing a television ad that could be the basis for misrepresentation if the statement made were untrue.

18. **HOT DEBATE** Write a letter for your friend to the credit card company. In the letter argue that the amount billed for the cell phone was incorrect and should be changed.

MAKE ACADEMIC CONNECTIONS

19. **ENGLISH** Read Frank Abagnale's book, *Catch Me If You Can*. Prepare a report on the nature and level of complexity of his fraudulent schemes. What, in your opinion, made them so successful?

THINK CRITICALLY ABOUT EVIDENCE

Study the situation, answer the questions, and then prepare arguments to support your answers.

20. In negotiations for the purchase of a ranch, Adler (the seller) discussed water rights with Folt, the buyer. Adler never mentioned an ongoing dispute she had over such rights with a neighboring rancher. After the purchase, Folt realized that he had "bought a lawsuit" when his neighbor sued him over the water rights. In turn, he therefore sued Adler for rescission of their contract. Who will prevail, and why?

21. During negotiations for the sale of a well to be used to water animals, Hutton said the well was free of gypsum and brine (salty water). In fact, the well did contain gypsum, although there was no brine. The gypsum made the well unusable for watering animals. Curry, the purchaser, refused to pay, claiming the contract was voidable because of misrepresentation. Was it?

22. Ashbery, a salesperson, told Gelman that a new computer and its accounting software should do the work of at least five employees. Relying on this statement, Gelman bought the products. When Gelman found that he could eliminate only three employees but needed a new specialist, he claimed fraud. Was fraud committed?

23. Moser had no automobile liability insurance, although it was required by state law. She negligently collided with Chang's car. Chang threatened to sue if Moser failed to pay $1,000 for pain and suffering and $2,000 for car repairs. Moser gave Chang a check for $3,000. Then she stopped payment on it, claiming duress. Was it duress?

24. Olga Mestrovic, the widow of the successful artist Ivan Mestrovic, died. 1st Source Bank was the representative of her estate. It entered into a contract for the sale of Olga's home to the Wilkins. There was a lot of personal property in the home including a stove, dishwasher, and other items. The contract of sale provided that these items of personal property also were being sold to the Wilkins. When the Wilkins took possession of the realty, they found it in a cluttered condition which would require substantial cleaning. When they complained to the bank, it sent a bank officer to the scene. That person offered the Wilkins two options: Either the bank would pay to have the rubbish removed or the Wilkins could remove it and, "keep any items of personal property they wanted." No one thought there were any works of art on the property. The Wilkins accepted the latter option and later found eight very valuable drawings by Ivan Mestrovic. Was there a mutual mistake? Was there a mistake about the subject matter of the transaction? (*Wilkin v. 1st Source Bank*, 548 N.E. 2d 170, Ind. Ct. App.)

25. Using a smuggled-in .38 caliber pistol, Gorham and Jones took control of their cell block in a District of Columbia (Washington, D.C.) jail. They and other prisoners released by them ultimately took several hostages and demanded to be freed. One hostage was Kenneth Hardy, the Director of Corrections for the District of Columbia. The hostages were threatened with violence and used as human shields. Ultimately the authorities reestablished control of the cell block. Gorham and Jones were then transferred to the maximum security part of the prison from which, with the use of smuggled-in hacksaw blades, they later escaped. After their recapture, they appealed their subsequent criminal convictions (on 22 counts) of charges relating to their efforts. They said that the transfer to maximum security was in violation of the agreement they had extracted from Hardy while he was a hostage. They said he promised they would not be punished for their first attempt at jailbreak. Should the court recognize the agreement as binding and overturn the convictions? (*United States v. Gorham and Wilkerson (a/k/a Jones)*, 532 F. 2d 1088)

26. Treasure Salvors, Inc. located a Spanish ship on the ocean bottom in 55 feet of water about 46 miles off the Florida coast. The ship, the Nuestra Señora de Atocha, sank in a hurricane while heading from Havana to Spain in 1622. It was carrying "a treasure worthy of Midas: 160 gold bullion pieces, 900 silver ingots, more than 250,000 silver coins, 600 copper planks, 350 chests of indigo and 25 tons of tobacco." On the mistaken assumption that the seabed where the Atocha lay was state land, Treasure Salvors made a series of contracts with Florida whereby the state was to receive 25 percent of all items recovered. After the U.S. Supreme Court, in another case, had decided that the continental shelf where the ship rested was federal land, Treasure Salvors sued to rescind its contract with Florida and to recover all items as the exclusive owner of the Atocha. Should Treasure Salvors be able to rescind? Why or why not? (*Florida v. Treasure Salvors, Inc.*, 621 F.2d 1340)

27. Snap-On manufactures and sells hand tools such as wrenches to professional mechanics. It sold a distributorship to Eulich, but he was not successful and encountered significant financial difficulties. In Eulich's view his sales territory was too small. As a result Eulich terminated the dealership agreement. That agreement included a clause stating that on termination of the agreement, Snap-On might buy back any new tools owned by the distributor. Eulich attempted to turn in his tools but Snap-On delayed. Eulich's financial situation deteriorated to the point where he was unable to pay his personal bills and his wife needed to be hospitalized, though he had no medical insurance. Snap-On knew this. Finally, Snap-On accepted the tools. Before paying for the tools, Snap-On asked Eulich to sign an agreement promising not to sue Snap-On for claims arising out of the distributorship. He signed but later sued. What factors do you think the court considered in deciding whether the agreement not to sue was based on duress? (*Eulich v. Snap-On Tool Corp.*, 853 P.2d 1350)

Case For Legal Thinking

NOBLE V. SMITH
164 CAL. APP. 3D 1001 (1985)

FACTS Noble contracted with the U.S. Navy to remodel the engine maintenance shop at El Toro Marine Corps Air Station. The contract price was some $647,500. The work included installation of heating, ventilating and air conditioning systems (HVAC) with a chilled water system.

In preparing his bid for the work, Noble totaled the informal bids he had received from subcontractors plus a percentage for his profit. In particular, he used $90,000 to cover the HVAC based on a bid for a subcontract by John Berry, president of American. Later the bid from Berry was reduced to $86,500.

Noble sent Berry a contract for the HVAC work to be performed by American at its bid price of $86,500. Learning this, Coast (another bidder) warned Noble the $86,500 was not a reasonable bid as Coast's $94,000 bid had excluded the chilled water system from the HVAC.

Four weeks later, Berry told Noble he would not sign the contract. He testified he had a number of questions and "I knew going in it was a low bid." [Then Berry recommended Smith as a contractor who might do the work.]

Berry told Smith his $86,500 bid had a 20 percent profit margin. Smith signed that same day a contract identical to that turned down by Berry. Smith told Noble he had

© GETTY IMAGES/PHOTODISC

not done "much examination" of the plans or specifications and Ruff was going to look the job over. After checking the job site and the plans, Ruff told Smith the cost of the job "far exceeded" the contract price. The plans included the chilled water system in the HVAC which cost an additional $16,000 not contemplated by the [bid]. Smith promptly told Noble the $86,500 price would not cover the HVAC with the chilled water system. Noble responded with the comment he would get another contractor and "sue [Smith] for the difference." Noble then awarded Coast two subcontracts, one for $94,000 and one for $16,000 for the chilled water system and sued Smith for the difference between his bid and the Coast bids.

REASONING Unilateral mistake is grounds for relief where the mistake is due to the fault of the other party or the other party knows or has reason to know of the mistake. Substantial evidence supports the conclusion Noble knew Smith's contract for the HVAC did not include the chilled water system.

To rely on a unilateral mistake of fact, Smith must demonstrate his mistake was not caused by his "neglect of a legal duty." This was Smith's first venture into contract waters deeper than $10,000. He told Noble the plans and specifications had not been reviewed by him; Ruff was to undertake that task after the contract was signed. Importantly, Smith related to Noble the profit assurance given him by Berry. In these circumstances, neither the trial court nor we could find Smith's conduct neglect of a legal duty.

While the [lower] court relied on mistake to void the contract, we find an alternative ground in fraud. Smith's consent was obtained by Noble's fraud in the suppression by Noble of the fact Berry's contract price for the HVAC did not include the cost of the chilled water system.

CONCLUSION Judgment affirmed that the contract should be voided.

PRACTICE JUDGING

1. Is the mistake material?
2. Is the mistake unilateral or bilateral?
3. What evidence supports the conclusion that fraud occurred?

Chapter 8
Consideration

8-1 Types of Consideration

8-2 Questionable Consideration

8-3 When Consideration Is Not Required

HOT DEBATE

For a college graduation present, a wealthy aunt promised to pay for Maureen and a friend to take a luxury ocean cruise along the "Mexican Riviera" between Long Beach, California, and Acapulco, Mexico. At the graduation exercises, however, her aunt gave her a kiss instead and said, "The stock market is down. Sorry, darling!"

WHERE DO YOU STAND?

1. State two reasons why you think the aunt is legally obligated to pay for the cruise.
2. State two reasons why you think the aunt should not have to pay.

8-1 Types of Consideration

GOALS
- Identify the three requirements of consideration
- Discuss the adequacy of consideration

KEY TERMS
consideration

gift

donor

donee

forbearance

promisor

promisee

legal value

nominal consideration

Consideration

WHAT'S YOUR VERDICT? John, a writer, gets a call from his editor and, consequently, has to leave immediately on a research trip to Hudson Bay and Newfoundland in Canada. As the trip should take a couple of weeks, he leaves a note offering to pay his neighbor, Jordan, $100 to watch his house and feed and walk his dog during the absence. John then leaves without ever speaking to Jordan. Jordan gets the note and complies.

Is there an enforceable contract? What is the consideration for each party?

Consideration is what a person demands and generally must receive in order to make her or his promise legally binding. There are three requirements of consideration.

1. Each party must make a promise, perform an act, or forbear (refrain from doing something).
2. Each party's promise, act, or forbearance must be in exchange for a return promise, act, or forbearance by the other party.
3. What each party exchanges must have legal value, that is, it must be worth something in the eyes of the law.

Consideration distinguishes a contractual promise from a promise to make a gift. A **gift** is a transfer of ownership without receiving anything in return. A promise to make a gift is generally not legally enforceable. Only after a **donor** (the person giving the gift) intentionally transfers the gift to the **donee** (the person receiving the gift) and the donee accepts it does the transaction become legally binding.

Promise, Act, or Forbearance

In *What's Your Verdict?* what Jordan contributed was watching John's house and feeding and walking the dog each day. These acts were consideration for John's consideration, that is, John's promise to pay the $100. Both the acts and promise have value in the eyes of the law. Therefore, there was consideration and a valid contract.

When looking for consideration, look for legal value in the underlying act that is promised. If someone promises **forbearance**—or, to not do something—look beneath the promise and ask if the forbearance has legal value.

In *What's Your Verdict?* was Jordan's consideration an act or a forbearance in the contract that was created? Explain.

© GETTY IMAGES/PHOTODISC

Contractual Exchanges

In a typical contract, one party in effect says to another, "If you do this for me (pick up my mail and watch the house), I shall do that for you (pay you $100)." A person promising an action or forbearance is the **promisor**. The person to whom the promise is made is the **promisee**. In most contracts, the consideration necessary to legally bind a would-be promisor to his or her promise is identified through bargaining leading up to a mutual exchange of promises. In certain instances, however, such as in *"What's Your Verdict?"* bargaining is not possible. Consequently, an offeror must make a blind offer hoping the offeree will accept by performing the consideration the offeror desires.

Consideration must be mutual. If either of the parties does not receive the required consideration, that party has no duty to perform as promised.

IN THIS CASE Tyrone, a ten-year-old boy, attended a mineral show in Dallas, Texas. He bought several different crystal-like stones there. One such stone was purchased from Edwards for the marked price of $5. Later the stone was identified as a diamond and valued at more than $50,000. Edwards sued to recover the stone alleging he had not received proper consideration for the purchase. The courts held in Tyrone's favor as Edwards had received what he had demanded for the stone.

Legal Value

Legal value means there has been a change in a party's legal position as a result of the contract. In *What's Your Verdict?* Jordan performed acts which involved a benefit to his neighbor (feeding and walking the dog and watching the house). There is legal value because this changed (benefited) the neighbor's legal position. John, as promisor, benefited Jordan's legal position by promising the $100. Because both the act and the promise (to pay $100) have legal value and were an exchange reasonably suitable to the parties, consideration is present and there is a contract. Legal value (a change in legal position) is most commonly found in this form—in the exchange of two benefits.

© GETTY IMAGES/PHOTODISC

After you ask for permission, your dad promises that he will let you go out tonight if you will clean your room to his satisfaction tomorrow. You agree. Who is the promisor and who is the promisee in this situation?

Legal value also can be found in the exchange of benefit for a detriment. With regard to legal value, the detriment is the forbearing of a legal right. A detriment always arises when you promise forbearance—that is, promise to refrain from doing what you have a right to do. If your uncle said on your eighteenth birthday, "Look, if you refrain from driving until your twenty-first birthday, I'll give you $25,000." You respond, "Yes, I accept." What you have promised is not a benefit to your uncle, but rather a detriment to yourself—you have given up a legal right. This is a change in your legal position and is thus valid consideration.

Legal value also can arise from the exchange of two detriments. If you say to your neighbor that you will forbear buying a dog if she will forbear building a fence and she agrees, both parties have changed their legal positions. Therefore, there is consideration for each party's promise.

Adequacy of Consideration

Generally, what the parties give and get as consideration need not be of equal economic value. This idea is sometimes expressed as, "The courts do not inquire into the adequacy of consideration."

The values that different people place on the same property may vary widely. For example, one person might gladly pay $60,000 for an original and exclusive high-fashion gown by a famous designer. Others would not be interested in owning such a gown for $60. A person also might place a higher value on a product at one time than at another. For example, when you have been baking for hours on the sunny side of a baseball stadium, you might willingly pay three times the grocery-store price for a cold soft drink.

Economic value is unimportant as long as there is genuine agreement. However, a big difference in economic value of what one gives and receives may be evidence of mutual mistake, duress, undue influence, or fraud. If the consideration received by one of the parties is so grossly inadequate so as to shock the conscience of the court, the contract will be declared *unconscionable* (grossly unfair or oppressive). In such a case, the contract or the unconscionable clause may not be enforceable.

Would you be willing to pay more for a slice of pizza if you were really hungry? If so, why might this be?

© GETTY IMAGES/PHOTODISC

Nominal Consideration

In certain written contracts, such as publicly recorded deeds, consideration from one party may be identified as "one dollar ($1) and other good and valuable consideration." In such situations, the actual consideration may be substantially more. However, the parties either cannot state the amount precisely or do not want to publicize it. The token amount (for example, the $1 mentioned above) stated instead is known as **nominal consideration**.

CHECKPOINT List the three requirements of consideration.

GLOBAL ISSUES

Contracts in Medieval England

Contracts have not always been as important as they are in today's society. The rigid hierarchy of the feudal society in medieval England required very few contracts. Nobles, knights, serfs, and peasants all knew their place in society and understood their rights.

Formal contracts, known as "solemn promises," were more common in England by the fourteenth century. The royal courts required that these promises be written down and sealed. In order to seal the contract, a noble would use the imprint of his signet ring in a wax seal. Today, you can seal a document by writing the word "seal" in parentheses after your name.

8-1 Assessment

Xtra!
Study Tools
school.cengage.com/blaw/lawxtra

THINK ABOUT LEGAL CONCEPTS

1. Forebearance cannot be consideration. **True or False?**

2. The presence or absence of consideration distinguishes a legally enforceable promise from a generally unenforceable promise to make a _?_.

3. The person who makes a gift is called the donee. **True or False?**

4. Consideration can be found in the exchange of benefits, or in the trading of a benefit for a detriment, but not in the exchange of two detriments. **True or False?**

5. Courts do not consider the _?_ of consideration.

6. Token amounts given as consideration are referred to as _?_ consideration. (a) nominal consideration (b) normal consideration (c) insufficient consideration

THINK CRITICALLY ABOUT EVIDENCE

Study the situation, answer the questions, and then prepare arguments to support your answers.

7. After graduation from high school in June, you and three classmates plan to travel around the United States. The plan is to visit the capital cities of all 48 contiguous states, taking numerous pictures along the way. The Sunnyside Camera Shop offers to give you a dozen rolls of 36-exposure color film for the trip free if you agree to let it develop and print all the rolls you use, for a stated price per roll. You agree. Are both you and the Sunnyside Camera Shop legally bound? What is the consideration for each party?

8. A three-piece high school rock band practiced for at least one hour most days of the week. Its studio was the cramped one-car garage of the drummer's home. Ultimately, several neighbors offered to pay the rent at a local mini-warehouse as a practice room for a year if the group agreed to stop practicing at the drummer's home. As the warehouse was much larger, the players agreed. Did the neighbors receive consideration? Did the rock band receive consideration? Did the rock band receive a benefit, endure a detriment, both, or neither? Was the contract enforceable?

9. Gil found a nearly new engine in his neighbor's garage. He was experienced enough to see that it was in good shape. When he asked the neighbor how much she wanted for it, she said "you can have it if you'll get it out of here by the weekend and clean up the oil and grease around where it was." Gil said, "Okay," even though he knew the engine was worth nearly $1,200. Is this a valid contract?

© GETTY IMAGES/PHOTODISC

8-2 Questionable Consideration

GOALS

■ Describe situations in which consideration is present only under limited circumstances

■ Recognize when what appears to be binding consideration is not

KEY TERMS

output contract
requirements contract
liquidated debt
accord and satisfaction

release
composition with creditors
past consideration

Circumstantial Consideration

WHAT'S YOUR VERDICT? LedLove, Inc., designed and intended to produce a large red heart-shaped candy box for Valentine's Day. The box was to have a row of one-inch LEDs imbedded in its front cover. The LEDs could be programmed to spell out any message the purchaser desired. In late June, LedLove contracted with a local electronics manufacturer, Diodor Inc., to buy all of the specially designed LEDs Diodor produced in the month of December. However, at the end of November, Diodor contracted with another firm to produce a different LED product. The production run for the other firm would take up all of Diodor's capacity for December and make it twice the amount of profit it could expect from the deal with LedLove.

Was Diodor able to do this without breaching its contract with LedLove? Why or why not?

Certain forms of consideration are only legally binding in the proper circumstances. If these circumstances, in the form of properly worded contract provisions or patterns of behavior are not present, what would appear to be valid consideration is not.

Illusory Promises

To be consideration, a promise must be binding. In other words, the promise must create a duty or impose an obligation. If a contract contains a clause that allows you to escape the legal obligation, the promise is said to be *illusory*. For example, you might have a clause stating that you will "paint the house—if you have time." This does not increase your legal obligation because you may never have time to paint the house.

TERMINATION CLAUSES Businesses often want the power to withdraw from a contract if business circumstances change. Therefore they include termination clauses in their contracts. If the clause gives one party the power to terminate the contract for any reason, the promise to perform would be illusory.

The promise is not illusory if termination is allowed only after a change in defined circumstances, after the passage of a certain length of time, or after a set period after a notice of termination is given. There is clearly a change in the party's legal obligations.

OUTPUT AND REQUIREMENTS CONTRACTS Buyers sometimes agree to purchase all of a particular

NETBookmark

Access school.cengage.com/blaw/lawxtra and click on the link for Chapter 8. Using the online dictionary, look up the terms *illusory promise, output contract,* and *requirements contract.* Think of an example for each of these concepts, and write your examples down on a sheet of paper. Share your examples in class.

school.cengage.com/blaw/lawxtra

If a lumber company agrees to supply all of the lumber needs of a builder, what kind of contract would the two parties enter into?

producer's production. For instance, a steel company may buy all of the output of a nearby coal mining company. This is an **output contract**. On the other hand, a seller may agree to supply all of the needs of a particular buyer. For instance, a carburetor manufacturer may agree to supply all the carburetors needed for the production of a certain make of vehicle. This is a **requirements contract**.

It may seem that one party could elect to stop production and thereby eliminate the obligation. However, courts recognize these contracts as supported by consideration because they imply a duty of fair dealing.

This means that production cannot be stopped arbitrarily. Instead any action terminating the obligation of an output or requirement contract must be taken in a way that constitutes *fair dealings*. By finding an implied duty of fair dealings, the courts have maintained the basis for the presence of consideration. In *What's Your Verdict?* the courts would imply the fair dealings standard against Diodor and find them in breach of their contract with LedLove.

Existing Duty

A person sometimes promises to do something that he or she already is obligated to do by law or by prior contract. Such a promise, or act, cannot serve as consideration to bind the other party to a later contract.

EXISTING PUBLIC DUTY If on your sixteenth birthday, your aunt promised to pay you $10,000 if you promised to not purchase alcohol for two years and you said, "Okay," this would not be a contract. There is no consideration because it is illegal for you to purchase alcohol when you are 16 and 17 years old. While the agreement creates a benefit for you ($10,000), you don't incur a detriment because you are not giving up a legal right.

EXISTING PRIVATE DUTY If a contract creates a duty, this duty cannot be the basis of consideration in a different contract. The same rule holds true when a person demands further compensation for carrying out a contractual promise already made.

SETTLEMENT OF LIQUIDATED DEBTS A **liquidated debt** is one where the parties agree that the debt exists and on the amount of the debt. When a *creditor* (a person to whom a debt is owed) agrees to accept less than the total amount due in full settlement from a *debtor* (a person who owes money to a creditor) there is no consideration if the debt is liquidated.

Assume that Shawver borrows $1,000 from Reno. The loan is to be paid in one year with interest at 10 percent per year, or a total amount of $1,100. On the due date, Shawver sends Reno a check for only $1,000, saying "Sorry, I'm strapped for cash. You will have to accept this in full payment." Reno endorses (signs) and cashes the check. Reno may later sue and recover the unpaid balance of $100. She has received no consideration for the suggested agreement to reduce the amount due.

A debtor can settle a claim by paying less than the full amount if additional consideration is given. For example payment of less than the full amount before the due date could be consideration. However, there must be mutual agreement between the creditor and debtor to do so. Valid consideration exists because the creditor receives the benefit of early payment. If something extra is given by the debtor, the new consideration supports a voluntary release by the creditor.

SETTLEMENT OF UNLIQUIDATED DEBTS When there is a genuine dispute between the parties about how much is owed, the debt is referred to as unliquidated. In such case, a payment offered in full settlement by the debtor and accepted by a creditor settles the claim. This process is called an **accord and satisfaction**. For example, a debtor may in good faith claim that a certain debt is $500. The creditor in good faith contends that it is $1,000. If the parties compromise on $750, their new agreement on that sum is referred to as the *accord*. Consideration for the accord is found in their mutual forbearance from litigating over the amount owed. When the subsequent agreement is performed, in this case the amount of $750 is paid, the act is referred to as the *satisfaction*.

RELEASE In most instances when a tort occurs, the liability is unliquidated because the extent of damages is uncertain. Often due to financial pressure, an injured party in the tort will agree to dis-

charge another from liability for the tort in return for a monetary payment or other consideration. This discharge agreement is termed a **release**.

COMPOSITION WITH CREDITORS Occasionally a group of creditors will cooperatively agree to accept less than what they are entitled to, in full satisfaction of their claims against a debtor. In return, the debtor agrees not to file for bankruptcy. This is called a **composition with creditors**. Consideration for the promise of each creditor to release the debtor from full payment is found in the reciprocal promises of the other creditors to refrain from suing for the entire amounts due them. If the creditors did not agree to this arrangement, the debtor could file for bankruptcy, and the creditors might receive much less as a consequence.

CHECKPOINT Why is consideration not binding in illusory contracts?

False Consideration

WHAT'S YOUR VERDICT? John's elderly friend, Lloyd, was a diabetic who had had a leg removed and was on dialysis. When John was in city hall one day paying his water bill, he overheard two clerks discussing the fact that Lloyd's water was about to be cut off due to nonpayment of his utility bill for the last five months. John inquired how much the bill was, and then, without a word to Lloyd, paid the full amount due, a sum of $973. When Lloyd found out what John had done, he immediately promised to pay John the amount as soon as possible.

If Lloyd dies before he can repay John, could John sue and recover the $973 from Lloyd's estate?

Unlike forms of consideration that are only legally binding in certain circumstances, certain acts or promises are falsely identified as consideration but can never be.

Mutual Gifts

When something of value is given by one party to another without demanding anything in return,

IN THIS CASE Fillmore loaned Grant his riding lawnmower. While mowing a sloping piece of ground, the right rear wheel came off and the lawnmower rolled over Grant causing severe injuries. Fillmore knew that the wheel had been wobbling but hadn't warned Grant. When Grant threatened to sue Fillmore and the lawnmower company, Fillmore offered Grant $5,000 for a release from the unliquidated claim. Grant, owing for his hospital stay, accepted and gave the release knowing she could still pursue suit against the lawnmower company. The question only remains as to whether or not it would be successful.

the something of value is not consideration for anything later promised or provided.

Past Performance

Contractual bargaining takes place in the present, for immediate or future performance by both parties. Therefore, an act that has already been performed cannot serve as consideration. Such act is called **past consideration**. In *What's Your Verdict?* John could always file suit for the money. However he could not recover because his paying the water bill was past consideration for Lloyd's promise.

CHECKPOINT What distinguishes a gift from a valid contract?

8-2 Assessment

Xtra!
Study Tools
school.cengage.com/blaw/lawxtra

THINK ABOUT LEGAL CONCEPTS

1. If a contractual obligation can be negated by a volitional action of the obligor, the contractual promise is said to be

2. Termination clauses always make a contract invalid for lack of consideration. **True or False?**

3. Output clauses make contracts invalid. **True or False?**

4. If you already owe a duty, that duty cannot be used as consideration. **True or False?**

5. Legal value means a change in one's legal position as a result of the contract. **True or False?**

6. When there is a dispute over the amount owed, a subsequent agreement stipulating that amount and promising its payment is referred to as a(n) (a) accord (b) satisfaction (c) output contract

THINK CRITICALLY ABOUT EVIDENCE

Study the situation, answer the questions, and then prepare arguments to support your answers.

7. Deb Tore let her credit card debt get out of hand and ended up owing 11 card companies more than $35,000. Knowing that Deb could not pay the full amount due, the card companies conferred with one another and offered to reduce their total claims to $17,500, if she would not seek to discharge the amount owed through bankruptcy. She agreed. What is such a group of creditors called? What consideration binds each credit card company to the agreement?

8. Georgia's neighbors approached her right after she received her driver's license and said they felt that she drove too fast on the roads where

their kids often played. They struck a deal with her that if she stayed within the speed limit for the next three months they would pay her $200. Georgia agreed. Is there a benefit to the neighbors? Is there a benefit to Georgia? Is there an enforceable contract?

9. Kamiar owed Rubio $5,000, which was due in one year. There was no dispute as to the amount. However, Rubio needed money immediately, so Kamiar offered to pay $4,000 early in full settlement of the debt. If Kamiar pays the $4,000 early, will Rubio be able to successfully sue and collect the $1,000 later.

8-3 When Consideration Is Not Required

GOALS

- Distinguish situations in which consideration is not needed
- Recognize when the doctrine of promissory estoppel can be applied

KEY TERMS

statute of limitations

promissory estoppel

Exceptions to the Requirement of Consideration

WHAT'S YOUR VERDICT? The Constantine children, in memory of their father who had died of cancer, promised to pay for the local hospital's purchase of new cancer-fighting equipment. As a consequence, the board of directors of the facility entered into a contract for more than $450,000 worth of advanced devices. When presented with the bill, the Constantine children, due to a decline in their financial positions, refused to pay saying they weren't contractually obligated.

Can they be held to their pledge?

There are important exceptions to the general rule that, under contract law, consideration is necessary to bind someone to their promise. These exceptions include promises made to a charitable organization, promises covered by the UCC, promises to renew a debt barred from collection by certain statutes, and promises enforceable under the doctrine of promissory estoppel.

Promises to Charitable Organizations

Individuals and business firms often contribute to charitable organizations, such as churches, schools, and hospitals not operated for profit. The contributions may be completed gifts or promises (pledges) to pay in the future. Because the party who makes the pledge receives nothing in return, one might assume that the pledge is unenforceable.

Courts, however, generally enforce such promises provided the charity states a specific use for the money and actually acts in reliance on the pledge. For example, a hospital may have contracted for new facilities, as in *What's Your Verdict?* As it would be unjust to deprive the hospital of the promised support it reasonably relied on, the Constantine children are legally obligated to make good on their pledge.

Promises Covered by the UCC

FIRM OFFERS Under the UCC, a merchant who makes an offer in a signed writing to buy or sell

A store owner promises to fund the building of an addition to her church. Then the economy takes a downturn, and the store's business decreases. Is she legally obligated to fulfill her promise to the church?

© GETTY IMAGES/PHOTODISC

goods and promises to leave the offer open is bound for the period of time stipulated or up to three months. This is called a *firm offer* and is enforceable even when no payment or other consideration has been given for the promise.

MODIFICATIONS At common law modification of a contract needs consideration. Under the UCC, however, a good-faith agreement that modifies an existing contract for the sale of goods needs no new consideration. For example, after a sale has been made, a seller could agree to give the buyers a valid warranty without further charge. This modification is enforceable though not supported by consideration.

Promises Barred from Collection by Statute

STATUTE OF LIMITATIONS A state's **statute of limitations** specifies a time limit for bringing a lawsuit. Once you become aware of a legal claim, you must sue before the statute of limitations passes or you lose the right to litigate the issue. In many states, the statute of limitations for breach of contract or torts is three years. If there is a breach of contract or a tort, you must bring suit within three years after the claim arises.

Some states will enforce a promise to pay a claim after the passage of the statute of limitations even though there is no consideration for the promise. These states do require that the promise be in writing.

DEBTS DISCHARGED IN BANKRUPTCY Sometimes, even after a debt has been discharged as a result of the debtor declaring bankruptcy, the obligation may be reaffirmed or (reinstated) by a promise of the debtor. This is often done when someone close to the debtor cosigned or guaranteed payment on the debt. Such a promise does not have to be supported

LEGAL Research

Determine the statute of limitations periods for contracts, torts, and crimes in your state codes. Locate a copy of your state statutes in your local library or online at www.(insert your state name).gov. (www.florida.gov, for example). Using the Word Index in the statutes, locate the "statute of limitations" or "limitation of actions" for contracts, torts, and crimes for your state. If searching online, put these same terms in the search engine.

by additional consideration to be legally binding. To avoid taking advantage of other creditors, however, the debts to be reaffirmed have to be listed with the bankruptcy court during the proceeding.

Promissory Estoppel

At times a rigid adherence to the letter of the law can produce injustice. As a consequence, the law allows courts to counteract this effect by taking certain actions in the name of equity, or basic fairness. One such action that the courts can take is to use the doctrine of **promissory estoppel**. When brought into use—or "invoked"—by the courts, promissory estoppel prevents promisors from stating in court that they did not receive consideration for their promises. Under the doctrine of consideration, if a person cannot claim they did not get what they demanded in return for being bound to their promises, then those promises can be enforced against them.

For the courts to invoke promissory estoppel, the following conditions must be met:

■ The promisor should reasonably foresee that the promisee will rely on the promise.

■ The promisee does, in fact, act in reliance on the promise.

■ The promisee would suffer a substantial economic loss if the promise is not enforced.

■ Injustice can be avoided only by enforcement of the promise.

CHECKPOINT Name four exceptions to the requirement of consideration.

THINK ABOUT LEGAL CONCEPTS

1. Promissory estoppel can be invoked even if enforcing the promise is not the only way to avoid injustice. **True or False?**

2. At common law, changes to a contract must be supported by consideration. **True or False?**

3. There is no time limit under a typical statute of limitations for lawsuits based on breaches of contract. **True or False?**

4. A promise of a contribution to a charity is termed a _?_.

5. Under the UCC a merchant's signed, written offer to buy or sell goods is binding for a limited time without consideration. **True or False?**

6. Debts discharged in bankruptcy can still be reaffirmed by the debtor. **True or False?**

THINK CRITICALLY ABOUT EVIDENCE

Study the situation, answer the questions, and then prepare arguments to support your answers.

7. Laura wanted to go to graduate school after college and she knew it would be very expensive. Her dad told her that if she would major in math instead of history, he would pay tuition in graduate school for a master's degree. Laura majored in math but her dad refused to pay for her graduate school tuition. Can Laura compel her father to pay?

8. Welt entered into a contract with Carbonaro, Inc. for the purchase of two dozen ultralight bike frames that he planned to resell from his retail bike shop. The price was $1,100 each. The parties wrote out all the terms of their contract and each signed. Later Welt learned that he could acquire similar frames for $725 each. Welt told Carbonaro that if it wanted to maintain Welt's goodwill it would reduce the price to $725. Carbonaro agreed. What is the consideration in the original contract? Is the price of $725 enforceable? Explain.

9. When they were both freshmen in college, Steiner borrowed $200 from Faber so he could attend a big game in Chicago. Steiner never repaid the debt, and after five years it was barred by the statute of limitations. Then Steiner accidently bumped into Faber in an airport lounge in Tampa. Embarassed, Steiner said, "I haven't forgotten those four 50's I borrowed from you for the big game. Now that I am working, I'll pay you. In addition, I'll take you to this year's big game at my expense." Is Steiner legally obligated to repay the $200?

10. Lemke's son, Arthur, bought a videocassette recorder from Dyer on an installment plan. When Arthur was unable to keep up the payments, Dyer came to repossess the recorder. Lemke promised in writing to make the payments if Dyer would allow her son to keep the recorder. If Dyer agreed, could Lemke hold him to his promise?

Chapter 8 Assessment

CONCEPTS IN BRIEF

8-1   Types of Consideration

1. Consideration is what a person demands and generally must receive in order to make her or his contractual promise legally binding.

2. Consideration may consist of a promise, an act, or a forbearance.

3. The adequacy, equality, or fairness of the consideration given and received is immaterial as long as the consideration has some value and is voluntarily agreed to by both parties.

8-2   Questionable Consideration

4. Performing or promising to perform an existing obligation is not consideration.

5. Past performance is not consideration for a promise given now or in the future.

8-3   When Consideration Is Not Required

6. Pledges to pay money to charitable organizations are usually enforceable even though no consideration was given in return.

7. Agreements between merchants modifying contracts for the sale of goods need no consideration to be binding.

8. Promises barred by statute may be enforceable if reaffirmed.

9. If basic fairness demands it, the courts may invoke the doctrine of promissory estoppel to prevent promisors from stating that they did not receive consideration for their promises.

YOUR LEGAL VOCABULARY

Match each statement with the term that it best defines. Some terms may not be used.

1. Agreement by all creditors to accept something less than the total amount of their claims in full satisfaction of a debtor's obligations

2. Token consideration, which bears no relation to the real value of the contract

3. What a person demands and generally must receive in order to make her or his promise legally binding

4. Refraining from doing what one has a right to do

5. Voluntary transfer of ownership of property without consideration

6. Change in the legal position of a party as a result of the contract

7. Act that has already been performed and thus cannot be consideration for a promise in the present

8. Enforcement of a promise to avoid injustice by denying to the promisor the defense of lack of consideration

9. Person who makes a promise

10. Person to whom a promise is made

11. Contractual situation in which a seller agrees to supply all the needs of a particular buyer

a. accord and satisfaction
b. composition with creditors
c. consideration
d. donee
e. donor
f. forbearance
g. gift
h. legal value
i. liquidated debt
j. nominal consideration
k. output contract
l. past consideration
m. promisee
n. promisor
o. promissory estoppel
p. requirements contract
q. release
r. statute of limitations

REVIEW LEGAL CONCEPTS

12. Give an example of an output contract associated with school.

13. Give an example of a requirements contract associated with school.

14. Think of three promises you've made to your family or friends today. Might they be enforceable in court? Why or why not?

WRITE ABOUT LEGAL CONCEPTS

15. Write an analysis of why a deputy sheriff should not be able to collect a standing reward for capturing a criminal.

16. **HOT DEBATE** Write a paragraph about whether or not the doctrine of promissory estoppel should be applied to the situation involving Maureen's promised graduation trip. Who would win if the doctrine were applied?

MAKE ACADEMIC CONNECTIONS

17. **PSYCHOLOGY** Contact a charity and ask how people are about fulfilling their pledges. Ask if the charity relies on the pledges or waits to get the money before budgeting expenditures and what steps, including lawsuits, the charity takes to enhance the receipt of the promised money.

THINK CRITICALLY ABOUT EVIDENCE

Study the situation, answer the questions, and then prepare arguments to support your answers.

18. Glenn contracted to provide the labor for an addition to Reid's home for $10,000. When Glenn was partially through, he realized that the job was more time-consuming than anticipated. Therefore he refused to continue until Reid promised to pay an additional $2,000. Reid did so. Is Glenn legally entitled to the extra $2,000?

19. Jericha promised to lease the Gnosters an unimproved store front in Jericha's newly constructed shopping center. The Gnosters, in reliance on Jericha's promise, installed the drywall, electrical and plumbing systems, and flooring in the storefront. When Jericha realized the value of the Gnosters' efforts, she changed her mind about entering into a lease with them. What will the court invoke to compel Jericha to lease the property as promised?

20. Mary received a diamond lapel pin from the estate of her maternal grandmother. It was appraised at $7,500. Because it did not fit in with her sports-oriented lifestyle, Mary sold the pin to a jeweler who told her, "The setting is old-fashioned, but the diamond is forever the same. I'll give you $3,500 cash." Later Mary wondered whether she received legally sufficient consideration. Did she? Can she rescind the transaction if she can prove that she received much less than the pin was worth?

21. When Bob began college at age 21, his godmother promised to give him $1,000 at the end of each of the following four years if he remained in school and refrained from smoking and/or chewing tobacco. She also promised a bonus of $1,000 if and when he received his bachelor of science degree. Are the godmother's promises legally enforceable? What are the ethical implications of her promises?

22. Marine Contractors Company, Inc., did various kinds of marine repair work within a 100-mile radius of Boston, Massachusetts. The company maintained a trust fund for the benefit of retired employees. The trust agreement provided that employees who resigned could withdraw their share of the fund after waiting five years. Hurley, general manager of the company, had accumulated $12,000 in the trust fund. When Hurley resigned, the president of Marine offered to pay his $12,000 immediately if he would agree not to compete with Marine directly or indirectly within 100 miles of Boston for five years. The parties made a written contract which set forth a "consideration of One Dollar and other good and valuable consideration." The contract also stated that the parties have "set their hands and seals" to the contract. Within four months after leaving Marine's employ, Hurley began doing repair work similar to that of Marine. Soon after, he organized his own company, hiring two of Marine's supervisors. Marine sued to stop Hurley from breaking his contract. Hurley defended with a plea of no consideration. Was there consideration, and was Hurley therefore bound to the agreement not to compete? Why or why not? (*Marine Contractors Company, Inc. v. Hurley*, 310 N.E.2d 915)

23. Under a written contract with the Robert Chuckrow Construction Company, Gough agreed to do the carpentry work on a commercial building. Gough was to supply all necessary labor, materials, and other requirements to complete the work "in accordance with the drawings and specifications." After Gough's employees had erected 38 trusses, 32 of them fell off the building. Gough did not claim that the plans or specifications were defective or that Chuckrow was to blame for the collapse. Gough was told by a Chuckrow representative to remove the fallen trusses and to rebuild and erect them. Gough also was told to submit an additional bill for this work. He completed the job and submitted the additional bill. However, Chuckrow paid only the amount promised under the original written contract. Therefore Gough sued Chuckrow for the extra costs of reconstruction. Is he entitled to the added money? (*Robert Chuckrow Construction Company v. Gough*, 159 S.E.2d 469, Ga.)

24. Hoffman and his wife owned a bakery in Wautoma, Wisconsin. Lukowitz, an agent for Red Owl Stores, Inc., represented to and agreed with Hoffman that Red Owl would erect a grocery store building for them in Chilton, Wisconsin, and stock it with merchandise. In return, the Hoffmans were to invest $18,000 and Hoffman was to operate the store as a Red Owl franchise. In reliance on Red Owl's assurances and advice, the Hoffmans sold their bakery, paid $1,000 down on a lot in Chilton, and rented a residence there. In negotiations over some seventeen months, Red Owl boosted the required investment to $24,100; then to $26,000; and finally to $34,000, which was to include $13,000 from Hoffman's father-in-law. Red Owl insisted the $13,000 must either be a gift or a loan that would be inferior in claim to all general creditors. Hoffman balked and sued for damages. Should the Hoffmans win? If so, on what grounds? (*Hoffman v. Red Owl Stores*, 133 N.W.2d 267, 26 Wis. 2d 683)

25. Petty, a general contractor, made a series of purchases from Field Lumber Company. Field's records showed a total price of $1,752.21. Petty admitted he owed $1,091.96, but denied liability for the difference of $660.25. He claimed the difference was a result of an unauthorized $292.60 purchase by an employee, plus related finance charges. Petty sent a check for $500 along with a letter stating that the check must be accepted in full settlement of the total claim or returned. Field phoned to say the lumber company required full payment, but nevertheless Field cashed the check and sued for the full balance it claimed was due. Can Field Lumber Company now recover the full amount? (*Field Lumber Company v. Petty*, 512 P.2d 764, Wash.)

26. Burt made two pledges of $50,000 each to the Mt. Sinai Hospital of Greater Miami. He made the pledges "in consideration of and to induce the subscriptions of others." Nothing was said as to how the funds were to be used. Mt. Sinai Hospital did not use his pledge to induce others to subscribe. Nor did the hospital undertake any work in reliance on Burt's pledge. Burt died in the following year. Up to the time of his death, he had paid $20,000 on his pledge. The executors of his estate now refuse to pay the balance. Must they do so? (*Mount Sinai Hospital of Greater Miami, Inc., v. Jordan*, 290 So. 2d 484, Fla.)

Sports & Entertainment Law
Downhill Racer Hits Buffaloes

JEREMY BLOOM V. NCAA 93 P.3D 621

BACKGROUND Jeremy Bloom was a competitive skiing star before he was recruited to play football for the University of Colorado's Buffaloes. Bloom had won various Olympic and professional World Cup skiing events. The stardom was not just in athletic events. He also appeared on MTV and had the opportunity to host a show on Nickelodeon. As a consequence, through an agent who had marketed Bloom as a multi-sport athlete, he had contracted to make paid endorsements of various ski equipment and to model for Tommy Hilfiger.

FACTS Concerned that his paid activities might prevent his eligibility to play football for the Buffaloes, Bloom and the University requested that the NCAA waive and/or modify its rules against student-athlete endorsement and media participation. In doing so they pointed out that the NCAA rules do allow endorsements, modeling, and media participation when necessary to support a professional skiing career. When

© DOUG PENSINGER/GETTY IMAGES

the NCAA refused these requests, Bloom dropped his endorsements, modeling commitments, and media affiliations for a football season. Afterwards, he brought suit against the NCAA alleging their rules in differentiating between sports were "arbitrary and capricious" and that the rules were improper and unconscionable restraints on trade. In his suit Bloom petitioned for relief in the form of a declaration by the court that the rules were inapplicable to his activities originating before his enrollment at the University or wholly unrelated to his prowess as a football player. He also requested that the NCAA and the University be enjoined from applying them against him.

THE LAW NCAA rules prohibit a student athlete from engaging in paid endorsement or entertainment endeavors. However, NCAA bylaw 12.1.2. allows "a professional athlete in one sport (to) represent a member institution in a different sport."

THE ISSUE Should Bloom be held eligible to play football as a Buffalo given the NCAA rules pertaining to the matter?

HOLDING The court declared that, as Bloom was represented by his agent as a multi-sport athlete, it would be impossible to determine whether he was being paid because of his ability and celebrity as a skier or a football player. Therefore, Bloom, although allowed by the court to appear on TV while participating in skiing, could not receive compensation for so doing or for any other modeling, endorsement, or media work and still retain his eligibility to play football for the University of Colorado.

PRACTICE JUDGING

1. Do you feel that the NCAA's rules against student athletes receiving compensation are fair?

2. What would have been your holding in this case? Support your decision.

Chapter 9
Legal Capacity to Contract

9-1 Contractual Capacity of Individuals and Organizations

9-2 Limits on the Rights of Those Without Capacity

HOT DEBATE

When John Eric turned 16 he received a new car for a birthday present. The same month, he responded to a magazine ad from a "club" offering his choice of 10 music CDs for only one penny. His response included his address and correct age. The ad noted that in return for this bargain, anyone who subscribed to it would have to buy one CD at full price for the next 6 months. The 10 CDs arrived and John Eric ignored any further letters from the club. The next month, however, he received a CD entitled "Bach's Bombs" and a bill for $23.99 from the club. John Eric ignored the bill and filed the CD in the back of his CD stack. Over the next several months, John Eric continued to receive a CD a month and notice of an ever-increasing amount owed to the club. Finally, when the bill reached over $200, John Eric talked to his dad about the situation. His dad, a lawyer, wrote a letter for John Eric telling the club that the sender was canceling the contract and would send back any CDs previously received if the club would pay for postage. John Eric signed the letter and sent it. The club didn't respond but the CDs and bills stopped coming.

WHERE DO YOU STAND?

1. Which party (or parties) has acted improperly in a legal sense? Explain.
2. Which party (or parties) has acted improperly in a moral sense? Discuss.

9-1 Contractual Capacity of Individuals and Organizations

GOALS

- Identify parties who lack contractual capacity
- Explain the role of capacity in organizations

KEY TERMS

contractual capacity

age of majority to contract

minor

minority

necessaries

emancipation

mental incapacity

intoxication

scope of authority

What Is Capacity?

WHAT'S YOUR VERDICT?
Alexis, 15, was a great movie fan. Right after the winter holidays, Alexis combined the money she received for Christmas with the money she earned baby sitting over the past year and went to a local electronics store to buy DVDs of her 50 most favorite films. At the store, a salesperson convinced her that she should purchase a new high definition DVD player first as it was "the way of the future." Excited at the picture clarity and resolution the new technology offered, Alexis spent almost all of her money on the player and two high definition DVDs to play on it. That evening at home, however, she realized that she had made a mistake in purchasing the player, as her television was not equipped to show the DVDs in the high definition mode.

Can Alexis get her money back?

Certain parties to contracts are assumed by the law to lack the maturity and experience to protect their self-interests in contractual negotiations. The law grants these parties special contractual protections designed to keep them from being cheated due to their lack of such contractual capacity. **Contractual capacity** is defined by the law to mean the ability to understand the consequences of a contract. Note that this definition does not require that a person understand the actual terms of the contract which may be written in technical legal terminology. Nor does the definition require that the person have merely the actual understanding of the terms whether expressed in legal terminology or not. Contractual capacity requires only that she or he possess the ability to understand them.

Parties who have special contractual rights due to a legally recognized lack of such capacity include minors, the intoxicated, and the mentally impaired. All of these parties are said to be *incapacitated*. For contract law purposes, minors are defined as individuals under the **age of majority to contract**. This is the age at which a person is entitled to the management of his or her own affairs. The age of majority is 18 in most states. In a few states, it is 19 or 21. A person who has not yet reached the age of majority is called a **minor**. **Minority**, or the state of being below the age of majority, ends the *day before* the birthday of the age set as the age of majority.

GLOBAL ISSUES

Current Age Limits

Around the world there are many differences in the ages youthful individuals are permitted to leave school, work, and be married. For example a child may leave school as early as 10 years of age in Bangladesh but no earlier than 16 in the United States and the Netherlands. There is no minimum age of employment in New Zealand, but it is set at 16 in Armenia. A 16-year-old Japanese woman may marry, but a male in India must wait until he turns 21.

Protections for Those Who Lack Capacity

The contracts of most parties who lack capacity are considered voidable. As a consequence, the primary protection granted to those who lack contractual capacity is disaffirmance. *Disaffirmance* in contract law means a refusal to be bound by a previous legal commitment. Generally, when a protected party disaffirms a contract, by law the protected party is to receive back whatever they have put into the contract. The other party may or may not get back their consideration. For example, assume a protected party bought a four-wheel ATV from a dealership and then wrecked it. He or she could disaffirm the contract and recover any payments made. The dealership would only be able to recover the damaged ATV. In *What's Your Verdict?* Alexis could disaffirm her contract, return the player and the DVDs, and receive back the money she paid for them.

The problem with giving certain parties, especially minors, the legal ability to disaffirm a contract and get back whatever they had given to the other party is that no one will want to contract with them. As a consequence, another protection was afforded those who lack capacity. It applies when protected parties purchase things classified as **necessaries**—things needed to maintain life—typically food, clothing, and shelter.

When the protected, or special, parties contract for such items they must at least pay a reasonable value for the necessaries even if they disaffirm the actual purchase contract. For example, if a minor purchased a fur coat for $5,000, she could disaffirm the contract. However she would still be

NETBookmark

Click on the link for Chapter 9 on school .cengage.com/blaw/lawxtra to access the web site of the National Conference of State Legislatures. Locate your state in the chart entitled "Termination of Child Support and Support Beyond Majority." Write down the age in your state at which parents can legally terminate support. Then write the description of parents' duty to provide post-majority support in your state. Compare your state's treatment with that in surrounding states. Write a paragraph describing any major differences you notice among the states, citing specific examples.

school.cengage.com/blaw/lawxtra

required to pay the cost of a good cloth coat (say $200, a reasonable price), for the fur if she chose to keep it. This price may be seemingly unfair to the seller. However, in the eyes of the law, receiving only $200 for the fur serves as punishment for taking advantage of minors in contractual dealings.

© DIGITAL VISION

If this minor decides to purchase this bottle of expensive perfume, could she later disaffirm the contract and get back the money she paid for it? Or, upon disaffirmance, would she still have to pay a reasonable price for it? Explain your answer.

LAW BRIEF

You may be surprised to learn that in addition to the normal list of food, clothing, and shelter considered necessaries in most states, the state of California tacks on cars and televisions. Cell phones are not considered necessaries anywhere as yet.

Minors

Minors' contracts are considered voidable, and they may disaffirm contracts during their minority. They also may disaffirm for a reasonable length of time after achieving their majority.

After the age of majority, the power to disaffirm is immediately cut off if the person ratifies the contract. Ratification is acting toward the contract as though one intends to be bound by it. Note that ratification can never occur before the age of majority.

Minors also may find themselves bound to their contracts if they are emancipated. **Emancipation** is the severing of the child-parent relationship. It ends the duty of the parent to support a child and the duty of the child to obey the parent. A minor naturally becomes emancipated upon reaching the age of majority. However, a minor also may be emancipated before that time.

Early emancipation can occur formally or informally. Formal emancipation occurs when a court decrees the minor emancipated. Informal emancipation arises from the conduct of the minor and the parent. The following are evidence of informal emancipation:

1. The parent and minor agree that the parent will cease support.

2. The minor marries.

3. The minor moves out of the family home.

4. The minor becomes a member of the armed forces.

5. The minor gives birth.

6. The minor undertakes full-time employment.

States differ greatly in their treatment of emancipated minors. Some give them full contractual capacity and others don't. If you become emancipated, you may lose your capacity protection.

Those Mentally Incapacitated

Mental incapacity is much less precisely defined than minority. Under contract law mental incapacity means that a person lacks the ability to understand the consequences of his or her contracts. Thus people with severe mental illness, severe mental retardation, or severe senility lack capacity.

If a judge rules that a person is permanently insane, then this person has a complete lack of capacity. All contracts executed by this person are void. However, the rules surrounding necessaries are applied to an insane person's purchases of food, clothing, and shelter. If the judge rules that a person was insane when the contract was made but the condition was only temporary, the contract is considered voidable.

The Intoxicated

Intoxication can arise from using alcohol in forms such as beer or vodka, from using drugs such as marijuana or crack cocaine, or inhaling products such as glue or aerosols. If a person's degree of

IN THIS CASE Emily was 88 years old when she contracted to sell her family home to her nurse, Gail, for about 15 percent of its value. At the time, she was suffering from advanced Alzheimer's disease and didn't understand the consequences of the transaction. Two months later Emily died. Her will provided for all her property to be split equally among her four children. Emily's children sued to have the deed set aside because Emily lacked the mental capacity to contract. As Emily did not understand the consequences when she deeded the home to Gail, the contract was voided.

A Question of ETHICS

Perkins is a regional sales manager for an automobile manufacturer. She is responsible for visiting 15 car dealerships in one state. Perkins' job is to "push" certain models at different times to compensate for oversupply from the manufacturer. As part of her job, she often takes the owner and salespeople of a dealership to lunch. Over lunch, Perkins' guests often order several drinks. After these lunches, Perkins then gets down to business. She often does not know if her guests are drunk or not when she begins her pitch. Does Perkins have an ethical obligation to determine whether the dealers have had too much to drink? Do the owners have an ethical obligation to refrain from drinking at lunch, knowing that they will be asked to commit to deals after lunch?

intoxication is high enough, the law holds she or he loses the capacity to contract. To determine if this state has been reached, the courts often refer to the same definition of incapacity as for the mentally impaired—that is, does the person have the ability to understand the consequences of his or her contracts. However, most courts are reluctant to consider a temporarily intoxicated party's contracts voidable. This would allow disaffirmance for intoxication even though it may injure an innocent party. Therefore courts typically allow disaffirmance only for those who are so temporarily intoxicated that they do not even know they are contracting. This stricter standard is used because intoxication is a voluntary act. If, in a court proceeding, a judge holds that a person is in a permanent state of alcoholism (a status that in most states is legally termed an "habitual drunkard"), that person's contracts are considered void. In addition, giving or selling intoxicating substances including alcohol to such an habitual drunkard is a misdemeanor in most states.

CHECKPOINT What three classifications of individuals lack contractual capacity?

This photo shows the manager (middle), a bagger (left), and a sales clerk (right) who work for a supermarket. Which of these employees do you think has the broadest scope of authority, and why?

© DIGITAL VISION

Who Has Contractual Capacity in Organizations?

WHAT'S YOUR VERDICT? Alicia was a wholesaler of flowers. Her friend, Caryn, worked for a grocery store as a checker. One day Alicia stopped by during Caryn's break and asked if she could sell her flowers through that store. Caryn said yes and signed a contract to purchase 10 dozen roses for the store. When Alicia tried to deliver the roses, they were refused by the store and Alicia sued.

Is the store bound by Caryn's contract?

Some people who work for businesses or other types of organizations have the capacity to bind the organizations to contracts. If someone has this capacity, it is said to be within his or her **scope of authority**, or within the range of contractual acts the organization has authorized him or her to be responsible for. Capacity to contract can be created when the employer tells an employee that they are authorized to bind the organization.

Capacity also can be created when the organization leads others to believe that a person has certain authority. For example a person who holds the title of purchasing agent in an organization is assumed to have the authority to make purchases in its behalf. As another example, a person selling shoes probably could not bind the shoe store to a contract for the lease of a new store in a shopping center. The salesperson has capacity to sell the shoes, but doesn't have the capacity to contract for the store in any other way. It would be within the shoe store owner's scope of authority to contract for the lease.

When doing business with organizations, it is important to ensure that the person signing the contract has the scope of authority to bind the organization. People acting outside the scope of their authority generally are personally liable when the organization isn't. In *What's Your Verdict?* the store is not bound by the contract but Caryn may be liable to Alicia for the lost profit on the sale of the roses.

CHECKPOINT In what two ways is capacity to contract on behalf of an organization created?

Although in mid-2004, the U.S. Supreme Court for the second time decided to put on hold the enforcement of the Child Online Protection Act of 1988, enforcement of the Act is once again being pursued by the U.S. Department of Justice. In its 2004 decision, the Court in its majority opinion stood behind First Amendment free-speech advocates who had maintained that there were less-restrictive means of preventing children's access to pornography on the web. The opinion by Justice Kennedy stated: "[c]ontent-based prohibitions, enforced by severe criminal penalties, have the constant potential to be a repressive force in the lives and thoughts of a free people. To guard against that threat, the Constitution demands that content-based restrictions on speech be presumed invalid and that the government bear the burden of showing their constitutionality." By content-based prohibitions, Justice Kennedy was pointing to the part of the law that made it a criminal act to knowingly and for commercial purposes make any material that is "harmful to minors" accessible to them. Justice Kennedy also noted that such a pervasive and ambiguous law would chill legitimate speech. A lawyer for the American Civil Liberties Union who agreed with the Court in putting enforcement of the Act on hold stated: "The Court has made it safe for artists, sex educators and Web publishers to communicate with adults about sexuality without risking jail time."

THINK ABOUT IT

Do you think the court struck the right balance between free speech and the danger of children accessing pornography on the Internet? Why or why not? Can you propose any other solutions to the problem?

9-1 Assessment

THINK ABOUT LEGAL CONCEPTS

1. The contracts of all those who lack capacity are void. **True or False?**

2. A temporarily intoxicated person who did not even know she was entering into a contract of marriage could avoid the contract. **True or False?**

3. Which of the following contracts are for necessaries? (a) a purchase of a high definition television (b) the purchase of groceries at a market (c) the rental of a truck for moving (d) all of the above are necessaries

4. What is the most common age of majority? (a) 21 (b) 18 (c) 16 (d) 9

5. The three most common necessaries are food, education, and shelter. **True or False?**

6. If a person acts within his or her scope of authority in entering into a contract for an organization, he or she is not personally liable for any losses that might occur. **True or False?**

THINK CRITICALLY ABOUT EVIDENCE

Study the situation, answer the questions, and then prepare arguments to support your answers.

7. Clare was age 17, a minor in her state, when she bought a week's worth of groceries at a local supermarket. Later she discovered she spent too much money and was going to be over her weekly budget. So she took the groceries back and asked for her money back. If she sues, will she get her money back?

8. Tanya bought a car two weeks before her 18th birthday. After making her fifth monthly payment, she decided the car was beyond her ability to afford and tried to avoid the contract on the basis that she had been a minor when she entered into it. Was she able to do so?

9-2 Limits on the Rights of Those Without Capacity

GOALS

- Recognize the time frame during which a contract can be disaffirmed
- Identify contracts that cannot be disaffirmed
- Discuss the effects of misrepresentation of age on contractual responsibilities

KEY TERMS

disaffirmance

ratification

When Can Disaffirmance Occur and What Must Be Done at That Time?

WHAT'S YOUR VERDICT?

While still a minor, Beach bought a stereo system on credit from McReam's Electronic Cloud for $500. Beach paid $100 down and promised to pay $50 a month on the unpaid balance until the debt was paid. After making four payments, two of which were made after he reached the age of majority, Beach decided to disaffirm the contract and return the equipment.

Can Beach do so?

As mentioned previously, in contract law, **disaffirmance** means a refusal to be bound by a previous legal commitment. Generally, a person lacking contractual capacity can disaffirm a contract for necessaries or goods or services that are not necessaries

1. any time while still under the incapacity, or
2. within a reasonable time after attaining capacity.

After attaining capacity, a person may ratify the contract made while under an incapacity. **Ratification** is action by the party indicating intent to be bound by the contract. For a minor, ratification must occur after achieving majority. Ratification may consist of either of the following:

1. giving a new promise to perform as agreed, or
2. any act (such as making payments to the seller) that clearly indicates the party's intention to be bound.

In *What's Your Verdict?* Beach ratified the contract by making payments after reaching majority. These actions cut off his power to disaffirm. Once ratification occurs, it may not be withdrawn.

What Must Be Done Upon Disaffirmance

In all states, when a minor disaffirms, anything of value the minor received and still has must be returned. The minor is then entitled to get back everything that was given to the other party.

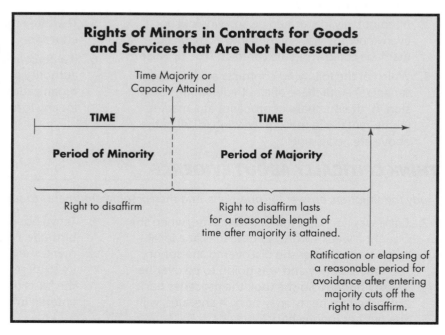

Rights of Minors in Contracts for Goods and Services that Are Not Necessaries

Time Majority or Capacity Attained

TIME — TIME

Period of Minority — Period of Majority

Right to disaffirm

Right to disaffirm lasts for a reasonable length of time after majority is attained.

Ratification or elapsing of a reasonable period for avoidance after entering majority cuts off the right to disaffirm.

LOSS OF VALUE In most states, if minors are unable to return exactly what was received under the contract, they can still get back everything they gave. This is true even if a minor returns used or damaged goods. It is also true even if a minor returns nothing because the goods have been lost, consumed, or destroyed.

In some states, however, a minor must return everything received in a condition as good as it was when it was received. If this cannot be done, the minor must pay the difference in value, or deduct the difference from the amount to be refunded.

OBLIGATIONS OF PARTY WITH CAPACITY Not only can the party lacking capacity generally disaffirm contracts for goods and services that are not necessaries, but, should he or she choose to, the party lacking capacity can enforce them against the party with capacity. On the other hand, generally the party with capacity can neither enforce against a party lacking capacity nor avoid on the basis of the other party's lack of capacity all or any part of a contract for goods or services that are not necessaries.

IN THIS CASE Lamon, a minor, bought a diamond engagement ring and a necklace for his fiancée, Morgan. He paid for the items in weekly installments of $10. One day while still a minor, he and Morgan quarreled. Morgan returned the ring to Lamon but refused to part with the necklace.

Morgan was legally entitled to keep the necklace because it was an ordinary gift not connected with the proposed marriage. Lamon could return the ring to the jeweler and demand a refund of the money he had paid for both pieces of jewelry. Lamon is entitled to the money he had paid on the ring. In most states, he is even entitled to what he had paid on the necklace. That is because he returned everything that was still in his possession. In some states, however, a minor must return everything received in a condition as good as it was when it was received. If this cannot be done, the minor must pay the difference in value, or deduct the difference from the amount to be refunded. In these states, Lamon could be unable to recover the price of the necklace.

CHECKPOINT When can a person who lacks contractual capacity disaffirm a contract?

Contracts That Cannot Be Disaffirmed

WHAT'S YOUR VERDICT? Upon graduation from high school, Robinson, age 17, began a business doing electrical work. He bought $375 in tools from Muller. The venture was a disappointing failure. Discouraged after a month, Robinson asked Muller to take back the tools and to return his $375 payment.

Must Muller do so?

Some contracts of minors for goods or services that are not necessaries cannot be disaffirmed. These exceptions to the general rule vary considerably from state to state. The statutes and cases of your state are the only definitive source on this topic. The most common examples follow.

COURT-APPROVED CONTRACTS In all states, minors cannot void any contracts approved for them by a court. For example, minors who are employed as actors or actresses or as professionals in sports usually have their contracts approved by a court. Once approved, these contracts may not be disaffirmed.

MAJOR COMMITMENTS In all states, contracts to enlist in the armed services and contracts for educational loans cannot be disaffirmed. Similarly, marriage contracts of minors cannot be disaffirmed.

BANKING CONTRACTS In most states, minors are permitted to make deposits in banks and in savings and loan associations. Most states also permit minors to make withdrawals as if they were adults, without any right to disaffirm these transactions.

INSURANCE CONTRACTS More than one-half of the states provide that minors who are over a certain age may not disaffirm certain contracts of life insurance.

WORK-RELATED CONTRACTS In most states, minors who engage in a business or trade cannot disaffirm agreements involving their businesses. In *What's Your Verdict?* Muller would not have to comply with Robinson's demands in such states as Robinson would not be able to avoid the purchase contract made for his business.

SALE OF REALTY In some states, a minor who owns real property and sells it or borrows money against it cannot disaffirm until after achieving majority.

APARTMENT RENTAL In a few states, the lease of an apartment cannot be disaffirmed even if the apartment is not a necessary.

> **CHECKPOINT** What contracts entered into by minors cannot be disaffirmed in any of the 50 states?

Contractual Effect of Misrepresenting Age

WHAT'S YOUR VERDICT? Ron, a mature-looking minor, lied about his age when he bought an extensive wardrobe of clothing from the Casuals Shop. Ron showed his older brother's driver's license as identification. He also used his brother's name on the installment contract. By October, Ron had paid $325 on the $785 contract. He then became bored with the wardrobe and returned it to the store and demanded the return of all payments.

Must the store return his money?

Minors have been known to misrepresent their ages. In most states, minors who lie about their age may nevertheless disaffirm their contracts. However, in these states, a minor who gives a false age may be held liable for the tort of false representation.

Minors are liable for their torts and delinquent or criminal conduct growing out of a contractual transaction, although typically they still have the right to disaffirm their contracts. Thus, the other party to the contract may collect from a minor any damages suffered because of the minor's fraud even though the minor may be able to disaffirm the contract.

In *What's Your Verdict?* Ron is within his rights as a minor in disaffirming the contract. However, he also committed the tort of fraud. Therefore in most states, the Casuals Shop probably could hold back from the refund an amount of money sufficient to cover the decrease in value of the wardrobe as returned. Or the store could hold back the full amount if nothing was returned. Ron could be held liable in damages under tort law for deceiving the seller. These damages could exceed the price of the goods he lied to get.

> **CHECKPOINT** If minors lie about their age, what happens in most states with regard to their ability to disaffirm contracts for goods and services that are not necessaries?

© GETTY IMAGES/PHOTODISC

Why do you think that most states permit minors to make deposits and withdrawals to their bank accounts without the right to disaffirm these transactions?

LEGAL *Research*

Investigate the effect in your state of using fake identification in contracts to purchase alcohol or tobacco, or for entering age-restricted areas. Summarize your findings in a paragraph. Note especially the effect on the ability to rescind the contract.

9-2 Assessment

school.cengage.com/blaw/lawxtra

THINK ABOUT LEGAL CONCEPTS

1. A disaffirmed contract for a necessary may still be enforced against a minor for a reasonable value. **True or False?**

2. A contract for goods or services that are not necessaries entered into while a minor can be disaffirmed (a) anytime (b) anytime after achieving majority (c) anytime during minority (d) within a reasonable time after achieving majority (e) both c and d

3. Generally, a minor who lies to appear in his or her majority loses the right to disaffirm a contract that might result. **True or False?**

4. Which of the following contracts can a minor disaffirm in most states? (a) bank depository contracts (b) enlistment contracts in the armed services (c) gambling contracts (d) none of the above can be disaffirmed by a minor

THINK CRITICALLY ABOUT EVIDENCE

Study the situation, answer the questions, and then prepare arguments to support your answers.

5. Richard bought car insurance while he was 16. He had a perfect driving record until he reached the age of majority for contracting, 18 in his state. The day after his birthday, Richard disaffirmed the insurance contract and asked for the return of his payments. In most states would he be legally entitled to the money?

6. Linda subscribed to a "Book of the Month" program on her sixteenth birthday. She received monthly books from the publisher until her eighteenth birthday. She continued receiving books for another six months, and then attempted to disaffirm. Will she succeed?

7. In Juan's state, the age of majority for contracting is 21. Three weeks after his eighteenth birthday, Juan joined the Marine Corps. After two weeks of boot camp, he decided he didn't like the lifestyle. He told the Marines he was disaffirming his contract to join. Can he do so?

8. Beverly was 14 when she bought a used motorcycle that wouldn't run. Beverly made repairs and got it going. She rode it illegally for more than six months. Then a leak developed in a gas line and the bike caught fire. It was a total loss. Beverly returned the burned-out motorcycle to the seller and asked for all her money back. Will she succeed?

Chapter 9 Assessment

CONCEPTS IN BRIEF

9-1 Contractual Capacity of Individuals and Organizations

1. Generally, the contracts of individuals lacking contractual capacity are voidable and can be disaffirmed by the incapacitated party. Upon so doing they are to receive back what they put into the bargain and must return what they received from it, if possible.

2. Necessaries are those things needed to sustain life. In most states, necessaries are limited to food, clothing, and shelter. Even after disaffirming a contract for these items, a party without capacity is liable for their reasonable value.

3. Minors are those under the age of majority.

4. If a court has held that an individual is permanently insane or is permanently addicted to alcohol, that person's contracts are void. However, the doctrine of necessaries will apply where appropriate.

5. The contractual party having capacity has no right to disaffirm the contract just because the party lacking capacity has the right to do so.

6. Employees bind their employers to contracts they execute on their behalf if they are acting within their actual or apparent scope of authority.

9-2 Limits on the Rights of Those Without Capacity

7. Generally, those lacking contractual capacity can only disaffirm contracts during the time of their incapacity and for a reasonable time thereafter.

8. Ratification of a contract cannot occur before capacity is attained or recovered.

9. Ratification may consist of either giving a new promise to perform as agreed, or any act (such as making payments to the seller) that clearly indicates the previously incapacitated party's intention to be bound.

10. In many states certain types of contracts, such as insurance and banking contracts, cannot be disaffirmed.

11. Generally, misrepresentation of age does not affect the right to disaffirm but may expose a minor to a subsequent lawsuit for tortious conduct.

YOUR LEGAL VOCABULARY

Match each statement with the term that it best defines. Some terms may not be used.

1. Severing of the parent-child relationship
2. Within the range of authorized contractual acts
3. Goods and services needed to sustain life
4. State of being unable to understand the consequences of a contract because of alcohol or drugs
5. Act after regaining capacity indicating an intent to be bound by the contract
6. Ability to understand that a contract is being made and the consequences thereof
7. Giving back what you have received under a contract and requesting the return of what you gave
8. Period of time when a young person lacks full contractual capacity
9. The inability to contract due to severe mental illness, retardation, or senility
10. Either 18, 19, or 21 in most states
11. One who has not yet reached the age of majority

a. **age of majority to contract**
b. **contractual capacity**
c. **disaffirmance**
d. **emancipation**
e. **intoxication**
f. **mental incapacity**
g. **minor**
h. **minority**
i. **necessaries**
j. **ratification**
k. **scope of authority**

REVIEW LEGAL CONCEPTS

12. Assume you were going to buy a two-year-old car at a bargain price from a woman who was 86 years old. Explain the steps you would take to create evidence that she has mental capacity.

13. Assume you were going to buy a two-year-old car at a bargain price from a man with alcohol on his breath. Explain the steps you would take to create evidence that he has capacity.

14. Identify three things you've bought recently that are necessaries and three things that are not.

15. If any of the three purchases in exercise 14 can be ratified, describe the exact conduct you might engage in after achieving majority to constitute ratification.

WRITE ABOUT LEGAL CONCEPTS

16. Write a one-paragraph summary of the law of capacity as it applies to minors.

17. Write a one-paragraph summary of the law of capacity as it applies to the intoxicated.

18. Write a one-paragraph description of what you would do to protect your legal interests if dealing with a 90-year-old man who wanted to rent an apartment to you.

19. **HOT DEBATE** John Eric kept a copy of the letter his father wrote. Thereafter, he subscribed to similar offers from several other clubs, and then cancelled the contracts with the letter. All of the other clubs responded in the same manner as the first. He amassed a large CD collection at almost no cost to himself. Should John Eric still be under the protection of the law in these later contractual circumstances?

THINK CRITICALLY ABOUT EVIDENCE

Study the situation, answer the questions, and then prepare arguments to support your answers.

20. A month after he turned 16, Chris, a resident of Missouri, answered a classified newpaper ad and, after prolonged negotiations, bought a used car from Dowdy. Chris spent $8,500 of the $10,000 in cash given to him by his father on his birthday on the purchase. Six months after buying the car, the crankshaft in the engine broke. The cost of a new engine would have been about $3,200 so Chris decided to disaffirm the contract to purchase the car. Legally, can he do so?

21. On her sixteenth birthday, Laurisa bought a used computer from Stuart for $100 cash. Laurisa is from a wealthy family and receives an allowance of $200 a week. Six months after buying the computer, the hard drive crashed so Laurisa decided to disaffirm. Legally, can she?

22. June stopped by a bar on the way home from work and drank three gin and tonics. Then she bought a six-pack of beer at the local grocery store and drank three cans before her husband came home. June and her husband then began drinking whiskey and water and each finished two drinks. A salesperson from Metropolitan Life Insurance came over and sold June a life insurance policy that cost $3,000 per year. Is there evidence indicating that June may be able to disaffirm?

23. Larson was 69 years old and trying to sell his home. He had it appraised, and the estimated value was $300,000. He listed the home with a local real estate broker for $330,000. When Perry offered him $305,000 he counteroffered at $320,000. When Perry balked at the price, he lowered his offer to $315,000 and she accepted. Is there evidence that Larson possesses the mental capacity to contract?

MAKE ACADEMIC CONNECTIONS

24. **MARKETING** Interview people who work in telemarketing, Internet sales, banking, insurance, and like industries to see how they determine if the parties they are dealing with have capacity to contract. Evaluate the methods and report to the class on those you consider effective and those that you consider ineffective. State why.

25. Sixteen-year-old Johnny Hays went to Quality Motors, Inc., in Tennessee, to buy a car. When a salesperson asked about his age, Johnny sidestepped the question. The salesperson refused to sell except to an adult. Hays left and returned shortly with a companion of 23, whom he had just met. The salesperson then sold Hays the car. The bill of sale was made out to the companion who, with the help of the salesperson, later transferred the title to Hays. When Hays' father, Dr. D. J. Hays, discovered the sale, he called Quality Motors and asked them to take the car back. The company refused. Dr. Hays tried to return the car on three more occasions. Finally, the car was put into storage. Johnny Hays found the keys to the car and took it on a trip, damaging it in two accidents. As a result, the car was not in running condition at the time of the trial. Can Johnny disaffirm? Who will bear the loss due to the damage? (*Masterson v. Sine,* 216 Ark. 264)

26. W. O. Lucy and J. C. Lucy, the plaintiffs, sued A. H. Zehmer and Ida Zehmer, the defendants, to force the Zehmers to transfer the title to the Ferguson Farm to the Lucys for $50,000. The Lucys alleged that the Zehmers had agreed to do so one night when Mr. Lucy had stopped in to visit the Zehmers in the combination restaurant, filling station, and motor court they operated. While there, Lucy tried to buy the Ferguson Farm just as he had tried many times before. This time he tried a new approach. Lucy said to Zehmer, "I bet you wouldn't take $50,000 for that place." Zehmer replied, "Yes, I would too; you wouldn't give fifty." Throughout the evening, the conversation returned to the sale of the Ferguson Farm for $50,000. At the same time, the parties continued to drink whiskey and engage in light conversation. Eventually Lucy got Zehmer to write up an agreement to the effect that Zehmer would sell to Lucy the Ferguson Farm for $50,000 complete. Later, Lucy sued Zehmer to go through with the sale. Zehmer argued that he had been drunk and that the offer had been made in jest and hence was unenforceable. What evidence supports the conclusion that Zehmer was intoxicated? What evidence supports the conclusion that Zehmer was not intoxicated? Is Zehmer bound? (*Lucy v. Zehmer,* 196 Va. 493)

27. Webster Street Partnership owned real estate in Omaha, Nebraska. It leased an apartment to Matthew Sheridan and Pat Wilwerding for one year at a rental of $250 per month. Although Webster Street did not know this, both Sheridan and Wilwerding were younger than the age of majority when the lease was signed. Both minors had moved out of their homes voluntarily and were free to return there at any time. Sheridan and Wilwerding paid $150 as a security deposit. They paid for two months, for a total of $500, then failed to pay for the next month on time. Webster Street notified them that they would be required to move out unless they paid immediately. Unable to pay rent, Sheridan and Wilwerding moved out of the apartment. Webster Street later demanded that they pay the expenses it incurred in attempting to re-rent the property and assorted damages and fees, amounting to $630.94. Sheridan and Wilwerding refused on the ground of minority to pay any of the amount demanded. Further, they demanded the return of their security deposit. Webster Street then sued. Is the apartment a necessary? Can Sheridan and Wilwerding disaffirm? (*Webster Street Partnership v. Sheridan,* 368 N.W. 2d 439, Neb.)

28. Kevin Green was 16 years old when he purchased a 1979 Camaro for $4,642.50 from Star Chevrolet. Shortly after the purchase, the car blew a head gasket and couldn't be driven. Thereafter Kevin informed Star that he was disaffirming the contract. He offered to return the car, but Star would not accept it unless it was repaired. In January 1982 Kevin brought suit for the purchase price. The car was not used for four or five months until Kevin repaired the blown head gasket himself. In June 1982 the car was in an accident which substantially reduced its value. In an insurance settlement arising out of the accident, Kevin received $1,500 as a salvage payment for the Camaro. He used the salvage money to buy another car. Star then sued Green. What resulted? (*Star Chevrolet v. Green,* 473 So. 2d 157, Miss.)

Sports & Entertainment Law

Home and Really Alone

COOGAN V. BERNSTEIN
CAL. SUPERIOR CT. NO. C426945

BACKGROUND In 1997, Macaulay Culkin, a minor and most notably the star of the *Home Alone* movies, sued to remove his finances from the control of his parents. In so doing, he joined the ranks of other child stars of the entertainment and sports worlds who have had to resort to the courts to protect or attempt to recover from their parents the monies they earned as children. Jackie Coogan, the first true child star of the movie industry, filed the landmark case in this area back in the 1930s.

FACTS Coogan, best known to current entertainment fans as Uncle Fester in the constantly rerun *Addams Family* television series, was a natural mimic. He was discovered in vaudeville at a young age by Charlie Chaplin. With Chaplin's support, Coogan initially gained fame while in his minority in many highly profitable silent and sound films of the 1920s and 1930s. He also was the first child star to be heavily merchandised with food

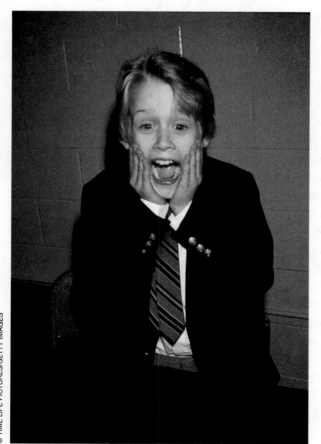

products, toys, figurines, and stationery all bearing his image or name. When he reached his majority, however, he discovered that most of his earnings were gone. Shortly thereafter he sued his mother and stepfather for the more than $4 million of those earnings they allegedly squandered.

THE LAW At the time of the lawsuit, the law regarding minors' earnings in the State of California was the same as it had always been under the common law and as it is today in the overwhelming majority of our states: all of a child's earnings belonged to his or her parents to do with as they wanted.

THE ISSUE Are the parents responsible to a child for the resources generated by the child during her or his minority?

HOLDING The court upheld the California Law and Coogan was rendered basically penniless at 18. However, shortly after the lawsuit, the negative publicity given the result in the case caused the California legislature to enact the "Coogan Law." This law required, in cases placed under a court's jurisdiction, parents to set aside a minimum of 15 percent of a child star's earnings for his or her use upon attaining majority. (Unfortunately, few child stars took their financial matters before the courts.) Other states with large entertainment industries, New York in particular, also passed statutes to remedy the problem. New York's statute required up to 50 percent of a minor's earnings to be set aside in contracts referred to the courts for administration.

PRACTICE JUDGING

1. Do you think it is fair that, in the states applying the common law rule (approximately 45 of the 50), the parents have complete and total claim to the earnings of their minor children? Why or why not?

2. What alternative rule(s) can you propose? Justify your proposal.

Chapter 10
Legal Purpose and Proper Form

10-1 Illegal Agreements
10-2 The Statute of Frauds

HOT DEBATE

"The winner is number 3913. Who's won this incredible classic? Who's got the winning ticket?" The voice echoed throughout the gym. Sanford Davis looked around. A man was running toward the stage from the other side of the floor. It was Brandon Johnson, the son of Michael Johnson. Michael Johnson was the owner of Johnson's Exotic Car Shop and the donor of the '67 Mustang that was the prize in the lottery. Odd, thought Sanford, that out of more than 2,000 purchasers of the $25 tickets, the son of the man who had donated the car had won it. Of course, buying new uniforms for the high school's Marching Terrapins band was a great cause. Still, it was too much of a coincidence. Sanford pushed his way through the crowd. Near the stage he found the band director carrying a box with the receipts in it. "I want my money back," said Sanford, "or I'll swear out a criminal complaint against everybody involved in this for holding an illegal lottery." Sanford knew that the state statute on gambling only allowed lotteries run by the state and bingo games run by licensed charitable organizations. The band director replied that it had been an honest lottery for a good cause and that she would not refund Sanford's money. Sanford immediately knew what he had to do. The next afternoon, after a lengthy session with Sanford, the local prosecutor called the school and said she would bring felony gambling charges against the band director and other school officials if the receipts were not refunded to the ticket purchasers.

WHERE DO YOU STAND?

1. Were Sanford's actions ethical?
2. Would a statute that allowed "honest lotteries for a good cause" be acceptable? Why or why not?

10-1 Illegal Agreements

GOALS

■ Identify various forms of unenforceable illegal agreements

■ Specify agreements that, although illegal, the courts will enforce

KEY TERMS

lottery

wager

compounding a crime

competency license

revenue license

price fixing

bid rigging

unconscionability

Which Agreements Are Illegal?

WHAT'S YOUR VERDICT? Razer agreed with several published articles that criticized laws prohibiting the production, possession, and use of marijuana. The authors of the articles claimed such legislation was unrealistic and often violated civil rights. Razer agreed so heartily that he bought several dozen marijuana plants from a friend, Sara. Then he rented a patch of isolated land and persuaded the owner, Tom, to accept a share of the proceeds from the sale of the anticipated crop as rent. After harvesting the first crop, Razer sold most of the product to a local drug dealer for $7,500.

Were any of Razer's agreements illegal?

Agreements that involve contracting for an illegal act generally are void and unenforceable. For example, almost any agreement to commit a felony (a serious crime) will be an illegal agreement. In *What's Your Verdict?* all of Razer's agreements were criminal and therefore void and unenforceable in court. Examples of the most frequently prosecuted types of illegal contracts are discussed next.

Illegal Lotteries

Most states either forbid or regulate gambling. Usually they have statutes which make gambling agreements, typically termed illegal lotteries, void. A **lottery** has three elements: a *prize* (something of value for one or more winners), *chance* (the winner determined solely by luck), and *consideration* (a payment is required to participate). A **wager**, one of the most common forms of gambling, is a bet on the uncertain outcome of an event, such as a football game.

Economic Impact

NATIVE AMERICANS AND TRIBAL GAMING

In many states that permit gambling or "gaming," casinos are being operated by Native American tribes. The tribes, recognized as "sovereign nations," depend on the revenue from the casinos as an important part of their tribal economy. Tribal gaming has stimulated community growth and economic development within many once-impoverished Native American nations. The large-scale tribal gaming operations began in the early 1980s, about the same time as the emergence of lotteries in many states. Since then, several court cases have shaped the relationship between the sovereign nations' gaming operations and the states. In 1987 in *California v. Cabazon* the Supreme Court upheld the tribes' rights as sovereign nations to conduct gaming on Native American lands. They may conduct the gaming free of state control if similar gaming is permitted outside the reservation. The Indian Gaming Regulatory Act, passed by Congress in 1988, affirms the tribes' right to conduct gaming on their lands.

THINK CRITICALLY

What is your opinion of Native American tribes raising revenue through casino gambling?

Most states have legalized various forms of gambling under regulated conditions:

- *Casinos*—where most forms of traditional gaming are permitted such as keno, blackjack, roulette and the like
- *Pari-mutuel betting*—a form of betting in which those who bet on the winner of a horse race share the total prize pool
- *State-run lotteries*—often with millions in the jackpot to be split between the winner(s) and state educational institutions
- *Bingo games and pull-tab betting*—permitted in many states when conducted by licensed institutions for financing charitable, religious, or educational projects.

Agreements to Pay Usurious Interest

Almost all states provide that, with certain exceptions, lenders of money may not charge more than a specified maximum rate of interest. Generally, the penalties specified by these statutes vary. In some states, the lender cannot collect some or all of the interest. However, the borrower usually must repay the principal. The maximum interest rate varies among the states, and 18 percent is a common maximum. Lending money at a rate higher than the state's maximum allowable rate is *usury*. Note, however, that, because of a U.S. Supreme Court decision, most state laws today allow higher interest rates to be charged on relatively small "payday" loans (under $1,500 in most states) with two week or monthly pay backs. The annualized interest rates on such cash-advance or paycheck loans generally are around 250 percent. Similarly, most pawn shops collect an annualized interest rate close to that on their secured loans. In comparison, a $100 overdraft at the bank with a $25 insufficient funds charge produces an annualized interest rate of around 300 percent.

Sometimes a person borrows money for which interest will be charged but no exact rate is stated. In such a case, the rate to be paid is the *legal rate of interest,* which is specified by state statute. In about one-half of the states, this rate is 7 percent or less per year. In most of the other states, the legal rate ranges between 8 and 12 percent.

Agreements Involving Illegal Discrimination

Some agreements are unenforceable because they violate anti-discrimination statutes. For example, an agreement between a motel chain and a local manager to not accept guests of a particular race or national origin would be unenforceable because it violates the federal Civil Rights Act of 1964.

Agreements also may be illegal as violations of the Constitution. For example, a contract between a residential subdivision developer and a home buyer providing that the buyer would not sell to a member of a particular race would be unenforceable because it violates the Fourteenth Amendment to the Constitution.

Agreements That Obstruct Legal Procedures

Agreements that delay or prevent justice are void. Examples include promises to

- pay non-expert witnesses in a trial to testify, or pay for false testimony
- bribe jurors
- refrain from informing on or prosecuting an alleged crime in exchange for money or other valuable consideration. This is called **compounding a crime**.

A court or prosecutor may make a penalty dependent upon a criminal's making restitution (for example, repairing a vandalized building). However, the victim may not make reporting a crime dependent upon restitution.

Who benefits from mandatory competency licensing of tradespeople and professionals?

Agreements Made Without a Required Competency License

All states require that persons in certain occupations and businesses pass exams and receive a **competency license** to ensure that they can perform adequately. Persons engaged in trades, such as barbers, plumbers, and electricians typically require a competency license. Professionals such as physicians, teachers, lawyers, and pharmacists also must have competency licenses. Real estate brokers, insurance agents, and building contractors are subject to such regulation as well. Persons who lack the required competency license may not enforce the contracts they make in doing the regulated work.

In contrast, if the license is a **revenue license**, whose purpose is only to raise revenue rather than to protect the public, contracts made by the unlicensed person are valid. Generally the only penalty for failure to get such a license is a higher fee when the license is obtained later.

Agreements That Affect Marriage Negatively

The law encourages marriage and family life by making agreements that harm or interfere with marriage unenforceable. For example, Mimi is an illegal immigrant and Bill is a U.S. citizen. It would be an illegal contract if Mimi agreed to pay Bill $5,000 in exchange for his promise to marry her so she could obtain citizenship. Similarly, a father's promise to pay his daughter for not marrying would be unenforceable. Also it would be illegal for a boss to agree to pay her assistant money in exchange for his promise to divorce his spouse.

LAWBRIEF

Licensing of computer users may be just around the corner. Already students at many universities are being required to pass computer classes covering copyright, security, password protection, and other subjects before being allowed on each school's system. One college now fines any student who passes on a virus $25.

Agreements That Restrain Trade Unreasonably

The U.S. economic system is based on the concept of free and open competition. This creates profits for producers who benefit consumers the most. Hence, both state and federal laws seek to prevent monopolies and combinations that restrict competition unreasonably.

PRICE FIXING When competing firms agree on the same price to be charged for a product or service, this injures consumers. It deprives them of the lower prices which competition would produce. **Price fixing** is a crime under federal law. Agreements to fix prices are therefore unenforceable.

One form of price fixing is **bid rigging**. This occurs when competitors who bid on jobs agree that one bidder will have the lowest bid for a particular job. It is illegal because typically the bid riggers take turns being the lowest bidder and set the bid price higher than if there were real competition.

IN THIS CASE

The three main providers of Internet access for the city of Miller met to discuss their problems. Chief among these problems was an overabundance of customers. As a consequence, all three were going to have to invest in expensive new hardware to maintain the transmission speed their customers required. One provider suggested that, instead of spending money, they all double their monthly fee. Such an action, she maintained, would reduce the number of their customers by about 30 percent. As a result, they could keep the Internet speed up but not have to buy the new hardware. Most importantly, it would actually result in more revenue. The providers agreed to do so. Because this agreement restrained free trade and controlled prices, it was illegal and void.

RESALE PRICE MAINTENANCE Manufacturers may engage in a legal form of *resale price maintenance* if they merely identify to retailers a "suggested retail price." They may even refuse to sell to retailers who will not charge that amount and still be legally proper in so doing. However, manufacturers may not agree or contract with retailers to sell the product at a particular price because that would involve two parties fixing the price.

ALLOCATION OF MARKETS The same injury to competition produced by price fixing can be achieved if competitors divide markets between themselves. This practice is known as *allocation of markets*. If the Ford dealers in a state agree that they will not sell to residents outside the county where their dealership is located, this eliminates price competition for Fords and injures consumers. Therefore agreements to allocate markets are illegal and unenforceable.

Agreements Not to Compete

Although agreements not to compete, such as those that fix prices and allocate markets, generally are unenforceable, the law will uphold some that are a part of termination clauses in employment contracts. In particular, when persons are hired they may agree that they will not compete with their employer after the employment terminates. However, these agreements become illegal if they are unreasonable in

■ time period for the limitation

■ geographic area to which the limitation applies

■ employer's interest protected by the limitation

The business executive in the middle is explaining the company's "non-compete" contract to two new salespeople. The contract states that upon termination of their employment, they are not to work in the same industry anywhere in the world for five years. Is this a legal agreement?

An agreement not to compete for 20 years would almost certainly be illegal as would an agreement not to compete anywhere in the United States. In contrast, an agreement not to engage in the printing business for a year in the city or county where the former employer is located probably would be legal and enforceable. The employer's interests protected by the agreement not to compete must be significant. Trade secrets are the most commonly recognized employer interests.

CHECKPOINT Name four of the eight illegal agreements discussed in this section.

When Will the Courts Enforce Illegal Agreements?

WHAT'S YOUR VERDICT? A young couple, the Guptas, wanted to provide for the college education of their infant daughter. They received an offer in the mail from the True Bonanza Mining Corporation, which seemed perfect for their need: "Join us now for only 10 cents a share of stock. Become part owner of a gold and silver mine with already proven mineral deposits. In ten years, you will be rich enough to retire!" The Guptas used all their savings to buy 250,000 shares of Bonanza stock. Months later they learned that Bonanza had violated the law. Its "proven mineral deposits" were commercially worthless aluminum oxides. The sales agreement was illegal.

Can the Guptas recover their $25,000?

Most illegal contracts are void and unenforceable. However, when the connection between the illegality and the agreement is slight or a party is relatively innocent of wrongdoing or both, the law will allow restitution (the restoring of the party involved to his or her original position) or the agreement to be enforced in court. Examples of the circumstances under which such treatment may be afforded include cases involving protected victims, the excusably ignorant, those who rescind before the prohibited act, and cases in which the contract is divisible.

Protected Victims

In some cases the law that was violated was designed to protect a party to the agreement. For example, state *blue-sky laws* prohibit sales of worthless stocks and bonds. Such securities have no more value than a section of the blue sky. The victim who purchases them may obtain restitution to recover money paid. Thus, in *What's Your Verdict?* restitution would be available to the Guptas.

Parties to an illegal agreement often are not equally to blame. For example, one party might be desperate enough to borrow money from another at a usurious rate of interest. To protect the innocent borrower, the agreement, although illegal, would be enforced by the court at the legal rate of interest. Any amount paid as interest over the legal rate would be restored to the victim of the usury.

The Excusably Ignorant

The excusably ignorant can either enforce the legal part of the contract or obtain restitution. A person is *excusably ignorant* who

- does not know the contract is illegal, but
- the other party knows the transaction is illegal, and
- the illegality is minor

Rescission Prior to Illegal Act

If a party rescinds before the illegal act occurs, then restitution will be available. For example, suppose you paid $50 to another student to steal an advance copy of a final exam. Then you changed your mind and called off the deal before the theft. You could recover the $50 payment. In this way, the law creates an incentive to stop illegal acts.

Divisible Contracts

Illegal contracts often contain a combination of legal and illegal provisions. Courts may enforce the legal part of a contract if it is divisible. *Divisible* generally means that separate consideration is given for the legal and illegal parts of the contract. Suppose a retailer contracts to sell camping and hunting supplies, including a pistol. If the seller fails to comply with a state law that requires a 30-day waiting period and a police clearance of sale of a handgun, this part of the contract is illegal. However, a court would probably enforce the legal provisions of the contract because the amount paid for the pistol (the illegal part) can be distinguished from the amount paid for everything else (the legal part).

On the other hand, suppose a single bid for all electrical contracting work on an office building specifies wiring and terminals in conflict with the building code. This contract probably would not be divisible because labor, wiring, terminals, and other costs were not broken out as separate items. This contract is *indivisible.*

A major provision in the UCC governing the sale of goods makes agreements or contract clauses that are unconscionable unenforceable. The UCC establishes an additional remedy for courts when dealing with such agreements. **Unconscionability** occurs when there is a grossly unfair contract that parties under ordinary circumstances would not accept. The UCC makes unconscionable contracts for the sale of goods subject to the rules for illegality.

To show unconscionability, a victim must show to the satisfaction of the court that (1) he or she was presented with a take it or leave it contract; (2) the other party had overwhelming bargaining power; (3) there was no viable alternative in the marketplace; and (4) injustice can only be avoided by holding certain terms or the whole contract unconscionable.

When the court finds a contract illegal for unconscionability, it can refuse to enforce the contract, or it can enforce the legal part and refuse to enforce the illegal part. In addition, courts also can modify the terms of an agreement to make it fair.

CHECKPOINT Under what circumstances will the courts enforce illegal agreements?

THINK ABOUT LEGAL CONCEPTS

1. Contracts in which one person pays another to commit a felony are unenforceable. **True or False?**

2. Charging interest on a loan of money at a rate higher than allowed by law is called (a) compounding a crime (b) wagering (c) loan kiting (d) usury

3. Typically, illegal contracts are held by the courts to be _?_ and unenforceable. (a) valid (b) voidable (c) void

4. A lottery has three elements: prize, chance, and consideration. **True or False?**

5. Restitution is (a) the enforcement of an agreement (b) the restoring of a party to his or her original position prior to contracting

6. If you agreed to pay a non-expert witness to make sure that she testified for you at a trial, this agreement would be unenforceable. **True or False?**

7. A party to an illegal contract may be able to either enforce the agreement or obtain restitution if he or she (a) is excusably ignorant (b) is a protected victim (c) rescinds before the illegal act occurs (d) all of the above

THINK CRITICALLY ABOUT EVIDENCE

Study the situation, answer the questions, and then prepare arguments to support your answers.

8. Crump was coming up for trial on felony charges. He paid the judge in the case $10,000 to make errors in conducting the trial so that Crump's conviction could be overturned on appeal. When the appeal failed, Crump sought to sue for restitution of the $10,000. Should he be allowed to recover the bribe? Why or why not?

9. Dixon, a wholesaler, was on the brink of bankruptcy. He bought fire insurance policies for more than twice the value of his warehouse and its contents from two companies. Then he arranged to pay a character known only as "Sparky" $5,000 to "torch" the structure. If Sparky did so but Dixon did not pay him, could Sparky enforce the contract for the $5,000? Could Dixon legally collect on his insurance policies if Sparky torched the building?

10. A new boss was scheduled to take over Patty's department in three weeks. Patty agreed to pay Nancy $600 to remove unflattering information from her personnel file so she would look good to the new boss. The day before Nancy was going to do it, Patty called and told her not to. She also asked for her money back. Nancy never took the information. Could Patty sue and recover her money?

11. Cliff worked as a site manager for an oil-drilling company. When a drill bit broke, he called Texas Bit Company, the only bit manufacturer in the area. Cliff told the salesperson that he had to have a replacement bit immediately as his company's drilling agreement with the landowner was about to expire. He then asked for a bit able to cut quickly through granite. The salesperson recommended their model 2123 which was described as a high carbon steel bit with diamonds embedded on the cutting edges. The salesperson quoted a price that was triple what Cliff had purchased a similar bit for a few months previously. She also said there were no warranties and that the product was being sold, "as is." Although selling "as is" was an unusual practice in the drilling industry, the salesperson said Cliff could take it or leave it as they only had one in stock and demand was high. It turned out that the bit was made only of low-carbon steel and it cut very slowly. Is this agreement unconscionable? What would the court likely do if it found the agreement to be unconscionable?

12. Glamorgan served a remote community as a doctor. When several patients refused to pay for treatment, she sued them. During the trial it was proven that, although she had a medical degree, Glamorgan had failed to pass the state examination required to be licensed to practice medicine. Will Glamorgan win the lawsuits?

13. Randy entered into a contract to provide a computer program to a New Jersey school district. He used without permission parts of a computer program copyrighted by another programmer. The portion of the program that violated the copyright law cost $12,000 and the part that didn't violate the copyright law cost $44,000. He delivered both parts to the school district. Can he recover anything for his work?

10-2 The Statute of Frauds

GOALS

- Explain why the Statute of Frauds is necessary and what it requires
- Identify the main instances when the Statute of Frauds requires a writing
- Understand the rules of contract interpretation

KEY TERMS

Statute of Frauds
executed contract
executory contract
quasi-contract
parol evidence

Why Have a Statute of Frauds?

WHAT'S YOUR VERDICT? While they were playing golf, Haka orally agreed to buy an apartment building from Simon. In a later telephone conversation, Haka promised Simon $100,000 as a down payment on the purchase price with the balance to be paid within five years. Simon promised to deliver the deed to the property at the time the balance of the purchase price was paid. Both parties were satisfied that all the terms had been completely negotiated. Later Haka found a better deal and told Simon he was backing out.

Is Haka's contract with Simon enforceable?

Although oral contracts are generally valid and binding, because they are subject to fraudulent claims, the law requires that several of the most important types of contracts be placed in writing to be enforceable in court. These types are determined in most states by a law entitled the **Statute of Frauds**. For example, under such a statute in every state, contracts to transfer an interest in *real property* (land, buildings, and things permanently attached to them) must be evidenced by a writing and signed by the party against whom enforcement is sought. In *What's Your Verdict?* the oral agreement between Haka and Simon would not be enforceable in court.

Note that most agreements, oral or written, are carried out without resort to the courts for enforcement. Nonetheless, it is always a good idea to put an important contract in writing whether it is required by the Statute of Frauds or not.

IN THIS CASE Sue orally agreed to provide interior decorating services for a law firm for two years at a rate she found attractive. She wrote and signed a letter to the law firm expressing her appreciation for the business, which she described as "interior decorating services, not to exceed 10 hours per week." The law firm replied with its own signed letter which described the transaction as, "services for 24 months at $3,500 per month." The two letters would be considered together by a court as evidence of a contract under the Statute of Frauds.

Contracts Within the Statute of Frauds

A contract is said to be *within the Statute of Frauds* if it is required to be in writing. It is *without the Statute of Frauds* if it is not required to be in writing. Contracts within the Statute of Frauds include

- contracts to buy and sell goods for a price of $500 or more
- contracts to buy and sell real property or any interest in real property
- contracts that require more than one year to complete
- promises to stand good for the debts of another or of an estate
- promises to give something of value in return for a promise of marriage

If a contract is within the Statute of Frauds, but there is either no writing or no signature, how courts will treat the parties depends on the extent of contractual performance.

EXECUTED CONTRACTS An **executed contract** is one that has been fully performed. Both parties have done all they promised to do. If an executed contract is within the Statute of Frauds, but there is either no writing or no signature, the courts leave the parties where they are. Neither party can reverse the contract.

EXECUTORY CONTRACTS An **executory contract** is one that has not been fully performed. Something agreed upon remains to be done by one or both of the parties.

An executory contract within the Statute of Frauds, but not signed or not in writing, is unenforceable. This means neither party can compel performance from the other.

An executory contract that does not comply with the Statute of Frauds is different from an illegal contract. One difference is that restitution is available in the former situation. Any consideration exchanged can be recovered by suing based on quasi-contract. A **quasi-contract** exists when some element of an enforceable contract is missing (such as a signed writing), yet courts award money to prevent the unjust enrichment of one party.

Requirements of the Writing

Generally a writing need not utilize any special form to satisfy the Statute of Frauds as long as the writing contains certain key elements. However, even within a state there usually are two sets of such requirements for a writing. One set of requirements is contained in each state's version of the Uniform Commercial Code and is typically applied only to sales of goods. The second set is applied to all other contracts and is contained in a state's Statute of Frauds.

STATUTE OF FRAUDS REQUIREMENTS Such statutes vary widely from state to state in their requirements. The least demanding Statutes of Frauds merely require that the writing indicate the existence of a contract. The most demanding standard used by states is that the writing must contain all the essential terms that would be required to create a valid offer. In general, this includes

1. names of the parties
2. a description of the subject matter
3. price
4. quantity
5. signature
6. other essential terms

"Other essential terms" can include time or method of delivery, terms of payment, methods of financing, date for transfer of possession and so on, depending on the nature of the

On a recent trip to Singapore, you fell in love with these statues of Tang Dynasty warriors, each worth at least $1,000. You then learn that an import-export business in the United States has several of these statues for sale. Write up a contract that contains all the essential terms required to create a valid offer for one of the statues. Assume that the sale is taking place in a state that uses the most demanding Statute of Frauds standard.

LEGAL Research

Assume you are about to get engaged. Research the issue of who gets to keep the ring if the engagement is called off. What rules are utilized to make the determination? Find out if the rules have stayed the same for many years, or if they change frequently.

transaction. Most states require contracts for the sale of real estate to provide a legal description (as opposed to a street address) of the realty.

UCC REQUIREMENTS Because the UCC is essentially the same in each state, it establishes a uniform content standard. Under the UCC, the writing must indicate only

- the quantity of goods
- that a contract has been created between the parties

SPECIAL RULES FOR SIGNATURES Note that, under the Statute of Frauds requirements, only the parties whose signatures actually appear on the contract may be sued for enforcement. The signature may be written, stamped, engraved, or printed. It may consist of any mark that is intended as a signature or authentication of the writing. Under the UCC, however, this rule is changed for those who regularly deal in the type of goods being sold in the contract. For such parties a contract proposal in writing signed by one party and sent to the other is enforceable against the other party unless the other party objects to the terms within 10 days of receipt.

CHECKPOINT Name the six essential elements in a writing required by the most demanding Statutes of Frauds standards.

How do the Statute of Frauds requirements for signatures differ from the UCC requirements?

© GETTY IMAGES/PHOTODISC

Types of Contracts Within the Statute of Frauds

To be enforceable under the Statute of Frauds, five types of executory contracts must be evidenced by a writing and signed by the party against whom the contract is to be enforced. As an alternative, the contract may be provable by some other writing, such as a letter signed by the party who is being sued. A plaintiff seeking to enforce the contract can readily sign if his or her signature is missing. Because either party might later want to sue for breach, both parties should sign when the contract is made.

The following sections discuss the five types of executory contracts within the Statute of Frauds, that is, those contracts that must be evidenced by a writing and signed by the party against whom the contract is to be enforced.

Contract for the Sale of Goods for $500 or More

Goods (such as a book, car, or TV) are items of *personal property* (any property other than real property) that are tangible. If parties agree to buy and sell goods for a price of $500 or more, their contract must be evidenced by a writing. If a contract for the sale of goods is for less than $500, then it need not be in writing. However, a modification of that contract which brings the total price above $500 must be in writing and signed.

The Uniform Commercial Code provides exceptions to the Statute of Frauds. In these cases, a writing and signature is not required

■ when goods are ordered to be specially manufactured and they are not suitable to be sold to others in the ordinary course of the seller's business

■ when goods have been ordered and paid for and the seller has accepted payment

■ when goods have been received and accepted by the buyer

■ when the party against whom enforcement is sought admits during legal proceedings that the oral contract was made

Contract to Sell an Interest in Real Property

Real property includes land and buildings permanently attached to land. Transfers of title, ownership of real property, or of lesser interests—such as possession in a lease or the right to profit from real property by pumping oil or cutting timber—must be in a properly signed writing to be enforceable. In most states, oral leases for one year or less are enforceable. Some states require that contracts employing real estate brokers satisfy the Statute of Frauds.

As an exception to the general rule, courts will enforce the oral contract if the seller has delivered the deed or if the buyer also has done all of the following: (1) made partial or full payment, (2) occupied the land, and (3) made substantial improvements to the land.

Contracts That Require More Than One Year to Complete

Courts will not enforce a contract that cannot be performed within one year unless there is a signed writing to prove the agreement. The year begins at the time the contract is made, not at the time contractual performance is to begin.

This time provision does not apply to agreements that might be executed within one year. This is true even if such agreements are not actually carried out within that time. The test is not whether the agreement is actually performed within one year, but whether there is a possibility of performance within one year. To illustrate, two persons, such as Cervante and Joan in *What's Your Verdict?* shake hands and orally agree to be business partners. But they do not specify a definite time period. Because either partner may quit or die within one year, their agreement does not require more than one year to complete, and it need not be in writing. Either party could withdraw at anytime.

Contract to Pay a Debt or Answer for Another's Debt or The Debts of an Estate

Another provision of the Statute of Frauds requires a writing for a promise to answer for the debt or default of another. For example, if a father tells his daughter's landlord that he will pay the rent if she defaults on a three-month lease, this promise is called a *collateral promise*. It must be in writing to be enforceable. This contrasts with a primary promise to pay. A *primary promise* exists if Dad says, "I'll cosign the rental agreement with my daughter. That way you can collect from which ever one of us you care to." This agreement is enforceable without a writing.

When a person dies, a party may be appointed by the court to settle the deceased's estate. In so doing, the party typically uses the estate's assets to satisfy the deceased person's unpaid obligations. However, as the appointed party often is a relative, and, as a consequence, does not want to sell off the assets to pay the debts, he or she

GLOBAL ISSUES

Writing Requirement

The laws regarding a writing requirement for contracts differ among nations. Stemming from the 1677 English Parliament law, some common law countries may still have writing requirements in effect. (England, however, repealed this law in 1954.) Countries with civil law codes have not required that contracts be in writing. The United Nations Convention on Contracts for the International Sale of Goods (CISG) is in effect in approximately 60 countries. Under the CISG, contracts for the sale of goods need not be in writing.

may agree to pay them personally. This promise to answer personally for the debts of the estate is not enforceable unless placed in writing.

EXCEPTION—MAIN PURPOSE RULE A third party is liable for an oral promise to pay another's debt if the main purpose of the promise serves the promisor's own interest. This is called the *main purpose rule.* Suppose an owner of a house under construction is anxious to see it completed. After the building contractor fails to pay on time, the driver of the delivery truck refuses to unload a shipment of lumber. If the homeowner orally promises to pay the lumberyard if the contractor does not pay for needed supplies, the homeowner cannot defend using the Statute of Frauds. The main purpose rule applies.

Contract for Which the Consideration Is Marriage

A signed writing is required for agreements in which one party promises to marry in return for something more than the other's promise to marry. If Sue and Bill agree to marry each other, this is outside the Statute of Frauds. If Alice agrees to marry Buck because he promised to deed his house to her, this is within the Statute of Frauds. In some U.S. subcultures, a parent of the woman may promise to pay a dowry to the man in return for his promise to marry. This agreement must be placed in writing to be enforceable.

In some states, if one party breaches either an oral or written contract to marry, the victim of the breach may successfully sue for damages. The trend, however, is to ban such "heart balm" suits.

CHECKPOINT Name the five types of executory contracts that require a writing.

How Are Contracts Interpreted?

At times parties to a written agreement claim that it does not include everything that was agreed upon or is not clear about such terms. In court these claims are settled either by an examination of the agreement itself or by a set of rules specifically devoted to the interpretation of contracts.

Acknowledgement of Final Agreement

Often, issues develop involving preceding oral agreements not reflected in the ultimate contract. As a consequence writings will include a contract clause stating that both parties agree that the terms in the written contract constitute the entire and final agreement.

Specific Rules of Interpretation

ANALYSIS The first thing a court will do is interpret the contract in terms of the parties' principal objective. By looking at the main objective, courts can see which clauses should prevail over others. Further, if an agreement can be interpreted in two ways, the courts will choose the way that renders the agreement a contract. Interpreting each clause in the light of all other provisions of the contract is another way to follow the parties' principal objective.

CONFLICTING TERMS If there is a conflict between a printed form contract and something typewritten or handwritten thereon, the later writings—not the conflicting typeset print—determine the contract's meaning. This is because the writing is likely to have occurred after the typesetting. Similarly a typewritten agreement which includes a conflicting handwritten statement or clause will be interpreted based on the handwritten portion.

When contracts refer to amounts of money, they often describe the amount with numerals, such as "10," and also with words such as "ten." If there is a conflict between the numeral and the word, and one of them is ambiguous, then the unambiguous expression will prevail. For example, "Two twenty-five dollars ($2.25)" will be interpreted by reliance on the numerals. When both the writing and the numerals are unambiguous, then the writing prevails. For example, "Two hundred twenty-five and 00/100 ($235.00)" will be interpreted in reliance on the words. The reason is that writing out amounts in longhand takes more deliberation than writing them in numerals.

IN THIS CASE Milo contracted with Corrigan for the installation of a complete burglar alarm system for $2,900. The printed standard form contract provided that Milo was to pay $900 down and the balance at $100 a month for 20 months. Failure to pay any installment when due would make the entire balance payable immediately. The payments were to be made on the first day of each month. Milo explained that he did not receive his paycheck until the tenth. Therefore, he said he would prefer to make the payments on that date. Corrigan agreed, and in the margin wrote in "tenth," and initialed it. However, Corrigan did not cross out the term calling for payment on the first in the printed form of the contract. Later, when Milo failed to make the first payment by the first day of the month, Corrigan demanded the full balance. The court ruled he was not entitled to it because the handwritten modification prevails over the conflicting typeset date.

Find the conflicting terms in this contract. Which numbers prevail?

REAL ESTATE MORTGAGE

THIS MORTGAGE made this _____20th_____ day of
_October_____, 20--, between
_Bernard and Mariah Easton (husband_____
_and wife), 6720 Observatory Lane,_____
_Cuyahoga Falls, Ohio_____,
Mortgagors, and the LAST NATIONAL BANK of Akron, Summit County, Ohio, a corporation doing business under the laws of the United States with its principal office in Akron, Ohio, Mortgagee.

WITNESSETH: That whereas, Mortgagors are jointly indebted to Mortgagee for money borrowed in the sum of $____one hundred_____
_thirty-four thousand, five_____
_hundred_____ Dollars ($_134,900_____) to secure the payment of which Mortgagors have executed their promissory note of even date herewith in the said amount together with interest as stated in said note, payable within ten (1) years.

WORDS The plain and normal meaning of ordinary words will be used to determine the meaning of the contract. Prior relationships of the parties may indicate how the words should be interpreted. Legal and other technical terms are given their technical meaning unless the contract as a whole shows that a different meaning is intended. Where both parties are members of a trade or profession, both parties are presumed to know the trade custom or practice, and the contract is interpreted in light of that trade custom or practice.

AMBIGUITIES Courts will interpret ambiguities (things that can be understood in two or more possible ways) against the party who drafted the contract. Often consumers are asked to accept and sign "take it or leave it" contracts.

These are contracts such as credit purchases or life insurance policies. They are prepared by the stronger parties (usually the sellers), with the help of skilled lawyers, who naturally favor the interests of their clients. Generally, the terms of such contracts are not negotiable. The weaker parties (usually the consumers) must "take it or leave it." In such contracts, courts interpret ambiguity against the author. Statutes in some states now require that the language of consumer contracts be clear, simple, and understandable to the average person.

IMPLIED REASONABLENESS Contracts often include implied terms as a matter of reasonableness. Thus, a clause requiring "payment in cash" usually may be satisfied by check. Promised services must be performed with reasonable care and skill even when this is not stated. When no time for performance is mentioned, a reasonable time is allowed.

Parol Evidence Rule

Generally, when a contract is placed in final written form, the courts feel that it is a reasonable expectation that the parties will consider the terms carefully. If a party to a contract does not understand it, he or she may exercise one of several options such as not entering the contract or getting the help of an attorney to interpret it. Certainly, given the volume of contracts that are made each

Consumers who purchase appliances on credit often are required to sign "take it or leave it" contracts. What can you do to protect yourself against contract terms that strongly favor the interests of the offering parties?

© GETTY IMAGES/PHOTODISC

day, we can never have enough judges to review and save parties from their contractual errors.

This wise conclusion is supported by the *parol evidence rule*. This rule makes the final writing the source of evidence about the terms of the contract. **Parol evidence** consists of words spoken prior to the execution of the final writing or at the time of signing. Parol evidence generally is inadmissible in court proceedings. For example, if a complete final written agreement for the sale of a house is signed, then a court will not admit oral testimony that, prior to the parties' signing the written agreement, the seller had said he would paint the exterior before vacating. The rule keeps out preliminary inquiries, initial proposals, negotiations, and other discussions that are not the final agreement.

In *What's Your Verdict?* Highman could not recover the refund. Evidence of the salesperson's oral promise would be parol evidence. In complete and final writings, both parties should carefully include all terms that they deem essential.

EXCEPTIONS TO THE PAROL EVIDENCE RULE Parol evidence may be admissible in the following exceptional instances:

1. to clarify ambiguities in the written agreement
2. if the written contract was not intended to be a complete agreement
3. if a condition necessary to the existence of the contract never occurred
4. if fraud, forgery, illegality, mistake, or misrepresentation occurred
5. to show the parties reached another agreement or terminated the contract under consideration after executing the written contract
6. to show that the contract is voidable because a party lacked contractual capacity

CHECKPOINT Explain the parol evidence rule.

© GETTY IMAGES/PHOTODISC

Stan and Lauretta attend an open house for a home they are interested in buying. They tell the agent that they would be serious about buying this house if the owner would remove some of the bushes in front of the house. The salesperson says that would not be a problem. Later, they sign a contract to buy the house, but it doesn't mention removing the bushes. If the couple later decided to sue to make the homeowners remove the bushes, would they win the case? Why or why not?

THINK ABOUT LEGAL CONCEPTS

1. Enforceable contracts can often be created without a writing. **True or False?**

2. Ambiguity in the terms of a written contract will be interpreted against the author. **True or False?**

3. Where there are contractual obligations unperformed, the contract is called _ ?_.

4. Parol statements can be admitted to prove which of the following? (a) fraud (b) illegality (c) a conflicting agreement existed before the signing (d) a and b

THINK CRITICALLY ABOUT EVIDENCE

Study the situation, answer the questions, and then prepare arguments to support your answers.

5. Jason's father, Phil, died. He left credit card bills totaling $17,000 and some additional small bills. His only asset at the time of death was a savings account with $6,000 in it. One of the credit card companies called Jason. In his grief, Jason orally promised to pay them the balance on his dad's account, $2,000. Is this promise enforceable in court?

6. A salesperson tries to persuade you to buy an electronic musical instrument. The price is $499, plus carrying charges of $72. The salesperson says, "You'll soon be the life of the party. If not, just return it and get your money back." You sign an installment payment contract, which says nothing about a return privilege. Can you hold the seller to the promise to accept a return?

7. Under a written contract, Cabrera bought a used sedan from Sharpe's Previously Owned Cars Inc. The salesperson had knowingly falsely assured her that the car was in "tip-top condition . . . with just 45,000 miles driven by only one previous owner." Later, in checking official registration records, Cabrera discovered that the sedan had three previous owners and that the odometer had been set back from 70,000 miles. In court, Sharpe's attorney claims that under the parol evidence rule, introduction of the salesperson's oral statements is barred. Is this parol evidence admissible?

CONCEPTS IN BRIEF

10-1 Illegal Agreements

1. To be valid, a contract must not violate the law (constitutional, statutory, or case), nor be contrary to public policy in its formation, purpose, or performance.

2. Among agreements that violate law or public policy and are therefore void and unenforceable are those that require committing a crime or tort, obstruct legal procedures, injure public service, are made by persons without a required competency license, involve usury, involve illegal lotteries, threaten marriage, involve price fixing or market allocation, include an unreasonable promise not to compete, or are unconscionable.

3. Illegal agreements usually are unenforceable and restitution is not available. Exceptions are made to this rule when the violated law was meant to protect one of the parties, one party is excusably ignorant, a party rescinds before the illegal act occurs, or the contract is divisible into legal and illegal parts.

10-2 The Statute of Frauds

4. Unless so required by the Statute of Frauds, contracts need not be in writing to be enforceable.

5. An express contract is stated in words—written or spoken. An implied contract is shown by conduct of the parties and by surrounding circumstances.

6. An executory contract has not been fully performed. When all required performances have been completed by all parties a contract is deemed executed.

7. A quasi-contract exists when some element of a valid contract is missing, yet it is enforced as if it were a contract. This is done to prevent unjust enrichment of one party.

8. To be enforceable, the following contracts must be in writing (or evidenced by some other written proof) and signed by the party against whom enforcement is sought: (1) contracts to buy and/or sell goods for a price of $500 or more, (2) contracts to buy and/or sell real property or any interest in real property, (3) contracts that cannot be performed within one year after being made, (4) contracts to pay a debt or fulfill a legal obligation of another person or an estate, (5) marriage contracts involving more consideration than just mutual promises to wed.

9. The writing required by the Statute of Frauds need not be in any special form. The requirements for the content of a writing under the common law vary greatly from state to state.

10. The terms of a written contract may not be changed by parol evidence unless the original writing is clearly ambiguous, incomplete, or modified by subsequent agreement. Parol evidence also may be used to show that a written agreement is not binding because of mistake, fraud, illegality, or because a party was a minor.

YOUR LEGAL VOCABULARY

Match each statement with the term that it best defines. Some terms may not be used.

1. To refrain from informing on or prosecuting an alleged crime in exchange for money or other valuable consideration

2. Contract that has been fully performed

3. Composed of prize, chance, and consideration

4. When competing firms agree on the same price to be charged for a product or service

5. A bet on the outcome of an event

6. License required of professionals certifying they can perform adequately

7. Created by court action to prevent unjust enrichment

8. Oral evidence

9. License granted only to earn revenue for the licensing body

a. bid rigging
b. competency license
c. compounding a crime
d. executed contract
e. executory contract
f. lottery
g. parol evidence
h. price fixing
i. quasi-contract
j. revenue license
k. Statute of Frauds
l. unconscionability
m. wager

REVIEW LEGAL CONCEPTS

10. Describe the ways courts handle contracts for which a required license is missing.

11. Assume the usury limit is 20 percent in your state. What is the annual dollar amount of interest charged on a loan of $1,000 where the interest rate is a legal 20 percent. Compare that with the dollar amount of interest on a $1,000 loan carrying a usurious 25 percent. Does the difference in the interest amounts indicate to society criminal behavior on one lender's part and not another? Does it indicate criminal behavior to you? What about a business that buys goods at $1,000 each and sells them with a 100 percent markup the same day for $2,000? Is that much markup criminal? Why or why not?

12. Describe the elements of unconscionability.

13. Name the categories of contracts that are within the Statute of Frauds.

14. Describe how the parol evidence rule affects the court's evaluation of the facts underlying a contractual dispute by identifying the times when parol evidence can be introduced to clarify a contract. What other rules help a court in such evaluations?

WRITE ABOUT LEGAL CONCEPTS

15. Select a type of local business. Next write three sentences that describe three different illegal agreements that might be entered into by such a business.

16. List four licenses that are held by people you know. For each license, indicate whether it is a revenue or competency license.

17. Invent a situation involving the sale of a used car. Write a related contract which includes the minimum content required to satisfy the UCC.

18. Write a dialogue between two people that creates some oral statements which would be admissible and some which would not be admissible for a contract of employment for three years.

19. **HOT DEBATE** Did the prosecutor act impartially by giving the organizers of the illegal lottery a way out without being indicted? What would you have done if you were the prosecutor?

THINK CRITICALLY ABOUT EVIDENCE

Study the situation, answer the questions, and then prepare arguments to support your answers.

20. Trent, a minor, bought a copyrighted CD from Shawn. After making a copy of the disc, Trent found a defect in the CD. He tried to return it to Shawn for a full refund. Shawn suspected the illegal copying and refused the refund. Can Shawn assert illegality as a defense here? Why or why not?

21. Moser had no automobile liability insurance, although state law required it. She negligently collided with Chang's car. He threatened to inform the police if Moser failed to pay $5,000 for pain and suffering and $2,000 for car repairs. Moser gave Chang a check for $7,000. Then he stopped payment on it. If Chang sues, will he recover?

22. During the final week of March in Al's junior year at East High, a recruiter from Granite Inc. offered him a job. "Complete your entire junior and senior years and then, after you get that diploma," the officer said, "show up ready for work." Al replied, "I'll be there." Was this a contract enforceable in court?

23. Kelley was admitted to University Hospital as an emergency heart transplant patient. The next day, the hospital's business manager discussed the cost of the surgery with Kelley's two sons. Both sons told the manager, "Do whatever is necessary to save his life, and we will pay you." When the hospital presented the staggering bill to the junior Kelleys, they said the contract was unenforceable. Are they correct? Explain your answer.

24. Cornelius, an elderly bachelor, was at the town cafe. In front of several witnesses who will vouch for the story, Cornelius made the following statement to Barbara, a young waitress: "I can't give you a castle in Spain. But if you marry me, I will deed to you a half interest in Meadowland Acres, the best farm in the county. And I'll give you 75 cows, 200 hogs, and 5,000 chickens." Barbara said, "I will," and they were married. Is Cornelius legally bound to keep his promise to transfer the property?

MAKE ACADEMIC CONNECTIONS

25. **LAW** Research the procedure by which a lawyer may lose her or his license in your state. Call the State Bar Association and obtain statistics about how many lawyers there are in your state and how many have been complained against, reviewed, brought up on charges, and disbarred in the last five years.

ANALYZE REAL CASES

26. Blubaugh, a farmer, leased a combine from John Deere Leasing (JDL). The lease document was preprinted on two sides of the paper, but one side was printed in very small, light type and could not be altered. Blubaugh read and signed the front side but did not notice or read the other side of the document. It contained unusual provisions making Blubaugh liable in the event of breach for much more money than the unpaid lease payments. When Blubaugh breached, JDL sued. The trial judge required a magnifying glass to read the fine print. Is the lease contract unconscionable? Why or why not? (*John Deere Leasing Company v. Blubaugh,* 636 F. Supp. 1569, Kan.)

27. Dixon, a motor vehicle purchaser, sued the Wisconsin Finance Company with which he had entered into an installment contract. He also sued its Illinois sister corporation, alleging that the contract was void under the Sales Finance Agency Act because the finance company was not licensed to do business in the state of Illinois. The license was not a competency license. Will Dixon prevail? (*Dixon v. Mercury Finance Company of Wisconsin,* 694 N.E.2d 693, Ill.)

28. For a nine-year period, Kiyosi served as a teaching associate and lecturer at Indiana University, Bloomington. Meanwhile, he continued to study and write to qualify for a Ph.D. degree. He relied on an oral promise by the defendant university that upon obtaining the degree, he would be appointed to a permanent position with perpetual renewals, starting at the rank of assistant professor. It was customary for the university to make such appointments for terms of three years. When Kiyosi received his Ph.D., he was appointed assistant professor. However, he was told that he would not be reappointed for the following year. He then sued for damages for breach of contract. The university officials claimed that the Statute of Frauds barred his action because a lifetime contract cannot be performed within one year. Who should win this case? (*Kiyosi v. Trustees of Indiana University,* 166 Ind. App. 34, 333 N.E.2d 886)

29. Franklin Life Insurance Co. issued a policy that named Burne as a beneficiary. The policy provided for double indemnity accidental death benefits because of the death of the insured. The insured had been struck by an automobile and was kept alive in a vegetative state for four and a half years before he died. The policy provided that the accidental death benefits would be paid only if death occurred within 90 days of the accident, and that such benefits would not be paid if death occurred during a time when premiums were being waived due to the insured's disability. Will the beneficiary be allowed to recover on the policy? (*Burne v. Franklin Life Ins. Co.,* 301 A.2d 799, Pa.)

30. For safekeeping, Kula deposited $18,300 with the cashier of a Nevada hotel casino and was given a receipt for the money. Kula and a friend, Goldfinger, gambled in the hotel's casino. (Casino gambling is legal in Nevada.) Kula made withdrawals and deposits from time to time with the casino cashier and at the time had a balance of $18,000. One evening Goldfinger lost $500 in gambling and was unable to pay it. He asked the shift boss, Ponto, to telephone Kula for a guarantee of the loss. Ponto did so and received Kula's authorization to give Goldfinger credit up to $1,000 but no more. Ponto confirmed this but stated that Kula had also said Goldfinger could gamble the entire deposit of $18,000. Goldfinger was permitted to gamble until he lost $18,000. The casino tried to collect the amount from Kula on his alleged oral promise to cover Goldfinger's debt to $18,000. The casino did this by refusing to return to Kula the amount he had on deposit. Kula was willing to honor his oral guarantee of Goldfinger's debt up to $1,000 but no more. Kula sued the hotel for return of his deposit. Should he get it? (*Kula v. Karat, Inc.,* 531 P.2d 1353)

Sports & Entertainment Law

Hollywood Handshakes

COPPOLA V. WARNER BROTHERS
2003 CAL. APP. UNPUB. B154280

BACKGROUND By the 1990s Francis Ford Coppola was a Hollywood legend both for his stunning successes and his disastrous failures. Coppola's success stories were everywhere in Hollywood. He initiated the "blockbuster" films *Godfather I* and *Godfather II* in the early 1970s. He promoted the careers of cutting-edge directors such as George Lucas, and introduced the acting talents of Matt Dillon, Mickey Rourke, Nicolas Cage, Patrick Swayze, Rob Lowe, and Tom Cruise. His failures at first were brought on by fate. His immediate follow-up to the *Godfather* successes, *Apocalypse Now,* suffered everything from typhoon Olga's destruction of its sets to the leading actor suffering a heart attack. However, Coppola's own personal flaws and indulgences interfered as well.

FACTS When Warner Brothers approached Coppola with an offer to allow him to carry out his vision of a new version of the movie Pinocchio, Coppola at first balked. Warner Brothers previously had lent tentative backing to a Coppola/Lucas project in the late 1960s, and then had pulled back their financial support leaving Coppola

heavily in debt. Nevertheless, Warner Brothers was persistent and, ultimately, a long-term "Producer's Agreement" based on various "handshake" (oral) agreements between the parties was circulated in draft form. However, the agreement, though the subject of intermittent negotiations between the parties, was never completed or signed. In the interim, however, a screenwriter approved by Coppola was hired by Warner Brothers and produced a screenplay. Nearly a year after serious negotiations on the project were initiated, Warner Brothers turned down the screenplay. Coppola then rejected Warner Brothers' final contract offer and broke off negotiations. He then wrote his own draft of the Pinocchio story and approached Columbia Pictures with the project. Hearing of this maneuver, Warner Brothers' Senior Vice President sent a letter to Coppola's agent indicating that any contract with Columbia on the project would be contested by Warner Brothers. Columbia Pictures then notified Coppola that it would not go further with the Pinocchio project until the matter with Warner Brothers was cleared up. Unable to conclude a settlement with Warner Brothers, Coppola eventually lost the project and sued Warner Brothers.

THE LAW Provable oral contracts are legally valid, binding, and enforceable as long as they are not required to be in proper written form under the Statute of Frauds.

THE ISSUE Was there an enforceable oral contract?

HOLDING The alleged oral contract was determined to be unenforceable, even if it could be proven in court, as it would have required more than a year to be completed. As a consequence of the lack of a contract with Coppola, Warner Brothers' action in impeding Coppola's contracting with Columbia pictures was tortious. The jury in the case awarded Coppola $20 million in compensatory damages and $60 million in punitive damages. (The latter were ultimately disallowed by the trial court, leaving the final damage award at $20 million.)

PRACTICE JUDGING

1. Should the contract have been under the Statute of Frauds? Why or why not?

2. Should the punitive damages award have been allowed? Why or why not?

Chapter 11
Contractual Obligations and their Enforcement

11-1 Transfer and Discharge of Obligations

11-2 Remedies for Breach of Contract

© GETTY IMAGES/PHOTODISC

HOT DEBATE

Tony, 12, wanted to begin saving for college as soon as possible. His parents helped him open a checking account with the First Predatory Bank. The Predator, as the bank was called, had just been formed and was conducting an aggressive campaign for new depositors. For opening his account, Tony received a new toaster oven and a set of carving knives, which he gave his parents. To earn money, Tony took a job delivering papers at 5 A.M. each day. By the time he was 14 Tony had $1,023 in his account. Tony then transferred $1,000 into a savings account but agreed to an overdraft protection plan so that, if he overdrew his checking account, the necessary amount would be transferred from savings thereby saving any overdraft charges. Tony did not notice the small print in the agreement concerning the overdraft coverage plan that limited such transfers to $50 per month for accounts under $10,000. When Tony bought his parents an anniversary gift for $70 and wrote a check for it, he almost exhausted his $50 transfer amount for the month. Thereafter, when he wrote several small checks all for $5 or less for incidental items, the Predator would pay the checks but debit his savings account for $50 for each one as an overdraft charge. By the time he received his statement, Tony's savings account was down to $37 having been debited some $950 in overdraft charges for a sequence of checks that totalled $48.

WHERE DO YOU STAND?

1. What legal remedies can Tony pursue? Will he likely be successful?
2. Has the Predator acted ethically in this situation?

11-1 Transfer and Discharge of Obligations

GOALS

- Identify what rights can be assigned and what duties delegated
- Describe the various ways in which contractual obligations may be discharged

KEY TERMS

assignment
obligor
performance
discharge
breach of contract

substantial performance
defaults
anticipatory breach
alteration
tender

The Transfer of Contract Rights and Duties

WHAT'S YOUR VERDICT?

Whipple bought a high-powered sports coupe from Boss Motors for $32,000. After a down payment of $2,000, the balance, plus a finance charge, was to be paid by mail in installments over the following 48 months. Boss Motors needed cash to restore its inventory of new cars. It immediately sold Whipple's contract to a finance company, Palmout Inc., and told Whipple to mail all installment payments to Palmout.

Is such a transfer of contract rights legal?

A transfer of a right a party may have under a contract to another is called an **assignment**. For example, one party may transfer to another the right to collect a payment. The party who transfers the contractual right is the *assignor*. The party who receives this contractual right is the *assignee*. An assignment does not need to be supported by consideration to be legally effective, although it often is. In *What's Your Verdict?* it was perfectly legal for Boss Motors to assign to the finance company its right to receive Whipple's payments in return for needed cash. When Whipple was notified of the assignment, he became obligated to pay the finance company instead of Boss Motors.

From the perspective of the courts the assignee "stands in the shoes of the assignor." This means that the assignee receives exactly the same contractual rights and duties as the assignor—no more and no less. If a contractual right is transferred, this does not change the legal rights of the other party to the contract. For example, if Whipple's newly purchased automobile is defective and it takes $2,000 to fix it, he may withhold that amount from Palmout, the assignee, if he would have had the right to withhold it from Boss.

In all assignments, the assignor guarantees to the assignee that the assignor has a right to assign and that the assigned right is legally enforceable. However, the assignor typically does not promise that the **obligor** (the one who owes a duty under a contract) will perform as

A restaurant assigns to credit card issuers the right to collect amounts due from customers who use the card. Which party is the assignor and which is the assignee?

© GETTY IMAGES/PHOTODISC

promised in the original contract. If the obligor breaches, the assignee, not the assignor, must sue for the breach. This means that, in *What's Your Verdict?*, if Whipple (the obligor) stops making payments, Palmout (the assignee) must bring suit instead of Boss (the assignor) to enforce against Whipple his duty to pay. Often, the assignment will include specific language making the assignor liable for breach by the obligor.

Assignable Rights

Generally, a party may assign contractual rights to another, provided performance will not be materially changed, that is, changed in an important way. **Performance** is the fulfillment of contractual promises as agreed. In *What's Your Verdict?* Whipple's payment was to be sent by mail regardless of to whom, so the assignment was proper. In a similar way, retailers and restaurants assign to issuers of credit cards the right to collect the amounts due from customers who have used the cards. In exchange, the credit card companies immediately pay the retailers and restaurants the face amount of the credit slips, less an agreed percentage.

Non-Assignable Rights

Contractual rights may not be assigned if performance requirements would be materially changed as a consequence. Other situations in which rights may not be transferred include

1. a right created under a contract that prohibits transfer of the contractual rights
2. claims for damages for personal injuries
3. claims against the United States
4. rights to personal services, especially those of a skilled nature, or when personal trust and confidence are involved
5. assignments of future wages, as limited by state statutes

Form of Assignments

Assignment of contractual rights usually is made voluntarily by the assignor. While an assignment usually is valid whether oral or written, putting an assignment in writing is always wiser. State statutes sometimes require that certain assignments be in writing. No consideration is necessary to make a valid assignment.

Notice of Assignments

Until notified that an assignment has occurred, the obligor may continue to pay the assignor. After notification, however, the obligor is liable to the assignee for performance. To protect newly acquired rights, the assignee should promptly notify the obligor of the assignment.

Delegation of Contractual Duties

The routine obligations of a party that must be performed to fulfill a contract often can be transferred to another to perform. This is known as *delegation of duties*. However a person who delegates contractual duties remains legally obligated and responsible for proper performance even though someone else may do the required work. A person cannot delegate to another any duty where performance requires unique personal skill or special qualifications. Also, a contract creating a duty can prohibit delegation.

CHECKPOINT Under what conditions may you assign contractual rights to another person?

Discharge of Contractual Obligations

WHAT'S YOUR VERDICT? Jan borrowed $2,000 from Effriham to buy a new keyboard for his band. Jan agreed to pay the money back plus interest on the first of December. When Jan did not pay, Effriham, who needed money to pay off Christmas bills, suggested that if Jan would pay $1,500 by January 15, he would call the loan paid in full. Jan agreed but then failed to make even the $1,500 payment. Effriham then brought suit for payment of the debt.

Will the court order Jan to pay the original amount or the $1,500?

By Performance

Discharge of a contract is a termination of duties that ordinarily occurs when the parties perform as promised. Most contracts are discharged by complete performance of the terms of the contract. Failure to provide complete performance is a **breach of contract**. The significance of the breach determines what the non-breaching party can do in response.

When one party fails to perform a crucial duty under a contract, the other party may treat such a failure as a major breach and regard her or his own obligation as discharged. In sales contracts under the Uniform Commercial Code (UCC) this is termed a *cancellation*.

When just about all the duties are performed, but a minor duty under the contract remains, **substantial performance** has occurred. In this case there has been only a minor breach. A minor breach does not discharge the duties of the non-breaching party the way a major breach does. The party who has substantially performed can sue and recover what is due, less the cost of completing the remaining work. If the failure to perform is deliberate, however, the non-breaching party may treat it as a major breach.

Sometimes a party who **defaults**, or fails to perform, notifies the other party to a contract before the time of performance has arrived that he or she will not perform. This is called an **anticipatory breach**. In this situation, the non-breaching party may wait until the promised time of performance, or may treat the notice as evidence of a breach of contract and immediately sue for damages.

TIMING OF PERFORMANCE Contracts often identify a duty but don't say when it must

IN THIS CASE

On January 5, Graham Roofers contracted to remove the old shingles and to install a new fire-proof roof on the home of the Sterlings. The job was to be completed "by March 30, at the latest," to be ready for anticipated heavy spring rains. Late in February, Graham notified the Sterlings that because of a rush of orders, his crews were "swamped" and he could not get to the job until late April or early May. This was an anticipatory breach. The Sterlings have the choice of waiting for performance or immediately proceeding as though Graham had breached the contract.

be performed. In these cases, the duty must be performed within a reasonable time. If it is not performed within a reasonable time, the non-performance is considered a breach. A judge or jury will determine what is a reasonable time after examining the circumstances at trial. Thus a contract to ship tomatoes—which rot quickly—might have a reasonable time for performance of several hours. Alternatively, a contract to ship furniture—which doesn't change in value as quickly—might have a reasonable time of several weeks.

In other instances, the contract identifies a date for performance. Most courts will rule that performance shortly after the date is only a minor breach. The circumstances in each case will influence how much time after the specified date will be allowed before the delay is treated as a major breach.

When a contract states that performance is to occur by a specified date, and that "time is of the essence," failure to perform by that

LAW BRIEF

The mere appearance of the words "time is of the essence" in a contract does not mean that the courts will accept the statement without inquiring as to whether it truly is essential for the performance to be rendered by a certain date. Note that, if time is truly of the essence, a lack of timely performance is a major breach.

date may be regarded as a major breach. If so, the duties of the non-breaching party are discharged. Time will be "of the essence" when a contract deals with property that rapidly fluctuates in value or property that is perishable. Courts look to the subject matter of the contract and the individual circumstances of the case to determine whether time is "of the essence." Just having the words placed in a contract is not the deciding factor.

By the Initial Terms

When the parties prepare their contract, they may agree that it will terminate

- on a specified date or upon the expiration of a specified period of time (for example, a fresh food supply contract with a school district to terminate on the last day of school)

- upon the occurrence of a specified event (for example, a contract to have someone mow your yard until you return from vacation and resume doing it yourself)

- upon the failure of a certain event to happen (for example, a construction loan contract upon failure to get a required building permit)

- at the free will of either party upon giving notice (for example, when one partner decides to retire from business and gives the required notice as specified in the business agreement with her associates)

By Subsequent Agreement

The parties who have made a contract may later mutually agree to change either the terms of the contract or the nature of their relationship. They may do so without any liability for breach in any of the following ways.

RESCISSION By rescission the parties may agree to unmake or to undo their entire contract from its very beginning. Each party returns any consideration already received. Both parties are placed in their original positions to the extent possible.

SUBSTITUTION Parties may decide that the present contract is not what they want, and so replace it with a new contract. This discharges their original contract by *substitution.*

ACCORD AND SATISFACTION As discussed in Chapter 8, an agreement to substitute a new contractual obligation for an existing one if the new obligation is satisfactorily performed is an *accord.* The actual performance of the new obligation is called a *satisfaction.* Thus, an accord and satisfaction discharges the previous obligation. However, if the performance in the accord is not

Two parties to a contract later mutually agree to change the terms of the contract. What are the four ways in which they can do so without any liability for breach?

rendered, the old contract remains in effect. That is the situation in *What's Your Verdict?* Jan failed to perform under the accord (to pay $1,500 by January 15), and so the original contract was not discharged. He still owes $2,000.

NOVATION A party entitled to receive performance under a contract may release the other party from the duty of performance and accept a substitute party. This is a *novation*. In effect, a new contract is formed by agreement of the three parties who are involved.

By Impossibility of Performance

Generally, impossibility of performance refers to extreme external conditions rather than an obligor's personal inability to perform. A surprise war or an unexpected embargo (the legal stoppage of commerce) may lead to impossibility of performance. On the other hand, increased prices of needed supplies, a strike of workers, difficulty in obtaining materials or equipment, or natural disasters (such as a flood or earthquake) that only delay performance do not discharge the contractual obligations.

Impossibility of performance also may be used to discharge contractual obligations when events

Inspectors determined that this bridge, damaged in an earthquake, would not be usable until it is repaired. The bridge provides your company's only connection for transporting goods. Would your company's contracts be discharged due to this situation? Why or why not?

on a smaller scale than wars or earthquakes interfere. For example,

- unique subject matter identified in the contract is destroyed before it can be delivered to the buyer (for example, a Picasso is burned to a crisp in a fire at an auction house)

- a performance becomes illegal before it can be rendered (for example, installing asbestos shingles on a new building)

- the death or disability of someone who was to provide a personal service that only that person could render

Parties commonly do include "escape hatch" language in their contracts. Such language permits modification, or even termination, of performance without liability for damages in the event of an inability to perform on schedule because of specified conditions.

By Operation of Law

A contract may be discharged or the right to enforce it may be barred by operation of law. This happens when the person's debts are discharged in bankruptcy. It also happens when the time allowed for enforcement of the contract has elapsed because of the statute of limitations.

Alteration of a written agreement also usually discharges the agreement by operation of law. **Alteration** is a material change in the terms of a written contract without the consent of the other party. To discharge the contract, the alteration must be

- material, thus changing the obligation in an important way

- made intentionally, and not by accident or mistake

- made by a party to the agreement, or by an authorized agent

- made without consent of the other party.

By Tender of Performance

A ready, willing, and able offer to perform an obligation is a **tender**. If the duty requires the doing of an act, a tender that is made in good faith but is rejected will discharge the obligation of the one offering to perform. However, if the obligation requires the payment of money, rejection of a tender to pay the money does not discharge the debt nor does it prevent the creditor from collecting later. It merely relieves the debtor of court costs or future interest charges that might otherwise become due. To be valid, the tender of money must consist of the exact amount due in currency or coins, or *legal tender*.

A tender of only part of the debt is not a valid tender. If the debtor offers less than the amount due, the creditor may refuse it without losing the right to later collect the entire amount due.

CHECKPOINT Identify the six ways in which contractual obligations can be discharged.

11-1 Assessment

Xtra!
Study Tools
school.cengage.com/blaw/lawxtra

THINK ABOUT LEGAL CONCEPTS

1. The party transferring a right in an assignment is called the (a) assignee (b) assignor (c) obligor

2. An assignment has to be supported by consideration. **True or False?**

3. Which of the following is the most frequent cause of a discharge of all contractual duties? (a) complete performance (b) major breach (c) accord and satisfaction

4. If the contract creating the rights prohibits assignment, the parties may still assign them. **True or False?**

5. An agreement in which the parties agree to substitute one obligor for another and to release the original obligor from her or his contractual obligations is called a(n) (a) novation (b) substitution (c) accord

6. If a valid tender of money to pay a monetary debt under a contract is rejected, the debt is discharged. **True or False?**

THINK CRITICALLY ABOUT EVIDENCE

Study the situation, answer the questions, and then prepare arguments to support your answers.

7. Tori operated a business that provided graphic design and printing services. Gerov contracted to have Tori design and print 25,000 brochures in full color promoting a variety of international tours. Under their contract, Tori also agreed to address and mail envelopes containing the brochures to a select list of prospects. Tori delegated the addressing, stuffing, and mailing of the envelopes. Is this a valid delegation? Does Tori remain liable to Gerov for proper completion of the entire job?

8. Your school orders 50 new uniforms for its marching band. The contract is with Quality Uniforms Inc., a firm with whom the school has done business for 12 years. A week before the first public performance

by the band, Quality states that it has overbooked its business and has delegated the sewing to New Era Uniforms. Is the delegation legally proper?

9. Your school orders 50 new uniforms for its marching band. The contract states that "time is of the essence," and if the goods are not received in time for the first performance by the band on September 1, the old uniforms will be used for another year. The performance is the major part of a contest to see which area band will go to New York City to take part in Macy's Thanksgiving Day Parade. The manufacturer does not deliver the uniforms until September 3. Can the school cancel the contract?

11-2 Remedies for Breach of Contract

GOALS

- Name and describe various remedies possible for minor or major breach of contract
- Discuss the factors that affect the choice of remedies

KEY TERMS

remedy

specific performance

mitigate the damages

waiver

statute of limitations

Remedies Possible for Breach

WHAT'S YOUR VERDICT? Liu contracted to buy 160 acres of land from McCall. She planned to build an amusement park on the land as it was near the junction of two interstates and had adequate utilities and population density. When McCall learned of her plan, he refused to transfer the title.

What remedies does Liu have from which to choose, and what is her optimal remedy?

A **remedy** is the legal means by which a right is enforced or a right's violation is prevented or redressed. Different remedies are available depending on whether a breach is a major or minor one. Whether a breach is major or minor is an issue of fact in a trial. The primary guideline in making the classification is the significance of the breach in relation to the entire contract.

Remedy for a Minor Breach

The only remedy generally available for a minor breach is money damages. The party injured by a minor breach generally must continue to perform the duties defined by the contract. The amount of damages would be whatever it took to complete the minor duty left undone by the breaching party. They could be recovered by suit if the victim had already paid. They could be deducted from the money due the breaching party under the contract if the victim had not yet paid.

Remedies for a Major Breach

If the breach is classified as a major breach, then the injured party need not continue performing

the duties defined by the contract. In addition, the victim, such as Liu in *What's Your Verdict?*, can choose among the following remedies:

1. *Rescission and restitution* Canceling the contract and returning whatever has been received under it
2. *Money damages* The payment of money to compensate for injury
3. *Specific performance* A court order commanding the breaching party to perform what was promised in the contract

RESCISSION AND RESTITUTION These remedies are intended to place the parties in the same

Do you think the contract breach in the *What's Your Verdict?* situation on this page would be a major breach or a minor breach? Explain your answer.

© GETTY IMAGES/PHOTODISC

legal position they were in before contracting. Rescission allows the parties to treat the contract as canceled. *Restitution* permits each party to recover money or property (or the value thereof) given to the other party. Thus, if a seller of realty committed a major breach by failing to deliver the deed, the buyer could sue for restitution and recover any money paid for the property. When rescission is granted, all the contractual obligations of the parties are canceled. Restitution also is usually available when the parties have attempted to contract, but failed, and in the process one party has delivered something of value to the other.

MONEY DAMAGES Money damages may be compensatory, consequential, punitive, liquidated, or nominal.

COMPENSATORY An award of *compensatory money damages* seeks to restore injured parties to the same financial position they were in prior to the breach. For example, consider a situation where, Charlotte, a home broker, contracted to buy a house from Ben for $65,000, knowing that the fair market value of the property was considerably higher. To facilitate the purchase Charlotte then spent $3,000 on a title search, a survey, an appraisal, loan origination fees, and other expenses. If Ben then committed a material breach for refusing to sell, a court would award Charlotte $2,000 as compensatory money damages. This would restore the broker to her financial position prior to the breach.

CONSEQUENTIAL In awarding *consequential money damages,* the court again tries to place injured parties in the same financial position they would have been in if the contract had been performed. This remedy grants money for the foreseeable injuries caused by the breach. Consequential damages generally are foreseeable when a reasonable person would know that a breach would cause the injury or has been explicitly notified of same.

For example, suppose that, in the above example, Charlotte brags to Ben that because they contracted, she has arranged the resale of his property for $85,000. Upon hearing this Ben refuses to go through with their contract. As a result of the time delay in getting a court to order Ben to pass title, Charlotte loses her potential buyer at $85,000. However, because of her telling Ben of the potential resale, the injury is specifically foreseeable to Ben. He will, therefore, be liable for consequential damages in the amount of Charlotte's lost profit of $20,000. Consequential damages may be granted for both major and minor breaches.

PUNITIVE Under certain circumstances, such as fraud or when an intentional tort is involved in a breach of contract, the courts will award *punitive damages.* Such damages are added to other money damages. Their purpose is to punish and to make an example of the defendant. This could happen, for example, when a dishonest seller cheats a buyer by falsely saying a necklace is made of solid, 18-carat gold when in fact it is gold-plated copper or highly polished brass.

LIQUIDATED Parties to a contract sometimes agree on a certain amount of monetary damages that will be paid if a particular contract breach occurs. These are termed *liquidated money damages.* They are typically placed in a contact when an actual damage amount would be too speculative or too difficult to arrive at in court. A liquidated damages clause might state.

> In the event there are insufficient funds in depositor's account to cover incoming checks, causing the bank to refuse to pay them, the bank shall be able to deduct $30 per such check from depositor's account.

Not all liquidated damages clauses are enforceable. When the liquidated damage amount is excessive in relation to the injury, the clause will not be enforced. A liquidated damages clause will be enforced only when it stipulates an amount reflecting a reasonable attempt to forecast the damages that would result from the breach. If it does reflect a reasonable forecast, it will be enforced even when no damages actually are suffered. When the liquidated damages clause is not enforceable, the injured party can collect damages only by proving other money damages.

NETBookmark

Access school.cengage.com/blaw/lawxtra and click on the link for Chapter 11. Surf the material in "Contract Law: The Basics" in the FindLaw for Small Business web site. Write two or three sentences explaining a fact you learned about contract law from the web site. Be prepared to read your sentences in class.

school.cengage.com/blaw/lawxtra

NOMINAL Failure to perform a duty under a contract is a legal wrong. Therefore courts, even when no substantial harm has been done, will still award a token amount called *nominal damages* to acknowledge that a wrong has been committed. This could happen when, after a breach, the plaintiff finds a replacement product at a lower price. Nominal damages are granted in recognition of the rights that have been violated.

SPECIFIC PERFORMANCE Sometimes the only appropriate remedy for breach of contract is to decree (order) that the breaching party do exactly what was required under the contract. This is termed the remedy of **specific performance**.

Specific performance generally is available when the subject of the contract is unique such as in the purchase of an antique custom made 1932 Rolls Royce or a specific parcel of land. In *What's Your Verdict?* Liu's optimal remedy would be specific performance. The court would order McCall to transfer title to the property with a properly signed deed delivered to Liu.

Courts are reluctant to grant specific performance in situations where they would have great difficulty in supervising the result. For example, watching over the construction of a home or other structure to be sure it was up to contract specifications would absorb too much of the court's time. Similarly, it is very difficult for courts to super-

vise personal service or employment contracts. Therefore these contracts usually are not specifically enforceable. However, a court may grant an injunction prohibiting the defaulting party, such as an athletic coach or a key laboratory scientist, from working for anyone else during the period of employment agreed to under the contract. The person who breached the contract still would be liable for any money damages suffered by the employer. In addition to personal service and employment contracts, courts will not specifically enforce contracts in which terms are vague or ambiguous.

Finally, note that specific performance is an equitable remedy. A court will not award the remedy unless the party seeking it is blameless and has acted reasonably and fairly throughout the transaction. This is often called "clean hands."

CHECKPOINT Explain the remedies available for a major breach of contract.

Factors Affecting Choice of Remedy

WHAT'S YOUR VERDICT? Jim "high and tight" Brushback, an unknown baseball pitcher, signed a contract to play his rookie year for a major league team for $120,000. After two months, Brushback had won all four games he'd started with 37 strikeouts and an earned-run average (ERA) of 1.75. He then contracted with a competing team for $4 million a year for the next five years, thereby breaching his rookie contract

What remedies are available to the original team?

Conflict of Remedies

A party injured by a breach of contract must elect, or choose, a remedy when suing. Often, electing to pursue one remedy will rule out pursuing another. For example, specific performance and damages cannot be recovered for the same breach because specific performance is not available when damages are an adequate remedy. Similarly, as rescission and restitution place the victim in the pre-contract position and damages place the victim in a post-contract financial

IN THIS CASE Rod McFink, a well-known rock and roll star, contracted with TickXX, Inc., a promotion company, to play in Springfield, Missouri's new convention center on December 15. TickXX had rented the venue, printed 15,000 tickets, and sold more than 1,000 in advance, when Rod announced that he would not be able to appear. TickXX personnel quickly found out that Rod had cancelled in order to play on the same date in Minneapolis for almost double the money. TickXX sued for its expenditures, lost profits on the 1,000 tickets (the potential sale of the other 14,000 was too speculative to get a lost profits award for them), and for a court order prohibiting Rod from playing anywhere other than Springfield on that weekend. Upon hearing of the suit, Rod called TickXX and agreed to perform in Springfield as scheduled. TickXX then dropped the suit.

position, the combining of these remedies is not permitted for most contracts. Under the UCC, however, these remedies can be combined for a breach of contract for the sale of goods.

Restitution and specific performance are essentially opposites, so you could not combine these remedies. In *What's Your Verdict?* Brushback's original team could recover the two months' wages ($20,000) as restitution. However, if the team elects this remedy, they would lose the ability to sue for damages and the ability to obtain an injunction to stop Brushback from playing for the competition.

Duty to Mitigate

A party injured by a breach of contract is required by law to take reasonable steps to minimize the harm done or, in legal terminology, to **mitigate the damages**. Suppose you contracted for a daily supply of 10-cent bolts used to assemble a car. If the supplier breached, you could not recover the consequential damages associated with the production line's being halted unless you made a reasonable attempt to find substitute bolts. Similarly, in most states, a landlord must take reasonable steps to re-rent an apartment vacated in breach of a lease. If an injured party fails to take reasonable steps to mitigate the damages, the amount of potential recovery is lessened by the amount that could have been mitigated.

Waivers

Sometimes a party intentionally and explicitly gives up a contractual right. This is called a **waiver**. If a creditor says, "I will accept your overdue payment without a late charge," this is a waiver. Waivers also arise by implication from conduct. For instance, if one party consistently sends late payments and is not charged the late fee specified in the contract, the rights to collect a late fee on future payments may be waived.

Statute of Limitations

Statutes in all states deny any remedy if suit is not brought within a certain time after a legal claim, such as breach of contract, arises. Such laws are called **statutes of limitations**. While the time period varies among the states, four years is a common time for contracts and three years is a common time for torts. About half of the states allow more time to sue on written contracts than on oral ones. The UCC provides that an action for breach of a contract for the sale of goods must be begun within four years after the cause of action arises. In their original agreement, the parties may shorten the period to not less than one year, but they may not lengthen it. The statute of limitations begins to run from the moment there is a right to sue for a breach or default.

LEGAL *Research*

Research the time period for the statute of limitations in contracts of sale in your state. When was this statute of limitations enacted?

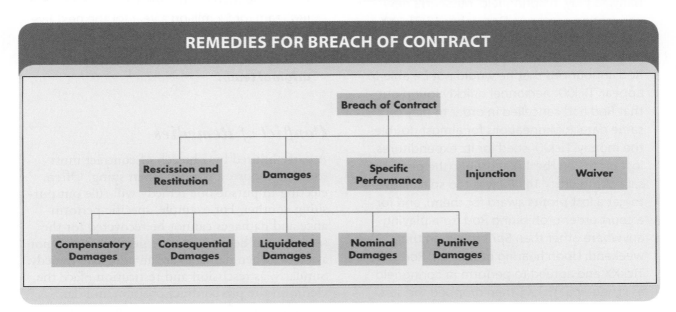

REMEDIES FOR BREACH OF CONTRACT

Breach of Contract
- Rescission and Restitution
- Damages
  - Compensatory Damages
  - Consequential Damages
  - Liquidated Damages
  - Nominal Damages
  - Punitive Damages
- Specific Performance
- Injunction
- Waiver

In the case of minors and others who lack capacity to contract, allowance is made for their period of incapacity. Thus, a minor is given a reasonable time after reaching majority to file suit.

Bankruptcy

Under the U.S. Constitution, Congress has established uniform laws on bankruptcies that permit the discharge (or excusing) of debts. Under these laws, debtors can get a fresh start, and creditors share fairly in whatever assets are available. *Bankruptcy* is a legal proceeding whereby a bankrupt's estate is distributed among various claimants in order to discharge many of the bankrupt's debts and give the bankrupt a fresh financial start. (See Chapter 33.)

CHECKPOINT What does it mean to "mitigate the damages"?

11-2 Assessment

Xtra!
Study Tools
school.cengage.com/blaw/lawxtra

THINK ABOUT LEGAL CONCEPTS

1. Which remedy seeks to place the parties in exactly the same position they would have been in if the contract had been performed? (a) liquidated damages (b) restitution (c) specific performance

2. If a liquidated damages clause is excessive, the clause will not be enforced and the injured party only can collect by proving other money damages. **True or False?**

3. Specific performance will be granted if (a) money damages are an adequate remedy (b) the subject matter of the contract is unique (c) the duty to be performed is difficult for the court to supervise (d) any of the above

4. Which of the following remedies can be pursued at the same time? (a) damages and restitution for services (b) specific performance and damages (c) specific performance and restitution (d) none of the above can be pursued at the same time

5. In contracts for the sale of goods, rescission can be combined with damages. **True or False?**

THINK CRITICALLY ABOUT EVIDENCE

Study the situation, answer the questions, and then prepare arguments to support your answers.

6. A college football coach has directed his team to division championships five times. With two years remaining in his current three-year employment contract, he notifies the college president that he is resigning in order to coach a professional team at a higher salary. Is the coach legally free to change employers? Is the professional team legally free to hire him? What can the college legally do?

7. The Bethlehem Steel Company contracted with the city of Chicago to supply and erect the steelwork for a certain section of an interstate highway. The price agreed upon was $1,734,200. The contract also provided that the steel company would pay as liquidated damages $1,000 for each day the work was extended and uncompleted beyond a specified date. The work was completed 52 days after the date agreed upon. Is the company liable for $52,000?

8. As she had in previous years, Rivera secured the concession rights to sell food, drinks, and souvenirs at a post-season football bowl game. Some 60,000 reserved seat tickets had been sold for the event. After consulting her records of previous years' sales, Rivera contracted with Ace Novelty Company for 10,000 pennants, noisemakers, and other items imprinted with the emblems and in the colors of the two competing teams. Although Rivera had emphasized the absolute necessity of delivery at least eight hours before game time, the goods arrived two days after the game had been played. Can Rivera recover lost profits from Ace? Why?

9. While under contract with the county, Pyramid Paving improperly applied asphalt to the public gravel road in front of your family's home. Soon after application, large cracks appeared and your family complained. It took the city six years to file suit. What defense can Pyramid assert?

CONCEPTS IN BRIEF

11-1 Transfer and Discharge of Obligations

1. A party may generally assign rights under a contract as long as the performance will not be materially changed. One is not released from contractual duties by making an assignment of them.

2. Duties may not be delegated when they involve personal judgment or skill, as with artists and professional experts.

3. Generally, an assignee acquires only such rights as the assignor has under the contract.

4. A material breach of contract generally permits the other party to regard his or her obligation to perform as discharged.

5. An obligation calling for an act, except that of paying money, is discharged by a tender of performance.

11-2 Remedies for Breach of Contract

6. In case of a breach of contract, the injured party has various remedies. An injured party may rescind or cancel the contract, recover the amount of loss through damages, and in certain cases, require specific performance or obtain an injunction.

7. Compensatory, consequential, nominal, and liquidated damages are all available where appropriate as remedies under contract law. Punitive damages are not available. However, should the breach of contract involve an intentional tort or crime, punitive damages may be obtained as a separate cause of action.

8. When the legal remedy of damages is not adequate, the court may grant the equitable remedy of specific performance, or of rescission, or it may grant an injunction prohibiting specified acts.

9. A remedy for breach of contract may be barred by the lapse of the time prescribed by a statute of limitations or by the debtor's discharge in bankruptcy.

YOUR LEGAL VOCABULARY

Match each statement with the term that it best defines. Some terms may not be used.

1. The fulfillment of contractual promises as agreed
2. A notification given by a defaulting party prior to initiation of performance that he or she is not going to perform
3. The intentional and explicit giving up of a contractual right
4. A ready, willing, and able offer to perform contractual obligations
5. One who owes a duty under a contract
6. The result of a court decree that the breaching party do exactly what was required under the contract
7. A termination of duties that ordinarily occurs when the parties perform as promised
8. The action or procedure followed to enforce a right or to get damages for an injury to a right
9. The injured party takes reasonable steps to minimize the harm done

a. alteration
b. anticipatory breach
c. assignment
d. breach of contract
e. default
f. discharge
g. mitigate the damages
h. obligor
i. performance
j. remedy
k. specific performance
l. statute of limitations
m. substantial performance
n. tender
o. waiver

REVIEW LEGAL CONCEPTS

10. Tell how to determine whether a right can be assigned.

11. Describe those situations where specific performance will not be granted.

12. Explain how a statute of limitations works.

13. Why aren't claims against the United States government assignable?

14. What is the difference between a novation and an accord and satisfaction?

WRITE ABOUT LEGAL CONCEPTS

15. Write a short contract for the fictitious sale of a car between two of your classmates. Stipulate that the money is to be paid in two weeks and the title is to be delivered in one week. Now for each of the two classmates, write a sentence describing the rights and duties created by this contract.

16. Under what circumstances would an embargo present a legitimate defense to a breach of contract suit?

17. Make a list of five things that might be the subject of a contract but where specific performance would not be available. After each item write one sentence which states why this remedy is not available.

18. **HOT DEBATE** In its defense, Predator notes that its system for paying overdrafts and then debiting accounts for $50 each is totally automated and run by computer. No bank official ever sees the overdrafts. How does this affect the ethical and legal evaluations of their actions in Tony's case?

THINK CRITICALLY ABOUT EVIDENCE

Study the situation, answer the questions, and then prepare arguments to support your answers.

19. The Conch Oil Company, located at Marathon in the Florida Keys, contracted to sell and to deliver 500 barrels of fuel oil on the first of each month for one year to the Monsoon Mushroom Factory, an indoor farm. Conch delivered the oil for the first two months, but only two barrels at the beginning of the third month. Conch said there was unprecedented demand due to hurricane Sunny heading their way and it was allocating available supplies to customers on a pro-rata basis. There was nothing in the contract covering such a circumstance. The hurricane missed Marathon, and the mushroom crop died for want of fuel to help the climate control system keep it at an even temperature and humidity. Monsoon sued Conch. How should Conch defend against the suit? Who would likely win?

20. Hoglund reneged on his promise to sell his car to Elsen. Elsen went to nearby Los Angeles and found the same model with lower mileage, in better condition, and priced $600 below Hoglund's. Nevertheless, Elsen was incensed by

Hoglund's conduct and wanted to sue him. To what damages, if any, would Elsen be entitled?

21. Good contracted to build a house for Stern according to Stern's plans. After the house was completed, there were several defects that Good refused to fix. Stern then contracted with Madden to do the necessary corrective work for $8,000 and then sued Good for $8,000 in compensatory damages. Stern also demanded $10,000 in punitive damages "to punish Good and set an example for others." Is Stern entitled to compensatory damages? Is Stern legally or ethically entitled to punitive damages?

22. Horatio opened a checking account at Bridge Bank. Month after month he verified his statement balance to the penny. In December, however, due to buying extra gifts for his sons, Horatio overdrew his account by thirteen cents. The Bridge Bank's computer then automatically refused to pay the check and charged Horatio the $50 overdraft fee agreed to in his checking account contract. What legal argument could Horatio make against paying the $50 overdraft fee?

MAKE ACADEMIC CONNECTIONS

23. **SCIENCE** Development of products to be used in the frontiers of space can be expensive. The process is often saddled with delays, cost overruns, and failures. Research how NASA writes its contracts for the

projects it funds. Be especially observant for liquidated damage clauses, waivers, assignment restrictions, testing, security precautions, and any unusual clauses that are specific to such undertakings. Keep in mind the legendary aside of an astronaut to another as the countdown neared an end. "Did you ever think we're about to blast off in a rocket built by a host of lowest bidders?"

ANALYZE REAL CASES

24. Eugene Plante was a general contractor who built a house for Frank and Carol Jacobs for a contract price of $26,765. The buyers paid $20,000 but refused to pay the balance, claiming that the contract had not been substantially performed. Plante sued, and the court ruled in his favor but first deducted the cost of repairing plaster cracks in the ceilings and a number of other defects. The buyers were dissatisfied with the judgment and appealed, notably because the trial court had allowed nothing for the misplacement of a wall between the kitchen and the living room. This enlarged the kitchen and narrowed the living room by one foot. Real estate experts testified during the trial that this did not affect the market price of the house, yet to move the wall would cost about $4,000. How should the appellate court decide? (*Plante v. Jacobs,* 103 N.W.2d 296, Wis.)

25. The Washington Trader was a giant oil tanker owned by the plaintiff, American Trading and Production Corporation. In March 1967, the defendant, Shell International Marine, Ltd., contracted for the ship to carry a load of oil from Texas to India. The total fee agreed upon was $417,327.36. No reference was made in the contract for the route to be taken; this was to be a decision of the shipping company. The route around Africa's Cape of Good Hope was an acceptable route. However, the price was based on passage through the Suez Canal (the invoice contained a Suez Canal toll charge). The Washington Trader headed for the Mediterranean Sea and the Suez. When the ship reached Gibraltar, it was warned of possible violence in the Middle East. Nevertheless, it continued. Upon reaching the Suez Canal, the ship found the canal closed by the Arab-Israeli War. The ship turned back and took the long route around Africa, at an added cost of $131,978.44. It arrived in Bombay some 30 days later than originally expected. American Trading then billed Shell for the full amount. When Shell refused to pay, American Trading sued. American claimed that the war made it impossible to perform as originally agreed. Shell, it said, should pay the extra cost because otherwise Shell would be unjustly enriched. You decide. (*American Trading and Production Corporation v. Shell International Marine, Ltd.,* 453 F.2d 939, 2d Cir.)

26. Under a written contract, plaintiff Shirley MacLaine Parker agreed to play the female singing-dancing lead in defendant 20th Century-Fox Film Corporation's planned production of a musical entitled "Bloomer Girl," to be filmed in Los Angeles. Fox Films was to pay MacLaine a minimum of $53,571.42 a week for 14 weeks, starting May 23. Before then, Fox decided not to produce the picture. In a letter dated April 4, Fox offered to employ MacLaine in a dramatic, western-type movie to be produced in Australia instead. She was given one week in which to accept. She did not, and the offer lapsed. She then sued for the agreed-upon $750,000 guaranteed compensation. Fox defended by saying MacLaine had unreasonably refused to mitigate damages by rejecting the substitute role. Is MacLaine entitled to receive the damages? (*Parker v. 20th Century-Fox Film Corporation,* 474 P.2d 689, Cal.)

27. Cingular Wireless bought out its rival AT&T Wireless in 2004 for some $41 billion. According to court filings, Cingular then launched an aggressive program to halve the broadcast tower rental amounts paid under contracts with more than 15,000 landlords. One such landlord, the City of Parma, Ohio, whose rent was $4,000 per month, subsequently brought a class action suit on behalf of tower owners for anticipatory breach of their contracts. Parma alleged that Cingular's buyout of AT&T necessitated that the wireless corporation reduce its expenses by some $900 million a year. Reducing tower rentals would provide a large part of the necessary revenue savings. As a consequence, Cingular threatened that, should landlords not allow the halving of their rentals they would be left out of the network it was forming by consolidating the coverage areas from its and AT&T's towers. Was the threat an anticipatory breach? Why or why not? (*Parma, City of, v. Cingular Wireless L.L.C.,* No. 05-4107, 6th Cir. Sept. 8, 2006)

Sports & Entertainment Law

Freedom Isn't Free

MIAMI DOLPHINS LTD. V. ERRICK L. "RICKY" WILLIAMS AND THE NFL PLAYERS ASSOCIATION 356 F. SUPP. 2D 1301

BACKGROUND His credentials were impeccable. Heisman Trophy winner in 1998, NFL leader in rushing with 1,853 yards in 2002, and rusher for another 1,372 yards in 2003 with less offensive support, Ricky Williams was the National Football League's premier running back. Williams also was the foundation for the team the Miami Dolphins hoped would take them back to the Super Bowl. Ricky was not the stereotypical football player, however. His passions included shopping and photography, and he was shy. So shy in fact that he habitually avoided eye contact and gave post-game interviews with his helmet on. Eventually he was diagnosed with social anxiety disorder.

FACTS It came as the paradoxical "expected surprise" when Williams retired in mid 2004 at age 27. As he boarded a plane that was to take him to India for several months of travel and self-discovery, Williams was quoted as saying, "You can't understand how free I feel." The Dolphins, however, felt that Williams' "freedom wasn't free" and sued him, citing a liquidated damage clause in Williams' seven-year contract. The clause read: "In the event Player fails or refuses to report to Club, or fails or refuses to practice or play with Club at any time for any reason . . . , or leaves Club without its consent during the duration of the above league years, or if Player is otherwise in breach of this Contract, then Player shall be in default. If Player is in Default, then upon demand by Club, Player shall . . . return and refund to the Club any and all incentive payments previously paid by Club . . . relinquish and forfeit any and all earned but unpaid incentives." The total amount ultimately to be repaid to the Dolphins under the clause totaled more than $8.6 million. Subject to the agreement between the NFL and its players' association, the dispute was referred to arbitration. When the arbitrator awarded the Dolphins the full amount as damages, Ricky brought an appeal before the U.S. District Court for the Southern District of Florida.

THE LAW A liquidated damage amount that is greatly disproportionate to the harm done should be voided as a penalty.

THE ISSUE Was the damage award certified by the arbitrator under the contract with the Dolphins a penalty instead of a valid estimation of the harm done to the NFL team by Ricky's departure?

HOLDING The District Court upheld the decision of the arbitrator after noting the speculative nature of any determination of damages under the circumstances.

© STEPHEN DUNN/GETTY IMAGES

PRACTICE JUDGING

1. Why is the court concerned about the damage award being a penalty?

2. What factors do you feel that the court should have considered in determining whether or not the $8.6 million liquidated damage award was a penalty?

Chapter 12
Contractual Aspects of Marriage and Divorce

12-1 Marriage and the Law of Contracts

12-2 Divorce and the Law of Contracts

HOT DEBATE

Ben, 16, had been dating Betsy for several months when he told his parents about the relationship. Ben's father had been in business with Betsy's dad and the partnership ended poorly. When his father heard the news, he told Ben to stop seeing Betsy. Ben refused, and his father took away the car Ben bought with his own money, stopped paying Ben's tuition, and spent the funds saved for Ben's college. With his mother's backing, Ben brought suit against his father for "improper parenting." Ben's father's attorney filed a motion to dismiss the suit. The motion stated that "improper parenting" was not a legitimate cause of action and that the father had acted within his powers as a parent under the law. The lower court dismissed the suit, and Ben appealed to the state court of appeals.

WHERE DO YOU STAND?

1. Make a persuasive argument that emphasizes the legal reasons supporting Ben's suit.
2. Make a persuasive argument that emphasizes the legal reasons supporting his father's actions.

12-1 Marriage and the Law of Contracts

GOALS

- Discuss how the law affects premarital relationships
- Explain how a marriage contract is formed and legalized
- Name the rights and duties of husbands and wives

KEY TERMS

marriage

common-law marriages

civil union

marital consortium

adoption

prenuptial agreement

Premarital Relationships and the Law

WHAT'S YOUR VERDICT? Jim and Mary are both 16 years old. While dating they have intimate relations, and Mary becomes pregnant.

Will the law compel them to marry?

Marriage is a legal union of a man and a woman as husband and wife. The law affects several areas of premarital relationships. These include the minimum age at which you are allowed to marry with or without parental permission, the responsibilities and rights of the parents when a child results from a premarital relationship, and couples living together outside of marriage.

Age and Premarital Relationships

Although no law specifies a minimum age for dating, nearly all states have laws setting minimum ages for marriage with or without parental permission. Typically, the minimum age for marriage without parental permission is 18. No law restricts the choice of marital partners, with one exception—close relatives may not marry.

If parents tell their minor child not to date or not to see a specific person, they can enforce that order only with the "reasonable force" that they may use to see that their other directions are carried out. If that fails, parents have no legal means to achieve their ends short of having their child

labeled "incorrigible" in a juvenile delinquency proceeding. Parental use of excessive force may result in charges of child abuse.

Premarital Pregnancy and Child Birth

Criminal laws against consensual premarital sexual intercourse between adults generally have been eliminated over the past couple of decades. However, if pregnancy results and the male responsible is identified, he will be required to pay his share of the female's medical bills and to contribute to the child's support until the child reaches adulthood. This is true even if the father is a minor. Beyond that requirement, no law

GLOBAL ISSUES

Marriage Rules in Muslim Cultures

In Muslim countries, such as Saudi Arabia and Kuwait, the Muslim religious rules of marriage are part of the legal rules as well. In these countries, arranged marriages are common. There may be little or no contact between the bride and groom prior to the marriage. A dowry—or payment from the groom to the bride's father—is made. (In some other cultures dowry payments are made by the bride's family to the groom or the groom's family.) Polygamy, the taking of multiple wives, is legal in some Muslim countries. In these situations the husband may take up to four wives, provided each wife shares equally in the husband's companionship and worldly goods.

exists to force the parents of an illegitimate child to marry. In *What's Your Verdict?* Mary and Jim may remain single.

Cohabitation

A man and woman who live together outside of marriage are said to *cohabitate*. Such living arrangements were considered illegal in most states until the late 1970s. Cohabitation is still illegal in some states, although such laws are seldom enforced.

CHECKPOINT Name the aspects of premarital relationships that are affected by the law.

The Marital Contract

WHAT'S YOUR VERDICT? Grady and Cheryl are engaged to be married. Grady's parents strongly disapprove of the upcoming marriage. They finally convince Grady to break the engagement.

Can Cheryl bring a successful lawsuit against Grady's parents for interfering with her contract to marry Grady?

If one party in a heterosexual relationship proposes marriage and the other accepts, a binding contract results. If both later mutually agree to end their engagement, the contract is *annulled*. This means that the law considers their agreement void and never to have existed.

Breach-of-Promise Lawsuits

If only one party wants out of the contract and refuses to perform, a breach-of-promise suit may be brought by the other party. At one time juries set abnormally high figures to compensate the jilted party (usually the woman) for the actual damages, humiliation, and hurt feelings that accompanied the breakup. Today, some states allow such suits only where the woman is pregnant and her ex-fiancé is the father. Other states have placed a cap on the amount of damages that can be awarded. Many states have banned breach-of-promise suits altogether.

If third parties interfere with the engagement, a few states allow damage suits against the intruders. Such suits, however, cannot be brought against the parents who try to prevent their son or daughter from marrying. In *What's Your Verdict?* Grady's parents may try to keep him from marrying Cheryl. Cheryl could not successfully sue them for interfering with her contract to marry Grady.

When a relationship breaks down, gifts given by one party to the other may create legal problems. If the gift, such as a ring, is given in expectation of marriage, the courts generally order it to be returned. However, some states allow the woman to keep the ring if the man breaks off the engagement. Gifts other than those given in expectation of marriage can be kept by the recipient.

IN THIS CASE When Amanda said yes to his proposal, Antonio gave her several gifts including a five-carat engagement ring, a new sports car, and some plastic surgery. Two months later, Amanda fell in love with the jeweler who appraised the ring for her. Consequently, she broke off the engagement to Antonio. In most states, she must return the ring but can keep the car (and the plastic surgery).

What happens, legally, if a couple mutually decides to end their engagement to be married?

© GETTY IMAGES/PHOTODISC

Legalizing the Marital Contract

Couples may get married by following the laws of the state in which they wish to marry. Alternative ways to marry include entering into a common-law marriage or a civil union.

STATE STATUTORY REQUIREMENTS Each state has its own requirements for marriage. Most couples begin the process by appearing before the city or town clerk. The couple must apply for and pay a fee for a marriage license. In the vast majority of states, if the parties are 18 years of age or older, they do not need their parents' consent. With parental consent, most states allow minors as young as 16 years old to marry.

Some states require a blood test before the license is issued to show that the applicants are free from various communicable diseases. A mandatory waiting period of three days from application to issuance is common. Once the license has been issued, any authorized religious or civil officials—court clerks, mayors, judges, rabbis, ministers, priests, and even ship captains at sea—can perform the ceremony.

An attempt has been made to standardize state laws for marriage and divorce. The Uniform Marriage and Divorce Act has been adopted by eight states. These states include Illinois, Kentucky, Missouri, Minnesota, Colorado, Montana, Arizona, and Washington. Marriage laws in the other states vary.

COMMON-LAW MARRIAGES Common-law marriages have their roots in the American frontier. Because of the absence of suitable authorities, many pioneers could not follow the legal methods for becoming husband and wife. As a consequence, the law recognized **common-law marriages** that occurred when a single woman and a single man lived together, shared common property, and held themselves out as husband and wife over a prolonged period of time (usually 10 years or longer). Today, about one-fourth of our states allow common-law marriages, although all states must recognize such a union if it is legal in the state in which it occurred. See the list above to see if your state recognizes common-law marriages.

CIVIL UNIONS During the last few decades in various countries around the world as well as in a few states of the United States, an alternative form of interpersonal legal union has developed that is similar to marriage. Generally referred to

States That Recognize Common-Law Marriages

Alabama

Colorado

Georgia (if formed before 1/1/97)

Idaho (if formed before 1/1/96)

Iowa

Kansas

Montana

New Hampshire (for inheritance purposes only)

Ohio (if formed before 10/10/91)

Oklahoma (if formed before 11/1/98)

Pennsylvania

Rhode Island

South Carolina

Texas (called an "informal relationship")

Utah

Washington, D.C.

as a **civil union**, it typically offers many of the rights, duties, and benefits as marriage to those who elect to form it. A civil union also is known by the term *same-sex marriage* in some areas. This is a misnomer, however, because it is open to opposite-sex couples in several jurisdictions.

First legitimized in the United States by Vermont in 2000, civil unions have since been made a legal alternative to marriage in Connecticut and New Jersey. Unlike the United

NETBookmark

Access school.cengage.com/blaw/lawxtra and click on the link for Chapter 12. Examine the table entitled "Marriage Laws of the Fifty States, the District of Columbia, and Puerto Rico." Locate the marriage laws for your state, and write a paragraph explaining them.

school.cengage.com/blaw/lawxtra

Kingdom, France, Germany, and most other European nations, the federal government of the United States has chosen not to recognize civil unions. In addition, under the federal Defense of Marriage Act of 1996, states other than adopting states do not have to recognize such unions.

CHECKPOINT What two actions result in a binding marital contract?

Marital Rights and Duties

WHAT'S YOUR VERDICT? Your friend Bill's mother died three years ago. Now his father plans to remarry. Bill is concerned that his father's fiancée will have a claim against the family home and other property.

Is there anything Bill can do to prevent such a claim?

Traditionally, the law sees husband and wife as parties to a marriage contract for life and for the benefit of each other. The practical and legally recognized purposes for marriage are procreation, raising children, and filling sexual, economic, and companionship needs.

Marital Consortium

The law recognizes these purposes as mutual duties of the wife and husband and calls them the **marital consortium**. In most states, if either spouse suffers an injury that prevents fulfillment of these marital duties, the other can sue the party who caused the harm for damages for "loss of consortium."

The most important duty of both spouses is to provide for the support, nurture, welfare, and education of their children. Other obligations jointly entered into, such as contracts, notes, and income tax returns, also are the mutual responsibility of the marital partners.

Parenthood Rights and Duties

Parents are obligated by state laws to support their children until they reach adulthood. An exception applies if a minor child takes legal measures to become "emancipated." Financial support of a couple's children is a joint obligation. This duty may be divided according to each spouse's financial position. Both parents in a married couple have custody rights to their children. Likewise, both have an equal voice in decisions that arise while raising them.

Some couples may choose to adopt children. The legal process of **adoption** creates a parent-child relationship. Adoptive parents have the same rights and duties to the adoptive child as they would to a child born of their union. Adoptions are governed by state law and must be approved by the courts.

Property Rights and Duties

Property acquired during the marriage may be kept in the name of the husband, the wife, or both. Either marital partner can buy and sell property of all types in her or his own name and have sole control of the respective earnings and credit. Such was not always the case, especially for the woman in the relationship.

Sometimes, spouses bring property into marriage that they want to keep in their own names. They don't want the other spouse to have claim over it, especially in the event of death or divorce. Keeping a spouse from getting rights in such property can be accomplished with a **prenuptial agreement**.

By entering into a prenuptial agreement, the marital partners-to-be typically give up any future claim they might have to part or all of

LEGAL *Research*

In 1851, Massachusetts passed a major adoption law—the first in the United States. Today adoption laws are the focus of attention in many states. Much of the attention is centered on access to adoption records. Laws vary from state to state but most states allow some access. As new adoption laws are enacted, they are also being challenged. In 1997 the U.S. Supreme Court let stand a decision by the U.S. Court of Appeals for the Sixth Circuit that Tennessee's open records statute does not violate the federal Constitution. Research the approach taken in your state's adoption law and its status.

the other's property. Such a contract is especially useful when one or both are entering into their second or subsequent marriage and want to reserve the property from a previous marriage for the children of that bond. In *What's Your Verdict?* Bill could recommend that his father enter a prenuptial agreement with his fiancée by which she would give up any claims on certain or all such property that she might acquire by the marriage. Note that prenuptial agreements are not limited in their scope and may cover practically anything. For example, "prenups" can stipulate everything from how the premarital debts of the marital parties are to be paid to when the in-laws can visit. However courts will only enforce terms that are of a monetary nature.

The actions of one spouse may incur liability for the other. For example, the wife or husband may take care of the household while the other works outside the home. This often happens when there are young children in the family. In such a circumstance, the wage-earning spouse is legally responsible for the debts incurred by the other spouse in purchasing food, clothing, medical care, furniture, and any other items necessary to run the household.

CHECKPOINT What is the collection of legal duties owed by the marital partners to one another called?

Prenuptial Agreement

Whereas the bonds of matrimony are about to surround and forever join them to one another and whereas they are of the belief that their commitments to one another should be explicit and known, the following agreement, whose terms shall have precedence over all otherwise applicable statutory requirements, is hereby entered into on this 17th day of June, 20—, by Ms. Monica Sacks of 900 Blind Tree Lane, West Amherst, N.Y., and Mr. Bernard Wells, no current address, of that same city.

It is, therefore, agreed, as Ms. Sacks has considerable property left to her by her deceased husband, Mr. Toby Sacks, and can expect to acquire more as a function of the sound management of said estate, that:

1. Mr. Wells hereby relinquishes any and all claims, rights, or other interests and estates that the forthcoming marriage might bestow upon him in Ms. Sacks' property with the exceptions as to those granted by the following terms of this agreement.

2. That Mr. Wells shall enjoy during the term of the marriage a monthly stipend of $5,000, to be spent as he deems necessary.

3. That, should the marital union be broken and divorce ensue, Mr. Wells should receive a lump sum payment of $1,000,000 in full settlement of any claims he might have for maintenance or other support.

4. That said payment shall be forthcoming within three months of the entering of a decree of divorce in a court of this state with appropriate authority.

5. That the terms of this agreement expressed in paragraphs 2, 3, and 4 above, shall be null and void if Mr. Wells is shown to have been unfaithful to Ms. Sacks from this time forward.

IN WITNESS HEREOF, we, the undersigned, have set our hands and seals on the day and year first above written.

Monica Sacks
Monica Sacks

Bernard Wells
Bernard Wells

THINK ABOUT LEGAL CONCEPTS

1. No law specifies a minimum age for dating. **True or False?**

2. Even if both parties agree to end their contract to marry, the contract is still valid. **True or False?**

3. The voiding of a marital contract is referred to as an (a) alleviation (b) allois (c) annulment (d) none of the above

4. If one party wants out of and refuses to perform the marital contract but the other party wants to go through with it, a _ ?_ suit may result.

5. In most states, parental consent to marry is required for any party under the age of 18. **True or False?**

6. Do all states have to recognize a common-law marriage as long as it is legal in the state in which it occurred? **Yes or No?**

7. Do all states have to recognize a civil union as long as it is legal in the state in which it occurred? **Yes or No?**

8. By entering into a(n) _ ?_ agreement, the marital partners-to-be typically give up any future claim they might have to any or all of the other's property.

9. A parent-child relationship is artificially created by the legal process of (a) adhesion (b) alignment (c) assignment (d) none of the above.

THINK CRITICALLY ABOUT EVIDENCE

Study the following situations, answer the questions, and then prepare arguments to support your answers.

10. Becky and Tom are engaged and have set a date for the ceremony. Becky has, at her own expense and with Tom's knowledge, rented a chapel for the wedding and a reception hall, bought a dress and invitations, contracted for flowers, a photographer, and a caterer. Now Tom has told her that he is breaking off the engagement. Does Becky have a legal recourse to recover her expenditures?

11. Maria is an only child. Her mother died when she was eight years old. Now, seven years later, her father is engaged to remarry, and Maria objects. She is afraid that her father's new wife will come between her and her father and that the new wife will end up with the family home after her father dies. Ethically, should Maria try to persuade her father not to marry? Is there a legal device that would help resolve part of her worries?

12. Michael was driving home late one night when a large truck ran a red light and struck his vehicle and he was critically injured. Several months later it became obvious that he was permanently paralyzed from the waist down. Michael has grounds for a negligence lawsuit against the trucking company and the driver of the truck. What cause of action does his wife have?

13. Ben and Tanya were married for several years before Tanya took her first job. Newly graduated from college, she was able to get a high-paying position in computer imaging. When she brought home her first paycheck, she announced to Ben that she was not going to put the check in their joint account, but instead keep it solely for her own use. Ben responded that, because they were married, the money belonged to them both. Who is correct and why?

14. Orlando and Mary lived together for 14 years in Wichita, Kansas. During their cohabitation, they both claimed to be married to one another. They added Mr. and Mrs. to their address and held a joint bank account in those names. Now they are living apart. Orlando currently lives in California. He has fallen in love with another woman and plans to marry her. He hires an attorney to determine whether he and Mary were legally married. What will the attorney check first? What other elements of common-law marriage might be significant in the determination? Is Orlando free to marry another?

12-2 Divorce and the Law of Contracts

GOALS

■ Discuss the ways by which a marriage can end
■ Explain the divorce procedure

KEY TERMS

annulment

voidable marriage

void marriage

bigamist

divorce

dissolution

no-fault divorce

separation

child custody

child support

alimony

Nullifying the Marriage Contract

WHAT'S YOUR VERDICT? After they were married a short time, Samuel told Rhonda that he did not want to have children. Despite several months of discussion, he remained firm.

Can Rhonda end their marriage due to his firm decision?

A marriage may end several ways. The death of either spouse, annulment, divorce, or a variety of illegalities may bring about the end of a marriage. Legal consequences of a spouse's death are discussed in Chapter 20.

Annulment ends many marriages. An **annulment** is a legal procedure for declaring that a voidable marriage is null and void. A **voidable marriage** results from a problem that existed from the beginning of the supposed union. Such a problem might involve a refusal to have children or fraudulent grounds for the marriage contract itself. Fraudulent grounds for marriage include either spouse lying to the other as to wealth, condition of pregnancy, freedom from disease, willingness to have a child, past marriage, or age. Such a marriage may be terminated within a reasonable time by an annulment proceeding. A voidable marriage stays valid until the annulment. In *What's Your Verdict?* Rhonda could void her marriage by annulment on the grounds that Samuel refused to have children.

A **void marriage**, on the other hand, creates no rights or duties for either party and is considered invalid from the beginning. A void marriage is automatically without effect. However, a *declaration of nullity* (not an annulment) must be sought from an appropriate court to confirm that status. Such a marriage typically occurs whenever laws are violated by the matrimonial union. For example, if one partner is already married when the second marriage occurs, the second is a void marriage. A person who knowingly marries a second spouse while still married to the first is a **bigamist**. Bigamy is a crime. A void marriage may also stem from an incestuous relationship (a marriage between close relatives) or mental incompetence of a party or parties.

CHECKPOINT Name the ways by which a marriage contract can end.

© BRAND/PICTURES

To avoid entering into a voidable marriage, what questions do you need to ask your partner before deciding to marry?

Terminating the Marriage Contract

WHAT'S YOUR VERDICT?

Jerry and Oprae married when they were very young. As the years passed, they grew apart. Oprae wanted a divorce so she could "move on with her life." However, she did not have any real grounds for requesting one. Jerry had not deserted her nor had he been been abusive, cruel, or adulterous. Oprae had just grown tired of living with him.

Could Oprae still get a divorce?

The method usually used to end a marriage is **divorce**. In many states the termination of marriage is called **dissolution**. Divorce and dissolution are court actions that end the marriage and divide the property and remaining responsibilities between the parties. Divorce rates increased greatly during the twentieth century. In fact, the divorce rate per year trebled in the United States from 1920 to 1990. Since 1990 the divorce rate has declined by 25 percent (as has the number of marriages).

No-Fault Divorces

Since the first statute allowing it was signed into law in 1969 by Governor Ronald Reagan of California, divorce has been made more available by **no-fault divorce** laws. In a no-fault divorce proceeding, the requesting spouse does not have to list a grievance, such as adultery, desertion, or cruelty, against the other. Instead the court recognizes the right of either the wife or the husband to terminate a marriage unilaterally or of both spouses to end the marriage by mutual agreement. In *What's Your Verdict?* Oprae could get a divorce even though there were no possible grounds for it other than being bored with Jerry.

A no-fault marriage dissolution may be initiated by either spouse. The dissolution is granted after testimony that there is no chance of repairing the marriage relationship. In most no-fault states *irreconcilable differences* are stated as the legal reason for dissolution. After the dissolution request is filed, the couple usually must wait about six months before it is final. In some states couples must meet with a marriage counselor to try to save their marriage.

Divorce Procedure

SEPARATION In some states, the first step toward divorce is **separation**. In such an event the spouses maintain separate living quarters, but their marital rights and obligations remain intact. To alter these rights and obligations, the parties or their lawyers must negotiate a legal separation agreement.

A separation agreement contains terms covering such items as child custody, child support, alimony, and property division. Often, if the parties fail to reconcile their differences during the period of separation and instead divorce, the separation agreement often becomes the basis for the final divorce decree.

COUNSELING Many jurisdictions today require that the couple undergo marital counseling before finalizing their divorce.

What do spouses cite as the legal reason for dissolution of marriage in states that have no-fault divorce laws?

Covenant Marriage

In 1997, the Louisiana state legislature enacted a "covenant marriage" law. The covenant marriage law was enacted in response to ever-increasing divorce rates in an effort to make divorces more difficult to obtain. The law states that before getting married, couples must choose between a standard marriage and a covenant marriage. With a standard marriage, the couple may obtain a no-fault divorce after a six-month separation. With the covenant marriage, couples may only divorce if one party can prove a particular fault in the other. The list of faults includes a felony conviction with a sentence of hard labor, one-year abandonment, physical cruelty, or an 18-month legal separation. A legal separation is only granted with proof of a chronic drinking problem, mental cruelty, or one of the grounds for divorce.

RESOLUTION OF ISSUES Either in the context of negotiating a separation agreement or later in the divorce procedure several crucial issues must be resolved.

DIVISION OF PROPERTY In most states marital property laws are based on the English common law. These laws typically prescribe that the property brought into a marriage by a spouse will remain that spouse's property should the marriage end. During the marriage, whatever is earned, inherited, or received as a gift also remains the property of the spouse who earned or received it. States that do not follow this common-law rule are called community property states. You will learn more about community property laws in Chapter 16.

Regardless of the law followed, most states provide some type of equitable distribution of marital property upon the dissolution of a marriage. Judges distribute property fairly between the spouses. They consider issues such as the age and earning power of each spouse, length of the marriage, and contributions of each spouse to the marriage. If one of the spouses has stayed home to raise children and or take care of the household, the value of those services are considered as well.

CHILD CUSTODY AND SUPPORT The issue of **child custody** is concerned with the division of the physical and other care and control responsibilities for a child. The welfare of the child is the most important consideration in determining who will have custody of the child. Under the provisions of the Uniform Marriage and Divorce Act adopted in most states, the factors a court must consider in awarding custody include

- parents' wishes as to custody
- child's wishes as to custody
- child's relationship with parents, siblings, and others who may affect the child's best interest
- child's adjustment to home, school, and community
- physical and mental health of all persons concerned.

Many divorcing couples are awarded *joint custody* of their children. In these situations the

© GETTY IMAGES/PHOTODISC

What do you see as the advantages of divorced parents having joint custody of their children rather than one or the other having full custody?

responsibility of raising the children is shared. With joint custody, both parents usually remain more interested and involved with their children.

Even if joint custody is not awarded, both parents have a duty to support minor children. The court typically orders the noncustodial parent to pay child support to the custodial parent. **Child support** is the monetary payment by a parent to provide a dependent child with appropriate economic maintenance. These payments help pay for the needs and wants of the child, including housing, food, clothing, and other expenses.

ALIMONY **Alimony** is the support paid by the wage earner of the family to the other spouse. Alimony is usually paid at regular intervals. It may, in some cases, be a lump-sum payment. Alimony is not intended to penalize the person ordered to pay it. The amount to be paid is set by the court. Factors considered by the court are the paying spouse's income, financial resources, earnings outlook, current debts, number of dependents, and number of spouses (former and subsequent).

ISSUANCE OF DECREE OF DISSOLUTION OF MARRIAGE This decree or judgment in the form of a court order officially declares that the marriage is over. It also makes final and legally binding the terms of the resolution of the issues that have developed or needed to be considered in the course of the divorce.

CHECKPOINT Name the steps in the divorce procedure.

A Question of ETHICS

Debra Cater had lived her whole life at the direction of others. As the oldest child, she had been controlled by her mother while growing up. Upon marriage, she had been ordered around by her husband who told her how to behave and dress. Finally, she became aware that her husband was having an affair with a woman at the business he owned. The affair had been long-running, but Debra felt that she had been blinded to it by the trust she placed in others' directions for her life. Ready to finally live life on her own terms, Debra filed for divorce at the age of 40. Her husband vowed that she would get no further support from him, even though the couple had a young son, Tony. To prepare for living on her own, Debra decided to finish college and then go to law school. Unfortunately, she realized that Tony would have to be without her a great deal, especially in the evenings. Debra would have to be in the library studying, when she should be focusing on him. Nonetheless, Debra felt she could not wait any longer to prepare herself for independence. What would you advise Debra to do? On what ethical grounds is your advice based?

12-2 Assessment

Xtra!
Study Tools
school.cengage.com/blaw/lawxtra

THINK ABOUT LEGAL CONCEPTS

1. A void marriage is considered to have never been valid. **True or False?**

2. A voidable marriage is considered to have never been valid. **True or False?**

3. The _ ?_ agreement often becomes the basis for the divorce decree.

4. Child support is a part of alimony. **True or False?**

5. Bigamy always produces a void marriage. **True or False?**

6. Which of the following is usually given as the legal reason in a no-fault marriage dissolution? (a) bigamy (b) irreconcilable differences (c) cruelty (d) desertion

Study the following situations, answer the questions, then prepare arguments to support your answers.

7. The night after Zeke and Shanda were married, Shanda admitted that she was pregnant by another man. Can Zeke end their marriage? How?

8. Ben Thomas was a writer. He was married to Agnes, a stockbroker. Ben stayed home to write and to take care of their two children. But because Ben's writing had not sold, Agnes provided the sole financial support to the family. If Ben and Agnes ever divorce, would Agnes have to pay for Ben's support?

9. After they had been married several months, Alfie admitted to his wife that he was not a secret agent of British Intelligence with a double zero "license to kill." She immediately sued to have their union annulled on the grounds he had lied to her about his profession. Will she be successful?

 Online Research> **Tom's Tribulation**

As he watched the judge enter the courtroom with her decision, Tom thought back over the last year. The incident was still as clear as though it were yesterday. There he stood by the roadside shaking his head as Josyln started to drive away. It was the third time in the last month that his wife had shown up drunk to drive him home after work. This time he had steadfastly refused to get in the car with her. It was the final straw. He had begged her to get help for her drinking problem, but she refused to admit that she had one. At that moment two things happened. First he decided to file for divorce immediately, and then Joslyn darted into traffic right in front of an oncoming pizza delivery vehicle which swerved and hit him. He had been thrown more than 30 feet by the impact and suffered several broken bones and a permanent painful back injury. The pizza delivery vehicle had been driving 20 miles over the speed limit according to the testimony of the driver of a vehicle following it. The personal injury suit which Tom filed shortly thereafter had been settled for $2.5 million two months ago.

Now in the context of the divorce litigation, Joslyn was claiming that she deserved half of the settlement. It was the only matter of contention in the entire proceeding: There were no children. They both had jobs paying about the same amount so there were no support payments due. They had divided their property amicably except for the settlement sum. They lived in a state where the judge could allocate personal injury awards as she or he saw fit.

THINK CRITICALLY

What legal rationales support Joslyn's claim for half the settlement amount? What legal rationales support Tom's position that he deserves the entire amount? If you were the judge, how would you rule in the matter?

GO TO FINDLAW.COM TO FIND THE ANSWERS

To find the material in FindLaw on this issue, go to Findlaw.com and click on the following sequence of hyperlinks: Divorce and Family Law, Divorce and Property, Personal Injury Awards.

CONCEPTS IN BRIEF

12-1   Marriage and the Law of Contracts

1. Parental consent to marry is generally required for individuals under age 18.

2. In most jurisdictions, a gift given by one party in a relationship to the other in anticipation of marriage must be returned to the giver if the parties do not marry.

3. Suits involving loss of consortium may succeed against individuals who cause harm that prevents a spouse from fulfilling marital duties.

4. In a prenuptial contract, marital partners-to-be may renounce any claim to their future spouse's property that they might otherwise acquire through marriage.

12-2   Divorce and the Law of Contracts

5. Annulments are available based upon fraud where either spouse lied about such things as freedom from diseases, past marriages, age, preference towards having children, and wealth.

6. The vast majority of marital terminations today are through no-fault divorces due to irreconcilable differences.

7. Even though a married couple may separate or divorce, each's marital obligations such as providing for the non-wage earning spouse and children, if appropriate, remain.

YOUR LEGAL VOCABULARY

Match each statement with the term that it best defines. Some terms may not be used.

1. Voiding of a marital contract
2. Marital union treated as valid by the law until terminated at the option of one or both parties due to improper grounds
3. Marital union considered invalid from the beginning
4. Person who is married to two or more people at the same time
5. Court action terminating a marriage
6. Divorce procedure in which no cause need be shown for termination of the union
7. Generally the first step towards divorce
8. Care and control of a minor
9. Legal process that creates a parent-child relationship
10. Legal union of a man and woman as husband and wife
11. Marital relationship legalized by a couple holding themselves out as husband and wife, sharing home and property for an extended period
12. Money paid by parent to provide child with economic maintenance
13. Mutual obligations of wife and husband undertaken to fulfill the purposes of their union
14. Legal contract resolving property and other claims that might result from a marriage
15. Term in some states for the ending of a marriage

a. adoption
b. alimony
c. annulment
d. bigamist
e. child custody
f. child support
g. civil union
h. common-law marriage
i. dissolution
j. divorce
k. marital consortium
l. marriage
m. no-fault divorce
n. prenuptial agreement
o. separation
p. void marriage
q. voidable marriage

REVIEW LEGAL CONCEPTS

16. What are the advantages of parental control over when and to whom a child marries?

17. What sort of "reasonable force" do parents have at their disposal for enforcing their decisions against their children? Can they refuse to feed them ("go to bed without your supper"), beat them, or imprison them ("you're grounded")?

18. Why does the government require parental consent for marriages of persons under 18 years old?

19. What is the purpose of breach-of-promise lawsuits?

WRITE ABOUT LEGAL CONCEPTS

20. Imagine that you are engaged to be married. Write a letter to your fiancée stating reasons for or against having a prenuptial agreement.

21. Write an essay explaining what you would most like to see changed about our divorce laws.

22. **HOT DEBATE** Write a persuasive opening argument that emphasizes the legal and ethical points in Ben's favor. Or, write a persuasive opening argument that emphasizes the legal and ethical points in his father's favor.

THINK CRITICALLY ABOUT EVIDENCE

Study the following situations, answer the questions, and then prepare arguments to support your answers.

23. Billy and his first cousin, Sally, were raised together as children. They have the same values, go to the same school, have the same friends and are extremely happy together. One day, Billy asks Sally for her hand in marriage. Sally says yes. They are both 17. What problems might they encounter in fulfilling their desires to marry?

24. Tom and Juanita are lovers. Several years into their relationship, Juanita has a child by Tom. They do not marry, however. Now, Juanita has broken off their relationship but expects Tom to help pay for the child's support. Must he do so by law? What rights does Tom have with the child? What interest does the government have in making sure that someone has responsibility for the child?

25. Alexandra and Thomas are engaged. Before they marry, Thomas meets Marcia and falls in love with her. He then breaks off his engagement. Alexandra is humiliated by the rejection. Further, she and her parents have already invested thousands of dollars in wedding preparations. What legal cause of action might she have against Thomas? Could she also sue Marcia in some states? Why?

26. Stephanie and Alfred moved to Missouri after 15 years of living in Oklahoma. All during the time they were together in Oklahoma, they held themselves out as husband and wife, lived together, and shared common property. Now Alfred wants to leave Stephanie. He has been the sole wage earner the whole time they have been together. Therefore, he wants to take all the property except a bed and an old car. Stephanie believes that Alfred owes her far more than that. She feels they have been married at common law and, therefore, she has the same rights as any other divorcing spouse. Alfred points out that Missouri does not have common-law marriage, so she has no such rights. Who is correct?

27. Antonio and Doris have been married a year when Antonio is injured in a freak chemical accident that leaves him unable to conceive a child. Antonio has sued the negligent parties for his loss. What cause of action does Doris have stemming from the same incident?

28. More than four years after they were married, George Woy sought an annulment of his marriage to Linda Woy on the basis of fraud. In his petition he alleged that at the time of the marriage ceremony he was unaware that she had a dependence on illegal drugs, and that, had she not concealed the fact from him, he would have refused to marry her. Should the court grant an annulment on this basis? (*Woy v. Woy*, 737 S.W.2d 769)

29. When they remarried each other, Robert Root owed Nila Root several thousand dollars of unpaid child support from their first marriage. A month and a half after their second marriage ceremony, Nila filed to dissolve their second marriage and demanded payment of the back child support. Should the court allow her to collect the money, as she is still married to Robert? (*In re Marriage of Root*, 774 S.W.2d 521)

30. James and Anna Nesbit were contemplating divorce. They entered into a property settlement agreement, but James died before the divorce became final. His will provided a greater amount of property for Anna than did the settlement agreement. Which document should be enforced? (*Crist v. Nesbit*, 352 S.W.2d 53)

31. Three days before their marriage, Donna Rinvelt and Arnold Rinvelt signed a prenuptial agreement drafted by the latter's attorney. The document stated that each party would keep all rights in their separate property and could dispose of it without any claims upon it by the other spouse. The document also contained the following clause:

    Divorce: In the event that the marriage of the parties shall end in divorce, annulment, or separate maintenance, it is hereby agreed that their respective rights in and to the property of the other spouse shall be limited as follows: (a) The Prospective Husband shall be entitled to ten percent (10%) of the net estate of the Prospective Wife, net estate meaning gross estate less all expenses. (b) The Prospective Wife shall be entitled to ten percent (10%) of the net estate of the Prospective Husband, net estate meaning gross estate less all expenses.

    As a consequence of this latter provision, Donna Rinvelt was awarded almost a quarter of a million dollars of Arnold's property by the divorce court. Arnold brought an appeal asking that the award be thrown out. What arguments could be made in this regard? What arguments could Donna make to the contrary? What do you think the court decided? (*Rinvelt v. Rinvelt*, 475 N.W.2d 478)

32. Thea Ella Curless brought an action for divorce against Timothy Dean Curless. The judgment and decree granted the divorce, awarded custody of the two children, a boy, Trist, age 13, and a girl, Tobi, age 10, to their father with rights of visitation to the mother. The court divided the personal property and debts according to the agreement between the parties and awarded the house to Timothy Curless with Thea Curless' equity secured by a second mortgage in the amount of $36,000, to be paid in installments of $600 per month with 10 percent interest. After entering judgment, the trial judge denied Mrs. Curless' motion for a new trial and denied the children's motion to intervene, as well as their motion to have a guardian appointed for them. Mrs. Curless is a junior high school teacher with a master's degree in education. Timothy Curless is employed by the Union Pacific Railroad. The court heard conflicting testimony as to how much time Mr. Curless' job keeps him away from home and how much time Mrs. Curless' employment and extracurricular activities kept her from attending to the children. The court also heard conflicting facts about which spouse did more or less than his or her share of household duties and attending of children. The court heard testimony to the effect that Mr. Curless is an alcoholic but that he has "quit drinking." Mr. Curless testified that he had not had a drink since he made a commitment to give up alcohol four years ago. There was evidence that Mr. Curless had been a user of marijuana and had a marijuana plant in his home. Mr. Curless testified that he had had "no involvement with any drugs for 45 days," and had not had a marijuana plant in his home for the last "eight or nine years." Finally, the court held, and the parties do not seriously contend otherwise, that both parties are "fit" and proper persons to have care and custody of the children. Because of the divorce court's rulings in the case, Thea Curless has brought an appeal before the Supreme Court of Wyoming. Should the court uphold the divorce court's determinations or reverse them? Why or why not? (*Curless v. Curless*, 708 P.2d 426)

Case For Legal Thinking

IVANA TRUMP V. DONALD J. TRUMP
SUPREME COURT OF NEW YORK, APPELLATE DIVISION, 582 N.Y.S.2D 1008

FACTS The Trumps were married in 1977. On December 24, 1987, they entered into a postnuptial agreement. Both spouses did so under the advice of separate counsel. The agreement of December 1987 superceded three previous agreements of 1977, 1979, and 1984, respectively.

Two paragraphs of the 1987 agreement are under primary scrutiny in this case. The first is paragraph 9(b) which sets out the parties' rights and obligations in the event of divorce. These rights and obligations included the husband's obligation to pay $350,000 per year to the wife as maintenance and $10,000,000 in a lump sum within 90 days after the entry of the final divorce decree.

The second paragraph (paragraph 10) provides that without obtaining Mr. Trump's advance written consent, Mrs. Trump can not publish, or cause to be published, any diary, memoir, letter, story, photograph, interview, article, essay, account, or description or depiction of any kind, whether fictionalized or not, concerning their marriage or any other aspect of Mr. Trump's personal, business, or financial affairs. She also could not assist or provide information to others in connection with the publication or dissemination of any such material or excerpts.

The agreement goes on to terminate any of Mr. Trump's obligations under paragraph 9(b) if a breach of the

agreement occurs. It also provides that, in the event of divorce, the terms and conditions of this agreement shall supercede any divorce decree.

In 1990, Mrs. Trump initiated a divorce action against Donald J. on the grounds of cruel and inhuman treatment. Concurrently, she brought suit to have the agreement voided as she maintained it violated her rights to a property division available under state law.

TRIAL COURT DECISION The court granted Mrs. Trump her divorce. Later, after extensive negotiations between the parties, the court issued a judgment that reflected the result of these negotiations, i.e., that Mrs. Trump would accept the lump sum payment of the $10 million in return for allowing the agreement to be enforceable. Regrettably, the court, although including all the other terms of the agreement by reference, did not include paragraph 10 of the agreement in its judgment. Mr. Trump appealed the court's unilateral action which was taken without explanation or notice to the parties.

APPELLATE COURT DECISION "Since it is clear that the trial court exceeded its limited authority to disturb the terms of a separation agreement and paragraph 10 does not, on its face, offend public policy as a prior restraint on protected speech, we modify to incorporate the terms of said agreement into the . . . judgment as agreed to by the parties."

© MICHAEL JACOBS/SAGA/LANDOV

PRACTICE JUDGING

1. What is the significance of the omitted term? Could you infer that Mrs. Trump gave up anything of value in the negotiations in return for its being omitted?

2. Do you think the courts should have the discretion to pick and choose what sections of a contract they are going to enforce, even though all sections are valid under the law?

3. Mrs. Trump argued against the reinclusion of the term by saying that it involved a "prior restraint" on what she might publish. This, she maintained, would be a violation of her Constitutional rights. Do you agree? Why or why not?

Entrepreneurs
AND THE LAW

Project 2 Contract Law

THE ROAD TEST Stacy and her father, Joe, walked around the 18 wheeler. The truck was fully loaded and ready to begin the test run. Joe stopped a moment and hit a couple of the tires with the short club he carried to test the level of inflation. "They look good, Stace." He gestured towards the tires with the club. "We'll just see how they do over the next 6,000 or so miles."

Stacy had to use all of the vacation days she had accrued with the DOT to allow for this crucial trip. To be beside her on what he called the "journey of their lives," Joe had finally taken a vacation after many years without one. Joe also had called in some favors to get a cross-country run from one of the local trucking firms for the road test of the "SecureSeal Tires," a name Stacy had coined. The tires now were mounted on every axle of the truck. During their trip they would expose the tires to extreme hot and cold temperatures, high and low elevations, and fast and crawling speeds. Ten spares were stored in a special rack attached to the trailer. They had rented it from a national leasing concern. Fortunately, both Joe and Stacy were licensed as Class A Commercial Drivers.

Stacy looked up at her father and said, "Then let's go find out."

EVALUATION AND REFINEMENT Following the 6,891-mile trip, the tires underwent laboratory evaluation for separation of the retread, cracks, tread wear, and the like. As they predicted from rough observations during the road test, the results were extremely favorable. Not one tire had had a problem, much less blown, over the entire trip.

Shortly after getting the results, Joe once again exercised a firm but gentle hand in the product's development. He arranged an appointment for Stacy with an attorney to clarify and resolve some issues. Now seated in the waiting room of the Don Blair law firm, Stacy noted that Blair was not the attorney Joe used for the shop. After a few minutes an interior door opened and a man poked his head in and said her name. When she rose in response, the man walked up to her, smiled and introduced himself as Brandon Jenkins, a paralegal who would do her initial interview.

It was an interview Stacy would never forget. The more they tried to talk over the legal issues involved in the product's development, the more personal the discussion became, and the more intriguing Brandon became to Stacy. It was obvious he was experiencing similar feelings. Just before the allotted hour was over, noting they had not covered all the necessary material, Brandon suggested they meet for dinner that evening to finish up. Stacy readily accepted.

At dinner, before the conversation could be diverted to other matters, Brandon quickly named off issues that needed to be resolved: formalization of Stacy's business relationship with her dad (considering his investment, guidance, and future position in the product's development) and her dad's shop of which he was part owner; ways to limit potential liability; division of income; responsibility for expenses for utilities, cleanup, and raw materials; non-disclosure agreements; and agreements not to compete. "Here," he said, and handed Stacy a list of what he'd just mentioned. "You can go over it with Mr. Blair when you meet him tomorrow. I was hoping we could talk about other things now."

Two weeks later Brandon proposed to Stacy. As a part of the proposal he revealed some other legal issues that needed to be resolved. He asked that they enter into a prenuptial agreement as he had two children by a previous marriage that he supported and wanted to have inherit the home in which Brandon and the two of them currently lived. Brandon also revealed that he, himself, was to inherit a large amount of money when he turned 30 that he wanted to retain to enable him to go back to school to obtain his law degree.

ACTIVITIES

Prepare Legal Documents

Divide into teams to represent the parties at interest in the business and personal issues noted. Prepare appropriate business and prenuptial contract(s) reflecting the best interests of your particular client.

Negotiate

Role-play negotiations over the proposed contracts to obtain the best result for your client.

POSITIVE PEER PRESSURE Motor vehicle crashes are the number one cause of death among youth ages 15 to 20 according to the National Highway Traffic Safety Administration. In 2005 there were 7,460 youth motor vehicle deaths. Of the drivers in this category who were killed, 28 percent, or 2,089, were under the influence of alcohol.

You can help combat these frightening statistics through an organization called SADD—Students Against Destructive Decisions. With thousands of chapters in middle schools, high schools, and colleges, SADD student volunteers help peers with destructive behaviors and attitudes including underage drinking, substance abuse, impaired driving, violence, and suicide. SADD offers a variety of peer-led educational projects including classes, workshops, conferences, rallies, and legislative work.

DO YOUR PART

1. Use the Internet to research a SADD chapter in or near your community. Contact them to learn how you can help.

2. If SADD is not already in your school or community, gather a group of your peers and go to work. Use the Internet for information on setting up a chapter.

3. Set a date and agenda for your first meeting. Arrange to hold the meeting at your school

4. Advertise the meeting with flyers and press releases.

5. At the meeting, provide information about SADD and your chapter, and invite students to become volunteers.

Multimedia Presentation

This event may be completed by one to three individuals. Using technology to support a presentation enhances a business leader's effectiveness. This event recognizes FBLA members who demonstrate the effective use of presentation technologies and software to prepare and deliver their message.

You have been asked to prepare a presentation that covers common types of contracts that young people sign (college loan, car loan, rental agreement, etc.) Your presentation must cover all elements of a contract (offer and acceptance, genuine agreement, consideration, capacity, legality, and proper form). The presentation should relate all of the contract elements to one type of contract entered into by a young person.

The presentation is an explanation of the Multimedia Presentation, not a viewing of the presentation.

Performance Indicators Evaluated

- Understand the elements of a contract.
- Describe common contracts that young people sign.
- Use multimedia effectively for thorough coverage of all elements of contracts.
- Design an effective multimedia presentation.
- Explain all aspects of the multimedia presentation.
- Involve all members in the multimedia project.

For more detailed information about performance indicators, go to the FBLA web site.

THINK CRITICALLY

1. Why is multimedia an effective means to cover the elements of a contract?

2. What effect does the use of pictures have in a multimedia presentation?

http://www.fbla-pbl.org/

Mock Trial Prep

CASE SCENARIO

WHAT HAPPENED

Robert Craig is a 17-year-old high school senior. He was stopped by the state police driving a car that wasn't his near the high school he attends. Unknown to Robert was the fact that the car recently had been reported stolen by its registered owner, Sam Perkins, age 45. Robert was arrested and charged with grand larceny, a felony. Following a search of the car, the police discovered Robert's backpack in the trunk. Upon searching the backpack the police found a black purse which seemed to match a description of one which had been reported stolen in a robbery earlier in the week. In a wallet inside the purse they found several credit cards and a driver's license with the name Mandy Martin. Mandy Martin had reported her purse stolen. The police then charged Robert with the additional count of robbery. He was read his rights and taken into custody.

Robert retained counsel. His defense attorney, upon reviewing the facts of the case, filed a Motion to Suppress the introduction of the purse found in Robert's backpack believing it to be the result of an illegal search. Without the purse as evidence it would be difficult for the Prosecution to prove a robbery.

Pre-Trial Hearings

There are many possible pre-trial hearings that may be held to determine if proper procedures were followed in obtaining evidence, conducting interrogations, and making searches. There also may be a hearing to determine a person's mental competency. Usually the judge presiding over the case will preside over the pre-trial hearings related to that case.

Motion to Suppress Evidence

The Defense in this case has filed a motion to suppress the introduction by the Prosecution of the purse and wallet obtained by the police when they searched the trunk of the car and then Robert's backpack. The Defense argues that the search of the backpack was an unreasonable search and seizure in that the police had no probable cause to indicate that the backpack had anything to do with the stolen car. Therefore the search is in violation of Robert's Fourth Amendment right against unreasonable search and seizure. The Defense argues that illegally obtained evidence cannot be introduced in court. A Motion to Suppress Evidence is a written request made to a judge to exclude certain evidence from being presented at trial. Once a Motion to Suppress is filed, the burden of proof is upon the state to produce testimony or evidence that the evidence seized was not the product of an illegal search.

A hearing has been granted. At the hearing the Defense will present its opening statement, followed by the opening statement of the Prosecution. The Defense will then have the first opportunity to convince the judge of the validity of its claims by the presentation of witness testimony and evidence. Once the Defense has presented its arguments, the Prosecution will present its side of the case to the judge. The hearing will conclude with the closing arguments of first the Defense followed by the Prosecution. The Defense may present a rebuttal if thought necessary.

Defense arguments   When the police determined that Robert was driving a reportedly stolen car he was removed from the car, read his rights, arrested, and put in the back of the police car. There was no reason to search the car, especially the trunk, to which Robert did not have access from the front seat. Once inside the trunk, the police had no probable cause to search the backpack. It was not ticking, nor did it smell funny, for example. It could have been part of the inventory of the vehicle, but there was no probable cause to search it.

Prosecution arguments   The Prosecution contends that the police had a legal obligation to search the vehicle and inventory all of the items found in the vehicle when it was recovered. Given the age of the driver and the reports of gang activity in the area, it was reasonable for the police to inventory the contents of the backpack for possible weapons.

Defense Witness Statements

Robert Craig   My girlfriend Michele Perkins picked me up as usual for school on that morning. Everything was cool. On the way to school I realized that I had forgotten my gym stuff and that I would be a heap of trouble if I forgot them again. So I asked Michele if I could borrow her car on my lunch hour and go home to get my stuff. She said okay but I had to be careful and not let her dad see me driving the car. When the police stopped me I was not doing anything wrong. I am a real good driver. When they told me I was driving a stolen car I could not

believe it. I was very polite and complied with all their directions. As far as the purse in the backpack, I hadn't seen that backpack in a week, and I thought I lost it.

Michele Perkins   Robert and I have been friends since fourth grade, and now I really like him. My parents are not happy about our relationship. My brother especially gives him a hard time. He is always taking things from him and hiding his stuff. I did tell Robert he could borrow my dad's car on the day in question. I know Robert is an excellent driver and would be very careful. My brother saw Robert driving the car, called my dad, and my dad reported the car stolen.

Virginia Goodheart   I am a guidance counselor at Dewey High School where Robert is a student. In my 25 years of professional service I have had few students with the honesty and integrity of Robert. He is a hard working young man who gets very good grades. He volunteers at a homeless shelter on the weekend and holds down a part-time job. I don't think he has a bad bone in his body.

Prosecution Witness Statements

Officer Tony Miranda   On the morning in question I was driving south on Route 9W at approximately 12:15 P.M. and I spotted a vehicle with license number 2850-UL approaching in the opposite direction. That plate matched one that was on a vehicle reported stolen 15 minutes previously. The driver was observing the speed limit. I made a U-turn and followed the vehicle. I then turned on my lights and the vehicle pulled over. When I approached the vehicle the driver offered his driver's license. I asked him to get out of the car. I then informed him that the vehicle was reported stolen, and upon reading him his rights I took him into custody. I then searched the interior of the car thoroughly taking inventory of its contents. I also looked in the trunk. Among the items in the trunk was the backpack which I also searched. I was looking for weapons.

Sam Perkins   My daughter Michele had no right allowing anyone to drive my car. She knows better. I have had this conversation with her many times and now maybe she will learn her lesson. That Robert kid didn't own the car he was driving, it's just that simple. I called the cops and reported the car stolen.

Bart Perkins   Imagine my surprise when I saw that punk Robert driving my dad's car. The kid just doesn't get it. We don't like him. I called my dad immediately to report what I had seen. Hey, I drive that car, too, and I didn't want any thing to happen to it.

Facts and Issues

As you prepare for a hearing or trial it is important that you understand both the facts and issues in the case. A fact is an event that took place—an act. A fact can be proven by believable trustworthy testimony by a witness or an expert in the field. A fact may be proven further by tangible evidence or scientific study. An issue is one single point in dispute between two sides in a lawsuit. There may be issues of fact as to whether the fact is indeed true or not. There may be issues of law as to how the law may apply to a particular case.

TEAMWORK

1. To prepare for the Motion to Suppress Hearing it is important to gather the facts and examine the issues in this case. Make a chart showing the facts and issues for each witness.

2. Robert has been charged with two crimes, grand larceny and robbery. In order for a person to be convicted all of the elements of the crime should be able to be proven. Study the definitions of both crimes and formulate an opinion as to whether there is enough evidence to support the charge. Be sure to list specific examples from the testimony that supports the charge.

Grand larceny   The unlawful taking and carrying away of the personal property of another with the intent to deprive him or her of it permanently. The difference between petit larceny and grand larceny is the value of the object taken. This is an offense against property.

Robbery   A trespass and taking away from the person, or in his presence, the personal property of another with violence or putting in fear with the intent to steal the property.

Unit 3
The Law of Sales

Chapters

13 Sales Contracts

14 Ownership and Risk of Loss in Sales

15 Consumer Protection

Border Patrol Agent

Are you interested in working outdoors in an exciting, fast-paced, and sometimes dangerous environment? Would you find it rewarding to help prevent illegal drugs and persons from entering the United States? If so, you might consider a career as a border patrol agent.

Border patrol agents work to prevent, detect, and apprehend people illegally entering the United States. They also are responsible for intercepting drug smugglers.

One of the most important activities of a border patrol agent is "line watch." This involves patrolling the areas along the U.S. border, particularly the border between the United States and Mexico. This is rigorous outdoor work, often in isolated areas and under extreme weather conditions. In addition to line watch, agents are responsible for city patrol, traffic, and transportation checks. Duties also include intelligence work, community relations, and acting as a liaison with other law enforcement agencies.

EMPLOYMENT OUTLOOK

- The current increase in drug-smuggling operations has meant rapid growth and more opportunities for talented individuals to put their skills to work for the border patrol. This work would require candidates to live in the southwest region of the United States.

- The level of government spending determines the number of jobs available for border patrol agents. Therefore, the number of job opportunities can vary from year to year.

NEEDED SKILLS AND EDUCATION

Border patrol agents must be U.S. citizens, be younger than 37 years of age at the time of appointment, possess a valid driver's license, pass a three-part examination on reasoning and language skills, and be physically fit. Applicants must be prepared to face challenges that are both mental and physical, and be proficient in using a firearm. Personal characteristics such as honesty, sound judgment, integrity, and a sense of responsibility are especially important.

A bachelor's degree or previous work experience that demonstrates the ability to handle stressful situations, make decisions, and take charge is required. Applicants may qualify through a combination of education and work experience. Knowledge of a foreign language is an asset.

How you'll spend your day

As a border patrol agent you will be challenged physically and mentally every day. Regardless of your assignment, you'll likely work outdoors and spend your day on a bike, boat, horse, or all-terrain vehicle.

Your most important activity will be line watch. Using intelligence collected from co-workers, you'll look for and apprehend undocumented aliens from entering the country. You'll also look for smugglers of drugs. You'll work surveillance from a covert position, follow up on leads, and respond to electronic sensor alarms.

You'll use some of the most technologically advanced equipment in law enforcement, including low-light television and detection systems, seismic metallic and infrared sensors, and a unique computerized identification and tracking system. During night operations you'll use infrared scopes. You'll use information obtained from this equipment, along with aircraft sightings and physical evidence like tracks and marks on the ground to locate suspects.

You may be asked to work overtime and may be sent on temporary assignments on short notice. Some assignments may involve performing traffic checks, traffic observation, city patrol transportation checks, and other administrative, intelligence, and anti-smuggling activities.

What about you?

Does the job of border patrol agent interest you? Why or why not? Which aspects of the job would you most enjoy? Which aspects would you least enjoy?

Chapter 13
Sales Contracts

13-1 Sales

13-2 Special Rules for Sales Contracts

© GETTY IMAGES/PHOTODISC

HOT DEBATE

Amanda and Bob, a successful young married couple, began the renovation of the kitchen in the antebellum house they had just purchased in New Orleans. They contracted with several artisans in the effort. Anton, the owner of a custom cabinet shop, worked closely with Amanda to develop a pattern in the period of the house. After taking measurements, Anton set about making the cabinets to fit the unique dimensions and style of the house's cooking area. As the work was nearing completion, Amanda and Bob decided to divorce. They notified Anton to stop work and told him he would not be paid as he had not completed the job. Anton sued.

WHERE DO YOU STAND?

1. Should Anton be able to recover? Why or why not?
2. Discuss the ethical reasons in Anton's favor.

13-1 Sales

GOALS

- Define sale and explain how the UCC governs the sale of goods
- Explain how the UCC treats unconscionable contracts and contracts of adhesion

KEY TERMS

sale	vendor
ownership	vendee
contract to sell	payment
goods	delivery
price	receipt of goods
barter	bill of sale

What Is a Sale?

WHAT'S YOUR VERDICT?

At the Dan-Dee Discount Department Store, Jack and Jean Medina signed a contract to buy a clothes washer and dryer set. The Dan-Dee salesperson explained that although the set on display was not in stock, "We will deliver and install it within two weeks." While shopping at the store, the Medinas left their car in the store's automobile service department to have the engine's idling speed adjusted and to have squeaks in the door eliminated. The charge for labor was $45. There was no charge for parts or supplies. The service attendant recommended replacing the car's tires, and the Medinas agreed. The cost of the tires was $300, plus $25 for balancing and installation. The Medinas also bought a new battery for $59. It was installed free of charge.

Were all of these agreements sales?

A **sale** is a contract in which ownership of goods transfers immediately from the seller to the buyer for a price. **Ownership** entails a collection of rights that allow the use and enjoyment of property. If the transfer of ownership is to take place in the future, the transaction is a **contract to sell** rather than a sale. **Goods** are *tangible* (touchable), movable *personal property* (items other than land or buildings), such as airplanes, books, clothing, and dogs. **Price** is the consideration for a sale or contract to sell goods. It may be expressed in money, in services, or in other goods. When parties exchange goods for goods, the sale is a **barter**.

The Uniform Commercial Code (UCC) governs sales of goods. It also governs contracts to sell goods in the future. By UCC definition, goods do not include the following:

1. Money (except rare currency or rare coins, which are collectible items with value that may exceed their face amounts)
2. Intangible (not touchable) personal property, such as legal rights to performance under a contract. Such rights are transferred by assignment rather than by sale

© DIGITAL VISION

This girl is listening to a song on a music CD. When she decides to buy the CD, will the transaction be considered a sale or a contract to sell? Explain your answer.

3. Patents and copyrights, which are exclusive rights granted by the federal government in the intellectual products of inventors and writers

4. Real property (generally land, buildings, and legal rights therein), the transfer of which is subject to special rules (as discussed in Unit 4 on Property)

Under the UCC a sales contract may be made in any manner sufficient to show agreement. The resulting contract suffices if the parties, by their actions, recognize the existence of a contract. This is true even though a court might not be able to determine precisely when the contract was made, and even though one or more terms are left open in accordance with customs of the trade.

In general, as applied to the sale of goods, the law of contracts (as discussed in Unit 2) has been simplified and made less strict. For example, although the price for goods usually is fixed in the contract, the parties may indicate that the price is to be set in a certain way at a later date. This method is used in long-term sales contracts due to the fluctuation of prices over time. Ordinarily, when nothing is said about the price, a sales contract results if all other essentials are present, and provided the parties do not express a contrary intent. In such a case, the buyer is required to pay the price that is reasonable when the goods are received.

Contracts That Are Not Sales

In some contractual situations, goods may be included, but the primary purpose of the contract is to provide a service. Such contracts are not sales because any goods supplied are merely incidental. In *What's Your Verdict?* the work on the car engine and the doors was a contract for services. Any goods supplied, such as lubricants, were incidental. Even if a specific charge was made for them, the contract would remain one for the services that were the dominant part of that agreement. Such a contract would not fall under the UCC rules and requirements as a consequence.

On the other hand, the transfer to the Medinas of title to the tires was a sale of goods, even

LEGAL Research

Determine how the tax laws treat sales for money versus barter contracts. What are the advantages and disadvantages of bartering?

A Question of ETHICS

Destiny Pharmaceuticals sponsored a great deal of research in the area of locating and developing new drugs from plants growing in isolated areas. A recent expedition to the central Amazon region of Brazil brought back several potentially beneficial discoveries. An exceptionally rare tree, known to be very beneficial to the life systems in the rain forest, could produce what the chemists at Destiny labeled "Revita." Revita had been shown to be able to completely cure even late-stage cases of breast and testicular cancer. Regrettably, it was found in the bark of a rare tree and harvesting it usually exposed the tree to invasion of parasites and, ultimately, death. Revita, however, would help millions of people and would produce large profits for Destiny. Should Destiny develop the drug for sale?

though a small charge was made for related labor. The battery also was acquired in a sale of goods, with no charge for labor. The Medinas' agreement to buy the washer and dryer at a later date was not a sale. Instead, it was a contract to sell—a contract in which ownership of goods is to transfer in a sale in the future. In both sales of goods and contracts to sell, the seller is known as a **vendor**. The buyer is known as the **vendee** or the purchaser.

Payment and Delivery

Payment occurs when the buyer transfers the agreed-upon consideration and the seller accepts it. **Delivery** is the act by which the subject matter of the contract is placed within the possession or control of the buyer. **Receipt of goods** means that the buyer takes physical possession or control of the goods. Receipt usually involves actual delivery. However, delivery may be constructive. This means that there is no actual transfer of possession of the goods, but the recipient has the power to control them, as intended by the parties involved. Examples would be when the buyer gets the keys to a car or receives a warehouse receipt for stored goods.

In the basic sales transaction, payment, delivery, and transfer of title take place simultaneously at the seller's place of business. Even if payment or delivery, or both, take place later, title still passes when the buyer selects and agrees to buy existing goods in the seller's store.

At the appropriate time fixed in the sales contract, the buyer has a duty to pay, and the seller has a duty to transfer possession. Generally neither is obligated to perform until the other does. Thus, unless it is otherwise agreed (as when the sale is on credit), or if it is the custom of the trade, the seller may retain the goods until the buyer makes payment in full. Similarly, the buyer may refuse to pay the price until the seller delivers all the goods. The buyer is entitled to a receipt when payment is made.

BILL OF SALE A **bill of sale** is a receipt that serves as written evidence of the transfer of ownership of goods. Such a document is sometimes required by statute, as in the case of automobile sales. Under the UCC's version of the Statute of Frauds, if a bill of sale is signed by the seller, buyer, or both, it might satisfy a requirement for a signed writing (See Lesson 13-2). However, neither a sales contract nor a bill of sale necessarily identifies the parties nor explains the terms of the transaction.

A bill of sale makes resale of the property easier because it provides the owner with written evidence of ownership. When goods are lost, stolen, or destroyed, as in a fire, the document can be used to help prove value. The bill of sale is not absolute proof of complete ownership because other persons may have acquired claims against the goods since the bill of sale was issued. Also, dishonest persons may forge such documents to help dispose of stolen property.

USE OF CREDIT To encourage business, most sellers extend credit to qualified buyers, including other business firms. Some retailers do most of their business selling to customers who use credit cards or charge accounts, or who pay in installments. Thus, the buyer may get both title and possession before payment.

ACCEPTANCE OF GOODS Acceptance of goods means that the buyer has agreed, by words or by conduct, that the goods received are satisfactory. Acceptance is shown when the goods are used,

© GETTY IMAGES/PHOTODISC

This candy retailer just received this bill of sale from Becksmith Candies, one of her vendors. What does the bill of sale indicate about the ownership of the candy she purchased?

resold, or otherwise treated as if they were owned by the buyer. Acceptance also may be indicated when a buyer fails to reject the goods within a reasonable time, if the buyer has had adequate opportunity to inspect them.

IN THIS CASE The Miller Trailer Manufacturing Company ordered three tons of steel reinforcing rods from a new supplier. The rods arrived on schedule but were not inspected by the company for more than a month. At that time, it was determined that the rods were not the expected diameter as provided by the previous supplier. When the Trailer Company tried to return the rods, the new supplier refused the effort as the Trailer Company had had adequate opportunity to inspect the shipment. The failure to inspect and consequently reject the shipment within a reasonable time would likely be considered acceptance by a court.

Other Ways to Contract

Sales contracts may be made through a traditional exchange of offer and acceptance. However, the

LAW BRIEF

Several important changes recently were proposed by the National Conference of Commissioners on Uniform State Laws to UCC Article 2: Sales. The changes represent the impact of e-commerce, inflation, and an increasing international focus. These changes, especially those relating to e-commerce, have met with great resistance. As of 2007, only two states, Virginia and Maryland, had adopted the proposed changes. The states are especially reluctant to accept the change that proposes to redefine "sign" to include electronic signatures and to create other definitions pertaining to electronic commerce such as "electronic agent," "electronic record," and others. The states also object to considering an electronic record of a transaction as the "writing" required by the Statute of Frauds.

UCC also recognizes alternative methods. Instead of telephoning, sending a facsimile (fax), or mailing an acceptance, the seller may simply ship the goods and thereafter notify the buyer of this action.

CHECKPOINT What is the definition of a sale?

Unconscionable Sales Contracts

WHAT'S YOUR VERDICT? Piotr, a recent immigrant, bought a refrigerator from a rent-to-own store that advertised its willingness to deal with people with unestablished credit. Piotr spoke, read, and wrote Russian and German, but only spoke a few words of English. The negotiations and sale of the refrigerator were conducted in German. However, although the seller knew that Piotr could not understand it, the written contract was entirely in English. The store had paid the manufacturer $348 for the refrigerator but the total cost to Piotr under the three-year installment contract was $2,567. When Piotr defaulted on his payments after more than a year, the store sued for the $1,805 left to be paid.

Why shouldn't the store recover the remainder due under the contract?

The UCC provides that a court may find that a contract or a clause of a contract is *unconscionable*, that is, grossly unfair. An unconscionable contract or clause offends an honest person's conscience and sense of justice, as does the contract in *What's Your Verdict?* The terms need not be criminal nor violate a statute, but they are unethical.

Contracts of adhesion are more likely to be unconscionable. This is so because in such contracts one of the parties dictates all the important terms. The weaker party must generally accept the terms as offered or not contract at all. A court that decides whether a clause of a contract is unconscionable may do any of the following:

■ refuse to enforce the contract
■ enforce the contract without the unconscionable clause

■ limit the clause's application so that the contract is no longer unfair.

In *What's Your Verdict?* Piotr would probably receive title to the appliance without further payment as it is the unconscionable result of a contract of adhesion and Piotr has paid double the cost to the store already. The law is not designed to relieve a person of a bad bargain. A person may be legally bound by the purchase of overpriced, poor quality, or unneeded goods.

CHECKPOINT Why are contracts of adhesion likely to be unconscionable?

13-1 Assessment

THINK ABOUT LEGAL CONCEPTS

1. Rare coins, even though currency, can be considered goods under the UCC. **True or False?**

2. Intellectual property, such as a patent or a copyright, is not considered a good under the UCC. **True or False?**

3. A(n) _?_ delivery occurs when there is no actual transfer of possession of the goods, but the recipient has the power to control them, as intended by the parties involved.

4. Contracts to sell are not governed by the UCC's law of sales. **True or False?**

5. Which of the following would not be considered goods under the UCC's law of sales? (a) passenger plane (b) computer (c) six acres of land (d) All of the above are goods under the UCC.

6. Can a court refuse to enforce an entire contract that it finds to be unconscionable? **Yes or No?**

THINK CRITICALLY ABOUT EVIDENCE

Study the situation, answer the questions, and then prepare arguments to support your answers.

7. Ashleigh wanted to buy an additional 1,000 shares of her employer's stock. To do so she placed an order with her stock broker to buy "1,000 shares at market price." While the order was pending a fellow employee, Benton, sold Ashleigh 1,000 of his shares. Shortly thereafter Ashleigh's stock broker reported the execution of her purchase order for 1,000 shares at a price $5 higher than what Ashleigh had paid Benton. Ashleigh therefore refused to pay the broker as she had not specified a price term in her offer. Was the contract to buy the stock at market enforceable in court?

8. As Brackston was examining a china plate in the Nook and Cranny Shoppe, it slipped from her hands. The plate smashed into countless pieces when it hit the floor. After the store owner swept up the mess, she pointed to a sign on the wall that said, "Handle with Care! If You Break It, You Buy It." She then rang up a sales charge of $300 plus $18 sales tax. Was Brackston the vendee in a sales contract?

9. After their business law class, Alexa and Ronald were discussing contracts of adhesion. Ronald insisted that when a "big-ticket item," such as a television, is sold on credit terms, the seller prepares the contract. "You agree to it as written or you're out of luck. No sale." Alexa argued, "That's the truth, but not the whole truth." Can you explain what Alexa meant by her comment? Is it ethical for a seller to use contracts of adhesion?

13-2 Special Rules for Sales Contracts

GOALS

- Compare the status of a casual seller with a merchant
- Explain how the Statute of Frauds is applied to sales

KEY TERMS

merchant
casual sellers

Special Rules for Merchants

WHAT'S YOUR VERDICT? During the week, Adonis would buy property at auctions and then sell it to others on weekends at one of his garage sales. As a result of his holding garage sales on 33 consecutive weekends, the city in which he lived claimed he was a merchant and therefore had to pay sales tax.

Is the city correct?

In most cases, the UCC treats all buyers and sellers alike. However, specialized rules may be applied to individuals who are merchants. A **merchant** is someone who deals regularly in the type of goods being exchanged or claims special knowledge or skill in the type of sales transaction being conducted. Individuals who do not qualify as merchants in a transaction are known as **casual sellers**.

You would be a casual seller if you sold your private automobile. A used-car dealer selling an identical car would be a merchant. In general, the UCC holds merchants to a higher standard of conduct than it does casual sellers. Merchants may be required to have licenses to sell. They also usually are subjected to special taxation and closer regulation by the government. In *What's Your Verdict?* Adonis was indeed a merchant and would have to pay sales tax.

Merchant Status in Sales Contracts

Under the UCC, an offeror may state that the offer to buy or to sell goods must be accepted exactly as made or not at all. Otherwise the offeree may accept and still change some terms of the contract or add new ones. Recall that in contract negotiations governed by the common law such changes would end the original offer and would be considered a counteroffer. Under the law of sales of goods, however, the new term is treated as a *proposal for addition* to the contract. What happens then depends on whether both parties are merchants.

When both parties are merchants, a new term inserted by the offeree automatically becomes part of the contract if the offeror fails to object within a reasonable time. However, the new term must not materially alter the offer. In addition,

Your cousin's hobby is making surfboards for friends. He makes three or four a year. Occasionally someone offers to buy one of the boards from him before he gives it away. Is your cousin a merchant or a casual seller of surfboards?

the original offer must not expressly bar such changes. If the new term is a *material* (important) alteration, it is included in the contract only if the original offeror expressly shows an intention to be bound by it.

Other special rules applying to merchants will be pointed out as the appropriate topic area is covered.

CHECKPOINT How do merchants differ from casual buyers in a sales situation?

How Does the Statute of Frauds Apply to Sales?

WHAT'S YOUR VERDICT? Chilton orally agreed to buy an imported camera from the Open Shutter Shop for $748.98. The camera she wanted was not in stock, but a shipment was expected any day. Therefore the salesclerk prepared a memorandum of the sale, signed it, and gave Chilton a copy. A week later the clerk phoned and said, "Your camera is ready." Chilton replied that she did not want it because she had learned that the identical model could be purchased for much less by mail from a New York City discount store.

Is Chilton liable to Open Shutter for breach of contract?

Sales contracts, like other contracts, are generally valid and enforceable in court whether they are oral, written, or implied from the conduct of the parties. However, as you may recall, under the Statute of Frauds, sales contracts for goods valued at $500 or more must be evidenced by a writing to be enforceable in court.

In good business practice, both parties sign a written sales contract and each party gets a copy. This provides both parties with a useful legal record, and it reinforces mutual good faith. Normally both parties expect to perform, but either party might choose to breach the contract. If that happens, the injured party can sue. In court, the written contract goes a long way towards proving the existence and terms of the agreement.

In *What's Your Verdict?* the price of the goods was more than $500. Therefore the sale was governed by the Statute of Frauds. Open Shutter is bound because its clerk signed the contract. Chilton is not bound because she did not sign, but she could enforce the agreement against Open Shutter if she so desired.

Not all the terms of a sales contract have to be in writing to satisfy the Statute of Frauds. Essentially, all that is required is a writing, signed by the party being sued, which satisfies the court that a contract to sell, or a sale, has been made. The number or quantity of goods involved in the transaction must be contained in the writing. The contract is not enforceable beyond the stated quantity.

However, the time and manner of performance; credit and warranty terms; packaging, labeling, and shipping instructions; and even the price need not be included for the writing to satisfy the statute. If necessary, this information can be provided later in oral testimony in court.

A variation of the Statute of Frauds applies only to contracts between merchants. The law generally requires a signature of the person being sued. Between merchants, however, the signature of the party who is suing may be enough to prove an otherwise unenforceable sales contract. If a merchant sends a written confirmation of an oral contract to another merchant within a reasonable time after this oral agreement was made, the confirmation binds both parties. If the second merchant sends a written objection to the confirmation within ten days, the confirmation is not binding.

Exceptions to the Statute of Frauds for Sales Contracts

Under certain circumstances, oral contracts for the sale of goods valued at $500 or more may be valid and enforceable. These exceptions to the requirements of the Statute of Frauds include the following:

GOODS RECEIVED AND ACCEPTED BY THE BUYER Receiving the goods does not in itself make an oral contract binding under the Statute of Frauds. Both receipt and acceptance are necessary. A buyer may receive goods without accepting them. Under the UCC a buyer can accept goods in three ways.

1. After a reasonable opportunity to inspect the goods, the buyer signifies to the seller that the goods conform to the contract or will be retained in spite of their nonconformity.

2. The buyer acts inconsistently with the seller's ownership (for example, uses, consumes, or resells the goods).

3. The buyer fails to make an effective rejection after having a reasonable opportunity to inspect the goods.

Note that if the buyer has received and accepted only some of the goods, the oral contract is enforceable only for those goods received and accepted.

BUYER PAYS FOR GOODS AND SELLER ACCEPTS PAYMENT When payment in full has been accepted by the seller, the oral contract is enforceable in full. When partial payment has been accepted by the seller, the oral contract is

The seller of this used car makes an oral agreement to sell the car and accepts partial payment for it. Is the contract enforceable in full?

IN THIS CASE At an auction, Zutto bought a handmade, oak rolltop desk from Winslow for $1,250. Zutto paid $250 and left to get a truck with the balance still due. When Zutto returned, Winslow told her the desk had been sold to another person who had paid $1,500 in cash for the desk and disappeared with it. He explained that the contract with her was oral and therefore not enforceable. Winslow was wrong; Zutto's partial payment for the indivisible goods (the oak desk) made the oral contract enforceable. If the goods had been divisible (for example, 50 reams of paper), the contract would be enforceable only for the quantity for which payment was made and accepted. Winslow is liable to Zutto for damages measured by the extra amount she must now pay someone else for an equivalent desk.

enforceable only for the goods paid for if the goods can be divided and the price can be apportioned fairly. If the goods are indivisible and there can be no dispute as to quantity, the contract is enforceable in full.

GOODS SPECIALLY MADE NOT SUITABLE FOR SALE TO OTHERS A seller can enforce an oral contract for non-resalable goods if

1. the seller has substantially begun to manufacture them, or

2. the seller has made contracts to obtain the goods from third parties.

PARTY AGAINST WHOM ENFORCEMENT SOUGHT ADMITS ORAL CONTRACT MADE A party against whom enforcement of an oral contract is sought may admit in legal pleadings or testimony that he or she agreed to part or all of a contract. In such a case, a signed writing is not necessary for the enforcement of the part of the contract that was admitted.

CHECKPOINT Name the four situations in which the Statute of Frauds does not apply to sales contracts.

THINK ABOUT LEGAL CONCEPTS

1. Generally, oral contracts are unenforceable in court. **True or False?**

2. Under the Statute of Frauds, sales of goods valued at _?_ or more need to be evidenced by a writing to be enforceable in court.

3. If a buyer resells the goods, the UCC treats the buyer's action as an acceptance. **True or False?**

4. Do both parties have to sign the writing to satisfy the Statute of Frauds? **Yes or No?**

5. If a party admits to agreeing to the terms of an oral contract during legal proceedings, the contract becomes enforceable against him or her. **True or False?**

6. Individuals involved in sales transactions are either classified as casual sellers or _?_ by the law.

THINK CRITICALLY ABOUT EVIDENCE

Study the situation, answer the questions, and then prepare arguments to support your answers.

7. A pottery manufacturer offered to sell red clay flowerpots in three different sizes to a garden supply store. The store accepted the offer but specified that the pots had to be packaged in sets of three (with one of each size) rather than in bulk as described in the offer. This was a material change in the terms. The pottery maker did not object or revoke the original offer. Instead the maker packaged and shipped in threes the goods as requested. Later, the pottery maker did a cost evaluation of shipping the pots in threes and stopped doing so. Could the maker be sued under the sales contract and be forced to ship in threes?

8. When Soule bought a sweater for his wife, the clerk deliberately lied to him. She said that the garment was a pure silk and mohair, hand-knitted import from Italy. In fact, it was a machine-made, domestic, polyester-and-wool mix. Did the clerk violate the Statute of Frauds by her conduct? Did the clerk act ethically?

9. Grant had long admired Kahn's collection of records featuring the big bands of the 1930s. One day Kahn orally agreed to sell the collection to Grant for $275. When Grant appeared with the money, however, Kahn said she had changed her mind and refused to deliver. Moreover, she insisted she was acting within her legal rights. Kahn said she had learned that her collection was worth at least $1,000. Therefore, she said, a signed writing was required to make the contract enforceable. Did Kahn state the law correctly?

10. Harrison orally agreed to buy two electric guitars and a matched set of drums from Rudolph. The price was $1,250, payable with $800 in cash and a large-screen television. Harrison paid the price in full. However, Rudolph refused to deliver the guitars and drums, and he sent television back and mailed a certified check for $800 to Harrison. He explained that he had decided to start another rock group. Rudolph claimed that their oral agreement was not enforceable. Is he right?

CONCEPTS IN BRIEF

13-1 Sales

1. Both sales of goods and contracts to sell goods are governed by a combination of basic contract law and special UCC provisions on sales.

2. Neither payment nor delivery is essential for transfer of title.

3. Price may consist of anything such as money, services, or goods—whatever was agreed upon by the parties as consideration.

4. Payment occurs when the buyer delivers the price and the seller accepts it.

5. Receipt of goods occurs when the buyer takes physical possession or control of the goods.

6. Acceptance of the goods occurs when the buyer indicates that the goods conform to the contract or will be retained in spite of non-conformity, the buyer acts inconsistently with the seller's ownership of the goods, or the buyer fails to reject the goods before a reasonable time to inspect them has passed.

7. A bill of sale may provide useful evidence of the transfer of title to goods.

13-2 Special Rules for Sales Contracts

8. Merchants generally are held to a higher standard of conduct by the UCC than are casual sellers.

9. Unless otherwise required by statute, sales or contracts to sell may be oral, written, or implied from the conduct of the parties.

10. To be enforceable, a sale or contract to sell goods for $500 or more must be evidenced by a writing. The writing must specify at least a quantity of goods involved and must be signed by the party who is sued or by that party's agent. A writing is not essential when the

   - buyer has received and accepted the goods
   - buyer has paid for the goods in full and the seller has accepted payment
   - goods custom-made for the buyer are not suitable for sale to others in the ordinary course of business, and the seller has begun manufacturing or has contracted to obtain the goods
   - party seeking to avoid the contract admits during legal proceedings that the oral agreement was made.

YOUR LEGAL VOCABULARY

Match each statement with the term that it best defines. Some terms may not be used.

1. Immediate transfer of ownership of goods from a seller to a buyer for a price

2. Consideration for a sale or a contract to sell

3. An exchange of goods for goods

4. Tangible, movable, personal property

5. Label for a seller who claims special knowledge in a certain type of sales transaction

6. Receipt showing evidence of a transfer of ownership of goods

7. Seller who does not meet the definition of a merchant

8. Occurs when the buyer transfers the agreed-upon consideration and the seller accepts it

9. Collection of rights that allow the use and enjoyment of property

10. Purchaser

11. The act by which the subject matter of the contract is placed within the possession or control of the buyer

a. barter
b. bill of sale
c. casual seller
d. contract to sell
e. delivery
f. goods
g. merchant
h. ownership
i. payment
j. price
k. receipt of goods
l. sale
m. vendee
n. vendor

REVIEW LEGAL CONCEPTS

12. Why should the law of sales be different from the law of contracts?

13. Give specific examples of a barter transaction, a sale for money transaction, and a transaction that combines the two. Identify the advantages and disadvantages of each kind of transaction.

14. Arguably, the law of sales helps facilitate the smooth transfer of goods in commerce. It also provides clear standards that are, in general, uniform from state to state. Why should the governments of the states devote their time and resources to accomplish such ends?

15. Compare the retail sale of 10,000 feet of irrigation pipe from a Farmer's Supply to a farmer with the commercial sale of that same amount of pipe from a wholesaler to the Farmer's Supply. Label the parties to each transaction. List the specialized knowledge of the law of sales that might be required by the various parties.

16. What is the justification for requiring a higher standard of knowledge and conduct from merchants than casual sellers? Would merchants likely agree with such a justification? Why or why not?

WRITE ABOUT LEGAL CONCEPTS

17. Consider the concept of ownership. What rights and duties do you think come with it?

18. Why is a bill of sale not considered a contract?

19. **HOT DEBATE** Would it make a difference if Anton had refused Bob's requests to put the contract in writing and the amount demanded by Anton is twice what Bob and Anton had shaken hands on?

MAKE ACADEMIC CONNECTIONS

20. **ART** Research how artists, sculptors, architects, composers, and other creative individuals handle contracting when they are commissioned to produce unique goods (portraits, statues, fountains, etc.).

THINK CRITICALLY ABOUT EVIDENCE

Study the situation, answer the questions, and then prepare arguments to support your answers.

21. Paul, a graduate student at the university, repeatedly sold his blood to a blood bank to pay for his tuition and books. Does the law of sales apply to these transactions?

22. One day, on his way back from selling his blood, Paul became light headed and crashed his car into a light pole. The car was repairable but the charges for parts and labor totalled more than $2,000. Should he have to pay sales tax on this whole amount? Why or why not?

23. When the economy turned sour and a large number of people sought to sell their blood, the blood bank wrote a term in its contracts that, in order to sell blood to the blood bank, each "donor" had to sell at least three pints a month to it or would have to refund any payments made to them in a month where the quota was not met. This meant that the donors would be very low on their own blood supply. What might a court do when confronted by such a term in a contract? What would be the result?

24. On one visit Paul could only bleed out three quarters of a pint of blood. The blood bank refused to pay anything for what had been donated until Paul could complete the donation of a full pint of blood that the sales contract called for. Paul maintained that he should be paid pro rata for the amount he had given. Who is correct under the law of sales?

25. When Paul returned to complete the delivery of blood, the blood bank refused to pay, yet kept the full pint and resold it to a hospital. Paul then maintained that the blood bank had accepted the goods he had for sale and should pay. Is he correct?

26. Paul had type B-negative blood. It is extremely rare. As a consequence, when the blood bank received a request for that type, it called Paul and orally promised to pay him $645 per pint. Paul gave two pints in less than three weeks, but the blood bank only paid him the standard $35 per pint. Was the oral contract enforceable? Why or why not?

27. Gillispie, a minor, was injured when two bottles of a soft drink exploded. The accident occurred as Gillispie was carrying the bottles to the checkout counter in the defendant's self-service store. If a sale had taken place even though Gillispie had not yet paid for the goods, the store could be partially liable for the injury. Has a sale taken place? (*Gillispie v. Great Atlantic and Pacific Tea Company*, 187 S.E.2d 441, N.C.)

28. In July of 1977 Dr. Sedmak read in Vett Vues, a Corvette fancier's magazine, that the Pace Car, a special edition of the Corvette, would soon be manufactured. He was a collector of Corvettes and wanted one of the 6,000 that were to be placed on sale. In January of 1978 Mrs. Sedmak gave Charlie's Chevrolet a $500 check as a deposit on a Pace Car and specified the options the Sedmaks desired. She was then informed that the purchase price of the car would be around $15,000. In April of 1978 the Sedmaks were notified that the Pace Car, equipped as specified, had arrived. However, because of the unanticipated high demand for the car, it would be put up for sale to the highest bidder. The Sedmaks did not submit a bid; instead they filed a suit for specific performance. The trial court found that the parties had entered into an oral contract. If that contract could be excepted from the application of the Statute of Frauds, the court would order specific performance as petitioned by the Sedmaks. Charlie's Chevrolet would then have to sell them the car at a reasonable price which, given the options added, would be around $15,000. What exception to the application of the Statute of Frauds would this transaction fall under? (*Sedmak v. Charlie's Chevrolet*, Inc. 622 S.W. 2d 694)

29. Cargill, Inc., the plaintiff, is a large grain company. Warren, an agent of Cargill, managed its grain elevator in Hingham, Montana. On August 24, Warren orally contracted to buy from Wilson, the defendant farmer, 28,000 bushels of wheat at $1.48 per bushel and 6,000 bushels of higher protein wheat at $1.63 per bushel. Warren prepared two standard grain purchase written contracts. He signed them for Cargill, as its agent, and he also signed Wilson's name. A few days later, he delivered copies to Wilson, who made no objection. On August 30, Wilson received a $10,000 loan from Cargill. The check was attached to a detachable part of the standard grain contract, and it incorporated the two contracts by specific references to their numbers. Wilson endorsed and cashed the check. The loan was interest-free because it was an advance payment for the wheat. During September and October, Wilson delivered 11,000 bushels of ordinary wheat at the agreed-upon price of $1.48, and 6,000 bushels at the then-current, higher market price. Then Wilson refused to deliver any more wheat. Cargill sued for damages. Wilson claimed he was not bound because of the Statute of Frauds. Who should win? (*Cargill, Inc. v. Wilson*, 532 P.2d 988, Mont.)

30. Jordan Paper Products, Inc., sued to recover $22,089.48 owed to it under an oral contract by Burger Man, Inc., an Indiana fast-food chain. The contract was for various paper products that Jordan had prepared at Burger Man's order, to specially identify the fast-food chain to its customers. Burger Man maintained that the oral contract was unenforceable because of the Statute of Frauds. Was the contract unenforceable? (*Burger Man, Inc. v. Jordan Paper Products,* Inc., 352 N.E.2d 821, Ind.)

31. Albert Reifschneider knew farming. Born and raised on a farm, he had been selling his crops for more than 20 years. He also had a lot of experience in farm futures (contracts made between farmers and buyers for the purchase of crops to be harvested at some future time). One year he orally contracted to sell more than 12,000 bushels of corn from the fall harvest to the Colorado-Kansas Grain Company. Treating Reifschneider as a merchant, the company sent him a written confirmation of the deal to which he did not respond. When Reifschneider refused to deliver the corn, the Grain Company sued him for breach of contract. Who won, and why? (*Colorado-Kansas Grain Co. v. Reifschneider*, 817 P. 2d 637)

32. The Palermos needed carpeting for their home. Colorado Carpet Installation, Inc., agreed to do the job for a price that, including carpet and labor, totalled more than $500. Mrs. Palermo did not like how the job was being done and so sought the services of another contractor. Colorado Carpet then sued for enforcement of the oral contract. The Palermos replied that, as the contract was for more than $500, it was unenforceable under the Statute of Frauds. The issue at trial became whether or not the contract was for the sale of goods or services. How do you think the court ruled? (*Colorado Carpet Installation, Inc. v. Palermo*, 668 P.2d 1384)

Case For Legal Thinking

ADVENT SYSTEMS, LTD., V. UNISYS CORPORATION U.S. COURT OF APPEALS, THIRD CIRCUIT, 925 F. 2D 670

FACTS In the pre-1990 developing world of computers, Unisys Corporation and IBM were major competitors. When Unisys was approached in the mid-1980s by Advent Systems, Ltd., a software developer, Unisys saw a chance to make a major improvement in its market position. Advent had developed a computer-based data management system that allowed engineering drawings and specialized documents to be transformed into a database. The database could then be improved, tailored, and reused again and again for different projects. In June of 1987, Unisys agreed with Advent to sell the system throughout the United States for an initial two-year period. Advent was required to provide the technical personnel that might be necessary to produce a successful installation of each individual system.

In the summer of 1987, however, Unisys failed in an attempt to sell the Advent-developed system to Arco, a large oil company. This cast a negative light on the properties and marketability of the Advent system. Regardless, progress continued on the product's joint sales and training programs in the United States.

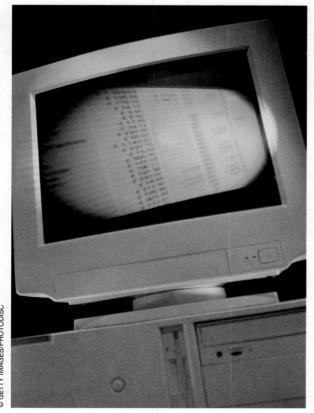

Finally, however, the relationship split apart. Unisys, in a period of downsizing, determined that it would be better off if it developed its own system. Therefore, in December, 1987, Unisys informed Advent that their relationship was at an end. Similarly, negotiations between Unisys' United Kingdom subsidiary and Advent came to an end. Advent promptly filed a complaint against Unisys alleging a breach of contract. Unisys defended by contending the sale of the software was, in essence, a sale of goods and, therefore, there was no breach of contract suit. Advent countered that software was not a good and that Advent was basically contracting to sell Unisys the services of its technical personnel.

LOWER COURT DECISION The trial court found in favor of Advent. A jury awarded Advent $4,550,000 as a result of Unisys' "breach of contract." The case was appealed to the U.S. Court of Appeals.

APPELLATE ARGUMENTS On appeal before the federal 3rd Circuit Court of Appeals, Advent continued to base its arguments on a breach of contract claim for the providing of services. Unisys also followed its previous line of reasoning in the lower court. Before the appellate court, it basically said that the transaction was a sale of goods and, therefore, subject to the Statute of Frauds in the Uniform Commercial Code. As the agreement lacked an explicit term on quantity, the Statute of Frauds would, therefore, preclude any suit and recovery.

DECISIVE ISSUE Was the transaction a sale of goods or a providing of services?

APPELLATE DECISION The court held that it was a sales contract.

PRACTICE JUDGING

1. As a consequence of the appellate court's holding that the contract was for a sale of goods, should the trial court's decision be reversed, or should the decision be affirmed?

2. What do you feel is the legal reasoning that led the appellate court to its conclusion?

3. Can you envision any circumstances when computer software would not be considered a good?

Chapter 14
Ownership and Risk of Loss in Sales

14-1 Transfer of Ownership

14-2 Risk of Loss and Insurable Interest in Sales

© GETTY IMAGES/PHOTODISC

HOT DEBATE

While you are having dinner one evening, your laptop computer is stolen from the front seat of your car. You do not report the theft for a week and a half. The police discover that the computer was sold to an innocent purchaser by a pawn shop that has since gone out of business. The new "owner" of the laptop is a pastor of a church that ministers to the homeless. She bought the laptop from the pawn shop before you reported the theft to the police. When you approach the pastor to get the computer back, she refuses. She says that the church needs it desperately to keep track of its "flock." It is especially important during the current winter season, when knowing where the homeless can seek shelter means life or death. You file suit for the return of the computer.

WHERE DO YOU STAND?

1. What are the legal reasons for your suit?
2. What legal arguments could you anticipate the attorney for the church making?

14-1 Transfer of Ownership

GOALS

■ Discuss who may transfer ownership of goods

■ Explain what is required for transfer of ownership of goods and when it occurs

KEY TERMS

good faith purchaser

existing goods

identified goods

future goods

tender of delivery

Who May Transfer Ownership?

WHAT'S YOUR VERDICT?
Brad was walking through a part of town near the docks for ocean going cargo vessels when he came upon an electronic goods store. Attracted by the goods and prices in the window, Brad went inside and eventually haggled Standon, the owner and only sales clerk, into selling a surround-sound system to him. Brad bought the system, available even in discount stores for more than $600, for $110. Standon turned out to be a dock worker who stocked his store with stolen goods. When police showed up to take back the surround-sound system, which had been stolen by Standon, Brad protested that he had paid for it in good faith and didn't know it was stolen property.

Who has title to the sound system?

As a general rule, only the true owner of goods may legally transfer ownership of those goods. Further, the buyer of goods receives only the property rights that the seller has in the goods and nothing more.

As with most general rules, there are exceptions to these rules about transfer of ownership. Such exceptions include the following.

1. Persons authorized to do so may transfer another's title.

2. Buyers in a sale induced by the fraud of the seller may transfer better title than they have to an innocent third-party purchaser.

3. Holders of negotiable documents of title may transfer better title than they have.

4. Merchants who keep possession of goods they have sold may transfer better title than they have.

Authorized Persons

Persons may sell what they do not own if the owner has authorized them to do so. Salespeople in retail stores are so authorized. Auctioneers and sheriffs also are authorized when they sell, under court order or when empowered by statute, stolen or repossessed goods or foreclosed property.

Buyers in a Sale Induced by Fraud

If an owner of goods is induced by fraud to sell the goods, the transfer of title is voidable by the seller. Upon discovering the fraud, the

What gives salespeople the ability to sell goods they don't own?

© DIGITAL VISION

victimized seller may cancel the contract and recover the goods unless an innocent third party already has given value and acquired rights in them. Such a third party is known as a **good faith purchaser**. Thus, a buyer with voidable title resulting from a sale induced by fraud may transfer valid title to a good faith purchaser. To act in good faith, the purchaser must not have reason to suspect the person who has the voidable title. The defrauded seller must seek damages from the original fraudulent buyer.

In contrast, the person who buys stolen goods from a thief receives possession, but not title, because the thief did not have good title to give. This is true whether the buyer is innocent or knows that the goods were stolen. In *What's Your Verdict?* Brad did not receive title to the surround-sound system.

Unfortunately, stolen goods are seldom recovered. If they are recovered, they often have been damaged or stripped of parts. Even when recovered in good condition by the police, stolen goods often cannot be identified clearly as property of the victim and therefore are not returned. The police are compelled by statute to sell such goods at public auction.

Holders of Negotiable Documents of Title

In business, certain documents often are used as a substitute for title to goods. One example is a warehouse receipt issued by public warehouses when goods are stored there. Other examples are bills of lading and air bills issued by common carriers when goods are shipped by them. These documents may be negotiable or nonnegotiable. If such a documents is negotiable, the goods are to be delivered to the bearer, who is the person in possession of the document, or to the order of a party named by the document. Such a person, also known as a *holder,* is deemed to have title to the goods. A holder may transfer title of the goods by merely transferring the document. A holder who is named in the negotiable document must sign as well as deliver the document to transfer it to a third party.

Merchants with Possession of Sold Goods

Occasionally a buyer will allow the merchant seller to temporarily retain possession of the goods after the sale. If, during this period, the merchant resells and delivers these goods to a good faith purchaser, the latter receives good title. However, the merchant must replace the resold goods or be liable to the original buyer.

CHECKPOINT Besides the owner, who may transfer ownership of goods?

GLOBAL ISSUES

Negotiable Bills of Lading

Negotiable bills of lading have been a part of commerce for centuries. Many European countries used them as early as the sixteenth century. In today's international transactions, ownership still is often transferred using negotiable bills of lading. These documents are bought and sold while cargo is literally floating on the open seas. When the document is sold, so is the cargo. It is not uncommon for oil to change hands 20 times between the time it leaves the Persian Gulf and arrives in the United States.

IN THIS CASE At the Consumer Electronics Show in Las Vegas, Millicent became convinced that an innovative new gaming system that allowed gamers to duel with one another using holograms that followed their body movements would be the hit of the Christmas season. As a consequence, she placed an order for one thousand of the systems, paying for them in full so as to receive one of the first shipments. In early November, she received by overnight mail a negotiable bill of lading indicating the systems had been loaded on a delivery truck in California and were on the way to a local warehouse. Once they arrived she could obtain them by presenting the document of title to the warehouse keeper and paying any shipping or storage fee that might be due.

Requirements for Ownership Transfer

WHAT'S YOUR VERDICT?

Chien Huang ordered electronic equipment worth more than $3 million from Inter-Continental Traders, a Seattle exporter. The equipment was to be shipped to a company in the People's Republic of China. The sales agreement, signed by both parties, stated that title and risk of loss would pass "when all necessary governmental permits are obtained." The Chinese government granted an import permit and necessary clearance to allow the exchange of Chinese currency into dollars to pay for the order. However, the U.S. State Department refused to grant an export permit because of the classified nature of some of the equipment

Did a sale take place?

Do you think this grain would be considered a fungible good? Why or why not?

© GETTY IMAGES/PHOTODISC

For ownership of goods to be transferred in a sale, the goods must be both existing and identified. **Existing goods** are physically in existence and owned by the seller. However, they need not be in a fully assembled and immediately deliverable condition. **Identified goods** are existing goods that have been designated specifically as the subject matter of a particular sales contract. The identification of such goods may be done by the buyer, the seller, both, or by a mutually agreed-upon third party. Typically, when identified, the goods are marked, separated, or in some way made distinct from similar goods that the seller might have on hand.

Unless goods are both existing and identified, they are **future goods**. Any contract for the sale of future goods is a contract to sell rather than a sale. Neither ownership nor risk of loss passes at the time of an agreement concerning future goods.

An important exception to the process of identification is made for *fungible goods*. These are goods of a homogeneous or essentially identical nature. With fungible goods, by nature or trade usage, each unit is regarded as equal to every other unit. Examples are a quantity of corn or oil of a given variety and grade, or thousands of cases of identical canned fruit in a warehouse. In many states, ownership and risk of loss in fungible goods pass without selection or identification of specific goods. The buyer therefore becomes the owner at the time of the agreement.

When Does Ownership Transfer?

Once goods are existing and identified, disputes still may arise over who has title and risk of loss to the goods at particular times. Sometimes creditors of the seller, or creditors of the buyer, may claim possession in order to collect money due. Other disputes may concern who bears the risk of loss if the goods are damaged, stolen, or destroyed before the transaction is completed. A risk-bearer may want or need the protection of casualty insurance. Generally, the person who has title to the goods will bear the loss, but this is not always the case.

In deciding when title transfers from seller to buyer, courts first examine the sales agreement to see if the parties have specified clearly when they intended for title to pass. If they have expressed such intent, courts generally will uphold their agreement. In *What's Your Verdict?* no sale took place. The agreement said that title and risk of loss would pass "when all necessary governmental permits" were obtained. Therefore Inter-Continental Traders would retain title to the goods because this condition had not been met.

If the parties do not specify when title is to pass, courts first determine if there is any applicable custom or usage in the particular trade that can settle the question. If there is no agreement on the matter and no available trade custom or usage, courts look to the UCC for a solution.

Common Situations

Common situations involving transfer of title are discussed below. Note that neither the method nor the time of payment governs the outcome.

SELLER DELIVERS GOODS TO THEIR DESTINATION If the contract requires the seller to deliver the goods to their destination, title passes when the goods are tendered at that specified destination. **Tender of delivery** means that the seller places (or authorizes a carrier to place) the proper goods at the buyer's disposal and notifies the buyer so that delivery can be received. The manner, time, and place for tender are determined by the agreement and the UCC. When the seller is required to do additional work, title does not pass until such work is completed.

SELLER SHIPS, BUT DOES NOT DELIVER, GOODS TO THEIR DESTINATION If the contract requires

or authorizes the seller to ship the goods but does not obligate the seller to deliver them to the destination, title passes to the buyer at the time and place of shipment, when possession is transferred to the carrier.

SELLER DELIVERS DOCUMENT OF TITLE When customary, or when the parties have agreed that the seller is to deliver a document of title (for example, an airbill), title passes when and where the document is delivered. For example, Degory bought 600 tons of oats from Delta. The oats were stored in a public grain elevator. Title passed when an authorized agent of Delta delivered a negotiable warehouse receipt for the oats to Degory.

SELLER TENDERS GOODS AT PLACE OF SALE If the seller is to tender the goods at the place of sale, title passes at the time and the place where the sales contract is made.

CHECKPOINT What two characteristics must goods have in order to have ownership of them transferred?

14-1 Assessment

Xtra!
Study Tools
school.cengage.com/blaw/lawxtra

THINK ABOUT LEGAL CONCEPTS

1. The buyer of stolen goods receives good title if he or she did not know the goods were stolen. **True or False?**

2. If an owner of goods is induced by fraud to sell the goods, the transfer of title is _?_ by the seller. (a) valid (b) voidable (c) void

3. If the seller is to tender the goods at the place of sale, title passes at the time and place where the sales contract is made. **True or False?**

4. Ownership of fungible goods can be transferred in a sale without the goods being identified. **True or False?**

THINK CRITICALLY ABOUT EVIDENCE

Study the situation, answer the questions, and then prepare arguments to support your answers.

5. Conch lied about his income and assets when he bought a dinette from Furniture World on credit. After making the first of 12 payments, Conch defaulted. Furniture World then checked Conch's credit record and discovered the fraud. Conch had already sold the dinette to Tilly, who honestly thought that Conch was the owner. Furniture World sued to recover the furniture from Tilly. Who wins? Why?

6. After Carr refurbished her home, she held a yard sale for things she did not need. Included was a large crosscut saw, which she sold to Sutro. She did not know that her husband had borrowed the saw from a neighbor. Did Sutro become the owner?

14-2 Risk of Loss and Insurable Interest in Sales

GOALS

- Explain the general rules for identifying when risk of loss transfers
- Identify the point at which insurable interest of goods transfers
- Identify when risk of loss and insurable interest transfer in specific situations

KEY TERMS

FOB

CIF

credit sale

COD

sale or return

sale on approval

sale of an undivided interest

auction

bulk transfer

When Does Risk of Loss Transfer?

WHAT'S YOUR VERDICT? Knowing that streaming video cell phones, extremely popular in Japan, would soon hit the American market, Correlone ordered 250 of each of the best-selling cell phone models with the streaming video feature for his high-end electronics store. He ordered them from a wholesaler in Osaka, Japan, to be shipped directly to his location by a carrier that the seller would select. Two weeks later the goods arrived and the carrier notified Correlone that they could be picked up at its local warehouse. When Correlone arrived at the warehouse's address the next day, he found the building a smoldering ruin. It had been hit by lightning and caught fire the previous evening destroying all of its contents.

Who has the risk of loss for the goods, Correlone or the wholesaler?

A wise buyer and seller of goods in a sales transaction will be sure to pay special attention to identifying the point at which the risk of loss transfers. At that point, insurance coverage can be terminated by the seller to minimize costs. By this time as well insurance coverage should also be in place for the buyer to minimize exposure to the consequences of damage to or destruction of the goods. The following discussions provide the general rules for identifying this important point.

If Seller Ships Goods by Carrier

If the seller is required to deliver the goods to a particular destination but is allowed to use a carrier, such as a railroad, to make the delivery, the risk of loss passes to the buyer at the destination, upon tender of delivery. This is true even if goods that are shipped by carrier are still in the possession of the carrier. In *What's Your Verdict?* Correlone had the risk of loss as soon as the shipper gave its tender of the goods by notifying him they were available for pickup. Hopefully, Correlone had insurance that covered property loss under these circumstances.

The seller of the goods in one of the containers being shipped on this vessel is required to deliver the goods to a particular destination. When and where would the risk of loss pass to the buyer?

© GETTY IMAGES/PHOTODISC

Suppose the seller is not required to deliver the goods to the buyer at a particular destination. If the seller then uses a carrier to transport the goods, the risk of loss passes to the buyer when the goods are delivered to the carrier.

Commercial buyers often use the shipment term **FOB**, which means "free on board." Assume that the seller is in Atlanta and the buyer is in New York City. In this case, "FOB Atlanta" means the seller agrees to deliver the goods no further than the carrier's freight station in Atlanta. Title and risk of loss transfer to the buyer at that point. On the other hand, if the terms are "FOB, buyer's warehouse, New York City," the seller must deliver the goods to the buyer's warehouse in New York City. The title and the risk of loss remain with the seller until delivery takes place. In the absence of contrary arrangements, the buyer pays the transportation charges in the first situation described and the seller pays the charges in the second.

In shipments from foreign countries, it is not uncommon for the seller to quote a **CIF** (cost, insurance, freight) price. This means that the seller contracts for adequate insurance and for proper shipment to the named destination and then adds these items to the price or cost of the goods. The risk of loss passes to the buyer when the seller delivers the goods to the carrier, such as a seagoing ship. However, the insurance provides protection against loss from any identified risks.

If the Goods are Held by a Bailee

Sometimes goods are held for a seller by a bailee. A *bailee* has temporary possession of another person's goods, holding them in trust for a specified purpose. A watch or computer repairperson is an example of a bailee. Note that if such a repairperson sells the entrusted goods in error, the innocent purchaser obtains good title. (Bailments are discussed more fully in Chapter 17.)

The goods may be sold by the owner, yet the contract may call for delivery to the buyer without the warehoused goods being moved. The risk of loss transfers to the buyer under such circumstances upon any of the following events:

■ when the buyer receives a negotiable document of title covering the goods (for example, a negotiable warehouse receipt)

■ when the bailee acknowledges the buyer's right to possession of the goods

■ after the buyer receives a non-negotiable document of title (for example, a non-negotiable warehouse receipt) or other written direction to a bailee to deliver the goods. (The buyer must have had a reasonable time to present the document to the bailee, who must have honored it.)

If Either Party Breaches after the Goods are Identified

The seller sometimes breaches by providing goods so faulty that the buyer rightly rejects them. The risk of loss then remains with the seller until the defects are corrected.

IN THIS CASE Galaxy Furniture Company shipped a truckload of chairs and sofas to Brenda's Bargain Basement. Without unloading the tractor-trailer, inspection disclosed that Galaxy had mistakenly shipped sofas and chairs upholstered in costly Italian leather. Brenda had ordered the durable but much cheaper vinyl upholstery models. Brenda promptly notified Galaxy of the error and asked for instructions on what to do with them. After a week, the loaded trailer was still parked in back of Brenda's warehouse. Then a fire of undisclosed origin destroyed the trailer and its contents (along with some other vehicles). Galaxy suffers the loss as the goods were faulty and risk of loss therefore remained with it.

In Other Cases

In any case not covered previously, the risk of loss falls on the buyer upon receipt of the goods if the seller is a merchant. If the seller is not a merchant, the risk of loss transfers to the buyer as soon as the seller makes a tender of delivery

CHECKPOINT Explain the point at which the risk of loss transfers from seller to buyer when the seller ships the goods by carrier.

When Does Insurable Interest Transfer?

WHAT'S YOUR VERDICT? Frosty-Frolic Company was a fresh-food packer and processor. In a sales contract with Goodman, Frosty-Frolic agreed to pack a quantity of head lettuce grown near Salinas, California, in specially marked "Soaring Eagle" brand cartons. The lettuce was routinely dehydrated, cooled, packaged, placed in the special cartons, and stacked on pallets in Frosty-Frolic sheds for daily shipment as ordered by Goodman.

At what point did Goodman obtain the right to insure the goods against possible loss?

The buyer obtains certain rights in goods at the time of their identification to a sales contract. One such right, called an *insurable interest,* gives the buyer the right to buy insurance on the goods. This often is necessary as, even though the risk of loss may still reside with the seller, the buyer may lose money should the goods be destroyed and the buyer cannot satisfactorily find them elsewhere. The physical act of identifying goods usually takes the form of setting aside, marking, tagging, labeling, boxing, branding, shipping, or in some other way indicating that specific goods are to be delivered or sent to the buyer in fulfillment of the contract. In *What's Your Verdict?* Goodman obtained an insurable interest when the lettuce was identified as hers (when placed in "Soaring Eagle" cartons).

If the goods already exist and have been identified to the contract when the contract is made, an insurable interest arises in the buyer at that time.

LAW BRIEF

The euro is now the only legal tender in the following European Union countries: Austria, Belgium, Finland, France, Germany, Greece, Republic of Ireland, Italy, Luxembourg, the Netherlands, Portugal, and Spain. These countries' old national currencies, such as the German mark and the French franc, have been withdrawn from circulation.

In addition to the insurable interest, the buyer has the following rights:

1. to inspect the identified goods at a reasonable hour
2. to compel delivery if the seller wrongfully withholds delivery
3. to collect damages from third persons who take or injure the goods.

CHECKPOINT When does a buyer obtain an insurable interest in the goods?

Transfer of Rights and Risks in Specific Sales

WHAT'S YOUR VERDICT? With a high bid of $145, Angelina and Tom bought a king-sized mattress at an auction held outside the house of a neighbor who had died the previous month. Before they could pay for and receive their goods, a sudden storm dumped an inch of rain on the mattress ruining it.

Who had the risk of loss at the time the mattress was ruined?

The following sales transactions merit special attention because of the frequency with which they occur or because of the uniqueness of the rules that apply to them.

Cash-and-Carry Sales

When the buyer in a sales contract is a consumer who pays cash and takes immediate delivery, title passes to the buyer at the time of the transaction. This is the most common type of transaction for groceries and other low-priced items. Risk of loss passes upon the buyer's receipt of the goods from a merchant and on tender of goods by a casual seller.

The seller may insist on payment in legal tender. Checks are commonly used but are not legal tender. Acceptance of a check by the seller is not considered payment until the check is paid at the bank. However, use of a check by the consumer in a cash-and-carry sale does not affect the timing of the transfer of title or risk of loss.

Sales on Credit

The fact that a sale is made on credit does not affect the passing of title or risk of loss. A **credit sale** is simply a sale that, by agreement of the parties, calls for payment for the goods at a later date. Ownership and risk of loss may pass even though the time of payment or delivery is delayed.

COD Sales

Goods often are shipped **COD**, which means collect on delivery. The carrier collects the price and transportation charges upon delivery and transmits this amount to the seller. If the buyer does not pay, the goods are not delivered. Thus, in effect, the seller retains control over the possession of the goods until the price is paid. In a COD arrangement, the buyer loses the right otherwise available to inspect the goods before payment. Nevertheless, ownership and risk of loss transfer just as though there were no such provisions.

Sale or Return

A **sale or return** is a completed sale in which the buyer has an option of returning the goods. When goods are delivered to a merchant buyer in a sale or return, the ownership and risk of loss pass to the buyer upon delivery. Such a transaction is a true sale. In a sale or return transaction, if the buyer returns the goods within the fixed or a reasonable amount of time, ownership and risk of loss pass back to the seller. This is true whether the sale is made for cash or on credit. The returned goods must essentially be in their original condition. Normally goods held on sale or return are subject to the claims of the buyer's creditors, who can seize the goods under court order.

The clothes these shop assistants are unloading were sold to the shop on a sale or return transaction. What would be the benefit of this type of sale to the store? What would be the benefit to the seller?

© GETTY IMAGES/PHOTODISC

The sale or return provision should not be confused with the return privilege granted to customers of some retail stores. These stores allow customers to return most purchases that have not been used, even if they are not defective. This return privilege is not required by law, but stores offer it to promote goodwill and increase sales in the long run.

A Question of ETHICS

Dorothy owned her own plumbing business. She bought her tools from a nationwide retailer that offered an unconditional guarantee that tools sold under its trademark could be returned and exchanged for new ones any time the customer was dissatisfied for any reason. Dorothy made it a policy to use the retailer's tools until they were worn out and then return them, demanding and receiving a new replacement. She did this even though the retailer's tools outlasted comparable tools by a wide margin. Are her actions legal? Ethical?

Sale on Approval

Sometimes goods are delivered to the buyer in a **sale on approval**, "on trial," or "on satisfaction." In such a case, ownership and risk of loss do not pass until the prospective buyer approves the goods. This may be done by words, payment, any conduct indicating approval, or retention of the goods beyond a specified or reasonable time. While in possession of the goods, the prospective buyer is liable for any damage to them caused by his or her negligence. Normally, the prospective buyer may reject the goods for any cause, whether or not it is reasonable.

Sale of an Undivided Interest

A person who sells a fractional interest in a single good or in a number of goods that are to remain together makes a **sale of an undivided interest**. Ownership and risk of loss pass to each buyer at the time of the sale of each undivided interest.

Auction

An **auction** is a public sale to the highest bidder. When an auctioneer decides that no one will bid any higher for the goods on sale, the bidding is closed, usually by the pounding of the auctioneer's gavel. In doing so, the auctioneer accepts the bid on behalf of the owner of the goods. Ownership passes to the buyer at that time. Risk of loss passes whenever the auctioneer acknowledges the buyer's right to possess the goods which generally follows payment. In *What's Your Verdict?*, as Tom and Angelina had not paid, they did not have the right to possess the mattress. Therefore, the risk of loss remained on the seller.

CyberLAW

Contract law's application to the Internet currently is in open dispute in most states of the union. An effort by the National Conference of Commissioners on Uniform State Laws (NCCUSL), whose efforts have produced many proposed statutes that are then offered to the states for adoption, recently resulted in UCITA—the Uniform Computer Information Transactions Act. However, as with other model statutes in the electronic business arena, only two states adopted its original version. The UCITA met with a lot of resistance by the states because, according to state authorities, it made most consumer-protection statutes irrelevant. It did this by failing to define "computer software" as goods. This is because most, if not all, consumer-protection statutes specifically apply to goods.

THINK ABOUT IT

Should the term *goods* be applied to software? Why or why not? Would defining software as such affect any other area of the law's application to it? If so, which area(s)?

© RISER/GETTY IMAGES

How does an auction sale with reserve differ from one that is without reserve?

Auction sales are "with reserve" unless specifically announced in advance to be "without reserve." "With reserve" means that if nothing to the contrary is stated, an auctioneer may withdraw the goods anytime before announcing completion of the sale. If "without reserve" the goods must be sold to the person who makes the highest bid—even if it is the first and only and ridiculously low.

Bulk Transfer

A **bulk transfer** is the transfer, generally by sale, of all or a major part of the goods of a business in one unit at one time. Such goods include materials, supplies, merchandise, and equipment if sold with the inventory.

The law protects creditors of the occasional dishonest merchant who would otherwise sell out secretly, keep the proceeds, and disappear. The UCC requires notice to the seller's creditors before the bulk transfer is made. The seller is required to list all creditors. The buyer is required to notify those creditors of the forthcoming transfer of ownership and to pay their claims or to make other arrangements with them. If the buyer does not do this, creditors of the seller may make claims against the inventory and equipment after the buyer takes possession.

An innocent third party who in good faith buys some or all of the goods from a bulk transferee gets good title. But if such third party pays no value or knows the buyer failed to comply with requirements of the bulk transfer law, the creditors can retake the goods.

CHECKPOINT What is the most common type of transaction for low-priced items such as groceries, and when does risk of loss pass from a merchant to a buyer for these sales?

Economic Impact

IMPACT OF THE EURO ON TRADE

The euro was first introduced as an electronic currency in 1999 in order to permanently tie together the exchange rates of the participating countries. It became the physical legal tender of the participating countries on January 1, 2002. (See the Law Brief on page 249 for a list of these countries.) A two-month change-over period followed, during which the national currencies such as the German mark and the French franc were phased out. Recently the first broadly based assessments of the effects on trade of the use of the euro have been published. These studies compared the trade levels of European Union euro users with the Union's non-users and concluded that the euro's impact was very positive.

THINK CRITICALLY

Why do you think the use of a common currency has been so beneficial for the participating members of the European Union?

THINK ABOUT LEGAL CONCEPTS

1. The transfer of the risk of loss from seller to buyer always occurs when title transfers. **True or False?**

2. If a buyer properly rejects faulty goods, the risk of loss stays with the seller until the defects are corrected. **True or False?**

3. An insurable interest is acquired by the seller when the goods are identified to the contract. **True or False?**

4. The seller is required to notify all of its creditors of an upcoming bulk transfer. **True or False?**

5. The buyer does not have the right to inspect the goods in which of the following sales situations? (a) cash-and-carry (b) auction (c) COD (d) The buyer can inspect the goods in all of the above situations.

THINK CRITICALLY ABOUT EVIDENCE

Study the situation, answer the questions, and then prepare arguments to support your answers.

6. Sondaya bought a camper trailer at a garage sale. The seller said that Sondaya could take the trailer home at any time. Sondaya went home to get a pickup with a trailer hitch. Upon returning, Sondaya was told that during her absence, an unidentified person had backed into the trailer, causing extensive damage to it. If the person cannot be found, who will have to bear the loss?

7. Donatti, of California, ordered 400 pounds of fresh blueberries from Margeson, a produce broker in New Zealand. The terms called for shipment by airfreight, FOB, to Donatti's cold-storage plant in Los Angeles. The blueberries were properly packed and shipped by airline common carrier, but they were mishandled upon arrival at the Los Angeles International Airport. Delivery was delayed, and when the fruit was finally delivered, it was not edible. Who must suffer the loss?

8. Thompson spotted a rare antique lamp worth more than $5,000 at a farm auction. When the item came up for bidding, Thompson started it off at $10. For several minutes the auctioneer tried to get a higher bid from anyone in the audience but failed. Just as the auctioneer was about to bring down her gavel to close the sale at $10, the owner rushed up and pulled the item out of the bidding. Thompson became irate and argued that the owner could not do so once the item was placed up for bids. Is Thompson correct?

Chapter 14 Assessment

CONCEPTS IN BRIEF

14-1 Transfer of Ownership

1. Generally the owner of goods is the only one who can legally transfer title to them. Exceptions are made for a party who
   - is authorized by the owner to sell the goods
   - has obtained good title to the goods by fraud and sells them to a good faith purchaser
   - is the holder of a negotiable document of title
   - is a merchant seller who has retained possession of previously sold goods

2. Before ownership in goods can pass, goods must be both existing and identified to the sales contract.

3. In determining when ownership and risk of loss pass in a sales transaction, the terms of the sales contract are given top priority. If those terms do not provide an answer, then trade customs and usage may provide the determining rule. If not, UCC rules are used to make the determination.

14-2 Risk of Loss and Insurable Interest in Sales

4. The buyer obtains an insurable property interest when goods are identified to the contract.

5. In cash-and-carry sales, title passes at the time of the transaction. If a check is used, the payment is conditional until the check is paid by the bank on which it is drawn.

6. COD terms by a seller do not affect the time of transfer of ownership or of risk of loss. But the terms do reserve control of the goods to the seller until payment is received.

7. In a sale or return, ownership and risk of loss generally pass to the merchant buyer upon delivery.

8. At an auction, title passes when the auctioneer signifies acceptance of the bidder's offer. Unless otherwise announced, the auctioneer may refuse all bids and withdraw the goods.

9. Notice of a bulk transfer of the inventory and equipment of a business must be given to creditors of the seller before the sale takes place.

YOUR LEGAL VOCABULARY

Match each statement with the term that it best defines. Some terms may not be used.

1. Completed sale in which the buyer has an option of returning the goods
2. Goods that are not both existing and identified
3. Goods specifically earmarked for a particular sales contract
4. To place the goods at the buyer's disposal
5. Sale that, by agreement, calls for payment for the goods at a later date
6. Public sale to the highest bidder
7. Collect on delivery
8. Innocent third party to a fraudulent transfer of goods who gives value and acquires rights in the goods
9. The transfer, generally by sale, of all or a major part of the goods of a business in one unit at one time
10. Goods delivered to the buyer "on trial," or "on satisfaction"

a. auction
b. bulk transfer
c. CIF
d. COD
e. credit sale
f. existing goods
g. FOB
h. future goods
i. good faith purchaser
j. identified goods
k. sale on approval
l. sale or return
m. sale of an undivided interest
n. tender of delivery

REVIEW LEGAL CONCEPTS

11. Why should an innocent purchaser from a thief receive only possession whereas an innocent purchaser of another's goods from a buyer of those goods in a fraudulent sale obtain good title?

12. What are the advantages and disadvantages to allowing ownership to be transferred by the passage of documents of title?

13. Why should the buyer rather than the seller have to notify creditors in a bulk sale?

14. Why should the courts give priority to the actual sales contract when determining when the ownership of goods passes from seller to buyer?

15. Why should the risk of loss to fungible goods pass at the time of the agreement instead of when the goods are existing and identified to the contract?

WRITE ABOUT LEGAL CONCEPTS

16. Should checks be considered "legal tender"? Write a paragraph stating arguments for both sides of the issue.

17. Are COD sales still useful? Make a list of instances in which they fill a need.

18. **HOT DEBATE** Write a paragraph contrasting the ethical positions of the church versus the owner from whom the laptop was stolen. Ethically, who should be allowed to have the laptop?

MAKE ACADEMIC CONNECTIONS

19. **FOREIGN LANGUAGE** Interview businesses in your area that buy and sell internationally. Prepare a report on problems they have encountered in making their orders and billings clear to their trading partners. Try to find trading partners who speak a variety of different languages.

THINK CRITICALLY ABOUT EVIDENCE

Study the situation, answer the questions, and then prepare arguments to support your answers.

20. Trina, a computer programmer, had her laptop computer stolen. She reported what had happened to the police and gave them its serial number. Three months later, the police recovered a laptop that was the same make and model as Trina's, but the serial number had been removed. Trina tried to obtain the computer from the police, but they declined her request. They put the computer up for sale at the next police auction. Trina sued to recover what she thought to be her computer. Who won and why?

21. Shortly after her lawsuit against the police department was resolved, Trina decided to buy a new laptop from a 1-800 phone order seller. As Trina and the seller agreed, the seller shipped Trina's new computer to a warehouse near Trina's home. The warehouse then notified Trina to come and pick up the computer. Through no fault of the warehouse, the computer was drenched with water and rendered inoperable during a minor fire. Trina tried to return the computer to the seller for a new one, saying that the seller had to bear the loss. The company refused to accept the return. Trina sued the computer company for her money back or another computer. Who won and why?

22. Shortly after her lawsuit against the computer company was resolved, Trina took her new laptop into a computer store for needed repairs. When Trina returned to pick it up, she found it had been sold by one of the store's salespeople to an innocent purchaser. Evidently, due to a bookkeeping error and its mint condition, Trina's laptop had been shelved with the store's regular stock after being repaired and was snapped up by the first customer who saw it. Before Trina's attorney could bring suit against the shop, it went out of business. She then sued to recover the laptop from the customer who purchased it from the store. Who won and why?

23. Trina's boyfriend, Serge, asked her over one summer evening to watch a movie on his deck using his new HD DVD projector and screen. Serge had been supplied the projector and screen through a sale on approval from BrightLite Industries. When Trina arrived, she and Serge decided to drive to the local grocery store to pick up some food and drink for their "night at the movies." While they were gone a rainstorm came up and destroyed the projector and screen. Who typically has the risk of loss in this type of sales transaction? Why? Who must bear the loss in this particular case? Why?

24. When his company developed financial trouble, Pais, a member of the legal staff, was suddenly transferred from Houston, Texas, to company headquarters in New York City. As a consequence, he bought with cash $50,000 worth of new Danish furniture for his apartment on Park Ave. When the furniture was tendered by the seller before the apartment was ready, Pais had to ask them to keep it in their warehouse in the Bronx. In the meantime, his employer had to suspend salary payments for a month. Pais sought to use the furniture as collateral for a loan. Did he have title to it even though he had not taken possession?

ANALYZE REAL CASES

25. Lane had a boat dealership in North Carolina. In February, he sold a new boat, a 120-HP motor, and a trailer to a man who represented himself to be "John Willis." Willis gave Lane a check for $6,285 and left with the goods. The check proved to be worthless. Less than six months later, Honeycutt bought the three items in South Carolina from a man whom he had known for several years as "John R. Garrett." In fact, this was Willis, using an alias. Later, while searching for Willis under the alias of "John Patterson," the Federal Bureau of Investigation contacted Honeycutt. Honeycutt said that (a) he had paid a full price of only $2,500; (b) Garrett had nothing to show he was the owner; (c) he did not know from whom Garrett got the boat; (d) Garrett said he was selling the boat for someone else; (e) Garrett signed what he called a "title" (the document was nothing more than a "Certificate of Number" issued by the state Wildlife Resources Commission, not the "certificate of title" required by statutes); (f) Garrett forged the signature of the purported owner, John F. Patterson, on the so-called title. Plaintiff Lane now claims that defendant Honeycutt was not a good-faith purchaser and therefore should return the boat to him, with damages for a wrongful detention. Who has title to the boat? You decide. (*Lane v. Honeycutt*, 188 S.E.2d 604, N.C)

26. Consolidated Chemical Industries purchased three heat exchangers from Falls Industries in Cleveland. The contract specified that after identification the machines were to be crated securely. They were then to be delivered, without breakage, to the Consolidated plant in East Baton Rouge. Because the machines were not crated securely, the exchangers were badly damaged in transit. Consolidated refused to accept them, and Falls sued. Falls claimed that risk of loss had passed when the goods were delivered to the carrier. Do you agree? (*Falls Industries, Inc. v. Consolidated Chemical Industries, Inc.*, 258 F.2d 277)

27. The plaintiff, a Los Angeles manufacturer of men's clothing, sold a variety of clothing to the defendant, a retailer in Westport, Connecticut. The plaintiff prepared four invoices covering the clothing and stamped them "FOB Los Angeles," and added the words "goods shipped at purchaser's risk." The plaintiff delivered the goods to the Denver-Chicago Trucking Company. When the truck arrived in Connecticut with the goods, the defendant's wife was in charge of the store. She ordered the driver to unload the cartons and place them inside the store. The driver refused and left with the goods. The defendant complained to the plaintiff, who filed a claim against the trucking company. No reimbursement was obtained by the plaintiff, and the defendant never received the goods. Now the plaintiff seller sues the defendant buyer for the purchase price. Who wins? You decide. (*Ninth Street East, Ltd. v. Harrison*, 259 A.2d 772, Conn.)

28. In June, plaintiff Multiplastics, Inc., contracted with defendant Arch Industries, Inc., to make and to ship 40,000 pounds of plastic pellets, which were to be delivered at the rate of 1,000 pounds a day after Arch gave "release instructions." Multiplastics produced the pellets within two weeks. Arch refused to give the release orders, citing labor difficulties and its vacation schedule. On August 18, Multiplastics wrote, "We have warehoused these products for more than 40 days . . . however we cannot warehouse . . . indefinitely, and request that you send us shipping instructions." Multiplastics followed this with numerous telephone calls seeking payment and delivery instructions. In response, on August 20, Arch agreed to issue the release orders but never did. On September 22, the Multiplastics factory, including the 40,000 pounds of this order, was destroyed by fire. The pellets were not covered by Multiplastics' fire insurance policy. Therefore Multiplastics sued Arch for breach of contract and also claimed that the risk of loss had passed to the buyer. You decide. (*Multiplastics, Inc. v. Arch Industries, Inc.*, 348 A.2d 618, Conn.)

Case For Legal Thinking

PREWITT V. NUMISMATIC FUNDING CORPORATION U.S. COURT OF APPEALS, EIGHTH CIRCUIT, 745 F. 2D 1175

FACTS Numismatic Funding Corporation sold rare collectible coins by mail throughout the United States. In general, buyers would request specific coins, and Numismatic would ship them on the terms discussed below. Typically, Numismatic would enclose with a shipment of solicited coins unsolicited coins for the recipient to also consider for purchase. Early one year, Numismatic mailed a sizeable shipment of solicited and unsolicited coins to Frederick Prewitt. Prewitt was a commodities broker in St. Louis, Missouri, with whom the Corporation had done business on at least two other occasions. The shipment of rare gold and silver coins was valued at over $60,000. The would-be sales transaction was partially governed by the terms set down in the documents that were enclosed with the coins. These terms stated that Prewitt could buy part or all of the shipment which was available to him on a "14-day approval basis."

The accompanying invoice stated that the title did not transfer until the seller was paid in full. Also the buyer was given 14 days from the receipt of the goods to settle the account in full. No directions were provided as to how to return the unwanted coins. After examining the coins, Prewitt told his wife to send them back to Numismatic by certified mail. She did so within the 14-day period. She insured each of the two packages the coins were returned in for $400.

Numismatic Funding Corporation never received the coins. Prewitt then sued to be declared free of responsibility for the loss.

REASONING At trial in Federal District Court it was noticed by the Court that Numismatic's sales technique was to not only mail out coins requested by a prospective retailer, but also to send out unsolicited merchandise at the same time. The Court then found for Prewitt, in effect, deciding that Prewitt had acted properly under the laws and, in doing so, avoided legal responsibility for the loss. Numismatic then appealed to the Eight Circuit Court of Appeals.

PRACTICE JUDGING

1. Assume you are the Eighth Circuit, how would you decide the issue of who must bear the loss for the solicited coins?

2. What legal theory prompted you to answer question 1 as you did?

3. What is the status of the unsolicited merchandise? What is the source of the law that decides the issue of the unsolicited merchandise?

© GETTY IMAGES/PHOTODISC

Chapter 15
Consumer Protection

15-1 Protection through Governmental Action

15-2 Protection through Action by the Consumer

HOT DEBATE

Edison buys a lawnmower from a department store. Because of a defect in design, a protective plastic flap binds the lawnmower whenever the lawnmower is pulled backwards. For efficiency's sake Edison removes the flap. Later, as his son is pulling the mower backwards, he trips and falls backwards. Due to the lack of the protective flap, his foot shoots upwards into the mower blade. Edison's son, who was only wearing tennis shoes, loses half his foot. Later, Edison brings suit against the manufacturer on behalf of his son.

© GETTY IMAGES/PHOTODISC

WHERE DO YOU STAND?

1. List and discuss the legal reasons supporting Edison's suit.
2. List and discuss the legal reasons supporting the manufacturer.

15-1 Protection through Governmental Action

GOALS

- Explain the need for governmental involvement in the marketplace
- Identify protections against substandard goods
- Recognize unfair trade practices

KEY TERMS

consumer

caveat emptor

caveat venditor

class actions

cease-and-desist order

consent order

restitution

unfair trade practice

bait and switch

Governmental Protection in Today's Marketplace

WHAT'S YOUR VERDICT? Eliza had a little more than 3,000 miles on his new car when he drove into Lester's Lightening Lube Center and ordered the all fluid replacement special for only $49.95. At the first stop light he encountered after turning out of Lester's Lightening Lube, Eliza's brakes failed and his car rammed the back of a garbage truck. When a mechanic checked the brake fluid, she found that Lester's had mistakenly replaced it with transmission fluid causing the brake failure. Eliza complained to Lester, but Lester refused to pay for the damages.

How can Eliza resolve the problem in his favor?

A **consumer** is an individual who acquires goods that are intended primarily for personal, family, or household use. Consumers are protected in the marketplace through actions they may take on their own behalf as well as through actions the government takes to protect them.

Consumer Caveats

The phrase that historically guided consumers in the marketplace was ***caveat emptor***, meaning "let the buyer beware." Consumers were thought to be adequately protected by their own ability to judge a product's safety and utility. The forces of supply and demand in a competitive marketplace were to keep product makers and sellers committed to producing the best product for the money. Consumers also could (and still can) seek help or advice from the state attorney general's office, the local Better Business Bureau, and, if appropriate, the customer service department of the company involved.

Unfortunately, relying mainly on consumers' individual initiative and resources has proved to be inadequate. In our affluent, technology-oriented society, it is very difficult for consumers to judge properly the quality or advantages and disadvantages of a product. The products often are offered by huge corporations which are not always responsive to consumer complaints.

Local, state, and federal governments have passed legislation to help put consumers on an equal footing with sellers in the marketplace. These laws fund agencies that add to the common-law based contract, tort, and criminal protection against such abuses. Today any

What would the phrase *caveat emptor* mean to this woman who is considering buying a used car?

seller who has deceived a consumer while contracting may be sued by the individual consumer as well as be subject to legal action by a governmental agency. This has led to the use of the phrase *caveat venditor*, meaning "let the seller beware."

Class Actions

The law also has recognized the fact that if the product in question costs little or the potential damage claims are low, court action by a consumer often is not worth the effort and expense. To help overcome this problem, **class actions** have been authorized by court rules. A class action allows one or several persons to sue not only on behalf of themselves, but also on behalf of many others similarly wronged. This ability to combine individual causes of action in one suit provides incentive for law firms to handle such cases. In *What's Your Verdict*, Eliza should try to solve his problem through renewed private negotiations with Lester. Those failing, he can initiate a small claims court suit and notify the appropriate government agencies and the Better Business Bureau of what happened.

Governmental Procedure

When a governmental agency acts on behalf of the injured consumer, it may investigate and issue a **cease-and-desist order** to a company. This is an order requiring the company to stop the specified conduct. If the defendant violates the order, heavy civil penalties may be imposed. Often a defendant will sign a consent order rather than resist the charge in a long legal battle. A **consent order** is a voluntary, court-enforceable agreement to stop

LEGAL *Research*

Current class actions include suits against: a famous rock group for $51 million due to the lead singer's sore throat forcing a show cancellation, the makers of a malfunctioning hernia patch, the manufacturers of an ATV due to the noise from its tires, and many more. Prepare a two-to-five page report on class actions in the United States today to include information on how they are generated and conducted, and their success rate.

an illegal or questionable practice. An agency also may order **restitution**, which permits a party to a contract to recover money or property (or the value thereof) given to the other party.

CHECKPOINT Define the terms *caveat emptor* and *caveat venditor*.

Protection Against Inferior Services and Goods

WHAT'S YOUR VERDICT? The Annihilator Pest Company developed and sold thousands of robot cockroach traps called the Terminator. The human user of the trap simply placed it on the floor of the room and the device would pursue, kill, and consume any roaches on the surface it occupied. Recent consumer reports have shown that the computer chip that controls the trap is too sensitive to vibration and causes the Terminator to go out of control and attack mice, house pets, and even furry house slippers.

What could the government require Annihilator to do?

Licensing

Protection of consumers by government often begins with licensing suppliers of consumer services. This is particularly true for those who provide health services, such as doctors, nurses, laboratory technicians, and pharmacists. Also, teachers, lawyers, accountants, construction professionals, realtors, insurance agents, and beauticians, among others, are licensed in most jurisdictions.

Certain businesses and institutions also must pass inspection before they receive operating licenses. Examples include hospitals, rest homes, private schools, check-cashing services, and insurance companies. Failure to maintain minimum standards may cause suspension or cancellation of the license.

Businesses offering repairs on cars, electronic equipment, watches, and the like often are required to give written estimates and detailed bills for all work performed. Similarly, states regulate special sales by retail businesses, such as bankruptcy sales and going-out-of-business sales. Often a special license is required and the businesses must shut down after the sale or be guilty of fraud.

Unsafe Products

Large numbers of people are injured or killed each year by products in use around the home. As a response, in 1972 the federal government passed the Consumer Product Safety Act. This law created the Consumer Product Safety Commission (CPSC) and gave it authority to issue and enforce safety standards for most consumer products.

The CPSC requires any manufacturer, distributor, or retailer discovering the failure of its products to comply with safety regulations to report that fact to the commission. The CPSC also receives reports from the nation's hospitals on product-caused injuries. If the CPSC determines that a product is substantially hazardous, the manufacturer, distributors, and retailers of the product must notify purchasers about the hazard and then either recall and repair the product, replace it, or refund the purchase price.

Often the mere threat of CPSC action causes responsible parties to recall their product "voluntarily." In *What's Your Verdict?* Annihilator could be required to notify those concerned and implement

Why do you think retailers must, in some cases, obtain a special license from the state in order to hold a "going-out-of-business sale"?

an appropriate remedy. Failure to comply could lead to a fine and imprisonment. If necessary, the CPSC has the power to seize the hazardous product and ban it from the market place.

Consumers who think the CPSC is not taking action where needed may sue in federal district court to have a protective rule established. If victorious, consumers may be awarded an amount to cover reasonable attorney's fees, as well as their court costs.

The CPSC maintains a toll-free telephone service and a web site. Consumers can call or use the Internet to contact the CPSC, and they also may report claims concerning unsafe products, find

LAW BRIEF

The CPSC recently responded to the publication of conclusive research that the CCA in treated lumber used in decks and children's play sets to preserve the wood leaks out of the wood for years. (CCA is 22% arsenic. One 12-foot section of such pressure-treated lumber contains about an ounce of arsenic, or enough to kill 250 people.) The CPSC noted in its response that it is currently performing studies of wood sealants to keep the arsenic off children's hands—and out of their mouths. They also have removed CCA from the list of approved pesticides and negotiated a phase-out of CCA in wood treatment.

NETBookmark

Access school.cengage.com/blaw/lawxtra and click on the link for Chapter 15. Click on one of the federal agencies' Recall Press Releases or Recall Announcements. Prepare a short oral report to the class that describes the nature of the product recall as explained in the announcement. Note that you can sign up on this web site to be notified by e-mail of new product recalls and class-action suits.

school.cengage.com/blaw/lawxtra

out about product recalls occurring in the last few months, and get information about unsafe children's products.

Additional protection is afforded to consumers in indirect ways. For example, laws govern the type of construction, location, accessibility, occupancy rate, and type of use of buildings where the public gathers. Detailed regulations apply to fire escapes, elevators, parking, sprinkler systems, exit location and marking, and sanitary facilities. All of these safety laws are designed to protect consumers and to assist them in deciding which products and services best meet their needs.

ADULTERATED FOOD, DRUGS, AND COSMETICS The federal Food and Drug Administration (FDA) requires that the production facilities for cosmetics, food, and drugs be clean. It also requires that the products be prepared from ingredients fit for human use or consumption. A product that does not meet the minimum standards for purity and quality set by the FDA is considered *adulterated.* Such a product may be confiscated, or seized, by the government.

The U.S. Department of Agriculture also inspects canners, packers, and processors of poultry and meat entering interstate commerce. Their actions help ensure that the products are free of disease and are processed under sanitary conditions.

In addition, the FDA requires that labels on regulated products give the name and address of the manufacturer, packager, or distributor, and reveal the quantity, such as the weight or the fluid ounces. Nutritional labeling also is required. Labels include information such as the calories, fat, cholesterol, sodium, carbohydrate, protein, vitamin A, and calcium amounts provided by a serving.

States and localities usually provide for the inspection of businesses where food is handled. Meat markets, bakeries, restaurants, hotels, and other businesses are rated on their cleanliness and are required to display their ratings. Food handlers may be subject to periodic health examinations. Laws also regulate the purity and quality of such products as milk, meat, fruit, and vegetables sold in such businesses.

Drugs are regulated by the FDA to ensure their safety for users and to be certain of their effectiveness for the purpose sold. Without FDA

What do you think would be the issues involved in the regulation of a fire escape?

© GETTY IMAGES/PHOTODISC

approval, new drugs cannot be marketed in this country. The FDA also determines which drugs are prescription and which may be sold "over-the-counter." The FDA has been both praised and criticized for its extremely cautious approach to granting new drug approval. Its procedures have led some Americans to go beyond the U.S. borders for certain drugs alleged to be life-saving and pain-easing.

IMPROPER WEIGHTS AND MEASURES The U.S. Constitution gives Congress the power to set standards for weights and measures. Currently the Weights and Measures Division of the National Institute of Standards and Technology promotes uniformity in U.S. weights and measures laws, regulations, and standards. With proper inspection, testing, and enforcement at state and local levels, the measurement of a gallon of gasoline, pound of bananas, or foot of rope is uniform throughout the country. Most states inspect and test weighing and measuring devices at least once a year. Seals certify the accuracy of such devices as gasoline pumps, supermarket scales, and taxicab meters. Violations of the weights and measures laws are punishable by fine, imprisonment, or both. The goods involved may be confiscated.

Protection Against Unfair Trade Practices

WHAT'S YOUR VERDICT?

A national magazine planned to increase subscriptions by giving away prizes of up to $1 million in a drawing. People contacted in a huge mail campaign could enter the drawing by return mail, whether or not they actually subscribed to the magazine. Instructions on how to enter would be placed in the text of the promotional material so a person contacted would not have to read about the magazine in order to find out how to enter the drawing. A senior officer of the magazine canceled the plans because she thought it was an illegal lottery.

Was she correct?

Generally, an **unfair trade practice** is any method of business that is dishonest or fraudulent or that illegally limits free competition. To protect consumers, the federal and state governments have enacted numerous laws prohibiting such practices. Chief among these are federal antitrust laws and the Federal Trade Commission Act. They are designed to prevent unfair trade practices in *interstate commerce* (business conducted between or among two or more states). States have similar laws for *intrastate commerce* (business conducted wholly within one state). Unfair trade practices take many forms including those discussed in the following sections.

Agreements to Control or Fix Prices

The part of the free market system that serves the consumer best is *competition*. Competition is the force that drives efficient businesses to create new and better products and services. Competition also drives inefficient firms out of business. Some individuals and companies enter into agreements to control or fix prices and thereby try to ensure their survival by eliminating competition. Such agreements are illegal and unenforceable. Violators are subject to criminal penalties.

False and Misleading Advertising

False and misleading advertising intentionally deceives, makes untrue claims of quality or effectiveness, or fails to reveal critically important facts. Claiming that a mouthwash prevents and cures colds and sore throats when it does not is one example of such advertising.

A store practices another form of improper advertising when it uses an understocked, abnormally low-priced "come on" to lure prospective buyers into the store. Once there, the would-be buyers find that the advertised item has been sold out and the customers are then redirected to a product with a greater profit margin. This practice is referred to as **bait and switch**.

The advertisement is not considered deceptive if it states how many of the advertised items are available or states that the supply of the item is limited. Many stores that want to maintain customer goodwill give rain checks when even reasonably stocked items are exhausted. Rain checks permit customers to purchase the items later at the advertised price.

The *Federal Trade Commission (FTC)* has the main responsibility for preventing false and misleading advertising. If necessary, the FTC may order an advertisement terminated. If the advertiser has created a false impression that will persist when the advertisement is no longer being run, the FTC may order corrective advertising. *Corrective advertising* requires the advertiser to admit the wrongdoing and state the truth in a prescribed number of future advertisements.

Illegal Lotteries and Confidence Games

As mentioned in Chapter 10, to be a lottery, a gambling scheme or game must have three elements:

1. a required payment of money or something else of value to participate
2. the winner or winners to be determined by chance rather than by skill
3. a prize to be won

Holding or participating in such a gambling scheme is illegal and violators are subject to fine and imprisonment. However, many states have exempted by statute certain religious and charity groups from the lottery prohibition. These groups are allowed to run bingo and other games to produce revenue for their activities. Also, some

Sending mass, unsolicited advertisements over the Internet is a practice known as *spamming*. Many receivers do not appreciate receiving these unsolicited e-mails. Initially, spammers maintained that they had an absolute First Amendment right to send e-mails and pop-up ads. However, as a consequence of laws passed in California and Washington allowing spammers to be sued by recipients, the spamming industry changed its position to agreement with those desiring regulation to produce the federal CAN-SPAM Act of 2003. This Act preempts state laws and allows unsolicited e-mails as long as they contain an opt-out mechanism, an adult content label if appropriate, and information identifying the sender.

THINK ABOUT IT

How would you distinguish Internet spam from the junk mail that is delivered to you at discount postage by the U.S. Postal Service? Is the contrast significant to resolving the issue of spam?

---

states hold their own lotteries to generate revenue for state projects.

The use of lotteries by businesses to promote sales remains an unfair method of competition. However, in *What's Your Verdict?* the promotion was legal because no payment was required to participate. Even so, the FTC would monitor such a game to ensure that all promised prizes are awarded.

Other prohibited schemes often are disguised as legitimate business undertakings. These are sometimes referred to as *confidence* games. Such games typically involve a fraudulent device whereby the victim is persuaded to trust the swindler with the victim's money or other valuables in hopes of a quick gain. One example of the confidence game is the pyramid sales scheme. A chain letter is one such pyramid scheme.

Unfair Pricing and Service

Some of the more common unfair pricing methods include intentionally misrepresenting that goods are being sold at a considerable discount and stating that the price charged for the goods is a wholesale price. Both of these unfair pricing schemes are illegal.

Representing goods or services as being free when purchased with another good that is sold at an inflated price to cover the cost of the first also is an unfair pricing method. Merchants may have legitimate "two-for-one" and "one-cent" sales as long as the cost of the main item is not artificially raised for the sale.

Consumers of repair services may have problems related to unfair pricing. These problems may occur when the estimated price of a repair is significantly less than the actual price. They may also occur when the repair service charges the consumer for repairs that were not authorized. Most states require businesses to provide consumers with written estimates of repair costs before the work is performed. As noted earlier, many service providers are required to obtain a license from a government body to further assure consumers of their legitimacy.

Mislabeled Goods

Mislabeling a good to make it more marketable is an unfair method of competition prohibited by law. Even the shape or size of a container must not mislead the consumer into thinking the package contains more than it does.

The law also requires that certain products carry warning labels. Poisons and insecticides must have appropriate "Danger" labels. Cigarette packaging and advertisements must carry warnings indicating the danger smoking poses to the health of the user and to others.

Mislabeling also involves marking used articles as new or in a better condition than they actually are. The most common instance occurs when no indication is given that the goods are secondhand. For example, in used cars, odometers (which show the total miles a car has traveled) are sometimes turned back, and the cars are then sold for a much higher price. This activity is illegal.

Other Unfair Trade Practices

There are many other forms of unfair trade practices and competition.

- Using a brand name or trademark so similar to a competitor's that it confuses the public.

- Sending unordered merchandise and demanding payment for it or its return. According to federal law, when someone deliberately sends unordered merchandise through the mail, the recipient is under no obligation to return it or to pay for it.

- Giving a corporation's purchasing agent money "under the counter" in exchange for an order from the supplier or paying a retail salesperson "push money" for extra effort in promoting the manufacturer's product.

- Conducting "industrial espionage" to find out a competitor's secrets.

- Conducting fraudulent telemarketing and Internet schemes.

- Figuring finance charges improperly.

- Failing to provide written warranties when required.

- In door-to-door *home solicitation sales,* failing to notify purchasers that they have until midnight of the third business day to cancel contracts for purchases of $25 or more.

CHECKPOINT List at least six forms of unfair trade practices.

15-1 Assessment

school.cengage.com/blaw/lawxtra

THINK ABOUT LEGAL CONCEPTS

1. Legally, a person buying goods for her or his business is not a "consumer." **True or False?**

2. If you took part in a chain letter would you have committed a crime? **Yes or No?**

3. Local governments do not have any consumer protection laws. **True or False?**

4. The elements of a lottery are _ ?_ , chance, and consideration. (a) price (b) money (c) luck (d) none of the above

5. Which of the following is regulated by the CPSC? (a) drugs (b) firearms (c) toys (d) cosmetics

6. The part of the free market system that best serves the consumer is (a) government regulation (b) informed consumer (c) competition

7. Consumers have three days to cancel home solicitation sales. **True or False?**

THINK CRITICALLY ABOUT EVIDENCE

Study the situation, answer the questions, and then prepare arguments to support your answers.

8. You properly terminated your membership in a CD club four months ago, yet you receive a compact disc through the mail from the club. It is the new release of your favorite artist. You play it repeatedly for more than a month before you receive a letter from the club stating that it made a mistake in sending the disc to you and asking that you either return the disc unused or pay for it. Do you have an ethical obligation to do so? Do you have a legal obligation to do so?

9. In a national television advertising campaign, FunTime fruit drink was said to contain "natural food energy." The FTC discovered that the "natural food" providing the energy was sugar and held that the advertisement therefore created a false impression. What remedy would you recommend that the FTC use to correct the situation?

15-2 Protection through Action by the Consumer

GOALS

■ Describe the protection afforded consumers by the law of product liability

■ Identify the various warranties that may apply to a sales transaction

KEY TERMS

product liability

warranty

privity of contract

express warranty

full warranty

limited warranty

puffing

implied warranty

encumbrances

warranty of merchantability

disclaimer

What Is Product Liability?

WHAT'S YOUR VERDICT?

Barsteel ran a lawn mowing business to earn money for college. To make her weed trimmer work faster, she removed the back shield from it. She also refused to wear safety goggles while operating the trimmer. One day, a piece of trimmer line broke and hit her in the cornea of an eye blinding her permanently in that eye. The remainder of the trimmer line was tested and shown to be only half as strong as advertised. Barsteel sued.

Can she recover for the injury caused by the defective product?

Instead of leaving consumers to rely on governmental agencies to prevent or remedy harm, today many states and the federal government give consumers rights allowing them to protect themselves. Using some of these rights in situations where an agency may or may not have acted, the victim may sue for damages and get a court order preventing future injuries.

Product liability means the affixing of responsibility to compensate buyers, users, and even those standing nearby for injuries caused by a defective product. A product liability suit may be based on the torts of fraud, negligence, or *strict liability*. Recall that strict liability is liability that exists even though the defendant was not negligent. A product liability suit also may be based on a breach of **warranty**, which is an assurance that the seller makes about the product's qualities or performance. Because they

involve sales of goods, warranties are governed by the Uniform Commercial Code (UCC).

Expansion of Product Liability

The legal requirements for affixing liability for injuries caused by a defective product have been relaxed in recent years. This was done in order to protect injured plaintiffs and enable them to recover. This has been especially effective in the

© GETTY IMAGES/PHOTODISC

In *What's Your Verdict?* do you think that Barsteel's removal of the safety guard and her failure to wear safety goggles will affect her chances of winning the lawsuit against the trimmer manufacturer?

areas of extent of warranty coverage and recovery for tortious conduct.

EXTENT OF WARRANTY COVERAGE At common law, warranty liability depended on the contract between the buyer and seller, who were said to be in privity of contract. **Privity of contract** is the relationship that exists between or among the contracting parties as a result of their legally binding agreement.

In the past only the immediate contracting buyer was permitted to sue, and suit could be brought only against the immediate contracting seller. Thus, an injured consumer could sue the retailer, but not the wholesaler or the manufacturer. This was true even if the wholesaler or manufacturer were primarily responsible for the defect and better able to pay. Now, however, the UCC broadens the common law rule so that all injured persons who are the buyer's family, household, or guests may sue. Moreover, courts in most states now permit the injured party, even a nonuser, to sue retailers, intermediate sellers, and manufacturers.

Today, a manufacturer or producer that makes inaccurate or misleading statements in advertising or labels is liable for resulting injuries to consumers. If the goods are defective and therefore dangerous, the maker is similarly liable for resulting harm. In either case, not only the manufacturer or producer but also intermediate sellers and the immediate supplier may be liable.

RECOVERY FOR TORTIOUS CONDUCT In addition to breach of warranty, a product liability suit may be based on the torts of fraud, negligence, or strict liability. Historically, however, regardless of which of these torts was used as a basis for attempted recovery, the injured consumer still had difficulty in winning the lawsuit and subsequently recovering damages.

For example, the alleged fraud of a seller or manufacturer was difficult to prove by proper evidence. In addition, negligence, even if present, was often difficult to show because the defective

If this teenage girl would be injured somehow as a result of proper use of the cooktop her family just purchased, could a lawsuit on her behalf be brought against the manufacturer? Why or why not?

© GETTY IMAGES/PHOTODISC

product may have been designed and made many months or years before in some distant factory by workers who could not be identified or located.

As a consequence of these problems, the area of strict liability has been and is continuing to be modified to allow qualified consumers to recover for their injuries. The trend in many states is to hold the manufacturer, wholesaler, and retailer strictly liable if someone is injured because of a defective condition in the product that caused it to be unreasonably dangerous to the user or consumer. The liability is imposed without reliance on warranties or on the presence or absence of fraudulent intent or negligence.

There is no liability if the injury was suffered while the product was used for a purpose for which it was not intended, for example, using gasoline to clean clothes. Likewise, there is no strict liability if the product is used for a purpose which could not reasonably be foreseen, for example, trying to climb a mountain using ropes made for tying packages. Liability may also be barred if the product has been altered by the user, for example, lengthening a ladder by nailing extensions to its legs.

Further, if the injured person is found guilty of improper conduct that causes the accident, he or she will not be allowed to recover. Examples of this include driving on a defective tire after discovering the defect, failing to service or to maintain an engine, or taking an overdose of medication. Finally, there generally is no liability if one is hurt

PUNITIVE DAMAGE AWARDS

Unlike Japan and other western countries, the U.S. legal system allows the recovery of punitive damages for various intentional torts such as fraud and for medical malpractice, drunk driving, and other injurious behaviors. In response, backed mainly by insurance companies, a tort reform movement has gained momentum to limit the amount of such punitive damage awards. This movement has emphasized the arbitrary and unfair costly nature of such awards. As a consequence, more than 19 states now have passed legislation that typically limits such awards to three times the amount of compensatory damages or a certain dollar figure such as $250,000. A recent Department of Justice study, however, pointed out that punitive damage awards only occur in 3.3 percent of the cases won by plaintiffs with a median award of $38,000. This is a far cry from the millions awarded in a few highly publicized cases.

THINK CRITICALLY

Would the amount of money typically awarded in punitive damages influence your decision to sue a manufacturer for an injury you received while using a product? Why or why not?

---

when improperly using a product, such as a knife or firearm, which may be dangerous when misused.

In *What's Your Verdict?* Barsteel's removal of the safety guard and the failure to wear safety goggles bar her recovery. Legally, the injury was the result of her choices, not the defect in the trimmer line.

CHECKPOINT Under what product liability approach is a person injured by a defective product most likely to recover damages?

How Important Are Warranties?

WHAT'S YOUR VERDICT? Bligh, a sales agent employed by Total Environments, persuaded the Fletchers to install a central air conditioning system. Bligh assured them that "this unit will keep all rooms at 68 degrees even on the hottest summer days and the coldest winter mornings." The unit failed to perform as promised.

Do the Fletchers have any rights against Total Environments?

Although strict liability often provides the best alternative for a cause of action in product liability cases, breach of warranty, if applicable, can be just as good. Warranties may be either express or implied. An assurance of quality or promise of performance explicitly made by the seller is an **express warranty**. An example is, "Use our brand of oil and you won't need to change your engine oil for 10,000 miles."

In *What's Your Verdict?* Bligh made an express warranty. Bligh's employer, Total Environments, is liable because the warranty was breached. A breach of warranty is a breach of contract. If there is no intent to deceive, it is not the tort of fraud for which punitive damages might be claimed and collected.

An express warranty may be oral or written. It may even be implied by conduct. If the contract is written, the warranty must be included in the writing, or it probably will be excluded from the agreement by the parol evidence rule. However, if the warranty is given after the sale, it may be oral even though the sales contract was written. A warranty or any other term may be added to a sales contract later by mutual agreement, and no new consideration is required.

Requirements of Express Warranties

Under the Magnuson-Moss Warranty Act, the Federal Trade Commission has established certain minimum standards that must be met by sellers who give written warranties on consumer products that cost more than $15 and that normally are used for personal, family, or household purposes. Note that sellers are not required to give warranties. If sellers do give warranties, however, they must make them available to consumers prior to the sale in a single document, written in simple, understandable language. The following information must be included:

1. to whom the warranty is extended (for example, if it is limited to the original buyer)
2. a description of the product and any excluded parts
3. what the *warrantor* (one who gives the warranty) will and will not do in the event of a breach of warranty
4. when the warranty begins (if different from purchase date) and when it ends
5. the step-by-step procedure to obtain performance of warranty obligations and a list of the expenses the warrantee must bear in the process
6. the availability of any informal methods of settling disputes
7. any limitation on how long implied warranties last
8. any exclusion or limitation on incidental or consequential damages
9. the words "This warranty gives you specific legal rights, and you may also have other rights which vary from state to state."
10. the clear identification of the names and addresses of the warrantors.

An express warranty that obligates the seller to repair or to replace a defective product without cost to the buyer and within a reasonable time is a **full warranty**. Any warranty that provides less protection than a full warranty is a **limited warranty**, and the seller must identify it as such.

Opinions v. Warranties

A positive statement about the value of goods or a statement that is just the seller's opinion does not create a warranty. Sellers often enthusiastically overstate the merits of the goods they are trying to sell. Making statements such as "superb quality," or "best on the market," is exaggerated sales talk called **puffing**. Such words are not warranties or statements of fact. They are merely personal opinions. Buyers should not—and generally do not—accept such opinions at face value. *Caveat emptor* or "let the buyer beware" provides the only measure of protection when sellers make such statements.

Sometimes, however, the buyer has good reason to believe that the seller is an expert. If a buyer asks for such a seller's opinion as an expert, the seller's word as to the quality of the article becomes part of the basis of the bargain. In such a case, it may be taken as a warranty. This is particularly true with merchants. For example, a statement by a jeweler that a diamond is flawless may be relied on as a warranty.

Express Warranties Made by All Sellers

Every seller is bound by any express statement of fact or promise that is part of the bargain. It is

If you ask this department store salesperson if a certain necklace is sterling silver, and she replies that it is, can you rely on her statement as a warranty? Why or why not?

desirable to have such statements in writing. When a description of the goods or a sample or model is made part of the contractual agreement, there is an express warranty that all the goods shall conform to the description, sample, or model used. This is true even if the words "warrant" or "guarantee" do not appear in the contract. It also is true even if the seller had no intention to give such a warranty.

Implied Warranties Given by All Sellers

Sellers are free to decide whether to give any express warranties. However, the law compels all sellers to honor certain implicit, or unstated, warranties, in order to ensure minimal standards of contractual performance. This rule applies whether or not explicit warranties are given by the seller. An implicit warranty obligation imposed by law on all sellers is called an **implied warranty**.

The three warranties discussed in the following sections are made to all purchasers by all sellers, including both casual sellers and professional merchants. These warranties are implied by law and need not be mentioned in the contract. Only if the parties specifically agree is any one or more of these warranties excluded.

WARRANTY OF TITLE Implicit in the act of selling, the seller warrants that he or she has title to the goods and the right to transfer them. This warranty is implied by law. Note, however, that it is excluded when it is obvious that the seller does not have title, such as when a sheriff, by court order, sells a debtor's goods to satisfy a judgment.

WARRANTY AGAINST ENCUMBRANCES Also implicit in the act of selling is the seller's

warranty that the goods shall be delivered free of all **encumbrances** (a claim of a third party, for example, for an unpaid balance) of which the buyer is not aware at the time of contracting. This warranty does not ensure that the goods are free of encumbrances at the time of the sale, but rather that they will be free at the time of delivery. This distinction enables the seller to comply with the warranty by paying off any third-party claimants before transferring ownership.

> **IN THIS CASE** Kresge sold a portable copying machine to Nansen and promised delivery in two weeks. Kresge did not mention that he owed $850 to the bank, with the machine as security. Kresge can avoid breaching the implied warranty against encumbrances by paying off the loan before delivering the machine.

WARRANTY OF FITNESS FOR A PARTICULAR PURPOSE A buyer who needs goods for a specific purpose often tells the seller about that purpose. Then the buyer relies on the seller's skill and judgment for a selection of appropriate goods.

In such circumstances, the seller makes an implied warranty that the goods delivered to the buyer are reasonably fit for the stated purpose. If they prove to be unfit, the buyer has a right of action for breach of warranty.

This warranty does not arise when the buyer

- personally selects the goods
- orders the goods according to the buyer's own specifications
- does not rely on the skill and judgment of the seller, because of independent testing or for other reasons

The warranty could arise even when the buyer asks for goods by patent or brand name. However, this variation applies only if the seller knows the purpose for which the goods are required and if the buyer relies on the seller's selection. For example, the buyer might ask for a "Buzzer" brand name chain saw to fell a stand of 30 trees with trunks two feet in diameter. When the seller selects the proper model, the buyer is relying on the seller's judgment, expertise, and implied warranty of fitness for a stated purpose.

A Question of ETHICS

While walking in the schoolyard, Stacy found an expensive gold necklace with an MP3 player built into it near the clasp. She posted notices of this find, but after three weeks without results, sold the necklace to her friend, Darleene, for $300. Is Darleene ethically obligated to return the ring if the true owner appeared and could prove ownership? Is she legally obligated to do so?

Why do you think it would be important for the buyer of a race horse to receive documentation of the lineage of the horse?

© GETTY IMAGES/PHOTODISC

sellers. This is certainly true in the area of warranties. In addition to the warranties made by all sellers, as previously discussed, the following warranties are, by law, also made by merchants.

WARRANTY AGAINST INFRINGEMENT A merchant makes an implied warranty that the goods in which she or he normally deals shall be delivered to a buyer free of any third party's claims for patent, copyright, or trademark infringement (unauthorized use). This warranty may be excluded by agreement between the parties. If the buyer furnishes specifications to the seller that lead to a claim of infringement against the seller, the buyer is obligated to indemnify the seller for any loss suffered because of the infringement.

WARRANTY OF MERCHANTABILITY Every merchant who customarily deals in goods of a particular kind makes an implied warranty of merchantability to all buyers of the goods. Basically, a **warranty of merchantability** requires that the goods be fit for the ordinary purposes for which such goods are used.

Also these goods must fit the sales contract description and meet the reasonable expectations of buyers in the seller's trade. If the goods are fungible, like grain, they must be at least of fair, average quality within the description. Within variations permitted by the contract, goods must be of even kind, quality, and quantity. If required by the contract, they must be adequately contained, packaged, and labeled. Finally, they must conform to any promises or statements of fact made on the label or on the container.

Implied Warranties Given Only by Merchants

Merchants typically are held to higher standards in their dealings with consumers than are casual

CyberLAW

Many businesses enter into contracts via the Internet that under the Statute of Frauds would require a "writing." Without such a paper representation of the contract—for example, for a sale of goods valued at more than $500—the agreement basically is unenforceable. Under UCITA such contracts are explicitly held to be valid as long as a record or authentication is available. Other issues that remain unresolved are the validity of electronic signatures, the effect of minority, and the requirements for proof of conditions that invalidate assent, such as intoxication, insanity, etc. Finally, under UCITA, tie-in sales using silence as acceptance would be legal unless a state's consumer protection statute renders them illegal. The terms in tie-in sales essentially state, "you bought our original version of the software, so we'll send you updates and charge you for them until you tell us not to."

THINK ABOUT IT

Elements of the Statute of Frauds and the UCC conflict with the terms suggested by the UCITA. Does knowledge of these conflicts affect your decision to make purchases over the Internet?

Food and drink sold for consumption on or off the premises of the seller must be wholesome and fit for human consumption. Otherwise it is considered *adulterated* and in violation of the warranty of merchantability. Drugs for human use also must be safe and wholesome.

Merchantability requires that any warranty protection that is customary in the trade be extended to all buyers. For example, the seller of a pedigreed animal, such as a dog or horse, is expected to provide documentation of the lineage of the animal because such proof is customary in the trade.

The warranty of merchantability may be expressly excluded by agreement of the parties. Also, when a buyer has examined the goods or a sample or model before contracting, there is no implied warranty of merchantability as to those defects that a reasonable examination would have revealed. This also applies if the buyer refused to examine the goods, sample, or model before contracting.

Exclusion of Warranties

A seller may offer to sell goods without any warranties. This is most likely to occur if the goods are known to have defects or if they are a new design or model. To sell goods without a warranty, the seller must refrain from making any express warranties, and use appropriate language that will exclude implied warranties.

For example, to exclude or modify the broad warranty of merchantability or any part of it, the seller must mention "merchantability" in a disclaimer. A **disclaimer** is a notice of exclusion. To exclude or modify any implied warranty of fitness, the exclusion must be in writing and be easily noticed. A statement such as the following would cover both merchantability and fitness: "There are no warranties of merchantability or fitness that extend beyond the description on the label." Unless otherwise indicated, all implied warranties are excluded by such expressions as "with all faults," "as is," or other similar words.

Lemon Laws

Warranties are augmented by consumer self-help laws called *lemon laws*. Typically, these laws protect consumers of vehicles, but they may extend to other consumer products in certain jurisdictions. Lemon laws are so called because chronically defective vehicles are referred to as "lemons." Lemon laws exist at both state and federal levels.

Lemon law protection works like this: A consumer returns a vehicle with a major defect to an authorized dealership for repair within the warranty period. If the dealership tries unsuccessfully to fix the vehicle several times (the number varies by statute—typically three visits are required), the consumer should then, in writing, request a refund or a replacement vehicle. If the request is not met, the consumer should seek the help of an attorney.

CHECKPOINT Distinguish express and implied warranties.

15-2 Assessment

Xtra!
Study Tools
school.cengage.com/blaw/lawxtra

THINK ABOUT LEGAL CONCEPTS

1. A warranty that obligates the seller to repair or replace the defective product with only a labor cost to the buyer is still a full warranty. **True or False?**

2. Strict liability is a tort cause of action. **True or False?**

3. The warranty of _?_ is implied against merchants of food products to be sure those products are not adulterated.

4. An express warranty may be given orally and still be legally effective. **True or False?**

5. *Caveat emptor* is Latin for (a) let the buyer beware (b) let the seller beware (c) let the ruler beware

Study the situation, answer the questions, and then prepare arguments to support your answers.

6. To install a brick walk in front of his home, Winslow bought three sacks of standard Pyramid-brand mortar mix from the U-Can-Do store. Instructions on the bags warned against direct contact with skin. Although Winslow had sensitive skin, he repeatedly touched the wet mix with his bare hands. This burned his hands, and he developed an allergic rash. Is either U-Can-Do or Pyramid liable to him under any theory of product liability?

7. When its new video game system developed problems after more than 150,000 had been sold, the maker repaired or replaced them. To induce sales it then extended the warranty on the unsold systems in retailer's stores for another two years. The maker also extended the warranty on the systems already sold. Can the maker be legally held to the extended warranty by the owners of the previously sold systems even if they gave no consideration for it? Why or why not?

8. Kent was critically injured when he dropped a running lawnmower on his foot. At the time he dropped it, Kent was using the lawnmower to trim the top of a three-foot-high hedge. He sued the retailer, wholesaler, and manufacturer of the lawnmower on a product liability theory. Kent claimed an automatic shutoff should have been built into the lawnmower for times when it was not in contact with the ground. Will Kent win? Why or why not?

9. While in Florida, Van Loon decided to go fishing for tarpon. Visiting Stanton's Sports Shop, Van Loon explained his specific need to the salesperson. Van Loon then bought the fishing gear the salesperson recommended. During the first trip out, Van Loon had repeated strikes, but the line was too light for the weight of the fish. The line broke every time even though handled properly. What legal rights, if any, does Van Loon have against Stanton's?

 ## Online Research> Anita's Attack

After the victory party for the big game between the Waynestown Pondfish and their cross-county rivals, Anita and the rest of the cheerleaders headed to Anita's for a slumber party. They were all hungry and there was only one place to go for a late night snack: TUPS, The Grand Taco Shack. Anita whipped into the drive-thru and bought 15 of TUPS' "Tasty Tacos." By the time she had driven the two miles to her house, she and the girls had devoured them all.

Four hours later, Anita and the other cheerleaders were all sick and throwing up. Anita's mother, a pediatrician, had just called for an ambulance to take Anita's co-captain, Antonia, to the hospital to be treated for food poisoning.

A week passed. Antonia was finally out of intensive care having almost died from Hemolytic Uremic Syndrome (HUS), a condition that can lead to permanent kidney damage and even death. The illness had been traced to lettuce in the tacos the girls consumed. It was infected with one of the most toxic forms of Escherichia coli, commonly known as E. coli. More than 100 similar cases in the outbreak had been reported, including the death of one young child.

THINK CRITICALLY

What governmental bodies respond to and are responsible for preventing and/or controlling such outbreaks? What implied warranty has been breached by TUPS? What legal options are open to individuals injured by the outbreak?

GO TO FINDLAW.COM FOR THE ANSWERS

To find the material in FindLaw on this issue, go to Findlaw.com and click on the following sequence of hyperlinks: Defective and Dangerous Products, Food Poisoning, Food Poisoning in the News.

Chapter 15 Assessment

CONCEPTS IN BRIEF

15-1 Protection through Governmental Action

1. The Latin phrase *caveat emptor* has long urged buyers to beware. The complexity of today's products and the inaccessibility of their makers now require consumers not only to beware but to be aware of the various federal, state, and local laws designed to inform and protect them.

2. Federal agencies and state and local governments work together to ensure safe products, services, and sanitary facilities for consumers.

3. Unfair trade practices include price fixing, false advertising, illegal lotteries, improperly labeling goods, and selling used articles as new.

4. Reports of substandard goods or services can be made to licensing authorities at the state and local levels.

15-2 Protection through Action by the Consumer

5. Generally, any person injured by a defective product may bring suit against any manufacturer or merchant in the distribution chain for that product. Depending on the circumstances, the suit may be based on warranty, fraud, negligence, or strict liability.

6. Warranties may be express or implied. Express warranties are oral or written promises by the seller about product quality or performance. Implied warranties are imposed by law and are effective even if not mentioned by the seller.

7. Merchant sellers normally are bound by the broad coverage of the implied warranty of merchantability unless explicitly disclaimed.

YOUR LEGAL VOCABULARY

Match each statement with the term that it best defines. Some terms may not be used.

1. Notice of exclusion of warranty
2. Permits a party to a contract to recover money or property (or the value thereof) given to the other party.
3. Individual who buys primarily for personal, family, or household use
4. Greatly exaggerated sales talk
5. Let the buyer beware
6. Let the seller beware
7. Obligation implicitly imposed on all sellers
8. Dishonest, fraudulent, or anti-competitive business method
9. Lawsuit made possible by the procedural joining of similarly situated plaintiffs
10. Explicit assurance of quality or performance by seller
11. Affixing of responsibility to compensate buyers, users, and others for injuries caused by a defective product.
12. Claims of third parties against property, for example, for an unpaid balance
13. The relationship that exists between or among the contracting parties as a result of their legally binding agreement

a. bait and switch
b. *caveat emptor*
c. *caveat venditor*
d. cease-and-desist order
e. class action
f. consent order
g. consumer
h. disclaimer
i. encumbrances
j. express warranty
k. full warranty
l. implied warranty
m. limited warranty
n. privity of contract
o. product liability
p. puffing
q. restitution
r. unfair trade practice
s. warranty
t. warranty of merchantability

REVIEW LEGAL CONCEPTS

14. What are the normal sanctions available to a consumer protection agency?

15. How would you prove a bait and switch had occurred?

16. Why is it a good idea to leave to local governments the inspection of restaurants and other establishments where food is handled? Why would more centralized state or federal standards not be a good idea?

17. Who can bring suit for product liability under the UCC?

18. Should a written contract include all express warranties?

19. Why are sellers not required to give warranties in every transaction?

20. How do the terms "puffing" and "*caveat emptor*" relate to one another?

WRITE ABOUT LEGAL CONCEPTS

21. Make a list of the reasons that *caveat emptor* does not work as well now as it once did in protecting consumers.

22. Write a paragraph stating your opinion on what is the most important implied warranty.

23. Would a company selling software that enabled the copying of movie DVDs be committing an unfair trade practice? Why or why not?

24. **HOT DEBATE** Write a persuasive opening statement that emphasizes the legal and ethical points in support of Edison's case. Or, write a persuasive opening statement that emphasizes the legal and ethical points in the manufacturer's favor.

MAKE ACADEMIC CONNECTIONS

25. **PSYCHOLOGY** Research and write a one-page paper on whether the use of subliminal (subconscious) techniques in advertising in movies, print, and television should be outlawed as false and misleading. Bring examples to class, if possible.

THINK CRITICALLY ABOUT EVIDENCE

Study the situation, answer the questions, and then prepare arguments to support your answers.

26. After an hour of persistent persuasion by a door-to-door salesperson, the Arnos signed a contract to buy magazine subscriptions. The next morning, the Arnos did some quick calculating and were appalled to discover that they had agreed to spend $257.40—a sum they could not afford—for magazines. Can the Arnos cancel the contract without being liable for damages?

27. Having seen several advertisements for WaterRocket engines, Vincent went to a nearby marina and told the salesperson that he had to have one for his 17-foot bass boat. The salesperson sold Vincent the smallest WaterRocket engine, a 345-horsepower dynamo. When Vincent fired it up on his boat for the first time, his bass boat did a water wheelie and flipped back over on him causing him severe injuries and humiliation among his fellow bassers. He sued the marina for breach of the warranty of fitness for a particular purpose. Will he recover?

28. Gallo, an experienced glider pilot, rented a glider from the owner of a commercial glider port. While in flight, she lost control because of a defect in the tail assembly. The glider crashed, and Gallo was permanently disabled. Although several years old, the glider had been properly maintained. However, due to the age of the aircraft, there was no warranty in effect on the glider. Does Gallo have any legal recourse?

29. Singer-Moser was thirty-nine years old when she had her first cavity. Unfortunately, the dentist treating her for the cavity had to do a root canal procedure. At the conclusion of the procedure, Singer-Moser was left with the shell of her tooth and a filling inside it. A week later, she was eating a hamburger at Carnivoracious, a franchised restaurant in her home town. She bit down on a piece of bone that shattered the remnants of her tooth and dislodged the filling. Now the dentist tells her she must have a cap that will cost $2,500. Her attorney tells her that Carnivoracious should pay for the work. Why?

30. Every week for a year and a half, Newmark was given a shampoo and set by employees of Gimbel's. Then a new product ("Candle Wave," made by the Helene Curtis company) was applied to Newmark's hair. As a result, Newmark suffered contact dermatitis of the scalp, with substantial hair loss. Newmark sued Gimbel's for breach of the implied warranty of fitness for a particular purpose. Gimbel's argued that it was providing a service and not selling goods in this transaction. Therefore it could not be held liable for breach of warranty with reference to the product of Helene Curtis. It could only be held liable, it claimed, if its own employees were proved negligent. Could a jury find Gimbel's liable if the wave solution was defective and caused the injury? (*Newmark v. Gimbel's Inc.*, 258 A.2d 679, N.J.)

31. Mahaney purchased a used car from Perry Auto Exchange. Mahaney was told that the car was in "perfect, A-1, and first-class condition." A written statement given to Mahaney at the time of the sale described the car as being in "good operating condition." Mahaney had no opportunity to investigate the truth of these statements. Later, it was determined that the car had a problem in the differential and had no brakes at the time of the sale. Mahaney sued for rescission. Were Perry's statements merely puffing or were they warranties upon which the rescission could be based? (*Mahaney v. Perry Auto Exchange*, 85 N.E.2d 558, Ohio)

32. On January 1, plaintiff Werner bought the *White Eagle,* a wooden sloop, from defendant Montana, and the parties signed a bill of sale. The previous October they had signed an intent to purchase and sell. During their negotiations, the seller had assured the buyer orally that the hull would "make up" from swelling when placed in the water and would be watertight. At the end of June, Werner put the boat in the water. He allowed more than six weeks—a sufficient time—for the planking to swell to form a watertight hull. But the hull still leaked. The boat could not be sailed. Werner then checked the hull and for the first time discovered extensive dry rot which required substantial repairs. In a letter in September, he demanded that Montana take the boat back and refund the purchase price of $13,250. The defendant refused, and so Werner sued for rescission. Montana argued that the oral assurances he had given that the boat was watertight could not be admitted at the trial because of the parol evidence rule. Who should win? (*Werner v. Montana*, 378 A.2d 1130, N.H.)

33. Through radio and television, the defendant's stores advertised a "top quality . . . Queen Anne Console Magic Stitcher" sewing machine, along with a sewing chair, for the "close-out price of just $29.50." Under the sales plan, a "lead person" would accept the customer's order, taking a deposit as small as 25 cents. After that, a demonstrator would visit the customer and "kill the sale" by having the machine jam in use. The demonstrator would also say that the customer could lose an eye if the machine jammed. Then the demonstrator would attempt to "step-up" the sale and persuade the customer to buy a higher-priced machine. In about 19 months, only 26 of the advertised machines were sold, although 10,951 customers entered into conditional sales contracts for such machines. The 26 advertised machines were sold at a time when the defendants had received complaints from a television station and the Better Business Bureau. The defendants were prosecuted for conspiring to sell merchandise by means of deceptive and misleading advertising. The prosecutor gave evidence that the defendants never intended to sell the advertised machines, which actually cost them $45 each. Are the defendants guilty as charged? (*People v. Glubo, Exelbert, Epstein, and Atlantic Sewing Stores, Inc.*, 158 N.E.2d 699)

34. Registration of a "MONOPOLY" trademark for use on clothing was sought by a New York-based corporation named Tuxedo Monopoly, Inc. The makers of the "MONOPOLY" board game, General Mills Fun Group, opposed the application. The Patent and Trademark Office Trademark Trial and Appeal Board sustained the opposition and would not allow the registration. On appeal to the U.S. Court of Customs and Patent Appeals, Tuxedo's attorneys argued that *monopoly* was a common term and that, regardless, there was very little likelihood of confusion between a trademark used on a game and one used on clothing. They also pointed out that the court had previously allowed the registration of the famous "DIXIE" cup mark by a company using it as its mark on waxed paper. If the court finds a likelihood of confusion exists, it will affirm the Board's decision. How should the court rule? (*Tuxedo Monopoly, Inc. v. General Mills Fun Group, Inc.*, 648 F.2d 1335)

Case For Legal Thinking

BLEVINS V. CUSHMAN MOTORS
SUPREME COURT OF MISSOURI, 551 S.W. 2D 602

FACTS Maxwell and Blevins teed off on hole number 13, and then hopped into their golf cart and motored out to Maxwell's ball. Maxwell fired his second shot, then drove the cart toward Blevins' ball. As the cart approached the ball at approximately 5 mph, it entered a shady area of the course on which a light dew lay. At that point the cart went into a 10- to 15-foot skid. It was like "being on ice." The cart then tipped over. Maxwell was thrown free. However, Blevins, who failed in his attempt to jump from the cart, was pinned under it when it came to rest. Blevins brought suit on product liability grounds based on strict liability in tort, not negligence. He sued for his personal injuries. In addition, his wife brought suit for loss of consortium (the fellowship of husband and wife in companionship and sexual relations).

TRIAL COURT'S DECISION The court found for Mr. and Mrs. Blevins. Both received very substantial awards.

APPELLATE COURT DECISION The Missouri Court of Appeals upheld the decision of the trial court and maintained the amount of the awards. An appeal was taken to the Missouri Supreme Court.

MISSOURI SUPREME COURT'S DECISION Cushman Motors, manufacturer of the cart, approached the Missouri Supreme Court arguing that although Missouri courts had used strict liability in tort to decide cases involving a defect in manufacturing, the courts of the state should not use such a standard to decide a case involving a defect in design. Instead, the negligence theory should be used to determine whether the maker of the product was liable.

The Supreme Court decided, "There is no rational distinction between design and manufacture in this context, since a product may be equally defective and dangerous if its design subjects protected persons to unreasonable risks as if its manufacture does so."

CONCLUSION Judgment affirmed.

PRACTICE JUDGING

1. What arguments can you make to justify Cushman's distinction between design and manufacture?

2. What arguments can you make against such a position?

3. According to the excerpted text of the Supreme Court's decision quoted above, was it correct to use strict liability in tort to determine the result in this case?

Entrepreneurs
AND THE LAW

Project 3 The Law of Sales

TESTING THE PRODUCT Stacy and Brandon were married less than two months after their meeting. Their prenuptial agreement allowed each to keep the rights they valued: Stacy's in the SecureSeal tires and process and Brandon's in his house and income for his children.

Stacy came to an amiable agreement with her dad and Bob over the rental of part of the retread shop for use in further developing and producing the tires. For her father's past, present, and future investment of money and expertise in the SecureSeal products, she agreed to share with him a portion of any future profits and to pay him a consulting fee on an hourly basis.

After a detailed review of the retread market and the results of their own test of the SecureSeals, Stacy and Joe decided to manufacture a small number of the tires for further testing by professional drivers. Joe regularly dealt with independent truckers in the ordinary running of the shop. He felt that, with proper compensation to Bob for any sales the shop might lose, he could find several potential customers willing to buy the SecureSeals at a discount price, run the tires, and then report back the results. Stacy cautioned that they had to be sure to get the drivers to sign non-disclosure agreements that included limitation of liability provisions.

Over the next four weeks, Stacy, Joe, and a couple of the shop employees who wanted extra income, worked late into the night producing the SecureSeal stock for the professional trucker road tests. The employees were made to sign non-disclosure agreements and agreements not to compete. Stacy kept careful records of production time and costs and worked on ways to lower both. Joe supervised the actual production efforts and recruited the test drivers. On the Saturday after a month of practically 24/7 labor, the ten trucks participating in the test were outfitted and sent on their way. Stacy and Joe took a few days off from manufacturing to receive reports from the drivers, and then to compile and calculate the results.

Reports from the drivers were uniformly supportive. The trucks used in the road test had satellite communications built into their cabs and so could send daily measurements on tread wear, cracks, and separations as well as descriptions of any total failures of the SecureSeals. The drivers had agreed in case of such a failure event they would collect all pieces of the tire and bring them back for lab evaluation. By the end of the test runs, however, no such event had occurred. Tread wear and the incidence of cracking or minor separations was far less than expected due to the excellent bond between the fresh cap and the old core.

MARKETING BEGINS After more than 2,000,000 miles, Stacy and Joe declared the test runs a success and turned their attention to marketing the tires. Stacy's data on material, labor, and other factors of production revealed that the SecureSeal tire's cost was about 25 percent more than the average recap produced in Joe and Bob's shop. They concluded that the best entry niche for the tire was with long-haul truckers whose jobs depended on timing and reliability of delivery. These truckers could least afford the disruption of a recap failure, repair, and potential collateral damage. They would, therefore, pay the premium price for the promise of the SecureSeal's performance. Joe suggested that, to secure their initial sale, they approach a small national hauler located in a nearby city. A week after making the sales presentation, the hauler placed orders for replacement tires for 120 over-the-road trucks. The size of the order surprised Stacy and Joe. Worried about being able to fill it on time, they decided to approach Bob to see if he would agree to convert the entire shop to manufacturing SecureSeals.

ACTIVITIES

Divide into teams and perform one or more of the following activities as directed by your teacher:

Prepare Legal Documents

Develop a sales contract with appropriate terms for payment, delivery, responsibility for loss or damage to the goods, warrantees, limitations of liability, etc.

Role-Play

Divide the class into two groups, one to represent Stacy's interests and the other to represent Joe's. Have each group define those interests and announce them to the class.

BECOME A CONSUMER ACTIVIST

In 1773 a group of patriots decided to take action against English taxation without representation by throwing a shipload of tea overboard into Boston Harbor. They were consumer activists. This long-standing tradition of citizen action aimed at influencing corporate and governmental decisions is taking on new and unprecedented power. The most popular forms of consumer activism include boycotts (not purchasing products for political reasons), buycotts (purchasing products for political reasons), and socially conscious investing. It also includes politically oriented shareholder tactics such as proposing a resolution, testifying at a shareholder meeting, disrupting a shareholder meeting, protests directed at corporate or governmental organizations, and protests that target businesses directly. Whether conservative or liberal, all political agendas have found their way into consumer activism.

DO YOUR PART

1. Make a list of three consumer-related concerns that you have about your community or the world. Research to find an organization that matches your concerns. For example, if you are concerned about the use of CCA in treated lumber, you could research the Consumer Product Safety Commission. If your concern is harvesting the world's rain forests or old-growth forests for lumber, you might research Greenpeace.

2. Join the organization and participate in any local activities.

3. Write letters to the editor for your school and local paper, state representatives, and any other governmental or corporate figures who could help your cause.

Public Speaking I

This event gives FBLA members the opportunity to demonstrate leadership through effective speaking skills.

The topic for your speech is Marriage, Divorce, and Prenuptial Contracts. Your business speech should be four minutes in length and must be developed from one or more of the nine FBLA-PBL goals found at the FBLA web site. Five points will be deducted for any time under 3:31 or over 4:20 minutes. A lectern will be available, but no microphone will be used. The participant may use notes or note cards when delivering the speech. However, no visual aids may be used.

Each participant's speech must be the result of his/her own efforts. Facts and working data may be secured from any source. Speeches must be well organized, contain verified statements, and written in an acceptable business style.

Performance Indicators Evaluated

- Understand the latest trends about marriage, divorce, and prenuptial contracts.
- Describe the role of contracts in marriages.
- Explain the latest marriage and divorce trends.
- Thoroughly defend/oppose prenuptial contracts with valid facts.

For more detailed information about performance indicators, go to the FBLA web site.

THINK CRITICALLY

1. What is the current divorce rate in the United States?
2. What is a prenuptial agreement?

http://www.fbla-pbl.org/

Mock Trial Prep

CASE LAW: SEARCH AND SEIZURE

WHAT IS CASE LAW?

Case law is the body of law created by the written opinions of judges. Case law provides an attorney with legal precedents. Legal precedents are adjudged cases or decisions of a court which furnish an example or authority for an identical or similar case afterwards arising out of or from a similar question of law. Case law provides attorneys a basis for how the courts interpret statutes and case law.

The following is a basic summation of the case law of the U.S. Supreme Court concerning search and seizure and the Fourth Amendment.

FOURTH AMENDMENT

The Fourth Amendment to the U.S. Constitution states:

> "The right of the people to be secure in their persons, houses, papers, and effects, against unreasonable searches and seizures, shall not be violated, and no Warrants shall issue, but upon probable cause, supported by Oath or affirmation, and particularly describing the place to be searched, and the persons or things to be seized."

The Fourth Amendment to the U.S. Constitution prohibits the government from conducting unreasonable searches and seizures of persons or their property. [*Terry v. Ohio* (1968), 392 U.S. 1, 88 S.Ct. 1868] All evidence obtained by searches and seizures in violation of the Constitution is inadmissible in a state court. [*Mapp v. Ohio* (1961), 367 U.S. 643, 655, 81 S.Ct. 1884.]

WARRANTS

State law generally requires that a warrant shall be issued only on an affidavit or affidavits sworn to before a judge of a court of record and establishing the grounds for issuing the warrant. The basis of knowledge and the truthfulness of the person supplying the knowledge under oath are considered to determine the value of the information and whether probable cause exists to issue the warrant. An affidavit is testimony that an individual gives in writing and under oath. A police officer or detective can be the affiant. Warrantless searches generally are considered unreasonable. Evidence obtained by means of a warrantless search is subject to exclusion, unless the circumstances of the search establish it as constitutionally reasonable.

PROBABLE CAUSE

Probable cause to issue a search warrant requires substantial evidence that items sought are connected with a crime and located at the place to be searched. [*Brinegar v. U.S.* (1949), 338 U.S. 160, 69 S.Ct. 1302]

To determine the sufficiency of "probable cause" in an affidavit submitted in support of a search warrant, the issuing magistrate must make a practical, common-sense decision whether, in light of all the circumstances set forth in the affidavit, including the veracity and the basis of knowledge of those persons who provide hearsay information, a fair probability exists that contraband or evidence of a crime will be found in a particular place. [*Illinois v. Gates* (1983), 462 U.S. 213, 238, 103 S.Ct. 2317] Probable cause to issue a search warrant requires substantial evidence that items sought are connected with a crime and located at the place to be searched. [*Brinegar v. U.S.* (1949), 338 U.S. 160, 69 S.Ct. 1302]

PLAIN VIEW DOCTRINE

The Plain View Doctrine is an exception to the warrant requirement for a lawful search. The Plain View Doctrine embodies the understanding that privacy must be protected by the individual, and if a police officer is lawfully on a person's property and observes objects in plain or open view, no warrant is required to look at them. [*Horton v. California* (1990), 496 U.S. 128, 134-37, 110 S.Ct. 2301] The U.S. Supreme Court has held that if police officers are at a lawful vantage point, they may use a flashlight to look through netting into a barn, even

though they do not have a warrant to search that building. [*United States v. Dunn* (1987), 480 U.S. 294, 305, 107 S.Ct. 1134]

In short, this doctrine allows law-enforcement officers to seize incriminating evidence or contraband when they discover it in plain sight in a place where they have a right to be. [*Coolidge v. New Hampshire* (1971), 403 U.S. 443, 466]

In *Payton v. New York* (1980), 445 U.S. 573, 100 S.Ct. 1371, 63 L.Ed.2d 639, the U.S. Supreme Court held that absent probable cause and exigent circumstances, warrantless arrests in the home are prohibited by the Fourth Amendment. Additionally, in *Horton v. California* (1990), 496 U.S. 128, 136, 110 S.Ct. 2301, 2307, 110 L.Ed.2d 112, 122, the Supreme Court pointed out that an officer's discovery of an object in plain view does not exempt the officer from complying with the Fourth Amendment. The officer must have a "lawful right of access" to the discovered object. Id. at 137, 110 S.Ct. at 2307, 110 L.Ed.2d at 123. The object, therefore, must be seized pursuant to a warrant or the seizure must be under circumstances that excuse the failure to get the warrant. Id. at 138, 110 S.Ct. at 2308, 110 L.Ed.2d at 123. Moreover, the burden is upon those seeking to justify a nonconsensual search without a warrant to show that it is properly done. [*McDonald v. United States* (1948), 335 U.S. 451, 69 S.Ct. 191, 93 L.Ed. 153]

Courts have held that the observation of an object in plain view is not a search under the law. If there is no search under the law, then there can be no violation of the Fourth Amendment.

CONSENT TO THE SEARCH

"[O]ne of the specifically established exceptions to the requirements of both a warrant and probable cause is a search that is conducted pursuant to consent." [*Schneckloth v. Bustamonte* (1973), 412 U.S. 218, 219, 93 S.Ct. 2041] The prosecution bears the burden of proving by clear and positive evidence that consent was voluntarily given. [*Schneckloth*, 412 U.S. at 222]

TEAMWORK

In the case of *People of Any State vs. Robert Craig*, Robert initially was arrested and charged with larceny and robbery. The larceny charge was related to the allegedly stolen car. The robbery charge stemmed from the fact that the police found a stolen purse and wallet in Robert's backpack, which was in the trunk of the car. Robert's defense attorney filed a motion to disallow the seized purse and wallet as evidence because they were obtained as a result of an improper search. Work in teams. It will be your team's job as a judge to make a ruling as to whether or not a search would be justified (reasonable) in the following circumstances.

A. Once stopped, the police searched the car and any place Robert reasonably could have reached while in the driver's seat.

B. Once the arrest was made, the police did an inventory on the car and listed all of the items found in the car and the trunk.

C. Police searched all of the contents of all items found in the trunk of the car.

D. Robert was given a pat-down search when asked to get out of the car and before he was arrested.

E. Robert was thoroughly searched after his arrest both at the scene and later at the station. This involved a strip search.

F. Michele was searched by the police when she accompanied her father to the station to pick up the car.

G. Bart is asked by the police at the station to empty his pockets, which he does, and the police discover he is carrying an illegal knife. It is confiscated, and he is arrested.

Unit 4
Property Law

Chapters

16 **Property and Its Acquisition**

17 **Bailments**

18 **Ownership and Leasing
of Real Property**

19 **Insurance Law**

20 **Wills, Trusts, and Estates**

Title Examiner

Titles are documents that show evidence of ownership to a piece of property. Title examiners make sure the title to a property is free of restrictions that may affect its sale or use. The work involves examining copies of records, such as deeds, mortgages, liens, judgments, easements, vital statistics, and land map books to determine ownership and legal restrictions. The work also is done to verify the legal description of a piece of property.

Such information is needed before the property can be bought, sold, or insured. Examination of a property's title also must be obtained before a buyer can obtain a loan to purchase the property.

Title examiners help to prepare mortgage agreements, trust deeds, and other contracts related to buying and selling property. They work for law firms, real estate agencies, or title insurance companies.

EMPLOYMENT OUTLOOK

Employment of title examiners is expected to grow more slowly than average through 2014. In the coming years, up until 2014, approximately 7,000 people are expected to be hired in the field. They will join the 61,000 who already work in this field in the United States.

NEEDED SKILLS AND EDUCATION

Title examiners typically receive training through on-the-job experience. A college degree usually is not required, but could be considered a superior credential when compared to job candidates who do not hold a college degree.

Title examiners need good reading and writing skills and must be good listeners. They compile reports based on the information they read and hear. The job involves critical thinking skills, the ability to solve problems, and attention to details. Computer skills are important for researching and writing reports. Knowledge of real estate, geography, law, and government are helpful but not a requirement for an entry-level position.

How you'll spend your day

As a title examiner you likely will work weekdays in an office-like setting. You'll spend time at your desk, using the computer for research and preparation of reports. You'll also spend time at the county courthouse examining public records.

Your company's client may want to purchase land to open a restaurant. Your job would be to verify the exact size of the lot to be purchased. You'll consult land map books at the courthouse to determine the precise measurement of the property. You'll also need to research information about the current owner of the property. Does the current occupant own the property, or does someone else own the property? Are there any unresolved legal issues involving the property? You'll search records to determine if there are liens on the property such as those stemming from unpaid income or real estate taxes.

You'll search the marital records of the property owner to determine who holds the rights to the land. Are the owners involved in any legal disputes that could jeopardize the sale?

Is the property zoned for the type of business the new owner wants to operate? Not all property is zoned for use as a restaurant.

Having gathered this information, you will review the data and submit a report. If any problems—such as the existence of unpaid property taxes—are identified, you'll meet with your client to discuss your findings.

What about you?

Does the job of title examiner interest you? Why or why not? Which aspects of the job would you most enjoy? Which would you least enjoy?

Chapter 16
Property and Its Acquisition

16-1 Types of Property

16-2 How Property Is
    Acquired and Held

HOT DEBATE

When he was 57, Neerow won $20 million in a state lottery. Upon receiving a lump sum after-tax payout of $13 million, he went on a spending spree. He had extensive plastic surgery, including a face lift. Then he bought a condominium in Florida, a new car which he soon wrecked, clothes he never even wore, a mink coat for a casual friend, and a large yacht. In the next year, he staged many parties including a wild New Year's Eve party on his yacht for 50 new friends. While pursuing his new lifestyle, Neerow totally neglected his business, which employed 10 people. The business weakened to the point of near bankruptcy.

WHERE DO YOU STAND?

1. Give the legal rationale as to why Neerow should be allowed to continue to spend his time and financial resources in this seemingly wasteful manner.
2. From society's standpoint, should his wastefulness be stopped? Why or why not?

16-1 Types of Property

GOALS

- Define property
- Identify the classifications of property

KEY TERMS

property
real property
personal property
intellectual property
copyright
infringement

fair use
trademark
service mark
patent
trade secret

Property and Its Classification

WHAT'S YOUR VERDICT? Needing a vacation after finishing a new edition of his book, Jon rented a house in Beach Haven, New Jersey, for a couple of weeks. He looked forward to relaxing and getting away from it all during that period.

Did Jon acquire property under the lease?

What Is Property?

When you hear the term *property*, you probably think of tangible things you can see or touch. Tangible things include this book, clothing, jewelry, buildings, land, cars, and boats. However, property also includes intangible things, or things you cannot see or touch.

For example, both the goodwill of a brand name and the secret formula by which a product is made are intangible property. Other examples include patents for inventions, the copyright of this book, the franchise to open a particular business in your town, and the right to collect money under an automobile insurance policy.

Technically, according to the law, **property** is defined as the rights and interests we recognize in one another in tangible and intangible things. For example, suppose you own some land with a house that you correctly call property. Legally, ownership of the land and house gives you a number of these rights and interests. These may include some or all of the following rights: title, possession, use, enjoyment, profit, and *alienation* (to dispose of it by sale, gift, consumption, or destruction).

Because he acquired possession of the beach house for two weeks by renting it, in *What's Your Verdict?* Jon acquired property in the transaction.

Classifications of Property

Property can be classified as real or personal. **Real property** is defined as rights and interests in land, buildings, and those things permanently affixed to them (*fixtures*). **Personal property** is basically defined as rights and interests in anything that is not real property. Personal property can be either tangible or intangible.

REAL PROPERTY Real property (sometimes called *realty*) includes not only the surface of the earth,

Name the types of real property pictured here.

© GETTY IMAGES/PHOTODISC

Ben rented a luxury apartment in the new Towers Complex on the south side of the city. He then bought more than $30,000 worth of audio-visual equipment and had it built into the walls of the apartment. When his lease expired two years later and he moved out, Ben could not take the equipment with him. The permanent way it was installed made the equipment a fixture and therefore part of the realty which belonged to the owners of the Towers.

but also the water and minerals on and below the surface. Real property in the form of land extends down to the center of the earth and, with certain limits, includes the airspace above the land. Real property also includes buildings and anything that becomes permanently attached to buildings and land. The rights to possess, use, profit from, and destroy such things also are considered real property.

PERSONAL PROPERTY Tangible personal property (sometimes called *personalty*) is something that has physical form. Intangible personal property comprises anything that does not have a physical form. Examples include the goodwill associated with a business and rights in intellectual property.

Intellectual property is intangible property created by the intellect and includes copyrights, service marks and trademarks, patents, and trade secrets. The creation, use, and transfer of interests in intellectual property generally are governed by federal statutes.

COPYRIGHTS A **copyright** protects the *expression* of a creative work, such as the work of an author, artist, or composer. Owners of the copyright have the exclusive right to reproduce, sell, perform, or display the work. For works created on or after January 1 of 1978, copyrights owned by the creator of the work last for the life of the creator plus 70 years. After a copyright period expires, the work can be used by anyone without cost or obtaining permission. An author can transfer ownership of the copyright to others.

Copyrighted works can include songs, books, computer programs, and architectural plans. The expression to be copyrighted must be *fixed* and *original.* Fixed means it is expressed in a permanent way others can understand, for example in writing, painting, computer language, or a blueprint. It is the fixed expression, not the idea, that is protected. If you wrote a book about the Civil War, it is only the way you used the words that would be protected.

Copyright protection is afforded by the common law from creation of the original work until it is spread to those outside of the author's circle. At that time the copyright will be lost unless the work has been registered with the U.S. Copyright Office. Damages may be collected for **infringement**, which is the unauthorized copying, sale, display, or performance of a copyright protected work.

CyberLAW

You probably view the e-mail you send as your own personal property. But what about the e-mail you send at work? Many companies now have e-mail policies about who owns the e-mail correspondence and whether the company considers the messages to be confidential. The courts have ruled that e-mails are the property of the company. However, in several states such as California, Delaware, Florida, Hawaii, Louisiana, Maryland, and Montana, statutes have superceded these court rulings. These statutes require the permission of all parties to the electronic transmission (e-mail) to enable the employer to read it. Other states allow the reading with only one party's permission while still others adhere to the original court ruling. The result is a confused state of the law. The bottom line: Be careful before you press the Send button. E-mail messages may not be confidential or your exclusive "private" property.

THINK ABOUT IT

Should you be able to send personal messages on your employer's computer system? What are the arguments for and against? Would it matter if you did so on your break time? What about searching the web or playing video games on the employer's computers? If you did any of these things, would you have an expectation of privacy?

Under the federal copyright law not all unauthorized uses of copyrighted works are infringements. **Fair use** is the very limited use of copyrighted works by critics, researchers, news reporters, and educators. The most important factor in determining whether the defense of fair use is available is the economic impact of the use.

Another factor is the quantity of the copied material in relation to the size of the whole copyrighted work. One novelist might quote a paragraph from another novelist's 300-page book. That would be fair use because it does not injure the first novelist by causing reduced sales of the quoted novel. Also, the paragraph is a small portion of the original, copyrighted novel. Teachers may reproduce very limited portions of copyrighted materials for use in their classes.

TRADEMARKS AND SERVICE MARKS Business firms may acquire property rights known as trademarks. A **trademark** is a word, mark, symbol, or device by which the products of a particular manufacturer or the commodities of a particular merchant can be distinguished from those of others. The trademark must be unique in its line of commerce. For example, the word "Kodak" is a trademark. It is included in the name of the owner, the Eastman Kodak Company, and it identifies products made by that company. However, descriptive words, such as "35mm camera," are not trademarks, and they may be used by any company. A **service mark** is a unique word, mark, or symbol that identifies a service as opposed to a product.

Registration of trademarks in the United States officially began in 1870. Internationally, beginning with the Paris Convention of 1883, a series of international treaties were entered into that guaranteed the protection of intellectual property, such as trademarks, patents, and copyrights,

LAW BRIEF

Trademarks have been used for centuries. Ancient Chinese potters and medieval sword makers used pictures and symbols as their trademarks. The American patriot and silversmith Paul Revere marked his work with his initials. Nonetheless, the rights of trademark owners were not clearly established in the United States until the late nineteenth century.

from infringers. Today this protection is enforced by the World Intellectual Property Organization of the United Nations and each of its 184 member states. The Lanham Act, enacted in 1946, is the current U.S. trademark law.

All states and the federal government have trademark registration laws. Registration is not essential. However, if a trademark is registered it is easier to prove ownership of the mark. Common law protection lasts without any required renewal filing or notification if a unique trademark establishes the product in the minds of the public and the trademark is used continuously. The originating company loses its exclusive property right to the trademark if either of the following occurs:

1. the company permits competitors to refer to similar products by the unique trademark, or

2. the trademark is used as a generic descriptive term of a class of products or services from more than one source

Examples of terms that have become generic are "shredded wheat" and "cellophane." In contrast, the terms "Xerox," "Levi's," and "Scotch Tape" remain the property of the original owners.

PATENTS A **patent** is the grant of the exclusive right to make, use, import, sell, and offer a novel or new, non-obvious, useful product or process. *Novel* means no one has ever thought of the product or process before. *Non-obvious* means that it was above the basic engineering standards in the field at the time. Useful means the product or process can help people do things. Like copyrights, patents can be transferred to others. A patent is good for up to 20 years and is not renewable.

An inventor will sometimes patent improvements to the original product and thereby extend the practical life of the initial patent. Patents are given for original designs, such as a unique chair, or original processes, such as one for refining oil into rubber. Patents also are given for certain new and distinct varieties of plants and other biological creations.

TRADE SECRETS Sometimes a business firm will have important ideas or knowledge that should not be revealed as required for patents and copyrights. These ideas can still be protected as trade secrets. A **trade secret** is commercially valuable information that the owner attempts to keep secret. If an employee leaves a company and sells a secret formula, process, or customer list, the former employee and the buyer of the trade secret will be liable to the employer.

CHECKPOINT What are the two main classifications of property?

FEATURES OF INTELLECTUAL PROPERTY

	What is protected?	Registration required?	Duration?	Examples
Patent	Ideas, designs, or processes that are novel, non-obvious, and useful	Yes	20 years	Industrial chemical manufacturing processes, prescription drugs
Copyright	Fixed expressions of creativity	Yes, before generally publicized, for federal protection.	70 years past the death of the creator	Novels, poems, songs, photographs
Trademark	Distinctive mark, word, or symbol associated with a particular product	No, but recommended	Indefinite	Logos, emblems, catch phrases

16-1 Assessment

Xtra!
Study Tools
school.cengage.com/blaw/lawxtra

THINK ABOUT LEGAL CONCEPTS

1. The ability to profit from real property is a property right. **True or False?**

2. Intellectual property is (a) tangible (b) intangible (c) not capable of ownership

3. To be protected by law, a trade secret (a) must be copyrightable (b) must be patentable (c) must be commercially valuable (d) must have had efforts to keep it secret (e) both c and d

4. Under current law, a book written in 1980, whose author died in 2000, would no longer be protected after the year (a) 2000 (b) 2030 (c) 2050 (d) none of the above

5. Patents are only available for new, useful, non-obvious products or processes. **True or False?**

6. Which of the following is not a property right? (a) use (b) possession (c) alienation (d) all of the above are property rights

THINK CRITICALLY ABOUT EVIDENCE

Study the situation, answer the questions, and then prepare arguments to support your answers.

7. Stephanie wrote an epic poem about teenage life for her English class. The idea was so novel that her teacher urged her to read it at a school assembly. Stephanie did so. Later, she noticed that large sections of the poem were being published on several web sites. Did Stephanie have the right to stop such publications?

8. Mary developed a hair dye, from natural ingredients, that could be washed with hot water without changing the color. She took the dye to a chemist who said that most chemists were

aware of the dye's properties. Which approach is most likely to help Mary protect her formula—a patent, copyright, or trade secret?

9. Steven was president of a successful chemical company. He developed a nonpatentable process for making soap better. At first, he treated his process as a secret. Later, however, his pride caused him to disclose the technique to a number of people. When one of these people started a competing business using his process, he sued claiming theft of a trade secret. Will Steven prevail?

16-2 How Property Is Acquired and Held

GOALS

- State the different ways of acquiring property
- Differentiate the various ways of holding ownership to property

KEY TERMS

constructive delivery

accession

lost property

mislaid property

occupancy

severalty

co-ownership

right of partition

joint tenancy

right of survivorship

tenancy in common

tenancy by the entireties

community property

Ways of Acquiring Property

WHAT'S YOUR VERDICT?

On a long trip to an away game, the five starters of the Allenton Tigerettes basketball team were talking about their MP3 players. Andrea bought hers with earnings from her job at a local animal shelter. Bridget received hers as a birthday gift. Caren inherited hers from a very "with-it" aunt who had recently passed away. Darlanda, a computer geek, made her own. Elzeena found hers on the street and, after months of trying, had been unable to find the owner.

Did each of the teammates have the same rights in her MP3 player?

Real or personal property is acquired most commonly by contract, gift, or inheritance. In addition, personal property legitimately may be acquired by accession, intellectual labor, finding, or occupancy. Real property may be acquired by adverse possession, dedication, and eminent domain. (See Chapter 17 to read about these means of acquiring real property.) In *What's Your Verdict?* even though the teammates acquired their MP3 players by a different means, each had the same ownership rights in her MP3 player except Elzeena. She only had the rights of a finder—mainly possession and use.

Acquiring Ownership by Contract

Any kind of property may be acquired and transferred, or bought and sold, by contract. People acquire most of their property by purchasing it.

Acquiring Ownership by Gift

As discussed in Chapter 8, a legally valid and binding gift is composed of three elements: intent, delivery, and acceptance. In particular, the donor must demonstrate two of them. First he or she must show an intent to transfer ownership. Note that a mere promise to make a gift creates no legal obligations. Secondly, the donor must

© GETTY IMAGES/PHOTODISC

Imagine that your parents give you the keys to a car as a graduation gift. What type of delivery are they utilizing?

GLOBAL ISSUES

The Domesday Book

In 1086, King William I of England ordered a survey done of all the lands in his kingdom. William wanted to definitively determine who owned every acre of land in England in order to collect property taxes more efficiently.

The king appointed several commissioners, each of whom conducted their survey in a specific circuit, which was separated into different counties. The commissioners' decisions on ownership were considered as final as the biblical "day of doom." The survey later became known as the Doomsday or Domesday Book.

The survey of land ownership conducted more than 900 years ago still survives today. It is an important source of historical and genealogical information.

deliver the property. Delivery is a shift of physical possession of the property to the new owner, the donee. Often the law allows a symbol of the subject matter of the gift to be substituted in delivery. Thus, the keys to a car or a deed to real property could be used in place of the car or realty itself. This is referred to as **constructive delivery**. Thirdly, the donee must then accept the gift either by not rejecting it within a reasonable time or expressly or impliedly showing acceptance by conduct.

IN THIS CASE Sturgeon Hamilton was diagnosed with a rare form of disease. His doctor told him he would have to be hospitalized immediately and would probably die in 48 to 72 hours. Sturgeon, knowing that he had not made a will, gave away his property to his friends from his hospital bed. He wrote Susie a check for the $34,000 in his banking and savings accounts and gave Tomee the keys to his brand new Jaguar. They thanked him profusely and left. An hour later, as Sturgeon was picking out the wording for his tombstone, his doctor came in and informed him that there had been a mistake at the lab. He really just had the flu and would probably live to be 100. Sturgeon will be able to void the gifts and get his money and car back.

Sometimes a gift is conditional, as when a man gives his fiancée an engagement ring. If the two mutually agree not to get married after all, or if the woman breaks the engagement, the man generally may reclaim the gift. In some states, if the man breaks the engagement the woman is entitled to keep the ring.

Another type of conditional gift is made when a donor expects to die soon. This is referred to as a gift *causa mortis* (in anticipation of death) and is distinguished from other gifts given *inter vivos* (during life). If the donor of a gift *causa mortis* recovers or dies of another cause or simply revokes the gift before death, the gift is not legally valid and may be recovered by the decedent's estate.

Acquiring Ownership by Intellectual Labor

You can acquire personal property rights by original production of intellectual property. As discussed in the preceding lesson, creators may take legal steps to acquire exclusive property rights in such property in the form of patents, copyrights, and the like.

On this sheep farm, by what means does the farmer acquire ownership of the newborn lambs?

Acquiring Ownership by Finding

Anyone who loses property has the right to recover it from any finder. However, one must prove true ownership. When a finder of property knows who the owner is, the finder must return the property or be guilty of theft. Under some laws, a finder must try (for example, by newspaper advertising) to locate the property owner. If the owner is unknown, either the finder or the owner of the place the property was found may keep the property until the true owner appears. Which one has this right depends on whether the property is lost or mislaid.

Finders of lost property and owners of the place where mislaid property is found both acquire possession and use of the property until the true owner is found. **Lost property** is created when the owner does not know when or where it disappeared from the owner's possession. If a $100 bill falls from your pocket as you are pulling out your keys and you don't notice it, the money is lost property.

Mislaid property is placed intentionally somewhere but then forgotten. If you hung your coat

Acquiring Ownership by Inheritance

Personal and real property can be acquired by inheritance. The legal methods involved in such an acquisition are discussed in Chapter 20.

Acquiring Ownership by Accession

Personal property also may be acquired by accession. **Accession** is the right of an owner of property to all that property produces, naturally or artificially, or to a significant *increase* in that property.

Thus, farm crops and the offspring of animals belong to the owner of the land or the animals. When new parts are put into an item of property, they generally become part of the property. For example, if a new hard drive is installed in your computer, it becomes part of the computer. If, by mistake, someone improves another's property, courts seek to do justice by letting the improver keep the property after paying fair value for the original item.

A Question of ETHICS

Jerry was eating at a restaurant near a large theme park. As he got up to pay, Jerry noticed an expensive camera a family of tourists had left behind a few minutes earlier in the booth next to his. What are Jerry's ethical obligations in this situation? What are Jerry's legal duties in this situation?

A salesperson has just lost a huge account, and, in disgust, throws his briefcase into a public waste can. Another person notices this and fishes it out. By what means does the finder acquire ownership of this briefcase?

on a coat rack in a restaurant while you ate, and then walked out without your coat, it would be mislaid. The finder of the coat would be required to turn it over to the restaurant. Because you may come back looking for the coat, this law helps owners find mislaid property.

Generally, the location and situation in which the items are discovered are used to infer whether they are lost or mislaid. Most states have statutes that detail how someone may become the owner of lost or mislaid property upon publication of the find and after a suitable waiting period passes for the true owner to appear.

Acquiring Ownership by Occupancy

Occupancy means acquiring title by taking possession of personal property that belongs to no one else. A common example is personal property that has been abandoned or discarded by the owner. In such a case, the finder who takes possession becomes the owner.

Like discarded or abandoned property, wildlife is considered to belong to no one. A properly licensed person who takes possession of a wild animal on public lands by killing or capturing it becomes the legal owner. Similarly, one may become the owner of sea shells by picking them up on a public beach. However, property on private lands belongs to the owner of the real property and may not be acquired by occupation.

CHECKPOINT Name the three most common means of acquiring property.

How Is Ownership of Property Held?

WHAT'S YOUR VERDICT? Beth and Maureen inherited a 12-acre tract of land from their parents. Beth moved onto the property, and Maureen stayed in her former home. Beth decided Maureen could have the back six acres and she would keep the front six acres.

Can Beth exclude Maureen from part of the tract of land they co-own?

There are two basic ways to own property—in severalty or by co-ownership. In either case, ownership rights are not absolute but limited as discussed below.

Ownership in Severalty

Ownership in **severalty** exists when one person owns all of the personal or real property involved. This is the most common form of ownership for personal property.

Co-Ownership

Co-ownership exists when two or more persons have ownership rights in the same property. Co-ownership may take one of several forms: joint tenancy, tenancy in common, tenancy by the entireties, or community property.

All forms of co-ownership have two attributes in common. The first is that all co-owners have equal rights of possession. Equal rights of possession means that no co-owner can exclude any other co-owner from any physical portion of the property. This is the most basic attribute of co-ownership.

The second attribute common to co-ownership is the right of partition. The **right of partition** allows any co-owner to legally compel the division of the property among the co-owners. Sometimes the partition is physical, as when a co-owned farm is divided into two parcels. Usually partition is financial. For example, a co-owned airplane could be sold and the proceeds of sale divided pro rata among the co-owners.

In *What's Your Verdict?* Beth had no right to exclude Maureen from the front six acres of their tract. They could, however, agree on a division, or ask a court to divide the property.

JOINT TENANCY **Joint tenancy** is the co-ownership of the same property with the *right of survivorship*. Each joint tenant is looked upon by the law as owning all of the subject property. The **right of survivorship** means that if one of the joint owners dies, the remaining owner or owners still retain their ownership right to the whole property. If the right of survivorship conflicts with provisions of a will, the property passes via the right of survivorship, not via the will.

Because the interest in a joint tenancy passes automatically on death, joint tenants often use this form of co-ownership to leave property to the other joint tenant(s). In this way, they do not have to incur the costs and delays of probate.

A joint tenant's interest may be transferred while the joint tenant is alive. However, the transfer would end the joint tenancy. The previous owners and the new co-owner would hold the property as tenants in common.

TENANCY IN COMMON In **tenancy in common** the number of shares owned may be equal or unequal, and there is no right of survivorship. Upon the death of any tenant in common, that person's interest passes to the heirs (relatives entitled to inherit) or to the beneficiaries designated in the will, if there is one. The heirs or beneficiaries then become tenants in common with the other owners. Any number of co-owners may be tenants in common of a particular piece of property. Tenants in common also may transfer their interest at any time without the other owners' consent.

TENANCY BY THE ENTIRETIES Some states also recognize a form of co-ownership between a husband and wife called **tenancy by the entireties**. A tenancy by the entireties can only be entered into by married couples, carries the right of survivorship, and one tenant cannot sell or mortgage the subject property without the spouse's consent. As a consequence, the claims of one spouse's creditors cannot be exercised against property held jointly in this form unless the other spouse consents.

A divorce or separation usually transforms a tenancy by the entirety into a tenancy in common. This exposes the property previously held in tenancy by the entireties to the claims of the creditors of the individual spouses. Both joint tenancy and tenancy by the entireties must be created with special language so the nature of the right of survivorship is communicated adequately.

COMMUNITY PROPERTY In some states, all property acquired by husband and wife during their marriage is presumed to be community property. With **community property**, each spouse owns a one-half interest in such property. Generally, while the spouses are alive, both must consent to disposal of community property. In some states, there is a right of survivorship. In other community property states, the spouse who dies may dispose of his or her half through a will.

Property owned by either spouse at the time of marriage or received as a gift or inheritance during the marriage is separate property. Such property becomes community property only if the owner formally or informally treats it as community property and mixes it with other community assets.

Limitations on Ownership

Ownership rights are not absolute. An owner of property is not permitted to use that property in an unreasonable or unlawful manner that injures another. The government may adopt laws to protect the public health, safety, morals, and general welfare. Such laws may limit the ownership rights and freedom of use.

Thus, a city may require that buildings be maintained at a certain level of livability. Cities or counties also may enact laws that prohibit the keeping of livestock or other animals in certain sections. Governments may regulate the purity of

Some local governments have laws that would prevent a property owner from keeping items such as this on the property. What is your opinion of such laws?

© GETTY IMAGES/PHOTODISC

food and drugs sold to the public. Governments even may destroy private property, such as shipments of canned fish that are infected with deadly botulism.

CHECKPOINT What are the two basic ways to hold property?

TYPES OF CO-OWNERSHIP						
Type of Co-ownership	May any number co-own?	Must interests be equal?	Is consent of co-owners required for sale?	Is there a right of survivorship?	Must co-owners be married?	Can a will replace survivorship?
Tenancy in common	Yes	No	No	No	No	N/A
Joint tenancy	Yes	Yes	No	Yes	No	No
Tenancy by the entireties	No, just 2	Yes	Yes	Yes	Yes	No
Community property	No, just 2	Yes	Yes	Yes*	Yes	In some states

*In some states a deceased spouse's one-half interest in community property passes automatically to the surviving spouse. In other states it can pass via a will to someone other than the surviving spouse; however, if there is no will, it then passes to the surviving spouse.

16-2 Assessment

Xtra!
Study Tools
school.cengage.com/blaw/lawxtra

THINK ABOUT LEGAL CONCEPTS

1. The donee must accept the gift for it to be legally complete. **True or False?**

2. The right of an owner of property to all that property produces or to a significant increase in that property is _ ?_ .

3. A gift of an engagement ring would typically be a (a) gift *causa vivos* (b) gift *causa mortis* (c) gift *inter vivos* (d) none of the above

4. Who has the right to possession of lost property when the true owner cannot be found? (a) the owner of the place where the property is found (b) the finder

5. If you were sailing off the coast of California and left a fishing line streaming behind the boat for three hours, and then you hooked a tuna and reeled it in, under which legal process would you become the owner of the fish? (a) accession (b) gift (c) occupancy (d) intestacy

6. When there is only one owner of property, that person is said to own it in _ ?_.

7. Which form(s) of co-ownership have the right of survivorship? (a) tenancy in common (b) joint tenancy (c) tenancy by the entireties (d) b and c

8. The right of survivorship allows property to pass on an owner's death to co-owners without a will. **True or False?**

9. Which form(s) of co-ownership require that the co-owners be married? (a) tenancy in common (b) joint tenancy (c) tenancy by the entireties (d) b and c

THINK CRITICALLY ABOUT EVIDENCE

Study the situation, answer the questions, and then prepare arguments to support your answers.

10. While on a two-week hiking vacation in Colorado, you (a) find an expensive pair of binoculars beside a trail, (b) pick up a worn pair of ski boots that someone has discarded, and (c) shoot two rabbits you plan to eat for dinner. What property rights have you acquired in each of these goods. Name the method by which you have done so.

11. Yvette gave her nephew, Jake, 100 shares of stock in Gold Stake Oil Co. for his twenty-first birthday. She handed the shares, worth about $2,000, to Jake right after Jake successfully blew out all his candles. Two days later, Gold Stake discovered a large oil field. The value of the stock increased 100 times to $200,000. As a result, Yvette demanded the return of the shares. Must Jake return the stock?

12. Dani worked as a server at Shift's Place, a restaurant and bar. Patrons frequently left things in the bar or cloakroom. Dani was responsible for closing Shift's. Closing required her to clean all the rooms and tables and lock the windows and doors before leaving. In closing, she discovered a full length fur coat in the cloakroom and one diamond earring under a bar stool. The fur coat had a label sewn into it with the name, address, and phone number of Tonya. Who is entitled to possession of the fur coat? The earring? Dani, Shift's, or Tonya?

CONCEPTS IN BRIEF

16-1 Types of Property

1. Property is a group of rights or interests in tangible and intangible things recognized by society and protected by law.

2. Real property is land, including surface and subsurface water and minerals, the airspace above, buildings, and fixtures.

3. Personal property is any intangible or movable tangible property.

4. Intangible personal property includes copyrights, patents, service marks, trademarks, and trade secrets.

16-2 How Property Is Acquired and Held

5. Rights and interests in personal property may be acquired by contract, gift, inheritance, accession, intellectual labor, finding, or occupancy.

6. Rights and interests in real property may be acquired by contract, gift, inheritance, adverse possession, dedication, and eminent domain.

7. The true owner of property is entitled to it over anyone who finds it. However, if the owner is not known, a finder is entitled to possession and use of lost property.

8. The owner of the property on which mislaid property is found is entitled to temporary possession.

9. When one person holds all the ownership rights in a subject property, the person owns it in severalty.

10. Co-ownership may take the form of joint tenancy or tenancy in common. In some states, husband and wife hold property by tenancy by the entireties. In other states, property acquired during marriage is community property.

YOUR LEGAL VOCABULARY

Match each statement with the term that it best defines. Some terms may not be used.

1. An item that is intentionally placed somewhere but then forgotten

2. Co-ownership of property without the right of survivorship

3. Ownership of property by one person alone

4. Right of an owner of property to an increase in the property

5. Exclusive, monopolistic right to make, use, and sell a novel, non-obvious, useful product or process

6. Means of acquiring title by taking possession of personal property that belongs to no one else

7. Exclusive right to produce, sell, copy, or publish the permanent expression of a creative work

8. Rights and interests in land, buildings, and fixtures

9. Co-ownership of property with the right of survivorship available to persons who are not husband and wife

10. Very limited utilization of copyrighted material allowed in certain circumstances

11. Unique word, mark, or symbol that identifies a service of a particular company or person

12. Rights and interests in tangible and intangible things

13. Unique word, mark, or symbol that identifies a product

14. Legal ability of a co-owner to require the physical or financial division of the property among the co-owners

a. accession
b. community property
c. constructive delivery
d. co-ownership
e. copyright
f. fair use
g. infringement
h. intellectual property
i. joint tenancy
j. lost property
k. mislaid property
l. occupancy
m. patent
n. personal property
o. property
p. real property
q. right of partition
r. right of survivorship
s. service mark
t. severalty
u. tenancy by the entireties
v. tenancy in common
w. trademark
x. trade secret

REVIEW LEGAL CONCEPTS

15. Identify items of property you can see in or from your classroom and classify them as real or personal.

16. Write a paragraph about how you would protect an original song you wrote.

17. Explain how the patent office distinguishes patentable and non-patentable inventions.

18. Describe the right of survivorship in joint tenancy.

19. List the various means of acquiring ownership of personal property. Give examples of how you have acquired or might acquire property in each case.

20. Identify and distinguish between the various forms of co-ownership of real property.

WRITE ABOUT LEGAL CONCEPTS

21. Write a paragraph describing tenancy in common.

22. Write a paragraph describing joint tenancy.

23. Write a paragraph describing tenancy by the entireties.

24. **HOT DEBATE** Through court action, relatives now seek to stop Neerow from using his money and goods so wastefully. Should they be allowed to do so?

MAKE ACADEMIC CONNECTIONS

25. **ARCHITECTURE** Research how various structures are attached to the ground so as to be able to determine when they actually become real property. Compare high-rise buildings, houses, mobile homes, yard buildings, fences, and various ground coverings.

THINK CRITICALLY ABOUT EVIDENCE

Study the situation, answer the questions, and then prepare arguments to support your answers.

26. Your mother operates a small lumber business. She owns a tract of land with a stand of trees on it. She cuts down the trees, saws them into construction lumber, and sells the wood to builders. She also is building a house as a business venture. The house is about one-third finished, and one-half of the framing for the walls is completed. Your mother is concerned about her insurance coverage because it covers only personal property. Which parts of her property are real property and which are personal property?

27. Jeff's school has a computer laboratory. Jeff also has a computer at home and decides to copy the school's word processing program for his personal use. The program is copyrighted. Is it legal for Jeff to make a copy for himself? Would it be ethical for Jeff to make a copy if he first obtains permission from the principal?

28. Michael carves and fashions furniture out of cherry wood. One day while walking on what he thought was a part of his forested acreage south of the city, he saw and then cut down a beautiful cherry tree. Later, his neighbor had a survey done of their communal property line and discovered that the cherry tree, which Michael had since fashioned into a magnificent cherry cabinet and sold for $10,000, actually was on his land. She sued Michael. Will the neighbor recover the value of the felled tree (approximately $750) or the value of the cherry cabinet?

29. Kurt and his best friend bought a 1964 Mustang convertible when they were roommates in college and took ownership as joint tenants with the right of survivorship. They have alternated possession by year ever since. When Kurt died his will stated that upon his death all of his personal property should go to his wife. Who owns Kurt's interest in the car?

30. You combine your savings with five friends to buy a large sailboat. What form of ownership makes the most sense for your group?

31. Foxx, Flynn, and Fish had equal shares as tenants in common in a drag racer. Foxx wants to get out of the arrangement. She proposes that she keep the engine as her share of the commonly owned racer. Is she entitled to it?

32. Joseph's aunt sent him $5,000 as a gift. Later, she sent a letter stating that upon her death the money was to be distributed among Joseph and his brothers and sisters. After the aunt died, Joseph kept the money and was sued. Joseph defended himself by claiming that a valid gift of the money occurred before the letter was sent, so the letter is of no legal significance. Is Joseph correct? (*In re Gordon's Will,* 27 N.W.2d 900, Iowa)

33. Betty Dolitsky was in a booth of the safe deposit room of the Dollar Savings Bank when she discovered a $100 bill in an advertising folder that the bank had placed in the booth. She turned the money over to the bank. A year later after the money had not been claimed by its true owner, Betty asked for it. The bank refused. Betty sued. Who prevails? (*Dolitsky v. Dollar Savings Bank,* 119 N.Y.S.2d 65)

34. Hamilton and Johnson were tenants in common of a parcel of land. Hamilton wanted to end the relationship and brought suit for partition of the property. A forced sale of the property would be inconvenient for Johnson and would cause him some loss. Must the court, nevertheless, divide the property? (*Hamilton v. Johnson,* 137 Wash. 92, 241 P. 672)

35. Alejo Lopez was a married man. Without divorcing, he married a second time. He and his second wife, Helen, purchased property and tried to take title as tenants by the entireties. Later Alejo divorced his first wife and then remarried Helen. When he died, a question arose as to whether the property was owned in tenancy by the entireties. Is it? (*Lopez v. Lopez,* 243 A.2d 588, Md.)

36. Bernice Paset went into the Old Orchard Bank to gain access to her safe deposit box. Once inside the vault, she went into an examining booth, which contained a small table and a chair. The chair was partially under the table. When Bernice pulled the chair out she discovered $6,325 in cash on the seat of the chair. Is this property abandoned, lost, or mislaid? Who, between Bernice and the bank, is entitled to possession of the property? (*Paset v. Old Orchard Bank,* 378 N.E.2d 1264)

37. On his wife's birthday, Leopold Cohn wrote, in the presence of his entire family, the following:

    West End, N.J., Sept. 20, 1911

    I give this day to my wife, Sara K. Cohn, as a present for her (46) forty-sixth birthday (500) five hundred shares of American Sumatra Tobacco Company common stock.

    Leopold Cohn

    That writing was immediately delivered to his wife. Six days later, Leopold died. At that time, Leopold owned 7,213 shares but the stock was in the name of and in the possession of his firm, A Cohn & Co., in which he was a partner. Is this a valid gift? (*Matter of Cohn,* 176 N.Y.S. 225)

38. E. I. DuPont de Nemours & Co. (DuPont) developed a new process for production of methanol. Although it had not patented the process, it had taken steps to keep the process secret. In order to implement the discovery, DuPont began construction of a refinery. During the construction process an aircraft was observed circling low above the construction site. When DuPont traced the aircraft by its numbers, they discovered that the occupants were photographers who had taken aerial pictures of the plant for an undisclosed client. DuPont believed the photographs might communicate the nature of its trade secret. Accordingly, it sued the photographers to obtain the identity of their client. DuPont then planned to sue the client for misappropriation of a trade secret. Would DuPont prevail in such a suit against the client? (*DuPont v. Christopher,* 621 F.2d 1012)

39. Roberts had an above-ground swimming pool installed on his land. It was not permanently attached to the realty and could be easily disassembled and moved to another location. Then Roberts received a real estate tax assessment bill with an increased assessed value because of the pool. Roberts sued for a deduction, claiming that the pool was personal property. Will he prevail? (*Roberts v. Assessment Board of Review of the Town of New Windsor,* 84 Misc. 2d 1017, N.Y.)

Case For Legal Thinking

MARCUS V. ROWLEY
695 F2D 1171

FACTS This is an appeal from a suit for copyright infringement. The plaintiff is a public school teacher who owns a registered copyright to a booklet on cake decorating. The defendant, also a public school teacher, incorporated a substantial portion of the copyrighted work into a booklet which she prepared for use in her classes.

Plaintiff, Eloise Toby Marcus was employed by San Diego Unified School District ("District") as a teacher of family and consumer science. Plaintiff wrote a booklet entitled "Cake Decorating Made Easy." Plaintiff's booklet consisted of 35 pages of which 29 were her original creation. Plaintiff properly registered the copyright for "Cake Decorating Made Easy," and 125 copies of the booklet were published.

Defendant, Shirley Rowley ("Rowley"), teaches culinary arts classes in the District. She enrolled in one of plaintiff's cake decorating classes and purchased a copy of plaintiff's book. During the following summer, Rowley prepared a booklet entitled "Cake Decorating Learning Activity Package (LAP)" for use in her culinary arts classes.

Rowley admits copying 11 of the 24 pages in her LAP from plaintiff's booklet. Rowley did not give plaintiff credit for the 11 pages she copied, nor did she acknowledge plaintiff as the copyright owner with respect to the pages. The lower court entered an order in favor of the defendant.

© GETTY IMAGES/PHOTODISC

REASONING In determining whether the use made of a work in any particular case is a fair use, the factors to be considered shall include:

1. the purpose and character of the use, including whether such use is of a commercial nature or is for non-profit educational purposes,
2. the nature of the copyrighted work,
3. the amount and substantiality of the portion used in relation to the copyrighted work as a whole,
4. the effect of the use upon the potential market for or value of the copyrighted work.

The facts that Rowley used the LAP for a nonprofit educational purpose and the LAP was distributed to students at no charge were not disputed. [Also] to be considered with respect to the fair use defense is the effect which the allegedly infringing use had on the potential market for or value of the copyrighted work. Under these circumstances . . . the fact that plaintiff suffered no pecuniary damage as a result of Rowley's copying [also underlies the finding of fair use by the lower court.]

These facts necessarily weigh in Rowley's favor. Nevertheless, a finding of a nonprofit educational purpose does not automatically compel a finding of fair use.

[Another] factor to be considered is the amount and substantiality of the portion used in relation to the copyrighted work as a whole. In this case, almost 50 percent of defendant's LAP was a verbatim copy of plaintiff's booklet and that 50 percent contained virtually all of the substance of defendant's book. This case presents a clear example of both substantial quantitative and qualitative copying.

CONCLUSION The order of the lower court is reversed. Summary judgment is entered for the plaintiff.

PRACTICE JUDGING

1. If only a page had been copied, would this be fair use?

2. If Rowley had given Marcus credit, would this be fair use?

3. If the 11 pages had been copied and credit given, but the plaintiff suffered financial injury, would this judge have concluded that the usage was fair?

Chapter 17
Bailments

17-1 Bailments

17-2 Bailor and Bailee Duties

© GETTY IMAGES/PHOTODISC

HOT DEBATE

The wind picked up as Abrahms turned into the discount store parking lot, as she had many times before. A big storm was approaching, and there were few cars in the huge lot surrounding the store. She pulled into a parking space near the front door of the store and locked her new car. Abrahms had to dodge wind-blown shopping carts that were sailing across the parking lot. She watched a cart hit a nearby car leaving dent marks in it. Forty-five minutes later, Abrahms pushed her full shopping cart out of the store to find the rain had stopped, but the wind was still howling. She put her purchases in the trunk of her car. Then, wanting to avoid stepping in a water puddle, she shoved her cart into the vacant adjacent parking slot rather than putting it in the cart corral some distance off. As she walked towards the driver's door, she saw the pattern of squares where a cart had obviously hit her car. Angrily, she glanced up at the store only to spy in the store window the large sign, yellowed with age: "NOT RESPONSIBLE FOR SHOPPING CART DAMAGE".

WHERE DO YOU STAND?

1. Ethically, who do you believe should be responsible for the damage to Abrahms car? Why?
2. What legal arguments can you make for and against Abrahms being able to recover for the damage from the store?

17-1 Bailments

GOALS

- Discuss the ways in which bailments are created and ended
- Identify common real-life bailments

KEY TERMS

bailment	custody
bailor	common carrier
bailee	demurrage
actual bailment	carrier's lien
constructive bailment	consignment

How Are Bailments Created and Ended?

WHAT'S YOUR VERDICT?

Posighdon was vacationing in Key West, Florida. Late one afternoon, she wanted to get a better view of the sunset. She rented a jet ski from Trident Rentals and rode it out beyond the harbor.

What is the legal relationship between Posighdon and Trident?

IN THIS CASE

Ruden pulled up behind a small flat-bed truck waiting at a stop sign to turn onto a busy road. As the truck accelerated away, a chain saw bounced out off the bed and into the road. Ruden got out, picked it up, and then tried to catch the truck but failed. When she returned home that evening a neighbor saw her lifting the chain saw out of the car and rented it from her for $30 to trim his trees. The bailment was legally enforceable as Ruden had acquired possession of the saw and, therefore, could be a bailor.

If you lend your pen to a friend, borrow a lawnmower from a neighbor, find a $20 bill, or rent a DVD, you become a party to a legal relationship called a bailment. The transaction is neither a sale nor a gift, because the personal property involved does not change ownership. The only change is one of possession. As the law defines it, a **bailment** is the transfer of possession and control of personal property subject to an agreement to return the property or deliver it to a third party. Note that the subject of the bailment can only be personal property. Real property, such as land or buildings, cannot be bailed. Real property is leased under different rules of law which will be discussed in Chapter 18.

The **bailor** is the party who gives up possession of the property. The **bailee** is the party who accepts possession. In *What's Your Verdict?* a bailment

was created between Posighdon and Trident, with Trident being the bailor and Posighdon the bailee. The rental agreement they entered into defined

What would determine if parking your car here was a bailment or a rental of space?

the rights and duties of the parties during the bailment and when and how it would end.

Transfer of Possession and Control

POSSESSION Usually property is bailed by the person who has title to the goods, but property may be bailed by any person in possession. This includes the owner's agent or employee, a finder, or even a thief.

There are two types of bailments. In **actual bailments**, bailees receive actual or constructive delivery of the subject matter of the bailment. *Actual delivery* consists of the transfer of the real possession of the book, car, or other item being bailed. *Constructive delivery* involves the transfer of a symbol of possession and control, such as the keys to a car. When you rent a car, get behind the steering wheel, and drive off, you receive and accept the car in bailment.

Constructive bailments occur when a person already in possession of personal property holds it in such a manner that the law imposes upon him or her a bailee's duty to deliver it to another. A bank holding money in dispute between two litigants would be a constructive bailee.

CONTROL In order for a bailment to arise, both possession and control of the goods must shift from the bailor to the bailee. Disputes often arise over cars left in parking lots. Suppose a car owner drives onto a lot, parks the car, but keeps the key. The owner can later drive the car away without permission of an attendant. The owner gave up possession but not control. In this case there is no bailment. There is a bailment, however, if an attendant takes possession of the car and gives the owner a claim check that must be turned in to get the car back. In this situation both possession and control are given to the bailee.

It is possible for a person to have temporary control of another's personal property yet not have a bailment. This occurs with **custody**. A person hired to guard the paintings in an art museum has custody of the art but is not a bailee. The owners of the art do not give complete control of the art to the guard. They authorize the guard to watch over the goods, but the owners retain control.

Disposition of the Goods

Typically, both bailor and bailee agree that the goods be returned to the bailor. In some bailments, however, the bailor identifies another party to whom the goods must be delivered. In addition, the bailee must return the identical goods absent reasonable wear and tear. The goods also may be modified somewhat, as a result of agreed-upon use, repairs, processing, or aging.

Finally, some goods are fungible. *Fungible* means there is no difference between one unit of the goods and another. A gallon of 87-octane gasoline is the same as, or fungible with, another gallon of 87-octane gasoline. When the subject of the bailment is fungible, the bailee need only return the same number of units of the goods.

Termination of the Bailment

The bailment ends when the time agreed upon by the parties has elapsed, when the agreed purpose has been achieved, or when the parties mutually agree to end it. If no termination time is stated, either party may end the bailment. Thus, the bailor might ask for return of the property. Or the bailee may no longer need the property and return it. If the bailed property is destroyed or damaged so badly that it is not fit for the intended purpose, the bailment ends.

Death, insanity, or bankruptcy of one party can end the relation when the bailee's duties cannot be performed by another, or the bailment is one that may be ended at will. Normally, however, if there is a contractual bailment for a fixed period, death or incapacity does not end the relation. The rights and duties of the deceased are transferred to the personal representative of the deceased's estate.

CHECKPOINT What are the three ways in which bailments are ended?

Common Examples of Bailments

WHAT'S YOUR VERDICT? Werner owned a retail sporting goods store. A supplier, Irresistible Lures, offered Werner a counter card that displayed a new type of fishing lure. Werner agreed to display the card when the sales agent said, "You pay nothing and return any lures not sold. Just deduct 50 percent of each sale for yourself and send the balance to us."

Was Werner a bailee?

The most common examples of bailments include bailments for transport, hire, services, and sale.

Bailments for Transport

A **common carrier** is an enterprise that agrees, for a fee, to transport goods for anyone who applies, provided the goods are lawful and fit for shipment. Although passengers may be transported by common carriers, only their baggage is governed by bailment law.

A common carrier has the right to do the following:

1. Enforce reasonable rules and regulations for the conduct of its business (for example, it may enforce rules stating how goods must be packed)

2. Charge an amount negotiated with the bailor or, if the carrier is regulated by the government, charge the scheduled rate

3. Charge **demurrage**, that is, a fee for use of the transportation vehicle when it is not loaded or unloaded at the agreed time

4. Enforce a **carrier's lien**, that is, retain the goods until charges for transportation and incidental services are paid or, if necessary after an appropriate period of time, sell the goods to recover the charges.

Bailments for Hire

A bailment for hire arises when the bailor, for a fee, provides personal property (such as a car, truck, tool, machine, or other equipment) for use by the bailee. Under the common law the bailee is required to take ordinary care of the bailed item(s). However, most rental contracts modify the duty of care making the bailee strictly liable for damage to the bailed property.

Typically the rental companies ask the bailee to initial those parts of the contract which modify the duty of care. The bailee must abide by the contract, using the property only for the stated purposes and returning it at the agreed time.

Bailments for Services

When a person delivers goods to be serviced, repaired, or made into a finished article, a bailment for services results. For example, the bailor may deliver wool cloth to a tailor to have a suit made.

Or a bailor may deliver clothes to a dry cleaner to be laundered or a watch to a jeweler to be repaired.

If the goods are damaged or destroyed, but the bailee has exercised ordinary care in their protection, the loss falls on the bailor who owns them. Moreover, the bailor must pay for any work done by the bailee before the accident.

Bailments for Sale

Goods may be bailed on consignment by a manufacturer or wholesaler to a retailer for sale by that retailer. In a **consignment**, ownership remains with the manufacturer or wholesaler (the bailor) until the goods are sold. The retailer then takes a certain percentage of the selling price for her or his services. Retailers who display and sell consigned goods (like Werner in *What's Your Verdict?*) are bailees.

A bailment also is created when a merchant sends goods "on approval" to a prospective buyer. In a sale on approval the prospective buyer may use the goods to decide whether to buy them. During this time the prospective buyer is a bailee of the goods.

Ownership shifts if the bailee agrees to buy the goods. At that point the bailment ends. If the bailee rejects the goods, they must be returned. This arrangement is common in merchandising books, cassettes, and compact disks.

CHECKPOINT Name four common examples of bailments.

NETBookmark

Access school.cengage.com/blaw/lawxtra and click on the link for Chapter 17. Read the web page, which is an advertisement for a book about starting an eBay consignment business. Explain the concept behind starting such a business. Which party is the bailee and which is the bailor in such a business? What do you think of the eBay consignment business owner's chance for success in this business? Explain your answer.

school.cengage.com/blaw/lawxtra

THINK ABOUT LEGAL CONCEPTS

1. If you rent a locker at an airport, put your luggage in it, and keep the key to the locker, a bailment of your luggage has been created. **True or False?**

2. If a farmer stores a particular grade of potatoes in a warehouse, the warehouse must return the same potatoes to the farmer. **True or False?**

3. The fees a common carrier receives for use of its vehicle in the event that it is not loaded or unloaded at the agreed upon time is called (a) a waiting fee (b) a carrier's lien (c) demurrage

4. A bailment that is imposed by law in certain situations, such as on the finder of a lost article, is referred to as an actual bailment. **True or False?**

5. In a bailment relationship, the party who accepts possession and control of the property is the (a) bailor (b) bailee

6. A publisher lent one of its authors a computer to use in producing her manuscript. Unfortunately, she suffered a severe personal loss several months into the job and was declared insane. Did the bailment end at that point? **Yes or No?**

7. In a consignment, the retailer is a bailee. **True or False?**

8. In a bailment for services, the person providing the services is strictly liable for any damage to the bailed property until it is returned to the bailor. **True or False?**

THINK CRITICALLY ABOUT EVIDENCE

Study the situation, answer the questions, and then prepare arguments to support your answers.

9. Lorant found a watch on the sidewalk. The watch was not accurate, but Lorant thought it was worth fixing. She took the watch to a jeweler's shop, where she left it for repairs. Were bailments created? If so, who were the parties?

10. Hoping to collect a reward, Moriarity stole a rare breed of dog from the fenced yard of a wealthy lady. He placed the dog in a kennel in another town. Were any bailments created?

11. Vernay found an old portrait of her grandparents that had been damaged from moisture and abrasion. She took the portrait to Stockhelm so that he could restore it. Stockhelm thought the process would take him several months, but before finishing the work, he was killed in an accident. What relationship was created between Vernay and Stockhelm? What effect, if any, did Stockhelm's untimely death have on this relationship?

12. Hanson bought and contracted to have delivered a large industrial stamping machine weighing 11,000 pounds. When a common carrier truck arrived with the machine, it took Hanson a week to locate a crane that could lift the stamping machine off the truck. Is he liable for the rental value of the truck while it waited to be unloaded?

13. Wingate took her chair to a local shop, Just Like New, to be reupholstered. Just Like New finished the work on May 22. It notified Wingate that the chair was ready and placed the reupholstered chair in a locked storage room at the rear of its building. Wingate planned to pick up the chair May 23, but on the night of May 22, someone broke into the storage room and stole some items, including Wingate's chair. What relationship existed between Wingate and Just Like New? Who bears responsibility for the loss? Must Wingate pay for the work already performed by Just Like New?

14. NewMark Co. sent Breggler a postal meter with the understanding that Breggler could try it out for 60 days. If at the end of the 60 days Breggler wanted to keep the postal meter, she was to pay for it. If she was dissatisfied or just decided she did not want it, she was to return it to NewMark before the end of the 60-day period. What relationship was created between NewMark and Breggler during the 60-day period? Who owned the postal meter during the 60-day period?

17-2 Bailor and Bailee Duties

GOALS

- Describe the duties owed by the bailee in a bailment
- State the bailor's duties in a bailment

KEY TERMS

extraordinary bailment

extraordinary care

gratuitous bailment

ordinary care

mutual-benefit bailment

involuntary bailment

minimal care

disclaimer

bailee's liens

Duties Owed by the Bailee in a Bailment

WHAT'S YOUR VERDICT? After taking a sailing class at her university, Patricia borrowed her friend Amy's small sailboat for the afternoon. While out on Lake Stockton with it, a strong wind came up unexpectedly and ripped the sail in two.

What type of bailment have Patricia and Amy created? Is Patricia liable for the damage to the sail?

Both the bailor and the bailee owe various duties at law in order to ensure the success of the bailment. However, most legal issues spring from the care or lack thereof that the bailee gives to the bailed property. When the property is damaged, whether or not the bailee is liable is determined by the type of bailment involved and the degree of care owed as a consequence. In general, there are three levels of care: extraordinary, ordinary, and minimal. In a trial, the burden of showing that the required level of care has been met rests with the bailee.

Duty to Care for the Property

When goods are bailed with common carriers and hotels an **extraordinary bailment** arises. The duty of care required as a result is extraordinary. **Extraordinary care** generally means the bailee will be strictly liable for any damage, loss, or injury to the goods. Thus a common carrier is strictly liable for injury to the bailed goods. The only time such a bailee is not liable is when the loss is caused by an act of war, unforeseeable acts of God, or acts of police.

When only one of the parties benefits from the bailment, a **gratuitous bailment** arises. When the party benefited is the bailee, it is termed a bailment for the sole benefit of the bailee. This applies if you lend your calculator to a classmate without charge. The bailee's duty of care for this type of bailment is extraordinary care.

In *What's Your Verdict?* Patricia is a gratuitous bailee. The bailment is for her sole benefit, so she must exercise extraordinary care. As high winds are not unforeseeable acts of God, she is liable for the damage to the boat. Damage caused by a tornado, however, would have been considered an act of God, and Patricia would not have been held liable.

Ordinary care means that the bailee will be liable if negligent in some way. A **mutual-benefit bailment**, in which consideration is given and received by both bailor and bailee, invokes the duty of ordinary care. Assume that you left your car at a repair shop and paid $27.99 for an oil change. You would receive the benefit of the oil change, and the repair shop would receive the benefit of the $27.99. Mutual-benefit bailments result from contracts, whereas gratuitous

LEGAL *Research*

Research the liability ceilings in your state for hotels, warehouses, common carriers, repair facilities, and other bailees. Are the ceilings reasonable? Would the average bailor know of or consider them in the bailment bargain? Do the limits impede or further the businesses involved?

Which of the six major requirements of contracts is crucial to establishing the relationship between the bailor and the bailee in a mutual-benefit bailments? Use the oil-change example in your answer. (Hint: See Lesson 6-1.)

bailments do not because there is no exchange of consideration.

Minimal care is called for with **involuntary bailments**, which typically arise accidentally and without the consent of the bailee. A finder of a ring, for example, would be an involuntary bailee and be required to take minimal care of the ring and return it to the true owner as appropriate. **Minimal care** generally means that the bailee will only be liable for harm to the bailed property if he or she ignores, wastes, or destroys it. For valuable property, the bailee must make a minimal effort to identify the owner.

A bailment for the sole benefit of a bailor also calls for minimal care. This type of bailment would arise if you agree to use a neighbor's riding lawn mower to mow his yard for him free of charge while he is gone on vacation.

Modification of the Level of Care

There are three common ways to modify the nature of the bailee's duty of care: (1) by legislation, (2) by contract, and (3) by disclaimer.

MODIFICATION BY LEGISLATION An industry may seek to avoid the duty of care established by the common law by lobbying for legislation with a state legislature or regulatory body.

For example, as common carriers, airlines would owe the duty of extraordinary care for passengers' luggage. However, the industry has persuaded the Federal Aviation Administration to adopt a regulation limiting liability for loss, delay, or damage to baggage to a set amount per passenger on U.S. domestic flights.

Laundries and dry-cleaning establishments often have special legislation limiting their duty of care. On the other hand, legislatures may increase the duty or limit the ability of the industry to modify the duty of care.

MODIFICATION BY CONTRACT When the bailor and bailee negotiate a contract, they usually can modify the duty of care. Suppose a large auto manufacturer negotiated with a transportation company to deliver cars to local auto dealers. The parties could agree in the contract that this mutual benefit bailment would create an extraordinary duty of

GLOBAL ISSUES

International Air Carrier Liability

The Warsaw Convention of 1929 governs many aspects of international aviation law. This international agreement was adopted in the United States in 1934. It is the law in more than 120 nations.

The Warsaw Convention determines whether an international air carrier can be held liable for personal injury or death of a passenger. It also determines whether the air carrier is liable for damage to luggage and personal belongings. The Warsaw Convention has been amended several times since 1929.

care for the transportation company. Or, they could agree that the duty would be minimal. The bailee cannot, however, be relieved of liability for willful or deliberate injury to the bailed property.

MODIFICATION BY DISCLAIMER Often merchants attempt to modify the duty of care with a disclaimer. A **disclaimer** is a sign, label, or warning reducing the bailee's duty of care. Thus, a garage may have a sign on the wall stating that it is not liable for loss of items left in a car. A restaurant may have a sign indicating that it is not responsible for loss of coats left on coat racks. A parking lot might have a ticket with small print on it stating that it is not liable for any loss or damage to the car.

Usually disclaimers only become a part of the contract when the bailor is aware of the limitation before the purchase. So a limitation in small print on a claim check or parking ticket is insufficient notice, unless the bailor has read it or was specifically told about the limitation in advance. Courts often find disclaimers to be unenforceable.

Duty to Return the Goods

The bailee is required to return or deliver the bailed property according to the terms of the bailment agreement. A bailee entitled to payment is granted the right under the law to enforce one of several types of **bailee's liens**. These allow the

bailee to retain possession of the goods until paid. If payment is delayed unreasonably, the bailee may sell the property to recover the fee and related costs. Note that, if the bailee gives the property back to the bailor without receiving payment, the bailor loses the right to force the sale of the bailed property to pay the amount due. (See also artisan's lien coverage in Chapter 33.)

CHECKPOINT Name the three levels of care owed bailed goods.

What Duties Are Owed by the Bailor in a Bailment?

Other than those prescribed by a contract or by statute, a bailor generally has duties relating to the condition of the property bailed. These duties depend upon the type of bailment involved.

Mutual-Benefit Bailments

In a mutual-benefit bailment, the bailor's main duty is to provide goods fit for the intended purpose. In addition, a bailor in a mutual-benefit bailment who fails to inform the bailee of defects which reasonably could be discovered is liable for any resulting injuries. Thus, the RV dealer in *What's Your Verdict?* would be liable to Hon's family for any injuries resulting from the failure to warn of the defective oven.

A bailee who has been told about or discovers a defect cannot collect damages if injured because of the defect. The bailee is held to have assumed the risk. This could happen, for example, if a bailee drives a rented truck with defective brakes after being told of the dangerous condition and has an accident.

Bailments for the Sole Benefit of Bailor

Suppose your friend goes on vacation and leaves her dog, house plants, and car with you to take care of as a favor to her. These are gratuitous bailments for the sole benefit of the bailor. The standard of care that the bailee has to maintain is minimal.

In a bailment for the sole benefit of the bailor, before transferring possession the bailor should examine the goods for possible defects. Failure to inform the bailee of known or reasonably discoverable defects or dangerous conditions, such as a vicious dog, makes the bailor liable for any possible resulting injury. Unless otherwise agreed, the bailee may not use the bailed items unless the use is necessary to preserve or maintain them.

Bailments for the Sole Benefit of Bailee

Friends or relatives often borrow equipment and other personal property from one another without charge. These transactions are gratuitous bail-

What kind of bailment is created when you leave your clothes with a dry cleaner? What level of care does the dry-cleaning establishment owe its customers?

ments for the sole benefit of the bailee. As such, they require that the bailee take extraordinary care of the bailed goods. The bailee borrower may use the goods, but only as agreed. Note that the bailor-lender is still obligated to inform the bailee of known defects. The bailor who knows of a loose rung in a ladder, yet says nothing, may be liable for any resulting injuries suffered by the bailee.

CHECKPOINT Name the types of bailments in which a bailor has duties.

17-2 Assessment

Xtra!
Study Tools
school.cengage.com/blaw/lawxtra

THINK ABOUT LEGAL CONCEPTS

1. The level of care a bailee must exercise over the goods is determined by (a) the value of the bailed property (b) whether a bailor is a merchant or not (c) the type of the bailment

2. When both parties benefit from a bailment, it is a mutual-benefit bailment and the bailee's duty of care is ordinary. **True or False?**

3. When the bailment is only for the sole benefit of the bailor, the duty of care is minimal. **True or False?**

4. The bailee in an extraordinary bailment is strictly liable for loss or damage to the bailed goods. **True or False?**

THINK CRITICALLY ABOUT EVIDENCE

Study the situation, answer the questions, and then prepare arguments to support your answers.

5. During the fall harvest, most of the Roman Beauty apples picked at Scott's Orchard were immediately placed in the Kool-Tech Storage Co. warehouse. Scott paid a monthly fee for the storage and informed Kool-Tech that the apples had to be stored at temperatures between 40 and 55 degrees to prevent spoilage. When Scott removed some of the apples three months later, many had begun to rot because Kool-Tech had failed to keep the building at the proper temperature. Who is liable for this loss?

6. Widdington inherited an old 90-foot navy-patrol boat. She delivered it to Ol' Jon Silver's Shipyard, located near the oceanfront. Widdington contracted with Jon Silver for a conversion of the patrol boat into a houseboat for $130,000. After the work was completed, but before Widdington came to get her boat, a tsunami from an undersea earthquake destroyed the shop and all the boats in the immediate vicinity. Is Jon Silver liable for the loss of Widdington's boat? Or must Widdington pay the $130,000?

7. Cararro rented a car and, because it wasn't his, treated it harshly. He gunned the engine while it was still cold, drag raced, and intentionally burned a cigarette hole in the upholstery. When a friend asked why he did it, he said, "The car isn't mine, so who cares? Besides, it's kind of fun. It makes me feel good, and kind of powerful." Is Cararro acting ethically? Why or why not? Is Cararro liable for the damage? Why or why not?

8. Boyd borrowed a lawn edger from her neighbor Enbanks. The edger's circular blade was defective, but Enbanks did not know this. While Boyd was using the edger, the blade snapped. A piece of metal lodged in Boyd's eye, blinding it. Was Enbanks liable for the injury?

9. J. Eric worked in a dry cleaners. While going through some costumes that had been turned in for cleaning, he found an expensive ring in a pocket. He turned the ring over to the shop owner. Shortly thereafter it disappeared even though the shop owner had been keeping it in a locked drawer in his office. The ring's owner has appeared asking for it. Who is liable, and why?

Chapter 17 Assessment

CONCEPTS IN BRIEF

17-1   Bailments

1. In a bailment, one party has possession and control of personal property belonging to another.

2. Every bailment has four characteristics: the subject is tangible personal property; the bailor transfers temporary possession to the bailee; the bailor transfers temporary control to the bailee; the goods must be returned to the bailor or to someone the bailor specifies.

3. A bailment may be terminated by agreement, an act of either party, destruction of the subject matter, or operation of law (such as by death of a party).

4. Common types of bailments are those for transport, for hire, for services, and for sale.

17-2   Bailor and Bailee Duties

5. Bailments created for the benefit of both parties are mutual-benefit bailments. Bailments created for the benefit of only one party are gratuitous bailments. Mutual-benefit bailments arise from contracts because there is an exchange of consideration.

6. In a mutual-benefit bailment, the bailee must exercise ordinary care. In a gratuitous bailment for the sole benefit of the bailee, the bailee must exercise extraordinary care. In a gratuitous bailment for the sole benefit of the bailor or in an involuntary bailment, the bailee need exercise only minimal care.

7. In a mutual-benefit bailment, the bailor is liable for damages caused by known or reasonably discoverable defects in the property unless the bailee has been informed of such defects.

8. A bailee may by law have a bailee's lien in the subject property to assist in the collection of repair or storage fees from the bailor if such are due.

YOUR LEGAL VOCABULARY

Match each statement with the term that it best defines. Some terms may not be used.

1. Party who accepts possession and control of another's personal property

2. Duty of care when the bailment is involuntary

3. Bailment in which a person with possession of personal property acquires or holds it in such a manner or situation that the law imposes upon him or her a bailee's duty to deliver it to another.

4. Allows a bailee to hold goods until paid

5. Enterprise that undertakes, for hire, to transport goods or passengers for anyone who applies

6. Fee for delay in loading or in unloading goods shipped by common carrier

7. Control of another's personal property, under the owner's direction

8. Bailment in which one party receives no benefit

9. Bailment that arises without the consent of the bailee

10. Party who gives up temporary possession and control of personal property

11. The type of bailment formed when a bailor leaves personal property with a hotelkeeper or a common carrier

12. Sign, label, or warning reducing the bailee's duty of care

a. actual bailment
b. bailee
c. bailee's lien
d. bailment
e. bailor
f. carrier's lien
g. common carrier
h. consignment
i. constructive bailment
j. custody
k. demurrage
l. disclaimer
m. extraordinary bailment
n. extraordinary care
o. gratuitous bailment
p. involuntary bailment
q. minimal care
r. mutual-benefit bailment
s. ordinary care

REVIEW LEGAL CONCEPTS

13. Create a factual scenario where property is mislaid.

14. Create a factual scenario where property is lost.

15. Create a factual scenario where the bailee's duty of care is ordinary care.

16. Create a factual scenario where the bailee's duty of care is extraordinary care.

WRITE ABOUT LEGAL CONCEPTS

17. You are headed for the lake pulling your boat. Suddenly your vehicle starts to veer to the right and you realize that your boat trailer tire on that side is going flat. You pull into a station to fix it. You borrow a tire tool from the station owner to take the tire off. As you do not have a spare, you then ask if you can leave the boat in her lot while you go to a nearby garage to have the tire repaired. She says fine. You lock the trailer hitch so that the boat cannot be towed, and then leave. Write a short paragraph about the bailment transaction(s) involved in this scenario.

18. **HOT DEBATE** As Abrahms pulls away from the store, angry and disgusted, the wind drives the cart she has just left into a little old lady using her walker to get to her car. She falls and breaks her hip. A store clerk, who was pushing the lady's cart, has observed Abrahms leaving the cart where she did and gets her plate number. Write a paragraph about who is ethically and legally responsible for the little old lady's injuries.

MAKE ACADEMIC CONNECTIONS

19. **ARCHAEOLOGY** One of the most valuable bailments in history took place when many of the treasures of King Tut were sent to the United States as an exhibit. Other exhibits of priceless artifacts and paintings regularly tour the country. Research the precautions taken against damage and theft, how the pieces are valued, and the type and provider of insurance associated with one such tour. Report your findings to the class.

THINK CRITICALLY ABOUT EVIDENCE

Study the situation, answer the questions, and then prepare arguments to support your answers.

20. Babbitt rented a paint-spraying outfit from Baron. The equipment was in good working condition, and Babbitt knew how to use it properly. However, when Babbitt was shifting position between two buildings, she carelessly sprayed the neighbor's building and the top of the neighbor's car parked below. The neighbor sued Baron. Is Baron liable?

21. Bortez, a sales representative, had a breakfast appointment with a prospective buyer. They were to meet in the restaurant of the Grand Prix Hotel. Bortez left his brief case, which contained almost $30,000 worth of sample watches, with the clerk in the hotel checkroom. The clerk gave him a receipt that stated in fine print: "Not liable for loss or damage from any cause beyond a maximum of $100." Bortez, in a hurry, stuffed the stub into his pocket without reading it. The clerk left his post briefly to go to the restroom. When he returned, the case was gone. Is the Grand Prix liable? If so, for how much?

22. Burg customized and sold new vans and serviced used ones. Jake and Jayne Slinker were trusted employees who had been carefully hired and trained and had worked for Burg for ten years. Jake did metalworking and woodworking; Jayne did upholstering. One holiday weekend, the Slinkers and an accomplice stole three vans and then disappeared. The first van belonged to Adams, who had brought it in to have the engine tuned. The second van belonged to Yates, a friend who had asked Burg if he could leave the van on the lot with a "For Sale" sign. Burg had agreed and did not charge Yates. The third van was a very valuable vehicle, built by Burg, and sold to Mox. Mox had loaned the van

to Burg, free, for display in the latter's exhibit at a Civic Auditorium show scheduled for the following week. What is Burg's liability, if any, to each of the three parties (Adams, Yates, and Mox)?

23. Mineo was a member of the state highway patrol working a stretch of I-44 near Springfield, MO. Late one night he stopped a brown west-bound sedan for not signalling a lane change. In interviewing the driver, Mineo became suspicious due to the driver's inconsistent answers to Mineo's questions. Finally Mineo asked if he could search the vehicle, and the driver consented. Mineo found $500,000 in small, unmarked bills in the trunk. The driver said that she had answered an ad in a Chicago paper wanting individuals to drive cars to Phoenix, and that the property was not hers. A phone call to the number the driver had in her possession was answered, but the party hung up upon Mineo identifying himself. Thereafter, no responsbile party could be reached to claim ownership of the $500,000. Who should retain the $500,000 until the true owner is found?

ANALYZE REAL CASES

24. Plaintiff Wall drove his car into a self-parking lot at O'Hare Airport in Chicago. He entered through an automatic gate and received a ticket bearing the date and time of arrival. He parked, locked the car, and left with the keys. Normally, when ready to depart, he would walk to his car and, using his keys, would enter the car and drive it to the exit. There an attendant would take the ticket and compute and collect the parking fee. This time his car had been stolen. He sued the defendant, Airport Parking Company of Chicago, for damages. Is the defendant liable? (*Wall v. Airport Parking Company of Chicago*, 244 N.E.2d 190, 41 Ill. 2d 506)

25. Mrs. Carter took her fur coat to Reichlin Furriers to be cleaned and stored. She was given a receipt for the coat. On the front of the receipt an employee had written the number "100." On the back of the receipt, the words, "the . . . amount recoverable for loss or damage to this article shall not exceed . . . the depositor's valuation appearing in this receipt . . ." Also on the front of the receipt was a place for the customer's signature, but Mrs. Carter had not signed it. The coat was lost. Is Reichlin liable for its market value of $450 or only for the $100? (*Carter v. Reichlin Furriers*, 386 A.2d 648)

26. A student enrolled in flight school. While 900 feet above the ground on a practice flight in the school's aircraft, the student discovered that the rudder was stuck. As a result the plane crashed into the ground, and the student was seriously injured. Is the school liable to the student for the injury? (*Aircraft Sales and Service v. Gannt*, 52 A.2d 388)

27. Loden shipped a quantity of perishable cucumbers from Yuma, Arizona, to Los Angeles via the Southern Pacific Company Railroad. However, the carrier failed to deliver the goods within the ordinary and usual time. On January 25, a railroad inspector was sent out to check the track structures. The inspector discovered that heavy rainfall had damaged two bridges. Repairs were started on January 26, and the tracks were joined on January 28. The making of these repairs further delayed the shipment of Loden's cucumbers. When the cucumbers finally arrived in Los Angeles on January 29, they were spoiled. Loden sued the railroad for $10,000 in damages. Which party is liable for the damages? (*Southern Pacific Company v. Loden*, 19 Ariz. App. 460, 508 P.2d 347)

28. Armored Car Service, Inc., had its employees pick up at the Miami Springs Junior High School a locked money bag containing $1,511.25. The money was supposed to be deposited in the proper cafeteria fund account at a certain bank. However, the bag was mistakenly delivered to the First National Bank of Miami. First National provided a receipt for the bag but made no record of the bag's handling or disposition. Presumably, the bag was stolen. Armored Car Service indemnified the high school and now seeks to recover its loss from First National. (a) What kind of bailment was created by the mistake? (b) Is the First National Bank of Miami liable as bailee? (*Armored Car Service, Inc. v. First National Bank of Miami*, 114 So. 2d 431)

Case For Legal Thinking

NUMISMATIC ENTERPRISE V. HYATT CORP.
797 F. SUPP. 687

FACTS Mark Teller was a partner with Norman Applebaum in Numismatic Enterprises. The business bought and sold rare coins. The partners traveled to Indianapolis, Indiana, for a convention of coin dealers. They brought a large black briefcase with a double lock on it containing rare coins worth more than $300,000.

When they arrived at the Hyatt Regency Hotel, an employee named Ms. Atkinson took them to the safe deposit room and assigned them a box. Atkinson gave them one of the two keys required to open the box. When this occurred, Teller told Atkinson that he was with the coin show. Then Teller signed a Safe Deposit Record form and Atkinson signed as a witness.

Later, when Teller opened the safe deposit box to retrieve the coins, the box was empty. The partners sued, claiming that Hyatt had breached its duty as a bailee.

REASONING The Indiana statute provides: "A hotel, apartment hotel, or inn, or the proprietor or manager thereof, shall not be liable for the loss of or damage to any merchandise samples or merchandise for sale, whether such loss or damage is occasioned by the negligence of such proprietor or manager or his agents or otherwise, unless the guest or other owner shall have given prior written notice of having brought such merchandise into the hotel and of the value thereof, the receipt of such notice shall have been acknowledged in writing by the proprietor, manager or other agent and in no event shall liability exceed the sum of four hundred dollars ($400.00) unless the manager or proprietor of such hotel, apartment hotel or inn shall have contracted in writing to assume a greater liability."

In the present case, there does not appear to be any dispute that the plaintiffs failed to comply with the statute's requirements. Although it might be argued that the hotel had sufficient notice under the statute as a result of its employee's observation of the coins and her conversation with the plaintiff.

The court found persuasive the defendant's argument that the Safe Deposit Record cannot be construed as sufficient notice under the Indiana Innkeeper's statute. It did not inform the Hyatt Regency of the fact that the plaintiffs were bringing their merchandise into the hotel or the estimated value thereof. Although the Hyatt Regency's agent (Atkinson) signed the Safe Deposit Record, thereby witnessing the Plaintiff's execution of the form (and at least implicitly, the fact that Teller had read the "Rules and Regulations Governing Safe Deposit Boxes"), her signature hardly constitutes a written acknowledgment that the Hotel had received sufficient notice under the statute. Even if Ms. Atkinson's signature could somehow be interpreted as the equivalent of a written acknowledgment that plaintiff Teller was bringing merchandise into the Hotel (on the theory that Teller provided Atkinson and her employer with "notice" of that fact when he (1) told her he was with the coin show, and (2) proceeded to place the partnership inventory in the safe deposit box while in her presence), it would nevertheless fail to constitute a valid acknowledgement. Under the statute, an innkeeper's agent must acknowledge notice which includes a declaration of the value of the guest's merchandise.

CONCLUSION Judgment for Hyatt Corporation

PRACTICE JUDGING

1. If there were not a special statute in Indiana, what duty of care would Hyatt owe?

2. How would this case have been decided if there were not a special statute for innkeepers in Indiana?

3. Which do you think is more fair, this innkeeper's statute or the bailee's usual duty?

© GETTY IMAGES/PHOTODISC

Chapter 18
Ownership and Leasing of Real Property

18-1 Ownership and Transfer of Real Property

18-2 Leasing Real Property

HOT DEBATE

Sally rented an apartment that had been constructed only a month before she moved in. After she had lived there for a week, she discovered the fan in her bathroom didn't work. Because she was knowledgeable about electrical work, Sally made the repair to the fan herself. Then she told her landlord about the problem and her solution. She asked to be compensated for her work at $55 per hour, the going rate for electricians in her community.

WHERE DO YOU STAND?

1. What, if any, are the legal reasons why Sally should be compensated for fixing the fan?
2. What, if any, are the legal reasons why the landlord should not have to compensate Sally for fixing the fan?

18-1 Ownership and Transfer of Real Property

GOALS

- Understand both the rights and limitations associated with ownership of real property
- Identify the forms of ownership and how they are transferred

KEY TERMS

doctrine of capture

easement

restrictive covenant

zoning ordinance

spot zoning

variance

trespass

estate

conveyance

fee simple absolute

deed

adverse possession

eminent domain

Rights and Limitations of Real Property Ownership

WHAT'S YOUR VERDICT? Herbert "Snowy" Bird drove his RV down to the Florida Keys every December and parked it on a lot he owned outside Marathon. In late April, Snowy would drive the RV back up to his home in New Hampshire where he spent the rest of the year. Last year the RV blew its engine 20 miles from Marathon. Snowy had it towed to the lot he owned, where he built a foundation and had the RV bolted to it. He then ran electricity to the RV and plumbed in water and sewer pipes. In April of this year, Snowy flew home leaving the RV in place. In early September Snowy was incensed to receive a real property tax bill not only on his lot but on the RV.

Must Snowy pay real property tax on the RV?

Real property was defined in Chapter 16 as rights and interests in land, buildings, and fixtures. Any piece of personal property that becomes permanently attached to land or a building is called a *fixture.*

For example, if a structure such as a portable tool shed is permanently attached to a foundation set into the land, the structure will be considered a fixture and taxed as real property. If instead the building is merely placed on the foundation but not permanently attached,

it remains personal property. In *What's Your Verdict?* the RV has been transformed into real property by Snowy's actions. As a consequence, he must pay tax on it as such. Items built into the structural members of realty which cannot be removed without permanent harm to the real property, become realty themselves as fixtures.

If the apples in this orchard are harvested each fall, would the apples be considered personal property or real property?

However, items of business property permanently attached to realty, such as a pizza oven bolted to the floor of a restaurant, are considered *trade fixtures*. These fixtures retain their identity as personal property. Finally, crops growing on land typically are considered personal property if they are harvested at least once a year. Crops harvested less frequently are considered realty until they are separated from the land.

Real Property Rights

The number of rights and interests in real property are many and varied. With land, for example, the buyer usually acquires surface rights, rights to the air space above the land and, in most states, the rights to the earth beneath the surface.

SURFACE RIGHTS *Surface rights* include the right to occupy the land, develop it with buildings and fixtures, and even to lay waste to it by destroying its resources such as timber or water.

RIGHTS TO THE AIR SPACE ABOVE THE LAND The air space above the surface of the land is also part of the realty. Ownership of that space is called the *right to air space*. The ownership power, except for the right to exclude aircraft from flying over, extends to the upper atmosphere. If the branch of a neighbor's tree grows into your air space you have the right to force its removal.

While surface rights and the right to air space usually are owned by the same party, occasionally one party owns the surface rights and another has rights in the air space. For example, in large cities, a company may acquire the right to build an aerial walkway between two of its corporate buildings from the owner of the land underneath.

MINERAL RIGHTS Realty also includes the earth beneath the surface. The right to dig or mine that earth is called a *mineral right*. In theory, ownership of mineral rights extends down from the land surface to the center of the earth. Note that in several states, the mineral rights are treated as distinct from the surface rights and may be transferred separately. This is especially true in mineral rich, oil-producing, and mining regions. The extent of the right to extract the resources below the surface, however, varies depending on the physical state of the resource.

SOLID MINERALS Ownership of solid minerals such as coal, iron ore, copper ore, nickel, and

This walkway was constructed by an office building owner to connect the offices to a parking garage belonging to the owner. What rights did the owner have to acquire in order to build it?

uranium usually extends downward from the perimeter of a surface parcel. The owner of the mineral right has the power to remove any mineral located within that area.

FLUIDS Ownership of fluids such as oil (a liquid) and natural gas (a vapor) also usually extends downward from a surface area. However, the **doctrine of capture** grants ownership of these fluid minerals to the party who extracts (or captures) them. Thus, if a person drilled an oil well on a quarter-acre lot and began pumping from a pool of oil that extended beneath a 25-acre area, all the oil could be removed under the doctrine of capture. This is so even though the oil originally was another's property and, because of the pumping, it flowed from one location to another. Note that the well shaft itself may not extend into realty owned by others.

WATER RIGHTS Water on the surface or under the ground is a part of the realty. Control of that water is called a *water right*. Control of water rights is governed by individual states. States use two systems for regulating the use of water. The most-used system grants the water rights to riparians. A *riparian* is someone who owns land abutting a body of water. Thus, ownership of the adjoining land and, in many cases, the land beneath the water, carries with it the right to use the water.

The other system, used by a minority of states, is called the *prior appropriation system.* Prior appropriation does not connect the right to use the water with the adjoining land. Rather, it grants the first party to use the water source priority in subsequent years over other potential users. The amount of the initial use determines the amount of water that may be used in later years.

Limitations on Ownership

Ownership of real property is at the heart of our economic system. However, some limitations on ownership rights are posed by the rights of others in the form of easements, restrictive covenants, zoning, and those who might simply enter upon it.

EASEMENTS Irrevocable rights to some limited use of another's land usually are called **easements**. Easements generally are given for substantial periods of time—for example, for five years, fifty years, or forever. To comply with the Statute of Frauds, easements should be in writing. Easements may be granted to allow a neighbor to drive across your land, for a utility company to bury a sewer pipe or hang power lines, or to make any other use that does not constitute exclusive possession. Easements may be appurtenant, in gross, by necessity, or by prescription.

EASEMENT APPURTENANT When easements are given to neighboring landowners and the easement benefits the neighbor's land, then it is called an *easement appurtenant.* Appurtenant means attached to the land. Thus an easement to drive farm equipment across a neighbor's land in order to farm an otherwise inaccessible parcel would be an easement appurtenant. Easements for access roads or water ditches are easements appurtenant. These easements are generally transferred when the land benefited by the easement is sold.

EASEMENTS IN GROSS Easements that do not benefit neighboring land but benefit a person or business are called *easements in gross.* Examples include access to your property for telephone lines and poles or access that you might give to a non-neighbor. The person benefited generally cannot transfer his or her rights.

EASEMENT BY NECESSITY An owner may sell part of his or her property, and the buyer can only gain access to it by crossing the seller's property, thus the buyer would be granted an easement by necessity. For example, the sale of a mineral right would impliedly transfer a right to the buyer to utilize an appropriate amount of the surface land in its mining operations.

EASEMENT BY PRESCRIPTION If someone makes systematic use of your property for a long period of time, typically 15 to 21 years, then the law will acknowledge an *easement by prescription* arising from the use.

RESTRICTIVE COVENANTS A **restrictive covenant** is a promise usually made in writing by the buyer to the seller. Usually the promise limits the use of the land in some way. For example, the buyer may contract with the seller, promising not to graze sheep on the land. If the buyer who gave the covenant resells, the new owner is bound only if the covenant is the kind that *runs with the land.* This means that the covenant must be intended to pertain to subsequent owners who are on notice of it and must affect the use or title of the property.

ZONING ORDINANCES The owner's use of his or her realty also can be restricted by zoning ordinances. **Zoning ordinances** are adopted by cities or counties to regulate the location of residential, business, and industrial districts. If the zoning reduces the value of the owner's land, the owner would bear the loss and could not recover from the local government for the financial injury.

Zoning is not enforceable if it exceeds the constitutional powers of the government. This occurs when the ordinance is clearly arbitrary, unreasonable, or without substantial relation to the public health, safety, morals, and general welfare. In addition, zoning cannot be used unreasonably to eliminate an existing use. Thus a zoning ordinance restricting use of an area to residential could not be used to eliminate an already existing cemetery. (The cemetery in a residential zone is called a *nonconforming use.*) Recently, however, some courts have begun to allow reasonable zoning ordinances that eliminate existing uses.

Spot zoning is the treatment of a single property in a manner inconsistent with the treatment of similar properties in the area. It is usually prohibited. However, a **variance** may be granted by a city or county to allow a landowner to make some use of his or her land that is inconsistent with the general zoning ordinance. Usually the applicant for a variance must appear before a variance board and establish hardship and lack of injury to others.

DUTIES OWED TO ENTRANTS ON LAND A person who has the right to possess land may owe certain tort duties to others who come on the land. Under the common law, the extent of the duties depends on whether the people are trespassers, licensees, or

invitees. Some courts ignore these distinctions and hold possessors liable if they fail to take reasonable steps to prevent harm to those entering their land.

TRESPASSERS A **trespass** is an unauthorized invasion of the private property or premises of another. Thus, when a neighbor walks upon your land without your consent, the neighbor is a trespasser. The only duty a landowner has to trespassers is to refrain from doing them intentional harm.

LICENSEE A *licensee* is a person whom the possessor of real property has permitted to be on that realty. Social guests and delivery persons are

Why is it a good idea to keep sidewalks free of hazards, such as ice and snow build-up?

examples of licensees. The possessor of realty has the duty to disclose to the licensee any known, non-obvious dangers on the realty and to refrain from doing them intentional harm.

INVITEE An invitee is either a public invitee or a business invitee. A *public invitee* is a member of the public invited by the land's possessor to enter or remain on the land for a public purpose. A *business invitee*, such as a shopper or a moviegoer, is invited on the realty to do business with the possessor. The possessor of realty has the duty to invitees to inspect the premises in a reasonable fashion so as to find dangers and correct them. The possessor also has a duty to warn invitees of dangers on the land of which the possessor should be aware and which are not reasonably discoverable by the invitee.

CHILDREN A person who, on his or her own premises, the premises of another, or in a public place, creates something that may be attractive and dangerous to small children, is required to take effective precautions against their injury. Typically, if children are injured regardless of precautions, it shows that those precautions were inadequate and the creator of the condition is strictly liable.

CHECKPOINT List four potential limitations on the ownership rights of real property.

IN THIS CASE John Elza and his son, JJ, entered a movie theater after the feature had begun. In the darkness, with JJ leading the way, they moved into a row of vacant seats headed for the middle two. Suddenly, JJ slipped on a box of popcorn that the previous crowd had left. His face collided with the seat back in the row ahead. An inch-long split opened under his right eye. John Elza rushed the child to a doctor who stitched up the cut. John Elza then took the child home and returned to the theater to take the names of witnesses to the incident and to the fact of how littered the theater floor was. He then notified the theater of his contention that they owed for his son's treatment and pain and suffering, as he was a business invitee. The theater agreed and its insurer paid. The insurer also required, from that time forward, that the theater clean the aisles after each showing of every movie.

Ownership Forms and Their Transfer

WHAT'S YOUR VERDICT? Susan gave her daughter Emily a deed to a five-acre lot next to her home with the hope that Emily would live there. In the deed, Susan wrote that the property was being deeded on the condition that Emily not keep any livestock on the property. If Emily did so, the ownership of the property would revert to Susan or the current owner of her home. Emily did build a home on the property, and, fifteen years later while Susan was still alive, she also built a stable and kept horses there.

Will Emily lose ownership of the realty because of the horses?

Forms of Real Property Ownership

Ownership of realty usually is acquired by the passage of rights via a purchase, gift, or inheritance. Regardless of how rights to real property are acquired, not all owners necessarily receive the same rights. The number of rights acquired in the transfer is determined by the estate in land that the new owner receives. Each **estate** is comprised of a certain set of these rights and interests. The words used in the deed, will, or lease determine which estate and thereby which rights and interests are transferred. The party who transfers rights and interests in real property is called the *grantor*. The party who receives these rights and interests is called the *grantee*. When an estate is transferred from a grantor to a grantee by deed, the transaction is called a **conveyance**.

The major types of estates in real property are the fee simple absolute, conditional estates, life estates, and non-freehold estates.

FEE SIMPLE ABSOLUTE A **fee simple absolute** is an estate that conveys all ownership rights and interests. If this estate is present, there can be no other estate in the same land as the holder in fee simple has all the possible rights and interests. Almost all buyers of homes and farms and commercial property purchase the fee simple absolute estate.

CONDITIONAL ESTATE A *conditional estate* makes the ownership conditional on some act or event.

For example, ownership may be conveyed to exist only "so long as no alcoholic beverages are served on the premises." Therefore, if beer were served, ownership would shift from the owner of the conditional estate to the grantor who conditionally conveyed the property. Similarly, if a deed made ownership conditional upon not having horses on the property, ownership of the realty would be lost by violating that condition. Thus, in *What's Your Verdict?* Emily would lose ownership of the five-acre lot.

Whenever there is an estate with powers less than fee simple absolute, there must be a second corresponding estate with the remaining powers. In the conditional estates, the second estate is made up of the ownership power retained by the grantor of the conditional estate. This non possessory estate is called a *future interest*. An example of a future interest would be the potential right of Susan to reclaim the property she deeded her daughter in *What's Your Verdict?* if livestock were kept on it.

LIFE ESTATE A *life estate* is ownership only for the length of a specified person's life. The owner of a life estate has the right of possession and exercises all the ownership powers except the right to waste or permanently dispose of the property. The length of the ownership period is generally conditioned on the life of the holder of the life estate but does not have to be. For example, a husband might convey his home "to my wife Julia, for the life of her mother." Julia would own the home only for her mother's lifetime. Upon Julia's mother's death, the property would go back to Julia's husband, or to whomever he specified such as their children.

NON-FREEHOLD ESTATE A *non-freehold estate*, sometimes called a tenancy, involves the transfer of only certain rights and interests (typically possession and use) for a limited period of time. Those who are renting real property own non-freehold estates. The length of ownership is either specified in the rental agreement, indicated by the payment period, or lasts only as long as the landlord desires.

Transfer of Ownership

Ownership of real property is transferred principally by sale, gift, or inheritance. Ownership also can be transferred by adverse possession, by dedication, and by eminent domain. A deed is the primary evidence of the transfer in most of these transactions.

DEED A **deed** is the legal document used to transfer ownership of real property. The two major types of deeds used to convey realty are the quitclaim deed and the warranty deed. The *quitclaim deed* transfers only whatever rights and interests the grantor may have in the real property. This doesn't guarantee that the grantor has any such rights and interests or that the grantee receives anything. A grantee has no legal claim against the grantor based on the quitclaim deed. The *warranty deed*, however, protects the grantee by providing several enforceable grantor's warranties enforceable against the grantor. The principal warranties include the following:

- The grantor has good title to the subject property.
- The grantor has the legal ability to transfer the realty described by the deed.

CyberLAW

You may have heard the phrase "buying swamp land in Florida." That phrase originated with get-rich-quick land deals in the 1920s. In most such transactions people invested in real estate that turned out to be swamp and wilderness land. Today, the Florida swamp land schemes have been replaced with Internet real estate offers. These offers claim you don't need money to start (or even need a real estate brokers' license) to get rich selling real estate. You just need to say yes—and then send money. These land deals typically don't even involve land. What you receive for your money is either a seminar or book on making money. All you learn is that your investment money now belongs to someone else. If such an e-mail offer comes to you, you may want to simply press the Delete key before trying to make quick money through real estate over the Internet.

THINK ABOUT IT

How would you determine if such a potential "good deal" is legitimate?

- There are no undisclosed claims or encumbrances (for example, liens, mortgages, or overdue taxes) against the property.

- The grantee shall have *quiet enjoyment* of the property (no one with superior title will disturb the grantee's possession).

GIFT, SALE, OR INHERITANCE The requirements of an enforceable gift or sale have been discussed elsewhere in the book. The laws of inheritance are discussed in Chapter 20.

ADVERSE POSSESSION In some situations, a person who publicly occupies another's land for a number of years may be treated by the law as the new owner of the realty. Suppose you bought a 600-acre farm and the legal description of its boundary inadvertently included 10 adjoining acres that belonged to an absentee neighbor. If you fenced your farm and included the 10 acres, or otherwise occupied this land for period set by state statute, you could become its owner. This is because of the doctrine of adverse possession.

Adverse possession occurs when you adversely and exclusively possess in an open and notorious way the land of another private person. Possession must be continuous for the statutory period of 5 to 21 years, depending on the law of the state in which the property is located.

- *Adverse* means that the occupation is without the consent of the owner. If an owner said you could occupy the land, either for rent or without charge, you could not become an adverse possessor.

- *Open and notorious* means that the occupation must be visible to the public, including the owners, upon inspection. Erecting fences, planting crops, building barns, and grazing cattle constitute open and notorious occupation.

- *Continuously* means that the occupation is uninterrupted. If a couple occupied your land for two years, then moved away, then returned two years later and occupied it for another six years, they would not satisfy a statutory requirement that the adverse possession occur for seven years.

Many states require the payment of property taxes on the occupied land before adverse possession can be asserted. Some states also require that adverse possessors have a legal basis for concluding that they own the property.

DEDICATION OR EMINENT DOMAIN Dedication typically involves giving real property to a governmental entity, such as a city, for use as a park or roadway. As with any other gift, the dedication is effective only if the government accepts the property.

In contrast with dedication, **eminent domain** is the power of the government to take private property for public use in exchange for the fair market price. If the owner is unwilling to sell at a price that the government thinks is fair, the government can initiate a condemnation proceeding.

A *condemnation proceeding* is a hearing to determine fair compensation for the owner and acquire ownership for the government. If not satisfied with the price offered, the owner may demand a trial by jury to set a just price.

Property taken under eminent domain must be for a public use, such as for highways, airports, parks, or schools. Although previously the use of eminent domain to directly benefit private interests other than railroads and utilities was not allowed, a 2005 decision of the U.S. Supreme Court allowed the power's use to condemn land to build a privately owned mall. This was permitted because the mall was part of the community's economic development plan.

CHECKPOINT Name the four major types of estates in real property.

NETBookmark

Sometimes local governments try to use eminent domain to acquire property they then resell to other private parties for redevelopment projects. Access school.cengage.com/blaw/lawxtra and click on the link for Chapter 18. The Castle Coalition is a group that helps people protect their ownership rights in these situations. What must the government prove in order to acquire property for purposes other than public use? What can you do if you are faced with such a situation?

school.cengage.com/blaw/lawxtra

18-1 Assessment

Xtra!
Study Tools
school.cengage.com/blaw/lawxtra

THINK ABOUT LEGAL CONCEPTS

1. Land is the only component of real estate. **True or False?**

2. The doctrine of _?_ grants ownership of fluid minerals to the party who extracts them.

3. The water in a river is treated by the law as real property. **True or False?**

4. Which of the following does not have the right of possession? (a) fee simple absolute (b) conditional estates (c) future interests

5. The length of a life estate can be measured by the life of anyone the grantor chooses. **True or False?**

6. Which of the following is the most common estate? (a) conditional estate (b) life estate (c) nonfreehold estate (d) fee simple absolute

7. The _?_ deed provides the most protection to grantees.

8. Adverse possession can occur in secret. **True or False?**

9. An estate is a particular bundle of legal rights and interests in real property. **True or False?**

10. Taking by eminent domain only can occur when there is a legitimate public purpose for the taking. **True or False?**

11. Easements appurtenant benefit nearby land. **True or False?**

12. The owner of land owes which of the following duties to a trespasser? (a) to refrain from doing the trespasser intentional harm (b) to warn them of known dangers (c) to conduct reasonable searches for dangers (d) all of the above

THINK CRITICALLY ABOUT EVIDENCE

Study the situation, answer the questions, and then prepare arguments to support your answers.

13. Clarence sold Delbert a parcel of land on which there was a house, a barn, unharvested crops, and a house trailer. The house trailer was on a cement foundation, connected to the city electricity line, and plumbed into the water and sewer systems. Delbert protested when Clarence removed the trailer, and Delbert sues to recover it. Who should prevail, Clarence or Delbert?

14. When oil was discovered on his neighbor's property, Slasher brought in a wildcat drilling company to drill on his. The wildcatters suggested that they drill on a slant so that they would stand a better chance of tapping the same pool of oil as his neighbor. Slant drilling would cause the hole to go directly below his neighbor's land. The wildcatters also stated that, even if they drilled straight down and hit the same pool as his neighbor had, they could pump as much as they wanted from it. Are either of these approaches legal? Why or why not?

15. Atushi conveyed a life estate for his lifetime to his niece, Tomomi, with a quitclaim deed. Three years later Atushi died. What estate is owned by Tomomi after Atushi's death?

16. With a warranty deed, Anistasio conveyed a life estate to his niece, Terresa, for her lifetime. Six months later Terresa died. What estate did Anistasio own during Terresa's lifetime? After Terresa's death?

17. Juan bought a farm and took title with a warranty deed. He then built a fence around the farm. He misjudged the boundary so that his fence ran 25 feet inside the property of his neighbor Swensen. The fence remained in place for 22 years, and Juan paid taxes on all the enclosed realty. Then Swensen died without a will. The statutes of his state specified his brother, Phil, would receive his real property in the event Swenson died without a will. Phil had a surveyor check the boundary of the farm and identified the misplaced fence. Phil then hired a bulldozer operator to level the fence. Juan obtained an injunction to halt this action. He filed suit asking a court to determine who owns the disputed land. Who will win, Juan or Phil?

18-2 Leasing Real Property

GOALS

- Compare the various types of leases
- Explain the rights and duties of landlords and tenants

KEY TERMS

lease
rent
landlord
tenant

leasehold estate
eviction
subletting

What Are the Types of Leases?

WHAT'S YOUR VERDICT? During lunch with several of his business associates, Jason orally agreed to rent Curtis' condo at the Jersey Shore for the month of July. He promised to give Curtis the $15,000 rent on the July 1 when he checked in. In late June Jason was assigned to a new project at work. Realizing that he could not utilize the condo during July, Jason told Curtis he would neither occupy the condo nor pay the rent. Curtis said that he didn't have time to re-rent the condo and that Jason owed him the $15,000. Jason replied that as the contract was orally made it was unenforceable.

Is Jason correct?

A **lease** is an agreement in which one party receives temporary possession and use of another's real property in exchange for rent. **Rent** is the consideration given in return. The lease creates a relationship between the person conveying possession and use of the realty (termed the **landlord** or *lessor*) and the person receiving possession and use (called the **tenant** or *lessee*). (Note that the occupant of real property who has the use but not the exclusive possession of it is termed a *lodger.*) The interest of the tenant is called a leasehold estate. A **leasehold estate** is similar to the other estates in land in that it grants certain rights and interests in the subject property to the tenant.

Most leases constitute a blending of the law of conveyance (that is, transferring rights and interests in realty) and the law of contracts. The conveyance aspect of the transaction is concerned with transferring a leasehold estate to the tenant. The contract aspects relate to the agreements between the parties on such issues as the amount of the rent, who shall repair the realty, and the amount of security or cleaning deposits.

A lease may be oral. However, under the Statute of Frauds in most states, leases that extend for more than one year must be in writing to be enforceable. Even if a writing is not required, it is a good idea to

One important issue for you to consider in renting an apartment might be whether or not you are allowed to keep a pet there. How can you be sure that your pet would be welcome?

© GETTY IMAGES/PHOTODISC

put the important terms of a lease in written form to avoid disputes. In *What's Your Verdict?* Jason is wrong. The oral lease would be enforceable, if its terms could be proven to the satisfaction of a court, as it was for a period of less than a year.

There are four basic types of leasehold estates that can be created. These estates are a periodic tenancy, a tenancy for years, tenancy at sufferance, and a tenancy at will.

Periodic Tenancy

A *periodic tenancy* arises when the leasehold is for a renewable period of time with rent due at stated intervals. Leases that create a periodic tenancy sometimes identify a rental period, such as from "week to week," "month to month," or "year to year." If the lease does not state the period, then the frequency with which rent is paid will be assumed to be the period.

In general, this tenancy continues for the length of the payment period and is automatically renewed unless one party gives adequate notice of termination. If no length of time is set for notice in the lease, then in most states the notice of termination must encompass one full payment period. Thus, where rent is paid on the first of every month and no length of time for notice of termination is set in the lease, a complete payment period, from the first of one month to the first of the next month, must expire between the date of the notice to the termination date.

Tenancy for Years

When a leasehold is for a definite period of time—such as six months, one year, or ninety-nine years—it creates a *tenancy for years*. It has this name even when the period of the lease is less than one year. The feature that distinguishes a tenancy for years from a periodic tenancy is the identification of a date for the ending of the lease. Thus, if a lease states that the rental period is from May 1 to August 15, this is a tenancy for years because August 15 is specified as the ending date. At the end of the lease period, a tenancy for years terminates automatically without a requirement of notice.

Tenancy at Sufferance

Tenants often have a hard time leaving the rented property on or before the day when the lease ends. If a tenant remains in possession after a lease has expired, a *tenancy at sufferance* arises. The tenant is then called a *holdover tenant*.

When there is a tenancy at sufferance, the landlord generally has a choice of remedies. The holdover tenant can be evicted—that is, be forcibly removed from the property by the sheriff. Further, the tenant is liable for reasonable rent for the holdover period. In some states the landlord can collect double or triple rent for the holdover period. If the tenant holds over, the landlord may—as an alternative to eviction—compel the tenant to pay rent for another lease period.

If the holdover tenant pays and the landlord accepts additional rent, a periodic tenancy is generally created for the same period or term as the prior lease. Therefore, if the prior lease were for one year, upon the payment of the rent the old lease would be placed back in effect for an additional year.

IN THIS CASE Anne rented an apartment to Clare, a college freshman. The lease was for a nine-month period from September 1 to May 31, and rent was due in advance every month. Clare paid the rent on May 1 for May. Then she decided she wanted to go to a summer school session which lasted two months. She paid a month's rent on June 1 without disclosing her plans. The payment was accepted by Anne. Clare and Anne initially created a tenancy for years because the termination date was identified. When Clare stayed in the apartment after the end of May, a tenancy at sufferance existed. When Anne accepted the rent in June, Clare ceased being a tenant at sufferance, and both Anne and Clare were bound to a lease for another nine-month period.

Tenancy at Will

If a party possesses land with the owner's permission but without an agreement as to the term of the lease or the amount of the rent, a *tenancy at will* results. Such a leasehold may be terminated at any time by either party with minimal notice.

CHECKPOINT Name the four types of leaseholds.

Rights and Duties of the Tenant and The Landlord

WHAT'S YOUR VERDICT?

Luis was a writer who often wrote for hours at a time. One Sunday, his landlord, Trip, called to ask if he could show Luis' apartment to some prospective tenants in the next few minutes. Luis knew the interruption would cause him to break the flow of his work. Quickly he checked his lease, but there wasn't a term in it that covered the situation.

Can Luis legally deny the landlord's request?

In *What's Your Verdict?* Luis is not legally obligated to allow his landlord to show the apartment to a prospective renter. What would you do if confronted by this situation?

© GETTY IMAGES/PHOTODISC

Tenant's Rights

The tenant in a leasehold has several rights, subject to the terms of the lease. These rights include the rights to the possession and use of the premises and the rights to assign the lease or sublet the premises.

RIGHT OF POSSESSION The tenant has a right to the possession of the real property starting at the time agreed upon in the lease. In addition, unless otherwise provided in the lease, the tenant's possession is to be exclusive of all other persons and is for the duration of the lease. Landlords generally do not have a right to enter leased premises for inspection unless this right is given in the lease.

Luis in *What's Your Verdict?* could legally deny Trip's request to show the apartment to a prospective renter. Even if a landlord is given the right to enter and inspect the leased premises, most states require that the landlord give reasonable advance notice and that the landlord inspect at a reasonable time of the day.

If the landlord deprives the tenant of the possession of the leasehold, an **eviction** has occurred. The tenant may recover damages from the landlord if the eviction is improper.

If, instead of directly depriving the tenant of possession, the landlord disturbs the tenant in the beneficial enjoyment of the leasehold thereby causing the tenant to abandon the premises, a *constructive eviction* has occurred.

For example, if the landlord fails to heat residential premises and this forces the tenant to move out, there has been a constructive eviction. If the lessor fails to keep residential premises in a condition fit for human habitation for other reasons, perhaps because of infestation by insects or rodents, this also could amount to a constructive eviction if the tenant leaves the premises because of such condition.

Upon being constructively evicted, the tenant may sue for the expenses incurred to include

GLOBAL ISSUES

In Mexico, a tenant who has been leasing real property for more than five years has preferential rights to the property if the owner decides to sell. What would be the impact of such a law in this country on the length of leases, the ability to sell real property, and the mobility of the population?

moving expenses and the increased cost of renting equivalent premises, if necessary.

RIGHT TO USE THE PROPERTY The tenant is allowed to use the leased property in the manner specified in the lease. If a particular use is not mentioned in the lease, the tenant may use the property for any purpose for which it is designed or customarily used.

RIGHT TO ASSIGN THE LEASE OR TO SUBLET THE PREMISES Unless restricted by the terms of the lease, a tenant may assign the lease or may sublet the premises. An assignment of a lease takes place when the tenant transfers his or her entire interest in the lease to a third person. Although the new tenant becomes liable to the landlord for the rent and performance of other conditions of the lease, the original tenant also remains liable should the assignee not pay.

Subletting occurs when the tenant does either of the following:

■ leases all of the property to a third person for a period of time that is less than that remaining on the lease, or

■ leases part of the property to a third person for part or all of the term remaining.

When the property is sublet, the original tenant continues to be directly liable to the landlord for performance of the lease. Leases often require the landlord's prior approval of assignment or subletting. However, courts have held that, regardless of a lease's provisions to the contrary, the landlord must have a valid reason if approval is withheld.

Tenant's Duties

With rights come duties such as the tenant's duties to pay rent, take care of the property, and be responsible for torts that occur on the property.

DUTY TO PAY RENT A tenant's most important duty is to pay the agreed-upon rent when it is due. Although rent usually is expressed as a fixed sum of money, it may consist of a share of the crops of a farm or a percentage of the profits of a business. The tenant may be evicted for failure to pay rent.

Before leasing property in a tenancy for years or a periodic tenancy from month to month, landlords sometimes require the payment of the first and last months' rent. Thus, if the tenant fails to make prompt payment for the next period's rent, the landlord can use the prepaid last month's rent to cover the lost rent for the month during which legal steps are taken to evict the tenant. In residential rentals, a "cleaning" or "security" deposit is almost always required as well. The amount of this deposit should be refunded at the end of the lease period if the property is left as clean and undamaged as it was when first occupied, less ordinary wear and tear.

DUTY TO TAKE CARE OF THE PROPERTY A tenant owes a duty of reasonable care to return the property in substantially the same condition it was in when the lease began. This ordinarily includes responsibility for making all minor repairs. The tenant is not liable for wear and tear caused by ordinary use. However, the tenant is liable for the destruction, damaging of, or substantial deterioration in value of the estate due to the tenant's unreasonable conduct. This is referred to as *wasting* the estate.

In some states by statute, and sometimes based on the lease, landlords make all repairs. This can include even minor repairs such as replacing faucet washers and electric fuses. The tenant normally is under no obligation—in fact, has no right—to make major structural changes or to make improvements without the consent of the landlord. For example, if the roof leaks, the necessary repair is the responsibility of the landlord.

However, the tenant is expected to act reasonably and to take appropriate steps to prevent avoidable damage until the landlord has been notified and can make needed repairs. The tenant also is obligated to notify the landlord when

A Question of ETHICS

Lynn rented a house from Bouvier. One January, when nighttime temperatures were dropping near zero, the furnace stopped working. Bouvier told Lynn that, because the furnace was so old, it would take two weeks until a replacement part could be obtained. Lynn tried to stay in the house but finally had to move into a motel with some of her possessions until the furnace was fixed. What ethical and legal obligations do Lynn and Bouvier have as a result of the situation?

major repairs are needed. In a few states, the tenant may apply up to a full month's rent toward essential repairs if the landlord does not make the repairs after reasonable notice.

RESPONSIBILITY FOR TORTS A business or residential tenant in possession of leased property has a duty of care to those who enter the property. An injury to a licensee or invitee caused by a tenant's negligence is the responsibility of the tenant in the areas under the tenant's control. The tenant even may be held liable if the landlord had the responsibility under the lease to make repairs, which, if they had been made, would have avoided the injury. A tenant can buy liability insurance to protect against loss from injury claims.

In the majority of states, lessees assume liability for injuries to themselves and to others (torts) that occur on the leased property. An exception to this rule exists when the landlord knows the defective condition but does not disclose it to the tenant, and the tenant would not be able to identify the problem after a reasonable inspection. The landlord is also liable for injuries occurring in common or public areas of the property. Common areas are those not under the specific control of any one tenant. Public areas include common hallways, stairs, elevators, yards, and swimming pools. Thus if a tenant's guest is injured because of a defective diving board in the pool area of an apartment complex, the landlord is likely to be liable.

Landlord's Rights

Generally, the rights of landlords find their complements in the corresponding duties of the tenant. The landlord's primary right is to receive the rent agreed upon in the lease. If the tenant fails to pay the rent, the landlord may take legal action to recover the rent and evict the tenant.

If a tenant vacates the property before the end of the lease, that tenant remains liable for the unpaid rent. In some states, the tenant is liable for the rent even if the landlord allows the property to remain empty. Most states, however, require that the landlord mitigate the damages by making a good-faith effort to rerent the property. If the property still cannot be rerented, the original tenant is liable for the rent remaining on the lease. If it is rerented, but at a lower rental amount, the original tenant is liable for the difference.

If the tenant fails to pay rent and remains in possession, the landlord may sue to evict the tenant. The landlord may include the claim for overdue rent in the same suit. However, the landlord may not take the law into his or her own hands, personally evicting the tenant and placing the tenant's belongings on the sidewalk. If the tenant refuses to leave the premises, a court order directing the sheriff or other official to evict the tenant must be obtained.

At the end of the lease term, the lessor also has the right to regain possession of the real property. If a tenant has added fixtures to the realty, they belong to the landlord. This general rule does not apply to trade fixtures added by business tenants.

Landlord's Duties

DUTY TO PROVIDE HABITABLE PREMISES The landlord's duties tend to complement the tenant's rights and reasonable expectations. These duties emphasize the providing and maintaining of habitable premises for the tenant. In addition, when a number of tenants rent portions of a building, the landlord is responsible for all the

Who is liable for injuries that occur in a public area of an apartment complex?

IMAGESOURCEPINK/JUPITERIMAGES

upkeep of the exterior and the public, or common, areas.

One who is injured because of the faulty condition of common areas could bring suit for damages against the landlord. In addition, a landlord may be held liable for injuries that result from defective conditions in the property in the tenant's exclusive possession if the conditions are concealed or are not readily apparent.

DUTY TO CONFORM TO GOVERNMENTAL REQUIREMENTS A landlord is required to provide residential property in a condition fit for human living. This sometimes is enforced by the courts in the form of an implied warranty of habitability. In other instances and especially in many large cities, the law—in the form of a *housing code*—may prescribe in detail the required condition of such properties. A representative city housing code makes provisions such as these:

- There should be no exposed electrical wiring.

- The roof should not leak.

- Every ceiling and wall should be smooth, free of loose plaster and wallpaper, and easily cleanable.

- Outside doors and windows should have tight-fitting screens.

- Every unit should have a private bathroom.

- Gas stoves should be properly vented and connected.

Often, violation of housing codes is a violation of the *warranty of habitability*. If that warranty is violated, the tenant may recover damages, become entitled to a reduction in rent, or terminate the lease.

In addition to conforming to the appropriate codes, the landlord must pay all property taxes and assessments on the leased property. However, long-term leases of commercial property commonly provide that the tenant will pay such taxes and assessments, as well as premiums for fire insurance.

Finally, the federal Fair Housing Act (Title VIII of the Civil Rights Act of 1968) makes it illegal for the lessor, or the lessor's agent, to discriminate on the basis of race, religion, sex, color, national origin, handicap, or family status (including pregnancy). A lessor must allow a handicapped person to pay for reasonable modification to the property on the condition that the property is returned to its original condition at the end of the lease. In addition, lessors may not discriminate against families with children unless the facility falls within the "housing for older persons" exception.

CHECKPOINT Name three rights a tenant has.

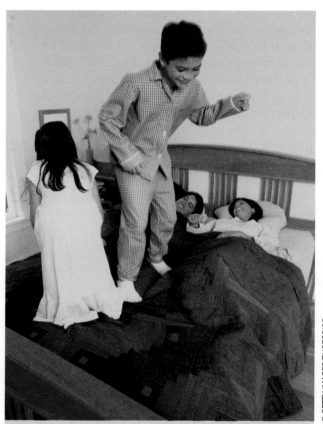

Why might a landlord attempt to discriminate against families with children?

18-2 Assessment

Xtra!
Study Tools
school.cengage.com/blaw/lawxtra

THINK ABOUT LEGAL CONCEPTS

1. Which of the following must be in writing to be enforceable by a court? (a) a lease for a period of two months (b) a lease for a period of six months (c) a lease for a period of one week or less (d) a lease for period of 24 months (e) both c and d

2. If the landlord and tenant do not identify an ending date for the lease, but they do identify a payment period, then the lease is a _?_.

3. If the landlord and tenant identify an ending date for the lease, then the lease is a (a) periodic tenancy (b) tenancy for years (c) tenancy at sufferance (d) tenancy at will

4. If a party possesses land with the owner's permission but without an agreement as to the term of the lease or the amount of the rent, that party has a tenancy _?_.

5. The landlord does not have the right to enter the premises even if the lease grants him or her that right. **True or False?**

6. If a tenant transfers her interest in the lease for all but the last month, which of the following has occurred? (a) subletting of the premises (b) assignment of the lease

7. Which of these is not one of the tenant's duties if a major repair becomes necessary? (a) to notify the landlord of the problem (b) to take reasonable steps to prevent avoidable damage (c) to make the necessary repairs

8. The lessor is responsible for all repairs for (a) common areas (b) the tenant's premises (c) both a and b

9. It is illegal to discriminate on the basis of sex in the rental of housing. **True or False?**

THINK CRITICALLY ABOUT EVIDENCE

Study the situation, answer the questions, and then prepare arguments to support your answers.

10. The written lease on your apartment specifies December 31 of the current year as its termination date. As required, you plan to move out as of December 31 but do not tell the landlord. Two days before the lease expires, while you are packing, your landlord appears and informs you that because you did not give notice of your intent to leave, you owe rent for an additional month. Is the landlord right?

11. Smith rented a furnished apartment from Jerry on a month-to-month basis for $700 per month. At the time Smith first saw the apartment, there was a large tear in the carpet right behind the entryway door. The carpet there often bunched up, and it was easy to trip on if you didn't notice it. On Saturday, Smith was entertaining guests when her boss arrived. The boss rang the doorbell and let herself in when no one answered. She then tripped on the torn rug, fell, and broke her arm. She sued both Smith and Jerry for her medical expenses, lost wages, and pain and suffering. Smith is nearly broke, but Jerry, her landlord, is a multi-millionaire. Is Jerry liable?

12. Buford moved into a high-rise university dormitory building in August in preparation for school to start. During his first month a hot snap with temperatures over 100 degrees at midday and no lower than 80 degrees at night occurred. When the air conditioning broke, Buford discovered that the windows in the building could not be opened. He thought about leaving but instead stayed in the dorm during the two-week period that the air conditioner wasn't working. When his rent was due, he refused to pay more than for two weeks out of the month saying he had been constructively evicted for the other two weeks by the heat and lack of air conditioning. Do you agree? Why or why not?

Chapter 18 Assessment

CONCEPTS IN BRIEF

18-1 Ownership and Transfer of Real Property

1. The rights that may accompany ownership in real property include surface rights, rights to air space, mineral rights, and water rights.

2. Personal property becomes realty when it is intentionally and permanently attached to the realty.

3. The grantee's rights and interests in real property are determined by the type of estate he or she receives. Fee simple absolute is the most common and greatest estate. Other major estates are conditional estates, life estates, non-freehold estates, and future interests.

4. Real property can be transferred by sale, gift, inheritance, adverse possession, dedication, or eminent domain. The transfer usually is evidenced by a quitclaim deed or a warranty deed.

5. The exercise of the rights of ownership of real property can be limited by licenses, easements, restrictive covenants, and zoning.

18-2 Leasing Real Property

6. The four types of leasehold estates are the tenancy for years, the periodic tenancy, the tenancy at will, and the tenancy at sufferance.

7. Generally the tenant is responsible for paying the rent, taking reasonable care of the premises, and using the premises only for the agreed purposes.

8. A tenant may assign the lease or sublet the premises unless there are restrictions on such activities in the lease.

9. The landlord must make major repairs, see that the tenant is not deprived of the possession or use of the leased property, and pay the taxes.

10. A lease may be terminated by expiration of the lease period, by agreement of the parties, or at the option of either party upon material breach by the other. In a periodic tenancy, either party seeking to terminate must give the other party proper notice.

YOUR LEGAL VOCABULARY

Match each statement with the term that it best defines. Some terms may not be used.

1. Greatest possible bundle of rights and interests in realty
2. Irrevocable rights to some limited use of another's land
3. Method of acquiring title to another's land by continuously occupying it in an adverse, open, and notorious fashion for a prescribed period of years
4. Document used to evidence transfer of ownership of real property
5. Power of the government to take private property for public use upon payment of the fair market price
6. Consideration given by a tenant
7. One who, through a lease, transfers to another exclusive possession and control of real property
8. Grants ownership of below-ground fluid minerals to the party that extracts them
9. An agreement that grants certain rights in the subject property to the tenant
10. Tenant's transfer of partial interest in the leasehold to a third person
11. Legal action taken to remove a tenant from possession of the landlord's real property

a. adverse possession
b. conveyance
c. deed
d. doctrine of capture
e. easement
f. eminent domain
g. estate
h. eviction
i. fee simple absolute
j. landlord
k. lease
l. leasehold estate
m. rent
n. restrictive covenant
o. spot zoning
p. subletting
q. tenant
r. trespass
s. variance
t. zoning ordinance

REVIEW LEGAL CONCEPTS

12. Define the differing duties owed by the owner to a trespasser, a licensee, and a business invitee on the owner's real property.

13. Describe the legal features of fee simple absolute.

14. Explain what a future interest is.

15. Describe a situation where tenancy at will is created.

16. Describe a situation where a tenancy at sufferance is created.

17. Describe how the house you own could be rented so that a periodic tenancy would arise.

18. Describe when a lease does not need to be placed in writing yet will still be enforceable in court.

WRITE ABOUT LEGAL CONCEPTS

19. Assume you own a fast-food restaurant with a leasehold in the local mall. Write a paragraph distinguishing the licensees from the business invitees that enter your premises at that location.

20. Write a paragraph describing the parts of a typical apartment complex where the landlord will be liable for injuries to guests.

21. Write a paragraph describing the parts of a typical apartment complex where the tenants will be liable for injuries to guests.

22. Write a paragraph describing the difference between an apartment at the end of a lease after "normal wear and tear" versus after deterioration because of willful misuse.

23. **HOT DEBATE** Suppose that Sally had instead made emergency repairs to a skylight in the apartment's living room. The skylight had been improperly installed and began leaking during a fierce rainstorm on her furniture and the apartment's rug and hardwood floor. How would your arguments differ for Sally and the landlord?

MAKE ACADEMIC CONNECTIONS

24. **HISTORY** Research the history of the estate in real property known as the "fee tail." Write a report on the conditions that caused it to come into and then go out of use.

THINK CRITICALLY ABOUT EVIDENCE

Study the situation, answer the questions, and then prepare arguments to support your answers.

25. Brand had been squatting on land adjacent to a local river for over three years. She had moved a mobile home onto it, fenced it, and farmed it. Alioto offered her $10,000 for it. What type of deed would best suit the transfer of "ownership"?

26. Purcey gave a written easement to her neighbor Pitzer allowing Pitzer to run a water ditch across Purcey's property to irrigate Pitzer's land. Purcey later sold her property to Riddell, who filled in the ditch because, "it's dangerous for my kids." Pitzer sued. Who prevailed?

27. Swit bought a single-family residence and converted it into a halfway house for delinquent teenagers. Neighbors objected to the increased risk of crime in the neighborhood. Then the neighbors filed suit claiming that the residents of the home were not, "a single family," as required by the applicable zoning ordinance. Who prevails, Swit or his neighbors?

28. The city of Westerly maintained an old-fashioned Merry-Go-Round near a beach. All summer both kids and adults would ride it. It was shut down during the winter. Occasionally, kids would climb the fence around the Merry-Go-Round, start the electrical motor, and ride it for free. Shelly, age 12, climbed the fence, started the motor, but had her hand crushed when it was caught between a v-belt and a pulley on the motor. Is the city of Westerly liable to Shelly?

29. Slovin entered into a month-to-month tenancy of an apartment for $450 per month. When he married, his wife moved in with him. The landlord did not discover this until three months later. The landlord told Slovin that he owed an extra $100 per month for the time during which the wife had also occupied the apartment. In addition, he told Slovin that the rent for the next month would be $600. What are Slovin's legal obligations to the landlord?

30. Romero rented a farmhouse under a three-year lease. At the end of the lease, Romero and the landlord walked through the farmhouse to inspect for damage. In an empty upstairs room the landlord found a window that was jammed open. It was obvious that rain and snow had come through the open window and damaged the curtains and carpeting. Who is liable for this damage, Romero or the landlord?

31. Rondale opened a mortgage loan refinancing office for a five-year term in a mall store near the food court. When interest rates rose and the refinancing market disappeared, she assigned the remaining two years on the lease to Constantine. When Constantine's business failed and he defaulted on the rent payments, the mall billed Rondale for them. Is Rondale liable?

ANALYZE REAL CASES

32. W. E. and Jennie Hutton executed a warranty deed conveying their interest in a parcel of land to the local school district. The words of conveyance stated: "This land to be used for school purposes only; otherwise to revert to grantors herein." The property was used for a school for 32 years. Then the property was used by the school district for storage purposes. When this occurred, the heirs of the Huttons filed suit to recover the property from the school district. Who owns the land? (*Mahrenholz v. County Board of School Trustees of Lawrence County,* 417 N.E.2d 138, Illinois)

33. Holmes was engaged in the business of raising and processing chickens. He bought property in Clackamas County, Oregon, on which he planned to erect a chicken-processing plant. To prepare for construction, he spent $33,000 to install a well system, plant special grass, and run soil tests to determine where drain fields for the plant's sewage should be located. Later Clackamas County enacted an ordinance zoning the property Rural Agricultural-Single Family Residential. The zoning prohibited further construction of the chicken-processing plant. Holmes continued work and the county sued. The trial court enjoined defendant from further construction. He appealed. What resulted? (*Clackamas County v. Holmes,* 508 P.2d 190, Oregon)

34. The Wakes operated a cattle ranch in Cassia County, Idaho. During the spring and fall, they drove their cattle over land owned by the Johnsons. Eventually the Wakes sold their cattle ranch to the Nelsons. The new owners continued to use the Johnsons' land as a cattle trail twice a year. This went on for about sixteen years before the Johnsons objected and locked the gates to the cattle trail. The Nelsons sued, claiming an easement by prescription. Is there an easement by prescription here? (*Nelson v. Johnson,* 679 P.2d 662) EOC ch. 21 #32

35. Smith bought two lots along the shore of Lake Pepin and built a cottage, which he mistakenly extended over the boundary line into a third lot, Parcel X8. Smith cleaned all three lots, seeded X8 with grass, and used it in the sporadic and seasonal manner associated with lakeshore property. Burkhardt had a warranty deed to X8 but did not challenge Smith's possession for more than twenty years. Now Smith claims title to X8 by adverse possession. Burkhardt argues that the entire parcel was not actually occupied nor was it usually cultivated. Burkhardt also argues that Smith's possession was not hostile because it was based on a mistaken boundary line and because Smith paid no taxes on X8. Does Smith get title to Parcel X8 by adverse possession? (*Burkhardt v. Smith,* 17 Wis. 2d 132)

36. Wallenberg leased certain property from Boyar in a tenancy from month to month, beginning October 1. The rent was payable in advance on the first of each month. On November 27, Wallenberg left without notifying the landlord. Is Boyar entitled to rent for the month of December? (*Boyar v. Wallenberg,* 132 Misc. 116, 228 N.Y.S. 358)

37. James Kreidel was engaged to be married and planned to attend school. He entered into a lease of an apartment from May 1, 1972, to April 30, 1974. Before the lease period began, Kreidel's engagement was broken. As a student, Kreidel then had no means of support and therefore had no way to pay the rent. On May 19, 1972, he wrote the landlord explaining his situation and stating that he was abandoning the lease. Although the landlord had the opportunity, he did not rerent the apartment until September 1, 1973. Is James liable for the rent from May 1, 1972, to September 1, 1973? (*Sommer v. Kreidel,* 378 A.2d 767, N.J.)

Case For Legal Thinking

CHERBERG V. JOSHUA GREEN CORPORATION, ET AL. 564 P.2D 1137

FACTS The Cherbergs leased a portion of the Lewis Building on Fifth Avenue in downtown Seattle and invested approximately $80,000 in the establishment of a restaurant business at that location. Joshua Green Corporation acquired the Lewis Building in February, subject to the Cherberg lease. In April Peoples National Bank of Washington, the owner of the property abutting the Lewis Building on the south, commenced demolition of the existing buildings on its property for the purpose of constructing a high-rise office tower. The demolition work resulted in the exposure of the south wall of the Lewis Building. It was found to be structurally unsafe and in need of substantial repairs to satisfy requirements of the City of Seattle Building Department. The premises here at issue were located within the Lewis Building but did not abut the south wall.

The lease between the parties required the lessee to make necessary repairs to maintain the premises, excepting the outside walls and other structural components of the building, and reserved to the lessor the use of the roof and outside walls of the building.

Upon learning of the problems with the south wall, the lessor contacted the Cherbergs, indicating that the Green Corporation would probably elect not to repair the wall and that the city might order the building closed. The Cherbergs responded that the lessor was obligated under the lease to make repairs and that they would suffer substantial damage should their tenancy be disrupted. James Cherberg and his wife brought suit claiming the tort of intentional interference with business expectations arising from the willful refusal of the Joshua Green Corporation, their landlord, to perform duties owed them under a commercial lease.

The trial court, at the conclusion of testimony, instructed the jury that Green Corporation was liable for damages caused by the failure to repair the outside wall. It further instructed the jury with regard to the elements of the tort of intentional interference with business expectations that, if the jury concluded that the defendant's actions were willful, damages for mental suffering, inconvenience, and discomfort would be compensable. The jury made a special finding of willful action and returned a verdict of $42,000. The defendant then appealed.

REASONING The first issue is the rights and duties of the parties with regard to the unsafe condition of the south wall of the building.

A landlord has a duty to maintain, control, and preserve retained portions of the premises subject to a leasehold in a manner rendering the rented premises adequate to the tenant's use. Failure to fulfill this duty results in liability on the part of the lessor for injury caused thereby, and failure to fulfill this duty, by omission to repair, can in a proper case constitute an actionable constructive eviction.

The willful refusal to adequately maintain retained portions of a building so as to allow the tenant to enjoy the beneficial use of the rented portion of the building is a breach of an implied duty owed by the landlord to the tenant under Washington law. On these facts, this breach of duty was sufficient to constitute an actionable constructive eviction and provides a basis for the conclusion that the landlord was liable for any damages stemming from that breach.

CONCLUSION The judgment in favor of the Cherbergs is upheld. It is so ordered.

PRACTICE JUDGING

1. Can the lease create a duty to repair, which differs from the duty presumed by the law?

2. Who had the duty to maintain the interior of the restaurant, the lessor or lessee? If the lessor had not retained control over the exterior walls, would the court have ruled differently?

Chapter 19
Insurance Law

19-1 Insurance Fundamentals

19-2 Property and Casualty Insurance

19-3 Life and Social Insurance

HOT DEBATE

You own and run a successful business. You apply for insurance that covers losses due to employee dishonesty. You do so knowing that Joan, one of your managers, has served a prison term for theft. She has had many opportunities to take money from your business, but she has not done so. You decide not to inform the insurance company about Joan's record, as your rates would then be set so high that you would have to fire her to stay in business. Two years after you take out the policy, another employee steals $50,000. The insurance company performs a background check on all your employees. It finds out you knew about but did not report Joan's record and refuses to pay the claim.

© GETTY IMAGES/PHOTODISC

WHERE DO YOU STAND?

1. If you sue to force the insurance company to adhere to the policy, what are the legal reasons supporting your suit?
2. What are the legal reasons in favor of the insurance company?

19-1 Insurance Fundamentals

GOALS

- Discuss the rationale for insurance
- Identify the common types of insurance
- Recognize when an insurable interest is present

KEY TERMS

insurance

indemnify

insurer

insured

beneficiary

policy

premium

risk

insurable interest

Why Have Insurance?

WHAT'S YOUR VERDICT?

Eric has a successful dry-cleaning business. His main competitor is about to be forced to move from its present location to one several miles away due to the sale of the building in which it is located. Eric wants to open another store near the competitor's soon-to-be-closed location. However, he is worried about the risks involved in expanding his business. Eric approaches his insurance agent to take out coverage for any losses he might suffer due to the expansion.

Will the agent be able to sell him a policy that insures against this risk of doing business?

Insurance is a contractual arrangement that protects against loss. One party—usually an insurance company—agrees to pay money to help offset a specified type of loss that might occur to another party. The loss may be the death of a person, property damage from earthquake, or injury resulting from exposure to many other risks.

When one party pays to compensate for such harm, that party is said to **indemnify**, or make good, the loss to the suffering party. The party who agrees to indemnify is called the **insurer**. The party covered or protected is the **insured**. The recipient of the amount to be paid is the **beneficiary**. In some cases, notably under life insurance contracts, the insured will not be the beneficiary.

Insurance makes an important contribution to society. By collecting relatively small premiums from many persons, an insurer builds a fund from which to pay insureds that suffer a covered loss. This process spreads losses among a greater number of people.

The written contract of insurance is called a **policy**. The *face value* of a policy is the stated maximum amount that could be paid if the harm a person is insured against occurs. However, a person who suffers a loss covered by insurance recovers no more than the actual value of the loss, even if this amount is less than the face value of the policy.

The consideration for a contract of insurance is called the **premium**. The potential for loss

What specific risks can you think of that this business owner might want to insure against?

arising from injury to or death of a person or from damage or destruction of property from a specified peril is called the **risk**.

Most risks can be covered by contracting for insurance. Certain risks, however, cannot be. In *What's Your Verdict?* Eric will not be able to find insurance against a business loss. The risk of doing business is too unpredictable and too subject to the control of the would-be insured. If he were insured, Eric could simply neglect the business and still collect on the insurance when the store failed. The best protection against the risk of doing business is found in hard work, good products, and excellent service.

CHECKPOINT What is the purpose of insurance?

Common Types of Insurance

WHAT'S YOUR VERDICT? To raise funds for a trip to the New Year's Day Parade in New Orleans, the Band Boosters planned a fall festival complete with contests and games. Some of the planned events involved a risk of injury to participants and spectators alike.

What kind of insurance would protect the Band Boosters against tortious conduct that might result in injury to individuals at the fundraiser?

There are seven major types of insurance. These are (1) life insurance, (2) fire insurance, (3) casualty insurance, (4) social insurance, (5) marine insurance, (6) inland marine insurance, and (7) fidelity and surety bonding insurance. These types will be discussed in the following paragraphs.

Life Insurance

Insurance that pays the beneficiary a set amount upon the death of a specified person is life insurance. There are three common types of life insurance: term, whole or ordinary, and endowment. In addition, insurance companies have developed combination policies to meet the changing needs of their customers. Life insurance will be discussed further in Lesson 19-3.

TERM INSURANCE *Term insurance* is written for a certain number of years—generally one, five, or ten years. If the insured dies within the policy term, the beneficiary receives the face value of the policy. If the term ends before the insured dies, the contract ends with no further obligation on the insured or the insurer. Term insurance is a relatively inexpensive type of life insurance.

WHOLE LIFE INSURANCE *Whole life insurance,* sometimes called *ordinary* or *straight life insurance,* requires the insured to pay premiums for as long as the insured lives or until age 100. The premiums remain constant, and a portion of the premium goes into a savings program against which the insured can borrow at a relatively low interest rate. If the insured dies, the face value less any outstanding loans against it is paid to the beneficiary.

A variation of whole life insurance is *limited pay life*. The policyholder pays higher premiums than under a straight whole life policy but over a shorter period of time (usually 10, 20, or 30 years). The beneficiary receives the face value of the policy when the insured dies, whether the death occurs during the period when premiums are being paid or after all payments have been made. Limited pay life has the advantage of enabling the insureds to pay premiums during their high-earning-power years.

ENDOWMENT LIFE INSURANCE *Endowment life insurance* requires the insurer to pay the beneficiary the policy's face amount if the insured dies within the period of coverage. This period usually extends from the time the policy is taken out for 20 years or until the insured reaches retirement age. If the insured lives to the end of the coverage period, the owner of the policy (usually the insured) is paid or endowed with the face value. Premiums for endowment policies are high. However, this type of policy has been attractive to people who need a large lump sum available at a set point in time. For example, the endowment could be used to buy a retirement home.

Fire Insurance

Insurance that indemnifies for loss or damage due to fire (and usually smoke as well) is *fire insurance.* The typical fire insurance policy coverage may be increased to cover losses due to perils such as rain, hail, earthquake, and windstorm.

Casualty Insurance

Casualty insurance provides coverage for a variety of specific situations in which the intentional, negligent, or accidental acts of others or mere chance may result in loss. Some of the most important types of casualty insurance include the following.

INSURANCE AGAINST CRIMINAL ACTIVITY Such insurance protects against losses resulting from identifiable criminal behavior such as embezzlement, burglary, fraud, theft, robbery, and larceny. In addition, this form of insurance may also protect against the mysterious disappearance of property, that is, when the reason the property disappeared cannot be determined.

AUTOMOBILE INSURANCE This type of insurance indemnifies for losses arising from or connected to the ownership and operation of motor vehicles. This important insurance coverage will be discussed in detail in Lesson 19-2.

LIABILITY INSURANCE Such insurance provides protection against claims of parties who suffer injury or other loss as a result of negligence or other torts committed by the insured. In *What's Your Verdict?* if the Band Boosters were insured under a suitable liability policy, the organization would be protected against tort claims arising from the fundraiser.

DISABILITY, ACCIDENT, OR HEALTH INSURANCE These policies protect the insured from the financial consequences of hospital bills and loss of income stemming from accident or illness.

Social Insurance

Under the provisions of the Social Security Act and related acts, millions of Americans insure themselves against unemployment, disability, poverty, and medical expense problems. This form of insurance is covered in Lesson 19-3.

Marine Insurance

Marine insurance indemnifies for loss of or damage to vessels, cargo, and other property exposed to the perils of the sea. It is perhaps the oldest type of insurance, dating back to ancient times.

Inland Marine Insurance

This type of insurance originally covered personal property only while it was being transported anywhere but on the ocean. Today it covers the property wherever it is located whether in transport or not.

Fidelity and Surety Bonding Insurance

Fidelity insurance provides coverage against financial loss caused by dishonesty. Such dishonest acts include embezzlement or failure of one person to perform a legal obligation to another, such as constructing a building as promised. Contracts of fidelity insurance are often known as surety bonds.

CHECKPOINT Name the seven major types of insurance.

The oldest known marine insurance policy written in English covered the voyage of a ship called the Santa Crux which sailed from Calicut, India, to Lisbon, Portugal, around 1555. What does the existence of marine insurance in ancient and medieval periods suggest about trade in those times?

© GETTY IMAGES/PHOTODISC

What Is an Insurable Interest?

WHAT'S YOUR VERDICT?

While the kids were in their teens, Iris Nelson took out an insurance policy on her husband, Clyde, naming herself as beneficiary. The policy was for a quarter of a million dollars. Now, seven years later, the kids are out of college and leading their own lives, and she and Clyde are divorced. Nonetheless, she has continued paying the premiums on the policy.

If Clyde dies, can she legally collect the $250,000?

A person with contractual capacity can acquire insurance if he or she would suffer loss if the insured property is damaged or destroyed or if the insured person is injured or dies. This potential to sustain loss is referred to as an **insurable interest**.

Insurable Interests in Property

Any person who would suffer a direct and measurable monetary loss if property were damaged or destroyed has an insurable interest in that property. Note, however, for the insurer to be legally obligated to pay, an insurable interest in property must exist not only at the time the insurance is contracted for but at the time of the loss. A person may not insure property, then sell it, and expect to be paid if the property is later damaged or destroyed.

A person need not hold all the property rights (title, possession, use, a security interest, or some future interest) in the insured property in order to have an insurable interest. Just one of these rights would be sufficient. Many individuals may therefore have an insurable interest in the same property at the same time.

IN THIS CASE Mansfield owned a limousine service. He leased the limo from the owner, Regal Motors. Regal Motors had financed the purchase of the limo through a loan from a local bank. Mansfield, Regal, and the bank all have insurable interests in the vehicle.

Insurable Interests in Life

A person has an insurable interest in her or his life. Everyone who meets the insurance company's requirements and is legally competent may acquire a life insurance policy on herself or himself. Would-be beneficiaries seeking to take out a policy on another person's life must demonstrate that there is a reasonable expectation they would suffer direct financial loss if the insured died.

Creditors may insure their debtors, business people may insure their partners or key employees, and husbands and wives may insure one

Could this woman have had an insurable interest in her husband before he died? Why or why not?

another. Courts frequently rule against adult children having insurable interests in their aging parents. Brothers and sisters ordinarily do not have insurable interests in each other.

Unlike property insurance, the insured has to demonstrate only an insurable interest at the time the policy is taken out, not at the time of the death of the person whose life is insured.

Therefore, in *What's Your Verdict?*, Iris could legally collect the $250,000 upon the death of her ex-husband.

CHECKPOINT What is an insurable interest?

19-1 Assessment

THINK ABOUT LEGAL CONCEPTS

1. The party who agrees to indemnify another is termed the (a) insurer (b) insured (c) beneficiary

2. The face value of a policy is always paid whenever the covered loss is sustained. **True or False?**

3. The consideration for a contract of insurance is called the _?_.

4. The risk of any and all financial losses can be covered by insurance. **True or False?**

5. The party taking out the life insurance policy does not have to be the beneficiary nor the party whose life is insured. **True or False?**

6. Which of the following types of insurance covers loss of or damage to property while it is being transported? (a) marine (b) surety (c) fidelity (d) none of the above

7. The three common types of life insurance are term, whole or ordinary, and _?_.

8. _?_ insurance provides coverage for a variety of specific situations in which the intentional, negligent, or accidental acts of others or mere chance may result in loss.

9. An insurable interest in property must exist at the time of loss for a fire insurance policy to pay. **True or False?**

THINK CRITICALLY ABOUT EVIDENCE

Study the situation, answer the questions, and then prepare arguments to support your answers.

10. Bentson's house was covered by an extensive fire insurance policy. One day Bentson had a grease fire in his kitchen. Thanks to the quick response of the fire department, the only damage from the fire itself was to the stove. However, several windows were broken by the fire department and much of the home's furnishings were damaged by water and smoke. Will the fire insurance policy cover these losses?

11. Your grandfather is retired and has taken out a large mortgage against his home to support his lifestyle. Your father, who grew up in the home, wants to take out life insurance on your grandfather to pay off the mortgage rather than let the loan company take the property when your grandfather dies. Can your father do so?

12. Lampson sold Stark a large recreational vehicle for $52,500. However, Lampson forgot to cancel the insurance he held on the vehicle. One

month after Stark bought the recreational vehicle, it was totally destroyed by fire. Shocked by the occurrence, Lampson then remembered the policy and immediately filed a claim for the loss of the recreational vehicle with his insurance company. Will he be able to collect?

13. Buck and Shannon formed a partnership to market a new type of computer memory device that Buck had developed. Shannon, who was in poor health, had all the business contacts that would make the venture a success. Buck worried that she would lose her $250,000 investment if Shannon died. Therefore, Buck insured Shannon's life for $250,000. A year later, Shannon quit the partnership and retired. Regardless, Buck decided to keep the insurance in force. When Shannon died eight months after she retired, Buck sought to collect the $250,000 from the insurance company. Will she be successful?

19-2 Property and Casualty Insurance

GOALS

■ Contrast the various types of property and casualty insurance

■ Recognize the risks covered by automobile insurance

KEY TERMS

property insurance

casualty insurance

exclusions

fire insurance

endorsements

coinsurance

liability insurance

automobile insurance

collision insurance

comprehensive insurance

no-fault insurance

Property and Casualty Insurance

WHAT'S YOUR VERDICT? Worriare noticed that, in the last hurricane season, several home insurance companies had declared bankruptcy because they could not pay for all the damage claims made against them. As a consequence he fully insured his home on the Florida coast with each of two insurance companies. When Hurricane Jeanne subsequently destroyed his home Worriare tried to collect the full amount of the loss, some $588,000 from both companies.

Is he legally entitled to do so?

The general type of insurance intended to indemnify for harm to the insured's personal or real property brought about by perils such as fire, theft, and windstorm is **property insurance**. The type of insurance that indemnifies for losses resulting from accident, chance, or negligence is **casualty insurance**. There is some overlap between these two. Certain types of casualty insurance (for example, automotive policies) are written to indemnify for both casualty and property losses. Examples of casualty insurance include workers' compensation, disability insurance, and health insurance.

Liability insurance, which protects the insured against other parties' claims of negligence or other tortious conduct, also is a type of casualty insurance.

The purpose of all property and casualty insurance is indemnification for loss. This means that a person who experiences a loss recovers no more than the actual value of the loss. In *What's Your Verdict?* Worriare's total recovery from both insurance companies could not exceed $588,000.

Although property and casualty insurance can be obtained to indemnify for almost any peril that might cause a loss, certain exceptions to coverage relieve the insurance company from paying. These exceptions, known as **exclusions**, are required to be expressly stated in the policy.

What general type of insurance would you need to purchase to protect yourself from damage caused by a tornado?

© GETTY IMAGES/PHOTODISC

Many states make certain that all exclusions are easily noticeable within a policy. States may require that exclusions be set in a different style and larger size of type, in a different color of print, or both. Examples of common exclusions include losses due to war, terrorism, invasion, rebellion, nuclear disaster, depreciation, and pollution.

Fire Insurance

The type of property insurance that covers the direct loss to property resulting from fire, lightning strike, or removal from premises endangered by fire is known as **fire insurance**.

STANDARD FIRE POLICY Generally, any one of the different forms of fire insurance policies will include coverage to protect against the basic risks mentioned above. In most states this basic coverage is specified by law. In addition, each form will have clauses that fulfill the specific needs of the insured. For example, for a residence, the insured may choose between a "homeowner's form" and a "dwelling form." The homeowner's form combines liability coverage with the basic risk coverage to property whereas the dwelling form insures only the property from the basic risks. Businesses and associations may choose between forms tailored to their needs such as shop, mercantile, nursing home, factory, warehouse, church, and like forms.

ENDORSEMENTS TO THE STANDARD FIRE POLICY The standard policy and forms may be modified by **endorsements**, also known as *riders*. Endorsements are attached to the policy and forms to provide for special and individual needs. Endorsements help, for example, in clarifying whether a loss was caused by fire, lightning, wind, explosion, or some other peril.

To illustrate this, suppose that a truck crashes into a building and explodes, causing a fire. In such a case, it would be hard to tell how much of the loss was caused by the impact of the truck, how much by the explosion, and how much by the resulting fire. To avoid this difficulty, a fire insurance policy may be issued with an extended coverage endorsement. This endorsement adds coverage for damage by windstorm, hail, explosion, riot, smoke, aircraft, and vehicles. Therefore, it would not be necessary to determine the exact cause of the damage, because all possible causes would be covered.

PROVING A LOSS SHOULD BE INDEMNIFIED Regardless of the particular form utilized or endorsements added to the standard fire policy, three steps must be taken to prove that a particular loss should be indemnified.

1. The insured must show that there was an actual fire. A glow or a flame is required. Damage to an item resulting from scorching, blistering, or smoke due to being too near to a heat source is not enough.

2. The actual fire has to be hostile. A *hostile fire* is either (a) a fire started by accident, negligence, or a deliberate act uncontrolled by the insured or (b) a *friendly fire* (a fire in its intended place) that becomes uncontrollable.

3. The hostile fire has to be the natural and foreseeable cause of the loss. This cause is referred to as being the proximate cause of the harm. Generally, a hostile fire is

"Wildfire" is the term used to describe any unwanted and unplanned fire burning in a forest, shrub, or grass. Nine out of ten "wildfires" are caused by humans. Explain, then, why most wildfires can be considered hostile.

considered the proximate cause of damage produced not only by the burning, but also produced by scorching, smoke, techniques used in extinguishing the fire, and actions in removing goods endangered by the fire.

As the capability of fire departments to respond to alarms and quickly suppress fires has increased over the years, the number of structures totally lost to fire has decreased markedly. In recognition of this fact and the needs of their insureds to keep premiums low, insurance companies developed coinsurance.

COINSURANCE **Coinsurance** is a clause in a fire insurance policy that requires the insured to maintain coverage equal to a certain percentage of the total current value of the insured property. The coverage amount, therefore, must be increased as the property value increases. In the event of loss, the insurance company will fully indemnify up to the face amount of the policy unless the insured has failed to keep that face amount at the proper level.

Inland Marine Insurance

Modeled after insurance covering goods being transported on the high seas, *inland marine insurance* was developed by fire insurance companies to indemnify for loss to most personal property while it is being transported across land or inland waterways. However, the carrier, such as the automobile, airplane, or railroad car, is not covered by this insurance. In response to the changing needs of insureds over time, the basic inland marine policy was altered to produce a second type, called a *personal property floater.* This was issued to cover any and all of an insured's personal property against practically any peril regardless of the location of the property. The term *floater* means that the protection floats with, or follows, the property.

Rather than have the policy written to cover all the insured's personal property, it also is possible to contract for coverage of scheduled (specifically identified) property, such as jewelry, furs, stamp collections, musical instruments, livestock, athletic

equipment, wedding presents, and computer and photographic equipment. One also can arrange to insure a single piece of personal property, such as an antique vase or a neon sign. Mail-order dealers frequently take out a blanket policy to cover all losses, including breakage and mysterious disappearances of shipped goods. Laundries and dry cleaners may take out policies covering possible losses to customers' property in their possession. Such a policy is known as *bailee insurance.*

Although the application of the personal property floater is quite broad, some losses are excluded from coverage. Examples include losses caused by wear and tear, repair efforts, dampness, temperature, war, confiscation, and dishonesty of a party to whom the goods have been entrusted.

Liability Insurance

Liability insurance is a type of casualty insurance that indemnifies against personal injury or property damage claims for which the insured is legally responsible. Generally, liability coverage is limited to harm accidentally caused by the insured. Intentional infliction of harm by the insured is not covered.

Liability coverage is a major part of most automobile insurance policies. Coverage for liability claims not arising out of the operation of a motor vehicle often is offered as part of a homeowner's or an apartment dweller's insurance policy.

Many persons engaged in providing personal services, such as beauty salon operators, and most businesses usually carry liability insurance.

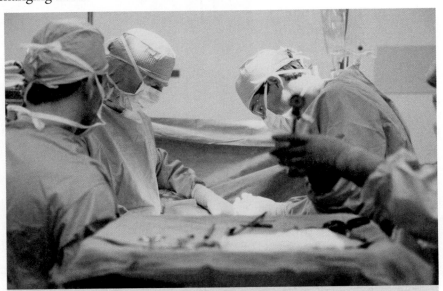

Why would surgeons need to purchase malpractice insurance?

Persons rendering professional services, such as hospital operators and physicians, usually purchase coverage for malpractice through liability insurance. Television and radio broadcasting companies also carry liability insurance to protect against liability for defamation.

CHECKPOINT What general type of insurance indemnifies for losses resulting from accident, chance, or negligence?

Automobile Insurance

WHAT'S YOUR VERDICT? Kim drove to work early in the morning. She had a favorite shortcut across a mall parking lot. One spring morning she was cutting across the mall lot when the sun peeked over one of the large department store buildings. Momentarily blinded, she drove into a concrete pillar supporting a handicapped sign. Kim was uninjured thanks to her seatbelt. The pillar was not damaged but Kim's small sports car was totaled.

What type of insurance would cover Kim for the loss of her vehicle in this situation?

A variety of coverages may be provided by the typical **automobile insurance** policy. These include liability coverage, medical payments coverage, collision and comprehensive coverage, and uninsured and underinsured coverage.

Liability Coverage

An automobile insurance policy's liability coverage obligates the insurer to represent and provide for the insured's defense if the insured is accused of or sued for negligent ownership, maintenance, or use of the motor vehicle. In addition, if necessary, the coverage indemnifies for the payment of damages resulting from such negligence.

Automobile liability insurance coverage may be augmented by an *omnibus clause*. An omnibus clause extends similar coverage to all members of the named insured's household and to any person not in the household who is given permission to drive the insured's car.

NETBookmark

Access school.cengage.com/blaw/lawxtra and click on the link for Chapter 19. Many web sites are available to help you become a wise consumer of automobile insurance. Click on "Auto Insurance Articles" under the Auto Insurance tab on the Insurance.com home page. Read one of the articles. Then prepare a one- to two-minute presentation to the class on what you learned.

school.cengage.com/blaw/lawxtra

Automobile liability insurance usually also provides coverage for the insured and members of the insured's family when such persons are operating non-owned vehicles with the owner's permission. This coverage applies to all borrowed or substitute automobiles. Examples include automobiles used when the car described in the policy has broken down or is being repaired or serviced. Also, if one purchases another automobile to replace the insured car, generally all the coverage under the policy automatically applies to the replacement car for a limited time as specified in the policy.

When one becomes liable for damage or injury while driving a vehicle he or she does not own, the car owner's policy provides the primary coverage. The driver's policy then provides coverage up to its face amount for any excess liability.

Insurers are contractually liable for legitimate claims against their insureds. Therefore, the insurers have the right to settle such claims out of court. This may be done even if their insured does not want to admit fault. In the alternative, the insurers may choose to defend their insureds in court. Because the insurer has potential liability under the policy, only the insurer can make a settlement with claimants against the insured. If the insurer requires the presence of the insured as a witness at any legal hearings, most automobile insurance policies provide for payment of lost wages to the insured.

Liability claims against the insured that the insurer may have to pay include bodily injury or death of third parties and damage to the property of third parties. Third parties are persons other than the insured or insurer and include passengers in the insured's vehicle.

Medical Payments Coverage

Medical payments coverage pays for the reasonable medical claims of occupants of the insured's vehicle who are injured in an automobile accident. An *occupant* is one who is in, upon, entering, or leaving a vehicle. The coverage also applies to the insured and the insured's family members while such persons are driving or riding in another's vehicle. This kind of coverage is mainly for vehicle occupants. However, it also covers the named insured and the family members if a vehicle strikes those persons while walking, riding bikes, roller skating, or sledding.

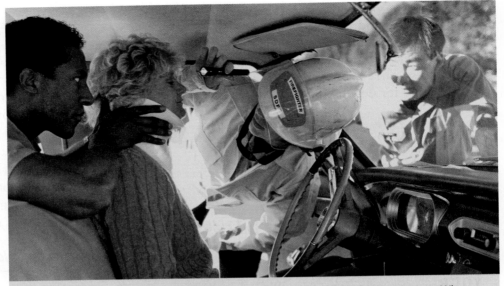

Imagine this woman was driving her sister's car when it collided with another car. What type of insurance would pay for any reasonable medical claims she might have as a result of the accident? Who would need to have this insurance?

IN THIS CASE Spielman was disabled due to the loss of his leg to diabetes. When his car broke down, Spielman borrowed a friend's car. Unfortunately, when he went to hit the brake while approaching a stop sign, he mistakenly hit the accelerator and the car ran the stop sign and hit another. Two occupants of the other car were seriously injured and the other car totaled. The friend's auto policy limit for liability was $100,000. Consequently, the friend's insurance company would have to pay up to that amount. Spielman's auto insurance company would pay everything over that amount up to the limit of his policy. He would be personally responsible for any excess.

Collision and Comprehensive Coverage

Two types of automobile insurance coverage indemnify insureds for damage to their own vehicles. The first, **collision insurance**, protects against direct and accidental damage to the vehicle caused by (a) colliding with another object, such as a tree or bridge abutment, and (b) overturning (upset). Kim in *What's Your Verdict?* would be covered for the loss of her vehicle by collision insurance because she collided with the concrete pillar.

Collision coverage pays only the actual cash value (the cost new minus an allowance for age and use) of the vehicle or its damaged parts less any deductible. Thus, for each loss the insured pays up to the amount of the deductible. The insurer pays the rest up to the policy limit.

The second type of automobile insurance coverage indemnifying insureds for damage to their own vehicles is **comprehensive insurance**. (Sometimes it is called *other than collision insurance*.) Comprehensive insurance indemnifies against all damage to the insured's car except that caused by collision or upset. The causes covered by comprehensive insurance, include fire, theft, water, vandalism, hail, and glass breakage. Theft includes loss of the car and any part of the car, such as hubcaps. However, loss of clothing and other personal property left in the car generally is not covered unless the loss is by fire. Similarly, most policies require extra premiums to cover compact disc players, radios, and stereos. Any damage done to a car, such as broken locks, is covered.

© GETTY IMAGES/PHOTODISC

LAW BRIEF

Vehicular homicide is the causing of the death of a human being by the unlawful and negligent operation of a motor vehicle. Unlike the crime of murder, vehicular homicide does not require intent. Under a typical state statute, the punishment depends on the severity of the incident. First-degree vehicular homicide usually is a felony punishable by five to fifteen years in prison. Such a charge stems from events where a death has been caused by the defendant who unlawfully passed a stopped school bus, left the scene of the accident, was driving under the influence, was trying to flee from a police officer, etc.

Imagine that this car accident victim does not survive the emergency airlift to the hospital. If the driver of the other car had been driving under the influence, what crime will he or she be guilty of, and what would the punishment likely be?

Uninsured and Underinsured Coverage

An accident may be caused by the negligence of a driver who is uninsured and potentially insolvent or one who leaves the scene and cannot be found. In these situations, innocent parties involved in the accident may have to bear their own losses. Certainly their collision and medical payments coverage may help, but significant amounts of loss, for example, lost wages and the medical payments that exceed the limit of their policy, may not be indemnified.

Consequently, many vehicle owners carry a supplemental coverage to their regular policy. This additional coverage, called *uninsured motorists coverage,* allows the insured to collect damages from his or her own insurance company when they are not collectible because the person who caused the harm is uninsured. In most states, the coverage is limited to compensation for bodily injury, death, lost wages or support, and pain and suffering. Indemnification for property damage generally is excluded from this coverage. A similar type of coverage is *underinsured motorists coverage,* which compensates the insured when the negligent driver may be insured but does not have sufficient insurance to cover damages. Like uninsured motorists coverage, underinsured motorists coverage excludes payment for property damage.

No-Fault Insurance

To cut back on the growing number of cases in our court systems, some states have instituted no-fault insurance systems. **No-fault insurance** requires that parties to an automobile accident be indemnified by their own insurance company regardless of who is at fault. Therefore, a court trial to determine who is at fault in an accident may be avoided. The indemnification of the losses by the insurance company takes the place of the damages that might have been awarded. However, if the medical claims of an injured person exceed a set amount or the injuries are permanent, a suit can be brought for all alleged damages, including pain and suffering.

Generally, property damage is not covered at all by a no-fault system. This is because it is not likely that people will sue for the amounts involved. Insurance companies tend to resolve such claims fairly and efficiently without court involvement.

CHECKPOINT What are the six major types of coverage found in a typical automobile insurance policy?

Economic Impact

NO-FAULT INSURANCE

The basic idea behind no-fault insurance was to lower premiums by saving the expenses and delays of court trials. However, today in most of the states that have adopted the idea, no-fault policies actually cost more than regular policies. In a true no-fault system, the driver's insurance company would pay for all their insured's losses in an auto accident up to the policy limits. No state has seen fit to adopt such a system, however. In the 12 states plus the District of Columbia that have no-fault systems at the current time (DC, FL, HI, KS, KY, MA, MI, MN, NJ, NY, ND, PA—note, however, that as of late 2007, Florida is set to repeal its no-fault law unless the legislature acts to extend it), the legislatures only adopted a part of the no-fault concept (called PIP for personal injury protection) into law. Typically these states have retained the right to sue the other driver under certain conditions. These conditions are based on the severity of the accident or the dollar level of the potential loss. As a consequence, liability insurance is mandated in all the no-fault states in addition to the no-fault policy.

THINK CRITICALLY

Why do you think the states did not adopt a pure no-fault system? Why might the automobile insurance costs for consumers be higher in the states that have adopted a partial no-fault system, than in those states that have not?

19-2 Assessment

school.cengage.com/blaw/lawxtra

THINK ABOUT LEGAL CONCEPTS

1. A _?_ clause in a fire insurance policy requires the insured to maintain coverage equal to a certain percentage of the total current value of the insured property.

2. Which of the following is not a common exclusion in a property and casualty policy? (a) loss due to depreciation (b) loss due to pollution (c) loss due to war (d) All of the above are common exclusions.

3. Which of the following is not covered in the standard fire policy? (a) losses due to fire (b) losses due to lightning strikes (c) losses due to inept attorneys (d) none of the above are covered.

4. A friendly fire that becomes uncontrollable is considered a hostile fire for fire insurance purposes. **True or False?**

5. A(n) _?_ clause extends auto insurance coverage to members of the insured's household.

THINK CRITICALLY ABOUT EVIDENCE

Study the situation, answer the questions, and then prepare arguments to support your answers.

6. Carben was involved in an accident with a negligent driver. Carben's medical treatment and property losses totaled more than $53,000. Unfortunately, the other driver was insolvent and carried only the minimum liability coverage of $10,000 as required by the state. What type of coverage in Carben's own auto policy would compensate him for the remaining $43,000?

7. To protect her inventory, Olivet, owner of an appliance store, carried a coinsurance fire policy. The policy required that Olivet carry insurance in the amount of 80 percent of the current inventory value. Late one night, fire totally destroyed the inventory, which was valued at $100,000 when the loss occurred. The face value of Olivet's policy was $80,000. For how much of the $100,000 loss will the insurance company pay?

19-3 Life and Social Insurance

GOALS

■ Explain the purpose of life insurance coverage

■ Recognize the types of social insurance coverage

KEY TERMS

life insurance

grace period

Life Insurance

Life insurance is a contractual arrangement under which an insurer promises to pay an agreed-upon amount of money to a named party upon the death of a particular person. Given the uncertainties of today's fast-paced world, such insurance is crucial to families, businesses, and responsible individuals throughout our society. The insurer of life agrees to pay to a named beneficiary or to the insured's estate the amount stated in the policy, in accordance with the policy provisions.

Exemptions

Life insurance policies typically contain *exemptions* that excuse the insurer from the obligation to pay the death benefit. These exemptions may include death caused by the crash of a private airplane, an act of terrorism, or during military service abroad or at home.

In cases where death occurs under an exemption, the insurer is liable for return of the premiums paid or cash value (less loans against the policy), instead of the proceeds. In *What's Your Verdict?* if an exemption for military service were in Edmonton's uncle's policy, the insurance company legally could not be forced to pay the $100,000.

Incontestability Clause

In addition to exemptions, a life insurance policy usually contains an *incontestability clause.* Such a clause prohibits the insurer from refusing to perform due to misrepresentation or fraud after the policy has been in effect for a specified period of time—usually one or two years. However, if the misrepresentation or fraud involves the age of the insured, the policy is not voided regardless of the length of time it has been in effect. Instead the insurer provides the face amount of insurance that the premium would have bought if the insured's correct age had been known.

Why might a life insurance policy contain an exemption for a policyholder's death due to the crash of a private airplane?

© GETTY IMAGES/PHOTODISC

A similar clause denies the insurer the right to contest paying the death benefit if the insured commits suicide after one or two years from the date the policy was issued. If the suicide occurs before the one- or two-year limit, the insurer is required to return only the premiums paid.

Grace Period

By statute, most life insurance contracts must also provide for a period of time, called the **grace period**, during which an overdue premium can be paid to keep the policy in force. Typically, this period is one month. If an insured fails to pay the premium before the grace period expires, the policy terminates, or lapses. A policyholder in good health who pays the back premiums can revive or reinstate a lapsed policy.

Additional Coverages

In addition to these common provisions, it is possible to pay for other favorable clauses to be written into a life insurance policy. For example, for an extra premium, a *double indemnity* provision can be written into a policy. Such a provision requires the insurer to pay twice the face amount of the policy if the death of the insured is accidental. Triple or quadruple indemnity also may be purchased, if desired. These indemnities usually excludes certain causes of death, such as suicide, illness or disease, wartime military service, certain airplane accidents and will not apply to an insured after a certain age, such as 65 or 70.

Another beneficial provision that can be added to a policy is disability coverage. It provides for protection against the effects of total permanent disability by cancelling the requirement for payment of policy premiums while the insured is totally disabled. It often provides money to replace lost wages.

CHECKPOINT To whom is a life insurance policy face amount paid when the insured dies?

Social Insurance

WHAT'S YOUR VERDICT? Johnny contracted diabetes late in life. After several years fighting the disease, he had to have first one leg and then the other amputated to the point where he was unable to work at all.

What social insurance program would assist him?

The primary source for social insurance coverage in this country is the federal government's Social Security Act. Coverage provided under the act frequently is labeled RSDHI (for Retirement, Survivors', Disability, and Health Insurance). Unemployment compensation, which is designed to lessen the financial hardship of losing one's job, also is provided indirectly through programs under the act but controlled and administered by the various states.

Retirement Insurance

An eligible person may elect to begin receiving social security retirement insurance checks as early as age 62. The amount of these checks, however, is just a percentage of the full retirement check available between 65 and 67 years of age. (Sixty-five is the full retirement age if you were born in 1937 or before. The age gradually increases to 67 if you were born in 1960 or later.) Regardless of when you retire, the checks

IN THIS CASE Elton's life insurance policy was for $500,000 when he died of pneumonia at the age of 57. His policy contained a triple indemnity clause. As a consequence, his wife anticipated a payout of $1.5 million dollars. However, as the death was by natural causes the company only had to pay the face amount of $500,000.

LEGAL *Research*

Unemployment benefits are a vital part of social insurance. However, they vary widely in eligibility, duration, and amount depending on the state. Research unemployment law of your state and a state in a different region and report your findings to the class. How well could you live on what your state provides?

The Social Security Administration (SSA) is the government agency that runs the social security program in the United States. The SSA has one of the most extensive web sites of any government agency. When you visit www.ssa.gov you can perform a number of functions. You can learn about the history of the SSA and its plans for the future. You can inquire about all of the benefits that the SSA offers, such as retirement income and Medicare medical insurance. You also can request many of the services the SSA offers directly from the web site. The SSA accepts requests from the web site for personal earnings and benefits summaries. Companies also can download forms used to report employees' earnings and wages to the SSA.

THINK ABOUT IT

Has use of the Internet increased or decreased the efficiency of the SSA programs? Explain.

are meant to provide supplemental income only. Too often, individuals rely solely on these checks for their retirement income. This is not the purpose of the program.

During the working years, each individual is responsible for accumulating savings. These savings should provide enough income that, when added to the social security retirement amount, will allow an adequate standard of living during the retirement years. All too often, people retire only to find that they have to return to some form of employment to make ends meet.

Survivor's Insurance

Survivors of a person eligible for benefits under the system also may receive benefits if they are

■ a widow or widower or ex-spouse (if married for at least 10 years to deceased recipient) age 60 or older (or, if disabled, age 50 or older),

■ a widow or widower of any age if caring for a child under age 16 or a child who is disabled,

■ dependent children under 18 (or 19 if still in high school); dependent parents 62 or older.

© GETTY IMAGES/PHOTODISC

What do you think about working during what are traditionally thought to be "the retirement years"? Should the federal government be responsible for paying for your entire livelihood when you retire through the social security program? Why or why not?

A Question of ETHICS

Under the current Social Security Act, all working people have a portion of their paychecks withheld as a FICA tax. (FICA stands for Federal Insurance Contributions Act.) These funds are used to pay social security retirement insurance benefits to current retirees. There is some debate about whether funds will be available to pay benefits to current contributors when they retire. Is it ethical of the federal government to deduct this tax from workers' paychecks when they can't guarantee the benefits?

Disability Insurance

A severe, long-lasting disability is one that prevents the eligible person from being able to do "any substantial work." Before any payments can be made, it must be established that the condition is physical or mental, and is expected to continue indefinitely or result in death. The disabled person must have earned a certain number of work credits within a specific time period. The eligible person must not refuse reasonable medical treatment.

The following conditions ordinarily are considered severe enough to meet the test of disability:

■ Loss of both arms, both legs, or a leg and an arm. In *What's Your Verdict?* the loss of both his legs to diabetes would make Johnny eligible for assistance under the disability coverage of the social security system.

■ Heart and lung diseases that cause pain or fatigue on slight exertion

■ Progressive cancer

■ Brain damage that results in loss of judgment or memory

■ Loss of vision, inability to speak, deafness

Health Insurance

In the last two decades, the costs of medical care have risen so dramatically that a major illness involving extended hospitalization and treatment threatens not only the physical well-being but also the financial livelihood of the patient and the patient's family. As a consequence, health insurance, which indemnifies against the cost of medical care necessary to regain physical well-being after an illness, has become very important. Medicare provides such coverage primarily for those age 65 and older. Private insurance companies provide similar coverage for those not protected by the Social Security Act.

MEDICARE Medicare consists of two basic programs. The first, hospital insurance, helps pay for hospital expenses and the costs of follow-up treatment. To receive payments under this program, an eligible person must enter a hospital for necessary treatment. Persons with enough work credits and who are age 65, those with permanent kidney failure, or those covered for extensive periods by the disability program if under age 65 are eligible.

Medical insurance, the second basic Medicare program, helps pay for items not covered by hospital insurance. These include services of physicians

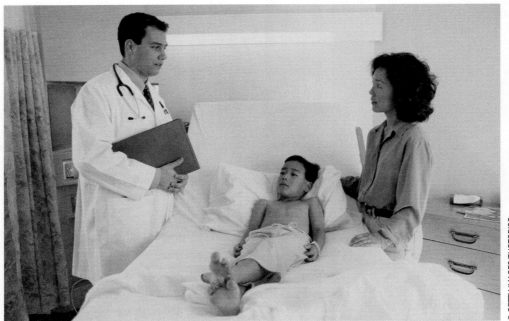

In 2005, an estimated 15.9 percent of the U.S. population was without health insurance coverage. Do you think that the U.S. government should be responsible for providing health insurance coverage for all U.S. citizens? Why or why not?

and surgeons. Also included are services such as ambulance charges, X-rays, radium treatments, laboratory tests, surgical dressings, casts, and home visits by nurses or therapists. The patient pays relatively small yearly deductibles, and then medical insurance generally pays either a large percentage or all of the costs of the covered services.

Unlike hospital insurance coverage, financed primarily from the social security tax, contracting and paying premiums for medical insurance coverage are voluntary. Each person enrolled in the medical insurance plan pays a monthly premium. The federal government pays an equal amount out of general revenues.

In November 2005, the largest expansion of Medicare since its inception took place when the sign-up period for prescription drug coverage opened. Unlike the relatively modest monthly premiums for the medical insurance described above, the typical drug plan offered by the private insurers certified by Medicare involved substantial costs to the insured. Under most plans, after the insured pays a deductible of $265, the insurance plans typically pay about 75 percent of costs up to $2,400. From $2,400 to approximately $5,450, the seniors must pay 100 percent of their medicine's costs. Finally, above the $5,400, the plans cover 95 percent of the insured's medicine's costs. Changes in the program are forecast to help deserving seniors with these higher costs.

CHECKPOINT What does RSDHI stand for?

19-3 Assessment

THINK ABOUT LEGAL CONCEPTS

1. Which of the following individuals would be eligible for survivor's insurance upon the death of the insured? (a) the widower who is 55 years of age (b) the widower caring for a child who is 19 years old (c) the ex-spouse who was married to the insured for 11 years and is 62 years old (d) none of the above are eligible for survivor's insurance.

2. Unemployment programs under the Social Security Administration are controlled directly by the federal government. **True or False?**

3. Which of the following types of social insurance provides health insurance and hospital insurance for people age 65 and older? (a) retirement insurance (b) survivor's insurance (c) disability insurance (d) Medicare

4. A(n) _?_ clause prohibits an insurer from refusing to perform due to fraud or misrepresentation after a policy has been in effect for one or two years.

5. Double-indemnity coverage requires the insurer to pay half the face amount of the policy if the death of the insured is accidental. **True or False?**

THINK CRITICALLY ABOUT EVIDENCE

Study the situation, answer the questions, and then prepare arguments to support your answers.

6. When Henecker took out his life insurance policy, he misrepresented his age as 27. In reality, he was 34. Will the insurance company be required to pay on the policy when Henecker dies?

7. When she turned 62, Shirly filed for her social security retirement benefits. Will she receive more money per month because she filed early?

8. Shuster had a $100,000 life insurance policy. Three years after contracting for it, she committed suicide. Will the insurance company have to pay $100,000?

9. A month after his release from jail, Bill Bravo insured his own life in a double indemnity policy. Two months later, he was killed while attempting to hold up a bank. The insurance company refused to pay the benefits to Bill's wife and son, even though the policy contained no provision excluding liability if the insured died as a result of violating the law. Under what legal grounds can the insurance company refuse to pay this claim?

CONCEPTS IN BRIEF

19-1   Insurance Fundamentals

1. Although insurance is an excellent way to protect against possible loss, coverage of certain risks such as that of doing business is not offered by insurance companies due to the potential for abuse.

2. Fire insurance policies can be augmented to cover other risks as well, such as hail, earthquake, and windstorm.

3. An insurable interest in property must exist both at the time the policy is taken out and at the time of the damage or destruction of the subject matter or the insurer is not obligated to pay for the loss.

4. An insurable interest in life need only exist at the time the policy was taken out.

19-2   Property and Casualty Insurance

5. Losses covered by a fire insurance policy will be indemnified only upon a showing that they were most likely caused by a hostile fire.

6. A property or casualty insurance policy can be assigned only with the consent of the insurer. The right to recover from an insurer a loss that already has been sustained may be assigned by the insured without consent of the insurer.

7. Coinsurance requires the insured to keep the face value of the policy equal to a certain percentage (usually 80 percent) of the current value of the insured property.

8. The basic purpose of automobile insurance is to provide coverage against liability. It also can provide medical payments coverage, collision and comprehensive coverage, and uninsured and underinsured coverage.

9. No-fault insurance indemnifies the insured for various losses sustained in an automobile accident regardless of who had legal responsibility for the accident. It is now required by some states.

19-3   Life and Social Insurance

10. Life insurance policies may be subject to exemptions for deaths related to military service, private airplane crashes, and others.

11. Federal disability insurance provides monthly benefits for a worker and dependents if a severe, long-lasting disability is suffered.

12. Social security retirement insurance provides monthly benefits for a worker and dependents when the worker retires at age 62 or later.

YOUR LEGAL VOCABULARY

Match each statement with the term that it best defines. Some terms may not be used.

1. To make good a loss

2. Party who will indemnify if loss occurs

3. Period of time during which an overdue premium can be paid to keep the policy in force

4. Consideration for a contract of insurance

5. The potential loss that has been insured against

6. Potential to sustain loss due to the covered risk

7. Indemnifies for loss from personal negligence, chance, and accident

8. Exceptions to insurance coverage

9. Modifications to the standard fire policy made to eliminate certain risks from coverage

10. Requires that, in the event of loss, insureds be indemnified by their own insurance companies

11. Clause in a fire policy that requires the insured to maintain coverage equal to a certain percentage of the total current value of the insured property

12. Recipient of the amount to be paid under an insurance policy

a. automobile insurance
b. beneficiary
c. casualty insurance
d. coinsurance
e. collision insurance
f. comprehensive insurance
g. endorsements
h. exclusions
i. fire insurance
j. grace period
k. indemnify
l. insurable interest
m. insurance
n. insured
o. insurer
p. liability insurance
q. life insurance
r. no-fault insurance
s. policy
t. premium
u. property insurance
v. risk

REVIEW LEGAL CONCEPTS

13. As a seasonal bonus you are planning a trip for your employees to the local casino. Each one is to be given $1,000 in credit and must share half of any earnings with the business. Is insurance available to cover your risk?

14. Why does the insurable interest in property have to be present at the time of loss?

15. What is the purpose of fidelity insurance?

16. The insurable interest in life only has to be present when the policy is taken out. Can you think of situations where this might lead to problems?

17. Why should renters and tenants have fire and liability insurance?

WRITE ABOUT LEGAL CONCEPTS

18. Compose a persuasive written statement for the editorial page of your newspaper as to why flight insurance should be no longer allowed.

19. **HOT DEBATE** Write a persuasive opening statement that emphasizes the legal and ethical points in your favor. Write a persuasive opening statement that emphasizes the legal and ethical points in the insurer's favor.

MAKE ACADEMIC CONNECTIONS

20. **POLITICAL SCIENCE** Research the issues surrounding the passage of the Medicare prescription drug program in November of 2003. Note especially how the program's passage, funding, and future were treated during the 2004 presidential election and the demographics among seniors regarding which candidate they voted for. Write a paper concerning your findings.

THINK CRITICALLY ABOUT EVIDENCE

Study the situation, answer the questions, and then prepare arguments to support your answers.

21. An abandoned store surrounded by high, dry weeds stood adjacent to a frequently traveled road near Ashleigh's home. She realized that the store would be destroyed if just one cigarette butt were thrown from a passing vehicle. Therefore, even though she did not own it, she decided to insure the building against loss by fire. After she obtained the insurance, there was a fire that destroyed the structure. Legally, will Ashleigh be allowed to collect?

22. Claudia James took out a $200,000 life insurance policy on her husband and named herself as beneficiary. Three months later they were divorced, and a month after that her ex-husband died in a car accident. Claudia sought to collect on the policy, but the insurance company refused to pay. The company said she lacked an insurable interest both at the time the policy was taken out and at the time of death. Is the company legally obligated to pay the $200,000?

23. McNeely owned a go-cart track on which the public was invited to race the small motorized carts that she provided. Collisions and upsets occurred relatively frequently. What type of insurance would it be advisable for McNeely to have?

24. Dr. Bray performed a tympanoplasty (eardrum replacement) on Azle. The operation appeared to be successful, but one year later another doctor found the ear canal to be completely closed due to the growth of scar tissue from areas where Dr. Bray had drilled improperly. What type of insurance would protect Dr. Bray if Azle files a malpractice suit against him?

25. Sarnof took a summer job to earn money for his college education. On his way home from work late one evening, a drunken driver ran a red light and smashed into Sarnof's car. Sarnof's medical bills were more than $45,000, and his injuries prevented him from working for the rest of the summer. Unfortunately, the drunken driver had only the minimum state-required liability coverage ($10,000). The driver's other known assets totaled less than $5,000. This will cause Sarnof to exhaust his college fund and take out a loan to pay his medical bills. What type of auto insurance coverage would have helped Sarnof cover the excess costs?

26. Antrell made an offer to purchase a building on the Leech Lake Indian Reservation for $300. He paid $100 in cash at the time he made the offer and received the keys to the structure. Without examining the property, his insurance company issued a policy with a face value of $16,000. Several months later, fire totally destroyed the structure. At the time of the loss, Antrell had not paid the balance of the purchase price nor had the title been transferred. The company claims that the plaintiff did not have the required insurable interest and that, therefore, the company was not liable on the policy. Do you think the company should pay? (*Antrell v. Pearl Assurance Company*, 89 N.W.2d 726)

27. Lakin sued the Postal Life and Casualty Insurance Company for its failure to pay him, as beneficiary, under an insurance policy on the life of his business partner, Hankinson. Evidence presented at the trial showed that Hankinson had contributed neither capital nor skills to the alleged partnership, that he could not issue partnership checks, and that he could not hire or fire employees. In addition, it was disclosed that Lakin paid the policy premiums and had made no settlement of "partnership" interests after Hankinson's death. Should the insurance company be ordered by the court to pay the $25,000 face amount to Lakin? (*Lakin v. Postal Life and Casualty Insurance Company*, 316 S.W.2d 542)

28. In the life insurance policy agreed to by James McElroy was a term that read, "if the insured is over the age of 54 years at the date hereof, this policy is void. . . ." McElroy was indeed over 54 at the time. When he died three years later, his beneficiary sued for the face amount of the policy claiming it should be paid because of a two-year incontestability clause in the same policy. Should the court order the insurance company to pay the policy's face amount? (*Hall v. Missouri Ins. Co.*, 208 S.W.2d 830)

29. Milburn carried automobile damage and theft insurance on his Cadillac sedan as required by the creditor on his car loan. Milburn could no longer make the payments. He turned the car over to an automobile salesperson to sell. The salesperson ultimately disappeared with the car. The insurer, Manchester Insurance Company, refused to pay, and World Investment Company, Milburn's creditor on the loan, sued Manchester. Manchester claimed the policy insured against theft which, as larceny, involved a taking against the owner's will. Because Milburn voluntarily delivered the car to the salesperson, no theft had occurred. World Investment Company claimed that the word "theft" should be given its common meaning of "steal," so the insurance company should pay. What do you think? (*World Investment Co. v. Manchester Insurance and Indemnity Co.*, 380 S.W.2d 487)

30. When Wilson and his passenger Davison were injured in an automobile accident, the insurance company stated that the policy on Wilson excluded coverage of more than one person in a single accident. Davison sued, contending that because the exclusion of coverage in the policy was not in a different color or type than the rest of the policy as required by state statute, the term was void. The insurance company pointed out that although the exclusion did not appear in a different color or type of print, it was in a section of the policy clearly labeled "exclusions." Should Davison be allowed to collect? (*Davison v. Wilson*, 239 N.W.2d 38)

31. Gary Stallings was on active duty with the National Guard when the three-quarter-ton truck he was driving overturned and caused a fellow Guard member and passenger, Robert Ward, bodily injury. Stallings was the named insured in Michigan Mutual Liability Company's "Auto-Guard" Family Insurance Policy. When Ward sued Stallings for the injuries, Michigan Mutual refused to defend Stallings and denied responsibility to pay any judgment that might result. In addition to other coverages, the policy obligated the company to defend and pay judgments up to the policy limit if the insured was driving a "nonowned automobile." The company maintained that the three-quarter-ton army truck with canvas top and doors was not an automobile. What do you think? (*Michigan Mutual Liability Company v. Stallings*, 523 S.W.2d 539)

Case For Legal Thinking

HALL V. WILKERSON
926 F.2D 311

BACKGROUND At the time of the automobile accident that is the origin of this suit, Wayne Wilkerson was residing in the home of Gwendolyn Hall. Before she left for France one spring, Hall gave permission to Wilkerson to continue to reside in her house and to drive her car under certain prescribed conditions. In particular, there were to be no drugs in her car, and she considered alcohol to be a drug just like any other.

FACTS Unfortunately, Wayne Wilkerson liked to drink—and he drank a lot. So after having consumed a large quantity of beer one day, he was involved in an accident. The accident involved only one vehicle. In the accident both of Wilkerson's passengers, Susan Kilmer and Richard Schock, were seriously injured. The car Wilkerson was driving in the accident was Gwendolyn Hall's.

LOWER COURT Gwendolyn Hall's insurance company and the injured parties brought this suit seeking a determination of whether or not Wayne Wilkerson was an insured at the time of the accident.

The lower court concluded that Wilkerson's use of alcohol was indeed a violation of the conditions imposed on his being able to use Hall's vehicle with permission. Therefore, he was not an "insured" under Hall's policy.

APPEALS The state law where the accident occurred requires that insurance coverage be maintained under such permissive use clauses in a policy if the driver's deviation is slight and inconsequential. It will not be permissive use if the deviation is substantial.

ISSUE Gwendolyn Hall's automobile insurance policy read:

"Who is an insured (under this policy)?"

The policy then answered its own question as follows:

"For YOUR car—YOU, any RELATIVE, and anyone else using YOUR CAR if the use is (or is reasonably believed to be) with YOUR PERMISSION, are INSUREDS."

PRACTICE JUDGING

1. Should the policyholder have the power to eliminate insurance coverage by imposing conditions on permission to drive, as Gwendolyn Hall did in this case? For example, what if Hall had granted Wilkerson permission to drive on the condition that he neither damage the car nor involve it in an accident?

2. If Wilkerson is not an insured, the injured parties lose a major source of funding to pay for the expenses of recovering from their injuries. This may prevent them from receiving treatment that would enable them to engage in gainful employment and/or may force them into conditions of financial hardship. On the other hand, holding that they are unable to recover from their injuries because Wilkerson is not an insured may send a warning to others to be careful about the persons from whom they accept rides under similar circumstances. From a societal standpoint, which alternative do you think should be chosen? Why?

3. How do you think the appellate court should hold? Why?

Chapter 20
Wills, Trusts, and Estates

20-1 Property Distribution Upon Death

20-2 Trusts

HOT DEBATE

Jewell Marie was 83 when she suffered her first stroke. She recovered well and went back to living on her own about three blocks from her son and his family. Two years later she had another, more serious, stroke. Her son then moved her into his home. The burden of caring for Jewell increased. She would seldom eat and usually threw the food on the server. She had little control of her bodily functions and had to be bathed each evening by her son. Finally, she suffered a massive stroke and was placed in intensive care in a local hospital. Jewell remained in a coma-like state for a week. Her doctor approached the son and suggested "off the record" that he could put Jewell to sleep peacefully but permanently before the hospitalization expenses ate up her financial resources.

WHERE DO YOU STAND?

1. Discuss the legal and ethical reasons in favor of keeping Jewell alive.
2. List the legal and ethical reasons for putting her to "sleep."

20-1 Property Distribution Upon Death

GOALS

- Differentiate between dying testate and dying intestate
- Describe how a decedent's property is distributed

KEY TERMS

decedent	testator
intestate	executor
administrator	codicil
estate	holographic will
testate	nuncupative will
will	escheats

Legal Alternatives in Property Distribution

WHAT'S YOUR VERDICT? Ethel had lived within 10 miles of her birthplace her entire life. She never married and worked in a local factory until retirement. Then she lived on her social security checks. Ethel was an avid and conservative saver. When she died the value of her property totaled more than $800,000, but she had never made a will.

How will her property be distributed?

When a person dies, the law looks for his or her instructions to resolve some basic legal issues that arise. These issues include how the debts of the person who dies, called the **decedent**, are to be paid and what is to be done with the remaining property. The necessary instructions are found either in the wishes of the decedent as expressed in a will, in statutes (especially if the decedent did not leave a will), or both.

Death Without a Will

Those who die without a valid will are said to have died **intestate**. When a person dies intestate, as Ethel did in *What's Your Verdict?*, a special type of court in the state court system, generally called a probate court (or surrogate's court in some states), has the power to settle the affairs of the decedent. Probate courts also settle the affairs of decedents who die without wills as well as administer guardianships and similar matters. When a person dies intestate the probate court with jurisdiction, appoints a personal representative known as an

administrator if male or administratrix if female. This person takes charge of the intestate's property. This representative uses the property of the deceased, called the **estate**, to pay all debts, including the costs of administering the estate. The remainder of the estate will then be distributed in accordance with the state's intestacy statute. Dying without a professionally drafted will can cause the beneficiaries to pay considerable administrative expenses and needlessly large estate taxes.

Why is dying with a will more beneficial to a person and his or her heirs than dying without a will?

© GETTY IMAGES/PHOTODISC

LAST WILL AND TESTAMENT
REBECCA BIRK FAULSTICH

I, Rebecca Birk Faulstich, of 1875 El Rey Way, San Francisco, California, declare that this is my will. I revoke all wills and codicils that I have previously made.

FIRST: I am married to Kevin Alan Faulstich and we have one child, Jeffrey Michael, born March 12, 2001.

SECOND: After payment of all my debts, I give my estate as follows:

(A) To my twin sister, Rachel Ann Wilson, I give my personal clothing, jewelry, and sporting equipment, if she should survive me.

(B) To my beloved husband, Kevin, I give all the residue if he should survive me for thirty (30) days.

(C) To our son, Jeffrey Michael, I give all the residue if my husband should not survive me for thirty days and if my son should survive me for thirty days.

(D) To the Regents of the University of California (to provide student scholarships and awards without reference to financial need, in order to encourage excellence of effort and achievement), I give all the residue if neither my husband nor my son should survive me for thirty days.

THIRD: I nominate my husband as the executor of this will. If for any reason he should fail to qualify or cease to act as such, I nominate my sister, Rachel, as executrix. If for any reason she should fail to qualify or cease to act as such, I nominate the Central City Bank, a California corporation, to act as executor. I direct that neither my husband nor my sister be required to post bond as executor or executrix.

IN WITNESS WHEREOF, I have hereunto set my hand this ____18th____ day of ____January____, 20_ _, in San Francisco, California.

Rebecca Birk Faulstich

_____
Rebecca Birk Faulstich

The foregoing instrument was subscribed on the date which it bears by the testatrix, Rebecca Birk Faulstich, and at the time of subscribing was declared by her to be her last will. The subscription and declaration were made in our presence, and being present at the same time; and we, at her request and in her presence and in the presence of each other, have affixed our signatures hereto as witnesses:

Diana P. Davis	residing at	_432 Third Street_
		San Francisco, California
Adam T. Price	residing at	_1644 Prospector's Point_
		San Francisco, California

Intestacy statutes vary from state to state. Generally, intestacy statutes call for a surviving spouse to receive one-third to one-half of the estate with the remainder divided equally among the children. A representative division of an intestate decedent's assets is presented in the Law Brief on page 361.

Death With a Will

All concerned usually benefit if the decedent dies **testate**, or leaving a valid will. A **will** is a legal expression, usually in writing, by which a person directs how her or his property is to be distributed after death. (See the example above of the "Last Will and Testament of Rebecca Birk Faulstich.") The maker of the will is called the **testator** if male or *testatrix* if female. A will generally allows a person to direct his or her estate's resources to where they can do the most good. This contrasts with the intestacy statutes, which distribute a decedent's estate without regard for need.

A will also allows its maker to name his or her own personal representative, called an **executor** if male or *executrix* if female, to carry out the directions in the will. The testatrix can specify that the executor be exempted from *posting bond*, as did Rebecca Faulstich. Such a posting involves making a pool of money available to reimburse anyone injured by the executor's improper handling of his duties. A will also may be used to name a guardian for minor children of the testator. Through the will, the named guardian also can be exempted from posting a bond.

Living will is a term used for a document directed to attending physicians regarding a person's choices about the use of life-support systems in treatment for terminal illness or vegetative state. Be sure to distinguish living wills from the wills described in this chapter. The term *living will* is a poor label. A more descriptive term for living will would be "Directive to Physicians." An alternative to achieve the same end would be using a *durable power of attorney,* which confers on a chosen or court-appointed individual the right to make health-care decisions, such as removal of life support.

CREATION AND EXECUTION OF A VALID WILL

To counteract the possibility of forgery, a will must strictly conform to the state laws regarding creation and execution, or it will be held to be invalid. The basic requirements in almost every state are the following:

1. The testator must have the clear intention that the document he or she is signing is to currently operate as his or her last will and testament. This is called *testamentary intent.* A person must not be pressured into signing the document against his or her desires by the undue influence of others. Likewise, the signer must not be misled into thinking that the document is something other than a will.

2. At the time the will is executed, the testator must have testamentary capacity to make the will. *Testamentary capacity* means the maker must know, at least in a general way, the kind and extent of the property in the estate he or she intends to dispose of, the recipients who stand to benefit, and that he or she is making arrangements to dispose of his or her property after death. Lapses into senility by the maker may bring the will of an elderly person into question due to the possible lack of capacity. In most states a person under age 18 does not have testamentary capacity.

3. Ordinarily the will must be in writing and, in most states, signed at the end of the document to prevent unauthorized additions. The signing must be witnessed by at least two adults. In some states, three witnesses must

sign. These witnesses should not be individuals who will inherit under the will. The witnesses must be advised that they are watching the testator's will being signed as they do so.

AMENDMENT OF A VALID WILL

A will takes effect only upon the death of the maker. Therefore, it can be changed or canceled at any time during the maker's life. However, this ability to change the document as often as desired, coupled with the fact that the contents of a will are proved only after the death of the maker, opens the way to potentially false claims under forged documents.

Regardless of the potential problems in making changes, it is, nonetheless, important that the maker of a will keep it current. Marriage, divorce, the birth of children, and other significant changes in a person's life should be reflected in the document by periodic amendments or by a new will. In states requiring a formal will, changes must be made using a **codicil**, which is a formal, written, and witnessed amendment. A codicil must be executed with the same formalities as a will.

SPECIAL TYPES OF WILLS

There are exceptions to the rules for the creation, execution, and altering of a valid will. For example, many states recognize a **holographic will** as valid even without witnesses. A holographic will is one that was written entirely by the decedent's own hand, signed by him or her, and not witnessed. Where a valid holographic will is used, changes require appropriate additions or deletions before witnesses, if necessary, in the handwriting of the maker.

A **nuncupative will**, or oral will, is recognized in some states if proclaimed during the maker's last illness or by service personnel on active duty. However, the will must be witnessed and reduced to writing. It often is limited to controlling the distribution of personal property.

IN THIS CASE While cleaning her rifle, Charleson accidentally shot herself. As she lay dying, she told the paramedics and the responding police officer that she was making an oral will. She then stated that she wanted her valuable collection of dolls to go to her only granddaughter, Annabelle. Charleson's state allowed nuncupative wills if the witnesses' recollections of the will agreed and were properly and promptly reduced to writing. Therefore, Charleson's dying wish would be carried out.

REVOCATION OF A WILL A will is subject to partial or total change at the desire of the testator. A will is only intended to take effect upon the testator's death. Anytime before that moment, as long as the testator has testamentary intent and testamentary capacity, the will can be amended or revoked. A will may be completely revoked, rather than being amended, in several ways. For example, doing something to the will that clearly indicates intent to revoke it, such as destroying it or defacing it, will accomplish this end.

According to some state statutes, the marriage of the maker or the birth or adoption of a child by that individual works an automatic termination of the will. Divorce, on the other hand, does not produce such an automatic revocation. However, a divorce settlement does revoke the parts of a will with which the settlement conflicts once the divorce occurs.

Finally, a will may be revoked by a written revocation in a later will. Such a document must either explicitly state, "I hereby revoke all prior wills," or contain provisions that conflict with the prior will so that it impliedly revokes the preceding document.

CHECKPOINT What does it mean to die intestate?

© GETTY IMAGES/PHOTODISC

Why do you think that the statutes in some states automatically terminate an existing will upon marriage of the testator?

Distribution of the Decedent's Estate

WHAT'S YOUR VERDICT? Strontiumm made a personal loan to his old business school buddy, Burser. The money, $45,000, was for Burser to start a frozen custard business in his hometown. The loan was due and payable in a year. Although he lived in another state, Strontiumm attended the grand opening of the business two months later. Strontiumm did not know, however, that Burser was killed a week after the opening while picking up trash in the business's drive-through. When, at the end of the year, Strontiumm tried to contact Burser to collect on the loan, he discovered Burser's death and that the six-month period for filing claims against Burser's estate had elapsed.

Can Strontiumm still collect the $45,000?

Procedure Prior to Distribution

Regardless of whether a person dies testate or intestate, the first item of business on the executor's or administrator's list is to offer proof of death to the appropriate court. This proof may be in the form of a death certificate, official notification of death from an armed service, or even testimony of the deceased's presence in a disaster that resulted in unidentifiable or irretrievable bodies. In the last case, the court can take judicial notice of the situation and issue a declaration of death.

If a person simply vanishes without a trace, after several years he or she can be declared dead under the "Enoch Arden laws." (These laws were named for a poem by Tennyson about a seaman who returns home after a long absence to find his "widow" married to another.) Almost without exception, the time required under such laws is either five or seven years of absence.

After proof of death is established, the personal representative's duties include the following:

1. assembling, preserving, inventorying, and appraising the assets of the estate and collecting the debts owed to it

2. giving public notice of the estate and the necessity for filing claims against it within the statutory period

3. paying valid claims against the estate
4. distributing the remaining property according to the will or statute

The personal representative will be liable for failure to reasonably carry out her or his duties. Depending on the size and types of property in the estate, the task can be quite complex. As indicated above, the personal representative must properly give public notice that all creditors of the estate have a set time, typically six months, to file a claim or go unpaid. He or she must then determine which claims are valid and pay them where possible. In *What's Your Verdict?* because Strontiumm did not file within the proper period, he cannot collect the loan from the estate. Note, however, that although six months are given to file such claims, the full procedure of settling an estate can take several months beyond this. This is true especially if the validity of the will is challenged or contested or if the meaning of the will is unclear in some of its provisions.

Distribution

WITHOUT A WILL As mentioned previously, intestate distributions are determined by the appropriate state statute. See the Law Brief feature in the next column.

WITH A WILL Where there is a valid will, its terms are to be followed as closely as possible by the executor. The probate or surrogate's court will supervise this procedure. Regardless, the personal representative often is assisted by an attorney whose fees are paid out of the estate. Following the will's directives frequently is complicated by paying valid claims from creditors against the estate for which the testator did not allow.

There also may be statutory provisions allowing certain relatives to override the will's terms and receive more of the estate than the will provided. For example, in most states the surviving spouse is able to elect to receive a set percentage of the decedent's property instead of what was allocated under the will. Usually this *right of election* is for one-third to one-half of the decedent's property.

Another complex issue has to do with how the testator has decided to split the property among the lineal descendants. The testator may specify that the living lineal descendents

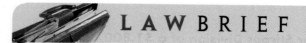

LAW BRIEF

Typical Intestate Distribution

If a person dies without a will . . .

- With no spouse but one or more children surviving, the children inherit equal shares in the real and personal property.
- With a spouse and one or more children or grandchildren surviving, the spouse gets one-half of the real and personal property and the children share equally in the remainder. If a child is deceased but has surviving children, those children share equally in the deceased child's share.
- With a spouse and no children or grandchildren surviving, the spouse gets one-half of the real and personal property and the deceased's parents receive the remainder. If the deceased's parents are not alive, the deceased's brothers and sisters receive equal shares in the remainder.
- With no spouse, no children, and no grandchildren surviving, the deceased's parents each receive one-half of the real and personal property or, if only one parent survives, he or she receives it all. If both of the deceased's parents are dead, the brothers and sisters of the deceased share equally.

split the property equally, be they children, grandchildren, or even further down the lineal tree. This is referred to as a *per capita* distribution. Or the testator may specify that the lineal descendants split equally what a deceased parent would have received but receive nothing if the parent still lives. This latter is referred to as a *per stirpes* distribution. These are illustrated in the charts on page 362.

IF THERE ARE NO INHERITORS If there are no inheritors, the property of the deceased **escheats** (or reverts) to the state.

CHECKPOINT What are the terms for the two ways in which the testator can distribute the estate among the lineal descendents?

Per Stirpes Division of a $1,800,000 Estate

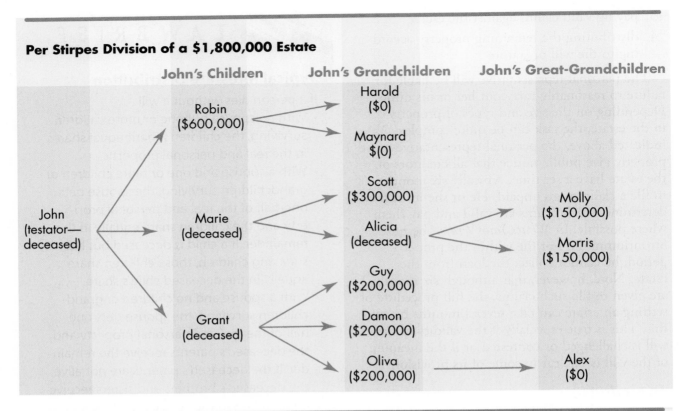

	John's Children	John's Grandchildren	John's Great-Grandchildren
John (testator—deceased)	Robin ($600,000)	Harold ($0)	
		Maynard $(0)	
	Marie (deceased)	Scott ($300,000)	
		Alicia (deceased)	Molly ($150,000)
			Morris ($150,000)
	Grant (deceased)	Guy ($200,000)	
		Damon ($200,000)	
		Oliva ($200,000)	Alex ($0)

Per Capita Division of a $1,800,000 Estate—the 10 lineal living descendants all share equally

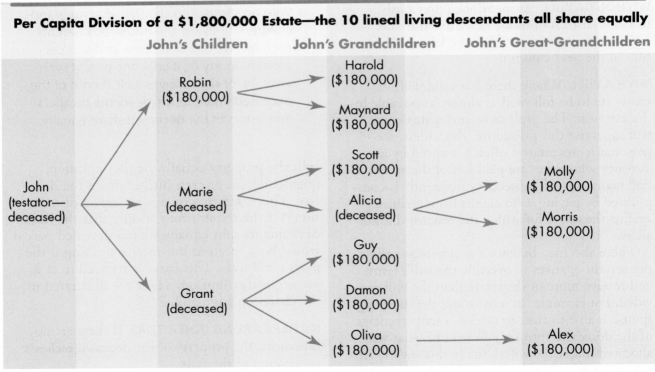

	John's Children	John's Grandchildren	John's Great-Grandchildren
John (testator—deceased)	Robin ($180,000)	Harold ($180,000)	
		Maynard ($180,000)	
	Marie (deceased)	Scott ($180,000)	
		Alicia (deceased)	Molly ($180,000)
			Morris ($180,000)
	Grant (deceased)	Guy ($180,000)	
		Damon ($180,000)	
		Oliva ($180,000)	Alex ($180,000)

20-1 Assessment

Xtra!
Study Tools
school.cengage.com/blaw/lawxtra

THINK ABOUT LEGAL CONCEPTS

1. Those who die without a valid will are legally termed to have died intestate. **True or False?**

2. If there are no inheritors of the decedent's estate, the property _?_ to the state.

3. The maker of a will, if female, is called (a) an administratrix (b) an executrix (c) a decedent (d) a testatrix.

4. A will can be amended at any time as long as the maker has testamentary intent and testamentary capacity. **True or False?**

5. The legal term for an oral will is a(n) _?_ will.

6. The execution of a codicil on a will does not have to be witnessed. **True or False?**

7. If the person making a will decides to split the property equally among all his or her living lineal descendents, he or she is specifying a _?_ distribution.

8. The typical time allowed for all creditors of the estate to file a claim against it is (a) four months (b) six months (c) ten months (d) twelve months

9. If a person vanishes without a trace, the person's estate can be probated after a year. **True or False?**

THINK CRITICALLY ABOUT EVIDENCE

Study the situation, answer the questions, and then prepare arguments to support your answers.

10. Sid went to his attorney's office and described in detail how he wanted his estate distributed upon his death. The lawyer made extensive notes and prepared a 12-page will. He called Sid and read it to him over the phone. Sid made a few minor changes. The lawyer then prepared a final copy. On his way to the lawyer's office to sign the document, Sid died of a heart attack. Was the final copy a valid will? Why or why not?

11. Toa was ill. She did not think she could afford an attorney, so she sat down and wrote on notebook paper what she wanted done with all of her property upon her death. She signed at the end and dated the document in front of four neighbors, who also signed as witnesses. Will Toa's estate be distributed according to her wishes or in some other manner?

12. Hilda executed a will on the first day of January. On the first day of June in the same year she executed a second will, which contained many provisions in conflict with the first will. She died on the first day of December. Which will governs the distribution of her estate?

13. Eric executed a valid will dividing his property among his wife, Amber, and their five children. The will was not altered for 22 years. Then Eric separated from his wife but did not divorce her. He wrote a second will, which left all his property to their children. Eric passed away before making any further changes. What can his wife do to receive a portion of Eric's estate?

14. Worried about the medical costs associated with a lingering terminal illness, Evangel Smith went to his attorney's office and dictated a document that he subsequently signed before witnesses. The document specified that, upon Evangel lapsing into a vegetative state, no life-prolonging methods were to be used upon him. It was the only legal provision Evangel made pertinent to his death or estate. Later his children became concerned about Evangel's declining health and the disposition of his property upon his death. When they asked him if he had a will, Evangel replied "certainly." Is Evangel correct?

15. Evander was the lineal descendant through his father, Eston, of his grandfather, Elias Fieldstone. When Elias died he left an estate worth $5,000,000. Elias' will called for the estate to be distributed per capita among his lineal descendants. These included four children and seven grandchildren, of which Evander was the youngest. Regrettably, Evander's father had died during the time between when the will was made and Elias' death. All the other lineal descendants were alive and well. How much will Evander receive from the distribution of Elias' estate (not considering taxes and administration charges)?

20-2 Trusts

GOALS
- Recognize the value of the trust instrument
- Identify the various types of trusts

KEY TERMS

trust

trustee

settlor

beneficiary

inter vivos trust

testamentary trust

revocable trust

charitable trust

private trust

spendthrift trust

express trust

resulting trust

constructive trust

Purpose and Creation of Trusts

WHAT'S YOUR VERDICT? Jan loved getting his family of five grown children together. As a consequence, he bought an estate in Key West that was large enough to accommodate him, all the children, and their families. He then extended an open invitation to them to visit any time but especially at Christmas. As he entered his seventies, he worried that the family would gradually grow apart if they didn't have the estate as a rallying point at which to come together. He wanted to be sure the children did not sell the property and split the proceeds after his death.

What legal device can Jan use to prevent that from happening?

For various reasons, people may wish to transfer the immediate control of some or all of their property to another party with instructions on how it is to be managed for the benefit of the transferor or a third party. When the transferee of the property is a separate legal entity a **trust** has been created.

A trust can be created for any conceivable legal purpose. The legal entity that has the title to the subject property is known as the **trustee**. The trustee must utilize the property in the trust in such a way as to accomplish the trust's objectives.

The creator of a trust is known as the **settlor**. The party for whose benefit the trust is managed in accordance with the settlor's wishes is the **beneficiary**. The trustee has a fiduciary duty (the highest

NETBookmark

Access school.cengage.com/blaw/lawxtra and click on the link for Chapter 20. Read "The Will versus Trust Debate" and then answer the questions.

1. Does life insurance go through probate?
2. When an estate goes through probate, does the public have access to information about how it is to be distributed?
3. Can trusts ever be open to public view? If so, under what circumstances?
4. Are the actions of a trustee supervised by a court?

school.cengage.com/blaw/lawxtra

Assume that the man in this photo has created a trust for his wife and daughters and their families. Identify the settlor and the beneficiaries in this photo.

© GETTY IMAGES/PHOTODISC

standard of duty implied by law requiring someone to subordinate her or his personal interests in order to act for the benefit of another) to the beneficiary. As a consequence, the trustee may become personally liable if he acts in "breach of trust." Actions that are considered breaches of trust include: spending the monetary resources of the trust on matters outside the trust's legal objects, fraud, serious negligence, failure to comply with relevant statutes, or receiving personal benefit other than assigned pay for services. The trustee cannot cause the beneficiary to acquire liability to third parties through the trust management. In addition, the trust does not usually terminate at the death of the trustee. Another person simply is appointed to fulfill the trustee's role, and the operation of the trust continues.

Finally, even if it is not mentioned in the trust document, trustees have the right to be paid for their services. The probate court or state law will determine just how much the trustee's fee might be in such a case. However, the settlor also may detail in the trust document how much the trustee will receive for her or his services. If the pay is inadequate, it is wise for the settlor to keep in mind that the person nominated for the trusteeship is free to decline it. In *What's Your Verdict?* Jan should create a trust to manage the property with the objective of prolonging his family's contact with one another.

CHECKPOINT What is the legal term for the creator of a trust?

IN THIS CASE Rensch loved a radio show concerning automobile problems that was broadcast weekly on National Public Radio (NPR). As a consequence, he placed $100,000 of his considerable estate into a trust to be managed by a trustee in the trust department of his local bank. The trust was to pay its proceeds to NPR as long as the show was broadcast by the network. After the show left the air, the trust property would revert back into Rensch's estate.

A Question of ETHICS

Marie's 82-year-old father, Isaac, mentioned that he wanted to see the western part of the United States before he died. Marie, his only child, didn't hesitate to help him fulfill this request. Late in May, they headed out from Maine in a recreational vehicle he purchased for the trip. Unfortunately, Isaac suffered a fatal heart attack walking some miles through rough terrain to a cliff dwelling in northern New Mexico. In going through Isaac's things, Marie found a valid holographic will that left half of his considerable estate to Estelle, his housekeeper of more than 35 years. The will was dated two days before the trip had begun. As far as Marie knew, no one else knew of it. Marie felt she deserved the full measure of the estate. Still, she wanted to respect her father's wishes. She wondered why he had not made the will public before leaving. Perhaps he was still considering whether or not to put it into effect, or maybe he was waiting until the end of the trip to tell her about it. Now she sat in her seat in the airplane, her father's casket in the hold below. She had to make a decision by the end of the flight. Should she probate the will or not?

Types of Trusts

Gleason was a wealthy financier brought up in the depression era. His son and daughter, however, had been raised after he had made his fortune. As a consequence, they quickly spent any money he gave them without saving a penny. Gleason loved them but knew he had to protect them from themselves after he died. If he did not, they would spend their inheritances quickly and could end up on the street.

What legal device would you recommend to Gleason?

Trusts basically are named according to the timing and purpose of their creation. A trust may be created during the lifetime of the settlor. This type of trust is known as an **inter vivos trust** also called a *living trust*. A trust created after the death of the settlor in accordance with directions in her or his will is labeled a **testamentary trust**. Testamentary trusts, once a mainstay of estate planning, are no longer considered a wise means of transferring property to others upon death. Instead, revocable living trusts are recommended. A **revocable trust** may be cancelled at any time prior to the death of the settlor(s) and the property taken back. Revocable trusts avoid the extended delays of probate (often two to five years) and are not subject to the relatively expensive fees usually paid to the attorney utilized by the administrator or executor of an estate.

A trust created for the fulfillment of an altruistic purpose is known as a **charitable trust**. Alternatively, a trust created for a private purpose is known as a **private trust**. One type of private trust is called a **spendthrift trust**. This trust protects the beneficiary's interest in the subject property from the beneficiary's creditors. As long as the beneficiary can have no control whatsoever in the trust arrangement, her or his creditors cannot reach the property in the trust. In *What's Your Verdict?* a testamentary spendthrift trust could be formed around Gleason's estate with his children as beneficiaries. The trustee, a local bank's trust department, could be instructed to pay the children's reasonable expenditures for their necessities and provide them some disposable income. Also, in most states, the children's creditors could not reach the income-generating assets of the estate.

The trusts mentioned previously usually are created by a written or oral statement in which the terms are clearly stated by the settlor. As a consequence, they are all properly labeled **express trusts**. The law, however, also makes provisions for at least two types of *implied trusts*. The first implied trust is known as a **resulting trust**. This trust is formed when the entity intended to receive the benefit of an express trust cannot do so. In such a case a resulting trust is formed to hold the property for its original owner.

The other type of implied trust is known as a **constructive trust**. Such a trust is created to require a person holding property to transfer it to another because retention of the property would be a wrongful and unjust enrichment of the holder. Property obtained through fraud, duress, or like means is deemed to be held by the wrongdoer in constructive trust for the person wronged.

CHECKPOINT What is the difference between an *inter vivos* trust and a testamentary trust?

LEGAL Research

Constructive trusts are used for a variety of purposes. They are imposed by a court to avoid someone profiting from fraud, duress, or other illicit means of acquiring money or other property. Constructive trusts also can be imposed in situations that have a legitimate base. For example, where someone purchases property with his or her resources but puts it in the name of a close relative or friend the former person is presumed by law to have that property held in a constructive trust in his or her favor. For example, if a person pays the purchase price of a large homestead and then puts the title in his or her spouse's name, a court will presume the payor has thereby established a constructive trust in the payor's favor.

Brainstorm and then research the potential uses of a constructive trust to insure that an elderly person lacking capacity or a child star receives the benefit of the money he or she acquired during his or her years of competency or minority respectively.

20-2 Assessment

Xtra! Study Tools
school.cengage.com/blaw/lawxtra

THINK ABOUT LEGAL CONCEPTS

1. A trust terminates at the death of the trustee. **True or False?**

2. Every type of trust terminates upon the death of the settlor. **True or False?**

3. A resulting trust may be created due to the death of a trust's beneficiary. **True or False?**

4. A trust created by the will of a deceased settlor is known as a(n) (a) *inter vivos* trust (b) end of vivos trust (c) testamentary trust (d) none of the above

5. Someone who is being unjustly enriched because of property he is holding may be required to transfer the property to another because of the enforcement of a(n) _?_ trust.

THINK CRITICALLY ABOUT EVIDENCE

Study the situation, answer the questions, and then prepare arguments to support your answers.

6. Terry was named in his parents' will as the trustee of the family farm. He does not want the position as he has little or no interest in farming. His brother, Harold, has worked the farm for the last five years and would be a far better trustee. His parents chose Terry, however, because he was older. What can Terry do in this situation?

 Online Research> Stanley's Situation

Langdon and Stanley had been running buddies for years. Langdon watched with pride as his friend slowly fought his way to success in the country music business. Stanley's big break came when he got a gig in Branson, Missouri, performing a music tribute show.

Just three years after Stanley hit the big time with his wildly popular show he was earning a six-figure income. It was then that a stagehand for the theater that sponsored Stanley's show made a near-fatal mistake: He improperly placed a light fixture above the place where Stanley stood throughout the show. During the grand finale in which Stanley sang a popular patriotic song, the vibrations of the stomping and clapping audience, combined with the reverberation of the many instruments and drums, worked the light fixture loose from its mounting, and it fell on Stanley's head.

After he got out of the hospital, a still partially paralyzed Stanley grew depressed and withdrew to a small room in his house, refusing to see his friends. Rick, his brother and only surviving relative, claimed to be caring for him. Langdon, seeing the pitiful conditions that Stanley was living in, grew suspicious that Rick had taken control of Stanley's finances.

Concerned that Rick would spend all Stanley's money, including the $2.5 million award from a lawsuit against the theater. Langdon knew that his old friend needed someone to intervene and obtain long-term rehabilitative physical and mental care for him and to institute sound financial management.

THINK CRITICALLY

What legal device could be utilized to help Stanley if he is no longer able to manage his financial or health environment or both? Would it be utilized? Why or why not? If it is utilized, who would likely be appointed to assume the responsibility for these matters? Why?

GO TO FINDLAW.COM TO FIND THE ANSWER

To find the material in FindLaw on this issue, go to Findlaw.com and click on the following sequence of hyperlinks: Estate Planning, Estate Planning, Wills & Trusts, More Topics, Conservatorships and Guardianships.

Chapter 20 Assessment

CONCEPTS IN BRIEF

20-1 Property Distribution Upon Death

1. An individual either dies testate (with a valid will) or intestate (without a will). An intestate death requires that the estate of the deceased be distributed in accordance with the state's intestacy statute. A testate death generally allows the distribution of the estate according to the will of the decedent.

2. The basic requirements for a valid, formal will are testamentary intent and capacity, a general knowledge of what is being done, and a signed writing with witnesses.

3. A will can be revoked or changed at any time prior to the testator's death.

4. Creditors' rights against the estate and the rights of a surviving spouse to a share of the estate may not be defeated by a will that attempts to give the property to others.

20-2 Trusts

5. In essence, a trust can be created to accomplish any conceivable legal purpose.

6. Trusts may either be created during the life of the settlor (termed an inter vivos trust) or after the settlor's demise through the execution of the provisions of settlor's will (termed a testamentary trust).

7. Inter vivos or testamentary trusts may either be charitable or private, express or implied.

8. A resulting trust holds the subject property for the true owner when the entity intended to receive the benefit of an express trust cannot do so.

9. A constructive trust is imposed to benefit the true owner on someone wrongfully holding the true owner's property.

10. A trustee who breaches his or her fiduciary duty may be held personally liable for any losses the trust sustains as a consequence.

YOUR LEGAL VOCABULARY

Match each statement with the term that it best defines. Some terms may not be used.

1. A deceased person
2. To die without a will
3. Intestate's personal representative appointed to settle the estate
4. Property of the deceased
5. To die with a valid will
6. Maker of a will
7. Orally made will
8. Creator of a trust
9. Trust created by the will of the settlor
10. A reversion of estate property to the state
11. Trust created for the fulfillment of an altruistic purpose
12. Trust in which the terms are explicitly stated by the settlor
13. Will written and signed by the maker
14. Legal vehicle used to transfer the immediate control of property to another party
15. Trust created during the lifetime of the settlor

a. administrator
b. beneficiary
c. charitable trust
d. codicil
e. constructive trust
f. decedent
g. escheat
h. estate
i. executor
j. express trust
k. holographic will
l. inter vivos trust
m. intestate
n. nuncupative will
o. private trust
p. resulting trust
q. revocable trust
r. settlor
s. spendthrift trust
t. testamentary trust
u. testate
v. testator
w. trust
x. trustee
y. will

REVIEW LEGAL CONCEPTS

16. What changes in the settlor's life should cause the updating of a will?

17. Why would a holographic will be disallowed?

18. What is the difference between a per stirpes and a per capita distribution?

19. Is a spendthrift trust fair to the creditors of the settlor? Why or why not?

20. What are the advantages of using a revocable living trust instead of a will to pass along property to would-be inheritors?

21. Does a resulting trust carry out the wishes of the settlor? Why or why not?

22. Could a constructive trust be used in situations in which the property is not wrongfully obtained from the true owner? Why or why not?

WRITE ABOUT LEGAL CONCEPTS

23. Is it fair for individuals under age 18 not to have testamentary capacity? Write a comparison of "legal ages" such as to drive and to consume alcoholic beverages and identify the traits necessary for capacity in each instance. What trait is more important for testamentary capacity than for the others? Should the age level be changed?

24 Draft a will for yourself.

25. How could you use a trust in your life? Draft a document to set it up.

26. What qualities would you want in the trustee of your estate? List them in order of importance.

27. **HOT DEBATE** Write a letter to your legislative representative taking a stand either for or against the government taking control of such situations and deciding when people in Jewell Marie's situation can be removed from life support and allowed to die. Consider especially the long-term potential of allowing the government to determine who, among law-abiding citizens, may live or die.

MAKE ACADEMIC CONNECTIONS

28. **MEDICINE** Read recent articles in medical journals to determine just how we currently define a vegetative state from a medical standpoint and, thereby, the standards the medical evaluations the courts use to determine who may be removed from life support. Report your findings to the class.

THINK CRITICALLY ABOUT EVIDENCE

Study the situation, answer the questions, and then prepare arguments to support your answers.

29. Tim had a considerable estate. He also had three children whom he loved dearly. He did not want to show any favoritism in the distribution of his estate after his death. Therefore, he decided not to make out a will and let the state handle the matter according to its rules. Is this a good idea? Explain.

30. On his deathbed, Tim's youngest child, Paula, finally persuades him to make a will. The other two children are rushing to be at Tim's bedside but have not arrived yet. A nurse overhears Paula telling Tim that the other two children died several years ago and that they should, therefore, receive nothing. Tim, nodding his head in agreement, then signed the will leaving everything to Paula. Two friends of Paula then signed as witnesses. Will the will stand up in probate court?

31. Not only was Tim's will attacked by the other two children as soon as it was filed in probate court but Tim's wife suddenly reappeared. They thought she had drowned two years before when a golf cart she was driving veered into a canal near their Florida home. She is extremely upset that Tim has willed away all the property. Does she have any rights in the matter?

32. Suspicious of the validity of the will, the probate court appointed a neutral party rather than Paula as executor. The executor discovered that, about two months before his death, Tim had placed $500,000 in a spendthrift trust for Paula. Should the amount in the trust be included in the estate for distribution? Why or why not?

33. Paula has a number of creditors mainly because of her gambling problem. Will these creditors want to have the $500,000 included in the estate if Tim's will is held to be valid? Will they want the amount to be included in the estate if the will is invalidated?

ANALYZE REAL CASES

34. Ralph Mangan was wounded by a gunshot in 1971. He was hospitalized and later moved to a nursing home. There, he executed a will dated February 23, 1972. After his release from the nursing home, he was cared for by his brother for a short time after which, because of Ralph's advanced age and medical problems, he was again hospitalized. In May 1972, he returned to the nursing home and in June was adjudicated incompetent. He died in August 1972. His will was filed for probate and was contested on the grounds that at the time of his death Ralph was disoriented because of his advanced age, heart disease, and the gunshot wound. The will left property to someone described as a nephew when there was no such nephew. Witnesses testified that during Ralph's first stay in the nursing home he was self-reliant and was able to handle his own business affairs. Ralph's attorney testified that Ralph appeared to be of sound mind at the time he executed the will. Ralph had discussed the details of the will with the attorney and had mentioned a number of nephews, cousins, and other distant relatives. Ralph's physicians testified that Ralph had periods of disorientation and periods of lucidity. Is Ralph's will valid? (*Edward L. Mangan v. Joseph J. Mangan, Jr.,* 554 S.W.2d 418)

35. Joyner wrote out her will and took it to the neighbors to type and sign as witnesses. She only told them that it was a "piece of paper" that she wanted "fixed up so as I can sign it so that [her son] could have a place to live." The neighbors knew that she was asking them to sign the paper so her property would be properly disposed upon her death. Did Joyner's failure to announce that it was her "last will and testament" render the will invalid? (*Faith v. Singleton,* 692 S.W.2d 239)

36. When the administrator of Courziel's estate opened the safe deposit box that contained a copy of Courziel's will, he found the will was missing the last page. Unfortunately this page contained Courziel's signature and those of the witnesses to the document. Courziel had sole control over the box. Should the "will" be enforced? (*Board of Trustees of the University of Alabama v. Calhoun,* 514 So. 2d 895)

37. Gillespie, during a visit to his bank, dictated a codicil to his will. It was typed and signed by Gillespie before he left the bank. However, it was not until later that two bank employees signed the document as witnesses. They were not present to see Gillespie actually sign the document. Would the probate court treat the codicil as valid? (*Brammer v. Taylor,* 338 S.E.2d 207)

38. Mr. Suarez purchased a $50,000 insurance policy on himself from Liberty National Insurance Company. As beneficiary, he designated his mother, Guarina Cardona. Months later Suarez met with his insurance agent to change the beneficiary on his policy from Cardona to Zeigler. At the meeting Suarez indicated that he wanted the policy payoff to be used for the benefit of his two children, Ebony and Antonio. After Zeigler agreed to carry out Suarez's wishes, Suarez changed the beneficiary to Zeigler. However, when the insurance agent submitted the change of beneficiary form to Liberty National, the company never actually changed the beneficiary. Not knowing this, Zeigler faithfully paid the premiums on the policy until Suarez's death. Afterwards this suit was brought to correct the matter. What sort of trust device could be used by the court to see that Suarez's wishes would be carried out? Why? (*Ziegler v. Cardona,* 830 F. Supp. 1395)

39. When Edwin Fickes died his will provided that a trust should be established and that it should be split "in equal portions between the grandchildren then living" upon the death of his last surviving child. When that occurred, there were eight surviving grandchildren. Four of these were adopted. Two of the adopted grandchildren had been adopted before Fickes died. The other two were adopted afterwards. Which grandchildren should receive a portion of the estate? (*Connecticut National Bank v. Chadwick,* 217 Conn. 260)

Case For Legal Thinking

MORSE V. VOLZ
164 CAL. APP. 3D 1001 (1985)

BACKGROUND The plaintiff, John Morse, son of the decedent, Marvin, brought this action to contest his father's will. He alleged that his father lacked testamentary capacity and was under the undue influence of his second wife when he made out the contested document. The Lower Court decided in favor of the son and ruled that it was not the father's legitimate last will and testament. Barbara Volz, the personal representative of the estate of John Morse's second wife, now deceased, brought this appeal.

FACTS When the father's first wife lay dying, he began to exhibit behavior that seemed questionable. He drank more and refused to visit her in the hospital. He would isolate himself in his study with a bottle of scotch and take long solitary walks. He was so irritable that he struck his granddaughter and yelled and screamed at family, friends, and neighbors.

This behavior struck his son, John, as exceptional as he had never seen his father act in such a way. After the death of his first wife, the father refused to make the funeral arrangements or attend the visitations. To John, he had always been a kind and understanding man. John and his wife, Claire, decided to live permanently near the father and had a caring relationship with him for several years after the first wife's death. Then the father's eyesight began to fail and he became depressed and reclusive. He began to drink heavily.

Obsessed with money, the father moved into the basement of his house and slept on a cot to save on utilities. He also experienced memory lapses and could not recall the events of past days or even hours. After his house was burglarized, the father began to prowl it at night carrying a .20 gauge shotgun.

Then he began seeing Inga, the woman who would become his second wife. Inga was at the time seeing another man named Eldon Zion. Following a luncheon with her friend Zelma and Marvin, Inga telephoned Zelma and said that, although she loved Eldon, she was going to date Marvin because Eldon "had no money and was not a Mason."

When Marvin announced his impending marriage to Inga, his son noted that the date for the wedding was during the time the son and his wife would be in Italy.

At the same time, the father also said that he had been to an attorney and "everything has been taken care of to protect all of our children."

After the wedding, the father made out the new, contested will. "At the time there was nothing at all unusual about him," testified the attorney chosen to craft the will and who took the decedent through it "rather carefully" afterward. The attorney also said "He was quite capable of making a will."

The will in question left everything to Inga, if she survived him, and to her children, if she predeceased him. The will expressly stated that the decedent left nothing to his son as "he does not have the need for what I may leave in my estate."

Various experts testified to the possibility that the decedent may have been subject to early senile degeneration or Alzheimer's Disease at the time of the making out of the will.

PRACTICE JUDGING

1. Did the decedent have testamentary capacity?

2. Did the decedent act of his own free will in cutting out his son and the son's family, or was Inga's influence too great?

3. How should the court rule in this case?

Entrepreneurs
AND THE LAW

Project 4 Property Law

RAPID GROWTH Six months after leasing and converting Joe and Bob's shop to production of the SecureSeals, the number of sales and the size of the resulting profits staggered Stacy. Even with the lease payments and paying for supplies to create new inventory, she was able to pay her dad back the amount of his initial investment and quit her job at the DOT. Word-of-mouth advertising brought customer after customer to the shop.

PATENT PROTECTION Due to this rapid growth, Brandon became concerned that Stacy had not taken the actions necessary to secure her long-term interests in the intellectual property involved in SecureSeal. He felt that relying on trade-secret protection aided by the non-disclosure agreements and common-law trademark rules was not enough. Acting on his advice, Stacy hired both an engineer and an intellectual property law firm. They quickly set about the tasks necessary for filing for patent protection on the SecureSeal process and the production machine. They also prepared a trademark filing to protect the name SecureSeal. In just two weeks the engineer completed the necessary drawings of the process and the production machine. The lawyer then began identifying the claims (the characteristics that set Stacy's process and machine apart from all others) that would be made on the SecureSeal system to obtain the patents.

POTENTIAL LIABILITY The wisdom of Brandon's advice became evident several months later. Shortly after the patent and trademark filings, reports began filtering back to Joe and Stacy of a product similar to the Secure-Seal being sold on the West Coast. Stacy and Joe hired a detective agency to investigate. The report that came back shocked them. Joe's former partner in the shop, Bob, had secretly made a video of the SecureSeal production line and process. He had sold the video as well as a copy of the design plans for Stacy's machine to a competitor on the coast, Teddy's Retreads, for $250,000. Scarcely a month later, Teddy's had begun marketing a similar product under the name SecurelySealed. Unfortunately for those using that product, the video did not show the true secret of the SecureSeal process and, as a consequence, the SecurelySealed tires were vastly inferior to the SecureSeal tires and dangerously defective. Several accidents had been attributed to the tendency of the SecurelySealed recaps not only to lose their tread at full speed but to do so in an explosive manner. Stacy realized that the similarity of the name as well as the connection between Bob and Stacy and Joe's operation might result in lost sales and even one or more lawsuits against them. When she discussed the matter with Brandon, he recommended that they immediately sue Teddy's for patent and trademark infringement as well as damages to their goodwill.

INSURANCE NEEDS Before he hung up, Brandon reminded Stacy to set up a meeting with a local business insurer. "You need a lot of insurance protection—for you and the business. There's too much riding on it now to take any further risks."

Stacy felt snowed under for a moment, but rebounded when Brandon said, "I know you're worried, Stace, and it's a lot to handle. But, I'll be there to help whenever you need me."

ACTIVITIES

Divide into teams and perform one or more of the following activities.

Prepare Legal Documents

Consider your team to be the firm of intellectual property attorneys that Stacy has hired to protect the SecureSeal name and system. Divide your team into two groups and have one draft the trademark application and the other a patent application for SecureSeal.

Argue

Divide your team into two groups, each representing a party in a potential lawsuit against Teddy's and Bob. Consider causes of action, remedies to be pursued, and likelihood of success of the suit. Each group should prepare an opening argument to use in event of a trial. After each side presents its argument the class should vote on which party is likely to prevail.

PROTECT YOUR ENVIRONMENT Did you know the nation's leading environmental protection club has youth programs that encourage young people to become actively involved in protecting the environment? The Sierra Club—nature's advocate in the United States—in partnership with Youth Services, has provided more than 500,000 young people nationwide with the opportunity to experience wilderness outings, learn about environmental issues, and engage in grassroots activism.

DO YOUR PART

1. Research to find a local environmental issue.
2. Use the Internet to find the closest chapter of the Sierra Club. Contact them to see if they are working on the issue.
3. Research the issue and make a fact sheet.
4. Ask to speak to local organizations, which may include the PTO, Rotary Club, Lions Club, and others. Pass out your fact sheet at the meeting.

Presentation Management

This event will assess your use of current desktop computing technologies and software to prepare and deliver an effective multimedia presentation.

You will design a computer-generated multimedia presentation. You have fifteen (15) minutes for preparation and setup. The presentation will last a minimum of seven (7) minutes and a maximum of ten (10) minutes. Up to five (5) minutes will be allowed for questions from the judges. The contestant must make effective use of current multimedia technology in the presentation. To prepare for the presentation, contestants should use space, color, and text as design factors. No VCR or laser disc may be used in the presentation. Charts and other graphics should be used in the presentation.

You are an attorney who specializes in wills and estates. Many individuals recognize the need for wills; however, they just don't seem to take time to create a will. Individuals without wills have not exercised their right to tell the government how to distribute their property when they die. You must prepare a multimedia presentation for young parents with children. The pre-

sentation must emphasize the importance of wills and discuss what happens to estates when individuals die.

Performance Indicators Evaluated

- Understand wills and estate planning.
- Explain strategies for developing a will.
- Explain what happens to property not covered by a will.
- Discuss the importance of a will.

For more detailed information about performance indicators, go to the BPA web site.

THINK CRITICALLY

1. What is a will?
2. Why is it important for a young, healthy family to have a will?
3. What can happen to an estate when no will exists?
4. Why should an individual consider hiring an attorney when drawing up a will?

Mock Trial Prep

WHAT IS AN OPENING STATEMENT?

A mock trial begins with an opening statement made by counsel for the Plaintiff, followed by an opening statement made by counsel for the Defense. An opening statement will explain what the evidence will be and what the attorney will try to prove. The goal is to acquaint the judge with the case and outline what you are going to prove through witness testimony and the admission of evidence.

PROCEDURAL MATTERS

The judge will ask counsel for the Plaintiff to make his or her opening statement to begin the trial. The judge will ask if counsel is ready to proceed. Stand up and say, "Yes, Your Honor." The judge usually will state either, "Counsel, present your opening argument" or "Counsel, are you prepared to make an opening statement?"

Typically, an opening statement is delivered from the podium. Opening statements should begin with the traditional opening phrase, "May it please the Court." Next, introduce yourself, your co-counsel, and state who you represent. This also is an appropriate time to introduce your witnesses.

For example, your opening statement will begin with the following statement:

> May it please the Court. My name is _____ and my co-counsel is _____. We represent the Defendant _____. Today the Court will hear testimony from (character name), portrayed by _____, and from (character name), portrayed by _____.

Co-counsel and the witnesses should stand when introduced so that the judge or jury can identify them.

COURTROOM ETIQUETTE

When the judge enters and leaves the courtroom, everyone in the courtroom stands. An attorney also should stand when addressing the court. An attorney should not interrupt the judge. Attorneys should address the judge as "Your Honor" or "Judge." When addressing opposing counsel, it is appropriate to refer to him or her as "Mr. Smith" or "Defendant's counsel." However, it is inappropriate to address opposing counsel during the trial. Arguments and objections should be made to the bench, not to opposing counsel.

Civility plays an important role in mock trial and within the practice of law. Every attorney should zealously represent his or her clients within the bounds of civility. Civility means courtesy, dignity, decency, and kindness. It is an element of professionalism. Treating opposing counsel, the court, and the witnesses with civility is an important component of mock trial.

DEVELOP YOUR THEORY OF THE CASE

The single most important aspect of your opening statement is the development and description of your theory of the case. Develop your theory of the case before writing your opening statement. Your theory of the case is a simple, logical story consistent with the evidence explaining your version of the facts. What really happened? You also will want to develop a theme in your theory of the case. Introduce this theme in your opening statement and continue the theme throughout the trial and closing arguments. For instance, the theme of your case might be jealousy, revenge, power, or tainted evidence.

TELL A STORY

Begin your opening statement by telling the court what your case is about by stating the facts of your client's case as developed by your theory of the case. Present the facts in a chronological fashion. There is no need to present every fact to the judge in your opening. Present just enough of the important facts to insure that the judge has an accurate overview of the case.

Introduce the key witnesses who will be testifying during the hearing or trial. Give the court a preview of their testimony. What will the witness testify to seeing, hearing, etc.? What will the witnesses tell the court? What will the testimony (evidence) prove? Remember never to promise to prove anything that you will not or cannot prove during the hearing or trial.

Be a vivid storyteller. Hold the attention of the court by presenting the opening statement with drama,

emotion, and passion. However, use an appropriate and sincere level of drama as the facts of your case warrant. Insincerity and "overacting" can result in a lack of credibility and persuasive power.

NO ARGUING!

Do not argue in the opening statement! The opening statement is not the time to argue case law or to argue the facts of the case. You should tell the court what the case is about, what witnesses the court will hear, and what the testimony will prove. You may say:

> The evidence will show…
>
> Mr. X will testify that….
>
> We intend to prove today…
>
> You will learn from (witness) that…

Argument, discussion of law, or objections by the opposing attorney are not permitted.

ASK FOR WHAT YOU SEEK

Conclude your opening statement by asking the court what remedy you are seeking. What do you want the court to do or how do you want the court to rule? Respectfully ask for the court to return a verdict or decision for your client. For instance:

> Therefore, the State of Ohio respectfully asks this Court deny Defendant's motion to eliminate the death penalty as a sentencing option for the Defendant. Thank you.
>
> Therefore, Defendant Jane Smith respectfully asks this Court to find the Defendant not guilty of all charges against him. Thank you.

PREPARATION IS KEY TO SUCCESS

Preparation and organization of your opening statement is critical. Write a clear, concise, and well-organized statement. An important part of the preparation is to familiarize yourself with all of the witness statements. You must have a working knowledge of the facts and of the testimony of each witness.

Never read the opening statement. Delivery of the statement is key to its success. Make eye contact with the judge. Speak with clarity, confidence and animation. This will insure a more compelling and persuasive presentation. Try to deliver the opening statement without the use of notes. However, it is common for most attorneys to use an outline of the key points to cover during the opening statement.

TEAMWORK

Work in small teams. Half the teams will represent the Defense and half will represent the Prosecution. Write an opening statement in the case of *The People of Any State vs. Robert Craig* for either the prosecution or the defense. Consider the following questions in composing your opening statements.

Defense

What is the theory of the case from the Defense's point of view?

What is your strongest argument in Robert's defense?

What witnesses will you interview to support this argument?

Prosecution

What is the theory of the case from the Prosecution's point of view?

Should you stress the reality of the fact that Robert was indeed driving a car that did not belong to him at the time of his arrest?

What witnesses will you call to develop this fact pattern?

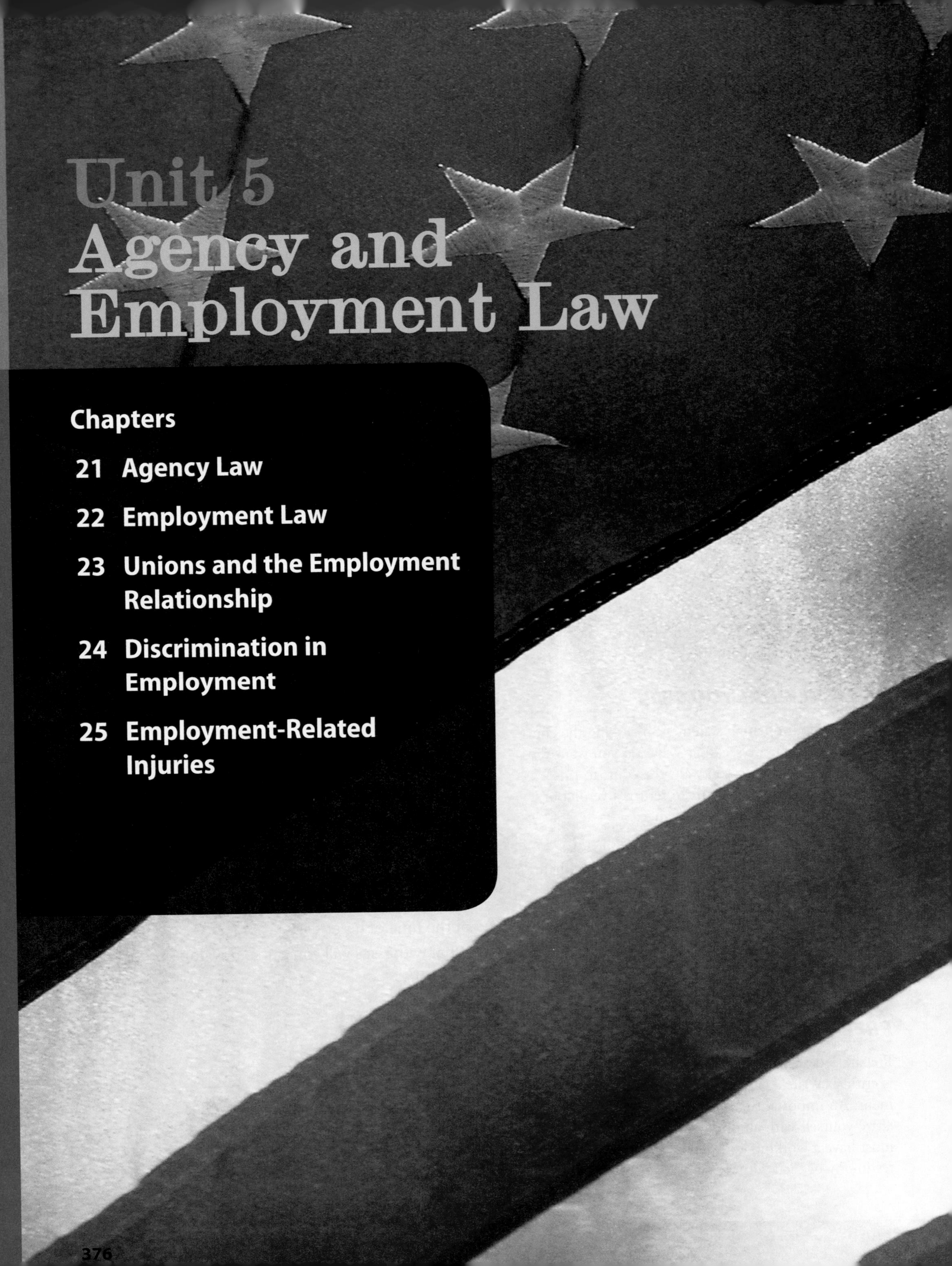

Unit 5
Agency and Employment Law

Chapters

21 Agency Law

22 Employment Law

23 Unions and the Employment Relationship

24 Discrimination in Employment

25 Employment-Related Injuries

Government & Public Administration

Pension Investigator

Pension investigators examine the activities of employee benefit plans to make sure employers are operating within the law. They review whether or not investments have been made wisely, if reports have been filed correctly, and if benefits and eligibility requirements are legitimate. They make sure that pension plans are being managed solely in the interests of the people who contribute to, and benefit from, the plan. In the course of their work they look for criminal violations including theft, embezzlement, and attempts to influence illegal actions related to a pension. Pension investigators use strong enforcement efforts to ensure workers receive the benefits they have been promised.

EMPLOYMENT OUTLOOK

- Employment by the federal government is projected to grow slowly through the year 2014.

- Most new employees will be hired in five major areas including inspectors and investigators.

- In general, federal employment is considered to be relatively stable because it is not affected when the economy fluctuates.

NEEDED SKILLS AND EDUCATION

- Pension investigators typically hold a bachelor's degree in accounting or a related field. Some hold graduate or law degrees.

- Special knowledge of pension laws, and experience in developing policies related to employee benefit plans, is a distinct advantage when searching for a job. This specialized knowledge is not learned in the classroom. It is acquired through on-the-job experience.

- Experience in financial auditing and accounting also is helpful.

- Pension investigators should have an aptitude for mathematics and be able to analyze, compare, and interpret facts and figures quickly. They must have a curious nature and the ability to think analytically.

- They need organizational skills that will allow them to sift through complex financial information and recognize something that is out of the ordinary.

How you'll spend your day

As a pension investigator you likely will work weekdays in an office setting. Periodically you may travel to other work sites to complete an investigation. Your work will involve sifting through company records, via computer files and hard copies. You'll make inquiries using the phone and e-mail in the course of your work.

As a pension investigator, you may be asked to carefully analyze a company's pension plan. Your job will be to determine if the plan is being properly managed and will result in a financial gain. When an employee of the company retires, you want to make sure that money will be available to them as outlined in their retirement package. To do so, you'll ask: Was the money in the pension fund invested wisely? Were investments diversified in order to limit the possibility of large losses?

By law, some plans can invest no more than 10 percent in employer securities and real property. But there are exceptions. It will be your job to make sure the law was followed in the pension plan you are analyzing. Some of the work may be sensitive or confidential. Results of your investigation could mean criminal charges for one or more persons involved in managing a pension fund. When your investigation is complete, you'll write a report on your findings. You may be asked to recommend actions to be taken as a result of your findings.

What about you?

Does the job of pension investigator interest you? Why or why not? Which aspects of the job would you most enjoy? Which aspects would you least enjoy?

© PHOTODISC/GETTY IMAGES

Chapter 21
Agency Law

21-1 Creation and Operation of Agencies

21-2 Agency Duties

HOT DEBATE

After two years of courtship, Alexis, the widow of a famous American diplomat, accepted an engagement ring from Osiris, a billionaire Russian businessman. Osiris desired not only Alexis, but also the prestige a marriage to her would bring. Alexis called in her attorneys to negotiate the prenuptial agreement with Osiris' attorneys. After a week of negotiations, the agreement was signed by both parties. The couple then said their vows of love and devotion in a simple ceremony at a Black Sea resort.

© GETTY IMAGES/PHOTODISC

WHERE DO YOU STAND?

1. Should agents (the lawyers) be used in such an intimate setting to put a price tag on feelings? Justify your answer.
2. Given the disruptive effects of "blinding" love on individuals, should any such prenuptial agreement be enforceable? Why or why not?

21-1 Creation and Operation of Agencies

GOALS

- Understand the agency concept
- Appreciate the scope of agency authority

KEY TERMS

agency
principal
agent
warranty of the
   principal's capacity
scope of authority

gratuitous agency
express authority
power of attorney
implied authority
apparent authority
ratification

What Is an Agency?

WHAT'S YOUR VERDICT? Ortiz, a minor, had a huge CD collection. In order to raise funds for college, she ripped the CDs onto her computer and downloaded the music onto her MP3 player. Then she agreed to pay Stems, a local shopkeeper, a 10 percent commission if he would sell the CDs for her. After he found a buyer, however, Ortiz's MP3 player was stolen, so she decided not to sell the CDs. She claimed that, as a minor, she could avoid both the agency contract and the sales contract even though it was made by an adult merchant.

Is she correct?

An **agency** is a relationship between two parties that allows one of the parties to act so as to legally bind the other. The person who authorizes another to enter into legal relationships in his or her behalf is the **principal**. The party so authorized is the **agent**.

The most common form of agency occurs when a salesperson in a store makes a contract with a customer on behalf of the store's owner. Note that the same salesperson who acts as an agent in a sales transaction may then turn around and perform other duties for the business that do not involve agency.

Agency is consensual. Even if you contract to make someone your agent, both parties always have the power to terminate the agency relationship. While there may be liability for breach of contract for ending the agency, no one can be forced to continue in an agency relationship.

Principals

Generally, almost anyone can be a principal. Minors and others who lack contractual capacity can be principals and act through agents. However, they retain their rights flowing from a lack of contractual capacity. Thus they may disaffirm contracts made with their agents for non-necessaries. In *What's Your Verdict?* Oritz may avoid her contract to pay Fischer the 10 percent commission. As a minor,

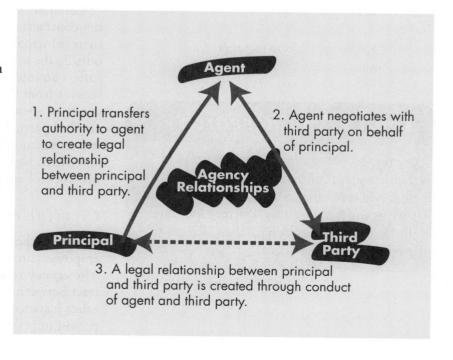

1. Principal transfers authority to agent to create legal relationship between principal and third party.

Agent

2. Agent negotiates with third party on behalf of principal.

Agency Relationships

Principal

Third Party

3. A legal relationship between principal and third party is created through conduct of agent and third party.

she also can avoid the contract with the buyer of her CDs because contracts made through agents can be avoided by principals who lack capacity.

As a general consequence of this potential for avoidance, the law tries to protect third parties with a warranty of capacity. A **warranty of the principal's capacity** is imposed by law on the agent. The law assumes that the agent promised the third party that the principal had capacity. If the principal lacked capacity, avoided the contract, and thus injured the third party, the third party can recover from the agent.

Agents

As far as who can qualify to be an agent is concerned, the general requirement is that an agent must be able to understand the transaction entered into on behalf of the principal. As a consequence, those who lack contractual capacity themselves still may be agents. Thus, minors who lack legal capacity to act for themselves generally can act for and bind adults in contracts. An adult principal cannot later avoid the resulting contract simply by showing the minority of her or his agent. Instead a principal must show that the individual agent lacked an ability to understand that particular transaction.

To protect the public, all states require that agents in certain occupations be licensed. This usually requires passing a professional examination. Licensing often is required of auctioneers, insurance agents, lawyers, stock brokers, and real estate brokers.

CHECKPOINT Define the agency relationship.

LEGAL *Research*

Contact several sports agents for copies of their standard contracts. Annual listings can be found in libraries or online in publications such as the *Sports Agents Directory*. Evaluate the contracts you obtain for their fairness to the athlete and the agent.

Scope of an Agent's Authority

WHAT'S YOUR VERDICT? Jared was shopping for a new car. One morning, while admiring a new Thunderhawk sedan on a dealer's lot, he was approached by Arnold, a salesperson for the dealership. After considerable negotiations, they arrived at an agreement for the sale of the car to Jared. However, Jared said he wanted to think about it overnight. Arnold then wrote down the terms of the deal they had agreed upon including a statement that the deal was good until 5 P.M. the next day. He signed the paper and gave it to Jared. When Jared returned the next day to take the deal, he found that Arnold had been fired for getting a traffic ticket while driving a dealership car at an excessive rate of speed.

Is the dealership bound by the terms of the deal for the sale of the Thunderhawk?

An agent must act within the granted **scope of authority** in order to bind the principal. The scope of authority is the range of acts authorized by the principal. If the agent has acted outside the scope of authority, the principal is not bound.

Generally, agents are not personally liable for the contracts that they negotiate on behalf of their principals. However, when the agent acts outside the scope of authority and the third party suffers an injury as a result, the third party can recover from the agent. Of course a person who is not an agent has no authority and cannot bind another party. In *What's Your Verdict?* Arnold was an agent and did bind the dealership to the agreement by his signature as it was well within his scope of authority.

Creation of Authority

Agency authority is created when a principal empowers an agent to represent the principal. The agency relationship may arise from a contract between the agent and the principal. In other instances, there may be no contract. One person may simply agree to help another in altering legal relationships with third parties. In cases where the agent receives no consideration and there is no contract, the agency is called a **gratuitous agency**.

Agency authority may be created in a variety of ways. These include an express grant of authority, an implied grant of authority, creation by apparent authority, and ratification.

EXPRESS GRANT OF AUTHORITY **Express authority** is communicated directly by the principal to the agent. It may be oral or written. If written, the grant may be in an informal letter or a carefully drafted document. Any writing that appoints someone as an agent is called a **power of attorney**. The agent empowered by such a document is termed an *attorney in fact*. Generally, a power of attorney is revoked by law upon the death of the principal. See the sample power of attorney document on page 382.

IMPLIED GRANT OF AUTHORITY **Implied authority** is the power to do anything that is reasonably necessary or customary to carry out the duties expressly authorized. Thus, an agent's implied authority flows out of the express authority. Implied authority may be expanded in an emergency. For example, suppose Taylor asks Logan to run an errand for her and gives Logan the keys to her car. If Taylor's car catches on fire while Logan is driving it on the errand, Logan would have implied authority to promise money to someone to assist in putting out the fire. Taylor would be liable to pay for this help.

APPARENT AUTHORITY Agency authority may sometimes result from the appearance created by the principal. This does not create a conventional agency because there has been no agreement between the principal and the agent. **Apparent authority** is created when a principal leads the third party to reasonably believe that a particular person has agency authority. The apparent authority must always come from the principal's words or conduct. It can never arise from the words or conduct of the agent alone.

IN THIS CASE Bob owned a hi-tech home theater business. One day the store, which had several suites where the prospective customers could preview the various screens and projectors, was especially busy. As Bob's salespeople were out doing installations, he was handling the customers himself. Bob recognized Jameel, a customer that he had been working with for several days, pulling into the parking lot. He knew he would have to deal directly with Jameel so as to close the sale. As a consequence, Bob went into the back of the store and pulled Doris, an employee he had hired the day before, away from her job of assembling new displays. He told her to keep showing the customers more equipment until he had closed the sale with Jameel. He then introduced Doris to the other customers and in so doing said, "She'll be able to help you." Before Bob could return, Doris had sold a $23,000 home theater system to the Pushkins for half the normal price. Because he had clothed Doris in apparent authority, Bob had to go through with the contract.

RATIFICATION As previously mentioned, if a person acts outside the scope of his or her authority, the principal is not bound. However, a principal who later agrees to the transaction can be bound. This approval of a previously unauthorized act, or an act outside the agent's scope of authority, is called **ratification**. A principal impliedly ratifies an agency transaction by knowingly accepting its benefits.

POWER OF ATTORNEY
GENERAL

Know All Men by These Presents: That I, _____

_____

the undersigned (jointly and severally, if more than one) hereby make, constitute and appoint _____

_____

as a true and lawful Attorney for me and in my name, place and stead and for my use and benefit:

(a) To ask, demand, sue for, recover, collect and receive each and every sum of money, debt, account, legacy, bequest, interest, dividend, annuity and demand (which now is or hereafter shall become due, owing or payable) belonging to or claimed by me, and to use and take any lawful means for the recovery thereof by legal process or otherwise, and to execute and deliver a satisfaction or release therefor, together with the right and power to compromise or compound any claim or demand;

(b) To exercise any or all of the following powers as to real property, any interest therein and/or any building thereon: To contract for, purchase, receive and take possession thereof and of evidence of title thereto; to lease the same for any term or purpose, including leases for business, residence, and oil and/or mineral development; to sell, exchange, grant or convey the same with or without warranty; and to mortgage, transfer in trust, or otherwise encumber or hypothecate the same to secure payment of a negotiable or non-negotiable note or performance of any obligation or agreement;

(c) To exercise any or all of the following powers as to all kinds of personal property and goods, wares and merchandise, choses in action and other property in possession or in action; To contract for, buy, sell, exchange, transfer and in any legal manner deal in and with the same; and to mortgage, transfer in trust, or otherwise encumber or hypothecate the same to secure payment of a negotiable or non-negotiable note or performance of any obligation or agreement;

(d) To borrow money and to execute and delivery negotiable or non-negotiable notes therefor with or without security; and to loan money and receive negotiable or non-negotiable notes therefor with such security as he shall deem proper;

(e) To create, amend, supplement and terminate any trust and to instruct and advise the trustee of any trust wherein I am or may be trustor or beneficiary; to represent and vote stock, exercise rights, accept and deal with any dividend, distribution or bonus, join in any corporate financing, reorganization, merger, liquidation, consolidation or other action and the extension, compromise, conversion, adjustment, enforcement or foreclosure, singly or in conjunction with others of any corporate stock, bond, note, debenture or other security; to compound, compromise, adjust, settle and satisfy and obligation, secured or unsecured, owing by or to me and to give or accept any property and/or money whether or not equal to or less in value than the amount owing in payment, settlement or satisfaction thereof;

(f) To transact business of any kind or class and as my act and deed to sign, execute, acknowledge and deliver any deed, lease, assignment of lease, covenant, indenture, indemnity, agreement, mortgage, deed of trust, assignment of mortgage or of the beneficial interest under deed of trust, extension or renewal of any obligation, subordination or waiver of priority, hypothecation, bottomry, charter-party, bill of lading, bill of sale, bill, bond, note, whether negotiable or non-negotiable, receipt, evidence of debt, full or partial release or satisfaction of mortgage, judgment and other debt, request for partial or full reconveyance of deed of trust and such other instruments in writing of any kind or class as may be necessary or proper in the premises.

Giving and Granting unto my said Attorney full power and authority to do and perform all and every act and thing whatsoever requisite, necessary or appropriate to be done in and about the premises as fully to all interests and purposes as I might or could do if personally present, hereby ratifying all that my said Attorney shall lawfully do or cause to be done by virtue of these presents. The powers and authority hereby conferred upon my said Attorney shall be applicable to all real and personal property or interests therein now owned or hereafter acquired by me and wherever situate.

My said Attorney is empowered hereby to determine in his sole discretion the time where, purpose for and manner in which any power herein conferred upon him shall be exercised, and the conditions, provisions and covenants of any instrument or document which may be executed by him pursuant hereto; and in the acquisition or disposition of real or personal property, my said Attorney shall have exclusive power to fix the terms thereof for cash, credit and/or property, and if on credit with or without security.

The undersigned, hereby further authorizes and empowers my said Attorney, as my duly authorized agent, to join in my behalf, in the execution of any instrument by which any community real property or any interest therein, now owned or hereafter acquired by my spouse and myself, or either or us, is sold, leased, encumbered, or conveyed.

When the contest so requires, the masculine gender includes the feminine and/or neuter, and the singular number includes the plural.

WITNESS my hand this _____ day of _____, 20_____

_____   _____

_____   _____

State of _____,
County of _____ } SS.

On _____, before me, the undersigned, a Notary Public in and for

said State, personally appeared _____

_____

known to me to be the person _____ whose name _____ subscribed

to the within instrument and acknowledged that _____ executed the same.

(Seal) _____

Notary Public in and for said State

Witness my hand and official seal.

For a valid ratification, the following conditions must be met:

- The third person must have believed that by dealing with the principal's agent, he or she was making a contract with the principal.
- Before ratification, the principal must have full knowledge of all material facts.
- The principal must show an intent to ratify.

- The principal must ratify the entire act, not just one part of the transaction.
- The principal must ratify before the third person withdraws from the unratified transaction.

CHECKPOINT List the ways in which agency authority can be created.

21-1 Assessment

school.cengage.com/blaw/lawxtra

THINK ABOUT LEGAL CONCEPTS

1. Every employee who is authorized to bind the employer to a contract is an agent. **True or False?**

2. If an agent acts outside the agent's authority, then (a) the principal is not bound (b) the agent is liable to the third party for any injury caused by acting outside the scope of authority (c) both a and b

3. A minor cannot under any circumstances be an agent. **True or False?**

4. Minors who act through agents have the same rights they would have if they acted directly. **True or False?**

5. A power of attorney generally contains a grant of what type of authority? (a) express authority (b) implied authority (c) apparent authority

6. When someone acts outside the scope of express authority, but the principal accepts the benefits of the transaction with knowledge of all its terms, the principal's action is termed a _?_.

THINK CRITICALLY ABOUT EVIDENCE

Study the situation, answer the questions, and then prepare arguments to support your answers.

7. Alonzo hired Lawrence to help him sell a valuable Persian rug. He authorized Lawrence to sell it for $400,000 cash. Lawrence did so. Later, Alonzo discovered that the rug was worth more than $600,000. Because Alonzo was a minor, he disaffirmed the contract, returned the $400,000 to the buyer, and got the rug back. The buyer sued Lawrence for $200,000—the difference between the $400,000 contract price and the $600,000 value. Will the buyer collect?

8. Sweet Store, Inc., hired Li to work in the store. Mrs. Sweet, the owner, asked Li to be in charge of the vegetable displays. This involved spraying the vegetables with water periodically and sorting out vegetables that no longer looked fresh. Another employee was in charge of ordering and taking deliveries of the vegetables. Cash register clerks were in charge of selling the veg-

etables. One day, Li was taking a break on the loading dock when a load of vegetables arrived. He signed the shipping receipt, although he was not authorized to do so. Unfortunately, about $600 worth of vegetables were missing from the shipment. Is the store liable for the loss because of Li's signature?

9. Jane asked Kroger to represent her in selling her farm. She signed a limited power of attorney authorizing Kroger to negotiate a sale and to execute all necessary documents to transfer title to her real property. Then Jane left for vacation. When she returned, she learned that Kroger had sold the farm at an attractive price. He also sold two tractors and a truck. Is Jane bound by Kroger's conduct in selling the farm? In selling the tractors and the truck?

21-2 Agency Duties

GOALS

- List the duties of an agent
- List the duties of a principal
- Identify when an agency is terminated

KEY TERMS

fiduciary duties

duty of loyalty

duty of obedience

duty of reasonable care and skill

duty of confidentiality

duty of accounting

commingling

trust accounts

undisclosed principal

What Are an Agent's Duties?

WHAT'S YOUR VERDICT? Medici had collected comic books since the late 1940s when she was a child. Now, needing retirement funds and seeing the interest shown in the movie versions of the comic book characters, she contracted with an agent to auction them off over the Internet. Medici had no computer skills, so she did not discover that the agent instead sold the collection directly to his uncle for half the average market price.

If Medici discovered what occurred, could she recover the rest of the collection's value from the agent?

Duties Owed the Principal

In many respects, the agent's duties to the principal are the same as those of an ordinary employee. However, the agent has the additional ability to bind the principal in dealings with third parties. Therefore, agents must be exceptionally honest and show good faith. The law encourages this by requiring fiduciary duties of the agent. **Fiduciary duties** in general require an agent to adhere to the highest standard of duty implied by law by subordinating her or his personal interests in order to act for the benefit of the principal.

The specific fiduciary duties owed by agents to principals are loyalty, obedience, reasonable care and skill, confidentiality, and accounting. If an agent violates a fiduciary duty and that injures the principal, the agent will be liable for the injury.

LOYALTY AND OBEDIENCE The agent's core duties are those of loyalty and obedience. The **duty of loyalty** means that the agent may not secretly benefit from the agency transaction. Thus, agents may neither buy from nor sell to themselves, their relatives, or their friends without prior approval from their principals. In *What's Your Verdict?*, due to the agent's breach of the duty of loyalty by selling the collection to his uncle, Medici could recover the shortfall from the sale from the agent. In addition any profits the agent earns in performing the agency duties belong to the principal, unless otherwise agreed.

The agent also owes the **duty of obedience** to the principal. This means that the agent must carefully obey the instructions of the principal. Of course an agent should not follow instructions to do an illegal or immoral act. For

LAW BRIEF

In late September of 2004, President Bush signed into law the Sports Agent Responsibility and Trust Act (SPARTA). SPARTA imposes higher standards on sports agents and mandates much stiffer penalties for agents who unethically sign amateur athletes in high school or college. The law requires that the agent disclose in writing that the athlete may lose NCAA eligibility after signing with an agent. The agent and the athlete also are required to notify the athlete's school so that it will not use an ineligible athlete and have to forfeit games. SPARTA also bars giving anything of value to the athlete or the athlete's family or friends. Penalties up to $11,000 per day can be levied for each offense.

example, a sales agent may not lie about a product even if the principal has ordered such fraudulent conduct. If a principal orders an agent to do something illegal or immoral, the agent should document the event (to protect from a potential breach of contract suit) and resign from the agency relationship.

REASONABLE CARE AND SKILL In representing one's principal, an agent must satisfy the **duty of reasonable care and skill**. This requires the agent to exercise the degree of care and skill that a reasonably prudent person would use in a similar situation. Failing to satisfy the fiduciary duty of reasonable care and skill renders the agent liable to the principal for the resulting loss or injury. At a minimum, reasonable care and skill requires the agent to communicate to the principal any information that would affect the principal's decisions.

CONFIDENTIALITY The **duty of confidentiality** requires the agent to treat information about the principal with great caution. Information that is obviously confidential must be kept confidential. Some information obviously is not confidential. If a principal asks an agent to treat any information as confidential, however, the agent must do so. This duty of confidentiality survives the agency relationship. The duty may bind the agent years after the agency relationship has ended.

ACCOUNTING Agents owe the **duty of accounting** to the principal. It requires an agent to account to the principal for all money and property of the principal that comes into the agent's possession. The agent must promptly notify the principal of the receipt of money from third parties and must make an accounting within a reasonable time. An *accounting* is a formal statement, usually in writing, that tells the principal what happened to all of the principal's money or property.

The duty of accounting prohibits the agent from commingling. **Commingling** is mixing the funds or property of a fiduciary such as an agent

The woman on the right (the principal) hired the woman on the left (the agent) to represent her in the sale of her business. The principal emphasized that it was important to her to keep the terms of the sale secret. Which fiduciary duty of the agent does this situation call for?

© GETTY IMAGES/PHOTODISC

with those of her or his client, employer, or principal. If commingling occurs and there is a loss, the agent bears that loss.

Money of the principal held by the agent usually must be deposited in a bank, in an account separate from that of the agent. The separate accounts for the funds of principals are called **trust accounts**. Professional agents such as lawyers, accountants, real estate brokers, and stockbrokers maintain trust accounts that are separate from their personal and office checking accounts. If an agent places a client's funds in the agent's personal or office account, it would be commingling. Such action would subject the agent to both professional sanctions, such as disbarring a lawyer, and liability to the principal for any loss.

Duties Owed to Third Parties

An agent owes two main duties to third parties. First, the agent must not act outside the scope of authority given him or her by the principal. Second, the agent must insure that the principal has capacity. A breach of either of these duties may result in the agent being liable to the third parties dealt with under the agency.

EXCEEDING THE SCOPE OF AUTHORITY If an agent acts without authority from the principal, the agent becomes personally liable to the third party for resulting injury. That is because the agent implies the promise that he or she has appropriate authority. This usually arises when an agent exceeds the authority given by the principal.

In some cases, a person will act as agent for an alleged principal when absolutely no authority has been given for any action. Again, only the "agent" is liable to the third party unless the "principal" ratifies or has given apparent authority.

PRINCIPAL'S LACK OF CAPACITY An agent warrants the principal's capacity to the third party. If it turns out that the principal does not exist, or that the principal is able to avoid the contract for lack of contractual capacity, the agent will be liable. Normally, to bind the principal and to avoid personal liability an agent will sign the name of the principal to a contract or commercial paper (see Chapter 29) and add words to indicate that the signature is by an agent.

LIABILITY DUE TO AN UNDISCLOSED PRINCIPAL Sometimes under the terms of the agency an agent is not allowed to reveal the principal's existence or identity. The principal in such a case is known as an **undisclosed principal**. The agent is liable on a contract entered into under such circumstances. However, in most contractual situations, when the third party learns the identity of the principal, the third party generally may elect to hold either the principal or the agent to the agreement. The third party may not enforce the agreement against both, however.

CHECKPOINT What are the duties of an agent to the principal?

What Are the Principal's Duties?

WHAT'S YOUR VERDICT? Thompson, a writer, wanted to move from New England to Costa Rica. As a consequence, he listed his million-dollar house for sale with Howie Houdeene of the Escape Real Estate Company. Under the listing contract, a commission of 10 percent was to be paid for producing a buyer. A month later Houdeene did produce such a ready, willing, and able buyer for the property at the asking price. Before the property sale was closed, however, Thompson's mother, who lived nearby, suffered a stroke. To be able to attend to her, Thompson decided not to move and refused to go through with the sale.

Is Houdeene entitled to the commission?

In an agency relationship, a principal has duties to both the agent and third parties. A failure to fulfill these duties can result in liability for the principal.

Duties Owed the Agent

The principal's main duty is to pay what was promised for the agency services. In addition, if an agent properly incurs expenses, the principal must reimburse the agent. If the agent suffers any loss because of the principal's instructions, the principal must indemnify, or repay, the agent the amount lost. In *What's Your Verdict?* Thompson must fulfill his duty to compensate Houdeene for his services as Houdeene fulfilled his duty under the agency agreement by producing a ready, willing, and able buyer.

Finally, after a principal gives an agent certain tasks to perform, the principal has a duty to cooperate with the agent so that the tasks can be performed. Failure of the principal to fulfill her or his obligations gives the agent the right to quit and recover any damages.

Duties Owed Third Parties

As long as agents act within the scope of their authority, principals are bound by the agreements with the third parties. Even when the agents exceed their authority, principals are bound when they ratify the unauthorized acts.

Principals also have a duty not to authorize or permit improper acts in carrying out the agency. If torts or fraud are committed by an agent, the agent is liable. The principal also will be liable if the principal directed the agent to engage in the illegal activity, or the agent was acting to advance the interests of the principal. For example, if a sales agent defrauds a customer to make a sale, the principal is liable for any damages that result.

Usually, the principal is not liable for an agent's crime unless the crime itself has been authorized or ratified. As an exception to this rule, the principal generally is liable for the illegal sale, by the agent, of intoxicating liquor or adulterated foods. Thus, a bar owner, the principal, would be liable if the agent, a bartender, illegally served liquor to a minor.

> **IN THIS CASE** Reepou, the credit manager for Suburban Motors, thought that Bently had fallen behind in her payments on her SUV. Early one Sunday morning, Reepou had Bently's vehicle towed back to the dealership. In reality, Bently had married, and her new checks bore her married name. She had, in fact, informed the dealership of the change. Even though her account had not been credited with the amounts of the payments, the checks had been received exactly on time and had been cashed by the dealership's credit office. As Reepou committed the tort of conversion while acting as an agent for his principal, Suburban Motors, it would be vicariously liable.

CHECKPOINT What is a principal's main duty?

How Is an Agency Terminated?

> **WHAT'S YOUR VERDICT?** Daisy entered into a one-year written contract with the Sweet Magnolia Nursery as its sales agent in North and South Carolina. After six months, company sales dropped far below expectations. Daisy was the last to be hired, and so she was the first to be fired—even though her manager admitted that her performance had been satisfactory.
>
> **Did the nursery have a legal right to terminate the agency?**

By Unilateral Action of a Party

Generally, both the agent and the principal have the power, but not the right, to terminate the agency at any time. The principal terminates by revoking the agent's authority. If the termination violates the agency agreement and the agent is injured, the principal may have to pay damages as a consequence.

In *What's Your Verdict?* the nursery's firing of Daisy terminated the agency and thereby revoked her power to contractually bind the nursery. However, although the nursery had the power to terminate the agency, it did not have the right. Daisy could bring suit for any damages she sustained due to the breach of the one-year agency contract.

In a similar way, the agent has the power to quit at any time. However, he or she may lack the right to do so unless the principal has breached the contract. If an agent wrongfully terminates the agency before the contract expires, the principal may sue for damages. Note that in a gratuitous agency, which exists when it is agreed that the agent will not receive any consideration, the agent cannot recover any damages if the authority is revoked. Likewise, a principal normally cannot recover any damages from a gratuitous agent who abandons the agency.

In *What's Your Verdict?* could Sweet Magnolia Nursery be liable for damages if the agency termination were improper?

By Agreement

Normally an agency expires at the time or under the circumstances provided in the contract that created it. This may be after a particular length of time, upon the occurrence of an event, or at the completion of certain tasks. If nothing is specified in the agency contract, the agency continues for a reasonable time. An agency can be ended at any time if both the principal and agent agree to terminate it.

By Operation of Law

An agency ordinarily is terminated upon the death, insanity, or bankruptcy of either the principal or the agent. Also, if it becomes impossible to perform the agency, such as if the subject matter of the agency is destroyed or if a change of law makes the agent's required actions illegal, the agency is ended.

When the authority of an agent is terminated by the principal's voluntary act, the principal should notify promptly each individual third party who has previously dealt with the agent. If the principal does not give individualized notice,

the agent is likely to have apparent authority to make binding contracts between the principal and third persons as long as the third persons do not know of the termination. Others who may have heard of the agency also are entitled to notice. This can be given by publishing the fact of the termination in a newspaper of general circulation in the area.

CHECKPOINT Name the three general ways in which an agency may be terminated.

GLOBAL ISSUES

Export Employees and Agents

Companies engaged in direct exporting—selling directly to overseas companies—may hire full-time employees. These employees include full-time export managers and international sales specialists. Their duties include developing new products for overseas markets, pricing, and packaging and labeling products for export, among others.

Instead of hiring its own employees to do so, companies also may conduct business with overseas companies through foreign sales agents. These are agents of the companies who work on commission, earning a percentage of the sales they make.

They also may conduct overseas business using independent contractors, such as foreign distributors or export management companies. Foreign distributors usually are located in the country with which the company is doing business. They assume the risks of buying and warehousing the goods. They typically also service the products they sell, train end users to use the product, extend credit to customers, and advertise the products.

Finally, an exporter may employ an export management company. These companies are consultants that advise manufacturers and other exporters. They conduct research targeted to specific countries, exhibit goods at foreign trade shows, prepare export documentation, handle language translations, and make shipping arrangements.

21-2 Assessment

Xtra!
Study Tools
school.cengage.com/blaw/lawxtra

THINK ABOUT LEGAL CONCEPTS

1. Fiduciary duties are owed to the agent by the principal. **True or False?**

2. Which of the following duties would be violated by the agent's commingling of funds?
(a) loyalty and obedience (b) reasonable care and skill (c) confidentiality (d) accounting

3. The duty of confidentiality lasts even after the agency relationship is terminated. **True or False?**

4. If an agent acts outside the scope of authority, the principal will still be bound if the principal _?_ the agent's unauthorized acts.

5. Both principals and agents have the power but not the right to terminate the agency before the end of the contracted-for period, but they may be liable for damages if they do so. **True or False?**

THINK CRITICALLY ABOUT EVIDENCE

Study the situation, answer the questions, and then prepare arguments to support your answers.

6. Jeff hired Sally, a real estate broker, to help sell his home. While she was trying to sell the home, a buyer asked Sally what Jeff's bottom price was. To insure the house sold, she told the buyer without Jeff's permission . The buyer then offered that amount and Jeff accepted. Has Sally done anything wrong legally?

7. Anita retained Lynn as her lawyer. When Lynn settled Anita's lawsuit for more than $200,000, the check was mailed to Lynn at her law office. Lynn deposited the check in her personal account, and she used the money to pay monthly bills. When Anita asked about the money, Lynn stalled her saying it might take another month to arrive. Anita eventually became suspicious and checked with the defendant only to learn the judgment had been paid. What should Anita do?

8. Kathy was Jon's agent in selling cattle. In the course of a sale Jon lied to her about the health of a herd. He denied that the cows had hoof and mouth disease when he knew they suffered from it. Kathy then represented to the buyer that the herd was in good health. Is Kathy liable for Jon's conduct?

9. Susan, a minor, hired an attorney to represent her in the sale of her car. The lawyer did not disclose to the buyer that Susan was a minor. Later Susan disaffirmed the sale. Will the lawyer be liable to the buyer?

© PHOTODISC/GETTY IMAGES

Chapter 21 Assessment

CONCEPTS IN BRIEF

21-1 Creation and Operation of Agencies

1. An agency is a relationship between two parties that allows one of the parties to act so as to legally bind the other.

2. In order to have capacity as an agent, a person must be able to understand the transaction entered into on behalf of the principal.

3. Generally, if the agent has acted outside the scope of authority granted by the principal, the principal is not bound.

4. Agency authority may be created by an express grant of authority, an implied grant of authority, apparent authority, and ratification.

5. An action taken by an agent that is outside the scope of authority still may be ratified and thereby made effective against the principal.

21-2 Agency Duties

6. An agent owes a general fiduciary duty to the principal to adhere to the highest standard of duty implied by law by subordinating her or his personal interests in order to act for the benefit of the principal.

7. The specific fiduciary duties owed by agents to principals are loyalty, obedience, care and skill, confidentiality, and accounting.

8. The principal's main duty is to pay what was promised for the agency services and to reimburse the agent for reasonable expenses and losses involved in carrying out the agency.

9. Either the principal or the agent has the power to terminate the agency at any time. If the termination violates the terms of the agency agreement, however, the terminating party may be liable.

YOUR LEGAL VOCABULARY

Match each statement with the term that it best defines. Some terms may not be used.

1. Requirements that an agent act in the principal's best interests
2. Agency that is not based on a contract
3. A written grant of agency authority
4. A person who authorizes another to enter into legal relationships in his or her behalf
5. A person who authorizes an agency but does not allow the revealing of his or her existence or identity
6. Mixing together the property of the agent and the principal
7. Principal's assent to unauthorized acts of an agent
8. Separate repository for the money of the agent's principal
9. Requirement that the agency respect the private nature of the information received from the principal
10. The range of acts authorized by the principal
11. A party authorized to enter into legal relationships on behalf of another
12. Duty prohibiting the agent from secretly benefitting from the agency transaction
13. At a minimum, requires the agent to communicate to the principal any information that would affect the principal's decisions

a. agency
b. agent
c. apparent authority
d. commingling
e. duty of accounting
f. duty of confidentiality
g. duty of loyalty
h. duty of obedience
i. duty of reasonable care and skill
j. express authority
k. fiduciary duties
l. gratuitous agency
m. implied authority
n. power of attorney
o. principal
p. ratification
q. scope of authority
r. trust account
s. undisclosed principal
t. warranty of the principal's capacity

REVIEW LEGAL CONCEPTS

14. Distinguish the effect of minority on the position of principal versus the position of agent.

15. Describe a transaction where a principal creates apparent authority. Describe a transaction where an agent acts outside the scope of authority.

16. Describe the fiduciary duty of confidentiality.

17. Explain the rationale for trust accounts.

18. Describe the fiduciary duty of loyalty.

WRITE ABOUT LEGAL CONCEPTS

19. Create a one-paragraph scenario where a principal ratifies conduct outside the scope of authority.

20. Create a one-paragraph scenario where the fiduciary duty of reasonable care and skill has been violated.

21. Create a one-paragraph scenario where the fiduciary duty of confidentiality has been violated.

22. **HOT DEBATE** Five years later, Osiris was killed in the crash of his private jet. Alexis then sought to enforce her rights under the prenuptial agree-

ment. Amile, Osiris' son, who stood to inherit Osiris' fortune, realized that the contract contained provisions that would result in a long legal battle. Such a battle would delay his being able to exercise control over his father's empire. He therefore offered to buy out Alexis' rights for 100 million dollars, but she held out for more. Finally, they settled on a quarter of a billion dollars. Does such a result justify the use of attorneys as agents to negotiate a prenuptial agreement? Write a short paragraph supporting your answer.

MAKE ACADEMIC CONNECTIONS

23. **ATHLETICS** Read a book on the marketing of athletes, such as *The Business of Sports Agents* by Shropshire and Davis. Then report to the class on the ethics and legalities of sports agency.

THINK CRITICALLY ABOUT EVIDENCE

Study the situation, answer the questions, and then prepare arguments to support your answers.

24. Susan celebrated her sixteenth birthday. Two weeks later she went shopping for a car using money she received. She became frustrated with the process and asked her father to select and purchase an appropriate car on her behalf. She trusted her dad to know what she would like and also thought he was more knowledgeable. He found a car and purchased it, signing as her agent. Unfortunately dad bought a large gray four-door sedan and Susan wanted something sporty. Can Susan disaffirm?

25. When Kraus discharged his purchasing agent, Stacey, and terminated their agency relationship, Stacey became angry. To get even, Stacey made two contracts that included terms that were unfavorable to Kraus, yet were reasonable in the competitive market. The first contract was with an old customer, A, who thought Stacey was still the purchasing agent for Kraus. The second contract was with a new customer, B, who

had never heard of Stacey or Kraus before. Is Kraus liable on either of these contracts?

26. Bud was a real estate broker. He was acting as the agent in finding a buyer for Crib's home. A seller made an offer of $250,000 for the property but said, "If Mr. Crib doesn't accept this offer, I will raise it by $15,000." Bud knew that the duty of loyalty compelled him to tell Crib of the buyer's statement. Is this fair to the buyer? Why or why not? What could Bud do in future transactions to allow him to treat buyers more fairly?

27. Baroni asked her boyfriend, Sid, to help her sell her car. She promised to pay Sid 10 percent of the sales price. Sid agreed. Later, when trying to sell the car, Sid stated that a rebuilt engine had just been installed. This was not true. Kate bought the car. When she discovered the deception, she sued Baroni. Is Baroni legally responsible?

28. Nissan Motor Corporation appointed McKnight as its Denver area agent and dealer for the sale of its automobiles. McKnight purchased automobiles and parts from Nissan. He then sold them as he desired and at prices he set without any control from Nissan. The question arose as to whether an agency existed. What is your judgment? (*United Fire and Casualty Company v. Nissan Motor Corporation,* 164 Colo. 42, 433 P.2d 769)

29. Serges owned a retail butcher shop. One of his managers borrowed $3,500 from David for use in the butcher shop. Serges claimed that the manager had no authority to borrow money. Nevertheless, Serges made payments of $200. Serges also told David on several occasions that the full sum would eventually be paid. Was Serges liable? (*David v. Serges,* 373 Mich. 442, 129 N.W.2d 882)

30. Mrs. Terry is dealing with Alice, a clerk in Peters Department Store. Mrs. Terry sees a cashmere sweater she likes, but she notices it is slightly soiled. Alice, pushing for a sale, agrees to mark it down from $25 to $15, which she has no authority to do. Mrs. Terry says, "fine," asks that the sweater be delivered, and promises to pay C.O.D. The manager of Peters sees the item being wrapped, corrects the bill, and sends it out to Mrs. Terry. On seeing her sweater accompanied by a bill for $25, Mrs. Terry calls the store. She is told by Peters that Alice had no authority to mark down the price. Mrs. Terry also is told that she should either pay the bill or return the sweater. Is Mrs. Terry entitled to her bargain? Why or why not? (From Mearns, "Vicarious Liability for Agency Contracts," 48 Virginia Law Review 76.)

31. Smith and Edwards operated a sporting goods shop in Brigham City, Utah. Sponsors of the Golden Spike Little League made arrangements with the store to purchase, at a substantial discount, the players' baseball uniforms and equipment. The sponsors picked up $3,900 worth of merchandise without making any payments. After a demand for full payment, Smith and Edwards sued the sponsors. The sponsors defended by asserting that they were agents of Golden Spike Little League, acting within the scope of their authority, and thus were not personally liable. The trial judge found that Golden Spike Little League was a loosely formed voluntary association and thus not a legal entity upon which liability could be imposed. Are the sponsors liable? If the sponsors avoided liability, do you think this would be ethical? (*Smith and Edwards v. Golden Spike Little League,* 577 P.2d 132, Utah)

32. MBank hired El Paso Recovery Services to repossess the Pontiac Trans-Am owned by Sanchez because she was late on her loan payments. The repossessor went to Sanchez's home with a tow truck and tried to hook the car to the tow truck. Sanchez, who was cutting her grass at the time, asked what they were doing. The repossessors didn't respond. Sanchez then locked herself in the car to try to stall them until the police arrived. The repossessor finally towed the Trans Am on a high-speed trip, with Sanchez inside, to a repossession lot where they left the car in a fenced and locked yard. Police later rescued Sanchez. She sued MBank. Will she recover? (*MBank of El Paso v. Sanchez,* 836 S.W.2d 151, Tex.)

33. Margaret Berry was admitted to the hospital in February. In March, she executed a power of attorney designating her niece, Irene Montanye, as her agent. In April, Margaret suffered a stroke. She remained in a comatose or semi comatose condition until her death in June. On April 30, Mrs. Montanye, acting under the power of attorney, transferred some $109,000 of the decedent's funds into a trust account in the name of the decedent in trust for Ann R. Scully, administrator of this estate. Heirs of the decedent maintained that the transfer of the funds was void because at the time of the transfer and thereafter the decedent was mentally incompetent by reason of being in a comatose or semi comatose state and, therefore, the agency was revoked. Is the transfer valid? (*In re Estate of Berry,* 329 N.Y.S.2d 915)

Case For Legal Thinking

Perkins v. Rich
415 N.E.2d 895 (Mass. 1980)

FACTS The First Parish Unitarian Church of East Bridgewater hired Rich as its minister. At this time a Church Committee ran the church. As Rich's role in the Church expanded, he began to perform many of the duties of the Committee. The Church also expanded, from 12 families to more than 400. After about 10 years the Committee stopped meeting. Rich then ventured into real estate and other unrelated business ventures. To finance these, he gave mortgages on the church property which he, but not the Church Committee, executed. When the businesses he established failed, the creditor sought to foreclose on the mortgages. Church members claimed the mortgages were invalid because the Committee did not authorize them. The lower court found for the mortgage holders and the Church appealed.

The Committee claims that it did not know of the existence of the mortgages. Thus its failure to repudiate the mortgages resulted not from a ratification of the transactions but from ignorance of essential facts. Generally, in order to establish ratification of unauthorized acts of an agent, a principal must have "knowledge of all material facts . . ." However, a qualification to this rule is that one cannot "purposefully shut his eyes to means of information within his own possession and control." This is especially true of the Committee that functioned as the "business center" of the Church and had a duty to keep itself informed of Church business.

Further, the Committee was not totally ignorant of Rich's actions. From the many indications of the radical physical and structural changes to the Church and surroundings, it should have been obvious to the Church that "something was afoot." The very nature of the construction and renovation indicated that large expenditures were being made. Although Rich was far from candid in his disclosures, he did inform Church members of various projects at Church events through annual reports and publications.

REASONING We conclude that the Committee's knowledge of substantial and costly physical changes at the Church should have provoked an investigation by the Committee which would have led to the discovery of the mortgages. In these circumstances, the Committee's failure to act "will be deemed to constitute actual knowledge." By failing to disavow the mortgages, the Church ratified the transactions, a ratification that may be inferred without a vote by the Committee.

VERDICT The mortgages are valid. The decision of the lower court is affirmed.

PRACTICE JUDGING

1. Do you think the Church or the mortgage holders should pay?

2. What specific conduct does the court point to as constituting the ratification?

© GETTY IMAGES/PHOTODISC

Chapter 22
Employment Law

22-1 Making and Terminating Employment Contracts

22-2 Duties of Employers and Employees

© GETTY IMAGES/PHOTODISC

HOT DEBATE

Justin wanted to be a chef. He was considering joining the Army to get training and experience in that field. A friend pointed out that in combat cooks often are made to take up their rifles and fight like infantry. Justin, who was strongly against killing under any circumstances, said that it was just a job. If ordered to fight in combat, he said, he would refuse to do so and quit the service.

WHERE DO YOU STAND?

1. Would Justin's proposed course of action be ethical? Who might be harmed by his refusal?
2. Would Justin's proposed course of action violate his contract with the Army? Why or why not?

22-1 Making and Terminating Employment Contracts

GOALS

■ Describe how employment contracts are made

■ Explain how employment contracts are terminated

KEY TERMS

employment

employer

employee

independent contractor

employment at will

wrongful discharge

discharged without cause

unemployment compensation

discharged for cause

How Are Employment Contracts Made?

WHAT'S YOUR VERDICT?
Andrewski hired on as a machinist in Zinton's fabricating shop. Her supervisor told Andrewski she would have to provide her own protective gloves, goggles, and protective apron. Andrewski complained to Zinton, saying that providing these items was not covered in the employment contract.

Must Andrewski supply these items to stay employed?

Employment is a legal relationship based on a contract that calls for one individual to be paid for working under another's direction and control. The parties to this contract are the employer and the employee. The party who pays someone in order to direct and control that person's activities is the **employer**. The party who is paid by the employer to serve under the employer's direction and control is the **employee**.

If there is no contract to pay for work, or if there is no direction and control, the relationship between the parties is not one of employment. If you hire someone merely to produce a specified result in the manner they see fit, you have hired what the law terms an **independent contractor**. In general, an independent contractor agrees to produce a finished job without being supervised. An example would be a small publishing house that is hired to write, print, and distribute a company's newsletter. On the other hand, an employee agrees to do a range of tasks under the direction and control of the employer. An example of this would be

a staff member of the company who is assigned the job of writing all of a company's newsletters and press releases under the supervision of the head of the company's public relations department.

Terms of The Employment Contract

Employment contracts are unusual because their terms can come from a variety of sources. The terms can be derived from

■ express agreements between the employer and employee

This man has just been hired as a customer service representative at a large consumer products company. The woman in the photo will be his supervisor, and he will work under her direction. Is he an employee or an independent contractor? Explain.

- implied agreements between the employee and employer
- state and federal laws

EXPRESS AGREEMENTS Express employment contracts are oral or written documents. Detailed written contracts are used with sports professionals, entertainers, top-level managers, and union members. These written contracts expressly describe all of the elements of the employment relationship. See the sample employment contract on page 399. A party who violates an express term is liable for breach of the contract.

Only a small percentage of employment contracts are completely in writing. Most express contracts are partly written and partly oral. Compensation is almost always an express term. So are fringe benefits. Often the employer and employee also expressly agree upon the duration of the job or the time required for advance notice of termination.

IMPLIED AGREEMENTS When hiring hourly workers, custom or trade practice determines whether length of employment is expressly stated. Generally, hourly wage jobs are impliedly considered to come under the doctrine of **employment at will**. This means that an employer can discharge an employee at any time for any cause or even without cause without being liable for breach of contract. This is because there has been no agreement about the length of the employment. It also means an employee may quit a job at any time without being liable for breach of contract. Employment contracts can always be identified as either "at will" or "for a specific period."

Frequently, other terms also are implied from the way individual employers supervise their employees. For example, in a particular restaurant there may be an implied term that requires waiters and waitresses to pool their tips and to share them with the people who clear tables. Factory workers may be required to provide their own safety shoes and gloves. Andrewski in *What's Your Verdict?* can be fired if she does not provide the items required by her employer.

TERMS IMPOSED BY LAW State and federal laws impose many important terms into each employment contract whether or not the employer and employee want them included. Terms requiring the payment of a minimum wage and the hiring of racial and other minorities over other more qualified applicants, if necessary, are examples.

CHECKPOINT Name three sources of the terms in employment contracts.

How Are Employment Contracts Terminated?

WHAT'S YOUR VERDICT? Jin was asked to stay after work one evening to assist in moving some barrels containing a toxic chemical onto a truck. A forklift tine punctured one of the drums causing a large spill. The company supervisor used a garden hose to wash the material down a city drain. No report was made of the incident to the EPA. When a fish kill resulted in a nearby river and an official investigation followed, the company asked Jin to lie about what he'd seen. When he refused, he was terminated.

In a state that allows employment contracts to be terminated at will, does Jin have any legal recourse against his ex-employer?

NETBookmark

Many federal laws have been passed to protect employees from wrongful termination. Access school.cengage.com/blaw/lawxtra and click on the link for Chapter 22. Read the article "Employment at Will: U.S. Federal Laws Limiting Employment at Will." Then click on one of the laws listed and read about it. Write a paragraph that explains how this law protects an employee from wrongful termination by his or her employer.

school.cengage.com/blaw/lawxtra

Generally, contracts of employment are terminated either by performance of a specific job or performance for a specific period, by termination at the will of one or both of the parties, or as the result of a material breach. Terminated employees may be eligible for government assistance during their subsequent unemployment.

By Performance

Most contracts of employment are terminated the way all other contracts are—by performance. Completion of the job or the running of the period of employment defined in the contract terms is the key to such performance. As mentioned previously, the courts will look at the express, implied, and terms defined by laws to determine the obligations owed by the parties to one another. If these obligations have been fulfilled, the employment contract is terminated.

By Termination at Will

As discussed, many employment contracts are terminable at the will of either the employer or the employee. This occurs because the employer and employee generally do not specify a length of time for the employment relationship. The law then assumes that either party may terminate employment at any time without liability.

For example, an automobile repair shop mechanic would incur no liability for quitting her job for a higher paying one. By the same token, the repair shop manager could fire the mechanic without giving any reason for doing so. It is important to note, however, that many employers ask for and check references of prospective employees. As a consequence, abruptly quitting a job and consequently leaving an employer without the ability to fulfill his or her contracted tasks, could diminish future opportunities for the departing employee.

WRONGFUL DISCHARGE There are limitations on this power to terminate without cause. Firing because of race, religion, gender, age, disability, pregnancy, veteran status, or national origin is job discrimination and illegal. Federal law also prohibits an employer from dismissing an employee for engaging in unionizing activities. Further, most states now deny the power to terminate at will when it is used to retaliate against those who

- refuse to commit perjury at the request of the company
- insist on filing a workers' compensation claim
- report violations of law by the company
- urge the company to comply with the law

When an employer fires an employee for one of the above reasons, it commits the tort of **wrongful discharge**. Jin in *What's Your Verdict?* would be able to sue his ex-employer for such a wrongful discharge.

VIOLATION OF CONTRACT TERMS Employers who make promises orally or in company documents such as employee handbooks to "treat employees fairly" may cause this promise to become a part of the employment contract. When such terms are part of the employment contract, the employer cannot fire an employee without a fair reason.

The Pregnancy Discrimination Act is a federal law that outlaws discrimination against employees based on pregnancy, childbirth, or related medical conditions. Do you think such protection for pregnant women is necessary? Why or why not?

© GETTY IMAGES/PHOTODISC

GOVERNMENT EMPLOYEES In general, employees who work for the government, often referred to as *public employees,* are entitled to due process before being discharged. This means that they are entitled to notice of the reasons for the discharge along with a hearing. In a hearing, they are given the opportunity to present their own evidence and to challenge the claims of the governmental employer. For this reason, it is more difficult to discharge public employees than private sector employees.

IN THIS CASE Waller accidentally discovered that the test results had been faked on the new body armor her company was developing for sale to various police departments around the country. She urged her superiors to withdraw the product from the market, but they refused. She then went to the media with documentation of their unlawful conduct. When she was fired as a result, she sued the employer for wrongful discharge and won.

By Material Breach

If the obligations of the employment contract are not fulfilled, breach of contract occurs. As mentioned, if the breach is material, it extinguishes the obligations of the other party to the contract.

Suppose an employer fails to pay the employee an agreed-upon monthly check. This would be a breach of the contract. Because it is material, the employee would be justified in quitting or in abandoning the job without liability for breach of contract. Similarly, if the employee fails to perform the daily required tasks for which she or he was hired, the employer may treat the contract as terminated and discharge the employee without liability.

Unemployment Compensation

Workers who have been terminated despite having complied with all the terms of their employment contract are said to have been **discharged without cause**. This means the cause of the discharge was not the employee's conduct. An employee who is discharged without cause is entitled to unemployment compensation benefits. **Unemployment compensation** is money paid by the government or a private insurance fund to workers who have lost their jobs through no fault of their own.

Workers who have been **discharged for cause**, however, are not eligible for unemployment compensation. Felonious conduct, participation in an unlawful strike, starting a prison sentence of longer than 30 days, disqualification under federal or state mandatory drug testing, engaging in willful misconduct in disregard of the employer's interest are all considered bases for being discharged for cause by the U.S. Department of Labor.

Unemployment compensation payments are made by the states in cooperation with the federal government under the Social Security Act of 1935. There usually is a period of one or two weeks after termination before payments begin. Then a percentage of the regular wage is paid to the unemployed person every week for a limited

Upon graduating from college later in life with a chemistry degree, Alexandra took a job as a lab technician. The job bored her, and she began to arrive late for work or not show up at all. Would the lab be justified in terminating her? Why or why not?

period of time. Unemployment compensation generally is not available to those who quit voluntarily, strike, or refuse to accept similar substitute work. It often is available to part-time workers.

CHECKPOINT What are the three main ways in which an employment contract is terminated?

EMPLOYMENT CONTRACT

The parties to this contract _____ ("Employer") and _____
("Employee") do hereby agree that the following terms shall govern their employment relationship:

1. The effective date of commencement of this contract is _____ at _____ A.M./P.M. and it shall continue in force until terminated as set forth below.

2. Employee's job description shall be _____ with the following duties to be performed at a location(s) to be determined after evaluation by employer:
   _____
   _____

3. After the initial probationary period of four weeks (during which time termination shall be at will and without notice by either party) termination of the contract can be effectuated by either party to it with a verbal or written notice of at least two weeks duration.

4. Employee's wages shall be paid by check/cash/direct deposit (circle appropriate method) on the last working day of every week. Employee's initial wage shall be $ _____ per hour with a $.50/hour raise at the end of the successful conclusion of the probationary period. Thereafter evaluations for wage increases and promotions will be held semi-annually.

5. A normal work day will consist of 8 hours of labor with a half-hour lunch break. More than 40 hours of labor per week (Monday through Saturday) will be paid at time and a half. For work performed on Sundays and public holidays double time will be paid.

6. All state and federal public holidays will be honored. Employees taking these holidays will receive normal pay for an 8-hour day as though it had been worked. Any actual work on these days will be voluntary and paid at the rate noted above.

7. A sick-leave period with pay of one week for each 6 months of continuous employment shall accrue after the probationary period for employee. Sick leave taken during employee's probationary period shall be without pay.

8. An annual leave entitlement of one week for each 6-month period of continuous employment shall be granted to employee. Said leave shall be taken at a time mutually agreeable and convenient to both employer and employee.

9. Each employee shall be entitled to 60 days maternity or family-care leave without pay for every 18-month period of continuous employment.

10. Additional term(s): _____
    _____

NOTE: ALTERATIONS TO THIS AGREEMENT TO BE LEGALLY VALID MUST BE IN WRITING AND SIGNED BY BOTH PARTIES.

DATE _____

_____   _____   _____
EMPLOYEE   FOR EMPLOYER   TITLE

22-1 Assessment

Xtra!
Study Tools
school.cengage.com/blaw/lawxtra

THINK ABOUT LEGAL CONCEPTS

1. Someone who is paid to perform a job but is not supervised or controlled in so doing is a(n) _?_.

2. Federal law is likely to supply which of the following terms in employment contracts? (a) job title (b) minimum wage (c) job location

3. When no length of employment is specified, the employer–employee relationship is known as employment _?_.

4. Firing an employee because he or she had served in the military would be employment discrimination. **True or False?**

5. Unemployment compensation will be denied if the employee was fired for cause. **True or False?**

6. Most _?_ employees are entitled to due process (notice and a hearing) before they can be discharged.

THINK CRITICALLY ABOUT EVIDENCE

Study the situation, answer the questions, and then prepare arguments to support your answers.

7. Susan contracted to park customers' cars at a local restaurant. All her pay was in the form of tips, and she worked whenever the restaurant was open. She had no direct supervisor and parked the cars in a lot nearby. When she was unable to work, the restaurant placed a sign at their entrance telling customers to self-park. Is Susan an employee?

8. Darrell, a high school student, was friends with an adult neighbor, Bill. Bill operated an auto tune-up business from his garage. Darrell often helped out. At first he would drop by for an hour in the evening and just watch. Then he started handing tools and parts to Bill. Occasionally Bill would give Darrell a $5 bill or take him to dinner. Darrell showed up about twice a week, but there was never any advance notice. Is Darrell an employee?

9. Sterling was the night clerk at the Monument Inn. He had several duties besides working at the main desk. Therefore, he was not allowed to sleep while on the job, even if business was slow. On several occasions, the manager of the inn found Sterling sleeping and warned him not to do so. If Sterling continued to fall asleep on the job, would the manager be justified in discharging him? If discharged, could Sterling collect unemployment compensation?

10. Belly T. Buckle, a famous rodeo bull rider, signed on for a rodeo tour of 15 shows. His employer, In the Dirt, Inc., featured him in all their advertisements. Halfway through the tour, Belly fell in love with an emergency room nurse. As a consequence, he quit the tour. In the Dirt had to hire a replacement rider on short notice at a premium of $75,000 over Belly's pay. At the close of the tour, In the Dirt sued Belly for the extra $75,000, $23,000 for the expense of changing its ad campaign, and more than $200,000 in projected attendance revenue lost due to Belly not being on the tour. Will Dirt recover? How much?

© GETTY IMAGES/PHOTODISC

22-2 Duties of Employers and Employees

GOALS

■ List an employer's duties
■ Name an employee's duties

KEY TERMS

payroll deductions

workers' compensation

duty of obedience

duty of reasonable skill

duty of loyalty and honesty

duty of reasonable performance

What Are an Employer's Duties?

WHAT'S YOUR VERDICT? Armstrong was a nurse at the local hospital and an Army reservist. When her unit was called to active duty for service in the Middle East, Armstrong left her job and family to serve her country. After she was honorably discharged from the Army, she sought to reclaim her job at the hospital. Upon her return, however, she found the job had been filled by another person.

Is she entitled to regain her job?

Employers owe a variety of duties to employees and others. Some of these duties arise out of the express terms of the contract of employment. Others are implied by law. Following are the principal duties that employers owe employees.

Duties Owed to Employees

REASONABLE TREATMENT An employer is required to treat workers in a reasonable manner. If the employer commits an assault or battery upon an employee, the employee may quit the job without liability. The injured employee also may sue for damages.

SAFE WORKING CONDITIONS An employee is entitled by law to reasonably safe working conditions, including safe tools, equipment, machinery, and the building itself. The working conditions must not be harmful to the employee's health, safety, morals, or reputation. If the employer does not provide safe working conditions, the employee may quit without being liable for breaching the contract.

FAIR LABOR STANDARDS The federal government enacted the Fair Labor Standards Act to establish the minimum wage and maximum hours for all employees under the jurisdiction of the act. Maximum hours that can be worked at regular rates of pay are 40 per week (with no daily maximum except for transportation employees). If more than 40 hours are worked in a week, overtime must be paid at one and a half times the regular rate. Note that American workers currently work almost 100 hours more per year than their Japanese counterparts and 350 hours more per year than their European counterparts.

Not all workers are covered by this act. The minimum wage and overtime requirements of the law do not apply to executives, administrators, and professional workers. In addition, the hourly provisions apply only partially to workers in seasonal industries. Special rules apply to trainees,

This metal-cutting tool was supplied by the employer of the man who is using it. If it malfunctions, the man is burned, and he quits his job over the incident, will he have breached his employment contract? Why or why not?

apprentices, student workers, and handicapped workers. In certain circumstances they may be paid at 85 percent of the minimum wage.

PAYROLL DEDUCTIONS Certain governmental programs are financed by payments made by employees. Typically the employer deducts money from the employee's paycheck. These are called **payroll deductions**. Thus, the employer is legally obligated to withhold a percentage of the paycheck to cover the employee's federal and state income tax obligations. Similarly, the employer must withhold certain amounts for the employee's portion of social security payments. The abbreviation FICA, which stands for Federal Insurance Contributions Act, on an employee's paycheck stub refers to these social security payments. Refer to Chapter 19 for a description of the programs supported by these payments.

Other payments often are made from the funds of the employer. **Workers' compensation** is an example. This is a payment into an insurance fund that compensates employees for their injuries on the job. It eliminates the need for employers to compensate employees directly for on-the-job injuries. See Chapter 25 for a detailed discussion of this program.

Similarly, employers must make payments for unemployment insurance. Unemployment insurance provides short-term income, or unemployment compensation, for people who have recently lost their jobs. This topic was discussed in Lesson 22-1.

MILITARY SERVICE The Military Selective Service Extension Act of 1950 requires that certain military persons be re-employed by their former employer after honorable discharge from the service. Persons who have been drafted, enlisted, or called to active duty receive this protection. To qualify for reemployment, veterans must still be able to perform the work. In *What's Your Verdict?* Armstrong is legally entitled to get her old job back.

VOTING More than one-half the states provide that workers must be given sufficient time off with pay, at a time convenient to the employer, to vote in regular primary and general elections.

FAMILY AND MEDICAL LEAVES The Family and Medical Leave Act requires that a covered employer grant to an eligible worker up to 12 weeks of unpaid leave in a year for the following: serious medical conditions, birth and care of a newborn child of the employee, care of an immediate family member with a serious health condition, or circumstances involved with the employee's receiving children for adoptive or foster care.

Duties Owed to Minors

Both state governments and the federal government have prescribed employer duties aimed at protecting minors from overextended working hours and dangerous working conditions. Although the federal and state laws vary, they are all based on the following principles:

- A person's early years are best used to obtain an education.
- Certain work is harmful or dangerous for young people.
- Child labor at low wages takes jobs from adults.

STATE LAWS Every state government regulates the conditions and types of employment permitted for persons under age 18. These are often termed child-labor laws. When state child-labor laws have stricter standards than federal laws, the state laws control.

GLOBAL ISSUES

Worst Forms of Child Labor

Children are exploited as cheap labor throughout the developing world. They are tied to looms in India while their elders work. They perform tasks among machinery and toxic substances in shoe factories in Mexico. In response, members of the United Nations (UN) have adopted either partially or completely the UN's Convention on the Rights of the Child (CRC). This document sets out the economic, social, and political rights of the young members of our societies. Only two UN member countries, the United States and Somalia, have not ratified the CRC.

The states usually specify a minimum age for employment. All states place a limit on the number of hours a young person may work. In calculating the maximum number of hours, the school hours often are combined with the hours on the job while school is in session. For example, a common maximum is 48 hours (school and outside work combined) in one week. Most states maintain controls over those hours, and most require a work permit if the individual is under the age of 18.

In addition, some states have child labor laws that

- set the maximum number of working hours in one day
- prohibit night work
- prescribe the grade in school that must be completed before being able to work
- set the required age for certain hazardous occupations
- restrict the hours of work to between 5 A.M. and 10 P.M.

Child labor laws in this country are written essentially to discourage child labor. Do you see any benefits of children working? If so, what are they?

LAW BRIEF

Occupations Prohibited by the FLSA for Certain Age Groups

Under 14 years of age
All occupations except entertainment and agriculture

14 and 15 years of age
Any manufacturing, any mining, most processing, any involving operating power-driven machinery (including lawn mowers and "weed whackers"), any involving operating motor vehicles or helping with same, any in the transportation, warehousing, communication, public utilities, and construction industries, any as public messengers.

16 and 17 years of age
Any occupation declared "particularly hazardous" by the Secretary of Labor to include (with some exemptions possible for apprentices and student learners) mining, manufacturing explosives, logging and saw milling, driving motor vehicles, slaughtering or meat packing, operating powered saws, demolition, roofing, and excavating.

FEDERAL LAW The Fair Labor Standards Act (FLSA) sets the minimum protection for most young workers. (FLSA exempts from its coverage youths delivering newspapers, making wreaths in the home, employment as actors or actresses, or employment by their parents in occupations other than mining and manufacturing or those declared hazardous by the Secretary of Labor.) This law makes it illegal for people under fourteen years old to work. Fourteen- and fifteen-year-olds are only permitted to work limited hours after school in non-hazardous jobs. Unless modified by state law, sixteen- and seventeen-year-olds can work unlimited hours in non-hazardous jobs.

Duties Owed to Those Injured by Employees

If an employee, acting within the *scope of employment,* commits a tort (injures persons or property), the employer is liable for the damages. It is immaterial that the employer did not authorize the act. If an employee commits a tort but is not acting within the scope of the employer's business, the employee alone is liable for any resulting injuries. Even if an employee intentionally causes damage, the employer may be held liable if the employee has acted with the intention of furthering the employer's interests

Generally, if a person is an independent contractor rather than an employee, the person who hired the contractor is not liable for the contractor's torts. If the job is inherently dangerous, such as blasting with dynamite, the party who hired the independent contractor may be liable to those injured.

CHECKPOINT Name the duties owed by employers to their employees.

What Are an Employee's Duties?

WHAT'S YOUR VERDICT? Mel was hired by the Critical Care Construction Company as an expert welder to help assemble the containment vessel for a new nuclear power plant. For safety each weld was x-rayed after being completed. When more than 70 percent of Mel's welds were found to be improperly done, he was discharged by Critical Care.

Did Critical Care act legally?

Duty to Fulfill the Employment Contract

An employee has a duty to fulfill the express terms of the employment contract and other implied agreements made with the employer. In addition to the duties acquired by personal consent to the employment agreement, the employee also has duties imposed by state law. These duties include the duties of obedience, reasonable skill, loyalty and honesty, and reasonable performance.

Duty of Obedience

Each employee is bound by the **duty of obedience**. This means the employee has a duty to obey the reasonable orders and rules of the employer. This duty exists whether or not the employee has expressly agreed to it. However, an employee cannot be required to act illegally, immorally, or contrary to public policy.

IN THIS CASE Ash was the assistant to the president of Pinos Point Properties. She had confidential information that her company was going to make an offer on a certain piece of land for $250,000 but would be willing to pay as much as $350,000 for it. Ash told this to the owners of the land, who agreed to give her one-half of any amount over $250,000 that they received. After the purchase was made for $350,000, Pinos Point learned of Ash's action. Pinos justifiably dismissed Ash and sued her for damages.

Duty of Reasonable Skill

The **duty of reasonable skill** requires that those who accept work possess the skill, experience, or knowledge necessary to do it. The employer need not keep the employee, nor pay damages for discharging the employee, if the employee does not perform with reasonable skill. Thus, a welder whose welds are consistently substandard, such as Mel's in *What's Your Verdict,* could be fired for the lack of reasonable skill.

Duty of Loyalty and Honesty

An employee owes the **duty of loyalty and honesty** to the employer. The employee is obligated to look out for the employer's best interest. By committing a fraud upon the employer, or by revealing confidential information about the business, an employee may be justifiably discharged. Such a worker also may be liable for damages.

A Question of **ETHICS**

Tuchbach was a coach at the University of Southern Missouri. In his third season of a five-year contract, he led his football team to an 10-1 record and a Division I-AA bowl bid. Two weeks after the game, Tuchbach received an offer from another school at double his current salary plus a weekly interview show and endorsement rights. Is it ethical to break his contract even if he pays damages?

Duty of Reasonable Performance

Employees owe the **duty of reasonable performance** to employers. This is the obligation to perform the job tasks with competence. An employer is justified in discharging an employee who fails to perform assigned duties at the prescribed time and in the prescribed manner. Occasional minor failure to perform as expected ordinarily is not sufficient grounds for dismissing an employee.

On the other hand, any employee may be discharged if unable to do the work because of illness or injury.

CHECKPOINT What duties are owed the employer by an employee?

22-2 Assessment

Xtra!
Study Tools
school.cengage.com/blaw/lawxtra

THINK ABOUT LEGAL CONCEPTS

1. Which of the following is not a duty owed by the employer to the employee? (a) duty of reasonable treatment (b) duty to provide safe working conditions (c) duty to follow Fair Labor Standards (d) all of the above are employer duties

2. If state laws designed to protect minors have stricter requirements than federal laws, the federal laws still prevail. **True or False?**

3. An employer is liable for the torts of an employee if the employee was acting within the _?_ when the tort occurred.

4. Any party who hires an independent contractor may be liable for the independent contractor's torts if the work (a) involves overtime (b) is inherently dangerous (c) requires professional skill

5. Which of the following is not a duty owed by employees to employers? (a) duty of obedience (b) duty of reasonable performance (c) duty to follow immoral but not illegal instructions (d) duty of loyalty and honesty (e) all of the above are employee duties

6. Generally, an employee may be discharged if unable to do the work because of illness or injury. **True or False?**

THINK CRITICALLY ABOUT EVIDENCE

Study the situation, answer the questions, and then prepare arguments to support your answers.

7. Socow's father was an operator of a backhoe. For three summers, the father trained his son to operate backhoes. When Socow turned 14 years old, he applied for a job with a local construction firm as a backhoe operator but was turned down because of his age. Was the construction company's conduct legal?

8. Your friend is hired as a ride operator with a traveling carnival. At a county fair, he carelessly fails to secure the safety bar over the seat on a small roller coaster. Two riders are thrown out and seriously injured. Who is liable for the injuries?

9. Holtz entered into a contract with Acme Pool Company for the construction of a pool in the back yard of his new country estate. As the pool was to be located on a rock bluff, Acme had to do a considerable amount of dynamiting. During one blast, a large portion of the bluff accidentally fell away and severely injured a neighbor below. The neighbor sued Acme and Holtz for $1,000,000. Acme's assets and insurance coverage equalled no more than $150,000. Is Holtz liable for the remainder?

10. Sharp worked for Silicompetent Inc., a computer chip design company. While developing applications for Silicompetent's hypersecret new bubblechip, Sharp copied its schematics and sold them to a competing microchip firm. Is this grounds for firing Sharp?

11. Francis was hired as a cook at a local restaurant. He said he was experienced in cooking breakfast items and could handle lunch, too. In fact, his only experience was as a dishwasher, although he had carefully watched cooks work. On the first day, he was fired because he was too slow. Was the employer acting legally?

CONCEPTS IN BRIEF

22-1 Making and Terminating Employment Contracts

1. In an employment relationship, an employee is paid for working under the direction and control of an employer.

2. If there is no contract to pay for work, or if there is no direction and control, the relationship between parties is not one of employment.

3. Express employment contracts may encompass terms agreed to orally or in writing. These may be augmented by terms implied from the work setting, environment, and applicable state and federal laws.

4. Many employment contracts are terminable at the will of either the employer or the employee. This applies primarily to those without a set duration or job to complete. Employment contracts also may be terminated by performance or material breach.

5. If they are discharged without cause, employees may be eligible for unemployment compensation.

22-2 Duties of Employers and Employees

6. An employer's primary duties are to treat the employee reasonably, provide safe working conditions, and comply with applicable laws and the contract of employment.

7. Both state and federal governments have child-labor laws that regulate conditions and types of employment for persons under age 18.

8. An employee must adhere to the fiduciary duties prescribed by law and comply with the contract of employment. Employees have duties that include fulfilling the employment contract, obedience, reasonable skills, loyalty and honesty, and reasonable performance.

YOUR LEGAL VOCABULARY

Match each statement with the term that it best defines. Some terms may not be used.

1. Governmental payments to those who recently lost their jobs
2. Payment for injuries that occur on the job
3. Party who engages another to work for pay under the former's control and direction
4. One who contracts to do something for another but is free of the latter's direction and control
5. Contractual relationship in which one party engages another to work for pay under the supervision of the party paying
6. Party who works under the supervision of another for pay
7. The obligation to look out for the best interests of the employer
8. The obligation to perform the job tasks with competence
9. Firing an employee in retaliation for reporting violations of law by the company
10. Obligation to obey the reasonable orders of the employer
11. Employment relationship whereby employee may be discharged at any time because no agreement was made about length of employment
12. Money withheld from an employee's paycheck

a. discharged for cause
b. discharged without cause
c. duty of loyalty and honesty
d. duty of obedience
e. duty of reasonable performance
f. duty of reasonable skill
g. employee
h. employer
i. employment
j. employment at will
k. independent contractor
l. payroll deductions
m. unemployment compensation
n. workers' compensation
o. wrongful discharge

REVIEW LEGAL CONCEPTS

13. Describe the difference between an independent contractor and an employee.

14. Evaluate the employer's exposure to liability due to employee and independent contractor activities.

15. Explain how courts will decide whether an employment contract is terminable at will.

16. What are the basic provisions of the Fair Labor Standards Act?

WRITE ABOUT LEGAL CONCEPTS

17. Write a short description of a job you know about. Next write two or three sentences describing an employment contract for that job that makes it terminable at will. Last, write another two or three sentences describing an employment contract for the job that makes it not terminable at will.

18. Write a short comparative essay on the origins and evolution of your state's unemployment compensation programs and the federal unemployment compensation programs. Include the social, economic, and political pressures that caused the enactment of each.

19. Investigate the actions and results of Canada's reaction to the UN Convention on the Rights of the Child. Compare Canada's overall response to that of the United States. Do you agree with the position of Canada or the United States in the matter? Justify your answer.

20. Contact the embassies of several foreign countries, being sure to include at least one country from each populated continent. Ask for a list of employee and employer rights and protections in the country. Compare them with the rights and protections of workers and employers in the United States. State your conclusions as to which countries provide better conditions and where the United States both excels and falls short.

21. **HOT DEBATE** What sanctions would the Army impose on Justin if he reacted in combat as he planned? Would these be ethical?

MAKE ACADEMIC CONNECTIONS

22. **ENGLISH** Consider how conditions of employment have changed since the turn of the twentieth century by reading *The Jungle* by Upton Sinclair. Sinclair, one of the famous authors dubbed "muckrakers" by President Theodore Roosevelt, investigated the working conditions of immigrants in the Chicago meat packing industry. Prepare a report for the class on the changes.

THINK CRITICALLY ABOUT EVIDENCE

Study the situation, answer the questions, and then prepare arguments to support your answers.

23. Chin interviewed Caroline for a position as a cashier in her grocery store. She described the job responsibilities, the days and hours Caroline would work, the attitude she wanted Caroline to communicate to customers, and the hourly pay. After the interview, Chin said she would hire Caroline and they shook hands. Describe three terms of this employment contract that are express and three that are imposed by law.

24. Myron owned Crossroads Service Station. He directed Pat, an employee, to put re-refined oil into the unlabeled oil jars displayed for sale. Pat knew that the law required re-refined oil to be labeled "re-refined." Therefore, Pat refused to fill or display the jars. Was Pat's disobedience grounds for discharge? If discharged, could Pat collect unemployment compensation?

25. Harrison was hired as an electrical engineer, but there was no agreement about the length of the employment period. At the time he was hired he was told that he would not be fired unless he failed to perform his job. The employee's handbook said the same thing. Later when the company changed product lines, it fired Harrison. Can Harrison recover for breach of the employment contract?

26. Cerney operated a computer programming business. Sharon began working for Cerney after school because she could program in a useful language. When she was hired, she was told she would be paid $14 per hour. However, her first paycheck had a third of the pay taken out for federal and state taxes, social security (FICA) taxes, and other deductions. Are the deductions legal?

ANALYZE REAL CASES

27. Thomas P. Finley worked for Aetna Life Insurance. Aetna had a company personnel manual that stated that employees would "not be terminated so long as their performance is satisfactory." Finley was fired. He sued and asserted that the language in the personnel manual meant that he was not terminable at will but rather entitled to employment as long as he performed satisfactorily. Can a personnel manual supply such terms of the employment contract? (*Finley v. Aetna Life and Casualty Company*, 202 Conn. 190)

28. Gale, an umpire, was a member of the Greater Washington Softball Umpires Association. During a game which Gale was officiating, a player objected to his decision on a play. The player then struck Gale with a baseball bat, causing injuries to Gale's neck, hip, and leg. Gale claimed that he was an employee of the association and, as such, sought workers' compensation for his injuries. The association asserted that its members were independent contractors. It based this assertion on the fact that the umpires had full charge and control of the games, and that the association did not direct the worker in the performance or manner in which the work was done. The evidence presented showed (a) that the umpires were paid by the association from fees collected from the teams; (b) that the umpires, while assigned to the games by the association, were not obligated to accept the assignments; (c) that the association conducted clinics, administered written examinations, and required members to wear designated uniforms while officiating; and (d) that the umpires had to meet with the approval of committees of the association who observed a member officiating during a probationary period. Under these circumstances, do you believe Gale was an employee of the association or an independent contractor? (*Gale v. Greater Washington Softball Umpires Association*, 311 A.2d 817)

29. Whirlpool operated a manufacturing facility that used overhead conveyors to transport parts around the plant. Because the parts sometimes fell from the overhead conveyor belt, Whirlpool installed a wire screen below the conveyor belts to catch them. Maintenance workers were required to retrieve fallen parts from the screen, which was about twenty feet above the floor of the plant. On two occasions, maintenance work- ers fell through the screen onto the floor. One of the workers was killed by the fall. Shortly there- after, Vergil Deemer and Thomas Cornwell asked that the screen be repaired. When repairs were not made, these men complained to OSHA. The next day they were told by their supervisor to climb out onto the screen to retrieve fallen parts. When they refused, they were sent home with- out pay. Was their refusal a violation of their duty of obedience? (*Whirlpool v. Marshall*, 445 U.S. 1)

30. Lucky Stores, Inc., owned a building with a large sign spelling out "ARDENS" on it. Lucky hired Q.R.I. Corporation as an independent contractor to remove the sign. The removal work was inherently dangerous because each letter was about six-feet high and two and one-half feet wide and weighed between fifty and sixty pounds. Q.R.I. workers safely removed the letter "A" and loaded it on their truck. They also safely removed the letter "R" and leaned it against the truck. Then, for a moment, one worker negligently released his hold on the letter. A gust of wind blew the letter into contact with 79-year-old Smith, injuring her seriously. Is Lucky liable to Smith for damages? (*Smith v. Lucky Stores, Inc.*, 61 Cal. App. 3d 826, 132 Cal. Rptr. 628)

31. Central Indiana Gas Co. hired Frampton. Later Frampton was required to serve on a jury. Because he missed work for jury duty, he was fired. He sued. Will he win? (*Frampton v. Central Indiana Gas Co.*, 297 N.E. 2d 425, Indiana)

32. Walgreen Company planned to open a restaurant in Duluth, Minnesota. A.J. Gatzke, a district man- ager for Walgreen, was sent to Duluth to supervise the opening. Gatzke obtained a room—paid for by Walgreen—in a motel owned by Edgewater Motels, Inc. One day after work, Gatzke and another Walgreen employee went to a bar near the motel. There Gatzke drank four brandy Manhattans in about one hour. Then Gatzke went back to his motel room where, apparently, he smoked several cigarettes after completing an expense account report. The butt of one cigarette was apparently thrown into a wastebasket in the room. The room caught on fire and the fire spread to the entire motel. Gatzke escaped uninjured, but the damage to the motel was more than $330,000. Edgewater Motels sued both Gatzke and his employer, Walgreen Company. Who is liable? (*Edgewater Motels, Inc. v. Gatzke*, 277 N.W.2d 11)

Sports & Entertainment Law

Say It Ain't So, Jason

JASON GIAMBI V. NEW YORK YANKEES

BACKGROUND According to newspaper reports of federal grand jury testimony, among baseball's active major leaguers, only three players have admitted using performance-enhancing drugs. However, Barry Bonds and Gary Sheffield have denied knowing that the "nutritional supplements" were steroids. Bonds in his testimony indicated that he thought the supplements were actually flaxseed oil.

In his December 2003 testimony, however, Jason Giambi did not quibble. Giambi—signed to a $120 million, seven-year contract by the New York Yankees in 2001—admitted using steroids both prior to and during playing for the Yankees in 2002 and 2003. His honesty, in fact, has become a thorn in the side of the administrators of the supposed "national pastime." In a *USA TODAY* article published in early 2007, Giambi commented on steroids and their use in professional baseball during the 1990s and early 2000s. He said, "What we should have done a long time ago was stand up—players, owners, everybody—and said, 'We made a mistake.' We should have apologized back then and made sure we had a rule in place and gone forward. . . . Steroids and all of that was a part of history. But it was a topic that everybody wanted to avoid. Nobody wanted to talk about it." In reality, Major League Baseball (MLB) did not put in a rule against the use of performance enhancers until 2004. That action was taken mainly as a result of a federal grand jury investigation into a lab in San Francisco

that had allegedly provided such substances to several top players. Reacting to Giambi's comments to *USA TODAY*, the Yankees were again said to be considering enforcing a clause in Giambi's contract allowing the club to void it if he had used illegal substances while with the team in 2002 and 2003.

THE LAW The avoidance would have terminated the $20-million-plus payments per year required under Giambi's contract. The Yankees had made a similar evaluation back in 2004 but did not act as terminating the contract would have been opposed by the Major League Baseball Player's Association (MLBPA). The MLBPA's collective bargaining agreement with baseball's ownership arguably precluded such independent action and was likely to be held by a court as superseding the conflicting terms in the Yankees' contract with Giambi.

THE ISSUE Can Giambi's contract with the Yankees be voided due to his steroid use?

HOLDING Case not litigated yet.

PRACTICE JUDGING

1. Would the failure of the club to act in 2004 in response to Giambi's admissions of steroid use in 2002 and 2003 have a bearing on the case?
2. Which contract would be held as superior, the Yankees' individual contract with Giambi or the collective bargaining agreement between the baseball ownership and the MLBPA? Explain your answer.

© AP PHOTO/RAY STUBBLEBINE

Chapter 23
Unions and the Employment Relationship

23-1 Establishment of Unions

23-2 Employment Relations in a Unionized Workplace

HOT DEBATE

Charlee Brawn is a laborer working at harvesting various crops throughout the western part of the United States. Her employer hires thousands of laborers and contracts their labor out to various farmers to pick vegetables and fruit. The hours are extremely long, typically spent in direct sunlight, and the pay is minimal. She decides to try and improve these conditions for all the workers.

WHERE DO YOU STAND?

1. Do you think it is likely that Charlee can get things changed as an individual worker?
2. Identify the problems Charlee might encounter in trying to form a union. Does such an action seem possible?

23-1 Establishment of Unions

GOALS

- Discuss the development of labor law
- Understand how a union is formed

KEY TERMS

yellow-dog contracts

ex-parte injunction

bargaining unit

authorization card

representative election

certification

decertification election

union shop

agency shop

open shop

closed shop

right-to-work laws

History of Labor Law

WHAT'S YOUR VERDICT? Tron, a news desk anchor for the Channel 39 news team, wanted to form a union for the employees of the station.

Would the process be governed by the National Labor Relations Board?

The current state of labor law in the United States is best understood through a brief look at relevant history. The early labor organizations in this country were mostly created in reaction to specific situations. When the need disappeared, typically so did the organization. In 1770, rope workers in Boston temporarily united to stop the use of off-duty British soldiers in their places. (The tension between the two groups resulted in the Boston Massacre.) In 1778, printers in New York City united and forced an increase in wages and then disbanded. In the 1800s, however, unions took permanent form and strikes, slowdowns, and other forms of organized efforts were utilized to achieve gains for the laborer. Employers and other vested interests then tried to use the law to curtail union activities.

Early Labor Law

One legal tactic utilized in this repressive campaign was to maintain that union activities were the result of criminal conspiracies. Unions were held to be organizing their members to extort higher wages at the expense of the consuming public. The courts supported this claim until about 1842. After that time, the courts ceased classifying unions as criminal conspiracies.

After union activities were decriminalized, the legal attack on them shifted to the civil law. Courts reasoned that, as employment contracts already existed between employers and workers, strikes were attempts to pressure employers into accepting terms they otherwise would reject. Courts therefore held that strikes, boycotts, and similar tactics were actions in breach of the employment contract. Consequently, companies felt justified in firing any employee suspected of sympathizing with unions. In most states,

NETBookmark

Access school.cengage.com/blaw/lawxtra and click on the link for Chapter 23. Read the details surrounding the Danbury Hatters Case, and then answer these questions:

1. What was the situation that prompted the suit against the hatters' union?
2. When did the U.S. Supreme Court decide the case?
3. What punishments did the Supreme Court hand down to the hatters' union?

school.cengage.com/blaw/lawxtra

companies could do this because employment contracts were terminable at will.

In other states, companies made employees agree as a condition of employment not to join a union. Therefore, union membership could legally justify immediate dismissal. Employment contracts that contained this term earned the name **yellow-dog contracts**. In addition, court-issued injunctions often were used to hinder union organization efforts aimed at employees already working under such contracts.

These and similar injunctions often were issued by a judge after hearing only one side of an argument, typically the employer's. An injunction issued in this manner is termed an **ex-parte injunction**. If the employer could show potential injury flowing from a strike, many judges would issue an injunction prohibiting the strike. If employees struck or continued to strike in the face of the injunction, they could be arrested and imprisoned for contempt of court.

In 1890, Congress passed the Sherman Antitrust Act, which prohibited restraints of trade and made business monopolies illegal. Federal judges came to interpret this act as making unions illegal as they monopolized the supply of labor. For example, in the Danbury Hatters case, the U.S. Supreme Court held that the Sherman Antitrust Act did apply to unions. Eventually, in 1914, in a portion of the Clayton Act, Congress responded by exempting unions from the Sherman Antitrust Act.

The Depression Era

When the pro-business climate of the post-World War I economy disintegrated in the wake of the Great Depression, unions came more into favor. As a part of its sweeping economic reforms under the leadership of President Franklin Roosevelt, the federal government solidified the status of unions in this country by assuming regulatory responsibility for labor relations.

Today most labor relations are governed by a federal administrative agency instead of through the courts and Congress. That agency, the National Labor Relations Board (NLRB), administers the rights and duties given to workers, employers, and unions. The NLRB was created by the National Labor Relations Act (NLRA, also known as the Wagner Act) in 1935. The NLRB supervises and controls all the

---

LAW BRIEF

Currently the NLRB will claim jurisdiction over labor relations only when the business involved exceeds a certain dollar amount in gross volume. In addition, the NLRB has refused to exert any jurisdiction over certain industries such as horse and dog racing. Some examples of NLRB jurisdictional minimums are

Non-retail businesses	$50,000
Radio, TV, telegraph and telephone companies	$100,000
Newspapers	$200,000
Hospitals	$250,000
Public utilities	$250,000
Retail business	$500,000
Taxicab companies	$500,000
Restaurants and country clubs	$500,000
Symphony orchestras	$1,000,000
Private educational institutions	$1,000,000

---

aspects of labor relations from the formation of a union, through representative bargaining, to the implementation and carrying out of the collective bargaining agreements. Representatives of the union, employers, and individual workers are entitled to file charges and to take part in hearings before the NLRB. A party that is dissatisfied with the board's order may seek review in the federal courts, but that review power is limited.

Although the potential jurisdiction of the NLRB is quite broad, reaching to any business that directly or indirectly affects interstate commerce, it restricts itself to larger enterprises. Control of labor relations in smaller businesses is left to the states. (See the Law Brief feature on this page for a sample of the current guidelines.) Whether or not Tron's efforts in *What's Your Verdict?* to unionize the station would be governed by the NLRB would be determined by the gross volume of the station's business. As most of the guidelines were set decades ago and have not been adjusted for inflation, there is a great likelihood that the answer is yes.

CHECKPOINT What federal agency currently exercises control over labor relations?

How Is a Union Established?

WHAT'S YOUR VERDICT?

John worked on the dock for Right of Way Truck Lines Company. When union organizers gathered enough signatures to force a vote, the NLRB conducted an election at the company. The majority of employees, John being a major dissenter, voted for union bargaining representation. John now finds that the contract negotiated by the union is lacking, especially where it creates an agency shop and requires union dues deducted from every worker's pay whether or not they join the union. Consequently, John wants to negotiate his own contract with the employer.

What are John's rights in this situation?

The formation of a union can be a long and difficult process. The following sections discuss the steps in this process.

Determining the Bargaining Unit

To establish union representation, a series of steps needs to be taken. One step involves determining which employees should be represented together. Within a unionized company, any group of employees whose employment contract is negotiated together is called a **bargaining unit**. The NLRB may determine the appropriate unit in accordance with statutory requirements.

Common employment interests such as training are important considerations in who should be included in the bargaining unit. Employees who have supervisory responsibilities or those who have a confidential role in creating management-labor policies cannot be in a bargaining unit.

Sometimes one union represents several bargaining units in negotiating with a single employer. Each unit is entitled to create its own union to bargain with the employer or to select an existing union to represent them.

Attempting Voluntary Recognition

To establish a union, the organizers obtain employee signatures on authorization cards. An **authorization card** indicates the worker wants to be represented by a particular union. If a sizable percentage of workers sign authorization cards for a particular union, it may approach management and ask to be recognized as the exclusive bargaining representative.

Holding a Certification Election

If management denies voluntary recognition, the union can ask the NLRB to conduct a **representation election**. If at least 30 percent of the employees in the proposed bargaining unit have signed authorization cards or a petition, the NLRB will conduct hearings to determine who is in the bargaining unit and who is eligible to vote. To select a bargaining representative (a union), workers in the bargaining unit vote secretly in an election conducted by the NLRB. Majority vote governs. If a union is selected, it becomes the exclusive negotiator for all the employees in the bargaining unit. The NLRB will then acknowledge that union as the exclusive bargaining agent. This is called **certification**.

The man in this photo is the woman's supervisor, and he is training her to do a job task. Is he eligible to be in a bargaining unit?

CERTIFICATION CAMPAIGNS Often management is hostile to the possibility that a union will represent workers. So labor law makes certain conduct illegal during organizing campaigns. Thus, it is illegal for an employer to fire or to threaten to fire union sympathizers to discourage unionization. Similarly, employers may not threaten to close a plant, to automate the workplace to reduce the number of workers, or to move work out of the country just to avoid unionization. In addition, management may not support one union over another. Labor unions are similarly regulated. During certification campaigns they may not picket, make threats, or engage in violence.

DECERTIFICATION If a union has been certified and later 30 percent of the employees decide they want different or no representation, they can petition the NLRB to conduct a **decertification election**. At this election, employees can reject union representation or select a different union. If a majority rejects representation, workers will negotiate individually with the employers. An employer cannot file a decertification petition. Managerial employees are not permitted to vote in certification or decertification elections or to be represented by a union.

Negotiating the Employment Contract

Once a union has been certified, it is the exclusive bargaining representative for everyone within the unit. Whether or not they are union members, all workers in each bargaining unit are bound by the collective agreement reached between the union and the employer. In *What's Your Verdict?* John could not negotiate

IN THIS CASE You live in a right-to-work state. Nonetheless, you have led a successful drive to form a union. Unfortunately, more than 40 percent of the work force in the bargaining unit have not joined and are not required to pay dues as it, by law, is an open shop. Regardless, the bargaining you do is for them as well as your members. They will receive the same pay and other benefits as though they were members themselves.

an individual employment contract with his employer. Whether or not he must join the union depends on the type of shop that has been authorized in the negotiation process.

UNION AND AGENCY SHOPS Workers are not required to join a union unless the employer has agreed to have a union shop. In a **union shop**, non-union employees may be hired, but they must join the union within a stated maximum period, usually 30 days. The **agency shop** is a variation of the union shop. In the agency shop, employees are not required to join the union, but if they do not, they must nevertheless pay union dues as a condition of employment.

OPEN AND CLOSED SHOPS In the **open shop**, employees are not required to belong to a union or to pay dues. The union bargains collectively with the employer and agrees to an employment contract binding union and nonunion workers.

In a **closed shop**, the employer agrees that workers must belong to the recognized union before they can be hired. The closed shop was outlawed by the Labor Management Relations Act (also known as the Taft-Hartley Act) of 1946. The Taft Hartley Act also allows individual states to pass right-to-work laws.

Right-to-work laws prohibit compulsory union membership and ban the union shop, closed shop, and agency shop. In states with right-to-work laws, unions may function, but only with open shops.

CHECKPOINT What is a bargaining unit?

These employees are working in an open shop. Some of them belong to the union, but others do not. Which employees are bound by the collective bargaining agreements reached by the union with management?

23-1 Assessment

THINK ABOUT LEGAL CONCEPTS

1. Yellow-dog contracts are legal in right-to-work states. **True or False?**

2. The group of workers for whom a union negotiates a common contract is called the _?_.

3. Who conducts the certification election? (a) the union (b) management (c) the petitioning workers (d) the NLRB

4. Who determines the membership in the bargaining unit? (a) the union (b) management (c) the petitioning workers (d) the NLRB

5. What percentage of workers in a bargaining unit must vote in favor to cause the NLRB to certify a bargaining representative for the unit? (a) 10% (b) 20% (c) 30% (d) a majority

6. What percentage of workers in a union must petition the NLRB to get it to conduct a decertification election? (a) 10% (b) 20% (c) 30% (d) a majority

7. In right-to-work states, unions may function but only with closed shops. **True or False?**

THINK CRITICALLY ABOUT EVIDENCE

Study the situation, answer the questions, and then prepare arguments to support your answers.

8. It is in the late autumn of 1852. Your textile plant in northern Massachusetts is working you 14 hours a day, 6 days a week, producing clothing for the upcoming winter. Several of your fellow employees are getting hurt due to the fatigue caused by the extended hours. In addition, word has reached you that several plants in Boston are paying their employees almost half again what yours is paying because they have unionized. You and three of your friends decide to try and form a union at your plant. When the owners of the plant discover this, they file for and receive an ex-parte injunction against your organizing activites. Nonetheless, you continue to recruit for the union. By doing so you (a) are likely to be sued by the company for breach of the employment contract (b) are likely to be fired by the company (c) are likely to be fined and imprisoned for contempt of court (d) all of the above

9. You are working as a printer at a small town newspaper which grosses about $185,000 per year in sales. You lead a unionization drive and file a petition with the NLRB for a certification election. What will happen?

10. At Alta Corporation, 5 of the 20 machinists and 20 of the 30 assembly workers favored unionizing. Describe how the petition for certification and the votes on certification would fare if the bargaining unit(s) were defined as (1) the machinists and the assembly workers as separate units, or (2) a combination of both.

23-2 Employment Relations in a Unionized Workplace

GOALS

- Explain how a collective bargaining agreement is negotiated
- Recognize unfair labor practices

KEY TERMS

collective bargaining

strike

lockout

mediation

unfair labor practices (ULPs)

featherbedding

picketing

boycott

How Is a Labor Contract Negotiated with a Union?

WHAT'S YOUR VERDICT? Ace Inc. manufactures automobile parts for several U.S. car companies. The same union represents all of its manufacturing employees. Historically, labor and Ace management negotiated five-year contracts. The current round of negotiations, however, was unsuccessful. During one session, union and management representatives became very angry with each other, and someone threw a chair across the bargaining table. Because of such incidents and the unlikelihood of reaching an agreement, Ace refused to continue negotiating. It said it was prepared to continue paying workers under the old contract but that it was unwilling to negotiate with the current leaders of the union.

What alternatives are available to solve this problem?

Collective bargaining is the process whereby the union and the employer negotiate a contract of employment that binds both sides. Unions choose their own negotiators. Management and/or company lawyers typically represent the company. Pay and fringe benefits are the most commonly negotiated issues. However, grievance procedures, hours, overtime, pensions, health care, working conditions, and safety issues also are frequently negotiated.

An employer is not required to bargain over such issues as product prices or designs, plant location, or quality of products. These are strictly management matters even though they do affect the company's ability to pay wages.

Should the union and management fail to reach an agreement, the union employees may choose to strike and the employer, to hold a lockout. A **strike** is a collective work stoppage intended to force an employer to alter its position on an issue. A **lockout** occurs when an employer temporarily closes down operations to induce the workers and their representatives to alter their position on an issue.

Great economic pressure confronts both sides if either a strike or a lockout occurs. Employee wages usually cease and production often stops. This economic pressure is reinforced by the NLRA which requires that the negotiators engage each other with open and fair minds intending to overcome the obstacles they face to producing a satisfactory agreement. As a consequence of this requirement, failure to bargain is a violation of NLRB rules. In

LEGAL Research

Contact the NLRB and the EEOC. Inquire about collective bargaining agreement terms that, when included in a negotiated contract, indicate the intent to comply with the legislated requirements of the ADA, affirmative action, and the various anti-discrimination laws. Ask about the current issues in these areas as well as the rates of actual compliance that the agencies find in their inspections, dispute resolution actions, and prosecutions. What conclusions can you draw from the results of your research?

What's Your Verdict? Ace committed such a violation by refusing to continue negotiations. The union could file a complaint with the NLRB, which might issue an order compelling management to negotiate in good faith.

When collective bargaining negotiations become *deadlocked* (stalemated) and a strike is imminent or in progress, the government may intervene. When this happens, a representative may be appointed by the government to try to bring the parties together and settle their differences. In **mediation** (also known as *conciliation*), a mediator (conciliator) talks with both sides and attempts to achieve a compromise. However, the result of mediation is not enforceable against the bargaining parties.

In other situations, the parties may submit their deadlocked dispute to binding arbitration if allowed under their labor contract. The arbitrator holds a hearing and then makes a determination that is enforceable at law against both employer and union.

CHECKPOINT Who are the parties to a collective bargaining agreement?

The signs these union employees are wearing indicate that they are on strike. What issues might their bargaining unit have failed to settle with management?

IN THIS CASE Educredit, a national lender of short-term loans for educational purposes, was secretly evaluating moving its collection services from Malibu, California, to Bangpoor, India. Local 1313 of the Phone Solicitors Union heard from an unidentified source of Educredit's interest in transferring its operations and wanted to negotiate over the matter. When Educredit refused, 1313 went on strike claiming to the NLRB it was an unfair labor practice not to negotiate over such a drastic measure that would take away more than 400 of its jobs. The NLRB noted that under the law the company did not have to negotiate over location and had made no threats to move. Therefore, its actions were legal and the union was acting illegally by striking. Reacting to the union action which had improperly cost it considerable business, Educredit then executed the move.

What Are Unfair Labor Practices?

WHAT'S YOUR VERDICT? Kiersten worked in a factory that manufactured uniforms. Upset by the low wages and poor working conditions at the plant, Kiersten began collecting certification petition signatures during her lunch hour and after work. Kiersten's employer noticed what she was doing. He met with her and stated that, since he paid better-than-union wages and the plant's working conditions were better than those in other plants in the area, he did not want to deal with unions. Nonetheless Kiersten continued her organizing efforts and was fired as a consequence.

Can Kiersten's employer legally fire her because of her organizing activities?

The National Labor Relations Act and other federal and state statutes require that employers treat unions fairly by allowing them to organize. These statutes also require that management engage in good-faith negotiations (collective bargaining) with unions. Such laws seek to ensure unions are fairly treated in these matters by prohibiting certain actions of employers. Similarly, unions are prohibited from taking certain actions against employers or their own members. In either case, these prohibited actions are referred to as **unfair labor practices (ULPs)**.

Management's Unfair Labor Practices

For employers the list of unfair labor practices includes (1) interfering with employees' efforts to form, join, or assist unions (2) dominating a union or giving it financial or other support (3) encouraging or discouraging union membership, and (4) refusing to bargain in good faith with the union.

INTERFERING WITH EMPLOYEES' EFFORTS TO FORM, JOIN, OR ASSIST UNIONS Such interference can take a variety of forms. For example, it would be an unfair labor practice to refuse to deduct union dues for union members, to disrupt organizing meetings, or to threaten to fire employees to keep them from organizing a union. In *What's Your Verdict?* Kiersten's employer was guilty of an unfair labor practice. The employer could be required to rehire Kiersten and to pay her the wages lost while barred from the job. Similarly, employers may not threaten to stop operations, replace workers with machines, or move the factory just to avoid unionization.

DOMINATING A UNION OR GIVING IT FINANCIAL OR OTHER SUPPORT Laws that prohibit management from dominating a union or giving it financial or other support preserve the independence of unions in representing the interests of employees. In the past, some companies tried to influence certification elections. Sometimes they wanted the least aggressive union to win. Other times they tried to win favor with union leaders by contributing money to their election campaigns.

What are management's responsibilities with regard to negotiating with union representatives?

ENCOURAGING OR DISCOURAGING UNION MEMBERSHIP Employers may not threaten to blacklist employees who join unions. Employers blacklist employees by placing their names on a list of pro-union persons and sending it to other employers with the purpose of making it difficult for the employees to find work.

REFUSING TO BARGAIN IN GOOD FAITH WITH THE UNION This means management must participate actively in attempting to reach an agreement. It must make honest and reasonable proposals and must listen to the arguments of the union. Management must attempt to find a common ground with the union. However, the law does not require that management agree to a union proposal. Management must only engage in good faith bargaining. Similarly, it is an unfair labor practice to discharge or otherwise discriminate against an employee for filing charges of labor law violations or for testifying about such charges.

Unfair Labor Practices by Unions

The Taft-Hartley Act and other statutes require that unions treat employees and management fairly. Unfair labor practices by unions include

1. Refusing to bargain collectively in good faith with the employer.

2. Attempting to force an employer to pay for featherbedding. **Featherbedding** is payment

for services not performed. If the work is performed, there is no featherbedding even though the work may be unnecessary.

3. **Picketing**, or patrolling near the employer's property with signs, by uncertified unions trying to force the employer to bargain with that union. Certifying elections are the appropriate method for compelling an employer to bargain with a particular union. It is also an unfair labor practice for a union to picket in an effort to force employees to select that union as their representative within 12 months after losing a valid representation election.

4. Engaging in strikes and boycotts prohibited by law. Most strikes are legal, however, if they are conducted without violence.

5. Requiring payment of an excessive or discriminatory fee for initiation into the union.

6. Forcing or attempting to force employees to support a union or to restrain employees from supporting competing unions. A union may, however, try to persuade employees to support it.

7. Causing or attempting to cause an employer to discriminate against an employee because of union-related activities.

After congressional testimony about corruption and violence in a few unions, Congress passed legislation designed to limit such abuses. The Labor-Management Reporting and Disclosure Act (also known as the Landrum-Griffin Act) requires that unions operate in a manner that gives members full voice in decision making. The law was intended to ensure that union members themselves could correct abuses of power by entrenched leadership through free and open elections.

The Union Bill of Rights on this page describes rights that union members have with regard to their unions.

Unfair Labor Practices in Strikes and Boycotts

STRIKES An *economic strike* is one where the dispute is over wages, hours, or conditions of employment. An employer may respond to an economic strike by giving any striking employee's job to someone else. However, when there is an economic strike, unions commonly refuse to settle unless striking members are rehired.

UNION BILL OF RIGHTS

ELECTIONS Union members have the right to equal opportunities for nominating candidates for union offices and the right to vote by secret ballot in union elections.

MEETINGS Union members have the right to meet with other members to express views about candidates or other business.

DUES Union members have the right to vote by secret ballot on increases in dues, initiation fees, and assessment levies.

LAWSUITS Union members have the right to sue, to testify in court or before any administrative agency or legislative body, and to communicate with any legislator.

DISCIPLINE Union members are protected from union disciplinary action, unless the member is served with written charges, given time to prepare a defense, and afforded a fair hearing. Members may be disciplined for nonpayment of dues without such elaborate due process.

MANAGEMENT Union members have the right to obtain information about union policies and financial matters, to recover misappropriated union funds for the union, to inspect union contracts, and to be informed of provisions of this act.

If the strike is over an unfair labor practice by management, the employer may not permanently give the striking worker's job to someone else. When such an *unfair labor practice strike* is over, the employer must reinstate the striking worker even if this requires transferring or discharging the replacement.

Strikes of public employees generally are prohibited even though such workers may unionize and bargain collectively. Sometimes public workers (including police officers, teachers, and fire fighters) strike or stay away from work claiming illness. In such cases, the workers and their leaders are subject to court orders directing them to return to work. If they ignore the court order, they may be fired or jailed.

The President of the United States has the power to obtain an injunction in federal court forcing a *cooling-off period* of 80 days when a national emergency strike is threatened. A *national emergency strike* is one that involves

What category of strike would an air traffic controllers' union strike be? Explain your answer.

national defense or major industries or would endanger national health or safety. Strikes and lockouts are illegal during the cooling-off period.

BOYCOTTS A **boycott** is a refusal to buy or to use someone's products or services. A *primary boycott* involves the employees' refusals to buy their employer's products or services. Primary boycotts are legal. Typically they are accompanied by a strike and by picketing at the employer's place of business. Usually the striking employees also encourage others, such as customers and suppliers, to boycott the employer.

Sometimes, however, striking employees try to get customers to stop buying the products or services of a third party. Such action against a third party is known as a *secondary boycott*. It generally is illegal. However, picketing is legal if the picketers had urged customers of the stores to stop buying only products made by a particular manufacturer, not all products.

In addition, secondary boycotts are legal when the National Labor Relations Act, or state statutes similar to the NLRA, do not apply. This would be the case with farm labor in most states. Thus, farm workers engaged in labor disputes with farmers have encouraged consumers to not buy anything at grocery stores carrying nonunion grapes and lettuce. This secondary boycott is legal because the farm workers are not covered by the National Labor Relations Act.

CHECKPOINT What is the difference between an economic strike and an unfair labor practice strike?

THINK ABOUT LEGAL CONCEPTS

1. A _?_ occurs when an employer temporarily closes down operations to induce the workers and their representatives to alter their position on an issue. (a) lockin (b) strike (c) shutout (d) none of the above

2. A compromise achieved by a mediator in a labor dispute is enforceable against the bargaining parties. **True or False?**

3. Management's First Amendment rights allow it to say anything in an attempt to defeat the union during a certification campaign. **True or False?**

4. In a collective bargaining session, which of the following is an employer not required to bargain over? (a) wages (b) working conditions (c) plant location (d) the employer must bargain over all of the above

5. Blacklisting an employee is an unfair labor practice. **True or False?**

6. After losing a certification election, a union must wait _?_ months before resuming picketing of a particular employer to be selected as the bargaining representative. (a) 6 (b) 12 (c) It may begin immediately after the loss.

7. In labor parlance, freeloading is payment for services not performed. **True or False?**

THINK CRITICALLY ABOUT EVIDENCE

Study the situation, answer the questions, and then prepare arguments to support your answers.

8. Sharpe worked in an auto plant. Due to a change in assembly lines she, along with several others, was moved to a new position that required welding skills she did not possess. Feeling that she deserved training before assuming the position, she asked at her local union office to see a copy of her union's contract with the employer. The request was refused. Sharpe persisted saying that she had a right to see the contract. Is she correct?

9. The Electrical Workers Union represented most of the workers in the General TV Plant. In a dispute over wages, the union went on strike and began picketing the plant. They also picketed nearby stores that carried the General televisions, asking that shoppers not purchase them. Is any of this conduct illegal?

10. Alonzo owns his own machine shop and has several close friends among his employees. The NLRB is about to conduct a certification election. Alonzo knows he could persuade his employee friends to spread rumors that if the union is certified, he would move his shop out of the country. He also is certain that such rumors could never be traced back to him. Would this action be legal? Would it be ethical for Alonzo to spread such rumors if they would cause the union to lose the election?

Chapter 23 Assessment

CONCEPTS IN BRIEF

23-1 Establishment of Unions

1. Labor law in this country has taken more than two centuries to evolve to its current state.

2. The National Labor Relations Board (NLRB) is the federal administrative agency that regulates union activity.

3. Organizing a union is an activity protected by law.

4. Steps in organizing a union include securing authorization card signatures from the employees, determination of the appropriate bargaining unit, holding a representation election, and receiving certification as the collective bargaining representative.

5. Right-to-work laws passed by individual states prohibit compulsory union membership.

23-2 Employment Relations in a Unionized Workplace

6. Where a union does represent the employees, they bargain collectively through it in hopes of obtaining better wages and working conditions, and other labor objectives.

7. Over the years, unfair labor practices for unions and employers have been spelled out by various laws.

8. Strikes and lockouts may occur where the parties cannot reach agreement in the collective bargaining sessions.

9. Mediation and binding arbitration may result in a compromise settlement in difficult labor negotiations so as to avoid the waste of resources characteristic of a strike or lockout.

YOUR LEGAL VOCABULARY

Match each statement with the term that it best defines. Some terms may not be used.

1. A process by which a union ceases to be the exclusive bargaining agent for employees

2. State laws that ban the union shop and the closed shop

3. Establishment in which all employees must belong to the union, either when they are hired or within a specified time after they are hired

4. Any group of employees whose employment contract is negotiated together within a unionized company

5. Concerted stoppage of work to force an employer to yield to union demands

6. Patrolling by union members with signs alongside the premises of the employer during a labor dispute

7. Union or employer actions that violate the rights of employees with respect to union activity

8. Attempt by a neutral third party to achieve a compromise between disputing parties

9. Employer's shutdown of operations to bring pressure on employees

10. Establishment in which employees do not have to belong to a union nor pay dues

11. The process whereby the union and the employer negotiate a contract of employment that binds both sides

12. Employment contracts in which employees agree not to join a union as a condition of employment

a. agency shop
b. authorization card
c. bargaining unit
d. boycott
e. certification
f. closed shop
g. collective bargaining
h. decertification election
i. ex-parte injunction
j. featherbedding
k. lockout
l. mediation
m. open shop
n. picketing
o. representation election
p. right-to-work laws
q. strike
r. unfair labor practices
s. union shop
t. yellow-dog contracts

REVIEW LEGAL CONCEPTS

13. Explain the history of labor law.

14. Explain the steps involved in establishing a new union.

15. How can members of a bargaining unit change their selection of the union that represents them?

16. Contrast the various types of "shops" that determine the nature of an employee's relationship with her or his union.

WRITE ABOUT LEGAL CONCEPTS

17. Invent four examples of unfair labor practices by a union. Describe each in a separate paragraph.

18. Invent four examples of unfair labor practices by management. Describe each in a separate paragraph.

19. Explain which boycotts are legal and which are not in a short paragraph.

20. **HOT DEBATE** Charlee discovers that the vast majority of the would-be members of her prospective union are not citizens. Write a paragraph analyzing why this should matter or not in forming a union.

MAKE ACADEMIC CONNECTIONS

21. **HISTORY** Research the strike called by John L. Lewis, the head of the United Mine Workers (UAW), during the height of World War II. More than half a million workers went out on strike and stayed out in defiance of government orders to return to work. As a consequence, steel mills stopped production and the war effort was hampered greatly. Write a paragraph analyzing the ethics of this action from both sides.

THINK CRITICALLY ABOUT EVIDENCE

Study the situation, answer the questions, and then prepare arguments to support your answers.

22. When a national union sent organizers to try to persuade Baker's workers to join the union, Baker called three of her most trusted employees to her office. She urged them to organize a new union limited to company employees. She offered to provide the union with office space and time for officers to conduct union business. Baker then gave the three workers money to buy printed notices and refreshments for an organizational meeting. Was Baker's action legal?

23. O'Donnell felt that management at the company where he worked was engaging in unfair labor practices. He complained in public and filed charges with the NLRB. Those charges were dismissed. Later he was called to testify about charges filed by the union. O'Donnell's bosses hinted that they would get even. About two months later, the company decided to eliminate O'Donnell's job. Does he have any recourse?

24. Joan and the other members of her union were striking for higher wages. Management made a public announcement that workers who failed to report on the following Monday would be permanently replaced. Can an employer permanently replace striking union members? Can a union continue striking until the employer agrees to rehire the striking employees?

25. A strike at the Titan Stone Works was in its fifth week when Paxton, a federal mediator, was called in. After long discussions with both sides, she persuaded the union representatives to accept certain terms. The terms were a major concession on the part of the union but seemed to her to be fair to all parties involved, including the buying public. Titan rejected the terms even though it was financially able to meet every demand. Can Paxton compel Titan to sign the proposed contract?

26. In August 1981, President Ronald Reagan, confronted by striking federal air-traffic controllers who threatened to shut down the nation's airlines, fired them all. The president justified his actions by noting the striking workers were in violation of the law. Their places were taken in the short term by military air traffic controllers and ultimately, after training, by new personnel. Did President Reagan act legally? Did he act ethically?

ANALYZE REAL CASES

27. The United Steelworkers of America, a national union, had a provision in its constitution that imposed requirements to be satisfied before a member could run for leadership positions in local affiliates. The limitation was that to be eligible to be a local officer, the union member must have attended at least one-half of the regular local meetings for the three years prior to the election. Is this restriction legal? (*Local 3489 United Steelworkers of America v. Usery*, 97 S. Ct. 611)

28. Mary Weatherman was the personal secretary to the president of Hendricks County Rural Electric Membership Corporation. One of her friends at the firm was involved in an industrial accident that resulted in the loss of one of his arms. Shortly after the accident, he was dismissed. Mary, concerned about the plight of her friend, signed a petition seeking his reinstatement. Because of this conduct Mary also was discharged. Mary filed a charge with the NLRB alleging an unfair labor practice. The company defended itself by claiming that because Mary was a confidential secretary, she was not covered by the National Labor Relations Act's definition of "employee." Who is right, Mary or the company? (*NLRB v. Hendricks County*, 102 S. Ct. 216)

29. During a union-organizing campaign at Portage Plastics Company, some members began wearing union buttons on the job. Because a button fell into a grinder and caused loss of material and because of the increasing division among the employees, the president of Portage prohibited the wearing of either union or nonunion badges at work. Other jewelry and hair attachments were still permitted even though such ornaments also had fallen into equipment and caused losses on prior occasions. Immediately after the president gave his order, a strike was started in protest. Was the company rule on union badges an unfair labor practice? Would it make any difference if the union agreed, after the order, that its members would not wear badges? (*Portage Plastics Company v. International Union, Allied Industrial Workers of America, AFL-CIO*, 163 NLRB No. 102)

30. Kuebler was a member in good standing of the lithographers union when it struck the Art Gravure Company. Several months after the strike began, Kuebler met in a non-secret meeting with 12 or 13 other strikers. Their purpose was to discuss "the widening gap" between the labor and management bargaining committees and to "try to straighten this thing out to where we could get back to work." Later, a three-person committee from the group communicated its views to the Union Negotiating Committee. Kuebler returned to the picket line. When the strike finally ended, the trial board of the local union charged and found Kuebler guilty of attending "a meeting . . . held for the purpose of undermining the Union Negotiating Committee." Kuebler was suspended from the union for three months and was fined $2,000. He filed a notice of appeal to the membership and requested several items: copies of charges against him, with supporting facts; names of the persons on the executive board who had accused and tried him; a copy of the decision in writing showing how each member had voted; and a copy of the transcript of the evidence and proceedings at his trial by the union trial board. This information was refused, and so Kuebler sued for relief in the U.S. district court. Had the union violated Kuebler's rights? Had Kuebler been denied a fair hearing? (*Kuebler v. Cleveland Lithographers and Photoengravers Union Local*, 473 F.2d 359)

31. The Greenpark Nursing Home hired First National Maintenance to maintain its facilities. First National in turn hired employees to work for it on the premises of the nursing home. These employees of First National formed a union. Shortly after, First National decided, for financial reasons, to cancel its maintenance contract with the nursing home. Anticipating a complete layoff, the union sought to negotiate with management over the decision to terminate this contract. Management refused to negotiate on this issue. Was this refusal to negotiate legal? (*First National Maintenance v. NLRB*, 452 U.S. 666)

Sports & Entertainment Law

A Tip of the Old Salary Cap

MAJOR LEAGUE BASEBALL PLAYERS' ASSOCIATION (MLBPA) V. OWNERS

BACKGROUND Collective bargaining in professional sports in the United States began where it had always been at issue: in baseball. Two major bargaining points were at the heart of the first attempt to organize the players: the reserve clause (a contractual clause that bound players for their playing lives to the team that signed them to it) and the prospect of a salary cap imposed on the teams. The Brotherhood of Professional Base Ball Players, the first in a long line of attempts to unionize the players in America's Pastime, was formed in 1885 mainly to battle the club owners on those two issues. However, the Brotherhood eventually disbanded in failure. Eighty-three years later, in 1968, another baseball players' union negotiated the first collective bargaining agreement (CBA) in U.S. professional sports. It did not eliminate the reserve clause, but did move the minimum salary of players up from $6,000 to $10,000. In 1970, subsequent negotiations between the players' union and the owners resulted in the CBA being amended to allow the resolution of grievances by arbitration. This finally led to an arbitrator in 1975 declaring that the reserve clause only allowed a club to hold onto a player for one additional year after his basic contract expired. The era of free agency had arrived. Echoing this major victory were unprecedented increases in players' base salaries, pension funds, and licensing rights and revenues. Drawing on the baseball example, football, basketball, hockey, and other professional sport leagues also unionized and met with similar success with one exception: the salary cap.

Today, only the MLBPA has successfully resisted the demands of the owners to install a salary cap. A salary cap would give teams equal chances of winning a championship trophy. With no salary cap, there is a wide disparity in salaries among the teams. For example, the Florida Marlins in 2006 had a total payroll less than the yearly salary of Alex Rodriguez, the third baseman of the New York Yankees for that season.

The latest players' union to surrender to such a cap was professional hockey. After a lockout centering on the issue ended play for the entire 2004–2005 season, the NHLPA agreed to an ongoing cap first set at $39 million per team for the 2005–2006 season, and currently set at $50.3 million for the 2007–2008 season. By comparison, the NBA's salary cap for 2007–2008 is set at almost $56 million and the NFL's at $109 million for the 2007 season.

THE ISSUE Should and can a salary cap be imposed on the MLB clubs when MLB's current CBA expires in 2011?

HOLDING Case not litigated yet.

PRACTICE JUDGING

1. Research and compare to MLB teams, team results in profitability, and-on-the-field success in the various other professional leagues.

2. What bargaining positions and potential trade-offs would you recommend to the players' union and the club owners in relation to the salary cap issue?

Chapter 24
Discrimination in Employment

24-1 Legal versus Illegal Discrimination

24-2 Proving Illegal Discrimination

HOT DEBATE

Phan's parents were born in Vietnam. They spoke Vietnamese in the home. Phan did not learn English until he began kindergarten. Upon graduating from high school, Phan's language skills were still below par. When Phan applied for a job as a dispatcher for an emergency ambulance service, he was asked to take an English grammar test. He took the test but failed, and therefore was denied employment. Phan contended that his life circumstance caused him to fail the test. The prospective employer said the company didn't care about Phan's life circumstance, only how well he could do the job.

WHERE DO YOU STAND?

1. Why did Phan deserve the job?
2. Why did Phan not deserve the job?

24-1 Legal versus Illegal Discrimination

GOALS

- Recognize the difference between legal and illegal employment discrimination
- List the various statutes governing employment discrimination

KEY TERMS

employment discrimination

protected classes

Equal Employment Opportunity Commission (EEOC)

affirmative action plan

Americans with Disabilities Act (ADA)

disability

When Is Discrimination Illegal?

WHAT'S YOUR VERDICT? Clare has been working at Rich Manufacturing for three years. Lisa has been working there for two months. They both operate computerized machine-tooling equipment. The machines perform many operations, such as drilling, cutting threads, turning, deburring, and surfacing metal objects. Lisa is faster. When a promotion opportunity came along, it was given to Lisa. Clare protested, saying that she was being discriminated against. She was angry because Lisa would be earning almost 30 percent more money than she would.

Is Clare correct? Is she a victim of unjustified discrimination?

Everyone discriminates for and against individuals. Choosing a team for a pick-up game of basketball, friends, a mate for marriage, a class officer, or a President of the United States are all actions that require discrimination. In employment, however, discrimination that is not work related is extremely harmful. The harm affects not only the individual discriminated against but all of society, as achieving efficient production and quality products depends on putting the best qualified person in the right job.

As a consequence, the government has become involved in making sure that choices within the workplace are made on the proper bases and do not reflect illegal **employment discrimination**. Such discrimination is defined as treating individuals differently on the basis of race, color, gender, pregnancy and pregnancy intention, age (40 or older), religion, disability, and national origin. Instead the law compels employers to judge each person according to their individual abilities to perform the work at hand.

Employees who are fairly judged to be more dependable, skilled, creative, smart, or hard working should receive more favorable treatment. They earn more money and have more job opportunities. Thus, in *What's Your Verdict?* Clare is being legally discriminated against. The employer has a work-related reason for the treatment (for example, Lisa works faster).

Protected Classes

The law attacks illegal discrimination in a practical way. It identifies group characteristics

Do you think it is fair for employers to treat more favorably employees who are dependable, skilled, and hardworking? Why or why not?

© GETTY IMAGES/PHOTODISC

that employers may not consider when making employment decisions. The courts have attached the label **protected classes** to people within these groups. Members of protected classes are often, but not always, minorities. Employment discrimination law is designed to ensure that membership in a protected class is not a significant factor in employment decisions. A variety of federal statutes define the criteria that employers cannot consider when making employment decisions. These criteria and the associated protected classes of persons are listed in the following paragraphs.

RACE AND COLOR The protected class based on race or color includes all persons who are not white. So, African Americans, Asians, Filipinos, Hispanics, Native Americans, and others are members of this protected class.

GENDER Employers may not discriminate against females or males based on their gender. In addition, sexual harassment is illegal.

PREGNANCY/PREGNANCY INTENTION Employers may not discriminate because of a person's childbearing condition or plans.

AGE People 40 years of age and older are protected against discrimination on the basis of their age.

RELIGION People who have religious beliefs of any kind are members of a protected class.

DISABILITY The physically and mentally disabled are afforded limited protection against discrimination.

NATIONAL ORIGIN People are protected against discrimination based on their country of origin. Those who do not speak English or who are not citizens of the United States are protected to a limited extent.

LAW BRIEF

Discrimination against the obese by employers may be based on health care and health insurance costs. A recent study published in the *American Journal of Health Behavior* showed that in the first years of the twenty-first century annual health care expenditures for those of normal weight averaged $114 compared to $620 for the obese.

IN THIS CASE Nadine was turned down for a job as a flight attendant even though she scored higher than the other applicants in her class. She alleged it was because of her obesity. She stood a little over five feet tall and weighed 258 pounds. Nadine complained to the Equal Employment Opportunity Commission about the alleged discrimination. The EEOC, noting that obesity was not a protected class under federal law, denied the complaint.

OTHER Certain other groupings of people are making a case for being a protected class. The obese are already such in the state of Michigan (as are those with height issues) and in scattered municipalities around the country, such as San Francisco. The morbidly and super obese (100 and 200 pounds overweight) have especially gained significant ground in this area over the past few years. Also aiming at protected class status are smokers and those not considered attractive.

Scope of Protection

The most obvious forms of employment discrimination arise out of the hiring decision. In the past, this country's employment advertisements often included such language as "men only," "no black people need apply," and "persons between the ages of 16 and 30 years only, please."

IN ALL ASPECTS OF EMPLOYMENT Today the law makes illegal not only discrimination against protected classes in hiring, but similar discrimination in any "term, condition, or privilege of employment." This means it is illegal to discriminate against protected classes in any aspect of the job. If such discrimination is displayed in pay, promotions, training, overtime, educational opportunities, travel requirements, shift rotations, firings, layoffs, post-employment letters of recommendation, or any other aspect of employment, it is illegal.

GOVERNING MOST EMPLOYERS Most employers that have 15 or more employees and are engaged in interstate commerce are subject to federal employment discrimination laws. This means that almost all employers except some small businesses are subject to the laws described in this chapter. Agencies of state governments, employment agencies, and labor unions generally also are subject to anti-discrimination laws.

CHECKPOINT Name the characteristics that, under federal law, employers may not consider in any employment-related decision.

Laws That Prohibit Employment Discrimination

WHAT'S YOUR VERDICT? Jannette was arguing with her friend Phil about the inequality of pay between men and women. Phil pointed out that the Equal Pay Act was signed into law 45 years previously and so pay for men and women surely had achieved parity by now.

Is Phil correct in his assumption?

The federal government has enacted a number of statutes to prohibit discrimination against protected classes in employment. These statutes are described in the following sections.

Title VII of The Civil Rights Act of 1964

With some exceptions, Title VII of the Civil Rights Act of 1964 forbids employers, employment agencies, and unions from discriminating in hiring, paying, training, promoting, or discharging employees on the basis of race, color, religion, national origin, or sex. An employer may discriminate in selecting one worker over another if the standard set is necessary for proper performance of the job. For example, a prospective airplane pilot may be required to understand radar and navigation equipment. That person also may be required to react quickly to emergencies and to be free of potentially fatal heart diseases.

Title VII of the Civil Rights Act also created the **Equal Employment Opportunity Commission (EEOC)** and gave it the authority to investigate and settle complaints of job discrimination. If necessary, it also can prosecute offenders. If an employer has discriminated in the past, the courts may mandate an **affirmative action plan** to remedy the past discrimination. The plan must include positive steps aimed at offsetting past discrimination by bringing the percentages of minorities and women in the workforce up to their corresponding percentages in the pool of qualified applicants. Most employers that contract with the federal government also must submit affirmative action plans. Because the federal government

CyberLAW

DISABILITIES UNDER THE SSA

The Social Security Administration (SSA) is the government agency that runs the social security program in the United States. The SSA has one of the most extensive web sites of any government agency. When you visit www.ssa.gov you can perform a number of functions. You can learn about the history of the SSA and its plans for the future. You can inquire about all of the benefits that the SSA offers, such as disability and retirement income and Medicare. You also can request many of the services the SSA offers directly from the web site. The SSA accepts requests from the web site for personal earnings and benefits summaries. Companies can download forms they need to report employees' earnings and wages to the SSA.

THINK ABOUT IT

Research the SSA web site to look into the disability status of a specific physical condition or problem, for example, obesity. Research the procedure to be followed for someone who has the condition or problem to establish their entitlement to disability income. Also check the web sites of attorneys willing to represent disability claimants for their fees and specialties.

is the biggest buyer of goods and services in the country, most large employers are directly affected by affirmative action.

Equal Pay Act of 1963

The Equal Pay Act prohibits wage discrimination on the basis of sex. Women who do the same work or substantially equal work as that of men must be paid at the same rate. This means that when the same skill, effort, and responsibility are required and when the job is performed under similar working conditions, women must be paid the same as men.

Differences in pay are allowed if based on any of the following:

1. merit system
2. seniority system
3. system basing pay on quantity or quality of production
4. system based on any factor other than gender

In *What's Your Verdict?* Phil is incorrect. When The Equal Pay Act was signed into law, women were making $.59 on average for every dollar a man earned doing the same job. In 2006, according to the Census Bureau, women were only earning $.77 per every dollar a man earned doing the same work.

Age Discrimination in Employment Act of 1967

The Age Discrimination in Employment Act forbids discrimination against workers 40 years of age and older in any employment practice (hiring, discharging, retiring, promoting, and compensating). Exceptions are made when age is a necessary consideration for job performance. Such occupations include bus drivers, fire fighters, and police officers.

Americans with Disabilities Act

The **Americans with Disabilities Act (ADA)** requires that employers not engage in unjustified discrimination against disabled persons on the basis of their disability. The act attempts to prevent employers from automatically assuming that disabled persons cannot perform work. A **disability** as defined by the ADA is a physical or mental impairment that substantially limits one or more of life's major activities. Such activities include seeing, hearing,

speaking, breathing, walking, learning, performing manual tasks, lifting, reproduction, eating, sleeping, driving, caring for oneself, and working. However, current use of illegal drugs is not a disability under ADA. Neither are sex-related traits or conditions such as homosexuality. A person with a contagious disease may be protected under the ADA, although the courts determine this based on individual medical judgments.

The ADA defines a qualified individual with a disability as one who can perform the essential functions of the job or who could perform those functions with a reasonable accommodation. Thus employers must make a reasonable accommodation for the qualified disabled worker. A reasonable accommodation is not required if it would produce an undue hardship for the employer. Factors considered in determining whether there would be undue hardships are the cost of the accommodation and the financial resources of the employer.

Pregnancy Discrimination Act

The Pregnancy Discrimination Act is a statute that makes it illegal to discriminate because of pregnancy, childbirth, or related medical conditions. Accordingly, an employer may not fire, refuse to hire, refuse to promote, or demote a woman because she is pregnant.

The act also makes it illegal to discriminate in the providing of fringe benefits on these bases. Thus, an employer cannot carry an insurance policy that insures all physical conditions except pregnancy.

Federal anti-discrimination laws such as those just discussed have been enacted because of past

LEGAL *Research*

Interview the manager responsible for compliance with ADA rules and regulations at a local business. Note and report on the manager's knowledge of the law and attitude towards the law and its enforcers. Then interview an employee who is disabled about the accommodations he or she has received. Note and report on the employee's knowledge of the law and attitude towards the law and its enforcers. Compare your notes on the two interviews. What conclusions can you draw? Compare your conclusions with those of your classmates.

injustices in the hiring, paying, training, transferring, and discharging of workers. Most states and many cities have enacted similar laws. In addition, the Supreme Court has interpreted the Fourteenth Amendment to apply to employment. The Supreme Court also has extended to employment the civil rights laws passed in 1866 and 1870.

These efforts have modified the old common-law concept that an employer has complete freedom in hiring and, subject to liability for breach of contract,

freedom in discharging workers. Essentially, current laws, regulations, and court decisions require that job applicants be judged on their merits as individuals, not as members of any group or class.

CHECKPOINT Name the laws discussed in this section that prohibit unjustified discrimination in employment.

24-1 Assessment

Xtra! Study Tools
school.cengage.com/blaw/lawxtra

THINK ABOUT LEGAL CONCEPTS

1. Any discrimination by an employer is illegal. **True or False?**

2. In general, employment law makes it illegal to consider a group characteristic when hiring individuals. **True or False?**

3. A group of individuals who exhibit characteristics against which it is illegal to discriminate are a part of a __?__.

4. Which of the following employees would not fit into a protected class? (a) pregnant female (b) 60-year-old white male (c) Buddhist monk (d) All of these would fit into a protected class.

5. Which law prohibits discrimination based on race, color, religion, sex, or national origin in any term, condition, or privilege of employment? (a) ADA (b) Equal Pay Act (c) Civil Rights Act of 1964

6. The law that protects workers age 40 and older from discrimination is called the _?_.

THINK CRITICALLY ABOUT EVIDENCE

Study the situation, answer the questions, and then prepare arguments to support your answers.

7. Sven immigrated to the United States at age 12 and obtained citizenship at age 18. He speaks with a thick accent. When he applied for a job as a bank clerk, someone else was selected because the other person was more accurate in counting money. Has Sven been the subject of illegal discrimination?

8. "We Wash Windows" is a company that washes windows in a commercial building where many windows are six or seven feet off the ground. Taller people can wash these windows more quickly. Atushi is Japanese. When he applied for a window washer job, the company told him they don't hire Japanese because most Japanese people are too short. Atushi is six feet, four inches tall. Has Atushi been the subject of illegal discrimination?

9. When Quality Furniture Manufacturing Company faced financial difficulties, it began laying off employees. The majority were over

the age of 40, although they constituted only 5 percent of the workforce. Young workers in their twenties were immediately hired to fill the jobs of those discharged. Quality justified this action by noting that increased health insurance costs were the overwhelming reason for its financial problems. As insurance coverage for older employees, especially those 50 and older, costs two to three times what coverage for younger employees costs, it only made common sense to discharge the older employees first. Is this ethical? What statute, if any, was violated?

10. Irene was a Mormon. She believed that other members of her religion were more honest than the general population. When she was asked to hire a bank teller for her employer, she advertised the job as one available only for members of her religion. Is Irene's action legal? Would it be legal if Irene could prove in court that members of her religion were in fact more honest?

24-2 Proving Illegal Discrimination

GOALS

- Discuss how a case based on unequal treatment is proven
- Describe how a case based on disparate impact is proven
- Recognize the forms of sexual harassment

KEY TERMS

unequal treatment

business necessity

bona fide occupational qualification (BFOQ)

bona fide seniority system

neutral on its face

disparate impact

applicant pool

workforce pool

quid pro quo

hostile environment

Unequal Treatment Cases

WHAT'S YOUR VERDICT?

After retiring from teaching at a college in another state, Harold was 62 when he applied for an assistant professor's position at a nearby university. His only competition came from Darlene, a person with far less experience, fewer publications, poorer class ratings, and a master's degree instead of the doctorate that Harold possessed. When Darlene was selected for the position, Harold brought suit for age discrimination saying the the local university had just experienced a large increase in costs for health insurance for its senior faculty. Harold also noted that the committee making the selection was asked to base its decision on which one of the two candidates would be more productive in the long run.

Will the court find that Harold has been discriminated against because of his age?

Unequal treatment (sometimes called *disparate treatment*) means that an employer intentionally treats members of a protected class less favorably than other employees.

Evidence of Unequal Treatment

Based on the nature of the evidence, cases based on unequal treatment have taken several forms.

CASES BASED ON DIRECT EVIDENCE In the past, unequal treatment often was both intentional and

open. Newspapers carried want ads that listed jobs as "men only." Some firms would refuse publicly to hire African Americans, Asians, Cajuns, Mexicans, mulattos, Puerto Ricans, or women. Flyers would sometimes state, "no Irish" or "no Jews need apply." Sometimes women would receive letters stating, "I am sorry, but we have a policy against hiring women in these positions."

To win a case where the discrimination is admitted, the employee need only prove that she or he was denied employment because of membership in a protected class. Today, most direct-evidence litigation focuses not on the decision to hire, but on decisions related to other aspects

© GETTY IMAGES/PHOTODISC

Kari applied for a job for which she believed she was well qualified, but she was rejected. She's not sure, but she thinks the employer objected to the fact that she was pregnant. What must she show in order to establish a discrimination case against this employer?

of the employment relationship. Thus, if an employer offered life insurance as a fringe benefit but the amount was less for women than for men (on the grounds that women outlive men), this would be intentional unequal treatment.

CASES BASED ON INDIRECT EVIDENCE Today most cases involve situations where the employer denies any intention to illegally discriminate. To establish a case against such an employer, an employee must show the following:

1. The person was a member of a protected class.
2. The person applied for the job and was qualified.
3. The person was rejected.
4. The employer held the job open and sought other persons with similar qualifications.

In *What's Your Verdict?* Harold was a member of a protected class. Given the disparity in qualifications, the direct evidence inherent in the selection criterion utilized by the committee, and the awarding of the position to someone of lesser qualifications, Harold would likely win his case. Note that the possibility that Darlene also was a member of a protected class would not disallow Harold's claim.

CASES BASED ON STATISTICS In some cases, the government can initiate proceedings against a company for employment discrimination when there is evidence of a pattern and practice of discrimination. In this type of litigation, the government merely shows a statistically significant difference between the protected class composition of the pool of qualified applicants and the workforce.

IN THIS CASE Beck wanted to be considered for advanced training at her company's headquarters. Their bosses nominated employees for the training. In Beck's job classification, there were about 80 men and 60 women. Beck's boss nominated her. Of the 20 people nominated for the home-office training, half were men and half were women. Of the 10 people selected for the training, all were men. If she filed a complaint, Beck's employer probably would be liable for employment discrimination due to the statistically significant difference between the protected class in the pool of applicants and those picked for training.

Employer's Defenses

BUSINESS NECESSITY Once the employee has shown, with either direct or indirect evidence, that unequal treatment occurred, the employer may defend by establishing one of several defenses. These defenses attempt to show that the unequal treatment was legally justifiable. Thus, in an indirect proof case, the employer's most common defense is that the employee's skills or work history was the reason for not hiring. This general defense is sometimes called business necessity or job relatedness. **Business necessity** means that the employer's actions were meant to advance the business rather than to create unjustified discrimination.

BONA FIDE OCCUPATIONAL QUALIFICATION Another defense available to an employer is called the **bona fide occupational qualification (BFOQ)**. A bona fide occupational qualification is a job requirement that compels discrimination against a protected class. Thus, if an employer hired actors to play parts in a stage show, some of the parts would be for men and so the employer justifiably could decide to hire only men for these parts. Similarly, employers could request only male or female models for a fashion show.

To establish the BFOQ, the discrimination must truly be essential to the business. The fact that discrimination is helpful is not enough.

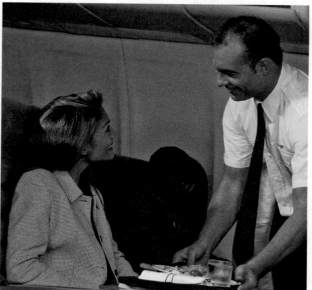

© GETTY IMAGES/PHOTODISC

When the airlines were attempting to preserve the tradition of female-only flight attendants, why do you think the courts rejected their argument that female flight attendants were necessary because most passengers preferred to be served by women?

When airlines were fighting to preserve female-only flight attendants, they presented surveys showing that a high proportion of their passengers preferred to be served by women. The courts rejected this argument and held that being female is not necessary to perform the job.

SENIORITY Seniority can be another justification for unequal treatment. A **bona fide seniority system** is one that rewards employees based on the length of employment rather than merit and is not intended to discriminate. If an employer pays union members on the basis of seniority, promotes on the basis of seniority, or lays employees off on the basis of seniority, unequal treatment of protected classes will be tolerated. The Supreme Court will permit seniority to be used even when it perpetuates past discrimination.

PRETEXTS Employers sometimes assert business necessity or BFOQ as a pretext, or a cover, for

discriminating. For example, a company hires a male instead of a female, Julie, for a job. The company says the reason is that the job involves a lot of travel. Because Julie is the mother of three children, the company says that would make travel harder for her to schedule. Julie could establish that this reason is not a business necessity but a pretext by showing that men with three or more children had been hired for the job.

CHECKPOINT What are the three main bases for unequal treatment cases?

Disparate Impact Cases

WHAT'S YOUR VERDICT? Sharon's Machine Shop manufactures fire hydrants. When finished, each hydrant weighs approximately 125 pounds. Part of the job description for hydrant assemblers states that a person hired for this job be able to lift 125 pounds ten times in two minutes. This requirement is similar to the actions required to assemble the hydrants.

Is this job requirement a form of illegal employment discrimination?

Many companies have a policy (like the one at Sharon's in *What's Your Verdict?*) that is regarded as **neutral on its face**. This means that the policy makes no reference to a protected class. In *What's Your Verdict?* more men probably will be able to satisfy this job requirement than women. So the policy has a disparate, or different, impact on a protected class. **Disparate impact** indicates that the policy eliminates more members of protected classes than members of the majority. If prison guards are required to be six feet tall, this would eliminate a higher proportion of Asians, Hispanics, and women than white and black males. Agility tests, height tests, weight tests, educational requirements, and tests of clerical abilities all may have a disparate impact on a protected class.

The courts treat cases involving job requirements quite differently from cases involving unequal treatment. To win a suit claiming

NETBookmark

Access school.cengage.com/blaw/lawxtra and click on the link for Chapter 24. Read the article entitled "Proving Business Necessity: The Disparate Impact Challenge." Then answer these questions.

1. What five factors have emerged as keys to assessing the legality of employment practices that create disparity?
2. A person who has demonstrated factually that they have been discriminated against due to disparate impact is said to have established a _?_ case.
3. Courts generally approve employment standards in the abstract rather than in relation to the requirements of a particular job. **True or False?**
4. The burden of proving business necessity varies based on the determination of whether a candidate's success is made by the employer or by an entity external to the employer. What is the underlying judicial concern?

school.cengage.com/blaw/lawxtra

disparate impact, the employee need not prove an intention to discriminate. However, the employee must identify a specific employment practice and show statistically that the practice excludes members of a protected class. Even then the employee will lose if the employer is able to show that there is a legitimate business necessity for the practice.

In *What's Your Verdict?* Sharon's weight-lifting test is neutral on its face. It can be statistically shown, however, that a smaller proportion of women will pass the test. Therefore, it has a disparate impact. However, the test is justified by business necessity because it is clearly job-related. In the past, such practices as requiring high school graduation, written aptitude tests, height and weight requirements, and subjective interviews have been attacked by employees on the basis of disparate impact.

By Statistical Proof

To win a case based on disparate impact, an employee must establish that fewer members of the protected class qualified for the job when the challenged employment practice is used than when it is not. This involves examining two groups:

1. the **applicant pool** (those qualified for the job when the challenged qualification practice is not considered)

2. the **workforce pool** (persons actually in the employer's workforce)

The percentage of protected class individuals in each pool is then compared. If the percentage in the applicant pool is statistically higher than the percentage in the workforce group, this suggests disparate impact. But one other element, *causation*, must be proven. Causation is a linking of the challenged practice and the difference in percentages of protected class persons. After causation is established, the employee has proven disparate impact.

Employer's Defenses

Employers can avoid liability even after the employee has shown disparate treatment. If the challenged practice is justified by business necessity, there is no liability. Thus, if weight lifting is required on the job, it does not legally matter that the requirement excludes a larger part of a protected class from the job. In addition, an employer can utilize the defenses of bona fide occupational qualification and seniority.

CHECKPOINT What does disparate impact mean?

Sexual Harassment Cases

WHAT'S YOUR VERDICT? Ben delivered the internal mail at the headquarters of Antonia's, a national chain of lingerie shops. Everyday when he entered the product design section, several of the female employees would whistle at him and call him "honey doo" and other similar terms of endearment. Occasionally, a female worker in the section would pinch him or caress him. Ben mentioned to their manager that the attention made him uncomfortable, but she refused to correct it.

What form of sexual harassment is taking place here? Would the company be liable for what is done by its employees and manager?

One unique form of sex discrimination is sexual harassment. Sexual harassment takes two forms: quid pro quo and hostile environment.

Quid Pro Quo

Quid pro quo means one thing is exchanged for another. The most vivid illustration of this form of sexual harassment is when a boss threatens to fire a subordinate unless the subordinate provides sexual favors. Sexual favors become the quid pro quo for continued employment. The employer may offer any term, condition, or privilege of employment, such as a raise, or a favorable evaluation.

Hostile Environment

A **hostile environment** arises when unwelcome sexual comments, gestures, or contact interfere with an employee's ability to work.

If the sexual harassment is a result of the conduct of a supervisor, the employer is strictly liable. If, instead, the conduct of non-supervisory employees causes the problem, the employer is liable only when the harassment is either known or should have been known to supervisors and they failed to act effectively to prevent further occurrences. In *What's Your Verdict?* the manager knew about the harassment but refused to take effective action to correct it. Therefore, Antonia's will be liable if Ben brings a hostile environment case.

 CHECKPOINT What are the two forms of sexual harassment?

Economic Impact

DEFENDING A SEXUAL HARASSMENT LAWSUIT

Business managers unfamiliar with the laws on discrimination and particularly sexual harassment often go into shock when confronted with the costs of defending against such a suit. The business is motivated to stage a good defense due to the potential of compensatory and even punitive damages they might incur. Consequently, the business will not utilize in-house counsel but will, at considerable expense, hire an attorney who specializes in the area. The employer often is ordered to pay the attorney's fees of the employee whereas, should the business win, the employee seldom is given a responsibility to pay those of the business. Also, as a consequence of being involved in a sexual harassment lawsuit, the business often loses the patronage of several of it customers, even if the resolution is in the business's favor. The business also loses the innumerable hours its managers and employees spend in hearings, depositions, searching for evidence, and trials. Finally, the business must face increased charges for its liability insurance.

THINK CRITICALLY

How might a company protect itself from sexual harassment suits?

24-2 Assessment

Xtra! Study Tools
school.cengage.com/blaw/lawxtra

THINK ABOUT LEGAL CONCEPTS

1. To win a case where the discrimination is admitted, the employee need only prove that she or he was denied employment because of membership in a(n) _?_.

2. Which of the following are grounds for illegal discrimination? (a) disparate treatment (b) disparate impact (c) pattern and practice (d) all of the above

3. If a restaurant does what it in good faith believes will be effective in ending sexual harassment of its waitresses by non-supervisory personnel working in its kitchen, it will not be liable if the harassment continues. **True or False?**

4. Employers may discriminate against protected classes if it is justified by business necessity. **True or False?**

5. If a member of a protected class proves disparate treatment, the employer will not be liable if it can show the defense of seniority or BFOQ. **True or False?**

6. A job requirement may be illegal although it appears on its face to be neutral towards a protected class. **True or False?**

THINK CRITICALLY ABOUT EVIDENCE

Study the situation, answer the questions, and then prepare arguments to support your answers.

7. Jennifer interviewed people to serve as clerks at her dry-cleaning business. She thought that she would get more repeat business if she hired attractive male clerks. Jennifer advertised and told females applicants that she was only interested in male clerks, so they need not bother with an interview. Would this form of discrimination be proved directly or indirectly? Would the case be one based on disparate impact or disparate treatment?

8. Finance America reimbursed employees for their job-related educational expenses. Janice applied for reimbursement for a course, but was told, "This isn't job related." She learned that another employee, Gail, had been turned down, too. Later, Janice met four men with similar jobs who had taken the same course and had been reimbursed. What type of discrimination occurred? What defense is Finance America most likely to employ in this case?

9. When Debbie won the job of administrative assistant to Toby Main, the president of Condorama, a time share company, she was told the position involved a lot of traveling with the president. Every week, Main flew to various places in the United States and the Caribbean. After a few weeks of this travel, several of her fellow employees started implying that Debbie was being intimate with her boss, which she was not. The gossip, however, made her very uncomfortable, and she was considering quitting her job as a consequence. What options are open to her instead of quitting?

 Online Research> **Ashleigh's Argument**

Ashleigh gazed down at her baby boy asleep in his crib. Everything had gone smoothly from conception to birth to this very day. Unfortunately, Ashleigh just received a call from Phyllis her boss at Universal Galaxy General (UGG) with some seriously bad news.

When Ashleigh and Ryan had decided that it was time to have a child, she had been at UGG for five years. She was the newly appointed product design department manager for a product line that UGG intended to introduce over the next two years. She had set the project in motion before giving the required 30-day notice that she was going to take leave shortly before the baby was born. As UGG had more than 50 employees and Ashleigh had worked for the company a minimum of 12 months and more than 1,250 hours in the last 12 months, she was covered by the Federal Family and Medical Leave Act (FMLA). It allowed her to take up to 12 weeks per year off for the birth of her child. Although the 12 weeks were without pay, FMLA did require that the company health insurance still remain in effect. Then, at the conclusion of the leave, with few exceptions, the person taking the leave was to be given her or his old job back or its equivalent.

Phyllis had just notified Ashleigh, however, that this last benefit under FMLA, the return to the previously held job, was not to be afforded Ashleigh. The new product line had been cancelled and all the personnel associated with it had been terminated. With just Ryan working, even in the short term, and with their savings low, the future looked bleak. After thinking for a moment, Ashleigh reached for the phone book and started scanning the business pages for an employment law attorney.

THINK CRITICALLY

Research FMLA to determine if Ashleigh has a basis for a lawsuit to recover her job, any pay she might lose due to her termination, and other damages. Evaluate her chances. What defenses could UGG use against such a lawsuit? Evaluate these defenses. Who would likely win the suit?

GO TO FINDLAW.COM TO FIND THE ANSWERS

To find the material in FindLaw on this issue, go to Findlaw.com and click on the following sequence of hyperlinks: Employee Rights, Employee Rights Center, Family and Medical Leave, Rights and Responsibilities Under the FMLA.

CONCEPTS IN BRIEF

24-1 Legal versus Illegal Discrimination

1. In the work environment illegal discrimination harms not only the individual discriminated against but all of society. Achieving efficient production and quality products depends on putting the best qualified person in the right job.

2. Illegal discrimination in employment is defined as treating individuals differently on the basis of race, color, gender, pregnancy and pregnancy intentions, age (40 and older), religion, disability, or national origin. These categories are referred to as protected classes.

3. A large number of statutes, especially at the federal level, make discrimination against a member of a protected class illegal.

24-2 Proving Illegal Discrimination

4. Generally, illegal discrimination in employment is proven by showing unequal treatment, disparate impact, or by statistics showing a pattern or practice.

5. Among an employer's potential defenses to charges of illegal discrimination are business necessity, BFOQs, and a bona fide seniority system.

6. An employment policy that has a disparate impact is one that eliminates more members of protected classes than members of the majority.

7. Sexual harassment claims generally take one of two forms: quid pro quo or hostile environment.

8. To avoid liability, action taken by an employer against sexual harassment must be immediate and effective.

YOUR LEGAL VOCABULARY

Match each statement with the term that it best defines. Some terms may not be used.

1. All the people who work for an employer that has been charged with employment discrimination
2. Interference with an employee's ability to work due to unwelcome comments, gestures, or touching of a sexual nature at work
3. Label for a workplace policy that does not seem on the surface to discriminate against any protected class
4. Legal remedy requiring employment of members of a protected class due to past discrimination in hiring
5. Employer's defense that actions were meant to advance the business rather than to create unjustified discrimination
6. Exchange of a sexual favor for better work status
7. Groups that employment law protects
8. System that rewards employees for length of employment rather than merit
9. Those qualified for the job
10. Has the authority to investigate and settle complaints of job discrimination and to prosecute suspected offenders
11. Condition that substantially limits a major life activity
12. Employer intentionally treats members of a protected class less favorably than other employees

a. affirmative action plan
b. ADA
c. applicant pool
d. BFOQ
e. bona fide seniority system
f. business necessity
g. disability
h. disparate impact
i. employment discrimination
j. EEOC
k. hostile environment
l. neutral on its face
m. protected classes
n. quid pro quo
o. unequal treatment
p. workforce pool

REVIEW LEGAL CONCEPTS

13. Explain the difference between legal and illegal discrimination.

14. Describe the elements of disparate treatment and the main defenses utilized by those charged with it.

15. Describe the elements of disparate impact and the way it is proven in court.

16. Describe how disparate treatment cases can still be proven even though there is no direct or indirect evidence.

WRITE ABOUT LEGAL CONCEPTS

17. Write an ad for a job as a server in a restaurant which creates direct evidence of disparate treatment.

18. Write a job description for a high school teacher which contains two types of job requirements. One type might create a disparate impact. Another type will not create a disparate impact.

Which requirements are likely to create a disparate impact?

19. **HOT DEBATE** Write a letter from the employer to Phan explaining the reasons he will not be hired for the job. Write a letter from Phan to the employer explaining why he should be hired.

MAKE ACADEMIC CONNECTIONS

20. **POLITICAL SCIENCE** The passage of the Americans with Disabilities Act was an important event in the political history of the United States. Without great fanfare and little opposi-tion from either party, the ADA became law. Research how the ADA was conceived and passed. Report to the class on the lessons learned.

THINK CRITICALLY ABOUT EVIDENCE

Study the situation, answer the questions, and then prepare arguments to support your answers.

21. When Angela almost miscarried in her sixth month of pregnancy, she was confined to total bed rest. As a consequence of her continuing absence, her employer fired her. Has the employer acted legally?

22. Suppose you were in charge of hiring workers to assemble very small electrical components to make a toy. If you thought that females of Asian ancestry were most likely to do this type of work well, would you limit your interviews to this group of persons only? Would your decision be different if you were certain there would be no legal risk?

23. Peter owned a small restaurant that specialized in Indian food. He had only 8 employees and therefore knew that most employment discrimination laws did not apply to him. Is Peter ethically obligated to follow these laws anyway?

24. Jerry had owned a small printing shop in the same location for over 25 years. For most of the quarter of a century he had had medical insurance coverage for all his employees. The policy was periodic, renewable once each year. As Jerry's employees aged, however, he found the insurance premiums on those 55 and over were extremely costly. As a consequence, he instituted a new rule that he would only pay an amount on each employee's premium equal to a 30 year old's premium. If the employees wanted health insurance through the company, they would have to pay the balance if there were one. What type of discrimination does this constitute? Identify the protected class and the form the discrimination takes.

25. Ann Hopkins worked for Price Waterhouse, a large accounting firm. It was a practice to make professional employees partners in the firm after several years. Ann had been distinctively successful in the performance of her job. Of about 600 partners in the firm, only eight were women. When Ann was being considered for partnership, a committee of all male partners evaluated her. Several members of the committee made comments such as the following: "She should go to charm school;" "She needs to learn to dress, walk, and talk like a woman;" and "She should wear jewelry and makeup." Ultimately the committee turned her down for partnership. When she was told the comments of the members of the committee, Ann sued, claiming unequal treatment. Will she prevail? (*Price Waterhouse v. Hopkins,* 109 S.Ct. 1775)

26. Wards Cove Packing Company operated canneries in remote areas of Alaska. The workers in the canneries were primarily Filipinos and native Alaskans. These jobs were unskilled, and the pay was low. The workers in non-cannery jobs were primarily white. These positions were highly skilled and highly paid. Antonio was a canner, and he sued for employment discrimination. He claimed that the difference in the composition of the cannery and non-cannery workforces established that Wards Cove was illegally discriminating. Will he prevail? (*Wards Cove Packing Company v. Antonio,* 109 S. Ct. 2115)

27. Henderson worked as a radio dispatcher for the Dundee, Florida, police department. The police chief, she alleged, subjected her to repeated sexual comments and requests that she have sexual relations with him. She said that because she refused, the chief refused to allow her to attend the police academy. Further, he suspended her for two days for violating a minor office policy that never before had been enforced. She interpreted the suspension as a threat that she would be fired unless she gave in to her boss's advances. Eventually Henderson quit and then sued the city claiming sexual harassment. Will she prevail? (*Henderson v. City of Dundee,* 682 F.2d 897)

28. The catastrophic Exxon Valdez oil spill, which arguably might have resulted because of the alcoholism of one of the ship's officers, occurred in 1989. As a consequence, Exxon Corporation adopted a preventive policy of terminating the employment of employees in safety-sensitive, minimally supervised positions who had undergone treatment for substance abuse. This safety-oriented policy intended to prevent relapses into substance abuse that might harm the public at large applied to approximately 10 percent of the company's workforce. The EEOC brought suit for a violation of the ADA's prohibition against broad-based discrimination against a protected class instead of reviewing each individual's case. Exxon maintained that such individual review would often come too late and at the expense of public safety. Should Exxon be held guilty of illegal discrimination under the ADA? Why or why not? (*EEOC v. Exxon Corporation,* 203 F. 3d 871, 5th Cir. 2000).

29. Shiela Grove and David Klink were both tellers for Frostburg National Bank. Both were high school graduates. They had worked for the bank for the same length of time performing the same duties. Occasionally, Klink performed miscellaneous tasks that were not assigned to Grove. A male supervisor, David Willetts, set the salaries for both tellers. Klink's salary was significantly higher than Grove's. Has the bank violated the Equal Pay Act? (*Grove v. Frostburg National Bank,* 549 F. Supp. 922)

30. Johnson Controls, Inc., manufactures batteries made primarily of lead. Lead is a dangerous substance for pregnant women because exposure to lead can harm the fetus. For this reason, Johnson Controls excluded women who are pregnant or who are capable of bearing children from jobs that involve exposure to lead. Numerous plaintiffs, including a woman who had chosen to be sterilized to avoid losing her job, entered a federal district court class action suit alleging that Johnson Controls' policy constituted illegal sex discrimination under Title VII of the Civil Rights Act. Is this illegal discrimination? (499 U.S. 187, U.S. Sup. Ct., 1991)

Sports & Entertainment Law

Title IX Takes Wrestlers and Techies to the Mats

AMY COHEN, ET AL., V. BROWN UNIVERSITY
101 F.3D 155

BACKGROUND   Title IX of the Education Amendments of 1972 to the Civil Rights Act of 1964 foreshadowed fundamental change in federally supported educational institutions. It read, "No person in the United States shall, on the basis of sex, be excluded from participation in, or denied the benefits of, or be subjected to discrimination under any educational program or activity receiving federal assistance." The Office of Civil Rights (OCR) of the federal government's Department of Education set down a three-part test to determine if a violation of Title IX existed. Colleges that receive federal assistance could prove compliance with Title IX if they (1) had substantially the same proportion of male and female athletes as males and females in the general student population, (2) had a "history and continuing practice" of expanding opportunities for women, or (3) were "fully and effectively accommodating the interests and abilities of women on campus." The ambiguity of the latter two criteria was seemingly intended to cover any decision that could be said to have been based on a simple quota-type proportional disparity. The result was a perfect record against court challenges by male teams and team members dropped by colleges to try and achieve compliance with

the standards. In fact, in the 1990s, for every woman who was newly provided an opportunity to play organized collegiate sports, 3.4 men had that chance taken from them. Especially hard hit were the wrestling programs.

FACTS   In the case of *Amy Cohen v. Brown University*, the decision came to turn on statistics and quotas. Cohen and others had sued to stop Brown from demoting women's volleyball, women's gymnastics, men's water polo, and men's golf teams from university-funded varsity status to the status of solely donor-funded teams. The federal appeals court in deciding the case found that Brown supported 12 men's and 13 women's teams in the funded, varsity status. However, the University had a 13 percent disparity between the percentage of women in varsity-funded sports and the percentage of women in the student body. It also found that, even though the number of female teams exceeded those of the male gender, the actual playing positions in the various sport offerings was heavily biased in favor of the men's programs, 479 to 312. Mainly as a result of these statistics, the court enjoined (prohibited) the demotion of the women's teams but did not halt the same action being taken against the male teams. As a consequence, since *Cohen v. Brown* the emphasis on comparative statistics in colleges and in the OCR administration has grown. To the shock of many, OCR recently has considered turning its attention to the male-dominated educational programs in math and science and, in particular, the hard sciences of engineering, physics, and computers. Investigations were threatened into the treatment of women as undergraduates, graduates, and faculty members in those areas. In fact the head of the OCR promised to not look exclusively "at the numbers" but at the environments in these areas that made women feel "unwelcome."

THE ISSUE   Should comparative statistics be the primary indicator of gender bias in education?

HOLDING   Brown was enjoined from demoting the status of subject women's programs.

PRACTICE JUDGING

1. Research the success of Title IX in eliminating disparity in gender in collegiate sports programs.

2. Should Title IX standards be applied to the areas of the hard sciences mentioned above. Why or why not?

Chapter 25
Employment-Related Injuries

25-1 Safety on the Job

25-2 Employer's Liability for Work-Related Injuries

© GETTY IMAGES/PHOTODISC

HOT DEBATE

Joaquim worked at a sandwich shop in lower Manhattan. The owner of the shop asked all her employees to wear costumes to work on Halloween. Despite a heavy rain, Joaquim, who loved Halloween, came in an elaborate wizard's costume that he owned. He had a long gray wig, a flowing robe, and a tall peaked hat. Unfortunately, while sneaking a cigarette in one of the restrooms during a break, which was against the shop's policies, Joaquim caught the wig on fire. He was unable to get the wig off immediately or to put out the fire, as the shop's fire extinguisher was empty. Instead he ran outside the shop where the rain eventually doused the fire. Joaquim's real hair was burned off and he suffered minor burns to his hands. When a daily newspaper covered the story with color photos shot by a passing tourist under the headline, "Wizard Wigs Out," the shop's business increased twofold. Now Joaquim is considering suing the shop for negligence.

WHERE DO YOU STAND?

1. Why should the store be required to pay for Joaquim's injuries?
2. Why should the store not be required to pay?

25-1 Safety on the Job

GOALS

- Recognize the two approaches taken to protect workers from on-the-job injuries
- Distinguish the role of OSHA in the effort to prevent such injuries

KEY TERMS

Occupational Safety and Health Administration (OSHA)

Occupational Safety and Health Act

general duty clause

Requiring a Safe Workplace

WHAT'S YOUR VERDICT? Browning Processing Company prepares fruits and vegetables for the market. An OSHA inspector ordered the company to install clutches on the prune-pitting machines and to provide electrical grounding of all electric typewriters and word processors.

Must Browning comply?

The system in place in the United States to protect workers from on-the-job injuries and their consequences utilizes two approaches. The first is a preventive approach utilized by federal and state agencies. These agencies make rules pertaining to safe working conditions and conduct inspections to discover and prosecute dangerous conditions and rule violations. The **Occupational Safety and Health Administration (OSHA)** is the most vital of all the federal agencies to the success of the preventative approach.

The second approach involves after-the-fact compensation for injuries sustained on the job. This compensation typically is obtainable through negligence lawsuits and the workers' compensation system and will be discussed in the next lesson. The remainder of this lesson focuses on the positive steps OSHA takes to prevent the injuries in the first place.

Legislative Background of OSHA

In 1970, the **Occupational Safety and Health Act** (OSH Act) became law. The groundbreaking policy put into force by this statute involved the federal government directly in the preventing of workplace injuries. The law created the Occupational Safety and Health Administration and empowered it to enact rules and regulations designed to achieve safety in the workplace. Read the provisions of the act on page 445 of this chapter.

OSHA's rules and regulations apply to firms with eleven or more employees that are engaged in interstate commerce. The Department of Labor enforces those rules. State administrative agencies often apply similar safety laws to smaller organizations or those not engaged in interstate commerce.

© GETTY IMAGES/PHOTODISC

What types of accidents could happen in this factory that would lead to injury? What types of preventive safety measures do these men appear to be taking while working here?

OSHA's Responsibilities

ASSURE A HAZARD-FREE WORKPLACE The OSH Act requires in its **general duty clause** that employers provide a place of employment free from recognized hazards that are likely to cause death or serious physical harm. If this general duty requirement is violated, the employer can be fined or shut down by OSHA and held liable to the injured employee in a court of law.

DEVELOP AND ENFORCE SPECIFIC REGULATIONS OSHA also is responsible for making specific workplace safety regulations. These regulations cover most aspects of work. They spell out safety training requirements; safety clothing and equipment to be worn by workers; and the construction, maintenance, and shielding of equipment.

Minimum standards are established for lighting, ventilation, and sanitation. For example, OSHA specifies that spray paint booths must be vented to the exterior of the building and that they must be constructed of metal rather than wood. Another example is the requirement that hair protection (hairnets) be worn when working near equipment such as drills.

Minor violations of OSHA regulations usually are resolved by bringing the workplace into compliance, although employers can be fined. In *What's Your Verdict?* Browning Processing would be required to comply with OSHA's demands because the lack of clutches and electrical grounding violates specific OSHA regulations. If the company did not comply, it could be fined.

CONDUCT WORKPLACE INSPECTIONS OSHA uses workplace inspections to ensure compliance with its general duty clause and specific regulations. While an employer may deny OSHA inspectors access to the workplace, inspectors easily can obtain a search warrant giving them authority to inspect.

Employers are required to file periodic safety reports describing work-related injuries. If there is an injury requiring hospitalization of three or more employees or resulting in a death, the employer must notify the Department of Labor within eight hours. These reports often prompt OSHA inspections.

Employees also may anonymously call OSHA to report safety violations. OSHA will then send inspectors to the workplace. Employers may not discriminate against workers who have informed OSHA of safety violations.

Dealing with OSHA Violations

In most simple cases, employers deal with OSHA officials without a lawyer. The problems usually involve technical engineering and safety issues rather than legal issues. Inspectors and company supervisors are best equipped to resolve these problems. However, some OSHA violations become serious because the cost of compliance can be prohibitive, pushing some companies into bankruptcy. In these situations, the employer needs immediate expert legal help. Unless a company acts quickly, some rights to appeal an OSHA action may be lost.

CHECKPOINT What are the two approaches taken to prevent on-the-job injuries in the United States?

IN THIS CASE During an OSHA visit to the St. Louis plant of a large dish-washing soap manufacturer, an inspector noticed that large portions of the production floor were extremely slippery. The company vice president, who was accompanying the inspector, said that the soap product occasionally spilled off the bottling line and caused the problem. She assured the inspector that the spills were cleaned up immediately. The inspector, however, stated that the clean up was not adequate, as it left a slippery film on the floor. He cited the company for a safety violation.

JOB SAFETY & HEALTH PROTECTION

The Occupational Safety and Health Act of 1970 provides job safety and health protection for workers by promoting safe and healthful working conditions throughout the Nation. Provisions of the Act include the following:

Employers

All employers must furnish to employees employment and a place of employment free from recognized hazards that are causing or are likely to cause death or serious harm to employees. Employers must comply with occupational safety and health standards issued under the Act.

Employees

Employees must comply with all occupational safety and health standards, rules, regulations and orders issued under the Act that apply to their own actions and conduct on the job.

The Occupational Safety and Health Administration (OSHA) of the U.S. Department of Labor has the primary responsibility for administering the Act. OSHA issues occupational safety and health standards, and its Compliance Safety and Health Officers conduct jobsite inspections to help ensure compliance with the Act.

Inspection

The Act requires that a representative of the employer and a representative authorized by the employees be given an opportunity to accompany the OSHA inspector for the purpose of aiding the inspection.

Where there is no authorized employee representative, the OSHA Compliance Officer must consult with a reasonable number of employees concerning safety and health conditions in the workplace.

Complaint

Employees or their representatives have the right to file a complaint with the nearest OSHA office requesting an inspection if they believe unsafe or unhealthful conditions exist in their workplace. OSHA will withhold, on request, names of employees complaining.

The Act provides that employees may not be discharged or discriminated against in any way for filing safety and health complaints or for otherwise exercising their rights under the Act.

Employees who believe they have been discriminated against may file a complaint with their nearest OSHA office within 30 days of the alleged discriminatory action.

Citation

If upon inspection OSHA believes an employer has violated the Act, a citation alleging such violations will be issued to the employer. Each citation will specify a time period within which the alleged violation must be corrected.

The OSHA citation must be prominently displayed at or near the place of alleged violation for three days, or until it is corrected, whichever is later, to warn employees of dangers that may exist there.

Proposed Penalty

The Act provides for mandatory civil penalties against employers of up to $7,000 for each serious violation and for optional penalties of up to $7,000 for each nonserious violation. Penalties of up to $7,000 per day may be proposed for failure to correct violations within the proposed time period and for each day the violation continues beyond the prescribed abatement date. Also, any employer who willfully or repeatedly violates the Act may be assessed penalties of up to $70,000 for each such violation. A minimum penalty of $5,000 may be imposed for each willful violation. A violation of posting requirements can bring a penalty of up to $7,000.

There are also provisions for criminal penalties. Any willful violation resulting in the death of any employee, upon conviction, is punishable by a fine of up to $250,000 (or $500,000 if the employer is a corporation), or by imprisonment for up to six months, or both. A second conviction of an employer doubles the possible term of imprisonment. Falsifying records, reports, or applications is punishable by a fine of $10,000 or up to six months in jail or both.

Voluntary Activity

While providing penalties for violations, the Act also encourages efforts by labor and management, before an OSHA inspection, to reduce workplace hazards voluntarily and to develop and improve safety and health programs in all workplaces and industries. OSHA's Voluntary Protection Programs recognize outstanding efforts of this nature.

OSHA has published Safety and Health Program Management Guidelines to assist employers in establishing or perfecting programs to prevent or control employee exposure to workplace hazards. There are many public and private organizations that can provide information and assistance in this effort, if requested. Also, your local OSHA office can provide considerable help and advice on solving safety and health problems or can refer you to other sources for help such as training.

Consultation

Free assistance in identifying and correcting hazards and in improving safety and health management is available to employers, without citation or penalty, through OSHA-supported programs in each State. These programs are usually administered by the State Labor or Health department or a State university.

Posting Instructions

Employers in States operating OSHA approved State Plans should obtain and post the State's equivalent poster.

Under provisions of Title 29, Code of Federal Regulations, Part 1903.2(a)(1) employers must post this notice (or facsimile) in a conspicuous place where notices to employees are customarily posted.

More Information

Additional information and copies of the Act, OSHA safety and health standards, and other applicable regulations may be obtained from your employer or from the nearest OSHA Regional Office in the following locations:

Atlanta, GA	(404) 562-2300
Boston, MA	(617) 565-9860
Chicago, IL	(312) 353-2220
Dallas, TX	(214) 767-4731
Denver, CO	(303) 844-1600
Kansas City, MO	(816) 426-5861
New York, NY	(212) 337-2378
Philadelphia, PA	(215) 596-1201
San Francisco, CA	(415) 975-4310
Seattle, WA	(206) 553-5930

Washington, DC
1997 (Reprinted)
OSHA 2203

Alexis M. Herman, Secretary of Labor

U.S. Department of Labor
Occupational Safety and Health Administration

This information will be made available to sensory impaired individuals upon request.
Voice phone: (202) 219-8615; TDD message referral phone: 1-800-326-2577

CyberLAW

It is now possible to download and file an OSHA complaint online. Such a complaint can be filed anonymously. However, anonymous filings are treated as non-employee complaints and given a lower priority as a consequence. The official form for complaint submission (OSHA-7) along with instructions on how to properly fill it out can be downloaded from the OSHA web site. Access the link through the Xtra! web site.

THINK ABOUT IT

Should someone be able to file such a complaint without being responsible for its allegations? What possible abuses do you think might occur with such a system?

25-1 Assessment

THINK ABOUT LEGAL CONCEPTS

1. Which of the following is a preventative means of dealing with the potential for employee injuries? (a) negligence suit (b) workers' compensation (c) job safety requirements

2. OSHA regulations control even very specific conditions of the workplace such as the type of shields that must be on equipment. **True or False?**

3. OSHA can shut down employers who fail to provide a "workplace free from recognized hazards." **True or False?**

4. Even minor violations of OSHA regulations can result in imprisonment of employers. **True or False?**

5. Most employers deal with OSHA violations without involving lawyers. **True or False?**

THINK CRITICALLY ABOUT EVIDENCE

Study the situation, answer the questions, and then prepare arguments to support your answers.

6. Bill operated a bakery with only 16 employees, selling bread in two states. Is the bakery subject to regulation by OSHA?

7. Circo-Pacific manufactured circuit boards—the base on which electrical components are mounted by soldering. Peery worked as a dip solderer, inserting the bare boards into a small tub of molten solder to coat the copper circuits. The building in which he worked leaked. Once when it rained, water dripped into the tub and splashed molten solder onto Peery's arm, causing numerous slight burns. The largest of the burns was about half the size of a pencil eraser. Peery complained to his boss about the problem several times but his boss dismissed the complaints saying, "Don't be such a sissy."

Peery finally complained to OSHA. An inspector arrived at the plant and cited the company. The fine was $500. A month later, Peery was transferred to a job that paid much less than that of dip solderer. He complained to OSHA that he was being discriminated against because of his complaint. Is he correct? What is the result?

8. AB Co. stored trichlorethelene in 55 gallon drums at floor level. A forklift nicked a drum, and the liquid spilled out without anyone immediately realizing it. Fumes spread throughout the plant. Five people fainted. The fire department was called, and ambulances took the workers to the hospital. The chemical was cleaned up within two hours and production was restored. What legal obligations remain for AB Co.?

25-2 Employer's Liability for Work-Related Injuries

GOALS

■ Recognize the importance of employee negligence suits and workers' compensation

■ Describe the procedure for handling workers' compensation cases

KEY TERMS

common-law defenses

assumption of risk

co-worker negligence

workers' compensation statutes

casual workers

vocational rehabilitation

Negligence Law and Workers' Compensation

WHAT'S YOUR VERDICT?

Crow was a steelworker working on the fifth story of a fifteen-story apartment project. His employer, Nu-Dimensions, Inc., provided all workers with helmets as required by law to protect from objects that frequently fall from the top floor of a construction project. One day, because of the intense heat, Crow removed his helmet and worked bareheaded while the supervisor was off-duty. A large bolt fell from the employer's construction crane and hit Crow on the head, fracturing his skull.

Could Crow recover any money for injuries due to this on-the-job incident?

If, regardless of OSHA's preventative efforts, worker injuries are sustained, there are two means of providing compensation and rehabilitation. The first and oldest method is a recovery from the employer based on negligence law. The second, covered later in this lesson, is through the system of workers' compensation.

Employee Negligence Suits

Under the common-law negligence approach used in this country for centuries, employees may sue their employers for injuries sustained on the job. Employees win their negligence suits if they prove in court that the employer's negligence caused their injury. By making employers liable for the injuries caused by their negligence, the common law encouraged employers to protect employees.

Negligence law imposes on employers the general duty to provide reasonably safe working conditions for employees. This duty may be violated in several ways. For example, an employer might fail to provide a safe workspace, safe tools, or safe machinery. Similarly, the employer would violate the duty if there were an insufficient number of co-workers to do a job safely or if employees were given inadequate safety instructions. When the employer violates the duty to provide safe working conditions and this causes injury to workers, the employee has grounds to recover for her or his injuries.

DIFFICULTIES FOR EMPLOYEES IN NEGLIGENCE SUITS The original common-law system placed many obstacles in the path of an employee seeking to recover from an employer. In particular the injured worker had several reasons for not suing the employer. First of all, the employee had to hire an attorney. Then, the employee who

LEGAL *Research*

Contact county, city, state, and federal departments, bureaus, and agencies responsible for overseeing the safety of workers in the workplace. Ask them for a list of the laws, ordinances, or regulations they enforce and what each covers. Compile a composite list. Evaluate your list from the standpoint of effectiveness and from the standpoint of the employer. Are there so many requirements that the employer cannot comply with them all, or has a commonsense balance been reached?

sued also risked being fired. Further, even if an employee proved that the employer's negligence caused the injury, the employee would not collect if the employer proved any one of the following **common-law defenses**:

- the employee had assumed the risk involved
- the employee was negligent
- the negligence of a co-worker caused the injury (fellow-servant rule)

Assumption of risk occurs when a person is aware of a danger that could cause injury, but voluntarily remains in the dangerous situation. In *What's Your Verdict?* Crow assumed the risk of being hurt by falling objects when he remained on the job without wearing a helmet knowing that objects often fall from the working areas above him.

Contributory negligence means that the employee carelessly did something that contributed to her or his injury or death. This defense can be effective even when the employee's negligence is very slight in relation to the employer's. In *What's Your Verdict?* Crow was contributorily negligent because he removed his safety helmet.

Co-worker negligence means simply that a co-worker is the cause of the injury. It also prevents recovery from an employer. In *What's Your Verdict?* if the employer could show that a co-worker caused the bolt to fall, the employer would not be liable, and Crow's only option would be to sue the co-worker.

The Compromise of Workers' Compensation

These common-law defenses prevented employees from winning most negligence suits. However, when an employee did win, the size of the recovery often threatened the very existence of the business. Therefore, between 1890 and 1910 state legislatures began enacting compromise laws intended to help more injured employees receive compensation for workplace injuries and be rehabilitated. At the same time, these **workers' compensation statutes** imposed limits on the amounts that injured employees could receive for their injuries. Thus the exposure of employers to potentially ruinous lawsuits was minimized.

Today these statutes require most employers to obtain insurance to pay benefits to injured employees. The benefits are paid without regard to fault. So the insurance pays even when the employer is not a cause of the injury.

The workers' compensation system was created as a substitute for negligence suits. If the injured employee is covered by workers' compensation, no negligence suit ordinarily is allowed against the employer. Also, because the amount an employer must pay for workers' compensation insurance is related somewhat to the firm's safety record, employers still have an incentive to maintain a safe workplace.

Recovering in Lieu of Workers' Compensation

As mentioned, the general rule is that an employee cannot sue the employer for on-the-job injuries if the employee is covered by workers' compensation.

Why do you think it would be a good idea for the employer of these workers to pay for workers' compensation insurance?

However there are several important exceptions. In these exceptional circumstances, an injured employee (or the family of an employee who is killed on the job) can still sue the employer for negligence. These circumstances are covered in the four paragraphs that follow.

IF EMPLOYER FAILS TO PROVIDE WORKERS' COMPENSATION INSURANCE

If state law requires that an employee be covered but the employer has not purchased workers' compensation insurance, the injured employee can sue the employer for negligence. In these cases, the employer generally may not use the employers' common-law defenses of assumption of the risk, contributory negligence, or co-worker negligence. Thus, the employee has the possibility of recovering large sums of money while the employer is almost defenseless. This possibility creates a great incentive for the employer to purchase workers' compensation coverage.

IF EMPLOYEE COVERAGE IS NOT REQUIRED

If an employee is not required to be covered by workers' compensation and is injured because of the employer's negligence, the employee may sue the employer. In these cases, the employer usually may use all the common-law defenses.

IF THE INJURY IS NOT COVERED BY WORKERS' COMPENSATION

In some cases, the employee is injured because of the negligence of the employer, but workers' compensation does not cover the injury. See this lesson's In This Case for an example. In such situations the law would allow the employer to assert the defenses of contributory negligence or assumption of the risk.

IN THIS CASE

Entertainer Tonight Inc. (ETI) hired performing artists as its employees and booked them for one-night gigs in various cities. It also contracted for private pilots and planes to fly the performers to their various venues. Rapper NoBonzBoutIt was aboard such a plane when it crashed on takeoff. NoBonz was severely injured. The pilot was shown to be well-known for his drinking on the job and had been intoxicated at the controls that evening. ETI could be sued for negligence in its selection of the pilot even though it had workers' compensation insurance.

EMPLOYER COMMITS AN INTENTIONAL TORT

In some states, even when covered by workers' compensation, an employee may sue the employer for intentional actions that the employer knows will cause injury. This most often occurs when the conduct of the employer is criminal, is an intentional tort, or is an intentional violation of a safety regulation.

CHECKPOINT Name the three common-law defenses utilized by employers against negligence cases by employees.

How Does the Workers' Compensation System Work?

WHAT'S YOUR VERDICT?

Johnson was a jailer for the Tarrant County Sheriff's Department. While off duty at his home, he cleaned his 9 mm service pistol, reinserted the magazine, and chambered a round. He then left the room. Upon his return, Johnson noticed oil dripping from the pistol. He picked it up, removed the magazine, and vigorously wiped the gun off, forgetting that he had chambered a round. In the process he pulled the trigger and shot himself in the left leg and foot.

Can Johnson recover workers' compensation for this self-inflicted injury?

Determination Made as to Whether Injured Employee Is Covered

Employees are generally protected by workers' compensation insurance if they are injured by accident or disease, including job-related stress, in the scope of employment and from the risks of that employment.

SCOPE OF EMPLOYMENT To recover from workers' compensation, the injured employee must have been acting within the scope of employment at the time of the injury. Scope of employment generally means acting for the benefit of the employer. For example, an auto accident while driving to or from work usually would

RISKS OF EMPLOYMENT There are risks associated with jobs, and these are the risks that workers' compensation generally covers. Thus, while a person assembling heavy fire hydrants could recover for a hernia, a clerical worker who suffered a hernia while picking a piece of paper off the floor might not collect benefits. That is because the injury may not have been caused by the job, but rather by weak abdominal muscles.

EXCLUDED EMPLOYEES Not all workers are required to be covered by a plan of workers' compensation. These vary by state but often include workers for companies with too few employees, casual workers, independent contractors, domestic workers, agricultural workers, and those covered by other systems.

WORKERS FOR COMPANIES NOT REQUIRED TO CARRY WORKERS' COMPENSATION INSURANCE A minority of states do not require companies with very few employees to provide workers' compensation insurance. In contrast, some employers are so large that they are allowed to be self-insuring.

not be within the scope of employment because you do that primarily for yourself. On the other hand, an employee doing an errand for the employer on the way home from work is likely to be within the scope of employment.

The facts in *What's Your Verdict?* were adapted from a Texas case containing typical scope of employment issues. Therein the court wrote:

The Texas Workers' Compensation Act provides a definition of scope of employment: "an activity performed by an employee while engaged in or about the furtherance of the affairs or business of the employer." All county jailers were required to own a weapon, and each officer had the responsibility for cleaning and maintaining his or her own weapon. Because the sheriff's department did not provide an area at the jail for officers to clean their weapons, officers were permitted to clean their weapons at home or "anywhere," as long as they showed up for work each day with a clean weapon. Johnson is entitled to workers' compensation. (*Esis, Inc. v. Johnson,* 908 S.W.2d 554)

© GETTY IMAGES/PHOTODISC

What risks of employment do you think would be associated with this job?

CASUAL WORKERS In most states, casual workers need not be covered. **Casual workers** are those who do not work regularly for one employer.

INDEPENDENT CONTRACTORS Independent contractors need not be covered. An independent contractor is someone hired to accomplish a task, but who is not supervised while doing so. If a dry cleaning business hires an expert from outside the company to fix the steam mechanism on its dry cleaning system, he or she would be an independent contractor, not an employee.

THOSE COVERED BY OTHER SYSTEMS Rather than being covered by state workers' compensation laws, employees of railroads, airlines, trucking firms, and other common carriers engaged in interstate commerce are governed by special federal laws. Longshore and harbor workers also operate under a different federal law and are not subject to state workers' compensation laws. A special statute also governs the crews on seagoing vessels.

What should independent contractors do to make sure that their medical costs will be covered if they are injured on the job?

the employer is grossly negligent or reduced if the employee is nominally negligent. A 10 percent increase or reduction is typical.

The Determination of Benefits

If a worker covered by workers' compensation is injured because of the job, the worker becomes entitled to benefits. Sometimes there is a lump-sum payment to cover such things as pain and suffering involved with injuries such as loss of a hand, or loss of life. All medical expenses usually are covered. Most states also will pay a percentage of lost wages. Compensation for lost wages typically is about 80 percent. In nearly every case, the payment is much less than if the injured party had won a negligence suit.

If an accident makes it impossible for a worker to continue in the former job, most states also pay for vocational rehabilitation. **Vocational rehabilitation** is training for another type of job. Often the amount of the benefit is increased if

LAW BRIEF

In most states both employers and insurers are required by statute to report suspected fraudulent injury claims to the local authorities and the state's department in charge of workers' compensation. Note that it is important to distinguish between "abuse" and "fraud." The former is defined as using the system for something other than it was intended. Fraud occurs when there is clear intent to misrepresent one's injuries or fabricate injuries. Criminal penalties for fraud include incarceration for one to five years, fines from $15,000 to $50,000, and repayment of fraudulently obtained benefits.

THE AWARD HEARING The decisions about whether a person is entitled to benefits and, if so, the types and amounts of those benefits, are made at a hearing conducted by a state administrative agency. This agency is often called the Workers' Compensation Board or the Industrial Accident Commission. Hearing procedures for the Workers' Compensation Board and the Industrial Accident Commission are much less complicated than those of a trial. For small claims, the injured worker does not need a lawyer. However, when the claim or injury is significant, a lawyer who is a specialist in the field should represent the person.

Paying for the Insurance

Workers' compensation benefits are paid from one of three sources. Employers may purchase a workers' compensation insurance policy from a private insurance company, participate in a state-administered workers' compensation fund, or be self-insured. Insurance companies and state funds charge amounts that reflect the riskiness of the business and each employer's safety history. The amount paid out by those that are self-insured depends on the number and severity of workplace injuries. As a consequence, employers have an incentive to make the workplace safe so as to reduce their costs of workers' compensation coverage.

CHECKPOINT What employees are generally excluded from the coverage of a workers' compensation system?

25-2 Assessment

school.cengage.com/blaw/lawxtra

THINK ABOUT LEGAL CONCEPTS

1. Which of the following is not a common-law defense to a negligence suit against an employer? (a) contributory negligence (b) fellow-servant rule (c) OSHA violations in the workplace (d) assumption of the risk

2. In general, can an employee who is covered by workers' compensation bring a suit against the employer for negligence? **Yes or No?**

3. If a worker cannot continue in the former job due to a covered injury, most workers' compensation systems provide for the worker's immediate retirement. **True or False?**

4. Acting for the benefit of the employer is generally referred to as (a) risk of employment (b) scope of employment (c) being an independent contractor (d) none of the above

5. Casual workers generally are covered by workers' compensation. **True or False?**

6. As private insurance companies go out of business occasionally, employers must only purchase workers' compensation insurance policies from the state. **True or False?**

THINK CRITICALLY ABOUT EVIDENCE

Study the situation, answer the questions, and then prepare arguments to support your answers.

7. Suppose you are working at a car wash. One day you are injured when you slip on the wet floor after a fellow worker throws a towel at your head. Which common-law defense would be most useful to the car wash owner in a subsequent negligence suit?

8. Wynett was a delivery driver for Express Delivery. One Friday, he departed from his delivery route to see his girlfriend, Latasha. Latasha lived nearly 60 miles away from Wynett's delivery area. As he pulled up to Latasha's home, his vehicle was hit in the back by a large tractor-trailer truck causing Wynett severe whiplash-related injuries. Was this injury a risk of the employment? Was Wynett acting within the scope of employment? Can Wynett recover workers' compensation for this injury?

9. Lambert hired Mayer, a casual worker, to apply anhydrous ammonia, a fertilizer, to the soil on her farm. Lambert was not required to provide workers' compensation insurance, so Mayer was not covered. Lambert said to Mayer, "Be careful when you handle this stuff; it might burn you." However, Mayer had never used this type of equipment before, and Lambert did not explain to him how to handle the tank or the hose or what to do if he was sprayed on his body. Mayer lost control of the hose and was sprayed in the face with the chemical, blinding him in one eye. Mayer wants to sue Lambert for negligence, claiming that he was not properly instructed in how to handle the equipment. Will he be prevented from doing so because of the state having a workers' compensation system?

10. Jerold hired an independent contractor to install a tile roof on his home. The work was to be completed within 30 days. All the decisions about materials, methods, and working hours were left to the contractor. Must Jerold purchase workers' compensation insurance for the contractor? Why or why not?

11. A 27-year-old retail store employee was raped twice by a store security guard. The security guard had been convicted of violent sex crimes before the store hired him. In her lawsuit the plaintiff sought $50 million, plus punitive damages. The store has asked a judge to dismiss the woman's lawsuit, contending that her only recourse is to pursue a workers' compensation claim. Is rape a risk of the job? What evidence of negligence by the employer is there here? If there is a negligence suit against the employer, what defenses could the employer assert?

© PHOTODISC/GETTY IMAGES

Chapter 25 Assessment

CONCEPTS IN BRIEF

25-1 Safety on the Job

1. The U.S. system to protect workers from on-the-job injuries and their consequences currently utilizes two approaches. The first is a preventive approach embodied by OSHA. The second is a post-injury system based on negligence law and workers' compensation insurance.

2. According to the OSH Act, it is the general duty of employers to provide a place of employment free from hazards that are likely to cause death or serious physical harm.

3. OSHA is empowered to develop specific rules and regulations to ensure workplace safety.

4. OSHA is also empowered to conduct inspections and to cite and prosecute violators.

25-2 Employer's Liability for Work-Related Injuries

5. Employees have long been able to sue employers for work-related injuries under the common law of negligence.

6. Unlike the law of negligence, the workers' compensation system is not fault based.

7. Employees are generally protected by workers' compensation insurance if, because of accident or disease, they are injured in the scope of employment and from the risks of that employment.

8. Workers can still sue employers for negligence in certain circumstances but, as a general rule, if the business has workers' compensation insurance, a negligence suit is prohibited.

YOUR LEGAL VOCABULARY

Match each statement with the term that it best defines. Some terms may not be used.

1. A worker's knowing assent to performing a dangerous job

2. Retraining of an injured worker

3. Laws that provide compensation for workers (or their dependents) when the workers are injured (or killed) in the course of employment

4. Federal agency that administers the Occupational Safety and Health Act

5. Persons who do not work regularly for a certain employer

6. Part of the Occupational Safety and Health Act requiring that employers provide a workplace free from hazards likely to cause serious harm or death

7. Assumption of risk, contributory negligence, and negligence of a co-worker

8. A fellow employee's conduct that is partially responsible for your injury

a. assumption of risk

b. casual workers

c. common-law defenses

d. co-worker negligence

e. general duty clause

f. Occupational Safety and Health Act (OSH Act)

g. Occupational Safety and Health Administration (OSHA)

h. vocational rehabilitation

i. workers' compensation statutes

REVIEW LEGAL CONCEPTS

9. Describe when an employee can maintain a negligence suit against an employer.

10. Describe the employer's general duty under the Occupational Safety and Health Act.

11. Invent a situation where an employer would be able to escape liability in a negligence suit by an injured employee by asserting the defense of contributory negligence.

WRITE ABOUT LEGAL CONCEPTS

12. Write a short paragraph describing the reasons why the creation of the workers' compensation system was a good compromise for employers and employees.

13. Write one paragraph describing how the employer's liability for negligence is determined. Write a second paragraph describing how an insurer's liability under a workers' compensation system is determined.

14. Write a short essay about your state's workers' compensation program. In the essay discuss the program's evolution as well as compare the level of awards the program provides for various injuries with programs of states in other parts of the country.

15. **HOT DEBATE** Write a short paragraph supporting Joaquim's ability to recover under the workers' compensation system. Write another paragraph arguing that he does not have the right to recover under the system.

MAKE ACADEMIC CONNECTIONS

16. **BUSINESS** Select a book advising small business owners about the finer points of the workers' compensation system. Compare the advice it offers with "how to" books on filing workers' compensation claims. Report to the class on the level of compromise and adversarial attitudes found in these publications.

THINK CRITICALLY ABOUT EVIDENCE

Study the situation, answer the questions, and then prepare arguments to support your answers.

17. Blake worked for West Oregon Lumber Company as a wood sorter. In violation of Oregon law, the company did not carry workers' compensation insurance. While sorting wood on a table, Blake knocked a very heavy piece off, and it fell and hit his foot. Blake sued the employer for negligence as the pieces for sorting should have been small enough to handle properly. The lumber company asserted contributory negligence as an employer's defense. Will Blake win?

18. Atlas Warehouse was equipped with an old-fashioned freight elevator that had a manually operated gate on each floor. When the elevator reached a floor, the employee had to raise the gate and then lower it after getting off. Lacey, a supervisor delivering a message to Ritter, stepped off the elevator after raising the gate. She did not lower the gate because she intended to get back on immediately. While she was talking with Ritter, the elevator was moved to another floor. After her conversation, Lacey returned to the elevator. Not noticing it had been moved, she stepped into the shaft and fell to her death. What would be the employer's liability in a negligence suit?

19. Fries, a farmer, received a notice from the manufacturer of a farm harvester that a cable on the machine was defective and likely to snap. Fries ignored the warning, and two weeks later the cable snapped and cut off one of his employee's arms. OSHA initiated proceedings to fine Fries for failure to correct the defect. Can it do so, as farming operations were exempted from OSHA regulation?

20. Randle worked at the Hide Tanning Company, which employed only two people. The company did not carry workers' compensation insurance because the state law did not apply to very small firms. A large wooden vat of acid with an open top was mounted on a wooden stand six feet off the ground. Because the stand was old and rickety, the person working near it was afraid that it would collapse and spill the acid on them. An OSHA inspector cited the company for violation

of the general duty clause. Two days after the citation, the vat broke, spilling acid on Randle. Randle sued the employer and introduced the citation as evidence of the company's negligence. The

company objected, claiming that OSHA inspections have nothing to do with suits for employer's negligence. Is the company correct?

ANALYZE REAL CASES

21. Abell and his brother had been hired as laborers to help prepare the grounds for the county fair. They were to be paid by the hour and were to furnish their own tools. No understanding was reached concerning the length of their employment, but it was understood that it would be "for one or two weeks." The work to be done consisted of "odd jobs," such as cleaning up and making minor repairs. Abell died when he was struck by a tractor while working. In light of these facts, were Abell's survivors entitled to workers' compensation benefits? (*Wood v. Abell,* 300 A.2d 665)

22. Thornton was employed as production foreman with the defendant corporation. On several occasions, Thornton had reprimanded an employee, Sozio, for failure to wear safety glasses and had reported this to the employer. On one occasion, Sozio threatened Thornton, saying, "I'll take care of your eyes later." Nine days after Sozio's employment had been terminated, Thornton saw him in a bar. At that time Sozio said, "Remember me, remember me?" and attacked Thornton, causing him to lose the sight of one eye. Thornton claims that he is entitled to workers' compensation benefits because his injuries arose out of and had their origin in his employment and because the injuries were in the course of the employment. His employer claims that the injuries did not occur on the job even though they did arise out of the employment. Sozio, no longer an employee, had deliberately inflicted the injuries. Therefore, the employer argues, Thornton is not entitled to workers' compensation benefits. Is Thornton entitled to benefits? (*Thornton v. Chamberlain Manufacturing Corporation,* 62 NJ. 235, 300 A.2d 146)

23. Bailey managed a gas station. He was required to use his station wagon to make emergency calls for the station. Tools were carried in the car, and the service station paid for the gas and oil it used. Bailey owned another car that was used as a "family car." One morning while driving to work, Bailey was struck and killed by a train. His wife filed a claim for workers' compensation benefits. The Industrial Commission denied the claim,

stating that travel to and from work is not covered by workers' compensation insurance. Was Bailey's death caused by his work? Is his widow entitled to the death benefit? (*Bailey v. Utah State Industrial Commission,* 16 P.2d 208, Utah)

24. Eckis, age 22, was a full-time employee of Sea World, an amusement park. Eckis served as secretary for Burgess, the director of animal training. Eckis, who was an excellent swimmer, had worked as a model. When Burgess asked her to ride "Shamu, the Killer Whale" in a bikini for some publicity pictures, she eagerly agreed. Burgess knew Shamu was conditioned to being ridden only by persons wearing wet suits and had attacked riders in bathing suits. Eckis was warned in general terms of the danger, and she fell off during one practice session while wearing a wet suit. When a trainer told Eckis he would not watch her ride Shamu "because it was really dangerous," Burgess reassured Eckis, and she rode Shamu three different times. Each time she wore a bikini instead of a wet suit. During the second ride, Shamu's tail was fluttering, indicating that the whale was upset. During the third ride, Eckis fell off and Shamu bit her on her legs and hips and held her in the tank until she was rescued. As an employee, Eckis qualified for modest workers' compensation payments but had no other insurance benefits. Therefore, she sued for more money in a civil action. She claimed that the employer was negligent, had defrauded her, and was liable for the acts of an animal with dangerous tendencies. The jury awarded Eckis damages of $75,000. Sea World appealed. Was workers' compensation Eckis's only remedy? (*Eckis v. Sea World Corporation,* 64 Cal. App. 3d 1)

25. Barlow's Inc. was an electrical and plumbing contractor. An OSHA inspector appeared at Barlow's place of business and asked to inspect the premises. There had been no injuries at Barlow's and the inspector did not possess a search warrant. Barlow's denied the inspector access to the business. OSHA sued to compel Barlow to admit the inspector without a warrant. Who prevails, Barlow or OSHA? (*Marshall v. Barlow's Inc.,* 436 U.S. 307)

Sports & Entertainment Law

Pro Cornerback Blocked by Workers' Comp

HENDY V. LOSSE 819 P. 2ND 1

BACKGROUND   A standout player for Long Beach State, third-round NFL draft pick, and selected to the League's All-Rookie Team for his play for the San Diego Chargers, John Hendy seemed unstoppable. Then he met the immovable object—the NFL-Players and Owners Collective Bargaining Agreement (CBA).

FACTS   While playing in an early 1986 football game, he suffered an injury to his right knee. Under the terms of the CBA, in order to continue to receive his salary and medical care at the expense of the Chargers, Hendy was required to consult the team physician, Dr. Gary Losse. The physician examined Hendy and advised him to continue playing football. Almost a year later, after yet another injury to the knee, Hendy again

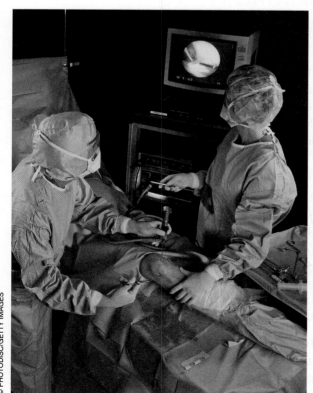

consulted Dr. Losse who again advised him to continue playing football. This resulted, according to the allegations in the complaint, in Hendy suffering "irreparable and permanent injury to his right knee." The complaint then alleges that, after finally consulting a physician who was not an employee of the Chargers, Hendy discovered that the cause of his injuries was Dr. Losse's lack of the knowledge and skill necessary to properly diagnose and treat Hendy's condition.

As a consequence Hendy filed this malpractice suit against Dr. Losse. Dr. Losse then filed a motion asking the court to recognize that, even if all Hendy's allegations were true, he could not recover from Dr. Losse in a civil action for malpractice. Instead, under California law, the motion argued that Hendy's sole and exclusive remedy for the employment-related injuries was within the workers' compensation system of the state. Hendy opposed the motion on the grounds that the injury was aggravated by the employer's "fraudulent concealment of the existence of the injury and its connection with the employment." In addition, Hendy indicated a willingness to amend his complaint to construe Dr. Losse not as an employee but as an independent contractor.

HOLDING   The California Supreme Court allowed the motion by Dr. Losse and did not grant plaintiff Hendy leave to amend his complaint to allege Dr. Losse was an independent contractor. As a consequence, the plaintiff's exclusive remedy for the injuries was through the state's workers' compensation system. He could not bring a civil suit for malpractice.

PRACTICE JUDGING

1. Why did plaintiff Hendy oppose the motion on the grounds of fraud?

2. Why did the plaintiff desire to allege the status of the team physician as being an independent contractor and not an employee of the club?

Entrepreneurs
AND THE LAW

Project 5   Agency and Employment Law

Stacy gazed out the window of her new office down onto the production floor. The volume of orders for SecureSeal tires was still growing rapidly. Although there had been a temporary dip due to the negative publicity surrounding the successful lawsuit against Teddy's Retreads, sales had rebounded to the point where the three-shift production line in Joe and Bob's old facility had been unable to meet the demand. To remedy this situation, Stacy approached the SBA and secured a loan to lease a much larger facility, buy new production machines and raw materials, and double the workforce. At the present time, two months after being brought on line, the new facility was running at 58 percent capacity. Stacy was pleased but somewhat apprehensive, as her sales projections called for an order volume that would have the plant running between 70 and 85 percent capacity. As a consequence, she was planning some changes in the marketing structure.

ADVERTISING AND SALES AGENTS   Stacy had relied solely on word of mouth to bring in new customers in the past. Her father's contacts with local over-the-road fleets and conversations among the truckers themselves had caused the past dynamic increases in sales. Now, however, she was entertaining the idea of funding an advertising campaign. To do so she had to select an ad agency and, consequently, had invited two different firms to make presentations to her next week as to the type of campaign they would recommend, its costs, and predicted results.

In addition, Stacy was getting ready to enter into marketing contracts with various potential sales agents around the country. Tire stores, truck stops, and maintenance establishments were the prime candidates as well as several independent distributors who responded to truckers' calls and drove to deliver tires on request.

EMPLOYMENT ISSUES   Due to the increase in her workforce and the accompanying scrutiny by government agencies and potential unions, Stacy had asked Brandon's firm to draft a written employment contract for managers, supervisors, and line workers. In addition,

Stacy wanted to prevent any potential form of illegal discrimination, especially that based on gender, in hiring, firing, and promotion. Therefore, she also asked Brandon's firm to review SecureSeal's hiring procedures all the way from the employment application, to the interview, to the composition of the workforce. She also asked the local office of the EEOC to speak to all employees periodically on sexual harassment and discrimination on the job. Finally, she invited an inspection by OSHA of the new production facilities and procedures to discover any health- and safety-related problems before they resulted in injuries or diseases.

ACTIVITIES

Divide into teams and perform one or more of the following activities.

Prepare Legal Documents

Draft a standard employment contract for Secure-Seal laborers, supervisors, and management. Consider the basic terms as well as potential benefit packages at each level. Draft agency contracts for the advertising campaigns as well as for the various sales agents that Stacy is intending to utilize.

Be Creative

Divide into two teams, each representing one of the two competing ad agencies. Prepare a presentation of a prospective ad campaign for Stacy. Identify the consumers you wish to target, the channels of communication you wish to use to reach them, the message you want to convey, and the means and methodology of testing the results.

Role-Play

Have representatives of the two teams make the ad agency presentation to Stacy. At the conclusion of the presentations role-play the contract negotiations with her as to the funding, timing, duration, etc., of your proposed campaign.

HOMELAND SECURITY AT SCHOOL Do you know the color codes of the Homeland Security Advisory System? The Department of Homeland Security is a federal government agency responsible for protecting the nation against terrorist attacks. Schools can use this system to prepare and respond to national threats and acts of terrorism.

DO YOUR PART

1. Obtain permission from your school administration to create and display posters that inform students about Homeland Security.

2. Make a poster of the Homeland Security Advisory System to post in the school hallway. Include the following information: Severe risk of terrorist attack (Red); High risk of terrorist attack (Orange); Elevated risk of terrorist attack (Yellow); Guarded or General risk of terrorist attack (Blue); Low risk of terrorist attack (Green).

3. Make a second poster titled "Terrorism at School: A Guide to Action." Find the information that needs to be on this poster at the National School Safety Center web site.

Human Resources Management

This event will assess interpretation of personnel policies and knowledge of human resource management.

You are the human resources director for a large hotel. You hire employees for all departments. Many individuals who apply for housekeeping positions are Mexican citizens who legally live in the United States and speak only Spanish. You do not speak Spanish. Labor unions are pressuring you not to hire the less expensive nonunion Mexican labor; however, you do not want to be guilty of discrimination. You are challenged to develop a human resources policy manual that states how employees are selected.

You also must prepare a presentation that will appease the labor union and Mexican citizens applying for positions at your hotel. Address the following issues: minimum wages, legal citizenship, and policies against discrimination.

Performance Indicators Evaluated

- Demonstrate understanding of human relations skills.
- Describe why professional development is the responsibility of the business and the employee.
- Demonstrate successful evaluation techniques.
- Discuss compensation, benefits, and incentive programs.
- Recognize how organized labor influences business.
- Demonstrate understanding of policies and procedures manuals.
- Demonstrate effective oral communication skills.
- Demonstrate understanding of policies and procedures manuals.

You have 30 minutes to prepare your event. Your presentation should not last more than seven (7) minutes and judges have three (3) minutes to ask questions.

For more detailed information about performance indicators, go to the BPA web site.

THINK CRITICALLY

1. Why is it important for a personnel director to be bilingual?

2. How is training and development affected by a staff that speaks several languages?

www.bpa.org

Mock Trial Prep

DIRECT AND CROSS EXAMINATION

WITNESSES IN MOCK TRIALS

Witnesses are integral to a successful mock trial. Witnesses present the evidence. Witnesses bring the fictitious story to life. Depending on the role being played, a witness should embody the language, demeanor, and persona of the character he or she is role playing. Appropriate emotional responses to the questions are key to the credibility and believability of a character.

In a mock trial competition each witness is provided a written affidavit, which is a statement of sworn testimony given under oath. The witness must testify to the facts as presented in the affidavit. These facts may not be altered or exaggerated. Therefore, a witness must thoroughly familiarize himself or herself with the facts as presented in the witness' affidavit. If a question is asked of a witness where the witness statement provides no factual answer to the question, the witness may answer the question based upon the character's reasonable extrapolation of the facts.

Every witness has his or her biases. Every witness has something damaging in his or her testimony.

WHAT IS DIRECT EXAMINATION?

Direct examination of a witness at trial is the questioning of a witness by the attorney for the party who called the witness to the stand. A witness on direct examination is generally a valuable witness to the party who called him or her.

On direct examination the witness should be the focal point of the examination. An attorney asks questions to allow the testimony of the witness to develop and for a story to be told. The witness should do most of the talking because it is the witness who is telling the story. The attorney will ask the questions that are necessary to guide the witness in their narrative. For instance, "What happened next?" and "Who was there, if anyone?" The attorney should be as unobtrusive as possible and allow the judge and jury to focus on the testimony of the witness.

Watch out for compound questions on direct examination. You can only ask one question of the witness at a time. Listen to your witness as the witness is answering

the question. You will need to listen carefully to the witness' answers to your questions in order to ask the appropriate follow-up questions.

After the cross examination, the attorney may redirect a witness. This is the process of asking follow-up questions about testimony presented during cross examination. An attorney should use redirect examination to rehabilitate a witness damaged or discredited in cross-examination.

PROCEDURAL MATTERS

Every courtroom is different, and every judge has different preferences involving witness examination. Some judges prefer attorneys to remain at the podium at all times. Others allow for the attorney to move about the courtroom. Attorneys should ask what the preference is of the presiding judge prior to the beginning of the mock trial.

Begin your questioning on direct examination with "Good morning/afternoon. Please state your name for the record." If you ask a question you wish to withdraw and the witness has yet to answer, simply say, "I withdraw the question" and proceed with your examination. Conclude your direct examination by stating "I have no further questions, Your Honor. Thank you."

WHAT IS CROSS EXAMINATION?

Cross examination is the interrogation of a witness called by the opposing party in a trial. Cross examination is not a questioning of the witness. Rather, it is a series of statements made by the attorney conducting the cross examination, followed by a request for the witness to either agree or disagree with the statement. For example: "You are the owner of the house, correct?" and "The window was broken, wasn't it?" These are examples of leading questions.

An attorney conducts a cross examination by the use of leading questions. A leading question is one which instructs the witness how to answer. A leading question suggests or coaxes the answer within the question itself. Other examples of a leading questions are, "You are

a police officer, correct?" or "You saw John when you
arrived, didn't you?" Leading questions should always
be used on cross examination. Conversely, on direct examination, leading questions are improper and are objectionable.

After the redirect by the witness' attorney, the cross-
examining attorney may conduct a re-cross examination. In a re-cross, the attorney can only ask follow-up
questions about testimony presented during the redirect
examination. Use the re-cross examination to help rehabilitate your witness or clarify testimony if your case is
harmed during the redirect examination.

On cross examination, an attorney should ask questions
which explore the witness' motives, memory, biases, ability to ascertain any facts, and inconsistencies in prior
testimony.

IMPEACHMENT

On cross examination, the cross-examining attorney may
impeach the witness and discredit him or her on the
witness stand. Impeachment is a cross-examination technique used to show that the witness is being untruthful
or has changed his or her testimony.

An example of how to impeach a witness:

Attorney: Witness, you testified today that the window
was in tact on the day of the robbery, correct?

Witness: Yes

Attorney: You gave a deposition in this case, correct?

Witness: Yes.

Attorney: Before you gave that deposition you were
sworn in by the court reporter to tell the
truth, weren't you?

Witness: Yes

Attorney: In your deposition, you testified that the window was broken on the day of the robbery,
isn't that true?

Witness: I don't remember.

The attorney should retrieve a copy of the witness' deposition from his or her trial notebook at this time. Show
the copy of the deposition to opposing counsel.

Attorney: Your Honor, may I approach the witness?

Judge: You may.

Attorney: Witness, I am handing you a copy of the
deposition you gave in this case. I'll ask you
to read along as I read the first full paragraph
of page 3, "I saw the window that day, the
day of the robbery. The window was broken.
It looked like someone had thrown a rock or
something at it. Most of the glass was missing." Did I read that correctly?

Witness: Yes

EXHIBITS

There may be one or more exhibits contained in the
mock trial materials. Exhibits are introduced by the
attorney though the questioning of the witness who is
familiar with the exhibit. This is an example of how you
introduce an exhibit during the trial:

Attorney: Your Honor, let the record reflect that I am
showing what has been previously stipulated
as Exhibit A to opposing counsel.

Walk over and show Exhibit A to opposing counsel.

Attorney: Your Honor, may I approach the witness?

Judge: You may.

Attorney: Witness, I'm showing you what has been
marked Exhibit A. Do you recognize this
exhibit?"

Witness: Yes.

Attorney: Please tell the Court what this Exhibit is.

Witness: It is a diagram of the house and garage. If
applicable, ask the following question:

Attorney: Is this a fair and accurate depiction of the scene?

TEAMWORK

Work in small teams. Half the teams will represent
the Defense and half will represent the Prosecution.
Develop a series of direct and cross-examination
questions to be used at trial for each of the witnesses in the case of *People of Any State vs. Robert
Craig*. The Defense team decides whether or not to
call the defendant, Robert Craig, to the stand.

Unit 6
Legal Forms of Business Organization

Chapters

26 Forms of Business Organization

27 The Law of Corporations

28 Organizational Forms for Small Business

Corporate Attorney

Business, Management & Administration

Corporate attorneys (also known as corporate lawyers) make sure a business is operating in a legal manner. A large corporation may employ them, or they may work for a law firm specializing in corporate law.

Corporate attorneys spend much of their time researching specific laws and regulations that pertain to the business of their employer (such as tax law, securities law, and licensing and zoning laws). Their work ensures that the company's business practices do not conflict with local, state, or federal laws.

Unlike some attorney jobs that involve arguing a case, corporate law is team-oriented. Everyone involved works toward an agreeable solution.

EMPLOYMENT OUTLOOK

- Employment of lawyers is expected to grow about as fast as average for all occupations through 2014.

- Demand is expected to increase in growing business sectors, such as health care.

- Demand in other areas will be limited as businesses, in an effort to reduce costs, increasingly use large accounting firms and paralegals to perform some of the same functions that lawyers do.

NEEDED SKILLS AND EDUCATION

- It usually takes seven years of full-time study after high school—four years of undergraduate study, followed by three years of law school—to become a lawyer.

- Admission to law school is competitive. Applicants must have a bachelor's degree to qualify. Some law schools have night or part-time divisions that usually require four years of study.

- There is no recommended "prelaw" major, but prospective lawyers should develop excellent communication skills and the ability to research, analyze, and think logically.

- Courses in English, business, foreign languages (especially Latin), government, philosophy, history, economics, mathematics, and computer science are useful.

How you'll spend your day

As a corporate attorney you will work in an office setting. You'll spend time at your desk, on the phone, and using the computer for research. Much of your workday will be spent meeting with heads of the corporation you represent, as well as others involved in resolving a particular issue. You also will be the corporate liaison officer with private, specialized, law firms that represent the corporation in lawsuits, before government agencies, and in other vital matters.

For example, your employer may want to purchase another company. As corporate attorney, you will help determine if the acquisition is a wise one. Is the company financially sound? Will the acquisition violate any antitrust laws? Does the company have any lawsuits pending? Can you retain the company's current employees, or will they need to be let go? Results of your research will help your employer determine if the acquisition is a good idea.

During the negotiation process you will constantly write and revise legal documents. This process can be time-consuming and will result in long work hours. Corporate attorneys often spend time traveling to the offices of other companies or to other locations of the company for whom they work. They also may spend some time in courtrooms.

What about you?

Does the job of corporate attorney interest you? Why or why not? Which aspects of the job would you most enjoy? Which aspects would you least enjoy?

© PHOTODISC/GETTY IMAGES

Chapter 26
Forms of Business Organization

26-1 Main Forms of Business Organization

26-2 Creating and Terminating Partnerships

26-3 Operating Partnerships

HOT DEBATE

One morning while shaving Bill felt a lump in his neck. The lump seemed to grow over the next few days, so Bill sought treatment in St. John's hospital emergency room. The emergency room physician, Dr. Compton, listened to Bill's worried statement. Then, after nothing more than a visual exam, the doctor told Bill not to worry and started to leave the examining room. Unsatisfied, Bill grabbed Compton's hand and placed it on the lump. The doctor shrugged his shoulders in disapproval but did order a set of x-rays to be taken. The x-ray request only covered the neck area above the lump and, as a consequence, the x-rays were read as negative. Bill was dismissed. Months passed, and the lump grew. Seeing the lump one day, a friend recommended Bill see another physician. That doctor and his partners diagnosed the lump as being a malignant growth on Bill's carotid artery and indicated he had but a few months to live.

© GETTY IMAGES/PHOTODISC

WHERE DO YOU STAND?

1. From an ethical standpoint, identify the parties and organizations that should share blame for what happened to Bill.
2. What parties should be held legally liable for what happened to Bill?

26-1 Main Forms of Business Organization

GOALS

■ State the definitions of the three basic forms of business organization

■ Contrast the attributes of the basic forms of business organization

KEY TERMS

sole proprietorship

partnership

corporation

Principal Business Forms

WHAT'S YOUR VERDICT? Shirley wants to open a sporting goods store catering solely to women. She hesitates because she thinks the expenses would be prohibitive. She lists the costs of renting or buying the required space; hiring help; buying a computer to keep records; buying a large inventory; obtaining a charter from the state; and paying for licenses, legal fees, and accounting fees.

Should these obstacles cause her to drop her plans?

There are three principal forms of business organization:

1. sole proprietorships
2. partnerships
3. corporations

Sole Proprietorships

Of the three principal forms, the simplest, most flexible, and easiest to start is the **sole proprietorship**, which is owned by one person. The owner of a sole proprietorship has relatively unlimited control over the business and keeps all the profits. However, the sole proprietor also has unlimited personal responsibility for all debts and for other liabilities that the business may incur. If the proprietor is sued for breach of contract or for a tort

the proprietor or her or his employees commit, the proprietor's own home, car, and belongings as well as all of his or her business property may be seized to pay the damages awarded by courts. Careful management, along with adequate public liability insurance, limits those risks and makes them tolerable.

Sole proprietorships are by far the most often used form of business organization. Most independent contractors listed in the business pages of telephone directories are sole proprietors. Many expand their businesses with the help of employees and agents. Corporations are fewer in number, but they have a much larger sales dollar volume and employ many more workers.

There are no significant legal requirements for organizing or conducting most sole proprietorships. When started, many sole proprietorships are conducted out of the owner's home, garage, or van. No workers need be hired to help the owner, no computer is required for the simple records, and inventory may be limited and often

Why might the owner of this new coffee shop have chosen to organize the business as a sole proprietorship?

purchased on credit. No charter is needed from the state, although a local business license and perhaps a permit to collect sales taxes for transmittal to the state may be required. Some types of businesses, such as those selling food or securities, are subject to special governmental regulations regardless of the legal form of organization.

In *What's Your Verdict?* Shirley should not necessarily drop her plans. She needs instead to investigate further. The obstacles that are causing her to hesitate can be and are routinely overcome by informed individuals. Specific information, well-qualified objective advisors, and other resources such as compilations of the experiences of other small business owners in her area of interest, can be found at small business development centers. These centers typically are state sponsored and located at institutions of higher learning throughout the country.

Partnerships

A **partnership** is an association of two or more persons to carry on, as co-owners, a business for profit. The most common type of partnership is referred to as a general partnership. Under the Uniform Partnership Act (UPA), the law that governs partnerships in most states, the general partners share all profits equally. They also equally share any losses that are suffered. The UPA also allows the partners to agree among themselves to different shares of either or both of the profits and losses. However, just as with a sole proprietor, each partner remains fully responsible for the firm's liabilities. This unlimited liability limits the popularity and utility of the general partnership form of business organization.

The positive feature of the partnership is that it combines the capital, labor, skill, and knowledge of two or more persons. Often the resulting combination serves to multiply the individual talents and productivity of the parties.

However, having a partner also greatly increases a businessperson's exposure to potential liability from that partner's actions. As a consequence, a partner needs to be carefully selected. If possible, they should be socially compatible, financially responsible, ethical and morally trustworthy, professionally competent, physically fit, and willing to work hard. As with sole proprietors, competence and integrity, coupled with adequate public liability insurance, make the risks of unlimited liability tolerable.

Corporations

A **corporation** is a legal entity that is treated as an artificial person by the law. It has an existence distinct or separate from the real persons who organize, own, and run it. Therefore, it is the corporation that makes or loses money. The corporation also may injure people and even commit crimes.

As a consequence of the corporation's being treated as an entity in its own right under the law, investors in a corporation only run the risk of losing what they have invested in it, not all their personal wealth. The corporation, but not the investors, may be hit with a large lawsuit. The corporation—not the investors—may lose money and go bankrupt as a consequence. This limit on the owners' potential risk makes the corporate form very attractive. Unlike the partnership, the corporate form also features free transferability of ownership. A corporation can have perpetual life as a result. A partnership, however, ends if a partner withdraws, dies, or goes bankrupt.

Limited liability, ease of transferring ownership interests, and perpetual life make the corporate form attractive to potential investors and professional managers alike. As a consequence,

NETBookmark

Access school.cengage.com/blaw/lawxtra and click on the link for Chapter 26. In the New York Loves Small Business home page, click on the arrow on the drop-down menu under "Starting Your Small Business." Then click on "business organization." Read the information and then answer these questions.

1. If you want to start operating a sole proprietorship in New York under a name other than your own, what document must you file with the state?
2. If you want to start operating a partnership in New York, what document must you file with the state?

school.cengage.com/blaw/lawxtra

IN THIS CASE

IN THIS CASE
Lenton and Meggin had operated a successful tow truck business for more than 30 years. Lately, however, they had been concerned that their profitable business would come to an end when they retired. As a consequence, they decided to reorganize the business as a corporation. In that form, the business could go on existing after they had left it and, with good professional management, continue providing them and their families with income.

it can acquire the financial strength and managerial expertise to attempt (and profit from) larger projects than other forms of business organization.

CHECKPOINT What are the three main forms of business organization?

A Question of ETHICS

Dennis Rice formed and owned 51 percent of the stock in Silver Veins Inc., a Delaware Corporation intended to invest in silver futures. The other 49 percent was owned by various charities and pension plans Dennis had solicited as investors. Once the investors paid in their money, Dennis hired himself as the chief executive officer. He then arranged a salary package that paid him so much each year that no funds were left to pay dividends. Consequently, the other investors received no return on their money. Is this ethical? Is this legal?

MAJOR FORMS OF BUSINESS ORGANIZATION

	Sole proprietorship	General partnership	Corporation
Requirements for organizing	None	Agreement of the parties	Obtain a charter from the state; organizational fees
Legal status	Owner is the business; not a separate entity	Not a separate entity in many states	Separate entity from owners
Liability of owners	Unlimited liability	Unlimited liability	Liability limited to amount of investment
Management	Owner makes all decisions	Partners have equal say in management unless otherwise specified in agreement	Directors (elected by shareholders) set policy and appoint officers who run the company
Dissolution	Terminates upon owner's decision or death	Terminates by agreement of partners or upon a partner's death, withdrawal, bankruptcy	Ends when charter terminated
Ease of formation	Just do it	Moderately difficult	Assistance of legal counsel required
Duration	Death or as proprietor determines	Death, bankruptcy, or withdrawal of any partner	Can be perpetual
Ability to attract professional managers	Poor	Moderate	Excellent

26-1 Assessment

Xtra!
Study Tools
school.cengage.com/blaw/lawxtra

THINK ABOUT LEGAL CONCEPTS

1. Which form of business organization does not involve unlimited personal liability for its owners? (a) sole proprietorship (b) partnership (c) corporation

2. Which form of business organization does not terminate upon the death of its owner(s)? (a) sole proprietorship (b) partnership (c) corporation

3. Which form of business is the easiest to set up? (a) sole proprietorship (b) partnership (c) corporation

4. Which form of business has the greatest potential to bring together large sums of capital? (a) sole proprietorship (b) partnership (c) corporation

5. Which form of business has the greatest potential for attracting professional managers? (a) sole proprietorship (b) partnership (c) corporation

6. Which form of business organization requires a charter from the state? (a) sole proprietorship (b) partnership (c) corporation

7. The UPA governs (a) proprietorships (b) partnerships (c) corporations

8. Which form of business organization is looked upon as being an artificial entity, separate from its owners? (a) sole proprietorship (b) partnership (c) corporation

THINK CRITICALLY ABOUT EVIDENCE

Study the situation, answer the questions, and then prepare arguments to support your answers.

9. One day Sol had an idea to make money. He took his savings and went out and bought large blocks of tickets for the main entertainment attractions in Branson, Missouri. He then called several tour directors to see if they would buy them. When they did, Sol charged them a dollar extra per ticket. He did nothing else. What form of business organization does Sol have?

10. Sol hired Nadine to deliver the tickets in his car to the theaters just as the tour buses arrived. If Nadine has an accident on such an errand, what are the potential consequences for Sol's business and his personal assets?

11. After several months of brokering tickets to tour directors, Sol thought it would be a good idea if he offered his ticket service to people on the Internet. His friend Tom was a computer programmer, and Sol made him an offer to join the business. Tom would control computer marketing of the tickets and, rather than a salary, would receive a percentage of the profits. What form of business organization exists between Sol and Tom?

12. If Nadine has another accident while delivering tickets, what might the consequences be for Sol and Tom's business and personal assets?

13. As Sol and Tom's business continued to grow, they decided to open a storefront on the main access road into Branson. Unfortunately, their business was still too new to get a loan from the bank, and their personal credit standings would not support a loan the size they needed. They did have some friends who were interested in investing in their business. However, the friends did not want to be exposed to unlimited personal liability. What type of business organization seems ideal in this situation, and why?

14. Sol and Tom decide to go forward with the new storefront and to organize as a corporation. Now another employee is delivering tickets and has an accident. What are the potential consequences for the owners' business and personal assets?

15. Sol and Tom have been running their business as a corporation for a decade. It has grown so much it is difficult to keep up with all the work. One day Sol mentions they could hire professional managers to run the business and live on the dividends from their stock ownership. Tom thought about this and said, "just because we want to hire a professional manager doesn't mean we could find one to work for us." "Actually, we're in the right business form to attract a good one," replied Sol. Is he correct?

26-2 Creating and Terminating Partnerships

GOALS

■ Describe how a partnership is formed

■ Explain how a partnership may be ended

KEY TERMS

partnership agreement

trading partnership

non-trading partnership

general partnership

general partner

silent partner

secret partner

dormant partner

nominal partner

limited partnership

limited partner

joint venture

dissolution

winding-up period

termination

partnership at will

Creation of a Partnership

WHAT'S YOUR VERDICT?
Abbie Pinegar and her sister Ashlee wanted to form a partnership to run a hot dog stand at this year's county fair. After talking about what was required, they agreed that each would pay for one half of the supplies and rental of space for the stand. They also agreed that they would alternate days spent running the booth and that the profits would be split equally. Any decisions they could not agree on would be made by their mother.

Does their partnership agreement have to be in writing?

"Strong fences good neighbors make" is the old adage. The same is certainly true about "good partners." The strong fences of a partnership are the terms and conditions that the partners agree on to guide them in managing the partnership. These terms and conditions comprise the **partnership agreement**.

Form and Content of the Partnership Agreement

Although best in an explicit written form, the partnership agreement need not be in writing unless required by the Statute of Frauds. As discussed previously, the Statute of Frauds requires a writing signed by the party being sued to make the contract enforceable if it cannot be performed within one year from the date it is made. Therefore, if two persons agree at the time they form their partnership that it is to last longer than one year, their agreement must be in writing and signed by both persons to be enforceable by both. In *What's Your Verdict?* the agreement to operate a booth in this year's fair does not have to be in writing.

Why is it a good idea to put a partnership agreement in writing?

© GETTY IMAGES/PHOTODISC

GENERAL PARTNERSHIP AGREEMENT FORMING "DOWN THE DRAIN"

Date, identity of partners, and purpose of partnership

Name, location, and records availability

Duration and termination procedure

Capitalization

Funding of reserve

Division of profits and losses, payout schedule

Account location, withdrawal procedure

Duties and limitations

Nonroutine decision-making procedure

Signatures

By agreement made this 18th day of September, 20--, we Amy Brock, Martin Espinoza, and Gerald Hunt, the undersigned, all of Castletown, Kansas, hereby join in general partnership to conduct a plumbing installation and repair business and mutually agree to the following terms:

1.   That the partnership shall be called "Down the Drain" and have its principal place of business at 166 Oak Street, Castletown, Kansas, at which address books containing the full and accurate records of partnership transactions shall be kept and be accessible to any partner at any reasonable time.

2.   That the partnership shall continue in operation for an indefinite time until terminated by 90 days' notice provided by one or more of the partners and indicating his, her, or their desire to withdraw. Upon such notice an accounting shall be conducted and a division of the partnership assets made unless a partner wishes to acquire the whole business by paying a price determined by an arbitrator whose selection shall be agreed to by all three partners. Said price shall include goodwill, and the paying of same shall entitle the payor to continue the partnership business under the same name.

3.   That each partner shall contribute to the partnership: $50,000 for initial working capital and the inventory and equipment (including trucks—which shall be marked with the partnership name, address, and logo) of their current individual plumbing businesses.

4.   That in return for the capital contribution in item 3, each partner shall receive an undivided one-third interest in the partnership and its properties.

5.   That a fund of $50,000 be set up and retained from the profits of the partnership business as a reserve fund. It being agreed that this fund shall be constituted on not less than 15 percent of the monthly profits until said amount has been accumulated.

6.   That the profits of the business shall be divided equally between the partners, that the losses shall be attributed according to subsequent agreement, and that a determination of said profits and losses shall be made and profit shares paid to each partner on a monthly basis.

7.   That the partnership account shall be kept in the First National Bank of Castletown and that all withdrawals from same shall be by check bearing the signature of at least one of the partners.

8.   That each partner shall devote his or her full efforts to the partnership business and shall not engage in another business without the other partners' permission.

9.   That no partner shall cause to issue any commercial paper or shall enter into any agreements representing the partnership outside the normal conduct of the plumbing business without notice to the remaining partners and the consent of at least one other partner and further that all managerial and personnel decisions not covered by another section of this agreement shall be made with the assent of at least two of the partners.

IN AGREEMENT HERETO, WE ARE

Amy Brock   Martin Espinoza   Gerald Hunt

Amy Brock   _Martin Espinoza_   _Gerald Hunt_

Using the Internet or library resources, determine what forms of business organization (for example, joint ventures, partnerships, or standalone entities) are available to U.S. businesses when they do business in the European Union or under NAFTA provisions in Mexico or Canada. What effects do the GATT requirements have on the choice of such business forms?

If the parties do not agree on a specific length of time for their partnership to continue, their agreement need not be in writing. This is because the partnership could be ended at any time during its first year by a partner's death, bankruptcy, or withdrawal. Regardless of the potential life of the partnership, the time, resources, and detail involved still make it highly desirable to put every partnership agreement in writing, preferably with the assistance of a lawyer. Doing so encourages thoughtful review of the many potential problems of the new business. It also helps to avoid future costly controversies by spelling out rights and duties of the partners in advance. A sample partnership agreement with terms addressing common concerns of a partnership is found on page 470.

Types of Partnerships

Partnerships may be classified according to their purpose and according to the extent of the liability of the partners.

CLASSIFICATION BY PURPOSE Classified by purpose, partnerships are either trading or non-trading. A **trading partnership** buys and sells goods and services commercially. A **non-trading partnership** provides professional and noncommercial assistance, such as legal, medical, or accounting advice.

CLASSIFICATION BY EXTENT OF LIABILITY Classified by the extent of the potential liability of the partners, partnerships are either general or limited.

GENERAL PARTNERS In a **general partnership**, all the partners exercise managerial control over the firm. Each one acting alone can bind it in contracts and perform other functions with full legal authority. As a consequence, each **general partner** has full personal liability for debts of the firm. (When the text refers simply to a "partnership," you may assume it means a general partnership. Otherwise the specific type of partnership under discussion will be identified.)

General partners may be classified as silent, secret, or dormant. A **silent partner** may be known to the public as a partner but takes no active part in management. A **secret partner** is not known to the public as a partner yet participates in management. A **dormant partner** is neither known to the public as a partner nor active in management. All such partners, when identified, can be held liable without limit for partnership debts.

Persons determined by a court to be nominal partners also may find themselves liable for the partnership debts. **Nominal partners** hold themselves out as partners, or let others do so, but are not truly partners. Parents sometimes become nominal partners to assist children who have taken over the family business. Consequently, if a partnership liability arises, they are liable as partners. A third party, acting in good faith, may rely

Assume that the man and woman on the right are celebrities and co-owners of a new restaurant with the man on the left. The public knows the couple has an ownership interest in the restaurant. However, the couple is not involved in its management. What type of partner would the couple most likely be?

© GETTY IMAGES/PHOTODISC

on the reputation of the nominal partner and therefore extend credit to the firm. If so, all partners who consented to the misrepresentation are fully liable. If all members consent, the firm is liable as well.

LIMITED PARTNERS In a **limited partnership**, at least one partner must be a general partner, with unlimited liability. However, one or more partners may be **limited partners**. A limited partner's liability for firm debts and losses is limited to the amount of capital the partner invested.

Why would it be wise for a limited partner to stay clear of any circumstance that might bring her or his status into question?

© GETTY IMAGES/PHOTODISC

The Uniform Limited Partnership Act (ULPA) governs limited partnerships and has been adopted with few amendments in almost all the states. Unlike a general partnership, a limited partnership can be created only by proper execution, recording, and publication of a certificate that identifies the partners and states basic facts about their agreement. Limited partners contribute capital and share profits and losses with general partners.

However, limited partners must not participate in the managerial control of the business. If they do so, they lose their status and become liable without limit as general partners. This rule has been relaxed and redefined of late by the Revised Uniform Limited Partnership Act (RULPA), which has been adopted by a majority of the states. Under RULPA, a limited partner does not participate in the managerial control of the business solely by doing such things as

1. being an independent contractor for, or an agent or employee of, the limited partnership
2. consulting with or advising a general partner
3. attending a meeting of the general partners
4. proposing, approving, or disapproving (by vote or otherwise) the dissolution, change in the nature of the business, admission or removal of a general or limited partner, or amendment to the partnership agreement.

Nonetheless, a limited partner is well-advised to stay clear of any circumstance that might bring her or his status into question.

Status of Minors

A minor who enters into a partnership agreement generally has special status. In most states, such a partner retains all of the rights and privileges of a minor. Thus, the minor normally can plead minority as a defense and not pay if sued by a creditor of the partnership. The minor may also withdraw and thus dissolve the partnership without being liable for breach of contract. Some states, however, do hold minors liable on contracts made as either an individual proprietor or as a partner in connection with business.

IN THIS CASE Ashlee and Abbie were so successful in running the hot dog stand at the county fair that they wanted to open a small restaurant on a main street in town specializing in hot dog "cuisine." To do so, they needed new capital. As a consequence, they invited their mother to invest in their business as a limited partner. As such she would share in the profits, yet her exposure to loss would be only for the amount of the investment she might make.

Powers of a Partnership

Under the UPA, a partnership, in some respects, is legally treated as an entity. This means that it is a distinct, real being in the eyes of the law. A partnership has the power to

1. take title to and transfer property in its own name
2. be regarded as a principal, for which each partner may act as agent, making contracts in the firm's name
3. use its own assets as security for loans and to pay its creditors before any individual partner's assets may be seized

Status of a Partnership

For most purposes, a partnership legally is treated as an aggregation or group of individual partners, with the following results.

1. Each partner must pay income taxes on her or his share of the net profits even if they are retained in the business rather than distributed. The firm pays no income tax but files an information return. This enables the Internal Revenue Service (IRS) to cross-check the accuracy of the partners' individual tax returns.
2. The firm must sue and be sued in the names of all the partners unless there is a state statute allowing such actions as an entity.
3. All debts of the firm not paid out of firm assets are chargeable to every partner. If, for example, only one partner is available in the jurisdiction to be sued for the partnership liabilities, he or she must pay the full amount and then recover on her or his own from the other partners.
4. When any partner withdraws, dies, becomes bankrupt, or otherwise leaves the partnership for any reason, the partnership is dissolved. However, prior arrangements can be made to continue the operation of the partnership business without interruption.
5. Because of the uncertain future of a partnership, it is handicapped when it comes to attracting large sums of new capital beyond the amount originally invested.

Note that a partnership is to be distinguished from a **joint venture**. A joint venture occurs when two or more persons or firms combine their resources and skills to do a specific project. Because

GLOBAL ISSUES

Joint Ventures with Firms in the CIS

Multinational corporations may form joint ventures with companies in other countries in order to do business in those countries. The Commonwealth of Independent States (CIS) was formed after the breakup of the Soviet Union. It is now comprised of 11 of the 15 former Soviet Republics. For multinational corporations, doing business there often involves forming joint ventures with companies in those countries. Because these formerly communist countries are new to capitalism, the joint ventures serve as a way to help the businesspeople there learn about doing business in a free market economy. The joint ventures also help the multinational corporation expand into new markets.

the joint venture is so similar to a general partnership (which also may be formed to do a single project), many courts, as well as the IRS, treat it as such. However, unlike the rule for general partnerships, death of a participant does not cause dissolution of the joint venture. The joint venture normally continues until the project is completed.

CHECKPOINT What is the difference between a general partner and a limited partner?

Termination of a Partnership

WHAT'S YOUR VERDICT? Chris and Chase had a successful manufacturing business in which they were equal and only partners. As they approached retirement age, Chase wanted to move the factory from Missouri to the Florida Keys. Chris, who had many investments in and around the current factory location, did not. After a year of disagreement, their relationship and then their business began to suffer losses. Finally, they brought suit over the issue.

What might a court do in this situation?

Termination of a partnership generally occurs in three distinct phases: dissolution, winding-up, and the legal termination of the partnership's existence. **Dissolution** refers to the change in the relationship of the partners due to the action of one or more of them in ceasing to be involved in operating the business. Dissolution also can occur by, operation of the law, or court decree. Dissolution is normally followed by a **winding-up period**, which concludes with the actual termination or ending of the partnership. During the winding-up period, all partnership business in process at the time of dissolution is concluded, creditors of the business are satisfied if possible, and each partner's share is accounted for and distributed. When the winding-up process is completed, **termination** of the legal existence of the partnership actually occurs.

By Action of One or More of the Partners

A partnership may be dissolved by agreement of the parties. For example, if the original agreement is for one year, the partnership concludes at the end of that year. Sometimes a firm is organized for a specific purpose, such as the development of a large tract of farmland into a subdivision for houses. Sale of the last lot and house would end the partnership. Also, the parties may unanimously agree at any time to terminate their relationship.

Withdrawal of a partner for any reason dissolves the partnership. The partnership agreement may permit such withdrawal without penalty, preferably after a reasonable advance notice. In such case, the withdrawing partner would not be liable to the remaining partner(s) for any drop in profits that might result. If the withdrawal violates their agreement, the withdrawing partner would be liable in damages for any injury resulting from the breach of the partnership contract. If the organization is a **partnership at will**, a partner normally may withdraw at any time without liability to associates. However, the withdrawing partner could be liable for resulting losses if the sudden withdrawal was unreasonable.

By Operation of Law

Death of any partner dissolves the partnership. This is a serious disadvantage of the partnership form of organization. Prudent partners simply anticipate this inevitable event and specify what action shall be taken when it happens. For example, they may agree that the surviving partner(s) will continue with the business and pay for the decedent's share over a period of years.

Bankruptcy, a kind of financial death, also automatically dissolves the partnership. This is true whether the bankruptcy is suffered by any of the partners or by the firm itself. Although rare, subsequent illegality also dissolves the partnership. For example, a professional partnership of doctors would be dissolved if any member lost the license to practice.

By Court Decree

Partners, if living, usually arrange for dissolution privately. If necessary, however, one partner may petition a court to order dissolution if another

Imagine that this woman is in the process of withdrawing from a partnership. If the business was organized as a partnership at will, what, if any, liability might she face?

partner has become insane, otherwise incapacitated, or guilty of serious misconduct affecting the business.

A court also may act if continuation is impractical or if the firm is losing money continuously and there is little or no prospect for success. This could happen when there are irreconcilable differences between the partners. For example, irreconcilable differences could be the result of stalemated decisions to add or drop a major line of merchandise or, as Chris and Chase in *What's Your Verdict?*, to move a factory to another location to reduce labor costs.

CHECKPOINT Name the three main ways a partnership may be terminated.

26-2 Assessment

school.cengage.com/blaw/lawxtra

THINK ABOUT LEGAL CONCEPTS

1. Which of the following is active in management of a partnership but unknown to the public? (a) silent partner (b) dormant partner (c) limited partner (d) none of the above

2. Which of the following is known to the public but does not participate in management? (a) silent partner (b) dormant partner (c) secret partner (d) none of the above

3. Can a partnership agreement be structured so as to continue the partnership business even if the partnership is dissolved? **Yes or No?**

4. Dissolution of a partnership is usually followed by what is referred to as a stepping-down period. **True or False?**

5. If a partner becomes insane the partnership is dissolved. **True or False?**

6. If you form a partnership to prepare income taxes for businesses over the next five years, does the agreement have to be in writing? **Yes or No?**

THINK CRITICALLY ABOUT EVIDENCE

Study the situation, answer the questions, and then prepare arguments to support your answers.

7. Tole and Hunt orally agreed to sell Christmas trees and share any profits or losses equally. What type of organization have they formed? Must they pay income taxes individually on any profits, or will the organization pay as a legal entity?

8. Peterson, Goebel, and seven other parents orally agree to fix up a park for the local children. What type of organization have they formed? Could Peterson and Goebel raise money for the group without changing to a different type of organization?

9. Brooke was 17 years old when he entered into a partnership with Beale, age 22. Their agreement to operate a dog-training school was for three years. After six months, Brooke decided to withdraw. Was he liable for breach of contract? Why or why not?

10. Sanferd and Sontag were partners in a very successful real estate development firm. After all the lots in their latest subdivision were sold, they decided to look around for another undeveloped part of town. Acting independently of one another one day, they both bought separate sections of land for the partnership to use for its next subdivision. Neither one had the other sign the contract for purchase. Is the partnership bound to buy both parcels of land? Why or why not?

11. Zeno, Smith, and Cospit were partners in Fly by Night, a small, overnight, parcel delivery service. In forming their partnership, they provided for continuation of the business if the partnership should end for any reason. Their written agreement specified that the business would continue uninterrupted, under the same name, with management and control by a new partnership composed of the surviving partners. The business is now showing a profit of more than $500,000 a year and has net assets valued at more than $5,000,000. If a partner dies, how should the deceased partner's share be valued? How will the partnership be able to pay it?

26-3 Operating Partnerships

GOALS

- List the powers of a partner
- Explain the duties and potential liabilities of a partner

KEY TERM

tenancy in partnership

A Partner's Powers

WHAT'S YOUR VERDICT? Jerico customarily bought the cleaning solvent for the Lake Country Cleaners from Solvent Solvers of Camdenton, Missouri. Unknown to Jerico, however, his two other partners in Lake Country Cleaners had voted to stop doing business with Solvent Solvers due to a dispute over a bill. Before finding out about their decision, Jerico contracted to buy five drums of solvent at $1,500 a barrel from Solvent Solvers.

Will the partnership be bound by Jerico's contract?

A partner's powers are far reaching. They are comprised of specific rights and the implied authority necessary to exercise those rights. In the absence of contrary agreement, each partner has the same rights as every other. Partners may, however, agree as to whom shall have particular rights and duties.

A Partner's Rights

The principal rights a partner has include the following:

RIGHT TO PARTICIPATE IN MANAGEMENT Every partner, as a co-owner of the business, has an equal right to participate in its management. Acting alone, a partner may buy, sell, hire, fire, and make other routine decisions in carrying on the ordinary day-to-day activities of the firm. In effect, each partner acts as an agent for the firm and for the other partners. All partners are bound by the result, unless the partner lacked the necessary authority, and the person with whom the contract was made knew this. In *What's Your Verdict?* the solvent contract resulted from a routine decision by Jerico, a partner with apparent authority. Consequently, the partnership is bound.

In addition to routine decisions, each partner has the right to do the things normally done by managers in similar firms. This includes the right to inspect the partnership books at all times, unless otherwise agreed.

When a difference of opinion arises as to ordinary matters connected with the business, a majority vote of the partners decides the issue. Unless otherwise agreed, each partner has one vote regardless of the amount of capital contributed. If there is an even number of partners and they split equally on a question, no action can be taken. A pattern of such deadlocks can eventually lead to dissolution. To forestall such an outcome,

When a difference of opinion among partners arises as to ordinary business matters, how is the issue typically resolved?

partnership agreements often provide that deadlocks over specified matters shall be settled by arbitration.

Unanimous agreement of all the partners is required to make any change in the written partnership agreement, however minor it may be. All partners also must agree to any fundamental change that affects the very nature of the business (for example, changing its principal activity or location). In addition, under the UPA, unanimous agreement is required for decisions to

- assign partnership property to creditors
- confess judgment (allow a plaintiff to obtain a judgment against the firm without a trial)
- submit a partnership claim or liability to arbitration
- do any act that would make it impossible to carry on the business

The preceding rules governing the use of managerial authority may be changed by agreement. Often, by agreement, work is divided according to talents and interests. Certain partners have exclusive control over specific activities, such as selling, purchasing, or accounting and finance. By specializing in this way, efficiency and productivity may increase.

RIGHT TO PROFITS Partners are entitled to all profits earned. In the absence of contrary

IN THIS CASE In addition to being a general partner in Spin-off, a weight loss and fitness salon, Falstaff independently made money as a dietary and exercise consultant to various Hollywood celebrities. In fact, in the most recent tax year, Falstaff made more than $200,000 in consulting fees while the partnership lost nearly $100,000. Fortunately for Falstaff, because she had provided all the start-up capital for Spin-off, the partners had agreed to assign to her all losses should they occur. As a consequence of being able to deduct the partnership's $100,000 in losses from her $200,000 income from consulting, Falstaff only showed $100,000 in taxable income on her tax return. Consequently she paid more than $35,000 less in income taxes for that year than she would have otherwise.

agreement, both profits and losses are shared equally regardless of different amounts of capital contributed or time spent. However, the partners may agree to divide the profits and/or the losses in any percentages desired. Often, profits will be shared equally, but a partner with a large amount of outside income may agree, for tax purposes, to take all the losses. Outsiders, however, are not bound by such internal agreements and may hold any or all general partners liable without limit for all partnership debts. If one partner is forced to pay an entire debt it is up to that partner to recover from the other partners their rightful share.

RIGHTS IN PARTNERSHIP PROPERTY Partnership property consists of all cash and other property originally contributed by the partners as well as all property later acquired and retained by the firm. The property is held in a special form of co-ownership called **tenancy in partnership**. In tenancy in partnership, each partner is a co-owner of all the partnership property and is not the sole owner of any specific piece. For example, if a firm of two partners owns two identical trucks, neither partner may claim exclusive ownership of either vehicle. Therefore, a partner has no salable or assignable interest in any particular item of property belonging to the partnership. However, the interest of a partner in the firm may be sold or assigned to another party. The buyer or assignee is not a partner but is entitled to that partner's share of the profits, and of the assets upon dissolution.

Each partner has an equal right to use firm property for partnership purposes. However, no partner may use firm property for personal purposes unless all other partners consent.

RIGHT TO EXTRA COMPENSATION A partner who invests more capital, brings in more business, or works longer and harder than his or her associates is not entitled to extra pay or a larger share of the profits unless all the partners so agree. Common sense and fairness often dictate that a partner who gives more should receive more, but all partners must agree to this.

A Partner's Authority

Generally, the law implies to each member the authority necessary to carry on the business.

This includes the authority to do the following:

MAKE BINDING CONTRACTS FOR THE FIRM Acting within the scope of the particular business, each partner can make binding contracts deemed by that partner to be necessary or desirable, regardless of the risk or result of the deals. Any internal agreement limiting powers of a partner is binding on the partners, but not on third parties that do not know about the limita-

Imagine that this woman is a partner and has just closed a deal with clients on behalf of the partnership. Under what circumstances would the other partners not be bound by the resulting contract?

tion. However, a partner who violates such internal agreement is liable to the other partners for any resulting loss.

No partner can bind the firm in contracts that are beyond the scope of the firm's business as publicly disclosed. Partners engaged in an aerial photography business, for example, would not be bound by a contract by one of the partners to use the plane for air ambulance service. Even if a partner has acted beyond authority in making a contract, the other partners may choose to ratify the act. If they do, the partnership is bound, as a principal would be in an ordinary agency.

RECEIVE MONEY OWED TO AND SETTLE CLAIMS AGAINST THE FIRM In the eyes of the law, all partners are assumed to have received any payments to the firm even if the partner who actually received the money disappears. Also, each partner may adjust debts of the firm by agreement with creditors. Each may compromise firm claims against debtors, settling for less than is due. However, a partner may not discharge a personal debt by agreeing to offset it against a debt owed to the partnership.

BORROW MONEY IN THE FIRM'S NAME In a trading partnership, any partner can borrow for partnership purposes. In such borrowing, the partner can execute promissory notes binding the firm

and can pledge or mortgage partnership property as security. Partners in a nontrading partnership generally do not have such power.

SELL A partner can sell in the regular course of business any of the firm's goods and give customary warranties. Acting alone, however, a partner may not sell the entire inventory in a bulk transfer because this could end the business.

BUY Any partner can buy for cash or credit any property within the scope of the business.

DRAW AND CASH CHECKS AND DRAFTS A partner can draw checks and drafts for partnership purposes and can endorse and cash checks payable to the firm.

HIRE AND FIRE EMPLOYEES AND AGENTS Each partner has the authority to hire and fire employees, agents, and independent contractors to help carry on the business.

RECEIVE NOTICE OF MATTERS AFFECTING THE PARTNERSHIP When one partner is served with a summons and complaint against the firm, all are deemed to have received the notice, even if they are not informed. Likewise, one partner's declarations and admissions in carrying on the business bind all partners even when contrary to the best interests of the firm.

A Partner's Duties and Liabilities

WHAT'S YOUR VERDICT? Finester was one of five partners in a firm of certified public accountants. Her duties included management of the office. As such, she bought all office equipment. Recently, she purchased an advanced photocopying system for $25,000, a competitive price. Several days later, she met the seller, Fisher, at a dinner party. Finester convinced Fisher to give her a 5 percent discount on the price because clients of her accounting firm might be inclined to buy similar equipment when they learned of its use from her. Finester now claims the $1,250 discount belongs to her alone because she obtained it on her own time after the original contract was signed.

Is she correct?

Inherent in the nature of a partnership are certain duties and liabilities. The duties have at their core the fiduciary concept that the interests of the partnership must be placed ahead of personal interests.

A Partner's Duties

By law or by agreement each partner has a duty to do the following.

COMPLY WITH PARTNERSHIP AGREEMENT AND DECISIONS Each partner must comply with the partnership agreement, including later provisions properly added and related decisions properly made.

USE REASONABLE CARE In performing partnership duties, partners must use reasonable care. However, they are not personally liable for the full loss caused by their own errors in judgment, mistakes, and incompetence. Any resulting financial burden rests on the firm and is shared by all

partners. This harsh reality affirms the importance of selecting competent persons as partners.

ACT WITH INTEGRITY AND GOOD FAITH A partnership is a fiduciary relationship of utmost trust and confidence. Each partner is legally bound to act with the highest integrity and good faith in dealing with the other partner(s). No partner may personally retain any profit or benefit unless the other partners are informed and consent. In *What's Your Verdict?* Finester was wrong in claiming the discount. All profits or benefits flowing from the firm's business belong to the firm, to be shared by all partners equally or as otherwise agreed.

NOT CONDUCT COMPETING BUSINESS Unless there is a contrary agreement, a partner may not do any business that competes with the partnership or prevents performance of duties for the firm. A partner may, however, attend to personal affairs for profit, as long as the firm's business is not sacrificed. A partner who withdraws from the firm may compete with it unless validly prohibited by the partnership agreement.

KEEP ACCURATE RECORDS A partner should keep accurate records of all business done for the firm and give the firm all money belonging to it. Moreover, every partner should disclose to the other partner(s) all important information that concerns the firm's business.

A Partner's Potential Liabilities

Between or among themselves, partners may make any agreements they choose regarding authority to run the business. Outsiders, however, may not be aware of such internal agreements. When this is the case, the partnership firm and all of its members are liable without limit for all obligations of the firm that arise out of contracts made by any partner within the scope of the firm's business.

The partnership and all partners are liable when any partner commits a tort (for example, negligence or fraud) while acting within the ordinary course of the business. The partner who is the wrongdoer would be obligated to indemnify the partnership for any damages it had to pay to the injured party. If the other partners had authorized or participated in the tort, all would share the blame and no indemnity would be payable.

Liability for certain crimes committed in the course of business, such as selling alcoholic beverages to minors, also is imposed on the partnership and all the partners. Generally, however, if the business of the firm does not require the criminal activity, neither the partnership nor the partners who do not authorize or take part in the crime are held criminally liable. Thus, a partner who kills a pedestrian while recklessly driving a company car on firm business will alone be criminally liable. However, the wrongdoer as well as the firm and the other partners are civilly liable for damages.

When a judgment is obtained against a partnership, and the partnership assets are exhausted, the personally owned property of the general partners, such as their houses and cars, legally may be seized and sold to pay the debt. Creditors of the respective individual partners, however, have first claim to such property. Any partner who pays an obligation of the firm with personal assets legally is entitled to recover a proportionate share from each of the other partners.

A partner cannot escape responsibility for firm debts by withdrawing from the partnership. One who withdraws remains liable for all debts incurred while a member. A new partner who joins the firm is liable for both existing and new debts of the business. However, creditors with claims that arose before the new partner joined the firm are limited, with respect to the new

partner, to action against only the new partner's share of partnership property. The new partner's personally owned property cannot be recovered against to satisfy such preexisting claims.

CHECKPOINT What are the duties of partners?

What is the limitation of a new partner's liability for creditor claims that arose before the new partner joined the firm?

THINK ABOUT LEGAL CONCEPTS

1. _?_ agreement of all the partners is required to make any change in a written partnership agreement.

2. Partnership property is held by the partners in a(n) _?_ in partnership.

3. A partner may engage in other businesses without the consent of the other partners, even if the businesses compete with the partnership. **True or False?**

4. Every general partner has an equal right to participate in management of the firm. **True or False?**

5. A partner who invests more time or money in the partnership has a right to a larger percentage of the profits. **True or False?**

6. Any general partner can buy for cash or credit any property within the scope of the partnership business. **True or False?**

7. Which of the following is not a duty of a partner? (a) comply with partnership decisions (b) not conduct competing business (c) keep accurate records (d) All of the above are duties.

THINK CRITICALLY ABOUT EVIDENCE

Study the situation, answer the questions, and then prepare arguments to support your answers.

8. Laird and Ball were partners in an indoor tennis center. Laird, a wealthy surgeon, contributed all the capital. Ball, a former tennis champion with an international reputation, contributed her name and agreed to work full time at the center. They agreed to split the profits equally. The losses, however, were all to be charged to Laird. Can the partners legally receive different proportions of the losses and the profits?

9. Adams, Starnes, and Williams were partners in a burglar and fire alarm service. Adams would mount his own camper cabin on the back of one of the company's pickup trucks every weekend and drive it into the country on overnight fishing trips. Starnes would take the company's laptop computer home every weekend to work on her

version of the "great American novel." On weekends, Williams used the company's photocopying machine to run off copies of the weekly bulletins for his church. No partner was aware of any other partner's action. Did each have a legal right to utilize the firm's equipment? Why or why not?

10. Aki, Degas, and Kline were partners in an air-conditioning business. They obtained a $275,000 contract to install units in a candy factory. Long before the job was finished, Kline accepted the final payment of $100,000 and disappeared with the money. Must Aki and Degas absorb the loss and complete the job for the $175,000 already paid to them, without being paid an additional $100,000 by the candy factory?

Chapter 26 Assessment

Xtra! Quiz Prep
school.cengage.com/blaw/lawxtra

CONCEPTS IN BRIEF

26-1 Main Forms of Business Organization

1. The owner of a sole proprietorship has relatively unlimited control over the business and keeps all the profits.

2. The sole proprietor also has unlimited personal responsibility for all debts and for other liabilities that the business may incur.

3. Unless they agree to another ratio, general partners share all profits and losses equally.

4. A corporation is treated as an artificial person by the law. As such it has an existence distinct or separate from the real persons who organize, own, and run it.

5. The major advantage of the corporate form of organization is that its owners risk losing only what they have invested in it. Due to this limited risk, corporations typically attract larger sums of capital than do other forms of business organization.

26-2 Creating and Terminating Partnerships

6. The time, resources, and detail involved make it highly desirable to put every partnership agreement in writing, preferably with the assistance of a lawyer.

7. Partnerships may be classified according to their purpose and according to the extent of the liability of the partners.

8. Under the UPA, a partnership, in some respects, is legally treated as an entity—a distinct, real being in the eyes of the law.

26-3 Operating Partnerships

9. A partner's powers are comprised of specific rights and the implied authority necessary to facilitate the exercise of those rights.

10. In the absence of contrary agreement, each partner has the same rights as every other.

YOUR LEGAL VOCABULARY

Match each statement with the term that it best defines. Some terms may not be used.

1. Simplest form of business organization

2. Association of two or more to do business as co-owners for profit

3. Partnership where all partners have full personal liability

4. Partner whose potential liability is restricted to his or her investment in the partnership

5. Partner who is publicly known but not actively managing

6. Partner who is not publicly known but is actively managing

7. Form of ownership by which partners hold partnership property

8. Conclusion of a partnership's legal existence

9. Partner who is not publicly known and not actively managing

10. Partnership that provides professional and noncommercial assistance or advice

11. The step in termination of a partnership that precedes the winding-up process

12. Artificial person created as a legal entity by the authority of federal or state law

a. corporation
b. dissolution
c. dormant partner
d. general partner
e. general partnership
f. joint venture
g. limited partner
h. limited partnership
i. nominal partner
j. non-trading partnership
k. partnership
l. partnership agreement
m. partnership at will
n. secret partner
o. silent partner
p. sole proprietorship
q. tenancy in partnership
r. termination
s. trading partnership
t. winding-up period

REVIEW LEGAL CONCEPTS

13. What are the major problems with the sole proprietorship form?

14. Why would someone want to be a limited partner?

15. If you were a professional manager looking for a lifetime or even a long-term position, under what terms would you consider a partnership or a sole proprietorship as a potential employer?

WRITE ABOUT LEGAL CONCEPTS

16. Design a form of business organization that would be especially useful to a small business owner. What would be its attributes?

17. What protection can you design into your business form in exercise 17 for small investors that have no part in the management of the business?

18. **HOT DEBATE** After experimental surgery saved his life, Bill filed suit against St. John's. He then discovered that the emergency room was not run by the hospital but by a subcontractor, Emergency

Physicians, Inc. Bill also found that at the time he was treated there, Dr. Compton was a recovering drug addict and had lost his license to practice in Texas, but he could still practice in Bill's state. The x-rays Dr. Compton had ordered only showed Bill's neck from the top of the lump up. St. John's hospital has petitioned the court to be dismissed as a defendant. It contends that only Dr. Compton and Emergency Physicians, Inc., should be held liable. Write a statement supporting St. John's position or one advocating it be held liable as well.

MAKE ACADEMIC CONNECTIONS

19. **ECONOMICS** Research and then write a one-page paper comparing the economic potential of the sole proprietorship to that of the partnership and corporation.

THINK CRITICALLY ABOUT EVIDENCE

Study the situation, answer the questions, and then prepare arguments to support your answers.

20. At the end of the school year, you hire the best students to write comprehensive study guides for the classes they have just completed. Over the summer you then compile these guides, print them out, and bind them. When school reopens in the fall, you offer your "Class Busters" for sale. The authors of the guides are paid a percentage royalty on each sale, and you pocket the profits. Which form of business organization would you choose for your enterprise?

21. Jonnas and Schmidt entered into a partnership for five years to conduct a catering business. After two years, Schmidt's husband's employer offered him a promotion and transfer to corporate headquarters 2,000 miles away. Schmidt and her husband decided he should accept the promotion and they would move. Could she sell out to Topper, a well-qualified assistant, transferring all duties and assigning all her rights, title, and interest in the firm? Could she simply assign her interest to Topper?

22. The written agreement of a professional partnership stated that, during the first year of operations, no partner could draw more than $300 earnings per week, and that no partner could take a vacation. All members would have to rely on personal savings and credit if they needed more funds. The business prospered beyond expectations. After six months, four of the five partners agreed to increase the permitted draw to $500 a week, and three of the five voted to permit up to one week of vacation without pay. Are these modifications legal and binding?

23. Stanton and Tokun agree to work together as partners for a year. Both are experienced in treating wooden shingle and shake roofs to make them fire resistant and waterproof. Stanton puts up the $20,000 capital needed for equipment and supplies. Both agree to work full time, and each draws a salary of $2,500 a month. Stanton does all of the difficult sales work, as well as helping on site. Tokun is slow

on the job and repeatedly fails to show up, falsely claiming to be sick. In fact, he goes fishing and hunting on long weekends. At the end of the year, the firm shows a net profit of $25,000 after all expenses and the return of Stanton's capital contribution. How should the net profit be divided? Why?

ANALYZE REAL CASES

24. Lewis owned a vacant building. He persuaded Dinkelspeel to open and to conduct a business called The Buffet in the property. Together, they purchased furniture, fixtures, and merchandise. They agreed that Dinkelspeel was to run the business and that profits were to be divided equally. Lewis's interest was not to be disclosed to the public, although he was to raise necessary funds and provide the building space. When the International Association of Credit Men sued both parties for goods sold to The Buffet, Lewis denied liability as a partner. Is he a partner? If so, what kind? If he is a partner, what is his liability? (*International Association of Credit Men v. Lewis,* 50 Wyo. 380, 62 P.2d 294)

25. On January 1 Vernon and Engel became partners in a food brokerage business. Later, they disagreed about the way profits were being divided and expenses were being paid. On August 1 they dissolved the partnership by mutual agreement. Vernon ran the business during the winding-up period. He claimed that Engel had violated their agreement and therefore was not entitled to his share of the profits. Vernon also argued that because he had carried on the business during the winding-up period, Engel was not entitled to any commissions collected during that time. Is Vernon right? (*Engel v. Vernon,* 215 N.W.2d 506)

26. Gast brought suit for back wages against a partnership headed by general partner Petsinger. To improve his chances of recovering a court award, Gast maintained that the limited partners in the business were really general partners and were fully liable along with Petsinger. Gast based his claim on the partnership agreement that gave the limited partners the rights and powers to receive distributions of profits and dissolution funds; prevent the transfer of assets of the firm; examine the books and records; attend meetings; hear reports of the general partner; and transfer, sell, or assign their interests to third parties. Should the limited partners in the agreement be considered general partners? (*Gast v. Petsinger,* 228 Pa. Super. 394, 323 A.2d 371)

27. Cooper and Isaacs were partners in a business that sold and distributed janitorial supplies. Their written agreement provided that the partnership "shall continue until terminated by sale of interests, mutual consent, retirement, death or incompetency of a partner." After eight years, Cooper filed an action seeking dissolution because of irreconcilable differences between the partners regarding matters of policy. He also asked for appointment of a receiver to manage the partnership property until the business was wound up. Isaacs claimed such dissolution was in violation of the partnership agreement. Was Cooper's action a wrongful dissolution? (*Cooper v. Isaacs,* 448 F.2d 1202, D.C.)

28. L.W. Clement and his brother Charles formed a partnership in the 1920s to run a plumbing business. The partnership lasted some 40 years. However Charles ultimately became suspicious of the way L.W., who had total control over the partnership finances, was handling partnership funds. He filed an equity suit maintaining that L.W. had used partnership funds to invest in personal real estate and insurance policies. The chancellor of equity heard the case and awarded Charles one-half interest in the real estate and insurance policies in question. The appellate court reversed the chancellor's decision saying that Charles had no claim as he could not trace the flow of partnership funds into L.W.'s investments. The Supreme Court of Pennsylvania then agreed to hear the case. The issue as perceived by the Pennsylvania Supreme Court was whether L.W. owed to Charles the duty of negating the inference that the source of the funds for the investment was the partnership coffers. Decide. (*Clement v. Clement,* 260 A.2d 728)

Case For Legal Thinking

LENKIN V. BECKMAN
575 A.2D 273

FACTS The law firm of Beckman and Kirstein was comprised of Robert Beckman and David Kirstein and located in Washington, D.C. Both partners were well schooled and had many years in education and government service between them, including teaching at Harvard Law, serving as counsel to the Civil Aeronautics Board, and working as a trial attorney for the Antitrust Division of the United States Department of Justice. After forming a law practice with another attorney, the resulting partnership signed a 10-year lease for office space in a Washington, D.C., building owned by Melvin Lenkin.

The lease had a clause that stated that the individual partners as well as their successors in interest in the lease could not be held personally liable under its terms. One year after entering into the lease, the third partner dissolved the partnership by withdrawing. The partnership of Beckman and Kirstein was then formed. A little more than a year after the new partnership began and nearly eight years before the lease was to expire, Lenkin received a letter from Beckman informing Lenkin that the lease was going to be terminated in a month as the partnership of Beckman and Kirstein was to be dissolved. Lenkin then filed suit against Beckman and Kirstein for the balance due on the lease.

Beckman and Kirstein immediately filed a motion to dismiss based on the prohibition in the lease against holding partners individually liable. The lower court granted the motion and also held that, as a partnership cannot be sued in the District of Columbia, Lenkin could not even get a judgment against the partnership of Beckman and Kirstein. As a consequence, Lenkin was left without a remedy. He then appealed.

REASONING The appellate court faced the following issues:
1. Should the assets be retained in the partnership of Beckman and Kirstein until the winding-up process for the partnership or did the assets become the personal property of the partners

immediately upon dissolution? 2. Should such assets be open to suit by such a creditor as Lenkin even given the prohibition in Washington, D.C., law against suing a partnership?

In resolving these issues the appellate court pointed out that the lower court's holding that the partnership property automatically becomes the personal property of the individual partners upon dissolution was incorrect. Instead, the property of the partnership became the personal property of the ex-partners only after the winding-up process was complete. Secondly, the court noted that although the partnership itself could not be sued under D.C. law, the business entity could be sued by serving both partners.

CONCLUSION Reversed and remanded to the lower court for proceedings according to the above opinion.

PRACTICE JUDGING

1. How would you rule on the first issue, and why?

2. If you rule that the property should remain in the partnership until the winding-up process is complete, how would you justify suing the partnership in conflict with D.C. law so that the assets could be properly used to satisfy partnership creditors?

Chapter 27
The Law of Corporations

27-1 **Founding a Corporation**

27-2 **Shareholders, Directors, and Officers**

27-3 **Corporate Powers and Termination**

© GETTY IMAGES/PHOTODISC

HOT DEBATE

A large American automobile manufacturer, responding to competition from small, gas efficient foreign cars, rushed a model through production to compete with them. This vehicle had a serious design defect that caused its gas tank to rupture and spray gas and fumes into the passenger compartment upon even a minor rear-end collision. As a consequence, the car would burst into flames almost instantaneously causing grievous burns and death for its occupants. When initially confronted in a civil case brought by a victim of the car's defect, the manufacturer's executives denied knowledge of any problem. This defense was quickly overcome by the testimony of a surprise witness, the manufacturer's ex-safety engineer. He stated that when he would not sign off on the car for production due to its problems, he was fired. He also presented as evidence memos of the executives' knowledge of and decision to market the car regardless of the defect. After this information became public, a Detroit prosecuting attorney brought criminal charges against the executives.

WHERE DO YOU STAND?

1. Should the corporation or its executives and shareholders or all of the above be held legally responsible in this situation? How would you punish your choice(s)?
2. Which parties are ethically responsible?

27-1 Founding a Corporation

GOALS

- Compare the advantages and disadvantages of the corporate form
- Explain the steps in corporate formation

KEY TERMS

promoters

articles of incorporation

incorporators

corporate charter

Attributes of the Corporate Form

> **WHAT'S YOUR VERDICT?**
>
> Several musicians in Branson, Missouri, formed a corporation, Chariots of Flair, and bought two motorized trolleys. The trolleys were used for tours of the country music theaters and, seasonally, for Christmas light tours. The musicians played, sang, sold CDs of their music, and acted as tour guides. They were the incorporators, officers, employees, directors, and shareholders in the corporation.
>
> *If a customer is injured during one of the tours and brings suit, who would have to pay any court judgment that results?*

The last chapter introduced the corporate form of business and a few of the reasons many businesses, large and small, utilize it. These businesses obtain the authority to exist in the corporate form by complying with the incorporation statutes of one of the 50 state governments. Congress, by special legislative acts, occasionally creates corporations (for example, the Federal Deposit Insurance Corporation, or FDIC) to serve specific national interests.

Advantages of the Corporate Form

Although corporations are far outnumbered by sole proprietorships and partnerships, corporations do most of the business in this country. This is because the corporation has advantages that are essential for large-scale enterprises. Some of these attributes are attractive to small business ventures, too. The advantages of corporations are perpetual life, limited liability, ease of transfer of ownership interests, ability to attract large sums of capital, and the ability to secure professional management.

PERPETUAL LIFE Unlike the sole proprietorship, a corporation is a legal entity separate and distinct from its owners and managers. Therefore it can continue to function after they die. Under the law, a corporation may continue indefinitely with new owners, managers, and employees.

LIMITED LIABILITY Although a corporation itself is liable without limit for its debts, creditors in the vast majority of instances cannot collect what is owed by the corporation from a corporation's shareholders. All of a corporation's assets may be seized under court order to pay delinquent claims. However, individual stockholders stand to lose only the amount they have invested in the corporation. It is this limited liability that makes the corporation an appropriate form of business organization for investors such as the musicians in *What's Your Verdict?* They are willing to assume risks entrepreneurs face. But they want a ceiling or limit on the amount they might lose if someone successfully sues and recovers a large amount of damages from the business or if the business fails and cannot pay its debts.

Under exceptional conditions, courts may hold the shareholders personally responsible for corporate

> **IN THIS CASE**
>
> Shortly after Chariots of Flair was incorporated, two of its major stockholders received lucrative long-term recording contracts. Because the two artists would have to move permanently to Nashville, Tennessee, they no longer wanted to own shares in Chariots of Flair. This was not a problem as, due to the transferability of ownership of corporate shares, they could sell their stock without causing the business to be dissolved. One of the other stockholders bought their shares to increase her ownership percentage.

debts. This practice is called "piercing the corporate veil." A court may take this extreme action, more likely with small corporations, if shareholders fail to keep corporate assets separate from their own or if they hide behind the corporate form for improper purposes, such as to avoid just debts.

TRANSFERABILITY OF OWNERSHIP INTERESTS

A major advantage of the corporate form over the partnership form is the ease of transferring ownership interests in the firm. In the vast majority of instances, individual owners can sell their interests in the corporation without requiring that the company be reformed (as a partnership would have to be), disturbing the company's operations, or getting the consent of other owners. The stock of most large corporations is traded (bought and sold) on the New York Stock Exchange or the American Stock Exchange. By contacting a stockbroker, any person financially able may buy or sell a reasonable number of shares of any listed stock within minutes when the exchanges are open.

ABILITY TO ATTRACT LARGE SUMS OF CAPITAL

Many investors feel comfortable and reasonably secure when buying stock in corporations. This is because their liability as owners of the corporation is limited to the amount they have invested. Moreover, as owners they may readily sell their individual shares, or buy more. Finally, the corporation may have perpetual life, outlasting present owners, directors, and employees, all of whom may be replaced without terminating the business. As a result of these attributes, large sums of money may be raised.

PROFESSIONAL MANAGEMENT Because they can and do raise substantial amounts of capital, efficient corporations generally have greater financial strength than do other forms of business organizations. This enables such corporations to attract superior workers and managers by offering generous salaries and fringe benefits. Moreover, because the corporation is not dissolved automatically by the death of any owner or manager, it usually provides better assurance of continued employment.

Disadvantages of the Corporate Form

There are some important disadvantages to the corporate form. One of the main disadvantages is double taxation. In essence, the federal government taxes net income of corporations when it is earned. What remains after taxes at the corporate level, if paid out as dividends, may then be taxed again as part of the income of the owners of the corporation. (Certain types of corporations can elect to be given special status under the Internal Revenue Code that allows them to avoid this double taxation. This special status will be discussed in detail in Chapter 28.) Some states also tax the corporation income and then the corporation's shareholders on the income they subsequently receive from the corporation. Note that the sole proprietorship and partnership forms are not subject to such double taxation.

In addition to the taxation disadvantage, it is costlier and more troublesome to organize a corporation than it is to organize a sole proprietorship or partnership. Further, large corporations are subject to extensive regulation of the sale of stocks and bonds to the public. Finally, juries

Economic Impact

SUCCESS OF INCORPORATION STATUTES

U.S. corporate formation laws allow limited liability protection, excellent capital formation potential, and perpetual life. These laws have paid off handsomely for the leading U.S. corporations. In the 2006 *Forbes Magazine* rankings of the top 2,000 companies worldwide according to market value, U.S. corporations occupy the top four positions and seven out of the top ten. Of the U.S. companies listed, ExxonMobil leads the way with $362.5 billion in worth followed closely by General Electric at $348.5 billion. Microsoft, Citigroup, Procter & Gamble, Pfizer, and finally Wal-Mart complete the list of U.S. enterprises.

THINK CRITICALLY

What common attributes do these U.S. corporations have? How are they dissimilar?

tend to favor individuals in legal disputes with corporations. Overall, however, the advantages of the corporation far outweigh its disadvantages, especially for big enterprises.

Types of Corporations

Corporations are classified according to their place of incorporation and purpose. If a corporation is chartered in a particular state, it is a *domestic corporation* in that state. A corporation doing business in one state but chartered in another is termed a *foreign corporation* in the state in which it is not chartered. Finally, a corporation chartered in another nation doing business in a state within the United States is an *alien corporation* in that state.

Legally when categorized in terms of purpose, a corporation is either public or private. A *public corporation* is established for a governmental purpose. Incorporated cities, state hospitals, and state universities are public corporations. A *private corporation* usually is established by individuals for business or charitable purposes. Note that sometimes a private corporation is said to be "publicly held" because its stock can be owned by the general public and typically is listed on a stock exchange. This availability for public ownership of stock differentiates such a company from a *closely held corporation* which is a private corporation that is owned by just a small number of shareholders. Generally a closely held corporation's stock is held by a family or like grouping of people.

Private corporations are further classified as profit-making, nonprofit, and public service corporations. A *profit-making corporation* is a private corporation organized to produce a financial return on the investment of its owners. Examples include banks, manufacturing and merchandising companies, and airlines.

A *nonprofit corporation* is organized for a social, charitable, or educational purpose. It may have revenues that exceed expenses, but it does not distribute to owners any earnings as profits. If a nonprofit corporation engages in business for profit, it must, like any other business, pay income taxes. Churches, colleges, fraternal societies, and charitable organizations typically are organized as nonprofit corporations.

Finally, a *public service corporation* (also called a *public utility*) generally is a private company that furnishes an essential public service. Electric, gas, and water companies are examples. However, they are regulated closely as to the quality of service they must provide, the prices they can charge, and the profit margin they may earn. Over time it has been shown that competition in providing such services needed by most persons would be wasteful of scarce resources. Therefore such public utilities usually receive monopolistic franchises and special powers of eminent domain to acquire needed real estate.

CHECKPOINT Explain the corporate advantage of limited liability.

© WOLFGANG KAEHLER/CORBIS

The Microsoft Corporation was incorporated in the state of Washington in 1975. The company's fiscal 2006 sales were $41 billion with profits of $13 billion. As of May 17, 2007, the company had 9.57 billion shares of stock outstanding. Based on this information, in terms of place of incorporation, what type of corporation is Microsoft in the state of Washington? In terms of purpose, is Microsoft a public or a private corporation? Is Microsoft a closely held corporation? Why or why not?

How Is a Corporation Formed?

WHAT'S YOUR VERDICT? The Chariots of Flair Company was incorporated in Delaware. It now wants to incorporate a subsidiary in Missouri to build and operate a country music theater.

Can Chariots of Flair be an incorporator of another corporation?

Typically, a corporation is formed as a result of the efforts of one or more persons called **promoters**. These individuals bring together interested parties and take preliminary steps to form a corporation. Note that the resulting corporation is not liable on any contract made on its behalf by the promoters. This is because they cannot bind an organization that is still to be created. Usually, though, once it comes into being the corporation adopts these preliminary contracts and is thereby bound by them. The promoters, however, also remain liable on such contracts.

To create a corporation in most states, an application for a corporate charter must be filed with a state. The application is submitted to the proper state official, usually the Secretary of State, in the state in which incorporation is sought. This application is accompanied by or consists of the articles of incorporation. The **articles of incorporation** contain the basic facts about the would-be corporation. (See the sample on page 491.)

GLOBAL ISSUES

Multinational Corporations

Corporations that have a significant investment of assets in foreign countries are called multinational corporations (MNCs). These firms operate production facilities and target markets for their products worldwide. In the late 1990s the largest 500 U.S. corporations earned more than half of their revenues from products sold outside the country. Examples of MNCs are Procter & Gamble, a consumer goods company, International Business Machines (IBM), Coca-Cola, and McDonalds.

The articles are signed and submitted by one or more persons called **incorporators**. At least one of the incorporators must have legal capacity to enter into a binding contract. Thus, the incorporators cannot all be minors. A corporation such as Chariots of Flair in *What's Your Verdict?* may, however, be an incorporator.

Articles of incorporation generally contain the following information:

1. Name of the corporation
2. Duration (definite time period or perpetual)
3. Purpose, or purposes, for which the corporation is organized, which may be broadly stated (for example, "any purposes legal for a corporation in this state")
4. Number and kinds of shares of capital stock to be authorized for issuance
5. Location of the corporation's principal office and the name of its agent to whom legal notices may be given
6. Number of directors or the names and addresses of the persons who are to serve as directors until the first annual meeting of shareholders or until their successors are elected (in some states, the incorporators serve as directors until the shareholders elect their replacements)
7. Name and address of each incorporator
8. Any other information required by law

If, after reviewing the articles of incorporation, the state approves, it will issue a certificate of incorporation, more commonly called a **corporate charter**. Once the corporation receives the corporate charter, shares of stock are sold. The shareholders (owners) then meet and elect a board of individuals to administer the corporation. This group then hires the managers who will run the company on a day-to-day basis. These managers use the capital collected in return for the sale of the shares of stock to begin doing business.

CHECKPOINT What is the difference between a promoter and an incorporator?

THE STATE OF MISSOURI
OFFICE OF THE SECRETARY OF STATE

ARTICLES OF INCORPORATION
(As required by revised statutes of Missouri, Section 351.055)

1. **THE NAME OF THE CORPORATION SHALL BE:** The Checkered Flag Company.

2. **THE ADDRESS, INCLUDING STREET AND NUMBER, IF ANY, AND ITS INITIAL REGISTERED OFFICE IN THIS STATE, AND THE NAME OF ITS INITIAL REGISTERED AGENT AT SUCH ADDRESS:** Omar Bradley Johnson, Agent, at 213 First Street North West, Miller, MO 56707.

3. **THE NUMBER, CLASS, AND RIGHT OF THE HOLDERS OF AUTHORIZED SHARES:** 100,000 common shares each with full ownership rights and voting authority.

4. **A CURRENT SHAREHOLDER'S RIGHT TO PURCHASE SHARES IN A NEW STOCK ISSUE:** Each current shareholder shall have the right to purchase a pro rata share equal to her or his ownership percentage of each subsequent issue at the public offering price of that issue.

5. **THE NAME AND PLACE OF RESIDENCE OF EACH INCORPORATOR:**
   Omar Bradley Johnson, Miller, MO 65707
   Charles Edgar Johnson, Miller, MO 65707

6. **THE NUMBER OF CORPORATE DIRECTORS AND THE NAMES AND ADDRESSES OF THOSE CHOSEN TO FILL THOSE POSITIONS UNTIL THE STOCKHOLDERS CAN ELECT THEIR REPLACEMENTS:** Three (3) directors shall constitute the initial Board of Directors of The Checkered Flag Company. They are:
   Omar Bradley Johnson, 213 First Street North West, Miller, MO 65707
   Charles Edgar Johnson, 1717 E. Delmar, Miller, MO 65707
   Jacqueline Alexis Johnson, 213 First Street North West, Miller, MO 65707

7. **THE NUMBER OF YEARS THE BUSINESS IS TO CONTINUE:** The business is to enjoy perpetual existence.

8. **THE PURPOSE(S) FOR WHICH THE BUSINESS IS FORMED:** The Checkered Flag Company is to involve itself in racing competitions with the hope of profiting thereby.

THINK ABOUT LEGAL CONCEPTS

1. Which form of business is most likely to attract large sums of capital? (a) sole proprietorship (b) partnership (c) corporation

2. Can a partnership continue on perpetually? **Yes or No?**

3. The _?_ sign the articles of incorporation.

4. Sole proprietorships and partnerships, like corporations, are subject to double taxation by the federal and some state governments. **True or False?**

5. In the event of problems, individual stockholders in a corporation generally stand to lose only what they have invested in the corporation. **True or False?**

6. A corporation that furnishes a utility, such as water, sewer, etc., is known as a public service corporation. **True or False?**

7. Which of the following is not required to be in the articles of incorporation? (a) name of the corporation (b) period of duration of the corporation (c) purpose, or purposes, for which the corporation is organized (d) all of the above are required

8. When courts take the action of holding shareholders personally responsible for the debts of the corporation, it is referred to as "piercing the corporate veil." **True or False?**

THINK CRITICALLY ABOUT EVIDENCE

Study the situation, answer the questions, and then prepare arguments to support your answers.

9. Several juniors at Metropolitan High School plan to organize a corporation named Teenage Noteworthy Talent, Inc. (TNT for short). Drawing on the talents of high school students, they hope to arrange part-time jobs and fulltime summer jobs as tutors, models, playground helpers, keyboard operators, tour guides, and clerks. What will prevent them, acting alone, from incorporating their business?

10. The Lacklands bought 5,000 out of the 100,000 outstanding shares of stock in Space Age Motion Pictures Inc., a speculative company created to imitate the fabulous success of producers of such space dramas as Star Wars. Of the other shares, 51,000 were held by officers of the company. Were the Lacklands correct when they said, "At $25 a share, we can't lose more than $125,000; one big hit and we're millionaires!"?

11. Excuses Corporation, named for the creative suggestion service it provides via an 800 number, earned more than $75,000 last year. It paid income taxes on that amount and was left with an after-tax gain of more than $50,000. $25,000 was then distributed in the form of dividends to the five shareholders. Will the shareholders have to pay taxes on the dividends?

12. Billy and Brady Anderson have just graduated from the University of Virginia with Masters in Business Administration degrees (MBAs). They are about to begin their careers as professional managers. In their final months in the MBA program they interviewed with some of the largest companies in the country. As graduation approached, they each had narrowed their choices down to two firms. Billy had job offers from a corporation and a large partnership. Brady had offers from a corporation and a sole proprietorship. The two brothers discussed the relative merits of each job offer. Billy said, "For professional managers like we will be, the form of the business does make a difference." What are the advantages and disadvantages of working for each of these business forms (sole proprietorship, partnership, corporation)?

13. Brady Anderson (see exercise 12) noted that he would like to have a share of the ownership in the business for which he would be working. It would motivate him as a manager. What he did to save or make money for the business would mean more money for him directly. Billy nodded in agreement. Which form of business organization would be the best in this regard? Why?

14. Billy noted that he wanted to put whatever organization he went to work for on the fast track for growth. Expansion into new areas with new stores and/or production facilities would be a necessity. Which form of business organization is best suited to attract the capital needed to fulfill Billy's desires for the future? Why?

27-2 Shareholders, Directors, and Officers

GOALS

- Understand the types of stock shareholders may own
- List the rights of shareholders
- Explain the roles of corporate directors and officers

KEY TERMS

shares of stock

shareholder

common stock

dividends

preferred stock

liquidation

proxy

preemptive right

directors

business judgement rule

The Role of Shareholders

WHAT'S YOUR VERDICT? Chariots of Flair's new corporation, County Flair Theater Inc., was capitalized with a $20 million dollar sale of stock to various investors. The money was used to build a theater in Branson, Missouri, and purchase equipment for the performances.

Who owns the theater and the equipment?

Typically, the promoters of a corporation sell not only the business idea but the corporate form for it. As a result of their sales efforts, they secure stock subscription agreements from the various potential investors with whom they have dealt. These subscription agreements commit the investors to providing a certain dollar amount of capitalization for the corporation. This commitment, however, is only legally binding against the prospective investors after a certain agreed-upon total of potential capitalization is reached through the accumulated stock subscriptions. Thereafter, as soon as the corporation is empowered to do so by the receipt of its charter, units of ownership called **shares of stock** will be transferred to the investors. These will be sold on a pro-rata basis to the new corporate owners in return for the payment of their monetary commitments under the stock subscription agreements. A person who owns one or more shares of stock in a corporation is termed a **shareholder** (or *stockholder*).

Stockholders today seldom recieve an actual *stock certificate*, which is physically written evidence of ownership and rights in the business. Instead the evidence of their ownership interest is merely recorded on the corporate books. Whatever form it takes, it is important to note that stock ownership does not transfer title to specific corporate property to the holder. The corporation, as a legal person, remains the owner of all corporate property. In *What's Your Verdict?* County Flair Theater Inc. owns the equipment and the theater itself.

The corporation uses the money received from the initial sale of stock to buy equipment, supplies, and inventory; to hire labor; and to pay other expenses. As goods and services are produced and sold, more income flows into the business. Often earnings are reinvested. Also more shares of stock may be sold and money may be borrowed to provide for further expansion.

What does possession of a stock certificate indicate?

© GETTY IMAGES/PHOTODISC

The Internet has had a major impact on investing in corporations. In the past, stock transactions could be made only through hiring the services of a stock broker. Now, those same transactions can be made from your home computer through an Internet brokerage. The advantages? With online trading you can make stock trades at any time of the day that a market is open. Even better, commissions on online trades are much lower. (For example, if you order 500 shares of stock at $25 per share from a full-service brokerage, the commission could be as much as $250, or 2 percent of the total. You could make the same trade online for about $30—a mere 0.24 percent.) Investors also can find a wealth of online information about corporations to help them make wise investment decisions. In addition, they can plug into sites that scroll stock market symbols with the day's current stock prices. Bottom line: if you invest in stocks, using the Internet could help your money grow faster.

THINK ABOUT IT

Use the Internet to research a local company whose stock is publicly traded. Then, do some firsthand research to verify the conclusions of your Internet research. Is the Internet information accurate? What does this suggest about the quality of investment information available on the Internet?

Types of Stock

Corporate stock comes in many varieties, each combining certain attributes to meet particular needs of the issuing corporation. The main types of stock include par and no-par stock, common stock, and preferred stock.

PAR AND NO-PAR STOCK Stock may have a *par value*, which is the face value printed on the certificate. If it does not have a par value, it is *no-par stock* and is originally sold at a price set by the board of directors of the corporation. When either par or no-par stock changes hands in later transfers, the price may be higher or lower. This market price is determined by many factors, including past and anticipated future profits.

COMMON STOCK Corporations may have one or more kinds of stock, each with its own rights and powers. **Common stock** is the basic type, with the right to vote in corporate elections. Shareholders of common stock typically have one vote per share owned. In addition, common shareholders may receive dividends. **Dividends** are distributions of some or all of the profits earned by the corporation in a particular time period. If the corporation does not earn a profit, typically it will not pay a dividend to its common shareholders.

PREFERRED STOCK To attract additional funds from investors who want greater assurance of payment of dividends, some corporations also issue **preferred stock**. Owners of preferred stock usually do not have the right to vote in corporate elections, but they legally are entitled to a stated dividend, if a dividend is paid before the common shareholders get one. For example, the preferred shareholder may be entitled to receive $2 per share each year before any distribution of dividends is made to the common shareholders. If profits are high, the common shareholders may get a bigger dividend than the preferred shareholders. Preferred shareholders also generally have a priority right to be repaid the face value of their stock from funds obtained in a corporate liquidation. **Liquidation** occurs when all of the business assets are sold, all debts are paid, and the corporate existence is ended.

NETBookmark

Access school.cengage.com/blaw/lawxtra and click on the link for Chapter 27. According to the web site, what issues should you consider when deciding on an online brokerage?

school.cengage.com/blaw/lawxtra

Preferred stock may be *cumulative*. With cumulative preferred stock, if the promised dividend is not paid in a given year, it remains due and payable in the future. Each year the unpaid dividends cumulate (add up) and must be paid in full before the common shareholders receive any dividends.

In some cases, the preferred stock also can be *participating*. For example, under a typical participating preferred plan, if dividends are distributed in a particular year, the participating preferred stock's shareholder receives the promised preferred dividend. Then once the common shareholder has received an amount per share equal to that received by the preferred shareholder, any remaining profit to be distributed that year is divided between the preferred and common shareholders on a pro rata basis.

Shareholder Rights

Ownership of stock in a company does not give shareholders the right to possess any corporate property or to participate directly in management. It does, however, confer on shareholders the following important rights.

RIGHT TO A STOCK CERTIFICATE If a corporation issues stock certificates, a shareholder has the right to receive a certificate as evidence of ownership of shares in the corporation. Today, however, with the blessing of the Security Exchange Commission (the government agency controlling stock offerings and trading), most major companies have done away with physical stock certificates. In fact, they have become collector's items in many cases. Instead the amount of shares owned by each investor is kept electronically. As a consequence, trading of these shares is done quickly and accurately without shuffling massive amounts of paper. In addition, the electronic system was proven extremely durable during the aftermath of 9/11 when a great deal of the financial district of NYC was destroyed. Because of backup data stored elsewhere, the ownership of the vast majority of shares was easy to reestablish.

RIGHT TO TRANSFER SHARES A shareholder generally has the right to sell or to give away any shares owned. This right sometimes is restricted in closely held corporations, where the owners may want to limit ownership to employees or to members of a given family. Accordingly, the corporation's articles of incorporation may provide that an owner who wants to sell shares must first offer them to the corporation or to the other stockholders.

RIGHT TO ATTEND SHAREHOLDER MEETINGS AND TO VOTE A shareholder may attend shareholder meetings and vote shares owned in any class of stock that has the right to vote. Regular meetings usually are held annually at the place and time designated in the corporation's articles or bylaws. Notice of the regular meetings usually is not required. Reasonable notice is required for special meetings.

In a corporate election, a shareholder usually is entitled to the number of votes that equals the number of shares of voting stock held. Having a *minority position* means owning less than 50 percent of the voting shares. To safeguard the interests of such shareholders, many states require the use of *cumulative voting* in the election of directors. Under this plan, each shareholder has the right to cast as many votes as the number of shares of stock held, multiplied by the number of directors to be elected. The shareholder may cast all available votes for one candidate or distribute them among two or more candidates with the top vote getters being elected.

A shareholder who does not wish to attend meetings and to vote in person ordinarily has the right to vote by **proxy** (see the illustration at the top of page 496). Most of the millions of people who individually own comparatively few shares of stock in various corporations cast their votes in this manner. The management, or anyone seeking control of the corporation, mails the necessary proxy forms to all shareholders and solicits their votes. The shareholders may then sign and return the forms. Shareholders who are satisfied with the corporation's performance typically give their proxies to incumbent directors, giving them authority to cast the votes. Federal law requires that the proxy form give the shareholder an opportunity to specify by ballot approval or rejection of particular proposals.

IN THIS CASE Berlin owned 301 of the 1,000 shares issued by County Flair Theater Inc. She wanted to be certain to elect at least one of her people as a director of the corporation out of the three to be elected by cumulative voting. To be certain of doing so, she would only have to concentrate her 903 votes on one candidate (301 shares × 3 positions). Therefore, no matter how the remaining 2,097 votes (699 × 3 positions) were voted, she would be sure one of her candidates would be in the top three vote getters and thereby be elected.

RIGHT TO INCREASE CAPITAL STOCK Shareholders alone have the right to increase the capital stock (total shares of stock) of the corporation. This usually is done by majority vote, on the recommendation of the board of directors. In some corporations, when the capital stock is increased, each shareholder may have a right to purchase additional shares to maintain the percentage of interest in the corporation owned before the increase. This is called the **preemptive right**.

RIGHT TO SHARE THE PROFITS Each share-holder is entitled to a proportionate share of the profits that are distributed on the class of stock owned. These dividends usually are paid in money, but they may be paid in shares of stock. Occasionally products of the corporation are distributed as dividends. Even when profits are earned, the board of directors may decide to retain them in the business for future needs of the firm. In effect, the stockholders are thus forced to make an additional investment in the business. Ideally, this additional capitalization should cause the price of stock to go up, and the stockholders can sell out if they so choose. Under unusual circumstances, courts will intervene to compel distribution of dividends at the request of shareholders who claim that there is an unreasonably large surplus of retained and unused or underutilized earnings.

RIGHT TO SHARE IN A DISTRIBUTION OF THE CAPITAL If a corporation is dissolved, its creditors have first claim upon the assets of the business. After their claims have been satisfied, any remaining assets or proceeds from the sale of assets are distributed to the shareholders. A preferred stockholder generally has priority over a common stockholder in such a distribution up to the amount of a preferred share's purchase price.

RIGHT TO INSPECT CORPORATE BOOKS OF ACCOUNT A shareholder has the right to inspect and to make appropriate records of the accounting books of the corporation. However, this inspection right may be denied if it is not carried out at a reasonable time and place, in good faith, and with proper motive. This restriction is understandable in light of the many thousands of shareholders in large corporations. Without restrictions, competitors could buy shares simply to gain an unfair advantage by inspection of company books.

CHECKPOINT Name the most significant powers of a common shareholder.

The Roles of Directors and Officers

WHAT'S YOUR VERDICT? Berlin was in Las Vegas when she heard a great new act, Vermillyon or "V" as he was called. V did country rap which Berlin believed to be the coming thing. As a consequence, Berlin, a major shareholder in County Flair Theater Inc., signed V to a year-long contract at the County Flair Theater.

Did Berlin's action legally bind the Theater?

As noted earlier, a corporation is a legal person in the eyes of the law. However, it must act through human agents elected by the shareholders, appointed by the directors, or hired by the officers. No shareholder, even one that owns most or all the stock, can act for the corporation or bind it by contract merely because of such ownership. In *What's Your Verdict?* Berlin had no authority to represent the corporation and therefore the Theater is not bound. The officers (appointed by directors) and their agents are the only parties that can bind the theater to contracts.

Directors

Although shareholders have the power to vote on major corporate issues such as changing the corporate articles or merging with another company, they do not directly control the running of the corporation. This is done through the directors whom the shareholders elect.

DIRECTORS AS FIDUCIARIES **Directors** are responsible for providing general guidance for the corporation. They are fiduciaries and as such are duty-bound to act in good faith, with due care, and in the best interests of the corporation. Directors oversee the corporation and formulate general policies. They must not act fraudulently or illegally. Most states apply the standard of the Model Business Corporation Act. This requires that directors act in a manner they "reasonably believe to be in the best interests of the corporation, and with such care as an ordinary prudent person in a like position would use under similar circumstances." Failure to do so can make a director liable to the shareholders.

REQUIREMENTS FOR DIRECTORS The number of directors varies among corporations. Most states allow the shareholders to determine the number. Some states require at least three. Other states require only one director, who also can be the sole officer and sole shareholder. This gives the corporation the attributes of a sole proprietorship while

retaining the advantage of limited liability for its owner.

Statutes sometimes require that directors be shareholders. A few states require that directors be adults. Some states require that the president of the company serve as a director. In many corporations all the directors are officers. This is called an *inside board* and is not considered ideal because the directors naturally tend to approve their conduct as officers. Better results sometimes are obtained from an *outside board,* which has no officers in its membership and which presumably scrutinizes corporate performance more objectively and critically. Probably the best form is a *mixed board,* with some officers to provide information and detailed understanding and some outsiders "to ask the embarrassing questions."

DUTIES OF DIRECTORS The directors are the top officials of the corporation. They set major goals, determine basic policies, and establish the rules for the internal governance of the corporation. They appoint, determine the duties, and set the salaries of the top officers of the company: typically the president, vice president, secretary, and treasurer. Acting together, the directors have the power to make contracts for the corporation, but they delegate the day-to-day duties of running the business to the officers they have selected.

The directors are expected to exercise their own best judgment in appointing the officers and in overseeing their work. The directors alone may declare dividends and authorize major policy decisions. Therefore they may not have others

Why do you think a mixed board of directors, consisting of both corporate officers (insiders) and outsiders, might provide the most effective guidance for a corporation?

serve as substitutes at board meetings to deliberate and vote for them.

Officers

Directors generally employ managing officers and delegate to them necessary authority to conduct the firm's day-to-day business. Corporate managing officers commonly include a president, a vice president, a secretary, and a treasurer. However, the duties of two or more of these positions may be combined. Other positions may be created as required. Many states and the Model Business Corporation Act permit one person to hold two or more offices, except that the president may not also serve as secretary. This helps to prevent falsification of records.

The board of directors usually appoints officers, although in some corporations they are elected by the shareholders. Generally there are no restrictions on the selection of officers. Thus, they do not necessarily have to be shareholders or directors, have certain qualifications, or be a certain age.

Because the officers of a corporation are its agents, they are fiduciaries governed by applicable principles of agency law. The articles of incorporation, the governing rules of the corporation, and the board of directors may impose limitations.

Officers are legally accountable to the corporation for willful or negligent acts that cause loss to it. However, neither shareholders, directors, officers, nor other corporate employees can be held personally to be criminally or civilly liable to parties outside the corporation for honest errors of judgment made in the course of business. This is referred to as the **business judgment rule**.

CHECKPOINT What is the importance of the business judgment rule?

LAW BRIEF

Two and one half years after the Enron scandal broke and the energy giant collapsed, the ex-CEO, Kenneth Lay, was finally indicted. Lay surrendered at the FBI office in Houston early one morning and was led away to the federal courthouse with his hands cuffed behind his back. There he pleaded not guilty to each of the 11 charges and was released on $500,000 bond. Lay later said that he took responsibility for Enron's collapse but denied that he did anything wrong. "I continue to grieve, as does my family, over the loss of the company and my failure to be able to save it," said Lay, speaking forcefully. "But failure does not equate to a crime." Enron's bankruptcy holds the record as the largest collapse in corporate history.

A Question of ETHICS

Mammoth Corporation had been one of the success stories of the 1960s. Mammoth was a conglomerate consisting of many unrelated companies in fields from high-tech agriculture to manufacturing children's clothing. Now its stock was at an all-time low. Bill Predator, president of Shark Inc., did some simple math. He figured that if he bought all the shares of Mammoth at their present market value, he would spend about $5 billion. Then he could break the company up and sell it in pieces to waiting buyers. The pieces would sell for more than $10 billion. However, this would leave the majority of Mammoth's 30,000 employees without jobs. Are Predator's plans legal? Are they ethical? Should the government allow him to go through with the plans?

27-2 Assessment

Xtra!
Study Tools
school.cengage.com/blaw/lawxtra

THINK ABOUT LEGAL CONCEPTS

1. Shareholders will always be paid dividends as long as the corporation makes a profit. **True or False?**

2. Unlike officers, directors do not have a fiduciary duty to the corporation. **True or False?**

3. If a cumulative preferred stock dividend is not paid in a particular period, it remains due and payable in full before the common shareholders receive any additional dividends. **True or False?**

4. No-par stock is sold originally at a price set by the market. **True or False?**

5. Directors have the ultimate control of corporate affairs. **True or False?**

6. A legal device that allows the current stockholders of a corporation to maintain their percentage of ownership even when new stock offerings occur is called (a) a permanent right (b) a percentage right (c) a preemptive right (d) none of the above

THINK CRITICALLY ABOUT EVIDENCE

Study the situation, answer the questions, and then prepare arguments to support your answers.

7. Ben invested $1 million in a company making computerized maps. The company was owned by its CEO who had a majority—more than 50 percent—of the stock. Each year Ben waited for dividends to be paid on the shares he owned. However, the CEO increased her pay each year to levels that cancelled out any possible earnings and, therefore, payment of dividends. Are the CEO's actions legal? Why or why not?

8. All directors of the ABC Avionics Corporation also were officers of the corporation. As directors, all were involved in the unanimous decision to follow the advice of De Moreal, the dynamic president. He had presented engineering and marketing studies in support of a proposal to build a small helicopter that also could be used as an automobile on public highways. After further study, the directors, as officers, proceeded with the plan to design, produce, and market the vehicle. Many problems caused abandonment of the project after the corporation had spent more than $25 million on it. Several stockholders sued the directors/officers for the full amount. Are they liable?

9. Fleener was employed as a director and vice president of Mt. Everest Productions, a manufacturer of outdoor sports equipment. Without informing the other directors of the corporation, she bought control of a small company that manufactured specialty nylon and composite fabrics. It sold large quantities of its products to Mt. Everest Productions at a profit. Its prices were fair and competitive, and the quality superior. Was Fleener's conduct legal? Was it ethical?

10. The CEO of the Consolidated Hands of Help, a nonprofit New York Corporation, was shown to be using corporate funds to maintain several limos and various houses for himself around the country. He responded that he needed these to enable him to better recruit donors. The board of directors agreed with his position. A shareholder brought suit claiming that more than 12,000 homeless people could be helped for what was being paid for the luxury items. The suit sought to recover the expenditures from the CEO and the board members. Will it be successful? Why or why not?

11. Bridges Inc., a large construction company dealing in federal highway construction contracts, showed earnings of $2 million for its latest fiscal year. The Board of Directors voted to pay out the $2 million in dividends. There are 2,000,000 preferred shares outstanding. Each preferred share has a stated dividend of $.50. There are 2,000,000 common shares outstanding. How much will each common shareholder receive per share?

27-3 Corporate Powers and Termination

GOALS
- Explain the powers of a corporation
- Relate the various ways that the dissolution of a corporation might be brought about

KEY TERMS
bonds

debentures

bylaws

consolidation

merger

The Powers of a Corporation

In general, a corporation can be formed to accomplish any lawful endeavor. The corporation then is allowed to exercise all powers that are necessary, convenient, and lawful in so doing. As a result powers vary among corporations, but some are inherent in almost every corporation. These powers are describe in the following section.

Power to Conduct Business

First and foremost, in order to achieve its basic purpose, a corporation may use any legal means to conduct its authorized business. Thus, the corporation has the power, in its own name, to

a. Make contracts.

b. Borrow money and incur other liabilities.

c. Lend money and acquire assets, including all forms of real and personal property.

d. Make, endorse, and accept commercial paper (orders or promises to pay money).

e. Issue various types of stock and bonds. **Bonds** are written promises to pay back money borrowed by the corporation. Bonds usually are secured by a mortgage or deposit of collateral. Unsecured bonds are **debentures**.

f. Mortgage, pledge, lease, sell, or assign property.

g. Buy back from its stockholders its own stock, unless this would make it impossible for the corporation to pay its debts or to pay off any superior class of stock. Such purchases are sometimes made to boost the market price of the stock, to eliminate protesting shareholders, to acquire shares for employee purchase and bonus plans, or to reduce the size of the corporation.

h. Acquire and hold stock in other corporations provided this does not violate antitrust laws.

i. Make reasonable donations or gifts for civic or charitable purposes to promote goodwill in accord with corporate social responsibility. In *What's Your Verdict?* the actions and expenditures for aid of the victims of the tornado were not only legal but commendable.

j. Hire and fire agents, independent contractors, and ordinary employees.

In your opinion, how seriously should a company take its corporate social responsibility?

© GETTY IMAGES/PHOTODISC

k. Establish pension, profit sharing, and other incentive plans for employees.

l. Sue and be sued.

Power to Continue Indefinitely

In most jurisdictions, the corporation is the only form of business organization that may be granted the power of perpetual succession. This means that regardless of changes in the identities of the shareholders (owners), directors, or officers, the corporation may continue indefinitely or for the period originally requested by the incorporators.

Power to Operate Under a Name of Its Own Choosing

A corporation can select any name to identify itself unless that name is identical or deceptively similar to the name of another business already operating in that geographical area. Most states require that the name selected indicate that the business is a corporation to alert the public of the owners' limited liability. Corporations do this by including a descriptive word in the name, such as Company, Corporation, or Incorporated (or Co., Corp., or Inc.).

Any business organization has the legal power to use a fictitious name. However, most states require that fictitious names be registered in a designated government office, along with information about the owners of the corporation.

Power to Make Rules to Govern Its Operation

A corporation can make its own reasonable rules and regulations for the internal management of its affairs. Called **bylaws**, these rules, for example, specify times for meetings of shareholders and directors, and define duties of officers.

Implied Powers

A corporation may do any legal act that is necessary or convenient for the execution of its express powers. This would extend to such matters as doing pure and applied research and development (R & D) work, leasing space and equipment, advertising, and buying life and health and liability insurance for officers and other employees.

CHECKPOINT What are bylaws?

Causes of Corporate Dissolution

WHAT'S YOUR VERDICT? A decade after its founding and against the objection of many performers who would be put out of work, a two-thirds majority of the stock of County Flair Theater Inc. was voted to terminate its existence. This contradicted the articles of incorporation which claimed a perpetual existence for the corporation.

Is the termination legal?

A variety of causes may bring about the dissolution or termination of a corporation. These include the following:

At a Time Specified in the Articles of Incorporation

The lifetime of the corporation can be set by the incorporators in the articles of incorporation for a certain number of years or the occurrence of a particular event.

By Agreement of the Shareholders

A corporation can be terminated by a set majority vote of its stockholders even before the time set in the articles of incorporation. In *What's Your Verdict?* the termination vote would legally bring County Flair Theater Inc. to an end.

By Forfeiture of the Charter

The state may bring judicial proceedings for the forfeiture of the charter of a corporation that has been guilty of certain acts. Examples of such acts are

1. fraudulent submission of articles of incorporation
2. obvious misuse of corporate powers
3. repeated violation of the law

Forfeiture is rare because the state does not monitor corporate affairs, and aggrieved persons can seek private relief in court.

IN THIS CASE When she turned 50, Berlin, who over the years had acquired over 70 percent of the stock in County Flair Theater Inc. decided to retire. She tried to sell her stock, but it would only bring approximately 40 percent of her share of the asset value in the corporation. She, therefore, decided to dissolve the corporation, liquidate the assets, and retire on the payout.

By Consolidation or Merger

A **consolidation** of corporations can occur with the approval of both boards of directors and a majority of the shareholders in each of the corporations involved. The two corporations cease to exist and a new corporation is formed.

In a **merger** one corporation absorbs the other. The surviving corporation retains its charter and identity; the other disappears. Again, approval must be given by the directors and by the shareholders of the merging corporations.

The combination brought about through either consolidation or merger of companies must not violate antitrust laws by interfering unreasonably with free competition. An illegal monopoly occurs when one company controls the supply of goods, excludes competitors, and sets prices. It also is illegal for two or more companies to conspire to set prices or to allocate marketing areas, as this reduces free competition.

U.S. antitrust laws have been amended to permit competing companies to form partnerships for joint research in order to meet global competition. Thus, for example, it is legal for General Motors, Ford, and Chrysler to do joint research on materials, oil and reformulated fuel, batteries, and electronic systems for control of vehicles.

As a Result of Bankruptcy

Bankruptcy of a corporation does not in itself cause dissolution. However, some bankruptcy proceedings leave the corporation without assets with which to do business. In addition, some state statutes provide that when a corporation is insolvent, its creditors may force dissolution.

By Court Order

Occasionally a corporation's assets are seriously threatened with irreparable harm because the board of directors or the shareholders cannot resolve an internal dispute. In some states a court can order dissolution if interested parties petition for it.

CHECKPOINT What is the difference between a consolidation and a merger?

27-3 Assessment

school.cengage.com/blaw/lawxtra

THINK ABOUT LEGAL CONCEPTS

1. A rule adopted by a corporation's board of directors that calls for a stockholder meeting every six months properly would be termed a corporate bylaw. **True or False?**

2. Corporate debentures are (a) secured (b) unsecured (c) government guaranteed

3. When two corporations merge, they both disappear and a new corporation is formed. **True or False?**

4. A corporation with perpetual life according to its articles of incorporation could still be dissolved by a vote of an appropriate majority of its shareholders. **True or False?**

5. Which of the following may result in a corporate dissolution? (a) corporate bankruptcy (b) irresolvable internal corporate dispute (c) state-ordered forfeiture of the corporate charter (d) all of the above

THINK CRITICALLY ABOUT EVIDENCE

Study the situation, answer the questions, and then prepare arguments to support your answers.

6. In order to attract a top manager away from another company, Scavengerr Corporation offered her a salary, profit sharing, and pension package that would cut deeply into prospective dividends to most shareholders for at least two years. Is this legitimately within the corporate powers?

7. KashKow Inc. is a very old, very profitable corporation with little debt. Recently its management has become aware of the possibility of a hostile takeover by an outside party. This outside investor, after buying a majority of KashKow's stock on the open market, would elect her own directors, fire all the corporate officers, and break up the company into salable pieces. Is such an action legal?

 Online Research> **Steve's Nonprofit**

Steve Boose, recently retired from his job and resettled in the town of his youth, spotted a run-down building that once had been the local playhouse. Steve knew there was no longer a playhouse in his community, and he had lots of extra time on his hands. He called the realtor listed on the for-sale sign and discovered that the building was priced at a mere $15,000.00. He made an on-the-spot decision to restore the old playhouse to its former glory. He stopped by the small local newspaper where he placed an advertisement announcing the first meeting of the Play House Preservation Society.

The meeting was well attended by enthusiastic locals, including young people hoping to hone their theater skills, and many retirees like Steve. The group discussed the many obstacles confronting them including how to raise the money to purchase and restore the building and how to pay the yearly property taxes that would increase once the building was restored. They also considered acquiring insurance to settle potential lawsuits if someone would be injured on the premises. The group discussed many options, but without any quick answers they elected Steve their leader and placed their trust in him hoping he would find solutions. The next morning, as Steve sat drinking his coffee, he wondered if there was a legal form the group could assume that would enhance their chances for success.

THINK CRITICALLY

Evaluate the advantages and the disadvantages of a non-profit corporation in this situation.

GO TO FINDLAW.COM TO FIND THE ANSWERS

Go to Findlaw.com and click on Small Business, Incorporation, Non-Profit Organizations, then Five Reasons to Incorporate Your Non-profit Association.

Chapter 27 Assessment

CONCEPTS IN BRIEF

27-1 Founding a Corporation

1. A corporation can be created only by government charter available by compliance with incorporation statutes in all states or through special legislative acts of the U.S. Congress.

2. In some states, corporate existence begins when properly prepared articles of incorporation are filed with the office of the Secretary of State. In some states, charters or certificates of incorporation are issued.

3. Corporations are a favored form of business organization because of advantages such as potential perpetual life, limited liability of shareholders, easy transferability of shares, better access to capital, and professional management. A major disadvantage is double taxation.

27-2 Shareholders, Directors, and Officers

4. Although status as a shareholder does not give one the right to possess any corporate property or to participate directly in management, it does convey many other rights.

5. Shareholder rights include the right to see the corporate books, the right to vote in corporate elections, and the right to share in whatever profits the corporation might produce.

6. The shareholders elect the directors who then select the officers of the corporation. The directors also create the bylaws of the corporation and monitor the day-to-day running of the business by the officers.

27-3 Corporate Powers and Termination

7. Corporate powers are many as a corporation is treated as an artificial person in our society. These powers include the abilities to buy and sell, sue and be sued, mortgage, and donate; all basically allow the corporation to carry out its mission to make a profit.

8. Corporate existence can be terminated in a number of ways. These include the expiration of time as specified in the articles of incorporation or when a majority of the stockholders vote to dissolve it.

YOUR LEGAL VOCABULARY

Match each statement with the term that it best defines. Some terms may not be used.

1. Signers of the articles of incorporation
2. Non-voting stock conveying the right to receive a stipulated dividend before any common shareholders receive their dividends
3. Application to a state for a corporate charter
4. Units of ownership in a corporation
5. Power to vote shares for shareholders
6. Distributions of corporate earnings
7. Rules for the internal organization and management of a corporation
8. Combination of two companies into one new one
9. Basic stock in a corporation conveying to the stockholder the right to vote and to receive dividends
10. Rule that protects management from being personally held criminally or civilly liable for a business decision made within the scope of power and authority granted by the corporate charter and applicable laws
11. Individuals elected by the shareholders to be responsible for the general guidance of the corporation

a. articles of incorporation
b. bond
c. business judgment rule
d. bylaws
e. common stock
f. consolidation
g. corporate charter
h. debentures
i. directors
j. dividends
k. incorporators
l. liquidation
m. merger
n. preemptive right
o. preferred stock
p. promoters
q. proxy
r. shareholder
s. shares of stock

REVIEW LEGAL CONCEPTS

12. To what other uses can profits be put instead of paying dividends?

13. Why is it important to pay dividends in the first place?

14. Are preemptive rights more important in a small corporation or a large publicly held corporation? Why?

15. Must dividends be paid to preferred shareholders regardless of whether or not the corporation has made a profit? Why or why not?

16. Why should preferred shareholders have priority over common shareholders in a corporate liquidation?

WRITE ABOUT LEGAL CONCEPTS

17. Devise a better way than cumulative voting of ensuring minority opinions are represented on a corporate board. Write an outline that sums up your plan.

18. Write an essay stating your opinion about whether it is ever appropriate for the courts to violate the business judgment rule and punish individual officers for their criminal actions on behalf of the corporation.

19. **HOT DEBATE** Write a letter to the editor of one of the Detroit papers discussing the business judgment rule and either supporting the prosecuting attorney's filing of charges or arguing against the action. Read the letter to the class. The letter should give the justification for the business judgment rule regardless of the side taken.

MAKE ACADEMIC CONNECTIONS

20. **HISTORY** Read a book on the development of the corporation, for example, Bruce Brown's *The History of the Corporation,* in which he cites the Benedictine Order of the Catholic Church, founded circa 529 A.D., as being the oldest surviving corporation. Draw conclusions and give a report to the class on your findings.

THINK CRITICALLY ABOUT EVIDENCE

Study the situation, answer the questions, and then prepare arguments to support your answers.

21. Hull organized a corporation to manufacture antibiotics for cattle. She owned most of the capital stock. All went well until a faulty batch of the drugs caused the serious illness or death of more than 3,000 cows. After a series of lawsuits, the corporation was forced into bankruptcy with some $200,000 in debts unpaid. Could Hull be held personally liable for these debts?

22. In its press release, Able Products, a Virginia corporation, announced that it was forming a joint venture with Hyallah, Inc., a toy-making corporation chartered in South Korea. In the release, Hyallah was referred to as a public, foreign corporation. Lin, the CEO of Hyallah, pointed out the terms "public and foreign" were legally incorrect. Is he correct, and why or why not?

23. Charlene Bertram owned 98 percent of the stock of Traces of Beauty, Inc. The company had been founded in the 1920s by her maternal grandmother. The company had been run by profes-sional managers after the grandmother died and left Charlene her stock. Traces imported cosmetics from France, England, and Sweden. The products were then sold directly to consumers by mail, 800 numbers, and on the Internet. While on a trip to Italy, Charlene found a new line of cosmetics that dazzled her. Without consulting any of the company officers, Charlene negotiated an exclusive distributorship for Traces with the Italian cosmetic maker. Upon her return to the states, Charlene met with the company president and told her about the deal. The president was shocked and noted that carrying the Italian line would breach an existing contract with the French cosmetic firm. This contract had made Traces millions of dollars over the last 10 years. The president then consulted the corporate legal staff to see if there was any way out of the contract with the Italian firm. Assume you are the company attorney. How would you answer the question posed by the president? Explain your answer.

24. As the testing of its new anti-arthritis drug showing results that exceeded anyone's expectations, JointEase Corporation bought back more than one third of its outstanding, publicly traded stock. As a consequence, because of the decreased supply, when the company announced the test results its stock price increased to more than double what would have been expected without the buyout. Feeling that they had been defrauded, the ex-shareholders who had sold their stock back to JointEase picketed outside company headquarters and complained to the media. Has the drug company done anything wrong?

ANALYZE REAL CASES

25. Pillsbury believed U.S. involvement in the Vietnam War was wrong. He learned that Honeywell, Inc., had a large contract to produce antipersonnel fragmentation bombs and he became determined to stop such production. He learned that a trust set up for his benefit owned 242 shares of the stock, but the shares were voted by a trustee. Pillsbury bought one share in his own name. As a shareholder, he petitioned the court to order Honeywell to produce its shareholder ledgers and all records dealing with weapons manufacture. He wanted to convince other shareholders to change the board of directors and have the corporation stop making munitions. Should the court grant his request? (*Pillsbury v. Honeywell, Inc.*, 291 Minn. 322, 191 N.W.2d 406)

26. A group of shareholders of the Manganese Corporation of America sued the corporation and four officers who also were directors. The group of shareholders sought to recover damages for the corporation and all its shareholders. Evidence indicated that the officers and directors negligently had caused the corporation's assets to drop from $400,000 to $30,000 in less than two years by being wasteful, careless, and unwise. Are the officers and directors liable for the losses? (*Selheimer v. Manganese Corporation of America*, 423 Pa. 563, 224 A.2d 634)

27. General Telephone Company of Florida owned more than 1 percent of the stock of Florida Telephone Corporation. General sought to examine the latter's stock records in order to make a list of the names, addresses, and holdings of all shareholders. Florida refused, claiming that General intended to use this information in order to buy more shares and thus get control of the corporation. Can General get a court order to compel the disclosure? (*Florida Telephone Corporation v. State ex ref. Peninsular Telephone Company*, 111 So. 2d 677, Fla.)

28. Years before lights were installed in Wrigley field in Chicago, Schlensky, a minority stockholder in the Chicago National League Ball Club (Inc.), owner of the Chicago Cubs, sued the corporation and its board of directors, including Philip K. Wrigley. Wrigley also was president and owned about 80 percent of the voting stock. Schlensky alleged negligence and mismanagement for failure to install floodlights to permit night games. He claimed that funds for the installation could be obtained and would be far more than recaptured by increased ticket sales. Allegedly Wrigley thought that baseball was a daytime sport and that night games would have a negative effect on the neighborhood surrounding the ball park, and the other directors gave in. The trial court dismissed the complaint, and Schlensky appealed. How should the appellate court rule? (*Schlensky v. Wrigley*, 237 N.E.2d 776, Ill.)

29. Two attorney-shareholders in Ched Realty sought to buy out the shares of two recently deceased shareholders in the company. The attorneys cited a clause in a shareholder agreement that allowed them to buy the shares at "book value or $200 per share, whichever was greater." At the time, the book value of the shares was negative, as the assets of the long-standing corporation had been depreciated to nothing. However, the market value of the shares was well over $40,000 per share. The estates of the two deceased shareholders sued to block the sale for $200 per share claiming that the deceased shareholders were not fully aware of what they were signing because they were older and had not completed high school. The lower court disallowed the shareholder agreement. The two attorneys appealed. Should the appeals court overturn the lower court's ruling? Why or why not? (*Rosiny v. Schmidt*, 587 N.Y.S.2d 929)

Sports & Entertainment Law

Who Do You Anti-Trust?

DENVER ROCKETS V. ALL-PRO MANAGEMENT
325 F. SUPP. 1049

BACKGROUND Spencer Haywood was the ultimate American rags-to-riches story. Born into a Mississippi sharecroppers' family of 10 children, he spent his first 15 years in a rural poverty only imagined today. Then he moved to Detroit to live with his brother and, for the next decade or so, created the foundation of what could have become a legend greater than Michael Jordan's. At 6 foot 9 inches and 225 pounds, he was not of remarkable size for the company he kept on the basketball court. He was just, in a word, unstoppable. At 19 years of age he led a decimated U.S. basketball team (at the time composed of all collegiate players) to a gold medal in the Mexico City Olympics. That same year, as a sophomore, he scored an average of 32 points AND pulled down an average of 21.5 rebounds for the Division I University of Detroit. Citing the hardship of his family he then left school to play for the Denver Rockets of the American Basketball Association (ABA). His first season he was named not only the ABA's rookie of the year but also its most valuable player. Unfortunately, the ABA was falling apart around him, and he sought to jump to the well-funded NBA to play for the Seattle Supersonics.

Standing in his way, however, was one of the rules that, along with its reserve clause and the exclusivity of its draft system, preserved the NBA's control over the supply of players that might run up and down its hardwoods. Simply put, the NBA prohibited any person to play in its system until their high school class had graduated college (a four-year period in those days).

FACTS In a lawsuit against the NBA, Haywood claimed that the NBA's employment of this rule was illegal as it violated the Sherman Antitrust Act's main provision: "Every contract, combination in the form of trust or otherwise, or conspiracy, in restraint of trade or commerce among the several States, or with foreign nations, is declared to be illegal."

ISSUE Is the prohibition by the NBA prohibiting anyone playing for its teams whose high school class has not had time to graduate college a restraint of trade and thereby illegal under the antitrust laws of this country?

HOLDING The court held that the four-year rule was a restraint on trade and illegal under the Sherman Antitrust Act.

PRACTICE JUDGING

1. Are all professional sports subject to the antitrust laws?

2. What was the effect of this ruling on the professional sport of basketball?

Chapter 28
Organizational Forms for Small Business

28-1 Traditional Small Business Forms

28-2 New and Evolving Small Business Forms

HOT DEBATE

Earl opened his recreational vehicle repair garage, Snowbird's Nest, in Florida in the late 1970s. He incorporated the garage as a C corporation. As the years wore on, Earl retained this status although his CPA told him he was losing money due to the double taxation. Now that his children are out of college and settled down, Earl has decided to take more risks. He plans to expand his garage operation into a couple of other locations, start selling accessories for RVs, and open an RV park. He also is considering taking a new business form. His CPA has advised him that he can elect to be taxed as a subchapter S corporation just by filing a one-page form with the IRS. The CPA even offered to do it for Earl for free. The CPA also told Earl that for around $750, an attorney could move his company into an LLC form.

WHERE DO YOU STAND?

1. List and discuss the reasons that Earl might want to assume the subchapter S form.
2. List and discuss the reasons that Earl might want to assume the LLC form.

28-1 Traditional Small Business Forms

GOALS

- Contrast the roles of general partners and limited partners in a limited partnership
- Explain why the owners of a C corporation would elect the S corporation status

KEY TERMS

double taxation

S corporation

Limited Partnerships

WHAT'S YOUR VERDICT? Melbourne, a wealthy financier, decided to invest as a limited partner in a business that manufactured a new form of collapsible luggage. The business did well. One day, when he was at the main office, the general partner mentioned that she was going to move the business into another field of manufacture. Melbourne, who had invested 80 percent of the capital to start it, blurted out, "Oh no, not with my money you're not." The general partner, in front of all the front office personnel, immediately retracted her decision. Later, one of the front-office secretaries, Jim, won his suit against the partnership for sexual harassment. He could only collect $500,000 of the $1,000,000 damage award from the business. Therefore, he went after Melbourne's private fortune. Jim cited the incident in the front office as proof that Melbourne was a general partner and, as a consequence, fully personally liable.

Will Jim be able to recover the remaining damages from Melbourne's private fortune?

Because today's economic giants all have their origins in small ventures, organizational forms have been created to help similar small businesses develop. These forms evolve constantly but have their roots in the limited partnership and the subchapter S corporation forms. This lesson discusses these two older forms, and the next lesson covers more recently developed forms.

Attributes of the Limited Partnership

In a limited partnership, there must be at least one general partner with unlimited liability. All the other partners may be limited partners. Limited partners are liable only to the extent of their investment in the business. The general partners in a limited partnership have full managerial control over running the business. They are the ultimate decision-makers concerning who has what responsibilities in making the business a success.

As with a general partnership, if the terms of the partnership agreement are not set out by the partners themselves, the law will impose its own terms. However, the government intrudes further into the domain of the partners in a limited partnership than it does in a general partnership. In the eyes of government, this additional intrusive behavior is warranted due to the limited liability provisions afforded the limited partners.

IN THIS CASE Fresh out of business school, Maltese formed a limited partnership with Dr. Falcon, the limited partner who supplied the capital. After five years of intense work by Maltese, during which she acquired many personal assets, the business was a roaring success. Finally, Maltese decided that it was time to do something she had put off for too long—to change the business from a limited partnership to the corporate form. Such a move would eliminate the full personal liability to which she had been exposed as the general partner since the business began. Dr. Falcon would continue to enjoy a limited liability protection.

Forming a Limited Partnership

Unlike a general partnership, a limited partnership can only be created by following the procedures set forth in the controlling state statute. Although most states originally enacted a controlling statute modeled after the Uniform Limited Partnership Act (ULPA), the majority have now amended their statutes to conform to the provisions of the Revised Uniform Limited Partnership Act (RULPA). Under either statute, unlike the general partnership, a limited partnership can be created only by proper execution, recording, and publication of a certificate that identifies the partners and states basic facts about their agreement.

The sample limited partnership certificate shown below is based on the RULPA requirements. Note that the limited partnership is legally formed at the time of the filing, usually with the Secretary of State. If the filing requirements of the controlling statute are not met, all business participants are treated as general partners.

Record Keeping for a Limited Partnership

In addition to the information contained in the Certificate of Limited Partnership, the RULPA requires certain records to be kept at the office specified in paragraph 2 of the certificate. These records include

1. A list of the last known addresses of the general and limited partners with each properly identified as general or limited

2. Copies of the certificate of limited partnership and its amendments

3. Copies of the limited partnership's local, state, and federal income tax returns for the three most recent years

4. Copies of any currently effective partnership agreement and any financial statements issued for the three most recent years

5. Unless contained in the partnership agreement, a listing of the amount of cash and property contributed or pledged by any partner, times of any future contributions by any partner, and agreed-to circumstances that might require the limited partnership's dissolution and winding up

Any of these records are obtainable by subpoena and are subject to inspection and copying by the reasonable request of any partner during ordinary business hours.

Status of the Partners

Under the ULPA, limited partners who participate in any managerial decisions lose their status and become liable without limit as general partners. This rule was relaxed and redefined by the RULPA. Under the provisions of the RULPA, a limited partner does not participate in the managerial control of the business solely by doing such things as consulting with the general partner(s), acting as an agent or employee for the partnership, attending meetings of the general partners, or by participating in the restructuring of the partnership.

CERTIFICATE OF LIMITED PARTNERSHIP

1. **Name** (must contain without abbreviation the words "Limited Partnership")—Burnin' Hot Charcoal, A Limited Partnership

2. **Address of Office** (need not be a place of business but must be located in the state where records required by RULPA are kept)—350 BarBQ Lane, Westown, NM

3. **Agent for Service of Process** (must be either a natural resident, domestic corporation, or foreign corporation authorized to do business in New Mexico)—Howard Fernandez, 1339 Savory Street, Liberty NM

4. **Name and Address of Each General Partner**—Margaret Whitaker, 1313 Hideaway Haven, Bluffton, NM

5. **Latest Date Upon Which the Limited Partnership is to Dissolve**—March 13, 2013

6. **Any Other Matters the General Partners Determine to Include Therein**—N/A

Filed with the Secretary of State, March 13, 2006,
and effective as of that date

In *What's Your Verdict?* the answer would depend on the state that had jurisdiction over the case. In a state that has not adopted the RULPA, Jim would be able to recover the remaining $500,000 against the private fortune of Melbourne. If the RULPA were in place, however, Melbourne would probably be able to keep his private fortune intact. This is because the RULPA does allow limited partners to participate in decisions that pertain to the structuring of the partnership. Consequently, if the lawyer for Melbourne could show how the move into another field of manufacture would necessitate such restructuring, his private fortune would be safe.

Under almost all controlling statutes, if a limited partner knowingly allows her or his name to be used in the name of the limited partnership, that limited partner is liable to creditors who extend credit without actual knowledge that she or he is a limited partner.

CHECKPOINT How do general partners differ from limited partners in a limited partnership?

Subchapter S Corporations

WHAT'S YOUR VERDICT? Juwon and Ennis founded a business partnership to remanufacture automobile engines. After several successful years, they adopted the C corporation form and have operated under it for almost a decade. Recently Juwon bought Ennis' stock and is now the sole owner of the corporation. Juwon wants to become a subchapter S corporation and avoid the double taxation.

Can Juwon elect the subchapter S corporation form?

Several decades ago, Congress authorized a new corporate form. It was intended to give small business owners a tax break by allowing them to choose an alternative to the traditional corporate form governed by subchapter C of the Internal Revenue Code. This was important as subchapter

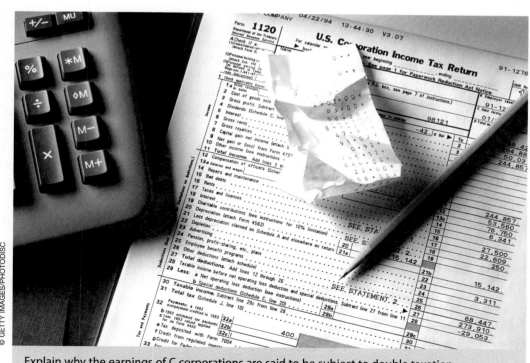

Explain why the earnings of C corporations are said to be subject to double taxation.

C corporations are subject to double taxation. **Double taxation** means that the corporation is taxed on corporate income and then corporate shareholders are taxed on dividends paid them out of the funds remaining after the corporate taxes are remitted. This alternative form provided by Congress is the **S corporation**, governed by subchapter S of the Internal Revenue Code. Subchapter S eliminated double taxation for small businesses formed according to subchapter S's rules by not taxing such corporations on their earnings.

Attributes of the Subchapter S Form

A corporation that qualifies under the subchapter S rules need only elect to be taxed as an S corporation. After it does so, corporate earnings are treated the same as a gain (or loss) from a partnership and only taxed at the individual owner's level. The elimination of double taxation in this manner resulted in many businesses adopting this form. Even though newer business forms with more attractive corporate and partnership attribute mixes are now available (see the next lesson), businesses still choose the subchapter S form due to its ease of entry from the C corporate form. Juwon in *What's Your Verdict?* could take advantage of this ease of entry by simply filing the one-page election form with the IRS before March 15 of the year in which he wants the business to be classified as a subchapter S corporation.

Electing to be taxed as an S corporation will allow Juwon's corporation to avoid paying income taxes at the corporate level. Instead he will be able to treat his business income or loss solely as personal income or loss on his taxes. In addition, the best elements of the corporate form, such as limited liability, perpetual life, and free transferability of ownership interests will be retained for his business.

Eligibility Requirements for an S Corporation

In order to qualify as an S corporation under the IRS code, the business must satisfy several requirements.

1. *Timely filing* A corporation wanting to be taxed as an S corporation must file the appropriate form indicating such an election with the IRS before March 15 of the tax year in which the election is to be effective. The election must reflect the unanimous choice

of the stockholders. Any election of an S-qualified company to resume being taxed as a C corporation also must be the unanimous decision of shareholders.

2. *Domestic corporation* The S corporation status is reserved for businesses incorporated in the United States.

3. *Identity of shareholders* Only natural persons, estates, or certain types of trusts can be shareholders in an S corporation. Other corporations, partnerships, and non-qualifying trusts cannot. In addition, nonresident aliens cannot be shareholders.

4. *Number of shareholders* The corporation must have 100 or fewer stockholders.

5. *Classes of stock* The corporation can have only one class of stock. Shareholders do not have to have the same voting rights.

Formation of an S Corporation

The S corporation is not so much a corporate form as it is a tax status. To form such an entity, one needs only to be in the form of a corporation and then make a qualified filing with the IRS.

CHECKPOINT Why would the owners of a C corporation elect to change the organizational form to an S corporation?

THINK ABOUT LEGAL CONCEPTS

1. There could be ten or more general partners in a limited partnership. **True or False?**

2. Which uniform act is more flexible in the governing of key issues of limited partnerships? (a) ULPA (b) RULPA

3. A limited partner might be held personally liable to the firm's creditors by letting her/his name be used in the limited partnership's name. **True or False?**

4. Which of the following records do not have to be kept in the limited partnership's designated office within the certifying state? (a) tax records

for the last five years (b) names and addresses of all the general partners (c) names and addresses of all the limited partners (d) all of the above

5. Another corporation can be a shareholder in a subchapter S corporation. **True or False?**

6. What is the maximum number of stockholders in a subchapter S corporation? (a) 15 (b) 50 (c) 100 (d) unlimited

7. All a corporation's shareholders must assent before the subchapter S status can be assumed. **True or False?**

THINK CRITICALLY ABOUT EVIDENCE

Study the situation, answer the questions, and then prepare arguments to support your answers.

8. Judith's brother, a famous actor, left her a fortune. She wanted to invest part of it in a start-up business venture. At a party, Judith met Hector, an electrical engineer with an invention that he wanted to market. Judith liked the idea and wanted to capitalize the venture with $150,000. However, she wanted to be able to maintain control over who had an ownership interest in the business and all the business losses for tax purposes, and keep her liability limited to what she had invested in the concern. Hector had no money to invest but did have the rights to the invention and some managerial skills. What business form would you recommend? Why?

9. In a state in which only the ULPA is in effect, Dee was a limited partner in a small manufacturing business. One day she insisted that the general partner hire her sister as his administrative assistant. Did her action make her as liable as a general partner for the debts of the business?

10. In exercise 9, if RULPA is in effect, would Dee be liable as a general partner for the business debts?

11. Eriq wanted to start a tennis court repair business. To get the supplies and capital equipment needed, he decided to form a corporation and issue stock. Some 103 investors, including a partnership in which his dad was a partner,

bought stock. Later, Eriq wanted to elect the subchapter S form of corporation. Can he do so? Why or why not?

12. Tracy wanted to start a company to make Christmas ornaments. Her mother agreed to help fund the company by buying stock in it. Tracy's attorney suggested that she utilize the subchapter S form for the business. Tracy knew that the subchapter S form only had one class of stock. She worried that if she and her mother both had the same level of ownership, her mother might try to manage the company. Tracy thought it might be a better idea to form a regular corporation and sell her mother preferred stock with no voting rights. The lawyer shook her head. "That means you'll likely have to pay thousands more in taxes. Instead, let me tell you some good news about the subchapter S stock." What was that good news?

13. Tracy (in exercise 12) mentioned to her lawyer that she wanted to be sure that, if her company were successful, she could pass its ownership on to either or both of her two daughters. She mentioned that she was worried that, like a partnership, the subchapter S corporation would end when she died. Is this correct? Why or why not?

28-2 New and Evolving Small Business Forms

GOALS

- Explain the attributes of the LLC that make it ideal for small businesses
- State why the LLP form is so useful to professional partnerships

KEY TERMS

limited liability corporation (LLC)

articles of organization

members

operating agreement

distributive shares

limited liability partnership (LLP)

The Limited Liability Corporation

> ### WHAT'S YOUR VERDICT?
>
> Jose wanted a business form that had the limited liability protection of the corporation, no double taxation, and no restrictions on ownership such as those imposed by the subchapter S rules.
>
> **Which form should he choose?**

For years, the best forms of business organization for small businesses were the limited partnership and the subchapter S corporation. These forms, however, had flaws and limitations that needed to be improved upon. These improvements began to appear in the American West in 1977. The Economic Impact feature on this page explains the introduction of the **limited liability corporation (LLC)** form of business organization in the United States. This form offers limited liability, taxation as a partnership, and few of the restrictions encountered in the S corporation or limited partnership.

Formation of an LLC

Similar to a corporation or limited partnership, a limited liability corporation (LLC) must be formed and operated in accordance with the law in the state in which it was organized. In most states, an LLC is formed by filing **articles of organization** in the appropriate state office (usually the Secretary of State's office). A typical "articles of organization" submission is shown on page 515.

Economic Impact

BIRTH OF THE LIMITED LIABILITY CORPORATION

In 1977 legislators in Wyoming took a bold step toward providing the ultimate in small business organization alternatives to Americans by passing a statute that authorized creating Limited Liability Corporations (LLCs) in their state. They based their statutory creation on forms of business organizations that existed in Europe and South America. In essence, the LLC offered limited liability protection and taxation as a partnership, but lacked the limitations of the subchapter S or limited partnership alternatives. For more than a decade, however, the LLC remained an alternative only in Wyoming and Florida. (Florida imitated Wyoming's creative action by passing a similar statute in 1982.) Interest in LLCs mushroomed in 1988, when the Internal Revenue Service ruled that LLCs would be taxed as partnerships at the federal level. By late 1997, every state in the union had an LLC-empowering statute. Today, small businesses throughout America are better protected and capitalized as a result.

THINK CRITICALLY

Why do you think it took so long for the United States to allow LLCs when they had been in existence in Europe and South America for an extended time?

State of _____

ARTICLES OF ORGANIZATION

1. **Name***—The Moot Point LLC

2. **Nature of Business**—Retailer of fine accessories for the successful attorney

3. **Office Address**—1339 W. Synchronicity Blvd., Coincidence, Colorado

4. **Agent for Service of Process**—John Acausal, 1339 W. Synchronicity Blvd., Coincidence, Colorado

5. **Name and Address of Organizers**—John Acausal, 1339 W. Synchronicity Blvd., Coincidence, Colorado

6. **Names of Initial LLC Members**—John and Jeanne Acausal, 1339 W. Synchronicity Blvd., Coincidence, Colorado

*Note that the business' name must include the LLC designation or the full Limited Liability Company title.

The owners of an LLC are known as **members**. Their liability is limited to the amount that they have invested in the business, and the earnings of the LLC are taxed as a partnership. However, some states allow certain members to declare themselves as fully personally liable at the time of organization. This can be a plus with potential creditors who want someone's personal assets at risk in addition to the corporation's.

The Operating Agreement

After the articles of organization, the most necessary document for an LLC is its **operating agreement**. This document is somewhat like the bylaws of a corporation but more far reaching. An operating agreement is required by many states but, whether required or not, is a good idea even in an LLC with just one member. When there is only one member, the operating agreement protects the LLC from appearing as a sole proprietorship and thus possibly being stripped of its limited liability protection in a court action.

An operating agreement should cover the following:

1. *Assignment of percentages of ownership* Most states have a "default" statute that will assign percentages of ownership according to the value of capital contributions. However, this statute only comes into play if the members do not assign the percentages in the operating agreement. Oftentimes, one member may not be able to contribute much in capital but deserves—and needs to be motivated by—a large ownership interest. The LLC

form allows such an assignment regardless of capital contribution percentages.

2. *Assignment of distributive shares* Although most often assigned in the same percentage as

When drawing up the operating agreement, what do the members of an LLC need to consider in assigning percentages of ownership?

capital contributions in the state's default statute, the members can allocate each member's shares of profits and losses as they see fit. These **distributive shares** do not have to be equal percentages for profits and for losses. Many times a person with outside income will want to take a much larger percentage of the LLCs losses than profits for tax purposes. It also is wise to note in the operating agreement if and when the distributive shares will be paid.

3. *Voting rights* The operating agreement should reflect the members' choice between whether each has a vote on important matters (called per capita voting) or if they have voting power proportional to their capital investment percentages.

4. *Member rights and duties* The operating agreement can specify which members have the power to bind the LLC to contracts of various kinds and which do not. Possession and use of LLC property also can be covered.

5. *Prohibitions on sale of interest* Any restrictions on members selling their interests should be explicitly stated in the operating agreement.

6. *Termination of ownership interests* Procedure on how to value and buy out the interests of members who die, retire, or withdraw for other reasons should be specified in the operating agreement.

Other stipulations can be included in the operating agreement. If the members do not formulate provisions for their agreement themselves, the state of organization likely will have a default

CyberLAW

Today a number of companies provide services that allow a business to be incorporated via the Internet. Basically, the provider of the service does the paperwork and filing of the documents. It also typically acts as the long-term representative, called a registered agent, for the new company in the jurisdiction awarding the charter. Of course, it has long been possible for a business of one state to incorporate in another—it has just not been this easy. Because of revenue generated, states vie for the position of "most hospitable" to foreign (out of state) incorporators. Delaware and Nevada are the most utilized jurisdictions at the moment. However, the Internet brings an international set of options to such a decision. Through the Internet it is possible to exercise the option of incorporating "offshore" with relative ease. Offshore typically refers to "safe financial havens" where privacy is as much the currency as the dollar and means out of the jurisdiction of the United States and the easy reach of its legal process. Currently a major shift in the availability of "safe havens" is underway. Many old havens associated with Great Britain, such as the Cayman Islands, Anguilla, Bermuda, British Virgin Islands, Montserrat, Turks and Caicos, the Isle of Man, and the British Channel Islands have had the privacy protection diminished by international accords. New havens, such as the Caribbean Island of Nevis, and assistance by the Internet, have moved in to take their place.

THINK ABOUT IT

One such Internet site offering offshore incorporations offers protection from "litigious attorneys, employers/employees, ex-spouses, ex-business partners, big brother and others" that might invade the privacy of their users. Are these ethical reasons for choosing the corporate form? For incorporating offshore?

statute to provide missing terms. These terms probably will not be as desirable as those the members could have created for themselves.

Advantages of LLCs

The most significant advantages that make LLCs more attractive than other small business forms are the following.

1. No limitation on the number of members (the S corporation currently limits the number of stockholders to 100).

2. No limitations as to whom or what can be a stockholder in an LLC. Therefore, foreign nationals, corporations, and other business entities can be shareholders.

3. Members are allowed to participate completely in managing the business. There are no worries of losing the limited liability status for those who do manage, as might be the case even under RULPA.

Disadvantages of the LLC

After several decades of modification, the LLC has become the ideal form for most small businesses. Tests imposed on it in the mid-1990s by the IRS to determine if it should be afforded limited liability status have been swept away. The only relative disadvantage to the form impacts those who encounter tax problems in transferring assets from a partnership or other type of corporation to the LLC. A partial solution to this remaining problem exists in the recently created form of the limited liability partnership which will be discussed in the next section.

Today, however, the attributes of the LLC are so suitable to small businesses that, unless a business entity is either a corporation formed under a state incorporation statute (not an LLC statute), a publicly traded corporation, or particular types of foreign-owned corporations, it will be presumed by the IRS to want to be taxed as an LLC. If the business entity wants to be taxed as a corporation, it can achieve this end by simply checking a box on the appropriate IRS form. With all this in mind, Jose in *What's Your Verdict?* would do well to choose the LLC form.

CHECKPOINT Why should an LLC with only one member still have an operating agreement?

The Limited Liability Partnership

WHAT'S YOUR VERDICT? Drs. Bryant, Rico, and Ferrar wanted to form a partnership. Dr. Rico, however, was concerned about the possibility of being held personally liable for any malpractice claims against her partners.

What business form could protect Dr. Rico from such claims?

With all the advantages of the LLC, it is hard to imagine a need for any other small business form. However, as mentioned previously, already-existing business entities might find it difficult to convert to an LLC form due to tax and asset appreciation issues. In addition, especially for partnerships constructed for professionals, the difficulty is not limited to these taxation problems but extends to the complexity of ending the partnership, valuing the interests, and then fairly reestablishing the concern as an LLC.

As a consequence, in 1991 Texas created the **limited liability partnership (LLP)**. This form offered ease of conversion from an existing partnership, avoidance of double taxation, and partial limited liability protection. Barely more than a decade later, almost all the states have enacted LLP statutes, mostly by simply amending already-existing partnership statutes.

Under the majority of the LLP statutes, the limited liability protection extends only to shield against the consequences of conduct involving the torts of others in the partnership. The Texas statute, for example, protects innocent partners from the consequences of errors, omissions, negligence, incompetence, or wrongdoing stemming from partnership operations.

Therefore, if a partner commits professional malpractice and the resulting damage claim exceeds the amount of liability insurance coverage the partnership or that individual carries, the other partners will not have their personal fortunes endangered. In *What's Your Verdict?* Dr. Rico would be protected from personal liability for malpractice claims against Drs. Bryant and Ferrar if they formed an LLP. The partners remain responsible for other debts such as wages or loans.

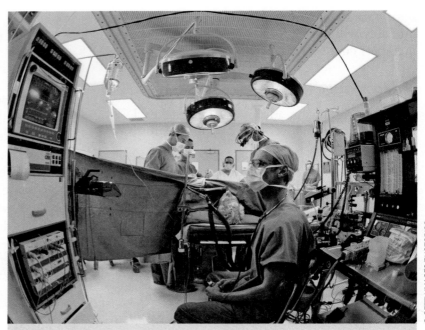

Imagine that one of these doctors is a member of an LLP with other doctors. The doctor makes a mistake during an operation, and the patient dies because of it. The patient's family sues the doctor, and they are awarded an amount that exceeds the doctor's and the LLP's liability insurance coverage. What is the extent of the other partners' liability for the mistake?

CHECKPOINT What limited liability protection does an LLP offer?

LEGAL Research

Compare and contrast the information required by your state for the formation of a sole proprietorship, a general partnership, a limited partnership, a corporation, a limited liability corporation, a limited liability partnership, and any other hybrid business form legally available. What does the information you find tell you about the state's regulatory emphasis in the area of forms of business organization?

LAW BRIEF

Medical malpractice is a form of professional malpractice in which a professional breaches his or her duty of ordinary care. An example of medical malpractice would be a surgeon amputating the wrong limb of a patient. Medical malpractice also may apply to misdiagnosing patients' medical problems. In the United States, about 80,000 people die each year due in part to medical malpractice. Only 2 percent of the patients who are victims of medical malpractice seek compensation through filing a lawsuit. Doctors are not required to purchase medical malpractice insurance.

THINK ABOUT LEGAL CONCEPTS

1. Restrictions that effectively prohibit the free transfer of LLC ownership interests can be placed in the operating agreement. **True or False?**

2. The members of an LLC can define the ownership percentages as they see fit regardless of capital contributions. **True or False?**

3. The members of an LLC can define the _?_ shares of the profits for the members.

4. The operating agreement is the same as the articles of organization of an LLC. **True or False?**

5. An LLC can have no more than 100 members. **True or False?**

6. Which of the following could not be an LLC member? (a) corporation (b) partnership (c) foreign, nonresident, national (d) all of the above can be members

7. LLCs are still subject to double taxation. **True or False?**

8. For professional partnerships, the main advantage of an LLP over an LLC is the ease of transferring to the LLP form. **True or False?**

THINK CRITICALLY ABOUT EVIDENCE

Study the situation, answer the questions, and then prepare arguments to support your answers.

9. Phil Rosato and his three brothers formed a business to manufacture baseball mitts. A minor league baseball club, the Carolina Copperheads, wanted to invest in the business so as to have specialty gloves made for it by the Rosatos. Also, due to the depreciation of the new equipment they purchased for the business, the Rosatos were sure to have losses for the first two years. Thereafter, the profits should be substantial. As far as their dealings with the Copperheads are concerned, why would the LLC form be better for the Rosatos than the S corporation?

10. All four Rosato brothers plan to continue working at their current jobs for the first year or so after the business starts up. How will the LLC form help them tax-wise? Once the Rosatos'

business starts to show a profit in the third year, how will the LLC form help them even more?

11. If the Rosatos' business grows, the likelihood of marketing their gloves in Japan seems great. The Rosatos feel that, should they decide to penetrate the Japanese market, they would want to bring in as a member their long-time friend, Mickie Hosaido. Mickie is a Japanese national living in Tokyo. How would the LLC form facilitate bringing Mickie into the business better than the S corporation form?

12. To facilitate going international, the Rosatos will probably have to "go public" and list their stock on a major stock exchange. How will this affect their choice of business form?

Chapter 28 Assessment

Xtra! Quiz Prep
school.cengage.com/blaw/lawxtra

CONCEPTS IN BRIEF

28-1   Traditional Small Business Forms

1. The primary advantages of the small business forms discussed in this chapter are the avoidance of double taxation and limited liability.

2. The limited partnership form requires one partner with full personal liability, but this is often required by lenders to LLCs as well.

3. Limited partnerships, like all partnerships, do not have perpetual life.

4. The subchapter S business form, while easy to assume, comes with several eligibility requirements.

28-2   New and Evolving Small Business Forms

5. The LLC has evolved from an obscure beginning to become the most chosen and optimal small business form in the United States.

6. The LLC has the desirable attributes of the subchapter S form but without the limitations.

7. The operating agreement is vital to the legal status of the LLC.

8. Tax problems encountered by professional partnerships trying to assume the LLC form have been alleviated by the LLP form.

YOUR LEGAL VOCABULARY

Match each statement with the term that it best defines. Some terms may not be used.

1. Owners of an LLC

2. Form of business organization that offers limited liability only to the consequences of conduct involving torts

3. Form of business organization offering limited liability and the elimination of double taxation but limiting the number and types of permitted shareholders

4. Document filed with the state to organize an LLC

5. Taxation of a corporation as an entity based on its earnings and then of the shareholders on corporate dividends

6. Form of business organization that avoids double taxation, affords limited liability protection, and is without limits imposed on other forms

7. The equivalent of corporate bylaws but for an LLC

8. Agreed-to percentage split of LLC profits and losses

a. articles of organization
b. distributive shares
c. double taxation
d. limited liability corporation (LLC)
e. limited liability partnership (LLP)
f. members
g. operating agreement
h. S corporation

REVIEW LEGAL CONCEPTS

9. What records are limited partnerships required by law to keep?

10. Why is there a prohibition against ownership of a subchapter S corporation by another corporation?

11. What is the financial effect for a business of organizing as an LLC?

12. Why is the operating agreement so important for an LLC?

WRITE ABOUT LEGAL CONCEPTS

13. Fill out an articles of organization form for an imaginary business or one that you are familiar with.

14. For the business in exercise 13, make up an operating agreement covering each of the suggested areas mentioned on pages 515 and 516. Presume there are at least two members.

15. Suppose you and a friend decide to start a business writing and selling computer programs. Make a list of the pros and cons of each form of business organization you are considering.

16. **HOT DEBATE** Discuss the disadvantages that the S and LLC forms pose for Earl. Choose the form you think Earl should utilize and justify your choice in a short paper.

MAKE ACADEMIC CONNECTIONS

17. **POLITICAL SCIENCE** The acceptance of the LLC business form by the IRS came after a power struggle between the states and the federal government. The federal government saw the potential for business growth in the new status. The states stood to lose large amounts of corporate tax revenue without any compensating funding from the federal level. Research the development of this conflict and how it was resolved within the political and legal systems.

THINK CRITICALLY ABOUT EVIDENCE

Study the situation, answer the questions, and then prepare arguments to support your answers.

18. West Virginia Tank and Tower Inc. (TnT) bought and sold used water towers. Metal Raincloud (Cloud) manufactured water towers. One of its suppliers, Gravity Flow Inc., an S corporation, developed and patented a new type of valve for such towers. Wanting to hasten the new valve's development but not wanting to cause Gravity Flow to lose its S corporation status, Cloud offered L. Quidity, the owner of Gravity Flow, $1,000,000 for her to invest in her corporation and its new product. In return Quidity agreed to pay half her earnings from Gravity Flow to Cloud. Will the IRS allow Gravity Flow to maintain its S corporation status as a result? Why or why not?

19. Minnie Octaves, a well-known opera singer, was a limited partner in "Octaves and Clark, a limited partnership." The Florida real estate development concern's only project was the construction and management of Octaves Upper Scale, a residential retirement complex for senior citizens. When the partnership approached a group of local banks for an expansion loan, it did not mention that Octaves was just a limited partner. The loan was for $1.5 million and is now in default. Can the banks collect what is due from Octaves' personal fortune?

20. Three doctors were in a limited liability partnership with Dr. S. Kay Bell. The practice's offices were in Dallas, Texas. During a minor plastic surgery, one of Dr. Bell's partners severed an artery of a patient, and the patient died. The family brought suit and recovered more than $4 million dollars. The financial resources of the negligent surgeon are financially exhausted after paying nearly $1.5 million dollars of the recovery. The partnership's liability policy has covered all but $1 million of the rest. Now the other doctors want to take out a loan in the partnership's name to cover the remaining million. Dr. Bell has come to you for advice as to whether or not she should go along with the idea. How would you advise her? Why?

21. Quiet Running, a closely held LLC, produces electric cars. It recently secured the rights to a patent that will allow it to produce such cars with a cruising range of nearly 500 miles. In order to meet the anticipated demand, it needs a large amount of capital to set up a new factory. You are the corporate counsel and are attending a board meeting when one of the company's financial advisors suggests that the company "go public" with their stock. What advice would you give as to the potential impact of doing so on the company's organizational form?

ANALYZE REAL CASES

22. A limited partnership was formed to promote a boxing match between professional football player Lyle Alzado and an ex-boxing heavyweight champion, Muhummad Ali. The limited partner in the deal was to be the firm of Blinder, Robinson and Co. with Alzado and others joined together in an organization known as Combat Associates to be the general partner. Alzado personally guaranteed that if the proceeds of the match were to be less than $250,000 he would make up the difference. In preparation for the match, Blinder, Robinson and Co.'s president participated in interviews and a promotional rally. In addition, the company allowed one of its offices to be used as a ticket office and also held parties. When the proceeds came to less than $250,000, Blinder sued Alzado for the shortfall. Alzado counterclaimed contending that Blinder, Robinson and Co. had acted in such a way that it had become a general partner. How should the court rule on the general partner issue? Why? (*Blinder, Robinson and Co. v. Alzado,* 713 P. 2d 1314)

23. Ward Parkway was a wholly owned subsidiary of Kroh Brothers Development Company. Ward Parkway was also the general partner in West Tech, a limited partnership. Boatmen's Bank made a $1.3 million loan to West Tech but deposited it in the Kroh Brothers Development Company accounts. Section 620.60(2) of the ULPA states that an act of a partner that is not apparently for the carrying on of the business of the partnership in the usual way does not bind the partnership unless authorized by the other partners. No such authority was forthcoming from any partner when Jacob D. Mondahein executed the note for the loan as vice president of West Parkway. Mondahein also directed Boatmen's to put the money in the Kroh Brothers account. Should Boatmen's be able to collect its money from West Tech? Why or why not? (*West Tech, Ltd. v. Boatmen's First National Bank of Kansas City,* 882 F. 2d 323)

24. Allright Missouri, Inc. (Allright), a Missouri corporation, was a limited partner in Downtown Development Associates, Ltd. (Downtown). The limited partnership was formed to develop two city blocks located in an area known as Lacledes Landing in downtown St. Louis, Missouri. When questions arose as to the transfer of some of Downtown's land to another limited partnership, Allright and many other limited partners sought to sue Downtown. Should limited partners be allowed to sue the partnership they are a part of? Why or why not? (*Allright Missouri, Inc. v. Billeter,* 829 F. 2d 635)

25. American National Insurance Co. had a foreclosure sale on a limited partnership's property to recover an amount owed. The proceeds fell short by almost $1.5 million. To recover the shortfall, American National sought to recover against individuals who became partners after the obligation was undertaken by the limited partnership. Can it do so? Why or why not? (*American National Insurance Co. v. Gilroy, Sims and Associates,* 874 F. Supp. 973)

26. Ramsey Homebuilders was a limited partnership that constructed residential properties in the state of Alabama. Ramsey was the general partner in the firm while two others were limited partners. Ramsey had a bad credit history. So, when funds were needed to increase the partnership business, his signature alone often was not enough. Flanagan Lumber Company at first denied credit to the partnership. Pitman was one of the two limited partners and the possessor of a longstanding credit account with Flanagan. Pitman contacted Flanagan's credit manager and was able to get an account opened in Ramsey Homebuilders' name. When the partnership failed to pay off its account, Flanagan sued Pitman, alleging that his vouching for the partnership's credit made him responsible for the partnership's debt. The trial court found that Pitman had exercised control of the business by securing credit for it. Therefore, Pitman was held personally liable for the Flanagan debt. Pitman appealed to the Supreme Court of Alabama. Control is defined as "the power or authority to manage, direct, superintend, regulate, govern, administer, or oversee" according to Black's Law Dictionary. Did Pitman exercise control and therefore become liable for the debt? Why or why not? (*Pitman v. Flanagan Lumber Co.,* 567 So. 2d 1335)

Sports & Entertainment Law

The Great White "Jaws" Gets Bitten

UNIVERSAL CITY STUDIOS INC. V. FILM VENTURES INTERNATIONAL INC. (FVI)

BACKGROUND   Sometimes, no matter how carefully you protect your resources, for example by limiting your potential liability using the corporate and limited partnership forms, the sharks of the legal system can still find you and strip you clean. Such was the case with Edward L. Montoro, notorious producer of exploitation and "derivative" films of major studios' blockbusters in the 1970s. Montoro made low-budget but relatively high-grossing "B" features such as *Beyond the Door,* a 1974 film that was allegedly a rip-off of the immensely successful *Exorcist.* With this film, Montoro held the record for independent film money-makers for more than a decade until another of his films bested it. That film was *Grizzly.* Allegedly a derivative of the 1975 blockbuster *Jaws,* Montoro's *Grizzly* was produced on a budget of less than $1,000,000. It grossed nearly $40 million worldwide. Success followed success for Montoro until he perhaps went back to the well, or more accurately to the surf, one too many times. He acquired the rights to an Italian film (and alleged *Jaws* rip-off in its own right) called *Great White* for distribution in the United States. Montoro laid out plans and money for a nationwide release that could put him in the big time. Perhaps realizing the risks, he enclosed Film Ventures inside the limited liability shield of a Georgia Corporation and then funded the large-scale distribution of *Great White* through FVI as a member of a limited partnership. It did little good. The movie scarcely had been playing a week when Universal City Studios (Universal) obtained a preliminary injunction that forced the movie to be withdrawn from theaters, never to appear again. The court found, based upon some 17 close similarities elaborated in its opinion, that "the basic story points, the major characters, the sequence of incident, and the development and interplay of the major characters and story points of *Great White*" were substantially similar to *Jaws.* As a result of the significant financial losses that ensued due to his being unable to recover his investment through the showing of *Great White,* Montoro subsequently disappeared with $1,000,000 of FVI funds and has not been heard from again to this day.

ISSUE   Should a preliminary injunction be issued against FVI to halt the exhibition of the film *Great White?*

HOLDING   The court concluded that *Great White* infringed Universal's copyright in *Jaws* and held that the likelihood of irreversible injury to Universal if *Great White* was allowed to be exhibited was substantial. As a consequence, it ordered FVI to deliver to the Clerk of the Court "all prints and negatives of *Great White* or any version thereof."

PRACTICE JUDGING

1. What legal means would you have suggested to Montoro to protect his investment?

2. What practical means would you have suggested to Montoro to protect his investment?

Entrepreneurs
AND THE LAW

Project 6 Legal Forms of Business Organization

Stacy smiled as she examined the new sales figures. The last 18 months had been amazing. The ad agency she had chosen had done its job and then some. Orders from the trade journal and other media ads were coming in steadily. Even the relatively high unit price on the SecureSeals hadn't deterred new potential buyers once they were informed about the benefits, long life, and safety of the tires. The independent salespeople and points of sale also were producing results. Even though the economy was in recession, sales were at an all-time high. The production lines were running at 86 percent capacity and deadlines were being met.

BUSINESS ORGANIZATION On a personal level, Stacy's dad had retired to Florida several months previous thanks to a generous buy-out that Stacy had offered him. Brandon's inheritance had come in and he had started law school two semesters ago. His enrollment in one class in particular had produced especially beneficial results. The class, a survey course on the various forms of business organizations, led Brandon to forcefully recommend that SecureSeal assume a more protective form of organization other than the current sole proprietorship. "Even with insurance," he commented, "in the sole proprietorship form one bad mistake by a company driver, injury to an employee, or defective SecureSeal, and you, the company, and our employees are all in serious trouble." Stacy nodded and asked if he would prepare a comparison of the alternative forms into which they could move the business.

GOVERNMENT AGENCIES Stacy also was very pleased with the relationships she had established with the EEOC and OSHA. The former had been quite cooperative in informing the employees about the various aspects of discrimination and sexual harassment law. In addition, the review of SecureSeal's hiring and promotion practices had resulted in some very important and timely changes to conform to all the law's requirements. Finally, the OSHA review of the new plant had pin-pointed several problems with safety and health practices that were corrected before they could produce harm. Still Stacy recognized the worrisome fact that, as the business continued to grow, more and more government bodies at the city, county, state and federal level would focus their attention on SecureSeal.

ACTIVITIES

Divide into teams and perform one or more of the following activities, as directed by your teacher.

Brainstorm

Project the likely future development of SecureSeal over the next several years. What likely hurdles will the business face? What potential opportunities should SecureSeal be ready to seize? What resources will have to be available to properly handle the various situations pin-pointed by the brainstorming session?

Prepare Legal Documents

Divide into teams and assign one or more potential business forms for SecureSeal to each team. Have each team prepare a briefing for Stacy on their form. Prepare the appropriate legal documents necessary for the assumption of each form. Have the teacher role-play Stacy and select the best form based on the presentations.

Research and Present

Brainstorm to develop a list of the various government bodies with which Stacy will have to deal as SecureSeal grows. Divide into teams and have each prepare a report about one or more of these entities. The reports should detail the areas of expertise, the types of regulations that each body imposes on businesses, their means of assuring compliance, and potential sanctions for improper behavior. Teams should then present their reports to the class. (At the federal level agencies to report on include the Interstate Commerce Commission, Federal Trade Commission, Securities and Exchange Commission, Federal Communications Commission, National Labor Relations Board, Equal Employment Opportunity Commission, Occupational Safety and Health Administration, and the Environmental Protection Agency. City, county, and state regulatory bodies also should be reported on as though SecureSeal's plant was located in the same area as the student's school.)

ETHICAL BUSINESS CONDUCT Ethics give you a system of moral principles that govern appropriate conduct, but not everyone agrees on what conduct is appropriate. One business owner might think it is ethical to lock out a renter who is late with the rent. Another business owner might think that is unethical. Your own moral code will help you determine what you think is ethical conduct.

DO YOUR PART

1. Interview a businessperson you admire who is in a position to set the ethical tone for his or her company.

2. Before the interview, write a list of questions that concern the ethics of the company. You might ask: What are the ethical issues you confront in your business? How do ethics play a role in the success of your company?

3. Call for an appointment. Explain to the person you want to interview that you are doing a research project on business ethics.

4. Write a report on your interview. Comment on whether you agree with the person's business ethics, and why or why not.

Business Plan

Business plans are the key to acquiring finances for a start-up business. The business plan is the entrepreneur's tool for evaluating, organizing, and selling a business concept.

Select a business to start in your community. Your business plan should include an Executive Summary, Company Description, Industry Analysis, Target Market, Competitive Analysis, Marketing Plan and Sales Strategy, Operation, Management and Organization, Long-Term Development, and Financials. *Pay special attention to the legal form of business ownership and the legalities involved with the form of ownership.*

Include attachments such as certifications, licenses, and tax requirements. The business plan can be single- or double-spaced but cannot be more than 30 pages in length. The oral presentation will include five minutes for set up and ten minutes to present your business plan. Visual aids may be used during the presentation.

Performance Indicators Evaluated
- Understand the complete business plan.
- Describe the form of business ownership and legal agreements.
- Present the business plan with confidence and authority.
- Reinforce the business plan with appropriate research.
- Reinforce the presentation with appropriate visual aids.
- Produce a clear and concise written document that follows grammar, punctuation, spelling, and business style rules.
- Demonstrate understanding of policies and procedures manuals.

For more detailed information about performance indicators, go to the FBLA web site.

THINK CRITICALLY

1. Why is the business plan so important for an entrepreneur?

2. Why is the form of business ownership important to a lending institution?

3. Why does a financial institution want to know the long-term goals for a business?

4. Why should an entrepreneur consider hiring an attorney when writing a business plan proposal?

www.fbla-pbl.org/

Mock Trial Prep

EVIDENTIARY QUESTIONS: OBJECTIONS

WHAT ARE OBJECTIONS?

Objections are grounds for expressing opposition in a trial. Objections are raised when an attorney believes that a particular line of questioning of a witness or the introduction of a piece of evidence or other matter is improper and should not be allowed. By objecting, the attorney asks the court to rule on this impropriety.

The admissibility of testimonial and physical evidence is governed by the rules of evidence. If evidence that violates the rules is introduced, that evidence is inadmissible. When an objection is raised by an attorney against the introduction of any testimonial or physical evidence, the judge rules on the objection. By objecting to a question, an attorney preserves the rights of the client on appeal no matter how the judge rules on the specific objection.

An attorney failing to object is allowing that evidence to be admitted, even if the evidence normally is objectionable. Once the judge has ruled on the admissibility of the question or evidence, the witness will be instructed to answer or not answer. Many times you hear an attorney object and the judge find against the objection.

Although an attorney's objection may be overruled, by raising the objection, the attorney makes the objection a matter of the trial record. Without the objection on record, the issue of whether or not the judge made the correct decision about the objection cannot be brought up on appeal.

Attorneys make objections during a trial in an effort to limit the testimony being presented. Objections are a legal and proper part of the trial process. If the judge sustains an objection, the evidence or testimony presented is not proper and cannot be introduced. If the judge overrules an objection, the introduction of the evidence may continue.

MAKING OBJECTIONS

It is essential to make the objection timely before the witness answers the question. Stand when you state "Objection" and then state the basis of your objection to the court. You should remain standing while the opposing side responds. The opposing side will argue why the objection should be overruled. The judge will then sustain the object (agree with it) or overrule the objection (deny

it). No matter what the outcome, you should thank the judge ("Thank you, Your Honor") and sit down.

OBJECT BEFORE THE DAMAGE IS DONE

Once an answer has been given to the objectionable question, the answer has been heard by the judge or jury. The damage has been done. Therefore, the objection must be made timely, that is, before the answer is given. This requires attorneys to listen carefully to each question and to make the objection as soon as possible.

COMMON OBJECTIONS

Leading   *Objection, the question is leading.* A leading question is one which instructs the witness how to answer. A leading question suggests or coaxes the answer within the question itself. An example of a leading question is, "You are a police officer, correct?" or "You saw John when you arrived?" Also, an attorney cannot recite information in a specific order or manner and request approval or rejection of the statement. Leading questions generally are improper on direct examination and are objectionable. Leading questions are permitted on cross examination.

Asked and Answered   *Objection, the question already has been asked and answered.* It is improper to ask a witness a question which previously has been asked and answered by that witness or if the question already has been asked in a different way.

Calls for Speculation   *Objection, calls for speculation.* A witness may not answer a question where the answer is based on conjecture or a guess. Anything that invites a witness to guess is objectionable. Speculation as to what possibly could have happened is of little probative value. An example would be, "What was the man thinking at the time?" or "What would have happened if two people had been at the counter?"

Calls for Improper Opinion   *Objection, counsel's question calls for an improper opinion.* Expert opinion testimony is proper only in the area of expertise or specialized knowledge in which an expert witness is qualified. Expert testimony is scientific, technical, or other specialized knowledge that will assist the trier of fact to

understand the evidence or to determine a fact in issue. For instance, it would be proper for a civil engineer to testify as to the flawed design of a bridge. If the witness is not testifying as an expert, the witness testimony in the form of opinions or inferences is limited to those opinions or inferences which are based on the perception of the witness and helpful to a clear understanding of the witness testimony or the determination of a fact in issue. For instance, a lay (non-expert) witness may testify as to what she saw, heard, or otherwise perceived.

Relevancy *Objection, the question calls for an irrelevant answer.* Testimony cannot be requested that does not have a bearing on the issues raised in the case. Something is irrelevant if it does not serve, by any natural pattern of inference, to establish an issue of fact. The court is bound by efficiency and must prevent distractions on extraneous issues that do not have a relationship to the trial.

Hearsay *Objection, the question calls for hearsay.* Information requested was not directly experienced by the witness. Hearsay is a statement made by someone other than the witness testifying and offered to prove its own truth. There are exceptions to the hearsay rule, but it exists because second-hand statements are unreliable and cannot be tested by cross examination.

Lack of Foundation *Objection, lack of foundation.* Foundation is the asking of preliminary questions to a witness to establish the admissibility of evidence. It is objectionable when an attorney fails to build a basis for the question asked, that is, to "lay a foundation" of facts necessary to be admitted prior to asking the objectionable question. For instance, it is objectionable to first ask, "What did you see at the bank that morning?" before establishing first that the witness was at the bank. (Q: "Where were you on the morning of June 18?" A: At the bank.)

Argumentative *Objection, the question is argumentative.* Attorneys are not permitted to ask argumentative questions of the witness. An argumentative question is when counsel states a conclusion and then asks the witness to argue with it, often in an attempt to get the witness to change their mind. This is sometimes called "badgering" the witness. The court, at its discretion, may allow limited argumentative questions during cross examination.

Compound Question *Objection, compound question.* A compound question asks two or more separate questions or addresses two or more issues within the framework of a single question. When the witness answers the questions, it is confusing as to which part of the question is being answered and may cause the witness to unknowingly admit to another part of the question. (Q: "Are you still robbing banks?" A: "No".) This single question requesting a single answer implies that the witness robbed banks in the past. The question is a combination of the two questions: (1) Are you currently robbing banks? (2) Have you ever robbed banks?

TEAMWORK

The following are a list of questions that may be asked in the trial of the *People of Any State vs. Robert Craig*. Working in teams of three, determine if each is a valid question or one that is objectionable. If objectionable, be sure to indicate what your objection is. On your team, one student asks the question, one student offers an objection with appropriate reasoning, and the third, playing the role of the judge, makes the ruling.

1. Asked during direct examination by the Defense: "So, Robert, have you always been a good citizen?"

2. Asked by the Prosecution during cross examination: "Michele, when you loaned Robert your car did you tell him your father told you not to do that?"

3. Asked by Defense during cross examination: "Mr. Perkins, why did you overreact and call the police on Robert?"

4. The first question asked by the Prosecution during direct examination: "Officer Miranda, after you took Robert into custody what did you do next?"

5. Asked by the Prosecution during direct examination: "Officer Miranda, what was the weather like on the day in question?"

6. Asked by the Defense during cross examination: "Bart, do you think Robert would have had an accident if he had driven longer?"

Unit 7
Borrowing Money and Paying Bills

Chapters

29 Commercial Paper

30 Negotiability and Negotiation of Commercial Paper

31 Discharge of Commercial Paper and Electronic Fund Transfers

32 Secured and Unsecured Credit Transactions

33 Creditors, Debtors, and Bankruptcy

Forensic Accountant

Forensic accountants are part accountant, part detective. They use their professional accounting skills and investigative skills to analyze financial evidence and assist in criminal investigations involving financial or insurance fraud. They provide support during a court trial and often testify as expert witnesses.

Forensic accountants can work in public practice or be employed by insurance companies, banks, police forces, government agencies, and other organizations.

EMPLOYMENT OUTLOOK

- Employment of forensic accountants is expected to grow faster than average through 2014.

- Increased awareness of financial crimes such as embezzlement, bribery, and securities fraud will increase the demand for forensic accountants.

- Computer technology has made these crimes easier to commit, and they are on the rise. At the same time, new computer software and electronic surveillance technology has made tracking down financial criminals easier.

- As success rates of investigations grow, demand for forensic accountants also will grow.

NEEDED SKILLS AND EDUCATION

- Most accountant positions require at least a bachelor's degree in accounting or a related field.

- Professional recognition through certification or licensure provides a distinct advantage in the job market.

- Many accountants learn about forensic accounting by attending seminars and obtaining designation offered by the Association of Certified Fraud Examiners.

- Accountants should have an aptitude for mathematics and be able to analyze, compare, and interpret facts and figures quickly.

- Forensic accountants must have the curiosity of an investigator and the analytical skills of an accountant. They need organizational skills that will allow them to take complex financial information and make it easy for others to understand.

- They will present their findings in reports and exhibits that may be used in court.

- Verbal communication skills also are needed to serve as an expert witness during a trial.

How you'll spend your day

As a forensic accountant, you'll work to resolve allegations of fraud. Your work will involve obtaining evidence, taking statements, writing reports, testifying to findings, and assisting in the detection and prevention of fraud.

You may be involved in a variety of cases at one time, including criminal investigations, personal injury and insurance claims, business and employee fraud, marriage disputes, and negligence. Each case is unique, but the work follows similar steps.

Once assigned a case, you'll perform an initial investigation to help you plan your next steps. If the case involves employee theft, you'll meet with the owners of the company to determine their objectives and to collect evidence. This may involve locating documents and information, as well as talking with individuals to help prove the theft took place. You'll analyze the information you've collected and calculate the damages suffered by the company as a result of the theft. You'll use computer software and your math and accounting skills to determine your findings. Your final report, along with any graphics that help explain your findings, likely will be used in the courtroom where you may be called to testify.

What about you?

Does the job of forensic accountant interest you? Why or why not? Which aspects of the job would you most enjoy? Which aspects would you least enjoy?

Chapter 29
Commercial Paper

29-1 Basic Types of Commercial Paper
29-2 Specialized Types of Commercial Paper

HOT DEBATE

When your sister returned home from college for Thanksgiving break, she brought her boyfriend with her. The boyfriend was given your room, and you slept in the den. Sunday after the holiday, after they had returned to school, you moved back into your room. Later that evening you looked for your checkbook, but it was not in the usual drawer of your desk. Finally you found it behind the dresser where you normally place it while undressing. Curious, you run through your check register and compare check numbers. It seems as though two are missing. However, you often forget to record them so you do nothing. When your next bank statement arrives, you find that the two checks were written on your account over the Thanksgiving weekend. You call the bank and they retrieve the photocopies of the checks. The signatures on the checks are not even close to yours, yet the bank, in violation of its contract with you, has paid them. When the bank refuses to credit your account, you bring suit against it requesting the court to order the amount of the checks credited to your account.

WHERE DO YOU STAND?

1. List the legal reasons supporting your demand that the bank credit your account for the amount of the checks.
2. State any justification the bank may have for not doing so.

29-1 Basic Types of Commercial Paper

GOALS

- Recognize the need for commercial paper
- Identify the various types of commercial paper

KEY TERMS

commercial paper	check
draft	honor
bill of exchange	dishonor
drawer	stop-payment order
drawee	promissory note
payee	maker
sight draft	collateral note
time draft	mortgage note
acceptance	certificate of deposit

What Is Commercial Paper?

WHAT'S YOUR VERDICT? It is 1789, London. Lord Bennington has just received word that his ne'er-do-well son, Anthony, had once again overspent his allowance and now had several creditors hot on his heels. Although disgusted by the news, Bennington knows he has to appease the creditors before they do in his only son. Anthony had been sent to University in Edinburgh, Scotland, both for the quality of the education and to get him away from the temptations in London. Instead he'd just gotten wilder. Now Bennington has to get enough gold sovereigns to a solicitor in Edinburgh to allow him to pay the creditors directly without Anthony getting his hands on it.

How can Lord Bennington get the necessary money safely to the solicitor?

Throughout history, there always has been a need for a safe way of transferring things of value without exposing them to loss. Gold, silver, jewels, and currency all were and are invitations to thieves to come and help themselves. As a consequence, commercial paper and the banking system were created. A person could deposit money in a banking institution at one location and then order it paid to another by an affiliated institution in another location. This was done by a written instrument validated by the signature of the depositor.

LAW BRIEF

You may be familiar with the horrible legends of debtor's prisons in England and the United States. These were places of indefinite imprisonment where those unable to meet their debts often wasted away their lives. Charles Dickens' father almost died in a debtor's prison in England. This gave Dickens the idea for several of his works centered on poverty in England in the early 1800s. Now there are serious articles and appeals to bring debtor's prisons back. In Canada, several protestors against the incarceration of those behind on their support checks suggest they already are in existence. One among many cases involved a Toronto man, a self-employed consultant. He went to a default hearing for failure to make his support payments with his financial records but without a lawyer. He intended to show the judge how the economic downturn made it impossible to meet the level of payments that had been set for him when he was riding high. The judge arrested him on the spot and hauled him off for a 90-day stretch. The consultant says it was an odd experience. He was a non-convict in a prison, and, as a result of not being convicted of anything, he was not afforded the same rights as a convict.

In *What's Your Verdict?* Lord Bennington would simply write an order to his bank in London to pay to the solicitor the appropriate number of gold sovereigns. He would sign and seal the order, and then send it by messenger to the solicitor in that faraway city. The solicitor would take it to his bank and collect the amount of gold sovereigns necessary to keep the son out of debtor's prison. In return the solicitor would, by signing the written order, transfer the right to collect the sovereigns to his bank. The Edinburgh bank would then collect the amount of the order from the London bank in which Lord Bennington had an account.

Today, such unconditional written orders or promises to pay money are collectively defined as **commercial paper**. Most of the laws governing the legitimacy and use of commercial paper are in the Uniform Commercial Code (UCC). However, other laws are important to commercial paper as well. For example, commercial paper is not valid if used in illegal transactions, such as gambling, as defined in criminal codes.

In the new revision of the UCC, the term *negotiable instrument* is used in place of *commercial paper*. However, due to these revisions not being widely adopted by the states and the possibility of confusion with other negotiable instruments, such as documents of title and stocks and bonds, we shall mainly use the term commercial paper in this text.

The check is the most common form of commercial paper. As implied above, like other forms of commercial paper, it was developed centuries ago to serve as a relatively safe substitute for money. In those times, a bank could tell if an order was authentic by comparing the signature on the order with the depositor's signature that it had on file. The bank then complied with the order because, once an individual had deposited the currency—gold or silver—the bank became the depositor's debtor. Consequently, if the depositor appeared and demanded the gold or silver, the bank had to give it back.

This is still true today. Banks are the debtors of their depositors. They compete with one another to borrow funds from their depositors and then lend what they have borrowed to others. Checks are called *demand instruments* because they enable depositors, whenever they desire, to withdraw their money or have it paid in accordance with their order.

CHECKPOINT Why are banks debtors of their checking account depositors?

In the depositor-bank relationship with regard to checking accounts, who is the debtor and who is the creditor?

Types of Commercial Paper

WHAT'S YOUR VERDICT? In order to take a two week pre-Christmas vacation in the Florida Keys, John borrowed money from his friend, Patrick. In exchange, John gave Patrick an IOU for that amount. He signed the IOU and dated it.

Is the IOU commercial paper?

Commercial paper can be grouped into two categories. The first consists of unconditional orders to pay money. The second category is composed of unconditional promises to pay money.

"Unconditional," as used to define commercial paper, means that the legal effectiveness of the order or promise does not depend on any other event. Accordingly, an instrument that reads in part "Pay to the order of Sam after he delivers the bike to me" would not be commercial paper because its enforceability is conditional upon delivery of the bike.

Unlike unconditional orders or promises to pay a sum of money, an IOU (such as the one John gave to Patrick in *What's Your Verdict?*) only acknowledges the debt. The law holds that such an acknowledgment is far short of a promise or order to repay. Therefore, an IOU is not enforceable as commercial paper.

Of the four main types of commercial paper, two—the draft and the check—are unconditional orders to pay money. The other two—the promissory note and the certificate of deposit—are unconditional promises to pay money. These four main types are discussed in the following sections.

Drafts

A **draft** or **bill of exchange** is an unconditional written order by one person that directs another person to pay money to a third. The person directed to pay may be a natural person or an artificial "legal" person, such as a corporation.

If it is not necessary to specify that a particular person receive the money, the order may be made payable to "cash" or to "bearer." Then the person in legal possession of the order may collect on it. However, the order must be either effective upon demand or at a definite date, such as the "thirty days after sight" as shown in the illustration.

The person who executes or "draws" the draft and orders payment to be made is the **drawer**. The **drawee** is the party ordered to pay the draft. The **payee** is the party to whom commercial paper is made payable. The drawee is usually the debtor of the drawer. Refer to In This Case where Jay Minton is the drawer, Margaret Sanford is the drawee, and Downtown Audio is the payee.

Drafts are sometimes classified in terms of the time of payment. A draft may be payable "at sight" (also termed being payable "on demand"). This is called a **sight draft**. The drawee on a sight draft is expected to pay immediately upon the draft being presented for payment.

DRAFT

$ *500.00*   Nashville, Tennessee *January 20* 20 *--*

Thirty days after sight

To: Margaret Sanford
1339 Salvage Ave.
Augusta, Georgia 30913

Payee — Pay to the Order of *Downtown Audio*

Five hundred and $\frac{no}{100}$ ———— Dollars

For Classroom Use Only

Accepted January 21, 20--
Drawee — *Margaret H. Sanford* } *Jay A Minton*

Drawer

If a draft is payable on a set date, at the end of a specified period after sight, or at the end of a specified period after the date of the draft, it is a **time draft**. Minton's draft in the example is a time draft. When a time draft is payable a number of days or months after sight, it must be presented to the drawee for acceptance in order to start the running of the specified time.

Acceptance is the drawee's promise to pay the draft when due. Such a promise usually is evidenced by the signature of the acceptor on the face of the instrument along with words indicating the acceptance. When a draft states it is

---

IN THIS CASE Margaret Sanford bought a used amplifier for her electric guitar from Jay Minton for $600. She paid Minton $100 down and promised to pay the remaining $500 by her next payday. A few days after the sale, Minton bought a state-of-the-art, low-distortion speaker system for $750 at a clearance sale at Downtown Audio. As partial payment to Downtown Audio, Minton drew a draft (see the illustration above) on the $500 Sanford owed him. To be sure Sanford had enough time to get the money, Minton made the draft payable to the order of Downtown Audio thirty days after sight. Upon receiving the draft, Downtown immediately presented it to Sanford who indicated her willingness to pay in 30 days by writing the date and her signature on the front of the paper along with the word "accepted."

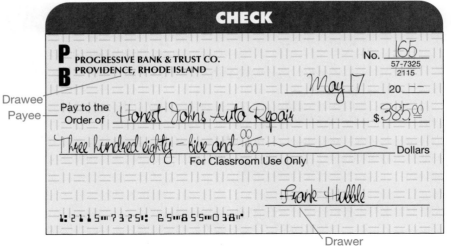

CHECK

Drawee
Payee

PROGRESSIVE BANK & TRUST CO.
PROVIDENCE, RHODE ISLAND

No. 165
57-7325
2115

May 17 20

Pay to the
Order of Honest John's Auto Repair $385.00

Three hundred eighty - five and 00/100 _____ Dollars

For Classroom Use Only

Frank Hubble

Drawer

1:2115 7325: 65 855 038

payable a number of days or months "after date," the time starts running immediately from the date of the draft.

Checks

A **check** is a type of draft by which a bank depositor orders the bank to pay money, usually to a third party (see the illustration above). Checks usually are written on special forms that are magnetically encoded to simplify check processing for the banking system. However, checks may be written on blank paper, on forms provided by the depositor, on rawhide, or on other materials and still be legally effective. The drawee, though, must always be a bank for the instrument to qualify as a check.

HONOR AND DISHONOR The bank, according to the contract between it and the depositor, agrees to **honor** (pay when due) each check as long as sufficient funds remain in the depositor's account. The bank owes that duty as a debtor of the depositor in return for being able to use the depositor's funds until the depositor demands their return. This means that the bank must retain a sizable percentage of the deposited funds so that it can pay properly drawn checks when presented. The remainder of the deposited funds is loaned at interest or invested to pay for the bank's operations and to return a profit to the bank's owners.

A person who deliberately issues a check knowing that there are insufficient funds in the account to pay the check when it is presented at the drawee bank is guilty of a crime. The bank will **dishonor** (refuse to pay when due) the instrument and the payee or current owner of the check will not get money for it from that source.

A Question of ETHICS

John Effriham is out of money. However, he will be paid in two days. John knows that he can cash a personal check with his employer at any time. He also has figured out that if he folds the check he's about to write many times and wets the crease over the electronic coding, the automatic check-routing machines will kick it out to be handled manually. Manual handling will cause at least another day's delay before the check gets to his bank. Therefore, he could cash a check late today and, in effect, use his employer's money to live on until payday. Is this ethical? Would anyone be injured by John's action? Is it illegal?

In addition, if a check is issued to pay a debt, the payoff is not effective until the check is presented to and honored by the drawee bank.

STOP-PAYMENT ORDERS When a check has been lost or stolen, the drawer should direct the bank not to pay it. Such an instruction is called a **stop-payment order**. If the drawee bank still pays the check, the bank must re-credit the account. The bank, not the depositor, must bear any loss. Oral stop-payment orders are good for only two weeks unless they are confirmed in writing. Written stop-payment orders are good for six months, but lapse at the end of that time unless renewed.

PRECAUTIONS AND CARE Care must be taken to prevent checks from being altered. When writing a check, do not leave space for someone to insert figures and words that would change the amount of the instrument. Certainly, never sign a blank check. Do not give anything of value in return for a check that appears to have been altered in any manner. In addition, be wary of a check that may have been issued in connection with illegal activities, for example, gambling. Courts usually consider such instruments void.

What is one precaution you can take to make sure that another party does not alter a check you have written?

© GETTY IMAGES/PHOTODISC

Promissory Notes

A **promissory note** is an unconditional written promise by a person or persons to pay money according to the payee's order or to pay money to the bearer of the instrument. The payment may have to be made on demand or at a definite time according to the stated terms on the face of the note (see the illustration on this page). The person who executes a promissory note is the **maker**. If two or more persons execute the note, they are termed "co-makers" and also may be liable for payment depending on the wording of the instrument.

Many financial institutions will not lend money unless some personal or real property is offered as security by the would-be borrower.

The security ensures that the loan will be paid when due. If the debtor fails to pay, the creditor can force the sale of the property and then take the proceeds of that sale to cover the amount the debtor owes. When personal property is offered as security and so indicated on the face of the note, the paper is a **collateral note**. When real property is the security for payment, the paper is a **mortgage note**.

Certificates of Deposit

A **certificate of deposit** is an instrument bearing a bank's written acknowledgment of the receipt of money, together with an unconditional promise to repay it at a definite future time (see the

---

PROMISSORY NOTE

$ *3,000.⁰⁰* Las Vegas, Nevada *December 20* 20 _ _

Sixty days _____ after date *I* promise to pay to

Payee —

the order of *First National Bank*

Three thousand and ⁿᵒ∕₁₀₀ _____ Dollars

For Classroom Use Only

Payable at *First National Bank, Building, LasVegas, Nevada*

with interest at *9* % a year.

No. *6* Due *February 18, 20--* *Eric Gordon*

Maker

illustration on this page). A certificate of deposit often is called a CD.

Federal law prohibits banks from paying out CDs and other long-term deposits before maturity without a penalty to the depositor. Usually the penalty is a sharp reduction in the amount of interest payable on the funds. This inhibits depositors from withdrawing funds before maturity and permits the banks to lend the funds to others on a long-term basis. Consequently, interest rates on CDs usually are significantly higher than the rates on savings or checking accounts (from which the depositor is far more likely to withdraw funds).

CERTIFICATE OF DEPOSIT

THE BANK OF LEWIS AND CLARK
St. Louis, Missouri   30431

March 15   20 __

Payee

Kimberly H. Crowson   has deposited in this bank

Ten thousand and no/100 ————————— Dollars $ 10,000.00

For Classroom Use Only

and this sum will be repaid to said depositor or order one year from date with interest at seven (7) percent per year.

THE BANK OF LEWIS AND CLARK

CERTIFICATE OF DEPOSIT   By: M.B. Burton, cashier

Maker

CHECKPOINT What is the difference between a check and a draft?

29-1 Assessment

THINK ABOUT LEGAL CONCEPTS

1. Unconditional written orders or promises to pay money are collectively known as (a) commercial promises (b) IOUs (c) ICIs (Intentional Credit Instruments) (d) none of the above

2. The Uniform Commercial Code is the exclusive source of the laws governing the use of commercial paper. **True or False?**

3. With checking accounts, banks are the creditors of their depositors. **True or False?**

4. A note secured by land is a mortgage note. **True or False?**

5. An oral stop payment order is only good for _____ days.

6. An instrument bearing a bank's written acknowledgment of the receipt of money, together with an unconditional promise to repay it at a definite future time, is a(n) (a) check (b) note (c) CD (d) promissory note

THINK CRITICALLY ABOUT EVIDENCE

Study the situation, answer the questions, and then prepare arguments to support your answers.

7. Hubble paid Honest Horace's Auto Repair $385 by check for the repair of his car's transmission. When the job proved defective, Hubble called the bank on his cell phone and ordered it to stop payment on the check. Three weeks later, however, the bank honored the check and paid Honest Horace's the $385 out of Hubble's account. Did the bank make a mistake?

8. Burger was the owner and president of a small surfboard manufacturing company. She also owned the land and building the company occupied. When she needed to raise cash to finance a major expansion, her financial advisers

told her that the best way to do so was by using the building and land as a source of funds. How could Burger do this?

9. Carl's son, Jared, wanted a new sports car. He convinced Carl to sign a promissory note in favor of the car dealership for the $47,000 purchase price. Jared also signed the note. Four months later, Jared stopped making payments and drove the car to Mexico and sold it. Jared has taken up permanent residence in Juarez, Mexico. Is Carl nonetheless obligated to pay off the balance of the note?

29-2 Specialized Types of Commercial Paper

GOALS

- Recognize the various specialized types of commercial paper
- Compare the functions of the specialized types of commercial paper

KEY TERMS

certified check
teller's check
cashier's check
money order
traveler's check

Specialized Types of Commercial Paper

WHAT'S YOUR VERDICT?

Dr. Pugh, of Santa Ana, California, needed expensive drugs to treat a patient with a rare nerve disease. Drugtek, the supplier of the drug, was a New York corporation. It would not ship COD, extend credit, or accept personal checks from customers outside the state.

What other means of payment could Dr. Pugh use to satisfy Drugtek?

The four types of commercial paper described in the previous lesson are the most frequently used. However, certain forms of commercial paper are available to meet specialized needs. Typically, these forms provide for an extremely safe, non-cash means of transfer of monetary value. Specialized forms that meet this need include those described in the following sections.

Certified Checks

A person offered another's personal check as payment may fear the bank will not honor the check because of insufficient funds in the drawer's account. However, if the bank already has agreed to pay the check, only if the bank fails will the payee or current owner of the check not receive the money due.

A personal check that has been accepted by a bank before payment is a **certified check**. At the time of certification, the bank draws funds from the depositor's account and sets them aside in a special account in order to pay the check when it is presented. In addition, the bank marks the front of the check with either the word "accepted" or "certified," along with the date and an authorized signature of the bank. In *What's Your Verdict?* Dr. Pugh could use a certified check if Drugtek will accept it.

Teller's Check

A draft drawn by a bank on funds that it has on deposit at another bank is a **teller's check**. Individuals and business firms may request their local bank to draft on its account with a bank near the third-party payee when a significant transaction is involved. A teller's check is another possibility open to Dr. Pugh.

Cashier's Check

A check that a bank draws on itself is a **cashier's check** (see the illustration below; note that the "drawer" is the First State Security Bank as represented by Assistant Manager Martha C. Todd).

CASHIER'S CHECK

First State Security Bank
Santa Ana, CA 92703

1203

Drawee

Pay to the Order of _Drugtek_

December 15 20 --

$ 1,375.50

Payee

Thirteen hundred and seventy-five and 50/100 ———— Dollars

For Classroom Use Only

CASHIER'S CHECK

⑆08 20⑈00 13⑇

Martha C. Todd

as ASSISTANT MANAGER of First State Security Bank

Drawer

Banks use such checks to pay their own obligations. Persons who wish to pay others but who do not have checking accounts or find it impractical to use their personal checks also may purchase them from a bank. Because it is relatively risk-free (only the bank may stop payment on the check), a payee usually is willing to take such a check. This could be the most appropriate type of check for Dr. Pugh.

Money Orders

Persons who do not have checking accounts often use money orders. A **money order** is a draft issued by a post office, bank, express company, or telegraph company for use in paying or transferring funds for the purchaser. Dr. Pugh also could use a money order.

Traveler's Checks

Travelers are rightfully wary of carrying a lot of cash. Retailers and hotelkeepers worldwide are understandably reluctant to take checks from people from other regions and other countries. The traveler's check was devised to overcome these problems and meet the needs of both groups. A **traveler's check** is a draft drawn by a well-known financial institution on itself or its agent.

The buyer signs the traveler's checks when purchased. Later, when used to pay for a purchase, the traveler writes in the name of the payee and then signs again, in the presence of the payee. The payee then deposits and collects the traveler's check in the same manner as other checks. The payee's ability to compare the two signatures, coupled with the payment guarantee and the reputation of the financial institution that issued the instrument, usually reduces the risk to the point where businesses worldwide accept traveler's checks.

CHECKPOINT What is the difference between a certified check and a cashier's check?

© PHOTODISC/GETTY IMAGES

What do you think is the benefit of paying for purchases with traveler's checks rather than cash while traveling?

CyberLAW

Services are now available online to allow the sending of money orders via the Internet. These services stem from the need to be able to eliminate fraud and forgeries in paying for purchases made during cyber auctions. Online auction houses now offer the successful bidder the alternative of sending a money order. This is done by going to the auction house's web site and entering the auction details and payment information. The amount is debited against whatever credit or debit card is on file for the bidder. The auction house will then send payment to the seller by mailing a Western Union® brand money order. It's quick, efficient, and the seller quickly has cash in hand as a result.

THINK ABOUT IT

Can you think of other transactions that this technique might facilitate?

29-2 Assessment

school.cengage.com/blaw/lawxtra

THINK ABOUT LEGAL CONCEPTS

1. A check that a bank draws on itself is termed a certified check. **True or False?**

2. Only the drawer of a cashier's check can stop payment on it. **True or False?**

3. The type of check that requires the owner to sign twice on its face is a (a) cashier's check (b) certified check (c) traveler's check

4. When a bank accepts liability on a personal check before it is presented for payment, the check is said to be certified. **True or False?**

5. A (n) _?_ is a draft drawn by a bank on favorable monetary balances it has in other banks.

6. Documentary letters of credit are typically used in international sales of goods. **True or False?**

THINK CRITICALLY ABOUT EVIDENCE

Study the situation, answer the questions, and then prepare arguments to support your answers.

7. Garrett owes Nosmada $250. Nosmada is driving through a subdivision one day when he spots a garage sale. At the sale, a nearly new titanium bicycle is marked for sale at a price that is one-fifth of its retail. Unfortunately, the price is still $200 more than Nosmada has. Luckily, the seller knows commercial paper law and the creditworthiness of Garrett. As a consequence, Nosmada writes out an order to Garrett to pay the seller the $200 needed to close the deal. What form of commercial paper has Nosmada utilized? Who are the drawer, drawee, and payee?

8. Howard ordered a new pair of running shoes from a discount seller via an 800 number. He paid by cashier's check. When he finds out that his new shoes are defective, he calls the bank to stop payment on the check. Can he stop payment? Who is liable on the instrument?

9. Henrietta has just moved to New York City. She doesn't have a bank account as yet and does not want to carry around much cash. She does have a check made payable to her by a car dealership to which she sold her car upon arriving in New York. What could she do with the check to make sure it will be honored when she cashes it?

10. Several months pass. Henrietta has become adjusted to the big city and wants to return home to Wisconsin to visit. She does not want to carry cash with her. What kind of commercial paper would you recommend that she use to carry her funds with her? It must be usable to pay many small amounts and be trusted by merchants in Wisconsin.

29-2 Specialized Types of Commercial Paper **539**

CONCEPTS IN BRIEF

29-1 Basic Types of Commercial Paper

1. Commercial paper was developed centuries ago to serve as a relatively safe substitute for money.

2. A promissory note is an unconditional written promise by a person or persons to pay money according to the payee's order or to pay money to the bearer of the instrument.

3. A certificate of deposit is an instrument bearing a bank's written acknowledgment of the receipt of money, together with an unconditional promise to repay it at a definite future time.

4. A draft or bill of exchange is an unconditional written order by one person that directs another person to pay money to a third.

5. A check is a type of draft by which a bank depositor orders the bank to pay money, usually to a third party.

29-2 Specialized Types of Commercial Paper

6. Specialized forms of commercial paper are available to provide for an extremely safe, non-cash means of transfer of monetary value.

7. A personal check, the liability on which has been accepted by a bank before payment, is a certified check.

8. A check that a bank draws on itself is a cashier's check.

9. A draft drawn by a bank on funds that it has on deposit at another bank is a teller's check.

10. A money order is a draft issued by a post office, bank, express company, or telegraph company for use in paying or transferring funds for the purchaser.

11. A traveler's check is a draft drawn by a well-known financial institution on itself or its agent that has attributes created to offer overwhelming assurance that it is a legitimate instrument.

YOUR LEGAL VOCABULARY

Match each statement with the term that it best defines. Some terms may not be used.

1. Unconditional written promise or order to pay money

2. Person to whom commercial paper is made payable

3. Drawee's promise to pay the obligee of a draft when the instrument is due

4. Draft written on bank by depositor

5. To pay a check when due

6. Person who executes a promissory note

7. Check drawn by bank on itself

8. Draft drawn by a bank on funds it has on deposit with another bank

9. Written instrument acknowledging a bank's receipt of money and promising to repay it at a definite future time

10. Draft issued by a post office, bank, or express company for use in transferring funds for the draft's purchaser

11. An unconditional written promise by a person or persons to pay money according to the payee's order or to pay money to the bearer of the instrument

a. acceptance
b. bill of exchange
c. cashier's check
d. certificate of deposit
e. certified check
f. check
g. collateral note
h. commercial paper
i. dishonor
j. draft
k. drawee
l. drawer
m. honor
n. maker
o. money order
p. mortgage note
q. payee
r. promissory note
s. sight draft
t. stop-payment order
u. teller's check
v. time draft
w. traveler's check

REVIEW LEGAL CONCEPTS

12. Why was commercial paper created?

13. Could you cash a check made out to you but written on an ordinary piece of paper?

14. What is the difference between a check and a draft?

15. Would a check or other piece of commercial paper be legally effective if written in pencil?

16. What is the purpose of having the purchaser sign the traveler's checks when buying them?

WRITE ABOUT LEGAL CONCEPTS

17. If a good customer comes into a bank and wants to stop payment on a cashier's check she had purchased and had the bank issue, how could the bank protect itself in doing so?

18. Would you rather hold a promissory note from a local retailer or a certificate of deposit from a local bank?

19. **HOT DEBATE** Write a persuasive opening statement that emphasizes the legal, ethical, and economic points in favor of your petition. Or, write a persuasive opening statement for the bank that encompasses the economic and legal reasons why the loss should fall on the depositor in this situation.

MAKE ACADEMIC CONNECTIONS

20. **ECONOMICS** Survey the Federal Reserve Board explanations, charts, and aggregate data to form an opinion as to how important commercial paper is to the U.S. economy. Compose a paragraph summarizing your findings and then read your paragraph to the class.

THINK CRITICALLY ABOUT EVIDENCE

Study the situation, answer the questions, and then prepare arguments to support your answers.

21. Joseph McReynolds gave the following signed instrument to Helen Harrison after borrowing $5,000 from her: "IOU Helen Harrison $5,000." It was dated and signed by McReynolds. Is the instrument commercial paper?

22. Chen wanted to order skis that she had seen advertised in a national magazine. The advertisement expressly said, "Do not send cash or personal checks. No COD orders accepted." How could Chen pay?

23. Thruster owns ID Data, Inc., a small company that manufactures facial recognition kits. The pocket size kits feature a button camera connected to a PDA. The camera automatically takes the facial measurements of approaching individuals, compares it to a data base on the PDA, and provides information to the wearer as to identity and other relevant material. Police departments, politicians, and the Department of Defense have ordered multiple units. Now Thruster wants to expand his operations. What types of promissory notes will be useful when:

    a. ID Data borrows $150,000 out of the $200,000 needed to pay for a shipment of integrated circuit chips for the PDAs and uses the chips as security for payment?

    b. ID Data borrows $650,000 out of the $1,000,000 needed to buy a building for a new assembly line and uses the real property as security for payment?

24. You are working as a checkout clerk at Surprise Discount, Inc., a local department store. Sarah Johnson, an elderly lady, comes through your line with what she describes as "the perfect gift for my great-grandson." She says that she never expected to find it for under $200 much less the $110 that it is marked at. She writes out a check for the purchase. After she has left the store, you realize that she has written the check for $17.50 rather than the $117.50 purchase price plus tax. However, there is plenty of room to alter the amount to the correct figure. Should you do so?

25. While in Shreveport, Louisiana, Claypool wanted to play poker for money stakes at the Crystal Bar. He persuaded Parker to stand good (pay) for any losses he might have. Before the night was over, Claypool's losses amounted to $6,000. Afterwards, Claypool gave Parker a promissory note for $10,473.14 to cover the $6,000 in gambling losses and a legitimate previous loan. When the note came due, Claypool refused to pay. Parker sued, and Claypool defended on the grounds that the note was illegal and void, because it originated in a gambling debt. Will Parker recover? (*Parker v. Claypool*, 78 So. 2d 124)

26. Purchasers of land developed by Holiday Intervals, Inc., signed writings in which they promised to pay a certain sum of money at a definite time in the future. However, according to the signed instruments, the payments were due only if specified structures were built in the complex within two years of the signings. Some of these instruments were labeled "promissory note." Were any of the writings commercial paper? (*In re Holiday Intervals, Inc.*, 94 Bankr. 594)

27. Gunn contracted to sell Tak, a broker from Hong Kong, 60,000 metric tons of UREA, a fertilizer, at $400 a ton. In connection with this $24 million sale, Gunn entered into another contract agreeing to pay Tak a commission for all Tak's sales of the fertilizer. After 10,000 tons of UREA had been sold, paid for, and delivered, Gunn bought and delivered to Tak a cashier's check from the Empire Bank of Springfield for $150,000 payable to Tak's order. Shortly after, Gunn learned that the balance of the order for the remaining 50,000 tons of UREA had been canceled by Tak. Consequently, Gunn went to court and obtained an injunction from the court to the bank to stop payment on the cashier's check. Shortly after the court acted, the cashier's check was transferred by Tak to Lai, who now claims the right to collect the face amount. Should the court order the bank to honor the stop-payment order, or must the bank pay Lai the face amount of the check? (*Lai v. Powell*, Judge, 536 S.W.2d 14)

28. In a Missouri circuit court, Kleen was convicted of issuing an insufficient funds check. He appealed, pointing out that he had merely signed a blank check form in Missouri and then given the form to his truck driver. The truck driver carried the signed blank check form to Memphis, Tennessee, where someone at the Herring Sales Company filled in the company name as the payee and also filled in the amount. Herring kept the check in return for a truckload of meal that was transported by Kleen's truck and driver back to Kleen's business in Nevada, Missouri. Kleen therefore contended that even though the check was drawn on the Citizen's Bank of Nevada, the alleged criminal act occurred in Tennessee, where the signed blank form was made a check and was issued. Consequently, Missouri had no jurisdiction, and his conviction should be overturned. You decide. (*State v. Kleen,* 491 S.W.2d 2)

29. General Motors Acceptance Corporation (GMAC) financed the purchase of a Jeep by Azevedo. It then held the positon of lienholder on the vehicle and was noted as such on the vehicle's title and car insurance policy. The policy was taken out by Azevedo but listed GMAC as the beneficiary. Therefore, if the vehicle was involved in an accident and damaged, the insurance company, Abington Casualty, was to pay GMAC the value of the loss. Later, after the Jeep was damaged in an accident, Azevedo submitted a claim on the policy. After suitable appraisals of the loss, Abington issued a check with joint payees, Azevedo and GMAC. Abington then delivered the check to Azevedo who deposited it in his bank with his indorsement but without GMAC's. The bank paid on the check in full to Azevedo even without the indorsement. GMAC never received the benefit of the funds. Now it has brought suit against Abington to recover for its loss. Is GMAC entitled to the insurance money? (*General Motors Acceptance Corporation v. Abington Casualty Insurance Co.,* 602 N.E.2d 1085)

Case For Legal Thinking

MEANS V. CLARDY
735 S.W. 2D 6

BACKGROUND Rick Means and Fred Barry owned an apartment building which they wished to sell. On July 18, 1980, they entered into a contract for deed with respondents, Joan and Gary Doerhoff. The agreement provided that the Doerhoffs would receive the apartment building and would give in exchange 6.81 acres of land in Maries County, Missouri, and a note purportedly executed almost a year earlier by Nancy Clardy, respondent Bruce Clardy's mother. At the time Means and Barry took the note in partial payment for the apartment building a required $5,000 payment had been made but several of the monthly installments were in arrears. Nonetheless the note's balance had been reduced to approximately $22,000 from its original $31,000. Curiously, the monthly payments according to the terms of the note had been and were to be in cabinets made in the Clardy cabinet shop with value "figured at the prevailing builders price for Jefferson City . . . until October 12, 1981, at which time the entire balance thereof is due and payable in cash . . ." When the note was not paid by Oct. 12, Means and Barry brought this lawsuit to collect the $22,000 still due plus interest and charges.

During the lower court trial, Nancy Clardy testified that she did not sign either the note or the bill of sale accompanying it. She alleged that her son, Bruce, had done so and had drawn $5,000 from a "remodeling" fund to make the initial payment on the note thereafter making payments in cabinets. Bruce took the Fifth Amendment (protection against self-incrimination) when asked about this at the trial.

Nancy Clardy's signature on the documents was notarized by John Gross. Gross later testified that Nancy Clardy had not signed any documents in his presence but that as a favor to Bruce he notarized them after Bruce told him that Nancy Clardy had signed them.

Under oath, Nancy Clardy stated that her son, Bruce, told her that he had signed her name to the documents. She did not remember exactly when he told her this. Mrs. Clardy testified that she did not contact Mr. Doerhoff or plaintiffs when she learned that Mr. Clardy had signed her name. She also testified that she had learned, after the fact, that Bruce Clardy used $5,000 from a remodeling fund in order to pay the initial $5,000 due on the note. Mrs. Clardy had authorized Mr. Clardy to draw upon the fund to remodel an investment property which she owned. She did not authorize him to use the money to pay the note for the cabinet shop.

The trial court held that Bruce Clardy had indeed signed the note for both parties. As a consequence, the trial court held that Nancy Clardy was not liable. Means and Barry then brought this appeal.

REASONING Means and Barry ask that the decision of the lower court be overturned and they be allowed to recover from Nancy Clardy because she had ratified her signature on the commercial paper by doing nothing to correct the situation. Means and Barry also ask that they be allowed to collect against the Doerhoffs as well because, on commercial paper, the UCC holds that "(2) Any person who transfers an instrument and receives consideration warrants to his transferee . . . that (b) all signatures are genuine or authorized." Therefore the Doerhoffs had breached the warranty and Means and Barry should be able to collect for the loss they suffered as a consequence.

CONCLUSION The appellate court ruled that Nancy Clardy did not ratify her signature and was not liable on the instrument. The court also determined that the note was not commercial paper and that, therefore, the UCC section upon which Means and Barry relied in their appeal did not apply. As a consequence they could not collect.

PRACTICE JUDGING

1. Do you agree with the court's conclusion that Nancy Clardy did not ratify the note? Why or why not?

2. Why did the court determine that the note was not commercial paper and that, consequently, Means and Barry could not recover?

3. Could Means and Barry recover on any other theory?

Chapter 30
Negotiability and Negotiation of Commercial Paper

30-1 Requirements of Negotiability

30-2 Proper Indorsement and Negotiation

HOT DEBATE

Souquer is president of his own company, SpringGen. Earlier this morning his secretary, Elizabeth, placed a stack of checks to pay the monthly bills on his desk for his signature. As he glanced through them he spotted a $5,000 check for electronic items to his old friend Bill Hutton's company. Later that week, he ran into Bill who mentioned that he hadn't sold SpringGen anything in ages and who expressed concern that his company had done something wrong. Souquer investigated and found that, over the last year and a half, Elizabeth had him sign more than $125,000 in checks made out to suppliers for goods they didn't provide. She then took the checks, forged a blank indorsement with the payee's signature and deposited them in her account to be used to cover gambling debts. Subsequent to the discovery, the company attorney sues both Elizabeth and the bank that cashed the checks against the company account over her forgeries. It is discovered that Elizabeth has few assets. She just sold her home and gambled away those proceeds as well.

WHERE DO YOU STAND?

1. From an ethical perspective, who besides Elizabeth is at fault for SpringGen's losses?
2. What legal right does SpringGen have to seek compensation for the losses from the bank?

30-1 Requirements of Negotiability

GOALS

- Explain the importance of negotiability
- Distinguish negotiable from non-negotiable instruments

KEY TERMS

negotiable
negotiable instrument
negotiation
antedated
postdated
money
acceleration clause

payable on demand
payable at a definite time
bearer paper
bearer
order paper

The Importance of Negotiation

WHAT'S YOUR VERDICT? Dwaynette was preparing to open her new business, a hardware store. However, in talking with her accountant, Dwaynette indicated that she wanted to do business on a cash-only basis because taking checks or promissory notes is too risky.

Is this advisable?

If commercial paper is to be accepted instead of cash, the person or business firm receiving it must be assured that there is a very high probability that the instrument will be paid. The UCC provides that assurance. It does so by empowering a qualified owner of commercial paper to overcome many of the legal defenses the person who is obligated to pay the instrument might raise to keep from paying.

To enable the owner to overcome most common defenses and collect on commercial paper, the instrument bearing the promise or order to pay money must be negotiable. **Negotiable** means that it must be in writing, be signed by the maker or drawer, contain an unconditional promise or order payable in a sum certain, be payable on demand or at a definite time, and be payable to the bearer or to someone's order. (These requirements are prescribed by statute and are discussed in the following

section.) An instrument must be negotiable in order to be classified as commercial paper. As mentioned in Chapter 29, another term generally referring to commercial paper is **negotiable instrument**. This latter term also is used to refer to various types of stocks, bonds, and documents of title.

In addition, the parties trying to secure the maximum number of rights to enable collection on pieces of commercial paper they hold must acquire the subject instruments in the correct manner. **Negotiation** means the proper transfer of a negotiable instrument so that the transferee acquires the rights to overcome many of the defenses that an obligor might raise to collection. If an instrument is not negotiated, it is considered to have been only assigned. In the case of assignment, the parties' rights are governed by contract law rather than the law of negotiable instruments. This means in most cases that the owner of commercial paper that has been

Why is it in this pharmacy's best interest to accept commercial paper from customers?

© GETTY IMAGES/PHOTODISC

transferred to the owner by assignment is subject to many if not all of the defenses the obligor on the paper can raise against being forced to pay. Therefore, a person would prefer to hold a negotiable instrument than an assigned instrument because the chances of collection are far greater.

In *What's Your Verdict?* the accountant would probably advise Dwaynette that significant protection would be afforded her by the UCC if she were to take properly transferred negotiable instruments. Such protection would drastically reduce the risk of not being able to collect. Refusing to accept commercial paper would probably mean losing customers. If they were denied the safety and convenience of using checks and notes in her store, they might not shop there at all.

CHECKPOINT Why would you prefer to hold a negotiable instrument rather than an assigned instrument?

What Makes an Instrument Negotiable?

WHAT'S YOUR VERDICT? As mayor of his small town, a position that paid $400 per year, Adamson also had to hold down a normal job. Thus he often could not be present to sign checks when needed. As a consequence, he had a signature stamp made up and gave it to the town clerk to be used at her discretion. The signature stamp read "by John Adamson, Mayor."

Were the checks signed in such a manner legal?

According to the UCC, whether or not an instrument is negotiable is determined by what appears on its face at the time it is issued. This does not mean that the instrument must state that something of value has been exchanged for the paper. However, doing so will not defeat negotiability.

Likewise, the ability to negotiate (but not the ability to collect on) an instrument is not affected by the fact that it is **antedated** (dated earlier than the date of issuance), **postdated** (dated later than the date of issuance), or even undated. If a date is not present, any owner who has possession and who knows the date on which the paper was issued may enter it.

Specifically, in order to be negotiable according to the UCC requirements, an instrument must

1. be in writing and be signed by the maker or drawer
2. contain an unconditional promise or order to pay
3. be payable in a sum certain in money
4. be payable on demand or at a definite time
5. be payable to the bearer or to someone's order

IN THIS CASE St. Benet received a check in the mail for payment of a debt. When she went to cash the instrument she noticed that the drawer had not entered a date on it. St. Benet, knowing the check was issued a week previous, wrote that date on the instrument and cashed it. Her action did not defeat the negotiability of the instrument.

In Writing and Signed by the Maker or Drawer

To be negotiable, commercial paper must be in writing and signed by the maker or drawer with the intent that it create a legal obligation. Because of the writing, commercial paper is subject to the parol evidence rule when its terms are challenged at law. (Under the parol evidence rule, oral testimony cannot be used to contradict the terms in a complete, final, written instrument.) However, oral evidence may be used to show fraud, incompleteness, forgeries, or illegalities, or to clarify ambiguities.

The writing may consist of a printed form with the terms typed or written in. Or, the paper may be totally handwritten. The law is very flexible in this regard. An ink pen, a typewriter, even a pencil may be used, although a pencil is not recommended because it invites unauthorized alteration. Any medium is satisfactory as a writing surface as long as the result is recognizable as a writing.

If there are conflicting terms within the writing, those written in by hand prevail over both typewritten and printed form terms. Similarly, typewritten terms prevail over printed form terms. Further, an amount expressed in words prevails over an amount expressed in figures.

As far as the signature is concerned, the form it takes does not alter its legal effectiveness as long as the writer placed it there with the intent to authenticate the instrument. For example, a legally effective signature may be made with a rubber stamp, as in *What's Your Verdict?*

A trade or assumed name may be used in signing if it is intended as one's signature. Also, one person may legitimately sign another person's name if authorized to do so as an agent. A manager may sign commercial paper as an agent for a corporation. Any individual who is unable to write her or his name because of illiteracy or a physical handicap may sign with a mark, typically an "X." However it is an advisable practice to have another person then insert the name of the signer next to the mark and sign as a witness.

The location of the signature generally is immaterial as long as it appears on the face of the instrument. Thus, the signature may appear scrawled diagonally across the face or even in the body of the instrument as long as the signer's status as maker or drawer is clear.

Unconditional Promise or Order

To be negotiable, a promissory note or a certificate of deposit must contain an unconditional promise to pay money. Similarly, a check or a draft must contain an unconditional order to pay money. Simply acknowledging a debt by saying "I owe you $1,000" is not enough. There is nothing in such a statement to indicate that the money will ever be repaid.

The use of the word "unconditional" means that the promise or order to pay money must be absolute, that is, free of any limits or restrictions. "I promise to pay Ann Kiersten $1,000 if my mare foals in the next year" would be conditional upon an event that might not occur. Therefore, the instrument that included the statement would not be negotiable.

Making payment subject to another agreement would make the obligation conditional on the agreement being properly performed. Such conditions would restrict the free flow of commercial paper. Conditions would require a prospective purchaser of the paper to deal with the uncertainty that the condition might not have been satisfied. This would mean that collection might not be legally possible. However, instruments that merely acknowledge the source of the obligation, as in "pay to the order of Merrick Miller as per contract," are negotiable.

A phrase entitling the holder to reasonable attorney's fees upon default or enhancing the possibility of collection, such as "secured by a mortgage," would improve the potential for negotiation by reducing the uncertainty of collection. Finally, courteous or considerate language, such as "please pay to the order of" or listing the obligor's bank account number (without the word "only" following) for the convenience of others, does not affect negotiability.

Payable in a Sum Certain in Money

To be negotiable, commercial paper must call for the payment of a sum certain in money. **Money**, for this purpose, is any official currency or coin acceptable as a medium of exchange either in the United States or in any foreign country at the time the commercial paper is written. Thus, commercial paper that is collectible in the United States but that has the amount expressed in an acceptable foreign currency is negotiable.

Often the foreign currency is simply changed into U.S. dollars on the day the paper is payable. However, if the paper requires that the foreign currency be used as the medium of payment, the commercial paper is payable in that currency.

Payment must be solely in money and not money plus a good or service. On the other hand, paper that gives the obligee (creditor) a choice of money or something else, for example, "I promise to pay to the order of Vera Spielman $10,000 or thirty-five ounces of gold at the obligee's option" would be negotiable because the obligee could choose money as payment. If the choice to pay in money or a good or service was the obligor's (debtor's), the instrument is not negotiable. In such a case the obligor could choose to make payment in something other than money.

An instrument still is negotiable if it requires that the amount be paid

- with interest or a discount. (The interest rate may vary. For example, if the instrument reads "interest to be set at the usury limit less 2%" the instrument would still be negotiable.)

- by installment, perhaps with an **acceleration clause** that makes the entire balance due and payable upon the happening of a certain event (for example, the obligor's default by missing an installment payment)

- with bank charges for exchanging one national currency into another

- with costs of collection and reasonable attorney's fees in case the paper is not paid

Most of these provisions usually tend to make the commercial paper more attractive to prospective owners.

NETBookmark

Commercial paper may be collectible in the United States even if the amount is expressed in a foreign currency. Often the foreign currency is changed into U.S. dollars on the day the paper is payable. Find the exchange rates for foreign currency by accessing school.cengage.com/blaw/lawxtra and clicking on the link for Chapter 30. Find today's exchange rate with the U.S. dollar for the currency of five different countries.

school.cengage.com/blaw/lawxtra

© GETTY IMAGES/PHOTODISC

When is commercial paper payable in a foreign currency in the United States?

Payable on Demand or at a Definite Time

Negotiability also requires that an instrument be payable on demand or at a definite time. **Payable on demand** means that the commercial paper is written so as to be payable immediately upon presentment (demand for payment) or at sight. If no time of payment is specified, an instrument is interpreted as being payable on demand.

Payable at a definite time means that the commercial paper is written payable on or before an identified calendar date. It is also acceptable for an instrument to be payable within a set period after an identified calendar date or a fixed period, such as 90 days after sight. An instrument is not negotiable if it is payable at or after an event that is sure to occur but whose date cannot be deter-mined beforehand. For example, a note payable "30 days after the death of Sam Larue" would not be negotiable. Such a promise might be honored by the person making it or it might be legally enforceable as part of a contract. However, that has nothing to do with whether the instrument is commercial paper and can therefore be negotiated.

Payable to Bearer or to Someone's Order

The final requirement is that the paper contain the words of negotiability by being made payable to bearer or to a specified person's order. When commercial paper is legally collectible by the party in possession of it, it is referred to as **bearer paper**. The party in possession of bearer paper is called the **bearer**. To qualify as bearer paper, the face of a piece of commercial paper can read "pay to the order of bearer," "pay to bearer," "pay to (a named party) or bearer," "pay to cash," or any other way that does not identify a specific payee, such as being made payable to a fictitious character like Superman or Santa Claus.

In contrast, when commercial paper is made payable to the order of a specified payee, it is called **order paper**. Such phrasing shows the intent of the maker or drawer to have the paper payable to the named payee or to anyone to whom the paper is subsequently negotiated by order of that payee. Order paper may read "pay to the order of Charles Blevins" or whatever specific party the maker or drawer intends. It also may read "pay to Charles Blevins or order." However, if it only reads "pay to Charles Blevins," it is not negotiable. An exception under the 1990 version of the UCC is a check. A check may be negotiable without being payable to order or bearer. However check forms ordinarily contain the pre-printed words "Pay to the order of."

Order paper may be made payable to the order of more than one party. These parties can be named either jointly ("pay to the order of Jeannette Edwards and Anthony Edwards") or

Would a note payable "on Christmas of next year" be negotiable? Why or why not?

© GETTY IMAGES/PHOTODISC

individually ("pay to the order of Emilio Morales or Daniel Elliott"). In the first example, both Jeannette and Anthony have to sign the instrument to negotiate it further. In the second example, either Emilio or Daniel acting alone can sign and cash it.

CHECKPOINT What requirements must be met for an instrument to be considered negotiable?

30-1 Assessment

THINK ABOUT LEGAL CONCEPTS

1. Is a check that fulfills all the other requirements of negotiablity but is written in pencil still negotiable? **Yes or No?**

2. A negotiable instrument dated later than the date of issuance is said to be _?_.

3. If there is a conflict between the amount of a check written in numerals and a different amount written out in words, the amount written in numbers will prevail, as numbers are easier to read. **True or False?**

4. A promissory note is physically issued on June 6 of this year. Which of the following dates, if actually entered on the face of the instrument as the date of issue, would make it antedated? (a) June 5 (b) June 7 (c) July 7 (d) June 6

5. If the signature of the maker of a promissory note only appears in the middle of the text on the face of the instrument, the note cannot be negotiable. **True or False?**

6. A(n) _?_ in a negotiable instrument makes the entire balance due and payable upon the happening of a certain event.

7. Commercial paper cannot be signed with an "X." **True or False?**

8. Which of the following wordings would not result in the paper being payable to the party in possession of it? (a) pay to bearer (b) pay to cash (c) pay to Sherlock Holmes (d) All of the above would result in the paper being payable to the possessor.

9. If the indorsement on a negotiable instrument reads "pay to the order of Michelle Holley" it is properly termed _?_ paper.

THINK CRITICALLY ABOUT EVIDENCE

Study the situation, answer the questions, and then prepare arguments to support your answers.

10. C.W. Bean wrote a check payable to Christopher John for the full purchase price of Christopher's used pickup. Bean put "$7,500" in numerals on the payee line for the amount of the check but wrote out "seven thousand eight hundred dollars" below it. If no other evidence were presented as to the sale price, what would a court hold as to the amount of the check?

11. On April Fool's Day, a friend gives you a $25 check that she has deliberately antedated to April 1 of the previous year. If she has adequate funds in her account when you present the check, can you still collect on it?

12. On August 7, you sell your car to pay for your college tuition. The buyer asks that you not cash the payoff check until his payday on the first of

September because he needs the money in his account for family expenses. You promise not to cash it, but when you go to register for classes you find that the tuition amount must be paid immediately or else you cannot enroll. Your only source of funds is the check, and you did tell the buyer that the money was to go for your tuition. You know that by law a check is a demand instrument. Can you cash it? Should you cash it?

13. Campbell wrote the following by hand: "I, Gary Campbell, promise to pay to the order of Allison J. Nagy $2,500." Campbell then delivered it to Nagy. In a dispute that arose later, it was argued that because the instrument lacked Campbell's signature, was not dated, and was without a time of payment, it was not negotiable. Do you agree?

30-2 Proper Indorsement and Negotiation

GOALS

- Describe how commercial paper is transferred
- Compare the functions of the various indorsements

KEY TERMS

indorsement

indorser

indorsee

holder

blank indorsement

special indorsement

qualified indorsement

unqualified indorsement

restrictive indorsement

accommodation party

How Is Commercial Paper Transferred?

WHAT'S YOUR VERDICT?

Every Friday, after being paid, Rainquest drove to a nearby grocery store and cashed her paycheck. Each time the store clerk would ask her to sign the back of the check. Finally, Rainquest complained to the store manager about having to do so, saying that her signature is private and others shouldn't see it as they might forge it later. The store manager just said if she didn't sign the check they couldn't give her the funds due on it.

Is Rainquest's signature necessary legally, or is the store just being overbearing?

Commercial paper usually is transferred by negotiation. As discussed previously, negotiation may give the transferee greater rights than if the paper is merely assigned. This is true because, in an assignment, the transferee receives only the rights of the transferor. In negotiation, the transferee, if qualified, may receive additional rights granted under the UCC.

In particular, negotiation for value may be to a party who has no knowledge of defects in the original transaction in which the paper was created. Negotiation could give that innocent transferee the power to overcome many defenses against payment that the party obligated to pay might have used otherwise. These defenses include breach of contract and failure of consideration, which are explained in the next chapter.

If the transfer of commercial paper does not qualify as a negotiation, it is legally considered as having been assigned. As such, it is subject to defenses that might stem from the application of contract law. To enable a transferee to receive the additional collection rights available under the UCC, it is critical to know the proper way to transfer commercial paper. The proper method of transfer in a specific instance depends on whether the instrument is order or bearer paper.

If the instrument is order paper (payable to the order of a named person), the named person or her or his agent must sign the paper on its reverse side. In *What's Your Verdict?* the store clerk and manager properly requested that Rainquest sign the back of the check. If she did not sign the check, the store could not collect the money due on it. After the signature is applied, the paper must be delivered to make the negotiation complete and proper.

A signature on the back of an instrument is termed an **indorsement** by the UCC. An owner of commercial paper who signs on its reverse indorses the paper and is an **indorser**. The party to whom the paper is indorsed is the **indorsee**. A party who has physical possession of commercial paper that is payable to his or her order or who is in possession of bearer paper is a **holder**. Therefore, a bearer is a holder, as is a person in possession of paper payable to his or her order.

LEGAL Research

Search law-related publications for descriptions of fraudulent schemes that have been committed against financial institutions. Report these to the class and discuss how businesses and individuals can protect themselves from similar problems.

If the paper is bearer paper, it may be negotiated by delivery alone. The bearer simply may hand the paper to the transferee. Many transferees, however, will require the bearer to indorse the paper. This generally allows the future holders to pursue the transferor for payment of the paper's value if there are problems collecting it from the maker or drawee.

> **CHECKPOINT** How does the proper way to negotiate order paper differ from that required to negotiate bearer paper?

Indorsements and Their Functions

WHAT'S YOUR VERDICT? Gordon Marshall paid his ex-wife, Gloria Marshall, her monthly alimony by indorsing his weekly paycheck with his name only and handing it to her. While shopping, Gloria had her purse stolen. The thief found the check and promptly bought goods with it at the Penny-Ante Quick Shoppe, which accepted it in good faith. Penny-Ante can legally collect on the check.

What kind of indorsement might have protected Gloria from this loss?

Indorsements are classified by whether any words, other than the indorser's signature, have been added to them and, if so, what those words are or what they direct.

Blank Indorsements

A **blank indorsement** consists of just the indorser's signature (see Gordon Marshall's signature in the illustration on this page). Because it is quickly written, the blank indorsement is the most common. It does not specify a particular person to whom the paper is being transferred. Therefore, it will transform order paper into bearer paper. Even a finder or a thief may negotiate an instrument with a blank indorsement. Therefore, Penny-Ante in *What's Your Verdict*, because it received the instrument through a proper negotiation even though it did so from

the thief, acquired the right to collect on the check. A blank indorsement is satisfactory and safe for the indorser if

1. value is immediately received for it, or
2. the paper is deposited in a bank at the time of indorsement.

Special Indorsements

A **special indorsement** makes the paper payable to the order of a designated party. Recall that, unless the instrument is a check, the words "Pay to the order of" must be used on the face of the instrument to achieve the same result. With an indorsement, the more concise wording "Pay to Gloria Marshall" is as effective as "Pay to the order of Gloria Marshall." The paper will be order paper as a result of either wording.

To be properly negotiated, order paper requires the signature of the party named in the indorsement. A forged signature used as an indorsement cannot transfer title. Therefore, unlike the situation with paper having a blank indorsement, a thief or a finder of the paper could not legally cash it.

Transferees who receive commercial paper with blank indorsements may protect themselves by writing that the paper is payable to them above the indorser's signature. This is perfectly legal and restores the order character of the instrument. For example, as shown in the illustration at the top of the next page, Gloria Marshall could have taken the blank indorsement of Gordon Marshall and written above it "Pay to the order of Gloria Marshall" or "Pay to Gloria Marshall." Then the thief would have had to forge her signature to pass the instrument. The law states that generally the loss falls on the

BLANK INDORSEMENT

Gordon Marshall

SPECIAL INDORSEMENT

Pay to the order of
Gloria Marshall
Gordon Marshall

person who takes from the forger. Therefore, if Penny-Ante had accepted the check with a forged special indorsement of Gloria Marshall's name, it would have been unable to collect.

It is important to note that there are exceptions to the above rule. These exceptions may allow innocent holders to collect despite the forgery. They are applied whenever there has been negligence on the part of the maker, drawer, or other holder of the instrument. For example, suppose that a dishonest employee fraudulently gets an employer to sign a check made payable to a frequent supplier of the business but for a nonexistent shipment. The employee then takes the check, forges the supplier's indorsement, and cashes it. The employer must pay it, because it was the employer's negligence that placed the employee in a position to commit the forgery. The employer can then try to recoup the loss from that dishonest employee.

Another exception occurs when an impostor tricks the maker or drawer of commercial paper into giving the impostor an instrument that is made payable to the person who is being impersonated. The impostor then forges the indorsement of the party being impersonated and cashes the check. The instrument is effective against the maker or drawer, who was negligent in not properly identifying the party to whom the paper was given.

Qualified Indorsements

If the maker or drawee of an instrument fails to pay it, the indorsers may be required to pay it. Adding "without recourse" or equivalent words such as "not liable for payment" over a blank or special indorsement can eliminate this potential secondary liability based on signature. The result

is a **qualified indorsement**. A qualified indorsement eliminates the indorser's secondary liability because of his or her signature appearing on the instrument. If the maker or the drawee does not add such wording, the result is an **unqualified indorsement**, and the indorser may be liable to subsequent holders.

Even though secondary liability is avoided by qualifying the indorsement, certain warranties still may bind a transferor. These warranties are implied by law against all transferors and may still require the indorser to pay if the instrument cannot be collected. The warranties guarantee that

1. the transferor is entitled to enforce the paper
2. all signatures are genuine
3. the instrument has not been altered
4. the transferor has no knowledge of a bankruptcy proceeding against the maker, drawer of an unaccepted draft, or an acceptor
5. there are no defenses of any type good against the transferor

The warranty liability of a qualified indorser is the same as the warranty liability of an unqualified indorser. The warranties are very broad in coverage.

The transferor of bearer paper who does not indorse it (and therefore does not acquire secondary liability on her or his signature as an indorser) still is accountable for these warranties. However, warranty liability runs only to the immediate transferee if not indorsed. If the transferor does indorse the bearer paper, the implied warranties are extended to protect the transferees beyond just the immediate transferee.

To be totally without potential liability on a piece of commercial paper, a qualified indorser

IN THIS CASE To pay Barrington back for a loan, Bill Austin made out a check to "cash" for the amount due and gave it to her. Barrington then drove to her bank and sought to receive funds for the check. When she passed it to the teller, the teller returned it and asked that she indorse the instrument. Barrington at first thought it strange as the check was a piece of bearer paper and could be negotiated by just a transfer of possession. Then she realized that the bank wanted her indorsement for warranty purposes.

restrictive indorsement, because it directs what is to be done with the proceeds of the paper. "For deposit only" and "for collection" also are restrictive indorsements.

In addition, a restrictive indorsement might impose conditions on payment such as "Pay to Kiersten Alexis upon her delivery of her 1965 Mustang to me." Such a condition, if on the face of the instrument, would destroy negotiability, but this is not true if included in an indorsement. However, a future holder is bound by the condition and cannot collect the instrument against the restrictive indorser until the condition is satisfied.

Accommodation Parties

Sometimes a person who desires to borrow money or to cash a check is not well known in the community or has not established credit. To make her or his commercial paper acceptable, the person might arrange for someone who is known and has a good credit rating to join in signing the paper. Such a cosigner is an **accommodation party**. Under such circumstances, a person who signs as an indorser, maker, drawer, or acceptor becomes primarily liable in that role. It is as though they received the value from the transfer of the instrument. The obligee of the instrument does not have to try to collect from the accommodated party before proceeding against the accommodation party.

might add "without warranties" and thus eliminate all warranty liability. However, it will be extremely difficult to find a transferee that will give significant value for the instrument to a potential transferor under such circumstances.

Restrictive Indorsements

A **restrictive indorsement** directs the use of the proceeds from the instrument or imposes a condition upon payment of the instrument by the indorser. For example, "Pay to Chase Larue to be held in trust for his oldest son, Tommy," would be a

Assume the man on the right is serving as an accommodation party for the woman sitting to his left. What is the extent of his liability for the instrument for which he is cosigning?

© GETTY IMAGES/PHOTODISC

However, if the accommodation party is collected against, he or she has the right to seek compensation from the accommodated party. On the other hand, if the party accommodated is collected against, he or she has no legal right to any contribution from the accommodation party simply because the latter was a cosigner.

CHECKPOINT List the four main types of indorsements.

30-2 Assessment

THINK ABOUT LEGAL CONCEPTS

1. A check made out to cash does not have to be indorsed in order to be negotiated. **True or False?**

2. The only two types of indorsements that determine how the instrument is to be negotiated are (a) blank and qualified (b) blank and special (c) qualified and blank (d) qualified and restrictive

3. An instrument that is payable on presentment is termed a _?_ instrument. (a) liquid (b) collateral (c) demand (d) none of the above

4. "Pay to Matt Jones" is a restrictive indorsement. **True or False?**

5. Could you use a restrictive indorsement to direct the use of the proceeds from the instrument. **Yes or No?**

THINK CRITICALLY ABOUT EVIDENCE

Study the situation, answer the questions, and then prepare arguments to support your answers.

6. An impostor came to Jean's door and stated he was the campaign chairman for Senator Walton Knudson's reelection. Without asking for identification and as she was a Knudson supporter, Jean made out a check to the "Walton Knudson Campaign Fund" for $500. The impostor forged the fund's indorsement and cashed the check at a dealership as partial payment for a new car. Can the car dealership enforce the instrument against Jean's checking account?

7. Lisa Pratt received a promissory note for $1,000 payable to bearer. She indorsed it "Pay to Vince Leonard, Lisa Pratt" and delivered it to him. Later Vince simply delivered the note to the Renaissance Record Shop for a portable CD player and a collection of greatest hits of the Sixties, Seventies, and Eighties. Was Vince's action a proper negotiation?

8. In return for repairing their car, you take a check from a couple in an old station wagon. The car is packed with what looks like all their worldly goods. You have a feeling that either the account is closed or that the check will not be paid or, most likely, both. How would you word an indorsement that would limit your liability to subsequent holders of the instrument?

9. If you also wrote in "without warranties" above your indorsement in exercise 8, would that help limit your liability?

10. Your friend wants to buy a car but his credit rating is poor. He asks you to cosign the note with him so that the transaction will go through. If you do so, could you later be required to pay the full amount of the note?

CONCEPTS IN BRIEF

30-1 Requirements of Negotiability

1. To be negotiable, an instrument must
   - be in writing and signed by the maker or drawer
   - contain an unconditional order (if it is a draft or a check) or promise (if it is a note or a CD)
   - call for payment of a sum certain in money
   - be payable on demand or at a definite time
   - be payable to the bearer or to the order of a specified person

2. In conflicts between terms written by various means, the handwritten version prevails over the typewritten version, and the typewritten version prevails over the printed version. Amounts expressed in words prevail over amounts expressed in figures.

3. Although the order or promise given in commercial paper must be unconditional, certain terms may be added to an instrument without destroying negotiability. An example is a provision for the recovery of collection costs and reasonable attorney's fees in case of default.

30-2 Proper Indorsement and Negotiation

4. Commercial paper payable to order may be negotiated only by the proper indorsement and delivery. Commercial paper payable to the bearer may be negotiated by delivery alone.

5. The four basic types of indorsements are blank, special, qualified, and restrictive.

6. Qualified indorsers will still have some potential liability on an instrument unless they add the words "without warranties" above their signatures, along with "without recourse."

7. An accommodation party is liable to all subsequent holders of the paper who give value for it, but an accommodation party is not liable to the party accommodated. If the accommodation party is forced to pay the liability, he or she may recover the amount paid from the accommodated party.

YOUR LEGAL VOCABULARY

Match each statement with the term that it best defines. Some terms may not be used.

1. Status of paper that is to be paid on presentment or at sight
2. Dated later than the date of issuance
3. Indorsement that eliminates the indorser's secondary liability to pay if the primarily liable party does not
4. Indorsement consisting only of the signature of the indorser
5. Someone who joins another in signing as a maker, drawer, acceptor, or indorser of an instrument in order to bolster the creditworthiness of the latter party
6. Indorsement that directs the use of the proceeds from an instrument or imposes a condition on payment
7. Indorsement that makes a paper payable to a particular party or to his or her order
8. Dated prior to the date of issuance
9. Official medium of exchange in the United States or a foreign country at the time a piece of commercial paper is issued
10. A signature rendered on the back of a piece of commercial paper
11. Commercial paper legally collectible by the party in possession

a. acceleration clause
b. accommodation party
c. antedated
d. bearer
e. bearer paper
f. blank indorsement
g. holder
h. indorsee
i. indorsement
j. indorser
k. money
l. negotiable
m. negotiable instruments
n. negotiation
o. order paper
p. payable at a definite time
q. payable on demand
r. postdated
s. qualified indorsement
t. restrictive indorsement
u. special indorsement
v. unqualified indorsement

REVIEW LEGAL CONCEPTS

12. In interpreting conflicting terms that appear on the face of commercial paper, why are handwritten terms given precedence over printed terms?

13. Explain why a finger or thumb print would be effective as a signature on a piece of commercial paper.

14. List and explain the importance of the necessary elements of a negotiable instrument.

15. Why are "reasonable attorney's fees" acceptable as part of a "sum certain"? Surely nothing can be less certain.

16. Why is it so important that the face of commercial paper bear the words "payable to order" or "payable to bearer"?

WRITE ABOUT LEGAL CONCEPTS

17. Why are holders allowed to eliminate their signature-based liability to future holders by using a qualified indorsement?

18. Why are warranties extended to all subsequent holders by a holder who indorses the paper?

19. **HOT DEBATE** Write the bank's attorney's opening statement to persuade the court that the loss should not fall on the bank.

MAKE ACADEMIC CONNECTIONS

20. **ART** Commercial art takes many forms, from the classic movie poster to the design of an ad showing a superhero endorsing cereal. Andy Warhol raised the common soup can to a level of consideration no one but its designer had given it. Collect several samples of checks and evaluate the background art on each. Formulate the requirements for such art and then create your own. Compose a report on the guidelines that should be used in these efforts and show a sample of your work to the class.

THINK CRITICALLY ABOUT EVIDENCE

Study the situation, answer the questions, and then prepare arguments to support your answers.

21. Parnell was the maker of a promissory note payable to LaSalle. The note was complete and legally correct in all respects except for the following additional terms. Do any of these terms destroy the negotiability of the note?

    ■ "This note is prepared as a result of a service contract between the parties dated 3/13/—"

    ■ "This note is secured by a mortgage on the maker's residence at 67 Park Central West, Pierre, South Dakota."

    ■ "This note is payable in Canadian dollars, with exchange."

22. Lasorda paid $7,500 for a $10,000 promissory note payable on the day the Chicago Cubs next win the World Series. Is the note negotiable? Can it still be collected?

23. Anton drew a check for $750 payable to bearer. Anton gave the check to Brewster. Brewster negotiated it by delivery to Charlois. Charlois negotiated it by delivery to Deltoid. Deltoid tried to collect but found that Anton's bank account lacked the necessary funds for payment. May Deltoid collect from either or both of the prior holders, and if so, under what circumstances?

24. Krosby was starting a new business and needed cash. He convinced the Finance Bank to lend him $10,000 against his new equipment. However, the bank insisted that his prominent friend, Hopper, or someone of equal financial means indorse the note as well. What would be the extent of Hopper's potential liability from such an act?

25. Associates Discount Corporation sought court enforcement of a note it held. The note stated that Fitzwater owed a large sum of money for a tractor that had been delivered to him. Fitzwater, the signer and obligor on the note, wanted to testify to the effect that the tractor was never delivered. May he do so? (*Associates Discount Corporation of Iowa v. Fitzwater*, 518 S.W.2d 474)

26. On May 8, 1957, Brookshire was convicted of issuing a check with intent to defraud. On January 1, 1957, Brookshire had given a check dated December 31, 1957, to pay his taxes for 1956. On January 7 or 8, 1957, Brookshire's bank dishonored the check due to insufficient funds. Under these circumstances, should an intent to defraud be inferred from Brookshire's issuing a postdated check? If not, should the conviction be overturned? (*State v. Brookshire*, 329 S.W.2d 252)

27. In May 1963, Ferri executed a note promising to pay $3,000 to Sylvia's order "within ten years after date." Two years later, Sylvia demanded payment. When refused, Sylvia sued Ferri. Is the note due at a definite time? If so, when? If not, why not? (*Ferri v. Sylvia*, 214 A.2d 470)

28. A $10,000 certificate of deposit (CD) "payable to the Registered Depositor hereof" was issued to John D. Cox by Commercial Bank of Liberty. Cox then used the CD as security for a loan made by the Kaw Valley Bank. When Cox defaulted on the loan, Kaw Valley sought to collect on the CD but Liberty refused to pay. Kaw Valley brought suit but could only collect if the CD was negotiable. Was it? (*Kaw Valley Bank Etc. v. Commercial Bank of Liberty*, 567 S.W.2d 710)

29. Haas, a trusted employee of a firm by the name of Trail Leasing, Inc., used her access to her employer's blank checks to defraud Trail Leasing of almost $40,000. She did this by making checks payable to the firm's bank, Drovers First American. She then had the checks signed by an authorized officer of the firm when she obtained cash for them. Once it discovered the fraud, Trail Leasing sued the Bank to recover its losses. Decide. (*Trail Leasing, Inc. v. Drovers First American Bank*, 447 N.W.2d 190)

30. When an employee of Epicycle cashed a payroll check at Money Mart Check Cashing Center, Inc., the instrument was deposited with others into Money Mart's bank account. Regrettably the check was subsequently returned marked, "payment stopped." When Money Mart attempted to collect on the check at a later date, Epicycle defended against the collection efforts by maintaining that Money Mart could not do so as it failed to even inquire about the validity of the check before taking it. Decide. (*Money Mart Check Cashing Center, Inc. v. Epicycle Corp.*, 667 P. 1372)

Case For Legal Thinking

FEDERAL DEPOSIT INSURANCE CORPORATION V. CULVER
640 F. SUPP. 725

FACTS When Texan Nasib Ed Kalliel entered into a business deal with the Rexford State Bank of Rexford, Kansas, the bank was in excellent financial shape. Kalliel suggested that he had a plan to rescue several farmers from the financial disaster that many in the farming industry at that time were experiencing. He suggested that if the bank would loan its money to farmers in trouble, he would guarantee the loan repayment through one of his companies. Unfortunately, the bank did not have enough capital to make adequate loans to all the farmers who needed them. Consequently, the bank agreed to take deposits from a New Jersey firm in the form of high-yield large certificates of deposits. Most of the new deposits went directly to farm loans. However, about 20 percent were "farmed out" to Kalliel himself and his companies.

Kalliel and a Missouri farmer, Gary Culver, agreed to a working relationship in which Kalliel would manage the business end and Culver the production end of the Culver farm. When Culver told Kalliel that he must have $30,000 to prevent foreclosure, the Rexford Bank provided the money. Shortly thereafter a Bank representative approached Culver and induced him to sign a blank promissory note form. The Bank's representative maintained to Culver that the note was nothing more than a receipt for the money. Later the amount, interest rate, and due date on the note were filled in. However $50,000 was entered as the amount instead of $30,000. When the Rexford Bank later became insolvent, the FDIC bought the note as it did the remaining outstanding Rexford Bank notes. The FDIC then sought to collect on the note as it was mature and no collection efforts had ever been started on it.

REASONING The FDIC moved for summary judgment. Culver defended that the circumstances surrounding the issuance of the note provided him with the defense of fraud which would be good even against the collection efforts of the FDIC. The FDIC maintained its right to collect, as under the UCC the defense of fraud is available only as long as there has not been "reasonable opportunity to obtain knowledge of its character or its essential terms" provided to the maker of the note. The FDIC maintained that Culver's failure to take notice of the nature of the form of the instrument that he was presented as a "receipt" was negligence and that, therefore, it could collect to the full value of the face of the note.

PRACTICE JUDGING

1. Should the FDIC's request for summary judgement against Culver be granted? Why or why not?

2. If Culver had just signed a blank piece of paper after being told that the bank would make a receipt out of it by printing the appropriate words around his signature, would he be able to avail himself of the defense of fraud? Why or why not?

3. If the Bank had made the note payable for an unreasonable amount, such as $1,000,000, could the FDIC have collected?

© GETTY IMAGES/PHOTODISC

Chapter 31
Discharge of Commercial Paper and Electronic Fund Transfers

31-1 Discharge of Commercial Paper

31-2 The Law of Electronic Fund Transfers

HOT DEBATE

Buanna Myers sat at her desk at the Commerce Bank of Statusville. She was deciding whether or not to buy a promissory note from Alyssia Thomas, the proprietor of Alyssia's Autos. The maker of the note was Televangelist Robert Shore, as president of Mercyland, a not-for-profit corporation that managed low-cost rental properties. Buanna knew that many of the transactions originating with Alyssia's Autos had resulted in lawsuits, mainly because the vehicles Alyssia sold were substandard and sold "as is." The note from Mercyland was for $78,000 for a bus just purchased. Buanna knew that her higher ups at the bank would insist on collecting, even from Mercyland. She also knew that if she didn't buy the note, someone else would.

WHERE DO YOU STAND?

1. Assume Buanna buys the note and the bus is defective. Ethically, should the bank be able to collect? Why or why not?
2. As the attorney for Mercyland, what arguments can you make to allow the cost for repairs to the bus, should it prove to have been defective when sold, to be offset from the amount due on the note?

31-1 Discharge of Commercial Paper

GOALS

- List the ways commercial paper can be discharged
- Recognize the importance of the status of a holder in due course
- Identify the limited and universal defenses

KEY TERMS

cancellation

holder in due course (HDC)

holder through a holder in course (HHDC)

limited defenses

universal defenses

alteration

consumer transaction

How Is Commercial Paper Discharged?

WHAT'S YOUR VERDICT? As partial payment for a scooploader bought from her heavy machinery company, Arianne took a promissory note in the amount of $100,000 from James Buus. Hurrying to make another meeting, Arianne placed the note on a stack of documents on her desk that were to be destroyed. While she was gone to the meeting, Arianne's secretary shredded the documents including the note.

Will the destruction of the note discharge Buus's debt?

The obligations assumed in commercial paper transactions may be discharged in a variety of ways.

By Payment

The vast majority of commercial paper is paid and discharged according to its terms. The maker usually pays a note or a certificate of deposit. A check usually is paid upon demand by the bank on which it is drawn. Other types of drafts usually are paid by the drawees who have accepted the drafts. Without such reliability the commercial paper system would not function.

By law the commercial paper terms must dictate that payment be made in money. At maturity or on demand, however, the holder (obligee/creditor) may agree to some form of substitution. For instance, the holder may agree to take different kinds of property, such as other commercial paper or anything else of value, instead of money.

IN THIS CASE Hofstra owed $7,700 on a note held by Duvall. On the due date Hofstra offered Duvall a prize quarter horse worth more than $7,700 as payment instead of cash. At that point, the holder, Duvall, had the right to demand payment in money or to consider the obligor, Hofstra, in default. Recognizing the value of the quarter horse, however, Duvall agreed to the substitution, and the note was discharged.

When an obligor pays a holder the amount due on commercial paper, the obligor should obtain possession of the paper. Otherwise, a dishonest holder who retains the paper might falsely claim that it had not been paid and demand a second payment. Such a dishonest

What is the most common method of payment and discharge for commercial paper?

holder also could negotiate it wrongfully to an innocent third party, who then also might be entitled to payment. Even if the amount due on paper is paid only in part, this fact should be shown by appropriate notation on the paper itself. Mistakenly marking a note paid and returning it to the maker does not discharge the obligation by itself. However, it is very difficult evidence for the obligee to overcome in order to be still allowed to collect.

By Cancellation

The obligation to pay commercial paper also may be discharged by cancellation. **Cancellation** in this context consists of any act by the current holder that indicates an intent to end the obligation of payment. Knowingly tearing up the paper, burning it, or just drawing a line through the name of a potential obligor, like an indorser, would be excellent evidence of an intent to discharge one or all obligations arising from the instrument. If the cancellation was the result of fraud, an accident, or a mistake, as in *What's Your Verdict?*, the action does not discharge the obligation.

By Alteration

A fraudulent change to or fraudulent completion of commercial paper by a party to the instrument will discharge the obligation of the other party. For example, suppose that it is shown to the satisfaction of a court that the holder of a note fraudulently changed the rate of interest due from 7 to 17 percent. In such a case, the maker would not be obligated to pay it. However, the original parties to the paper still might be bound to make payment in accordance with the original terms under certain circumstances. These circumstances will be discussed in the next section.

By Impairment of Collateral

If a holder extends the time of payment, releases the principal debtor, or impairs collateral provided as security for payment of the negotiable instruments, any party whose rights are affected and who did not consent is discharged.

As a Contract

A negotiable instrument may be discharged in the same ways as an ordinary contract for the payment of money. For example, a discharge could occur by novation, by accord and satisfaction, by operation of law, such as in bankruptcy, or because of the running of the statute of limitations.

CHECKPOINT Name four means of discharging commercial paper.

Collection of Commercial Paper Obligations

WHAT'S YOUR VERDICT? Donna paid Alanna $500 for a promissory note with a face value of $10,000. The note was bearer paper, and Alanna refused to indorse it, saying that she had to leave town and therefore her indorsement would not do any good. Donna knew Alanna recently had been indicted for participation in a blackmail scheme. When Donna tried to collect on the note, the maker refused to pay claiming he had signed it only because Alanna had threatened to reveal certain incriminating facts to the Internal Revenue Service.

Is Donna a holder in due course and thereby able to overcome the obligor's defense and collect?

If payment of commercial paper according to its terms is not voluntarily forthcoming, the obligee must try and collect what is due. Standing in the way may be one or more of a variety of defenses raised by the obligor. These defenses may be effective or not depending on their validity and the status of the obligee. To maximize the chances of collection, an obligee should try and attain the status of a holder in due course.

Holder in Due Course

As defined in the last chapter, a *holder* is a person who has physical possession of bearer paper or order paper payable to the order of that person as a payee or indorsee. All holders have the right to assign, negotiate, enforce payment, or discharge the paper, with or without payment in return. However, when trying to collect on an instrument, a party who qualifies as either a holder in due course or a holder through a holder in due course is legally placed in a much better position than a mere holder or an assignee.

To be a **holder in due course (HDC)**, a person must qualify as a holder and, in addition, take the commercial paper in good faith, give value for it, and not have knowledge of any defense, adverse claim to, or dishonor of the instrument.

For example, if the instrument is overdue and the acquirer knew or should have known of its status, a person cannot be an HDC. Such a person could still qualify as a **holder through a holder in due course (HHDC)**. An HHDC is a holder who takes commercial paper anytime after an HDC. An HHDC normally has the same rights as an HDC. Note, however, that according to the Uniform Commercial Code (UCC), persons cannot improve their position on commercial paper through reacquisition.

In other words, if an individual had been a mere holder the first time she had an instrument and she then sold it to a person who qualified as an HDC, reacquiring the instrument from that HDC would still leave her with only her original rights as a mere holder, not those of an HHDC. In collecting, either an HDC or an HHDC can overcome more of the defenses that the obligor on an instrument might raise against payment than a mere holder can overcome.

Defenses that are good against everyone except an HDC or an HHDC are termed **limited defenses**. (These were labeled *personal defenses* under pre-UCC law, and this terminology may still be used in some jurisdictions.) Defenses that are good against all potential plaintiffs, including HDCs and HHDCs, that might sue to collect on a negotiable instrument are called **universal defenses**. (These were known as *real defenses* under pre-UCC law, and this term inology also may still be used in some jurisdictions.) These defenses will be discussed in detail later in this section.

Qualifications of an HDC

For a holder to be considered an HDC and thereby able to overcome limited defenses, the holder must take the paper in good faith and give value without notice of defense, adverse claim to, or dishonor of the instrument.

TAKE IN GOOD FAITH AND GIVE VALUE Taking paper in good faith requires that the holder act honestly, not just in the immediate transaction, but in relation to the complete set of circumstances surrounding the paper. In addition, although the courts generally do not consider the adequacy of the value given for commercial paper, the amount given may affect the court's judgment as to the good faith of the parties involved. For example, if the value given is small in relation to the face value of the instrument, fraud or some other unconscionable act that would prevent the holder from being considered an HDC may be implied by the court.

In *What's Your Verdict?* Donna's knowledge of Alanna's alleged criminal activities and the small value given probably will disqualify her from being an HDC. A court would likely imply a lack of good faith in the situation.

WITHOUT KNOWLEDGE OF DEFENSE OR DISHONOR Besides giving value in good faith, an HDC must not know the paper is overdue. For example, a time instrument is overdue the day after the maturity date. If payments are to be made in installments, the paper is overdue if even a single installment is late. If an instrument is due on demand, it is overdue a reasonable time after it is issued. However, the UCC specifies that a check is overdue 90 days after issue. Also every holder is charged with knowledge of what is on the instrument, so failing to notice the date is no excuse. Similarly, if the date has been altered, as from May 5 to May 15, and if the alteration is not recognizable by a reasonable person, an innocent holder is accountable only for the date as altered (May 15).

Finally, to qualify as an HDC a holder must not know of any defenses against enforcement of the paper, any claims of ownership from third parties, or any previous dishonors of the paper. Any such knowledge attributable to the holder when he or she acquired the paper would prevent that holder from being considered an HDC. As a consequence, that holder legally might be unable to overcome an obligor's limited defenses against payment of the paper.

CHECKPOINT What must a mere holder do to be considered an HDC?

What Are the Limited and Universal Defenses?

WHAT'S YOUR VERDICT?

Spynal owned "Hello, Cleveland!" a business that provided touring rock groups with transportation from one concert to another. He bought a large used recreational vehicle (RV) to convert for such a purpose from Trail's Used Car and RV Center. Trail assured Spynal that the odometer reading of 25,275 on the RV was correct. Spynal paid for the vehicle with $15,000 in cash and by issuing a $45,000 promissory note payable to Trail's order. Spynal later learned from state authorities that the true odometer reading was 125,275 miles. Spynal wanted to avoid the contract because of the fraud. In the meantime, Trail had negotiated the note to the Continental Bank, an HDC, for $41,000.

Must Spynal pay Continental the $45,000 as promised?

Even though the emphasis in this section is on defenses, it is once again important to realize that most commercial paper is enforceable according to its terms and is promptly paid. Only in the exceptional case do defenses to collection come into play. In such instances, however, the holder's risk of not being able to collect is greatly reduced if he or she is an HDC and thereby is able to overcome the limited, but not the universal, defenses that might be raised against such collection.

The Limited Defenses

Limited defenses are good against all holders except an HDC or an HHDC. Against ordinary holders and assignees they are just as effective in barring collection as the universal defenses discussed later in this section. The following are the limited defenses.

BREACH OF CONTRACT OR FAILURE OF CONSIDERATION Often commercial paper is issued as a result of a contractual agreement, as in *What's Your Verdict?* Ordinary or mere holders are subject to defenses that arise when the terms of such a contract are not fulfilled or the consideration (or partial consideration) is not given as bargained for by the person who issued the instrument. In *What's Your Verdict?* for example, if Trail had failed to deliver the RV on time, it would have been a breach of contract or, if the RV were defective, a failure of consideration. In either instance only an HDC or an HHDC could have collected on the note. An ordinary holder, like Trail, could not have overcome the defenses.

FRAUD IN THE INDUCEMENT If a person uses fraud to induce another to issue commercial paper, as Trail did to Spynal in *What's Your Verdict?,* the party defrauded has a limited defense to use against holders who try to collect. However, in *What's Your Verdict?* Continental Bank is an HDC. Therefore, Spynal must pay the note. Spynal can then seek to recover from Trail.

Fraud in the inducement occurs when the issuer is aware that an obligation based on commercial paper is being created and knows the essential terms. However, the person is persuaded to issue the paper because of fraudulent statements. This should not be confused with fraud in the execution, where the issuer is unaware that an obligation based on commercial paper is being created or is unaware of the nature or essential terms of the commercial paper. Fraud in the execution is a universal defense covered later in this section.

TEMPORARY INCAPACITY TO CONTRACT— EXCLUDING MINORITY Contractual obligations made when a person is experiencing a temporary loss of capacity, such as through insanity or intoxication, are voidable. The law establishes a limited defense against commercial paper issued during such periods of temporary loss of capacity.

ORDINARY DURESS Duress can be either a limited or a universal defense depending on its severity. Ordinary duress, typically from severe economic threat or a legitimate threat of criminal prosecution, does not strip away a person's capacity to contract. It does force the person to enter into a contract improperly. As a consequence, ordinary duress provides a limited defense against collection of any commercial paper that originates in such a contractual setting.

PRIOR PAYMENT OR CANCELLATION If the obligee pays the amount due on a piece of commercial paper but does not obtain the instrument or at least have it marked "paid," the instrument

could continue circulating. If it does, and it ends up in the hands of an HDC, that party could then enforce it against the obligor a second time because prior payment or cancellation only produces a limited defense.

CONDITIONAL DELIVERY OR NONDELIVERY Assume that a check or a note is delivered under a separate agreement that the instrument is to be negotiated only upon the occurrence of a certain event. Before the condition is satisfied, the paper is negotiated regardless. The resulting defense of conditional delivery is good only against ordinary holders.

Nondelivery also is merely a limited defense. In such a case, an instrument is prepared or indorsed properly but only circulated as a result of theft or negligence. If the instrument is in bearer form, a later HDC could enforce it, but a mere holder could not.

UNAUTHORIZED COMPLETION A maker or drawer who signs a negotiable instrument but leaves the amount blank runs a great risk. In such an instance, someone else typically is authorized to complete the paper when, for example, a final price is negotiated. If the amount actually entered is not within authorized limits and the instrument is transferred to a holder in due course, the amount would have to be paid to the HDC because unauthorized completion is only a limited defense.

THEFT A mere holder cannot collect on the instrument if the holder or a person through whom she or he obtained the instrument acquired it by theft. An HDC can require payment in such circumstances, however.

The Universal Defenses

Defenses that are good against all kinds of holders, including HDCs and HHDCs, are universal defenses. They include the following.

PERMANENT INCAPACITY TO CONTRACT AND MINORITY If a person is declared permanently insane or a habitual drunkard by judicial proceeding, the person is not responsible for any obligation incurred thereafter on commercial paper. Either status poses a universal defense to the making, drawing, accepting, indorsing, or accommodating of another party on an instrument.

Just as a minor may avoid contractual responsibilities, her or his refusal to pay on a piece of commercial paper is a universal defense. This is true whether the minor signs as maker, drawer, acceptor, indorser, or in any other capacity.

ILLEGALITY Commercial paper issued in connection with illegal conduct, such as illegal gambling or prostitution in most states, is unenforceable even by an HDC or an HHDC.

FORGERY OR LACK OF AUTHORITY When one person signs the name of another with the intent to defraud, a forgery has been committed. Such an act is a crime. Forgery on commercial paper produces a universal defense for the person whose signature has been forged. If the intent to defraud is lacking, but a person signs another's signature without authorization, the signer does not commit forgery. However, the effect on an HDC would be the same unless the person whose name was signed later ratified (approved) the signing. Both the forger and the unauthorized signer would be liable for the instrument regardless.

ALTERATION An **alteration** is a party's unauthorized change to or completion of a negotiable instrument intended to change the obligation of a party. If the alteration was made fraudulently, the person whose obligation is affected no longer has liability on the instrument. Other alterations do not discharge a party, and the instrument may be enforced according to its original terms.

Even if the alteration was fraudulent, a payor bank, a drawee, or a person taking the instrument for value, in good faith and without notice of the alteration, can enforce the instrument according to its original terms. These parties also can enforce the terms as filled in on an incomplete instrument altered by unauthorized completion. If the $15 amount payable on a check is altered to read $150, an HDC or HHDC could collect on the instrument, but only $15. If, by negligence, the person sued on the check substantially contributed to making the alteration possible, that person cannot use the defense of alteration.

FRAUD IN THE EXECUTION OF THE PAPER OR AS TO THE ESSENTIAL TERMS Sometimes trickery is used in such a way that even a careful person who signs does not know and has no reasonable opportunity to learn of the nature or essential terms of the document. Such a person has a defense of fraud against even an HDC or an

HHDC. For example, a celebrity signs an autograph on a blank sheet of paper. The "fan" then prints or writes a promissory note around the signature. Or suppose the signer of the paper is not able to read because he or she is illiterate in English or has broken glasses, and the person planning to defraud gives a false explanation of the essential terms or substitutes one paper for another before the signing. Not even an HDC or an HHDC can collect in these cases.

DURESS DEPRIVING CONTROL While ordinary duress is a limited defense, duress that deprives a person of control is a universal one. For example, a person who signs a note or draft because another person is threatening to shoot him with a gun has a defense good against even an HDC or an HHDC.

CLAIMS AND DEFENSES STEMMING FROM A CONSUMER TRANSACTION Although not defined as a universal defense by the UCC, by Federal Trade Commission (FTC) rule any defense a consumer could raise against the seller of a good or service can be raised against commercial paper originating in the same transaction. Defenses such as breach of contract, failure of consideration, and fraud in the inducement are thereby made good even against an HDC or HHDC in

Imagine this woman has asked the celebrity to sign his autograph on a blank piece of paper. If she then creates a promissory note around the signature, what defense does the celebrity have?

the proper circumstances. A **consumer transaction** is one in which a party buys goods or services for personal or household use. A notice stating that a piece of commercial paper originated in a consumer transaction and that the debtor's defenses are good against holders must be given in bold print on the instrument.

Prior to the "consumer revolt" of the 1960s, the holder in due course doctrine allowed collection in both consumer transactions and business transactions. For example, if you purchased a defective car to drive back and forth to school

and whose transmission fell out on the way out of the used car lot, you would still have to pay off in full any promissory note that you signed in order to buy the car if the note was held by an HDC. You could seek compensation only from the used car dealer.

CHECKPOINT What is the difference between a universal and a limited defense?

31-1 Assessment

Xtra! Study Tools
school.cengage.com/blaw/lawxtra

THINK ABOUT LEGAL CONCEPTS

1. A mere holder can improve his or her status to that of an HHDC by selling the instrument to an HDC and then reacquiring it. **True or False?**

2. Which of the following would not discharge an instrument? (a) payment (b) alteration (c) unintentional destruction (d) All of the above would discharge the instrument.

3. A holder who takes paper in good faith, gives value, and does so without notice of defense or dishonor can become an HDC. **True or False?**

4. Can a mere holder discharge a potential obligor such as an indorser before the instrument is paid? **Yes or No?**

5. The vast majority of commercial paper is paid and discharged according to its terms. **True or False?**

6. Permanent incapacity to contract is a limited defense. **True or False?**

7. Fraud in the inducement is a universal defense. **True or False?**

THINK CRITICALLY ABOUT EVIDENCE

Study the situation, answer the questions, and then prepare arguments to support your answers.

8. On December 1, Sven Bollinger took a third-party check from Tim Wallace in partial payment for a used stereo Sven sold Tim. The check was made out on August 31 payable to Tim. He indorsed it in blank upon transfer. Can Sven be a holder in due course on the instrument?

9. Ficklin was an unqualified indorser on a note for $10,000. Dixon, the holder of the note, mistakenly believed that Ficklin was in financial ruin. Thinking that she could not collect on the note, Dixon struck out Ficklin's indorsement. Is Ficklin still potentially liable on the instrument?

10. A 17-year-old student contracts to pay $3,000 for a 12-month modeling course. She pays $500 down and gives a note for the balance, payable in 23 monthly installments. Advertisements for the course promise "exciting, high-paying jobs."

However, it becomes clear that the only jobs offered are to model clothes at local schools. The student decides to avoid the contract but is told that the note has been transferred to a bank that is a holder in due course. Must she pay as promised?

11. You contract for aluminum siding to be installed on the building of your skateboard manufacturing business. You sign a promissory note for $10,000 payable to the order of the siding company. Later, although the siding company has gone out of business without doing the job, a bank demands payment of the note. The bank purchased the instrument from the siding company for $9,500 and is a holder in due course. Are you legally required to pay the note?

31-2 The Law of Electronic Fund Transfers

GOALS
■ Distinguish the financial transactions that are electronic fund transfers

■ State the rules controlling electronic fund transfers

KEY TERMS
electronic fund transfer (EFT)

Electronic Fund Transfers Act (EFTA)

Electronic Fund Transfers

WHAT'S YOUR VERDICT? As Snyder used her ATM card at her bank's drive up machine, her PIN was observed by a man parked nearby using binoculars. He then followed Snyder and, later in the day, while she ran into a convenience store to grab a soda, stole her purse with the card in it from her car. Snyder immediately notified the police of the theft but she did not notify her financial institution for three days. During that time the thief took out $2,100 in cash advances using the card.

Who is liable for the loss?

A transfer of funds that requires a financial institution to debit or credit an account and that is initiated by the use of an electronic terminal,

© GETTY IMAGES/PHOTODISC

To prevent what happened to Snyder in *What's Your Verdict?* from happening to you, what safety precautions can you take when using an ATM machine?

LAW BRIEF

A new law, called Check 21, went into effect in late 2004 to eliminate the problems caused by the grounding of airlines during the 9/11 crisis. What did that tragic incident have to do with checks? It prevented the quick transfer by air of tens of millions of paper checks. As a consequence millions of consumers got the use of hundreds of millions of dollars for a few more days of "float time" (the time between writing a check and when it is deducted from your account). Check 21 eliminates that ever occurring again by allowing such checks to be immediately taken electronically (as a debit card expenditure is) against an account. This will result in the elimination of "float time" and, according to consumer groups, result in seven million more checks being returned for insufficient funds each year. The law also allows the destruction of cashed paper checks as long as an electronic image of the check is retained. This will cause problems not only in identifying forgeries but also, because of the lack of fingerprint identification, in catching the forgers. In addition Check 21 will not speed up the time in which the funds from deposited funds become available to you.

computer, telephone, or magnetic tape is an **electronic fund transfer (EFT)**.

EFTs basically are conducted without such paper instruments as checks or drafts. Automated teller machines, point-of-sale terminals in stores, pay-by-phone systems that eliminate check writing, and automated clearinghouse networks that credit payroll checks directly to accounts are examples of devices that facilitate EFTs.

Electronic Fund Transfers Act

Commercial paper law, due to its emphasis on the need for a writing, was generally inapplicable to EFTs. Therefore, the federal government enacted the **Electronic Fund Transfers Act (EFTA)** to protect consumers making such transfers. The EFTA emphasizes that the use of such transfers is to be purely voluntary. When an EFT is used, the consumer must immediately receive a written receipt and later must receive a statement of all transfers during a particular period. If the consumer detects an error of overbilling, it must be reported within 60 days of the date the statement was sent. The error is reported to the institution responsible for the EFT. The institution then has 10 business days to investigate and to report the results in writing. If the institution needs more time, it can use up to 45 days, but during this latter period the funds must be made available to the consumer.

IN THIS CASE In preparation for their world cruise, the Penguinns bought a large set of luggage at a discount store in a Florida port city. The luggage had detachable pricing bar-code labels on the packaging. As they were going through the checkout, Mr. Penguinn gave the pricing label for the luggage to the sales clerk who then ran it under the bar code reader. Mr. Penguinn then reattached it to the packaging. Not noticing, Mrs. Penguinn did the same, resulting in the Penguinn's paying twice for the luggage. They did not notice the error until they returned from their cruise three months later. As the deadline (60 days after the statement was sent) was long since passed, the Penguinn's could not reclaim the over-billed amount from the financial institution.

In the case of unauthorized transfers, Congress rejected the idea present in commercial paper law requiring full liability on the part of a depositor who negligently allows such a transfer (by losing a check, for example). Instead, Congress chose to divide the risk of unauthorized transfers between the consumer and the financial institution, even if the depositor is negligent. As a consequence,

In your opinion, do the safeguards provided by the EFTA provide adequate protection for consumers who transfer funds electronically? Would you feel safe transferring funds electronically from your bank accounts? Why or why not?

© GETTY IMAGES/PHOTODISC

What are the basic differences between consumer EFTs and business EFTs?

as long as the financial institution is notified within two business days of learning of the loss or theft of the card, the consumer is responsible only for the lesser of $50 or the value obtained in unauthorized transfers prior to the notification. However, if more than two days have elapsed before notification, the consumer may be responsible for up to a maximum of $500.

In *What's Your Verdict?* because three days went by before Snyder gave notification of her loss, she will probably have to pay $500 and the financial institution will have to absorb the other $1,600.

UCC Article 4A

While consumer electronic fund transfers are governed by the EFTA as administered by the Federal Reserve Board, electronic fund transfers by businesses are governed by Article 4A of the

UCC. These transfers generally involve large sums of money between highly sophisticated parties. Speed in making the transfer often is very important.

CHECKPOINT Name the laws that govern consumer EFTs and business EFTs.

CyberLAW

A form of electronic fund transfer used widely in international transactions is *electronic data interchange (EDI)*. With EDI, transport documents such as bills of lading, and others, such as import-export papers and invoices, are sent via computer to their destinations. Use of EDI helps to speed up international transactions for multinational corporations and other companies that do business internationally. Rules governing the EDI transfer of bills of lading and other transport documents have been adopted by an international trade organization, the Comite

Maritime International (CMI). The rules govern the problem of negotiating the transport documents. The party who has the right to control and transfer the goods is designated as the "holder" in the computer records. According to CMI, EDI can be used for transport documents only upon agreement of all parties involved in the transaction.

THINK ABOUT IT

What are the incentives for businesses to use this method of transfer of documents?

THINK ABOUT LEGAL CONCEPTS

1. Checks are not covered by the Electronic Fund Transfers Act. **True or False?**

2. When an EFT takes place the consumer must immediately receive a(n) _?_.

3. If, upon receiving an account statement, an error of overbilling is detected by a consumer in an EFT, it must be reported within _?_ days from the date the statement was sent. (a) 15 (b) 30 (c) 60 (d) none of the above

4. Electronic fund transfers by businesses are covered by state law. **True or False?**

5. If negligent, the consumer can be held liable for up to $5,000 of the losses that result from a lost or stolen ATM card. **True or False?**

THINK CRITICALLY ABOUT EVIDENCE

Study the situation, answer the questions, and then prepare arguments to support your answers.

6. In one day, Barbara bought a new couch and paid by check, bought lunch and paid with her credit card, took out cash from an ATM at her bank, and transferred funds by phone from her savings to her checking account. Which of these transactions are EFTs?

7. When she bought lunch, Barbara was double charged. When she received her statement, she noted what had happened and notified the credit card company immediately. Her financial institution took 44 days to investigate the matter and recredited her account on the 45th day. Has the institution acted properly?

© PHOTODISC/GETTY IMAGES

Chapter 31 Assessment

Xtra! Quiz Prep
school.cengage.com/blaw/lawxtra

CONCEPTS IN BRIEF

31-1 Discharge of Commercial Paper

1. The vast majority of commercial paper is paid and discharged according to its terms.

2. Discharge of commercial paper obligations can occur as a result of payment, cancellation, alteration, impairment of collateral, and in the manner of contracts as by novation, accord and satisfaction, or operation of law.

3. When trying to collect on an instrument, a party who qualifies as either a holder in due course or a holder through a holder in due course is legally placed in a much better position than a mere holder or assignee.

4. Limited defenses are good against all holders or assignees except an HDC or an HHDC.

5. Universal defenses are good against all kinds of holders, including HDCs and HHDCs.

31-2 The Law of Electronic Fund Transfers

6. An electronic fund transfer (EFT) is a transfer of funds that requires a financial institution to debit or credit an account and that is initiated by the use of an electronic terminal, computer, telephone, or magnetic tape.

7. Congress chose to divide the risk of unauthorized EFTs between the consumer and the financial institution, even if the consumer is negligent in the matter.

YOUR LEGAL VOCABULARY

Match each statement with the term that it best defines. Some terms may not be used.

1. One who takes commercial paper after an HDC and thereby acquires the same rights

2. Holder who takes commercial paper in good faith without knowledge of any defect or overdue status and who gives value for it

3. Defenses good against all obligees

4. Defenses good against all obligees except HDCs and HHDCs

5. An act, such as drawing a line through an indorser's signature, done with the intent to discharge that person's obligation on a negotiable instrument

6. A debit or credit to an account that is initiated by the use of a terminal, computer, telephone, or magnetic tape

7. A party's unauthorized change to or completion of a negotiable instrument intended to change the obligation of a party

a. alteration
b. cancellation
c. consumer transaction
d. electronic fund transfer (EFT)
e. Electronic Fund Transfers Act (EFTA)
f. holder in due course (HDC)
g. holder through a holder in due course (HHDC)
h. limited defenses
i. universal defenses

REVIEW LEGAL CONCEPTS

8. Why would a holder be able to cancel the obligation of an indorser on an instrument but not be required to cancel the obligation of the primary obligor at the same time?

9. Why might the payment of a nominal amount for an instrument relative to its face value effect the holder's chances of becoming an HDC?

10. Why does an HHDC have the same rights as an HDC?

11. In what ways can electronic transfers benefit (a) consumers and (b) the banking industry? Do you see any disadvantages to using electronic transfers rather than commercial paper?

WRITE ABOUT LEGAL CONCEPTS

12. Explain the importance of the status of holder in due course.

13. Why should a holder be denied the chance to acquire the rights of an HDC by reacquisition?

14. What is the purpose of the Electronic Fund Transfers Act, and how does it accomplish that purpose?

15. **HOT DEBATE** Write a persuasive letter from the Reverend Robert Shore to the president of the Commerce Bank of Statusville asking for more time to pay the note.

MAKE ACADEMIC CONNECTIONS

16. **ETHICS** A remarkably high percentage of commercial paper is paid off on time. Such instruments and their electronic substitutes have become the backbone of our commerce. Cash, once the unquestionable medium of exchange, has become suspect, requiring all manner of reports to the government if used in only moderate amounts. Do you feel that this shift has occurred because of the legal protections (such as those discussed in this chapter) provided those who take commercial paper in return for goods and services? Or is the shift grounded in an ethical basis? Write a paragraph answering this question and supporting your answer.

THINK CRITICALLY ABOUT EVIDENCE

Study the situation, answer the questions, and then prepare arguments to support your answers.

17. Abbiatti operated her own computer repair business. To work on the newer models, she purchased a set of advanced instruments for $2,300 from CompRepare, Inc. She paid $300 down and signed a 180-day negotiable note payable to CompRepare for the balance. After using the tools, she realized they were not of the precision required or promised. She refused to pay. In the meantime, the note had been sold to the People's Commercial Bank, an HDC, for $1,850. Can the bank overcome Abbiatti's defense and collect?

18. When Rebel T. Clef, a rock star, landed at the local airport, a young woman persuaded him to sign his autograph on a blank sheet of paper. The woman was a skilled typesetter. She went home and printed all the essential language of a promissory note around the signature. After filling in the amount of $15,000 and inserting her name as payee, she sold the note to an HDC. Is Rebel legally obligated to pay the $15,000?

19. Eaton owed Fobair $1,500 for supplies he purchased the year before for his business. Fobair had sold the supplies to Eaton on credit even though he knew that Eaton's business was on the ropes and he would likely not be able to pay. Months later Fobair met Eaton in a restaurant and loudly demanded either cash or a signature on a promissory note with an extremely high interest rate or he would "haul you into court and sue you for all you've got." Eaton signed, and Fobair promptly sold and assigned the note to Livingston. Now Eaton refuses to pay the note, claiming it was signed under duress. Will this be a valid defense to payment?

20. If, in exercise 19, Livingston sold the note to the Hometown Bank, Inc., an HDC, and then Fobair bought it from the Bank, could Fobair collect on the note?

21. Instead of receiving a paycheck every two weeks, Allessandro runs her payroll card through a machine as she leaves work. The card is thereby electronically credited with the amount of her pay and then used in the same way as any other EFT card. One pay day, right after work, Allessandro played third base for the company softball team. After the game, the team went to a local diner. As Allessandro went to pay for her meal, she discovered that her card was missing. She immediately reported the situation to the issuer. Only a few minutes later the card was used to purchase a $2,000 set of golf clubs. What is the extent of Allessandro's liability for the purchase?

22. On May 2, as part of the $96,500 purchase price of some real estate, Collins issued a 30-day note for $66,500. Just before the due date, Collins ordered his attorney, Sanders, to have money available from Collins' account to pay the note. The attorney had the money and did pay the note, but directed the payees to indorse the instrument in blank rather than mark the note paid. Sanders then, without Collins' knowledge, took the note and, on June 3, pledged it as security to the Oswego Bank for a loan the bank had made to the attorney. When Sanders defaulted on the loan, the bank tried to collect against Collins. Was the Oswego Bank an HDC and therefore able to overcome Collins' defense of prior payment? (*Collins v. First National Bank of Oswego, Kansas,* 746 S.W.2d 424)

23. The Pierces purchased siding for their home from the Globe Remodeling Company, Inc. They gave a promissory note for $3,044.40 in payment. In exchange, they were to receive sufficient siding for the job, properly installed, together with $1,200 in cash. Globe indorsed the note to the Gramatan Company, Inc. Gramatan then sold it without indorsement to its affiliate, the plaintiff, Gramatan National Bank, for $2,250. The bank had previously placed Globe on its "precautionary list" because it knew that in other sales, Globe had not performed as promised. The bank also knew that similar Globe notes were being litigated and that federal law enforcement officials had been investigating Globe's activities. In this case, only about $400 had been paid to the Pierces. In addition, only about one-half the siding had been delivered, and none had been installed. The Pierces refused to pay the note, and the bank sued. Is the bank a holder in due course? (*Gramatan National Bank and Trust Co. v. Pierce,* 159 A.2d 781)

24. A vacuum cleaner sales representative approached the Charltons and offered them a deal called the "club plan." Under its terms, the Charltons were to make appointments in their area for sales representatives to demonstrate the cleaners. For each appointment leading to a sale, the Charltons were to receive $25. After some discussion, the couple read and signed the club plan. Then the sales representative mentioned that because they were to be agents for the company, he wanted to leave a vacuum cleaner with them. He then had them sign a "receipt" for the cleaner. Taking his word for the nature of the document (although they could have read the instrument), the Charltons then signed the receipt. Only later, when approached by the Local Finance Company for payment, did the Charltons find out that the receipt was actually a promissory note. Can they successfully defend against payment by claiming fraud in the execution? (*Local Finance Co. v. Charlton,* 289 S.W.2d 157)

25. Cameo State Bank mistakenly believed that a credit life insurance policy had paid an $8,000 note it held. Consequently, it marked it "paid" and returned it to the heirs of the deceased maker. Having discovered the mistake, the bank now asks the court to void the release and enforce the note against the estate. Will the bank be able to recover the amount due from the estate? Why or why not? (*Cameron State Bank v. Sloan,* 559 S.W.2d 564)

26. Ognibene withdrew $20 at an automated teller machine (ATM) through the use of his Citibank card and the entry of his confidential personal identification number. As he did so, he was evidently observed by an individual who was using a telephone located between Ognibene's ATM and an adjacent ATM. The individual was seemingly reporting to the bank that the adjacent ATM was not working. The person, speaking into the telephone said, "I'll see if his card works in my machine." He then borrowed Ognibene's card and inserted it in the other ATM several times, finally stating, "Yes, it seems to be working." Then he returned Ognibene's card. Later, Ognibene discovered $400 had been withdrawn from his account by the person. Ognibene then sued the bank to have the $400 recredited to his account claiming it was an unauthorized transaction under the EFTA. The bank refused, stating that by giving the other person the card, Ognibene had "authorized" the transaction and was fully liable even though Ognibene had obviously not benefited from the transaction at all. Do you agree with the bank or with Ognibene? (*Ognibene v. Citibank N.A.,* 446 N.Y.S. 2d 845)

Case For Legal Thinking

KRAEMER V. LEBER
267 S.W. 2D 333

FACTS The Kraemers needed money. They owned certain pieces of real estate in Jefferson County, Missouri, and decided to use them as collateral for a loan. To accomplish this, they went to the office of George Pickles, a real estate dealer in the area. There they executed a negotiable promissory note in the principal sum of $50,000, payable five years after date. The note bore the interest rate of 8 percent. They then executed a deed of trust on their real estate as security for the loan.

The promissory note and the deed of trust were in favor of Grace A. Wheeler, the daughter of George Pickles. Ms. Wheeler was merely acting as a "straw party" for her father. As a consequence, she claimed no interest in the notes and indorsed them without recourse to her father, George Pickles. The note provided that payments thereon were to be made at the office of George Pickles. The deed of trust also allowed that the debtors could make payments in multiples of $1,000 at any time on the note.

During the next three years, plaintiffs made more than $12,000 in payments on the note. Whenever these payments were made, Mr. Pickles would hand to the plaintiffs a printed form of receipt showing the date of payment, the amount paid on the principal, and the amount of the principal remaining to be paid. No indorsement of payment on the note itself was ever made.

Ultimately, Mrs. J. C. Leber purchased the note for $45,000. At that time no notice was given to her of the payments rendered by the Kraemers. Later Mr. Pickles received two other payments on the note but did not remit them to Mrs. Leber.

When Mr. Pickles died before the note matured, Mrs. Leber contacted the Kraemers and for the first time advised them that the note had been purchased by her and that she had been advised by Mr. Pickles' business associate that now "she could do her own collecting."

When the Kraemers and Mrs. Leber could not agree on the amount due on the note, she began foreclosure proceedings. Ultimately, the property was sold and the proceeds deposited in the office of the circuit clerk for disposition by the court. The lower court then refused to give the Kraemers full credit for their payments. They appealed.

REASONING The note was a negotiable instrument of such a character that plaintiffs were bound to have known that it could and probably would be negotiated and passed into the hands of a third party. As a consequence plaintiffs in making payments on this note should have ascertained that the person to whom payment was made either owned the note or had possession thereof for the purpose of collection.

CONCLUSION Judgment of the lower court is affirmed as to the Kraemers not receiving credit for their payments against the face of the note.

PRACTICE JUDGING

1. Should the Kraemers have to pay the full face amount to Mrs. Leber? Why or why not?

2. What other alternatives do the Kraemers have in this situation?

3. Who could the Kraemers sue for their losses in this matter if they must pay the full amount on the note to Mrs. Leber? What legal barriers might they have to overcome to successfully recover their funds in each instance?

Chapter 32
Secured and Unsecured Credit Transactions

32-1 What Is a Secured Credit Transaction?

32-2 How Are Security Interests Perfected and Terminated?

HOT DEBATE

Zenobia owned several rental properties in Walnut Grove. When they were unoccupied, she had to mow their yards. If she didn't, the city would mow them and bill her. As a consequence, she bought a $3,500 riding lawnmower from the local hardware store. She financed $3,000 of the purchase price, and the hardware store took a security interest in the lawnmower and properly filed their financing statement to perfect it. A year later, Zenobia still owed $2,400 on the lawnmower but had sold her rental properties. Just before moving out of state, she held a garage sale and sold the lawnmower for $2,000 to her neighbor, Susan, who bought it in good faith and without knowledge of the lien against it. Susan intended to use it to mow her home's one-and-a-half acre lawn. Zenobia then stopped making payments and left no forwarding address. Two months later the hardware store repossessed the lawnmower from Susan.

© GETTY IMAGES/PHOTODISC

WHERE DO YOU STAND?

1. As Susan was not a businessperson, but a consumer, should the hardware store legally be able to repossess the mower? Why or why not?
2. Ethically, is it right to favor an experienced commercial entity over an inexperienced consumer?

32-1 What Is a Secured Credit Transaction?

GOALS

■ Assess the importance of secured credit transactions

■ Discuss how a security interest is created

KEY TERMS

credit

debt

debtor

creditor

secured transaction

security interest

collateral

right of repossession

secured party

pledge

security agreement

Importance of Secured Credit Transactions

WHAT'S YOUR VERDICT? The First National Bank of Bassland held a security interest in Sinquer's fishing boat. When Sinquer spent too much time on the water and lost her job, the bank repossessed the boat. Unfortunately, the boat sold for $5,000 but the amount of the debt secured by it was $7,000.

How can the bank collect the remaining $2,000?

In the U.S. economy, all purchases are made either with cash or credit. No debt is involved in a cash transaction. In a purchase on **credit**, however, whole or partial payment is delayed and whatever is owed as payment is referred to as a **debt**. A **debtor** is a person or a business that owes

LAW BRIEF

A bad check is a check written when the amount of money in a checking account is not enough to cover it. Writing a bad check is a crime in all states. Under typical bad-check statutes, it is a crime to write a check with intent to defraud, knowing that the funds are not sufficient to cover the check when presented for payment.

money, goods, or services to another as a consequence of such a credit transaction. The **creditor** is the one to whom the debt is owed.

In a sale on credit, the seller is understandably concerned about getting paid in full and on time, as promised by the buyer. The more reassurance society can offer possible extenders of credit, the more business activity and general prosperity in the economy. One legal device that encourages such performance by buyers and is used frequently by sellers on credit is called a secured transaction.

A **secured transaction** is a contractual exchange that creates a security interest in personal

For what types of purchases do you think consumers should be willing to enter into a secured transaction?

property or fixtures. As discussed in the chapters on property, *fixtures* are items of personal property that have become permanently attached to realty. A **security interest** is the interest in or claim against the debtor's property created for the purpose of assuring payment of the debt. **Collateral** is the term given to the property that is subject to the security interest of the creditor.

In a secured transaction, if the debtor-buyer defaults by failing to pay as promised, the creditor-seller, or lender, may exercise the legal **right of repossession**. This means the seller on credit (or the finance company that has provided money for the purchase) takes the goods back, resells them, and uses the net proceeds (after expenses of the repossession and resale are taken out) to pay against the balance due. If there is any excess, it is returned to the original debtor-buyer. If there is still a remaining balance due, as in *What's Your Verdict?*, the seller can sue the original debtor-buyer to collect against her or his other assets. Creditors, be they sellers on credit or lenders of money, are thus more likely to be paid if they are secured parties. A **secured party** is a person who has a security interest in collateral owned by the debtor.

In contrast, a creditor holding a defaulted unsecured claim must first sue, get a court judgment, and then execute (enforce) that judgment against the debtor's property. In doing so the creditor may run into several problems. For example, it may be difficult to determine the identity and location of that property. In addition, other creditors of the debtor may have equal or superior rights in it. If the debtor's financial obligations are discharged in bankruptcy, the unsecured creditor may receive nothing or only a few cents for each dollar of the unpaid debt rightly claimed. In contrast, in a bankruptcy proceeding, a secured

A Question of ETHICS

In the Middle Ages it was unethical for anyone to loan money at interest. The practice was forbidden by the Church and punished in the Church's courts. Why do you think charging interest was considered unethical? Do you agree? Why is charging too much interest (as with usury or loan sharking) considered illegal today? Do you think these practices should be illegal? Why or why not?

IN THIS CASE

When Phil Slither of Debtor Dogs Inc. showed up to repossess Altous Hammond's pickup truck, Altous drove it into his garage, slammed the garage door, and locked it. Altous then stood in front of the door and told Phil that he wouldn't give him the truck until they pried the keys from his cold, dead fingers. Slither then called the local sheriff's office and had a deputy report to the scene. The deputy inspected Slither's credentials and documents, and then ordered Altous to peacefully allow the repossession, which he did.

creditor typically will be able to repossess the collateral, sell it, and keep the proceeds up to the amount of the debt. If the proceeds do not extinguish the debt, the secured creditor can then file for the remainder as an unsecured creditor.

CHECKPOINT What is collateral?

Creation of Security Interests

WHAT'S YOUR VERDICT?

Earl needed new false teeth but had a bad credit standing. The Smile Center made a new set for Earl but, under an agreement with him, kept possession of them until Earl had paid in full.

What kind of a secured transaction was this?

Before the Uniform Commercial Code (UCC) was enacted, many types of legal transactions gave creditors special rights in the property of debtors. Each type had distinct rules for its creation, maintenance, and execution. These rules varied from state to state. Their number and technical nature created a situation that enabled unscrupulous individuals to take advantage of the unsuspecting or the uninformed.

The UCC, however, solved many of the problems by making secured transactions the only legal means of giving a creditor a security interest in another's property. These UCC provisions apply only to personal property and fixtures. Contracts involving real property as security, such as mortgages and deeds of trust, are still governed by a variety of other state laws.

A security interest under the UCC can be created only with the consent of the debtor. Such consent usually is given if suitable collateral is available because otherwise the creditor simply refuses to deal.

A security interest is created when three things take place. First, there must be an agreement between the debtor and creditor by which the debtor creates in the creditor a valid security interest. Second, the creditor must give value. Third, the debtor must have rights (either ownership or possession) in the collateral. These three things can occur in any order but when all three have occurred, the security interest becomes enforceable against the debtor. Note that the agreement may be expressed orally or in writing, depending on which of two basic types of secured transactions is used.

When the Creditor Has Possession of the Collateral

In the first type of secured transaction, the creditor obtains possession of the collateral. This transaction, which may be based on an oral or written agreement, is called a **pledge**. To be a pledge, the creditor must have possession of the collateral until the loan is discharged. Earl's teeth were the collateral for a pledge in *What's Your Verdict?*

Should the debtor default, the creditor has a legal right to sell the property and apply the proceeds of the sale to the debt. Any surplus is returned to the debtor. Any deficit remains an obligation of the debtor and is collectible as an unsecured claim through a lawsuit.

When the Debtor Retains Possession of the Collateral

In the second type of secured transaction, the debtor retains possession of the collateral under written

contract with the secured party. This contract, which must explicitly create or provide for a security interest in the creditor, is termed a **security agreement**. The security agreement must contain sufficient information to clearly identify the collateral, and the debtor must sign it.

It is this second type of secured transaction that typically is used to enable a consumer to buy an automobile, major kitchen appliance, or other costly item on credit. The debtor gets immediate possession and use of the goods. But the seller (or the bank or finance company) that lends money needed for the credit sale has the right to take the goods back if a payment is missed or if the contract is breached.

In a similar manner, a retail merchant can buy a shipment of goods on credit from a wholesaler or manufacturer. The retailer then routinely sells the goods to customers who get clear title. When the goods are sold to such consumers, the merchant gets paid and in turn pays the supplier. The supplier continues to be protected by the security interest that remains in all of the goods in the shipment that are still unsold.

This second type of secured transaction also is used in lending money because a lender often demands the security of collateral. Suppose you want to borrow $1,000 from a bank. By giving the bank a security interest in your car or other valuable personal property, such as your personal computer, your promise to repay the loan is strengthened. This is true because the bank has

Assume that this homeowner purchased the appliances for this newly remodeled kitchen by borrowing money from a finance company. What likely will happen to the appliances if the homeowner misses several payments?

the legal right to repossess the collateral in case of default and then to sell it and apply the proceeds of the sale to repay the loan. If the bank approves the loan, which it is likely to do with this added security, you obtain the desired money and still have the use of your property.

When the borrower retains possession of the collateral, the secured party may have problems repossessing the goods in case of default. Repossession must be accomplished without committing a breach of the peace (that is, without violence, actions likely to produce violence, or other violation of the law). Also the secured party

may find that the collateral has been improperly maintained, subjected to the claims of other creditors, or even sold. Even so, the UCC gives the secured party maximum protection against most such occurrences, provided the security interest has not only been properly created but also has been "perfected." How a security interest is perfected is discussed in the next lesson.

CHECKPOINT What types of property can be collateral for secured transactions under the UCC?

32-1 Assessment

Xtra! Study Tools
school.cengage.com/blaw/lawxtra

THINK ABOUT LEGAL CONCEPTS

1. A security interest is the interest in or claim against a creditor's property, created for the purpose of assuring payment of the debt. **True or False?**

2. A *secured party* is a person who has a security interest in collateral owned by the creditor. **True or False?**

3. When collateral is legally repossessed, the creditor has a legal right to sell the property and apply

the proceeds of the sale to the debt and the costs involved in the repossession and sale. Any surplus is returned to the (a) obligee (b) state (c) creditor (d) none of the above

4. In a pledge does the debtor retain possession of the collateral? **Yes or No?**

5. Repossession must be accomplished without committing a breach of the peace. **True or False?**

THINK CRITICALLY ABOUT EVIDENCE

Study the situation, answer the questions, and then prepare arguments to support your answers.

6. When Dodrill started her own copying and duplicating business, she entered into several contractual arrangements. First, she bought $900 worth of paper from Springfield Business Supply, promising to pay the money within 30 days. Then, using her bank credit card, she purchased spreadsheet and word processing software. In addition, she bought several desktop-copying units from the manufacturer on a 24-month installment purchase plan. The plan permitted the seller to repossess the machines if Dodrill defaulted on payments. Finally, Dodrill borrowed $2,000 from the Ozark Region National Bank to meet current expenses, giving a U.S. Treasury bond as security for repayment. Which of the transactions entered into by Dodrill involved a debtor-creditor relationship? Which relationships were secured? Which were unsecured?

7. Fanno pondered the pros and cons of buying versus leasing a costly computer system for his business. "There are so many improvements coming along," he said, "that I could be stuck with an obsolete white elephant if I buy. On the other hand, leasing eventually costs more because the lessor earns a profit too." Finally Fanno bought the needed machine in a five-year secured transaction. He told a friend, "If something better comes along while we're still making payments, I'll simply default and let the seller repossess the obsolete equipment." Could Fanno legally default as planned? Would it be ethical if this shifted the loss on the obsolete gear to the seller? How would the seller "have the last laugh" in this situation?

32-2 How Are Security Interests Perfected and Terminated?

GOALS

- Explain how a security interest is perfected
- Describe the ways in which security interests can be terminated

KEY TERMS

perfected security interest

financing statement

constructive notice

purchase money security interest

intangible property

termination statement

Perfecting a Security Interest

WHAT'S YOUR VERDICT?
When Horton defaulted on his loan to the Zuesstown Bank, the bank repossessed the collateral, Horton's collection of rare musical instruments. When they did so, they discovered that another bank also had a security interest in the instruments, and it had perfected before Zuesstown.

When the collateral is sold, how will the proceeds be used?

It is possible for a debtor to agree to give many different creditors, each unaware of the others, a security interest in the same goods. As a consequence, the sale of the collateral upon default and repossession might not produce enough proceeds to satisfy all the secured parties. The UCC therefore specifies that the first creditor to perfect a security interest is able to satisfy the entirety of her or his debt before the other creditors receive a penny of any left over proceeds. In *What's Your Verdict?* the Zuesstown Bank would only receive what proceeds, if any, were left over after the other bank had its loan completely paid.

If it were somehow guaranteed there would be only one creditor, there would be no need to perfect the security interest. This is because a security interest is valid against a debtor whether or not it has been perfected. A **perfected security interest**

Economic Impact

"CHIPPED" PASSPORTS AND IDENTITY THEFT

In August of 2006, the U.S. government began issuing a new type of passport with an embedded microchip containing a facial image and current data on the passport holder. At the instigation of the United States, similar chipped passports have now been issued by 24 of the 27 foreign governments whose citizens are not required to have a visa to enter the United States. There are recorded instances, however, of the British and other chipped passports being remotely stripped of their data by laptop computers connected to commercially available chip readers. Privacy advocates have expressed concerns about the ability of anyone in the vicinity to read the chips' signals and collect data on the owners. They also cited other potential problems including the ease with which terrorists could spot American tourists abroad. Suggestions that the information be protected by PIN numbers as with debit and credit cards were dismissed.

THINK CRITICALLY

Has the U.S. government taken adequate steps to prevent the stripping of vital personal information from the new passports? What further steps would be advisable in the fight against identity theft?

exists whenever the secured party has provided sufficient notice to other potential creditors of the existence of his or her secured position in particular collateral.

Notice Through Possession

A perfected security interest results when the creditor gives proper notice of the existence of her or his security interest to all other potential creditors. Such notice may be given in a number of ways. For example, a creditor in possession of the collateral, as in a pledge, needs to take no additional steps for protection. Possession alone is notice to any possible subsequent buyer or creditor of the debtor that a security interest may exist. The creditor who has possession, thereby, has a perfected security interest. If a creditor is able to repossess collateral upon default, the act of retaking possession also perfects the security interest even though the interest had not been perfected previously.

Notice Through Filing a Financing Statement

When the debtor has the goods, it may be necessary for the creditor to file a financing statement to perfect the creditor's interest. A **financing statement** is a brief, written notice of the existence of a

---

UNIFORM COMMERCIAL CODE—FINANCING STATEMENT—UCC-1

This FINANCING STATEMENT is presented to a filing officer for filing pursuant to the Uniform Commercial Code. 3 Maturity date (if any):

1 Debtor(s) (Last Name First) and address(es)	2 Secured Party(ies) and address(es)	For Filing Officer (Date, Time, Number, and Filing Office)
Daley, John C. and Ava G. 116 Seashore Drive Biloxi, MS 39534	Adam Cranston 485 Magnolia Street Gulfport, MS 39501	

4 This financing statement covers the following types (or items) of property:

"Smooth Sailin" Houseboat

Check ☒ if covered   ☐ Proceeds of Collateral are also covered   ☐ Products of Collateral are also covered   No. of additional sheets presented

Filed with _____

By: _John C. Daley_ _Ava G. Daley_   By: _Adam Cranston_
Signature(s) of Debtor(s)   Signature(s) of Secured Party(ies)

Filing Officer Copy—Alphabetical

This form of financing statement is approved by the Secretary of State.

STANDARD FORM—UNIFORM COMMERCIAL CODE—UCC-1

security interest in the identified property. (See the example on the previous page.) It must, to comply with UCC requirements, include the following:

1. the names and addresses of both the debtor and the creditor
2. the signature of the debtor (although the creditor also may sign and commonly does)
3. a statement describing the items of collateral

If crops or things attached to buildings or land are involved, the land where such property is located also must be described. If the security agreement extends to products to be derived from the original collateral, such as the calves of cows, or proceeds from the resale of such collateral, these facts must be stated. The security agreement itself may be filed instead of the financing statement if it meets the necessary requirements.

On the financing statement, any description that identifies the collateral reasonably well suffices even though it might be necessary to ask questions to determine exactly what property was intended. Of course, a debtor who possesses two automobiles, a motorcycle, a racing bicycle, and a mountain bicycle should be more specific than listing an unspecified one of these vehicles as "my favorite wheels."

Filing a financing statement with the required governmental office gives **constructive notice** that a security interest in specific property exists. This means that the law presumes everyone has knowledge of the facts on file. Anyone sufficiently concerned may get actual notice by checking the public records. The place of filing varies from state to state and is specified in the state's version of the UCC. Depending on the type of collateral, filing may be required centrally in the office of the secretary of state, or locally in the office of the clerk in the county where the collateral is located, or both.

As explained in the following paragraphs, there are special provisions for perfecting the security interest that depend on whether the property in question is tangible or intangible.

Tangible Property

When tangible property is used as collateral, the procedure for perfecting the creditor's security interest depends on whether the goods are

- **consumer goods** used primarily for personal, family, or household purposes

- **farm products** crops, livestock, unmanufactured products of the farm, and farm supplies
- **inventory** business goods that are intended for sale or lease, or if they are raw materials, work in process, or materials used or consumed in a business
- **equipment** goods used by a business in performing its function, such as telephone equipment or computers

Goods can be in only one of these four classes at a given time. Their classification may change, however, if their use changes. For example, a television is classified as inventory if held by an electronics store for sale. If used as a part of a closed-circuit system in the store for security, it is equipment. If installed in the buyer's home for entertainment, it is a consumer good.

CONSUMER GOODS Filing is not required to protect a seller's security interest in consumer goods against other creditors of the buyer. This is known as a **purchase money security interest** and relieves retail merchants, who sell many thousands of articles on installment plans, of what would be a heavy burden in paperwork and in payment of filing fees. In case of default in payment, the creditor may repossess the goods from the original buyer. Although not legally obligated, most creditors tolerate late payment for perhaps ten or more days. They typically impose a penalty charge for use of this privilege.

© GETTY IMAGES/PHOTODISC

What type of goods would the instruments these professional musicians are playing be considered?

Filing would be required for consumer goods if the consumer already owned the goods and was simply borrowing against them as security. Filing also is necessary, even in initial purchases, if the seller wants protection against a third person who might innocently buy the good for personal, family, or household use from a dishonest debtor. Such a buyer of consumer goods, who gives value and does not know of the security interest, acquires clear title if there has been no filing.

On the other hand, if a filing is in the public records, the innocent purchaser of consumer goods is subject to the filed security interest in them due to the constructive notice the filing provides.

Because there are so many motor vehicles on the roads, some states provide that instead of filing as described above, a special office and procedure must be utilized. Thus, the security interest in motor vehicles often is perfected by noting its existence on the certificate of title to the vehicle that is registered in the proper state office. The certificate of title is then held by the creditor until paid.

An exception to the filing requirement also is made when fixtures are sold on credit. Fixtures are items of personal property that are permanently attached to real property in a manner that makes the law treat them like real property. A filing to protect a security interest in fixtures must include in the financing statement a description of the real property involved.

FARM PRODUCTS A security interest in farm products is perfected by filing or by taking possession of the products upon default. This applies to farm products bought on credit and to those used as security for loans. Most states require filing a

IN THIS CASE

Furrow, a Missouri farmer, took out a loan to buy seed from the Urbane Bank in a nearby city. In the security agreement with Urbane, he gave the creditor bank a security interest in his thresher and farm tractor. Because the Urbane Bank was not used to dealing in farm equipment, it misfiled the financing statement pertaining to the security interest by filing it only with the Secretary of State of Missouri and not with Furrow's county clerk. As a consequence, when Furrow took out another loan from a local bank to buy a stock car so as to live out his childhood dream of racing, the local bank just checked the records at the county courthouse. When no lien against Furrow's tractor and thresher was found, the local Bank took a secured interest in them. The local bank then filed properly with the appropriate county clerk. When Furrow crashed the stock car on the first turn of his first race and later defaulted on both loans, the local bank had the only perfected security interest in the tractor and thresher. Whatever proceeds that might have been left after the local bank forced the sale of Furrow's equipment and satisfied its lien fully, if possible, would go to the Urbane Bank.

financing statement for farm products with the clerk at the courthouse of the county where the products are stored.

What does the In This Case scenario suggest about the importance of filing the financing statement with the correct governmental office?

INVENTORY A security interest in inventory is perfected by filing or by taking possession of the inventory upon default. This is true whether the inventory is bought on credit or is put up as security for a loan. However, because inventory generally is purchased by business firms for the very purpose of reselling, a person buying from such a debtor in the ordinary course of business gets clear title to the goods even if aware of the security interest. For example, if you buy a stove at an appliance store, you get title to it free of the security interest held by the unpaid manufacturer or wholesaler who originally sold it to the store on credit.

EQUIPMENT A security interest in equipment is perfected by filing or by taking possession of the equipment upon default. This applies whether the equipment is bought on credit or is put up as security for a loan. If the equipment is a motor vehicle, a notation on the certificate of title may substitute for filing in perfecting the interest. As with inventory, perfection of a security interest in equipment requires filing with the state government, usually in the office of the secretary of state.

If inventory that has been put up as security for a loan is sold to a consumer, does the consumer get clear title to the goods if aware of the security interest? Why or why not?

Intangible Property

The second major classification of collateral—**intangible property**—represents value in rights to money, goods, or promises to perform specified contracts. Legal documents or other writings are generally evidence of intangible property. Intangible property includes the accounts receivable of a business, the rights to performance under a contract, bills of lading or airbills, warehouse receipts, commercial paper, and bonds or stocks.

The procedure used in perfecting a security interest in intangible property depends on the classification of that property. A security interest in accounts receivable or contractual rights that cannot be possessed in a physical sense must be perfected by filing unless the transaction does not cover a significant part of the debtor's accounts receivable or other contractual rights.

For documents used in bailments, such as bills of lading, airbills, and warehouse receipts, the creditor may either file a financing statement or take possession of the goods upon default. To perfect a security interest in commercial paper (promissory notes, stock certificates, or bonds), possession by the creditor, upon default of the debtor, is essential.

CHECKPOINT What is a financing statement?

Terminating a Security Interest

Most secured transactions are routinely terminated when the debtor pays the debt in full and the creditor releases the security interest in the collateral. If the creditor has filed a financing statement, this release is made when the creditor files an acknowledgment of the full payment, called a **termination statement**, with the governmental office that has the financing statement. Filing the termination statement informs potential buyers and creditors that the property is no longer collateral. For consumer goods, the termination statement must be filed within 30 days of the payoff or within ten days of a written request by the debtor. Otherwise the creditor must pay $100 plus damages to the debtor.

If the debtor defaults by failing to pay as promised, the secured creditor who does not have possession of the collateral may take possession of it. This may be done without legal proceedings, provided it does not involve a breach of the peace. The creditor may then sell, lease, or otherwise dispose of the collateral. This right of sale also applies after default for the benefit of the secured creditor who has retained possession of the property. The proceeds at disposition are applied to the reasonable expenses of retaking, holding, preparing for resale, and reselling. They also are applied to payment of reasonable attorney's fees and other legal expenses incurred. What remains of the proceeds then goes to pay off the secured debt. In some cases, other credi-

tors may have subordinate or secondary security interests in the collateral, and these are now paid off if proper claims have been made. Finally, if any surplus remains, it goes to the debtor. If there is any deficiency, the debtor is obligated to pay it unless otherwise agreed.

Even when in default as to payment or other performance of the security agreement, the debtor does not forfeit all rights. For example, the debtor may pay the balance due and the expenses of the creditor and redeem the collateral any time before the creditor has disposed of it or contracted for its disposal.

As an alternative to resale, the secured creditor may retain the collateral in full settlement of the debt. Written notice of the creditor's intention to keep the collateral must be given to the debtor. If the debtor (or any other person entitled to receive notice) objects in writing within 21 days,

The law firm of Frazier and Cataldo LLP purchased this yacht for the purpose of entertaining potential clients. Unfortunately, many of the firm's existing clients failed to pay for the legal services they received, so the firm was unable to make the payments on the yacht. If the company that made the loan takes possession of the yacht, what can it do with this collateral?

© PHOTODISC/GETTY IMAGES

the creditor must dispose of the collateral in a commercially reasonable manner by a public or private sale.

Additional protection is given to a consumer who has paid 60 percent or more of a secured debt. In these situations, the creditor may not keep the collateral in satisfaction of the debt unless the consumer agrees in writing. In the absence of such a written agreement, the creditor must sell the collateral within 90 days after the repossession. This law seeks to protect consumers in situations where the value of the goods exceeds the amount of the debt.

In *What's Your Verdict?* Tom had paid more than 60 percent of the amount due. Therefore, Sillitech must obtain Tom's written consent before Sillitech can keep the mower. Without that consent, the mower must be resold in a commercially reasonable manner within 90 days of the date of the repossession.

CHECKPOINT What significance does the termination statement have for the debtor?

32-2 Assessment

school.cengage.com/blaw/lawxtra

THINK ABOUT LEGAL CONCEPTS

1. A perfected security interest exists whenever the debtor has provided sufficient notice to other potential creditors of the existence of his or her secured position in particular collateral. **True or False?**

2. A _?_ is a brief, written notice of the existence of a security interest in the identified property. (a) statement of perfection (b) termination abatement (c) repossession agreement (d) none of the above

3. Computers used by a business in performing its function would be classified as equipment by the UCC. **True or False?**

4. Computers purchased for resale or lease by a business also would be classified as equipment by the UCC. **True or False?**

5. A termination statement in a consumer goods secured transaction must be filed within _?_ days of the payoff unless the consumer requests a quicker filing in writing. (a) 30 (b) 60 (c) 10 (d) none of the above

6. If a consumer has paid _?_ percent or more of the debt before having the collateral repossessed, the creditor may not keep the collateral in satisfaction of the debt unless the consumer agrees in writing. (a) 15% (b) 18% (c) 20% (d) 60%

THINK CRITICALLY ABOUT EVIDENCE

Study the situation, answer the questions, and then prepare arguments to support your answers.

7. Taft borrowed $50 from a friend, agreeing to repay $5 each week. Although the agreement was informal and oral, Taft gave the friend her high school class ring to hold until the debt was paid in full. Did the friend have a perfected security interest in the ring?

8. The Hunts need money for corrective surgery for their young son. They decided to borrow the money from Desperation Finance, from whom they had taken another loan three years before. As in the previous instance, the Hunts put up their boat and cars for collateral. Desperation, however, said that, although the previous loan was paid off,

a termination statement had not been filed on it and demanded $100 to file the appropriate paperwork in addition to the loan charges for the new loan. Do the Hunt's have to pay the $100?

9. Cuisine International sold kitchen equipment on credit to the Shoreline Resort. In the security agreement and in the financing statement the collateral was identified as "food service equipment delivered to the Shoreline Resort." When Shoreline was unable to pay its creditors, including Cuisine, some creditors claimed that the collateral description was too vague to create a valid security interest. Were they correct?

Chapter 32 Assessment

CONCEPTS IN BRIEF

32-1   What Is a Secured Credit Transaction?

1. A secured transaction is a contractual exchange in which a security interest in personal property or fixtures is created as assurance to a creditor that an underlying debt or other obligation will be paid.

2. In a secured transaction, upon default by the debtor, the creditor may obtain the collateral, sell it, and use the net proceeds (after expenses of the repossession and resale are taken out) to pay against the balance due.

3. A creditor holding a defaulted unsecured claim must first sue, get a court judgment, and then execute (enforce) that judgment against the debtor's property.

4. In a pledge, the creditor must have possession of the collateral.

5. In order for a creditor to obtain a security interest in a transaction where the debtor is to retain possession of the collateral, a written security agreement signed by the debtor is required.

32-2   How Are Security Interests Perfected and Terminated?

6. The first creditor to perfect a security interest is, upon default, able to repossess and sell the collateral and satisfy the entirety of her or his debt before the other creditors receive a penny of any left over proceeds.

7. A perfected security interest exists whenever the secured party has provided actual or constructive notice to other potential creditors of the existence of his or her secured position in particular collateral.

8. A creditor in possession of the collateral, as in a pledge, needs to take no additional steps for perfection as possession alone should be legally sufficient notice to any possible subsequent buyer or creditor of the debtor that a security interest may exist.

9. When the debtor has the goods, it may be necessary for the creditor to file a financing statement to perfect the creditor's interest.

10. In a consumer transaction when a purchase money security interest is involved, a filing is not required to perfect.

YOUR LEGAL VOCABULARY

Match each statement with the term that it best defines. Some terms may not be used.

1. Contract that creates or provides for a security interest

2. A person or business that owes money, goods, or services to another

3. An interest in or claim against specified property of the debtor, such interest being created in favor of the creditor to assure payment of the debt

4. Secured party's right to take back collateral to use in satisfying a debt

5. Property that is subject to the security interest of the creditor

6. Filing by a creditor releasing a security interest in collateral

7. A legal filing that makes subsequent creditors aware of a lien against potential collateral

8. Transfer of possession of property to a creditor to insure payment of a debt

9. Rights to money, goods, or promises to perform specified contracts

10. Document filed to provide notice of an established security interest to other potential creditors

a. collateral
b. constructive notice
c. credit
d. creditor
e. debt
f. debtor
g. financing statement
h. intangible property
i. perfected security interest
j. pledge
k. purchase money security interest
l. right of repossession
m. secured party
n. secured transaction
o. security agreement
p. security interest
q. termination statement

REVIEW LEGAL CONCEPTS

11. Why is the law of secured transactions so important to prospective debtors?

12. Why is an unsecured creditor at a disadvantage?

13. Why is possession alone a suitable notice to other creditors who might take a security interest in the collateral.

WRITE ABOUT LEGAL CONCEPTS

14. Why is a debtor allowed to force a sale in a commercially reasonable manner by objecting to the creditor's intent to retain the collateral as full settlement of the debt?

15. Why is it important to have a termination statement filed promptly?

16. **HOT DEBATE** Write a paragraph justifying the difference between a neighbor's purchase of a mower with the filing of a financing statement and a like purchase by a neighbor of a mower on which the seller holds only a purchase money security interest.

MAKE ACADEMIC CONNECTIONS

17. **SCIENCE** What could secured transactions have to do with the advancement of science, you ask. Research the availability of startup loans for companies wanting to develop marketable technology or research and development loans to established companies. Write a report on how the potential lenders evaluate their prospective investment opportunites and what they want to receive in return for a loan.

THINK CRITICALLY ABOUT EVIDENCE

Study the situation, answer the questions, and then prepare arguments to support your answers.

18. D'Artole, an accountant, bought for her personal use a new SUV for $47,500. She paid $10,000 down and then paid $1,250 per month for several months under a security agreement she had signed with the dealer, Where the Pavement Ends, Inc. Finally, she paid off the remaining balance with her Christmas bonus. The next May she needed a $25,000 loan to take advantage of a business opportunity. She offered the SUV as collateral, but the lender refused, saying there was a financing statement showing a security interest in the vehicle in favor of Where the Pavement Ends still on file. D'Artole did not get the loan as a result. What are her rights in this situation?

19. At a county fair in southwest Nebraska, Gull used cash to buy two cows and a bull, all purebred Holsteins. The seller was Spane, who had just moved to the area from another corner of the state bringing his livestock with him. Soon after, Gull was surprised and annoyed when he discovered that Spane had defaulted on a loan given to Spane in a secured transaction in his previous county. The bank in that county had a perfected security interest in the animals. When it repossessed them, Gull protested: "How was I

supposed to know that? I never had any notice of the bank's interest. Where's the proof?" Did Gull actually have legal notice of the bank's interest in, and prior claim to, the animals? Did Spane act ethically in their deal? What can Gull do now?

20. You buy a new jet ski on credit for your use at your vacation home at the lake. The seller properly files a financing statement evidencing its security interest in the jet ski. If you sell it to a friend before you have paid for it in full, does the friend get clear title? Why or why not?

21. Burney loaned Sampson $4,000 to buy a car. Sampson issued a promissory note in favor of Burney for that amount. Also, when he registered the new car, Sampson had Burney's name entered on the title as lienholder. Later Sampson took out a loan from the First National Bank of Pennsboro. After a few months, he defaulted on both the bank loan and the promissory note. The bank filed suit and obtained a judgment against Sampson that it sought to execute against the car. Burney maintained his security interest in the car took precedence over the Bank's claim. Who won?

ANALYZE REAL CASES

22. Shelton purchased an automobile on credit from Erwin. Both Shelton and Erwin clearly intended to create a security interest in the car in favor of Erwin. As a consequence, they signed a bill of sale that set out the terms of payment of the balance due and that also required that Shelton insure the auto until paid for in full. Shelton later obtained a title certificate from the state that clearly showed Erwin as the holder of a first lien on the car. Did these actions and documents give Erwin a security interest in the car? (*Shelton v. Erwin*, 472 F.2d 1118)

23. Speigle fell behind in his car payments to Chrysler Credit Corporation. He had made 14 monthly payments on a 36-month contract, and Chrysler had accepted several late payments. Then Speigle found himself out of both work and money. He was almost a month in default on a current payment. Speigle went to the Chrysler office to negotiate a solution to his problem. While there, a Chrysler employee parked a car behind Speigle's car, blocking it so it could not be moved. Another employee told him it was repossessed. Speigle sued, claiming Chrysler's conduct was inequitable and in breach of the peace. Do you agree? (*Speigle v. Chrysler Credit Corporation*, 56 Ala. App. 469, 323 So. 2d 360)

24. The Uniform Commercial Code excludes "money" from its definition of goods. As a consequence, a perfected security interest cannot be obtained in money merely by the creditor's taking possession of it. Midas Coin Company transferred possession of some rare U.S. coins to the St. John's Community Bank as security for a loan. Did the bank have a perfected security interest? (*In re Midas Coin Co.*, 264 F. Supp. 193)

25. The Franklin State Bank repossessed the Parkers' automobile because of the Parkers' delinquency in payments. At the time, Mr. Parker and his son were giving the engine of the car a tune-up in their garage. The vehicle was not mechanically operational because the spark plugs, points, condenser, and air filter had been removed. Franklin State Banks did not try to determine why the car was not mechanically operational. Instead, after a three-day notice to the Parkers, the bank sold the car at a private sale to an auto parts dealer for $50. The bank then sued the Parkers to recover the substantial balance of the purchase price remaining and unpaid. Which party should win the suit? Why? (*Franklin State Bank v. Parker*, 136 N.J. Super. 476, 346 A.2d 632)

26. When Ziluck submitted the application for his Radio Shack credit card, he signed an application that had the following statement above the signature line: "I have read the Radio Shack Credit Account and Security Agreement, including the notice provision in the last paragraph thereof. . . . And I agree to the terms of the Agreement and acknowledge receipt of a copy of the agreement." The Security Agreement referred to was on the back of the application and read in part: "We retain a security interest under the Uniform Commercial Code in all merchandise charged to your Account. If you do not make payments on your Account as agreed, the security interest allows us to repossess only the merchandise that has not been paid in full." Ziluck later filed for bankruptcy. The bankruptcy court had to determine whether or not this was a valid security agreement. It decided that it was not because (1) the signature was on the opposite side of the form from the "Agreement," and (2) any collateral subject to the agreement would be improperly described. Radio Shack appealed the decision of the bankruptcy court. Does Radio Shack have a case? Why or why not? (*In re Ziluck*, 139 Bankruptcy Reporter 44)

27. Calcote bought a car using a loan from Citizens & Southern National Bank. The bank obtained a security interest in the car. Calcote later defaulted on the loan and the bank repossessed the car. The bank then sent notice of the repossession, the bank's plans to sell the repossessed car at a private auction, and Calcote's right to demand a public sale to her at the last known address that the bank had. Calcote did not get the certified letter, yet the car was thereafter sold at a private sale with more than 150 dealers invited to participate. Calcote then brought suit against the bank due to its failure to properly notify her and dispose of the vehicle in a commercially reasonable fashion. Do you think the bank acted improperly? Why or why not? (*Calcote v. Southern National Bank*, 345 S.E.2d 616)

Case For Legal Thinking

IN RE HOLIDAY INTERVALS, INC.
931 F.2D 500

FACTS Holiday Intervals sold "time share" deeds for the Holiday Shores resort it was developing at the Lake of the Ozarks, Missouri. These deeds entitled buyers to spend one week per year at one of Holiday's units. Many of the buyers agreed to pay the purchase price through installment contracts. Some of these installment contracts contained a separate promissory note section that repeated the buyer's installment obligations in the form of a promissory note, while other contracts contained no promissory note section. Holiday obtained financing for construction of the units by assigning its copies of the installment contracts and promissory notes to the banks. The banks did not seek to perfect their security interests in these installment contracts and promissory notes. Instead they assumed that they had perfected their security interests by possession of the buyers' installment contracts and promissory notes.

After Holiday ran into financial difficulties, Holiday Owners (one of Holiday's creditors) and various other creditors filed an involuntary bankruptcy petition against Holiday. Holiday Owners took over operation of the resort afterwards.

When a bankruptcy petition is filed, claims against the debtor's estate are automatically stayed. In order to obtain the installment contract proceeds, the banks separately moved for relief from this automatic stay.

REASONING The banks sought relief on the ground that they held perfected security interests through possession of the installment contracts. In the alternative, the creditors claimed that even if they had not perfected their security interests as to all installment contracts, they had at least done so to those installment contracts

containing promissory notes. The bankruptcy court rejected both arguments and denied the banks' motion for relief from the automatic stay. The banks then appealed to the Federal District Court.

CONCLUSION OF THE FEDERAL DISTRICT COURT DECISION The district court affirmed the bankruptcy court's decision in part and reversed in part, holding that the banks had perfected their security interests in those installment contracts which contained promissory notes, but not in the other installment contracts which did not. All parties then appealed to the Federal Court of Appeals.

PRACTICE JUDGING

1. In reaching its decision, the federal appeals court noted the rule that the seller's interest in a land sale contract is a general intangible. If this is so, how is perfection to be achieved?

2. Given your answer to the above question, have the creditors perfected or are their interests to be treated the same as any other unsecured creditor and, therefore, subject to the stay?

Chapter 33
Creditors, Debtors, and Bankruptcy

33-1 Legal Protection of Creditors

33-2 Legal Protection of Debtors and Credit Card Users

33-3 Bankruptcy

HOT DEBATE

Norm was a foreign correspondent for a large national television network. One afternoon he took his expensive watch to a jewelry shop to be repaired. The jeweler recognized Norm and told him he watched his network. The jeweler said the watch would be ready the next day. Norm left the store. He then received a call telling him to pack and head for Western Russia. When he went to get his watch, almost four months later, the jeweler told him he had sold it after sending Norm ten reminders. Norm responded that there was no mail service where he had been. The jeweler shrugged and said he was just following the state's artisan's lien laws. Norm's attorney ultimately brought suit against the jewelry store for damages.

© GETTY IMAGES/PHOTODISC

WHERE DO YOU STAND?

1. What are the jewelry store's reasons for selling the watch?
2. What legal reasons support Norm's suit?

33-1 Legal Protection of Creditors

GOALS

- Recognize the value of a security interest
- Contrast a secured loan with an unsecured loan

KEY TERMS

pledgor	suretyship
pledgee	principal debtor
pawn	surety
lien	guarantor
mechanic's lien	unsecured debt
artisan's lien	garnishment

Laws That Protect Creditors

WHAT'S YOUR VERDICT? To finance her divorce, Quinlan pawned her engagement ring for $300. Three months later, when she and her husband made up, she went back to redeem the ring and was told that she now owed almost $350. Shocked, she realized that the interest rate she was being charged was nearly 72 percent a year.

Is this high rate of interest legal?

The primary concern of a typical creditor is that the loan be paid promptly when due. If it is not paid, and especially if costly efforts to collect it prove fruitless, the creditor usually suffers a significant financial loss. When feasible, such bad debt losses are shifted to other borrowers through higher fees and charges. Thus, it is in the interest of all society that fair and honest loans be collectible with minimum difficulty and expense. Laws that assist creditors in their collection efforts will be discussed in the following sections.

Laws Allowing Secured Debts

Taking a security interest in personal property and fixtures or a mortgage on real property are common ways the law allows creditors to protect themselves. If a default occurs, the creditor may then exercise the right under a mortgage to obtain a court order for sale of the property or, if the collateral is personal property or a fixture, the creditor may peacefully repossess it, if possible, and sell it to satisfy the loan.

PLEDGES Some secured debt arrangements permit the creditor to have possession of the property until the debt is paid. In the pledge, for example, the possession of personal property is transferred to a creditor as security for the payment of a debt or for the performance of an obligation. The property may be either goods or documents representing property rights (for example, corporate stock). The **pledgor** (debtor) voluntarily gives up possession of the property. The **pledgee** (creditor) gets possession. Normally, the debt is paid when due or the legal obligation is performed. Then the property is returned to the pledgor.

While the pledge lasts, the pledgee must treat the property with reasonable care. The property may, however, be repledged to a third party on

Would a coin collection be suitable as collateral for a pawn? Why or why not?

terms that do not prevent the pledgor from getting the property back when the debt is paid.

A **pawn** is a legally regulated pledge of tangible personal property, usually of small size and comparatively high value. Collateral for this type of pledge includes such durable and readily resalable items as jewelry, cameras, and musical instruments. It excludes intangible property rights, stocks and bonds, as well as other valuable documents. A pawnbroker lends money at interest and takes possession of tangible personal property from the borrower as security for repayment. The borrower who pawns goods gets a receipt known as a pawn ticket. When the borrower repays the debt together with interest due and turns in the pawn ticket, the pawnbroker returns the goods. As a pawn shop operation faces many risks, the law allows what would otherwise be a very high interest rate to be charged. In most states, as in *What's Your Verdict?*, this rate is between 5 and 6 percent per month or between 60 and 72 percent per year.

Because thieves sometimes convert stolen goods into cash by pawning them, special statutes regulate the business. These laws require that the pawnbroker be licensed, post a bond, and keep accurate records open to police inspection. If stolen goods are found in the pawn shop, they may be seized without compensation to the pawnbroker. Also, maximum limits are imposed on the rate of interest pawnbrokers may charge.

Goods that are pawned must be held by the pawnbroker for a time prescribed by law (four months is typical) before they can be sold. In most states, the rights of the parties to the proceeds of the sale are the same as for ordinary pledges. In some states, the pawnbroker automatically gets title to pawned and unclaimed goods at the end of a specified time.

INVOLUNTARY LIENS A **lien** is a claim, encumbrance, or charge against property that gives the creditor the right, in case of default on a payment that is due, to sell the property and to use the proceeds from the sale to pay the debt. Although most liens are created with the consent of the debtor-owner, statutes in many states create liens in favor of the creditor without such consent. These involuntary liens include the mechanic's lien and the artisan's lien.

The **mechanic's lien** allows a person who has not been paid for labor or materials furnished to build a home, building, or other real property improvement to file a legal claim against the property. If the debt

is not paid, the realty may be sold. The holder of the mechanic's lien then gets the amount owed from the proceeds of the sale. Thus, such a lien holder is entitled to the amount owed from the sale proceeds even before other claimants, such as a bank with a mortgage on the property, gets any money.

The **artisan's lien** allows persons who have not been paid for services, such as repairing a car or watch, to retain possession of the serviced items until the service charges are paid. A *hotelkeeper's*

If this carpenter does not receive the contractually agreed-to payment for the deck he is building, what kind of lien would be placed on the homeowner's real property?

lien, which is utilized against luggage or other items brought onto the premises by the guest, fulfills a function similar to an artisan's lien for those providing temporary quarters for short-term rental. If payment for room and board is not made, these retained goods may be sold to pay the debts that are due. An artisan's or hotelkeeper's lien holder who gives up possession of the property before the debtor pays for the services loses the lien.

Laws Involving Third Parties

In addition to liens, other means of protection are available to creditors. These means involve third parties and are known as suretyship and guaranty.

SURETYSHIP A creditor who wishes assurance beyond the debtor's promise to pay may demand that a creditworthy third party assume the liability. This is **suretyship**, a contractual relation in which a third party agrees to be primarily liable for the debt or obligation if payment or performance becomes overdue. Three parties are involved. The **principal debtor** owes the debt or obligation. The *creditor* is the one to whom the obligation is owed. The **surety** is the third party who promises to be liable in case of default by the principal debtor. The surety may be bound by an oral contract because a suretyship is a primary obligation. Nevertheless, such agreements usually are put in writing.

Suretyship contracts are discharged in much the same way as other contracts. If the debtor pays off the debt in full, the surety is discharged. The surety also is discharged if the creditor releases the debtor or alters the obligation, as by extending the time of performance, without the surety's consent. But a surety, who has to pay the obligation because the principal debtor does not, has a legal right to collect from the principal debtor.

If there are cosureties, any cosurety who pays the full debt may get a judgment against the other cosureties for their proportionate share of the debt. This is called the *right of contribution.*

GUARANTY The guaranty relationship also protects the creditor. In it, the third party, the **guarantor**, agrees to pay if the principal debtor fails to do so. Unlike a surety, therefore, the guarantor is only secondarily liable. In effect, the guarantor merely promises that the debtor will pay when the debt comes due. However, this means that the creditor must first sue the defaulting debtor and get a judgment that proves to be uncollectible.

In contrast, in a suretyship, such a suit is not necessary. The surety has primary liability equal to that of the debtor. Also unlike the suretyship, the contract creating the guaranty relationship must be in writing and signed by the guarantor to be enforceable under the Statute of Frauds.

Laws Concerning Unsecured Debts

When the debt is small or the credit standing of the borrower is very good, the creditor may be willing to take an **unsecured debt**. This is a debt based only on the oral or written promise of the debtor.

Upon default, an unsecured creditor is in a much weaker position than a secured creditor, because in order to collect, the unsecured creditor must sue the debtor for breach of contract. Then, upon obtaining judgment, the creditor must take legally prescribed steps to collect. This is costly and time consuming. Moreover, some debtors may prove to be dishonest and may move without

Imagine that the man on the left owes at least 100 creditors amounts between $250 and $500. Because he cannot pay them, his solution is to move to another state and not give anyone a forwarding address. Would the creditors likely pursue this man for payment of his outstanding balances? Why or why not?

leaving a forwarding address. Or they may have no assets that the creditor can take.

In other instances, debtors may discharge their obligations by going through bankruptcy. In a bankruptcy proceeding, secured creditors may sell the collateral and satisfy their entire claim with the proceeds before any unsecured creditor gets a dime.

Laws Allowing Garnishment of Wages

One other method for creditor protection is the **garnishment** of wages. Once a creditor's claim is shown to be legally valid and fair in a court hearing, the creditor may receive a portion of the debtor's wages directly from the debtor's employer. The total amount that can be garnished by all creditors, however, generally is limited by the Consumer Credit Protection Act to 25 percent of the debtor's take-home pay.

CHECKPOINT What is the primary difference between a surety and a guarantor?

33-1 Assessment

school.cengage.com/blaw/lawxtra

THINK ABOUT LEGAL CONCEPTS

1. While the pledge lasts, the pledgee must treat the property with reasonable care. **True or False?**

2. Is it possible for a debtor to pawn her or his house? **Yes or No?**

3. In a bankruptcy proceeding, unsecured creditors generally stand a better chance of being paid in full than secured creditors. **True or False?**

4. In a surety relationship, before the debt can be collected, a creditor first must sue the defaulting debtor and get a judgment that proves to be uncollectible. **True or False?**

5. An auto repair garage would be able to retain the car it has worked on until it was paid for the service because of its (a) mechanic's lien (b) artisan's lien (c) repairperson's lien (d) none of the above

THINK CRITICALLY ABOUT EVIDENCE

Study the situation, answer the questions, and then prepare arguments to support your answers.

6. After graduating from high school, Jack Tern decided to become a truck driver. The A-OK Truck Driving Academy offered a two-week, intensive, one-on-one (instructor-student) course with training on two- and three-axle tractors and on 45-foot single and double trucks, for $4,000 cash. Because Jack had no money, A-OK agreed to take his written promise to pay the tuition fee in monthly installments of $130 for four years provided he could get a surety or guarantor to promise to pay if he defaulted. Jack's Uncle Joe signed a guaranty agreement, and Jack enrolled and completed the course. After six months, however, he lost his job as a truck driver and could not continue making the monthly payments. Can A-OK immediately demand payment from Jack's Uncle Joe?

7. Gary Meter took his very expensive watch in for repair to Mike's service center. The bill for the repair came to more than $375. When Gary heard how much it was, he told Mike that he could pay him at the first of the month. Gary also informed Mike that the watch had been given to him by his grandmother who was celebrating her hundredth birthday in two days. Gary then asked if he could take the watch with him without paying, so that he could wear it to his grandmother's birthday party. Mike sympathized with Gary and let him do so. When the first of the month came around, Gary did not pay. Mike waited until the end of the month. Then he decided to try and collect by legal means. Does Mike still have an aritsan's lien he can enforce against Gary? Why or why not? What are his other alternatives? Are they as effective as the lien?

8. Garrett took several items into the HiDollar Pawn Shop to get a loan. The items were an expensive guitar, 100 shares of stock in a large auto maker, and a large horseshoe-shaped ring set with diamonds. Which of these items would the pawn shop loan on?

33-2 Legal Protection of Debtors and Credit Card Users

GOALS

■ Discuss the various areas of debtor protection available under the law

■ Relate the protections afforded credit card users under the law

KEY TERMS

finance charge   credit rating

Debtor Protection

WHAT'S YOUR VERDICT? Bill complained that he was not getting his cell phone bill in time to pay for it. As a consequence, the cell phone company was charging him a $20 late fee each month. Thomas asked him what date his account came due. Bill replied that it was the first of each month. Thomas then had Bill look at the date the cell phone company mailed the last bill. Thomas noted that it was the 25th of the month. "Aha!" said Thomas.

What is Thomas about to say about the dates?

The law tries to protect debtors from unfair practices and situations by

1. setting maximum interest rates
2. requiring clear and complete advance disclosure of loan and lease terms
3. changing the terms of unconscionable contracts
4. correcting specific abuses of the credit system
5. requiring the creditor to record a public notice when certain debts have been paid
6. allowing the debtor to take bankruptcy and thereby cancel most debts and start afresh

Laws Setting Maximum Interest Rates

Usury laws that set maximum interest rates were discussed in the chapters on contracts. Usually such laws apply only to loans of money. They do not govern carrying charges imposed on credit purchases of goods and services "on time." A few states do regulate such charges as interest. They do this on the theory that the store, in effect, borrows money and re-lends it to the customer-debtor to finance the purchase on credit.

Laws Requiring Disclosure of Terms

A consumer loan arises when a person borrows money primarily for personal, family, household, or agricultural purposes. It often is called a personal loan to distinguish it from a business or commercial loan.

The federal Truth in Lending Act (part of the Consumer Credit Protection Act) was designed to protect consumers when they become debtors. This law requires complete and clear disclosure of loan terms by creditors. Note that the law does not limit the percentage amounts that may be charged. However, it requires creditors to make a full disclosure of interest and finance charges whenever the consumer loan is repayable in four or more installments or carries a finance charge.

A **finance charge** is the total added cost when one pays in installments for goods or services. The creditor also must declare the true equivalent annual interest rate or annual percentage rate (APR). Thus, 1 1/2 percent a month must be stated as 18 percent a year. Under the law, a credit sales contract also must state such details as the cash price of the item; the down payment or trade-in allowance, if any; an itemized list of finance charges; and the total amount to be financed.

The Truth in Lending Act does not apply to first mortgage loans on homes. Fortunately, interest rates on home loans usually are comparatively low. No doubt this is true because the risk associated with such loans also tends to be low and the property used as security can be protected by insurance.

Any creditor who willfully and knowingly violates the Truth in Lending Act in a sales or lease transaction or in billing for same may be fined, imprisoned, or both. The violator also must pay the debtor twice the finance charge (but no less than $100 nor more than $1,000) plus court costs and attorney's fees.

An increasing number of consumers lease automobiles and other equipment instead of buying the items. A big advantage of leasing for some persons is that it requires no down payment. However, in the end, the total price paid in leasing usually is higher than a cash or credit purchase would be. This is especially true for those who maintain their automobiles properly and keep them for perhaps five or more years.

The federal Consumer Leasing Act extends the protection of the Consumer Credit Protection Act to consumer lessees. Before the contract is signed, the lessor must comply fully with the disclosure requirements in the act.

Laws Challenging Unconscionable Contracts

The UCC provides that a court may find that a contract or a clause of a contract is unconscionable, that is, grossly unfair and oppressive. An unconscionable contract or clause offends an honest person's conscience and sense of justice. The terms need not be criminal nor violate a statute. They may simply be unethical. Contracts of adhesion are more likely to be unconscionable because one of the parties dictates all the important terms and the weaker party either must take it as offered or not contract. An example is a contract for emergency repairs in which a dishonest mechanic may take unfair advantage and grossly overcharge a motorist who is unfamiliar with automotive repair and has no viable alternative from which

to obtain repair service. If the contract is challenged in court, a judge who decides that a clause of the contract is unconscionable may

- refuse to enforce the contract
- enforce the contract without the unconscionable clause
- limit the clause's application so that the contract is no longer unfair

The law is not designed to relieve a person of a bad bargain. One still may be legally bound by the purchase of overpriced, poor quality, or unneeded goods.

Laws Prohibiting Abuses in the Credit System

Laws have been enacted to correct specific problems such as the relative inability of women to get credit, unfair debt-collection practices, and inaccurate credit reports.

FEDERAL EQUAL CREDIT OPPORTUNITY ACT This act makes it unlawful for any creditor to discriminate against an applicant because of sex or marital status. In the past, women had difficulty obtaining credit. This was true even for women who had jobs. It was especially true for married women who worked as homemakers. The act

This couple has just had an emergency repair made to the transmission of their car. After paying for the repair work and traveling only five miles, the transmission locks up again. If they take the case to court, and a judge finds the contract unconscionable, what, at a minimum, do you think the repair company will be required to do?

was created to make such discriminations illegal. Major provisions of the act are the following:

1. A creditor may not refuse, on the basis of sex or marital status, to grant a separate account to a creditworthy applicant.

2. A creditor may not ask the applicant's marital status if the applicant applies for an unsecured separate account.

3. A creditor may not prohibit a married female applicant from opening or maintaining an account in her maiden name.

4. A creditor shall not request information about birth control practices or childbearing intentions or capability.

5. Married persons who have joint accounts have the right to have credit information reported in both their names in order to provide a credit history for both. In the past, upon divorce or upon death of the husband, the wife often would be denied credit because the joint account had been listed in the husband's name only.

FEDERAL FAIR DEBT COLLECTION PRACTICES ACT

This act makes abusive and deceptive debt collection practices illegal. The act applies to professional bill collectors or agencies that regularly try to collect consumer debts for clients. Prohibited practices include

1. harassment of debtors (as with a series of letters that contain menacing or threatening language, or with repeated telephone calls, especially at night)

2. abusive and profane language

3. threats of violence

4. contact with third parties (relatives, neighbors, friends, and employers)

5. communication with the debtor at work

The act is aimed at aggressively insensitive and irresponsible professional collection agencies. It does not apply to individual creditors who personally try to collect money due them. Nor does it apply to "in-house" debt collection efforts of the creditor or of employees of the creditor. However, a seriously abused debtor may sometimes succeed in a civil action against any debt collector for damages. The intentional torts of defamation, assault, invasion of privacy, or intentional infliction of mental suffering often provide the cause(s) of action in such matters.

FEDERAL FAIR CREDIT BILLING ACT

This act provides the following protections to credit card holders:

1. Creditors must mail bills at least 14 days before the due date, must acknowledge billing inquiries within 30 days, and must settle any complaints within 90 days. In *What's Your Verdict?* Thomas is about to tell Bill that the cell phone company is violating the Fair Credit Billing Act and that he should report it. Complaints in such matters should be taken to the nearest FTC Regional Office. If they concern national creditors, they should be sent in writing to the Correspondence Branch, Federal Trade Commission, Washington, D.C., 20580.

2. Creditors may not send repeated, insistent letters demanding payment until disputes over the billing are settled.

3. Credit card holders may withhold payment for items that prove defective without being held liable for the entire amount owed. This applies only in case of purchases of more than $50 made in the buyer's state or within 100 miles of the buyer's home.

The Fair Credit Billing Act also permits merchants to offer discounts to customers who pay cash instead of using credit cards. Thus, gasoline service stations may charge a few cents less per gallon to customers who pay cash. This is fair because extending credit is costly for sellers even though it may increase sales volume.

NET Bookmark

Access school.cengage.com/blaw/lawxtra and click on the link for Chapter 33. Read the Federal Trade Commission press release about the provisions of the new Fair and Accurate Credit Transactions Act that address the problem of identity theft. Choose the provision that you think will be especially helpful in dealing with identity theft. Then write a paragraph about the provision explaining why you think it is helpful.

school.cengage.com/blaw/lawxtra

FEDERAL FAIR CREDIT REPORTING ACT This act regulates credit-rating service companies that review personal financial records of credit applicants. Aided by computers, these companies or agencies maintain voluminous files covering pertinent information about millions of individuals and business firms that buy goods and services on credit. Retailers, wholesalers, and manufacturers routinely supply such credit-rating agencies with data about their experience with customers. In turn, credit-rating agencies relay relevant information to cooperating member firms that request it when someone asks them for a credit purchase.

The Retailers Credit Association, composed of retail merchants who sell on credit, is an example of a credit-rating agency. It determines the prospective buyer's credit rating. A **credit rating** reflects the evaluation of one's ability to pay debts. Under the law, if credit is denied because of information in a credit report, the company denying credit must tell the applicant. The applicant then may demand that the reporting agency disclose the general nature of the contents of its file (except medical information) and the names of parties who were given this information. However, names of those who provided the information need not be disclosed.

If there is any demonstrated error in the report, the credit-reporting agency must correct it. Upon request, it must notify the inquirers who had been misinformed. The agency must make the disclosures and reports without charge if the applicant acted within 30 days of getting notice of a denial of credit. Similar rules apply when an individual is denied an insurance policy or employment contract because of an unfavorable credit report.

CREDIT REPAIR ORGANIZATIONS ACT The Credit Repair Organizations Act (CROA), passed in April 1997, governs companies that help consumers "repair" their credit histories. By law, these organizations must notify you of your rights (by providing a copy of the government document entitled "Consumer Credit File Rights Under State and Federal Law") before you sign a contract with them. The law states that a credit repair company cannot

- make false claims about its services
- charge you until they complete the promised services
- perform any services until you have signed a written contract and completed a three-day waiting period during which time you may

cancel the contract without being obligated to pay any fees

Any contract you make with a credit repair service must specify

- the payment terms for services, including the total cost of these services
- a detailed description of the services they will perform
- how long it will take them to achieve the results
- guarantees they offer
- repair company's name, business address, and contact information

Individuals who have been injured by violations of the CROA can sue to recover the greater of the amount paid to the credit repair company or actual damages, punitive damages, costs, and attorney's fees.

Laws Requiring Notice of Debt Payment to Be Recorded

As a practical matter, debtors should always request receipts, especially when paying in cash. In some states, a debtor is not required to pay a debt unless such a receipt is given. Financial institutions either return paid and cancelled checks to the drawers (writers) of the checks or keep an electronic image of them in their database. In either form, such canceled checks can serve as receipts. It often is helpful to indicate on the face of each check the purpose for the payment. Even without such notation, it can serve as evidence of payment. When a secured debt is paid in full, the law generally permits the debtor to require the creditor to record that fact in the public records.

Laws Allowing Debtors to Cancel Debts and Start Over

Bankruptcy laws have been enacted to help debtors who have become overburdened with debts. These laws are described in detail in the next lesson. Also, state statute of limitations laws will, after a suitable period, require that all efforts to enforce debts through the court system cease. Generally, unsecured debts have a statute of limitations of three to six years, written obligations six years, and court judgments up to 20 years. Note also that federal student loans, fines, and overdue child support payments typically do not have a statute of limitations.

CHECKPOINT Name at least four of the six approaches the law takes to protect debtors.

Protections for Credit Card Users

WHAT'S YOUR VERDICT? Beatrice was grocery shopping with her two young children, Barney and Bernice, when Barney knocked a liquid dish detergent display over. Several bottles broke and Beatrice quickly notified the management and apologized. When she turned back to her cart, she noticed that her purse had been taken in the confusion. Alarmed, she immediately notified all four of her credit card companies using a list she kept at home. Later that day unauthorized charges were made on each card, maxing them out. The unauthorized use totaled over $13,000.

How much of the $13,000 in losses is Beatrice responsible for?

Millions of consumers buy goods and services by using credit cards. A credit card identifies the holder as a person entitled to obtain goods or services on credit. The issuer of the card specifies the limit of available credit, and before a large sale is made, the seller can contact the issuer to determine if this limit has been exceeded.

Usually a credit card is made of plastic, is embossed with the holder's name and identification number, and has a space on the back for the holder's signature. As further protection against misuse, the card may have the holder's picture on the front and other security information, such as a number key, on the back. Annually, billions of dollars of credit purchases are made with this "plastic money." Some credit cards are intended for specialized purchases such as gasoline or oil. Some are limited to use in specific retail outlets, such as department stores or gas stations. Some are all-purpose cards, usually issued by banks, and intended for purchases from any cooperating seller. Examples are MasterCard, Visa, and Discover cards. A credit card usually is issued

IN THIS CASE Because of a recent divorce, Allee Mony's credit standing had slipped to such a low point that she knew she could not get a mortgage loan. The situation seemed hopeless as it would likely take years to rebuild her creditworthiness. Then LifeRing Credit Repair Services called and promised that they would repair her credit practically overnight to a point where it would be better than ever—for a price tag of more than $1,000 up front. Even though she was suspicious of their claims, Allee agreed to let them try. Three months later her credit had not improved, and she sorely needed the $1,000 she had given LifeRing. Frustrated and angry, she sought legal counsel. She was told that LifeRing had violated a number of provisions of the Credit Repair Organizations Act (CROA) by taking payment up front, working without a written contract, and not advising her of her rights in the situation. As a consequence she could sue to recover the greater of the amount paid or actual damages, punitive damages, costs, and attorney's fees. When she brought suit, LifeRing settled out of court for $15,000.

Why do people choose to use credit cards rather than pay for purchases with cash or checks?

© GETTY IMAGES/PHOTODISC

in response to a consumer's written application. The consumer who signs the card is bound in a contractual relation with the issuer and is liable for all purchases made with the card by the holder or by others with the holder's permission.

Under federal law, the cardholder also is liable for unauthorized use of the credit card by any other person, such as a thief or a dishonest finder. This liability is limited to $50 and is imposed only under the following conditions:

1. Cardholder had asked for and received the credit card or had signed or used it.

2. Card issuer had given adequate notice of the possible liability for unauthorized use.

3. Card issuer had provided the cardholder with a description of how to notify the card issuer if the card is lost or stolen.

4. Card issuer had provided positive means for identification on the card, such as space for the holder's signature or photograph.

5. Unauthorized use happened before cardholder notified issuer that card was lost or stolen.

Thus, the loss or theft of a credit card should be reported immediately to the issuer. In *What's Your Verdict?* because of her quick action, Beatrice would not be liable for any of the losses. Even if she had given her notification after the unauthorized charges, her maximum liability would have been $50 per card or a total of $200.

Most credit card agreements require the cardholder to pay the amount charged on the card within a specified number of days after the closing date shown on the billing statement. If the cardholder fails to do so, he or she is contractually obligated to pay interest or finance charges on the unpaid balance.

Most states set limits on the rates that can be charged credit card holders. A few states, notably South Dakota, have no set limits on interest charges. As a result, major card issuers, such as Citibank, the issuer of MasterCard, have moved their headquarters there. In addition, as a result of the recent U.S. Supreme Court decision in *Smiley v. Citibank,* there are no limits on late charges. As a consequence, such charges have soared and are predicted to reach the $50 level shortly.

A Question of ETHICS

Patricia Blakemore's husband often abused her after coming home drunk late at night. Finally, she reported him to the police.

For a while, with the help of intensive counseling, he had not attempted to harm her. But she could tell he was returning to his old ways. Sooner or later, she knew he would beat her again. She needed to get away. However, he kept the checkbook and money under his control and signature. If she could just take one of the credit cards, she could get enough cash advances to live on until she could get a job. The problem was that she was not a cosigner on the cards. Nonetheless, she knew the personal identification numbers for each card and had used them before at his direction. Of course, this time the money was solely for her own use. Patricia paused. Should she go ahead with what she was contemplating?

What effect do you think credit cards have on the television "home shopping" industry?

Not only does the consumer pay charges to the credit card company but so does the vendor. The vendor must pay for the credit card company's service in bookkeeping and prompt payment for purchases made. Commonly, this cost to the seller is a charge of between 3 percent and 6 percent of the sales prices. Such amounts paid to the credit card company are passed on to customers, both cash and credit, through higher prices for goods sold.

In addition, credit cards have a great potential for abuse through overuse by owners and misuse by thieves or finders of lost cards. Some consumers fail to plan and save for their purchases. Instead, they often use their credit cards for impulse purchases they do not really need. Sometimes, the payments for these purchases, when added to other living expenses, total more than their income. Debtors who find themselves in this situation may consult debt-counseling services that now operate in many cities. These services assist debtors in budgeting their income and expenses in a disciplined plan to pay off creditors and to avoid being forced into bankruptcy.

CHECKPOINT What is the liability limit for unauthorized credit card charges?

33-2 Assessment

THINK ABOUT LEGAL CONCEPTS

1. The federal Truth in Lending Act does not limit the percentage amounts that may be charged for interest on consumer loans. **True or False?**

2. The Truth in Lending Act does not apply to first mortgage loans on homes. **True or False?**

3. If a person owes $10,000 on a credit card that has a 36% annual interest rate, and she makes only a minimum payment each month equal to the interest charge, how much is the monthly payment? (a) $30 (b) $300 (c) $360 (d) $3,600

4. The federal Fair Credit Billing Act provides that creditors must mail bills at least _?_ days before the due date, must acknowledge billing inquiries within _?_ days, and must settle any complaints within _?_ days. (a) 14, 30, 90 (b) 15, 30, 90 (c) 15, 30, 60 (d) none of the above

5. Under federal law, a credit card holder may be liable for part of the unauthorized use of the credit card by a thief. **True or False?**

6. Both the consumer and the seller of goods or services in a credit card transaction pay charges to the credit card company in most cases. **True or False?**

THINK CRITICALLY ABOUT EVIDENCE

Study the situation, answer the questions, and then prepare arguments to support your answers.

7. During the warranty period, the Arnaudos returned their home computer for repair to the seller, Computerville Inc. Later, after the express warranty period had expired, the Arnaudos stopped making their regular monthly $100 payments for the computer because the problem continued. Computerville then gave its claim for the $900 balance to Bulldog Services, a collection agency. Bulldog had a clerk telephone the Arnaudos at least once a day and once a night, usually after 1 A.M. Every Sunday, a uniformed Bulldog agent would park the company truck in front of the Arnaudos' house. The truck had these words in large type on both side panels: "Bulldog Services. We Chase Deadbeats." The agent would then try to talk about the claim with any person entering or leaving the house. Was Bulldog Services acting legally? Was Bulldog Services acting ethically?

8. Shortly after graduation from college, Matilda Smith applied for credit at a local department store. The store denied her application, citing the unfavorable credit report it had received from the Alpha-Omega Credit Bureau. Matilda assumed that the negative report stemmed from a prolonged dispute with a major retail chain over goods she had not ordered. Recently the retail store acknowledged its error. What can Matilda do to clear her name?

33-3 Bankruptcy

GOALS

- Differentiate between the various types of bankruptcy filings
- List the stages of the Chapter 7 bankruptcy procedure

KEY TERMS

bankruptcy   insolvent

voluntary bankruptcy   involuntary bankruptcy

The Bankruptcy Act

WHAT'S YOUR VERDICT? Malcolm Eric, owner of Lake Cleaners, decided he had to face the fact that he was overextended. The new store in the Hollistown Mall had such an expensive monthly payment on its five-year lease that it was about to cause Malcolm to close down the whole chain. This would mean the loss of jobs for his 9 employees as well as his own financial ruin. In fact, he had been unable to make his monthly payments on the company truck and to his suppliers for the last three months. Several suppliers had stopped deliveries to him. He had discussed the situation with his attorney, and they were to meet later today to consider filing bankruptcy.

If bankruptcy is Malcolm Eric's only alternative, what form of bankruptcy would you recommend?

Many American colonists came from England at a time when debtors had to go to prison if they could not pay their debts. Therefore, at our country's founding, the ability to avoid such harsh treatment through a process of bankruptcy was considered important enough to be included in the U.S. Constitution. Even today, bankruptcy laws in the United States are more lenient than those in other countries.

By Article I, Section 8, of the U.S. Constitution Congress was given exclusive power to establish "uniform laws on the subject of bankruptcies throughout the United States." The bankruptcy law created as a result and in force in its modern form today has a dual purpose. First of all, **bankruptcy** protects creditors by setting up a framework to provide fair treatment in their competition for the debtor's assets. Secondly, and most importantly, it protects debtors by giving them an opportunity for a new economic start, free from most creditors' claims.

To accomplish these purposes, the federal Bankruptcy Code in its Chapters 7, 11, 12, and

Economic Impact

THE COST OF BANKRUPTCIES

In an effort to reduce the rising number of bankruptcies and eliminate the consumer abuse and loopholes burdening the then-current bankruptcy statute, Congress passed and the President signed into law the Bankruptcy Abuse Prevention and Consumer Protection Act (BAPCPA) of 2005. Although the immediate effect was a significant decrease in the number of bankruptcy filings from 2005 to 2006 (70 percent in some months), critics pointed out that this was because of the tidal wave of bankruptcies filed in 2005 in anticipation of the tougher standards about to be imposed by BAPCPA.

They also noted that the real test of BAPCPA would be in the latter part of 2007 and early 2008. In addition, constitutional challenges to BAPCPA's requirements that law firms must advertise as "debt relief agencies" and cannot advise clients to take on more debt in preparation for filing bankruptcy have been successful.

THINK CRITICALLY

Research the impact of BAPCPA. Has the Act achieved its goals? What are its unintended consequences? What changes would you recommend be made to the current form of the Act as a consequence?

13 provides a variety of possible ways for debtors to seek relief.

Chapter 7 Liquidation, or "Straight Bankruptcy"

Chapter 7 involves the sale for cash of the nonexempt property of the debtor and the distribution of the proceeds to creditors. Nonexempt property includes such assets as bank accounts, stocks, and bonds. Lists of exempt property exist at the state and federal level and will be discussed in the section on bankruptcy procedure. Utilizing Chapter 7 will result in the discharge of most of the debtor's financial obligations. However under the provisions of BAPCPA, relief under Chapter 7 will be denied if the debtors have income above the median income for similarly sized families in their state.

Chapter 11 Reorganization

This option for debtor relief is designed to keep a business organization such as a corporation, partnership, or sole proprietorship in operation with no liquidation. The debtor or a committee of creditors files a plan for reorganization. The bankruptcy court must approve this plan and will do so if it is reasonable and if it was created in good faith. In *What's Your Verdict?* a Chapter 11 plan probably would be optimal.

Under Chapter 11, claims of both secured and unsecured creditors, as well as the interests of the owners of the business, may be "impaired," meaning reduced. The plan to reorganize must be in the best interests of the creditors. In addition, under the BAPCPA changes, the court may dismiss the plan due to mismanagement, lack of proper insurance, unauthorized use of cash collateral, and failure to meet reporting requirements. Each class of creditors that is affected adversely must accept it. A class of creditors accepts the plan when a majority that represents two-thirds of the amount of that group's total claim votes to approve the plan. Even when only one class (for example, the bondholders) accepts the plan, the Bankruptcy Court may approve it under a so-called "cramdown provision." This requires that the creditors or the owners who object are either unaffected by the plan, or are paid in full before any junior (or lower) class of claimant is paid. Note that one significant change under BAPCPA was the creation of a

streamlined Chapter 11 procedure for small businesses whose debt does not exceed $2,000,000.

Chapter 12 Debt Relief for Family Farms

Congress added Chapter 12 relief to the Bankruptcy Code in 1986 for family farm owners. Under this chapter an individual or couple or, sometimes, a corporation or a partnership can be eligible to file a petition for relief. This petition entitles them to a court order protecting them from their creditors. Contrary to other Chapters in the Bankruptcy code, the requirements of Chapter 12 under BAPCPA were made much more friendly to the debtor/farmer. The limit on total debt for the party filing was increased from $1.5 million to more than $3 million. In addition, the percentage of that debt that must come from the farming operation was decreased from 80 percent to 50 percent. Finally, the Chapter 12 provisions themselves were made permanent. Those provisions previously had been only temporary and therefore subject to the necessity of repeated approval by Congress lest they expire. The Chapter 12 plan is similar in operation to the Chapter 13 proceeding for other debtors.

Chapter 13 Extended Time Payment Plan

Chapter 13 relief is available only to individuals who have regular income. This plan also avoids liquidation of assets. The debtor must have regular income, unsecured debts of less than $336,900, and/or secured debts of less than $1,010,650. The debtor must submit a plan for the installment payment of debts within three years with a possible extension to five years.

During this time, the creditors may not file suit for payment of any debts. Both secured and unsecured debts (other than a claim, such as a promissory note and mortgage, secured by the debtor's principal residence) may be reduced in amount or extended in time for payment. The plan must be "in the best interests of the creditors," who might otherwise receive even less in a Chapter 7 liquidation.

A major advantage of the Chapter 13 proceeding is that upon completion of payments called for under the plan, the court grants a discharge for almost all debts. The only exceptions are for certain long-term debts, such as payments for a house and payments of alimony and child support.

CHECKPOINT Of the various bankruptcy plans, which one involves total liquidation of the debtor's nonexempt assets?

Bankruptcy Procedure Under Chapter 7

WHAT'S YOUR VERDICT? Jack Gilbert was talking to his fellow law school student, Chase Adamson, about finances and said, ". . . after I graduate, I'm going to declare bankruptcy and get rid of all these student loans." Chase looked at Jack and said, "Whoa, man. I just finished the course on bankruptcy, and there's something about the law you should know that might change your plan."

What does Chase know about bankruptcy that Jack does not?

LEGAL Research

Research the connection between bankruptcy and student loans in two situations. First, research the effect on a student loan application where the applicant has previously taken bankruptcy. Secondly, research the availability of bankruptcy to someone wanting to discharge the obligations imposed by student loans he or she has received in the past.

As liquidation under Chapter 7 is at the very heart of the Bankruptcy Act, it is important to look at the procedure followed to carry out Chapter 7's provisions.

The Bankruptcy Petition

Bankruptcy under Chapter 7 may be either voluntary or involuntary. Once the process is begun by either a voluntary or involuntary filing of a petition under Chapter 7, the procedure is basically the same.

VOLUNTARY BANKRUPTCY With a few exceptions, any person, business, or other association may petition for protection from creditors under Chapter 7. This is the beginning of a **voluntary bankruptcy**. A person does not have to be **insolvent** (unable to pay debts when they are due) to file the petition. Husbands and wives may file jointly.

INVOLUNTARY BANKRUPTCY Any person or business, except farmers, financial and charitable institutions, and insurance companies owing at least $11,625 to their petitioning unsecured creditor(s) and unable to pay debts when they come due may be forced into **involuntary bankruptcy**. However, if a person has more than 12 creditors with unsecured claims totaling at least $11,625, at least three must sign the involuntary bankruptcy petition.

REQUIRED INFORMATIONAL FILING In either voluntary or involuntary bankruptcy proceedings, the debtor, under oath, must file the following information with the court:

- a list of all creditors and amounts owed to each
- a list of all property owned, including property claimed to be exempt from seizure
- a statement explaining the debtor's financial affairs
- a list of current income and expenses

To conceal or fraudulently transfer assets or to provide false information knowingly is a crime under the bankruptcy laws.

Selection of the Trustee in Bankruptcy

After the petition is filed, a trustee is then selected. The trustee's duties are to find and to protect the assets of the debtor, liquidate them, and pay the claims against the debtor's estate with the proceeds. Such claims would include court costs, back wages owed to the debtor's employees, taxes, and claims of the general creditors. Secured creditors would seek payment of the secured debts directly against the collateral. Secured debts would be enforced ahead of any other claims.

Non-Dischargeable Debts

There are certain types of claims that cannot be discharged by bankruptcy. These include any debts not listed in the bankruptcy petition and

- certain taxes
- alimony and child support
- claims against the debtor for property obtained by fraud, embezzlement, or larceny
- judgments against the debtor for willful and malicious injury to the person or property of another (but claims for injuries caused by negligence can be discharged)
- student loans owed to the government or to a nonprofit school of higher learning, unless the loan became due more than seven years before the bankruptcy, or an undue hardship would be imposed on the debtor or on his or her dependents (In *What's Your Verdict?* this is the information Chase thought Jack should have.)
- judgments against the debtor resulting from driving while intoxicated
- claims not listed by debtor

Exempt Property

Certain assets of the debtor are exempt from liquidation to satisfy creditor's claims. These exemptions are specified in the federal bankruptcy laws which are revised every three years. Individual states have been empowered to disallow the use of these exemptions and substitute their own. The states also can create their own list and let the petitioner choose between state and federal exemptions. Under the federal law, exempt property currently includes

- real property (homestead), including co-op or mobile home, to $18,450; any unused portion of this exemption up to $9,250 may be applied to any property
- life insurance payments for person the debtor depended on for support
- life insurance policy with loan value, in accrued dividends or interest to $9,850
- alimony and child support
- pensions and retirement benefits
- $475 per item of household goods up to a total of $9,850
- health aids
- jewelry to $1,225
- motor vehicle to $2,950
- personal injury compensation payments to $18,450
- wrongful death payments

What two categories of exempt property do this condo and car represent?

- crime victims' compensation
- public assistance
- social security
- unemployment compensation
- veterans' benefits
- tools of the debtor's trade, books, and equipment to $1,850
- unused portion of homestead exemption
- $925 of any property plus up to $9,250 of any amount of unused homestead exemption

What is your opinion of using bankruptcy as a tool if you find yourself in trouble financially? What do you see as the pros and cons of filing bankruptcy?

Liquidation and Distribution of Proceeds

Once the assets of the debtor not subject to a security interest are brought under the trustee's control, they are liquidated. The proceeds of the liquidation then are used to pay the creditors. After secured creditors have received either the value of their collateral or the collateral itself, the law provides an order of priority for payment of claims against the bankruptcy estate. The following list contains those recipients of general interest in priority order.

1. Unsecured claims for domestic support orders

2. Expenses of the administration of the bankruptcy case, including trustee's fees and attorney's fees

3. Claims for wages, salaries, and commissions with a maximum of $10,950 per creditor

4. Claims for contributions to employee benefit plans up to $10,950 per employee

5. Up to $2,425 per claim on unsecured claims for money deposited with the debtor for purchase or lease of property or for services contemplated for the personal, household, or family use of the debtor that were not provided

6. Unsecured claims of governmental units for taxes and penalties

7. Claims of all general unsecured creditors and those with residual unsatisfied claims from the above categories

If any amount is left after all the classes of claimants have been satisfied, it is turned over to the debtor. After the procedure is concluded, all eligible debts of the debtor are considered discharged. The debtor cannot file a petition in bankruptcy again until 6 years have elapsed. Bankruptcy stays on a credit report for 10 years.

CHECKPOINT What are the two types of bankruptcy under Chapter 7?

THINK ABOUT LEGAL CONCEPTS

1. "Straight bankruptcy" is obtained under what chapter of the Bankruptcy Act? (a) 7 (b) 11 (c) 12 (d) 13

2. A major advantage of the Chapter 13 proceeding is that upon completion of payments called for under the plan, the court grants a discharge for almost all debts. **True or False?**

3. Can involuntary petitions be filed against farmers under Chapter 7? **Yes or No?**

4. The U.S. Constitution specifies that _?_ has exclusive power to establish "uniform laws on the subject of bankruptcies throughout the United States." (a) the President (b) the U.S. Supreme Court (c) the Federal Trade Commission (d) none of the above.

THINK CRITICALLY ABOUT EVIDENCE

Study the situation, answer the questions, and then prepare arguments to support your answers.

5. Under the state exemptions to the bankruptcy act allowable under the law of a large southwestern state, there is a one-acre exemption for the debtor's home. Two brothers, Robert and Lyle Quest, are forced into involuntary bankruptcy due to losing a great deal of money in precious metal speculations. Robert lives in a penthouse atop a $62 million office building he owns. Lyle's penthouse is atop a $71 million building that he owns. Each claims the one acre due under the state law. The creditors claim that they should be able to reach all the value in the one acre except for the $15,000 exemption allowed by the federal law. Who wins?

Online Research> Ronald's Rehabilitation

Ronald Burton tried to regain his composure before entering his home. They were expecting him to announce the big news and had doubtlessly prepared a celebration. The Vice President's position at the bank had opened up a month ago and the President and majority owner of the First National Bank of Pennsboro, Charles "Nessie" Inverness, had announced that they were going to promote from inside. Because Ronald not only had seniority but also had the best performance reviews of all of the other candidates, he knew the job was likely his. His hopes spiked when the President had scheduled a meeting with Ronald for earlier this afternoon. However, instead of announcing Ronald's promotion, Nessie told him that Charles Inverness II, an accounting clerk, was going to receive the position. Nessie said that a major factor in his decision was the fact that one of the business loans Ronald had made to a local contractor had gone into default. In addition, Nessie said, "That time you took bankruptcy 15 years ago really hurt your chances. I realize that was due to your wife losing her job after the baby was born prematurely, but the cause is immaterial to my decision."

Ronald knew that, even with the lost loan to the contractor, his loan success rate was far better than any other loan officer's. Suddenly a wave of anger swept over him. Maybe he should consult an attorney in the matter.

THINK CRITICALLY

Does Ronald have a cause of action stemming from this situation. Why or why not?

GO TO FINDLAW.COM TO FIND THE ANSWERS

To find the material in FindLaw on this issue, go to Findlaw.com and click on the following sequence of hyperlinks: Bankruptcy & Debt, More Bankruptcy & Debt Topics, Bankruptcy and Discrimination.

CONCEPTS IN BRIEF

33-1 Legal Protection of Creditors

1. It is in the interest of all society that fair and honest loans be collectible with minimum difficulty and expense.

2. Taking a security interest in personal property and fixtures or a mortgage on real property are common ways the law allows creditors to protect themselves.

3. Some secured debt arrangements protect the creditor by allowing the creditor possession of the collateral until the debt is paid.

4. Other means of protection are available to creditors. These means involve third parties and are known as suretyship and guaranty.

33-2 Legal Protection of Debtors and Credit Card Users

5. The law tries to protect debtors from unfair practices and situations by setting maximum interest rates, requiring disclosure of loan terms, changing the terms of unconscionable contracts, correcting specific abuses of the credit system, requiring the creditor to record a public notice when certain debts have been paid, and providing a procedure to allow canceling most debts so as to give the debtor's financial life a fresh start.

33-3 Bankruptcy

6. The ability to avoid harsh treatment for unpaid debts through a process of bankruptcy was considered important enough to be included in the U.S. Constitution.

7. Bankruptcy laws in the United States are more lenient and the costs thereof to society far greater than those in other countries.

8. The federal Bankruptcy Code in its Chapters (7 for liquidation, 11 for reorganization, 12 for family farms, and 13 for an extended payment plan) provides a variety of possible ways for debtors to obtain relief from an oppressive load of debt.

YOUR LEGAL VOCABULARY

Match each statement with the term that it best defines. Some terms may not be used.

1. Repairperson's right to retain possession of the item of personal property being repaired until paid or if not paid, to sell the item to pay the repair bill

2. Status of being unable to pay debts when they become due

3. A debt in which the creditor lacks a secured interest in collateral

4. A claim against real property given to a builder, carpenter, plumber, or others involved in construction or repair of the real property

5. A court-ordered procedure by which a portion of a delinquent debtor's wages are paid to satisfy the debt

6. The total added cost when one pays in installments for goods or services

7. Procedure based on federal law that protects creditors and debtors in cases in which the latter are unable or unwilling to pay their debts

8. An objective evaluation of a party's ability to pay debts

9. Party who agrees to be primarily liable for the obligations of the principal debtor

10. A party who agrees to be secondarily liable for the obligations of the principal debtor

a. artisan's lien
b. bankruptcy
c. credit rating
d. finance charge
e. garnishment
f. guarantor
g. insolvent
h. involuntary bankruptcy
i. lien
j. mechanic's lien
k. pawn
l. pledgee
m. pledgor
n. principal debtor
o. surety
p. suretyship
q. unsecured debt
r. voluntary bankruptcy

REVIEW LEGAL CONCEPTS

11. What makes the artisan's lien so powerful?

12. What makes the mechanic's lien so powerful?

13. What is the legal difference between a surety and a guarantor?

14. What does a signature on a credit card indicate? If the card is lost or stolen, generally what is the cardholder's liability?

15. Why do usury laws not govern interest charges imposed on credit purchases of goods and services?

WRITE ABOUT LEGAL CONCEPTS

16. Contrast the differences between bankruptcy liquidation and dissolution for the various types of businesses, including sole proprietorship, partnership, and corporation.

17. Compare the bankruptcy options available to a business debtor versus an individual debtor. Compare especially the list of exemptions and the priority of payout of liquidated funds.

18. **HOT DEBATE** Write a persuasive opening statement that emphasizes the legal, ethical, and economic points in Norm's favor. Or, write a persuasive opening statement for the jeweler that encompasses the economic and legal reasons why the loss should fall on Norm.

MAKE ACADEMIC CONNECTIONS

19. **ENGLISH** Read the sections about debtor's prisons in *Little Dorrit, David Copperfield,* and the *Pickwick Papers* by Charles Dickens. Each refers to a different debtor's prison in London in the nineteenth century many years after the United States took a stance against them.

Realize Dickens' father had been imprisoned in one of them during the son's childhood. Write a paragraph contrasting your feelings about punishment of debtors with those of nineteenth century England. Identify why your feelings coincide with or differ from those of that period.

THINK CRITICALLY ABOUT EVIDENCE

Study the situation, answer the questions, and then prepare arguments to support your answers.

20. You are thinking of buying an automobile and plan to borrow money from a financial institution to help you pay cash for the purchase. Is there a limit on how much interest a lender can charge you? Suppose you decide to rely on dealer financing, paying the dealer or finance company a series of monthly installments. Is there any limit on the annual percentage rate (APR) of the financing charge the seller may add to the price of the car?

21. An acquaintance brags that she will finance her college education with government-insured student loans and then go bankrupt after graduation to avoid paying them. Is this possible? Is this ethical?

22. All five of your credit cards are stolen from your motel room while you are skiing. Fortunately you discover the loss within a few hours and immediately notify the credit card companies by telephone. On the following day, you also notify them by mail. However, later in the week, the thief uses your credit cards to charge $1,875 in purchases. Eventually, each credit card company bills you for $50 of the purchases made with its card. By what authority did they do this? Must you pay these bills?

23. Garrotte took his new flat screen TV to Tesla Technology Inc. for repairs. The bill came to more than $500. As Garrotte was short of money, he gave Tesla a 90-day promissory note for the amount due. Tesla then returned the TV to Garrotte. Has Tesla improved his position as a creditor by so doing? Why or why not?

24. When Lola came home from college for spring break, her mother gave her a credit card. "You can sign my name, but don't spend more than $100," she told Lola. Lola went on a buying spree with her friend Joyce and together they bought $575 worth of clothing using the credit card. Now her mother refuses to pay more than $150, stating, "I authorized $100, and $50 is the legal maximum for unauthorized purchases." The credit card company sues for $575. Who wins?

25. Medias and other pawnbrokers objected to an Indianapolis city ordinance that regulated their business. The ordinance required an applicant for a pawnbroker's license to establish good character by the certificate of three landowners. The ordinance also provided that the licensee keep specified records and supply information to the chief of police. Finally, the ordinance specified that the licensee hold all pledged articles for 96 hours, and it required that the licensee take the thumbprints of all persons from whom he or she bought or received goods. Are these regulations arbitrary and unreasonable? (*Medias v. City of Indianapolis,* 216 Ind. 155, 23 N.E.2d 590)

26. Sniadach owed the Family Finance Corporation (FFC) $420 under a written promise to pay. When this debt became overdue, the creditor obtained a court order that summarily garnished her wages. Her employer had $63 in wages earned by her but not yet paid, and it agreed to hold one-half of them subject to the court order. Sniadach sued the FFC and asked the court to reverse the garnishment order, claiming that it violated her right to due process under the Fourteenth Amendment. She had received the summons and complaint on the same day that her employer was notified and froze her wages. Thus, she had no opportunity to be heard and to present her side of the case before the garnishment took effect. The trial court denied her motion, and the Wisconsin Supreme Court affirmed. She now appeals to the U.S. Supreme Court. How should it rule? (*Sniadach v. Family Finance Corporation,* 395 U.S. 337)

27. In his divorce decree, Elliot was ordered to pay $102 of his weekly wages of $467.47 from his job at a General Motors plant for child support. Months later, U.S. Life Credit Corporation (USLC) recovered a judgment against Elliot in municipal court. With court approval, USLC then garnished 25 percent of Elliot's $467.47 per week to pay off the judgment amount. The U.S. Secretary of Labor then filed a lawsuit against the municipal court and USLC contending that the payments to USLC and for child support, taken together, violated the 25 percent of disposable income restriction on garnishments imposed by law. You decide. (*Donovan v. Hamilton County Municipal Court,* 580 F. Supp. 554)

28. When Hardison filed for bankruptcy, one of his main creditors was General Finance Corporation (GFC) to which he owed $2,800. After the GFC debt and others were discharged as a result of the bankruptcy procedure, he received a letter from GFC informing him that his credit was still good with it. By telephone, Hardison then arranged for a $1,200 loan from GFC. However, when he appeared to pick up the money, GFC informed him that it was going to make the loan only if he agreed to pay back not only the $1,200, but also an additional $1,200 from the first loan. Hardison then signed a consumer credit contract agreeing to those terms. Later, Hardison filed a lawsuit claiming that GFC should have included the amount from the previously discharged debt in the "total finance charge" in the truth-in-lending statement shown him at the time of the transaction, rather than as a part of the "total amount financed." Hardison wanted damages available under the Truth in Lending Act. Should he receive them? (*Hardison v. General Finance Corporation,* 738 F.2d 893)

29. When the Richmonds filed for Chapter 7 liquidation under the Bankruptcy Code, their unsecured debts totaled a little more than $19,000. All but $225 of the unsecured debts was owed on credit cards. The trustee in bankruptcy noted that the Richmond's monthly expenses included voluntary payments in support of their grandchildren. The trustee also pointed out to the court that, if these payments were stopped, the Richmonds would have an additional $300 per month with which to pay off the credit cards. In fact, under a three year Chapter 13 plan, the Richmonds could pay off more than 90 percent of the credit card debt in 36 months. As a consequence, the trustee filed a motion to dismiss the Richmond's case, contending that to grant relief to them would be an abuse of Chapter 7. The court noted that in making such a decision, it must decide whether the debtors are seeking an advantage or are truly needy in the sense that their financial situation warrants dismissal of the debts. How should the judge decide this case, and why? (*In Re Richmond,* 144 Bankruptcy Reporter 539)

Case For Legal Thinking

IN RE BAKER, U.S. BANKRUPTCY COURT
10 BANKRUPTCY REPORTER 870

FACTS Prior to 1976, a student could attend school on student loans guaranteed by the government and then discharge them immediately upon graduation, before starting employment, under the terms of the Bankruptcy Act. Congress ultimately closed the loophole except for those for whom paying back the loans posed an "undue hardship."

Mary Lou Baker filed for bankruptcy protection under the "undue hardship" provisions to relieve her of the burden of repaying educational loans totalling some $6,635. The loans were from three institutions of higher learning: The University of Tennessee at Chattanooga, Cleveland State Community College, and the Baroness Erlanger School of Nursing.

Mary Lou Baker was a mother of three with a monthly take-home pay of less than $650. Her monthly expenses for herself and the children (her husband had left town) were nearly $1,000. She did not receive any public aid and had no other income according to the record. However, just prior to filing this action, her church had paid her January heating bill to prevent her from being without heat in her home.

Of her three children, one had difficulty reading and another required special and expensive shoes. Baker herself had not been well and her medical bills had gone unpaid prior to the bankruptcy filing. In the bankruptcy petition she filed, Mrs. Baker seeks a discharge of her educational loans based on the hardship provision.

REASONING Ralph Kelley, Bankruptcy Judge, rendered the court's decision:

"In 1976 the Congress passed the Educational Amendments which restricted a discharge in bankruptcy (of student loans). The restriction was designed to remedy an abuse by students who, immediately upon graduation, would file bankruptcy to secure a discharge of educational loans. These students often had no other indebtedness and could easily repay their debts from future wages . . .

In passing the Educational Amendments of 1976 and including these amendments in the Bankruptcy Reform Act of 1978, Congress intended to correct an abuse. It did not intend to deprive those who have truly fallen on hard times of the 'fresh start' policy of the new Bankruptcy Code."

CONCLUSION The court concludes that under the circumstances of this case, requiring the debtor to repay the debts owed to the three defendants of $6,635 plus interest would impose upon her and her dependents an undue hardship.

PRACTICE JUDGING

1. What sort of standard does the court identify here for future debtors when it says petitioner Baker had "truly fallen on hard times"? What sort of standard would you propose?

2. Presume Mrs. Baker did her best at each institution but still ended up either without the soughtafter degree or without a job commensurate with the money expended to qualify for it. Does the government, as guarantor of such educational loans, find itself being forced into evaluating how successful each applicant may be before issuing them the money?

© GETTY IMAGES/PHOTODISC

Entrepreneurs
AND THE LAW

Project 7   Borrowing Money and Paying Bills

FINANCIAL SETBACK   The next few years at Secure Seal went well. Then disaster struck. After the new production facility was brought online, Stacy had seen an opportunity to move into even more lucrative fields such as contracts with the Department of Defense and overseas trucking companies. Unfortunately, using money retained from then-current profits did not produce a sufficient amount to allow her to build yet another new production plant for those markets without borrowing. Knowing the risk debt entailed, Stacy nonetheless used it for the construction financing. Unexpected delays soon depleted even the borrowed funds. So, to finish the plant, Stacy committed her personal "fortune," as she called it, by mortgaging her home and liquidating all her savings. Then the overall business environment worsened. Finding herself seemingly out of options, Stacy wrote her father with the bad news that she was preparing for an exploratory meeting with a bankruptcy attorney.

FINANCIAL SOLUTION   Two weeks later Stacy found herself listening in total dismay to the bankruptcy attorney's final report. Not only would she go down in flames, but she probably would take SecureSeal with her. When the bankruptcy attorney stopped speaking, Stacy asked him some pointed questions and then informed him that she would get back to him with a final decision within a week.

As Stacy escorted the attorney out of her offices, she noticed a middle-aged woman sitting in one of the nearby conference rooms with, of all people, Stacy's father. Overcome with joy, she gave him a big hug.

Her dad smiled. "I had a feeling that the conference you wrote me about with the bankruptcy attorney might not go the way you'd like. So, I contacted an old friend of mine who runs the local office of a national stock brokerage. He directed me to an expert in corporate finance, Ms. Darden here."

After shaking Stacy's hand, Ms. Darden gave a small stack of papers to Stacy. "A well-run business like yours with an excellent profit history and long-term contracts can most always find a way out of its problems. From what I've gathered from your reports and the tour of your facilities that your dad gave me, your capital equipment and other assets are still unencumbered by debt. So, we could set up a financing package that will basically take your company public and probably replace the current debt with bonds and secured positions for your current creditors. The funds from the public offering also will let you complete your current expansion and even give you surplus capital to buy whatever supplies and equipment you need to fully utilize the new facility. Perhaps the best news is that you should end up personally solvent once again. The only downside is that you will have to give up part of your ownership of SecureSeal. But you will still end up running it and owning the majority interest."

ACTIVITIES

Divide into teams and perform one or more of the following activities as directed by your teacher.

Present

Assume members of your team are the law firm's associates accompanying the bankruptcy attorney who explained the bankruptcy issues to Stacy. Each team member should consider one of the following issues and prepare a short presentation on it.

1. Which form of bankruptcy might be most helpful to Stacy? Why? What would she be able to salvage?

2. What form of bankruptcy would you recommend for SecureSeal? Why? What could be saved? How?

Prepare an overall plan for Stacy based on the presentations.

Brainstorm

Brainstorm a list of financing options for the business—a public stock or bond issue, mortgaging real or personal property, debentures, etc. Consider both the short-term and long-term impact of each.

Debate

Debate the pros and cons of each alternative from your list, given Stacy's current position. Make a recommendation about which financing option seems best for Stacy's company.

PROTECT AGAINST IDENTITY THEFT Did you know your identity can be stolen? Whenever someone uses your name, address, phone number, credit card, driver's license, or other personal information without your permission to commit fraud or another crime, they are guilty of identity theft. You can help protect yourself and others against identity theft.

DO YOUR PART

1. Create a multimedia presentation titled Protecting Against Identity Theft. Offer the presentation to your whole school.

2. Use the Internet for information to include in your presentation. Modify your research to be school and age appropriate.

3. Make an outline of your presentation before you write the full presentation.

4. Assign different aspects of the presentation to different students.

5. Arrange with the administration for a date the auditorium will be available for your presentation and a date for dress rehearsal.

6. Draw up a timeline that details each step that must be taken from beginning of the project to the date of presentation.

7. Write press releases for the school newspaper and radio station.

Extemporaneous Speaking

Participants will choose to prepare a speech about "Legal Aspects of Bankruptcy" or "Credit—Good, Bad, Legal Responsibilities."

Each participant will be provided ten (10) minutes to develop a speech for the topic they choose. Notes can be taken on the cards provided by the teacher. The length of the speech will be no less than one (1) minute and no more than three (3) minutes. The contestant will speak before a panel of judges and a timekeeper. No audience will be allowed. One-minute and 30-second warnings will be given during the speech.

Performance Indicators Evaluated
- Demonstrate effective communication skills.
- Describe the legal requirements and responsibilities for credit.

- Demonstrate effective speech presentation.
- Define bankruptcy.

For more detailed information about performance indicators, go to the BPA web site.

THINK CRITICALLY

1. What is bankruptcy?
2. Why do so many people declare bankruptcy?
3. What are long-term effects of bankruptcy?
4. What are the responsibilities of using credit?

www.bpa.org/

Mock Trial Prep

CLOSING ARGUMENTS

WHAT IS A CLOSING ARGUMENT?

A mock trial concludes with the closing argument presented by counsel for the Plaintiff, followed by a closing argument presented by counsel for the Defense. The counsel for the Plaintiff generally has the burden of proof in the hearing or trial, and, therefore, is the last to present his or her argument through a rebuttal.

A closing argument does not merely summarize the evidence presented during the trial. A closing argument is just that—argument. An attorney should discuss the evidence, summarize the testimony of the witnesses, and discuss the law that applies. Moreover, an attorney will argue how the evidence presented satisfies or fails to satisfy the elements of the applicable charge or cause of action. The goal of the closing argument is to provide a strong and persuasive argument to prove your case and highlight the weaknesses of your opponent's case.

OUTLINE OF A CLOSING ARGUMENT

A. **Introduction**   Repeat your theory of the case and theme. This should parallel the opening statement.

B. **Identify for the court what issues or discussion points you will be discussing in your closing**   For instance, "I will address three issues which prove that my client is not liable." Describe briefly each of your issues. In other words, provide a "roadmap" to the judge as to the three or four issues you will be addressing during your closing.

C. **Walk the road**   Discuss each issue and the legal and factual support for that point on your "roadmap." For each issue, you will need to argue the following:

  1. **Facts presented**   Review the testimony of the witnesses. Discuss the truthfulness (or lack thereof) and demeanor of the witness. Discuss the witness' statements, biases, and recollections. Outline the strengths of each witness whose testimony supports your case or weakens the opposing side's arguments.

  2. **Argue the law**   Identify and explain the applicable law. If there is case law which bolsters your case, discuss the facts and the holding of the case. Then compare the facts and holding of the case to your case.

  3. **Refute other side's arguments**   Mention the other side's arguments and refute them.

D. **Conclusion**   Reiterate your issues and restate the "roadmap" to the judge. Finally, request a proper verdict or decision from the judge.

CASE LAW AND STATUTES

Case law and statutes provide the legal reasoning in a mock trial competition. Case law is the law as reflected in the written decisions of the courts. Statutes are laws written and adopted by elected officials (Congress, state legislatures, city councils, etc.) Statutes also are referred to as legislation. Case law and applicable statutes are generally provided to the mock trial participants within the case materials. Reference to case law and statutes generally is limited to only that material. Therefore, no other legal citations may be presented outside the case law.

RESTATE YOUR THEORY OF THE CASE

It is now time to tie the theory of your case and theme given in your opening statement to the closing statement. Restate your theory of the case. Remember to continue your theme.

ARGUE YOUR CASE

You began your opening statement by telling the court what your case is about by stating the facts of your client's case as developed by your theory of the case. In your closing argument, reiterate only the facts that are important to your theory of the case and the "roadmap" points you are discussing.

Recall as well that in your opening statement you told the court what testimony to expect from each of the witnesses. Credibility is vital to a closing argument. Remember to never promise to prove anything that you will not or cannot prove during the hearing or trial.

DELIVER YOUR CLOSING ARGUMENT

Do not read your closing argument. There is nothing more tedious than a closing argument read in a monotonous voice by the attorney. Certainly, an outline is highly recommended to refresh your memory of the key points

you wish to touch upon. However, you must engage the judge through eye contact. Your delivery of the closing argument must hold the attention of the court in order to be effective. Belief in your argument is crucial and will project confidence and credibility. Remember to use inflection in your voice. Use pauses, silences, and the appropriate emotional cues.

THINK ON YOUR FEET

Closing arguments must be based on the actual evidence and testimony presented during the trial. No matter how much an attorney prepares, there is no way to anticipate the surprises and twists which may occur during the hearing or trial. It is vitally important to think on your feet, note the surprises, and incorporate the unexpected into your closing argument.

Witness testimony is not always predictable. You will need to adapt your closing arguments to reflect what the witnesses actually said at trial as opposed to the predicted testimony. Keep your closing statement outline with you during the trial. Check off the points as they are presented in evidence as the trial progresses. If you have a fact in your prepared closing that did not come out in trial, you need to take it out and modify your closing statement accordingly. If there is a contradiction or weakness of the other side exposed at trial, capitalize on it in your closing argument.

ASK AND YOU MAY RECEIVE

Conclude your closing statement by asking the court for the remedy you are seeking. What do you want the court to do? How do you want the court to rule? Respectfully ask for the court to return a verdict or decision for your client. For instance:

> Therefore, the State of Ohio respectfully asks this Court to deny the Defendant's motion to eliminate the death penalty as a sentencing option for the Defendant. Thank you.

> Therefore, Defendant Jane Smith respectfully asks this Court to find the Defendant not guilty of all charges against her. Thank you.

REBUTTAL

The rebuttal is the final part of a mock trial. The Plaintiff is given the opportunity to rebut (refute or disprove) the defense's closing argument. The rebuttal is limited to the scope of the Defense's closing argument. This means that the Plaintiff can only refute arguments actually made by the defense counsel in his or her closing. The rebuttal is not permitted to raise new arguments or expand on arguments raised in the Plaintiff's closing but not argued in the Defendant's closing. The most effective rebuttal will touch upon one or two points in Defendant's closing argument.

TEAMWORK

Work in small teams. Half the teams will represent the Defense and half will represent the Prosecution.

Larceny is defined as (1) the wrongful (2) taking (3) and carrying away (4) the personal property (5) of another (6) with the intent to deprive them of that property permanently.

One important part of your closing argument is an analysis of whether or not all of the elements of larceny have been satisfied by both witnesses and the evidence. Provide a closing statement by the Prosecution or the Defense that reflects this analysis.

Appendix A

Constitution of the United States

We the People Of the United States, in Order to form a more perfect Union, establish Justice, insure domestic Tranquility, provide for the common defence, promote the general Welfare, and secure the Blessings of Liberty to ourselves and our Posterity, do ordain and establish this Constitution for the United States of America.

Article I

Section 1. All legislative Powers herein granted shall be vested in a Congress of the United States, which shall consist of a Senate and House of Representatives.

Section 2. The House of Representatives shall be composed of Members chosen every second Year by the People of the several States, and the Electors in each State shall have the Qualifications requisite for Electors of the most numerous Branch of the State Legislature.

No Person shall be a Representative who shall not have attained to the Age of twenty five Years, and been seven Years a Citizen of the United States, and who shall not, when elected, be an inhabitant of that State in which he shall be chosen.

Representatives and direct Taxes shall be apportioned among the several States which may be included within this Union, according to their respective. Numbers, which shall be determined by adding to the whole Number of free Persons, including those bound to Service for a Term of Years, and excluding Indians not taxed, three fifths of all other Persons. The actual Enumeration shall be made within three Years after the first Meeting of the Congress of the United States, and within every subsequent Term of ten Years, in such Manner as they shall by Law direct. The number of Representatives shall not exceed one for every thirty Thousand, but each State shall have at Least one Representative; and until such enumeration shall be made, the State of New Hampshire shall be entitled to chuse three, Massachusetts eight, Rhode Island and Providence Plantations one, Connecticut five, New-York six, New Jersey four, Pennsylvania eight, Delaware one, Maryland six, Virginia ten, North Carolina five, South Carolina five, and Georgia three.

When vacancies happen in the Representation from any State, the Executive Authority thereof shall issue Writs of Election to fill such Vacancies.

The House of Representatives shall chuse their Speaker and other Officers; and shall have the sole Power of Impeachment.

Section 3. The Senate of the United States shall be composed of two Senators from each State, chosen by the Legislature thereof for six Years; and each Senator shall have one Vote.

Immediately after they shall be assembled in Consequence of the first Election, they shall be divided as equally as may be into three Classes. The Seats of the Senators of the first Class shall be vacated at the Expiration of the second Year, of the second Class at the Expiration of the fourth Year, and of the third Class at the Expiration of the sixth Year, so that one third may be chosen every second Year; and if Vacancies happen by Resignation, or otherwise, during the Recess of the Legislature of any State, the Executive thereof may make temporary Appointments until the next Meeting of the Legislature, which shall then fill such Vacancies.

No Person shall be a Senator who shall not have attained to the Age of thirty Years, and been nine Years a Citizen of the United States, and who shall not, when elected, be an Inhabitant of that State for which he shall be chosen.

The Vice-President of the United States shall be President of the Senate, but shall have no Vote, unless they be equally divided.

The Senate shall chuse their other Officers, and also a President pro tempore, in the Absence of the Vice-President, or when he shall exercise the Office of President of the United States.

*Sections on the Constitution which are crossed out in this text have been amended and are no longer in effect.

The Senate shall have the sole Power to try all Impeachments. When sitting for that Purpose, they shall be on Oath or Affirmation. When the President of the United States is tried, the Chief Justice shall preside: And no Person shall be convicted without the Concurrence of two thirds of the Members present.

Judgment in Cases of Impeachment shall not extend further than to removal from Office, and disqualification to hold and enjoy any Office of honor, Trust or Profit under the United States: but the Party convicted shall nevertheless be liable and subject to Indictment, Trial, Judgment and Punishment, according to Law.

Section 4. The Times, Places and Manner of holding Elections for Senators and Representatives, shall be prescribed in each State by the Legislature thereof; but the Congress may at any time by Law make or alter such Regulations, except as to the Places of chusing Senators.

The Congress shall assemble at least once in every Year, and such Meeting shall be on the first Monday in December unless they shall by Law appoint a different Day.

Section 5. Each House shall be the Judge of the Elections, Returns and Qualifications of its own Members, and a Majority of each shall constitute a Quorum to do Business; but a smaller Number may adjourn from day to day, and may be authorized to compel the Attendance of absent Members, in such Manner, and under such Penalties as each House may provide.

Each House may determine the Rules of its Proceedings, punish its Members for disorderly Behaviour, and, with the Concurrence of two thirds, expel a Member.

Each House shall keep a Journal of its Proceedings, and from time to time publish the same, excepting such Parts as may in their Judgment require Secrecy; and the Yeas and Nays of the Members of either House on any question shall, at the Desire of one fifth of those Present, be entered on the Journal.

Neither House, during the Session of Congress, shall, without the Consent of the other, adjourn for more than three days, nor to any other Place than that in which the two Houses shall be sitting.

Section 6. The Senators and Representatives shall receive a Compensation for their Services, to be ascertained by Law, and paid out of the Treasury of the United States. They shall in all Cases, except Treason, Felony and Breach of the Peace, be privileged from Arrest during their Attendance at the Session off their respective Houses, and in going to and returning from the same; and for any Speech or Debate in either House, they shall not be questioned in any other Place.

No Senator or Representative shall, during the Time for which he was elected, be appointed to any civil Office under the Authority of the United States, which shall have been created, or the Emoluments whereof shall have been increased during such time; and no Person holding any Office under the United States, shall be a Member of either House during his Continuance in Office.

Section 7. All Bills for raising Revenue shall originate in the House of Representatives; but the Senate may propose or concur with Amendments as on other Bills.

Every Bill which shall have passed the House of Representatives and the Senate, shall, before it becomes a Law, be presented to the President of the United States; If he approve he shall sign it, but if not he shall return it, with his Objections to that House in which it shall have originated, who shall enter the Objections at large on their Journal, and proceed to reconsider it.

If after such Reconsideration two thirds of that House shall agree to pass the Bill, it shall be sent, together with the Objections, to the other House, by which it shall likewise be reconsidered, and if approved by two thirds of that House, it shall become a Law. But in all such Cases the Votes of both Houses shall be determined by yeas and Nays, and the Names of the Persons voting for and against the Bill shall be entered on the Journal of each House respectively. If any Bill shall not be returned by the President within ten Days (Sundays excepted) after it shall have been presented to him, the Same shall be a Law, in like Manner as if he had signed it, unless the Congress by their Adjournment prevent its Return, in which Case it shall not be a Law.

Every Order, Resolution, or Vote to which the Concurrence of the Senate and House of Representatives may be necessary (except on a question of Adjournment) shall be presented to the President of the United States; and before the Same shall take Effect, shall be approved by him, or being disapproved by him, shall be repassed by two thirds of the Senate and House of Representatives, according to the Rules and Limitations prescribed in the Case of a Bill.

Section 8. The Congress shall have Power To lay and collect Taxes, Duties, Imposts and Excises, to pay the Debts and provide for the common Defence and general Welfare of the United States; but all Duties, Imposts and Excises shall be uniform throughout the United States;

To borrow Money on the credit of the United States;

To regulate Commerce with foreign Nations, and among the several States, and with the Indian Tribes;

To establish an uniform Rule of Naturalization, and uniform Laws on the subject of Bankruptcies throughout the United States;

To coin Money, regulate the Value thereof, and of foreign Coin, and fix the Standard of Weights and Measures;

To provide for the Punishment of counterfeiting the Securities and current Coin of the United States;

To establish Post Offices and post Roads;

To promote the Progress of Science and useful Arts, by securing for limited Times to Authors and Inventors the exclusive Right to their respective Writings and Discoveries;

To constitute Tribunals inferior to the supreme Court;

To define and punish Piracies and Felonies committed on the high Seas, and Offenses against the Law of Nations;

To declare War, grant Letters of Marque and Reprisal, and make Rules concerning Captures on Land and Water;

To raise and support Armies, but no Appropriation of Money to that Use shall be for a longer Term than two Years;

To provide and maintain a Navy;

To make Rules for the Government and Regulation of the land and naval Forces;

To provide for calling forth the Militia to execute the Laws of the Union, suppress Insurrections and repel Invasions;

To provide for organizing, arming, and disciplining, the Militia, and for governing such Part of them as may be employed in the Service of the United States, reserving to the States respectively, the Appointment of the Officers, and the Authority of training the Militia according to the discipline prescribed by Congress;

To exercise exclusive Legislation in all Cases whatsoever, over such District (not exceeding ten Miles square) as may, by Cession of particular States, and the Acceptance of Congress, become the Seat of the Government of the United States, and to exercise like Authority over all Places purchased by the Consent of the Legislature of the State in which the Same shall be, for the Erection of Forts, Magazines, Arsenals, dock-Yards and other needful Buildings; And

To make all Laws which shall be necessary and proper for carrying into Execution the foregoing Powers, and all other Powers vested by this Constitution in the Government of the United States, or in any Department or Officer thereof.

Section 9. The Migration or Importation of such Persons as any of the States now existing shall think proper to admit, shall not be prohibited by the Congress prior to the Year one thousand eight hundred and eight, but a Tax or duty may be imposed on such Importation, not exceeding ten dollars for each Person.

The Privilege of the Writ of Habeas Corpus shall not be suspended, unless when in Cases of Rebellion or Invasion the public Safety may require it.

No Bill of Attainder or ex post facto Law shall be passed.

No Capitation, or other direct, Tax shall be laid, unless in Proportion to the Census or Enumeration herein before directed to be taken.

No Tax or Duty shall be laid on Articles exported from any State.

No Preference shall be given by any Regulation of Commerce or Revenue to the

Ports of one State over those of another: nor shall Vessels bound to, or from, one State, be obliged to enter, clear, or pay Duties in another.

No Money shall be drawn from the Treasury, but in Consequence of Appropriations made by Law; and a regular Statement and Account of the Receipts and Expenditures of all public Money shall be published from time to time.

No Title of Nobility shall be granted by the United States: And no Person holding any Office of Profit or Trust under them, shall, without the Consent of the Congress, accept of any present, Emolument, Office, or Title, of any kind whatever, from any King, Prince, or foreign State.

Section 10. No State shall enter into any Treaty, Alliance, or Confederation; grant Letters of Marque and Reprisal; coin Money; emit Bills of Credit; make any Thing but gold and silver Coin a Tender in Payment of Debts; pass any Bill of Attainder, ex post facto Law, or Law impairing the Obligation of Contracts, or grant any Title of Nobility.

No State shall, without the Consent of the Congress, lay any Imposts or Duties on Imports or Exports, except what may be absolutely necessary for executing its inspection Laws: and the net Produce of all Duties and Imposts, laid by any State on Imports or Exports, shall be for the Use of the Treasury of the United States; and all such Laws shall be subject to the Revision and Controul of the Congress.

No State shall, without the Consent of Congress, lay any Duty of Tonnage, keep Troops, or Ships of War in time of Peace, enter into any Agreement or Compact with another State, or with a foreign Power, or engage in War, unless actually invaded, or in such imminent Danger as will not admit of delay.

Article II

Section 1. The executive Power shall be vested in a President of the United States of America. He shall hold his Office during the Term of four Years, and, together with the Vice-President, chosen for the same Term, be elected, as follows

Each State shall appoint, in such Manner as the Legislature thereof may direct, a Number of Electors, equal to the whole Number of Senators and Representatives to which the State may be entitled in the Congress: but no Senator or Representative, or Person holding an Office of Trust or Profit under the United States, shall be appointed an Elector.

~~The Electors shall meet in their respective States, and vote by Ballot for two Persons, of whom one at least shall not be an Inhabitant of the same State with themselves. And they shall make a List of all the Persons voted for, and of the Number of Votes for each; which List they shall sign and certify, and transmit sealed to the Seat of the Government of the United States, directed to the President of the Senate. The President of the Senate shall, in the Presence of the Senate and House of Representatives, open all the Certificates, and the Votes shall then be counted. The Person having the greatest Number of Votes shall be the President, if such Number be a Majority, of the whole Number of Electors appointed; and if there be more than one who have such Majority and have an equal Number of Votes, then the House of Representatives shall immediately chuse by Ballot one of them for President, and if no Person have a Majority, then from the five highest on the List the said House shall in like Manner chuse the President. But in chusing the President, the Votes shall be taken by States, the Representation from each State having one Vote; A quorum for this Purpose shall consist of a Member or Members from two thirds of the States, and a Majority of all the States shall be necessary to a Choice. In every Case, after the Choice of the President, the Person having the greatest Number of Votes of the Electors shall be the Vice-President. But if there should remain two or more who have equal Votes, the Senate shall chuse from them by Ballot the Vice President.~~

The Congress may determine the Time of chusing the Electors, and the Day on which they shall give their Votes; which Day shall be the same throughout the United States.

No Person except a natural born Citizen, or a Citizen of the United States, at the time of the Adoption of this Constitution, shall be eligible to the Office of the President; neither shall any person be eligible to that Office who shall not have attained to the Age of thirty five Years, and been fourteen Years a Resident within the United States.

~~In Case of the Removal of the President from Office, or of his Death, Resignation, or Inability to discharge the Powers and Duties of the said Office, the Same shall devolve on the Vice-President, and the Congress may by Law provide for the Case of Removal, Death, Resignation or Inability, both of the President and Vice-President, declaring what Officer shall then act as President, and such Officer shall act accordingly, until the Disability be removed, or a President shall be elected.~~

The President shall, at stated Times, receive for his Services, a Compensation, which shall neither be increased nor diminished during the Period for which he shall have been elected and he shall not receive within that Period any other Emolument from the United States, or any of them.

Before he enter on the Execution of his Office, he shall take the following Oath or Affirmation: "I do solemnly swear (or affirm) that I will faithfully execute the Office of President of the United States, and will to the best of my Ability, preserve, protect and defend the Constitution of the United States."

Section 2. The President shall be Commander in Chief of the Army and Navy of the United States, and of the Militia of the several States, when called into the actual Service of the United States; he may require the Opinion, in writing, of the principal Officer in each of the executive Departments, upon any Subject relating to the Duties of their respective Offices, and he shall have Power to grant Reprieves and Pardons for Offenses against the United States, except in Cases of Impeachment.

He shall have Power, by and with the Advice and Consent of the Senate, to make Treaties, provided two thirds of the Senators present concur; and he shall nominate, and by and with the Advice and Consent of the Senate, shall appoint Ambassadors, other public Ministers and Consuls, judges of the supreme Court, and all other Officers of the United States, whose Appointments are not herein otherwise provided for, and which shall be established by Law: but the Congress may by Law vest the Appointment of such inferior Officers, as they think proper, in the President alone, in the Courts of Law, or in the Heads of Departments. The President shall have Power to fill up all Vacancies that may happen during the Recess of the Senate, by granting Commissions which shall expire at the End of their next Session.

Section 3. He shall from time to time give to the Congress Information of the State of the Union, and recommend to their Consideration such measures as he shall judge necessary and expedient; he may, on extraordinary Occasions, convene both Houses, or either of them, and in Case of Disagreement between them, with Respect to the Time of Adjournment, he may adjourn them to such Time as he shall think proper; he shall receive Ambassadors and other public Ministers; he shall take Care that the Laws be faithfully executed, and shall Commission all the Officers of the United States.

Section 4. The President, Vice-President and all civil Officers of the United States, shall be removed from Office on Impeachment for, and Conviction of, Treason, Bribery, or other high Crimes and Misdemeanors.

Article III

Section 1. The judicial Power of the United States, shall he vested in one supreme Court, and in such inferior Courts as the Congress may from time to time ordain and establish. The Judges, both of the supreme and inferior Courts, shall hold their Offices during good Behaviour, and shall, at stated Times, receive for their Services, a Compensation, which shall not be diminished during their Continuance in Office

Section 2. The judicial Power shall extend to all Cases, in Law and Equity, arising, under this Constitution, the Laws of the United States, and Treaties made, or which shall be made, under their Authority; to all Cases affecting Ambassadors, other public Ministers and Consuls; to all Cases of admiralty and maritime Jurisdiction; to Controversies to which the United States shall be a Party; to Controversies between two or more States; between a State and Citizens of another State; between Citizens of different States between Citizens of the same State claiming Lands under Grants of different States, and between a State, or the Citizens thereof; and foreign States, Citizens or Subjects.

In all Cases affecting Ambassadors, other public Ministers and Consuls, and those in which a State shall be Party, the supreme Court shall have original Jurisdiction. In all the other Cases before mentioned, the supreme Court shall have appellate Jurisdiction, both as to Law and Fact, with such Exceptions, and under such Regulations as the Congress shall make.

The Trial of all Crimes, except in Cases of Impeachment, shall be by Jury; and such Trial shall be held in the State where the said Crimes shall have been committed; but when not committed within any State, the Trial shall be at such Place or Places as the Congress may by Law have directed.

Section 3. Treason against the United States, shall consist only in levying War against them, or in adhering to their Enemies, giving them Aid and Comfort. No Person shall be convicted of Treason unless on the Testimony of two Witnesses to the same overt Act, or on Confession in open Court.

The Congress shall have Power to declare the Punishment of Treason, but no Attainder of Treason shall work Corruption of Blood, or Forfeiture except during the Life of the Person attained.

Article IV

Section 1. Full Faith and Credit shall be given in each State to the public Acts, Records, and judicial Proceedings of every other State; And the Congress may by general Laws prescribe the Manner in which such Acts, Records and Proceedings shall be proved, and the Effect thereof.

Section 2. The Citizens of each State shall be entitled to all Privileges and Immunities of Citizens in the several States.

A Person charged in any State with Treason, Felony, or other Crime, who shall flee from Justice, and be found in another State, shall on Demand of the executive Authority of the State from which he fled, be delivered up, to be removed to the State having Jurisdiction of the Crime.

~~No Person held to Service or Labour in one State, under the Laws thereof, escaping into another, shall, in Consequence of any Law or Regulation therein, be discharged from such Service or Labour, but shall be delivered up on Claim of the Party to whom such Service or Labour may be due.~~

Section 3. New States may be admitted by the Congress into this Union; but no new State shall be formed or erected within the Jurisdiction of any other State; nor any State be formed by the Junction of two or more States, or Parts of States, without the Consent of the Legislatures of the States concerned as well as of the Congress.

The Congress shall have Power to dispose of and make all needful Rules and Regulations respecting the Territory or other Property belonging to the United States; and nothing in this Constitution shall be so construed as to Prejudice any Claims of the United States, or of any particular State.

Section 4. The United States shall guarantee to every state in this Union a Republican Form of Government, and shall protect each of them against Invasion; and on Application of the Legislature, or of the Executive (when the Legislature cannot be convened) against domestic Violence.

Article V

The Congress, whenever two thirds of both Houses shall deem it necessary, shall propose Amendments to this Constitution, or, on the Application of the Legislatures of two thirds of the several States, shall call a Convention for proposing Amendments, which, in either Case, shall be valid to all Intents and Purposes, as Part of this Constitution, when ratified by the Legislatures of three fourths of the several States, or by Conventions in three fourths thereof, as the one or the other Mode of Ratification may be proposed by the Congress; Provided that no Amendment which may be made prior to the Year One thousand eight hundred and eight shall in any Manner affect the first and fourth Clauses in the Ninth Section of the first Article; and that no State, without its Consent, shall be deprived of its equal Suffrage in the Senate.

Article VI

All Debts contracted and Engagements entered into, before the Adoption of this Constitution, shall be as valid against the United States under this Constitution, as under the Confederation.

This Constitution, and the Laws of the United States which shall be made in Pursuance thereof; and all Treaties made, or which shall be made, under the Authority of the United States, shall be the supreme Law of the Land; and the Judges in every State shall be bound thereby, any Thing in the Constitution or Laws of any State to the Contrary notwithstanding.

The Senators and Representatives before mentioned, and the Members of the several State Legislatures, and all executive and judicial Officers, both of the United States and of the several States, shall be bound by Oath or Affirmation, to support this Constitution; but no religious Test shall ever be required as a Qualification to any Office or public Trust under the United States.

Article VII

The Ratification of the Conventions of nine States, shall be sufficient for the Establishment of this Constitution between the States so ratifying the Same.

Done in Convention by the Unanimous Consent of the States present the Seventeenth Day of September in the Year of our Lord one thousand seven hundred and Eighty seven and of the Independence of the United States of America the Twelfth In Witness whereof We have hereunto subscribed our Names,

G.o Washington Presid.
and deputy from Virginia

Amendment I

Congress shall make no law respecting an establishment of religion, or prohibiting the free exercise thereof; or abridging the freedom of speech, or of the press, or the right of the people peaceably to assemble, and to petition the Government for a redress of grievances.

Amendment II

A well regulated Militia, being necessary to the security of a free State, the right of the people to keep and bear Arms, shall not be infringed.

Amendment III

No Soldier shall, in time of peace be quartered in any house, without the consent of the Owner, nor in time of war, but in a manner to be prescribed by law.

Amendment IV

The right of the people to be secure in their persons, houses, papers, and effects, against unreasonable searches and seizures, shall not be violated, and no Warrants shall issue, but upon probable cause, supported by Oath or affirmation, and particularly describing the place to be searched, and the persons or things to be seized.

Amendment V

No person shall be held to answer for a capital, or otherwise infamous crime, unless on a presentment or indictment of a Grand Jury, except in cases arising in the land or naval forces, or in the Militia, when in actual service in time of War or public danger; nor shall any person be subject for the same offence to be twice put in jeopardy of life or limb, nor shall be compelled in any criminal case to be a witness against himself, nor be deprived of life, liberty, or property, without due process of law; nor shall private property be taken for public use without just compensation.

Amendment VI

In all criminal prosecutions, the accused shall enjoy the right to a speedy and public trial, by an impartial jury of the State and district wherein the crime shall have been committed; which district shall have been previously ascertained by law, and to be informed of the nature and cause of the accusation; to be confronted with the witnesses against him; to have compulsory process for obtaining witnesses In his favor, and to have the assistance of counsel for his defence.

Amendment VII

In Suits at common law, where the value in controversy shall exceed twenty dollars, the right of trial by jury shall be preserved, and no fact tried by a jury shall be otherwise reexamined in any Court of the United States, than according to the rules of the common law.

Amendment VIII

Excessive bail shall not be required, nor excessive fines imposed, nor cruel and unusual punishments inflicted.

Amendment IX

The enumeration in the Constitution of certain rights shall not be construed to deny or disparage others retained by the people.

Amendment X

The powers not delegated to the United States by the Constitution, nor prohibited by it to the States, are reserved to the States respectively, or to the people.

Amendment XI

The Judicial power of the United States shall not be construed to extend to any suit in law or equity, commenced or prosecuted against one of the United States by Citizens of another State, or by Citizens or Subjects of any Foreign State.

Amendment XII

The Electors shall meet in their respective states, and vote by ballot for President and Vice-President, one of whom, at least, shall not be an inhabitant of the same state with themselves; they shall name in their ballots the person voted for as President, and in distinct ballots the person voted for as Vice-President, and they shall make distinct lists of all persons voted for as President, and of all persons voted for as Vice-President, and of the number of votes for each, which lists they shall sign and certify, and transmit sealed to the seat of the government of the United States, directed to the President of the Senate; The President of the Senate shall, in the presence of the Senate and House of Representatives, open all the certificates and the votes shall then be counted; The person having the greatest number of votes for President shall be the President, if such number be a majority of the whole number of Electors appointed; and if no person have such majority, then from the persons having the highest numbers not exceeding three on the list of those voted for as President, the House of Representatives shall choose immediately, by ballot, the President. But in choosing the President, the votes shall be taken by states, the representation from each state having one vote; a quorum for this purpose shall consist of a member or members from two-thirds of the states, and a majority of all the states shall be necessary to a choice. ~~And if the House of Representatives shall not choose a President whenever the right of choice shall devolve upon them, before the fourth day of March next following, then the Vice-President shall act as President, as in the case of the death or other constitutional disability of the President~~ The person having the greatest number of votes as Vice-President, shall be the Vice-President, if such number be a majority of the whole number of Electors appointed, and if no person have a majority, then from the two highest numbers on the list, the Senate shall choose the Vice-President; a quorum for the purpose shall consist of two-thirds of the whole number of Senators, and a majority of the whole number shall be necessary to a choice. But no person constitutionally ineligible to the office of President shall be eligible to that of Vice-President of the United States.

Amendment XIII

Section 1. Neither slavery nor involuntary servitude, except as a punishment for a crime whereof the party shall have been duly convicted, shall exist within the United States, or any place subject to their jurisdiction.

Section 2. Congress shall have power to enforce this article by appropriate legislation.

Amendment XIV

Section 1. All persons born or naturalized in the United States and subject to the jurisdiction thereof, are citizens of the United States and of the State wherein they reside. No State shall make or enforce any law which shall abridge the privileges or immunities of citizens of the United States; nor shall any State deprive any person of life, liberty, or property, without due process of law; nor deny to any person within its jurisdiction the equal protection of the laws.

Section 2. Representatives shall be apportioned among the several States according to their respective numbers, counting the whole number of persons in each State, excluding Indians not taxed. But when the right to vote at any election for the choice of electors for President and Vice-President of the United States, Representatives in Congress, the Executive and Judicial officers of a State, or the members of the Legislature thereof, is denied to any of the male inhabitants of such State, being twenty-one years of age, and citizens of the United States, or in any way abridged, except for participation in rebellion, or other crime, the basis of representation therein shall be reduced in the proportion which the number of such male citizens shall bear to the whole number of male citizens twenty-one years of age in such State.

Section 3. No person shall be a Senator or Representative in Congress, or elector of President and Vice-President, or hold any office, civil or military, under the United States, or under any State, who, having previously taken an oath, as a member of Congress, or as an officer of the United States, or as a member of any State legislature, or as an executive or judicial officer of any State, to support the Constitution of the United States, shall have engaged in insurrection or rebellion against the same, or given aid or comfort to the enemies thereof. But Congress may by a vote of twothirds of each House, remove such disability.

Section 4. The validity of the public debt of the United States, authorized by law, including debts incurred for payment of pensions and bounties for services in suppressing insurrection or rebellion, shall not be questioned. But neither the United States nor any State shall assume or pay any debt or obligation incurred in aid of insurrection or rebellion against the United States, or any claim for the loss or emancipation of any slave; but all such debts, obligations and claims shall be held illegal and void.

Section 5. The Congress shall have power to enforce, by appropriate legislation, the provisions of this article.

Amendment XV

Section 1. The right of citizens of the United States to vote shall not be denied or abridged by the United States or by any State on account of race, color, or previous condition of servitude.

Section 2. The Congress shall have power to enforce this article by appropriate legislation.

Amendment XVI

The Congress shall have power to lay and collect taxes on incomes, from whatever source derived, without apportionment among the several States, and without regard to any census or enumeration.

Amendment XVII

The Senate of the United States shall be composed of two Senators from each State, elected by the people thereof, for six years; and each Senator shall have one vote. The electors in each State shall have the qualifications requisite for electors of the most numerous branch of the State legislatures.

When vacancies happen in the representation of any State in the Senate, the executive authority of such State shall issue writs of election to fill such vacancies; Provided, That the legislature of any State may empower the executive thereof to make temporary appointments until the people fill the vacancies by election as the legislature may direct.

This amendment shall not be so construed as to affect the election or term of any Senator chosen before it becomes valid as part of the Constitution.

~~Amendment XVIII~~

Section 1. ~~After one year from the ratification of this article the manufacture, sale, or transportation of intoxicating liquors within, the importation thereof into, or the exportation thereof from the United States and all territory subject to the jurisdiction thereof for beverage purposes is hereby prohibited.~~

Section 2. ~~The Congress and the several States shall have concurrent power to enforce this article by appropriate legislation.~~

Section 3. ~~This article shall be inoperative unless it shall have been ratified as an amendment to the Constitution by the legislatures of the several States, as provided in the Constitution, within seven years from the date of the submission hereof to the States by the Congress.~~

Amendment XIX

The right of citizens of the United States to vote shall not be denied or abridged by the United States or by any State on account of sex. Congress shall have power to enforce this article by appropriate legislation.

Amendment XX

Section 1. The terms of the President and Vice-President shall end at noon on the 20th day of January, and the terms of Senators and Representatives at noon on the 3rd day of January, of the years in which such terms would have ended if this article had not been ratified; and the terms of their successors shall then begin.

Section 2. The Congress shall assemble at least once a year, and such meeting shall begin at noon on the 3rd day of January, unless they shall by law appoint a different day.

Section 3. If, at the time fixed for the beginning of the term of the President, the President elect shall have died, the Vice-President elect shall become President. If a President shall not have been chosen before the time fixed for the beginning of his term, or if the President elect shall have failed to qualify, then the Vice-President elect shall act as President until a President shall have qualified; and the Congress may by law provide for the case wherein neither a President elect nor a Vice-President elect shall have qualified, declaring who shall then act as President, or the manner in which one who is to act shall be elected, and such person shall act accordingly until a President or Vice-President shall have qualified.

Section 4. The Congress may by law provide for the case of the death of any of the persons from whom the House of Representatives may choose a President whenever the right of choice shall have devolved upon them, and for the case of the death of any of the persons from whom the Senate may choose a Vice-President whenever the right of choice shall have devolved upon them.

Section 5. Sections 1 and 2 shall take effect on the 15th day of October following the ratification of this article.

Section 6. This article shall be inoperative unless it shall have been ratified as an amendment to the Constitution by the legislatures of three-fourths of the several States within seven years from the date of its submission.

Amendment XXI

Section 1. The eighteenth article of amendment to the Constitution of the United States is hereby repealed.

Section 2. The transportation or importation into any State, Territory, or possession of the United States for delivery or use therein of intoxicating liquors, in violation of the laws thereof, is hereby prohibited.

Section 3. This article shall be inoperative unless it shall have been ratified as an amendment to the Constitution by conventions in the several States, as Provided in the Constitution, within seven years from the date of the submission hereof to the States by the Congress.

Amendment XXII

Section 1. No person shall be elected to the office of the President more than twice, and no person who has held the office of President, or acted as President, for more than two years of a term to which some other person was elected President shall be elected to the office of the President more than once. But this Article shall not apply to any person holding the office of President when this Article was proposed by the Congress, and shall not prevent any person who may be holding the office of President, or acting as President, during the term within which this Article becomes operative from holding the office of President or acting as President during the remainder of such term.

Section 2. This article shall be inoperative unless it shall have been ratified as an amendment to the Constitution by the legislatures of three-fourths of the several States within seven years from the date of its submission to the States by the Congress.

Amendment XXIII

Section 1. The District constituting the seat of Government of the United States shall appoint in such manner as the Congress may direct:

A number of electors of President and Vice-President equal to the whole number of Senators and Representatives in Congress to which the District would be entitled if it were a State, but in no event more than the least populous State;

they shall be in addition to those appointed by the States, but they shall be considered, for the purposes of the election of President and Vice-President, to be electors appointed by a State; and they shall meet in the District and perform such duties as provided by the twelfth article of amendment.

Section 2. The Congress shall have power to enforce this article by appropriate legislation.

Amendment XXIV

Section 1. The right of citizens of the United States to vote in any primary or other election for President or Vice-President, for electors for President or Vice-President, or for Senator or Representative in Congress, shall not be denied or abridged by the United States or any State by reason of failure to pay any poll tax or other tax.

Section 2. The Congress shall have power to enforce this article by appropriate legislation.

Amendment XXV

Section 1. In case of the removal of the President from office or of his death or resignation, the Vice-President shall become President.

Section 2. Whenever there is a vacancy in the office of the Vice-President, the President shall nominate a Vice-President who shall take office upon confirmation by a majority vote of both Houses of Congress.

Section 3. Whenever the President transmits to the President pro tempore of the Senate and the Speaker of the House of Representatives his written declaration that he is unable to discharge the powers and duties of his office, and until he transmits to them a written declaration to the contrary, such powers and duties shall be discharged by the Vice-President as Acting President.

Section 4. Whenever the Vice-President and a majority of either the principal officers of the executive departments or of such other body as Congress may by law provide, transmit to the President pro tempore of the Senate and the Speaker of the House of Representatives their written declaration that the President is unable to discharge the powers and duties of his office, the Vice-President shall immediately assume the powers and duties of the office as Acting President.

Thereafter, when the President transmits to the President pro tempore of the Senate and the Speaker of the House of Representatives his written declaration that no inability exists, he shall resume the powers and duties of his office unless the Vice-President and a majority of either the principal officers of the executive department or of such other body as Congress may by law provide, transmit within four days to the President pro tempore of the Senate and the Speaker of the House of Representatives their written declaration that the President is unable to discharge the powers and duties of his office. Thereupon Congress shall decide the issue, assembling within forty-eight hours for that purpose if not in session. If the Congress, within twenty-one days after receipt of the latter written declaration, or, if Congress is not in session, within twenty-one days after Congress is required to

assemble, determines by twothirds vote of both Houses that the President is unable to discharge the powers and duties of his office, the Vice-President shall continue to discharge the same as Acting President; otherwise, the President shall resume the powers and duties of his office.

Amendment XXVI

Section 1. The right of citizens of the United States, who are eighteen years of age or older, to vote shall not be denied or abridged by the United States or by any State on account of age.

Section 2. The Congress shall have power to enforce this article by appropriate legislation.

Amendment XXVII

No law, varying the compensation for the services of the Senators and Representatives, shall take effect, until an election of Representatives shall have intervened.

Appendix B

The Declaration of Independence

IN CONGRESS, JULY 4, 1776. A DECLARATION BY THE REPRESENTATIVES OF THE UNITED STATES OF AMERICA, IN GENERAL CONGRESS ASSEMBLED.

WHEN in the Course of human Events, it becomes necessary for one People to dissolve the Political Bands which have connected them with another, and to assume among the Powers of the Earth, the separate and equal Station to which the Laws of Nature and of Nature's God entitle them, a decent Respect to the Opinions of Mankind requires that they should declare the causes which impel them to the Separation.

WE hold these Truths to be self-evident, that all Men are created equal, that they are endowed by their Creator with certain unalienable Rights, that among these are Life, Liberty, and the Pursuit of Happiness That to secure these Rights, Governments are instituted among Men, deriving their just Powers from the Consent of the Governed, that whenever any Form of Government becomes destructive of these Ends, it is the Right of the People to alter or to abolish it, and to institute new Government, laying its Foundation on such Principles, and organizing its Powers in such Form, as to them shall seem most likely to effect their Safety and Happiness. Prudence, indeed, will dictate that Governments long established should not be changed for

light and transient Causes; and accordingly all Experience hath shewn, that Mankind are more disposed to suffer, while Evils are sufferable, than to right themselves by abolishing the Forms to which they are accustomed. But when a long Train of Abuses and Usurpations, pursuing invariably the same Object, evinces a Design to reduce them under absolute Despotism, it is their Right, it is their Duty, to throw off such Government, and to provide new Guards for their future Security. Such has been the patient Sufferance of these Colonies; and such is now the Necessity which constrains them to alter their former Systems of Government. The History of the present King of Great-Britain is a History of repeated Injuries and Usurpations, all having in direct Object the Establishment of an absolute Tyranny over these States. To prove this, let Facts be submitted to a candid World.

HE has refused his Assent to Laws, the most wholesome and necessary for the public Good.

HE has forbidden his Governors to pass Laws of immediate and pressing Importance, unless suspended in their Operation till his Assent should be obtained; and when so suspended, he has utterly neglected to attend to them.

HE has refused to pass other Laws for the Accommodation of large Districts of People, unless those People would relinquish the Right of Representation in the Legislature, a Right inestimable to them, and formidable to Tyrants only.

HE has called together Legislative Bodies at Places unusual, uncomfortable, and distant from the Depository of their public Records, for the sole Purpose of fatiguing them into Compliance with his Measures.

HE has dissolved Representative Houses repeatedly, for opposing with manly Firmness his Invasions on the Rights of the People.

HE has refused for a long Time, after such Dissolutions, to cause others to be elected; whereby the Legislative Powers, incapable of Annihilation, have returned to the People at large for their exercise; the State remaining in the mean time exposed to all the Dangers of Invasion from without, and Convulsions within.

HE has endeavoured to prevent the Population of these States; for that Purpose obstructing the Laws for Naturalization of Foreigners; refusing to pass others to encourage their Migrations hither, and raising the Conditions of new Appropriations of Lands.

HE has obstructed the Administration of Justice, by refusing his Assent to Laws for establishing Judiciary Powers.

HE has made Judges dependent on his Will alone, for the Tenure of their Offices, and the Amount and Payment of their Salaries.

HE has erected a Multitude of new Offices, and sent hither Swarms of Officers to harrass our People, and eat out their Substance.

HE has kept among us, in Times of Peace, Standing Armies, without the consent of our Legislatures.

HE has affected to render the Military independent of and superior to the Civil Power.

HE has combined with others to subject us to a Jurisdiction foreign to our Constitution, and unacknowledged by our Laws; giving his Assent to their Acts of pretended Legislation:

FOR quartering large Bodies of Armed Troops among us:

FOR protecting them, by a mock Trial, from Punishment for any Murders which they should commit on the Inhabitants of these States:

FOR cutting off our Trade with all Parts of the World:

FOR imposing Taxes on us without our Consent:

FOR depriving us, in many Cases, of the Benefits of Trial by Jury:

FOR transporting us beyond Seas to be tried for pretended Offences:

FOR abolishing the free System of English Laws in a neighbouring Province, establishing therein an arbitrary Government, and enlarging its Boundaries, so as to render it at once an Example and fit Instrument for introducing the same absolute Rule into these Colonies:

FOR taking away our Charters, abolishing our most valuable Laws, and altering fundamentally the Forms of our Governments

FOR suspending our own Legislatures, and declaring themselves invested with Power to legislate for us in all Cases whatsoever.

HE has abdicated Government here, by declaring us out of his Protection and waging War against us.

HE has plundered our Seas, ravaged our Coasts, burnt our Towns, and destroyed the Lives of our People.

HE is, at this Time, transporting large Armies of foreign Mercenaries to compleat the Works of Death, Desolation, and Tyranny, already begun with circumstances of Cruelty and Perfidy, scarcely paralleled in the most barbarous Ages, and totally unworthy the Head of a civilized Nation.

HE has constrained our fellow Citizens taken Captive on the high Seas to bear Arms against their Country, to become the Executioners of their Friends and Brethren, or to fall themselves by their Hands.

HE has excited domestic Insurrections amongst us, and has endeavoured to bring on the Inhabitants of our Frontiers, the merciless Indian Savages, whose known Rule of Warfare, is an undistinguished Destruction, of all Ages, Sexes and Conditions.

IN every stage of these Oppressions we have Petitioned for Redress in the most humble Terms. Our repeated Petitions have been answered only by repeated Injury. A Prince, whose Character is thus marked by every act which may define a Tyrant, is unfit to be the Ruler of a free People.

NOR have we been wanting in Attentions to our British Brethren. We have warned them from Time to Time of Attempts by their Legislature to extend an unwarrantable Jurisdiction over us. We have reminded them of the Circumstances of our Emigration and Settlement here. We have appealed to their native Justice and Magnanimity, and we have conjured them by the Ties of our common Kindred to disavow these Usurpations, which, would inevitably interrupt our Connections and Correspondence. They too have been deaf to the Voice of Justice and of Consanguinity. We must, therefore, acquiesce in the Necessity, which denounces our Separation, and hold them, as we hold the rest of mankind, Enemies in War, in Peace, Friends.

WE, therefore, the Representatives of the UNITED STATES OF AMERICA, in GENERAL CONGRESS, Assembled, appealing to the Supreme Judge of the World for the Rectitude of our Intentions, do, in the Name, and by Authority of the good People of these Colonies, solemnly Publish and Declare, That these United Colonies are, and of Right ought to be, FREE AND INDEPENDENT STATES; that they are absolved from all Allegiance to the British Crown, and that all political Connection between them and the State of Great-Britain, is and ought to be totally dissolved; and that as FREE AND INDEPENDENT STATES, they have full Power to levy War, conclude Peace, contract Alliances, establish Commerce, and to do all other Acts and Things which INDEPENDENT STATES may of right do. And for the support of this Declaration, with a firm Reliance on the Protection of divine Providence, we mutually pledge to each other our Lives, our Fortunes, and our sacred Honor.

Signed by ORDER and in BEHALF of the CONGRESS,
JOHN HANCOCK, PRESIDENT.

ATTEST.
CHARLES THOMSON, SECRETARY.

PHILADELPHIA: PRINTED BY JOHN DUNLAP.

Glossary of Legal Terms

A

Acceleration clause clause making the entire balance of a debt due and payable upon a certain event, typically default

Acceptance in contracts, occurs when a party to whom an offer has been made agrees to the proposal; in commercial paper, drawee's promise to pay the obligee of a draft when the instrument is due

Accession right of an owner of property to an increase in that property

Accommodation party party lending his or her credit standing to insure the payment of an instrument

Accord agreement between the parties to a contract to change the obligation required

Accord and satisfaction parties' agreement to change the obligation required by their original contract and the performance of the new obligation

Actual bailment bailee's receipt and acceptance of the goods themselves

Administrative agency governmental body formed to carry out particular laws

Administrator/administratrix court-appointed representative for a decedent (male/female)

Adoption legal process that creates a parent-child relationship

Adverse possession method of acquiring title to another's land by continuously occupying it in an adverse, open, and notorious fashion for a prescribed period of years

Affirmative action plan legal remedy requiring employment of members of a protected class due to past discrimination in hiring

Age of majority age at which a person can be legally bound to contracts

Agency legal relationship in which one person is authorized to alter another's legal relationships

Agency shop establishment in which nonunion members are not required to join the union but must pay union dues

Agent one who is authorized to alter the legal relations of another

Alien corporation corporation chartered in another nation

Alteration in contracts, material change in the terms of a contract made intentionally by one party without consent of the other; in commercial paper, party's unauthorized change to or completion of a negotiable instrument intended to change the obligation of a party

Amendment change or alteration

Americans with Disabilities Act of 1990 (ADA) prevents employers from engaging in unjustified discrimination against people based on their disabilities

Annulment court order that cancels a marriage because of a problem that existed from the beginning of the marriage

Antedated dated earlier than the date of issuance

Anticipatory breach notification, before the scheduled time of performance, of refusal to perform contractual terms as agreed

Antitrust laws laws that prohibit competing companies from price fixing or dividing up sales regions

Apparent authority agency authority created when a principal leads the third party to believe that someone has particular agency authority

Appellate brief written argument on the issues of law submitted by opposing attorneys

Appellate court reviews decisions of lower courts to determine if a significant error of law was made during trial

Applicant pool people qualified for a particular job

Arbitrator independent third party who develops a binding and enforceable resolution to a dispute

Arson willful and illegal burning of a building

Articles of Confederation loose form of charter for common government adopted by the thirteen colonies prior to adoption of the Constitution

Articles of incorporation application to a state for a corporate charter

Articles of organization document filed with the state to organize an LLC

Artisan's lien lien for unpaid services assessed against personal property that has been improved

Assault intentional threat to physically or offensively injure another

Assignment transaction by which a party transfers contractual rights to another

Assignment of a lease tenant transfers to a third party his or her interest in a lease

Associate circuit court court that hears minor criminal cases, state traffic offenses, and lawsuits involving amounts of no more than $25,000

Assumption of risk person is aware of a danger on the job but agrees to do it anyway

Attractive nuisance something that attracts children to trespass

Auction public sale to the highest bidder

Authorization card signature on card indicates that a worker wants to be represented by a particular union

Automobile insurance insurance providing liability and other coverages for the operation of a motor vehicle

B

Bailee person having temporary possession and control of another person's goods, holding them in trust for a specified purpose

Bailee's lien right of a bailee to retain possession of the bailed property until payment is made

Bailment transfer of possession of personal property without transfer of ownership

Bailor party who gives up possession of the property

Bait and switch improper business practice involving luring buyers to the store with an understocked, low-priced good and then redirecting them to a more expensive product

Bankruptcy legal proceedings discharging debts and distributing assets

Bargaining unit any group of employees whose employment contract is negotiated together

Barter exchange of goods for goods

Battery harmful or offensive touching

Bearer party in possession of bearer paper

Bearer paper commercial paper legally collectible by the party in possession

Beneficiary party for whose benefit a trust is managed; also, recipient of the amount to be paid under an insurance policy

Bid rigging competitors' agreement that one bidder will have the lowest bid for a particular job

Bilateral contract offeree can accept offer by giving a promise to the offeror instead of performing the contracted-for act

Bill of exchange (also called **draft**) unconditional written order from one person directing another to pay money to a third person

Bill of Rights first ten amendments to the U.S. Constitution

Bill of sale receipt that serves as written evidence of the transfer of ownership of goods

Blank indorsement indorsement consisting only of the indorser's signature

Blue-sky laws laws prohibiting the sale of worthless stocks and bonds

Bona fide occupational qualification (BFOQ) job requirement that compels discrimination against a protected class

Bona fide seniority system system that rewards employees for length of employment rather than merit

Bonds written promises to pay back money borrowed by the corporation

Boycott refusal to buy or use someone's goods or services

Breach of contract failure to provide complete performance of contractual obligations

Bribery offering or giving something of value to improperly effect performance of another party

Bulk transfer transfer, generally by sale, of all or a major part of the goods of a business in one unit at one time

Burglary entering a building without permission when intending to commit a crime

Business ethics ethical principles used in making business decisions

Business judgment rule rule that protects management and other parties involved in a corporation from being held personally liable (criminally or civilly) for honest errors in judgment made in the course of business

Business law group of laws that governs business situations and transactions

Business necessity defense to a disparate treatment employment discrimination case showing that an employer's actions were meant to advance the business rather than to create unjustified discrimination

Bylaws rules and regulations for the internal management of corporate affairs

C

Cancellation ending a contract for sale of goods because of breach, while retaining other remedies; also, any act that shows an intent to end the obligation of payment of commercial paper

Capacity ability to understand

Carrier's lien carrier's right to retain possession of the goods until the charges for transportation and incidental services are paid

Case law made when an appellate court endorses a rule to be used in deciding court cases

Cashier's check check drawn by a bank on itself

Casual seller seller who does not meet the definition of a merchant

Casualty insurance insurance that covers for losses due to accident, chance, or negligence

Casual workers persons who do not work regularly for a certain employer

Causation linking a job requirement with underrepresentation of a protected class in the workforce

Caveat emptor let the buyer beware

Caveat venditor let the seller beware

Cease-and-desist order governmental order requiring that certain improper conduct be stopped

Certificate of deposit (CD) bank's written acknowledgement of the receipt of money with an unconditional promise to repay it at a definite future time

Certification selecting a bargaining representative by a majority secret vote of the workers in the bargaining unit; NLRB then recognizes that union as the exclusive negotiator for employees in the bargaining unit

Certified check check upon which liability has been accepted by the drawee bank

Charitable trust created for the fulfillment of an altruistic purpose

Check draft written on a bank by a depositor

Child custody care and control of a minor

Child support money paid by a parent to provide a child with economic maintenance

CIF "cost, insurance, freight" price

Civil disobedience open, peaceful violation of a law to protest its alleged injustice

Civil law group of laws used to provide remedy for wrongs against individuals

Civil rights personal, human rights recognized and guaranteed by the U.S. Constitution

Class action court procedure allowing a party to bring suit on his or her behalf and for those similarly situated

Closed shop employer agrees that workers must belong to the recognized union before they can be hired

Closely held corporation private corporation whose stock is held by only one or a small number of shareholders

COD collect on delivery

Code laws grouped into an organized form

Codicil formal, written, and witnessed amendment to a will

Coinsurance clause in a fire policy that requires the insured to maintain coverage equal to a certain percentage of the total current value of the insured property

Collateral property subject to the security interest of the creditor

Collateral note note on which personal property is offered for collateral

Collateral promise promise to pay a debt or default of another

Collective bargaining process by which the union and employer negotiate a contract of employment that binds both sides

Collision insurance automobile insurance that protects against upset and direct and accidental damage due to colliding with another object

Commercial paper unconditional written promise or order to pay a sum of money

Commingling mixing the money of the agent and the principal together

Common carrier enterprise that agrees, for a fee, to transport goods that are lawful and fit for shipment for anyone who applies

Common law law based on current standards or customs of the people

Common-law defenses defenses in a negligence suit that include the employee's assumption of risk, the employer's contributory negligence, and coworker negligence

Common-law marriage marital relationship legalized by the couple holding themselves out as husband and wife and sharing home and property for an extended period

Common stock basic stock in a corporation conveying to its owner the right to vote and to receive dividends

Community property property owned equally by spouses

Compensatory damages amount of money awarded to place an injured party in the position he or she was in prior to a loss

Competency license state requirement for people in certain occupations and businesses to pass exams and receive a license

Composition of creditors agreement by all creditors to accept something less than the total amount of their claims as full payment

Compounding a crime accepting something of value for a promise not to inform on or prosecute a suspected criminal

Comprehensive insurance insurance that covers against all damage to the insured's car except that caused by collision or upset

Condemnation proceeding forcing a property owner to transfer property to a government in exchange for just reasonable compensation

Conditional estate estate where continued ownership is dependent upon some act or event

Consent order voluntary, court-enforceable agreement between the government and an offender requiring the termination of an illegal or questionable practice

Consequences-based reasoning form of ethical reasoning that evaluates the results of an action

Consequential damages money awarded to a party for foreseeable injuries caused by the other party's breach

Consideration what a person demands and generally must receive in order to make his or her promise legally binding

Consignment bailment in which ownership remains with the manufacturer or wholesaler until the goods are sold

Consolidation two or more corporations combine to form a new one

Conspiracy agreement between two or more persons to commit a crime

Constitution document that sets forth the framework of the government and its relationship to the people it governs

Constitutional law law made when the fundamental, supreme law of the land is adopted, amended, or interpreted

Constructive bailment occurs when a person already in possession of the personal property holds it in such a manner that the law imposes upon him or her a bailee's duty to deliver it to another

Constructive delivery having a symbol of a gift substituted in its delivery

Constructive eviction tenant moves out of leased premises because the landlord caused the premises to become unfit for its intended use

Constructive notice legal presumption that everyone has knowledge of facts on public file

Constructive trust created to require a person holding property to transfer it to another because retention would be a wrongful and unjust enrichment of the holder

Consumer individual who acquires goods primarily for personal, family, or household use

Consumer Product Safety Commission (CPSC) agency regulating the safety of various products including toys

Consumer transaction transaction in which a party buys goods or services for personal or household use

Contempt of court action that hinders the administration of justice in court

Contract agreement between two parties that creates an obligation

Contract of adhesion contract in which the more powerful party dictates all the important terms

Contract to sell transaction in which transfer of ownership is to take place in the future

Contractual capacity ability to understand that a contract is being made and its general meaning

Contributory negligence in personal injury law, plaintiff's own negligence is a partial cause of an injury; in employment law, employee does something carelessly to contribute to her or his injury or death

Conversion using property in a manner inconsistent with the owner's rights

Conveyance transfer of an estate from a grantor to a grantee by a deed

Cooling-off period stopping a labor dispute by federal court order for a period of 80 days when a national emergency strike is threatened

Co-ownership ownership existing when two or more persons have the same ownership rights in the same property

Copyright protects the expression of a creative work, such as the work of an artist, author, or composer

Corporate charter certificate of incorporation

Corporation legal entity treated as an artificial person by the law and created by the authority of federal or state law

Corrective advertising advertising to correct improper and false impressions

Counteroffer offeree's response to an offer which modifies it

County court See **Associate circuit court**

Court governmental forum that administers justice under the law

Court of record accurate, detailed report of what went on at trial

Co-worker negligence one worker causes the injury of another

Credit purchase by which whole or partial payment is delayed

Creditor party to whom a debt is owed

Credit rating evaluation of a party's ability to pay debts

Credit sale sale that, by agreement of the parties, calls for payment for the goods at a later date

Crime punishable offense against society

Criminal act specific conduct that violates a criminal statute

Criminal insanity defense based on the accused's inability to know right from wrong

Criminal intent intent to commit an evil act in violation of a statute

Criminal law group of laws that defines and sets punishments for offenses against society

Cumulative preferred stock preferred stock whose dividends remain due and payable beyond one corporate fiscal year

Custody care and present control of another's personal property under the owner's direction

Cyberlaw law that is intended to govern the use of computers in e-commerce and the Internet

D

Damages monetary award by the court to a person who has suffered loss or injury because of the act or omission of another

Deadlock collective bargaining situation in which the union and employer cannot agree on important issues

Debenture unsecured bond

Debt that which is owed on a purchase on credit

Debtor person or business that owes money, goods, or services to another

Decedent person who dies

Decertification election process by which employees can reject union representation or select a different union

Declaration of Independence document drafted by representatives of the 13 original colonies that asserts the rights desired by the colonists

Dedication transferring real property by donating it to the government, such as to a city for use as a park or roadway

Deed legal document used to transfer ownership of real property

Defamation false statement that injures one's reputation

Default failure to perform a legal duty or failure to perform an agreement

Defendant party complained against in a civil or criminal lawsuit

Defense at criminal law, a legal position that allows the defendant to escape criminal liability

Delegation of duties turning over to another party one's duties under a contract

Delivery subject matter of the contract is placed within the possession or control of the owner

Democracy governmental system in which citizens vote directly to decide issues

Demurrage fee for delay by party shipping goods in loading or by party receiving goods in unloading

Department of Homeland Security (DHS) controls an agency formed by the merger of 22 separate agencies into one with the mission of protecting the United States from terrorist attack

Directors individuals elected by the shareholders to be responsible for the overall direction of a corporation

Disability physical or mental condition that substantially limits a major life activity

Disaffirmance both parties to a contract return the consideration

Discharge termination of contractual duties that ordinarily occurs when the parties perform as promised

Discharged for cause employee is discharged due to the violation of an employment obligation

Discharged without cause employee's discharge is not due to his or her conduct

Disclaimer sign, label, or warning reducing a bailee's duty of care; also, notice of exclusion in a warranty

Dishonor bank's refusal to pay a check when due

Disparate impact employer treats members of a protected class less favorably than other employees; has the effect of eliminating members of a protected class

Dissolution step in termination of a partnership that precedes the winding-up process; also, term for divorce or the ending of a marriage in some states

Distributive shares each member's share of profits and losses in an LLC

Dividends distributions of corporate earnings

Divisible contracts contracts for which separate consideration is given for the legal and illegal parts

Divorce court action terminating a marriage

Doctrine of capture grants ownership of fluid minerals to the party who extracts them

Domestic corporation corporation doing business in the state in which it is chartered

Donee person receiving a gift

Donor person giving a gift

Dormant partner partner neither known to the public nor active in management

Double taxation taxation of a corporation as an entity based on its earnings and then of the shareholders on corporate dividends

Draft (also called **bill of exchange**) unconditional written order from one person directing another to pay money to a third person

Drawee party ordered to pay a draft

Drawer party that executes a draft and orders payment to be made

Due process of law constitutional requirement for fundamental fairness in our legal and court system

Duress occurs when one party uses an improper threat or act to obtain an expression of agreement

Duty of accounting requires agent to account to the principal for all money and property of the principal that comes into the agent's possession

Duty of confidentiality requires agent to treat information about the principal very carefully

Duty of loyalty agent may not secretly benefit from the agency transaction

Duty of loyalty and honesty requires employee to look out for the best interests of the employer

Duty of obedience requires employee to follow the reasonable orders and rules of the employer; requires agent to carefully obey the instructions of the principal

Duty of reasonable care and skill requires agent to exercise the degree of care and skill any reasonably prudent person would use in a similar situation

Duty of reasonable performance requires employee to perform assigned duties at the prescribed time and in the prescribed manner

Duty of reasonable skill requires employee to perform job tasks with competence

E

Easement irrevocable right to the limited use of another's land

Economic strike work stoppage in which the dispute is over wages, hours, or conditions of employment

Electronic fund transfer (EFT) debit or credit to an account initiated by the use of a terminal, computer, telephone, or magnetic tape

Emancipation severing the child-parent relationship

Embezzlement taking of another's property or money by a person to whom it has been entrusted

Eminent domain power of the government to take private property for public use in exchange for the fair market price

Employee party who works under the supervision of another for pay

Employer party who engages another to work for pay

Employment contractual relationship in which one party engages another to work for pay under the supervision of the party paying

Employment at will employment relationship whereby employee may be discharged at any time because no agreement was made about length of employment; alternately, employee may quit the job at any time without liability for breach of contract

Employment discrimination treating individuals differently on the basis of race, color, gender, national origin, or religion

Encumbrances claims of third parties against the property

Endorsements (also called **riders**) modifications made to the standard fire policy to eliminate certain risks for coverage

Environmental Protection Agency (EPA) agency regulating the creation, marketing, and use of hazardous chemicals, as well as the disposal of toxic waste

Equal Employment Opportunity Commission (EEOC) agency charged with eliminating workplace discrimination based on race, religion, sex, color, national origin, age, or disability

Equity basic fairness

Escheat reversion of property to the state

Estate bundle of ownership rights in, and powers over, realty; also, property of the deceased

Ethics deciding what is right or wrong action in a reasoned, impartial manner

Eviction legal action taken to remove a tenant from possession of all the landlord's real property

Evidence materials presented to prove or disprove alleged facts

Ex parte injunction injunction issued by a judge after hearing only one side of an argument

Exclusions exceptions to insurance coverage

Executed contract contract that has been fully performed

Executor/executrix intestate's personal representative appointed to settle the estate (male/female)

Executory contract contract that has not been fully performed

Existing goods physically existing goods owned by the seller

Express authority agency authority directly communicated by the principal to the agent

Express trust trust in which the terms are explicitly stated by the settlor

Express warranty assurance of quality or performance explicitly made by the seller

Extortion improperly obtaining money or other things of value by use of force, fear, or the power of office

Extraordinary bailment bailment formed when a bailor leaves personal property with a hotelkeeper or a common carrier

Extraordinary care duty arising from an extraordinary bailment in which the bailee is liable for all damage, loss, or injury

F

Face value stated maximum amount that could be paid under an insurance policy

Fair use limited use of copyrighted works by critics, researchers, news reporters, and educators

False imprisonment depriving a person of freedom of movement without consent and without privilege

False pretenses obtaining property by lying about a past or existing fact

Featherbedding forcing an employer to pay for services not performed

Federal Communications Commission (FCC) agency regulating all interstate and international channels of communication

Federal Reserve System's Board of Governors agency that regulates interest rates

Federal Trade Commission (FTC) agency that regulates unfair trade practices

Fee simple absolute greatest possible bundle of rights and interests in realty

Felony crime punishable by more than one year in jail, a fine of more than $1,000, or both

Fidelity bond insurance policy that pays the employer money in the case of employees' theft

Fidelity insurance provides coverage against financial loss caused by dishonesty

Fiduciary duties legal requirement that the agent serve the best interests of the principal; specific fiduciary duties are loyalty and obedience, reasonable care and skill, confidentiality, and accounting

Finance charge total added cost when one pays in installments for goods or services

Financing statement brief, written notice of the existence of a security interest in the identified property

Fire insurance insurance that covers for loss or damage due to fire (and usually smoke as well)

Firm offer contractual proposal in writing by a merchant stating how long the offer is to stay open

Fixture item of personal property that has become permanently attached to realty and is thus transformed from personalty into realty

FOB shipping term meaning "free on board"

Food and Drug Administration (FDA) agency regulating safety of food and drugs on the market

Forbearance refraining from doing what one has a right to do

Foreign corporation corporation doing business in a state other than the one in which it was chartered

Forgery falsely making or materially altering a writing to defraud another

Fraud intentional misrepresentation of an existing, important fact

Fraudulent misrepresentation party to a contract knows that a statement he or she made is untrue

Full warranty express warranty that obligates the seller to repair or replace a defective product without cost to the buyer within a reasonable time

Fungible goods goods of an essentially identical nature

Future goods goods that are not both existing and identified

Future interest nonpossessory estate made up of ownership power retained by the grantor of a conditional estate

G

Garnishment court-ordered procedure by which a portion of a delinquent debtor's wages are paid to satisfy the debt

General duty clause OSHA requirement that employers provide a place of employment free from hazards likely to cause death or serious physical harm

General jurisdiction court that can hear almost any kind of case

General partner assumes full personal liability for debts of the firm

General partnership all partners assume full liability for debts of the firm

Genuine assent agreement to enter into a contract that is evidenced by words or conduct between the parties

Gift voluntary transfer of ownership without consideration

Good faith purchaser innocent third party to a fraudulent transfer of goods who gives value to the goods and acquires rights in them

Goods items of tangible, movable, personal property

Grace period period of time during which an overdue insurance premium can be paid to keep the policy in force

Grantee person receiving ownership with a deed

Grantor person giving up ownership with a deed

Gratuitous agency agency relationship where the agent receives no consideration

Gratuitous bailment arises when only one of the parties benefits from the bailment

Guarantor party agreeing to be secondarily liable in case of default by the principal debtor

H

Heir person who, by statute, is entitled to property disposed of by a decedent's will

Holder party in possession of commercial paper payable to his or her order or to bearer

Holder in due course (HDC) party that takes commercial paper in good faith without knowledge of any defect or overdue status and gives value for it

Holder through a holder in due course (HHDC) party that takes commercial paper after an HDC and thereby acquires the same rights

Holographic will will written and signed entirely by the maker

Honor bank's promise to the depositor to pay checks when presented if sufficient funds are available in the depositor's account

Hostile environment interference with an employee's ability to work through unwelcome comments, gestures, or touching of a sexual nature

I

Identified goods designated subject matter of a particular sales contract

Immunity freedom from prosecution for a crime

Impartiality idea that the same ethical standards apply to everyone

Impeachment case trying a government official for misconduct in office

Implied authority agency authority that is implied from the grant of express authority or because of an emergency

Implied warranty warranty obligation implicitly imposed by law on all sellers

Incorporators signers of the articles of incorporation

Indemnify to make good a loss

Independent contractor one who contracts to do something for another but is free of the latter's direction and control

Indorsee party to whom commercial paper is indorsed

Indorsement signature on the reverse side of commercial paper

Indorser owner of commercial paper who signs it on the reverse

Infraction minor misdemeanor

Infringement unauthorized copying, sale, display, or performance of a copyrighted work

Injunction court order for a person to do or not do a particular act

Inland marine insurance insurance that covers against loss or damage to personal property where the property is located or while it is being transported by any means other than by sea

Innocent misrepresentation party to a contract does not know that a statement he or she made is untrue

Insolvent status of being unable to pay debts when they become due

Insurable interest potential to sustain loss if the insured property is damaged or destroyed or if the insured person is injured or dies

Insurance agreement under which one party will pay to offset a loss to another

Insured party protected or covered if the loss occurred

Insurer party who will indemnify if loss occurs

Intangible property classification of collateral that represents value in money, goods, or promises to perform specific contracts

Integrity doing what is right even under pressure to act otherwise

Intellectual property purely intangible personal property that one cannot touch or move

Intentional tort tort in which the defendant means to commit the injurious act

Interference with contractual relations enticing or encouraging a person to break a contract

Interstate commerce trade and other commercial intercourse between or among businesses in different states

Inter vivos trust trust created during the lifetime of the settlor

Intestate to die without a will

Intoxication mental impairment caused by voluntary use of alcohol, drugs, or inhalants

Intrastate commerce commerce conducted wholly within one state

Invasion of privacy unwelcome and unlawful intrusion into one's private life so as to cause outrage, mental suffering, or humiliation

Involuntary bailment arises without consent of the bailee; raises issue of whether the goods are lost or misplaced

Involuntary bankruptcy occurs when a person or business (except farmers and charities) owe at least $11,625 to petitioning unsecured creditor(s) and are unable to pay debts when they come due

J

Joint tenancy co-ownership of property with equal interests and the right of survivorship

Joint venture partnership formed by two or more persons or firms combining resources and skills for one complex project

Judgment final result of a trial

Jurisdiction power of a court to decide a case

Jury panel of citizens sworn by a court to decide issues of fact in court cases

Justice title of a judge on the state supreme court or federal Supreme Court

Juveniles individuals over 13 and under 18 years of age who have special status under the criminal law

L

Land basic physical element of realty

Landlord (also called **lessor**) one who, through a lease, transfers to another exclusive possession and control of real property

Larceny wrongful taking of another's property with the intent to deny them possession

Laws enforceable rules of conduct in a society

Lease agreement in which one party receives temporary possession of another's real property in exchange for rent

Leasehold estate tenants' ownership interest in real estate

Legal rate of interest rate specified by statute when interest is called for but no percentage is stated in the contract

Legal tender currency or coins

Legal value change in the legal position of a party as a result of a contract

Liability insurance insurance that covers personal injury or property damage claims for which the insured is legally responsible

License in real property, a temporary, revocable right to some limited use of another's land

Licensee person whom the possessor of land has permitted to be on that land

Lien legal right in another's property as security for the performance of an obligation such as the repayment of a loan

Life estate estate that lasts only for the grantee's life

Life insurance insurance that pays to a named beneficiary or the deceased's estate upon the death of the insured

Limited defenses defenses good against all obligees except HDCs and HHDCs

Limited liability corporation (LLC) form of business organization offering limited liability, taxation as a partnership, and few of the restrictions for use encountered in the S corporation or limited partnership

Limited liability partnership (LLP) form of business organization easily converted to a partnership that avoids double taxation and affords partial limited liability protection

Limited partner partner whose potential liability is restricted to his or her investment in the partnership

Limited partnership partnership form authorized by state statute requiring at least one general partner but allowing limited liability for the rest

Limited warranty warranty providing a level of protection less than a full warranty

Liquidated damages damages agreed upon before a possible breach of contract

Liquidated debt debt for which the parties agree that the debt exists and on the amount of the debt

Liquidation process by which a corporation's life is ended

Litigate to place a dispute before a court of law for resolution

Lockout employer shutdown of operations to force a union to agree to the employer's position

Lost property property that the owner unknowingly leaves somewhere or accidentally drops

Lottery game involving the three elements of prize, chance, and consideration

M

Main purpose rule exception to a Statute of Frauds provision making a third party liable for an oral promise to pay another's debt if the main purpose of the promise serves the promisor's own interest

Maker person who executes a promissory note

Marine insurance insurance that covers for loss of or damage to vessels, cargo, and other property exposed to the perils of the sea

Marital consortium mutual obligations of wife and husband undertaken to fulfill the purposes of their union

Marriage legal union of a man and woman as husband and wife

Material facts important facts that influence both parties' decisions about a contract

Mechanic's lien lien against realty available to one who has supplied labor or materials to improve it

Mediation attempt by a neutral third party to achieve a compromise between two parties in a dispute

Mediator independent third party who tries to develop a non-binding solution acceptable to both sides of a dispute

Members owners of an LLC

Mental incapacity condition in which a party to a contract is unable to understand the consequences of the contractual act

Merchant seller who deals regularly in a particular type of goods or who claims special knowledge in a certain type of sales transaction

Merger combination of corporations in which one absorbs another

Mineral rights ownership of the minerals on and beneath a parcel of realty

Minimal care duty arising from a bailment in which the bailee must not ignore, waste, or destroy the property

Minor individual under the age of majority (18 in most states)

Minority minor part of a person's life (typically under the age of 18)

Mirror image rule requires that the terms in the acceptance must exactly match the terms contained in the offer

Misdemeanor crime punishable by up to one year in jail, a fine of less than $1,000, or both

Mislaid property property that is intentionally placed somewhere but then forgotten

Mitigate the damages to act to minimize one's injury

Money official medium of exchange in the United States or any foreign country

Money order draft issued by a post office, bank, express company, or telegraph company for use in transferring funds for the draft's purchaser

Mortgage note note on which real property is used as security for payment

Multinational corporation (MNC) corporation that has a significant investment of assets in foreign countries

Municipal court city court, usually divided into traffic and criminal divisions

Mutual mistake both parties to a contract have an incorrect belief about an important fact

Mutual-benefit bailment consideration is given and received by both bailor and bailee

N

National emergency strike work stoppage that involves national defense or major industries or that would imperil national health or safety

National Labor Relations Board (NLRB) agency regulating collective bargaining

Necessaries things needed to maintain life and lifestyle

Negligence most common tort based on carelessness

Negligence suit suit brought by an employee against an employer that claims the employer's carelessness caused the employee's injury

Negotiable written unconditional promise or order for a sum certain payable on demand or at a definite time

Negotiable instrument another term for commercial paper

Negotiation proper transfer of a negotiable instrument so that the person receiving the instrument has the power to collect on it by overcoming defenses of the person who must pay it off

Neutral on its face label for a workplace policy that does not seem on the surface to discriminate against any protected class

No-fault insurance insurance that requires that the parties to an automobile accident be covered by their own insurance company, regardless of who is at fault

Nominal consideration token amount identified in a written contract when parties either cannot or do not wish to state the amount precisely

Nominal damages token amount awarded when rights have been violated but there is no actual injury

Nominal partner person who is not a partner but who is held out as such

Nonfreehold estate (also called **tenancy**) estate that involves ownership for a limited period of time

Nonprofit corporation business organization for a social, charitable, or educational purpose

Non-trading partnership partnership that provides professional and noncommercial assistance or advice

Novation contractual party's release of the other party from the duty of performance and the acceptance of a substitute party

Nuclear Regulatory Commission (NRC) agency charged with insuring safety of nuclear power plants

Nuncupative will orally made will

O

Obligor one who owes a duty under a contract

Occupancy acquisition of title by taking possession of personal property that belongs to no one else

Occupational Safety and Health Administration (OSHA) federal agency that administers the Occupational Safety and Health Act of 1970 by enacting safety regulations and inspecting workplaces

Offer proposal by an offeror to do something, provided the offeree does something in return

Offeree party to whom an offer is made

Offeror party who makes an offer to form a contract

Open shop establishment in which nonunion members are not required to join the union or to pay union dues

Operating agreement equivalent of corporate bylaws for an LLC

Option separate contract arising when the offeree gives the offeror something of value in return for a promise to leave an offer open

Order paper commercial paper made payable to the order of a specified payee

Ordinance legislation enacted by a town, city, or county board or commission

Ordinary care duty created by mutual-benefit bailment in which bailee is liable only if negligent in some fashion

Original jurisdiction power to hear the case in full for the first time

Output contract agreement to purchase all of a particular producer's production

Ownership a collection of rights that allow the use and enjoyment of property

Ownership in severalty ownership of all property rights by oneself

P

Parol evidence spoken words inadmissible in court

Parol evidence rule oral testimony cannot be used to contradict terms in a complete, final, written contract

Participating preferred stock preferred stock whose holder, after the preferred dividends are paid, shares in remaining dividends as a common shareholder

Partnership association of two or more persons, as co-owners, to carry on a business for profit

Partnership agreement explicit statement, orally or in writing, of the terms and conditions agreed to by the partners for running the partnership

Partnership at will partnership in which a partner may withdraw at any time without liability to other partners

Past consideration act that has already been performed cannot be consideration for a promise in the present

Patent government grant of exclusive right to make, use, and sell a product or process which is novel, nonobvious, and useful

Pawn pledge of tangible personal property

Payable at a definite time commercial paper payable on or before an identified calendar date

Payable on demand commercial paper payable on sight or when presented

Payee party to whom commercial paper is made payable

Payment delivery of the agreed-upon price and the concurrent acceptance of it by the seller

Payroll deductions money deducted from an employee's paycheck

Perfected security interest exists when the security interest is superior to all other claims in the collateral

Performance fulfillment of contractual promises as agreed

Periodic tenancy arises when the leasehold is for a renewable period of time with rent due at stated intervals

Perjury crime of lying under oath

Personal property (also called **personalty**) tangible, movable property and intangible property

Picketing members of uncertified unions patrolling near the employer's property with signs, trying to force the employer to bargain with that union

Plaintiff party that initiates a civil lawsuit by filing a complaint

Plea bargaining agreement with prosecutor allowing defendant to plead guilty to a lesser crime than the more serious one he or she likely would be charged with

Pledge secured transaction in which the creditor has possession of the collateral

Pledgee creditor in a pledge who takes possession of property given up by pledgor

Pledgor debtor in a pledge who voluntarily gives up possession of the property

Policy written contract of insurance

Political party private organization of citizens who select and promote candidates for public office

Positive law law based on the dictates of a central political authority

Postdated dated later than the date of issuance

Power of attorney any writing that appoints someone as an agent

Preemptive rights enable shareholders to protect their proportionate voting power and interest in past and future profits

Preferred stock non-voting stock conveying the right to receive a stipulated dividend before any common shareholders receive their dividends

Premium consideration for insurance contract

Prenuptial agreement legal contract resolving property and other claims that might result from a marriage

Price consideration for a contract to sell or sale of goods

Price fixing competitors agree to charge the same amount for a product or service

Primary promise promise to pay another's debt that is not conditioned upon the other person's failure to pay

Principal one who authorizes another to enter into legal relationships in his or her behalf

Principal debtor person who owes the debt or obligation

Private corporation corporation established for a private purpose

Private trust trust created for private reasons

Privity of contract relationship or connection between parties to a legally binding agreement

Probable cause a reasonable ground for belief

Probate court administers wills and estates

Procedural defense defense based on problems with the way evidence is obtained or the way the accused person is arrested, questioned, tried, or punished

Procedural law group of laws that define the methods for enforcing legal rights and duties

Procedural unconscionability element of unconscionability shown by how the contract is created

Product liability the fixing of responsibility to compensate buyers, users, and bystanders for injuries caused by a defective product

Profit-making corporation private corporation organized to produce a profit for its owners

Promisee person to whom the promise or action is given in exchange for the other person's promise or action

Promisor person who gives the promise or action in exchange for the promise or action of another

Promissory estoppel enforcement of a promise to avoid injustice by denying to the promisor the defense of lack of consideration

Promissory note unconditional written promise to pay money to order or to bearer

Promoters those who sell a business idea and the corporate form for it

Property tangible and intangible things and their corresponding legal rights and interests

Property insurance insurance that covers for losses resulting from perils such as fire, theft, or windstorm

Protected classes groups that employment law protects

Proximate cause legally recognizable cause of harm

Proxy power to vote shares for shareholder

Public corporation corporation established for a governmental purpose

Public service corporation private company that furnishes an essential public service

Puffing greatly exaggerated sales talk

Punishment penalty provided by law and imposed by a court

Punitive damages money a court requires a defendant to pay in order to punish a person who inflicted an injury; generally only awarded in intentional tort cases

Purchase money security interest filing is not required to protect a seller's security interest in consumer goods against other creditors of the buyer

Q

Qualified indorsement indorsement limiting or eliminating signature-based liability for the indorser

Quasi-contract obligation that is enforced as if it were a contract in order to prevent unjust enrichment of one party

Quid pro quo one thing exchanged for another; type of sexual harassment case in which a supervisor seeks sexual favors from a subordinate in exchange for continued employment or a favorable term or condition of employment

Quitclaim deed transfers any interest the grantor may have in the real property, but doesn't guarantee that the grantor owns anything or that the grantee receives anything

R

Ratification acting toward the contract as though one intends to be bound by it; principal's assent to unauthorized acts of an agent

Real property (also called **realty**) land, water, and minerals in the earth; airspace above the land; and things permanently attached to the land

Receipt of goods buyer takes physical possession or control of the goods

Receiving stolen property receiving or buying property known to be stolen from another so as to deny the rightful owner of possession

Release party settles a claim at the time the tort occurs, and the liability is unliquidated because the extent of damages is uncertain

Remedy action or procedure followed to enforce a right or to compensate for an injury

Rent consideration given by a tenant in return for temporary possession of a property

Representation election conducted by a union if workers wish to be represented by a union but management will not voluntary recognize it

Republic governmental system in which citizens elect representatives to decide issues

Requirements contract seller agrees to supply all of the needs of a particular buyer

Resale price maintenance manufacturer attempts to influence the retail price of its product

Rescission backing out of the transaction by asking for the return of what you gave and offering to give back what you received

Restitution permits a party to a contract to recover money or property (or the value thereof) given to the other party

Restrictive covenant promise as a part of a contract or deed limiting the owner's use of the realty

Restrictive indorsement directs the use of the proceeds from a negotiable instrument or imposes a condition upon its payment by the indorser

Resulting trust implied trust formed to hold property for its original owner

Revenue license required license imposed by governments on certain occupations for the sole purpose of raising money

Revocation withdrawing an offer before it is accepted

Rider (also called **endorsement**) modification made to the standard fire policy to satisfy an insured's needs

Right of contribution cosurety who pays the full debt is entitled to judgment against the other cosureties for their proportionate share of the debt

Right of partition attribute of co-ownership which allows any co-owner to require the division, usually financial, of the property among the co-owners

Right of repossession right of a secured party to take back collateral to use in satisfaction of the debt

Right of survivorship right of one joint tenant to ownership of property when the other joint tenant dies

Right-to-work laws state laws which prohibit compulsory union membership and ban the union shop, the closed shop, and the agency shop

Riparian rights water ownership system in which those abutting the water own the right to use it

Risk potential loss that is insured against

Robbery wrongful taking of another's property from their person or presence by threat of force of violence

S

Sale contract in which ownership of goods transfers from the seller to a buyer for a price

Sale of an undivided interest selling a fractional interest in a single good or in a number of goods that are to remain together

Sale on approval goods are delivered to the buyer in an "on trial" or "on satisfaction" basis

Sale or return completed sale in which the buyer has the option of returning the goods

Satisfaction performance of the new contractual obligation parties have agreed to substitute for their original obligation

Scope of authority in employment law, range of contractual acts an organization has authorized an employee to do; in agency, range of contractual acts authorized by the principal

S corporation form of business organization governed by subchapter S of the Internal Revenue Code, under which earnings are treated the same as a gain (or loss) from a partnership and only taxed at the individual owner's level

Secret partner partner not known to the public but active as a manager

Secured party person who has a security interest in collateral owned by the debtor-buyer

Secured transaction legal method or device creating a security interest in personal property or fixtures in order to protect creditors

Securities and Exchange Commission (SEC) agency regulating the disclosure of information pertinent to buying and selling stocks as well as the national stock exchanges themselves

Security agreement contract that creates or provides for a security interest

Security interest interest in or claim against specified property of the debtor created for the purpose of assuring payment of the debt

Self-defense use of force that appears reasonably necessary for the self-protection of an intended victim

Separation stage in the divorce process in which the spouses maintain their marital rights and obligations but do not live together

Service mark word, mark, or symbol that identifies a service as opposed to a product

Settlor creator of a trust

Severalty see **Ownership in severalty**

Shareholder (also called **stockholder**) person owning share of stock in a corporation

Shares of stock units of ownership in a corporation

Sight draft draft on which payment is due immediately when presented to the drawee

Silent partner partner known to the public but who takes no active managerial role

Small claims courts state courts that handle disputes in which small amounts, generally $2,500 or less, are involved

Social insurance government-sponsored insurance protecting against financial problems related to retirement, survivorship, disability, and declining health

Sole proprietorship form of business owned by one person who has total unlimited control and liability

Sovereignty freedom from external control

Special indorsement indorsement making the paper payable to the order of a designated party

Special jurisdiction court that hears only one specific type of case

Specific performance remedy for breach of contract that orders the breaching party to do exactly what was required under the contract

Spendthrift trust trust created to protect the beneficiary's interest in a property from the beneficiary's creditors

Spot zoning treatment of a single property in a manner inconsistent with the treatment of similar properties in the area

Standard fire policy fire insurance contract that covers for losses resulting from fire, lightning strike, or removal from premises endangered by fire

Stare decisis doctrine that requires lower courts to follow existing case law in deciding similar cases

Statute law enacted by state or federal legislatures

Statute of Frauds law stating that certain agreements are not enforceable in court unless they are evidenced by a signed writing

Statute of limitations state laws setting time limit for bringing a lawsuit

Stockholder (also called **shareholder**) person who owns a share or shares of stock in a corporation

Stop-payment order instruction by the depositor to a financial institution not to pay a particular instrument drawn on it

Strict liability holding a defendant liable without a showing of negligence

Strike collective work stoppage by employees to pressure the employer to give in to union demands

Subletting tenant transfers to a third party all the property for a period less than the remaining time of the lease or part of the property for part or all of the remaining term of the lease

Subpoena written court order compelling a person to appear and testify

Substantial performance performance of all but a minor contractual duty

Substantive defense defenses that disprove, justify, or otherwise excuse the alleged crime

Substantive law group of laws that define rights and duties

Substantive unconscionability element of unconscionability established by the terms of the agreement

Substitution parties' replacement of their original contract with a new contract

Surety third party agreeing to be primarily liable for debt in case of default by the principal debtor

Suretyship contractual relation in which a third party agrees to be primarily liable for a debt created in favor of the principal debtor

System of checks and balances division and allocation of the powers of government between its various branches

T

Teller's check draft drawn by a bank on its balance with another bank

Tenancy at sufferance tenant remains in possession after a lease has expired

Tenancy at will results if a party possesses land with the owner's permission but without an agreement as to the term of the lease or the amount of the rent

Tenancy by the entireties usual form of co-ownership between husband and wife, carrying equal interest and the right of survivorship

Tenancy for years leasehold that is for a definite period of time, such as six months, one year, or ninety-nine years

Tenancy in common form of co-ownership in which the shares may be unequal and there is no right of survivorship

Tenancy in partnership form of co-ownership by which the partners hold partnership property

Tenant (also called **lessor**) one who, through a lease, is given possession of real property

Tender offer to perform an obligation

Tender of delivery to place the goods at the buyer's disposal or to give notice to the buyer that delivery can be received

Termination following the winding-up process, the ending of the legal existence of the partnership

Termination statement filing by a creditor releasing a security interest in collateral

Testamentary capacity testator must know the kind and extent of property involved, persons who stand to benefit, and that he or she is making an arrangement to dispose of his or her property after death

Testamentary intent clear intention to make a will

Testamentary trust trust created after the death of a settlor in accordance with directions in the person's will

Testate to die with a valid will

Testator/testatrix maker of a will (male/female)

Testimony statements by witnesses under oath

Third party one who deals with an agent who represents the principal

Time draft draft payable on a date set on the instrument or one that is payable after the running of a specified period after the draft's date

Tort private or civil wrong for which the law grants a remedy

Trademark unique word, mark, symbol, or device that identifies a product of a particular manufacturer or merchant

Trade secret unpatented formula or process not known to others and which is valuable in business

Trading partnership partnership that buys and sells goods and services commercially

Transcript verbatim record of what went on at trial

Traveler's check draft drawn by a financial institution on itself and signed by purchaser who must sign again in presence of payee for validation

Trespass (also called **trespass to land**) to be on the land of another without right or permission of the owner

Trial court first court to hear a dispute

Trust legal vehicle used to transfer the immediate control of property to another party

Trust account separate account for the funds of principals

Trustee legal entity having title to the property named in a trust

U

U.S. Constitution document that consists of seven articles that provide a workable framework for our federal government

Unconscionable term or contract that, under the UCC, is grossly unfair and oppressive

Unconscionable contract grossly unfair contract for the sale of goods

Unconstitutional law that conflicts with a constitution and is therefore invalid

Underinsured motorists coverage compensates the insured when the negligent driver does not have sufficient insurance to cover damages

Undisclosed principal principal whose identity is kept secret from the third party by the agent

Undue influence occurs when one party to a contract is in a position of trust and wrongfully dominates the other party

Unemployment compensation government payments to those who recently lost their jobs through no fault of their own

Unequal treatment (also called **disparate treatment**) employer treats members of a protected class less favorably than other employees

Unfair labor practices union or employer actions which violate the rights of employees with respect to union activity

Unfair trade practice dishonest, fraudulent, or anticompetitive business method

Uniform Commercial Code (UCC) widely adopted uniform business law

Unilateral contract offeror promises something in return for the offeree's performance and indicates that this performance is the way acceptance must be made

Unilateral mistake occurs when one party holds an incorrect belief about the facts related to a contract

Uninsured motorists protection allows the insured to collect damages from his or her own insurance company when they are not collectible from the person who caused the harm

Union shop establishment in which all workers must join the union within a stated period

Universal defenses defenses good against all plaintiffs suing on a negotiable instrument

Universalizing mental test to identify irrational, illogical, or demeaning actions

Unqualified indorsement indorsement without wording limiting or eliminating liability for the indorser

Unsecured debt debt in which the creditor lacks a secured interest in collateral

Usury lending money at a rate higher than the state's maximum allowable rate

V

Variance granted by a city or county to allow a landowner to make some use of his or her land that is inconsistent with the general zoning ordinance

Vendee buyer in sales of goods and contracts to sell

Vendor seller in sales of goods and contracts to sell

Verdict jury's decision in a case

Vicarious criminal liability substituted criminal liability

Vicarious liability legal doctrine by which one party is held liable for the torts of another

Vocational rehabilitation retraining an injured worker for a different job

Void without legal effect

Voidable contract contract in which the injured party can withdraw, thus cancelling the contract

Voidable marriage valid marriage that can be terminated by one or both parties due to improper grounds

Void marriage marriage considered invalid from the beginning

Voluntary bankruptcy option that offers a person, business, or other association protection from creditors under Chapter 7

W

Wager bet on the uncertain outcome of an event

Waiver contractual party's intentional and explicit giving up of a contractual right

Warranty statement about the product's qualities or performance that the seller assures the buyer is true

Warranty deed transfers grantor's interest in the property and protects the grantee by providing several enforceable grantor's warranties

Warranty of habitability requires a landlord to provide residential property in a condition fit for human living

Warranty of merchantability warranty requiring that the goods fit the ordinary purposes for which goods are used

Warranty of the principal's capacity assumption of the law that the agent promises the third party that the principal has capacity

Water right ownership of water running over or under a parcel of realty

White-collar crime crime typically committed in the workplace that does not involve violence or force nor does it cause injury to people or physical damage to property

Will legal expression by which a person directs how his or her property is to be distributed after death

Winding-up period period following dissolution in which the ongoing business of the partnership is concluded, its obligations are satisfied, and each partner's share is distributed

Witness individual with personal knowledge of important facts

Work permit document obtained from the state allowing a person under 18 years old to work

Workers' compensation payment employer makes to an insurance fund that compensates employees for injuries that occur on the job

Workers' compensation statutes laws that require most employers to buy insurance to pay benefits to injured employees

Workforce pool persons actually in the workforce

Writ of certiorari order to a lower court to produce the record of a case for the Supreme Court to review

Wrongful discharge firing an employee in retaliation for reporting violations of law by the company

Y

Yellow-dog contract employment contract in which new employees promise not to join a union

Z

Zoning ordinance law adopted by a city or county to regulate the location of residential, business, and industrial districts

Case Index

A

Advent Systems, Ltd., v. Unisys Corporation, 241

Aircraft Sales and Service v. Gannt, 312

Allen v. Whitehead, 100

Allright Missouri, Inc., v. Billeter, 522

American National Insurance Co. v. Gilroy, Sims and Associates, 522

American Trading and Production Corp v. Shell International Marine, Ltd., 204

Amy Cohen et al v. Brown University, 441

Antrell v. Pearl Assurance Company, 354

Armored Car Service Inc. v. First National Bank of Miami, 312

Ashcroft v. American Civil Liberties Union, 41

Associates Discount Corporation of Iowa v. Fitzwater, 558

B

Bailey v. Utah State Industrial Commission, 456

Baldwin v. Peters, Writer, and Christensen, 122

Blevins v. Cushman Motors, 277

Blinder, Robinson and Co. v. Alzado, 522

Board of Trustees of the University of Alabama v. Calhoun, 370

Boyar v. Wallenberg, 332

Brammer v. Taylor, 370

Brown v. Board of Education, 15

Bunting v. Mellen, 62

Burger King Corporation v. Rudzewick, 41

Burger Man, Inc., v. Jordan Paper Products, Inc., 240

Burkhardt v. Smith, 332

Burne v. Franklin Life Ins., 188

C

Calcote v. Southern National Bank, 590

California v. Cabazon, 171

Cameron State Bank v. Sloan, 574

Cargill, Inc. v. Wilson, 240

Carter v. Reichlin Furriers, 312

Cherberg v. Joshua Green Corporation, et al., 333

City of Chicago v. Commonwealth Edison Company, 22

Clackamas County v. Holmes, 332

Clement v. Clement, 483

Collins v. First National Bank of Oswego, Kansas, 574

Colorado Carpet Installation, Inc., v. Palermo, 240

Colorado-Kansas Grain Co. v. Reifschneider, 240

Commission v. A Juvenile, 62

Commonwealth v. Feinberg, 78

Connecticut National Bank v. Chadwick, 370

Coogan v. Bernstein, 169

Cooper v. Isaacs, 483

Coppola v. Warner Brothers, 189

Costanza v. Seinfeld, 47

Crist v. Nesbit, 220

Curless v. Curless, 220

Cyber Promotions, Inc., v. America Online, Inc., 46

D

David v. Serges, 392

Davison v. Wilson, 354

Denver Rockets v. All Pro Management, 507

Dixon v. Mercury Finance Company of Wisconsin, 188

Dolitsky v. Dollar Savings Bank, 298

Donnelly v. Yellow Freight System, Inc., 62

Donovan v. Hamilton County Municipal Court, 612

DuPont v. Christopher, 298

E

Eckis v. Sea World Corporation, 456

Edgewater Motels, Inc., v. Gatzke, 408

Edward L. Mangan v. Joseph J. Mangan, Jr., 370

EEOC v. Exxon Corporation, 440

Engel v. Vernon, 483

Epton v. CBC Corporation, 124

Esis, Inc., v. Johnson, 450

Eulich v. Snap-On Tool Corp., 38

F

Faith v. Singleton, 370

Falls Industries, Inc., v. Consolidated Chemical Industries, Inc., 256

Federal Deposit Insurance Corporation v. Culver, 559

Ferri v. Sylvia, 558

Field Lumber Company v. Petty, 154

Finley v. Aetna Life and Casualty Company, 408

First National Maintenance v. NLRB, 424

Florida Telephone Corp v. State ex ref. Peninsular Telephone Co., 506

Florida v. Riley, 62

Florida v. Treasure Salvors, Inc., 138

Fortay v. University of Miami, 125

Frampton v. Central Indiana Gas Co., 408

Franklin State Bank v. Parker, 590

G

Gale v. Greater Washington Softball Umpires Association, 408

Galella v. Onassis, 79

Gast v. Petsinger, 483

General Motors Acceptance Corporation v. Abington Casualty Insurance Co., 542

Gillispie v. Great Atlantic and Pacific Tea Company, 240

Gramatan National Bank and Trust Co. v. Pierce, 574

Grove v. Frostburg National Bank, 440

H

Hall v. Missouri Ins. Co., 354

Hall v. Wilkerson, 355

Hamilton v. Johnson, 298

Hardison v. General Finance Corporation, 612

Heart of Atlanta Motel, Inc., v. United States, 46

Henderson v. City of Dundee, 440

Hendy v. Losse, 457

Hicklin v. Orbeck, 22

Hoffman v. Red Owl Stores, 154

I

In re Baker, U.S. Bankruptcy Court, 613

In re Estate of Berry, 392

In re Gordon's Will, 298

In re Holiday Interval, Inc., 542, 591

In re Marriage of Root, 220

In re Midas Coin Co., 590

In re Richmond, 612

In re Ziluck, 590

International Airport Ctrs. L.L.C. v. Citrin, 78

International Association of Credit Men v. Lewis, 483

Ivana Trump v. Donald J. Trump, 221

J

Jason Giambi v. New York Yankees, 409

Jeremy Bloom v. NCAA, 155

John Deere Leasing Company v. Blubaugh, 188

Johnson Controls, 440

K

Kaw Valley Bank Etc. v. Commercial Bank of Liberty, 558

Kraemer v. Leber, 575

Kuebler v. Cleveland Lithographers and Photoengravers Union Local, 424

Kula v. Karat, Inc., 188

L

Lai v. Powell, 542

Lakin v. Postal Life and Casualty Insurance Company, 354

Lambi v. Atkins, 124

Lane v. Honeycutt, 256

Lenkin v. Beckman, 484

Lewis v. Dayton Hudson Corporation, 100

Local 3489 United Steelworkers of America v. Usery, 424

Local Finance Co. v. Charlton, 574

Lopez v. Lopez, 298

Lucy v. Zehmer, 168

M

Mahaney v. Perry Auto Exchange, 276

Mahrenholz v. County Board of School Trustees of Lawrence County, 332

Major League Baseball Players Association v. Owners, 425

Mapp v. Ohio, 46

Marchiondo v. Scheck, 124

Marcus v. Rowley, 299

Marine Contractors Company, Inc., v. Hurley, 154

Marshall v. Barlow's Inc., 456

Masterson v. Sine, 168

Matter of Cohn, 298

MBank of El Paso v. Sanchez, 392

McCollum v. Board of Education, 46

Means v. Clardy, 543

Medias v. City of Indianapolis, 612

Miami Dolphins Ltd. v. Errick L. "Ricky" Williams and the NFL Players Association, 205

Michigan Mutual Liability Company v. Stallings, 354

Miller v. California, 40–41

Money Mart Check Cashing Center, Inc., v. Epicycle Corp., 558

Morse v. Volz, 371

Mount Sinai Hospital of Greater Miami, Inc., v. Jordan, 154

Multiplastics, Inc., v. Arch Industries, Inc., 256

N

Nelson v. Johnson, 332

Newmark v. Gimbel's Inc., 276

Ninth Street East, Ltd. v. Harrison, 256

NLRB v. Hendricks County, 424

Numismatic Enterprise v. Hyatt Corp., 313

O

Ognibene v. Citibank N.A., 574

P

Palsgraf v. Long Island Railroad Company, 100

Parker v. 20th Century-Fox Film Corporation, 204

Parker v. Claypool, 542

Parma, City of, v. Cingular Wireless L.L.C., 204

Paset v. Old Orchard Bank, 298

People v. Glubo, Exelbert, Epstein, and Atlantic Sewing Stores, Inc., 276

Perkins v. Rich, 393

Pillsbury v. Honeywell, 506

Pitman v. Flanagan Lumber Co., 522

Plante v. Jacobs, 204

Plessy v. Ferguson, 15

Portage Plastics Co. v. International Union, Allied Industrial Workers of America, 424

Prewitt v. Numismatic Funding Corporation, 257

Price Waterhouse, v. Hopkins, 440

R

Rinvelt v. Rinvelt, 220

Robert Chuckrow Construction Company v. Gough, 154

Roberts v. Assessment Board of Review of the Town of New Windsor, 298

Rosiny v. Schmidt, 506

Roth v. United States, 40–41

S

Schlensky v. Wrigley, 506

Sedmak v. Charlie's Chevrolet, Inc., 240

Selheimer v. Manganese Corporation of America, 506

Shelton v. Erwin, 590

Smiley v. Citibank, 602

Smith and Edwards v. Golden Spike Little League, 392

Smith v. Lucky Stores, Inc., 408

Sniadach v. Family Finance Corporation, 612

Sommer v. Kreidel, 332

Southern Pacific Company v. Loden, 312

Speigle v. Chrysler Credit Corporation, 590

Spurlock v. United Airlines, Inc., 440

Star Chevrolet v. Green, 168

State v. Brookshire, 558

State v. Kleen, 542

Stratton Oakmont, Inc., v. Prodigy Services Co., 100

T

Taylor v. Fitz Coal Company, 62

Texas v. Johnson, 63

Thornton v. Chamberlain Manufacturing Corporation, 456

Town Finance Corporation v. Hughes, 100

Trail Leasing, Inc., v. Drovers First American Bank, 558

Tuxedo Monopoly, Inc., v. General Mills Fun Group, Inc., 276

2 Live Crew Raps Roy Orbison's "Oh, Pretty Woman," 23

U

United Fire and Casualty Company v. Nissan Motor Corporation, 392

United States v. Basic Construction Company, 78

United States v. Douglas Aircraft Company, 62

United States v. Gorham and Wilkerson, 138

United States v. Hilton Hotels Corporation, 78

United States v. John W., Hinckley, Jr., 22

United States v. Pack, 78

United States v. Price, 78

Universal Studios Inc. v. Film Ventures International Inc., 523

W

Wall v. Airport Parking Company of Chicago, 312

Wards Cove Packing Company v. Antonio, 440

Weber v. Jolly, 46

Webster Street Partnership v. Sheridan, 168

Werner v. Montana, 276

West Tech, Ltd. v. Boatmen's First National Bank of Kansas City, 522

Whirlpool v. Marshall, 408

White v. Samsung Electronics Am., Inc., 101

Wilkin v. 1st Source Bank, 138

Wood v. Abell, 456

World Investment Co. v. Manchester Insurance and Indemnity Co., 354

Woy v. Woy, 220

Z

Zeller v. First National Bank, 124

Ziegler v. Cardona, 370

Index

A

Abagnale, Frank, 137
Academic connections
  archaeology, 311
  architecture, 297
  art, 239, 556
  athletics, 391
  biology, 61
  business, 455
  economics, 483, 541
  English, 137, 407, 611
  environmental science, 123
  ethics, 573
  foreign language, 255
  history, 45, 123, 331, 423, 505
  law, 188
  marketing, 167
  medicine, 22, 369
  political science, 353, 439, 521
  psychology, 99, 153, 275
  science, 203, 589
  social studies, 77
  social survey, 45
Acceleration clause, 548
Acceptance, 118–121
  bilateral, 119
  communicated to the offeror, 119–121
  defined, 118, 533
  effective, 120–121
  matching the offer, 118
  oral, 120
  requirements of, 118–121
  silence as, 119
  unilateral, 119
Accession, 291
Accident insurance, 337
Accommodation party, 554
Accord, 194
Accord and satisfaction, 147, 194
Active concealment, 131
Actual bailment, 302
Actual damages, 93
Administrative agencies, 11
Administrative law, 11–13
Administrator, 357
Adoption, 210, 360
Adult, age tried as an, 58
Adulterated food, warranty of merchantability and, 272
Adulterated food, drugs, and cosmetics, 262
Advanced Research Projects Agency (ARPA), 37
Adverse possession, 321
Advertising
  corrective, 263

false and misleading, 111, 263
  inaccurate or misleading, 267
  as invitation to negotiate, 111
Affirmative action plan, 429
Affirmed (court decision), 50
Age
  contractual effect of misrepresenting, 164
  criminal intent and, 66
  denial of right to vote by, 29
  minimum, for marriage, 207
  minority and, 157
  protected class based on, 428
  tried as an adult, 58
Age Discrimination in Employment Act, 430
Age of majority, 157
Agency
  defined, 379
  federal regulatory, 34
  gratuitous, 381
Agency law, 378–393
  agency duties, 384–389
  agents, 380
  creation and operation of agencies, 379–383
  scope of authority, 380–383
  termination of agency, 387–388
Agency relationships, 379
Agency shop, 414
Agent
  for corporation, signing commercial paper, 547
  defined, 379
  duties of, 384–386. *See also* Agent's duties
  export, 388
  scope of authority, 380–383
  duties of, 384–386
Agreements
  illegal, 171–176
  security, 579
  See also Contracts
Airlines, duty of care, 306
Air space, rights to, 316
"Alaska Hire," 22
Alcoholic. *See* Habitual drunkard
Alien corporation, 489
Alimony, 216, 607
Allocation of markets, 174
Alteration
  defined, 195, 566
  discharge of commercial paper by, 562
  as universal defense, 566
Amazon.com, CDA and, 41
Amended (court decision), 50

Amendment
  constitutional, 32
  defined, 32
  to U.S. Constitution. *See* U.S. Constitution
American Bar Association (ABA), Bankruptcy Reform Act and, 605
American Civil Liberties Union, 41, 161
Americans with Disabilities Act (ADA), 66, 430
American Stock Exchange, 488
American War of Independence, 26
America Online
  CDA and, 41
  spamming and, 46
Anger, statements made in, 110
Animals, ownership of dangerous, 91–92
Annual percentage rate (APR), 597
Annulled (contract), 208
Annulment, 213
Antedated, 546
Anticipatory breach, 193
Antitrust laws, 68, 502
Apparent authority, 381
Appellate briefs, 50
Appellate court, 50
  federal, 53
  King's Bench, 8
  state, 56
Applicant pool, 435
A Question of Ethics features
  agent's duties, 385
  anticipatory breach, 193
  business conglomerate, 498
  changing to subchapter S corporation, 512
  conflicting terms, 183
  credit card temptation, 602
  death as felony punishment, 65
  divorce, 216
  Emancipation Proclamation, 29
  entertaining business clients, 159
  ethics, culture, and values, 17
  FICA tax, 349
  fulfilling employment contract, 404
  harvesting a rare tree, 230
  holographic will, 365
  income tax evasion, 133
  indorsed check, 554
  interest during Middle Ages, 578
  investors' return, 467
  juvenile rehabilitation, 57
  liability disclaimer, 307
  mislaid property, 291
  obligation for whistleblowing, 450

personal check fraud, 534
promise keeping, 148
promissory note, 563
return policies, 250
reward advertisement, 112
sexual harassment, 436
slanderous clerk, 87
tenant's duties, 326
union dues, 414
warranty of title, 270
Arbitrator, 49
ARPANET, 37
Arson, 70
Articles of Confederation, 31
  defined, 26
  Supreme Court and, 52
Articles of incorporation, 490
  lifetime of corporation specified in,
    501
  sample, 491
Articles of organization, 514–515
Artisan's lien, 594–595
Assault, 85
Assignable rights, 192
Assignee, 191
Assignment, 191–192
Assignor, 191
Associate circuit courts, 57
Assumption of risk, 91, 448
Atocha, 138
Attorney
  corporate, 463
  See also Lawyer
Attractive nuisance, 318
Auction
  defined, 251
  online, 539
Austria, Franz Joseph, 32
Authority
  apparent, 381
  creation of, 380–381
  express, 381
  implied, 381
  lack of, as universal defense, 566
  scope of, 160, 380–383
Authorization card, 413
Automobile insurance, 337, 343–345
  collision coverage, 344
  comprehensive coverage, 344
  defined, 343
  liability coverage, 343–344
  medical payments coverage, 344
  no-fault, 345–346
  uninsured and underinsured
    coverage, 345

B

Bailee
  bailments for sole benefit of, 308
  defined, 301
  duty of care, 305–306
  goods held by, risk of loss and, 248
Bailee insurance, 342
Bailee's liens, 307

Bailiff, 50
Bailments, 300–313
  actual, 302
  common examples, 302–303
  constructive, 302
  creation of, 301–302
  defined, 301
  disposition of the goods, 302
  documents used in, perfected security
    interest in, 585
  duties owned by bailee in, 305–307
  extraordinary, 305
  gratuitous, 305
  for hire, 303
  involuntary, 306
  mutual-benefit, 305, 308
  for sale, 303
  for services, 303
  for sole benefit of bailee, 308
  for sole benefit of bailor, 308
  termination of, 302
  transfer of control, 302
  transfer of possession and control,
    302
  for transport, 303
Bailor
  bailment for sole benefit of, 308
  defined, 301
  duties owned by, 307–308
Bait and switch, 263
Banking contract, disaffirmance and,
    163
Bankruptcy
  bankruptcy petition, 606
  Chapter 7 (procedure), 606–608
  Chapter 7 (straight bankruptcy), 605
  Chapter 11 reorganization, 605
  Chapter 12 debt relief for family
    farms, 605
  Chapter 13 extended time payment
    plan, 606
  corporation termination as result of,
    502
  cost of, 604
  cramdown provision, 605
  debts discharged in, 150
  defined, 604
  exempt property, 607–608
  involuntary, 606
  liquidation and distribution of
    proceeds, 608
  non-dischargeable debts, 607
  partnership and, 474
  as remedy, 201
  selection of trustee, 607
  voluntary, 606
Bankruptcy Abuse Prevention and
    Consumer Protection Act
    (BAPCPA), 604–605
Bankruptcy Code, 604–606
Bankruptcy laws, for overburdened
    debtors, 600
Bankruptcy Reform Act, 605
BAPCPA. See Bankruptcy
Bargaining unit, 413

Barter, 229
Battery, 85–86
Bearer, 549
Bearer paper, 549
Beneficiary, 335, 364
Berners-Lee, Tim, 37
Better Business Bureau, 259
BFOQ. See Bona fide occupational
    qualification
Bid rigging, 173
Bigamist, 213
Bilateral contract, 119
Bilateral mistake, 130
Bill of exchange, 533. See also Draft
Bill of Rights. See U.S. Bill of Rights
Bill of sale, 231
Bills of lading, negotiable, 244
Binding arbitration, labor disputes and,
    417
Bingo games, 172
Blackmail, 70
Blank indorsement, 552
Blue-sky laws, 175
Bona fide occupational qualification
    (BFOQ), 433–434
Bona fide seniority system, 434
Bond
  corporate, 500
  posting, 358–359
Bonding insurance, fidelity and surety,
    337
Border patrol agent, 227
Boycott, 420
Brady, James, 22
Brand name, unfair trade practices and,
    265
Breach of contract
  anticipatory, 193
  defined, 193
  employment contract, 398
  as limited defense, 564–565
  remedies for, 197–199
Breach of duty, 65, 90
Breach-of-promise lawsuits, 208
Bribery, 69
Browser, 37
Bulk transfer, 252
Burger, Warren E. (Chief Justice
    USSC), 31
Burger King Corporation, 41
Burglary, 69, 72, 337
Bush, George W. (President)
  passport chip controversy, 581
  Sarbanes-Oxley Act, 501
  sports agency bill, 384
Business ethics, 16
Business invitee, 319
Business judgment rule, 498
Business law, 14
Business necessity, 433
Business organization
  corporations, 466–467. See
    Corporations
  main forms of, 465–467
  partnerships, 466. See Partnerships

Business organization *(cont.)*
    sole proprietorship, 465–466. *See*
        Sole proprietorship
    subchapter S corporations, 511–512
Business organizations
    limited liability corporation,
        514–517
    limited partnerships, 509–511
Business of Sports Agents, The
    (Shropshire and Davis), 391
Bylaws, 501

C

Canada
    debtor's prisons in, 531
    Quebec, civil law code of, 6
Cancellation
    discharge of commercial paper
        by, 562
    as limited defense, 565
    of sales contracts, 193
CAN-SPAM Act of 2003, 264
Capacity
    as contract requirement, 109
    intoxication and, 159–160
    limits on rights of those without,
        162–165
    mental incapacity, 159
    minors and, 159
    principal's lack of, 386
    protections for those who lack, 158
    warranty of the principal's, 380
    what is?, 157–160
Career Clusters
    Law, Public Safety, Corrections, and
        Security, 3
    Marketing, Sales, and Service, 107
    Government and Public
        Administration, 227, 377
    Business, Management, and
        Administration, 283, 463
    Finance, 529
Carelessness, torts based on, 82. *See also*
    Negligence
Carrier, seller ships goods by, 247–248
Carrier's lien, 303
Cars, rental, 303
Case law, 11
    validity and, 13
Cases for Legal Thinking
    Advent Systems Ltd. v. Unisys
        Corporation, 241
    Blevins v. Cushman, 277
    Cherberg v. Joshua Green Corporation,
        et al., 333
    Federal Deposit Insurance Corporation
        v. Culver, 559
    Hall v. Wilkerson, 355
    In re Baker, 613
    In re Holiday Intervals, Inc., 591
    Ivana Trump v. Donald J. Trump, 221
    Kraemer v. Leber, 575
    Lenkin v. Beckman, 485

    Marcus v. Rowley, 299
    Means v. Clardy, 543
    Morse v. Volz, 371
    Noble v. Smith, 139
    Numismatic Enterprise v. Hyatt
        Corporation, 313
    Perkins v. Rich, 393
    Prewitt v. Numismatic Funding
        Corporation, 257
    Texas v. Johnson, 63
Cash-and-carry sales, transfer of rights
    and risks in, 250
Cashier's check, 537–538
Casinos, 171–172
Castle Coalition, 321
Casual sellers, 234
Casualty insurance, 337, 340. *See also*
    Property and casualty insurance
Casual workers, 451
Catch Me If You Can (Abagnale), 137
Catholic Church, Benedictine Order
    of, 505
Causation
    disparate impact and, 435
    as element of tort, 83
    negligence and, 90
Caveat emptor, 259, 269
Caveat venditor, 260
CCA-treated lumber, 261
CDA. *See* Communications Decency
    Act
Cease-and-desist order, 260
Certificate of deposit (CD), 535–536
Certification (union), 413
Certified check, 537
Charitable organizations, promises
    to, 149
Charitable trust, 366
Charter, forfeiture of corporate, 502
Check
    bad, 577
    defined, 534
    as demand instrument, 532
    float time of, 568
    history of, 532
    honor and dishonor, 534–535
    partners' writing of, 478
    payment of, 561
    precautions and care, 535
    stop-payment order, 535
Check 21, 568
Checks and balances, system of, 11,
    31–33
Child birth, premarital, 207
Child custody, 215
Child-labor laws, 402–403
Child Online Protection Act (COPA),
    41, 43, 161
Children
    birth of, revocation of will and, 360
    criminal intent and, 66
    housing discrimination against
        families with, 312
    negligence and, 89
    See also Minors

Child support, 216, 607
China, contract law in, 116
CIF (cost, insurance, freight) price, 248
CIS. *See* Commonwealth of
    Independent States
CISG. *See* Convention on Contracts for
    the International Sale of Goods
City courts, 57
Civil damages, collection of, 96
Civil disobedience, 18
Civil law, 13, 80–92
    common intentional torts, 85–86
    negligence, 89–91
    strict liability, 91–92
    torts, 82–83
Civil offenses, 13. *See* Torts
Civil procedure, 14, 93–96
    remedies for civil suit, 95
    steps in, 94–95
Civil rights, 28–30
Civil Rights Act of 1964, 46, 62
    Title VII of, 328, 429–430
Civil union, 209
Civil War, Thirteenth Amendment
    and, 29
Class actions, 260
Clayton Act, 412
Clerk, 50
Closed shop, 414
Closely held corporation, 489
Closing arguments, in civil
    procedure, 95
CMI. *See* Comite Maritime
    International
Coca-Cola, as multinational
    corporation, 490
COD (collect on delivery) sales, 250
Code, 5
Codicil, 359
Cohabitation, 208
Coinsurance, 342
Collateral
    consumer goods as, 583–584
    defined, 578
    equipment as, 583, 585
    farm products as, 583
    impairment of, discharge of
        commercial paper by, 562
    inventory as, 583, 585
    pawn as, 594
    security interest perfection and,
        581–582
    tangible property as, 583–585
    See also Security interest
Collateral note, 535
Collateral promise, 180
Collective bargaining
    deadlocked, 417
    defined, 416
    union negotiation and, 416
Collision coverage, 344
Colonies, thirteen original, 26
Color, protected class based on, 428
Comite Maritime International
    (CMI), 570

Commercial paper, 530–543
  accommodation party and, 554
  cashier's check, 537–538
  certificate of deposit, 535–536
  certified checks, 537
  check, 534–535
  conflicting terms in, 547
  defined, 532
  discharge of. *See* Discharge of
    commercial paper
  draft, 533–534
  holder in due course of, 562–563
  indorsements, 552–555
  limited defenses against holders of,
    563–565
  money order, 538
  negotiation of, 544–549
  obligations, collection of, 562–564
  payable in sum certain in money,
    547–548
  payment in money, 561
  payable on demand or at definite
    time, 549
  payable to bearer or someone's order,
    549–550
  perfected security interest in, 585
  promissory note, 535
  teller's checks, 537
  transfer of, 551–552
  traveler's check, 538
  types of, 532–536
  unconditional promise or order, 547
  universal defenses against holders of,
    565–567
  what is?, 531–532
  writing requirements for, 546
  See also Negotiable instrument
Commingling, 385
Common carrier, bailments and, 303
Common law
  defined, 6
  disadvantages of, 8
  English, 7–8
  equity as alternative to, 8–9
Common-law defenses, for negligence
  suits, 448
Common-law marriage, 209
Common stock, 494
Commonwealth Edison Company, 22
Commonwealth of Independent States
  (CIS), 473
Communication, contractual, modes
  of, 119–120
Communications Decency Act (CDA),
  40–41, 86
Community Action activities
  Become a Consumer Activist, 279
  Ethical Business Conduct, 525
  Get Out the Vote, 103
  Homeland Security at School, 459
  Positive Peer Pressure, 223
  Protection against Identity Theft,
    615
  Protect Your Environment, 373
Community property, 215, 293–294

Community standards (for obscenity),
  40–41
Comparative negligence, 90
Compensatory damages, 93
Compensatory money damages, 198
Competency license, 173
Competition
  illegal agreements affecting, 174
  role in free market system, 263
Composition with creditors, 147
Compounding a crime, 172
Computer crime, 69–70
Computer Fraud and Abuse Act, 43, 70
Conciliation, 417
Condemnation proceeding, 321
Conditional estate, 319–320
Confidence games, 264
Consent order, 260
Consequences-based ethical
  reasoning, 17
Consequential money damages, 198
Consideration, 140–155
  adequacy of, 143
  circumstantial, 145–147
  as contract requirement, 109
  contractual exchange and, 142
  defined, 141
  exceptions to requirement of,
    149–150
  existing duty and, 146–147
  failure of, as limited defense,
    564–565
  false, 147–148
  legal value and, 142
  in lottery, 171
  nominal, 143
  past, 148
  as promise, act, or forbearance, 141
  promissory estoppel and, 150
  questionable, 145–148
  requirements of, 141
Consignment, 303
Consolidation, defined, 502
Conspiracy, 70
Constitution
  defined, 10
  powers allocated by, 10–11
Constitutional Convention, 25
Constitutional law, 10
Constitutional rights, 24–47
Constitutions, validity and, 12
Constructive bailment, 302
Constructive delivery, 290
Constructive eviction, 325
Constructive notice, 583
Constructive trust, 366
Consumer, 259
Consumer Credit Protection Act,
  596–598
Consumer goods, as collateral,
  583–585
Consumer Leasing Act, 598
Consumer Product Safety Act, 261
Consumer Product Safety Commission
  (CPSC), 34, 261–262

Consumer protection, 258–277
  by consumers, 266–273
  through governmental action,
    259–265. *See also* Governmental
    protection
Consumer transaction, claims
  stemming from, 566–567
Contacts, indivisible, 175
Contempt of court, 74
Continental Congress, 25
Contingency fee basis, 93
Contract
  acquiring property ownership by, 289
  breach of, 193
    as limited defense, 564–565
    remedies for, 197–199
  conflicting terms in, 182
  court-approved, disaffirmance
    and, 163
  defined, 109
  discharge of commercial paper as, 562
  discharge of obligations. *See*
    Contractual obligations,
    discharge of
  divisible, 175
  employment, 395–396
  executed, 178
  executory, 178
  illegal. *See* Illegal agreements
  interpretation of, 181–184
  mistakes in, 130
  modification of bailee's duty of care
    by, 306–307
  modifications of, 150
  online, tie-in sales and, 271
  output, 146
  partnership and, 478
  privity of, 267
  requirements of, 109–113, 146
  temporary incapacity to, as limited
    defense, 565
  termination clauses, 145
  transfer of rights and duties, 191–192
  unconscionable, 143, 175, 598
  writing requirement for. *See* Statute
    of Frauds
Contract law
  consideration, 140–155
  discharge of contractual obligations,
    192–196
  genuineness of assent, 126–139
  legal capacity to contract, 156–169
  legal purpose and proper form,
    170–189
  offer and acceptance, 108–125 *See
    also* Acceptance; Offer
  transfer and discharge of obligations,
    191–196
Contracts of adhesion, 232–233, 598
Contract to sell, 229
Contractual capacity, 156–169
  defined, 157
  disaffirmance and, 162–163
  in organizations, 160
  See also Capacity

Contractual exchanges, consideration and, 142
Contractual obligations, discharge of
  by impossibility of performance, 195
  by initial terms, 194
  by operation of law, 195–196
  by performance, 193–194
  by subsequent agreement, 194–195
  by tender of performance, 195–196
Contractual relations, interference with, 88
Contributory negligence, 90, 448
Convention on Contracts for the International Sale of Goods (CISG), 180, 231
Conversion, 88
Conveyance, 319
Cooling-off period, 419
Co-ownership, 293–294
Copyright, 286–287, 230
Corporate attorney, 463
Corporate charter, 490
Corporate powers, 500–501
Corporations, 486–507
  advantages of, 487–488
  agent for, signing commercial paper, 547
  criminal intent of employees, 66
  defined, 466
  directors of, 497–498
  disadvantages of, 488–489
  dissolution of, 501–502
  double taxation of, 488, 512
  formation of, 490
  founding, 487–492
  limited liability of, 487–488, 514–517
  nonprofit, 480
  officers of, 498
  "offshore," 516
  perpetual life of, 487
  powers of. See Corporate power
  professional management of, 488
  shareholders of, 493–496
  subchapter S, 511–512
  transferability of ownership interests in, 488
  types of, 489
Corrective advertising, 263
Cosigner, accommodation party as, 554
Cosmetics, adulterated, 262
Counteroffer, 115
County courts, 57
Court
  appellate, 50
  defined, 49
  trial, 50
Court of record, 55
Court systems, 48–63
  dispute resolution and, 49–50
  federal, 52–54. See also Federal court system
  state court systems, 55–58
Covenant marriage, 215
Co-worker negligence, 448

CPSC. See Consumer Product Safety Commission
Credit
  defined, 577
  secured transactions, 577–580
Credit card, 601
  abuse and, 603
  protections for users, 601–603
Creditor, 146, 593
  composition with, 147
  defined, 577
  insurable interest of, 338
  laws that protect, 593–596
  of partnership, 480
  possession of collateral by, 579
  in suretyship, 595
Credit rating, 600
Credit-rating service companies, 600
Credit Repair Organizations Act (CROA), 600
Credit sale, 250
Credit system, laws prohibiting abuses in, 598–600
Crime
  business-related, 68–70
  classification of, 67–68
  compounding a, 172
  computer, 69–70
  defined, 13, 65
  punishment for, 74
  threats to report, duress and, 128
  tort vs., 81
  white-collar, 68
Criminal act, 65
Criminal activity, liabilities for partners', 479
Criminal insanity, 73
Criminal intent, 65–67
Criminal law, 13, 65–70
  classification of crimes, 67–68
  defenses to criminal charges, 72–74
  elements of criminal acts, 65–66
  premarital sexual intercourse and, 207
Criminal procedure, 14, 71–75
  in France, 71
  procedural defenses, 73
  punishments for crimes, 74
  rights of the accused, 71–72
  substantive defenses, 73
CROA. See Credit Repair Organizations Act
Crops, 316
Culture, 17
Cumulative preferred stock, 495
Cumulative voting, 495
Currencies, hard vs. soft, 548
Custody, 302
Cyberlaw, defined, 36
Cyberlaw features
  Child Online Protection Act, 161
  defamation issue, 86
  disabilities under the Social Security Administration, 429

  electronic data interchange (EDI), 570
  e-mail flames, 8
  foundations of, 36
  Internet fraud, 134
  Internet real estate offers, 320
  offshore incorporation, 516
  online contracts and tie-in sales, 271
  online money orders, 539
  online trading, 494
  OSHA complaint hotline, 446
  personal e-mail at work, 286
  Social Security Administration web site, 349
  spamming, 264
  statutes of importance to, 43
  UCITA, 251
  See also Internet
Cyberspace, evolving legal issues in, 37–39

D

Damages
  actual, 93
  collection of civil, 96
  compensatory, 93
  for copyright infringement, 286
  defined, 81, 93
  fraud and, 134
  mitigate the, 200
  money, 197–199
  nominal, 199
  punitive, 93, 134, 198, 268
  recovering, with product liability, 267–268
Danbury Hatters case, 411–412
Deadlocked, 417
Death
  of offeror or offeree, 115
  of partner, 474
  property distribution upon, 357–363
  without a will, 357, 358, 361
  with a will, 358–361
Debentures, 500
Debt
  defined, 577
  discharged in bankruptcy, 150
  non-dischargeable, in bankruptcy, 607
  secured, laws allowing, 593–595
  settlement of liquidated, 146–147
  settlement of unliquidated, 147
  unsecured, 595–596
Debt-counseling services, 603
Debtor, 146, 593
  defined, 577
  legal protection of. See Debtor protection
  possession of collateral by, 579
  principal, in suretyship, 595
Debtor protection, 597–601
  disclosure of terms, 597–598
  usury laws, 597
Debtor's prisons, 531

Decedent
  defined, 357
  distribution of estate of, 360–362
Decertification election, 414
Declaration of Independence, 24–26
"Declaration of Independence"
     (Trumbull painting), 25
Dedication, 321
Deed, 320
Defamation, 86
Default, 193
Defendant, 13, 94
Defense, 72
Delegation of duties, 192
Delivery
  conditional, as limited defense, 565
  constructive, 290
  defined, 230
  tender of, 246
Demand instrument. *See* Check
Democracy
  pure, 32
  U.S. system of, 17–18, 32
Demurrage, 303
Department of Homeland Security
     (DHS), 34
Detriment, 142
Dickens, Charles, 611
Directors
  corporate, 497–498
  defined, 497
  duties of, 497
  requirements for, 497
Disability, 430
  protected class based on, 428
Disability coverage, 348
Disability insurance, 337, 350
Disaffirmance
  contractual capacity and, 162–163
  defined, 158
Discharge, 193
Discharged for cause, 398
Discharged without cause, 398
Discharge of commercial paper
  by alteration, 562
  by cancellation, 562
  as a contract, 562
  by impairment of collateral, 562
  by payment, 561–562
Disclaimer, 272, 307
Disclosure of terms, laws requiring,
     597–598
Discover Card, 601
Discrimination
  disability and, 66
  employment, 426–441
Dishonor (check), 534
Disparate impact, 434–435
Disparate treatment, 432
Dispute resolution, 49–51
Dissolution
  corporate, 501–502
  decree of, 216
  of partnerships, 474
Distributive shares (LLC), 515–516

Diversity of citizenship, 53
Dividends, 494
Divisible contracts, 175
Divorce, 214
  no-fault, 214
  procedure, 214–216
  resolution of issues, 215–216
  revocation of will and, 360
  tenancy by the entirety and, 293
Doctrine of capture, 316
Documentary letters of credit, 538
Domesday Book, 290
Domestic corporation, 489, 512
Donee, 141
Donor, 141
Dormant partner, 471
Double indemnity coverage, 348
Double taxation, 512
Draft, 533–534
  payment of, 561
  partners' writing of, 478
  See also Bill of exchange
Drawee, 533
Drawer, 533
Drugs
  adulterated, 262
  warranty of merchantability
     and, 272
Due process, for public employee
     termination, 398
Due process of law, 28–29
Durable power of attorney, 359
Duress
  defined, 127
  depriving control, as universal
     defense, 566
  economic threats and, 128
  ordinary, as limited defense, 565
  threats of illegal or tortious conduct
     and, 127–128
  threats to report crimes and, 128
  threats to sue and, 128
Duties
  agent's, 384–386
  breach of, 65, 90
  contract, transfer of, 191–192
  contractual delegation of, 192
  as element of tort, 82
  of employer, 401–404
  existing, consideration and,
     146–147
  fiduciary, 384
  imposed by negligence, 89–90
  to know the law, 65
  owed to entrants on land, 318–319
  violation of (with tort), 82
Duty of accounting (agency), 385
Duty of confidentiality (agency), 385
Duty of loyalty (agency), 384
Duty of loyalty and honesty
     (employee's), 404
Duty of obedience (agency), 384
Duty of obedience (employee's), 404
Duty of reasonable care and skill
     (agency), 385

Duty of reasonable performance
     (employee's), 405
Duty of reasonable skill (employee's),
     404

E

Easement, 317
Easement appurtenant, 317
Easement by necessity, 317
Easement by prescription, 317
Easements in gross, 317
Eastman Kodak Company, 287
eBay
  CDA and, 41
  as consignment business, 303
E-commerce
  jurisdiction issue, 38
  UCC Article 2 and, 232
Economic Impact features
  ADA accessibility guidelines, 66
  cost of bankruptcies, 604
  impact of euro on trade, 252
  incorporation statutes, 488
  limited liability corporation, 514
  Native Americans and tribal
     gaming, 171
  No Child Left Behind Act
     (NCLBA), 115
  no-fault insurance, 346
  passport chips and identity theft, 581
  punitive damage awards, 268
  sexual harassment lawsuits, 436
Economic strike, 419
Economic threats, 128
EDI. *See* Electronic data interchange
EEOC. *See* Equal Employment
     Opportunity Commission
Electronic data interchange (EDI), 570
Electronic fund transfer (EFT),
     568–571
Electronic Fund Transfers Act (EFTA),
     569–570
E-mail, personal, at work, 42, 286
E-mail flames, 8
Emancipation, 159
Emancipation Proclamation, 29
Embezzlement, 66
Eminent domain, 321
Employees
  covered by workers' compensation,
     449–451
  criminal intent of corporate, 66
  defined, 395
  duties of, 404–405
  duties owed by employer to,
     401–402
  employer's duties owed to those
     injured by, 403–404
  excluded from workers'
     compensation, 450
  export, 388
  government, termination of, 398
  negligence suits by, 447–448

Employer
  defined, 395
  duties of, 401–404. *See also*
    Employer's duties
  failure to provide workers'
    compensation insurance, 449
  OSHA safety reports, 444
  unfair labor practices, 418
Employer's duties
  owed to employees, 401–402
  owed to minors, 402–403
  owed to those injured by employees,
    403–404
Employment
  defined, 395
  discrimination in, 426–441. *See also*
    Employment discrimination
  Fourteenth Amendment applied
    to, 431
  risks of, workers' compensation
    and, 450
  scope of, 403
Employment at will, 396
Employment contract
  employee's duty to fulfill, 404
  express agreement in, 396
  implied agreement in, 396
  termination of, 396–399
  terms of, 395–396
  terms imposed by law, 396
  union negotiating, 414. *See also*
    Labor contract
  yellow-dog, 412
Employment discrimination
  defined, 427
  disparate impact cases, 434–435
  employer's defenses, 433–434
  illegal, 427–431
  laws that prohibit, 429–431
  protected classes, 427–428
  proving illegal, 432–436
  scope of protection, 428–429
  sexual harassment cases, 435–436
  unequal treatment cases, 432–436
Employment law, 394–409. *See also*
  Employment contract
Employment-related injuries, 442–457
Encumbrances, 270
Endorsements, to standard fire policy, 341
Endowment life insurance, 336
England
  contracts in medieval, 143
  Domesday Book, 290
  writing requirements in, 180
English common law, 7–8
Enoch Arden laws, 360
Enron scandal, 498
Entrepreneurs and the Law projects
  Agency and Employment Law
    (Project 5), 458
  Borrowing Money and Paying Bills
    (Project 7), 614
  Contract Law (Project 2), 222
  Law of Sales (Project 3), 278
  Law, Justice & You (Project 1), 102

Legal Forms of Business
    Organizations (Project 6), 52
  Property Law (Project 4), 372
Environmental Protection Agency
  (EPA), 34
Equal Credit Opportunity Act,
  598–599
Equal Employment Opportunity
  Commission (EEOC), 34,
  62, 429
Equal Pay Act, 430
Equal Rights Amendment (ERA), 35
Equipment, as collateral, 583, 585
Equity
  as common law alternative, 8–9
  defined, 8
Escheats, 361
Estate
  conditional, 319–321
  decedent's, distribution of, 360–362
  defined, 319
  defined (property of the deceased),
    357
  leasehold, 323
  life, 320
  non-freehold, 320
  wasting, 326
Ethics
  defined, 16
  forms of ethical reasoning, 16–17
  law and, 16–19, 17–18
Euro
  impact on trade, 252
  as legal tender, 249
European Union, information about
  online users in, 42
Eviction, 325
Exclusionary rule, 77
Exclusions (insurance policy), 340
Excusably ignorant, 175
Executed contract, 178
Executive branch, 31–32
Executor, 358
Executory contract, 178
Exemptions, life insurance policies, 347
Exempt property, in bankruptcy,
  607–608
Existing goods, 245
Ex-parte injunction, 412
Expert witness, 94
Express authority, 381
Express trust, 366
Express warranty, 269–270
Extortion, 70
Extraordinary bailment, 305
Extraordinary care, 305
ExxonMobil Corporation, 488

F

FAA. *See* Federal Aviation
    Administration
Face value, 335
Fair and Accurate Credit Transactions
  Act, 599

Fair Credit Billing Act, 599
Fair Credit Reporting Act, 600
Fair dealings, 146
Fair Debt Collection Practices Act, 599
Fair Housing Act, 328
Fair Labor Standards Act (FLSA),
  401, 403
Fair use, 287
False consideration, 147–148
False imprisonment, 86
False pretenses, 69
Farm products, as collateral, 583
Farms, Chapter 12 debt relief for
  family, 605
Fax transmission of acceptance, 120
FCC. *See* Federal Communications
    Commission
FDA. *See* Food and Drug
    Administration
FDIC. *See* Federal Deposit Insurance
    Corporation
Featherbedding, 418
Federal Aviation Administration
  (FAA), 306
Federal Communications Commission
  (FCC), 34
Federal courts of appeals, 53
Federal court system, 52–54
  federal courts of appeals, 53
  federal district courts, 52–53
  illustration, 53
  jurisdiction of, 52–54
  origin of, 52
  U.S. Supreme Court, 53–54
Federal Deposit Insurance Corporation
  (FDIC), 487, 559
Federal district courts, 52–53
Federal government
  allocation of power between states
    and, 11
  powers of, 33–35
Federal Insurance Contributions Act,
  349, 402
Federal Judiciary Act, 52
Federal law, child labor, 403
Federal regulatory agencies, 34
Federal Reserve System's Board of
  Governors, 34
Federal Trade Commission (FTC), 34,
  263, 566
  Operation Trip-Up, 134
  standards for written warranties,
    268–269
Federal Trade Commission Act, 263
Fee simple absolute, 319
Fee tail, 331
Felony, 67–68
Fence, 69
FICA tax, 349, 402
Fidelity bond, 18
Fiduciary duties, 384
Finance charge, 265, 597
Financing statement, 582–585
Finding, acquiring ownership
  by, 291

Fire
  friendly, 341
  hostile, 341
Fire insurance, 336, 341
Firm offer, 116, 149–150
Fixture, 285, 315, 578
Flag burning, 39, 63
Floater, 342
Fluids, ownership of, 316
FOB (free on board), 248
Food
  adulterated, 262
  warranty of merchantability and, 272
Food, Drug, and Cosmetics Act, 78
Food and Drug Administration (FDA),
    34, 262
Forbearance, 141
Foreign corporation, 489
Foreign Corrupt Practices Act, 69
Forensic accountant, 529
Forgery, as universal defense, 566
France
  criminal procedure in, 71
  Napoleonic Code, 6
Franchisee, 107
Fraud
  buyers in a sale induced by,
    243–244
  contract rescission and, 134
  damages and, 134
  defined, 88, 133
  remedies for, 133–135
  voidable marriage and, 213
  workers' compensation, 452
Fraud in the execution, 566
Fraud in the inducement, 565
Fraudulent misrepresentation, 131
Fraudulent Online Identity Sanctions
    Act of 2004, 10, 43
Freedom of speech
  as Internet-related issue, 39–41
  See also U.S. Constitution, First
    Amendment
Friendly fire, 341
FTC. See Federal Trade Commission
Full warranty, 269
Fungible goods
  bailments, 302
  transfer of ownership and, 245
  warranty of merchantability
    and, 271
Future goods, 245
Future interest, 320

G

Gambling Enforcement Act, 91
Gaming, tribal, 171
Gang wars, 6
Garnishment of wages, 596
Gender
  denial of right to vote by, 29
  protected class based on, 428
General Electric, world ranking of, 488

General jurisdiction
  defined, 52
  in state court systems, 55
General partner, 471
General partnership, 471
Genuine assent, 126–139
  as contract requirement, 109
  contractual mistakes and, 130
  defined, 127
  duress and, 127–128
  fraud and, 133–135
  misrepresentation and, 131–132
  undue influence and, 128–129
George II (King of England), 25
Gift
  acquiring ownership by, 289–290
  causa mortis, 290
  defined, 141
  mutual, 147–148
  of real property, 321
Global Issues feature
  child labor in Mexico, 402
  CISG, 231
  contract law in China, 116
  contracts in medieval England, 143
  criminal procedure in France, 71
  current age limits, 157
  democratic representation in
    Hungary, 32
  Domesday Book, 290
  European contract law, 132
  export employees and agents, 388
  hard v. soft currencies, 548
  international air carrier liability, 306
  joint ventures with firms in CIS, 473
  labor relations in Mexico, 420
  letters of credit, 538
  marriage rules in Muslim
    countries, 207
  multinational corporations, 490
  Napoleonic Code, 6
  negotiable bills of lading, 244
  tenants in Mexico, 325
  writing requirement, 180
Good faith purchaser, 244
Goods
  bailee's duty to return, 307
  defective, 267
  defined, 229
  existing, 245
  fungible, 245, 302
  future, 245
  identified, 245
  inferior, protection against, 260–263
  mislabeled, 264
  receipt of, 230
  sales of, 229–230. See also Sales
    contracts
Google, CDA and, 41
Government, federal. See Federal
    government
Governmental protection
  against inferior services and goods,
    260–263
  against unfair trade practices, 263–265

class actions, 260
consumer caveats and, 259–260
licensing, 260–261
procedure for, 260
unsafe products, 261–263
Government employees, termination
    of, 398
Grace period, 348
Grantee, 319
Grantor, 319
Gratuitous agency, 381
Gratuitous bailment, 305
Great Depression
  agencies formed during, 34
  labor unions and, 412
Guarantor, 595
Gun law, "Make My Day," 74

H

Habitual drunkard, 565
Hammurabi (King of Babylon), 5
Hard currencies, 548
HDC. See Holder in due course
Health insurance, 337, 350–351
Henry II (King of England), 7
HHDC. See Holder through a holder
    in due course
Hilton Hotels Corporation, 78
Hinckley, John, 22
History of the Corporation (Brown), 505
Hit-and-run driving, 73
Holder, 244, 551
  dishonest, 561–562
  in electronic data interchange, 570
  limited defenses against, 564–565
Holder in due course (HDC),
    562–564
Holder through a holder in due course
    (HHDC), 563
Holdover tenant, 324
Holographic will, 359
Home solicitation sales, 265
Homicide, 72
  vehicular, 67, 345
Honor (check), 534
Hostile environment, 435–436
Hostile fire, 341
Hot Debate scenarios
  Unit 1, 4, 24, 48, 64, 80
  Unit 2, 108, 126, 140, 156, 170,
    190, 206
  Unit 3, 228, 242, 258
  Unit 4, 284, 300, 314, 334, 356
  Unit 5, 378, 394, 410, 426, 442
  Unit 6, 464, 486, 508
  Unit 7, 530, 544, 560, 576, 592
Housing code, 328
HTML. See Hypertext markup
    language
HTTP. See Hypertext transfer protocol
Hungary, democratic representation
    in, 32
Hypertext, 37

Hypertext markup language
  (HTML), 37
Hypertext transfer protocol
  (HTTP), 37

I

IBM, 241
Identified goods, 245
Identity theft, 581
Ignorant, excusably, 175
Illegal agreements, 171–176
  allocation of markets, 174
  bid rigging, 173
  competency license and, 173
  court-enforcement of, 174–175
  divisible contracts, 175
  excusably ignorant and, 175
  illegal lotteries, 171–172
  involving discrimination, 172
  marriage and, 173
  not to compete, 174
  to pay usurious interest, 172
  price fixing, 173
  protected victims and, 175
  resale price maintenance, 173–174
  restraint of trade and, 173–174
  that obstruct legal procedures, 172
Illegality, as universal defense, 566
Illegal lotteries, 263–264
Illusory promises, 145–146
Immunity, 73
Impartiality, 16
Impeachment cases, 31
Implied authority, 381
Implied reasonableness, 183
Implied trust, 366
Implied warranties, 270–272
Incapacitated, 157
Incapacity
  permanent, as universal defense, 565
  temporary, as limited defense, 565
Income tax
  partnership income and, 473
  Sixteenth Amendment and, 12
Incontestability clause, 347
Incorporators, 490
Indemnify
  defined, 335
  proving loss to, 341–342
Independent contractor, 395
  in export business, 388
  workers' compensation and, 451
Indian Gaming Regulatory Act, 171
Indorsee, 551
Indorsement
  blank, 552
  defined, 551
  qualified, 553
  restrictive, 554
  special, 552–553
Indorsement of commercial paper,
  552–555
Indorser, 551

Industrial Accident Commission,
  452
Industrial espionage, 265
Infraction, 68
Infringement, 286
Inheritance
  acquiring ownership by, 291
  of real property, 321
Injunction, 9
  defined, 93
  ex-parte, 412
Injury
  as element of tort, 82
  negligence and, 90
Inland marine insurance, 337,342
Innocent misrepresentation, 131
Insanity, criminal, 73
Inside board, 497
Insolvent, 606
Insurable interest, 338–339
  defined, 338
  in life, 338–339
  in property, 338
  transfer of, 249
Insurance
  accident, 337
  automobile, 337. *See also* Automobile
    insurance
  bailee, 342
  casualty, 337, 340
  common types of, 336–337
  defined, 335
  disability, 350
  endowment life, 336
  fidelity and surety bonding, 337
  fire, 336, 341
  health, 337, 350–351
  inland marine, 337, 342
  liability, 337, 342–343
  life, 336, 347
  malpractice, 343
  marine, 337
  no-fault, 345–346
  property, 340. *See also* Property
    insurance
  property and casualty, 340–346
  retirement, 348–349
  social, 337, 348–351
  survivor, 349
  term, 336
  whole life, 336
  workers' compensation, 449–452
  See also Insurance law
Insurance contracts, disaffirmance
  and, 163
Insurance law, 334–355
  fundamentals of, 335–337
  insurable interest, 338–339
  See also Insurance
Insured, 335
Insurer, 335
Intangible personal property, 229
Intangible property, 585
Integrity, 18
  of partners, 479

Intellectual property, 286
  acquiring ownership by production
    of, 290
  copyright, 286–287
  features of, 288
  patent, 287
  trademarks and service marks, 287
  trade secrets, 287–288
Intent, contractual, 110
Intentional torts, 82, 85–86
Interest
  legal rate of, 172
  usurious, agreements to pay, 172
Interference with contractual
    relations, 88
Internal Revenue Code, 488
  subchapter C, 511
  subchapter S, 511–512
Internal Revenue Service (IRS),
    partnership taxes, 473
International Business Machines
    (IBM), 490
International jurisdiction, in
    e-commerce cases, 38–39
Internet
  birth of, 36–37
  Constitutional rights and, 36–43
  domain name registration, 10
  fraudulent schemes, 265
  gambling, 91
  jurisdiction issues, 38
  offshore incorporation and, 516
  spamming, 264
  stock transactions via, 494
  who controls?, 36–39
  World Wide Web, 37
  See also Cyberlaw
Interstate commerce, 11, 34
Inter vivos trust, 366
Intestate, 357
Intestate distribution, 361. *See also*
    Death, without a will
In This Case scenarios
  Unit 1, 11, 16, 42, 54, 70, 73, 83,
    85, 93
  Unit 2, 109, 115, 119, 127, 130,
    142, 147, 159, 163, 173, 177,
    181, 182, 193, 199, 208
  Unit 3, 232, 236, 244, 248, 270
  Unit 4, 286, 290, 301, 307, 319,
    324, 344, 348, 359, 365
  Unit 5, 381, 387, 398, 404, 414,
    417, 428, 433, 444, 449
  Unit 6, 467, 472, 477, 487, 495,
    502, 509, 516
  Unit 7, 533, 546, 553, 561, 569,
    578, 584, 594, 601
Intoxication, capacity and, 159–160
Intrastate commerce, 11, 34
Invasion of privacy, 87
Inventory, as collateral, 583
Invitations to negotiate, 111
Invitee, 318
Involuntary bailment, 306
Involuntary bankruptcy, 606

IOU, 533
Irreconcilable differences, 214
Islamic societies, women in, 17
Italy, civil law code of, 6

J

Japan, punitive damage awards in, 268
Jefferson, Thomas (President), 25
Jests, contractual intent and, 110
Job safety, 443–446
Joint custody, 215
Joint tenancy, 293
Joint venture, 473
Joseph, Franz (Austrian emperor), 32
Judges
    in civil procedure, 94
    King's Bench, 7–8
    state courts of appeals, 56
Judgment, 95
Judicial branch, 32
Jungle, The (Sinclair), 407
Jurisdiction
    defined, 7
    of federal courts, 52–54
    general, 52
    as Internet issue, 38–39
    original, 50
    special, 52
    of U.S. Supreme Court, 53–54
Jury, 7, 50
    in civil procedure, 94, 95
    for negligence cases, 89
Justice, as title for Supreme Court
    judge, 56
Juvenile
    rehabilitation vs. punishment for, 58
    See also Children; Minor
Juvenile courts, 57–58
Juvenile delinquency, 66

K

King, Dr. Martin Luther, Jr., 18–19
King's Bench, 7

L

Labels
    inaccurate or misleading, 267
    mislabeled goods, 264
    nutritional, 262
    warning, 264
Labor contract, negotiation by union,
    416–417
Labor law, history of, 411–412
Labor Management Relations Act, 414,
    416. *See also* Taft-Hartley Act
Labor-Management Reporting and
    Disclosure Act, 419
Labor unions. *See* Unions
Land
    duties owed to entrants on, 318–319
    as exception to goods, 230

Landlord
    defined, 323
    duties of, 327–328
    rights of, 327
Landrum-Griffin Act, 419
Lanham Act, 43, 287
Larceny, 68–69
    insurance to protect against, 337
Last will and testament, 358. *See
    also* Will
Law
    constitutional, 10
    criminal, 13, 65–70
    ignorance of the, 73
    procedural, 14
    sources of, 10–12
    stages in growth of, 5–6
    substantive, 14
    types of, 15
    See also Laws
Law Brief features
    acceptance by certified mail, 120
    adoption records, 210
    age tried as an adult, 58
    bad check, 577
    Bankruptcy Reform Act, 605
    Check 21, 568
    covenant marriage, 215
    CPSC and CCA-treated lumber, 261
    debtor's prisons, 531
    Enron scandal, 498
    euro, 249
    expert witnesses, 94
    law-equity courts, 9
    licensing computer users, 173
    medical malpractice, 518
    mineral rights, 318
    necessaries, 158
    NLRB jurisdiction, 412
    obesity as protected class?, 428
    occupations prohibited for
        minors, 403
    passport signatures, 547
    seller's duty to inform, 132
    sports agents, 384
    standard of reasonable care, 306
    state workers' compensation
        department, 452
    "time is of the essence," 193
    trademarks, 287
    typical intestate distribution, 361
    unincorporated nonprofit
        associations, 480
    vehicular homicide, 345
    women's right to vote in
        Wyoming, 29
Laws
    administrative, 11–12
    antitrust, 68
    case law, 11–12
    conflicting, 12–13
    defined, 5
    ethical bases for, 16–19
    main types of, 13–14
    statutes, 11

types of, 10–15
    See also Law
Lawsuit
    class action, 260
    threats of, 128
Lawyer
    contingency fees, 93
    trial, 3
    See also Attorney
Lay, Kenneth, 498
Lease
    defined, 323
    periodic tenancy, 324
    tenancy at sufferance, 324
    tenancy at will, 324
    tenancy for years, 324
    types of, 323–324
Leasehold estate, 323
Legality, as contract requirement, 109
Legal rate of interest, 172
Legal Research activities
    bankruptcy and student loans, 606
    business organizations, 518
    class actions, 260
    collective bargaining terms, 416
    community property states, 293
    compliance with ADA rules, 430
    computer-related crimes, 69
    constructive trust, 366
    Electronic Fund Transfers Act, 570
    fake IDs, 164
    financing statement, 584
    Fraudulent Online Identity Sanctions
        Act, 10
    fraudulent schemes, 134
    fraudulent schemes against financial
        institutions, 551
    Gambling Enforcement Act, 91
    GATT requirements and business
        forms, 471
    government body of Internet, 38
    legal resource inventory, 110
    letters of credit, 538
    liability ceilings for bailors, 305
    money vs. barter contracts, 230
    original jurisdiction, 50
    paycheck withholding, 402
    real or personal property, 317
    Sarbanes-Oxley Act, 501
    Sports Agency Directory, 380
    statute of limitations, 150, 200
    unemployment benefits, 348
    who keeps the engagement ring?, 178
    workplace safety, 447
Legal system
    common law vs. positive law, 6
    origin of U.S., 5–9
    stages in forming, 5
Legal tender, 196
Legal value, 142
Legislative branch, 31
Lemon laws, 272
Lessee, 323
Lessor, 323
Letters of credit, 538

Liabilities, partner's potential, 479–480
Liability
  limited. *See* Limited liability
  product, 266–268
  strict, 91–92, 266
  vicarious, 83
Liability coverage, automobile
    insurance, 343–344
Liability insurance, 337, 342–343
Libel, 86
License
  competency, 173
  marriage, 209
  revenue, 173
Licensee, 318
Licensing, 260–261
Lien
  artisan's, 594–595
  bailee's, 307
  defined, 594
  involuntary, as secured debt,
      594–595
  mechanic's, 594
Life, insurable interest in, 338–339
Life estate, 320
Life insurance, 336, 347–348
  additional coverages, 348
  defined, 347
  endowment, 336
  exemptions, 347
  as exempt property in
      bankruptcy, 607
  grace period, 348
  incontestability clause, 347–348
  whole, 336
Limited defenses, 563–565
Limited liability, corporations and,
    487–488
Limited liability corporation (LLC),
    514–517
  advantages of, 517
  birth of, 514
  disadvantages of, 517
  operating agreement, 515–517
  formation of, 514–515
Limited liability partnership (LLP),
    517–518
Limited partner, 472
Limited partnership (LLP), 472,
    509–511
  certificate of, 510
  status of partners in, 510–511
  attributes of, 509
  forming, 510
  record keeping for, 510
Limited pay life insurance, 336
Limited warranty, 269
Liquidated debt, 146
Liquidated money damages, 198
Liquidation, 494
Litigate, 49
Living will, 359
LLC. *See* Limited liability corporation
LLP. *See* Limited liability partnership
Loan sharking, 578

Lockout, 416
Lodger, 323
Long-arm statutes, 38
Lost property, 291
Lottery, 171
  illegal, 171–172, 263–264
  state-run, 172
Louisiana, legal system in, 6–7

M

Magna Carta, 27
Magnuson-Moss Warranty Act, 268
Main purpose rule, 181
Majority, age of, 157
"Make My Day" gun law, 74
Maker (promissory note), 535
Malpractice insurance, 343
Management
  of corporations, 488
  right of partners to participate in,
      476–477
Marine insurance, 337
Marital consortium, 210
Marital contracts
  breach of promise lawsuits and,
      208–209
  legalizing, 209–210
Marriage
  common-law, 209
  community property in, 293–294
  contracts and, 207–210. *See also*
      Marriage contracts
  illegal agreements and, 173
  insurable interest and, 338
  marital consortium, 210
  minimum age for, 207
  parenthood and, 210
  property rights and duties and,
      210–211
  revocation of will and, 360
  same-sex, 209
  Statute of Frauds and contracts
      for, 181
  statutory requirements for, 209
  void, 213
  voidable, 213
Marriage contracts
  nullifying, 213
  premarital relationships, 207–208
  prenuptial agreement, 210–211
  terminating, 214–216
Marriage and Divorce Act, 215
Marshal, federal court, 50
MasterCard, 601, 602
Material facts, 130
Materiality, misrepresentation and, 132
McDonalds Corporation, 490
Mechanic's lien, 594
Mediation
  defined, 417
  union negotiations, 417
Mediator, 49
Medical malpractice, 518

Medical payments coverage, automobile
    insurance, 344
Medicare, 350–351, 429
Members (LLC), 515
Mental incapacity, 159
Merchant, 234
  implied warranties given only by,
      271–272
  with possession of sold goods, 244
  special sales contracts rules for,
      234–235
Merger, 502
Mexico
  child labor in, 402
  labor relations in, 420
  tenants in, 325
Microsoft Corporation
  corporate facts, 489
  world ranking of, 488
Military Selective Service Extension
    Act, 402
Mineral rights, 316, 318
Minerals, ownership of solid, 316
Minimal care, 306
Minimum wage law, 396
Minor
  capacity and, 159
  defined, 157
  employer's duties owed to, 402–403
  liability for serving liquor to, 387
  misrepresenting age, 164
  occupations prohibited for, 403
  partner's liability for selling alcoholic
      beverages to, 480
  rights of, in contracts, 162
  status of, partnership agreement
      and, 473
Minority
  defined, 157
  as universal defense, 565
Minority position, 495
Miranda rights, *Hinckley* case and, 22
Mirror image rule, 118
Misdemeanor, 68
Mislaid property, 291
Misrepresentation, 131–132
  active concealment and, 131
  of age, contractual effect of, 164
  fraud and, 133
  materiality and, 132
  reasonable reliance and, 132
  silence and, 131–132
  untrue statement of fact for,
      131–132
Mitigate the damages, 200
Mixed board, 497
MNC. *See* Multinational corporations
Mock Trial Prep
  Case Law, 280–281
  Case Scenario, 224–225
  Closing Arguments, 616–617
  Concepts of Advocacy,
      104–105
  Direct and Cross Examination of a
      Witness, 460–461

Objections, 526–527
Opening Statements, 374–375
Model Business Corporation Act, 497
Money
    commercial paper payable in sum
        certain in, 547–548
    defined, 547
    federal coining of, 33
    lending, secured transaction in,
        579–580
    payment of commercial paper in, 561
Money damages
    compensatory, 198
    consequential, 198
    liquidated, 198
    as remedy for major breach of
        contract, 197–199
Money order, 538
Monopoly, illegal, 502
Mortgage, real estate, conflicting terms
    in, 182
Mortgage note, 535
Motor vehicles, perfection of security
    interest in, 584
Multinational corporations
    (MNC), 490
Municipal courts, 57
Mutual-benefit bailment, 305, 308
Mutual gifts, 147–148
Mutual mistake, 130

N

National Conference of Commissioners
    on Uniform Sate Laws
    (NCCULS)
    UCC Article 2, 232
    UCITA, 251
National Conference of State
    Legislatures, 158
National Consumers League, Internet
    Fraud Watch project, 134
National emergency strike, 419–420
National Fraud Information
    Center, 134
National Institute of Standards and
    Technology, Weights &
    Measures Division, 262
National Labor Relations Act, 412, 420
National Labor Relations Board
    (NLRB), 34, 412–413,
    416–417, 424
National origin, protected class based
    on, 428
National Science Foundation (NSF),
    Internet and, 37
Native Americans, tribal gaming
    and, 171
NCAA eligibility, 384
Necessaries, 158
Negligence
    breach of duty and, 90
    causation and injury and, 90
    comparative, 90

contributory, 90, 448
co-worker, 448
defenses to, 90
defined, 82
duty imposed by, 89–90
proving in product liability cases, 267
Negligence law
    common-law defenses, 448
    employee negligence suits, 447–449
    workers' compensation compromise,
        448
Negotiable, 545
Negotiable bills of lading, 244
Negotiable documents of title, holders
    of, 244
Negotiable instrument, 532, 545. See
    also Commercial paper
Negotiations, preliminary, contractual
    intent and, 111
Net Bookmark
    automobile insurance, 343
    blue sky laws, 175
    business necessity, 434
    check processing, 534
    commercial paper, 548
    contract of adhesion, 233
    contract law, 198
    contracts concepts, 145
    Danbury Hatters case, 411
    Dr. Martin Luther King, Jr., 19
    eBay consignment business, 303
    eminent domain, 321
    employment at will, 396
    failed or recently proposed
        amendments, 32
    Fair and Accurate Credit Transactions
        Act, 599
    federal agencies' Recall Press
        Releases, 261
    HDC of social security check, 564
    limited liability companies, 517
    marriage laws, 209
    National Conference of State
        Legislatures, 158
    NCCULS, 251
    online brokerage, 494
    power of attorney, 381
    retail web sites, 111
    rights abuses in U.S. and France, 72
    starting a small business, 466
    subpoena, 95
    tax fraud cases, 133
    U.S. Copyright Office, 290
    U.S. Supreme Court, 53
    UCC revised Article 9, 582
    will versus trust debate, 364
    Workers' Compensation Boards, 451
Netherlands, civil law code of, 6
Neutral on its face, 434
New York Stock Exchange, 488
9/11 crisis, Check 21 and, 568
NLRB. See National Labor Relations
    Boards
No Child Left Behind Act
    (NCLBA), 115

No-fault divorce, 214
No-fault insurance, 345–346
Nominal consideration, 143
Nominal damages, 199
Nominal partner, 471
Nonconforming use, 318
Nondelivery, as limited defense, 565
Non-freehold estate, 320
Nonprofit corporation, 480, 489
Non-trading partnership, 471
No-par stock, 493
Novation, 195
NRC. See Nuclear Regulatory
    Commission
Nuclear Regulatory Commission
    (NRC), 34
Nuncupative will, 359
Nutritional labeling, 262

O

Obligor
    defined, 191
    possession of commercial paper
        and, 561
Obscenity, Internet and, 40–41
Occupancy
    acquiring ownership by, 292
    defined, 292
Occupant, 344
Occupational Safety and Health Act,
    443, 445
Occupational Safety and Health
    Administration (OSHA), 34,
    443–444
Offer
    advertisement as, 111
    communicated to offeree, 112
    contractual intent and, 110–112
    counteroffer, 115
    creation of, 109–113
    defined, 110
    essential terms of, 112
    firm, 116, 149–150
    length of time of, 114–115
    rejection of, by offeree, 115
    requirements of, 110–113
    termination of, 114–117
    tests for valid, 110
    time stated in, 114
    ways to keep open, 116
Offeree
    acceptance by, 118
    death of, 115
    defined, 109
    offer communicated to, 112
    rejection of offer by, 115
Offeror
    acceptance communicated to,
        119–121
    death of, 115
    defined, 109
    revocation of offer by, 114
Omnibus clause, 343

Online auction houses, 539
Online money orders, 539
Online Research
    Anita's Attack, 273
    Ashleigh's Agreement, 437
    Becky's Battle, 97
    Ronald's Rehabilitation, 609
    Stanley's Situation, 367
    Steve's Nonprofit, 503
    Tom's Tribulation, 217
Online trading, 494
Opening statement, in civil
        procedure, 94
Open shop, 414
Operating agreement (LLC), 515–517
Option, 116
Oral acceptance, 120
Oral will, 359
Order paper, 549
Ordinance
    defined, 11
    zoning, 318
Ordinary care, 305
Organizations, contractual capacity
        in, 160
Original jurisdiction, 50, 53
OSHA. See Occupational Safety and
        Health Administration
Output contract, 146
Outside board, 497
Ownership
    acquiring, 289–292
    co-ownership, 293–294
    of dangerous animals, 91–92
    defined, 229
    limitations on, 294
    of real property. See Real property,
        ownership of
    in severalty, 292
    transfer of, in sales, 243–246

P

Pari-mutuel betting, 172
Paris Convention of 1883, 287
Parking violation, 68
Parol evidence, 184
Parol evidence rule, 183–184, 546
Participating preferred stock, 495
Partners
    authority of, 477–478
    binding contracts by, 478
    duties of, 479
    limited. See Limited partners
    potential liabilities of, 479–480
    rights of, 476–477
    See also Partnerships
Partnership
    creation of, 469–475
    defined, 466
    judgment obtaining against, 480
    limited, 509–511. See also Limited
        partnerships
    limited liability, 517–518

operating, 476–481
partner's powers in, 476–479
powers of, 473
property of, 477
status of, 473
termination of, 473–475
types of, 471–472
See also Partners
Partnership agreement
    defined, 469
    example, 470
    form and content of, 469–471
    minors and, 472
Partnership at will, 474
Par value, 493
Passport
    microchips in, 581
    signature, 547
Past consideration, 148
Patent
    defined, 287
    as exception to goods, 230
Pawn, 594
Payable at a definite time, 549
Payable on demand, 549
Payee, 533
Payment
    defined, 230
    prior, as limited defense, 565
Payroll deductions, 402
PDA. See Pregnancy Discrimination
        Act
Pension, as exempt property in
        bankruptcy, 607
Pension investigator, 377
People, governmental power of, in U.S.,
        34
Per capita distribution, 361–362
Per capita voting, 516
Perfected security interest, 581–582
    defined, 581–582
    in intangible property, 585
    notice through filing financing
        statement, 582–583
    notice through possession, 582
    tangible property, 583–585
    See also Collateral
Performance
    defined, 192
    discharge of contractual obligations
        by, 193–194
    specific, 199
    substantial, 193
    tender of, discharge of contracts by,
        195–196
    timing of, 193
Periodic tenancy, 324
Peripheral rights, 30
Personal defenses, 563
Personal property, 286
    defined, 285
    insurance for, 342
    intangible, 230
Personal property floater, 342
Personalty, 286. See also Personal property

Per stirpes distribution, 361–362
Persuasion, unfair, 129
Petition of Right, 27
Pfizer, world ranking of, 488
Picketing, 419
Piercing the corporate veil, 488
Plaintiff, 13, 94
Planning a Career in Law features
    border patrol agent, 227
    corporate attorney, 463
    forensic accountant, 529
    franchisee, 107
    pension investigator, 377
    title examiner, 283
    trial lawyer, 3
Plea bargaining, 74
Pledge, 579, 593–594
Pledgee, 593. See also Creditor
Pledgor, 593. See also Debtor
Policy, 335
Political party, 31
Poll tax, 29
Positive law, 6
Possession, tenant's right of, 325–326
Postdated, 546
Posting bond, 358–359
Power of attorney
    defined, 381
    durable, 359
    example, 382
Precedent, 8
Preemptive right, 496
Preferred stock, 494
Pregnancy
    premarital, 207
    protected class based on, 428
Pregnancy Discrimination Act (PDA),
        397, 430–431
Premium, 335
Prenuptial agreement, 210–211
Price
    CIF, 248
    defined, 229
Price fixing, 173
Prices, agreements to control or
        fix, 263
Pricing, unfair, 264
Primary boycott, 420
Primary promise, 180
Principal
    agency law, 379–380
    defined, 379
    duties agent owes, 384–386
    duties owed agent, 386–387
    duties owed third parties, 387
    lack of capacity, 386
    undisclosed, 386
Principal debtor, in suretyship, 595
Prior appropriation system, 317
Privacy
    invasion of, 87
    passport microchips and, 581
    right of, 30, 41–43
Private corporation, 489
Private trust, 366

Privity of contract, 267
Probable cause, 71
Probate court, 58, 357
Procedural defenses, 73
Procedural law, 14
Procter & Gamble, 488, 490
Product liability, 266–268
    defined, 266
    expansion of, 266–268
    recovery for tortious conduct,
        267–268
    warranties and, 268–272
Products, unsafe, 261–263
Professionals, negligence and, 89
Profit-making corporation, 489
Profit maximization, 16
Profits
    partner's rights to, 477
    shareholders' right to share, 496
Prohibition, 46
Promise
    to charitable organizations, 149
    collateral, 180
    covered by the UCC, 149–150
    illusory, 145–146
    primary, 180
Promisee, 142
Promisor, 142
Promissory estoppel, 153
Promissory note, 535
Promoters, 490
Property
    bailee's duty to care for, 305–306
    classifications of, 285–288
    defined, 285
    distribution of, upon death,
        357–363
    division of, in divorce, 215
    exempt, in bankruptcy, 607–608
    insurable interest in, 338
    intangible, 585
    intellectual, 286, 286–287
    lost vs. mislaid, 291
    partnership, 477
    personal. See Personal property real.
        See Real property
    receiving stolen, 69
    selling stolen, 69
    tangible, as collateral, 583–585
    ways of acquiring, 289–292
Property distribution upon death
    without a will, 357–358, 361
    with a will, 358–360
Property insurance, 340
Property law
    acquisition of property, 289–295
    bailments, 300–313
    insurance law, 334–355
    real property, 314–333
    wills, trusts, and estates, 356–371
Protected class, 427–428, 432
Proximate cause, 83
Proxy, 495–496
Public auction, goods sold at, 244
Public corporation, 489

Public employees, termination of, 398
Public service corporation, 489
Public utility, 489
Puffing, 269
Pull-tab betting, 172
Punishment
    for crimes, 74
    defined, 74
    for felony, 67
    rehabilitation vs., for juveniles, 58
    for white-collar crimes, 68
Punitive damage awards, 268
Punitive damages, 93, 134, 198
Purchase money security interest,
        583–584
Push money, 265

Q

Qualified indorsement, 553
Quasi-contract, 178
Queen's Bench, 7
Quid pro quo, 435
Quitclaim deed, 320

R

Race, protected class based on, 428
Ratification
    of agency authority, 381, 383
    defined, 127, 381
    minors and, 159
Reagan, Ronald (President), 22, 423
Real estate, transfer ownership,
        320–321
Real property, 314–333
    defined, 285
    as exempt in bankruptcy, 607
    intangible, 230
    leasing, 323–324
    ownership of
        duties owed to entrants on
            land, 318–319
        forms of, 319–321
        limitations of, 317–319
        rights of, 315–317
    quiet enjoyment of, 321
    Statute of Frauds and, 177, 180
    tenant's duty to take care of,
        326–327
    tenant's right to sublet, 326
    tenant's right to use, 326
Realty, 285
    sale of, disaffirmance and, 164
    See also Real property
Reasonable care
    as partnership duty, 479
    standard of, 306
Reasonable doubt, 72
Reasonable-person standard, 89
Reasonable reliance, 132
Receipt of goods, 230
Receiving stolen property, 69
Regulations, administrative, 12

Regulatory agencies, federal, 34
Release, 147
Religion
    freedom of, 28
    protected class based on, 428
Remanded (court decision), 50
Remedy
    bankruptcy as, 201
    conflict of, 199–200
    defined, 197
    duty to mitigate and, 200
    factors affecting choice of, 199–201
    statute of limitations and, 200–201
    waivers and, 200
Rent
    defined, 323
    tenant's duty to pay, 326
Rental, apartment, disaffirmance
        and, 164
Repossession, 580
Representation election, 413
Republic, 32
Requirements contract, 146
Resale price maintenance, 173–174
Rescission
    defined, 127
    discharge of contractual obligation
        by, 194
    fraud and contract, 134
    as remedy for major breach of
        contract, 197
Restitution
    defined, 260
    as remedy for major breach of
        contract, 197–199
Restrictive covenant, 317–318
Restrictive indorsement, 554
Resulting trust, 366
Retailers Credit Association, 600
Retirement insurance, 348–349
Revenue license, 173
Reversed (court decision), 50
Revised Uniform Limited Partnership
        Act (RULPA), 472,
        510–511, 517
Revocable trust, 366
Revocation, 114
Revolutionary War. See American War
        of Independence
Riders, 341
Right of contribution, 595
Right of election (to decedent's
        property), 361
Right of partition, 293
Right of possession, 578
Right to privacy, 30, 87–88
    Internet and, 41–43
Rights
    of the accused, 71
    contract, 191–192
    of those without capacity,
        162–165
Right of survivorship, 293
Right-to-work laws, 414
Riparian, 317

Risk
  assumption of, 91, 448
  defined, 336
  of employment, workers'
    compensation and, 450
Risk of loss
  auction and, 251–252
  breaches after goods are
    identified, 248
  bulk transfer and, 252
  COD sales and, 250
  goods held by bailee, 248
  goods shipped by carrier and,
    247–248
  sale on approval and, 251
  sale or return and, 250
  sales on credit and, 250
  sale of an undivided interest and, 251
  transfer of, 247–248
Robbery, 69
  insurance to protect against, 337
Roosevelt, Franklin (President), 412
Roosevelt, Theodore (President), 407
RSDHI, 348
Rule-based ethical reasoning, 17
Rules, administrative, 12
RULPA. *See* Revised Uniform Limited
  Partnership Act

S

Sale(s)
  bailments for, 303
  bill of, 231
  COD, 250
  defined, 229
  of real property, 321
  tie-in, 271
  transfer of insurable interest in, 249
  transfer of ownership, 243–246
  transfer of rights and risks in specific,
    249–252
  transfer of risk of loss in, 247–248
  See also Sales contracts
Sale on approval, 251
Sale or return, 250
Sales contract, 228–241
  acceptance of goods and, 231–232
  bill of sale, 231
  cancellation of, 193
  exceptions to Statute of Frauds for,
    235–236
  law of contracts vs., 230
  material alteration, 235
  payment and delivery,
    230–231
  proposal for addition, 234
  special rules for merchants, 234–235
  Statute of Frauds and, 235–236
  unconscionable, 232–233
  use of credit and, 231
Salesperson, as agent, 379
Same-sex marriage, 209
Sarbanes-Oxley Act, 501
Satisfaction, accord and, 147, 194

Scofflaws, 18
Scope of authority, 160, 380–383, 386
Scope of employment, 403
  workers' compensation and, 449–451
S corporation
  defined, 512
  eligibility requirements for, 512
  formation of, 512
SEC. *See* Securities and Exchange
  Commission
Secondary boycott, 402
Secret partner, 471
Secured debts
  involuntary liens, 594–595
  laws allowing, 593–595
  pledges, 593–594
Secured party, 578
Secured transaction, 577
  creation of security interests,
    578–580
  importance of, 577–578
  See also Security interest
Securities and Exchange Commission
  (SEC), 34
Security agreement, 579
Security deposit, 326
Security interest, 578
  creation of, 578–580
  perfecting, 581–585
  terminating, 586–587
  when creditor has possession of
    collateral, 579
  when debtor has possession of
    collateral, 579–580
  See also Collateral
Self-defense, 73
Self-incrimination, 73
Sellers
  express warranties by, 269–270
  implied warranties by, 270
Selling stolen property, 69
Separation agreement, 214
Service, unfair, 264
Service mark, 287
Services, bailment for, 303
Settlor, 364–365
Severalty, ownership in, 292
Sexual harassment cases, 435–436
Shareholder
  defined, 494
  rights of, 495–496
  role of, 493–496
  of S corporation, 512
  termination of corporation by
    agreement of, 501–502
Shares of stock, 493
  right to transfer, 495
  See also Stock
Sheriff, 50
Sherman Antitrust Act, 78, 412
Sight draft, 533
Signature
  forged, 552–553
  Statute of Frauds requirements
    for, 179

Silence, misrepresentation and,
  131–132
Silent partner, 471
Slander, 86
Slavery, abolition of, 29
Small claims courts, 57
Social agreements, contractual intent
  and, 111–112
Social insurance, 337, 348–351
  disability insurance, 350
  health insurance, 350–351
  retirement insurance, 348–349
  survivor's insurance, 349
Social Security Act (SSA), 348,
  349, 398
  as administrative agency, 12
  disabilities under, 429
  reimbursing for social security
    checks, 564
Society
  crime and, 65
  laws of, 6
Soft currencies, 548
Sole proprietorship, 465–466
Sovereign (leader or authority), 6
Sovereignty (state), 33
Spain, civil law code of, 6
Spamming, 41–42
Special indorsement, 552–553
Specialized jurisdiction, state courts
  with, 55, 57–58
Special jurisdiction, 52
Specific performance
  defined, 199
  as remedy for major breach of
    contract, 199
Speech, freedom of, 39–41
Spendthrift, trust, 366
Sports & Entertainment Law cases
  *Amy Cohen et al v. Brown
    University*, 441
  Coogan v. Bernstein, 169
  Coppola v. Warner Brothers, 189
  Costanza v. Seinfeld, 47
  *Denver Rockets v. All-Pro
    Management*, 507
  Fortay v. University of Miami, 125
  Galella v. Onassis, 79
  Hendy v. Losse, 457
  *Jason Giambi v. New York
    Yankees*, 409
  Jeremy Bloom v. NCAA, 155
  *Major League Baseball Players
    Association v. Owners*, 425
  *Miami Dolphins Ltd. v. Errick L.
    "Ricky" Williams and the NFL
    Players Association*, 205
  *2 Live Crew Raps Roy Orbison's "Oh,
    Pretty Woman,"* 23
  *Universal City Studios Inc. v. Film
    Ventures International Inc.*, 523
  White v. Samsung Electronics, 101
Sports Agency Directory, 380
Sports Agent Responsibility and Trust
  Act (SPARTA), 384

Spot zoning, 318
SSA. *See* Social Security Administration
Standard fire policy, 341
Standby letters of credit, 538
Stare decisis, 11, 14
State court system
  associate circuit courts in, 57
  city or municipal courts, 57
  courts of appeals, 56
  courts with specialized jurisdictions
    in, 57–58
  illustration of typical, 56
  juvenile courts, 57–58
  small claims courts, 57
  supreme courts, 56
State court systems
  probate courts, 58
  trial courts, 55–56
  typical, 55–56
State laws, child labor, 402–403
State-run lotteries, 172
States
  legal systems in 49, 7
  limiting powers of, 33
  "minimum contacts" with, as
    e-commerce issue, 38
  sovereignty of, 33
Statute
  defined, 11
  false or misleading advertising, 111
  long-arm, 38
  validity and, 12–13
  worker's compensation, 448
Statute of Frauds, 177–181
  bill of sale and, 231
  contract creating guaranty
    relationship and, 595
  contract for sale of goods for $500 or
    more, 179–181
  contracts to pay a debt and, 180
  contracts requiring more than one
    year and, 180
  contracts within, 177–178
  defined, 177
  electronic records and, 232
  leases and, 323
  main purpose rule and, 181
  marriage contracts and, 181
  online contracts and, 271
  purpose of, 177–179
  real property contracts and, 180
  sales contracts and, 235–236
  writing requirements, 178–179
Statute of limitations, 150, 200
Stock
  capital, right to increase, 496
  common, 494
  no-par, 493
  online trading, 494
  preferred, 494
  of S corporation, 512
  types of, 494–495
  See also Shares of stock
Stock certificate, 493, 495
Stock exchanges, 488

Stockholder. *See* Shareholders
Stop-payment order, 535
Straight bankruptcy. *See* Bankruptcy,
    Chapter 7
Straight life insurance, 336
Strict liability, 91–92, 266
Strike, 416
Subchapter S corporations, 511–512
Subletting, 326
Subpoena, 94–95
Substantial performance, 193
Substantive defenses, 73–74
Substantive law, 14
Substitution, discharge of contractual
    obligation by, 194
Supremacy rules, 12
Surety, 595
Suretyship, 595
Surface rights, 316
Surrogate's court, 357. *See also* Probate
    court
System of checks and balances, 11,
    31–33

T

Taft-Hartley Act, 414, 418
Tangible property, as collateral,
    583–585
Tax
  federal, on imports and exports, 33
  income. *See* Income tax
Tax fraud, 133
Telecommunications Act of 1996, 43
Telemarketing, fraudulent
    schemes, 265
Teller's check, 537
Tenancy at sufferance, 324
Tenancy at will, 324
Tenancy by the entireties, 293
Tenancy for years, 324
Tenancy in common, 293
Tenancy in partnership, 477
Tenant
  defined, 323
  duties of, 326–327
  holdover, 324
  rights of, 325–326
Ten Commandments, 17
Tender, 195
Tender of delivery, 246
Tender of performance, 195–196
Termination, of partnership, 473–475
Termination statement, 586
Term insurance, 336
Terror, statements made in, 110
Testamentary capacity, 359
Testamentary intent, 359
Testamentary trust, 366
Testate, 358
Testator
  changes to will by, 360
  defined, 358
  intention of, 359

Testimony
  in civil procedure, 94
  defined, 94
Texas, limited liability partnership, 517
Texas Workers' Compensation Act, 450
Theft, 68
  insurance to protect against, 337
  as limited defense, 565
Tie-in sales, Internet and, 271
Time draft, 533
Title, warranty of, 270
Title examiner, 283
Tort, 13
  crime vs., 81
  defined, 81
  elements of, 82–83
  employer commits intentional, 449
  intentional, 85–86
  liabilities for partners', 479
  recovery in product liability suit for,
    267–268
  responsibility for another's, 83
  tenant's responsibility for, 327
Trade
  impact of euro on, 252
  restraint of, illegal agreements and,
    173–174
Trade fixtures, 316
Trademark
  defined, 287
  unfair trade practices and, 265
Trademark Dilution Act of 1996, 43
Trade secret, 287
Tradespersons, negligence and, 89
Trading partnership, 471
Traffic offenses
  criminal intent and, 66–67
  state courts and, 57
Transcript, 50
Traveler's check, 538
Trespass, 318
Trespass to land, 88
Trial court, 50, 55–56
Trial lawyer, 3
Trumbull, John, 25
Trust, 364–367
  charitable, 366
  constructive, 366
  defined, 364
  express, 366
  implied, 366
  inter vivos, 366
  private, 366
  purpose and creation of, 364–365
  revocable, 366
  resulting, 366
  spendthrift, 366
  testamentary, 366
  types of, 366
Trust accounts, 386
Trustee
  bankruptcy, 607
  defined, 364
Truth in Lending Act, 597

U

U.S. Bill of Rights, 10, 27
  applied to the states, 33
  emphasis on basic rights in, 33
  ethics based on rules and, 17
U.S. Congress
  as legislative branch, 31
  powers of, 11
  power to lay and collect income
    tax, 12
  See also entries for specific acts
U.S. Constitution
  abolition of slavery and, 29
  Article I, 29
  Article I, Section 8 (on
    bankruptcy), 604
  Article III, 52
  Article IV, 29
  Article VI, 10, 12, 33
  Bill of Rights in, 27. *See also* U.S.
    Bill of Rights
  changing, 32
  civil rights and, 28
  defined, 27
  Eighteenth Amendment, 45
  Eighth Amendment, 27, 29
  emphasis on basic rights in, 33
  Fifteenth Amendment, 29
  Fifth Amendment, 27, 28, 33, 38, 73
  First Amendment, 27, 28, 39–40,
    46, 161, 264
  foundations of, 25–30
  Fourteenth Amendment, 29, 33, 38,
    39, 431
  Fourth Amendment, 27, 28, 62
  as guardian of greatest good, 18
  Internet and, 36–43
  Nineteenth Amendment, 29
  Ninth Amendment, 27, 33
  right of privacy and, 87
  Second Amendment, 27
  Seventh Amendment, 27, 29
  Sixteenth Amendment, 12
  Sixth Amendment, 27, 29
  on standards for weights and
    measures, 262
  states' ratification of, 26
  as "supreme law of the land," 10, 12
  system of checks and balances
    and, 31
  Tenth Amendment, 27, 33
  Third Amendment, 27
  Thirteenth Amendment, 29
  Twenty-First Amendment, 46
  Twenty-Fourth Amendment, 29
  Twenty-Sixth Amendment, 29
  U.S. Supreme Court as interpreter
    of, 10
U.S. Copyright Office, 286, 290
U.S. Courts of Appeals, 53
U.S. Department of Agriculture, 262
U.S. Department of Defense, 37
U.S. Department of Labor, 443–444
U.S. Foreign Corrupt Practices Act, 70

U.S. government
  branches of, 31–32
  consumer protection by, 259–265
  powers of, 33–35
  as representative democracy, 32
U.S. House of Representatives, 31
U.S. legal system, origin of, 6–9
U.S. Postal Service, acceptances by, 120
U.S. Post Office, 33
U.S. Senate, 31
U.S. Supreme Court (USSC)
  adoption laws, 210
  Child Online Protection Act
    and, 161
  constitutionality of Civil Rights Act
    of 1964, 46
  Danbury Hatters case, 411–412
  on due process of law, 28
  exclusionary rule, 77
  in federal court system, 53–54
  Federal Judiciary Act and, 52
  as final interpreter of
    Constitution, 10
  as head of judicial branch, 32
  as highest authority, 12
  interest rates, 172
  jurisdiction of, 53–54
  limits on credit card late charges, 602
  obscenity law, 39–40
  Plessy v. Ferguson, 15
  right of privacy and, 30, 41
  separation of church and state, 62
UCC. *See* Uniform Commercial Code
UCITA. *See* Uniform Computer
  Information Transactions Act
ULPA. *See* Uniform Limited
  Partnership Act
Unconscionability, 175
Unconscionable contract, 143,
  175, 598
Unconscionable sales contracts,
  232–233
Unconstitutional, 12
Under the counter payments, 265
Underinsured motorists coverage, 345
Undisclosed principal, 386
Undue influence, 128
Unemployment benefits, 348
Unemployment compensation,
  398–399
Unequal treatment
  bona fide occupational qualification
    and, 433–434
  business necessity and, 433
  cases based on direct evidence,
    432–433
  cases based on indirect evidence,
    432–433
  cases based on statistics, 433
  defined, 432
  evidence of, 432–433
  pretexts for, 434
  seniority and, 434
Unfair labor practices, 417–420
  in boycotts, 420

defined, 418
  in strikes, 419–420
  by unions, 418–419
Unfair labor practice strike, 419–420
Unfair persuasion, 129
Unfair trade practice
  agreements to control or fix
    prices, 263
  confidence games, 264
  defined, 263
  false and misleading advertising, 263
  illegal lotteries, 263–264
  mislabeled goods, 264
  other, 265
  unfair pricing and service, 264
Uniform Commercial Code
  (UCC), 14
  acceptance of goods, 235–236
  acceptance of offer, 120
  additional negotiation rights
    with, 551
  Article 2: Sales, proposed changes
    to, 232
  Article 4A (electronic fund
    transfers), 570
  attempted acceptance of offer, 119
  bulk transfer, 252
  cancellation of sales contracts, 193
  commercial paper, 532
  financing statement, 582–583
  firm offers, 116
  HDC or HHDC, 563
  innocent misrepresentation and, 134
  negotiable instrument, 532
  negotiation of commercial paper,
    545–546
  promises covered by, 149–150
  remedy for breach of contract, 200
  revised Article 9, 582
  sales of goods, 229–230
  secured transactions, 578–579
  special rules for merchants, 234–235
  tender of delivery and, 246
  unconscionable contracts, 175, 598
  warranties, 266–267
  writing requirement, 178–179
Uniform Computer Information
  Transactions Act (UCITA),
  251, 271
Uniform Limited Partnership Act
  (ULPA), 472, 510
Uniform Marriage and Divorce Act,
  209
Uniform Partnership Act (UPA),
  466–467
Unilateral contract, 119
Unilateral mistake, 130
Uninsured motorists coverage, 345
Union
  bargaining unit, 413
  establishment of, 411–415
  labor contract negotiation,
    416–417
  unfair labor practices, 417–420
Union Bill of Rights, 419

Union shop, 414
Unisys Corporation, 241
United Mine Workers, 423
United Nations
  Convention on Contracts for the
    International Sale of Goods
    (CISG), 180, 231
  Convention on the Rights of the
    Child (CRC), 402
United States
  debtor's prisons in, 531
  President of, national emergency
    strike and, 419
  punitive damage awards in, 268
Universal defenses, 565–567
Universalizing, 17
Unqualified indorsement, 553
Unsafe products, 261–263
  adulterated food, drugs, and
    cosmetics, 262
  improper weights, 262
Unsecured debts
  defined, 595
  laws concerning, 595–596
UPA. *See* Uniform Partnership Act
Usury, 172, 578, 597

V

Validity
  administrative law and, 13
  case law and, 13
  constitutions and, 12
  statutes and, 12–13
Values, 17
Variance, 318
Vehicular homicide, 67
Vendee, 230
Vendor, 230
Verdict
  in civil procedure, 95
  defined, 50, 95
Vicarious criminal liability, 66
Vicarious liability, 83
Victims, protected, of illegal
    agreements, 175
Violation, parking, 68
Visa, 601
Void, 130
Voidable, 127
Voidable marriage, 213
Void marriage, 213
Voluntary bankruptcy, 606
Vote, right to, 29
Voting, workers' time off for, 402

W

Wager, 171
Wages, garnishment of, 596
Wagner Act, 412. *See also* NLRA
Waiver, 200
Wal-Mart, 488
Warehouse, public, 248

Warrantor, 269
Warranty
  against encumbrances, 270
  against infringement, 271
  defined, 266
  exclusion of, 272
  express, 268, 269–270
  failure to provide, 265
  full, 269
  implied, 270
  importance of, 268–272
  lemon laws and, 272
  limited, 269
  of title, 270
  opinions v., 269
  qualified indorsers and, 553
Warranty deed, 320
Warranty of fitness for a particular
    purpose, 270
Warranty of habitability, 328
Warranty of merchantability,
    271–272
Warranty of the principal's
    capacity, 380
Warsaw Convention of 1929, 306
Washington, George (President), 52
Wasting the estate, 326
Water rights, 316–317
Weights and measures, improper, 262
What's Your Verdict? scenarios
  Unit 1, 5, 6, 10, 12, 13, 16, 25,
    28, 31, 32, 33, 36, 39, 49, 52,
    55, 57, 65, 67, 68, 71, 72, 74,
    81, 82, 83, 85, 89, 91, 93,
    94, 96
  Unit 2, 109, 110, 114, 116, 118,
    127, 128, 130, 131, 133, 141,
    145, 147, 149, 157, 160, 162,
    163, 164, 171, 174, 177, 179,
    181, 191, 192, 197, 199, 207,
    208, 210, 213, 214
  Unit 3, 229, 232, 234, 235, 243,
    245, 247, 249, 259, 260, 263,
    266, 268
  Unit 4, 285, 289, 292, 301, 302,
    305, 307, 315, 319, 323, 325,
    335, 336, 338, 340, 343, 347,
    348, 357, 360, 364, 366
  Unit 5, 379, 380, 384, 386, 387,
    395, 396, 401, 404, 411, 413,
    416, 417, 427, 429, 432, 434,
    435, 443, 447, 449
  Unit 6, 465, 469, 473, 476, 479,
    487, 490, 493, 496, 500, 501,
    509, 511, 514, 517
  Unit 7, 531, 532, 537, 545, 546,
    551, 552, 561, 562, 564, 568,
    577, 578, 581, 586, 593, 597,
    601, 604, 606
White-collar crimes, 68
Whole life insurance, 336
Wildfire, 341
Will
  amendment of valid, 359
  death with, 358–361

  death without, 357, 358, 361
  defined, 358
  example, 358
  holographic, 359
  nuncupative (oral), 359
  revocation of, 360
William I (King of England), 290
Winding-up period, 474
Winning Edge activities
  Business Plan (FBLA), 525
  Emerging Business Issues
    (FBLA), 103
  Extemporaneous Speaking
    (BPA), 615
  Human Resource Management
    (BPA), 459
  Multimedia Presentation
    (FBLA), 223
  Presentation Management
    (BPA), 373
  Public Speaking I (FBLA), 279
Witness
  in civil procedure, 94
  in court, 50
  defined, 94
  expert, 94
Workers' compensation, 402
  compromise of, 448
  employer's intentional tort, 449
  recovering in lieu of, 448–449
Workers' Compensation Boards,
    451–452
Workers' compensation insurance,
    paying for, 452
Workers' compensation statutes, 448
Workers' compensation system
  award hearing, 452
  paying for benefits, 452
  who's covered?, 449–450
Workforce pool, 435
Working conditions, employer's duty to
    provide safe, 401
Workplace
  OSHA safety regulations for, 444
  requirements for safe, 434–444
Work-related contracts, disaffirmance
    and, 164
Work-related injuries, employer's
    liability for, 447–452
World Trade Organization (WTO),
    Internet gambling, 91
World Wide Web, 37
World Wide Web consortium, 37
Writ of certiorari, 53
Writ of execution, 96
Writing requirements, 178
  for commercial paper, 546
  for contracts, 109
  See also Statute of Frauds
Wrongful discharge, 397
Wyoming
  limited liability corporations
    and, 514
  teachers' contracts in, 115
  women's right to vote in, 29

X

Xtra! Quiz Prep, 20, 44, 60, 76, 98,
122, 136, 152, 166, 186, 202,
218, 238, 254, 274, 296, 310,
330, 352, 368, 390, 406, 422,
438, 454, 482, 504, 520, 540,
556, 572, 588, 610
Xtra! Study Tools
Unit 1, 9, 15, 19, 30, 35, 43, 51, 54,
59, 70, 75, 84, 92, 96
Unit 2, 113, 117, 121, 129, 135,
144, 148, 151, 161, 165, 176,
185, 196, 201, 212, 216, 218
Unit 3, 233, 237, 246, 253,
265, 272
Unit 4, 288, 295, 304, 309, 322,
329, 339, 346, 351, 363, 367
Unit 5, 383, 389, 400, 405, 415,
421, 431, 436, 446, 452
Unit 6, 467, 475, 481, 492, 499,
502, 513, 519
Unit 7, 536, 539, 550, 555, 567,
571, 580, 587, 596, 603, 609

Y

Yahoo, CDA and, 41
Yellow-dog contracts, 412

Z

Zoning ordinance, 318